THINKING AND WRITING ABOUT LITERATURE

A Text and Anthology

SECOND EDITION

THINKING AND WRITING ABOUT LITERATURE

A Text and Anthology

Michael Meyer

University of Connecticut

BEDFORD / ST. MARTIN'S

Boston ♦ New York

FOR BEDFORD/ST. MARTIN'S

Developmental Edior: Alanya L. Harter
Production Editor: Stasia Zomkowski
Production Supervisor: Catherine Hetmansky
Marketing Manager: Karen Melton
Editorial Assistant: Amy Thomas
Production Assistant: Catherine E. Sheehan
Copyeditor: Jane Zanichkowsky
Text Design: Claire Seng-Niemoeller
Cover Design: Trudi Gershenov
Cover Art: Hera #1 (1968), Cleve Gray
Composition: Stratford Publishing Services, Inc.
Printing and Binding: Quebecor Printing

President: Charles H. Christensen
Editorial Director: Joan E. Feinberg
Editor in Chief: Karen S. Henry
Director of Editing, Design, and Production: Marcia Cohen
Managing Editor: Elizabeth M. Schaaf

Library of Congress Control Number: 00-103103

For information write: Bedford/St. Martin's, 75 Arlington Street, Boston, MA 02116

ISBN: 0-312-24874-1 (paperback)

Acknowledgments

Diane Ackerman. "A Fine a Private Place" from *Jaguar of Sweet Laughter* by Diane Ackerman. Copyright © 1991 by Diane Ackerman. Reprinted by permission of Random House, Inc.

Elizabeth Alexander. "Harlem Birthday Party" from *The Body of Life* by Elizabeth Alexander (Tia Chucha Press, 1996). Originally appeared in *Ploughshares* 22.1 (Spring 1996), p. 6. Reprinted by permission of the author.

Isabel Allende. "The Judge's Wife" from *The Stories of Eva Luna* by Isabel Allende, translated from the Spanish by Margaret Sayers Peden. Copyright © 1989, 2000 by Isabel Allende. English translation Copyright © 1991 by Macmillan Publishing Company, a Division of Macmillan, Inc. Reprinted with permission of Scribner, a Division of Simon & Schuster, and Key Porter Books.

Julia Alvarez. "Queens, 1963" from *The Other Side/El Otro Lado*. Copyright © 1995 by Julia Alvarez. Published by Plume Penguin, an imprint of Dutton, a Division of Penguin USA, and originally in hardcover by Dutton Signet. "Woman's Work" from *Homecoming*. Copyright © 1984, 1996 by Julia Alvarez. Published by Plume, an imprint of Dutton Signet, a Division of Penguin USA; originally published by Grove Press. Both poems reprinted by permission of Susan Bergholz Literary Services, New York. All rights reserved.

Katerina Angheláki-Rooke. "Jealousy" from *Daughters of Sappho: Contemporary Greek Women Poets*. Ed. and trans. Rae Dalven. Associated University Presses, Fairleigh Dickinson UP, 1994. Reprinted with permission of Associated University Presses.

Acknowledgments and copyrights are continued at the back of the book on pages 1407–1411, which constitute an extension of the copyright page. It is a violation of the law to reproduce these selections by any means whatsoever without the written permission of the copyright holder.

For My Wife
Regina Barreca

Preface for Instructors

Thinking and Writing about Literature, Second Edition, combines three texts in one—a writing about literature text, an introduction to literature, and a thematic anthology—all designed to help students become better writers and better readers of literature. This much-expanded version of the first edition grew out of *The Bedford Introduction to Literature*, which has been class-tested in thousands of literature courses and carefully revised and refined over five editions. Common to both books are the assumptions that understanding literature—through reflection, discussion, and writing—enhances its enjoyment, and that reading literature offers a valuable and unique means of apprehending life in its richness and diversity. Over the years scores of instructors have generously offered valuable comments on questionnaires indicating that any book with such high aspirations had also better provide clear, practical advice on thinking and writing about literature. This book is designed to do just that.

The second edition of *Thinking and Writing about Literature* accommodates a variety of teaching styles. This rich collection of 41 stories, 152 poems, 12 plays, and 17 essays represents a wide range of periods, nationalities, and voices. Each selection has been carefully chosen for its appeal to students and for its usefulness in demonstrating the effects, significance, and pleasures of literature. These selections are also chosen to assist instructors in achieving the goals of introductory courses as they are taught today. Introductory courses in reading and writing about literature vary more than ever before from school to school and from instructor to instructor.

Even the traditional course emphasizing the elements of literature and a broad range of works from the Western canon is changing in response to important developments in literary studies and, more generally, in higher education and in American society. The course is now viewed by many teachers as a rich opportunity to supplement classics of Western literature with the work of writers previously excluded from the traditional canon. Increasingly, it now also serves as an introduction to the discipline of literary study, a challenging development that brings to the undergraduate classroom important trends in literary theory and provocative new readings of both familiar and unfamiliar texts. Finally, and perhaps most often, the introduction to literature course is now also taught as a course in composition in which the critical thinking and writing that students do are as important as the reading that they do. This text and anthology responds to these developments with distinctive features that address the needs of instructors who teach a traditional course but who are also concerned about canonical issues, literary theory, and writing about literature.

Literature and the Writing Process

The book's concern with helping students write about literature is pervasive. The second edition of *Thinking and Writing about Literature* is especially suited for courses in which writing in response to literature is a central component. Part One, "Literature and the Writing Process," is a free-standing composition text consisting of four chapters that cover every step of the writing process. These chapters include practical, detailed information and advice about responsive reading, annotating a text, brainstorming, generating a topic, developing a thesis, building an argument, organizing the paper, writing the first draft, and revising and editing, as well as finding, using, and documenting sources. Coverage of these essential steps is followed by discussions of the different types of papers usually assigned in an introductory course, including personal response, explication, analysis, comparison and contrast, literary critical analysis, and research. A detailed chapter on the literary research paper, including a student model with a discussion of using and documenting print and online sources in the MLA style, provides the necessary information for finding, evaluating, and documenting sources.

The chapter titled "Applying a Critical Strategy" deepens the introductory discussion of active reading by focusing on the different reading strategies employed by contemporary literary theorists. This chapter, which can be assigned at any point in the course, introduces students to a wide variety of major contemporary theoretical approaches — formalist, biographical, psychological, historical (including literary history criticism, Marxist criticism, new historicist criticism, and cultural criticism), gender strategies (including feminist criticism and gay and lesbian criticism), mythological, reader-response, and deconstructionist approaches. In brief examples the approaches are applied in analyzing Kate Chopin's short story "The Story of an Hour," as well as other works, so that students will have a sense of how to use these strategies in their own reading and writing. A selected bibliography for the approaches concludes this chapter.

Each of the four chapters in Part One concludes with a "Writing in Process" casebook that demystifies the steps students need to follow when thinking and writing about literature (indeed all of the book's thirteen chapters include "Writing in Process" casebooks on student writing). Each casebook consists of sample student writing that includes first response and brainstorming lists, illustrating the process by which the student composed a paper. The casebook topics include reading and responding to literature, writing and revising a thesis statement, applying a critical strategy to a literary work, and writing a paper based on secondary sources.

Literature and Its Elements

Part Two, "Literature and Its Elements," consists of a comprehensive introduction to four genres: fiction, poetry, drama, and the essay. These four chapters introduce students to the key elements of each genre so that they can read critically and think and write about literature. Although the emphasis in this text is on critical reading and understanding rather than on critical terminology, terms such as *symbol, irony,* and *metaphor* are defined and illustrated to equip students with a basic working vocabulary for talking and writing about literature. When first defined in the text, these terms appear in boldface italic type. An "Index of Terms" appears inside the back cover of the book for easy reference, and a "Glossary of Literary Terms" provides thorough explanations of more than two hundred terms central to the study of literature.

The discussions of literary elements are complemented by examples from a rich and wide variety of short stories, poems, plays, and essays drawn from classical to contemporary works that illustrate the traditions and conventions of literary art while simultaneously demonstrating that literary art remains a vital part of the cultural landscape of students' lives.

In addition, each genre chapter includes a "Writing in Process" section that consists of a sample student paper that serves as a model for frequently assigned types of student writing. Each of the papers—comparison and contrast, explication, character analysis, and argument—is accompanied by samples of first response writing, brainstorming, or drafts that emphasize the process of how the student achieved the final paper. Also included for each genre are "Questions for Writing" about fiction, poetry, drama, or essays that will help students conceptualize topics and issues related to a particular genre.

Literature and Life

Part Three, "Literature and Life," offers a thematic anthology organized around five enduring themes that are familiar and appealing to students: "Home and Family," "Love and Its Complications," "Lessons from Life," "The Natural and Unnatural," and "Culture and Identity." This anthology gives students the opportunity to explore thematic links in a wide array of literary works by classic and contemporary writers—from Shakespeare, Melville, and Dickinson to David Henry Hwang, Alice Munro, and Wislawa Szymborska, to name but a few. The short stories, poems, plays, and essays found here speak to each of these themes and offer extensive opportunities for class discussion as works are compared and contrasted with respect to subject matter and style. Moreover, these motivating points of departure for student writers provide a wide variety of approaches to potential topics for writing exercises in each of the four genres. Like those in Parts One and Two, the five chapters in Part Three provide "Writing in Process" casebooks and samples of student writing. These include a feminist analysis of Henrik Ibsen's play *A Doll House;* a personal response to Katie Roiphe's essay "The Independent Woman"; an analysis of the setting in John Updike's short story "A&P"; a comparison and contrast study of four poems by Emily Dickinson; and a cultural analysis of a poem by Julia Alvarez, "Queens, 1963," that draws upon a series of cultural and historical documents to shed light on the poem.

Resources for Teaching THINKING AND WRITING ABOUT LITERATURE, *Second Edition*

This thorough and practical instructor's manual — more than 200 pages long and spiral bound — discusses every selection, suggests answers to many of the questions posed in the text, and provides teaching tips from instructors who have taught from *The Bedford Introduction to Literature*. The manual also gives suggestions for teaching thematic units and an annotated list of videos, films, and recordings related to the works of literature in the text.

Moreover, additional works of literature from any of Bedford Books' literary reprint series are available at a special price with *Thinking and Writing about Literature*. Titles from the highly praised Case Studies in Contemporary Criticism include *The Awakening, The Dead, Death in Venice, Frankenstein, Great Expectations, Gulliver's Travels, Hamlet, Heart of Darkness, The House of Mirth, Howards End, Jane Eyre, A Portrait of the Artist as a Young Man, The Rime of the Ancient Mariner, The Scarlet Letter, The Secret Sharer, Tess of the D'Urbervilles, The Turn of the Screw, The Wife of Bath,* and *Wuthering Heights*. Volumes from the Bedford Cultural Editions, the Bedford Shakespeare Series, and Case Studies in Critical Controversy include *Adventures of Huckleberry Finn, The Blithedale Romance, The Commerce of Everyday Life: Selections from THE SPECTATOR and THE TATLER, Evelina, The First Part of King Henry the Fourth, Life in the Iron-Mills, Macbeth, A Midsummer Night's Dream, The Rape of the Lock, Reading the West: An Anthology of Dime Westerns, The Taming of the Shrew,* and *The Yellow Wallpaper.*

Literature Aloud and Videotapes

An audio ancillary, available on either double CD or audiocassette, offers recordings of contemporary and classic short stories, poems, and selected scenes from the book. *Literature Aloud* features the voices of celebrated writers and actors — including several exclusive Bedford/St. Martin's recordings — and is available to any instructor who adopts the text. A selection of videotapes of plays and short stories are also available to qualified adopters.

Robert Frost: Poems, Life, Legacy

This comprehensive CD-ROM on the life and works of Robert Frost includes searchable text of his poetry, audio performances of Frost reading sixty-nine of his finest poems, over 1,500 pages of biography and literary criticism, and a new documentary film narrated by Richard Wilbur. It is available to qualified adopters of *Thinking and Writing about Literature*.

LitLinks and Companion Web Site

Because researching literary topics on the Web can be a daunting task for an undergraduate, Bedford/St. Martin's has compiled LitLinks — research links annotated to show students what kinds of information about a work, its author, or literary period they'll find on each site. LitLinks are organized alphabetically by author within five genres (fiction, poetry, drama, the essay, and literary criticism), and include links and brief biographies for almost every author included in the book. In addition to LitLinks, a Web site for *Thinking and Writing about Literature* provides additional online resources for instructors and students who use the book. Both can be accessed at <http://www.bedfordstmartins.com>.

Acknowledgments

This book has benefited from the ideas, suggestions, and corrections of careful readers who helped transform various stages of an evolving manuscript into a finished book, especially Shari Horner, Arnold Talentino, David Charlson, and Marianne Werner. I remain grateful to those I have thanked in the prefaces of *The Bedford Introduction to Literature* and *The Compact Bedford Introduction to Literature,* particularly Robert Wallace of Case Western Reserve University.

I would also like to give special thanks to the following instructors who contributed teaching tips to the fifth edition of *Resources for Teaching* THE BEDFORD INTRODUCTION TO LITERATURE, many of which appear in the *Thinking and Writing* Instructor's Manual: Sandra Adickes, Winona State University; Helen J. Aling, Northwestern College; Sr. Anne Denise Brennan, College of Mt. St. Vincent; Robin Calitri, Merced College; James H. Clemmer, Austin Peay State University; Robert Croft, Gainesville College; Thomas Edwards, Westbrook College; Elizabeth Kleinfeld, Red Rocks Community College; Olga Lyles, University of Nevada; Timothy Peters, Boston University; Catherine Rusco, Muskegon Community College; Robert M. St. John, De Paul University; Richard Stoner, Broome Community College; Nancy Veiga, Modesto Junior College; Karla Walters, University of New Mexico; and Joseph Zeppetello, Ulster Community College.

I am also indebted to those who cheerfully answered questions and generously provided miscellaneous bits of information. What might have seemed to them like inconsequential conversations turned out to be important leads. Among these friends and colleagues are Raymond Anselment, Ann Charters, Karen Chow, John Christie, Eleni Coundouriotis, Irving Cummings, William Curtin, Patrick Hogan, Lee Jacobus, Thomas Jambeck, Bonnie Januszewski-Ytuarte, Greta Little, George Monteiro, Brenda Murphy, Joel Myerson, Thomas Recchio, William Sheidley, Stephanie Smith, Milton Stern, Kenneth Wilson, and the dedicated reference librarians at the Homer Babbidge Library, University of Connecticut.

I continue to be grateful for what I have learned from teaching my students and for the many student papers I have received over the years that I have used in various forms to serve as good and accessible models of student writing. I am also indebted to Julie Nash for her extensive work on *Resources for Teaching* Thinking and Writing about Literature.

At Bedford/St. Martin's, my debts once again require more time to acknowledge than the deadline allows. Charles H. Christensen and Joan Feinberg initiated this project and launched it with their intelligence, energy, and sound advice. Karen Henry and Kathy Retan tirelessly steered earlier editions of *The Bedford Introduction to Literature* through rough as well as becalmed moments; their work was as first-rate as it was essential. Alanya Harter flawlessly carried on that tradition as developmental editor for the fifth edition of *The Bedford Introduction to Literature* and for this edition of *Thinking and Writing about Literature;* her savvy and quick takes were matched by her patience and prodigious appetite for work, qualities that helped to make this project both a success and a pleasure. Editorial Assistant Amy Thomas oversaw *Thinking and Writing about Literature* with clearheaded intelligence and welcomed enthusiasm. Her quiet determination and instinct for excellence added immeasurably to the quality of *Thinking and Writing about Literature,* especially in its crucial final stages. The unflappable Arthur Johnson performed the Herculean labor of clearing permissions. Ellen Thibault developed the CD/audiotape to accompany the text, *Literature Aloud.* The difficult tasks of production were skillfully managed by Stasia Zomkowski, whose attention to details and deadlines was essential to the completion of this project. Jane Zanichowsky provided careful copyediting, and Janet Cocker and Jocelyn Humelsine proofread. Numerous other people at Bedford Books — including Donna Lee Dennison and Zenobia Rivetna — helped to make this enormous project a manageable one.

Finally, I am grateful to my sons Timothy and Matthew for all kinds of help, but mostly I'm just grateful they're my sons. And always for making all the difference, I dedicate this book to my wife, Regina Barreca.

Contents

2. Writing and Revising   29

3. Applying a Critical Strategy   56

WRITING IN PROCESS

Critical Analysis 83

8. Reading and Writing about the Essay   511

PART THREE

LITERATURE AND LIFE   559

9. Home and Family   561

┌─ WRITING IN PROCESS ─────────────────────────────

Feminist Analysis 759

10. Love and Its Complications   775

WRITING IN PROCESS

Personal Response   917

11. Life and Its Lessons 924

Fiction 924

Poetry 986

Drama 1004

Essays 1073

— WRITING IN PROCESS —

Critical Analysis 1088

12. The Natural and Unnatural   1094

13. Culture and Identity   1225

Drama 1294

Essays 1342

WRITING IN PROCESS

Cultural Analysis 1363

Glossary of Literary Terms 1381

THINKING AND WRITING ABOUT LITERATURE

A Text and Anthology

INTRODUCTION

Reading Literature

THE NATURE OF LITERATURE

Literature does not lend itself to a single tidy definition because the making of it over the centuries has been as complex, unwieldy, and natural as life itself. Is literature everything that has been written, from ancient prayers to graffiti? Does it include songs and stories that were not written down until many years after they were recited? Does literature include the television scripts from *Seinfeld* as well as Shakespeare's *King Lear*? Is literature only writing that has permanent value and continues to move people? Must literature be true or beautiful or moral? Should it be socially useful?

Although these kinds of questions are not conclusively answered in this book, they are implicitly raised by the stories, poems, plays, and essays included here. No definition of literature, particularly a brief one, is likely to satisfy everyone because definitions tend to weaken and require qualification when confronted by the uniqueness of individual works. In this context it is worth recalling Herman Melville's humorous use of a definition of a whale in *Moby-Dick* (1851). In the course of the novel Melville presents his imaginative and symbolic whale as inscrutable, but he begins with a quotation from Georges Cuvier, a French naturalist who defines a whale in his nineteenth-century study *The Animal Kingdom* this way: "The whale is a mammiferous animal without hind feet." Cuvier's description is technically correct, of course, but there is little wisdom in it. Melville understood that the reality of the whale (which he describes as the "ungraspable phantom of life") cannot be caught by isolated facts. If the full meaning of the whale is to be understood, it must be sought on the open sea of experience, where the whale itself is, rather than in exclusionary definitions. Facts and definitions are helpful; however, they do not always reveal the whole truth.

Despite Melville's reminder that a definition can be too limiting and even comical, it is useful for our purposes to describe literature as a work consisting of carefully arranged words designed to stir the imagination. Stories, poems, plays, and some essays are fictional. They are made up — imagined — even when based on actual historic events. Such imaginative writing differs from other kinds of writing because its purpose is not primarily to transmit facts or ideas. Imaginative literature is a source more of pleasure than of information, and we read it for basically the same reasons we listen to music or view a dance: enjoyment, delight, and satisfaction. Like other art forms, imaginative literature offers pleasure and usually attempts to convey a perspective, mood, feeling, or experience. Writers transform the facts the world provides — people, places, and objects — into experiences that suggest meanings.

Consider, for example, the difference between the following factual description of a snake and a poem on the same subject. Here is *Webster's Tenth New Collegiate Dictionary* definition:

> any of numerous limbless scaled reptiles (suborder Serpentes or Ophidia) with a long tapering body and with salivary glands often modified to produce venom which is injected through grooved or tubular fangs.

Contrast this matter-of-fact definition with Emily Dickinson's poetic evocation of a snake in "A narrow Fellow in the Grass":

A narrow Fellow in the Grass
Occasionally rides —
You may have met Him — did you not
His notice sudden is —

The Grass divides as with a Comb —   5
A spotted shaft is seen —
And then it closes at your feet
And opens further on —

He likes a Boggy Acre
A floor too cool for Corn —   10
Yet when a Boy, and Barefoot —
I more than once at Noon

Have passed, I thought, a Whip lash
Unbraiding in the Sun
When stooping to secure it   15
It wrinkled, and was gone —

Several of Nature's People
I know, and they know me —
I feel for them a transport
Of cordiality —   20

But never met this Fellow
Attended, or alone
Without a tighter breathing
And Zero at the Bone —

The dictionary provides a succinct, anatomical description of what a snake is, while Dickinson's poem suggests what a snake can mean. The definition offers facts; the poem offers an experience. The dictionary would probably allow someone who had never seen a snake to sketch one with reasonable accuracy. The poem also provides some vivid subjective descriptions — for example, the snake dividing the grass "as with a Comb" — yet it offers more than a picture of serpentine movements. The poem conveys the ambivalence many people have about snakes — the kind of feeling, for example, so evident on the faces of visitors viewing the snakes at a zoo. In the poem there is both a fascination with and a horror of what might be called snakehood; this combination of feelings has been coiled in most of us since Adam and Eve.

That "narrow Fellow" so cordially introduced by way of a riddle (the word *snake* is never used in the poem) is, by the final stanza, revealed as a snake in the grass. In between, Dickinson uses language expressively to convey her meaning. For instance, in the line "His notice sudden is," listen to the *s* sound in each word and note how the verb *is* unexpectedly appears at the end, making the snake's hissing presence all the more "sudden." And anyone who has ever been surprised by a snake knows the "tighter breathing / And Zero at the Bone" that Dickinson evokes so successfully by the rhythm of her word choices and line breaks. Perhaps even more significant, Dickinson's poem allows those who have never encountered a snake to imagine such an experience.

A good deal more could be said about the numbing fear that undercuts the affection for nature at the beginning of this poem, but the point here is that imaginative literature gives us not so much the full, factual proportions of the world as some of its experiences and meanings. Instead of defining the world, literature encourages us to try it out in our imaginations.

THE VALUE OF LITERATURE

Mark Twain once shrewdly observed that a person who chooses not to read has no advantage over a person who is unable to read. In industrialized societies today, however, the question is not who reads, because nearly everyone can and does, but what is read. Why should anyone spend precious time with literature when there is so much reading material available that provides useful information about everything from the daily news to personal computers? Why should a literary artist's imagination compete for attention that could be spent on the firm realities that constitute everyday life? In fact, national best-seller lists much less often include collections of stories, poems, plays, or exploratory essays than they do cookbooks and, not surprisingly, diet books. Although such fare may be filling, it doesn't stay with you. Most people have other appetites too.

Certainly one of the most important values of literature is that it nourishes our emotional lives. An effective literary work may seem to speak directly to us, especially if we are ripe for it. The inner life that good writers reveal in their characters often gives us glimpses of some portion of ourselves. We can be moved to laugh, cry, tremble, dream, ponder, shriek, or rage with a character by simply turning a page instead of turning our lives upside down. Although the experience itself is imagined, the emotion is real. That's why the final chapters of a good adventure novel can make a reader's heart race as much as a 100-yard dash, or why the repressed love of Hester Prynne in *The Scarlet Letter* by Nathaniel Hawthorne is painful to a sympathetic reader. Human emotions speak a universal language regardless of when or where a work was written.

In addition to appealing to our emotions, literature broadens our perspectives on the world. Most of the people we meet are pretty much like ourselves, and what we can see of the world even in a lifetime is astonishingly limited. Literature allows us to move beyond the inevitable boundaries of our own lives and culture because it introduces us to people different from ourselves, places remote from our neighborhoods, and times other than our own. Reading makes us more aware of life's possibilities as well as its subtleties and ambiguities. Put simply, people who read literature experience more life and have a keener sense of a common human identity than those who do not. It is true, of course, that many people go through life without reading imaginative literature, but that is a loss rather than a gain. They may find themselves troubled by the same kinds of questions that reveal Daisy Buchanan's restless, vague discontentment in F. Scott Fitzgerald's *The Great Gatsby:* "What'll we do with ourselves this afternoon?" cried Daisy, "and the day after that, and the next thirty years?"

Sometimes students mistakenly associate literature more with school than with life. Accustomed to reading it in order to write a paper or pass an examination, students may perceive such reading as a chore instead of a pleasurable opportunity, something considerably less important than studying for the "practical" courses that prepare them for a career. The study of literature, however, is also practical because it engages you in the kinds of problem solving important in a variety of fields, from philosophy to science and technology. The interpretation of literary texts requires you to deal with uncertainties, value judgments, and emotions; these are unavoidable aspects of life.

People who make the most significant contributions to their professions — whether in business, engineering, teaching, or some other area — tend to be challenged rather than threatened by multiple possibilities. Instead of retreating to the way things have always been done, they bring freshness and creativity to their work. F. Scott Fitzgerald once astutely described the "test of a first-rate intelligence" as "the ability to hold two opposed ideas in the mind at the same time, and still retain the ability to function." People with such intelligence know how to read situations, shape questions, interpret details, and evaluate competing points of view. Equipped with a healthy respect for facts, they also understand the value of pursuing hunches and exercising their imaginations. Reading literature encourages a suppleness of mind that is helpful in any discipline or work.

Once the requirements for your degree are completed, what ultimately matters are not the courses listed on your transcript but the sensibilities and habits of mind that you bring to your work, friends, family, and, indeed, the rest of your life. A healthy economy changes and grows with the times; people do too if they are prepared for more than simply filling a job description. The range and variety of life that literature affords can help you to interpret your own experiences and the world in which you live. You'll find ample opportunities to explore some of the breadth and depth of human experience in the thematic chapters of this book. Part Three, Literature and Life, consists of five chapters with a broad range of stories, poems, plays, and essays that explore themes we're all familiar with: Home and Family, Love and Its Complications, Lessons from Life, The Natural and Unnatural, and Culture and Identity. These literary perspectives on what it means to be a human being are certainly specific to their time and place, but they also suggest the universal concerns of people engaged in life, regardless of when or where they were written.

To discover the insights that literature reveals requires careful reading and sensitivity. One of the purposes of a college introduction to literature class is to cultivate the analytic skills necessary for reading well. Class discussions often help establish a dialogue with a work that perhaps otherwise would not speak to you. Analytic skills can also be developed by writing about what you read. Writing is an effective means of clarifying your responses and ideas because it requires you to account for the author's use of language as well as your own. This book is based on two premises: that reading literature is pleasurable and that reading and understanding a work sensitively by thinking, talking, or writing about it increase the pleasure of the experience of it.

Understanding its basic elements — such as point of view, symbol, theme, tone, irony, and so on — is a prerequisite to an informed appreciation of literature. This kind of understanding allows you to perceive more in a literary work in much the same way that a spectator at a tennis match sees more if he or she understands the rules and conventions of the game. But literature is not simply a spectator sport. The analytic skills that open up literature also have their uses when you watch a television program or film and, more important, when you attempt to sort out the significance of the people, places, and events that constitute your own life. Literature enhances and sharpens your perceptions, and writing about literature offers opportunities to develop and demonstrate the clarity of your thoughts.

THE CHANGING LITERARY CANON

Perhaps the best reading creates some kind of change in us: We see more clearly; we're alert to nuances; we ask questions that previously didn't occur to us. Henry David Thoreau had that sort of reading in mind when he remarked in *Walden* that the books he valued most were those that caused him to date "a new era in his life from the reading." Readers are sometimes changed by literature, but it is also worth noting that the life of a literary work can also be affected by its readers. Melville's *Moby-Dick*, for example, was not valued as a classic until the 1920s, when critics rescued the novel from the obscurity of being cataloged in many libraries (including Yale's) not under fiction but under cetology, the study of whales. Indeed, many writers contemporary to Melville who were important and popular in the nineteenth century — William Cullen Bryant, Henry Wadsworth Longfellow, and James Russell Lowell, to name a few — are now mostly unread; their names appear more often on elementary schools built early in this century than in anthologies. Clearly, literary reputations and what is valued as great literature change over time and in the eyes of readers.

Such changes have accelerated during the past forty years as the literary **canon** — those works considered by scholars, critics, and teachers to be the most important to read and study — has undergone a significant series of shifts. Writers who previously were overlooked, undervalued, neglected, or studiously ignored have been brought into focus in an effort to create a more diverse literary canon, one that recognizes the contributions of the many cultures that make up American society. Since the 1960s, for example, some critics have reassessed writings by women who had been left out of the standard literary traditions dominated by male writers. Many more female writers are now read alongside the male writers who traditionally populated literary history. Hence, a reader of Mark Twain and Stephen Crane is now just as likely to encounter Kate Chopin in a literary anthology. Until fairly recently Chopin was mostly regarded as a minor local colorist of Louisiana life. In the 1960s, however, the feminist movement helped to establish her present reputation as a significant voice in American literature owing to the feminist concerns so compellingly articulated by her female characters. This kind of enlargement of the canon also resulted from another reform movement of the 1960s. The civil rights movement sensitized literary critics to the political, moral, and aesthetic necessity of rediscovering African American literature, and more recently Asian and Hispanic writers have been making their way into the canon. Moreover, on a broader scale the canon is being revised and enlarged to include the works of writers from parts of the world other than the West, a development that reflects the changing values, concerns, and complexities of the recent past, when literary landscapes have shifted as dramatically as the political boundaries of Eastern Europe and the former Soviet Union.

No semester's reading list — or anthology — can adequately or accurately echo all the new voices competing to be heard as part of the mainstream literary canon, but recent efforts to open up the canon attempt to sensitize readers to the voices of women, minorities, and writers from all over the world. This development has not occurred without its urgent advocates or passionate dissenters. It's no surprise that issues about race, gender, and class often get people off the fence and on their feet (these controversies are discussed further in Chapter 3, "Applying a Critical Strategy"). Although what we regard as literature—whether it's called great, classic, or canonical—continues to generate debate, there is no question that such controversy will continue to reflect readers' values as well as the writers they admire.

PART ONE

Literature and the Writing Process

1

Reading and Responding

THE PURPOSE AND VALUE
OF WRITING ABOUT LITERATURE

Introductory courses concerned with writing about literature typically include three components — reading, discussion, and writing. Students usually find the readings a pleasure, the class discussions a revelation, and the writing assignments — at least initially — a little intimidating. Writing an analysis of Melville's use of walls in "Bartleby, the Scrivener" (p. 944), for example, may seem considerably more daunting than making a case for animal rights or analyzing a campus newspaper editorial that calls for grade reforms. Like Bartleby, you might want to respond with "I would prefer not to." Literary topics are not, however, all that different from the kinds of papers assigned in nonliterary composition courses; many of the same skills are required for both. Regardless of the type of paper, you must develop a thesis and support it with evidence in language that is clear and persuasive.

Whether the subject matter is a marketing survey, a political issue, or a literary work, writing is a method of communicating information and perceptions. Writing teaches. But before writing becomes an instrument for informing the reader, it serves as a means of learning for the writer. An essay is a process of discovery as well as a record of what has been discovered. One of the chief benefits of writing is that we frequently realize what we want to say only after trying out ideas on a page and seeing our thoughts take shape in language.

More specifically, writing about a literary work encourages us to be better readers because it requires a close examination of the elements and themes of a short story, poem, play, or essay. To determine how plot, character, setting, point of view, style, tone, irony, or any number of other literary elements function in a work, we must study them in relation to one another as well as separately. Speed-reading won't do. To read a text accurately and validly — neither ignoring nor distorting significant details — we must return to the work repeatedly to test our responses and interpretations. By paying attention to details and being sensitive to the author's use of language, we develop a clearer understanding of how the work conveys its effects and meanings.

Nevertheless, students sometimes ask why it is necessary or desirable to write about a literary work. Why not allow the work to speak for itself? Isn't it presumptuous to interpret Hemingway, Dickinson, or Shakespeare? These writers do, of course, speak for themselves, but they do so indirectly. Literary criticism seeks not to replace the text by explaining it but to enhance our readings of works by calling attention to elements that we might have overlooked or only vaguely sensed.

Another misunderstanding about the purpose of literary criticism is that it crankily restricts itself to finding faults in a work. Critical essays are sometimes mistakenly equated with newspaper and magazine reviews of recently published works. Reviews typically include summaries and evaluations to inform readers about a work's nature and quality, but critical essays assume that readers are already familiar with a work. Although a critical essay may point out limitations and flaws, most criticism — and certainly the kind of essay usually written in a composition and literature course — is designed to explain, analyze, and reveal the complexities of a work. Such sensitive consideration increases our appreciation of the writer's achievement and significantly adds to our enjoyment of a short story, poem, or play. In short, the purpose and value of writing about literature are that doing so leads to greater understanding and pleasure.

READING THE WORK RESPONSIVELY

Reading a literary work responsively can be an intensely demanding activity. Henry David Thoreau — about as intense and demanding a reader and writer as they come — insists that "books must be read as deliberately and reservedly as they were written." Thoreau is right about the necessity for a conscious, sustained involvement with a literary work. Imaginative literature does demand more from us than, say, browsing through *People* magazine in a dentist's waiting room, but Thoreau makes the process sound a little more daunting than it really is. For when we respond to the demands of responsive reading, our efforts are usually rewarded with pleasure as well as understanding. Careful, deliberate reading — the kind that engages a reader's imagination as it calls forth the writer's — is a means of exploration that can take a reader outside whatever circumstance or experience previously defined his or her world. Just as we respond moment by moment to people and situations in our lives, we also respond to literary works as we read them, though we may not be fully aware of how we are affected at each point along the way. The more conscious we are of how and why we respond to works in particular ways, the more likely we are to be imaginatively engaged in our reading.

In a very real sense both the reader and the author create the literary work. How a reader responds to a story, poem, or play will help to determine its meaning. The author arranges the various elements that constitute his or her craft — elements such as plot, character, setting, point of view, symbolism, theme, and style, which you will be examining in subsequent chapters and which are defined in the Glossary of Literary Terms (p. 1381) — but the author cannot completely control the reader's response any more than a person can absolutely predict how a remark or action will be received by a stranger, a friend, or even a family member. Few authors *tell* readers how to respond. Our sympathy, anger, confusion, laughter, sadness, or whatever the feeling might be is left up to us to experience. Writers may have the talent to evoke such feelings, but they don't have the power and authority to enforce them. Because of the range of possible responses produced by imaginative literature, there is no single, correct, definitive response or interpretation. There can be readings that are wrongheaded or foolish, and some readings are better than others — that is, more responsive to a work's details and more persuasive — but that doesn't mean there is only one possible reading of a work.

Experience tells us that different people respond differently to the same work. Consider, for example, how often you've heard Melville's *Moby-Dick* described as one of the greatest American novels. This, however, is how a reviewer in *New Monthly Magazine* described the book when it was published in 1851: it is "a huge dose of hyperbolical slang, maudlin sentimentalism and tragic-comic bubble and squeak." Melville surely did not intend or desire this response; but there it is, and it was not a singular, isolated reaction. This reading — like any reading — was influenced by the values, assumptions, and expectations that the readers brought to the novel from both previous readings and life experiences. The reviewer's refusal to take the book seriously may have caused him to miss the boat from the perspective of many other readers of *Moby-Dick,* but it indicates that even "classics" (perhaps especially those kinds of works) can generate disparate readings.

READING THE WORK CLOSELY

Know the piece of literature you are writing about before you begin your essay. Think about how the work makes you feel and how it is put together. The more familiar you are with how the various elements of the text convey effects and meanings, the more confident you will be explaining whatever perspective on it you ultimately choose. Do not insist that everything make sense on a first reading. Relax and enjoy yourself; you can be attentive and still allow the author's words to work their magic on you. With subsequent readings, however, go more slowly and analytically as you try to establish relations between characters, actions, images, or whatever else seems important. Ask yourself why you respond as you do. Think as you read, and notice how the parts of a work contribute to its overall nature. Whether the work is a short story, poem, play, or essay, you will read relevant portions of it over and over, and you will very likely find more to discuss in each review if the work is rich.

It's best to avoid reading other critical discussions of a work before you are thoroughly familiar with it. There are several good reasons for following this advice. By reading interpretations before you know a work, you deny yourself the pleasure of discovery. That is a bit like starting with the last chapter in a mystery novel. But perhaps even more important than protecting the surprise and delight that a work might offer is that a premature reading of a critical discussion will probably short-circuit your own responses. You will see the work through the critic's eyes and have to struggle with someone else's perceptions and ideas before you can develop your own.

Reading criticism can be useful, but not until you have thought through your own impressions of the text. A guide should not be permitted to become a tyrant. This does not mean, however, that you should avoid background information about a work — for example, that Hemingway's story "Soldier's Home" is, to a degree, informed by the author's own experiences in World War I. Knowing something about the author as well as historic and literary contexts can help to create expectations that enhance your reading.

ANNOTATING THE TEXT AND JOURNAL NOTE TAKING

As you read, get in the habit of making marginal notations in your textbook. If you are working with a library book, use note cards and write down page or line numbers so that you can easily return to annotated passages. Use these cards to record reactions, raise questions, and make comments. They will freshen your memory and allow you to keep track of what goes on in the text.

Whatever method you use to annotate your texts — whether writing marginal notes, highlighting, underlining, or drawing boxes and circles around important words and phrases — you'll eventually develop a system that allows you to retrieve significant ideas and elements from the text. Another way to record your impressions of a work — as with any other experience — is to keep a journal. By writing down your reactions to characters, images, language, actions, and other matters in a reading journal, you can often determine why you like or dislike a work or feel sympathetic or antagonistic to an author or discover paths into a work that might have eluded you if you hadn't preserved your impressions. Your journal notes and annotations may take whatever form you find useful; full sentences and grammatical correctness are not essential (unless they are to be handed in and your instructor requires that), though they might allow you to make better sense of your own reflections days later. The point is simply to put in writing thoughts that you can retrieve when you need them for class discussion or a writing assignment. Consider the following student annotation of the first twenty-four lines of Andrew Marvell's "To His Coy Mistress" (p. 230) and the journal entry that follows it:

Annotated Text

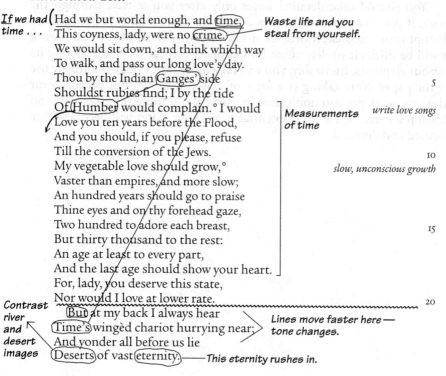

If we had time . . .

Had we but world enough, and **time,**
This coyness, lady, were no **crime.** — *Waste life and you steal from yourself.*
We would sit down, and think which way
To walk, and pass our long love's day.
Thou by the Indian **Ganges'** side   5
Shouldst rubies find; I by the tide
Of **Humber** would complain.° I would — **Measurements of time**   *write love songs*
Love you ten years before the Flood,
And you should, if you please, refuse
Till the conversion of the Jews.   10
My vegetable love should grow,°   *slow, unconscious growth*
Vaster than empires, and more slow;
An hundred years should go to praise
Thine eyes and on thy forehead gaze,
Two hundred to adore each breast,   15
But thirty thousand to the rest:
An age at least to every part,
And the last age should show your heart.
For, lady, you deserve this state,
Nor would I love at lower rate.   20

Contrast river and desert images

But at my back I always hear
Time's wingèd chariot hurrying near; — *Lines move faster here — tone changes.*
And yonder all before us lie
Deserts of vast **eternity.** — *This eternity rushes in.*

Journal Note

He'd be patient and wait for his "mistress" if they had the time--sing songs, praise her, adore her, etc. But they don't have that much time according to him. He seems to be patient but he actually begins by calling patience--her coyness--a "crime." Looks to me like he's got his mind made up from the beginning of the poem. Where's her response? I'm not sure about him.

This journal note responds to some of the effects noted in the annotations of the poem; it's an excellent beginning for making sense of the speaker's argument in the poem.

Taking notes will preserve your initial reactions to the work. Many times first impressions are the best. Your response to a peculiar character in a story, a striking phrase in a poem, a subtle bit of stage business in a play, or the author's tone in an essay might lead to larger perceptions. The student paper on John Updike's "A & P" (p. 981), for example, began with the student writing "how come?" next to the story's title in her textbook. She thought it strange that the title didn't refer to a character or the story's conflict. That annotated response eventually led her to examine the significance of the setting, which became the central idea of her paper.

You should take detailed notes only after you've read through the work. If you write too many notes during the first reading, you're likely to disrupt your response. Moreover, until you have a sense of the entire work it will be difficult to determine how connections can be made among its various elements. Inevitably, you will take more notes than you finally use in the paper. Note taking is a form of thinking aloud, but because your ideas are on paper you don't have to worry about forgetting them. As you develop a better sense of a potential topic, your notes will become more focused and detailed.

WRITING IN PROCESS

Reading and First Response

This casebook invites you to follow one student, Wally Villa, as he moves through responsive reading, annotating the text, writing a first response, and writing a more formal essay. He starts by reading the following brief story by Kate Chopin, a writer whose fiction (like Melville's) was sometimes met with indifference or hostility in her own time. As you read, keep track of your responses to the central character, Mrs. Mallard—you may want to write about the story yourself, using the Questions for Responsive Reading and Writing as a starting point. How do you respond to the emotions she expresses concerning news of her husband's death? What do you think of her feelings about marriage? Do you think you would react the way she does under similar circumstances?

KATE CHOPIN (1851–1904)

Born in St. Louis, Missouri, Kate Chopin was raised by her Creole mother's family after her father died when she was only four. In 1870 she married Oscar Chopin, and they lived in Louisiana, first in New Orleans and then on his cotton plantation on the Mississippi River. Her husband died only twelve years later in 1882, and she moved back to St. Louis with her children, after which she first began to write seriously. Her first novel *At Fault* was published in 1890, when she was forty-one years old. She also wrote many short stories, which were collected in *Bayou Folk* (1894) and *A Night in Arcadie* (1897). Her last, and greatest, novel, *The Awakening* (1899), scandalized readers and critics at the time for its frank and sympathetic portrayal of adultery and female sexuality.

Because her work challenged reigning social conventions for women's relations and behavior, when it was rediscovered in the 1960s after a half

Kate Chopin, featured in the periodical St. Louis Life *in 1894 — the same year she published "The Story of an Hour." She was seen at the time as a talented, if somewhat rebellious writer, and was yet to write her 1899 novel,* The Awakening, *which was considered shocking and scandalous. The photo is reprinted courtesy of the Missouri Historical Society.*

century of neglect, it was championed by feminist critics. Her novels and stories continue to provoke heated discussion about the issues, which are central to "The Story of an Hour," of marriage, gender conventions, and women's victimization and freedom.

The Story of an Hour 1894

Knowing that Mrs. Mallard was afflicted with a heart trouble, great care was taken to break to her as gently as possible the news of her husband's death.

It was her sister Josephine who told her, in broken sentences; veiled hints that revealed in half concealing. Her husband's friend Richards was there, too, near her. It was he who had been in the newspaper office when intelligence of the railroad disaster was received, with Brently Mallard's name leading the list of "killed." He had only taken the time to assure himself of its truth by a second telegram, and had hastened to forestall any less careful, less tender friend in bearing the sad message.

She did not hear the story as many women have heard the same, with a paralyzed inability to accept its significance. She wept at once, with sudden, wild abandonment, in her sister's arms. When the storm of grief had spent itself she went away to her room alone. She would have no one follow her.

There stood, facing the open window, a comfortable, roomy armchair. Into this she sank, pressed down by a physical exhaustion that haunted her body and seemed to reach into her soul.

She could see in the open square before her house the tops of trees that 5 were all aquiver with the new spring life. The delicious breath of rain was in the air. In the street below a peddler was crying his wares. The notes of a distant song which some one was singing reached her faintly, and countless sparrows were twittering in the eaves.

There were patches of blue sky showing here and there through the clouds that had met and piled one above the other in the west facing her window.

She sat with her head thrown back upon the cushion of the chair, quite motionless, except when a sob came up into her throat and shook her, as a child who has cried itself to sleep continues to sob in its dreams.

She was young, with a fair, calm face, whose lines bespoke repression and even a certain strength. But now there was a dull stare in her eyes, whose gaze was fixed away off yonder on one of those patches of blue sky. It was not a glance of reflection, but rather indicated a suspension of intelligent thought.

There was something coming to her and she was waiting for it, fearfully. What was it? She did not know; it was too subtle and elusive to name. But she felt it, creeping out of the sky, reaching toward her through the sounds, the scents, the color that filled the air.

Now her bosom rose and fell tumultuously. She was beginning to recognize this thing that was approaching to possess her, and she was striving to beat it back with her will — as powerless as her two white slender hands would have been.   10

When she abandoned herself a little whispered word escaped her slightly parted lips. She said it over and over under her breath: "free, free, free!" The vacant stare and the look of terror that had followed it went from her eyes. They stayed keen and bright. Her pulses beat fast, and the coursing blood warmed and relaxed every inch of her body.

She did not stop to ask if it were or were not a monstrous joy that held her. A clear and exalted perception enabled her to dismiss the suggestion as trivial.

She knew that she would weep again when she saw the kind, tender hands folded in death; the face that had never looked save with love upon her, fixed and gray and dead. But she saw beyond that bitter moment a long procession of years to come that would belong to her absolutely. And she opened and spread her arms out to them in welcome.

There would be no one to live for her during those coming years; she would live for herself. There would be no powerful will bending hers in that blind persistence with which men and women believe they have a right to impose a private will upon a fellow-creature. A kind intention or a cruel intention made the act seem no less a crime as she looked upon it in that brief moment of illumination.

And yet she had loved him — sometimes. Often she had not. What did it   15 matter! What could love, the unsolved mystery, count for in face of this possession of self-assertion which she suddenly recognized as the strongest impulse of her being!

"Free! Body and soul free!" she kept whispering.

Josephine was kneeling before the closed door with her lips to the keyhole, imploring for admission. "Louise, open the door! I beg; open the door — you will make yourself ill. What are you doing, Louise? For heaven's sake open the door."

"Go away. I am not making myself ill." No; she was drinking in a very elixir of life through that open window.

Her fancy was running riot along those days ahead of her. Spring days, and summer days, and all sorts of days that would be her own. She breathed a quick prayer that life might be long. It was only yesterday she had thought with a shudder that life might be long.

7. Did a single reading allow you to arrive at a satisfactory understanding of the work? How accessible or difficult is the text?

8. If you weren't satisfied with your understanding of the work on the first reading, what specifically created difficulties for you?

9. Have you looked up any words, references, or allusions that you don't understand?

10. What does a second reading yield that a first reading doesn't provide? How do subsequent readings improve your understanding of the work?

11. What passages seem especially important and revealing? Is there a single passage that seems to summarize the point of the work?

12. What range of emotions does the work evoke in you? If you find your emotions or perspectives changing during the course of the reading, what in the work caused the shift?

13. What kinds of devices such as connotation, images, figures of speech, symbols, or tone does the author use to create effects?

14. What seems to be the author's perspective on the subject matter of the work? What do you take to be the author's intended meaning? Do you derive the same significance from the work? To what extent do you agree or disagree with the author?

15. Can you use your marginal notations or journal entries to generate a written first response to the work?

16. If a writing assignment is to be based on your reading of the work, what reactions, questions, insights, or ideas might be worth pursuing in the paper?

A Sample Annotation

Only after you've read carefully are you ready to respond — and taking notes as you reread can be an important step toward actively engaging with the text. The following annotations show you the notes made by one student, Wally Villa, on the end of "The Story of an Hour" — notes that he will develop into a paper at the end of this Casebook.

What is she waiting for?

She sat with her head thrown back upon the cushion of the chair, quite motionless, except when a sob came up into her throat and shook her, as a child who has cried itself to sleep continues to sob in its dreams.

She was young, with a fair, calm face, whose lines bespoke repression and even a certain strength. But now there was a dull stare in her eyes, whose gaze was fixed away off yonder on one of those patches of blue sky. It was not a glance of reflection, but rather indicated a suspension of intelligent thought.

She's numb with grief

Notice repetition of "she" emphasizing feminine pronoun, not Mrs. M.

There was something coming to her and she was waiting for it fearfully. What was it? She did not know it was too subtle and elusive to name. But she felt it, creeping out of the sky, reaching toward her through the sounds, the scents, the color that filled the air.

"it" = from nature

Now her bosom rose and fell tumultuously. She was 10
beginning to recognize this thing that was approaching to
possess her, and she was striving to beat it back with her
will—as powerless as her two white slender hands would
have been.

When she abandoned herself a little whispered word
escaped her slightly parted lips. She said it over and over
under her breath: "free, free, free!" The vacant stare and
the look of terror that had followed it went from her eyes.
They stayed keen and bright. Her pulses beat fast, and the
coursing blood warmed and relaxed every inch of her
body.

She did not stop to ask if it were or were not a monstrous joy that held her. A clear and exalted perception
enabled her to dismiss the suggestion as trivial.

She knew that she would weep again when she saw
the kind, tender hands folded in death; the face that had
never looked save with love upon her, fixed and gray and
dead. But she saw beyond that bitter moment a long procession of years to come that would belong to her
absolutely. And she opened and spread her arms out to
them in welcome.

There would be no one to live for her during those
coming years; she would live for herself. There would be no
powerful will bending hers in that blind persistence with
which men and women believe they have a right to impose
a private will upon a fellow-creature. A kind intention or a
cruel intention made the act seem no less a crime as she
looked upon it in that brief moment of illumination.

And yet she had loved him—sometimes. Often she 15
had not. What did it matter! What could love, the unsolved mystery, count for in face of this possession of self-
assertion which she suddenly recognized as the strongest
impulse of her being!

"Free! Body and soul free!" she kept whispering.

Margin annotations:
more "she" repetition

"it" = powerful

she feels "free"

"it" = freedom

no guilt

free of marriage

marriage a kind of slavery

as if it's a secret

A Sample First Response

After active reading, the next step towards an assignment is often
informal writing. Wally's professor asked him to write an informal answer
to the first question after the story, *Did you find Mrs. Mallard a sympathetic
character?*

Initially I was sympathetic to Mrs. Mallard's sense of
relief over her husband's death, because she describes her
marriage as a kind of emotional slavery. But I also think that
she didn't do much to make her marriage better. I can't imagine
my older married sister suffering silently like that.

Because this story is so brief, I had no trouble getting
my father and my grandmother to read it. For some reason it was
easier to ask them than my mother. My father didn't think much
of Mrs. M. and identified a lot with the husband. He saw the
wife as keeping too much to herself and as selfish too. He
found even more fault in her than I did. My grandmother said
she could understand why Mrs. M. felt so trapped in her dutiful
marriage, because she remembers women like Mrs. M. when she was
young. It seems that readings of Mrs. M. have a lot to do with
the readers themselves.

A Sample Student Response Paper

After Wally actively read and started writing, it was easier for him to
approach his next task, which was to *Write a three- to four-page discussion of
how different readers might interpret Mrs. Mallard's character.* As you've learned
from his first response, he has also asked his father and his grandmother
to read the story — and he was interested to learn that they both had different takes on Mrs. Mallard's character. He also read the discussion of
reader-response criticism (74–76) in Chapter 3, "Applying a Critical Strategy." As that discussion indicates, reader-response criticism is a critical
approach that focuses on the reader rather than on the work itself in order
to describe how the reader creates meaning from the text.

Wally Villa
Professor Brian
English 210
March 12, 20--
                    Differences in Responses to
              Kate Chopin's "The Story of an Hour"
       Kate Chopin's "The Story of an Hour" appears merely
to explore a woman's unpredictable reaction to her husband's assumed death and reappearance, but actually Chopin
offers Mrs. Mallard's bizarre story to reveal problems
that are inherent in the institution of marriage. By offering this depiction of a marriage that stifles the
woman to the point that she celebrates the death of her
kind and loving husband, Chopin challenges her readers
to examine their own views of marriage and relationships
between men and women. Each reader's judgment of Mrs.
Mallard and her behavior inevitably stems from his or her
own personal feelings about marriage and the influences
of societal expectations. Readers of differing genders,
ages, and marital experiences are, therefore, likely to
react differently to Chopin's startling portrayal of the
Mallards' marriage, and that certainly is true of my response to the story compared to my father's and grandmother's responses.
       Marriage often establishes boundaries between people
that make them unable to communicate with each other. The
Mallards' marriage was evidently crippled by both their
inability to talk to one another and Mrs. Mallard's conviction that her marriage was defined by a "powerful will
bending hers in that blind persistence with which men and
women believe they have a right to impose a private will
upon a fellow-creature." (19; all page references are to
the class text, Thinking and Writing about Literature: A
Text and Anthology, 2nd ed.).

Villa 2

Yet she does not recognize that it is not just men who impose their will upon women and that the problems inherent in marriage affect men and women equally. To me, Mrs. Mallard is a somewhat sympathetic character, and I appreciate her longing to live out the "years to come that would belong to her absolutely" (19). However, I also believe that she could have tried to improve her own situation somehow, either by reaching out to her husband or by abandoning the marriage altogether. Chopin uses Mrs. Mallard's tragedy to illuminate aspects of marriage that are harmful and, in this case, even deadly. Perhaps the Mallards' relationship should be taken as a warning to others: sacrificing one's own happiness in order to satisfy societal expectations can poison one's life and even destroy entire families.

When my father read "The Story of an Hour," his reaction to Mrs. Mallard was more antagonistic than my own. He sees Chopin's story as a timeless "battle of the sexes," serving as further proof that men will never really be able to understand what it is that women want. Mrs. Mallard endures an obviously unsatisfying marriage without ever explaining to her husband that she feels trapped and unfulfilled. Mrs. Mallard dismisses the question of whether or not she is experiencing a "monstrous joy" (19) as trivial, but my father does not think that this is a trivial question. He believes Mrs. Mallard is guilty of a monstrous joy because she selfishly celebrates the death of her husband without ever allowing him the opportunity to understand her feelings. He believes that, above all, Brently Mallard should be seen as the most victimized character in the story. Mr. Mallard is a good, kind man, with friends who care about him and a marriage that he thinks he can depend on. He "never looked save with love" (19) upon his wife, his only "crime" was coming home from work one day, and yet he is the one who is bereaved at the end of the story, for reasons he will never understand. Mrs. Mallard's passion for her newly discovered freedom is perhaps understandable, but according to my father, Mr. Mallard is the character most deserving of sympathy.

Maybe not surprisingly, my grandmother's interpretation of "The Story of an Hour" was radically different from both mine and my father's. My grandmother was married in 1936 and widowed in 1959 and therefore can identify with Chopin's characters, who live at the turn of the century. Her first reaction, aside from her unwavering support for Mrs. Mallard and her predicament, was that this story demonstrates the differences between the ways men and women related to each other a century ago and the way they relate today. Unlike my father, who thinks Mrs. Mallard is too passive, my grandmother believes that Mrs. Mallard doesn't even know that she is feeling repressed until after she is told that Brently is dead. In 1894, divorce was so scandalous and stigmatized that it simply wouldn't have been an option for Mrs. Mallard, and so her only way "out" of the marriage would have been one of their deaths. Being relatively young, Mrs. Mallard probably considered herself doomed to a long life in an unhappy marriage. My grandmother also feels that, in spite of all we know of Mrs. Mallard's feelings about her husband and her marriage, she still manages to live up to everyone's expectations of her as a woman both in life and in death. She is a dutiful wife to Brently, as she is expected to be, she weeps "with sudden, wild abandonment" (18) when she hears the news of his death, she locks herself in her room to cope with her new situation, and she has a fatal heart attack upon seeing her husband arrive home. Naturally the male doctors would

Villa 4

think that she died of the "joy that kills" (20); nobody
could have guessed that she was unhappy with her life,
and she would never have wanted them to know.

Interpretations of "The Story of an Hour" seem to
vary according to the gender, age, and experience of the
reader. While both male and female readers can certainly
sympathize with Mrs. Mallard's plight, female readers--as
was evident in our class discussions--seem to relate more
easily to her predicament and are quicker to exonerate
her of any responsibility for her unhappy situation. Conversely, male readers are more likely to feel compassion
for Mr. Mallard, who loses his wife for reasons that will
always remain entirely unknown to him. Older readers
probably understand more readily the strength of social
forces and the difficulty of trying to deny societal
expectations concerning gender roles in general and marriage in particular. Younger readers seem to feel that
Mrs. Mallard is too passive and that she could have improved her domestic life immeasurably if she had taken
the initiative to either improve or end her relationship
with her husband. Ultimately, how each individual reader
responds to Mrs. Mallard's story reveals his or her own
ideas about marriage, society, and how men and women communicate with each other.

2

Writing and Revising

FROM READING TO WRITING

There's no question about it: Writing about literature is a different experience than reading it. The novelist William Styron amply concedes that writing to him is not so much about pleasure as it is about work: "Let's face it, writing is hell." Although Styron's lament concerns his own feelings about writing prose fiction, he no doubt speaks for many other writers, including essayists. Writing is, of course, work, but it is also a pleasure when it goes well—when ideas feel solid and the writing is fluid. You can experience that pleasure as well, if you approach writing as an intellectual and emotional opportunity rather than merely a sentence.

Just as reading literature requires an imaginative, conscious response, so does writing about literature. Composing an essay is not just recording your interpretive response to a work because the act of writing can change your response as you explore, clarify, and discover relationships you hadn't previously considered or recognized. Most writers discover new ideas and connections as they move through the process of rereading and annotating the text, taking notes, generating ideas, choosing a topic, developing a thesis, and organizing an argumentative essay. To become more conscious of the writing process, read the following discussion about composing a paper on a literary topic. If you approach this kind of writing assignment systematically and confidently, the work will be more manageable and less mysterious. Then examine the student casebook on developing and revising a thesis; this offers a student's efforts to choose a topic and create a thesis for a paper about David Updike's short story "Summer."

CHOOSING A TOPIC

If your instructor assigns a topic or offers a choice from among an approved list of topics, some of your work is already completed. Instead of being asked to come up with a topic about *Oedipus the King,* you may be asked to write a three-page essay that specifically discusses whether Oedipus's downfall is a result of fate or foolish pride. You also have the assurance that a specified topic will be manageable within the suggested number of pages. Unless you ask your instructor for permission to write on a different or related topic, be certain to address yourself to the assignment. An essay that does not discuss Oedipus's downfall but instead describes his efforts to save Thebes would be missing the point. Notice too that there is room even in an assigned topic to develop your own approach. One question that immediately comes to mind is whether Oedipus is simply a predestined pawn or personally responsible for the suffering and death in the play. Assigned topics do not relieve you of thinking about an aspect of a work, but they do focus your thinking.

At some point during the course, you may have to begin an essay from scratch. You might, for example, be asked to write about a short story that somehow impressed you or that seemed particularly well written or filled with insights. Before you start considering a topic, you should have a sense of how long the paper will be because the assigned length can help to determine the extent to which you should develop your topic. Ideally, the paper's length should be based on how much space you deem necessary to present your discussion clearly and convincingly, but if you have any doubts and no specific guidelines have been indicated, ask. The question is important; a topic that might be appropriate for a three-page paper could be too narrow for ten pages. Three pages would probably be adequate for a discussion of why Emily murders Homer in Faulkner's "A Rose for Emily." Conversely, it would be futile to try to summarize Faulkner's use of the South in his fiction in even ten pages; this would have to be narrowed to something like "Images of the South in 'A Rose for Emily.'" Be sure that the topic you choose can be adequately covered in the assigned number of pages.

Once you have a firm sense of how much you are expected to write, you can begin to decide on your topic. If you are to choose what work to write about, select one that genuinely interests you. Too often students pick a story, poem, play, or essay because it is mercifully short or seems simple. Such works can certainly be the subjects of fine essays, but simplicity should not be the major reason for selecting them. Choose a work that has moved you so that you have something to say about it.

Brainstorming

One means of discovering what you want to say about a work is called *brainstorming.* This technique consists of listing ideas as they come to you as you read or immediately after your reading. A student working on John

Updike's "A & P" (p. 981) quickly listed a series of impressions produced by her reading:

— *sound of cash registers*

— *girls in bathing suits*

— *all kinds of shoppers, young and old*

— *narrator looks at girls*

— *aisles of groceries*

— *manager's rules and store policy*

— *working at A & P is a horrible job*

— *Sammy quits because he's had it with the rules*

— *he doesn't know what his parents will think or what happens next*

This list prompted the student to see that she was responding most to the A & P itself—the story's setting. This was hardly surprising since she was initially attracted to the story's title because she had once worked in a similar store. After reading the story and doing some brainstorming, she became fascinated with its setting, because Updike's descriptions seemed so accurate. Her paper then grew out of her curiosity about the setting's purpose. When a writer is engaged in a topic, the paper has a better chance of being interesting to a reader.

After you have settled on a particular work, your notes and annotations of the text should prove useful for generating a topic. The paper entitled "The A & P as a State of Mind" (p. 1091) developed naturally from the notes that the student jotted down about the setting and antagonist. If you think with a pen in your hand, you are likely to find when you review your notes that your thoughts have clustered into one or more topics. Perhaps there are patterns of imagery that seem to make a point about life. There may be scenes that are ironically paired or secondary characters who reveal certain qualities about the protagonist. Your notes and annotations on such aspects can lead you to a particular effect or impression. Having chuckled your way through "A & P," you may discover that your notations about the story's humor point to a serious satire of society's values.

DEVELOPING A THESIS

When you are satisfied that you have something interesting to say about a work and that your notes have led you to a focused topic, you can formulate a **thesis,** the central idea of the paper. Whereas the topic indicates what the paper focuses on (the setting in "A & P"), the thesis explains what you have to say about the topic (because the intolerant setting of

persuasion. In developing a thesis, remember that you are expected not merely to present information but to argue a point.

ARGUING ABOUT LITERATURE

An argumentative essay is designed to make persuasive your interpretation of a work. Arguing about literature doesn't mean that you're engaged in an angry, antagonistic dispute (though controversial topics do sometimes engender heated debates; see, for example, Joan Templeton's comments in the casebook on Ibsen's *A Doll House* [p. 767]). Instead, argumentation requires that you present your interpretation of a work (or a portion of it) by supporting your discussion with clearly defined terms, ample evidence, and a detailed analysis of relevant portions of the text.

If you have a choice, it's generally best to write about a topic that you feel strongly about. If you're not fascinated by Bartleby the Scrivener's haunting presence in Melville's short story, then perhaps you'll find chilling Emily Grierson's behavior in Faulkner's "A Rose for Emily," or maybe you can explain why Bartleby's character is so excruciatingly boring to you. If your essay is to be interesting and convincing, what is important is that it be written from a strong point of view that persuasively argues your evaluation, analysis, and interpretation of a work. It is not enough to say that you like or dislike a work; instead you must give your reader some ideas and evidence that can be accepted or rejected based on the quality of the answers to the questions you raise.

One way to come up with persuasive answers is to generate good questions that will lead you further into the text and to critical issues related to it. Notice how the Considerations for Critical Thinking and Writing in this anthology raise significant questions and issues about texts from a variety of points of view. The critical strategies for reading summarized in Chapter 3 can be a resource for raising questions that can be shaped into an argument, and the Questions for Writing: Incorporating Secondary Sources (p. 123) can help you to incorporate a critic's perspective into your own argument. Moreover, the lists of questions for the critical approaches covered in Chapter 3 should be useful for discovering arguments you might make about a short story, poem, play, or essay.

ORGANIZING A PAPER

Using the Thesis as an Organizing Principle

After you have chosen a manageable topic and developed a thesis, a central idea about it, you can begin to organize your paper. Your thesis, even if it is still somewhat tentative, should help you decide what information will need to be included and provide you with a sense of direction.

Consider again the sample thesis in the section on developing a thesis:

On the surface, "To His Coy Mistress" is a celebration of the pleasures of the flesh, but this witty seduction is tempered by a chilling recognition of the reality of death.

This thesis indicates that the paper can be divided into two parts — the pleasures of the flesh and the reality of death. It also indicates an order: because the central point is to show that the poem is more than a simple celebration, the pleasures of the flesh should be discussed first so that another, more complex, reading of the poem can follow. If the paper began with the reality of death, its point would be anticlimactic.

Having established such a broad and informal outline, you can draw on your underlinings, margin notations, and note cards for the subheadings and evidence required to explain the major sections of your paper. This next level of detail might look something like the following:

1. Pleasures of the flesh
   Part of the traditional tone of love poetry
2. Recognition of death
   Ironic treatment of love
      Diction
      Images
      Figures of speech
      Symbols
      Tone

This list was initially a jumble of terms, but the student arranged the items so that each of the two major sections leads to a discussion of tone. (The student also found it necessary to drop some biographical information from his notes because it was irrelevant to the thesis.) The list indicates that the first part of the paper will establish the traditional tone of love poetry that celebrates the pleasures of the flesh, while the second part will present a more detailed discussion about the ironic recognition of death. The emphasis is on the latter because that is the point to be argued in the paper. Hence, the thesis has helped to organize the parts of the paper, establish an order, and indicate the paper's proper proportions.

The next step is to fill in the subheadings with information from your notes. Many experienced writers find that making lists of information to be included under each subheading is an efficient way to develop paragraphs. For a longer paper (perhaps a research paper), you should be able to develop a paragraph or more on each subheading. On the other hand, a shorter paper may require that you combine several subheadings in a paragraph. You may also discover that while an informal list is adequate for a brief paper, a ten-page assignment could require a more detailed outline. Use the method that is most productive for you. Whatever the length of the essay, your presentation must be in a coherent and logical order that allows your reader to follow the argument and evaluate the evidence. The quality of your reading can be demonstrated only by the quality of your writing.

WRITING A DRAFT

The time for sharpening pencils, arranging your desk, and doing almost anything else instead of writing has ended. The first draft will appear on the page only if you stop avoiding the inevitable and sit, stand up, or lie down to write. It makes no difference how you write, just so you do. Now that you have developed a topic into a tentative thesis, you can assemble your notes and begin to flesh out whatever outline you have made.

Be flexible. Your outline should smoothly conduct you from one point to the next, but do not permit it to railroad you. If a relevant and important idea occurs to you now, work it into the draft. By using the first draft as a means of thinking about what you want to say, you will very likely discover more than your notes originally suggested. Plenty of good writers don't use outlines at all but discover ordering principles as they write. Do not attempt to compose a perfectly correct draft the first time around. Grammar, punctuation, and spelling can wait until you revise. Concentrate on what you are saying. Good writing most often occurs when you are in hot pursuit of an idea rather than in a nervous search for errors.

To make revising easier, leave wide margins and extra space between lines so that you can easily add words, sentences, and corrections. Write on only one side of the paper. Your pages will be easier to keep track of that way, and, if you have to clip a paragraph to place it elsewhere, you will not lose any writing on the other side.

Using a Word Processor

If you are working on a word processor, you can take advantage of its capacity to make additions and deletions as well as move entire paragraphs by making just a few simple keyboard commands. Some software programs can also check spelling and certain grammatical elements in your writing. It's worth remembering, however, that though a clean copy fresh off a printer may look terrific, it will read only as well as the thinking and writing that have gone into it. Prudent writers store their data on disks and print their pages each time they finish a draft to avoid losing any material because of power failures or other problems. These printouts are also easier to read than the screen when you work on revisions.

Once you have a first draft on paper, you can delete material that is unrelated to your thesis and add material necessary to illustrate your points and make your paper convincing. The student who wrote "The A & P as a State of Mind" wisely dropped a paragraph that questioned whether

Sammy displays chauvinistic attitudes toward women. Although this is an interesting issue, it has nothing to do with the thesis, which explains how the setting influences Sammy's decision to quit his job. Instead of including that paragraph, she added one that described Lengel's crabbed response to the girls so that she could lead up to the A & P "policy" he enforces.

Remember that your initial draft is only that. You should go through the paper many times — and then again — working to substantiate and clarify your ideas. You may even end up with several entire versions of the paper. Rewrite. The sentences within each paragraph should be related to a single topic. Transitions should connect one paragraph to the next so that there are no abrupt or confusing shifts. Whether you're using a pen, typewriter, or word processor, awkward or wordy phrasing or unclear sentences and paragraphs should be mercilessly poked and prodded into shape.

Writing the Introduction and Conclusion

After you have clearly and adequately developed the body of your paper, pay particular attention to the introductory and concluding paragraphs. It's probably best to write the introduction — at least the final version of it — last, after you know precisely what you are introducing. Because this paragraph is crucial for generating interest in the topic, it should engage the reader and provide a sense of what the paper is about. There is no formula for writing effective introductory paragraphs because each writing situation is different — depending on the audience, topic, and approach — but if you pay attention to the introductions of the essays you read, you will notice a variety of possibilities. The introductory paragraph to "The A & P as a State of Mind," for example, is a straightforward explanation of why the story's setting is important for understanding Updike's treatment of the antagonist. The rest of the paper then offers evidence to support this point.

Concluding paragraphs demand equal attention because they leave the reader with a final impression. The conclusion should provide a sense of closure instead of starting a new topic or ending abruptly. In the final paragraph about the significance of the setting in "A & P," the student brings together the reasons Sammy quit his job by referring to his refusal to accept Lengel's store policies. At the same time she makes this point, she also explains the significance of Sammy ringing up the "No Sale" mentioned in her introductory paragraph. Thus, we are brought back to where we began, but we now have a greater understanding of why Sammy quits his job. Of course, the body of your paper is the most important part of your presentation, but do remember that first and last impressions have a powerful impact on readers.

Using Quotations

Quotations can be a valuable means of marshaling evidence to illustrate and support your ideas. A judicious use of quoted material will make your points clearer and more convincing. Here are some guidelines that should help you use quotations effectively.

I. Brief quotations (four lines or fewer of prose or three lines or fewer of poetry) should be carefully introduced and integrated into the text of your paper with quotation marks around them:

> According to the narrator, Bertha "had a reputation for strictness." He tells us that she always "wore dark clothes, dressed her hair simply, and expected contrition and obedience from her pupils."

For brief poetry quotations, use a slash to indicate a division between lines:

> The concluding lines of Blake's "The Tyger" pose a disturbing question: "What immortal hand or eye / Dare frame thy fearful symmetry?"

Lengthy quotations should be separated from the text of your paper. More than three lines of poetry should be double spaced and centered on the page. More than four lines of prose should be double spaced and indented ten spaces from the left margin, with the right margin the same as for the text. Do *not* use quotation marks for the passage; the indentation indicates that the passage is a quotation. Lengthy quotations should not be used in place of your own writing. Use them only if they are absolutely necessary.

2. If any words are added to a quotation, use brackets to distinguish your addition from the original source:

> "He [Young Goodman Brown] is portrayed as self-righteous and disillusioned."

Any words inside quotation marks and not in brackets must be precisely those of the author. Brackets can also be used to change the grammatical structure of a quotation so that it fits into your sentence:

> Smith argues that Chekhov "present[s] the narrator in an ambivalent light."

If you drop any words from the source, use an ellipsis with brackets around it to indicate the omission:

> "Early to bed [. . .] makes a man healthy, wealthy, and wise."

Use an ellipsis following a period to indicate an omission at the end of a sentence (again, with brackets around it):

> "Early to bed and early to rise makes a man healthy.[. . .]"

Use a single line of spaced periods to indicate the omission of a line or more of poetry or more than one paragraph of prose:

> Nothing would sleep in that cellar, dank as a ditch,
> Bulbs broke out of boxes hunting for chinks in the dark,
>
> . . . . .
>
> Nothing would give up life:
> Even the dirt kept breathing a small breath.

3. You will be able to punctuate quoted material accurately and confidently if you observe these conventions.

Place commas and periods inside quotation marks:

> "Even the dirt," Roethke insists, "kept breathing a small breath."

Even though a comma does not appear after "dirt" in the original quotation, it is placed inside the quotation mark. The exception to this rule occurs when a parenthetical reference to a source follows the quotation:

> "Even the dirt," Roethke insists, "kept breathing a small breath" (11).

Punctuation marks other than commas or periods go outside the quotation marks unless they are part of the material quoted:

> What does Roethke mean when he writes that "the dirt kept breathing a small breath"?
>
> Yeats asked, "How can we know the dancer from the dance?"

REVISING AND EDITING

Put some distance — a day or so if you can — between yourself and each draft of your paper. The phrase that seemed just right on Wednesday may be revealed as all wrong on Friday. You'll have a better chance of detecting lumbering sentences and thin paragraphs if you plan ahead and give yourself the time to read your paper from a fresh perspective. Through the process of revision, you can transform a competent paper into an excellent one.

Begin by asking yourself if your approach to the topic requires any rethinking. Is the argument carefully thought out and logically presented? Are there any gaps in the presentation? How well is the paper organized? Do the paragraphs lead into one another? Does the body of the paper deliver what the thesis promises? Is the interpretation sound? Are any relevant and important elements of the work ignored or distorted to advance the thesis? Are the points supported with evidence? These large questions should be addressed before you focus on more detailed matters. If you uncover serious problems as a result of considering these questions, you'll probably have quite a lot of rewriting to do, but at least you will have the opportunity to correct the problems — even if doing so takes several drafts.

A useful technique for spotting awkward or unclear moments in the paper is to read it aloud. You might also try having a friend read it aloud to you. If your handwriting is legible, your friend's reading — perhaps accompanied by hesitations and puzzled expressions — could alert you to passages that need reworking. Having identified problems, you can readily correct them on a word processor or on the draft, provided you've skipped lines and used wide margins. The final draft you hand in should be neat and carefully proofread for any inadvertent errors.

The following checklist offers questions to ask about your paper as you revise and edit it. Most of these questions will be familiar to you; however, if you need help with any of them, ask your instructor or review the appropriate section in a composition handbook.

QUESTIONS FOR WRITING: REVISING

1. Is the topic manageable? Is it too narrow or too broad?
2. Is the thesis clear? Is it based on a careful reading of the work?
3. Is the paper logically organized? Does it have a firm sense of direction?
4. Is your argument persuasive?
5. Should any material be deleted? Do any important points require further illustration or evidence?
6. Does the opening paragraph introduce the topic in an interesting manner?
7. Are the paragraphs developed, unified, and coherent? Are any too short or long?
8. Are there transitions linking the paragraphs?
9. Does the concluding paragraph provide a sense of closure?
10. Is the tone appropriate? Is it unduly flippant or pretentious?
11. Is the title engaging and suggestive?
12. Are the sentences clear, concise, and complete?
13. Are simple, complex, and compound sentences used for variety?
14. Have technical terms been used correctly? Are you certain of the meanings of all the words in the paper? Are they spelled correctly?
15. Have you documented any information borrowed from books, articles, or other sources? Have you quoted too much instead of summarizing or paraphrasing secondary material?
16. Have you used a standard format for citing sources (see p. 111)?
17. Have you followed your instructor's guidelines for the manuscript format of the final draft?
18. Have you carefully proofread the final draft?

Proofreading

Before handing in your paper, be sure to proofread it carefully. A good many potentially excellent papers have been defeated by inadequate proofreading. You may overlook missing words or entire lines simply because you are familiar with your own work. Meticulous proofreading is essential to catch everything from misspelled words to missing pages. Many writers proofread aloud (including the punctuation) to slow themselves down in order to overcome the tendency to see what they intended to write rather than what they've actually written. However you proofread, you can be certain that this crucial final effort will not only spare your reader annoying distractions but also make clear that you think well enough about your ideas to provide a finely tuned vehicle for them.

When you proofread your final draft, you may find a few typographical errors that must be corrected but do not warrant retyping an entire page. Provided there are not more than a handful of such errors throughout the page, they can be corrected as shown in the following passage. This example condenses a short paper's worth of errors; no single passage should be this shabby in your essay:

```
To add a letter or word, use a caret on the line where the
addition is needed. To delete a word draw a single line through
through it. Run-on words are separated by a vertical/line, and
inadvertent spaces are closed like this. Transposed letters
are indicated this way. New paragraphs are noted with the
sign ¶ in front of where the next paragraph is to begin.
¶Unless you . . .
```

These sorts of errors can be minimized by using correction fluids or tapes while you type. If you use a word processor, you can eliminate such errors completely by simply entering corrections on the screen after you have proofread the printed draft.

MANUSCRIPT FORM

The novelist and poet Peter De Vries once observed that he very much enjoyed writing but that he couldn't bear the "paper work." Behind this playful pun is a half-serious impatience with the mechanics of it all. You may feel some of that too, but don't let your thoughtful, carefully revised paper trip over minor details. The final draft you hand in to your instructor should not only read well but look neat. If your instructor does not provide specific instructions concerning the format for the paper, follow these guidelines:

1. Papers (particularly long ones) should be typed on 8½ by 11-inch paper in double space. Avoid thin or transparent paper such as onionskin; it is difficult to read and write comments on. The ribbon should be dark and the letters on the machine clear. If you compose on a word processor with a dot-matrix printer, be certain that the dots are close enough together to be legible. And don't forget to separate your pages and remove the strips of holes on each side of the pages if your printer uses a continuous paper feed. If

your instructor accepts handwritten papers, write legibly in ink on only one side of a wide-lined page.

2. Use a one-inch margin at the top, bottom, and sides of each page. Unless you are instructed to include a separate title page, type your name, instructor's name, course number and section, and date on separate lines one inch below the upper-left corner of the first page. Double space between these lines and then center the title two spaces below the date. Do not underline or put quotation marks around your paper's title, but do use quotation marks around the titles of poems, short stories, or other brief works, and underline the titles of books and plays (for instance, Racial Stereotypes in "Battle Royal" and *Raisin in the Sun*). Begin the text of your paper two spaces below the title. If you have used secondary sources, list them on a separate page at the end of the paper. Center the heading "Notes" or "Works Cited" one inch from the top of the page and then double space between it and the entries.

3. Number each page consecutively, beginning with page 2, a half inch from the top of the page in the upper-right corner.

4. Gather the pages with a paper clip rather than staples, folders, or some other device. That will make it easier for your instructor to handle the paper.

TYPES OF WRITING ASSIGNMENTS

For papers assigned in composition courses that focus on literature, the most common types of assignments are (1) personal response, (2) explication, (3) analysis, (4) comparison and contrast, (5) applying a critical strategy, and (6) writing from sources. Most writing about literature involves some combination of these techniques. Each type of assignment is briefly described below so that you have a clear sense of the range of writing that might be expected of you. In addition, each type of assignment is cross-referenced to a student casebook that provides further discussion and a sample paper that can be used as a model for your own writing.

Personal Response

A personal response paper typically focuses on the reader's reaction to a text as well as the text itself. Recording your initial emotions and ideas about a work can be a valuable method for determining an approach to a work that culminates in a more formal paper for an assigned or unassigned topic. See Writing in Process: Reading and Your First Response (p. 17).

Explication

The purpose of this approach to a literary work is to make the implicit explicit. *Explication* is a detailed explanation of a passage of poetry or prose. Because explication is an intensive examination of a text line by line, it is mostly used to interpret a short poem in its entirety or a brief passage from a long poem, short story, or play. Explication can be used in any kind of paper when you want to be specific about how a writer achieves a certain effect. An explication pays careful attention to language – the connotations of words, allusions, figurative language, irony, symbol, rhythm, sound, and so on. These elements are examined in relation to one another and to the overall effect and meaning of the work.

The simplest way to organize an explication is to move through the passage line by line, explaining whatever seems significant. It is wise to avoid, however, an assembly-line approach that begins each sentence with "In line one (two, three). . . ." Instead, organize your paper in whatever way best serves your thesis. You might find that the right place to start is with the final lines, working your way back to the beginning of the poem or passage.

You might also find it useful to structure a paper by discussing various elements of literature, so that you have a paragraph on connotative words followed by one on figurative language and so on. However your paper is organized, keep in mind that the aim of an explication is not simply to summarize the passage but to comment on the effects and meanings produced by the author's use of language in it. An effective explication (the Latin word *explicare* means "to unfold") displays a text to reveal how it works and what it signifies. Although writing an explication requires some patience and sensitivity, it is an excellent method for coming to understand and appreciate the elements and qualities that constitute literary art.

Analysis

While an explication discusses in detail all the important literary elements in a work and explains how they contribute to the whole, an analysis typically concentrates on a single element such as tone, point of view, image, or rhythm in order to explain how it contributes to the entire work. An analysis focuses on a particular part of the work to determine how it creates meaning for the whole. An analysis of Updike's "A & P," for example, might examine how the setting relates to the entire work, or it might analyze the store manager's character or the narrator's humor. Because analysis is an efficient means of shedding light on an entire work by examining a single important element, it's a particularly useful and frequently assigned type of paper. See Writing in Process: Character Analysis (p. 494).

Comparison and Contrast

Comparison and contrast assignments require you to write about similarities and differences between or within works. You might be asked to discuss the treatment of fathers in Andre Dubus's "Killings" and John Cheever's "Reunion" or Sammy's and Stokesie's attitudes about conformity in John Updike's "A & P." A comparison of either topic would emphasize their similarities, while a contrast would stress their differences. It is possible, of course, to include both perspectives in a paper if you find significant likenesses and differences. A comparison of "Popular Mechanics" and "Reunion" would yield, for example, similarities, because each story describes a father-and-son relationship; however, important differences also exist in the tone and theme of each story that would constitute a contrast. (You should, incidentally, be aware that the term *comparison* is sometimes used inclusively to refer to both similarities and differences. If you are assigned a comparison of two works, be sure that you understand what your instructor's expectations are; you may be required to include both approaches in the essay.)

Choose a topic that encourages you to ask significant questions about each work; the purpose of a comparison or contrast is to understand the works more clearly for having examined them together. Despite the obvious differences between Karen van der Zee's *A Secret Sorrow* and Gail Godwin's "A Sorrowful Woman," the two are closely related if we ask how marriage is treated in each work.

There is no single way to organize comparative papers since each topic is likely to have its own particular issues to resolve, but it is useful to be aware of two basic patterns that can be helpful with a comparison, a contrast, or a combination of both. One method that can be effective for relatively short papers consists of dividing the paper in half, first discussing one work and then the other. Here, for example, is a partial informal outline for a discussion of Updike's "A & P" and Mark Halliday's "Young Man on Sixth Avenue"; the topic is a comparison and contrast: "Sammy and the Young Man as Heroic Figures."

1. Sammy
   a. The nature of the conflict
   b. Strengths and stature
   c. Weaknesses and mistakes
   d. What is learned
2. Young Man
   a. The nature of the conflict
   b. Strengths and stature
   c. Weaknesses and mistakes
   d. What is learned

This organizational strategy can be effective provided that the second part of the paper combines the discussion of the Young Man with references to Sammy so that the thesis is made clear and the paper unified without being repetitive. If the two characters were treated entirely separately, then the discussion would be merely parallel rather than integrated. In a lengthy paper, this organization probably would not work well because a reader would have difficulty remembering the points made in the first half as he or she reads on.

Thus, for a longer paper it is usually better to create a more integrated structure that discusses both works as you take up each item in your outline. Here is the second basic pattern using the elements in the partial outline just cited:

1. The nature of the conflict
   a. Sammy
   b. Young Man
2. Strengths and stature
   a. Sammy
   b. Young Man
3. Weaknesses and mistakes
   a. Sammy
   b. Young Man
4. What is learned
   a. Sammy
   b. Young Man

This pattern allows you to discuss any number of topics without requiring that your reader recall what you first said about the conflict Sammy confronts before you discuss the Young Man's conflicts fifteen pages later. However you structure your comparison or contrast paper, make certain that a reader can follow its elements and keep track of its thesis. See Writing in Process: Comparison and Contrast (p. 175).

Applying a Critical Strategy

There are many ways to write about a literary work. A wide variety of contemporary theoretical approaches exist: among them are formalist, biographical, psychological, historical (including literary history criticism, new historicist criticism, and cultural criticism), gender strategies (including feminist criticism and gay and lesbian criticism), mythological, reader-response, and deconstructionist approaches. Applying a critical strategy to a work allows you to explain more consciously and clearly how your perspective helps to inform your discussion of a text. A historical approach to Updike's "A & P," for example, might reveal how life in a small New England town in the early 1960s is revealed in the story and helps set the tone for the story. A feminist approach to the same work would offer a very different lens through which you read the story. Perhaps a feminist critic would emphasize how Sammy's character reveals particular kinds of male assumptions about women in our culture. Being aware of the critical approach you take allows you to understand how different readings of the same text can be both valid and intriguing. See Chapter 3 and its Writing in Process: Critical Analysis (p. 83).

Writing from Sources

Papers that draw upon commentary by critics and scholars to help shed light on a work are research papers. Writing from sources involves not only the text — the primary source — and your own ideas about it but also information, comments, and interpretations — secondary sources — that are incorporated into your paper to support your thesis. Secondary sources can be used to support your own arguments or as a means of clarifying or qualifying their points about the literary work. You don't have to agree with your sources to make use of them in your own argument. In addition to developing a thesis and organizing an argument, a research paper requires that you find, evaluate, document, and incorporate secondary sources. Chapter 4 provides detailed information about these matters; see also Writing in Process: The Research Paper (p. 120).

WRITING IN PROCESS

The Thesis Statement

This casebook offers an example of how one student, Rose Vanderman, arrives at a thesis for an assigned topic on David Updike's short story "Summer," by brainstorming, drafting, and using the Questions for Writing to develop her thesis into a statement that makes a definite claim about a specific idea and provides a clear sense of direction for the paper to come. As you read "Summer," think about what you would want to say about the relationship—or lack thereof—between Homer and Sandra.

DAVID UPDIKE (B. 1957)

Born in Ipswich, Massachusetts, David Updike is the son of John Updike. David received his B.A. in art history at Harvard and his M.A. from Teachers College, Columbia University. His acclaimed children's books include *An Autumn Tale* (1988), *A Spring Story* (1989), *Seven Times Eight* (1990), *The Sounds of Summer* (1993), and *A Helpful Alphabet of Friendly Objects* (1998), which he co-authored with his father. "Summer," a poignant tale for adults, is part of *Out on the Marsh: Stories* (1988), a collection of his short fiction; his short stories have also appeared in *The New Yorker*. Updike resides in Cambridge, Massachusetts.

Summer   1985

It was the first week in August, the time when summer briefly pauses, shifting between its beginning and its end: the light had not yet begun to change, the leaves were still full and green on the trees, the nights were still warm. From the woods and fields came the hiss of crickets; the line of distant mountains was still dulled by the edge of summer haze, the echo of fireworks was replaced by the rumble of thunder and the hollow premonition of school, too far off to imagine though dimly, dully felt. His senses were consumed by the joy of their own fulfillment: the satisfying swat of a tennis ball, the dappled damp and light of the dirt road after rain, the alternating sensations of sand, mossy stone, and pine needles under bare feet. His days were spent in the adolescent pursuit of childhood pleasures: tennis, a haphazard round of golf, a variant of baseball adapted to the local geography: two pine trees as foul poles, a broomstick as the bat, the apex of the small, secluded house the dividing line between home runs and outs. On rainy days they swatted bottle tops across the living room floor, and at night vented budding cerebral energy with games of chess thoughtfully played over glasses of iced tea. After dinner they would paddle the canoe to the middle of the lake, and drift beneath the vast, blue-black dome of sky, looking at the stars and speaking softly in tones which, with the waning summer, became increasingly philosophical: the sky's blue vastness, the distance and magnitude of stars, an endless succession of numbers, gave way to a rising sensation of infinity, eternity, an imagined universe with no bounds. But the sound of the paddle hitting against the side of the canoe, the faint shadow of surrounding mountains, the cry of a nocturnal bird brought them back to the happy, cloistered finity of their world, and they paddled slowly home and went to bed.

Homer woke to the slant and shadow of a summer morning, dressed in their shared cabin, and went into the house where Mrs. Thyme sat alone, looking out across the flat blue stillness of the lake. She poured him a cup of coffee and they quietly talked, and it was then that his happiness seemed most tangible. In this summer month with the Thymes, freed from the complications of his own family, he had released himself to them and, as interim member — friend, brother, surrogate son — he lived in a blessed realm between two worlds.

From the cool darkness of the porch, smelling faintly of moldy books and kerosene and the tobacco of burning pipes, he sat looking through the screen to the lake, shimmering beneath the heat of a summer afternoon: a dog lay sleeping in the sun, a bird hopped along a swaying branch, sunlight came in through the trees and collapsed on the sandy soil beside a patch of moss, or mimicked the shade and cadence of stones as they stepped to the edge of a lake where small waves lapped a damp rock and washed onto a sandy shore. An inverted boat lay decaying under a tree, a drooping American flag hung from its gnarled pole, a haphazard dock started out across the cove toward distant islands through which the white triangle of a sail silently moved.

The yellowed pages of the book from which he occasionally read swam before him: ". . . Holmes clapped the hat upon his head. It came right over the forehead and settled on the bridge of his nose. 'It is a question of cubic capacity' said he . . ." Homer looked up. The texture of the smooth, unbroken air was cleanly divided by the sound of a slamming door, echoing up into the woods around him. Through the screen he watched Fred's sister Sandra as she came ambling down the path, stepping lightly between the stones in her bare feet. She held a towel in one hand, a book in the other, and wore a pair of pale blue shorts — faded relics of another era. At the end of the dock she stopped, raised her hands above her head, stretching, and then sat down. She rolled over onto her stomach and, using the book as a pillow, fell asleep.

Homer was amused by the fact, that although she did this every day, she 5 didn't get any tanner. When she first came in her face was faintly flushed, and there was a pinkish line around the snowy band where her bathing suit strap had been, but the back of her legs remained an endearing, pale white, the color of eggshells, and her back acquired only the softest, brownish blur. Sometimes she kept her shoes on, other times a shirt, or sweater, or just collapsed onto the seat of the boat, her pale eyelids turned upward toward the pale sun; and as silently as she arrived, she would leave, walking back through the stones with the same, casual sway of indifference. He would watch her, hear the distant door slam, the shower running in the far corner of the house. Other times he would just look up and she would be gone.

On the tennis court she was strangely indifferent to his heroics. When the crucial moment arrived — Homer serving in the final game of the final set — the match would pause while she left, walking across the court, stopping to call the dog, swaying out through the gate. Homer watched her as she went down the path, and, impetus suddenly lost, he double faulted, stroked a routine backhand over the back fence, and the match was over.

When he arrived back at the house she asked him who won, but didn't seem to hear his answer. "I wish I could go sailing," she said, looking distractedly out over the lake.

At night, when he went out to the cottage where he and Fred slept, he could see her through the window as she lay on her bed, reading, her arm folded beneath her head like a leaf. Her nightgown, pulled and buttoned to her chin, pierced him with a regret that had no source or resolution, and its imagined texture floated in the air above him as he lay in bed at night, suspended in the surrounding darkness, the scent of pine, the hypnotic cadence of his best friend's breathing.

Was it that he had known her all his life, and as such had grown up in the shadow of her subtle beauty? Was it the condensed world of the lake, the silent reverence of surrounding woods, mountains, which heightened his sense of her and brought the warm glow of her presence into soft, amorous focus? She had the hair of a baby, the freckles of a child, and the sway of motherhood. Like his love, her beauty rose up in the world which spawned and nurtured it, and found in the family the medium in which it thrived, and in Homer distilled to a pure distant longing for something he had never had.

One day they climbed a mountain, and as the components of family and 10 friends strung out along the path on their laborious upward hike, he found himself tromping along through the woods with her with nobody else in sight. Now and then they would stop by a stream, or sit on a stump, or stone, and he would speak to her, and then they would set off again, he following her. But in the end this day exhausted him, following her pale legs and tripping sneakers over the ruts and stones and a thousand roots, all the while trying to suppress a wordless, inarticulate passion, and the last mile or so he left her, sprinting down the path in a reckless, solitary release, howling into the woods around him. He was lying on the grass, staring up into the patterns of drifting clouds when she came ambling down. "Wher'd you go? I thought I'd lost you," she said, and sat heavily down in the seat of the car. On the ride home, his elbow hopelessly held in the warm crook of her arm, he resolved to release his love, give it up, on the grounds that it was too disruptive to his otherwise placid life. But in the days to follow he discovered that his resolution had done little to change her, and her life went on its oblivious, happy course without him.

His friendship with Fred, meanwhile, continued on its course of athletic and boyhood fulfillment. Alcohol seeped into their diet, and an occasional cigarette, and at night they would drive into town, buy two enormous cans of Australian beer and sit at a small cove by the lake, talking. One night on the ride home Fred accelerated over a small bridge, and as the family station wagon left the ground their heads floated up to the ceiling, touched, and then came crashing down as the car landed and Fred wrestled the car back onto course. Other times they would take the motorboat out onto the lake and make sudden racing turns around buoys, sending a plume of water into the air and everything in the boat crashing to one side. But always with these adventures Homer felt a pang of absence, and was always relieved when they headed back toward the familiar cove, and home.

As August ran its merciless succession of beautiful days, Sandra drifted in and out of his presence in rising oscillations of sorrow and desire. She worked at a bowling alley on the other side of the lake, and in the evening Homer and Fred would drive the boat over, bowl a couple of strings, and wait for her to get off work. Homer sat at the counter and watched her serve up sloshing cups of coffee, secretly loathing the leering gazes of whiskered truck drivers, and loving her oblivious, vacant stare in answer, hip cocked, hand on counter, gazing up into the neon air above their heads. When she was finished, they would pile into the boat and skim through darkness the four or five miles home, and it was then, bundled beneath sweaters and blankets, the white hem of her waitressing dress showing through the darkness, their hair swept in the wind and their voices swallowed by the engine's slow, steady growl, that he felt most powerless to her attraction. As the boat rounded corners he would close his eyes and release himself to gravity, his body's warmth swaying into hers, guising his attraction in the thin veil of centrifugal force. Now and then he would lean into the floating strands of her hair and speak into her fragrance, watching her smile swell in the pale half-light of the moon, the umber glow of the boat's rear light, her laughter spilling backward over the swirling "V" of wake.

Into the humid days of August a sudden rain fell, leaving the sky a hard, unbroken blue and the nights clear and cool. In the morning when he woke, leaving Fred a heap of sighing covers in his bed, he stepped out into the first rays of sunlight that came through the branches of the trees and sensed, in the cool vapor that rose from damp pine needles, the piercing cry of a blue jay, that something had changed. That night as they ate dinner—hamburgers and squash and corn-on-the-cob—everyone wore sweaters, and as the sun set behind the undulating line of distant mountains—burnt, like a filament of summer into his blinking eyes—it was with an autumnal tint, a reddish glow. Several days later the tree at the end of the point bloomed with a sprig of russet leaves, one or two of which occasionally fell, and their lives became filled with an unspoken urgency. Life of summer went on in the silent knowledge that, with the slow, inexorable seepage of an hourglass, it was turning into fall. Another mountain was climbed, annual tennis matches were arranged and played. Homer and Fred became unofficial champions of the lake by trouncing the elder Dewitt boys, unbeaten in several years. "Youth, youth," glum Billy

Dewitt kept saying over iced tea afterward, in jest, though Homer could tell he was hiding some greater sense of loss.

And the moment, the conjunction of circumstance that, through the steady exertion of will, minor adjustments of time and place, he had often tried to induce, never happened. She received his veiled attentions with a kind of amused curiosity, as if smiling back on innocence. One night they had been the last ones up, and there was a fleeting, shuddering moment before he stepped through the woods to his cabin and she went to her bed that he recognized, in a distant sort of way, as the moment of truth. But to touch her, or kiss her, seemed suddenly incongruous, absurd, contrary to something he could not put his finger on. He looked down at the floor and softly said goodnight. The screen door shut quietly behind him and he went out into the darkness and made his way through the unseen sticks and stones, and it was only then, tripping drunkenly on a fallen branch, that he realized he had never been able to imagine the moment he distantly longed for.

The Preacher gave a familiar sermon about another summer having run its course, the harvest of friendship reaped, and a concluding prayer that, "God willing, we will all meet again in June." That afternoon Homer and   15
Fred went sailing, and as they swept past a neighboring cove Homer saw in its sullen shadows a girl sitting alone in a canoe, and in an eternal, melancholy signal of parting, she waved to them as they passed. And there was something in the way that she raised her arm which, when added to the distant impression of her fullness, beauty, youth, filled him with longing as their boat moved inexorably past, slapping the waves, and she disappeared behind a crop of trees.

The night before they were to leave they were all sitting in the living room after dinner — Mrs. Thyme sewing, Fred folded up with the morning paper, Homer reading on the other end of the couch where Sandra was lying — when the dog leapt up and things shifted in such a way that Sandra's bare foot was lightly touching Homer's back. Mrs. Thyme came over with a roll of newspaper, hit the dog on the head and he leapt off. But to Homer's surprise Sandra's foot remained, and he felt, in the faint sensation of exerted pressure, the passive emanation of its warmth, a distant signal of acquiescence. And as the family scene continued as before it was with the accompanying drama of Homer's hand, shielded from the family by a haphazard wall of pillows, migrating over the couch to where, in a moment of breathless abandon, settled softly on the cool hollow of her arch. She laughed at something her mother had said, her toe twitched, but her foot remained. It was only then, in the presence of the family, that he realized she was his accomplice, and that, though this was as far as it would ever go, his love had been returned.

CONSIDERATIONS FOR CRITICAL THINKING AND WRITING

1. FIRST RESPONSE. How do you respond to this love story? Would the story be more satisfying if Homer and Sandra openly acknowledged their feelings for each other and kissed at the end? Why or why not?

2. What details in the first paragraph evoke particular feelings about August? What sort of mood is created by these details?

3. How is Homer's attraction to Sandra made evident in paragraphs 5 through 9?

4. Why do you think August is described as a "merciless succession of beautiful days" (para. 12)?

5. Analyze the images in paragraph 13 that evoke the impending autumn. What does Billy Dewitt's lament about "youth, youth" add to this description?

6. Discuss the transition between paragraphs 14 and 15. How is the mood effectively changed between the night and the next day?

7. What effect does Homer's friendship with Fred and his relationship with the Thyme family have on your understanding of his reticent attraction to Sandra?

8. What, if any, significance can you attach to the names of Homer, Sandra, Thyme, and the Dewitt boys?

9. How successful do you think Updike is in evoking youthful feeling about summer in this story? Explain why you responded positively or negatively to this evocation of summer.

Did you come up with a paper topic as you read "Summer"? Annotating the text and brainstorming are both good ways to identify moments in a text that you will feel moved to write about, if your instructor does not assign a paper topic to you. Even after you come up with a topic—say, the relationship between Homer and Sandra—you still need to turn it into a thesis. The following questions should prove useful in choosing a topic that you can develop into a thesis, the central idea of your paper. As you become increasingly engaged in your topic, you're likely to discover and perhaps change your ideas, so at the beginning stages it's best to regard your thesis as tentative. This will allow you to remain open to unexpected insights along the way.

QUESTIONS FOR WRITING: DEVELOPING A TOPIC INTO A REVISED THESIS

1. If the topic is assigned, have you specifically addressed the prescribed subject matter?

2. If you choose your own topic, have you used your annotations, notes, and first response writing to help you find a suitable topic?

3. Is the topic too broad or too narrow? Is the topic focused enough to be feasible and manageable for the assigned length of the paper?

4. Is the topic too difficult or specialized for you to write about successfully? If you need information and expertise that goes well beyond the scope of the assignment, would it be better to choose another topic?

5. Is the topic too simple or obvious to allow you to develop a strong thesis?

6. Once you have focused your topic, what do you think you want to say about it? What is the central idea—the tentative thesis—of the paper?

7. Have you asked questions about the topic to help generate a thesis?

8. Have you tried brainstorming or freewriting as a means of producing ideas that would lead to a thesis?

9. Have you tried writing a rough outline or simply jotting down ideas to see if your tentative thesis can be supported or qualified and made firmer?

10. Is your thesis statement precise or vague? What is the central argument that your thesis makes?

11. Does the thesis help provide an organizing principle — a sense of direction — for the paper?

12. Does the thesis statement consist of one or more complete declarative sentences (not framed as a question) written in clear language that express a complete idea?

13. Is the thesis supported by specific references to the text you are discussing? Have you used brief quotations to illustrate important points and provide evidence for the argument?

14. Is everything included in the paper in some way related to the thesis? Should any sentences or paragraphs be deleted because they are irrelevant to the central point?

15. Does the thesis appear in the introductory paragraph? If not, is there a particular reason for including it later in the paper?

16. If during the course of writing the paper you shifted direction or changed your mind about its central point, have you revised (or completely revamped) your thesis to reflect that change?

17. Have you developed a thesis that genuinely interests you? Are you interested enough in the thesis to write a paper that will also engage your reader?

A Sample of Brainstorming

After Rose has read carefully the story twice, she is ready to start working on turning the assigned topic into a defined thesis. Her instructor asked the class to answer the first question in the Considerations for Critical Thinking and Writing: *Would the story be more satisfying if Homer and Sandra openly acknowledged their feelings for each other and kissed at the end?* Rose uses the technique of brainstorming to come up with a more specific approach to the topic, trying to think carefully about elements of the story like plot, setting, and action.

— *plot with subtle drama — why?*

— *"blessed realm between two worlds" — adolescence, the school years, real home-life (Homer with another family), state of desire before culmination*

— *setting: tranquil, idyllic, familiar, warm, unabrasive, "happy, cloistered finity of their world" — unthreatening, known; things happen as they're expected to; navigable, happy*

— *action: regular, familiar, relatively uneventful, savoring state of vague desire*

A Sample First Thesis

Reviewing her brainstorming list, Rose sees a connection between the plot and the setting that helps her to address the question and to draft a thesis.

```
David Updike's short story "Summer" is a love story with
little drama or complication. This lack of action in the plot
is mirrored by Updike's rendering of the setting and general
atmosphere, which are evoked by the description of the pictur-
esque cabin on a lake, the season of summer, and the symbolic
"season" of adolescence. The fact that there is no great culmi-
nation to Homer's reticent attraction to Sandra is not a fail-
ure of the characters or of the fiction's drama. Instead, this
nearly actionless plot captures and reflects the sense of ado-
lescence and summer as a state of protected happiness.
```

A Sample Revised Thesis

After this initial attempt at a thesis, Rose asks herself several of the Questions for Writing on pages 52–53 and writes out her responses, realizing along the way how she needs to revise her thesis.

Is the topic (that the action reflects the setting to create a sense of "happy, cloistered finity") too simple? I could discuss whether the story succeeds in creating this sense. It does — through description of setting and of Homer's thoughts.

Is the thesis statement precise? Not quite; I think I need to say in the thesis what would be appealing about "between two worlds." Updike describes it in positive tones, but suggests with the word "cloistered" that there's something they're closing themselves away from, implies there's a world outside. Why is the cloistered state happy and blessed? (I should also comment on the religious terminology, but maybe not in the thesis statement, since it's not the most important descriptive technique in the story.)

Does my thesis offer a direction for the paper, an organizing principle? I think that if I add onto the last sentence something about why the "realm between two worlds" is blessed, I'd be able to organize the paper as a discussion moving between action and setting to argue that the lack of action isn't a failure but a kind of fulfillment or contentment.

Is the thesis supported by specific references to the text you are discussing? Instead of saying "protected happiness" I should use one of the quotes I've been mentioning: "the happy, cloistered finity of their world" (para. 1) and "a blessed realm between two worlds" (para. 2).

David Updike's short story "Summer" involves little action or complication, but this lack of action in the plot is made meaningful by the rendering of the idyllic setting. Combined, these create a particular sense of summer, the symbolic "season" of adolescence, and of adolescent love. The fact that there is no great culmination to Homer's reticent attraction to Sandra is not a failure of the characters or of the plot. Instead, this nearly actionless plot captures and reflects the sense of adolescence and summer as a "blessed realm between two worlds" (para. 2), in which the characters are relatively free of the constraints of more complex adult relationships but may enjoy something of adult consciousness of feeling.

Compare the two thesis statements. Does the revised version seem more effective to you? Why or why not? Can you think of ways of further improving the revised version?

3

Applying a Critical Strategy

CRITICAL THINKING

Maybe this has happened to you: The assignment is to write an analysis of some aspect of a work — let's say, Nathaniel Hawthorne's *The Scarlet Letter* — that interests you and takes into account critical sources that comment on and interpret the work. You cheerfully begin research in the library but quickly find yourself bewildered by several seemingly unrelated articles. The first traces the thematic significance of images of light and darkness in the novel; the second makes a case for Hester Prynne as a liberated woman; the third argues that Arthur Dimmesdale's guilt is a projection of Hawthorne's own emotions; and the fourth analyzes the introduction, "The Custom-House," as an attack on bourgeois values. These disparate treatments may seem random and capricious — a confirmation of your worst suspicions that interpretations of literature are hit-or-miss excursions into areas that you know little about or didn't know even existed. But if you understand that the four articles are written from four different perspectives — formalist, feminist, psychological, and Marxist — and that the purpose of each is to enhance your understanding of the novel by discussing a particular element of it, then you can see that the articles' varying strategies represent potentially interesting ways of opening up the text that might otherwise never have occurred to you. There are many ways to approach a text, and a useful first step is to develop a sense of direction, an understanding of how a perspective — your own or a critic's — shapes a discussion of a text.

This chapter offers an introduction to critical approaches to literature by outlining a variety of strategies for reading fiction, poetry, drama, or essays, and the chapter concludes with a student casebook on applying a particular critical strategy to "Barn Burning," a short story by William

Faulkner. These strategies include approaches that have long been practiced by readers who have used, for example, the insights gleaned from biography and history to illuminate literary works as well as more recent approaches, such as those used by gender, reader-response, and deconstructionist critics. Each of these perspectives is sensitive to point of view, symbol, tone, irony, and other literary elements, but each also casts those elements in a special light. The formalist approach emphasizes how the elements within a work achieve their effects, whereas biographical and psychological approaches lead outward from the work to consider the author's life and other writings. Even broader approaches, such as historical and cultural perspectives, connect the work to historic, social, and economic forces. Mythological readings represent the broadest approach because they discuss the cultural and universal responses readers have to a work.

Any given strategy raises its own types of questions and issues while seeking particular kinds of evidence to support itself. An awareness of the assumptions and methods that inform an approach can help you to understand better the validity and value of a given critic's strategy for making sense of a work. More important, such an understanding can widen and deepen the responses of your own reading.

The critical thinking that goes into understanding a professional critic's approach to a work is not foreign to you because you have already used essentially the same kind of thinking to understand the work itself. You have developed skills to produce a literary *analysis* that, for example, describes how a character, symbol, or rhyme scheme supports a theme. These same skills are also useful for reading literary criticism because they allow you to keep track of how the parts of a critical approach create a particular reading of a literary work. When you analyze a story, poem, play, or essay by closely examining how its various elements relate to the whole, your *interpretation* — your articulation of what the work means to you as supported by an analysis of its elements — necessarily involves choosing what you focus on in the work. The same is true of professional critics.

Critical readings presuppose choices in the kinds of materials that are discussed. An analysis of the setting of John Updike's "A & P" (p. 981) would probably focus on the oppressive environment the protagonist associates with the store rather than, say, the economic history of that supermarket chain. (For a student's analysis of the setting in "A & P," see p. 1091.) The economic history of a supermarket chain might be useful to a Marxist critic concerned with how class relations are revealed in "A & P," but for a formalist critic interested in identifying the unifying structures of the story, such information would be irrelevant.

Critics use a wide variety of approaches to analyze and interpret texts. In the casebook on Ibsen's *A Doll House* (Chapter 9), for instance, Carol Strongin Tufts (p. 764) offers a psychoanalytic reading of Nora that characterizes her as a narcissistic personality rather than as a feminist heroine. The criteria she uses to evaluate Nora's behavior are drawn from the language used by the American Psychiatric Association. In contrast, Joan Templeton (p. 767) places Nora in the context of women's rights issues to argue that Nora must be read from a feminist perspective if the essential meaning of the play is to be understood. Each of these critics raises different questions, examines different evidence, and employs different assumptions to interpret Nora's character. Being aware of those differences—teasing them out so that you can see how they lead to competing conclusions—is a useful way to analyze the analysis itself. What is left out of an interpretation is sometimes as significant as what is included. As you read the critics, it's worth reminding yourself that your own critical thinking skills can help you to determine the usefulness of a particular approach.

The following overview of critical strategies for reading is neither exhaustive in the types of critical approaches covered nor complete in its presentation of the complexities inherent in them, but it should help you to develop an appreciation of the intriguing possibilities that attend literary interpretation. The emphasis in this chapter is on ways of thinking about literature rather than on daunting lists of terms, names, and movements. Although a working knowledge of critical schools may be valuable and necessary for a fully informed use of a given critical approach, the aim here is more modest and practical. This chapter is no substitute for the shelves of literary criticism that can be found in your library, but it does suggest how readers using different perspectives organize their responses to texts.

The summaries of critical approaches that follow are descriptive, not evaluative. Each approach has its advantages and limitations. In practice, many critical approaches overlap and complement each other, but those matters are best left to further study. Like literary artists, critics have their personal values, tastes, and styles. The appropriateness of a specific critical approach will depend, at least in part, on the nature of the literary work under discussion as well as on your own sensibilities and experience. However, any approach, if it is to enhance understanding, requires sensitivity, tact, and an awareness of the various literary elements of the text, including, of course, its use of language.

Successful critical approaches avoid eccentric decodings that reveal so-called hidden meanings that are not only hidden but totally absent from the text. Literary criticism attempts, like any valid hypothesis, to account for a phenomenon—the text—without distorting or misrepresenting what it describes.

THE LITERARY CANON: DIVERSITY AND CONTROVERSY

Before looking at the various critical approaches discussed in this chapter, it makes sense to consider first which literature has been traditionally considered worthy of such analysis. The discussion in the Introduction called The Changing Literary Canon (p. 5) may have already alerted you to the fact that in recent years many more works by women, minorities, and writers from around the world have been considered by scholars, critics, and teachers to merit serious study and inclusion in what is known as the literary canon. This increasing diversity has been celebrated by those who believe that multiculturalism taps new sources for the discovery of great literature while raising significant questions about language, culture, and society. At the same time, others have perceived this diversity as a threat to the established, traditional canon of Western culture.

The debates concerning who should be read, taught, and written about have sometimes been acrimonious as well as lively and challenging. Bitter arguments have been waged recently on campuses and in the press over what has come to be called *political correctness.* Two main camps have formed around these debates — liberals and conservatives (the appropriateness of these terms is debatable, but the oppositional positioning is unmistakable). The liberals are said to insist on encouraging tolerant attitudes about race, class, gender, and sexual orientation, and opening up the curriculum to multicultural texts from Asia, Africa, Latin America, and elsewhere. These revisionists, seeking a change in traditional attitudes, are sometimes accused of trying to substitute ideological dogma for reason and truth and to intimidate opposing colleagues and students into silence and acceptance of their politically correct views. The conservatives are also portrayed as ideologues; in their efforts to preserve what they regard as the best from the past, they fail to acknowledge that Western classics, mostly written by white male Europeans, represent only a portion of human experience. These traditionalists are seen as advocating values that are neither universal nor eternal but merely privileged and entrenched. Conservatives are charged with ignoring the political agenda that their values represent and that is implicit in their preference for the works of canonical authors such as Homer, Virgil, Shakespeare, Milton, Tolstoy, and Faulkner. The reductive and contradictory nature of this national debate between liberals and conservatives has been neatly summed up by Katha Pollitt: "Read the conservatives' list and produce a nation of sexists and racists — or a nation of philosopher kings. Read the liberals' list and produce a nation of spiritual relativists — or a nation of open-minded world citizens" ("Canon to the Right of Me . . . ," *The Nation,* Sept. 23, 1991, p. 330).

These troubling and extreme alternatives can be avoided, of course, if the issues are not approached from such absolutist positions. Solutions to these issues cannot be suggested in this limited space, and, no doubt, solutions will evolve over time, but we can at least provide a perspective. Books — regardless of what list they are on — are not likely to unite a fragmented nation or to disunite a unified one. It is perhaps more useful and accurate to see issues of canonicity as reflecting political changes rather than being the primary causes of them. This is not to say that books don't have an impact on readers — that *Uncle Tom's Cabin,* for instance, did not galvanize antislavery sentiments in nineteenth-century America — but that book lists do not by themselves preserve or destroy the status quo.

It's worth noting that the curricula of American universities have always undergone significant and, some would say, wrenching changes. Only a little more than one hundred years ago there was strong opposition to teaching English, as well as other modern languages, alongside programs dominated by Greek and Latin. Only since the 1920s has American literature been made a part of the curriculum, and just five decades ago including twentieth-century writers such as James Joyce, Virginia Woolf, Franz Kafka, and Ernest Hemingway in the curriculum was regarded with raised eyebrows. New voices do not drown out the past; they build on it and eventually become part of the past as newer writers take their place beside them. Neither resistance to change nor a denial of the past will have its way with the canon. Though both impulses are widespread, neither is likely to dominate the other because there are too many reasonable, practical readers and teachers who instead of replacing Shakespeare, Melville, and other canonical writers have supplemented them with neglected writers from Western and other cultures. These readers experience the current debates about the canon not as a binary opposition but as an opportunity to explore important questions about continuity and change in our literature, culture, and society.

FORMALIST STRATEGIES

Formalist critics focus on the formal elements of a work — its language, structure, and tone. A formalist reads literature as an independent work of art rather than as a reflection of the author's state of mind or as a representation of a moment in history. Historic influences on a work, an author's intentions, or anything else outside the work are generally not treated by formalists (this is particularly true of the most famous modern formalists, known as the **New Critics,** who dominated American criticism from the 1940s through the 1960s). Instead, formalists offer intense examinations of the relationship between form and meaning within a work, emphasizing the subtle complexity of how a work is arranged. This kind of close reading pays special attention to what are often described as *intrinsic* matters in a literary work, such as diction, irony, paradox, metaphor, and symbol, as well as larger elements, such as plot, characterization, and narrative technique. Formalists examine how these elements work together to give a coherent shape to a work while contributing to its meaning. The answers to the questions formalists raise about how the shape and effect of a work are related come from the work itself. Other kinds of information that go beyond the text — biography, history, politics, economics, and so on — are typically regarded by formalists as *extrinsic* matters, which are considerably less important than what goes on within the autonomous text.

Poetry especially lends itself to close readings because a poem's relative brevity allows for detailed analyses of nearly all its words and how they achieve their effects. For a student's formalist reading of a sonnet by John Donne, see "The Use of Conventional Metaphors for Death in 'Death Be Not Proud'" (p. 278). Formalist strategies are also useful for analyzing drama and fiction. In his well-known essay "The World of *Hamlet,*" Maynard Mack explores Hamlet's character and predicament by paying close attention to the words and images that Shakespeare uses to build a world in which appearances mask reality and mystery is embedded in scene after scene. Mack points to recurring terms, such as *apparition, seems, assume,* and *put on,* as well as repeated images of acting, clothing, disease, and painting, to indicate the treacherous surface world Hamlet must penetrate to get to the truth. This pattern of deception provides an organizing principle around which Mack offers a reading of the entire play:

> Hamlet's problem, in its crudest form, is simply the problem of the avenger: he must carry out the injunction of the ghost and kill the king. But this problem . . . is presented in terms of a certain kind of world. The ghost's injunction to act becomes so inextricably bound up for Hamlet with the character of the world in which the action must be taken — its mysteriousness, its baffling appearances, its deep consciousness of infection, frailty, and loss — that he cannot come to terms with either without coming to terms with both.

Although Mack places *Hamlet* in the tradition of revenge tragedy, his reading of the play emphasizes Shakespeare's arrangement of language rather than literary history as a means of providing an interpretation that accounts for various elements of the play. Mack's formalist strategy explores how diction reveals meaning and how repeated words and images evoke and reinforce important thematic significances.

For an example of a work in which the shape of the plot serves as the major organizing principle, let's examine Kate Chopin's "The Story of an Hour" (p. 18), a two-page short story that takes only a few minutes to read. With the story fresh in your mind, consider how you might approach it from a formalist perspective. A first reading probably results in surprise at the story's ending: a grieving wife "afflicted with a heart trouble" suddenly dies of a heart attack, not because she's learned that her kind and loving husband has been killed in a terrible train accident but because she discovers that he is very much alive. Clearly, we are faced with an ironic situation since there is such a powerful incongruity between what is expected to happen and what actually happens. A likely formalist strategy for analyzing this story would be to raise questions about the ironic ending. Is this merely a trick ending, or is it a carefully wrought culmination of other elements in the story so that in addition to creating surprise the ending snaps the story shut on an interesting and challenging theme? Formalists value such complexities over simple surprise effects.

A second, closer reading indicates that Chopin's third-person narrator presents the story in a manner similar to Josephine's gentle attempts to break the news about Brently Mallard's death. The story is told in "veiled hints that [reveal] in half concealing." But unlike Josephine, who tries to protect her sister's fragile heart from stress, the narrator seeks to reveal Mrs. Mallard's complex heart. A formalist would look back over the story for signs of the ending in the imagery. Although Mrs. Mallard grieves immediately and unreservedly when she hears about the train disaster, she soon begins to feel a different emotion as she looks out the window at "the tops of trees . . . all aquiver with the new spring life." This symbolic evocation of renewal and rebirth — along with "the delicious breath of rain," the sounds of life in the street, and the birds singing — causes her to feel, in spite of her own efforts to repress her thoughts and emotions, "free, free, free!" She feels alive with a sense of possibility, with a "clear and exalted perception" that she "would live for herself" instead of for and through her husband.

It is ironic that this ecstatic "self-assertion" is interpreted by Josephine as grief, but the crowning irony for this "goddess of Victory" is the doctors' assumption that she dies of joy rather than of the shock of having to abandon her newly discovered self once she realizes her husband is still alive. In the course of an hour, Mrs. Mallard's life is irretrievably changed: her husband's assumed accidental death frees her, but the fact that he lives and all the expectations imposed on her by his continued life kill her. She does, indeed, die of a broken heart, but only Chopin's readers know the real ironic meaning of that explanation.

Although this brief discussion of some of the formal elements of Chopin's story does not describe all there is to say about how they produce an effect and create meaning, it does suggest the kinds of questions, issues, and evidence that a formalist strategy might raise in providing a close reading of the text itself.

BIOGRAPHICAL STRATEGIES

A knowledge of an author's life can help readers understand his or her work more fully. Events in a work might follow actual events in a writer's life just as characters might be based on people known by the author. Ernest Hemingway's "Soldier's Home" (p. 579) is a story about the difficulties of a World War I veteran named Krebs returning to his small hometown in Oklahoma, where he cannot adjust to the pious assumptions of his family and neighbors. He refuses to accept their innocent blindness to the horrors he has witnessed during the war. They have no sense of the brutality of modern life; instead they insist he resume his life as if nothing has happened. There is plenty of biographical evidence to indicate that Krebs's unwillingness to lie about his war experiences reflects Hemingway's own responses on his return to Oak Park, Illinois, in 1919. Krebs, like Hemingway, finds he has to leave the sentimentality, repressiveness, and smug complacency that threaten to render his experiences unreal: "the world they were in was not the world he was in."

An awareness of Hemingway's own war experiences and subsequent disillusionment with his hometown can be readily developed through available biographies, letters, and other works he wrote. Consider, for example, this passage from *By Force of Will: The Life and Art of Ernest Hemingway*, in which Scott Donaldson describes Hemingway's response to World War I:

> In poems, as in [*A Farewell to Arms*], Hemingway expressed his distaste for the first war. The men who had to fight the war did not die well:
>
> > Soldiers pitch and cough and twitch —
> >   All the world roars red and black;
> > Soldiers smother in a ditch,
> >   Choking through the whole attack.
>
> And what did they die for? They were "sucked in" by empty words and phrases —
>
> > King and country,
> > Christ Almighty,
> > And the rest,
> > Patriotism,
> > Democracy,
> > Honor —
>
> which spelled death. The bitterness of these outbursts derived from the distinction Hemingway drew between the men on the line and those who started the wars that others had to fight.

This kind of information can help to deepen our understanding of just how empathetically Krebs is presented in the story. Relevant facts about Hemingway's life will not make "Soldier's Home" a better written story than it is, but such information can make clearer the source of Hemingway's convictions and how his own experiences inform his major concerns as a storyteller.

Some formalist critics — some New Critics, for example — argue that interpretation should be based exclusively on internal evidence rather than on any biographical information outside the work. They argue that it is not possible to determine an author's intention and that the work must stand by itself. Although this is a useful caveat for keeping the work in focus, a reader who finds biography relevant would argue that biography can at the very least serve as a control on interpretation. A reader who, for example, finds Krebs at fault for not subscribing to the values of his hometown would be misreading the story, given both its tone and the biographical information available about the author. Although the narrator never *tells* the reader that Krebs is right or wrong for leaving town, the story's tone sides with his view of things. If, however, someone were to argue otherwise, insisting that the tone is not decisive and that Krebs's position is problematic, a reader familiar with Hemingway's own reactions could refute that argument with a powerful confirmation of Krebs's instincts to withdraw. Hence, many readers find biography useful for interpretation.

However, it is also worth noting that biographical information can complicate a work. Chopin's "The Story of an Hour" presents a repressed wife's momentary discovery of what freedom from her husband might mean to her. She awakens to a new sense of herself when she learns of her husband's death, only to collapse of a heart attack when she sees that he is alive. Readers might be tempted to interpret this story as Chopin's fiction-alized commentary about her own marriage because her husband died twelve years before she wrote the story and seven years before she began writing fiction seriously. Biographers seem to agree, however, that Chopin's marriage was evidently satisfying to her and that she was not oppressed by her husband and did not feel oppressed.

Moreover, consider this diary entry from only one month after Chopin wrote the story (quoted by Per Seyersted in *Kate Chopin: A Critical Biography*):

> If it were possible for my husband and my mother to come back to earth, I feel that I would unhesitatingly give up everything that has come into my life since they left it and join my existence again with theirs. To do that, I would have to forget the past ten years of my growth — my real growth. But I would take back a little wisdom with me; it would be the spirit of perfect acquies-cence.

This passage raises provocative questions instead of resolving them. How does that "spirit of perfect acquiescence" relate to Mrs. Mallard's insis-tence that she "would live for herself"? Why would Chopin be willing to "forget the past ten years of . . . growth" given her protagonist's desire for "self-assertion"? Although these and other questions raised by the diary entry cannot be answered here, this kind of biographical perspective cer-tainly adds to the possibilities of interpretation.

Sometimes biographical information does not change our under-standing so much as it enriches our appreciation of a work. It matters, for instance, that much of John Milton's poetry, so rich in visual imagery, was written after he became blind; and it is just as significant — to shift to a musical example — that a number of Ludwig van Beethoven's greatest works, including the Ninth Symphony, were composed after he suc-cumbed to total deafness.

PSYCHOLOGICAL STRATEGIES

Given the enormous influence that Sigmund Freud's psychoanalytic theories have had on twentieth-century interpretations of human be-havior, it is nearly inevitable that most people have some familiarity with his ideas concerning dreams, unconscious desires, and sexual repression, as well as his terms for different aspects of the psyche — the id, ego, and superego. Psychological approaches to literature draw on Freud's theories and other psychoanalytic theories to understand more fully the text, the writer, and the reader. Critics use such approaches to explore the motivations of characters and the symbolic meanings of events, while biographers speculate about a writer's own motivations — conscious or unconscious — in a literary work. Psychological approaches are also used to describe and analyze the reader's personal responses to a text.

Although it is not feasible to explain psychoanalytic terms and concepts in so brief a space as this, it is possible to suggest the nature of a psychological approach. It is a strategy based heavily on the idea of the existence of a human unconscious — those impulses, desires, and feelings that a person is unaware of but that influence emotions and behavior.

Central to a number of psychoanalytic critical readings is Freud's concept of what he called the **Oedipus complex,** a term derived from Sophocles' tragedy *Oedipus the King* (p. 293). This complex is predicated on a boy's unconscious rivalry with his father for his mother's love and his desire to eliminate his father in order to take his father's place with his mother. The female version of the psychological conflict is known as the **Electra complex,** a term used to describe a daughter's unconscious rivalry for her father. The name comes from a Greek legend about Electra who avenged the death of her father, Agamemnon, by plotting the death of her mother. In *The Interpretation of Dreams,* Freud explains why *Oedipus the King* "moves a modern audience no less than it did the contemporary Greek one." What unites their powerful attraction to the play is an unconscious response:

> There must be something which makes a voice within us ready to recognize the compelling force of destiny in the *Oedipus*. . . . His destiny moves us only because it might have been ours — because the oracle laid the same curse upon us before our birth as upon him. It is the fate of all of us, perhaps, to direct our first sexual impulse towards our mother and our first hatred and our first murderous wish against our father. Our dreams convince us that this is so. King Oedipus, who slew his father Laius and married his mother Jocasta, merely shows us the fulfillment of our own childhood wishes . . . and we shrink back from him with the whole force of the repression by which those wishes have since that time been held down within us.

In this passage Freud interprets the unconscious motives of Sophocles in writing the play, Oedipus in acting within it, and the audience in responding to it.

A further application of the Oedipus complex can be observed in a classic interpretation of *Hamlet* by Ernest Jones, who used this concept to explain why Hamlet delays in avenging his father's death. This reading has been tightly summarized by Norman Holland, a recent psychoanalytic critic, in *The Shakespearean Imagination*. Holland shapes the issues into four major components:

> One, people over the centuries have been unable to say why Hamlet delays in killing the man who murdered his father and married his mother. Two, psychoanalytic experience shows that every child wants to do just exactly that. Three, Hamlet delays because he cannot punish Claudius for doing what he

himself wished to do as a child and, unconsciously, still wishes to do: he would be punishing himself. Four, the fact that this wish is unconscious explains why people could not explain Hamlet's delay.

Although the Oedipus complex is, of course, not relevant to all psychological interpretations of literature, interpretations involving this complex do offer a useful example of how psychoanalytic critics tend to approach a text.

The situation in which Mrs. Mallard finds herself in Chopin's "The Story of an Hour" is not related to an Oedipus complex, but it is clear that news of her husband's death has released powerful unconscious desires for freedom that she had previously suppressed. As she grieved, "something" was "coming to her and she was waiting for it, fearfully." What comes to her is what she senses about the life outside her window; that's the stimulus, but the true source of what was to "possess her," which she strove to "beat . . . back with her [conscious] will" is her desperate desire for the autonomy and fulfillment she had been unable to admit did not exist in her marriage. A psychological approach to her story amounts to a case study in the destructive nature of self-repression. Moreover, the story might reflect Chopin's own views of her marriage — despite her conscious statements about her loving husband. And what about the reader's response? How might a psychological approach account for different responses in female and male readers to Mrs. Mallard's death? One needn't be versed in psychoanalytic terms to entertain this question.

HISTORICAL STRATEGIES

Historians sometimes use literature as a window onto the past because literature frequently provides the nuances of a historic period that cannot be readily perceived through other sources. The characters in Harriet Beecher Stowe's *Uncle Tom's Cabin* (1852) display, for example, a complex set of white attitudes toward blacks in mid-nineteenth-century America that is absent from more traditional historic documents, such as census statistics or state laws. Another way of approaching the relationship between literature and history, however, is to use history as a means of understanding a literary work more clearly. The plot pattern of pursuit, escape, and capture in nineteenth-century slave narratives had a significant influence on Stowe's plotting of action in *Uncle Tom's Cabin*. This relationship demonstrates that the writing contemporary to an author is an important element of the history that helps to shape a work. There are many ways to talk about the historical and cultural dimensions of a work. Such readings treat a literary text as a document reflecting, producing, or being produced by the social conditions of its time, giving equal focus to the social milieu and the work itself. Four historical strategies that have been especially influential are literary history criticism, Marxist criticism, new historicist criticism, and cultural criticism.

Literary History Criticism

Literary historians shift the emphasis from the period to the work. Hence a literary historian might also examine mid-nineteenth-century abolitionist attitudes toward blacks to determine whether Stowe's novel is representative of those views or significantly to the right or left of them. Such a study might even indicate how closely the book reflects racial attitudes of twentieth-century readers. A work of literature may transcend time to the extent that it addresses the concerns of readers over a span of decades or centuries, but it remains for the literary historian a part of the past in which it was composed, a past that can reveal more fully a work's language, ideas, and purposes.

Literary historians move beyond both the facts of an author's personal life and the text itself to the social and intellectual currents in which the author composed the work. They place the work in the context of its time (as do many critical biographers, who write "life and times" studies), and sometimes they make connections with other literary works that may have influenced the author. The basic strategy of literary historians is to illuminate the historic background in order to shed light on some aspect of the work itself.

In Hemingway's "Soldier's Home" we learn that Krebs had been at Belleau Wood, Soissons, the Champagne, St. Mihiel, and the Argonne. Although nothing is said of these battles in the story, they were among the bloodiest battles of the war; the wholesale butchery and staggering casualties incurred by both sides make credible the way Krebs's unstated but lingering memories have turned him into a psychological prisoner of war. Knowing something about the ferocity of those battles helps us account for Krebs's response in the story. Moreover, we can more fully appreciate Hemingway's refusal to have Krebs lie about the realities of war for the folks back home if we are aware of the numerous poems, stories, and plays published during World War I that presented war as a glorious, manly, transcendent sacrifice for God and country. Juxtaposing those works with "Soldier's Home" brings the differences into sharp focus.

Similarly, a reading of William Blake's poem "London" (p. 237) is less complete if we do not know of the horrific social conditions — the poverty, disease, exploitation, and hypocrisy — that characterized the city Blake laments in the late eighteenth century.

One last example: the repression expressed in the lines on Mrs. Mallard's face is more distinctly seen if Chopin's "The Story of an Hour" is placed in the context of "the women's question" as it continued to develop in the 1890s. Mrs. Mallard's impulse toward "self-assertion" runs parallel with a growing women's movement away from the role of long-suffering housewife. This desire was widely regarded by traditionalists as a form of dangerous selfishness that was considered as unnatural as it was immoral.

It is no wonder that Chopin raises the question of whether Mrs. Mallard's sense of freedom owing to her husband's death isn't a selfish, "monstrous joy." Mrs. Mallard, however, dismisses this question as "trivial" in the face of her new perception of life, a dismissal that Chopin endorses by way of the story's ironic ending. The larger social context of this story would have been more apparent to Chopin's readers at the end of the nineteenth century than it is to readers at the beginning of the twenty-first. That is why an historical reconstruction of the limitations placed on married women helps to explain the pressures, tensions, and momentary — only momentary — release that Mrs. Mallard experiences.

Marxist Criticism

Marxist readings developed from the heightened interest in radical reform during the 1930s, when many critics looked to literature as a means of furthering proletarian social and economic goals, based largely on the writings of Karl Marx. *Marxist critics* focus on the ideological content of a work — its explicit and implicit assumptions and values about matters such as culture, race, class, and power. Marxist studies typically aim at revealing and clarifying ideological issues and also correcting social injustices. Some Marxist critics have used literature to describe the competing socioeconomic interests that too often advance capitalist money and power rather than socialist morality and justice. They argue that criticism, like literature, is essentially political because it either challenges or supports economic oppression. Even if criticism attempts to ignore class conflicts, it is politicized, according to Marxists, because it supports the status quo.

It is not surprising that Marxist critics pay more attention to the content and themes of literature than to its form. A Marxist critic would more likely be concerned with the exploitive economic forces that cause Willy Loman to feel trapped in Miller's *Death of a Salesman* (p. 1007) than with the playwright's use of nonrealistic dramatic techniques to reveal Loman's inner thoughts. Similarly, a Marxist reading of Chopin's "The Story of an Hour" might draw on the evidence made available in a book published only a few years after the story by Charlotte Perkins Gilman titled *Women and Economics: A Study of the Economic Relation between Men and Women as a Factor in Social Evolution* (1898). An examination of this study could help explain how some of the "repression" Mrs. Mallard experiences was generated by the socioeconomic structure contemporary to her and how Chopin challenges the validity of that structure by having Mrs. Mallard resist it with her very life. A Marxist reading would see the protagonist's conflict as not only an individual issue but part of a larger class struggle.

New Historicist Criticism

Since the 1960s a development in historical approaches to literature known as *new historicism* has emphasized the interaction between the historic context of a work and a modern reader's understanding and interpretation of the work. In contrast to many traditional literary historians, however, new historicists attempt to describe the culture of a period by reading many different kinds of texts that traditional historians might have previously left for economists, sociologists, and anthropologists. New historicists attempt to read a period in all its dimensions, including political, economic, social, and aesthetic concerns. These considerations could be used to explain the pressures that destroy Mrs. Mallard. A new historicist might examine the story and the public attitudes toward women contemporary to "The Story of an Hour" as well as documents such as suffragist tracts and medical diagnoses to explore how the same forces — expectations about how women are supposed to feel, think, and behave — shape different kinds of texts and how these texts influence each other. A new historicist might, for example, examine medical records for evidence of "nervousness" and "hysteria" as common diagnoses for women who led lives regarded as too independent by their contemporaries.

Without an awareness of just how selfish and self-destructive Mrs. Mallard's impulses would have been in the eyes of her contemporaries, twentieth-century readers might miss the pervasive pressures embedded not only in her marriage but in the social fabric surrounding her. Her death is made more understandable by such an awareness. The doctors who diagnose her as suffering from "the joy that kills" are not merely insensitive or stupid; they represent a contrasting set of assumptions and values that are as historic and real as Mrs. Mallard's yearnings.

New historicist criticism acknowledges more fully than traditional historical approaches the competing nature of readings of the past and thereby tends to offer new emphases and perspectives. New historicism reminds us that there is not only one historic context for "The Story of an Hour." Those doctors reveal additional dimensions of late-nineteenth-century social attitudes that warrant our attention, whether we agree with them or not. By emphasizing that historical perceptions are governed, at least in part, by our own concerns and preoccupations, new historicists sensitize us to the fact that the history on which we choose to focus is colored by being reconstructed from our own present moment. This reconstructed history affects our reading of texts.

Cultural Criticism

Cultural critics, like new historicists, focus on the historical contexts of a literary work, but they pay particular attention to popular manifestations of social, political, and economic contexts. Popular culture — mass-produced and consumed cultural artifacts, today ranging from advertising to popular fiction to television to rock music — and "high" culture are given equal emphasis. A cultural critic might be interested in looking at how Baz Luhrmann's movie version of *Romeo and Juliet* (1996) was influenced by the fragmentary nature of MTV videos. Adding the "low" art of everyday life to "high" art opens up previously unexpected and unexplored areas of criticism. Cultural critics use widely eclectic strategies drawn from new historicism, psychology, gender studies, and deconstructionism (to name only a handful of approaches) to analyze not only literary texts but radio talk shows, comic strips, calendar art, commercials, travel guides, and baseball cards. Because all human activity falls within the ken of cultural criticism, nothing is too minor or major, obscure or pervasive, to escape the range of its analytic vision.

Cultural criticism also includes *postcolonial criticism,* the study of cultural behavior and expression in relationship to the formerly colonized world. Postcolonial criticism refers to the analysis of literary works written by writers from countries and cultures that at one time were controlled by colonizing powers — such as Indian writers during or after British colonial rule. The term also refers to the analysis of literary works written about colonial cultures by writers from the colonizing country. Many of these kinds of analyses point out how writers from colonial powers sometimes misrepresent colonized cultures by reflecting more their own values: Joseph Conrad's *Heart of Darkness* (published in 1899) represents African culture differently than Chinua Achebe's *Things Falling Apart* does, for example. Cultural criticism and postcolonial criticism represent a broad range of approaches to examining race, gender, and class in historical contexts in a variety of cultures.

A cultural critic's approach to Chopin's "The Story of an Hour" might emphasize how the story reflects the potential dangers and horrors of train travel in the 1890s or it might examine how heart disease was often misdiagnosed by physicians or used as a metaphor in Mrs. Mallard's culture for a variety of emotional conditions. Each of these perspectives can serve to create a wider and more informed understanding of the story. For a sense of the range of documents used by cultural critics to shed light on literary works and the historical contexts in which they are written and read, see the casebook on using cultural documents to write about Julia Alvarez's poem "Queens, 1963" (p. 1365).

GENDER STRATEGIES

Gender critics explore how ideas about men and women — what is masculine and feminine — can be regarded as socially constructed by particular cultures. According to some critics, sex is determined by simple biological and anatomical categories of male or female, and gender is determined by a culture's values. Thus, ideas about gender and what constitutes masculine and feminine behavior are created by cultural institutions and conditioning. A gender critic might, for example, focus on Chopin's characterization of an emotionally sensitive Mrs. Mallard and a rational, composed husband in "The Story of an Hour" as a manifestation of socially constructed gender identity in the 1890s. Gender criticism expands categories and definitions of what is masculine or feminine and tends to regard sexuality as more complex than merely masculine or feminine, heterosexual or homosexual. Gender criticism, therefore, has come to include gay and lesbian criticism as well as feminist criticism. Although there are complex and sometimes problematic relationships among these approaches because some critics argue that heterosexuals and homosexuals are profoundly biologically different, gay and lesbian criticism, like feminist criticism, can be usefully regarded as a subset of gender criticism.

Feminist Criticism

Like Marxist critics, *feminist critics* reading "The Story of an Hour" would also be interested in Charlotte Perkins Gilman's *Women and Economics: A Study of the Economic Relation between Men and Women as a Factor in Social Evolution* (1898) because they seek to correct or supplement what they regard as a predominantly male-dominated critical perspective with a feminist consciousness. Like other forms of sociological criticism, feminist criticism places literature in a social context, and, like those of Marxist criticism, its analyses often have sociopolitical purposes — explaining, for example, how images of women in literature reflect the patriarchal social forces that have impeded women's efforts to achieve full equality with men.

Feminists have analyzed literature by both men and women in an effort to understand literary representations of women as well as the writers and cultures that create them. Related to concerns about how gender affects the way men and women write about each other is an interest in whether women use language differently from the way men do. Consequently, feminist critics' approach to literature is characterized by the use of a broad range of disciplines, including history, sociology, psychology, and linguistics, to provide a perspective sensitive to feminist issues.

A feminist approach to Chopin's "The Story of an Hour" might explore the psychological stress created by the expectations that marriage imposes on Mrs. Mallard, expectations that literally and figuratively break her heart. Given that her husband is kind and loving, the issue is not her being married to Brently but her being married at all. Chopin presents marriage as an institution that creates in both men and women the assumed "right to impose a private will upon a fellow-creature." That "right," however, is seen, especially from a feminist perspective, as primarily imposed on women by men. A feminist critic might note, for instance, that the protagonist is introduced as "Mrs. Mallard" (we learn that her first name is Louise only later); she is defined by her marital status and her husband's name, a name whose origin from the Old French is related to the word *masle,* which means "male." The appropriateness of her name points up the fact that her emotions and the cause of her death are interpreted in male terms by the doctors. The value of a feminist perspective on this work can be readily discerned if a reader imagines Mrs. Mallard's story being told from the point of view of one of the doctors who diagnoses the cause of her death as a weak heart rather than as a fierce struggle.

Gay and Lesbian Criticism

Gay and lesbian critics focus on a variety of issues, including how homosexuals are represented in literature, how they read literature, and whether sexuality and gender are culturally constructed or innate. Gay critics have produced new readings of and discovered homosexual concerns in works by writers such as Herman Melville and Henry James, while lesbian critics have done the same for the works of writers such as Emily Dickinson and Toni Morrison. A lesbian reading of "The Story of an Hour," for example, might consider whether Mrs. Mallard's ecstatic feeling of relief—produced by the belief that her marriage is over owing to the presumed death of her husband—isn't also a rejection of her heterosexual identity. Perhaps her glimpse of future freedom, evoked by feminine images of a newly discovered nature "all aquiver with the new spring of life," embraces a repressed new sexual identity that "was too subtle and elusive to name" but that was "approaching to possess her" no matter how much she "was striving to beat it back with her will." Although gay and lesbian readings often raise significant interpretative controversies among critics, they have opened up provocative discussions of seemingly familiar texts.

MYTHOLOGICAL STRATEGIES

Mythological approaches to literature attempt to identify what in a work creates deep universal responses in readers. Whereas psychological critics interpret the symbolic meanings of characters and actions in order to understand more fully the unconscious dimensions of an author's mind, a character's motivation, or a reader's response, mythological critics (also frequently referred to as *archetypal critics*) interpret the hopes, fears, and expectations of entire cultures.

In this context myth is not to be understood simply as referring to stories about imaginary gods who perform astonishing feats in the causes of love, jealousy, or hatred. Nor are myths to be judged as merely erroneous, primitive accounts of how nature runs its course and humanity its affairs. Instead, literary critics use myths as a strategy for understanding how human beings try to account for their lives symbolically. Myths can be a window onto a culture's deepest perceptions about itself because myths attempt to explain what otherwise seems unexplainable: a people's origin, purpose, and destiny.

All human beings have a need to make sense of their lives, whether they are concerned about their natural surroundings, the seasons, sexuality, birth, death, or the very meaning of existence. Myths help people organize their experiences; these systems of belief (less formally held than religious or political tenets but no less important) embody a culture's assumptions and values. What is important to the mythological critic is not the validity or truth of those assumptions and values; what matters is that they reveal common human concerns.

It is not surprising that although the details of mythic stories vary enormously, the essential patterns are often similar because these myths attempt to explain universal experiences. There are, for example, numerous myths that redeem humanity from permanent death through a hero's resurrection and rebirth. The resurrection of Jesus symbolizes for Christians the ultimate defeat of death and coincides with the rebirth of nature's fertility in spring. Features of this rebirth parallel the Greek myths of Adonis and Hyacinth, who die but are subsequently transformed into living flowers; there are also similarities that connect these stories to the reincarnation of the Indian Buddha or the rebirth of the Egyptian Osiris. Important differences exist among these stories, but each reflects a basic human need to limit the power of death and to hope for eternal life.

Mythological critics look for underlying, recurrent patterns in literature that reveal universal meanings and basic human experiences for readers regardless of when or where they live. The characters, images, and themes that symbolically embody these meanings and experiences are called **archetypes.** This term designates universal symbols, which evoke deep and perhaps unconscious responses in a reader because archetypes bring with them our hopes and fears since the beginning of human time. Surely one of the most powerfully compelling archetypes is the death and rebirth theme that relates the human life cycle to the cycle of the seasons. Many others could be cited and would be exhausted only after all human concerns were catalogued, but a few examples can suggest some of the range of plots, images, and characters addressed.

Among the most common literary archetypes are stories of quests, initiations, scapegoats, meditative withdrawals, descents to the underworld, and heavenly ascents. These stories are often filled with archetypal images — bodies of water that may symbolize the unconscious or eternity or baptismal rebirth; rising suns, suggesting reawakening and enlightenment; setting suns, pointing toward death; colors such as green, evocative of growth and fertility, or black, indicating chaos, evil, and death. Along the way are earth mothers, fatal women, wise old men, desert places, and paradisal gardens. No doubt your own reading has introduced you to any number of archetypal plots, images, and characters.

Mythological critics attempt to explain how archetypes are embodied in literary works. Employing various disciplines, these critics articulate the power a literary work has over us. Some critics are deeply grounded in classical literature, whereas others are more conversant with philology, anthropology, psychology, or cultural history. Whatever their emphases, however, mythological critics examine the elements of a work in order to make larger connections that explain the work's lasting appeal.

A mythological reading of Sophocles' *Oedipus the King,* for example, might focus on the relationship between Oedipus's role as a scapegoat and the plague and drought that threaten to destroy Thebes. The city is saved and the fertility of its fields restored only after the corruption is located in Oedipus. His subsequent atonement symbolically provides a kind of rebirth for the city. Thus, the plot recapitulates ancient rites in which the well-being of a king was directly linked to the welfare of his people. If a leader was sick or corrupt, he had to be replaced in order to guarantee the health of the community.

These kinds of archetypal patterns exist potentially in any literary period. Consider how in Chopin's "The Story of an Hour" Mrs. Mallard's life parallels the end of winter and the earth's renewal in spring. When she feels a surge of new life after grieving over her husband's death, her own sensibilities are closely aligned with the "new spring life" that is "all aquiver" outside her window. Although she initially tries to resist that renewal by "beat[ing] it back with her will," she cannot control the life force that surges within her and all around her. When she finally gives herself to the energy and life she experiences, she feels triumphant—like a "goddess of Victory." But this victory is short-lived when she learns that her husband is still alive and with him all the obligations that made her marriage feel like a wasteland. Her death is an ironic version of a rebirth ritual. The coming of spring is an ironic contrast to her own discovery that she can no longer live a repressed, circumscribed life with her husband. Death turns out to be preferable to the living death that her marriage means to her. Although spring will go on, this "goddess of Victory" is defeated by a devastating social contract. The old, corrupt order continues, and that for Chopin is a cruel irony that mythological critics would see as an unnatural disruption of the nature of things.

READER-RESPONSE STRATEGIES

Reader-response criticism, as its name implies, focuses its attention on the reader rather than the work itself. This approach to literature describes what goes on in the reader's mind during the process of reading a text. In a sense, all critical approaches (especially psychological and mythological criticism) concern themselves with a reader's response to literature, but there is a stronger emphasis in reader-response criticism on the reader's active construction of the text. Although many critical theories inform reader-response criticism, all *reader-response critics* aim to describe the reader's experience of a work: In effect we get a reading of the reader, who comes to the work with certain expectations and assumptions, which are either met or not met. Hence the consciousness of the reader—produced by reading the work—is the subject matter of reader-response critics. Just as writing is a creative act, reading is, since it also produces a text.

Reader-response critics do not assume that a literary work is a finished product with fixed formal properties, as, for example, formalist critics do. Instead, the literary work is seen as an evolving creation of the reader's as he or she processes characters, plots, images, and other elements while reading. Some reader-response critics argue that this act of creative reading is, to a degree, controlled by the text, but it can produce many interpretations of the same text by different readers. There is no single definitive reading of a work, because the crucial assumption is that readers create rather than discover meanings in texts. Readers who have gone back to works they had read earlier in their lives often find that a later reading draws very different responses from them. What earlier seemed unimportant is now crucial; what at first seemed central is now barely worth noting. The reason, put simply, is that two different people have read the same text. Reader-response critics are not after the "correct" reading of the text or what the author presumably intended; instead they are interested in the reader's experience with the text.

These experiences change with readers; although the text remains the same, the readers do not. Social and cultural values influence readings, so that, for example, an avowed Marxist would be likely to come away from Miller's *Death of a Salesman* with a very different view of American capitalism than that of, say, a successful sales representative, who might attribute Willy Loman's fall more to his character than to the American economic system. Moreover, readers from different time periods respond differently to texts. An Elizabethan — concerned perhaps with the stability of monarchical rule — might respond differently to Hamlet's problems than would a contemporary reader well versed in psychology and concepts of what Freud called the Oedipus complex. This is not to say that anything goes, that Miller's play can be read as an amoral defense of cheating and rapacious business practices or that *Hamlet* is about the dangers of living away from home. The text does, after all, establish some limits that allow us to reject certain readings as erroneous. But reader-response critics do reject formalist approaches that describe a literary work as a self-contained object, the meaning of which can be determined without reference to any extrinsic matters, such as the social and cultural values assumed by either the author or the reader.

Reader-response criticism calls attention to how we read and what influences our readings. It does not attempt to define what a literary work means on the page but rather what it does to an informed reader, a reader who understands the language and conventions used in a given work. Reader-response criticism is not a rationale for mistaken or bizarre readings of works but an exploration of the possibilities for a plurality of readings shaped by the readers' experience with the text. This kind of strategy can help us understand how our responses are shaped by both the text and ourselves.

Chopin's "The Story of an Hour" illustrates how reader-response critical strategies read the reader. Chopin doesn't say that Mrs. Mallard's marriage is repressive; instead, that troubling fact dawns on the reader at the same time that the recognition forces its way into Mrs. Mallard's consciousness. Her surprise is also the reader's because although she remains in the midst of intense grief, she is on the threshold of a startling discovery about the new possibilities life offers. How the reader responds to that discovery, however, is not entirely controlled by Chopin. One reader, perhaps someone who has recently lost a spouse, might find Mrs. Mallard's "joy" indeed "monstrous" and selfish. Certainly that's how Mrs. Mallard's doctors — the seemingly authoritative diagnosticians in the story — would very likely read her. But for other readers — especially readers steeped in feminist values — Mrs. Mallard's feelings require no justification. Such readers might find Chopin's ending to the story more ironic than she seems to have intended because Mrs. Mallard's death could be read as Chopin's inability to envision a protagonist who has the strength of her convictions. In contrast, a reader in 1894 might have seen the ending as Mrs. Mallard's only escape from the repressive marriage her husband's assumed death suddenly allowed her to see. A reader today probably would argue that it was the marriage that should have died rather than Mrs. Mallard, that she had other alternatives, not just obligations (as the doctors would have insisted), to consider.

By imagining different readers we can imagine a variety of responses to the story that are influenced by the readers' own impressions, memories, or experiences with marriage. Such imagining suggests the ways in which reader-response criticism opens up texts to a number of interpretations. As one final example, consider how readers' responses to "The Story of an Hour" would be affected if it were printed in two different magazines, read in the context of either *Ms.* or *Good Housekeeping.* What assumptions and beliefs would each magazine's readership be likely to bring to the story? How do you think the respective experiences and values of each magazine's readers would influence their readings? For a sample reader-response student paper on "The Story of an Hour," see page 25.

DECONSTRUCTIONIST STRATEGIES

Deconstructionist critics insist that literary works do not yield fixed, single meanings. They argue that there can be no absolute knowledge about anything because language can never say what we intend it to mean. Anything we write conveys meanings we did not intend, so the deconstructionist argument goes. Language is not a precise instrument but a power whose meanings are caught in an endless web of possibilities that cannot be untangled. Accordingly, any idea or statement that insists on being understood separately can ultimately be "deconstructed" to reveal its relations and connections to contradictory and opposite meanings.

Unlike other forms of criticism, deconstructionism seeks to destabilize meanings instead of establishing them. In contrast to formalists such as the New Critics, who closely examine a work in order to call attention to how its various components interact to establish a unified whole, deconstructionists try to show how a close examination of the language in a text inevitably reveals conflicting, contradictory impulses that "deconstruct" or break down its apparent unity.

Although deconstructionists and New Critics both examine the language of a text closely, deconstructionists focus on the gaps and ambiguities that reveal a text's instability and indeterminacy, whereas New Critics look for patterns that explain how the text's fixed meaning is structured. Deconstructionists painstakingly examine the competing meanings within the text rather than attempting to resolve them into a unified whole.

The questions deconstructionists ask are aimed at discovering and describing how a variety of possible readings are generated by the elements of a text. In contrast to a New Critic's concerns about the ultimate meaning of a work, a deconstructionist is primarily interested in how the use of language — diction, tone, metaphor, symbol, and so on — yields only provisional, not definitive, meanings. Consider, for example, the following excerpt from an American Puritan poet, Anne Bradstreet. The excerpt is from "The Flesh and the Spirit" (1678), which consists of an allegorical debate between two sisters, the body and the soul. During the course of the debate, Flesh, a consummate materialist, insists that Spirit values ideas that do not exist and that her faith in idealism is both unwarranted and insubstantial in the face of the material values that earth has to offer — riches, fame, and physical pleasure. Spirit, however, rejects the materialistic worldly argument that the only ultimate reality is physical reality and pledges her faith in God:

> Mine eye doth pierce the heavens and see
> What is invisible to thee.
> My garments are not silk nor gold,
> Nor such like trash which earth doth hold,
> But royal robes I shall have on,
> More glorious than the glist'ring sun;
> My crown not diamonds, pearls, and gold,
> But such as angels' heads enfold.
> The city where I hope to dwell,
> There's none on earth can parallel;
> The stately walls both high and strong,
> Are made of precious jasper stone;
> The gates of pearl, both rich and clear,
> And angels are for porters there;
> The streets thereof transparent gold,
> Such as no eye did e'er behold;
> A crystal river there doth run,
> Which doth proceed from the Lamb's throne.

A deconstructionist would point out that Spirit's language — her use of material images such as jasper stone, pearl, gold, and crystal — cancels the explicit meaning of the passage by offering a supermaterialistic reward to the spiritually faithful. Her language, in short, deconstructs her intended meaning by employing the same images that Flesh would use to describe the rewards of the physical world. A deconstructionist reading, then, reveals the impossibility of talking about the invisible and spiritual worlds without using materialistic (that is, metaphoric) language. Thus Spirit's very language demonstrates a contradiction and conflict in her conviction that the world of here and now must be rejected for the hereafter. Her language deconstructs her meaning.

Deconstructionists look for ways to question and extend the meanings of a text. A deconstructionist might find, for example, the ironic ending of Chopin's "The Story of an Hour" less tidy and conclusive than would a New Critic, who might attribute Mrs. Mallard's death to her sense of lost personal freedom. A deconstructionist might use the story's ending to suggest that the narrative shares the doctors' inability to imagine a life for Mrs. Mallard apart from her husband.

SELECTED BIBLIOGRAPHY

Given the enormous number of articles and books written about literary theory and criticism in recent years, the following bibliography is necessarily highly selective. Even so, it should prove useful as an introduction to many of the issues associated with the critical strategies discussed in this chapter. For a general encyclopedic reference book that describes important figures, schools, and movements, see *The Johns Hopkins Guide to Literary Theory and Criticism,* edited by Michael Grodin and Martin Kreiswirth (Baltimore: Johns Hopkins UP, 1994); and for its concise discussions, see Ross Murfin and Supryia M. Ray, *The Bedford Glossary of Critical and Literary Terms* (Boston: Bedford/St. Martin's, 1998).

Canonical Issues

"The Changing Culture of the University." Special Issue. *Partisan Review* 58 (Spring 1991): 185–410.

Gates, Henry Louis, Jr. *The Signifying Monkey.* New York: Oxford UP, 1988.

Greenblatt, Stephen, and Giles Gunn. *Redrawing the Boundaries: The Transformation of English and American Literary Studies.* New York: MLA, 1992.

Lauter, Paul. *Canons and Contexts.* New York: Oxford UP, 1991.

"The Politics of Liberal Education." Special Issue. *South Atlantic Quarterly* 89 (Winter 1990): 1–234.

Sykes, Charles J. *The Hollow Men: Politics and Corruption in Higher Education.* Washington, D.C.: Regnery Gateway, 1990.

Formalist Strategies

Brooks, Cleanth. *The Well Wrought Urn: Studies in the Structure of Poetry.* New York: Reynal and Hitchcock, 1947.

Crane, Ronald Salmon. *The Languages of Criticism and the Structure of Poetry.* Toronto: U of Toronto P, 1953.

Eliot, Thomas Stearns. *The Sacred Wood: Essays in Poetry and Criticism.* London: Methuen, 1920.

Fekete, John. *The Critical Twilight: Explorations in the Ideology of Anglo-American Literary Theory from Eliot to McLuhan.* London: Routledge, 1977.

Lemon, Lee T., and Marion J. Reis, eds. *Russian Formalist Criticism: Four Essays.* Lincoln: U of Nebraska P, 1965.

Ransom, John Crowe. *The New Criticism.* Norfolk, CT: New Directions, 1941.

Wellek, René, and Austin Warren. *Theory of Literature.* New York: Harcourt, Brace and World, 1949.

Biographical and Psychological Strategies

Bleich, David. *Subjective Criticism.* Baltimore: Johns Hopkins UP, 1978.

Bloom, Harold. *The Anxiety of Influence.* New York: Oxford UP, 1975.

Brennan, Teresa. *The Interpretation of the Flesh: Freud and Femininity.* New York: Routledge, 1994.

Crews, Frederick. *Out of My System: Psychoanalysis, Ideology, and Critical Method.* New York: Oxford UP, 1975.

——. *The Sins of the Fathers: Hawthorne's Psychological Themes.* New York: Oxford UP, 1966.

Felman, Shoshana. *Writing and Madness (Literature/Philosophy/Psychoanalysis).* Ithaca: Cornell UP, 1985.

——, ed. *Literature and Psychoanalysis: The Question of Reading: Otherwise.* Baltimore: Johns Hopkins UP, 1981.

Freud, Sigmund. *The Standard Edition of the Complete Psychological Works.* 24 vols. 1940–1968. London: Hogarth Press and the Institute of Psychoanalysis, 1953.

Holland, Norman. *The Dynamics of Literary Response.* New York: Oxford UP, 1968.

Jones, Ernest. *Hamlet and Oedipus.* New York: Doubleday, 1949.

Lacan, Jacques. *Écrits: A Selection.* Trans. Alan Sheridan. New York: Norton, 1977.

——. *The Four Fundamental Concepts of Psychoanalysis.* Trans. Alan Sheridan. London: Penguin, 1980.

Lesser, Simon O. *Fiction and the Unconscious.* Chicago: U of Chicago P, 1957.

Skura, Meredith Anne. *The Literary Use of the Psychoanalytic Process.* New Haven: Yale UP, 1981.

Zizek, Slavoj. *Looking Awry: An Introduction to Jacques Lacan through Popular Culture*. Cambridge: MIT P, 1991.

Historical Strategies, Including Marxist, New Historicist, and Cultural Strategies

Ang, Ien. *Watching Television*. New York: Routledge, 1991.

Armstrong, Nancy. *Desire and Domestic Fiction*. New York: Oxford UP, 1987.

Ashcroft, Bill, Ga Breth Griffiths, and Helen Tiffin, eds. *The Post-Colonial Studies Reader*. New York: Routledge, 1995.

Bhabha, Homi K. *The Location of Culture*. New York: Routledge, 1994.

Dollimore, Jonathan. *Radical Tragedy: Religion, Ideology and Power in the Drama of Shakespeare and His Contemporaries*. Brighton, Eng.: Harvester, 1984.

Frow, John. *Marxist and Literary History*. Cambridge: Harvard UP, 1986.

Geertz, Clifford. *The Interpretation of Cultures: Selected Essays*. New York: Basic, 1973.

Greenblatt, Stephen. *Renaissance Self-Fashioning: From More to Shakespeare*. Chicago: U of Chicago P, 1980.

——. *Shakespearean Negotiations: The Circulation of Social Energy in Renaissance England*. Berkeley: U of California P, 1985.

Lindenberger, Herbert. *Historical Drama: The Relation of Literature and Reality*. Chicago: U of Chicago P, 1975.

McGann, Jerome. *The Beauty of Inflections: Literary Investigations in Historical Method and Theory*. Oxford: Clarendon, 1985.

Storey, John, ed. *What Is Cultural Studies?* New York: St. Martin's, 1996.

White, Hayden. *Tropics of Discourse: Essays in Cultural Criticism*. Baltimore: Johns Hopkins UP, 1978.

Williams, Raymond. *Marxism and Literature*. Oxford: Oxford UP, 1977.

Gender Strategies, Including Feminist and Gay and Lesbian Strategies

Ablelove, Henry, Michèle Aina Barale, and David M. Halperin, eds. *The Lesbian and Gay Studies Reader*. New York: Routledge, 1993.

Baym, Nina. *Feminism and American Literary History*. New Brunswick: Rutgers UP, 1992.

Beauvoir, Simone de. *The Second Sex*. Trans. H. M. Parshley. New York: Knopf, 1972. Trans. of *Le deuxième sexe*. Paris: Gallimard, 1949.

Benstock, Shari, ed. *Feminist Issues and Literary Scholarship*. Bloomington: Indiana UP, 1987.

Cixous, Hélène, and Catherine Clément. *The Newly Born Woman*. Trans. Betsy Wing. Minneapolis: U of Minnesota P, 1986.

Edelman, Lee. *Homographesis: Essays in Gay Literary and Cultural Theory*. New York: Routledge, 1994.

Fetterley, Judith. *The Resisting Reader: A Feminist Approach to American Fiction*. Bloomington: Indiana UP, 1978.

Flynn, Elizabeth A., and Patrocino P. Schweickert. *Gender and Reading: Essays on Readers, Texts, and Contexts*. Baltimore: Johns Hopkins UP, 1986.

Gilbert, Sandra M., and Susan Gubar. *The Madwoman in the Attic: The Woman Writer and the Nineteenth-Century Literary Imagination*. New Haven: Yale UP, 1979.

Irigaray, Luce. *This Sex Which Is Not One*. Ithaca: Cornell UP, 1985. Trans. of *Ce sexe qui n'en est pas un*. Paris: Éditions de Minuit, 1977.

Jagose, Annamarie. *Queer Theory*. Victoria: Melbourne UP, 1996.

Kolodny, Annette. "Some Notes on Defining a 'Feminist Literary Criticism.'" *Critical Inquiry* 2 (1975): 75–92.

Millett, Kate. *Sexual Politics*. New York: Avon, 1970.

Sedgwick, Eve Kosofsky. *Epistemology of the Closet*. Berkeley: U of California P, 1990.

Showalter, Elaine. *A Literature of Their Own: British Women Novelists from Brontë to Lessing*. Princeton: Princeton UP, 1977.

Smith, Barbara. *Toward a Black Feminist Criticism*. New York: Out and Out, 1977.

Mythological Strategies

Bodkin, Maud. *Archetypal Patterns in Poetry*. London: Oxford UP, 1934.

Frye, Northrop. *Anatomy of Criticism: Four Essays*. Princeton: Princeton UP, 1957.

Jung, Carl Gustav. *Complete Works*. Ed. Herbert Read, Michael Fordham, and Gerhard Adler. 17 vols. New York: Pantheon, 1953–.

Reader-Response Strategies

Booth, Wayne C. *The Rhetoric of Fiction*. 2nd ed. Chicago: U of Chicago P, 1983.

Eco, Umberto. *The Role of the Reader: Explorations in the Semiotics of Texts*. Bloomington: Indiana UP, 1979.

Escarpit, Robert. *Sociology of Literature*. Painesville, OH: Lake Erie College P, 1965.

Fish, Stanley. *Is There a Text in This Class? The Authority of Interpretive Communities*. Cambridge: Harvard UP, 1980.

Freund, Elizabeth. *The Return of the Reader: Reader-Response Criticism*. London: Methuen, 1987.

Holland, Norman N. *The Critical I*. New York: Columbia UP, 1992.

———. *Five Readers Reading*. New Haven: Yale UP, 1975.

Iser, Wolfgang. *The Implied Reader: Patterns of Communication in Prose Fiction from Bunyan to Beckett*. Baltimore: Johns Hopkins UP, 1974.

Jauss, Hans Robert. "Literary History as a Challenge to Literary Theory." *Toward an Aesthetics of Reception.* Trans. Timothy Bahti. Minneapolis: U of Minnesota P, 1982. 3–46.

Rosenblatt, Louise. *Literature as Exploration.* 1938. New York: MLA, 1983.

Suleiman, Susan, and Inge Crosman, eds. *The Reader in the Text: Essays on Audience and Interpretation.* Princeton: Princeton UP, 1980.

Tompkins, Jane P., ed. *Reader-Response Criticism: From Formalism to Post-Structuralism.* Baltimore: Johns Hopkins UP, 1980.

Deconstructionist and Other Poststructuralist Strategies

Barthes, Roland. *The Rustle of Language.* New York: Hill and Wang, 1986.

Culler, Jonathan. *On Deconstruction: Theory and Criticism after Structuralism.* Ithaca: Cornell UP, 1982.

de Man, Paul. *Blindness and Insight.* New York: Oxford UP, 1971.

Derrida, Jacques. *Of Grammatology.* 1967. Baltimore: Johns Hopkins UP, 1976.

—— *Writing and Difference.* 1967. Chicago: U of Chicago P, 1978.

Foucault, Michel. *Language, Counter-Memory, Practice.* Ithaca: Cornell UP, 1977.

——. *The Order of Things: An Archaeology of the Human Sciences.* 1966. London: Tavistock, 1970.

Gasche, Rodolphe. "Deconstruction as Criticism." *Glyph* 6 (1979): 177–216.

Hartman, Geoffrey H. *Criticism in the Wilderness.* New Haven: Yale UP, 1980.

Johnson, Barbara. *The Critical Difference: Essays in the Contemporary Rhetoric of Reading.* Baltimore: Johns Hopkins UP, 1980.

Martin, Bill. *Humanism and Its Aftermath: The Shared Fate of Deconstructionism and Politics.* Atlantic Highlands, NJ: Humanities, 1995.

Melville, Stephen W. *Philosophy Beside Itself: On Deconstruction and Modernism. Theory and History of Literature* 27. Minneapolis: U of Minnesota P, 1986.

Royle, Nicholas. *After Derrida.* Manchester: Manchester UP, 1995.

Said, Edward W. *The World, the Text, and the Critic.* Cambridge: Harvard UP, 1983.

Smith, Barbara Herrnstein. *On the Margins of Discourse: The Relation of Literature to Language.* Chicago: U of Chicago P, 1979.

Critical Analysis

This casebook shows one student, Peter Campion, using a particular critical strategy to approach William Faulkner's well-known short story "Barn Burning." He first reads the story carefully, then moves through brainstorming, a first response, and uses the Questions for Writing: Applying a Critical Strategy (p. 97) to determine which strategy best fits "Barn Burning" and his own initial response to it. Finally, he uses a Marxist approach to develop a thesis and to write his paper. Peter's approach to this challenging story results in an interesting perspective on southern society. As you read "Barn Burning" and follow Peter through his process, think about which strategy you would choose to write about the story, why you'd choose it, and how you'd use it to ask different questions of the text than Peter has in his paper.

WILLIAM FAULKNER (1897–1962)

Born into an old Mississippi family that had lost its influence and wealth during the Civil War, William Faulkner lived nearly all his life in the South writing about Yoknapatawpha County, an imagined Mississippi county similar to his home in Oxford. Among his novels based on this fictional location are *The Sound and the Fury* (1929), *As I Lay Dying* (1930), *Light in August* (1932), and *Absalom, Absalom!* (1936). Although his writings are regional in their emphasis on local social history, his concerns are broader. In his 1950 acceptance speech for the Nobel Prize for literature, he insisted that the "problems of the human heart in conflict with itself . . . alone can make good writing because only that is worth writing about, worth the agony and the sweat." This commitment is evident in his novels and in *The Collected Stories of William Faulkner* (1950). In "Barn Burning" Faulkner portrays a young boy's love and revulsion for his father, a frightening man who lives by a "ferocious conviction in the rightness of his own actions."

William Faulkner (May 6, 1955) in the spot where he did most of his writing—his living room—bent over a glass-topped table with a pen. Reprinted by permission of Corbis-Bettmann.

Barn Burning 1939

The store in which the Justice of the Peace's court was sitting smelled of cheese. The boy, crouched on his nail keg at the back of the crowded room, knew he smelled cheese, and more: from where he sat he could see the ranked shelves close-packed with the solid, squat, dynamic shapes of tin cans whose labels his stomach read, not from the lettering which meant nothing to his mind but from the scarlet devils and the silver curve of fish—this, the cheese which he knew he smelled and the hermetic meat which his intestines believed he smelled coming in intermittent gusts momentary and brief between the other constant one, the smell and sense just a little of fear because mostly of despair and grief, the old fierce pull of blood. He could not see the table where the Justice sat and before which his father and his father's enemy (*our enemy* he thought in that despair; *ourn! mine and hisn both! He's my father!*) stood, but he could hear them, the two of them that is, because his father had said no word yet:

"But what proof have you, Mr. Harris?"

"I told you. The hog got into my corn. I caught it up and sent it back to him. He had no fence that would hold it. I told him so, warned him. The next time I put the hog in my pen. When he came to get it I gave him enough wire to patch up his pen. The next time I put the hog up and kept it. I rode down to his house and saw the wire I gave him still rolled on to the spool in his yard. I told him he could have the hog when he paid me a dollar pound fee. That evening a nigger came with the dollar and got the hog. He was a strange nigger. He said, 'He say to tell you wood and hay kin burn.' I said, 'What?' 'That whut he say to tell you,' the nigger said. 'Wood and hay kin burn.' That night my barn burned. I got the stock out but I lost the barn."

"Where is the nigger? Have you got him?"

"He was a strange nigger, I tell you. I don't know what became of him."   5

"But that's not proof. Don't you see that's not proof?"

"Get that boy up here. He knows." For a moment the boy thought too that the man meant his older brother until Harris said, "Not him. The little one. The boy," and, crouching, small for his age, small and wiry like his father, in patched and faded jeans even too small for him, with straight, uncombed, brown hair and eyes gray and wild as storm scud, he saw the men between himself and the table part and become a lane of grim faces, at the end of which he saw the Justice, a shabby, collarless, graying man in spectacles, beckoning him. He felt no floor under his bare feet; he seemed to walk beneath the palpable weight of the grim turning faces. His father, stiff in his black Sunday coat donned not for the trial but for the moving, did not even look at him. *He aims for me to lie,* he thought, again with that frantic grief and despair. *And I will have to do hit.*

"What's your name, boy?" the Justice said.

"Colonel Sartoris Snopes," the boy whispered.

"Hey?" the Justice said. "Talk louder. Colonel Sartoris? I reckon anybody   10
named for Colonel Sartoris in this country can't help but tell the truth, can they?" The boy said nothing. *Enemy! Enemy!* he thought; for a moment he could not even see, could not see that the Justice's face was kindly nor discern that his voice was troubled when he spoke to the man named Harris: "Do you want me to question this boy?" But he could hear, and during those subsequent long seconds while there was absolutely no sound in the crowded little room save that of quiet and intent breathing it was as if he had swung outward at the end of a grape vine, over a ravine, and at the top of the swing had been caught in a prolonged instant of mesmerized gravity, weightless in time.

"No!" Harris said violently, explosively. "Damnation! Send him out of here!" Now time, the fluid world, rushed beneath him again, the voices coming to him again through the smell of cheese and sealed meat, the fear and despair and the old grief of blood:

"This case is closed. I can't find against you, Snopes, but I can give you advice. Leave this country and don't come back to it."

His father spoke for the first time, his voice cold and harsh, level, without emphasis: "I aim to. I don't figure to stay in a country among people who . . ." he said something unprintable and vile, addressed to no one.

"That'll do," the Justice said. "Take your wagon and get out of this country before dark. Case dismissed."

His father turned, and he followed the stiff black coat, the wiry figure   15
walking a little stiffly from where a Confederate provost's man's musket ball had taken him in the heel on a stolen horse thirty years ago, followed the two backs now, since his older brother had appeared from somewhere in the crowd, no taller than the father but thicker, chewing tobacco steadily, between the two lines of grim-faced men and out of the store and across the worn gallery and down the sagging steps and among the dogs and half-grown boys in the mild May dust, where as he passed a voice hissed:

"Barn burner!"

Again he could not see, whirling; there was a face in a red haze, moonlike, bigger than the full moon, the owner of it half again his size, he leaping in the red haze toward the face, feeling no blow, feeling no shock when his head struck the earth, scrabbling up and leaping again, feeling no blow this time either and tasting no blood, scrabbling up to see the other boy in full flight and himself already leaping into pursuit as his father's hand jerked him back, the harsh, cold voice speaking above him: "Go get in the wagon."

It stood in a grove of locusts and mulberries across the road. His two hulking sisters in their Sunday dresses and his mother and her sister in calico and sunbonnets were already in it, sitting on or among the sorry residue of the dozen and more movings which even the boy could remember — the battered stove, the broken beds and chairs, the clock inlaid with mother-of-pearl, which would not run, stopped at some fourteen minutes past two o'clock of a dead and forgotten day and time, which had been his mother's dowry. She was crying, though when she saw him she drew her sleeve across her face and began to descend from the wagon. "Get back," the father said.

"He's hurt. I got to get some water and wash his . . ."

"Get back in the wagon," his father said. He got in too, over the tail-gate.   20 His father mounted to the seat where the older brother already sat and struck the gaunt mules two savage blows with the peeled willow, but without heat. It was not even sadistic; it was exactly that same quality which in later years would cause his descendants to over-run the engine before putting a motor car in motion, striking and reining back in the same movement. The wagon went on, the store with its quiet crowd of grimly watching men dropped behind; a curve in the road hid it. *Forever* he thought. *Maybe he's done satisfied now, now that he has* . . . stopping himself, not to say it aloud even to himself. His mother's hand touched his shoulder.

"Does hit hurt?" she said.

"Naw," he said. "Hit don't hurt. Lemme be."

"Can't you wipe some of the blood off before hit dries?"

"I'll wash to-night," he said. "Lemme be, I tell you."

The wagon went on. He did not know where they were going. None of   25 them ever did or ever asked, because it was always somewhere, always a house of sorts waiting for them a day or two days or even three days away. Likely his father had already arranged to make a crop on another farm before he . . . Again he had to stop himself. He (the father) always did. There was something about his wolflike independence and even courage when the advantage was at least neutral which impressed strangers, as if they got from his latent ravening ferocity not so much a sense of dependability as a feeling that his ferocious conviction in the rightness of his own actions would be of advantage to all whose interest lay with his.

That night they camped, in a grove of oaks and beeches where a spring ran. The nights were still cool and they had a fire against it, of a rail lifted from a nearby fence and cut into lengths — a small fire, neat, niggard almost, a shrewd fire; such fires were his father's habit and custom always, even in freezing weather. Older, the boy might have remarked this and wondered why not a big one; why should not a man who had not only seen the waste and extravagance of war, but who had in his blood an inherent voracious prodigality with material not his own, have burned everything in sight? Then he might have gone a step farther and thought that that was the reason: that niggard blaze was the living fruit of nights passed during those four years in the woods hiding from all men, blue or gray, with his strings of horses (captured horses, he called them). And older still, he might have divined the true reason: that the element of fire spoke to some deep mainspring of his father's being, as the element of steel or of powder spoke to other men, as the one weapon for the preservation of integrity, else breath were not worth the breathing, and hence to be regarded with respect and used with discretion.

But he did not think this now and he had seen those same niggard blazes all his life. He merely ate his supper beside it and was already half asleep over his iron plate when his father called him, and once more he followed the stiff back, the stiff and ruthless limp, up the slope and on to the starlit road where, turning, he could see his father against the stars but without face or depth — a shape black, flat, and bloodless as though cut from tin in the iron folds of the frockcoat which had not been made for him, the voice harsh like tin and without heat like tin:

"You were fixing to tell them. You would have told him."

He didn't answer. His father struck him with the flat of his hand on the side of the head, hard but without heat, exactly as he had struck the two mules at the store, exactly as he would strike either of them with any stick in order to kill a horse fly, his voice still without heat or anger. "You're getting to be a man. You got to learn. You got to learn to stick to your own blood or you ain't going to have any blood to stick to you. Do you think either of them, any man there this morning, would? Don't you know all they wanted was a chance to get at me because they knew I had them beat? Eh?" Later, twenty years later, he was to tell himself, "If I had said they wanted only truth, justice, he would have hit me again." But now he said nothing. He was not crying. He just stood there. "Answer me," his father said.

"Yes," he whispered. His father turned.   30

"Get on to bed. We'll be there tomorrow."

Tomorrow they were there. In the early afternoon the wagon stopped before a paintless two-room house identical almost with the dozen others it had stopped before even in the boy's ten years, and again, as on the other dozen occasions, his mother and aunt got down and began to unload the wagon, although his two sisters and his father and brother had not moved.

"Likely hit ain't fitten for hawgs," one of the sisters said.

"Nevertheless, fit it will and you'll hog it and like it," his father said. "Get out of them chairs and help your Ma unload."

The two sisters got down, big, bovine, in a flutter of cheap ribbons; one of   35 them drew from the jumbled wagon bed a battered lantern, the other a worn broom. His father handed the reins to the older son and began to climb stiffly over the wheel. "When they get unloaded, take the team to the barn and feed them." Then he said, and at first the boy thought he was still speaking to his brother: "Come with me."

"Me?" he said.

"Yes," his father said. "You."

"Abner," his mother said. His father paused and looked back — the harsh level stare beneath the shaggy, graying, irascible brows.

"I reckon I'll have a word with the man that aims to begin tomorrow owning me body and soul for the next eight months."

They went back up the road. A week ago — or before last night, that is — he   40
would have asked where they were going, but not now. His father had struck
him before last night but never before had he paused afterward to explain why;
it was as if the blow and the following calm, outrageous voice still rang, reper-
cussed, divulging nothing to him save the terrible handicap of being young,
the light weight of his few years, just heavy enough to prevent his soaring free
of the world as it seemed to be ordered but not heavy enough to keep him
footed solid in it, to resist it and try to change the course of events.

Presently he could see the grove of oaks and cedars and the other flowering
trees and shrubs where the house would be, though not the house yet. They
walked beside a fence massed with honeysuckle and Cherokee roses and came
to a gate swinging open between two brick pillars, and now, beyond a sweep of
drive, he saw the house for the first time and at that instant he forgot his father
and the terror and despair both, and even when he remembered his father again
(who had not stopped) the terror and despair did not return. Because, for all the
twelve movings, they had sojourned until now in a poor country, a land of small
farms and fields and houses, and he had never seen a house like this before. *Hit's
big as a courthouse* he thought quietly, with a surge of peace and joy whose reason
he could not have thought into words, being too young for that: *They are safe
from him. People whose lives are a part of this peace and dignity are beyond his touch, he
no more to them than a buzzing wasp: capable of stinging for a little moment but that's
all; the spell of this peace and dignity rendering even the barns and stable and cribs which
belong to it impervious to the puny flames he might contrive . . .* this, the peace and joy,
ebbing for an instant as he looked again at the stiff black back, the stiff and
implacable limp of the figure which was not dwarfed by the house, for the reason that it had never looked big anywhere and which now, against the serene
columned backdrop, had more than ever that impervious quality of something
cut ruthlessly from tin, depthless, as though, sidewise to the sun, it would cast
no shadow. Watching him, the boy remarked the absolutely undeviating course
which his father held and saw the stiff foot come squarely down in a pile of
fresh droppings where a horse had stood in the drive and which his father could
have avoided by a simple change of stride. But it ebbed only for a moment,
though he could not have thought this into words either, walking on in the
spell of the house, which he could even want but without envy, without sorrow,
certainly never with that ravening and jealous rage which unknown to him
walked in the ironlike black coat before him: *Maybe he will feel it too. Maybe it will
even change him now from what maybe he couldn't help but be.*

They crossed the portico. Now he could hear his father's stiff foot as it
came down on the boards with clocklike finality, a sound out of all proportion
to the displacement of the body it bore and which was not dwarfed either by
the white door before it, as though it had attained to a sort of vicious and
ravening minimum not to be dwarfed by anything — the flat, wide, black hat,
the formal coat of broadcloth which had once been black but which had now
that friction-glazed greenish cast of the bodies of old house flies, the lifted
sleeve which was too large, the lifted hand like a curled claw. The door opened
so promptly that the boy knew the Negro must have been watching them all
the time, an old man with neat grizzled hair, in a linen jacket, who stood bar-
ring the door with his body, saying, "Wipe yo foots, white man, fo you come in
here. Major ain't home nohow."

"Get out of my way, nigger," his father said, without heat too, flinging the door back and the Negro also and entering, his hat still on his head. And now the boy saw the prints of the stiff foot on the doorjamb and saw them appear on the pale rug behind the machinelike deliberation of the foot which seemed to bear (or transmit) twice the weight which the body compassed. The Negro was shouting "Miss Lula! Miss Lula!" somewhere behind them, then the boy, deluged as though by a warm wave by a suave turn of the carpeted stair and a pendant glitter of chandeliers and a mute gleam of gold frames, heard the swift feet and saw her too, a lady — perhaps he had never seen her like before either — in a gray, smooth gown with lace at the throat and an apron tied at the waist and the sleeves turned back, wiping cake or biscuit dough from her hands with a towel as she came up the hall, looking not at his father at all but at the tracks on the blond rug with an expression of incredulous amazement.

"I tried," the Negro cried. "I tole him to . . ."

"Will you please go away?" she said in a shaking voice. "Major de Spain is 45 not at home. Will you please go away?"

His father had not spoken again. He did not speak again. He did not even look at her. He just stood stiff in the center of the rug, in his hat, the shaggy iron-gray brows twitching slightly above the pebble-colored eyes as he appeared to examine the house with brief deliberation. Then with the same deliberation he turned; the boy watched him pivot on the good leg and saw the stiff foot drag round the arc of the turning, leaving a final long and fading smear. His father never looked at it, he never once looked down at the rug. The Negro held the door. It closed behind them, upon the hysteric and indistinguishable woman-wail. His father stopped at the top of the steps and scraped his boot clean on the edge of it. At the gate he stopped again. He stood for a moment, planted stiffly on the stiff foot, looking back at the house. "Pretty and white, ain't it?" he said. "That's sweat. Nigger sweat. Maybe it ain't white enough yet to suit him. Maybe he wants to mix some white sweat with it."

Two hours later the boy was chopping wood behind the house within which his mother and aunt and the two sisters (the mother and aunt, not the two girls, he knew that; even at this distance and muffled by walls the flat loud voices of the two girls emanated an incorrigible idle inertia) were setting up the stove to prepare a meal; when he heard the hooves and saw the linen-clad man on a fine sorrel mare, whom he recognized even before he saw the rolled rug in front of the Negro youth following on a fat bay carriage horse — a suffused, angry face vanishing, still at full gallop, beyond the corner of the house where his father and brother were sitting in the two tilted chairs; and a moment later, almost before he could have put the axe down, he heard the hooves again and watched the sorrel mare go back out of the yard, already galloping again. Then his father began to shout one of the sisters' names, who presently emerged backward from the kitchen door dragging the rolled rug along the ground by one end while the other sister walked behind it.

"If you ain't going to tote, go on and set up the wash pot," the first said.

"You, Sarty!" the second shouted. "Set up the wash pot!" His father appeared at the door, framed against that shabbiness, as he had been against that other bland perfection, impervious to either, the mother's anxious face at his shoulder.

"Go on," the father said. "Pick it up." The two sisters stopped, broad, 50
lethargic; stooping, they presented an incredible expanse of pale cloth and a
flutter of tawdry ribbons.

"If I thought enough of a rug to have to git hit all the way from France I
wouldn't keep hit where folks coming in would have to tromp on hit," the first
said. They raised the rug.

"Abner," the mother said. "Let me do it."

"You go back and git dinner," his father said. "I'll tend to this."

From the woodpile through the rest of the afternoon the boy watched
them, the rug spread flat in the dust beside the bubbling wash pot, the two sisters stooping over it with that profound and lethargic reluctance, while the
father stood over them in turn, implacable and grim, driving them though
never raising his voice again. He could smell the harsh homemade lye they
were using; he saw his mother come to the door once and look toward them
with an expression not anxious now but very like despair; he saw his father
turn, and he fell to with the axe and saw from the corner of his eye his father
raise from the ground a flattish fragment of field stone and examine it and
return to the pot, and this time his mother actually spoke: "Abner. Abner.
Please don't. Please, Abner."

Then he was done too. It was dusk; the whippoorwills had already begun. 55
He could smell coffee from the room where they would presently eat the cold
food remaining from the midafternoon meal, though when he entered the
house he realized they were having coffee again probably because there was a
fire on the hearth, before which the rug now lay spread over the backs of the
two chairs. The tracks of his father's foot were gone. Where they had been were
now long, water-cloudy scoriations resembling the sporadic course of a lil-
liputian mowing machine.

It still hung there while they ate the cold food and then went to bed, scattered without order or claim up and down the two rooms, his mother in one
bed, where his father would later lie, the older brother in the other, himself,
the aunt, and the two sisters on pallets on the floor. But his father was not in
bed yet. The last thing the boy remembered was the depthless, harsh silhouette
of the hat and coat bending over the rug and it seemed to him that he had not
even closed his eyes when the silhouette was standing over him, the fire almost
dead behind it, the stiff foot prodding him awake. "Catch up the mule," his
father said.

When he returned with the mule his father was standing in the black
door, the rolled rug over his shoulder. "Ain't you going to ride?" he said.

"No. Give me your foot."

He bent his knee into his father's hand, the wiry, surprising power flowed
smoothly, rising, he rising with it, on to the mule's bare back (they had owned
a saddle once; the boy could remember it though not when or where) and with
the same effortlessness his father swung the rug up in front of him. Now in
the starlight they retraced the afternoon's path, up the dusty road rife with
honeysuckle, through the gate and up the black tunnel of the drive to the
lightless house, where he sat on the mule and felt the rough warp of the rug
drag across his thighs and vanish.

"Don't you want me to help?" he whispered. His father did not answer and 60
now he heard again that stiff foot striking the hollow portico with that
wooden and clocklike deliberation, that outrageous overstatement of the

weight it carried. The rug, hunched, not flung (the boy could tell that even in the darkness) from his father's shoulder struck the angle of wall and floor with a sound unbelievably loud, thunderous, then the foot again, unhurried and enormous; a light came on in the house and the boy sat, tense, breathing steadily and quietly and just a little fast, though the foot itself did not increase its beat at all, descending the steps now; now the boy could see him.

"Don't you want to ride now?" he whispered. "We kin both ride now," the light within the house altering now, flaring up and sinking. *He's coming down the stairs now,* he thought. He had already ridden the mule up beside the horse block; presently his father was up behind him and he doubled the reins over and slashed the mule across the neck, but before the animal could begin to trot the hard, thin arm came around him, the hard, knotted hand jerking the mule back to a walk.

In the first red rays of the sun they were in the lot, putting plow gear on the mules. This time the sorrel mare was in the lot before he heard it at all, the rider collarless and even bareheaded, trembling, speaking in a shaking voice as the woman in the house had done, his father merely looking up once before stooping again to the hame he was buckling, so that the man on the mare spoke to his stooping back:

"You must realize you have ruined that rug. Wasn't there anybody here, any of your women . . ." he ceased, shaking, the boy watching him, the older brother leaning now in the stable door, chewing, blinking slowly and steadily at nothing apparently. "It cost a hundred dollars. But you never had a hundred dollars. You never will. So I'm going to charge you twenty bushels of corn against your crop. I'll add it in your contract and when you come to the commissary you can sign it. That won't keep Mrs. de Spain quiet but maybe it will teach you to wipe your feet before you enter her house again."

Then he was gone. The boy looked at his father, who still had not spoken or even looked up again, who was now adjusting the logger-head in the hame.

"Pap," he said. His father looked at him—the inscrutable face, the shaggy   65
brows beneath which the gray eyes glinted coldly. Suddenly the boy went toward him, fast, stopping as suddenly. "You done the best you could!" he cried. "If he wanted hit done different why didn't he wait and tell you how? He won't git no twenty bushels! He won't git none! We'll gether hit and hide hit! I kin watch . . ."

"Did you put the cutter back in that straight stock like I told you?"

"No, sir," he said.

"Then go do it."

That was Wednesday. During the rest of that week he worked steadily, at what was within his scope and some which was beyond it, with an industry that did not need to be driven nor even commanded twice; he had this from his mother, with the difference that some at least of what he did he liked to do, such as splitting wood with the half-size axe which his mother and aunt had earned, or saved money somehow, to present him with at Christmas. In company with the two older women (and on one afternoon, even one of the sisters), he built pens for the shoat and the cow which were part of his father's contract with the landlord, and one afternoon, his father being absent, gone somewhere on one of the mules, he went to the field.

They were running a middle buster now, his brother holding the plow   70
straight while he handled the reins, and walking beside the straining mule, the

rich black soil shearing cool and damp against his bare ankles, he thought *Maybe this is the end of it. Maybe even that twenty bushels that seems hard to have to pay for just a rug will be a cheap price for him to stop forever and always from being what he used to be;* thinking, dreaming now, so that his brother had to speak sharply to him to mind the mule: *Maybe he even won't collect the twenty bushels. Maybe it will all add up and balance and vanish—corn, rug, fire; the terror and grief, the being pulled two ways like between two teams of horses—gone, done with for ever and ever.*

Then it was Saturday; he looked up from beneath the mule he was harnessing and saw his father in the black coat and hat. "Not that," his father said. "The wagon gear." And then, two hours later, sitting in the wagon bed behind his father and brother on the seat, the wagon accomplished a final curve, and he saw the weathered paintless store with its tattered tobacco- and patent-medicine posters and the tethered wagons and saddle animals below the gallery. He mounted the gnawed steps behind his father and brother, and there again was the lane of quiet, watching faces for the three of them to walk through. He saw the man in spectacles sitting at the plank table and he did not need to be told this was a Justice of the Peace; he sent one glare of fierce, exultant, partisan defiance at the man in collar and cravat now, whom he had seen but twice before in his life, and that on a galloping horse, who now wore on his face an expression not of rage but of amazed unbelief which the boy could not have known was at the incredible circumstance of being sued by one of his own tenants, and came and stood against his father and cried at the Justice: "He ain't done it! He ain't burnt . . ."

"Go back to the wagon," his father said.

"Burnt?" the Justice said. "Do I understand this rug was burned too?"

"Does anybody here claim it was?" his father said. "Go back to the wagon." But he did not, he merely retreated to the rear of the room, crowded as that other had been, but not to sit down this time, instead, to stand pressing among the motionless bodies, listening to the voices:

"And you claim twenty bushels of corn is too high for the damage you did 75 to the rug?"

"He brought the rug to me and said he wanted the tracks washed out of it. I washed the tracks out and took the rug back to him."

"But you didn't carry the rug back to him in the same condition it was in before you made the tracks on it."

His father did not answer, and now for perhaps half a minute there was no sound at all save that of breathing, the faint, steady suspiration of complete and intent listening.

"You decline to answer that, Mr. Snopes?" Again his father did not answer. "I'm going to find against you, Mr. Snopes. I'm going to find that you were responsible for the injury to Major de Spain's rug and hold you liable for it. But twenty bushels of corn seems a little high for a man in your circumstances to have to pay. Major de Spain claims it cost a hundred dollars. October corn will be worth about fifty cents. I figure that if Major de Spain can stand a ninety-five dollar loss on something he paid cash for, you can stand a five-dollar loss you haven't earned yet. I hold you in damages to Major de Spain to the amount of ten bushels of corn over and above your contract with him, to be paid to him out of your crop at gathering time. Court adjourned."

It had taken no time hardly, the morning was but half begun. He thought 80 they would return home and perhaps back to the field, since they were late, far behind all other farmers. But instead his father passed on behind the wagon, merely indicating with his hand for the older brother to follow with it, and crossed the road toward the blacksmith shop opposite, pressing on after his father, overtaking him, speaking, whispering up at the harsh, calm face beneath the weathered hat: "He won't git no ten bushels neither. He won't git one. We'll . . ." until his father glanced for an instant down at him, the face absolutely calm, the grizzled eyebrows tangled above the cold eyes, the voice almost pleasant, almost gentle:

"You think so? Well, we'll wait till October anyway."

The matter of the wagon — the setting of a spoke or two and the tightening of the tires — did not take long either, the business of the tires accomplished by driving the wagon into the spring branch behind the shop and letting it stand there, the mules nuzzling into the water from time to time, and the boy on the seat with the idle reins, looking up the slope and through the sooty tunnel of the shed where the slow hammer rang and where his father sat on an upended cypress bolt, easily, either talking or listening, still sitting there when the boy brought the dripping wagon up out of the branch and halted it before the door.

"Take them on to the shade and hitch," his father said. He did so and returned. His father and the smith and a third man squatting on his heels inside the door were talking, about crops and animals; the boy, squatting too in the ammoniac dust and hoof-parings and scales of rust, heard his father tell a long and unhurried story out of the time before the birth of the older brother even when he had been a professional horsetrader. And then his father came up beside him where he stood before a tattered last year's circus poster on the other side of the store, gazing rapt and quiet at the scarlet horses, the incredible poisings and convolutions of tulle and tights and the painted leers of comedians, and said, "It's time to eat."

But not at home. Squatting beside his brother against the front wall, he watched his father emerge from the store and produce from a paper sack a segment of cheese and divide it carefully and deliberately into three with his pocket knife and produce crackers from the same sack. They all three squatted on the gallery and ate, slowly, without talking; then in the store again, they drank from a tin dipper tepid water smelling of the cedar bucket and of living beech trees. And still they did not go home. It was a horse lot this time, a tall rail fence upon and along which men stood and sat and out of which one by one horses were led, to be walked and trotted and then cantered back and forth along the road while the slow swapping and buying went on and the sun began to slant westward, they — the three of them — watching and listening, the older brother with his muddy eyes and his steady, inevitable tobacco, the father commenting now and then on certain of the animals, to no one in particular.

It was after sundown when they reached home. They ate supper by lamp- 85 light, then, sitting on the doorstep, the boy watched the night fully accomplish, listening to the whippoorwills and the frogs, when he heard his mother's voice: "Abner! No! No! Oh, God. Oh, God. Abner!" and he rose, whirled, and saw the altered light through the door where a candle stub now burned in a bottle neck on the table and his father, still in the hat and coat, at once formal and burlesque as though dressed carefully for some shabby and ceremonial violence, emptying the reservoir of the lamp back into the five-gallon kerosene can from which it had been filled, while the mother tugged at his arm until he shifted the lamp to the other hand and flung her back, not savagely or viciously, just hard, into the wall, her hands flung out against the wall for balance, her mouth open and in her face the same quality of hopeless despair as had been in her voice. Then his father saw him standing in the door.

"Go to the barn and get that can of oil we were oiling the wagon with," he said. The boy did not move. Then he could speak.

"What . . ." he cried. "What are you . . ."

"Go get that oil," his father said. "Go."

Then he was moving, running, outside the house, toward the stable: this the old habit, the old blood which he had not been permitted to choose for himself, which had been bequeathed him willy nilly and which had run for so long (and who knew where, battening on what of outrage and savagery and lust) before it came to him. *I could keep on,* he thought. *I could run on and on and never look back, never need to see his face again. Only I can't. I can't,* the rusted can in his hand now, the liquid sploshing in it as he ran back to the house and into it, into the sound of his mother's weeping in the next room, and handed the can to his father.

"Ain't you going to even send a nigger?" he cried. "At least you sent a nig- 90 ger before!"

This time his father didn't strike him. The hand came even faster than the blow had, the same hand which had set the can on the table with almost excruciating care flashing from the can toward him too quick for him to follow it, gripping him by the back of his shirt and on to tiptoe before he had seen it quit the can, the face stooping at him in breathless and frozen ferocity, the cold, dead voice speaking over him to the older brother who leaned against the table, chewing with that steady, curious, sidewise motion of cows:

"Empty the can into the big one and go on. I'll catch up with you."

"Better tie him up to the bedpost," the brother said.

"Do like I told you," the father said. Then the boy was moving, his bunched shirt and the hard, bony hand between his shoulder-blades, his toes just touching the floor, across the room and into the other one, past the sisters sitting with spread heavy thighs in the two chairs over the cold hearth, and to where his mother and aunt sat side by side on the bed, the aunt's arms about his mother's shoulders.

"Hold him," the father said. The aunt made a startled movement. "Not 95 you," the father said. "Lennie. Take hold of him. I want to see you do it." His mother took him by the wrist. "You'll hold him better than that. If he gets loose don't you know what he is going to do? He will go up yonder." He jerked his head toward the road. "Maybe I'd better tie him."

"I'll hold him," his mother whispered.

"See you do then." Then his father was gone, the stiff foot heavy and measured upon the boards, ceasing at last.

Then he began to struggle. His mother caught him in both arms, he jerking and wrenching at them. He would be stronger in the end, he knew that. But he had no time to wait for it. "Lemme go!" he cried. "I don't want to have to hit you!"

"Let him go!" the aunt said. "If he don't go, before God, I am going up there myself!"

"Don't you see I can't?" his mother cried. "Sarty! Sarty! No! No! Help me, 100 Lizzie!"

Then he was free. His aunt grasped at him but it was too late. He whirled, running, his mother stumbled forward on to her knees behind him, crying to the nearer sister. "Catch him, Net! Catch him!" But that was too late too, the sister (the sisters were twins, born at the same time, yet either of them now gave the impression of being, encompassing as much living meat and volume and weight as any other two of the family) not yet having begun to rise from the chair, her head, face, alone merely turned, presenting to him in the flying instant an astonishing expanse of young female features untroubled by any surprise even, wearing only an expression of bovine interest. Then he was out of the room, out of the house, in the mild dust of the starlit road and the heavy rifeness of honeysuckle, the pale ribbon unspooling with terrific slow-ness under his running feet, reaching the gate at last and turning in, running, his heart and lungs drumming, on up the drive toward the lighted house, the lighted door. He did not knock, he burst in, sobbing for breath, incapable for the moment of speech; he saw the astonished face of the Negro in the linen jacket without knowing when the Negro had appeared.

"De Spain!" he cried, panted. "Where's . . ." then he saw the white man too emerging from a white door down the hall. "Barn!" he cried. "Barn!"

"What?" the white man said. "Barn?"

"Yes!" the boy cried. "Barn!"

"Catch him!" the white man shouted.   105

But it was too late this time too. The Negro grasped his shirt, but the entire sleeve, rotten with washing, carried away, and he was out that door too and in the drive again, and had actually never ceased to run even while he was screaming into the white man's face.

Behind him the white man was shouting, "My horse! Fetch my horse!" and he thought for an instant of cutting across the park and climbing the fence into the road, but he did not know the park nor how high the vine-massed fence might be and he dared not risk it. So he ran on down the drive, blood and breath roaring; presently he was in the road again though he could not see it. He could not hear either: the galloping mare was almost upon him before he heard her, and even then he held his course, as if the very urgency of his wild grief and need must in a moment more find him wings, waiting until the ulti-mate instant to hurl himself aside and into the weed-choked roadside ditch as the horse thundered past and on, for an instant in furious silhouette against the stars, the tranquil early summer night sky which, even before the shape of the horse and rider vanished, strained abruptly and violently upward: a long, swirling roar incredible and soundless, blotting the stars, and he springing up and into the road again, running again, knowing it was too late yet still run-ning even after he heard the shot and, an instant later, two shots, pausing now without knowing he had ceased to run, crying "Pap! Pap!," running again before he knew he had begun to run, stumbling, tripping over something and scrabbling up again without ceasing to run, looking backward over his shoul-der at the glare as he got up, running on among the invisible trees, panting, sobbing, "Father! Father!"

At midnight he was sitting on the crest of a hill. He did not know it was midnight and he did not know how far he had come. But there was no glare behind him now and he sat now, his back toward what he had called home for four days anyhow, his face toward the dark woods which he would enter when breath was strong again, small, shaking steadily in the chill darkness, hugging himself into the remainder of his thin, rotten shirt, the grief and despair now no longer terror and fear but just grief and despair. *Father. My father,* he thought. "He was brave!" he cried suddenly, aloud but not loud, no more than a whisper: "He was! He was in the war! He was in Colonel Sartoris' cav'ry!" not knowing that his father had gone to that war a private in the fine old European sense, wearing no uniform, admitting the authority of and giving fidelity to no man or army or flag, going to war as Malbrouck° himself did: for booty—it meant nothing and less than nothing to him if it were enemy booty or his own.

The slow constellations wheeled on. It would be dawn and then sun-up after a while and he would be hungry. But that would be tomorrow and now he was only cold, and walking would cure that. His breathing was easier now and he decided to get up and go on, and then he found that he had been asleep because he knew it was almost dawn, the night almost over. He could tell that from the whippoorwills. They were everywhere now among the dark trees below him, constant and inflectioned and ceaseless, so that, as the instant for giving over to the day birds drew nearer and nearer, there was no interval at all between them. He got up. He was a little stiff, but walking would cure that too as it would the cold, and soon there would be the sun. He went on down the hill, toward the dark woods within which the liquid silver voices of the birds called unceasing—the rapid and urgent beating of the urgent and quiring heart of the late spring night. He did not look back.

Malbrouck: John Churchill, duke of Marlborough (1650-1722), English military commander who led the armies of England and Holland in the War of Spanish Succession.

CONSIDERATIONS FOR CRITICAL THINKING AND WRITING

1. FIRST RESPONSE. Who is the central character in "Barn Burning"? Explain your choice.

2. How are Sarty's emotions revealed in the story's opening paragraphs? What seems to be the function of the italicized passages there and elsewhere?

3. What do we learn from the story's exposition—background information—that helps us understand Abner's character? How does his behavior reveal his character? What do other people say about him?

4. How does Faulkner's physical description of Abner further our understanding of his personality?

5. Explain how the justice of the peace, Mr. Harris, and Major de Spain contrast with Abner's character.

6. Explain how the description of Major de Spain's house helps to frame the main conflicts that Sarty experiences in his efforts to remain loyal to his father.

7. Describe Sarty's attitudes toward his father as they develop and change throughout the story.

8. What do you think happens to Sarty's father and brother at the end of the story? How does your response to this question affect your reading of the last paragraph?

9. How does the language of the final paragraph suggest a kind of resolution to the conflicts Sarty has experienced?

"Barn Burning" is a difficult story in many respects; even identifying the central character in the narration is debatable. Using a particular critical strategy can often help you read and write about a complicated text because it raises a particular set of questions and issues, gives you a particular lens through which to read. Peter uses the following set of questions—and his own interests—to pick a strategy with which to read "Barn Burning," asking himself Which of these seems to fit the story best? *And* Which strategy do I feel most comfortable using? *You could use the following questions to discover an argument you might want to make about "Barn Burning," or about any of the other short stories, poems, plays, and essays in the book. The page number that follows each heading refers to the discussion of that particular approach covered in this chapter.*

QUESTIONS FOR WRITING: APPLYING A CRITICAL STRATEGY

Formalist Questions *(p. 60)*

1. How do various elements of the work—plot, character, point of view, setting, tone, diction, images, symbol, and so on—reinforce its meanings?
2. How are the elements related to the whole?
3. What is the work's major organizing principle? How is its structure unified?
4. What issues does the work raise? How does the work's structure resolve those issues?

Biographical Questions *(p. 62)*

1. Are facts about the writer's life relevant to your understanding of the work?
2. Are characters and incidents in the work versions of the writer's own experiences? Are they treated factually or imaginatively?
3. How do you think the writer's values are reflected in the work?

Psychological Questions *(p. 64)*

1. How does the work reflect the author's personal psychology?
2. What do the characters' emotions and behavior reveal about their psychological states? What types of personalities are they?
3. Are psychological matters such as repression, dreams, and desire presented consciously or unconsciously by the author?

Historical Questions *(p. 66)*

1. How does the work reflect the period in which it is written?
2. What literary or historical influences helped to shape the form and content of the work?
3. How important is the historical context to interpreting the work?

(continued)

Marxist Questions *(p. 68)*

1. How are class differences presented in the work? Are characters aware or unaware of the economic and social forces that affect their lives?
2. How do economic conditions determine the characters' lives?
3. What ideological values are explicit or implicit?
4. Does the work challenge or affirm the social order it describes?

New Historicist Questions *(p. 68)*

1. What kinds of documents outside the work seem especially relevant for shedding light on the work?
2. How are social values contemporary to the work reflected or refuted in the work?
3. How does your own historical moment affect your reading of the work and its historical reconstruction?

Cultural Studies Questions *(p. 69)*

1. What does the work reveal about the cultural behavior contemporary to it?
2. How does popular culture contemporary to the work reflect or challenge the values implicit or explicit in the work?
3. What kinds of cultural documents contemporary to the work add to your reading of it?
4. How do your own cultural assumptions affect your reading of the work and the culture contemporary to it?

Gender Studies Questions *(p. 70)*

1. How are the lives of men and women portrayed in the work? Do the men and women in the work accept or reject these roles?
2. Is the form and content of the work influenced by the author's gender?
3. What attitudes are explicit or implicit concerning heterosexual, homosexual, or lesbian relationships? Are these relationships sources of conflict? Do they provide resolutions to conflicts?
4. Does the work challenge or affirm traditional ideas about men and women and same-sex relationships?

Mythological Questions *(p. 72)*

1. How does the story resemble other stories in plot, character, setting, or use of symbols?
2. Are archetypes presented, such as quests, initiations, scapegoats, or withdrawals and returns?
3. Does the protagonist undergo any kind of transformation such as a movement from innocence to experience that seems archetypal?
4. Do any specific allusions to myths shed light on the text?

Reader-Response Questions *(p. 74)*

1. How do you respond to the work?
2. How do your own experiences and expectations affect your reading and interpretation?
3. What is the work's original or intended audience? To what extent are you similar to or different from that audience?
4. Do you respond in the same way to the work after more than one reading?

Deconstructionist Questions *(p. 76)*

1. How are contradictory and opposing meanings expressed in the work?
2. How does meaning break down or deconstruct itself in the language of the text?
3. Would you say that ultimate definitive meanings are impossible to determine and establish in the text? Why? How does that affect your interpretation?
4. How are implicit ideological values revealed in the work?

A Sample First Response

After reading "Barn Burning" Peter uses informal writing to record how he personally responded to the story—how he felt as if the characters were doomed to act as they did. By the end of his first response, he realizes that he's really interested in exploring how the social class of the characters dictated their actions.

When I first read "Barn Burning" I was appalled by Abner's violence and guessed that Sarty's flight was an escape from that violence. Reading the story again, however, I was affected by the sense that Abner and Sarty were doomed. I came to believe that the story's plot depended on a sense of inevitability. Then I saw that what made these characters' actions inevitable was the society around them.

Harris's legitimate claim that he was an innocent victim of violence, and Abner's evident violence against the de Spain family's property, certainly left me convinced of Abner's legal guilt. But then I realized that this legality was dictated by economic forces. Faulkner's mention of Abner's history in the Civil War, in which he was a mere economic pawn, convinced me that class oppression was at work.

Guessing that Faulkner's story does more than detail the morals of individuals, I'm eager to explore the role society has in determining the actions of these individuals.

A Sample of Brainstorming

Peter had already identified class issues as particularly important to "Barn Burning" when he was reading the story and writing his first response, so he starts thinking about his paper by using the discussion of Marxist criticism (p. 68) and the questions raised by that approach (p. 98) to brainstorm. Below are his general observations about how class differences are presented in the work, and how those differences determine what happens to the characters — both how they act and react to each other.

SOCIETAL CONTEXT

— oppressive situation of poverty

— inability to compete economically because of conditions such as illiteracy

— Civil War history. Abner required to act violently as a soldier. Abner's lack of economic investment in the war

— race Baiting. Abner's disdain for the de Spain's house, built with "Nigger sweat"

— initial loss of respect for Abner based on social context

— realization in front of de Spain's house

— de Spain's anger toward Sarty, even given Sarty's confession

— Sarty condemns his father

A Sample Student Marxist Analysis

As you read Peter's final paper, think about how he uses different tools to come up with a sophisticated argument: critical strategy, personal response, and close reading. Each stage of the process — his first response, brainstorming, and planning of the paper — has been part of building and changing the final paper.

Peter Campion
Professor Hale
English 115
November 12, 20--

                    Class Issues in "Barn Burning"
     William Faulkner's "Barn Burning" tells the story of
Sarty Snopes and his doomed father, Abner. As Abner violently repeats his mistakes by burning the de Spain's
barn, even after being driven from another county for
suspected barn-burning, Sarty comes to realize hard
facts about the southern agrarian society around him.
"Barn Burning," however, is not the story of Sarty's
liberation. An examination of Sarty's and his father's
responses to their society's economically controlled idea
of justice, an idea of justice that ultimately dooms even
Sarty's struggle for freedom, proves "Barn Burning" to be
an indictment of that society.
     Consider first Abner's cycle of violence as it is
perpetuated by the very society that condemns it. Describing the meager campfire the Snopes light as they
flee from Abner's crime against Harris, Faulkner calls
the element of fire itself Abner's "one weapon for the
preservation of integrity" (para. 26). Although Abner's
use of this weapon appalls the reader, Faulkner's portrayal of Abner shrewdly conserving fire, which he has
used so recklessly, shows that fire is not merely his
means to express rage; it is a form of currency. Unable
to protect his integrity in normal economic competition,
Abner resorts to barn-burning as his final means of
exchange. His society, which never even provided him with
literacy, has produced in him this unavailing rage, so he
gives it back. This is nothing if not exchange.
     This violence makes Abner an outcast, yet he
learned it, as Faulkner tells us, in that central event

of southern society, the Civil War. Abner's renegade conduct in the war might tempt the reader to consider him a
cowardly deserter from civilization and its rules. But
Abner's acts, impotent though they were, were his form of
resisting his status as a pawn of the slaveholding society in which he had no investment. When he leaves the de
Spain house after trashing the carpet, he looks back at
the grand house, doubtless built by slaves, and tells
Sarty, "'That's sweat. Nigger sweat. Maybe it ain't white
enough yet to suit him. Maybe he wants to mix some white
sweat with it'" (para. 46). However doomed Abner is to
repeat his violence, he is not ignorant of the violence
on which his society has been built.

While Abner's violence against the de Spains, and
against the exploitation they represent, eventually has
him condemned, Sarty's slow realization of the economic
situation allows him to escape. Watching his father
approaching the de Spain's, Sarty thinks Abner's figure
"was not dwarfed by the house, for the reason that it
had never looked big anywhere" (para. 41). At this moment, Sarty figures out that his father, and his father's
actions, are infinitesimal compared to the towering power
of the rich. When the second barn-burning occurs, Sarty
decides to side with this powerful economic order.

His escape, however, shows Sarty to be as much of an
economic pawn as his father. When he learns of Abner's
determination to burn the de Spains' barn, he runs to
Major de Spain, but de Spain is just as intent on catching this valuable informer as the Snopes are, and Sarty
knows this, for he "had actually never ceased to run
even while he was screaming into the white man's face"
(para. 106). Sarty succeeds in physically freeing himself, but only at the cost of his father's condemnation.

Running away, Sarty hears the gunshots. His father is hardly given a reasonable defense. None of this would have occurred without Sarty's honesty, honesty that his society reduced to a bartering tool.

Faulkner shows us that Sarty has not liberated himself: alone in the woods, he has become as much a fugitive as Abner was from the war onward. Although Sarty initially gained more insight than Abner had, his action, whether he knew it or not, also made him more of a victim of economic oppression. Sarty exchanged his valuable information for his own father's condemnation. By showing us the painful results of this brutal barter, Faulkner implicitly accuses the society that accepts it.

4

Writing from Sources

A close reading of a primary source such as a short story, poem, play, or essay can give insights into a work's themes and effects, but sometimes you will want to know more. A published commentary by a critic who knows the work well and is familiar with the author's life and times can provide insights or information about the context in which a work was written. Such comments and interpretations — known as *secondary sources* — are, of course, not a substitute for the work itself, but they often can take you into a work further than if you made the journey by yourself.

After imagination, good sense, and energy, perhaps the next most important quality for writing a research paper is the ability to organize material. A research paper on a literary topic requires a writer to take account of quite a lot at once: The text, ideas, sources, and documentation techniques all make demands on one's efforts to present a topic clearly and convincingly.

The following list should give you a sense of what goes into creating a research paper. Although some steps on the list can be folded into one another, they offer an overview of the work that will involve you:

1. Choosing a topic
2. Finding sources
3. Evaluating sources
4. Taking notes
5. Developing a thesis
6. Organizing an outline
7. Writing drafts
8. Revising
9. Documenting sources
10. Preparing the final draft and proofreading

Even if you have never written a research paper, you most likely have already had experience choosing a topic, developing a thesis, organizing an outline, and writing a draft that you then revised, proofread, and handed in. Those skills represent six of the ten items on the list. This chapter — including a student casebook on the research paper — focuses on the remaining tasks, unique to research paper assignments: finding sources, evaluating sources, taking notes, and documenting sources.

CHOOSING A TOPIC

Chapter 1 discussed the importance of reading a work closely and taking careful notes as a means of generating topics for writing about literature. If you know a work well and record your understanding of it in notes, you'll have impressions and ideas to choose from for potential topics. You may find it useful to review the information on pages 14–16 before reading the advice about putting together a research paper in this chapter.

FINDING SOURCES

Whether your college library is large or small, its reference librarians can usually help you locate secondary sources about a particular work or author. Unless you choose a very recently published story, poem, play, or essay about which little or nothing has been written, you should be able to find out more about a literary work efficiently and quickly. Even if a work has been published recently, you can probably find relevant information on the Internet (see Electronic Sources, p. 107). Here are some useful reference sources that can help you to establish both an overview of a potential topic and a list of relevant books and articles.

Annotated List of References

> *American Writers.* 4 vols. New York: Scribner's, 1979–87. Chronological essays offer biography and criticism of major American writers.
> Baker, Nancy L., and Nancy Huling. *A Research Guide for Undergraduate Students: English and American Literature.* 4th ed. New York: MLA, 1995. Especially designed for students; a useful guide to reference sources.
> Bryer, Jackson, ed. *Sixteen Modern American Authors: A Survey of Research and Criticism.* New York: Norton, 1973. Extensive bibliographic essays on Sherwood Anderson, Willa Cather, Hart Crane, Theodore Dreiser, T. S. Eliot, William Faulkner, F. Scott Fitzgerald, Robert Frost, Ernest Hemingway, Eugene O'Neill, Ezra Pound, Edwin

Arlington Robinson, John Steinbeck, Wallace Stevens, William Carlos Williams, and Thomas Wolfe.

Contemporary Literary Criticism. 106 vols. to date. Detroit: Gale, 1973–. Brief biographies of contemporary authors along with excerpts from reviews and criticism of their work.

Corse, Larry B., and Sandra B. Corse. *Articles on American and British Literature: An Index to Selected Periodicals, 1950–1977.* Athens, OH: Swallow, 1981. Specifically designed for students using small college libraries.

Dictionary of Literary Biography. Detroit: Gale, 1978–. A multivolume series in progress of American, British, and world writers that provides useful biographical and critical overviews.

Eddleman, Floyd E., ed. *American Drama Criticism: Interpretations, 1890–1977.* 2nd ed. Hamden, CT: Shoe String, 1979. Supplement 1984.

Elliot, Emory, et al. *Columbia Literary History of the United States.* New York: Columbia UP, 1988. This updates the discussions in Spiller (p. 107) and reflects recent changes in the canon.

Harner, James L. *Literary Research Guide: A Guide to Reference Sources for the Study of Literature in English and Related Topics.* 3rd ed. New York: MLA, 1998. A selective but extensive annotated guide to important bibliographies, abstracts, databases, histories, surveys, dictionaries, encyclopedias, and handbooks; an invaluable research tool with extensive, useful indexes.

Holman, C. Hugh, and William Harmon. *A Handbook to Literature.* 8th ed. New York: Macmillan, 1999. A thorough dictionary of literary terms that also provides brief, clear overviews of literary movements such as Romanticism.

Kuntz, Joseph M., and Nancy C. Martinez. *Poetry Explication: A Checklist of Interpretation since 1925 of British and American Poems Past and Present.* Boston: Hall, 1980.

MLA International Bibliography of Books and Articles on Modern Language and Literature. New York: MLA, 1921–. Compiled annually; a major source for articles and books. Also available online and on CD-ROM.

The New Cambridge Bibliography of English Literature. 5 vols. Cambridge, Eng.: Cambridge UP, 1967–77. An important source on the literature from A.D. 600 to 1950.

Ousby, Ian, ed. *The Cambridge Guide to English Literature.* 2nd ed. Cambridge, Eng.: Cambridge UP, 1994. A valuable overview.

The Oxford History of English Literature. 13 vols. Oxford, Eng.: Oxford UP, 1945–, in progress. The most comprehensive literary history.

The Penguin Companion to World Literature. 4 vols. New York: McGraw-Hill, 1969–71. Covers classical, Asian, African, European, English, and American literature.

Preminger, Alex, and T. V. F. Brogan, eds. *The New Princeton Encyclopedia of Poetry and Poetics.* Princeton: Princeton UP, 1993. Includes entries on technical terms and poetic movements.

Rees, Robert, and Earl N. Harbert. *Fifteen American Authors before 1900: Bibliographic Essays on Research and Criticism.* Madison: U of Wisconsin P, 1971. Among the writers covered are Stephen Crane and Emily Dickinson.

Spiller, Robert E., et al. *Literary History of the United States.* 4th ed. 2 vols. New York: Macmillan, 1974. Coverage of literary movements and individual writers from colonial times to the 1960s.

Walker, Warren S. *Twentieth-Century Short Story Explication.* 3rd ed. Hamden, CT: Shoe String, 1977. A bibliography of criticism on short stories written since 1800; supplements appear every few years.

These sources are available in the reference sections of most college libraries; ask a reference librarian to help you locate them or to help you use their electronic resources.

Electronic Sources

Researchers can locate materials in a variety of sources, including card catalogs, specialized encyclopedias, bibliographies, and indexes to periodicals. Most libraries now also provide computer searches that are linked to a database of the libraries' holdings; you can even access many of these databases from home. This can be an efficient way to establish a bibliography on a specific topic. If your library has such a service, consult a reference librarian about how to use it and to determine whether it is feasible for your topic. If a computer service is impractical, you can still collect the same information from printed sources.

In addition to the many electronic databases ranging from your library's computerized holdings to the many specialized CD-ROMs available, such as *MLA International Bibliography* (a major source for articles and books on literary topics), the Internet also connects millions of sites with primary sources (the full texts of stories, poems, plays, and essays) and secondary sources (biography or criticism). If you have not had practice with research on the Web, it is a good idea to get guidance from your instructor or a librarian. Browsing on the Net can be absorbing as well as informative, but unless you have plenty of time to spare, don't wait until the last minute to locate your electronic sources. You might find yourself trying to find reliable, professional sources among thousands of sites if you enter an unqualified entry such as "Charles Dickens." Once you are familiar with the Net, however, you'll find its research potential both fascinating and rewarding.

Do remember that your own college library offers a broad range of electronic sources. If you're feeling uncertain, intimidated, and profoundly unplugged, your reference librarians are there to help you to get started. Once you take advantage of their advice and tutorials, you'll soon find that negotiating the World Wide Web can be an efficient means of researching almost any subject.

Online Resources for Research and Writing

The details you'll need to conduct research on the Web go beyond the scope of this chapter, but Bedford/St. Martin's offers several online resources for researching and writing about literature that can help you find what you need on the Web—and then use it once you find it. Visit <**www.bedfordstmartins.com/literature**>, and explore the resources we offer to help you research online.

Citing sources correctly in a final paper is often a challenge, and the Web has made it even more complex. *Research and Documentation Online,* the online version of the popular booklet *Research and Documentation in the Electronic Age,* by Diana Hacker, provides clear, authoritative advice on documentation in every discipline. It also covers conducting library and online research and includes links to Internet research sources.

The English Research Room is a good starting place for any research project, large or small. *Research Web guides* will answer questions you may have about doing research, conducting electronic searches, using the Web and other online resources, and evaluating and citing sources. *Interactive tutorials* give you the opportunity to practice common electronic search techniques in a live environment. *Research links* make it easy to find hundreds of useful research sites, including search engines and reference sites.

Organized alphabetically by author within five genres, *LitLinks* offers links to sites about many of the authors in *Thinking and Writing about Literature.* Clear, concise annotations and links to more than five hundred professionally maintained sites help you browse with direction, whether you're looking for a favorite text, additional biographical or critical information about an author, critical articles, or conversation with other students and scholars.

Once you're on the Web—or in the library—*Research Assistant,* a stand-alone application, can help you manage your research sources. Functioning as a smart file cabinet, *Research Assistant* helps you collect, evaluate, and cite your sources. It works not only with text but also with graphics, audio clips, and video clips. If you're writing a paper, *Research Assistant* will help you sort and organize your sources, moving you from researching into writing.

EVALUATING SOURCES AND TAKING NOTES

Evaluate your sources for their reliability and the quality of their evidence. Check to see whether an article or book has been superseded by later studies; try to use up-to-date sources. A popular magazine article will probably not be as authoritative as an article in a scholarly journal. Sources that are well documented with primary and secondary materials usually indicate that the author has done his or her homework. Books printed by university presses and established trade presses are preferable to books privately printed. But there are always exceptions. If you are uncertain about how to assess a book, try to find out something about the author. Are there any other books listed in the card catalog that indicate the author's expertise? What do book reviews say about the work? Three valuable indexes to book reviews of literary studies are *Book Review Digest, Book Review Index,* and *Index to Book Reviews in the Humanities.* Your reference librarian can show you how to use these important tools for evaluating books. Reviews can be a quick means to gain a broad perspective on writers and their works because reviewers often survey previous approaches to the topic under discussion.

A cautionary note: assessing online sources can be more problematic than evaluating print sources because anyone with a computer and online access can publish on the Internet. Be sure to determine the nature of your sources and their authority. Is the site the work of a professional or an amateur? Is the information likely to be reliable? Is it biased? Is it documented? Before placing your trust in an Internet source, make sure that it warrants your confidence.

As you prepare a list of reliable sources relevant to your topic, record the necessary bibliographic information so that it will be available when you make up the list of works cited for your paper. (See the sample bibliography card below.) For a book include the author, complete title, place of publication, publisher, and date. For an article include author, complete title, name of periodical, volume number, date of issue, and page numbers. For an Internet source, include the author, complete title, database title, periodical or site name, date of posting of the site (or last update), name of institution or organization, date when you accessed the source, and the network address (URL).

> *Minter, David.*
>> *William Faulkner: His Life and Work.*
>> *Baltimore, MD: Johns Hopkins UP, 1980.*

Sample bibliography card for a book.

Once you have assembled a tentative bibliography, you will need to take notes on your readings. If you are not using a word processor, use 3 by 5-, 4 by 6-, or 5 by 8-inch cards for note taking. They are easy to manipulate and can be readily sorted after you establish subheadings for your paper. Be sure to keep track of where the information comes from by writing the author's name and page number on each note card. If you use more than one work by the same author, include a brief title as well as the author's name. (See the sample note card below.)

The sample note card records the source of information (the complete publishing information is on the bibliography card) and provides a heading that will allow easy sorting later on. Notice that the information is summarized rather than quoted in large chunks. The student also includes a short note asking himself whether this will be relevant to the topic — the meaning of the title of "A Rose for Emily." (As it turned out, this was not directly related to the topic, so it was dropped.)

Note cards can combine quotations, paraphrases, and summaries; you can also use them to cite your own ideas and give them headings so that you don't lose track of them. As you take notes, try to record only points relevant to your topic, and don't include notes merely because you recorded them.

On the publication of "A Rose for Emily" Minter 116

Minter describes "A Rose" as "one of Faulkner's finest short stories" yet it was rejected at Scribner's when Faulkner submitted it.

[Can I work this in?]

Sample note card.

DEVELOPING A THESIS AND ORGANIZING THE PAPER

As you take notes on the sources you've found, you should begin to sort them into topics. To some degree, developing your thesis and organizing your paper is the same process when you're working on a research paper as it is when you're writing any other kind of assignment, and you should review the advice in Chapter 2 for help with these general steps (p. 31–36). What makes developing a thesis different for a research paper is that you want to make sure that you have support for the points that you want to make — you may well find after sorting your notes that your original topic is not supported by the outside reading you've done. If you're writing a longer paper, you may want to write a rough outline and mark down how many cards will fit under each of the points you want to make in your paper. If your cards don't match up to your points, you either need to do more research or you need to revise your thesis.

REVISING

After writing your first draft, you should review the advice on revising and the Questions for Revising on pages 39–40 so that you can read your paper with an objective eye. Two days after writing her next-to-last draft, the writer of the Frost paper realized that she had allotted too much space for discussions of Frost's poetic reputation that were not directly related to her approach. She wanted to demonstrate a familiarity with these studies, but it was not essential that she summarize or discuss them. She corrected this by simply deleting them. Her earlier draft had included summaries of these studies that were tangential to her argument. The point is that she saw this herself after she took some time to approach the paper from a fresh perspective.

DOCUMENTING SOURCES

You must acknowledge the use of a source when you (1) quote someone's exact words, (2) summarize or borrow someone's opinions or ideas, or (3) use information and facts that are not considered to be common knowledge. The purpose of this documentation is to acknowledge your sources, to demonstrate that you are familiar with what others have thought about the topic, and to provide your reader access to the same sources. If your paper is not adequately documented, it will be vulnerable to a charge of *plagiarism* — the presentation of someone else's work as your own. Conscious plagiarism is easy to avoid; honesty takes care of that for most people. However, there is a more problematic form of plagiarism that is often inadvertent. Whether inadequate documentation is conscious or not, plagiarism is a serious matter and must be avoided. Papers can be evaluated only by what is on the page, not by their writers' intentions.

Let's look more closely at what constitutes plagiarism. Consider the following passage quoted from John Gassner's introduction to *Four Great Plays by Henrik Ibsen* (New York: Bantam, 1959), p. viii:

> Today it seems incredible that *A Doll's House*° should have created the furor it did. In exploding Victorian ideals of feminine dependency the play seemed revolutionary in 1879. When its heroine Nora left her home in search of self-development it seemed as if the sanctity of marriage had been flouted by a playwright treading the stage with cloven-feet.

Now read this plagiarized version:

> *A Doll's House* created a furor in 1879 by blowing up Victorian ideals about a woman's place in the world. Nora's search for self-fulfillment outside her home appeared to be an attack on the sanctity of marriage by a cloven-footed playwright.

Though the writer has shortened the passage and made some changes in the wording, this paragraph is basically the same as Gassner's. Indeed, several of his phrases are lifted almost intact. Even if a parenthetical reference had been included at the end of the passage and the source included in "Works Cited," the language of this passage would still be plagiarism because it is presented as the writer's own. Both language and ideas must be acknowledged.

Here is an adequately documented version of the passage:

> John Gassner has observed how difficult it is for today's readers to comprehend the intense reaction against *A Doll's House* in 1879. When Victorian audiences watched Nora walk out of her stifling marriage, they assumed that Ibsen was expressing a devilish contempt for the "sanctity of marriage" (viii).

This passage makes absolutely clear that the observation is Gassner's, and it is written in the student's own language with the exception of one quoted phrase. Had Gassner not been named in the passage, the parenthetical reference would have included his name: (Gassner viii).

Some mention should be made of the notion of common knowledge before we turn to the standard format for documenting sources. Observations and facts that are widely known and routinely included in many of your sources do not require documentation. It is not necessary to cite a source for the fact that Alfred, Lord Tennyson, was born in 1809 or that

---

° Rolf Fjelde, whose translation is included in Chapter 9, renders the title as *A Doll House* in order to emphasize that the whole household, including Torvald as well as Nora, lives an unreal, doll-like existence.

Ernest Hemingway loved to fish and hunt. Sometimes it will be difficult for you to determine what common knowledge is for a topic that you know little about. If you are in doubt, the best strategy is to supply a reference.

There are two basic ways to document sources. Traditionally, sources have been cited in footnotes at the bottom of each page or in endnotes grouped together at the end of the paper. Here is how a portion of the sample paper would look if footnotes were used instead of parenthetical documentation:

```
By refusing to think about the speaker's question and choosing
to hide behind his own father's words, he closes any possible
window of communication between them.[1]
```

[1]George Monteiro, Robert Frost and the New England Renaissance (Lexington: UP of Kentucky, 1988) 127.

Unlike endnotes, which are double spaced throughout under the title of "Notes" on separate pages at the end of the paper, footnotes appear four spaces below the text. They are single spaced with double spaces between notes.

No doubt you will have encountered these documentation methods in your reading. A different style is recommended, however, in the Modern Language Association's *MLA Handbook for Writers of Research Papers,* Fifth Edition (1999). This style employs parenthetical references within the text of the paper; these are keyed to an alphabetical list of works cited at the end of the paper. This method is designed to be less distracting for the reader. Unless you are instructed to follow the footnote or endnote style for documentation, use the parenthetical method explained in the next section.

The List of Works Cited

Items in the list of works cited are arranged alphabetically according to the author's last name and indented five spaces after the first line. This allows the reader to locate quickly the complete bibliographic information for the author's name cited within the parenthetical reference in the text. The following are common entries for literature papers and should be used as models. If some of your sources are of a different nature, consult the *MLA Handbook for Writers of Research Papers,* Fifth Edition (New York: MLA, 1999); or, for the latest updates, check MLA's Web site at <http://www.mla.org>.

A BOOK BY ONE AUTHOR

Hendrickson, Robert. The Literary Life and Other Curiosities. New York: Viking, 1981.

Notice that the author's name is in reverse order. This information, along with the full title, place of publication, publisher, and date, should be taken from the title and copyright pages of the book. The title is underlined to indicate italics and is also followed by a period. If the city of publication is well known, it is unnecessary to include the state. Use the publication date on the title page; if none appears there, use the copyright date (after ©) on the back of the title page.

A Book by Two Authors

> Horton, Rod W., and Herbert W. Edwards. <u>Backgrounds of</u>
>
> <u>American Literary Thought</u>. 3rd ed. Englewood Cliffs:
>
> Prentice, 1974.

Only the first author's name is given in reverse order. The edition number appears after the title.

A Book with More than Three Authors

> Gates, Henry Louis, Jr., et al., eds. <u>The Norton Anthology</u>
>
> <u>of African American Literature</u>. New York: Norton,
>
> 1997.

The abbreviation *et al.* means "and others." It is used to avoid having to list all the editors of this work.

A Work in a Collection by the Same Author

> O'Connor, Flannery. "Greenleaf." <u>The Complete Stories</u>. By
>
> O'Connor. New York: Farrar, 1971. 311-34.

Page numbers are given because the reference is to only a single story in the collection.

A Work in a Collection by Different Writers

> Frost, Robert. "Mending Wall." <u>Thinking and Writing about</u>
>
> <u>Literature: A Text and Anthology</u>. Ed. Michael Meyer.
>
> 2nd ed. Boston: Bedford/St. Martin's, 2000. 121-22.

A Translated Book

> Grass, Günter. <u>The Tin Drum</u>. Trans. Ralph Manheim. New
>
> York: Vintage-Random, 1962.

An Introduction, Preface, Foreword, or Afterword

> Johnson, Thomas H. Introduction. <u>Final Harvest: Emily Dick-</u>
>
> <u>inson's Poems</u>. By Emily Dickinson. Boston: Little,
>
> Brown, 1961. vii-xiv.

This cites the introduction by Johnson. Notice that a colon is used between the book's main title and subtitle. To cite a poem in this book use this method:

> Dickinson, Emily. "A Tooth upon Our Peace." <u>Final Harvest:</u>
>
> > <u>Emily Dickinson's Poems</u>. Ed. Thomas H. Johnson. Boston:
> >
> > Little, Brown, 1961. 110.

AN ENCYCLOPEDIA

> "Wordsworth, William." <u>The New Encyclopedia Britannica</u>.
>
> > 14th ed. 1984.

Because this encyclopedia is organized alphabetically, no page number or other information is given, only the edition number (if available) and date.

AN ARTICLE IN A MAGAZINE

> Morrow, Lance. "Pressing the Germy Flesh." <u>Time</u> 8 Nov.
>
> > 1999: 164.

The citation for an unsigned article would begin with the title and be alphabetized by the first word of the title other than "a," "an," or "the."

AN ARTICLE IN A SCHOLARLY JOURNAL WITH CONTINUOUS PAGINATION BEYOND A SINGLE ISSUE

> Axelrod, Stephen Gould. "Robert Lowell and the Cold War."
>
> > <u>New England Quarterly</u> 72 (1999): 339-61.

Because this journal uses continuous pagination instead of separate pagination for each issue, it is not necessary to include the month, season, or number of the issue. Only one of the quarterly issues will have pages numbered 339–61. If you are not certain whether a journal's pages are numbered continuously throughout a volume, supply the month, season, or issue number, as in the next entry.

AN ARTICLE IN A SCHOLARLY JOURNAL WITH SEPARATE PAGINATION FOR EACH ISSUE

> Updike, John. "The Cultural Situation of the American
>
> > Writer." <u>American Studies International</u> 15 (Spring
> >
> > 1977): 19-28.

By noting the spring issue, the entry saves a reader looking through each issue of the 1977 volume for the correct article on pages 19 to 28.

AN ARTICLE IN A NEWSPAPER

> Ziegler, Philip. "The Lure of Gossip, the Rules of
>
> > History." <u>New York Times</u> 23 Feb. 1986, sec. 7: 1+.

This citation indicates that the article appears on page 1 of section 7 and continues onto another page.

A Lecture

> Tilton, Robert. "The Beginnings of American Studies." Eng-
>
> lish 270 class lecture. University of Connecticut,
>
> Storrs, 12 Mar. 1999.

Letter, E-Mail, or Interview

> Vellenga, Carolyn. Letter to the author. 9 Oct. 1999.
>
> Harter, Stephen P. E-mail to the author. 28 Dec. 1999.
>
> McConagha, Bill. Personal interview [or Telephone
>
> interview]. 4 Mar. 1998.

If a source appears in print as well as in an electronic format, provide the same publication information you would for printed sources — the title of the electronic source, the medium (such as "CD-ROM"), the name of the distributor, and the date of publication. If it does not appear in print form, or if you don't have all or some of the information, provide as much as you have along with the date of access and the electronic address. You need to provide all the information necessary for your readers to find the source themselves.

CD-ROM Issued Periodically

> Aaron, Belèn V. "The Death of Theory." Scholarly Book
>
> Reviews 4.3 (1997): 146-47. ERIC. CD-ROM. Silver-
>
> Platter. Dec. 1997.

CD-ROM Issued in a Single Edition

> Sideman, Bob, and Donald Sheehy. "The Risk of Spirit."
>
> Robert Frost: Poems, Life, Legacy. CD-ROM. Vers. 1.0.
>
> New York: Holt, 1997.

Electronic Web Site

> Cody, David. "Dickens: A Brief Biography." World Wide Web.
>
> 13 Feb. 1998. <http://www.stg.brown.edu/projects/
>
> hypertext/landow/victorian/dickens/dickensbio1.html>.

Electronic Newsgroup

> Kathman, David. "Shakespeare's Literacy--or Lack of." 3
>
> Mar. 1998. Newsgroup. <humanities.lit.authors.shake-
>
> speare>.

Parenthetical References

A list of works cited is not an adequate indication of how you have used sources in your paper. You must also provide the precise location of quotations and other information by using parenthetical references within the text of the paper. You do this by citing the author's name (or the source's title if the work is anonymous) and the page number:

```
Collins points out that "Nabokov was misunderstood by early
reviewers of his work" (28).
```
or
```
Nabokov's first critics misinterpreted his stories
(Collins 28).
```

Either way a reader will find the complete bibliographic entry in the list of works cited under Collins's name and know that the information cited in the paper appears on page 28. Notice that the end punctuation comes after the parenthesis.

If you have listed more than one work by the same author, you would add a brief title to the parenthetical reference to distinguish between them. You could also include the full title in your text:

```
Nabokov's first critics misinterpreted his stories
(Collins, "Early Reviews" 28).
```
or
```
Collins points out in "Early Reviews of Nabokov's Fiction"
that his early work was misinterpreted by
reviewers (28).
```

There can be many variations on what is included in a parenthetical reference, depending on the nature of the entry in the list of works cited. But the general principle is simple enough: provide enough parenthetical information for a reader to find the work in "Works Cited." Examine the sample research paper for more examples of works cited and strategies for including parenthetical references. If you are puzzled by a given situation, ask your reference librarian to show you the *MLA Handbook* or use the link within MLA's Web site at <http://www.mla.org>.

The Research Paper

Writing a research paper can be a big undertaking involving many stages—choosing a topic, finding sources, evaluating sources and taking notes, developing a thesis and organizing the paper, and documenting sources. This casebook shows you how one student, Stephanie Tobin, developed a research paper around a comparison of two poems by Robert Frost. Stephanie was asked to write a five-page paper that drew on what she had learned about Frost's poetry and life from the published work of other writers and scholars. Before looking at what others had written about Robert Frost, however, she chose the poems she wanted to learn more about—"Mowing" and "Mending Wall"—and read each several times, taking notes and making comments in the margin of her textbook on each poem. As you read the poems, think about the aspects of Frost's life or work you would want to explore further if you were assigned a research paper.

ROBERT FROST (1874–1963)

Few poets have enjoyed the popular success that Robert Frost achieved during his lifetime, and no twentieth-century American poet has had his or her work as widely read and honored. Frost is as closely associated with New England as the stone walls that help define its landscape; his reputation, however, transcends regional boundaries. Although he was named Poet Laureate of Vermont only two years before his death, he was for many years the nation's unofficial poet laureate. Frost collected honors the way some people pick up burrs on country walks. Among his awards were four Pulitzer Prizes, the Bollingen Prize, a congressional medal, and dozens of honorary degrees. Perhaps his most moving appearance was his recitation of "The Gift Outright" for millions of Americans at the presidential inauguration of John F. Kennedy in 1961. Frost's recognition as a poet is especially remarkable because his career as a writer did not attract any sig-

Robert Frost at his writing desk in Franconia, New Hampshire, 1915. Reprinted by permission of The Jones Library.

nificant attention until he was nearly forty years old. He taught himself to write while he labored at odd jobs, taught school, or farmed.

Frost's early identity seems very remote from the New England soil. Although his parents were descended from generations of New Englanders, he was born in San Francisco and was named Robert Lee Frost after the Confederate general. After his father died in 1885, his mother moved the family back to Massachusetts to live with relatives. Frost graduated from high school sharing valedictorian honors with the classmate who would become his wife three years later. Between high school and marriage, he attended Dartmouth College for a few months and then taught. His teaching prompted him to enroll in Harvard in 1897, but after less than two years he withdrew without a degree (though Harvard would eventually award him an honorary doctorate in 1937, four years after Dartmouth conferred its honorary degree on him). For the next decade, Frost read and wrote poems when he was not chicken farming or teaching. In 1912, he sold his farm and moved his family to England, where he hoped to find the audience that his poetry did not have in the United States.

Three years in England made it possible for Frost to return home as a poet. His first two volumes of poetry, *A Boy's Will* (1913) and *North of Boston* (1914), were published in England. During the next twenty years, honors and awards were conferred on collections such as *Mountain Interval* (1916), *New Hampshire* (1923), *West-Running Brook* (1928), and *A Further Range* (1936). These are the volumes on which most of Frost's popular and critical reputation rests. Later collections include *A Witness Tree* (1942), *A Masque of Reason* (1945), *Steeple Bush* (1947), *A Masque of Mercy* (1947), *Complete Poems* (1949), and *In the Clearing* (1962). He also taught at a number of schools, including Amherst College, the University of Michigan, Harvard University, Dartmouth College, and Middlebury College.

Frost's countless poetry readings generated wide audiences eager to claim him as their poet. The image he cultivated resembled closely what the public likes to think a poet should be. Frost was seen as a lovable, wise old man; his simple wisdom and cracker-barrel sayings appeared comforting and homey. From this Yankee rustic, audiences learned that "There's a lot yet that isn't understood" or "We love the things we love for what they are" or "Good fences make good neighbors."

In a sense, Frost packaged himself for public consumption. "I am . . . my own salesman," he said. When asked direct questions about the meanings of his poems, he often winked or scratched his head to give the impression that the customer was always right. To be sure, there is a simplicity in Frost's language, but that simplicity does not fully reflect the depth of the man, the complexity of his themes, or the richness of his art.

The folksy optimist behind the lectern did not reveal his private troubles to his audiences, although he did address those problems at his writing desk. Frost suffered from professional jealousies, anger, and depression. His family life was especially painful. Three of his four children died: a son at the age of four, a daughter in her late twenties from tuberculosis, and another son by suicide. His marriage was filled with tension. Although Frost's work is landscaped with sunlight, snow, birches, birds, blueberries, and squirrels, it is important to recognize that he was also intimately "acquainted with the night," a phrase that serves as the haunting title of one of his poems.

Among the major concerns that appear in Frost's poetry are the fragility of life, the consequences of rejecting or accepting the conditions of one's life, the passion of inconsolable grief, the difficulty of sustaining intimacy, the fear of loneliness and isolation, the inevitability of change, the tensions between the individual and society, and the place of tradition and custom. Frost's eye for strong, telling details was matched by his ear for natural speech rhythms. His flexible use of what he called "iambic and loose iambic" enabled him to create moving lyric poems that reveal the personal thoughts of a speaker and dramatic poems that convincingly characterize people caught in intense emotional situations. The language in his poems appears to be little more than a transcription of casual and even rambling speech, but it is in actuality Frost's poetic creation, carefully crafted to reveal the joys and sorrows that are woven into people's daily lives. What is missing from Frost's poems is artificiality, not art.

Mowing   1913

There was never a sound beside the wood but one,
And that was my long scythe whispering to the ground.
What was it it whispered? I knew not well myself;
Perhaps it was something about the heat of the sun,
Something, perhaps, about the lack of sound —   5
And that was why it whispered and did not speak.
It was no dream of the gift of idle hours,
Or easy gold at the hand of fay or elf:
Anything more than the truth would have seemed too weak
To the earnest love that laid the swale in rows,   10
Not without feeble-pointed spikes of flowers
(Pale orchises), and scared a bright green snake.
The fact is the sweetest dream that labour knows.
My long scythe whispered and left the hay to make.

CONSIDERATIONS FOR CRITICAL THINKING AND WRITING

1. FIRST RESPONSE. Describe the tone of "Mowing." How does reading it aloud
   affect your understanding of it?
2. Discuss the image of the scythe. Do you think it has any symbolic value?
   Explain why or why not.
3. Paraphrase the poem. What do you think its thematic significance is?
4. Describe the type of sonnet Frost uses in "Mowing."

Mending Wall   1914

Something there is that doesn't love a wall,
That sends the frozen-ground-swell under it,
And spills the upper boulders in the sun;
And makes gaps even two can pass abreast.
The work of hunters is another thing: 5
I have come after them and made repair
Where they have left not one stone on a stone,
But they would have the rabbit out of hiding,
To please the yelping dogs. The gaps I mean,
No one has seen them made or heard them made,   10
But at spring mending-time we find them there.
I let my neighbor know beyond the hill;
And on a day we meet to walk the line
And set the wall between us once again.
We keep the wall between us as we go.   15
To each the boulders that have fallen to each.
And some are loaves and some so nearly balls
We have to use a spell to make them balance:
"Stay where you are until our backs are turned!"

We wear our fingers rough with handling them. 20
Oh, just another kind of outdoor game,
One on a side. It comes to little more:
There where it is we do not need the wall:
He is all pine and I am apple orchard.
My apple trees will never get across 25
And eat the cones under his pines, I tell him.
He only says, "Good fences make good neighbors."
Spring is the mischief in me, and I wonder
If I could put a notion in his head:
"*Why* do they make good neighbors? Isn't it 30
Where there are cows? But here there are no cows.
Before I built a wall I'd ask to know
What I was walling in or walling out,
And to whom I was like to give offense.
Something there is that doesn't love a wall, 35
That wants it down." I could say "Elves" to him,
But it's not elves exactly, and I'd rather
He said it for himself. I see him there
Bringing a stone grasped firmly by the top
In each hand, like an old-stone savage armed. 40
He moves in darkness as it seems to me,
Not of woods only and the shade of trees.
He will not go behind his father's saying,
And he likes having thought of it so well
He says again, "Good fences make good neighbors." 45

Considerations for Critical Thinking and Writing

1. FIRST RESPONSE. What might the "Something" be that "doesn't love a wall"? Why does the speaker remind his neighbor each spring that the wall needs to be repaired? Is it ironic that the *speaker* initiates the mending? Is there anything good about the wall?

2. How do the speaker and his neighbor in this poem differ in sensibilities? What is suggested about the neighbor in lines 41 and 42?

3. The neighbor likes the saying "Good fences make good neighbors" so well that he repeats it (lines 27, 45). Does the speaker also say something twice? What else suggests that the speaker's attitude toward the wall is not necessarily Frost's?

4. Although the speaker's language is colloquial, what is poetic about the sounds and rhythms he uses?

5. This poem was first published in 1914; Frost read it to an audience when he visited Russia in 1962. What do these facts suggest about the symbolic value of "Mending Wall"?

6. CRITICAL STRATEGIES. Read the section on literary history criticism (pp. 67–68) in Chapter 3, "Applying a Critical Strategy." "Mending Wall" was originally published in 1914, when the world was on the verge of collapsing into the violent landscape of World War I. How does this historical context affect your reading of the poem?

The following questions can help you to incorporate materials from critical or biographical essays into your own writing about a literary work.

You may initially feel intimidated by the prospect of responding to the arguments of professional writers in your own paper. However, the process will not defeat you if you have clearly formulated your own response to the literary work and are able to distinguish it from the critics' perspectives. Reading what other people have said about a work can help you to develop your own ideas — perhaps, to cite just two examples, by using them as supporting evidence or by arguing with them in order to clarify or qualify their points about the literary work. As you write and discover how to advance your thesis, you'll find yourself participating in a dialogue with the critics. This sort of conversation will help you to improve your thinking and hone your argument.

Keep in mind that the work of professional critics is a means of enriching your understanding of a literary work rather than a substitution for your own analysis and interpretation of that work. Quoting, paraphrasing, or summarizing someone else's perspective does not relieve you of the obligation of choosing a topic, organizing information, developing a thesis, and arguing your point of view by citing sufficient evidence from the text you are examining. These matters are discussed in further detail in Chapters 2 and 3. You should also be familiar with the methods for documenting sources that are explained in this chapter; and keep in mind how important it is to avoid plagiarism.

No doubt you won't find everything you read about a work equally useful: Some critics' arguments won't address your own areas of concern; some will be too difficult for you to get a handle on; and some will seem wrong-headed. However, much of the criticism you read will serve to make a literary work more accessible and interesting to you, and disagreeing with others' arguments will often help you to develop your own ideas about a work. When you use the work of critics in your own writing, you should consider the following questions. Responding to these questions will help you to ensure that you have a clear understanding of what a critic is arguing about a work, to what extent you agree with that argument, and how you plan to incorporate and respond to the critic's reading in your own paper. The more questions you can ask yourself in response to this list or as a result of your own reading, the more you'll be able to think critically about how you are approaching both the critics and the literary work under consideration.

QUESTIONS FOR WRITING:
INCORPORATING SECONDARY SOURCES

1. Have you read the literary work carefully and taken notes of your own impressions before reading any critical perspectives so that your initial insights are not lost to the arguments made by the critics? Have you articulated your own responses to the work in a journal entry prior to reading the critics?

(continued)

2. Are you sufficiently familiar with the literary work that you can determine the accuracy, fairness, and thoroughness of the critic's use of evidence from the work?

3. Have you read the critic's piece carefully? Try summarizing the critic's argument in a brief paragraph. Do you understand the nature and purpose of the critic's argument? Which passages are especially helpful to you? Which seem unclear? Why?

4. Is the critic's reading of the literary work similar to or different from your own reading? Why do you agree or disagree? What generational, historical, cultural, or biographical considerations might help to account for differences between the critic's responses and your own?

5. How has your reading of the critic influenced your understanding of the literary work? Do issues that previously seemed unimportant now seem significant? What are these issues, and how does a consideration of them affect your reading of the work?

6. Are you too quickly revising or even discarding your own reading because the critic's perspective seems so polished and persuasive? Are you making use of your reading notes and the responses in your journal entries?

7. How would you classify the critic's approach? Through what kind of lens does the critic view the literary work? Is the critical approach formalist, biographical, psychological, sociological, mythological, reader-response, deconstructionist, or some combination of these or possibly other strategies? (For a discussion of these approaches, see Chapter 3, "Applying a Critical Strategy.")

8. What biases, if any, can you detect in the critic's approach? How might, for example, a southern critic's reading of "Mending Wall" differ from a northern critic's?

9. Can you determine how other critics have responded to the critic's work? Is the critic's work cited and taken seriously in other critics' books and articles? Is the work dated by having been superseded by subsequent studies?

10. Are any passages or topics that you deem important left out by the critic? Do these omissions qualify or refute the critic's argument?

11. What judgments does the critic seem to make about the work? Is the work regarded, for example, as significant, unified, representative, trivial, inept, or irresponsible? Do you agree with these judgments? If not, can you develop and support a thesis about your difference of opinion?

12. What important disagreements do critics reveal in their approaches to the work? Do you find one perspective more convincing than another? Why? Is there a way of resolving their conflicting views that could serve as a thesis for your paper?

13. Can you extend or qualify the critic's argument to matters in the literary text that are not covered by the critic's perspective? Will this allow you to develop your own topic while acknowledging the critic's useful insights?

14. Have you quoted, paraphrased, or summarized the critic accurately and fairly? Have you avoided misrepresenting the critic's arguments in any way?

15. Are the critic's words, ideas, opinions, and insights adequately acknowledged and documented in the correct format? Do you understand the difference between common knowledge and plagiarism? Have you avoided quoting excessively? Are the quotations smoothly integrated into your own text?

16. Are you certain that your incorporation of the critic's work is for the purpose of developing your paper's thesis rather than for name-dropping or padding your paper? How can you explain to yourself why the critic's work is useful for your argument?

A Sample First Response

Before starting to do outside research, Stephanie reads the first Question for Writing and realizes that she needs to articulate her own response to the work. She uses the technique of freewriting to help her choose a paper topic, recording her response to the class discussion that focused on the individuality of the speakers in each poem.

In class, most everybody seemed to think that the speaker in "Mowing" was pretty much saying the same thing as the speaker in "Mending Wall," that being a farmer is about one guy putting his shoulder to the scythe sort of thing — but I don't think that's right. I like both these poems because they really convey a sense of the individual speaker (maybe Frost himself?) behind the words, but it seems to me like "Mowing" is more about being a tough guy on your own and "Mending Wall" is more about being part of a larger community. I wonder what other people have said about these poems?

A Sample of Notetaking

Once Stephanie has a broad topic — individuality versus community in "Mowing" versus "Mending Wall" — she is ready to start reading outside sources. She goes to the library and looks for books and periodicals in the stacks; she goes online and uses LitLinks to look up what people have published about these poems on the World Wide Web; and she finds a CD-ROM on Robert Frost that contains a wide range of primary and secondary sources. As she reads through each of these sources, she keeps careful notes on note cards. One set of cards records complete bibliographic information for each source; this set will be invaluable when it's time to prepare her works cited page. You'll see an example of one such bibliography card on the next page.

Another set of cards records what each source says that she might be able to work into her final paper; this set will be invaluable as she shapes and writes her argument. She also uses the "Questions for Writing: Incorporating Outside Sources" to determine whether or not a source is worth recording. You'll see an example of a sample note card on the next page.

Parini, Jay
    Robert Frost: A Life.
    New York: Holt, 1997.

Sample bibliography card for a book.

                                                  Parini 121

Parini describes "Mowing" as contemplative,
private, and solitary — a poem in which the "poet
cultivates a private motion."

[Can I work this in?]

Sample note card.

A Sample of Brainstorming after Research

As her notes on "Mowing" and "Mending Wall" accumulate, Stephanie sorts them into related stacks and then makes a list, along with notes about whether or not they are directly related to her comparison of the poems. Because the assignment is relatively brief, she does not write a formal outline but instead organizes her stacks of usable note cards and proceeds to write the first draft from them.

1. publication history of the poems — not relevant

2. isolation in "Mowing"

3. the Soviet response to "Mending Wall"

4. *community in mending wall*

5. *the speaker in each poem*

6. *individuality in each poem*

7. *Frost's attempts at farming*

8. *Frost's growing reputation as a poet*

9. *the meaning of walls*

After reading through all my notes again and looking at this list as a whole, I can see that 3, 7, and 8 aren't really relevant to my topic. That leaves the notes I have in stacks 1, 2, 4, 5, 6, and 9. I started reading secondary sources because I thought that the speaker in each poem had a different view about individuality, and I had kind of thought that I'd discover that something happened in Frost's life that changed the way he thought about individuality versus community. But the more I read, the more it seems as if I can really only focus on how the speakers of the poems reflect a shift in emphasis from individuality to community rather than Frost's biography. I think I'll go with a revised thesis: "The speaker in Mowing strongly reflects Frost's emphasis on individuality, but the speaker in Mending Wall reflects Frost's recognition of the necessity for community while simultaneously preserving the basic need for human boundaries." It's less exciting than my original thesis but easier to support with my research.

A Sample Student Research Paper

As you read Stephanie's final paper, pay special attention to how she documents outside sources and incorporates other people's ideas into her own argument. How strong do you think her final thesis is? Is it effectively supported by the sources? Has she integrated the sources fully into the paper? How does the paper enhance your understanding of the two poems?

Stephanie's paper follows the format described in the *MLA Handbook for Writers of Research Papers,* Fifth Edition. This format is discussed in the preceding section on documentation in this chapter (p. 111) and in Chapter 2 in the section on manuscript form (p. 41). Though the sample paper is short, it illustrates many of the techniques and strategies useful for writing an essay that includes secondary sources — including a CD-ROM, a Web site, books, and journals.

Stephanie Tobin

Professor Bass

Poetry 100

November 19, 20--

Individuality and Community in

Frost's "Mowing" and "Mending Wall"

We think of Robert Frost as a poet of New England who provides portraits of the rural landscape and communities. But it was not until Frost's second book, <u>North of Boston</u> (1914), that he truly gave voice to a community--in dramatic monologues, dialogues, and narrative poems. The poems in his first book, <u>A Boy's Will</u> (1913), are mainly personal lyrics in which the poet encounters the world and defines it for himself through the writing of poetry, establishing both an individual perspective and an aesthetic. A poem from the first book, "Mowing," illustrates the theme of individualism, against which a poem from the second book, "Mending Wall," can be seen as a widening of the thematic lens to include other perspectives.

In <u>A Boy's Will</u>, Frost explores the idea of man as a solitary creature, alone, at work in the natural world. Poems such as "Mowing" capture the essence of this perspective in the very first lines: "There was never a sound beside the wood but one, / And that was my long scythe whispering to the ground" (lines 1-2). Jay Parini describes "Mowing" as a poem in which the "poet cultivates a private motion" (121)--the motions both of farm work, done to support oneself, and the motion of the individual mind expressed in the poem as it moves down the page. The sense of privacy and of an individually defined world captured in "Mowing" is central to the book itself.

The dramatic change in perspective evident in <u>North of Boston</u> illustrates Frost's development as a writer.

Although the second collection was published just one
year later, Frost expresses a different perception and
understanding of human nature in North of Boston.
W. S. Braithwaite wrote in 1915, in a review of the two
books, that A Boy's Will and North of Boston "represent a
divergent period of development. The earlier book
expresses an individuality, the later interprets a community" (2). The focus on community is best demonstrated by
the poem "Mending Wall," which presents the reader with
an image of two men, separated literally and metaphorically by a wall, yet joined by their dedication to the
task they must undertake and the basic human need for
boundaries that compels them. The speaker in "Mending
Wall" does not forfeit his own individuality, but rather
comes to understand it more fully in the context of the
society in which he lives, with its traditions and
requirements, some of which he tries to see as a game:
"Oh, just another kind of outdoor game, / One on a
side" (lines 21-22), while still allowing for deeper
implications.

Individuality can be defined by one's differences
from others, as well as by the creative work of defining,
and self-defining, done in poetry. Frost's own experience
of life in New England helped shape the perspectives of
both individualism and community exemplified in his first
two books. When Frost wrote "Mowing" his perspective on
life in New England leaned more toward isolation than
community. The first few years of farm life were arduous
and lonely, and the stark environment provided an atmosphere far more suitable for self-realization than socialization. Prior to the publication of A Boy's Will, Frost
had spent "five years of self-enforced solitude" (Meyers
99). "Mowing," which Frost considered to be the best poem
in the collection, exemplifies this feeling of isolation

and the need for self-exploration. While the poem is, in
the literal sense, about the act of cutting grass in
order to make hay, it is metaphorically rooted in the
idea that man finds meaning and beauty in the world,
alone. Jay Parini suggests that the idea that "a man's
complete meaning is derived alone, at work [. . .] is a
consistent theme in Frost and one that could be explored
at length in all his work" (14).

"Mowing" begins with the speaker's observation of
the silence that surrounds him as he works. The only
sound is the hushed whisper of his scythe as he mows. He
writes, "What was it it whispered? I knew not well
myself" (line 3). The possibility that its meaning could
be found in some fanciful imagination of the task is dismissed: "It was no dream of the gift of idle hours, / Or
easy gold at the hand of fay or elf" (lines 7-8). For
Frost, an exaggeration of the action would imply that
meaning cannot be found in objective reality, an idea
continually argued by his poems.

Instead, this poem asserts a faith in nature as it
is, and in the labor necessary to support and define one-
self--labor in the natural world, and in the making of
poems. This idea is brought forth in the next line: "Anything more than the truth would have seemed too weak /
To the earnest love that laid the swale in rows" (lines
9-10). Whether the "fact" that is the "sweetest dream
that labour knows" (line 13) is the actual act of
cutting the grass or the verse that is inspired by the
simple action, it is something that must be achieved in
solitude.

This faith in the work of the individual
demonstrated in A Boy's Will is not lost in North of
Boston but is redefined. Meyers writes that North of
Boston "signaled Frost's change of emphasis from solitary

to social beings" (112). In Frost's dedication to his
wife he called North of Boston "This Book of People." The
poems in this collection demonstrate an understanding of
the individual, as well as the community in which he
lives. This shift seems a natural development after a
book in which Frost so carefully established his sense of
self and his particular poetic vision and aims.

"Mending Wall," a poem in North of Boston, illustrates Frost's shift in focus from the solitary individual to the interacting society. In the poem, the speaker
and his neighbor set out to perform the annual task of
mending a wall that divides their properties. From the
very beginning, the speaker's tone--at once humorous and
serious--indicates that the real subject of the poem is
not the mending of the wall, which he describes almost
lightheartedly, but the "mending" of the subtle boundaries between the speaker and his neighbor. The poem
begins, "Something there is that doesn't love a wall, /
That sends the frozen-ground-swell under it" (lines 1-2),
yet this "something," mentioned twice in the poem, refers
to more than the seasonal frost that "spills the upper
boulders in the sun" (3). Peter Stanlis writes in a commentary on "Mending Wall" that "the central theme falls
within the philosophical polarities of the speaker and
his neighbor" (1). The man's statement that "good fences
make good neighbors" (26) implies his belief that boundaries between people will maintain the peace between
them, but the speaker questions this need for boundaries:
"Before I built a wall I'd ask to know / What I was
walling in or walling out" (31-32). With this he brings
the wall into the figurative realm to decipher its
meaning.

His neighbor feels no need for such analysis. But
while articulating a figurative barrier of noncommunica-

tion, and different values, between the men, the poem is
as much about community as individuality; the wall is
what connects as well as separates them. Marie Borroff
argues that "the story told in the poem is not about a
one-man rebellion against wall mending but about an
attempt to communicate" (66). However individuated the
men may perceive themselves to be, the common task they
must undertake and the ethos it represents join them in a
particular social community, the assumptions of which
Frost articulates in this poem by both participating in
and questioning them.

For the speaker, the task of mending the wall provides an opportunity for thought and questioning rather
than serving a utilitarian purpose. While the tradition
unites the men "by marking their claims to private property through mutual respect," it is still a barrier
(Stanlis 3). Both joined and separated by the fence, the
two neighbors walk together and alone, isolated by the
physical boundary but connected by their maintenance of
the relationship and tradition that created it. As James
R. Dawes points out, these "men can only interact when
reassured by the constructed alienation of the wall"
(300). They keep the wall in place, and thereby keep in
place their separate senses of self.

While the speaker is explicitly and lightheartedly
critical of the ritual, it is he who "insists on the
yearly ritual, as if civilization depends upon the collective activity of making barriers.[. . .] One senses a
profound commitment to the act of creating community in
the speaker" (Parini 139). Unwilling to placate his
neighbor by performing the task in silence, the speaker
makes a playful attempt at communication. Explaining that
"My apple trees will never get across / And eat the cones

Tobin 6

under his pines" (24-25), he asks why the wall is necessary. But rather than contemplate the logic behind the boundary, the neighbor rejects the invitation to communicate: "He only says, 'Good fences make good neighbors'" (26). By refusing to think about the speaker's question, and choosing to hide behind his own father's words, he closes any possible window of communication between them (Monteiro 127), not crossing the barrier of the wall literally or psychologically. And even while the speaker jokes about the wall's uselessness, he keeps his deeper questions to himself. Rather than threaten the agreed-upon terms of community, he is complicit in keeping them there in actuality, only privately articulating and upending them, in poetry.

Mark Van Doren wrote in 1951 that Robert Frost's poems "are the work of a man who has never stopped exploring himself" (2); he never stopped exploring the psychology of others, either. "Mowing," which illustrates his initial focus on individualism, was only a starting point in Frost's understanding of his place in the world as a poet. The change of perspective evident in "Mending Wall" demonstrates his enriched idea of man as an individual within a community. Having established a singular voice and his own moral aesthetic--"The fact is the sweetest dream that labour knows" (line 13)--Frost has the confidence to incorporate different voices into his poems and to allow his "facts" and values to encounter those of others, as the two men in "Mending Wall" do across the wall, each maintaining his own and the other's sense of personal identity.

Works Cited

Borroff, Marie. "Robert Frost's New Testament: The
    Uses of Simplicity." Modern Critical Views:
    Robert Frost. Ed. Harold Bloom. New York: Chelsea
    House, 1986. 63-83.

Braithwaite, W. S. "A Poet of New England." The Boston
    Evening Transcript 28 April 1915. From Robert
    Frost: Poems, Life, Legacy. CD-ROM. New York:
    Holt, 1997.

Dawes, James R. "Masculinity and Transgression in
    Robert Frost." American Literature 65 (June
    1993): 297-312.

Meyer, Michael. Thinking and Writing about Literature:
    A Text and Anthology, 2nd ed. Boston: Bedford/St.
    Martin's, 2000.

Meyers, Jeffrey. Robert Frost: A Biography. New York:
    Houghton, 1996.

Monteiro, George. Robert Frost and the New England
    Renaissance. Lexington: UP of Kentucky, 1988.

Parini, Jay. Robert Frost: A Life. New York: Holt,
    1999.

Stanlis, Peter J. "Commentary: Mending Wall." Robert
    Frost: Poems, Life, Legacy. CD-ROM. New York:
    Holt, 1997.

Van Doren, Mark. "Robert Frost's America." Atlantic
    Monthly June 1951. Atlantic Unbound
    <http://www.theatlantic.com/unbound/poetry/frost/
    vand.htm>.

PART TWO

Literature and Its Elements

5

Reading and Writing about Fiction

THE ELEMENTS

Plot

Plot is the author's arrangement of incidents in a story. It is the organizing principle that controls the order of events. This structure is, in a sense, what remains after a writer edits out what is irrelevant to the story being told. We don't need to know, for example, what happens to Rip Van Winkle's faithful dog, Wolf, during his amiable master's twenty-year nap in the Catskill Mountains in order to be enchanted by Washington Irving's story of a henpecked husband. Instead, what is told takes on meaning as it is brought into focus by a skillful writer who selects and orders the events that constitute the story's plot.

Events can be presented in a variety of orders. A chronological arrangement begins with what happens first, then second, and so on, until the last incident is related. That is how "Rip Van Winkle" is told. The events in William Faulkner's "A Rose for Emily," however, are not arranged in chronological order because that would give away the story's surprise ending; instead, Faulkner moves back and forth between the past and present to provide information that leads up to the final startling moment (which won't be given away here either; the story begins on p. 144).

Some stories begin at the end and then lead up to why or how events worked out as they did. If you read the first paragraph of Ralph Ellison's "Battle Royal" (p. 931), you'll find an example of this arrangement that will make it difficult for you to stop reading. Stories can also begin in the middle of things (the Latin term for this common plot strategy is *in medias res*). In this kind of plot we enter the story on the verge of some important moment. John Updike's "A & P" (p. 981) begins with the narrator, a teenager working at a checkout counter in a supermarket, telling us: "In walks these three girls in nothing but bathing suits." Right away we are brought into the middle of a situation that will ultimately create the conflict in the story.

Another common strategy is the *flashback,* a device that informs us about events that happened before the opening scene of a work. Nearly all of Ellison's "Battle Royal" takes the form of a flashback as the narrator recounts how his identity as a black man was shaped by the circumstances that attended a high-school graduation speech he delivered twenty years earlier in a hotel ballroom before a gathering of the town's leading white citizens, most of whom were "quite tipsy." Whatever the plot arrangement, you should be aware of how the writer's conscious ordering of events affects your responses to the action.

EDGAR RICE BURROUGHS (1875–1950)

Most of the sixty books Edgar Rice Burroughs wrote recorded bedtime stories he had told his children. In addition to the enormously popular Tarzan series, Burroughs wrote a good deal of science fiction, most notably a series of books that chronicle the adventures of John Carter of Mars. Before making his fortune as a writer, Burroughs was a cowboy, gold miner, policeman, and store manager. His books include *The Princess of Mars* (1917), *Tanar of Pellucidar* (1930), and *Tarzan and the Foreign Legion* (1947). *Tarzan of the Apes* (1914), the first of the Tarzan series, has been translated into more than fifty languages.

A great many stories share a standard plot pattern. The following excerpt from Edgar Rice Burroughs's novel *Tarzan of the Apes* provides a conventional plot pattern in which the *character,* an imagined person in the story, is confronted with a problem leading to a climactic struggle that is followed by a resolution of the problem. The elements of a conventional plot are easily recognizable to readers familiar with fast-paced, action-packed mysteries, spy thrillers, westerns, or adventure stories. These page-turners are carefully plotted so that the reader is swept up by the action. More serious writers sometimes use similar strategies, but they do so with greater subtlety and for some purpose that goes beyond providing a thrill a minute. The writer of serious fiction is usually less concerned with what happens next to the central character than with why it happens. In Burroughs's adventure story, however, the emphasis is clearly on action.

Burroughs's novel, published in 1914 and the first of a series of enormously popular Tarzan books and films, charts the growth to manhood of a child raised in the African jungle by great apes. Tarzan struggles to survive his primitive beginnings and to reconcile what he has learned in the jungle with his equally powerful instincts to be a civilized human being. One of the more exciting moments in Tarzan's development is his final confrontation with his old enemy, Terkoz, a huge tyrannical ape that has kidnapped Jane, a pretty nineteen-year-old from Baltimore, Maryland, who has accompanied her father on an expedition to the jungle.

In the chapter preceding this excerpt, Tarzan falls in love with Jane and writes this pointed, if not eloquent, note to her: "I am Tarzan of the Apes. I want you. I am yours. You are mine." Just as he finishes the note, he hears "the agonized screams of a woman" and rushes to their source to find Esmeralda, Jane's maid, hysterical with fear and grief. She reports that Jane, the fair and gentle embodiment of civilization in the story, has been carried off by a gorilla. Here is the first half of the next chapter, which illustrates how Burroughs plots the sequence of events so that the emphasis is on physical action.

From Tarzan of the Apes   *1914*

From the time Tarzan left the tribe of great anthropoids in which he had been raised, it was torn by continual strife and discord. Terkoz proved a cruel and capricious king, so that, one by one, many of the older and weaker apes, upon whom he was particularly prone to vent his brutish nature, took their families into the quiet and safety of the far interior.

But at last those who remained were driven to desperation by the continued truculence of Terkoz, and it so happened that one of them recalled the parting admonition of Tarzan:

"If you have a chief who is cruel, do not do as the other apes do, and attempt, any one of you, to pit yourself against him alone. But, instead, let two or three or four of you attack him together. Then, if you will do this, no chief will dare to be other than he should be, for four of you can kill any chief who may ever be over you."

And the ape who recalled this wise counsel repeated it to several of his fellows, so that when Terkoz returned to the tribe that day he found a warm reception awaiting him.

There were no formalities. As Terkoz reached the group, five huge, hairy   5
beasts sprang upon him.

At heart he was an arrant coward, which is the way with bullies among apes as well as among men; so he did not remain to fight and die, but tore himself away from them as quickly as he could and fled into the sheltering boughs of the forest.

Two more attempts he made to rejoin the tribe, but on each occasion he was set upon and driven away. At last he gave it up, and turned, foaming with rage and hatred, into the jungle.

For several days he wandered aimlessly, nursing his spite and looking for some weak thing on which to vent his pent anger.

It was in this state of mind that the horrible, manlike beast, swinging from tree to tree, came suddenly upon two women in the jungle.

He was right above them when he discovered them. The first intimation   10
Jane Porter had of his presence was when the great hairy body dropped to the earth beside her, and she saw the awful face and the snarling, hideous mouth thrust within a foot of her.

One piercing scream escaped her lips as the brute hand clutched her arm. Then she was dragged toward those awful fangs which yawned at her throat. But ere they touched that fair skin another mood claimed the anthropoid.

The tribe had kept his women. He must find others to replace them. This hairless white ape would be the first of his new household, and so he threw her roughly across his broad, hairy shoulders and leaped back into the trees, bearing Jane away.

Esmeralda's scream of terror had mingled once with that of Jane, and then, as was Esmeralda's manner under stress of emergency which required presence of mind, she swooned.

But Jane did not once lose consciousness. It is true that that awful face, pressing close to hers, and the stench of the foul breath beating upon her nostrils, paralyzed her with terror; but her brain was clear, and she comprehended all that transpired.

With what seemed to her marvelous rapidity the brute bore her through 15 the forest, but still she did not cry out or struggle. The sudden advent of the ape had confused her to such an extent that she thought now that he was bearing her toward the beach.

For this reason she conserved her energies and her voice until she could see that they had approached near enough to the camp to attract the succor she craved.

She could not have known it, but she was being borne farther and farther into the impenetrable jungle.

The scream that had brought Clayton and the two older men stumbling through the undergrowth had led Tarzan of the Apes straight to where Esmeralda lay, but it was not Esmeralda in whom his interest centered, though pausing over her he saw that she was unhurt.

For a moment he scrutinized the ground below and the trees above, until the ape that was in him by virtue of training and environment, combined with the intelligence that was his by right of birth, told his wondrous woodcraft the whole story as plainly as though he had seen the thing happen with his own eyes.

And then he was gone again into the swaying trees, following the high- 20 flung spoor which no other human eye could have detected, much less translated.

At boughs' ends, where the anthropoid swings from one tree to another, there is most to mark the trail, but least to point the direction of the quarry; for there the pressure is downward always, toward the small end of the branch, whether the ape be leaving or entering a tree. Nearer the center of the tree, where the signs of passage are fainter, the direction is plainly marked.

Here, on this branch, a caterpillar has been crushed by the fugitive's great foot, and Tarzan knows instinctively where that same foot would touch in the next stride. Here he looks to find a tiny particle of the demolished larva, ofttimes not more than a speck of moisture.

Again, a minute bit of bark has been upturned by the scraping hand, and the direction of the break indicates the direction of the passage. Or some great limb, or the stem of the tree itself has been brushed by the hairy body, and a tiny shred of hair tells him by the direction from which it is wedged beneath the bark that he is on the right trail.

Nor does he need to check his speed to catch these seemingly faint records of the fleeing beast.

To Tarzan they stand out boldly against all the myriad other scars and 25 bruises and signs upon the leafy way. But strongest of all is the scent, for

Tarzan is pursuing up the wind, and his trained nostrils are as sensitive as a hound's.

There are those who believe that the lower orders are specially endowed by nature with better olfactory nerves than man, but it is merely a matter of development.

Man's survival does not hinge so greatly upon the perfection of his senses. His power to reason has relieved them of many of their duties, and so they have, to some extent, atrophied, as have the muscles which move the ears and scalp, merely from disuse.

The muscles are there, about the ears and beneath the scalp, and so are the nerves which transmit sensations to the brain, but they are underdeveloped because they are not needed.

Not so with Tarzan of the Apes. From early infancy his survival had depended upon acuteness of eyesight, hearing, smell, touch, and taste far more than upon the more slowly developed organ of reason.

The least developed of all in Tarzan was the sense of taste, for he could eat 30 luscious fruits, or raw flesh, long buried, with almost equal appreciation; but in that he differed but slightly from more civilized epicures.

Almost silently the ape-man sped on in the track of Terkoz and his prey, but the sound of his approach reached the ears of the fleeing beast and spurred it on to greater speed.

Three miles were covered before Tarzan overtook them, and then Terkoz, seeing that further flight was futile, dropped to the ground in a small open glade, that he might turn and fight for his prize or be free to escape unhampered if he saw that the pursuer was more than a match for him.

He still grasped Jane in one great arm as Tarzan bounded like a leopard into the arena which nature had provided for this primeval-like battle.

When Terkoz saw that it was Tarzan who pursued him, he jumped to the conclusion that this was Tarzan's woman, since they were of the same kind — white and hairless — and so he rejoiced at this opportunity for double revenge upon his hated enemy.

To Jane the strange apparition of this godlike man was as wine to sick 35 nerves.

From the description which Clayton and her father and Mr. Philander had given her, she knew that it must be the same wonderful creature who had saved them, and she saw in him only a protector and a friend.

But as Terkoz pushed her roughly aside to meet Tarzan's charge, and she saw the great proportions of the ape and the mighty muscles and the fierce fangs, her heart quailed. How could any vanquish such a mighty antagonist?

Like two charging bulls they came together, and like two wolves sought each other's throat. Against the long canines of the ape was pitted the thin blade of the man's knife.

Jane — her lithe, young form flattened against the trunk of a great tree, her hands tight pressed against her rising and falling bosom, and her eyes wide with mingled horror, fascination, fear, and admiration — watched the primordial ape battle with the primeval man for possession of a woman — for her.

As the great muscles of the man's back and shoulders knotted beneath 40 the tension of his efforts, and the huge biceps and forearm held at bay those mighty tusks, the veil of centuries of civilization and culture were swept from the blurred vision of the Baltimore girl.

When the long knife drank deep a dozen times of Terkoz's heart's blood, and the great carcass rolled lifeless upon the ground, it was a primeval woman who sprang forward with outstretched arms toward the primeval man who had fought for her and won.

And Tarzan?

He did what no red-blooded man needs lessons in doing. He took his woman in his arms and smothered her upturned, panting lips with kisses.

For a moment Jane lay there with half-closed eyes. For a moment — the first in her young life — she knew the meaning of love.

But as suddenly as the veil had been withdrawn it dropped again, and an 45 outraged conscience suffused her face with its scarlet mantle, and a mortified woman thrust Tarzan of the Apes from her and buried her face in her hands.

Tarzan had been surprised when he had found the girl he had learned to love after a vague and abstract manner a willing prisoner in his arms. Now he was surprised that she repulsed him.

He came close to her once more and took hold of her arm. She turned upon him like a tigress, striking his great breast with her tiny hands.

Tarzan could not understand it.

A moment ago, and it had been his intention to hasten Jane back to her people, but that little moment was lost now in the dim and distant past of things which were but can never be again, and with it the good intention had gone to join the impossible.

Since then Tarzan of the Apes had felt a warm, lithe form close pressed to 50 his. Hot, sweet breath against his cheek and mouth had fanned a new flame to life within his breast, and perfect lips had clung to his in burning kisses that had seared a deep brand into his soul — a brand which marked a new Tarzan.

Again he laid his hand upon her arm. Again she repulsed him. And then Tarzan of the Apes did just what his first ancestor would have done.

He took his woman in his arms and carried her into the jungle.

This episode begins with **exposition,** the background information the reader needs to make sense of the situation in which the characters are placed. The first eight paragraphs let us know that Terkoz has been overthrown as leader of the ape tribe and that he is roaming the jungle "looking for some weak thing on which to vent his pent anger." This exposition is in the form of a flashback. (Recall that the previous chapter ended with Esmeralda's report of the kidnapping; now we will see what happened.)

Once this information supplies a context for the characters, the plot gains momentum with the **rising action,** a complication that intensifies the situation: Terkoz, looking for a victim, discovers the vulnerable Esmeralda and Jane. His first impulse is to kill Jane, but his "mood" changes when he remembers that he has no woman of his own after having been forced to leave the tribe (more exposition). Hence, there is a further complication in the rising action when he decides to carry her off. Just when it seems that the situation could not get any worse, it does. The reader is invited to shudder even more than if Terkoz had made a meal of Jane because she may have to endure the "awful face," "foul breath," and lust of this beast.

At this point we are brought up to the action that ended the preceding chapter. Tarzan races to the rescue by unerringly following the trail from the place where Jane was kidnapped. He relentlessly tracks Terkoz. Unfortunately, Burroughs slows down the pursuit here by including several paragraphs that abstractly consider the evolutionary development of human reliance on reason more than on their senses for survival. This discussion offers a rationale for Tarzan's remarkable ability to track Jane, but it is an interruption in the chase.

When Tarzan finally catches up to Terkoz, the ***conflict*** of this episode fully emerges. Tarzan must save the woman he loves by defeating his long-standing enemy. For Terkoz seeks to achieve a "double revenge" by killing Tarzan and taking his woman. Terkoz's assumption that Jane is Tarzan's woman is a ***foreshadowing,*** a suggestion of what is yet to come. In this conflict Tarzan is the ***protagonist*** or ***hero,*** the central character who engages our interest and empathy. *Protagonist* is often a more useful term than *hero* or ***heroine,*** however, because the central character of a story can be despicable as well as heroic. In Edgar Allan Poe's "The Tell-Tale Heart," for example, the central character is a madman and murderer. Terkoz is the ***antagonist,*** the force that opposes the protagonist.

The battle between Tarzan and Terkoz creates ***suspense*** because the reader is made anxious about what is going to happen. Burroughs makes certain that the reader will worry about the outcome by having Jane wonder, "How could any vanquish such a mighty antagonist?" If we are caught up in the moment, we watch the battle, as Jane does, with "mingled horror, fascination, fear, and admiration" to see what will happen next. The moment of greatest emotional tension, the ***climax,*** occurs when Tarzan kills Terkoz. Tarzan's victory is the ***resolution*** of the conflict, also known as the ***dénouement*** (a French word meaning the "untying of the knot"). This could have been the conclusion to the episode except that Jane and Tarzan simultaneously discover their "primeval" selves sexually drawn to each other. Burroughs resolves one conflict — the battle with Terkoz — but then immediately creates another — by raising the question of what a respectable professor's daughter from Baltimore is doing in the sweaty arms of a panting, half-naked man.

Consider how William Faulkner uses plot in the following short story, "A Rose for Emily," to create a particularly powerful ending.

WILLIAM FAULKNER (1897–1962)

Born into an old Mississippi family that had lost its influence and wealth during the Civil War, William Faulkner lived nearly all his life in the South writing about Yoknapatawpha County, an imagined Mississippi county similar to his home in Oxford. Among his novels based on this fictional location are *The Sound and the Fury* (1929), *As I Lay Dying* (1930), *Light in August* (1932), and *Absalom, Absalom!* (1936). Although his writings are regional in their emphasis on local social history, his concerns are broader. In his 1950 acceptance speech for the Nobel Prize for literature, he insisted that the "problems of the human heart in conflict with itself . . . alone can make good writing because only that is worth writing about, worth the agony and the sweat." This commitment is evident in his novels and in *The Collected Stories of William Faulkner* (1950). "A Rose for Emily," about the mysterious life of Emily Grierson, presents a personal conflict rooted in her southern identity.

A Rose for Emily   *1931*

I

When Miss Emily Grierson died, our whole town went to her funeral: the men through a sort of respectful affection for a fallen monument, the women mostly out of curiosity to see the inside of her house, which no one save an old manservant—a combined gardener and cook—had seen in at least ten years.

It was a big, squarish frame house that had once been white, decorated with cupolas and spires and scrolled balconies in the heavily lightsome style of the seventies, set on what had once been our most select street. But garages and cotton gins had encroached and obliterated even the august names of that neighborhood; only Miss Emily's house was left, lifting its stubborn and coquettish decay above the cotton wagons and the gasoline pumps—an eyesore among eyesores. And now Miss Emily had gone to join the representatives of those august names where they lay in the cedar-bemused cemetery among the ranked and anonymous graves of Union and Confederate soldiers who fell at the battle of Jefferson.

Alive, Miss Emily had been a tradition, a duty, and a care; a sort of hereditary obligation upon the town, dating from that day in 1894 when Colonel Sartoris, the mayor—he who fathered the edict that no Negro woman should appear on the streets without an apron—remitted her taxes, the dispensation dating from the death of her father on into perpetuity. Not that Miss Emily would have accepted charity. Colonel Sartoris invented an involved tale to the effect that Miss Emily's father had loaned money to the town, which the town, as a matter of business, preferred this way of repaying. Only a man of Colonel Sartoris' generation and thought could have invented it, and only a woman could have believed it.

When the next generation, with its more modern ideas, became mayors and aldermen, this arrangement created some little dissatisfaction. On the first of the year they mailed her a tax notice. February came, and there was no reply. They wrote her a formal letter, asking her to call at the sheriff's office at her convenience. A week later the mayor wrote her himself, offering to call or to send his car for her, and received in reply a note on paper of an archaic shape, in a thin, flowing calligraphy in faded ink, to the effect that she no longer went out at all. The tax notice was also enclosed, without comment.

They called a special meeting of the Board of Aldermen. A deputation 5
waited upon her, knocked at the door through which no visitor had passed
since she ceased giving china-painting lessons eight or ten years earlier. They
were admitted by the old Negro into a dim hall from which a stairway mounted
into still more shadow. It smelled of dust and disuse — a close, dank smell. The
Negro led them into the parlor. It was furnished in heavy, leather-covered furniture. When the Negro opened the blinds of one window, they could see that the
leather was cracked; and when they sat down, a faint dust rose sluggishly about
their thighs, spinning with slow motes in the single sun-ray. On a tarnished gilt
easel before the fireplace stood a crayon portrait of Miss Emily's father.

They rose when she entered — a small, fat woman in black, with a thin gold
chain descending to her waist and vanishing into her belt, leaning on an ebony
cane with a tarnished gold head. Her skeleton was small and spare; perhaps
that was why what would have been merely plumpness in another was obesity
in her. She looked bloated, like a body long submerged in motionless water,
and of that pallid hue. Her eyes, lost in the fatty ridges of her face, looked like
two small pieces of coal pressed into a lump of dough as they moved from one
face to another while the visitors stated their errand.

She did not ask them to sit. She just stood in the door and listened quietly
until the spokesman came to a stumbling halt. Then they could hear the invisible watch ticking at the end of the gold chain.

Her voice was dry and cold. "I have no taxes in Jefferson. Colonel Sartoris
explained it to me. Perhaps one of you can gain access to the city records and
satisfy yourselves."

"But we have. We are the city authorities, Miss Emily. Didn't you get a
notice from the sheriff, signed by him?"

"I received a paper, yes," Miss Emily said. "Perhaps he considers himself 10
the sheriff . . . I have no taxes in Jefferson."

"But there is nothing on the books to show that, you see. We must go by
the —"

"See Colonel Sartoris. I have no taxes in Jefferson."

"But, Miss Emily —"

"See Colonel Sartoris." (Colonel Sartoris had been dead almost ten years.)
"I have no taxes in Jefferson. Tobe!" The Negro appeared. "Show these gentlemen out."

II

So she vanquished them, horse and foot, just as she had vanquished their 15
fathers thirty years before about the smell. That was two years after her
father's death and a short time after her sweetheart — the one we believed
would marry her — had deserted her. After her father's death she went out very
little; after her sweetheart went away, people hardly saw her at all. A few of the
ladies had the temerity to call, but were not received, and the only sign of life
about the place was the Negro man — a young man then — going in and out
with a market basket.

"Just as if a man — any man — could keep a kitchen properly," the ladies
said; so they were not surprised when the smell developed. It was another link
between the gross, teeming world and the high and mighty Griersons.

A neighbor, a woman, complained to the mayor, Judge Stevens, eighty years old.

"But what will you have me do about it, madam?" he said.

"Why, send her word to stop it," the woman said. "Isn't there a law?"

"I'm sure that won't be necessary," Judge Stevens said. "It's probably 20 just a snake or a rat that nigger of hers killed in the yard. I'll speak to him about it."

The next day he received two more complaints, one from a man who came in diffident deprecation. "We really must do something about it, Judge. I'd be the last one in the world to bother Miss Emily, but we've got to do something." That night the Board of Aldermen met—three graybeards and one younger man, a member of the rising generation.

"It's simple enough," he said. "Send her word to have her place cleaned up. Give her a certain time to do it in, and if she don't . . ."

"Dammit, sir," Judge Stevens said, "will you accuse a lady to her face of smelling bad?"

So the next night, after midnight, four men crossed Miss Emily's lawn and slunk about the house like burglars, sniffing along the base of the brickwork and at the cellar openings while one of them performed a regular sowing motion with his hand out of a sack slung from his shoulder. They broke open the cellar door and sprinkled lime there, and in all the outbuildings. As they recrossed the lawn, a window that had been dark was lighted and Miss Emily sat in it, the light behind her, and her upright torso motionless as that of an idol. They crept quietly across the lawn and into the shadow of the locusts that lined the street. After a week or two the smell went away.

That was when people had begun to feel really sorry for her. People in our 25 town, remembering how old lady Wyatt, her great-aunt, had gone completely crazy at last, believed that the Griersons held themselves a little too high for what they really were. None of the young men were quite good enough for Miss Emily and such. We had long thought of them as a tableau, Miss Emily a slender figure in white in the background, her father a spraddled silhouette in the foreground, his back to her and clutching a horsewhip, the two of them framed by the back-flung front door. So when she got to be thirty and was still single, we were not pleased exactly, but vindicated; even with insanity in the family she wouldn't have turned down all of her chances if they had really materialized.

When her father died, it got about that the house was all that was left to her; and in a way, people were glad. At last they could pity Miss Emily. Being left alone, and a pauper, she had become humanized. Now she too would know the old thrill and the old despair of a penny more or less.

The day after his death all the ladies prepared to call at the house and offer condolence and aid, as is our custom. Miss Emily met them at the door, dressed as usual and with no trace of grief on her face. She told them that her father was not dead. She did that for three days, with the ministers calling on her, and the doctors, trying to persuade her to let them dispose of the body. Just as they were about to resort to law and force, she broke down, and they buried her father quickly.

We did not say she was crazy then. We believed she had to do that. We remembered all the young men her father had driven away, and we knew that with nothing left, she would have to cling to that which had robbed her, as people will.

III

She was sick for a long time. When we saw her again, her hair was cut short, making her look like a girl, with a vague resemblance to those angels in colored church windows — sort of tragic and serene.

The town had just let the contracts for paving the sidewalks, and in the 30 summer after her father's death they began the work. The construction company came with niggers and mules and machinery, and a foreman named Homer Barron, a Yankee — a big, dark, ready man, with a big voice and eyes lighter than his face. The little boys would follow in groups to hear him cuss the niggers, and the niggers singing in time to the rise and fall of picks. Pretty soon he knew everybody in town. Whenever you heard a lot of laughing anywhere about the square, Homer Barron would be in the center of the group. Presently we began to see him and Miss Emily on Sunday afternoons driving in the yellow-wheeled buggy and the matched team of bays from the livery stable.

At first we were glad that Miss Emily would have an interest, because the ladies all said, "Of course a Grierson would not think seriously of a Northerner, a day laborer." But there were still others, older people, who said that even grief could not cause a real lady to forget *noblesse oblige*° — without calling it *noblesse oblige*. They just said, "Poor Emily. Her kinsfolk should come to her." She had some kin in Alabama; but years ago her father had fallen out with them over the estate of old lady Wyatt, the crazy woman, and there was no communication between the two families. They had not even been represented at the funeral.

And as soon as the old people said, "Poor Emily," the whispering began. "Do you suppose it's really so?" they said to one another. "Of course it is. What else could . . ." This behind their hands; rustling of craned silk and satin behind jalousies closed upon the sun of Sunday afternoon as the thin, swift clop-clop-clop of the matched team passed: "Poor Emily."

She carried her head high enough — even when we believed that she was fallen. It was as if she demanded more than ever the recognition of her dignity as the last Grierson; as if it had wanted that touch of earthiness to reaffirm her imperviousness. Like when she bought the rat poison, the arsenic. That was over a year after they had begun to say "Poor Emily," and while the two female cousins were visiting her.

"I want some poison," she said to the druggist. She was over thirty then, still a slight woman, though thinner than usual, with cold, haughty black eyes in a face the flesh of which was strained across the temples and about the eyesockets as you imagine a lighthouse-keeper's face ought to look. "I want some poison," she said.

"Yes, Miss Emily. What kind? For rats and such? I'd recom —"   35

"I want the best you have. I don't care what kind."

The druggist named several. "They'll kill anything up to an elephant. But what you want is —"

"Arsenic," Miss Emily said. "Is that a good one?"

"Is . . . arsenic? Yes, ma'am. But what you want —"

"I want arsenic."   40

The druggist looked down at her. She looked back at him, erect, her face like a strained flag. "Why, of course," the druggist said. "If that's what you want. But the law requires you to tell what you are going to use it for."

---

noblesse oblige: The obligation of people of high social position.

Miss Emily just stared at him, her head tilted back in order to look him eye for eye, until he looked away and went and got the arsenic and wrapped it up. The Negro delivery boy brought her the package; the druggist didn't come back. When she opened the package at home there was written on the box, under the skull and bones: "For rats."

IV

So the next day we all said, "She will kill herself"; and we said it would be the best thing. When she had first begun to be seen with Homer Barron, we had said, "She will marry him." Then we said, "She will persuade him yet," because Homer himself had remarked—he liked men, and it was known that he drank with the younger men in the Elks' Club—that he was not a marrying man. Later we said, "Poor Emily" behind the jalousies as they passed on Sunday afternoon in the glittering buggy, Miss Emily with her head high and Homer Barron with his hat cocked and a cigar in his teeth, reins and whip in a yellow glove.

Then some of the ladies began to say that it was a disgrace to the town and a bad example to the young people. The men did not want to interfere, but at last the ladies forced the Baptist minister—Miss Emily's people were Episcopal—to call upon her. He would never divulge what happened during that interview, but he refused to go back again. The next Sunday they again drove about the streets, and the following day the minister's wife wrote to Miss Emily's relations in Alabama.

So she had blood-kin under her roof again and we sat back to watch devel-   45
opments. At first nothing happened. Then we were sure that they were to be married. We learned that Miss Emily had been to the jeweler's and ordered a man's toilet set in silver, with the letters H. B. on each piece. Two days later we learned that she had bought a complete outfit of men's clothing, including a nightshirt, and we said, "They are married." We were really glad. We were glad because the two female cousins were even more Grierson than Miss Emily had ever been.

So we were not surprised when Homer Barron—the streets had been finished some time since—was gone. We were a little disappointed that there was not a public blowing-off, but we believed that he had gone on to prepare for Miss Emily's coming, or to give her a chance to get rid of the cousins. (By that time it was a cabal, and we were all Miss Emily's allies to help circumvent the cousins.) Sure enough, after another week they departed. And, as we had expected all along, within three days Homer Barron was back in town. A neighbor saw the Negro man admit him at the kitchen door at dusk one evening.

And that was the last we saw of Homer Barron. And of Miss Emily for some time. The Negro man went in and out with the market basket, but the front door remained closed. Now and then we would see her at a window for a moment, as the men did that night when they sprinkled the lime, but for almost six months she did not appear on the streets. Then we knew that this was to be expected too; as if that quality of her father which had thwarted her woman's life so many times had been too virulent and too furious to die.

When we next saw Miss Emily, she had grown fat and her hair was turning gray. During the next few years it grew grayer and grayer until it attained an even pepper-and-salt iron-gray, when it ceased turning. Up to the day of her death at seventy-four it was still that vigorous iron-gray, like the hair of an active man.

From that time on her front door remained closed, save for a period of six or seven years, when she was about forty, during which she gave lessons in china-painting. She fitted up a studio in one of the downstairs rooms, where the daughters and granddaughters of Colonel Sartoris' contemporaries were sent to her with the same regularity and in the same spirit that they were sent to church on Sundays with a twenty-five-cent piece for the collection plate. Meanwhile her taxes had been remitted.

Then the newer generation became the backbone and the spirit of the 50 town, and the painting pupils grew up and fell away and did not send their children to her with boxes of color and tedious brushes and pictures cut from the ladies' magazines. The front door closed upon the last one and remained closed for good. When the town got free postal delivery, Miss Emily alone refused to let them fasten the metal numbers above her door and attach a mailbox to it. She would not listen to them.

Daily, monthly, yearly we watched the Negro grow grayer and more stooped, going in and out with the market basket. Each December we sent her a tax notice, which would be returned by the post office a week later, unclaimed. Now and then we would see her in one of the downstairs windows — she had evidently shut up the top floor of the house — like the carven torso of an idol in a niche, looking or not looking at us, we could never tell which. Thus she passed from generation to generation — dear, inescapable, impervious, tranquil, and perverse.

And so she died. Fell ill in the house filled with dust and shadows, with only a doddering Negro man to wait on her. We did not even know she was sick; we had long since given up trying to get information from the Negro. He talked to no one, probably not even to her, for his voice had grown harsh and rusty, as if from disuse.

She died in one of the downstairs rooms, in a heavy walnut bed with a curtain, her gray head propped on a pillow yellow and moldy with age and lack of sunlight.

V

The Negro met the first of the ladies at the front door and let them in, with their hushed, sibilant voices and their quick, curious glances, and then he disappeared. He walked right through the house and out the back and was not seen again.

The two female cousins came at once. They held the funeral on the second 55 day, with the town coming to look at Miss Emily beneath a mass of bought flowers, with the crayon face of her father musing profoundly above the bier and the ladies sibilant and macabre; and the very old men — some in their brushed Confederate uniforms — on the porch and the lawn, talking of Miss Emily as if she had been a contemporary of theirs, believing that they had danced with her and courted her perhaps, confusing time with its mathematical progression, as the old do, to whom all the past is not a diminishing road but, instead, a huge meadow which no winter ever quite touches, divided from them now by the narrow bottle-neck of the most recent decade of years.

Already we knew that there was one room in that region above stairs which no one had seen in forty years, and which would have to be forced. They waited until Miss Emily was decently in the ground before they opened it.

The violence of breaking down the door seemed to fill this room with pervading dust. A thin, acrid pall as of the tomb seemed to lie everywhere upon this room decked and furnished as for a bridal: upon the valance curtains of faded rose color, upon the rose-shaded lights, upon the dressing table, upon the delicate array of crystal and the man's toilet things backed with tarnished silver, silver so tarnished that the monogram was obscured. Among them lay a collar and tie, as if they had just been removed, which, lifted, left upon the surface a pale crescent in the dust. Upon a chair hung the suit, carefully folded; beneath it the two mute shoes and the discarded socks.

The man himself lay in the bed.

For a long while we just stood there, looking down at the profound and fleshless grin. The body had apparently once lain in the attitude of an embrace, but now the long sleep that outlasts love, that conquers even the grimace of love, had cuckolded him. What was left of him, rotted beneath what was left of the nightshirt, had become inextricable from the bed in which he lay; and upon him and upon the pillow beside him lay that even coating of the patient and biding dust.

Then we noticed that in the second pillow was the indentation of a head. 60 One of us lifted something from it, and leaning forward, that faint and invisible dust dry and acrid in the nostrils, we saw a long strand of iron-gray hair.

CONSIDERATIONS FOR CRITICAL THINKING AND WRITING

1. FIRST RESPONSE. What is the effect of the final paragraph of the story? How does it contribute to your understanding of Emily? Why is it important that we get this information last rather than at the beginning of the story?

2. What details foreshadow the conclusion of the story? Did you anticipate the ending?

3. Faulkner uses a number of gothic elements in this plot: the imposing decrepit house, the decayed corpse, and the mysterious secret horrors connected with Emily's life. How do these elements forward the plot and establish the atmosphere?

4. How does the information provided by the exposition indicate the nature of the conflict in the story? What does Emily's southern heritage contribute to the story?

5. Who or what is the antagonist of the story? Why is it significant that Homer Barron is a construction foreman and a northerner?

6. In what sense does the narrator's telling of the story serve as "A Rose for Emily"? Why do you think the narrator uses *we* rather than *I*?

7. Explain how Emily's reasons for murdering Homer are related to her personal history and to the ways she handled previous conflicts.

8. Discuss how Faulkner's treatment of the North and South contributes to the meaning of the story.

9. Provide an alternative title and explain how the emphasis in your title is reflected in the story.

10. CRITICAL STRATEGIES. Read the section on formalist criticism (pp. 60–62) in Chapter 3, "Applying a Critical Strategy." How might a formalist critic contrast the order of events as they happen in the story with the order in which they are told? How does this plotting create interest and suspense?

Character

Character is essential to plot. Without characters Burroughs's *Tarzan of the Apes* would be a travelogue through the jungle and Faulkner's "A Rose for Emily" little more than a faded history of a sleepy town in the South. If stories were depopulated, the plots would disappear because characters and plots are interrelated. A dangerous jungle is important only because we care what effect it has on a character. Characters are influenced by events just as events are shaped by characters. Tarzan's physical strength is the result of his growing up in the jungle, and his strength, along with his inherited intelligence, allows him to be master there.

The methods by which a writer creates people in a story so that they seem actually to exist are called **characterization.** Huck Finn never lived, yet those who have read Mark Twain's novel about his adventures along the Mississippi River feel as if they know him. A good writer gives us the illusion that a character is real, but we should also remember that a character is not an actual person but instead has been created by the author. Though we might walk out of a room in which Huck Finn's Pap talks racist nonsense, we would not throw away the book in a similar fit of anger. This illusion of reality is the magic that allows us to move beyond the circumstances of our own lives into a writer's fictional world, where we can encounter everyone from royalty to paupers, murderers, lovers, cheaters, martyrs, artists, destroyers, and, nearly always, some part of ourselves. The life that a writer breathes into a character adds to our own experiences and enlarges our view of the world.

A character is usually but not always a person. In Jack London's *Call of the Wild*, the protagonist is a devoted sled dog; in Herman Melville's *Moby-Dick*, the antagonist is an unfathomable whale. Perhaps the only possible qualification to be placed on character is that whatever it is — whether an animal or even an inanimate object, such as a robot — it must have some recognizable human qualities. The action of the plot interests us primarily because we care about what happens to people and what they do. We may identify with a character's desires and aspirations, or we may be disgusted by his or her viciousness and selfishness. To understand our response to a story, we should be able to recognize the methods of characterization the author uses.

CHARLES DICKENS (1812–1870)

Charles Dickens was the author of numerous novels, travel books, and sketches. Many of his most memorable characters are inspired by his memories of childhood, during which time his father was imprisoned for debt.

Dickens later acted in amateur theatricals and performed public readings of his work. His novels and other later writings were serialized in both English and American periodicals. Among his works are *Oliver Twist, Bleak House, Great Expectations, A Christmas Carol,* and *A Tale of Two Cities.* He is buried in Poet's Corner, Westminster Abbey.

Dickens is well known for creating characters who have stepped off the pages of his fictions into the imaginations and memories of his readers. His characters are successful not because readers might have encountered such people in their own lives, but because his characterizations are vivid and convincing. He manages to make strange and eccentric people appear familiar. The following excerpt from *Hard Times* is the novel's entire first chapter. In it Dickens introduces and characterizes a school principal addressing a classroom full of children.

From Hard Times   *1854*

"Now, what I want is, Facts. Teach these boys and girls nothing but Facts. Facts alone are wanted in life. Plant nothing else, and root out everything else. You can only form the minds of reasoning animals upon Facts: Nothing else will ever be of any service to them. This is the principle on which I bring up my own children, and this is the principle on which I bring up these children. Stick to Facts, sir!"

The scene was a plain, bare, monotonous vault of a schoolroom, and the speaker's square forefinger emphasized his observations by underscoring every sentence with a line on the schoolmaster's sleeve. The emphasis was helped by the speaker's square wall of a forehead, which had his eyebrows for its base, while his eyes found commodious cellarage in two dark caves, overshadowed by the wall. The emphasis was helped by the speaker's mouth, which was wide, thin, and hard set. The emphasis was helped by the speaker's voice, which was inflexible, dry, and dictatorial. The emphasis was helped by the speaker's hair, which bristled on the skirts of his bald head, a plantation of firs to keep the wind from its shining surface, all covered with knobs, like the crust of a plum pie, as if the head had scarcely warehouse-room for the hard facts stored inside. The speaker's obstinate carriage, square coat, square legs, square shoulders — nay, his very neckcloth, trained to take him by the throat with an unaccommodating grasp, like a stubborn fact, as it was — all helped the emphasis.

"In this life, we want nothing but Facts, sir; nothing but Facts!"

The speaker, and the schoolmaster, and the third grown person present, all backed a little, and swept with their eyes the inclined plane of little vessels then and there arranged in order, ready to have imperial gallons of facts poured into them until they were full to the brim.

Dickens withholds his character's name until the beginning of the second chapter; he calls this fact-bound educator Mr. Gradgrind. Authors sometimes put as much time and effort into naming their characters as parents invest in naming their children. Names can be used to indicate qualities that the writer associates with the characters. Mr. Gradgrind is precisely what his name suggests. The "schoolmaster" employed by Gradgrind is Mr. M'Choakumchild. Pronounce this name aloud and you have the essence of this teacher's educational philosophy. In Nathaniel Hawthorne's *The Scarlet Letter,* Chillingworth is cold and relentless in his single-minded quest for revenge. The innocent and youthful protagonist in Herman Melville's *Billy Budd* is nipped in the bud by the evil Claggart, whose name simply sounds unpleasant.

Names are also used in films to suggest a character's nature. One example that is destined to be a classic is the infamous villain Darth Vader, whose name identifies his role as an invader allied with the dark and death. On the heroic side, it makes sense that Marion Morrison decided to change his box-office name to John Wayne in order to play tough, masculine roles because both the first and last of his chosen names are unambiguously male and to the point, while his given name is androgynous. There may also be some significance to the lack of a specific identity. In Godwin's "A Sorrowful Woman" (p. 189), the woman, man, boy, and girl are reduced to a set of domestic functions, and their not being named emphasizes their roles as opposed to their individual identities. Of course, not every name is suggestive of the qualities a character may embody, but it is frequently worth determining what is in a name.

The only way to tell whether a name reveals character is to look at the other information the author supplies about the character. We evaluate fictional characters in much the same way we understand people in our own lives. By piecing together bits of information, we create a context that allows us to interpret their behavior. We can predict, for instance, that an acquaintance who is a chronic complainer is not likely to have anything good to say about a roommate. We interpret words and actions in the light of what we already know about someone, and that is why keeping track of what characters say (and how they say it) along with what they do (and don't do) is important.

Authors reveal characters by other means too. Physical descriptions can indicate important inner qualities; disheveled clothing, a crafty smile, or a blush might communicate as much as or more than what a character says. Characters can also be revealed by the words and actions of others who respond to them. In literature, moreover, we have one great advantage that life cannot offer; a work of fiction can give us access to a person's thoughts. Although in Herman Melville's "Bartleby, the Scrivener" (p. 944) we learn about Bartleby primarily through descriptive details, words, actions, and his relationships with the other characters, Melville allows us to enter the lawyer's consciousness.

Authors have two major methods of presenting characters: ***showing*** and ***telling.*** Characters shown in dramatic situations reveal themselves indirectly by what they say and do. In the first paragraph of the excerpt from *Hard Times,* Dickens shows us some of Gradgrind's utilitarian educational principles by having him speak. We can infer the kind of person he is from his reference to boys and girls as "reasoning animals," but we are not told what to think of him until the second paragraph. It would be impossible to admire Gradgrind after reading the physical description of him and the school that he oversees. The adjectives in the second paragraph make the author's evaluation of Gradgrind's values and personality clear: everything about him is rigidly "square"; his mouth is "thin, and hard set"; his voice is "inflexible, dry, and dictatorial"; and he presides over a "plain, bare, monotonous vault of a schoolroom." Dickens directly lets us know how to feel about Gradgrind, but he does so artistically. Instead of simply being presented with a statement that Gradgrind is destructively practical, we get a detailed and amusing description.

Characters can be convincing whether they are presented by telling or showing, provided their actions are *motivated*. There must be reasons for how they behave and what they say. If adequate motivation is offered, we can understand and find *plausible* their actions no matter how bizarre. In "A Rose for Emily" (p. 144), Faulkner makes Emily Grierson's intimacy with a corpse credible by preparing us with information about her father's death along with her inability to leave the past and live in the present. Emily turns out to be *consistent*. Although we are surprised by the ending of the story, the behavior it reveals is compatible with her temperament.

In most stories we expect characters to act plausibly and in ways consistent with their personalities, but that does not mean that characters cannot develop and change. A *dynamic* character undergoes some kind of change because of the action of the plot. Huck Finn's view of Jim, the runaway slave in Mark Twain's novel, develops during their experiences on the raft. Huck discovers Jim's humanity and, therefore, cannot betray him because Huck no longer sees his companion as merely the property of a white owner. On the other hand, Huck's friend, Tom Sawyer, is a *static* character because he does not change. He remains interested only in high adventure, even at the risk of Jim's life. As static characters often do, Tom serves as a foil to Huck; his frivolous concerns are contrasted with Huck's serious development. A *foil* helps to reveal by contrast the distinctive qualities of another character.

The protagonist in a story is usually a dynamic character who experiences some conflict that makes an impact on his or her life. Less commonly, static characters can also be protagonists. Rip Van Winkle wakes up from his twenty-year sleep in Washington Irving's story to discover his family dramatically changed and his country no longer a British colony, but none of these important events has an impact on his character; he continues to be the same shiftless and idle man that he was before he fell asleep. The protagonist in Faulkner's "A Rose for Emily" is also a static character; indeed, she rejects all change. Our understanding of her changes, but she does not. Ordinarily, however, a plot contains one or two dynamic characters with any number of static characters in supporting roles. This is especially true of short stories, in which brevity limits the possibilities of character development.

The extent to which a character is developed is another means by which character can be analyzed. The novelist E. M. Forster coined the terms *flat* and *round* to distinguish degrees of character development. A *flat character* embodies one or two qualities, ideas, or traits that can be readily described in a brief summary. For instance, Mr. M'Choakumchild in Dickens's *Hard Times* stifles students instead of encouraging them to grow. Flat characters tend to be one-dimensional. They are readily accessible because their characteristics are few and simple; they are not created to be psychologically complex.

Some flat characters are immediately recognizable as **stock characters.** These stereotypes are particularly popular in television programs, action movies, and *formula fiction* — such as adventure, western, detective, science fiction, and romance novels. Stock characters are types rather than individuals. The poor but dedicated writer falls in love with a hard-working understudy, who gets nowhere because the corrupt producer favors his boozy, pampered mistress for the leading role. Characters such as these — the loyal servant, the mean stepfather, the henpecked husband, the dumb blonde, the sadistic army officer, the dotty grandmother — are prepackaged; they lack individuality because their authors have, in a sense, not imaginatively created them but simply summoned them from a warehouse of clichés and social prejudices. Stock characters can become fresh if a good writer makes them vivid, interesting, or memorable, but too often a writer's use of these stereotypes is simply weak characterization.

Round characters are more complex than flat or stock characters. Round characters have more depth and require more attention. They may surprise us or puzzle us. Although they are more fully developed, round characters are also more difficult to summarize because we are aware of competing ideas, values, and possibilities in their lives. As a flat character, Huck Finn's alcoholic, bigoted father is clear to us; we know that Pap is the embodiment of racism and irrationality. But Huck is considerably less predictable because he struggles with what Twain calls a "sound heart and a deformed conscience."

In making distinctions between flat and round characters, you must understand that an author's use of a flat character — even as a protagonist — does not necessarily represent an artistic flaw. Moreover, both flat and round characters can be either dynamic or static. Each plot can be made most effective by its own special kind of characterization. Terms such as *round* and *flat* are helpful tools to use to determine what we know about a character, but they are not an infallible measurement of the quality of a story.

For a story that offers especially intriguing character studies, read Herman Melville's "Bartleby, the Scrivener" on page 944. The questions following the story in the "Considerations for Critical Thinking and Writing" should help you to explore more fully Melville's characterizations.

Setting

Setting is the context in which the action of a story occurs. The major elements of setting are the time, place, and social environment that frame the characters. These elements establish the world in which the characters act. In most stories they also serve as more than backgrounds and furnishings. If we are sensitive to the contexts provided by setting, we are better able to understand the behavior of the characters and the significance of their actions. It may be tempting to read quickly through a writer's descriptions and ignore the details of the setting once a geographic location and a historic period are established. But if you read a story so impatiently, the significance of the setting may slip by you. That kind of reading is similar to traveling on interstate highways: A lot of ground gets covered, but very little is seen along the way.

Settings can be used to evoke a mood or atmosphere that will prepare the reader for what is to come. In "Young Goodman Brown" (p. 1246), Nathaniel Hawthorne has his pious protagonist leave his wife and village one night to keep an appointment in a New England forest near the site of the seventeenth-century witch trials. This is Hawthorne's description of Brown entering the forest:

> He had taken a dreary road, darkened by all the gloomiest trees of the forest, which barely stood aside to let the narrow path creep through, and closed immediately behind. It was all as lonely as could be; and there is this peculiarity in such a solitude, that the traveler knows not who may be concealed by the innumerable trunks and the thick boughs overhead; so that with lonely footsteps he may yet be passing through an unseen multitude.

The atmosphere established in this descriptive setting is somber and threatening. Careful reading reveals that the forest is not simply the woods; it is a moral wilderness, where anything can happen.

If we ask why a writer chooses to include certain details in a work, then we are likely to make connections that relate the details to some larger purpose, such as the story's meaning. There is usually a reason for placing a story in a particular time or location. Katherine Mansfield has the protagonist in "Miss Brill" (p. 1270) discover her loneliness and old age in a French vacation town, a lively atmosphere that serves as a cruel contrast to an elderly (and foreign) lady's painful realization.

Time, location, and the physical features of a setting can all be relevant to the overall purpose of a story. So too is the social environment in which the characters are developed. In Faulkner's "A Rose for Emily" (p. 144) the changes in her southern town serve as a foil for Emily's tenacious hold on a lost past. She is regarded as a "fallen monument," as old-fashioned and peculiar as the "stubborn and coquettish decay" of her house. Neither she nor her house fits into the modern changes that are paving and transforming the town. Without the social context, this story would be mostly an account of a bizarre murder rather than an exploration of the conflicts Faulkner associated with the changing South. Setting enlarges the meaning of Emily's actions.

Not every story uses setting as a means of revealing mood, idea, meaning, or characters' actions. Some stories have no particularly significant setting. It is entirely possible to envision a story in which two characters speak to each other about a conflict between them and little or no mention is made of the time or place they inhabit. If, however, a shift in setting would make a serious difference to our understanding of a story, then the setting is probably an important element in the work. For a story whose meaning is significantly related to its small town setting, read Ernest Hemingway's "Soldier's Home" on page 579.

Point of View

Because one of the pleasures of reading fiction consists of seeing the world through someone else's eyes, it is easy to overlook the eyes that control our view of the plot, characters, and setting. *Point of view* refers to who tells us the story and how it is told. What we know and how we feel about the events in a story are shaped by the author's choice of a point of view. The teller of a story, the **narrator,** inevitably affects our understanding of the characters' actions by filtering what is told through his or her own perspective. The narrator should not be confused with the author who has created the narrative voice because the two are usually distinct (more on this point later).

The possible ways of telling a story are many, and more than one point of view can be worked into a single story. However, the various points of view that storytellers draw on can be conveniently grouped into two broad categories: (1) the third-person narrator and (2) the first-person narrator. The third-person narrator uses *he, she,* or *they* to tell the story and does not participate in the action. The first-person narrator uses *I* and is a major or minor participant in the action. A second-person narrator, *you,* is possible but rarely used because of the awkwardness in thrusting the reader into the story, as in "You are minding your own business on a park bench when a drunk steps out of the bushes and demands your lunch bag."

Let's look now at the most important and most often used variations within first- and third-person narrations.

THIRD-PERSON NARRATOR (Nonparticipant)

1. Omniscient (the narrator takes us inside the character[s])
2. Limited omniscient (the narrator takes us inside one or two characters)
3. Objective (the narrator is outside the characters)

No type of third-person narrator appears as a character in a story. The **omniscient narrator** is all-knowing. From this point of view, the narrator can move from place to place and pass back and forth through time, slipping into and out of characters as no human being possibly could in real life. This narrator can report the characters' thoughts and feelings as well as what they say and do. In the excerpt from *Tarzan of the Apes* (p. 139), Burroughs's narrator tells us about events concerning Terkoz in another part of the jungle that long preceded the battle between Terkoz and Tarzan. We also learn Tarzan's and Jane's inner thoughts and emotions during the episode. And Burroughs's narrator describes Terkoz as "an arrant coward" and a bully, thereby evaluating the character for the reader. This kind of intrusion is called ***editorial omniscience.*** In contrast, narration that allows characters' actions and thoughts to speak for themselves is known as ***neutral omniscience.*** Most modern writers use neutral omniscience so that readers can reach their own conclusions.

The ***limited omniscient narrator*** is much more confined than the omniscient narrator. With limited omniscience the author very often restricts the narrator to the single perspective of either a major or a minor character. Sometimes a narrator can see into more than one character, particularly in a longer work that focuses, for example, on two characters alternately from one chapter to the next. Short stories, however, frequently are restricted by length to a single character's point of view. The way people, places, and events appear to that character is the way they appear to the reader. The reader has access to the thoughts and feelings of the characters revealed by the narrator, but neither the reader nor the character has access to the inner lives of any of the other characters in the story. The events in Katherine Mansfield's "Miss Brill" (p. 1270) are viewed entirely through the protagonist's eyes; we see a French vacation town as an elderly woman does. Miss Brill represents the central consciousness of the story. She unifies the story by being present through all the action. We are not told of anything that happens away from the character because the narration is based on her perception of things.

The most intense use of a central consciousness in narration can be seen in the ***stream-of-consciousness technique*** developed by modern writers such as James Joyce, Virginia Woolf, and William Faulkner. This technique takes a reader inside a character's mind to reveal perceptions, thoughts, and feelings on a conscious or unconscious level. A stream of consciousness suggests the flow of thought as well as its content; hence, complete sentences may give way to fragments as the character's mind makes rapid associations free of conventional logic or transitions.

The following passage is from Joyce's *Ulysses,* a novel famous for its extended use of this technique. In this paragraph Joyce takes us inside the mind of a character who is describing a funeral:

> Coffin now. Got here before us, dead as he is. Horse looking round at it with his plume skeowways [askew]. Dull eye: collar tight on his neck, pressing on a bloodvessel or something. Do they know what they cart out of here every day? Must be twenty or thirty funerals every day. Then Mount Jerome for the protestants. Funerals all over the world everywhere every minute. Shovelling them under by the cartload doublequick. Thousands every hour. Too many in the world.

The character's thoughts range from specific observations to speculations about death. Joyce creates the illusion that we are reading the character's thoughts as they occur. The stream-of-consciousness technique provides an intimate perspective on a character's thoughts.

In contrast, the ***objective point of view*** employs a narrator who does not see into the mind of any character. From this detached and impersonal perspective, the narrator reports action and dialogue without telling us directly what the character feels and thinks. We observe the characters in much the same way we would perceive events in a film or play: We supply the meanings; no analysis or interpretation is provided by the narrator. This point of view places a heavy premium on dialogue, actions, and details to reveal character. A brief but powerful example of the objective point of view can be found in Raymond Carver's very short story "Popular Mechanics" (p. 169).

FIRST-PERSON NARRATOR (Participant)

1. Major character
2. Minor character

With a ***first-person narrator,*** the *I* presents the point of view of only one character's consciousness. The reader is restricted to the perceptions, thoughts, and feelings of that single character. This is Melville's technique with the lawyer in "Bartleby, the Scrivener" (p. 944). Everything learned about the characters, action, and plot comes from the unnamed lawyer. Bartleby remains a mystery because we are limited to what the lawyer knows and reports. The lawyer cannot explain what Bartleby means because he does not entirely know himself. Melville's use of the first person encourages us to identify with the lawyer's confused reaction to Bartleby so that we pay attention not only to the scrivener but to the lawyer's response to him. We are as perplexed as the lawyer and share his effort to make sense of Bartleby.

The lawyer is a major character in Melville's story; indeed, many readers take him to be the protagonist. A first-person narrator can, however, also be a minor character. Faulkner uses an observer in "A Rose for Emily" (p. 144). His *we,* though plural and representative of the town's view of Emily, is nonetheless a first-person narrator.

One of the primary reasons for identifying the point of view in a story is to determine where the author stands in relation to the story. Behind the narrative voice of any story is the author, manipulating events and providing or withholding information. It is a mistake to assume that the narrative voice of a story is the author. The narrator, whether a first-person participant or a third-person nonparticipant, is a creation of the writer. A narrator's perceptions may be accepted, rejected, or modified by an author, depending on how the narrative voice is articulated.

Faulkner seems to have shared the fascination, sympathy, and horror of the narrator in "A Rose for Emily," but Melville must not be so readily identified with the lawyer in "Bartleby, the Scrivener." The lawyer's description of himself as "an eminently *safe* man," convinced "that the easiest way of life is the best," raises the question of how well equipped he is to fathom Bartleby's protest. To make sense of Bartleby, it is also necessary to understand the lawyer's point of view.

The lawyer is an ***unreliable narrator,*** whose interpretation of events is different from the author's. We cannot entirely accept the lawyer's assessment of Bartleby because we see that the lawyer's perceptions are not totally to be trusted. The lawyer's perceptions frequently do not coincide with those Melville expects his readers to share. Hence, the lawyer's unreliability preserves Bartleby's mysterious nature while revealing the lawyer's sensibilities. The point of view is artistically appropriate for Melville's purposes because the eyes through which we perceive the plot, characters, and setting are also the subject of the story.

Narrators can be unreliable for a variety of reasons: They might lack self-knowledge, like Melville's lawyer, or they might be innocent and inexperienced, like Ralph Ellison's young narrator in "Battle Royal" (p. 931). Youthful innocence frequently characterizes a ***naive narrator*** such as Mark Twain's Huck Finn or Holden Caulfield, J. D. Salinger's twentieth-century version of Huck in *The Catcher in the Rye*. These narrators lack the sophistication to interpret accurately what they see; they are unreliable because the reader must go beyond their understanding of events to comprehend the situations described. Huck and Holden describe their respective social environments, but the reader, with more experience, supplies the critical perspective that each boy lacks. In "Battle Royal" that perspective is supplemented by Ellison's dividing the narration between the young man who experiences events and the mature man who reflects back on those events.

Few generalizations can be made about the advantages or disadvantages of using a specific point of view. What can be said with confidence, however, is that writers choose a point of view to achieve particular effects because point of view determines what we know about the characters and events in a story. We should, therefore, be aware of who is telling the story and whether the narrator sees things clearly and reliably.

Symbolism

A ***symbol*** is a person, object, or event that suggests more than its literal meaning. This basic definition is simple enough, but the use of symbol in literature makes some students slightly nervous because they tend to regard it as a booby trap, a hidden device that can go off during a seemingly harmless class discussion. "I didn't see that when I was reading the story" is a frequently heard comment. This sort of surprise and recognition is both natural and common. Most readers go through a story for the first time getting their bearings, figuring out what is happening to whom and so on. Patterns and significant details often require a second or third reading before they become evident — before a symbol sheds light on a story. Then the details of a work may suddenly fit together, and its meaning may be reinforced, clarified, or enlarged by the symbol. Symbolic meanings are usually embedded in the texture of a story, but they are not "hidden"; instead, they are carefully placed. Reading between the lines (where there is only space) is unnecessary. What is needed is a careful consideration of the elements of the story, a sensitivity to its language, and some common sense.

Common sense is a good place to begin. Symbols appear all around us; anything can be given symbolic significance. Without symbols our lives would be stark and vacant. Awareness of a writer's use of symbols is not all that different from the kinds of perceptions and interpretations that allow us to make sense of our daily lives. We know, for example, that a ring used in a wedding is more than just a piece of jewelry because it suggests the unity and intimacy of a closed circle. The bride's gown may be white because we tend to associate innocence and purity with that color. Or consider the meaning of a small polo pony sewn on a shirt or some other article of clothing. What started as a company trademark has gathered around it a range of meanings suggesting everything from quality and money to preppiness and silliness. The ring, the white gown, and the polo pony trademark are symbolic because each has meanings that go beyond its specific qualities and functions.

Symbols such as these that are widely recognized by a society or culture are called ***conventional symbols.*** The Christian cross, the Star of David, a swastika, or a nation's flag all have meanings understood by large groups of people. Certain kinds of experiences also have traditional meanings in Western cultures. Winter, the setting sun, and the color black suggest death, while spring, the rising sun, and the color green evoke images of youth and new beginnings. (It is worth noting, however, that individual cultures sometimes have their own conventions; some eastern cultures associate white rather than black with death and mourning. And obviously the polo pony trademark would mean nothing to anyone totally unfamiliar with American culture.) These broadly shared symbolic meanings are second nature to us.

Writers use conventional symbols to reinforce meanings. Kate Chopin, for example, emphasizes the spring setting in "The Story of an Hour" (p. 18) as a way of suggesting the renewed sense of life that Mrs. Mallard feels when she thinks herself free from her husband.

A ***literary symbol*** can include traditional, conventional, or public meanings, but it may also be established internally by the total context of the work in which it appears. In "Soldier's Home" (p. 579), Hemingway does not use Krebs's family home as a conventional symbol of safety, comfort, and refuge from the war. Instead, Krebs's home becomes symbolic of provincial, erroneous presuppositions compounded by blind innocence, sentimentality, and smug middle-class respectability. The significance of Krebs's home is determined by the events within the story, which reverse and subvert the traditional associations readers might bring to it. Krebs's interactions with his family and the people in town reveal what home has come to mean to him.

A literary symbol can be a setting, character, action, object, name, or anything else in a work that maintains its literal significance while suggesting other meanings. Symbols cannot be restricted to a single meaning; they are suggestive rather than definitive. Their evocation of multiple meanings allows a writer to say more with less. Symbols are economical devices for evoking complex ideas without having to resort to painstaking explanations that would make a story more like an essay than an experience.

When a character, object, or incident indicates a single, fixed meaning, the writer is using *allegory* rather than symbol. Whereas symbols have literal functions as well as multiple meanings, the primary focus in allegory is on the abstract idea called forth by the concrete object. John Bunyan's *Pilgrim's Progress,* published during the seventeenth century, is a classic example of allegory because the characters, action, and setting have no existence beyond their abstract meanings. Bunyan's purpose is to teach his readers the exemplary way to salvation and heaven. The protagonist, named Christian, flees the City of Destruction in search of the Celestial City. Along the way he encounters characters who either help or hinder his spiritual journey. Among them are Mr. Worldly Wiseman, Faithful, Prudence, Piety, and a host of others named after the virtues or vices they display. These characters, places, and actions exist solely to illustrate religious doctrine. Allegory tends to be definitive rather than suggestive. It drives meaning into a corner and keeps it there. Most modern writers prefer the exploratory nature of symbol to the reductive nature of pure allegory.

Stories often include symbols that you may or may not perceive on a first reading. Their subtle use is a sign of a writer's skill in weaving symbols into the fabric of the characters' lives. Symbols may sometimes escape you, but that is probably better than finding symbols where only literal meanings are intended. Allow the text to help you determine whether a symbolic reading is appropriate. Once you are clear about what literally happens, read carefully and notice the placement of details that are emphasized.

By keeping track of the total context of the story, you should be able to decide whether your reading is reasonable and consistent with the other facts; plenty of lemons in literature yield no symbolic meaning even if they are squeezed. Be sensitive to the meanings that the author associates with people, places, objects, and actions. You may not associate home with provincial innocence as Hemingway does in "Soldier's Home," but a close reading of the story will permit you to see how and why he constructs that symbolic meaning. If you treat stories like people — with tact and care — they ordinarily are accessible and enjoyable.

The next story, "The Hand" by Colette, relies on symbols to convey meanings that go far beyond the specific incidents described in its plot.

COLETTE (Sidonie-Gabrielle Colette / 1873–1954)

Born in Burgundy, France, Sidonie-Gabrielle Colette lived a long and remarkably diverse life. At various points during her career she supported herself as a novelist, music hall performer, and journalist. Her professional life and three marriages helped to shape her keen insights into modern love and women's lives. She is regarded as a significant feminist voice of the twentieth century, and her reputation is firmly fixed by her having been the first woman admitted to the Goncourt Academy and by the continued popularity of her work among readers internationally. Her best-known works include *Mitsou, or, How Girls Grow Wise* (1919), *Chéri* (1920), *Claudine's House* (1922), and *Gigi* (1944). "The Hand" signals a telling moment in the life of a young bride.

The Hand   1924

He had fallen asleep on his young wife's shoulder, and she proudly bore the weight of the man's head, blond, ruddy-complexioned, eyes closed. He had slipped his big arm under the small of her slim, adolescent back, and his strong hand lay on the sheet next to the young woman's right elbow. She smiled to see the man's hand emerging there, all by itself and far away from its owner. Then she let her eyes wander over the half-lit room. A veiled conch shed a light across the bed the color of periwinkle.

"Too happy to sleep," she thought.

Too excited also, and often surprised by her new state. It had been only two weeks since she had begun to live the scandalous life of a newlywed who tastes the joys of living with someone unknown and with whom she is in love. To meet a handsome, blond young man, recently widowed, good at tennis and rowing, to marry him a month later: her conjugal adventure had been little more than a kidnapping. So that whenever she lay awake beside her husband, like tonight, she still kept her eyes closed for a long time, then opened them again in order to savor, with astonishment, the blue of the brand-new curtains, instead of the apricot-pink through which the first light of day filtered into the room where she had slept as a little girl.

A quiver ran through the sleeping body lying next to her, and she tightened her left arm around her husband's neck with the charming authority exercised by weak creatures. He did not wake up.

"His eyelashes are so long," she said to herself.   5

To herself she also praised his mouth, full and likable, his skin the color of pink brick, and even his forehead, neither noble nor broad, but still smooth and unwrinkled.

Her husband's right hand, lying beside her, quivered in turn, and beneath the curve of her back she felt the right arm, on which her whole weight was resting, come to life.

"I'm so heavy . . . I wish I could get up and turn the light off. But he's sleeping so well . . ."

The arm twisted again, feebly, and she arched her back to make herself lighter.

"It's as if I were lying on some animal," she thought.   10

She turned her head a little on the pillow and looked at the hand lying there next to her.

"It's so big! It really is bigger than my whole head."

The light, flowing out from under the edge of a parasol of bluish crystal, spilled up against the hand, and made every contour of the skin apparent, exaggerating the powerful knuckles and the veins engorged by the pressure on the arm. A few red hairs, at the base of the fingers, all curved in the same direction, like ears of wheat in the wind, and the flat nails, whose ridges the nail buffer had not smoothed out, gleamed, coated with pink varnish.

"I'll tell him not to varnish his nails," thought the young wife. "Varnish and pink polish don't go with a hand so . . . a hand that's so . . ."

An electric jolt ran through the hand and spared the young woman from   15 having to find the right adjective. The thumb stiffened itself out, horribly long and spatulate, and pressed tightly against the index finger, so that the hand suddenly took on a vile, apelike appearance.

"Oh!" whispered the young woman, as though faced with something slightly indecent.

The sound of a passing car pierced the silence with a shrillness that seemed luminous. The sleeping man did not wake, but the hand, offended, reared back and tensed up in the shape of a crab and waited, ready for battle. The screeching sound died down and the hand, relaxing gradually, lowered its claws, and became a pliant beast, awkwardly bent, shaken by faint jerks which resembled some sort of agony. The flat, cruel nail of the overlong thumb glistened. A curve in the little finger, which the young woman had never noticed, appeared, and the wallowing hand revealed its fleshy palm like a red belly.

"And I've kissed that hand! . . . How horrible! Haven't I ever looked at it?"

The hand, disturbed by a bad dream, appeared to respond to this startling discovery, this disgust. It regrouped its forces, opened wide, and splayed its tendons, lumps, and red fur like battle dress, then slowly drawing itself in again, grabbed a fistful of the sheet, dug into it with its curved fingers, and squeezed, squeezed with the methodical pleasure of a strangler.

"Oh!" cried the young woman.   20

The hand disappeared and a moment later the big arm, relieved of its burden, became a protective belt, a warm bulwark against all the terrors of night. But the next morning, when it was time for breakfast in bed — hot chocolate and toast — she saw the hand again, with its red hair and red skin, and the ghastly thumb curving out over the handle of a knife.

"Do you want this slice, darling? I'll butter it for you."

She shuddered and felt her skin crawl on the back of her arms and down her back.

"Oh, no . . . no . . ."

Then she concealed her fear, bravely subdued herself, and, beginning her   25 life of duplicity, of resignation, and of a lowly, delicate diplomacy, she leaned over and humbly kissed the monstrous hand.

Considerations for Critical Thinking and Writing

1. FIRST RESPONSE. Where is "The Hand" set? How significant is the setting of the story?

2. How well did the young woman know her husband before she married him? What attracted her to him?

3. How does the wife regard the hand at the very beginning of the story? At what point does she begin to change her attitude?

4. Explain how the wife's description of the hand affects your own response to it. What prompts her "Oh!" in paragraphs 16 and 20? What do you suppose the wife is thinking at these moments?

5. What powerful feelings does the hand evoke in the wife? How do her descriptions of the hand suggest symbolic readings of it?

6. Describe the conflict in the story. Explain whether there is a resolution to this conflict.

7. Do you think the story is more about the husband or about the wife? Who is the central character? Explain your choice. Consider also whether the characters are static or dynamic.

8. Why do you think the narrator mentions that the husband was "recently widowed"?

9. Why do you think the wife kisses her husband's hand in the final paragraph? Write an essay explaining how the kiss symbolizes the nature of their relationship.

10. Describe the point of view in the story. Why do you suppose Colette doesn't use a first-person perspective that would reveal more intimately the wife's perceptions and concerns?

Style

Style is a concept that everyone understands on some level because in its broadest sense it refers to the particular way in which anything is made or done. Style is everywhere around us. The world is saturated with styles in cars, clothing, buildings, teaching, dancing, music, politics — in anything that reflects a distinctive manner of expression or design. Consider, for example, how a tune sung by the Beatles differs from the same tune performed by a string orchestra. There's no mistaking the two styles.

Authors also have different characteristic styles. **Style** refers to the distinctive manner in which a writer arranges words to achieve particular effects. That arrangement includes individual word choices and matters such as the length of sentences, their structure and tone, and the use of irony.

Diction refers to a writer's choice of words. Because different words evoke different associations in a reader's mind, the writer's choice of words is crucial in controlling a reader's response. The diction must be appropriate for the characters and the situations in which the author places them. Consider how inappropriate it would have been if Melville had had Bartleby respond to the lawyer's requests with "Hell no!" instead of "I would prefer not to." The word *prefer* and the tentativeness of *would* help reinforce the scrivener's mildness, his dignity, and even his seeming reasonableness — all of which frustrate the lawyer's efforts to get rid of him. Bartleby, despite his passivity, seems to be in control of the situation. If he were to shout "Hell no!" he would appear angry, aggressive, desperate, and too informal, none of which would fit with his solemn, conscious decision to die. Melville makes the lawyer the desperate party by carefully choosing Bartleby's words.

Sentence structure is another element of a writer's style. Hemingway's terse, economical sentences are frequently noted and readily perceived. Here are the concluding sentences of Hemingway's "Soldier's Home" (p. 579), in which Krebs decides to leave home:

He had tried so to keep his life from being complicated. Still, none of it had touched him. He had felt sorry for his mother and she had made him lie. He would go to Kansas City and get a job and she would feel all right about it. There would be one more scene maybe before he got away. He would not go down to his father's office. He would miss that one. He wanted his life to go smoothly. It had just gotten going that way. Well, that was all over now, anyway. He would go over to the schoolyard and watch Helen play indoor baseball.

Hemingway expresses Krebs's thought the way Krebs thinks. The style avoids any "complicated" sentence structures. Seven of the eleven sentences begin with the word *He.* There are no abstractions or qualifications. We feel as if we are listening not only to *what* Krebs thinks but to *how* he thinks. The style reflects his firm determination to make, one step at a time, a clean, unobstructed break from his family and the entangling complications they would impose on him.

Contrast this straightforward style with Vladimir Nabokov's description of a woman in his short story "The Vane Sisters." The sophisticated narrator teaches French literature at a women's college and is as observant as he is icily critical of the woman he describes in this passage:

Her fingernails were gaudily painted, but badly bitten and not clean. Her lovers were a silent young photographer with a sudden laugh and two older men, brothers, who owned a small printing establishment across the street. I wondered at their tastes whenever I glimpsed, with a secret shudder, the higgledy-piggledy striation of black hairs that showed all along her pale shins through the nylon of her stockings with the scientific distinctness of a preparation flattened under glass; or when I felt, at her every movement, the dullish, stalish, not particularly conspicuous but all-pervading and depressing emanation that her seldom bathed flesh spread from under weary perfumes and creams.

This portrait — etched with a razor blade — is restrained but devastating. The woman's fingernails are "gaudily painted." She has no taste in men either. One of her lovers is "silent" except for a "sudden laugh," a telling detail that suggests a strikingly odd personality. Her other lovers, the two brothers (!), run a "small" business. We are invited to "shudder" along with the narrator as he vividly describes the "striation of black hairs" on her legs; we see the woman as if she were displayed under a microscope, an appropriate perspective given the narrator's close inspection. His scrutiny is relentless, and its object smells as awful as it looks (notice the difference in the language between this blunt description and the narrator's elegant distaste). He finds the woman "depressing" because the weight of her unpleasantness oppresses him.

The narrator reveals nearly as much about himself as about the woman, but Nabokov leaves the reader with the task of assessing the narrator's fastidious reactions. The formal style of this description is appropriately that of an educated, highly critical, close observer of life who knows how to convey the "dullish, stalish" essence of this woman. But, you might ask, what about the curious informality of "higgledy-piggledy"? Does that fit the formal professorial voice? Given Nabokov's well-known fascination with wit and, more important, the narrator's obvious relish for verbally slicing this woman into a slide specimen, the term is revealed as appropriately chosen once the reader sees the subtle, if brutal, pun on *piggledy*.

Hemingway's and Nabokov's uses of language are very different, yet each style successfully fuses what is said with how it is said. We could write summaries of both passages, but our summaries, owing to their styles, would not have the same effect as the originals. And that makes all the difference.

Tone

Style reveals **_tone_,** the author's implicit attitude toward the people, places, and events in a story. When we speak, tone is conveyed by our voice inflections, our wink of an eye, or some other gesture. A professor who says "You're going to fail the next exam" may be indicating concern, frustration, sympathy, alarm, humor, or indifference, depending on the tone of voice. In a literary work that spoken voice is unavailable; instead we must rely on the context in which a statement appears to interpret it correctly.

In Chopin's "The Story of an Hour" (p. 18), for example, we can determine that the author sympathizes with Mrs. Mallard despite the fact that her grief over her husband's assumed death is mixed with joy. Though Mrs. Mallard thinks she's lost her husband, she experiences relief because she feels liberated from an oppressive male-dominated life. That's why she collapses when she sees her husband alive at the end of the story. Chopin makes clear by the tone of the final line ("When the doctors came they said she had died of heart disease — of joy that kills") that the men misinterpret both her grief and joy, for in the larger context of Mrs. Mallard's emotions we see, unlike the doctors, that her death may well have been caused not by a shock of joy but by an overwhelming recognition of her lost freedom.

If we are sensitive to tone, we can get behind a character and see him or her from the author's perspective. In Melville's "Bartleby, the Scrivener" (p. 944) everything is told from the lawyer's point of view, but the tone of his remarks often separates him from the author's values and attitudes. When the lawyer characterizes himself at the beginning of the story, his use of language effectively allows us to see Melville disapproving of what the lawyer takes pride in:

> The late John Jacob Astor, a personage little given to poetic enthusiasm, had no hesitation in pronouncing my first grand point to be prudence; my next, method. I do not speak it in vanity.

But, of course, he is vain and a name-dropper as well. He likes the "rounded and orbicular sound" of Astor's name because it "rings like unto bullion." Tone, here, helps to characterize the lawyer. Melville doesn't tell us that the lawyer is status conscious and materialistic; instead, we discover that through the tone. This stylistic technique is frequently an important element for interpreting a story. An insensitivity to tone can lead a reader astray in determining the meanings of a work. Regardless of who is speaking in a story, it is wise to listen for the author's voice too.

Irony

One of the enduring themes in literature is that things are not always what they seem to be. What we see — or think we see — is not always what we get. The unexpected complexity that often surprises us in life — what Herman Melville in *Moby-Dick* called the "universal thump" — is fertile ground for writers of imaginative literature. They cultivate that ground through the use of *irony,* a device that reveals a reality different from what appears to be true.

Verbal irony consists of a person saying one thing but meaning the opposite. If a student driver smashes into a parked car and the angry instructor turns to say "You sure did well today," the statement is an example of verbal irony. What is meant is not what is said. Verbal irony that is calculated to hurt someone by false praise is commonly known as **sarcasm.** In literature, however, verbal irony is usually not openly aggressive; instead, it is more subtle and restrained though no less intense. In Faulkner's "A Rose for Emily" (p. 144), Emily buys arsenic from a druggist who — because the law requires an indicated use — writes on the package that it is "For rats." The druggist doesn't realize, of course, that she's going to feed it to Homer Barron rather than to rodents, but the phrase is a fine example of verbal irony that allows us to understand (retrospectively) how Emily thinks of Homer.

Situational irony exists when there is an incongruity between what is expected to happen and what actually happens. For instance, in Chopin's "The Story of an Hour" (p. 18) our expectations concerning Mrs. Mallard's grieving for her husband are completely disrupted when at the end of the story Mr. Mallard turns out to be very much alive and Mrs. Mallard dies of heart failure. The ironic situation creates a distinction between appearances and realities and brings the reader closer to the central meaning of the story.

Another form of irony occurs when an author allows the reader to know more about a situation than a character knows. **Dramatic irony** creates a discrepancy between what a character believes or says and what the reader understands to be true. In "The Story of an Hour," a careful reading of the final sentence reveals how little Mrs. Mallard is understood by those around her. After she dies, the doctors assume that "she had died of heart disease — of joy that kills" because she was overwhelmed by the shock of seeing her husband alive. The reader recognizes, however, that her husband's continued life — rather than his presumed death — has killed the possibility of joy in her life. The doctors have no idea how fatally wrong their diagnosis is. Dramatic irony can be an effective way for an author to have characters unwittingly reveal themselves.

As you read Raymond Carver's "Popular Mechanics," pay attention to the author's artful use of style, tone, and irony to convey meanings.

RAYMOND CARVER (1938–1988)

Born in 1938 in Clatskanie, Oregon, to working-class parents, Carver grew up in Yakima, Washington, was educated at Humboldt State College in California, and did graduate work at the University of Iowa. He married at age nineteen and during his college years worked at a series of low-paying jobs to help support his family. These difficult years eventually ended in divorce. He taught at a number of universities, among them the University of California at Berkeley, the University of Iowa, the University of Texas at El Paso, and Syracuse University. Carver's collections of stories include *Will You Please Be Quiet, Please?* (1976); *What We Talk about When We Talk about Love* (1981), from which "Popular Mechanics" is taken; *Cathedral* (1984); and *Where I'm Calling From: New and Selected Stories* (1988). Though extremely brief, "Popular Mechanics" describes a stark domestic situation with a startling conclusion.

Popular Mechanics — 1981

Early that day the weather turned and the snow was melting into dirty water. Streaks of it ran down from the little shoulder-high window that faced the backyard. Cars slushed by on the street outside, where it was getting dark. But it was getting dark on the inside too.

He was in the bedroom pushing clothes into a suitcase when she came to the door.

I'm glad you're leaving! I'm glad you're leaving! she said. Do you hear?

He kept on putting his things into the suitcase.

Son of a bitch! I'm so glad you're leaving! She began to cry. You can't even 5 look me in the face, can you?

Then she noticed the baby's picture on the bed and picked it up.

He looked at her and she wiped her eyes and stared at him before turning and going back to the living room.

Bring that back, he said.

Just get your things and get out, she said.

He did not answer. He fastened the suitcase, put on his coat, looked 10 around the bedroom before turning off the light. Then he went out to the living room.

She stood in the doorway of the little kitchen, holding the baby.

I want the baby, he said.

Are you crazy?

No, but I want the baby. I'll get someone to come by for his things.

You're not touching this baby, she said.   15

The baby had begun to cry and she uncovered the blanket from around his head.

Oh, oh, she said, looking at the baby.

He moved toward her.

For God's sake! she said. She took a step back into the kitchen.

I want the baby.   20

Get out of here!

She turned and tried to hold the baby over in a corner behind the stove.

But he came up. He reached across the stove and tightened his hands on the baby.

Let go of him, he said.

Get away, get away! she cried.   25

The baby was red-faced and screaming. In the scuffle they knocked down a flowerpot that hung behind the stove.

He crowded her into the wall then, trying to break her grip. He held on to the baby and pushed with all his weight.

Let go of him, he said.

Don't, she said. You're hurting the baby, she said.

I'm not hurting the baby, he said.   30

The kitchen window gave no light. In the near-dark he worked on her fisted fingers with one hand and with the other hand he gripped the screaming baby up under an arm near the shoulder.

She felt her fingers being forced open. She felt the baby going from her.

No! she screamed just as her hands came loose.

She would have it, this baby. She grabbed for the baby's other arm. She caught the baby around the wrist and leaned back.

But he would not let go. He felt the baby slipping out of his hands and he 35
pulled back very hard.

In this manner, the issue was decided.

CONSIDERATIONS FOR CRITICAL THINKING AND WRITING

1. FIRST RESPONSE. Discuss the story's final lines. What is the "issue" that is "decided"?

2. Though there is little description of the setting in this story, how do the few details that are provided help to establish the tone?

3. How do small actions take on larger significance in the story? Consider the woman picking up the baby's picture and the knocked-down flowerpot.

4. Why is this couple splitting up? Do we know? Does it matter? Explain your response.

5. Discuss the title of the story. The original title was "Mine." Which do you think is more effective?

6. What is the conflict? How is it resolved?

7. Read I Kings 3 in the Bible for the story of Solomon. How might "Popular Mechanics" be read as a retelling of this story? What significant differences do you find in the endings of each?

8. Explain how Carver uses irony to convey meaning.

Theme

Theme is the central idea or meaning of a story. It provides a unifying point around which the plot, characters, setting, point of view, symbols, irony, and other elements of a story are organized. In some works the theme is explicitly stated. Nathaniel Hawthorne's "Wakefield," for example, begins with the author telling the reader that the point of his story is "done up neatly, and condensed into the final sentence." Most modern writers, however, present their themes implicitly (as Hawthorne does in the majority of his stories), so determining the underlying meaning of a work often requires more effort than it does from the reader of "Wakefield." One reason for the difficulty is that the theme is fused into the elements of the story, and these must be carefully examined in relation to one another as well as to the work as a whole. But then that's the value of determining the theme, for it requires a close analysis of all the elements of a work. Such a close reading often results in sharper insights into this overlooked character or that seemingly unrelated incident. Accounting for the details and seeing how they fit together result in greater understanding of the story. Such familiarity creates pleasure in much the same way that a musical piece heard more than once becomes a rich experience rather than simply a repetitive one.

Themes are not always easy to express, but some principles can aid you in articulating the central meaning of a work. First distinguish between the theme of a story and its subject. They are not equivalents. Many stories share identical subjects, such as fate, death, innocence, youth, loneliness, racial prejudice, and disillusionment. Yet each story usually makes its own statement about the subject and expresses some view of life. Hemingway's "Soldier's Home" (p. 579) and Faulkner's "Barn Burning" (p. 84) both describe young men who are unhappy at home and decide that they must leave, but the meaning of each story is quite different. A thematic generalization about "Soldier's Home" could be something like this: "The brutal experience of war can alienate a person from those — even family and friends — who are innocent of war's reality." The theme of Faulkner's story could be stated this way: "No matter how much one might love one's father, there comes a time when family loyalties must be left behind in order to be true to one's self."

These two statements of theme do not definitively sum up each story — there is no single, absolute way of expressing a work's theme — but they do describe a central idea in each. Furthermore, the emphasis in each of these themes could be modified or expanded because interpretations of interesting, complex works are always subject to revision. People have different responses to life, and so it is hardly surprising that responses to literature are not identical. When theme is considered, the possibilities for meaning are usually expanded and not reduced to categories such as "right" or "wrong."

Although readers may differ in their interpretations of a story, that does not mean that *any* interpretation is valid. If we were to assert that the soldier's dissatisfactions in Hemingway's story could be readily eliminated by his settling down to marriage and a decent job (his mother's solution), we would have missed Hemingway's purposes in writing the story; we would have failed to see how Krebs's war experiences have caused him to reexamine the assumptions and beliefs that previously nurtured him but now seem unreal to him. We would have to ignore much in the story in order to arrive at such a reading. To be valid, the statement of the theme should be responsive to the details of the story. It must be based on evidence within the story rather than solely on experiences, attitudes, or values the reader brings to the work—such as personally knowing a war veteran who successfully adjusted to civilian life after getting a good job and marrying. Familiarity with the subject matter of a story can certainly be an aid to interpretation, but it should not get in the way of seeing the author's perspective.

Sometimes readers too hastily conclude that a story's theme always consists of a moral, some kind of lesson that is dramatized by the various elements of the work. There are stories that do this—Hawthorne's "Wakefield," for example. Here are the final sentences in his story about a middle-aged man who drops out of life for twenty years:

> He has left us much food for thought, a portion of which shall lend its wisdom to a moral, and be shaped into a figure. Amid the seeming confusion of our mysterious world, individuals are so nicely adjusted to a system, and systems to one another and to a whole, that, by stepping aside for a moment, a man exposes himself to a fearful risk of losing his place forever. Like Wakefield, he may become, as it were, the Outcast of the Universe.

Most stories, however, do not include such direct caveats about the conduct of life. A tendency to look for a lesson in a story can produce a reductive and inaccurate formulation of its theme. Consider the damage done to Colette's "The Hand" (p. 163) if its theme is described as this: "Adolescents are too young to cope with the responsibilities of marriage." Colette's focus in this story is on the young woman's response to her husband's powerful sexuality and dominance rather than on her inability to be a good wife.

Determining the theme of a story can be a difficult task because all the story's elements may contribute to its central idea. Indeed, you may discover that finding the theme is more challenging than coming to grips with the author's values as they are revealed in the story. There is no precise formula that can take you to the center of a story's meaning and help you to articulate it. However, several strategies are practical and useful once you have read the story. Apply these pointers during a second or third reading:

1. Pay attention to the title of the story. It often provides a lead to a major symbol (Faulkner's "Barn Burning," p. 84) or to the subject around which the theme develops (Godwin's "A Sorrowful Woman," p. 189).

2. Look for details in the story that have potential for symbolic meanings. Careful consideration of names, places, objects, minor characters, and incidents can lead you to the central meaning — for example, think of the hand in Colette's story (p. 163). Be especially attentive to elements you did not understand on the first reading.

3. Decide whether the protagonist changes or develops some important insight as a result of the action. Carefully examine any generalizations the protagonist or narrator makes about the events in the story.

4. When you formulate the theme of the story in your own words, write it down in one or two complete sentences that make some point about the subject matter. Revenge may be the subject of a story, but its theme should make a statement about revenge: "Instead of providing satisfaction, revenge defeats the best in one's self" is one possibility.

5. Be certain that your expression of the theme is a generalized statement rather than a specific description of particular people, places, and incidents in the story. Contrast the preceding statement of a theme on revenge with this too-specific one: "In Nathaniel Hawthorne's *The Scarlet Letter*, Roger Chillingworth loses his humanity owing to his single-minded attempts to punish Arthur Dimmesdale for fathering a child with Chillingworth's wife, Hester." Hawthorne's theme is not restricted to a single fictional character named Chillingworth but to anyone whose life is ruined by revenge. Be certain that your statement of theme does not focus on only part of the story. The theme just cited for *The Scarlet Letter*, for example, relegates Hester to the status of a minor character. What it says about Chillingworth is true, but the statement is incomplete as a generalization about the novel.

6. Be wary of using clichés as a way of stating theme. They tend to short-circuit ideas instead of generating them. It may be tempting to resort to something like "Love conquers all" as a statement of the theme of Chekhov's "The Lady with the Pet Dog" (p. 776); however, even the slightest second thought reveals how much more ambiguous the ending of that story is.

7. Be aware that some stories emphasize theme less than others. Stories that have as their major purpose adventure, humor, mystery, or terror may have little or no theme. In Edgar Allan Poe's "The Pit and the Pendulum," for example, the protagonist is not used to condemn torture; instead, he becomes a sensitive gauge to measure the pain and horror he endures at the hands of his captors.

What is most valuable about articulating the theme of a work is the process by which the theme is determined. Ultimately, the theme is expressed by the story itself and is inseparable from the experience of reading the story. Tim O'Brien's explanation of "How to Tell a True War Story" (p. 1149) is probably true of most kinds of stories: "In a true war story, if there's a moral [or theme] at all, it's like the thread that makes the cloth. You can't tease it out. You can't extract the meaning without unraveling the deeper meaning." Describing the theme should not be a way to consume a story, to be done with it. It is a means of clarifying our thinking about what we've read and probably felt intuitively.

Comparison and Contrast

This casebook shows you how one student, Maya Leigh, develops a comparison and contrast paper—from her first response through two drafts and her final paper—about two contemporary pieces of fiction about a woman who experiences deep sorrow. The first, from A Secret Sorrow *by Karen van der Zee, is an excerpt from a romance by Harlequin Books, a major publisher of formula fiction that has sold well over a billion copies of its romance titles—enough for about 20 percent of the world's population. The second piece, Gail Godwin's "A Sorrowful Woman," is a complete short story that originally appeared in* Esquire; *it is not a formula story. These two stories are presented in the context of formula fiction, and Maya was also asked to read the following two contextual documents: the composite of a romance tip sheet and a romance novel cover. As you read each selection, look for evidence of formulaic writing. Pay particular attention to the advice on plotting and characterization offered in the composite tip sheet. As you read Godwin's short story, think how it is different from van der Zee's excerpt; note also any similarities. What would you want to focus on in a paper that compared the two?*

FORMULA FICTION

Many publishers of formula fiction—such as romance, adventure, or detective stories—issue a set number of new novels each month. Readers can buy them in stores or subscribe to them through the mail. These same publishers send "tip sheets" on request to authors who want to write for a particular series. The details of the formula differ from one series to another, but each tip sheet covers the basic elements that go into a story.

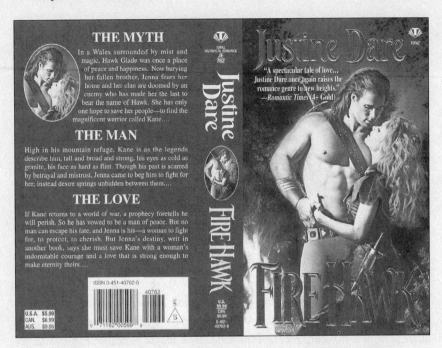

The cover for FireHawk *(Penguin, 1997) illustrates another convention of romance formula fiction: Its packaging demands an image of a man clasping a passionate beauty to his manly chest. As the back-cover copy suggests, this Topaz novel is a historical romance — a subcategory of the romance formula — and so a few of the guidelines on the tip sheet are modified (the setting is medieval Wales rather than contemporary America, for example). But most of the guidelines apply: Kane is strong and so is Jenna's powerful love. Reprinted by permission of Topaz Books, a division of Penguin Putnam.*

There are many kinds of formulaic romance novels; some include psychological terrors, some use historical settings, and some even incorporate time travel so that the hero or heroine can travel back in time and fall in love, and still others create mystery and suspense. Several publishers have recently released romances that reflect contemporary social concerns and issues; multicultural couples and gay and lesbian relationships as well as more explicit descriptions of sexual activities are now sometimes featured in these books. In general, however, the majority of romance novels are written to appeal to a readership that embraces more traditional societal expectations and values.

The following composite tip sheet summarizes the typical advice offered by publishers of romance novels. These are among the most popular titles published in the United States; it has been estimated that four out of every ten paperbacks sold are romance novels. The categories and the tone of the language in this composite tip sheet are derived from a number of publishers and provide a glimpse of how formula fiction is written and what the readers of romance novels are looking for in their escape literature.

A Composite of a Romance Tip Sheet

Plot

The story focuses on the growing relationship between the heroine and hero. After a number of complications, they discover lasting love and make a permanent commitment to each other in marriage. The plot should move quickly. Background information about the heroine should be kept to a minimum. The hero should appear as early as possible (preferably in the first chapter and no later than the second), so that the hero's and heroine's feelings about each other are in the foreground as they cope with misperceptions that keep them apart until the final pages of the story. The more tension created by their uncertainty about each other's love, the greater the excitement and anticipation for the reader.

Love is the major interest. Do not inject murder, extortion, international intrigue, hijacking, horror, or supernatural elements into the plot. Controversial social issues and politics, if mentioned at all, should never be allowed a significant role. Once the heroine and hero meet, they should clearly be interested in each other, but that interest should be complicated by some kind of misunderstanding. He, for example, might find her too ambitious, an opportunist, cold, or flirtatious; or he might assume that she is attached to someone else. She might think he is haughty, snobbish, power hungry, indifferent, or contemptuous of her. The reader knows what they do not: that eventually these obstacles will be overcome. Interest is sustained by keeping the lovers apart until very near the end so that the reader will stay with the plot to see how they get together.

Heroine

The heroine is a modern American woman between the ages of nineteen and twenty-eight who reflects today's concerns. The story is told in the third person from her point of view. She is attractive and nicely dressed but not glamorous; glitter and sophistication should be reserved for the other woman (the heroine's rival for the hero), whose flashiness will compare unfavorably with the heroine's modesty. When the heroine does dress up, however, her beauty should be stunningly apparent. Her trim figure is appealing but not abundant; a petite, healthy appearance is desirable. Both her looks and her clothes should be generously detailed.

Her personality is spirited and independent without being pushy or stubborn because she knows when to give in. Although sensitive, she doesn't cry every time she is confronted with a problem (though she might cry in private moments). A sense of humor is helpful. Because she is on her own, away from parents (usually deceased) or other protective relationships, she is self-reliant as well as vulnerable. The story may begin with her on the verge of an important decision about her life. She is clearly competent but not entirely certain of her own qualities. She does not take her attractiveness for granted or realize how much the hero is drawn to her.

Common careers for the heroine include executive secretary, nurse, teacher, interior designer, assistant manager, department store buyer, travel agent, or struggling photographer (no menial work). She can also be a doctor, lawyer, or other professional. Her job can be described in some detail and made exciting, but it must not dominate her life. Although she is smart, she is not extremely intellectual or defined by her work. Often she meets the hero through work, but her major concerns center on love, marriage, home, and family. White wine is okay, but she never drinks alone — or uses drugs. She may be troubled, frustrated, threatened, and momentarily thwarted in the course of the story, but she never totally gives in to despair or desperation. She has strengths that the hero recognizes and admires.

Hero

The hero should be about ten years older than the heroine and can be foreign or American. He needn't be handsome in a traditional sense, but he must be strongly masculine. Always tall and well built (not brawny or thick) and usually dark, he looks as terrific in a three-piece suit as he does in sports clothes. His clothes reflect good taste and an affluent life-style. Very successful professionally and financially, he is a man in charge of whatever work he's engaged in (financier, doctor, publisher, architect, business executive, airline pilot, artist, etc.). His wealth is manifested in his sophistication and experience.

His past may be slightly mysterious or shrouded by some painful moment (perhaps with a woman) that he doesn't want to discuss. Whatever the circumstance — his wife's death or divorce are common — it was not his fault. Avoid chronic problems such as alcoholism, drug addiction, or sexual dysfunctions. To others he may appear moody, angry, unpredictable, and explosively passionate, but the heroine eventually comes to realize his warm, tender side. He should be attractive not only as a lover but also as a potential husband and father.

Secondary Characters

Because the major interest is in how the heroine will eventually get together with the hero, the other characters are used to advance the action. There are three major types:

(1) *The Other Woman:* Her vices serve to accent the virtues of the heroine; immediately beneath her glamorous sophistication is a deceptive, selfish, mean-spirited, rapacious predator. She may seem to have the hero in her clutches, but she never wins him in the end.

(2) *The Other Man:* He usually falls into two types: (a) the decent sort who is there when the hero isn't around and (b) the selfish sort who schemes rather than loves. Neither is a match for the hero.

(3) *Other Characters:* Like furniture, they fill in the background and are useful for positioning the hero and heroine. These characters are familiar types such as the hero's snobbish aunt, the heroine's troubled younger siblings, the

loyal friend, or the office gossip. They should be realistic, but they must not be allowed to obscure the emphasis on the lovers. The hero may have children from a previous marriage, but they should rarely be seen or heard. It's usually simpler and better not to include them.

Setting

The setting is usually contemporary. Romantic, exciting places are best: New York City, London, Paris, Rio, the mountains, the ocean — wherever it is exotic and love's possibilities are the greatest. Marriage may take the heroine and hero to a pretty suburb or small town.

Love Scenes

The hero and heroine may make love before marriage. The choice will depend largely on the heroine's sensibilities and circumstances. She should reflect modern attitudes. If the lovers do engage in premarital sex, it should be made clear that neither is promiscuous, especially the heroine. Even if their relationship is consummated before marriage, their lovemaking should not occur until late in the story. There should be at least several passionate scenes, but complications, misunderstandings, and interruptions should keep the couple from actually making love until they have made a firm commitment to each other. Descriptions should appeal to the senses; however, detailed, graphic close-ups are unacceptable. Passion can be presented sensually but not clinically; the lovemaking should be seen through a soft romantic lens. Violence and any out-of-the-way sexual acts should not even be hinted at. No coarse language.

Writing

Avoid extremely complex sentences, very long paragraphs, and lengthy descriptions. Use concise, vivid details to create the heroine's world. Be sure to include full descriptions of the hero's and heroine's physical features and clothes. Allow the reader to experience the romantic mood surrounding the lovers. Show how the heroine feels; do not simply report her feelings. Dialogue should sound like ordinary conversation, and the overall writing should be contemporary English without slang, difficult foreign expressions, strange dialects, racial epithets, or obscenities (*hell, damn,* and a few other mild swears are all right).

Length

55,000 to 65,000 words in ten to twelve chapters.

CONSIDERATIONS FOR CRITICAL THINKING AND WRITING

1. FIRST RESPONSE. Given the expectations implied by the tip sheet, what generalizations can you make about those likely to write formula fiction? Does the tip sheet change the way you think about romantic fiction or other kinds of formula fiction?

2. Who is the intended audience for this type of romance? Try to describe the audience in detail: How does a romance novel provide escape for these readers?

3. Why is it best that the heroine be "attractive and nicely dressed but not glamorous"? Why do you think publishers advise writers to include detailed descriptions of her clothes? Do you find the heroine appealing? Why or why not?

4. Why should the hero be "about ten years older than the heroine"? If he is divorced, why is it significant that "it was not his fault"?

5. Why do you think the hero and heroine are kept apart by complications until the end of the story? Does the outline of the plot sound familiar to you or remind you of any other stories?

6. Why do you think restrictions are placed on the love scenes?

7. Why are "extremely complex sentences, very long paragraphs, and lengthy descriptions" discouraged?

8. To what extent does the tip sheet describe the strategies used in popular television soap operas? How do you account for the appeal of these shows?

9. Explain how the tip sheet confirms traditional views of male and female roles in society. Does it accommodate any broken traditions?

10. Carefully examine the Topaz Historical Romance cover. How do the cover's images and copy reinforce what readers can expect from a romance novel?

11. Included in the marketing material that accompanies the Topaz Historical Romance is this notation: "Topaz is an Official Sponsor of the Mrs. America Pageant." Why do you suppose the publishers support this contest?

12. Write a tip sheet for another kind of popular formula story, such as a western or a detective story, that you have observed in a novel, television show, or film. How is the plot patterned? How are the characters made familiar? How is the setting related to the story? What are the obligatory scenes? How is the overall style consistent? To get started, you might consider an Agatha Christie novel, an episode from a police series on television, or a James Bond film.

13. Try writing a scene for a formula romance, or read the excerpt from Edgar Rice Burroughs's *Tarzan of the Apes* (p. 139) and try an adventure scene.

Karen van der Zee (b. 1947)

Born and raised in Holland, Karen van der Zee lives in the United States, where she has become a successful romance writer, contributing more than fifteen novels to the popular Harlequin series. This excerpt consists of the final two chapters of *A Secret Sorrow.* This is what has happened so far: The central character, Faye, is recuperating from the psychological effects of a serious car accident in which she received a permanent internal injury. After the accident, she quits her job and breaks her engagement to Greg. She moves into her brother Chuck's house and falls in love with Kai, a visiting Texan and good friend of her brother. At the end of Chapter 10,

Kai insists on knowing why she will not marry him and asks, "Who is Doctor Jaworski?"

From A Secret Sorrow   *1981*

Chapter Eleven

Faye could feel the blood drain from her face and for one horrifying moment she thought she was going to faint right in Kai's arms. The room tilted and everything swirled around in a wild madman's dance. She clutched at him for support, fighting for control, trying to focus at some point beyond his shoulder. Slowly, everything steadied.

"I . . . I don't know him," she murmured at last. "I. . . ."

He reached in the breast pocket of his shirt, took out a slip of paper, and held it out for her to see. One glance and Faye recognized it as the note from Doctor Martin with Doctor Jaworski's name scrawled on it, thickly underlined.

"How did you get that?" Her voice was a terrified whisper. She was still holding on, afraid she would fall if she let go.

"I found it on the floor in my bedroom. It must have fallen out of your   5 wallet along with everything else on Saturday morning."

Yes — oh God! Her legs were shaking so badly, she knew it was only his arms that kept her from falling.

"Who is Doctor Jaworski, Faye?" His voice was patiently persistent.

"I . . . he. . . ." Her voice broke. "Let me go, please let me go." She felt as if she were suffocating in his embrace and she struggled against him, feebly, but it was no use.

"He's a psychiatrist, isn't he?" His voice was gentle, very gentle, and she looked up at him in stunned surprise.

He knew, oh God, he knew. She closed her eyes, a helpless sense of   10 inevitability engulfing her.

"You know," she whispered. "How do you know?"

"Simple. Two minutes on the phone to Chicago." He paused. "Doctor Martin — was he one of the doctors who treated you at the hospital?"

"Yes."

"Why did he give you Doctor Jaworski's name? Did he want you to make an appointment with him?"

"Yes." Despondency overtook her. There was no going back now. No   15 escape from the truth. No escape from his arms. Resistance faded and she felt numbed and lifeless. It didn't matter any more. Nothing mattered.

"Did you?" Kai repeated.

"Did I what?"

"See him — Doctor Jaworski."

"No."

"Why did Doctor Martin want you to see a psychiatrist?"   20

"I. . . ." Faye swallowed miserably. "It's . . . it's therapy for grieving . . . mourning." She made a helpless gesture with her hand. "When people lose a . . . a wife, or husband for instance, they go through a more or less predictable pattern of emotions. . . ." She gave him a quick glance, then looked away. "Like denial, anger. . . ."

". . . depression, mourning, acceptance," Kai finished for her, and she looked back at him in surprise.

"Yes."

His mouth twisted in a little smile. "I'm not totally ignorant about subjects other than agronomy." There was a momentary pause as he scrutinized her face. "Why did you need that kind of therapy, Faye?"

And then it was back again, the resistance, the revolt against his probing 25
questions. She stiffened in defense — her whole body growing rigid with instinctive rebellion.

"It's none of your business!"

"Oh, yes, it is. We're talking about our life together. Your life and mine."

She strained against him, hands pushing against his chest. "Let me go! Please let me go!" Panic changed into tears. She couldn't take his nearness any more, the feel of his hard body touching hers, the strength of him.

"No, Faye, no. You're going to tell me. Now. I'm not letting you go until you've told me everything. Everything, you hear?"

"I can't!" she sobbed. "I can't!" 30

"Faye," he said slowly, "you'll *have* to. You told me you love me, but you don't want to marry me. You have given me no satisfactory reasons, and I'll be damned if I'm going to accept your lack of explanations."

"You have no right to demand an explanation!"

"Oh, yes, I have. You're part of me, Faye. Part of my life."

"You talk as if you own me!" She was trembling, struggling to get away from him. She couldn't stand there, so close to him with all the pent-up despair inside her, the anger, the fear of what she knew not how to tell him.

His hands were warm and strong on her back, holding her steady. Then, 35
with one hand, he tilted back her head and made her look at him. "You gave me your love — I own that," he said softly. "True loving involves commitment, vulnerability, trust. Don't you trust me, Faye?"

New tears ran silently down her cheeks. "If I told you," she blurted out, "you wouldn't . . . you wouldn't. . . ."

"I wouldn't *what*?"

"You wouldn't want me any more!" The words were wrenched from her in blind, agonizing grief. "You wouldn't *want* me any more!"

He shook his head incredulously. "What makes you think you can make that decision for me? Do you have so little trust in my love for you?"

Faye didn't answer, couldn't answer. Through a mist of tears he was noth- 40
ing but a blur in front of her eyes.

"What is so terrible that you can't tell me?"

She shrank inwardly, as if shriveling away in pain. "Let me go," she whispered. "Please let me go and I'll tell you."

After a moment's hesitation Kai released her. Faye backed away from him, feeling like a terrified animal. She stood with her back against the wall, glad for the support, her whole body shaking. She took a deep breath and wiped her face dry with her hand.

"I'm afraid . . . afraid to marry you."

"Afraid?" He looked perplexed. "Afraid of what? Of me? Of marriage?" 45

Faye closed her eyes, taking another deep breath. "I can't be what you want me to be. We can't have the kind of life you want." She looked at him, standing only a few feet away, anguish tearing through her. "I'm so afraid . . . you'll be disappointed," she whispered.

"Oh God, Faye," he groaned, "I love you." He came toward her and panic surged through her as he held her against the wall, his hands reaching up to catch her face between them.

"Don't," she whispered. "Please, don't touch me." But it was no use. His mouth came down on hers and he kissed her with a hard, desperate passion.

"I love you," he said huskily. "I love you."

Faye wrenched her face free from his hands. "Don't touch me! Please don't touch me!" She was sobbing now, her words barely audible. Her knees gave way and her back slid down along the wall until she crumpled onto the floor, face in her hands.

Kai took a step backward and pulled her up. "Stand up, Faye. For God's sake stand up!" He held her against the wall and she looked at him, seeing every line in his dark face, the intense blue of his eyes, and knew that this was the moment, that there was no more waiting.

And Kai knew it too. His eyes held hers locked in unrelenting demand. "Why should I be disappointed, Faye? *Why?*"

Her heart was thundering in her ears and it seemed as if she couldn't breathe, as if she were going to drown.

"Because . . . because I can't give you children! Because I can't get pregnant! I can't have babies! That's why!" Her voice was an agonized cry, torn from the depths of her misery. She yanked down his arms that held her locked against the wall and moved away from him. And then she saw his face.

It was ashen, gray under his tan. He stared at her as if he had never seen her before.

"Oh my God, Faye. . . ." His voice was low and hoarse. "Why didn't you tell me, why. . . ."

Faye heard no more. She ran out the door, snatching her bag off the chair as she went by. The only thought in her mind was to get away—away from Kai and what was in his eyes.

She reached for Kai's spare set of car keys in her bag, doing it instinctively, knowing she couldn't walk home alone in the dark. How she managed to get the keys in the door lock and in the ignition she never knew. Somehow, she made it home.

The phone rang as Faye opened the front door and she heard Chuck answer it in the kitchen.

"She's just got in," he said into the mouthpiece, smiling at Faye as she came into view. He listened for a moment, nodded. "Okay, fine with me."

Faye turned and walked up the stairs, taking deep breaths to calm her shattered nerves. Kai hadn't wasted any time checking up on her. She didn't care what he was telling Chuck, but she wasn't going to stand there listening to a one-sided conversation. But only a second later Chuck was behind her on the stairs.

"Kai wanted to know whether you'd arrived safely."

"I did, thank you," she said levelly, her voice surprisingly steady.

"I take it you ran out and took off with his car?"

"Did he say that?"

"No. He was *worried* about you. He wanted to make sure you went home."
He sounded impatient, and she couldn't blame him. She was making life
unbearable for everyone around her. Everybody worried about her. Everybody
loved her. Everything should be right. Only it wasn't.

"Well, I'm home now, and I'm going to bed. Good night."

"Good night, Faye."

Faye lay in bed without any hope of sleep. Mechanically she started to sort
through her thoughts and emotions, preparing mentally for the next confrontation. There would be one, she didn't doubt it for a moment. But she
needed time—time to clear her head, time to look at everything in a reasonable, unemotional way.

It was a temptation to run—get in the car and keep driving, but it would   70
be a stupid thing to do. There was no place for her to go, and Kai would find
her, no matter what. If there was one thing she knew about Kai it was his stubbornness and his persistence. She had to stick it out, right here, get it over
with, deal with it. Only she didn't know how.

She lay listening to the stillness, just a few sounds here and there—the
house creaking, a car somewhere in the distance, a dog barking. She had to
think, but her mind refused to cooperate. She *had* to think, decide what to say
to Kai the next time she saw him, but she couldn't think, she *couldn't think.*

And then, as she heard the door open in the silence, the quiet footsteps
coming up the stairs, she knew it was too late, that time had run out.

Without even knocking he came into her room and walked over to the
bed. She could feel the mattress sag as his weight came down on it. Her heart
was pounding like a sledgehammer, and then his arms came around her and
he drew her against him.

"Faye," he said quietly, "please marry me."

"No," she said thickly. "No." She could feel him stiffen against her and she   75
released herself from his arms and slid off the bed. She switched on the light
and stood near the window, far from the bed, far from Kai. "I don't expect you
to play the gentleman, I don't expect you to throw out a life of dreams just for
the sake of chivalry. You don't have to marry me, Kai." She barely recognized
her own voice. It was like the cool calm sound of a stranger, unemotional, cold.
"You don't have to marry me," she repeated levelly, giving him a steady look.

Her words were underlined by the silence that followed, a silence loaded
with a strange, vibrating energy, a force in itself, filling the room.

Kai rose to his feet, slowly, and the face that looked at her was like that of a
stranger, a dangerous, angry stranger. Never before had she seen him so angry,
so full of hot, fuming fury.

"Shut up," he said in a low, tight voice. "Shut up and stop playing the
martyr!"

The sound of his voice and the words he said shocked Faye into silence.
She stared at him open-mouthed, and then a slow, burning anger arose inside her.

"How dare you! How. . . ."   80

He strode toward her and took her upper arms and shook her. "Shut up
and listen to me! What the hell are you thinking? What the hell did you expect
me to do when you told me? You throw me a bomb and then walk out on me!
What did you expect my reaction to be? Was I supposed to stay cool and calm
and tell you it didn't matter? Would you have married me then? Well, let me

tell you something! It matters! It matters to me! I am not apologizing for my reaction!" He paused, breathing hard. "You know I always wanted children, but what in God's name makes you think you're the only one who has the right to feel bad about it? I have that right too, you hear! I love you, dammit, and I want to marry you, and if we can't have children I have all the right in the world to feel bad about it!"

He stopped talking. He was still breathing hard and he looked at her with stormy blue eyes. Faye felt paralyzed by his tirade and she stared at him, incapable of speech. She couldn't move, she couldn't think.

"Why do you think I want you for my wife?" he continued on a calmer note. "Because you're some kind of baby factory? What kind of man do you think I am? I love *you,* not your procreating ability. So we have a problem. Well, we'll learn to deal with it, one way or another."

There was another silence, and still Faye didn't speak, and she realized she was crying, soundlessly, tears slowly dripping down her cheeks. She was staring at his chest, blindly, not knowing what to think, not thinking at all.

He lifted her chin, gently. "Look at me, Faye."   85

She did, but his face was only a blur.

"Faye, we're in this together—you and I. Don't you see that? It's not just *your* problem, it's *ours.*"

"No," she whispered. "No!" She shook her head wildly. "You have a choice, don't you see that? You don't have to marry me. You could marry someone else and have children of your own."

"Oh, God, Faye," he groaned, "you're wrong. Don't you know? Don't you see? I *don't* have a choice. I never did have a choice, or a chance. Not since I met you and fell in love with you. I don't *want* anybody else, don't you understand that? I want you, only you."

She wanted to believe it, give in to him. Never before had she wanted 90 anything more desperately than she wanted to give in to him now. But she couldn't, she couldn't. . . . She closed her eyes, briefly, fighting for reason, common sense.

"Kai, I . . . I can't live all my life with your regret and your disappointment. Every time we see some pregnant woman, every time we're with somebody else's children I'll feel I've failed you! I. . . ." Her voice broke and new sobs came unchecked.

He held her very tightly until she calmed down and then he put her from him a little and gave her a dark, compelling look.

"It's not *my* regret, or *my* disappointment," he said with quiet emphasis. "It's *ours.* We're not talking about *you* or *me.* We're talking about *us.* I love you, and you love me, and that's the starting point, that comes first. From then on we're in it together."

Faye moved out of his arms, away from him, but her legs wouldn't carry her and she sank into a chair. She covered her face with her hands and tried desperately to stop the crying, to stop the tears from coming and coming as if they would never end.

"How . . . how can I ever believe it?"   95

"Because I'm asking you to," he said quietly. He knelt in front of her, took her hands away from her wet face. "Look at me, Faye. No other woman can give me what you can—yourself, your love, your warmth, your sense of humor. All the facets of your personality that make up the final you. I've known other women, Faye, but none of them have ever stirred in me any feelings that come close to what I feel for you. You're an original, remember? There's no replacement for an original. There are only copies, and I don't want a copy. To me you're special, and you'll have to believe it, take it on faith. That's what love is all about."

He was holding her hands in his, strong brown hands, and she was looking down on them, fighting with herself, fighting with everything inside her to believe what he was saying, to accept it, to give in to it.

Leaning forward, Kai kissed her gently on the mouth and smiled. "It's all been too much too soon for you, hasn't it? You never really got a chance to get over the shock, and when I fell in love with you it only made things worse." He smiled ruefully and Faye was surprised at his insight.

"Yes," she said. "It all happened too fast."

"Bad timing. If only we could have met later, after you'd sorted it all out in 100 your mind, then it would never have been such a crisis."

She looked at him doubtfully. "It wouldn't have changed the facts."

"No, but it might have changed your perspective."

Would it have? she wondered. Could she ever feel confident and secure in her worth as a woman? Or was she at this moment too emotionally bruised to accept that possibility?

"I don't understand," he said, "why I never guessed what was wrong. Now that I know, it all seems so obvious." He looked at her thoughtfully. "Faye," he said gently, "I want you to tell me exactly what happened to you, what Doctor Martin told you."

She stared at him, surprised a little. A thought stirred in the back of her 105 mind. Greg. He had never even asked. The why and the what had not interested him. But Kai, he wanted to know. She swallowed nervously and began the story, slowly, word for word, everything Doctor Martin had said. And he listened, quietly, not interrupting. "So you see," she said at last, "we don't have to hope for any miracles either."

"We'll make our own miracles," he said, and smiled. "Come here," he said then, "kiss me."

She did, shyly almost, until he took over and lifted her up and carried her to the bed. He looked down on her, eyes thoughtful. "I won't pretend I understand your feelings about this, the feelings you have about yourself as a woman, but I'll try." He paused for a moment. "Faye," he said then, speaking with slow emphasis, "don't *ever,* not for a single moment, think that you're not good enough for me. You're the best there is, Faye, the very best."

His mouth sought hers and he kissed her with gentle reassurance at first, then with rising ardor. His hands moved over her body, touching her with sensual, intimate caresses.

"You're my woman, Faye, you're mine. . . ."

Her senses reeled. She could never love anyone like she loved him. No one 110 had ever evoked in her this depth of emotion. This was real, this was forever. Kai wanted her as much as ever. No chivalry, this, no game of pretense, she was very sure of that. And when he lifted his face and looked at her, it was all there in his eyes and the wonder of it filled her with joy.

"Do you believe me now?" he whispered huskily. "Do you believe I love you and want you and need you?"

She nodded wordlessly, incapable of uttering a sound.

"And do you love me?"

Again she nodded, her eyes in his.

"Okay, then." In one smooth flowing movement he got to his feet. He crossed to the closet, opened it, and took out her suitcases. He put one on the end of the bed and began to pile her clothes in it, taking armfuls out of the closet.

Faye watched incredulously. "What are you doing?" she managed at last.

Kai kept on moving around, opening drawers, taking out her things, filling the suitcase until it could hold no more. "Get dressed. We're going home."

"Home . . . ?"

For a moment he stopped and he looked at her with a deep blue glitter in his eyes. "Yes, *home* — where you belong. With me, in my house, in my bed, in my arms."

"Oh, Kai," she said tremulously, smiling suddenly. "It's midnight!"

His eyes were very dark. "I've waited long enough, I'm not waiting any more. You're coming with me, now. And I'm not letting you out of my sight until we're safely married. I don't want you getting any crazy ideas about running off to save me from myself, or some such notion."

Her throat was dry. "Please, let's not rush into it! Let's think about it first!"

Calmly he zipped up the full suitcase, swung it off the bed, and put it near the door. "I'm not rushing into anything," he said levelly. "I've wanted to marry you for quite a while, remember?"

He crossed to the bed, sat down next to her, and put his arm around her. "Faye, I wish you wouldn't worry so. I'm not going to change my mind. And I haven't shelved my hopes for a family, either." There was a brief silence. "When we're ready to have kids, we'll have them. We'll adopt them. There are orphanages the world over, full of children in need of love and care. We'll do whatever it takes. We'll get them, one way or another."

Faye searched his face, faint hope flickering deep inside her.

"Would you want that?"

"Why not?"

"I don't know, really. I thought you . . . it isn't the same."

"No," he said levelly, "it isn't. Adoption is a different process from pregnancy and birth, but the kids will be ours just the same and we'll love them no less."

"Yes," she said, "yes." And suddenly it seemed as if a light had been turned on inside her, as if suddenly she could see again, a future with Kai, a future with children.

A bronzed hand lifted her face. "Look, Faye, I'll always be sorry. I'll always be sorry not to see you pregnant, not to see you with a big stomach knowing you're carrying my child, but I'll live."

Faye lowered her eyes and tears threatened again. With both his hands he cupped her face.

"Look at me, Faye. I want you to stop thinking of yourself as a machine with a defect. You're not a damaged piece of merchandise, you hear? You're a living, breathing human being, a warm-blooded female, and I love you."

Through a haze of tears she looked at him, giving a weak smile. "I love you too." She put her arms around him and he heaved an unsteady breath.

"Faye," he said huskily, "you're my first and only choice."

Chapter Twelve

Kai and Faye had their family, two girls and a boy. They came to them one at a time, from faraway places, with small faces and large dark eyes full of fear. In their faces Faye could read the tragedies of war and death and poverty. They were hungry for love, hungry for nourishment and care. At night they woke in terror, screaming, their memories alive in sleep.

Time passed, and in the low white ranch house under the blue skies of Texas they flourished like the crops in the fields. They grew tall and straight and healthy and the fear in the dark eyes faded. Like their father they wore jeans and boots and large-brimmed hats, and they rode horses and played the guitar. They learned to speak English with a Southern twang.

One day Kai and Faye watched them as they played in the garden, and joy and gratitude overflowed in Faye's heart. Life was good and filled with love.

"They're all ours," she said. Even now after all these years she sometimes still couldn't believe it was really so.

Kai smiled at her. His eyes, still very blue, crinkled at the corners. "Yes, and 140 you're all mine."

"They don't even look like us," she said. "Not even a tiny little bit." No blondes, no redheads.

Taking her in his arms, Kai kissed her. "They're true originals, like their mother. I wouldn't want it any other way."

There was love in his embrace and love in his words and in her heart there was no room now for doubt, no room for sorrow.

Sometimes in the night he would reach for her and she would wake to his touch, his hands on her breast, her stomach, searching. In the warm darkness of their bed she would come to him and they would hold each other close and she knew he had been dreaming.

She knew the dream. She was walking away from him, calling out that she 145 couldn't marry him, the words echoing all around. *"I can't marry you! I can't marry you!"* And Kai was standing there watching her go, terrified, unable to move, his legs frozen to the ground. He wanted to follow her, keep her from leaving, but his legs wouldn't move.

Kai had told her of the dream, of the panic that clutched at him as he watched her walk out of his life. And always he would wake and search for her in the big bed, and she knew of only one way to reassure him. And in the warm afterglow of lovemaking, their bodies close together, she knew that to him she was everything, to him she was the only woman, beautiful, complete, whole.

GAIL GODWIN (B. 1937)

Born in Birmingham, Alabama, Gail Godwin was educated at the University of North Carolina and the University of Iowa, where she earned a Ph.D. in English in 1971. She is a full-time writer who has won grants from the National Endowment for the Arts, the Guggenheim Foundation, and the American Institute for the Arts and Letters. Among her novels are *Glass People* (1971), *A Mother and Two Daughters* (1981), *The Finishing School* (1985), and *Evensong* (1999). Her short stories have been collected in several volumes including *Dream Children* (1976) and *Mr. Bedford and the Muses* (1983).

A Sorrowful Woman   1971

Once upon a time there was a wife and mother one too many times

One winter evening she looked at them: the husband durable, receptive, gentle; the child a tender golden three. The sight of them made her so sad and sick she did not want to see them ever again.

She told the husband these thoughts. He was attuned to her; he understood such things. He said he understood. What would she like him to do? "If you could put the boy to bed and read him the story about the monkey who ate too many bananas, I would be grateful." "Of course," he said. "Why, that's a pleasure." And he sent her off to bed.

The next night it happened again. Putting the warm dishes away in the cupboard, she turned and saw the child's gray eyes approving her movements. In the next room was the man, his chin sunk in the open collar of his favorite wool shirt. He was dozing after her good supper. The shirt was the gray of the child's trusting gaze. She began yelping without tears, retching in between. The man woke in alarm and carried her in his arms to bed. The boy followed them up the stairs, saying, "It's all right, Mommy," but this made her scream. "Mommy is sick," the father said, "go wait for me in your room."

The husband undressed her, abandoning her only long enough to root beneath the eiderdown for her flannel gown. She stood naked except for her bra, which hung by one strap down the side of her body; she had not the impetus to shrug it off. She looked down at the right nipple, shriveled with chill, and thought, How absurd, a vertical bra. "If only there were instant sleep," she said, hiccupping, and the husband bundled her into the gown and went out and came back with a sleeping draught guaranteed swift. She was to drink a little glass of cognac followed by a big glass of dark liquid and afterwards there was just time to say Thank you and could you get him a clean pair of pajamas out of the laundry, it came back today.

The next day was Sunday and the husband brought her breakfast in bed ⁵ and let her sleep until it grew dark again. He took the child for a walk, and when they returned, red-cheeked and boisterous, the father made supper. She heard them laughing in the kitchen. He brought her up a tray of buttered toast, celery sticks, and black bean soup. "I am the luckiest woman," she said, crying real tears. "Nonsense," he said. "You need a rest from us," and went to prepare the sleeping draught, find the child's pajamas, select the story for the night.

She got up on Monday and moved about the house till noon. The boy, delighted to have her back, pretended he was a vicious tiger and followed her from room to room, growling and scratching. Whenever she came close, he would growl and scratch at her. One of his sharp little claws ripped her flesh, just above the wrist, and together they paused to watch a thin red line materialize on the inside of her pale arm and spill over in little beads. "Go away," she said. She got herself upstairs and locked the door. She called the husband's office and said, "I've locked myself away from him. I'm afraid." The husband told her in his richest voice to lie down, take it easy, and he was already on the phone to call one of the baby-sitters they often employed. Shortly after, she heard the girl let herself in, heard the girl coaxing the frightened child to come and play.

After supper several nights later, she hit the child. She had known she was going to do it when the father would see. "I'm sorry," she said, collapsing on the floor. The weeping child had run to hide. "What has happened to me, I'm not myself anymore." The man picked her tenderly from the floor and looked at her with much concern. "Would it help if we got, you know, a girl in? We could fix the room downstairs. I want you to feel freer," he said, understanding these things. "We have the money for a girl. I want you to think about it."

And now the sleeping draught was a nightly thing, she did not have to ask. He went down to the kitchen to mix it, he set it nightly beside her bed. The little glass and the big one, amber and deep rich brown, the flannel gown and the eiderdown.

The man put out the word and found the perfect girl. She was young, dynamic, and not pretty. "Don't bother with the room, I'll fix it up myself." Laughing, she employed her thousand energies. She painted the room white, fed the child lunch, read edifying books, raced the boy to the mailbox, hung her own watercolors on the fresh-painted walls, made spinach soufflé, cleaned a spot from the mother's coat, made them all laugh, danced in stocking feet to music in the white room after reading the child to sleep. She knitted dresses for herself and played chess with the husband. She washed and set the mother's soft ash-blonde hair and gave her neck rubs, offered to.

The woman now spent her winter afternoons in the big bedroom. She made a fire in the hearth and put on slacks and an old sweater she had loved at school, and sat in the big chair and stared out the window at snow-ridden branches, or went away into long novels about other people moving through other winters. 10

The girl brought the child in twice a day, once in the later afternoon when he would tell of his day, all of it tumbling out quickly because there was not much time, and before he went to bed. Often now, the man took his wife to dinner. He made a courtship ceremony of it, inviting her beforehand so she could get used to the idea. They dressed and were beautiful together again and went out into the frosty night. Over candlelight he would say, "I think you are better, you know." "Perhaps I am," she would murmur. "You look . . . like a cloistered queen," he said once, his voice breaking curiously.

One afternoon the girl brought the child into the bedroom. "We've been out playing in the park. He found something he wants to give you, a surprise." The little boy approached her, smiling mysteriously. He placed his cupped hands in hers and left a live dry thing that spat brown juice in her palm and leapt away. She screamed and wrung her hands to be rid of the brown juice. "Oh, it was only a grasshopper," said the girl. Nimbly she crept to the edge of the curtain, did a quick knee bend, and reclaimed the creature, led the boy competently from the room.

"The girl upsets me," said the woman to her husband. He sat frowning on the side of the bed he had not entered for so long. "I'm sorry, but there it is." The husband stroked his creased brow and said he was sorry too. He really did not know what they would do without that treasure of a girl. "Why don't you stay here with me in bed," the woman said.

Next morning she fired the girl who cried and said, "I loved the little boy, what will become of him now?" But the mother turned away her face and the girl took down the watercolors from the walls, sheathed the records she had danced to, and went away.

"I don't know what we'll do. It's all my fault, I know. I'm such a burden, I know that." 15

"Let me think. I'll think of something." (Still understanding these things.)

"I know you will. You always do," she said.

With great care he rearranged his life. He got up hours early, did the shopping, cooked the breakfast, took the boy to nursery school. "We will manage," he said, "until you're better, however long that is." He did his work, collected the boy from the school, came home and made the supper, washed the dishes, got the child to bed. He managed everything. One evening, just as she was on the verge of swallowing her draught, there was a timid knock on her door. The little boy came in wearing his pajamas. "Daddy has fallen asleep on my bed and I can't get in. There's not room."

Very sedately she left her bed and went to the child's room. Things were much changed. Books were rearranged, toys. He'd done some new drawings. She came as a visitor to her son's room, wakened the father and helped him to bed. "Ah, he shouldn't have bothered you," said the man, leaning on his wife. "I've told him not to." He dropped into his own bed and fell asleep with a moan. Meticulously she undressed him. She folded and hung his clothes. She covered his body with the bedclothes. She flicked off the light that shone in his face.

The next day she moved her things into the girl's white room. She put her 20 hairbrush on the dresser; she put a note pad and pen beside the bed. She stocked the little room with cigarettes, books, bread, and cheese. She didn't need much.

At first the husband was dismayed. But he was receptive to her needs. He understood these things. "Perhaps the best thing is for you to follow it through," he said. "I want to be big enough to contain whatever you must do."

All day long she stayed in the white room. She was a young queen, a virgin in a tower; she was the previous inhabitant, the girl with all the energies. She tried these personalities on like costumes, then discarded them. The room had a new view of streets she'd never seen that way before. The sun hit the room in late afternoon and she took to brushing her hair in the sun. One day she decided to write a poem. "Perhaps a sonnet." She took up her pen and pad and began working from words that had lately lain in her mind. She had choices for the sonnet, ABAB or ABBA for a start. She pondered these possibilities until she tottered into a larger choice: she did not have to write a sonnet. Her poem could be six, eight, ten, thirteen lines, it could be any number of lines, and it did not even have to rhyme.

She put down the pen on top of the pad.

In the evenings, very briefly, she saw the two of them. They knocked on her door, a big knock and a little, and she would call Come in, and the husband would smile though he looked a bit tired, yet somehow this tiredness suited him. He would put her sleeping draught on the bedside table and say, "The boy and I have done all right today," and the child would kiss her. One night she tasted for the first time the power of his baby spit.

"I don't think I can see him anymore," she whispered sadly to the man. 25 And the husband turned away, but recovered admirably and said, "Of course, I see."

So the husband came alone. "I have explained to the boy," he said. "And we are doing fine. We are managing." He squeezed his wife's pale arm and put the two glasses on her table. After he had gone, she sat looking at the arm.

"I'm afraid it's come to that," she said. "Just push the notes under the door; I'll read them. And don't forget to leave the draught outside."

The man sat for a long time with his head in his hands. Then he rose and went away from her. She heard him in the kitchen where he mixed the draught in batches now to last a week at a time, storing it in a corner of the cupboard. She heard him come back, leave the big glass and the little one outside on the floor.

Outside her window the snow was melting from the branches, there were more people on the streets. She brushed her hair a lot and seldom read anymore. She sat in her window and brushed her hair for hours, and saw a boy fall off his new bicycle again and again, a dog chasing a squirrel, an old woman peek slyly over her shoulder and then extract a parcel from a garbage can.

In the evening she read the notes they slipped under her door. The child 30 could not write, so he drew and sometimes painted his. The notes were painstaking at first; the man and boy offering the final strength of their day to her. But sometimes, when they seemed to have had a bad day, there were only hurried scrawls.

One night, when the husband's note had been extremely short, loving but short, and there had been nothing from the boy, she stole out of her room as she often did to get more supplies, but crept upstairs instead and stood outside their doors, listening to the regular breathing of the man and boy asleep. She hurried back to her room and drank the draught.

She woke earlier now. It was spring, there were birds. She listened for sounds of the man and the boy eating breakfast; she listened for the roar of the motor when they drove away. One beautiful noon, she went out to look at her kitchen in the daylight. Things were changed. He had bought some new dish towels. Had the old ones worn out? The canisters seemed closer to the sink. She got out flour, baking powder, salt, milk (he bought a different brand of butter), and baked a loaf of bread and left it cooling on the table.

The force of the two joyful notes slipped under her door that evening pressed her into the corner of the little room; she had hardly space to breathe. As soon as possible, she drank the draught.

Now the days were too short. She was always busy. She woke with the first bird. Worked till the sun set. No time for hair brushing. Her fingers raced the hours.

Finally, in the nick of time, it was finished one late afternoon. Her 35 veins pumped and her forehead sparkled. She went to the cupboard, took what was hers, closed herself into the little white room and brushed her hair for a while.

The man and boy came home and found: five loaves of warm bread, a roast stuffed turkey, a glazed ham, three pies of different fillings, eight molds of the boy's favorite custard, two weeks' supply of fresh-laundered sheets and shirts and towels, two hand-knitted sweaters (both of the same gray color), a sheath of marvelous watercolor beasts accompanied by mad and fanciful stories nobody could ever make up again, and a tablet full of love sonnets addressed to the man. The house smelled redolently of renewal and spring. The man ran to the little room, could not contain himself to knock, flung back the door.

"Look, Mommy is sleeping," said the boy. "She's tired from doing all our things again." He dawdled in a stream of the last sun for that day and watched his father roll tenderly back her eyelids, lay his ear softly to her breast, test the delicate bones of her wrist. The father put down his face into her fresh-washed hair.

"Can we eat the turkey for supper?" the boy asked.

CONSIDERATIONS FOR CRITICAL THINKING AND WRITING

1. FIRST RESPONSE. How did you respond to the excerpt from *A Secret Sorrow* and to "A Sorrowful Woman"? Do you like one more than the other? Is one of the women — Faye or Godwin's unnamed wife — more likable than the other? Why do you think you respond the way you do to the characters and the stories — is your response intellectual, emotional, a result of authorial intent, a mix of these, or something else entirely?

2. Describe what you found appealing in each story. Can you point to passages in both that strike you as especially well written or interesting? Was there anything in either story that did not appeal to you? Why?

3. How do the two women's attitudes toward family life differ? How does that difference constitute the problem in each story?

4. How is the woman's problem in "A Sorrowful Woman" made more complex than Faye's in *A Secret Sorrow*? What is the purpose of the husband and child in Godwin's story?

5. How would you describe the theme — the central point and meaning — in each story?

6. To what extent might "A Sorrowful Woman" be regarded as an unromantic sequel to *A Secret Sorrow*?

7. Can both stories be read a second or third time and still be interesting? Why or why not?

8. Explain how you think a romance formula writer would end "A Sorrowful Woman," or write the ending yourself.

9. Contrast what marriage means in the two stories.

10. Discuss your feelings about the woman in "A Sorrowful Woman." How does she remain a sympathetic character in spite of her refusal to be a traditional wife and mother? (It may take more than one reading of the story to see that Godwin does sympathize with her.)

11. The happy ending of *A Secret Sorrow* may seem like that of a fairy tale, but it is realistically presented because there is nothing strange, mysterious, or fabulous that strains our ability to believe it could happen. In contrast, "A Sorrowful Woman" begins with an epigraph ("*Once upon a time . . .*") that causes us to expect a fairy-tale ending, but that story is clearly a fairy tale gone wrong. Consider the two stories as fairy tales. How might "A Sorrowful Woman" be read as a dark version of "Sleeping Beauty"?

12. CRITICAL STRATEGIES. Read the section on feminist criticism (71–72) in Chapter 3, "Applying a Critical Strategy." Based on that discussion, what do you think a feminist critic might have to say about these two stories?

The following questions can help you consider important elements of fiction that reveal your responses to a story's effects and meanings. The questions are general, so they will not always be relevant to a particular story. Many of them, however, should prove useful for thinking, talking, and writing about a work of fiction. Maya used these questions, for example, to help her think about the similarities and differences between A Secret Sorrow *and* "A Sorrowful Woman." *If you are uncertain about the meaning of a term used in a question, consult the Glossary of Literary Terms beginning on page 1381 of this book. You should also find useful the discussion of various critical approaches to literature in Chapter 3, "Applying a Critical Strategy."*

QUESTIONS FOR WRITING ABOUT FICTION

Plot

1. Does the plot conform to a formula? Is it like those of any other stories you have read? Did you find it predictable?

2. What is the source and nature of the conflict for the protagonist? Was your major interest in the story based on what happens next or on some other concern? What does the title reveal now that you've finished the story?

3. Is the story told chronologically? If not, in what order are its events told, and what is the effect of that order on your response to the action?

4. What does the exposition reveal? Are flashbacks used? Did you see any foreshadowings? Where is the climax?

5. Is the conflict resolved at the end? Would you characterize the ending as happy, unhappy, or somewhere in between?

6. Is the plot unified? Is each incident somehow related to some other element in the story?

Character

7. Do you identify with the protagonist? Who (or what) is the antagonist?

8. Did your response to any characters change as you read? What do you think caused the change? Do any characters change and develop in the course of the story? How?

9. Are round, flat, or stock characters used? Is their behavior motivated and plausible?

10. How does the author reveal characters? Are they directly described or indirectly presented? Are the characters' names used to convey something about them?

---

11. What is the purpose of the minor characters? Are they individualized, or do they primarily represent ideas or attitudes?

Setting

12. Is the setting important in shaping your response? If it were changed, would your response to the story's action and meaning be significantly different?

13. Is the setting used symbolically? Are the time, place, and atmosphere related to the theme?

14. Is the setting used as an antagonist?

Point of View

15. Who tells the story? Is it a first-person or third-person narrator? Is it a major or minor character or one who does not participate in the action at all? How much does the narrator know? Does the point of view change at all in the course of the story?

16. Is the narrator reliable and objective? Does the narrator appear too innocent, emotional, or self-deluded to be trusted?

17. Does the author directly comment on the action?

18. If a different point of view had been used, how would your response to the story change? Would anything be lost?

Symbolism

19. Did you notice any symbols in the story? Are they actions, characters, settings, objects, or words?

20. How do the symbols contribute to your understanding of the story?

Style, Tone, and Irony

21. Do you think the style is consistent and appropriate throughout the story? Do all the characters use the same kind of language, or did you hear different voices?

22. Would you describe the level of diction as formal or informal? Are the sentences short and simple, long and complex, or some combination?

23. How does the author's use of language contribute to the tone of the story? Did it seem, for example, intense, relaxed, sentimental, nostalgic, humorous, angry, sad, or remote?

24. Do you think the story is worth reading more than once? Does the author's use of language bear close scrutiny so that you feel and experience more with each reading?

Theme

25. Did you find a theme? If so, what is it?

26. Is the theme stated directly, or is it developed implicitly through the plot, characters, or some other element?

27. Is the theme a confirmation of your values, or does it challenge them?

Critical Strategies

28. Is there a particular critical approach that seems especially appropriate for this story? (See Chapter 3, "Applying a Critical Strategy," p. 56.)

29. How might biographical information about the author help you to determine the central concerns of the story?

30. How might historical information about the story provide a useful context for interpretation?

31. What kinds of evidence from the story are you focusing on to support your interpretation? Have you left out any important elements that might undercut or qualify your interpretation?

32. To what extent do your own experiences, values, beliefs, and assumptions inform your interpretation?

33. Given that there are a variety of ways to interpret the story, which one seems the most useful to you?

A Sample First Response

After Maya has carefully read the romance formula tip sheet, the excerpt from *A Secret Sorrow,* and "A Sorrowful Woman," she's ready to start writing. Her instructor has asked her to write an informal response to the following questions: *How did you respond to each story? Do you like one more than the other? Is one of the women more likeable than the other? Why do you think you respond the way you do? Is your response to the characters and the stories primarily intellectual, emotional, a result of authorial intention, a mix of these, or something else entirely?*

Reading the excerpt from the Harlequin, I was irritated by the seeming helplessness of Faye; in the first chapter she is constantly on the edge of hysteria and can hardly stand up. I could do without all of the fainting, gasping, and general theatrics. I've read Harlequins before, and I usually skim through that stuff to get to the good romantic parts and the happy ending. What I like about these kinds of romance novels is the happy ending. Even though the ending is

kind of clichéd with the white fence and blue skies, there is
still something satisfying about having everything work out
okay.

The Godwin story, of course, does not have a happy ending.
It is a much more powerful story, and it is one that I could
read several times, unlike the Harlequin. The Godwin woman
bothers me too, because I can't really see what she has to complain about. Her husband is perfectly accommodating and understanding. It seems that if she were unhappy with her life as a
wife and mother and wanted to work or do something else, he
wouldn't have a problem with it. She seems to throw away her
life and hurt her family for nothing.

I enjoyed reading the Godwin story more just because it is
well written and more complex, but I liked the ending of the
Harlequin more. I think on an emotional level I liked the Harlequin better, and on an intellectual level I liked the Godwin
story more. It is more satisfying emotionally to see a romance
develop and end happily than it is to see the deterioration of
a marriage and the suicide of a depressed woman. I don't really
find either character particularly likable; toward the end when
the Godwin woman comes out of her room and starts doing things
again I begin to feel sympathy for her--I can understand her
having a period of depression, but I want her to pull herself
out of it, and when she doesn't, I am disappointed. Even though
Faye is annoying in the beginning, because everything ends happily I am almost willing to forgive and forget my previous
annoyance with her. If the Godwin woman hadn't killed herself
and had returned to her family life, I would have liked her
better, but because she doesn't I leave the story feeling discouraged.

A Sample of Brainstorming

By listing these parallel but alternate treatments of marriage in each
story, Maya begins to assemble an inventory of relevant topics related to
the assignment. What becomes clear to her is that her approach will
emphasize the differences in each story's portrayal of marriage.

<u>Marriage</u>

<u>Godwin</u>	<u>Harlequin</u>
marriage as <u>end</u> of life — confining, weighty	marriage as end, goal — dreamlike, idyllic
husband — durable, receptive, understanding	husband — understanding, <u>manly</u>
p. 189 sight of family makes her sad and sick	p. 188 watching kids she feels that life is good + filled with love
house in winter — <u>girl</u> paints room white	white house in Texas under blue skies
the power of his baby spit and looking at arm p. 191 & 192	in husband's embrace no room for doubt or sorrow p. 188
family makes her sad	family makes her happy
weight pressing on her	weight lifted off her
impersonal — the husband, the child	Kai, Faye, our children
emphasis on roles	
dead in the end	beautiful, whole, complete in the end
crisis due to fear of <u>always</u> having husband and kid	crisis due to fear of <u>never</u> having husband and kids
feels incomplete and depressed as only wife and mother	feels incomplete and depressed not being wife and mother

A Sample Revision: First and Second Drafts

Maya's first draft of the paper pursues and develops many of the topics she noted while brainstorming. She explores the differences between each story's treatment of marriage in detail by examining each protagonist's role as wife and mother, her husband's response, the role played by her children, and the ending of each story. The second draft's annotations indicate that Maya has been able to distance herself enough from her first draft to critique its weak moments. In the annotations she recognizes, for example, that she needs a clearer thesis, some stronger transitions between paragraphs, some crisper and more detailed sentences to clarify points, and a more convincing conclusion as well as a more pointed title. (Spelling and grammatical errors have been silently corrected so as not to distract from her developing argument.)

Separate Sorrows

In both the excerpt from A Secret Sorrow and "A Sorrowful Woman," by Gail Godwin, the story is centered around ideas of marriage and family. However, marriage and family are presented in very different lights in the two stories. Karen van der Zee presents marriage with children as perfect and somewhat dreamlike; it is what Faye, the heroine of A Secret Sorrow, wants, and what is necessary for her happiness. For Godwin's heroine, marriage and family are almost the antithesis of happiness; her home life seems to suffocate her and eventually leads her to commit suicide.

Both of the female protagonists in the two stories experience a crisis of sorts. In A Secret Sorrow Faye's crisis comes before marriage. She is distraught and upset because she cannot have children and fears that this will prevent her from marrying the man she loves. Both she and her beloved, Kai, have always wanted a marriage with children, and it is assumed that only under these circumstances will they truly be happy. Faye feels that her inability to have children is a fatal flaw. "Every time we see some pregnant woman, every time we're with somebody else's children I'll feel I've failed you!" (185). In "A Sorrowful Woman," however, the crisis comes after the marriage, when the woman has already procured her husband and child. Faye would be ecstatic in this woman's situation. The protagonist of the Godwin story, however, is not. Her husband and son bring her such sorrow that eventually she is unable to see them at all, and communicates only through notes stuck under her bedroom door. Faye's anxiety and fear is based on the thought of losing her man and never having children. In contrast, Godwin's character has a loving husband and child and is still filled with grief. In a Harlequin such as A Secret Sorrow, this is unimaginable; it goes against every formula of romance writing, where books always end with a wedding, and happiness after that is just assumed.

In A Secret Sorrow, marriage is portrayed as the end, as in the goal. It is what the heroine wants. The author works to let the reader know that only in this way will Faye be fulfilled and happy; it is what the entire story, with all the plot twists and romantic interludes, has been working toward. In "A Sorrowful Woman," marriage is the end, but not as in the goal--it is quite literally the end of the woman's life. Though we don't see what her life was like before her emotional crisis, there are hints of it. When she moves into the new room she men- tions seeing the streets from a whole new perspective, suggesting the previous monotony of her daily life. In addition, in the final paragraphs of the story when the character bakes pies and bread and washes and folds the laundry, her son says, "she's tired from doing all our things again" (193), giving us an idea of what "our things" were, and what the woman did with her time before becoming ill.

In A Secret Sorrow Faye's inability to have children does not end Kai's love for her, and the two go on to get married and adopt children. Faye's married life is described in a very idyllic way--she raises her son and two daughters in a "white ranch house under the blue skies of Texas" (188). In other words, once she is mar- ried and has children there is no more anxiety, nothing more to fear. The author leads us to the conclusion that marriage solves all problems and is a source of unending happiness for all. This is a great difference from the Godwin tale, which takes place in the winter and main- tains a sense of cold throughout the whole thing. When- ever Godwin describes the family it is not in the light, glowing terms of van der Zee, but always with a sense of weight or guilt or failure about it. The child's trusting gaze makes the protagonist begin "yelping without tears" (189).

Any sign of life or love increases her sorrow and makes her want to be rid of it. For example, when the hired girl brings her son to visit her with a grasshopper he's found--something both alive and from the outside world--she gets very upset and forces her husband to fire her. The girl is too much of an infringement on her space, and too much of a reminder of what she can no longer be.

Never is the difference between the two authors' portrayals of marriage more apparent than when both the women are viewing their families. Faye, sitting with her husband and watching her children play, felt that "life was good and filled with love" (188). Godwin's protagonist, on the other hand, says, "The sight of them made her so sad and sick she did not want to see them ever again" (189). When Kai, now her husband, embraces Faye, she feels that, "There was love in his embrace and love in his words and in her heart there was no room now for doubt, no room for sorrow" (188). When Godwin's heroine feels the loving touch of her husband's arm and the kiss of her child she cannot bear it and cuts off all direct contact with them. The situation of her marriage pushes her into a self-imposed imprisonment and lethargy. She feels unbearably sad because she can no longer be who they want and need her to be. She avoids them not because she does not love them, but rather because she loves them so much that it is too painful to see them and feel her failure.

When Faye's fears of losing Kai are assuaged, and she is happily married, it is as though a great weight has been lifted off of her. Godwin's character, on the other hand, feels her marriage as a great weight pressing in on her. The love of her husband and child weighs on her and immobilizes her. When she leaves her room for a day and leaves out freshly baked bread for her husband and son, they express their happiness in the notes they write to her that night, and "the force of the two joyful notes . . . pressed her into the corner of the little room; she hardly had space to breathe" (192). Faye can be a traditional wife and mother, so her family is a source of joy. Godwin's character can no longer do this, and so her family is a representation of her failure, and the guilt presses her further and further into herself, until she can retreat no further and ends her life.

The endings of the two stories are powerful illustrations of the differences between them. In the end of A Secret Sorrow the author shows us Faye feeling "beautiful, complete, whole" (188) in her role as wife and mother. Godwin, on the other hand, shows us her heroine dead on her bed. Godwin first gives the reader hope, by showing all that the woman has done, and saying that "the house smelled redolently of renewal and spring" (193). This makes the blow even harder when we then discover, along with the husband and child, the woman's suicide.

Karen van der Zee creates a story full of emotional highs and lows, but one that leads up to--and ends with-- marriage. After the marriage all plot twists and traumas come to a halt. Faye is brought to new life by her marriage and children; in it she finds completion of herself and total happiness. Godwin's tale, on the other hand, is full of anguish and emotion, but it all takes place after the marriage. The character she creates is stifled and killed by her marriage. There is no portrayal of unending happiness in her tale, but rather unending woe.

Maya Leigh
Professor Herlin
English 104
October 10, 20--

title works for Godwin—but does it for van der Zee?

Separate Sorrows ⟩→

Karen van der Zee's novel   *Gail Godwin's short story*

In both the excerpt from A Secret Sorrow and "A Sorrowful Woman," ~~by Gail Godwin,~~ the ~~story is~~ centered
                                        plot   *s*
around ideas of marriage and family. However, marriage and

family are presented in very different lights in the two

stories. Karen van der Zee presents marriage with children
                    totally fulfilling
as perfect and ~~somewhat dreamlike~~; it is what Faye, the
protagonist
~~heroine~~ of A Secret Sorrow, wants/ and what is necessary
                              unnamed protagonist
for her happiness. For Godwin's ~~heroine~~, marriage and

family are almost the antithesis of happiness; her

home life seems to suffocate her and eventually leads

her to commit suicide.

need a clear thesis here—is it that SS endorses marriage while SW problematizes it?

s she? s she sumed er e?

Both of the female protagonists in the two stories

experience a crisis ~~of sorts~~. In A Secret Sorrow Faye's

crisis comes before marriage. She is distraught and upset

because she cannot have children and fears that this will

prevent her from marrying the man she loves. Both she and

her beloved, Kai, have always wanted a marriage with chil-
                unclear referent
dren, and (it) is assumed that only under these

circumstances will they truly be happy. Faye feels that
                        that cuts her off from Kai's love
her inability to have children is a fatal flaw. "Every

time we see some pregnant woman, every time we're with

somebody else's children I'll feel I've failed you!" (185).

ert from xt page
In "A Sorrowful Woman," however, the crisis comes after
                                            secured
the marriage, when the woman has already ~~procured~~ her

husband and child. Faye would be ecstatic in this woman's
Unlike who

situation. The protagonist of ~~the~~ Godwin's story, ~~however,~~
's

is not. Her husband and son bring her such sorrow that
Inexplicably,

eventually she is unable to see them at all, ~~and~~ communi-

cates only through notes stuck under her bedroom door.
‿ing

Faye's anxiety and fear is based on the thought of losing
her man and never having children. ~~In contrast~~, Godwin's
insert
← first
page

character has a loving husband and child ~~and~~ is still
, yet she

filled with grief. I~~n a Harlequin such as A Secret Sorrow,~~
this ~~is~~ unimaginable, it goes against ~~every~~ formulas of
sense of defeat would be in a Harlequin romance because one of the most popular

romance writing: ~~where books~~ always ends with a wedding,
The plot

~~and happiness after that is just assumed.~~
with the assumption that the rest is happily ever after.

    In A Secret Sorrow, marriage is portrayed as ~~the end,~~
~~as in~~ the goal. ~~It is what the heroine wants.~~ ~~The author~~
Van der Zee

works to let the reader know that only in this way will

Faye be fulfilled and happy; it is what the entire story,

with all the plot twists and romantic interludes, ~~has been~~

working toward. In "A Sorrowful Woman," marriage is the end,
‿s   *also*

but not as in the goal: It is quite literally the end of
the woman's life. Though we don't see what her life was
I like
this!

like before her emotional crisis, there are hints of it.

When she moves into the new room, she mentions seeing the

streets from a whole new perspective, suggesting the pre-
need p. ref

vious monotony of her daily life. In addition, in the

final paragraphs of the story--when the character bakes

pies and bread and washes and folds the laundry--her son

says, "She's tired from doing all our things again" (193),

giving us an idea of what "our things" were, and what the

woman did with her time before becoming ill.
is she really
ill? or just
withdrawing
from her
life?

*need
transition* | In A Secret Sorrow Faye's inability to have children

does not end Kai's love for her, and the two go on to get

married and adopt children. Faye's married life is

described in a very idyllic way--she raises her son and two

daughters in a "white ranch house under the blue skies of

Texas" (188). In other words, once she is married and has

because the plot

children there is no more anxiety, nothing more to fear.

The author leads us to the conclusion that marriage solves

all problems and is a source of unending happiness, for

ly   *is*

all. This is a great difference from the Godwin's tale,

which takes place in the winter and maintains a sense of

cold, throughout the whole thing. Whenever Godwin

describes the family it is not in the light, glowing terms

that suggest

of van der Zee, but always with a sense of weight, or

guilt, or failure about it. The child's trusting gaze

makes the protagonist begin "yelping without tears" (189),

while

Any sign of life or love increases her sorrow and makes

unclear referent

her want to be rid of (it). For example, when the hired

girl brings her son to visit her with a grasshopper he's

found something both alive and from the outside world,

the girl.

she gets very upset and forces her husband to fire her.

Apparently,

The girl is too much of an infringement on her space, and

too much of a reminder of what she can no longer be.

Never is the difference between the two authors' por-

trayals of marriage more apparent than when both the women

are viewing their families. Faye, sitting with her husband

and watching her children play, felt that "life was good

and filled with love" (188). Godwin's protagonist, on the

other hand, says, "The sight of them made her so sad and

sick she did not want to see them ever again" (189). When

Kai, now her husband, embraces Faye, she feels "There was

love in his embrace and love in his words and in her heart

there was no room now for doubt, no room for sorrow" (188).

When Godwin's heroine feels the loving touch of her hus-

band's arm and the kiss of her child she cannot bear it

and cuts off all direct contact with them. The situation

of her marriage pushes her into a self-imposed imprison-

ment and lethargy. She feels unbearably sad because she

can no longer be who they want and need her to be. She

avoids them not because she does not love them but rather

because she loves them so much that it is too painful to

see them and feel her failure.

shoul
use ep
gram
here?
work i
the
thesis

need → When Faye's fears of losing Kai are assuaged, and she
transition
is happily married, it is as though a great weight has

been lifted off her. Godwin's character, on the other

hand, feels her marriage as a great weight pressing ~~in~~ on
and
her~~.~~ ~~The love of her husband and child weighs on her and~~
ɾing
immobiliz~~ed~~ her. When she leaves her room for a day and
puts
~~leaves~~ out freshly baked bread for her husband and son,

they express their happiness in the notes they write to

her that night, and "the force of the two joyful notes . . .

pressed her into the corner of the little room; she had
the
hardly space to breathe" (192). Faye can be ~~a~~ traditional

wife and mother, so her family is a source of joy.

Godwin's character can no longer do this, and so her fam-
s   *own*
ily ~~is a~~ representation ~~of~~ her failure, and the guilt

presses her further and further into herself/ until she

can retreat no further and ends her life.

The endings of the two stories are powerful illustrations of the differences between them. In the end of
<u>A Secret Sorrow</u> the author shows us Faye feeling "beauti-
ful, complete, whole" (188) in her role as wife and mother.
                                         protagonist
Godwin, on the other hand, shows us her ~~heroine~~ dead on
                  seems to
her bed. Godwin ~~first~~ gives/ the reader hope/ by showing
all that the woman has done/ and saying that "the house
smelled redolently of renewal and spring" (193). This makes
the blow even harder when we then discover, along with the
                                   death
husband and child, the woman's ~~suicide~~.

Karen van der Zee creates a story full of emotional
highs and lows/ but one that leads up to--and ends with--
marriage. After the marriage all plot twists and traumas
come to a halt. Faye is brought to new life by her mar-
                      ^   *fulfillment*
riage and children; ~~in it~~ she finds ~~completion of herself~~
                                       story, however,
and total happiness. Godwin's ~~tale, on the other hand,~~ is
                              confusion (?) that
full of anguish and ~~emotion, but it~~ all takes/ place after
the marriage. The character she creates is stifled and
killed by her marriage. There is no portrayal of unending
happiness in her tale, but rather unending (woe) *is this the right*
                                                 word, since she
                                                 dies?

Margin annotations (left):
me / llic / rround- / gs as / Z's / e / es?

ed / me / ry / ief / otes / make / nclu- / n / ronger?

A Sample Student Comparison and Contrast

The changes noted in Maya's annotations on her second draft are put to good use in the following final draft. By not insisting that Godwin's protagonist actually commits suicide, Maya shifts her attention away from this indeterminable death to the causes and effects of it. This shift leads her to a stronger thesis—that Godwin raises questions about the efficacy of marriage rather than endorsing it as a certain recipe for happiness the way van der Zee does. Maya also incorporates additional revisions, such as transitions (see, for example, the revision between paragraphs 3 and 4), sentence clarity, and a fuller and more persuasive concluding paragraph. She also looked at the Questions for Revising (p. 40) before writing her final draft.

Maya Leigh
Professor Herlin
English 104
October 10, 20--

Fulfillment or Failure?

Marriage in A Secret Sorrow and "A Sorrowful Woman"

In both the excerpt from Karen van der Zee's novel A Secret Sorrow and in Gail Godwin's short story "A Sorrowful Woman," the plots center around ideas of marriage and family. However, marriage and family are presented in very different lights in the two stories. Karen van der Zee presents marriage with children as perfect and totally fulfilling; it is what Faye, the protagonist of A Secret Sorrow, wants and what is necessary for her happiness. For Godwin's unnamed protagonist, marriage and family are almost the antithesis of happiness; her home life seems to suffocate her and eventually leads to her death. A Secret Sorrow directly endorses and encourages marriage, whereas "A Sorrowful Woman" indirectly questions and discourages it.

Both of the female protagonists in the two stories experience a crisis. In A Secret Sorrow Faye's crisis comes before the marriage. She is distraught and upset because she cannot have children and fears that this will prevent her from marrying the man she loves. Both she and her beloved, Kai, desire marriage with children, and van der Zee suggests that only with these things will they truly be happy. Faye feels that her inability to have children is a fatal flaw that cuts her off from Kai's love. "Every time we see some pregnant woman, every time we're with somebody else's children I'll feel I've failed you!" (185). Faye's anxiety and fear are based on the thought of losing her man and never having children. In

Leigh 2

"A Sorrowful Woman," however, the crisis comes after the
marriage, when the woman has already secured her husband
and child. Unlike Faye, who would be ecstatic in this
woman's situation, the protagonist of Godwin's story is
not. Inexplicably, her husband and son bring her such
sorrow that eventually she is unable to see them at all,
communicating only through notes stuck under her bedroom
door. Godwin's character has a loving husband and child,
yet she is still filled with grief. This sense of defeat
would be unimaginable in a Harlequin romance because it
goes against one of the most popular formulas of romance
writing: The plot always ends with a wedding, with the
assumption that the rest is happily ever after.

    In A Secret Sorrow, marriage is portrayed as the
goal. Van der Zee works to let the reader know that only
in this way will Faye be fulfilled and happy; it is what
the entire story, with all the plot twists and romantic
interludes, works toward. Marriage is also the end in "A
Sorrowful Woman" but not as in the goal: It is quite literally the end of the woman's life. Though we don't see
what her life was like before her emotional crisis, there
are hints of it. When she moves into a new bedroom--away
from her husband--she mentions seeing the streets from a
whole new perspective (191), suggesting the previous
monotony of her daily life. In addition, in the final
paragraphs of the story--when the character bakes pies
and bread and washes and folds the laundry--her son says,
"She's tired from doing all our things again" (193), giving us an idea of what "our things" were and what the
woman did with her time before her crisis.

    This monotony of marriage is absent in A Secret Sor-
row. Faye's inability to have children does not end Kai's
love for her, and the two go on to marry and adopt

children. Faye's married life is described in a very
idyllic way: She raises her son and two daughters in a
"white ranch house under the blue skies of Texas" (188).
Once she is married and has children, there is no more
anxiety because the plot leads us to the conclusion that
marriage solves all problems and is a source of unending
happiness. This greatly differs from Godwin's tale, which
takes place in winter and maintains a sense of cold.
Whenever Godwin describes the family, it is in terms that
suggest weight, guilt, or failure. The child's trusting
gaze makes the protagonist begin "yelping without tears"
(189), and any sign of life or love increases her sorrow
and makes her want to be alone. For example, when the
hired girl brings her son to visit her with a grasshopper
he's found (190)--something both alive and from the outside world--she gets very upset and forces her husband to
fire the girl. Apparently, the girl is too much of an
infringement on her space, too much of a reminder of what
she can no longer be.

Never is the difference between the two authors'
portrayals of marriage more apparent than when both women
are viewing their families. Faye, sitting with her husband and watching her children play, feels that "life was
good and filled with love" (188). Godwin's narrator, on
the other hand, says of her "The sight of them made her
so sad and sick she did not want to see them ever again"
(189). When Kai, now her husband, embraces Faye, she
feels, "There was love in his embrace and love in his
words and in her heart there was no room now for doubt,
no room for sorrow" (188). When Godwin's heroine feels
the loving touch of her husband's arm and the kiss of her
child, she cannot bear it and cuts off all direct contact
with them. The situation of her marriage pushes her into
a self-imposed imprisonment and lethargy. She feels

unbearably sad because she can no longer be who they want
and need her to be. She avoids them not because she does
not love them but rather because she loves them so much
that it is too painful to see them and feel her failure.
The epigram to Godwin's story tells us that "Once upon a
time there was a wife and a mother one too many times"
(189). The addition of "one too many times" to this traditional story opening forces the idea of repetition and
monotony: It suggests that it is not that state of being
a wife and mother that is inherently bad but rather the
fact that that is all Godwin's character is. Day in and
day out, too many times over, the woman is just a wife
and a mother, and it isn't enough for her.

    In van der Zee's story there could be no such thing
as too much motherhood or too much of being a wife. When
Faye's fears of losing Kai are assuaged, and she is happily married, it is as though a great weight has been
lifted off her. Godwin's character, on the other hand,
feels her marriage as a great weight pressing on her and
immobilizing her. When she leaves her room for a day and
puts out freshly baked bread for her husband and son,
they express their happiness in the notes they write to
her that night, and "the force of the two joyful
notes . . . pressed her into the corner of the little room;
she hardly had space to breathe" (192). Faye can be the
traditional wife and mother, so her family is a source of
joy. Godwin's character can no longer be the traditional
wife and mother, and so her family represents her own
failure, and the guilt presses her further and further
into herself until she can retreat no further and ends
her life.

    The endings of the two stories are powerful illus-
trations of the differences between them. In the end of
A Secret Sorrow the author shows us Faye feeling

"beautiful, complete, whole" (188) in her role as wife and mother. Godwin, on the other hand, shows us her protagonist dead on her bed. Godwin seems to give the reader hope by showing all that the woman has done and saying that "the house smelled redolently of renewal and spring" (193). This makes the blow even harder when we then discover, along with the husband and child, the woman's death. The ambiguous way the death of Godwin's unnamed protagonist is dealt with reinforces the author's negative portrayal of marriage. It isn't explicitly written as a suicide, and Godwin seems to encourage her readers to see it as the inevitable consequence of her marriage.

Van der Zee creates a story full of emotional highs and lows, but one that leads up to and ends with marriage. After the marriage all of the plot twists and traumas come to a halt, replaced with peace and happiness. Faye is brought to new life by her marriage and children; she finds fulfillment of all of her desires in them. Godwin's story, however, is full of postmarital anguish and confusion. The character she creates is stifled and most definitely unfulfilled by her marriage. A burst of creative energy right before her death produces, among other things, "a sheath of marvelous watercolor beasts accompanied by mad and fanciful stories nobody could ever make up again, and a tablet full of love sonnets addressed to the man" (192-193). It is clear that the woman had talents and desires not met by the routine duties of her marital life. For Faye, the protagonist of A Secret Sorrow, marriage is the happily-ever-after ending she has wanted all of her life; for Godwin's protagonist, on the other hand, marriage is just a monotonous and interminable ever after.

6

Reading and Writing
about Poetry

READING POETRY RESPONSIVELY

Perhaps the best way to begin reading poetry responsively is not to allow yourself to be intimidated by it. Come to it, initially at least, the way you might listen to a song on the radio. You probably listen to a song several times before you hear it all, before you have a sense of how it works, where it's going, and how it gets there. You don't worry about analyzing a song when you listen to it, even though after repeated experiences with it you know and anticipate a favorite part and know, on some level, why it works for you. Give yourself a chance to respond to poetry.

Try reading the following poem aloud. Read it aloud before you read it silently. You may stumble once or twice, but you'll make sense of it if you pay attention to its punctuation and don't stop at the end of every line where there is no punctuation. The title gives you an initial sense of what the poem is about.

MARGE PIERCY (B. 1936)

The Secretary Chant   *1973*

My hips are a desk.
From my ears hang
chains of paper clips.
Rubber bands form my hair.
My breasts are wells of mimeograph ink.   5
My feet bear casters.
Buzz. Click.
My head is a badly organized file.

My head is a switchboard
where crossed lines crackle.   10
Press my fingers
and in my eyes appear
credit and debit.
Zing. Tinkle.
My navel is a reject button.   15
From my mouth issue canceled reams.
Swollen, heavy, rectangular
I am about to be delivered
of a baby
Xerox machine.   20
File me under W
because I wonce
was
a woman.

What is your response to this secretary's chant? The point is simple
enough — she feels dehumanized by her office functions — but the pleasures are manifold. Piercy makes the speaker's voice sound mechanical by
using short bursts of sound and by having her make repetitive, flat, matter-
of-fact statements ("My breasts . . . My feet . . . My head . . . My navel").
"The Secretary Chant" makes a serious statement about how such women
are reduced to functionaries. The point is made, however, with humor
since we are asked to visualize the misappropriation of the secretary's
body — her identity — as it is transformed into little more than a piece of
office equipment, which seems to be breaking down in the final lines, when
we learn that she "wonce / was / a woman." Is there the slightest hint of
something subversive in this misspelling of "wonce"? Maybe so, but the
humor is clear enough, particularly if you try to make a drawing of what
this dehumanized secretary has become.

The next poem creates a different kind of mood. Think about the title,
"Those Winter Sundays," before you begin reading the poem. What associations do you have with winter Sundays? What emotions does the phrase
evoke in you?

ROBERT HAYDEN (1913–1980)

Those Winter Sundays   *1962*

Sundays too my father got up early
and put his clothes on in the blueblack cold,
then with cracked hands that ached
from labor in the weekday weather made
banked fires blaze. No one ever thanked him.   5

I'd wake and hear the cold splintering, breaking.
When the rooms were warm, he'd call,
and slowly I would rise and dress,

fearing the chronic angers of that house,
Speaking indifferently to him,   10
who had driven out the cold
and polished my good shoes as well.
What did I know, what did I know
of love's austere and lonely offices?

Does the poem match the feelings you have about winter Sundays? Either way your response can be useful in reading the poem. For most of us Sundays are days at home; they might be cozy and pleasant experiences or they might be dull and depressing. Whatever they are, Sundays are more evocative than, say, Tuesdays. Hayden uses that response to call forth a sense of missed opportunity in the poem. The person who reflects on those winter Sundays didn't know until much later how much he had to thank his father for "love's austere and lonely offices." This is a poem about a cold past and a present reverence for his father — elements brought together by the phrase "Winter Sundays." *His* father? You may have noticed that the poem doesn't use a masculine pronoun; hence the voice could be a woman's. Does the sex of the voice make any difference to your reading? Would it make any difference about which details are included or what language is used?

What is most important about your initial readings of a poem is that you ask questions. If you read responsively, you'll find yourself asking all kinds of questions about the words, descriptions, sounds, and structures of a poem. The specifics of those questions will be generated by the particular poem. We don't, for example, ask how humor is achieved in "Those Winter Sundays" because there is none, but it is worth asking what kind of tone is established by the description of "the chronic angers of that house." The remaining discussions in this part will help you to formulate and answer questions about a variety of specific elements in poetry, such as speaker, image, metaphor, symbol, rhyme, and rhythm. For the moment, however, read the following poem several times and note your response at different points in the poem. Then write down a half dozen or so questions about what produces your response to the poem.

JOHN UPDIKE   (B. 1932)

Dog's Death   *1969*

She must have been kicked unseen or brushed by a car.
Too young to know much, she was beginning to learn
To use the newspapers spread on the kitchen floor
And to win, wetting there, the words, "Good dog! Good dog!"

We thought her shy malaise was a shot reaction.   5
The autopsy disclosed a rupture in her liver.
As we teased her with play, blood was filling her skin
And her heart was learning to lie down forever.

Monday morning, as the children were noisily fed
And sent to school, she crawled beneath the youngest's bed. 10
We found her twisted and limp but still alive.
In the car to the vet's, on my lap, she tried

To bite my hand and died. I stroked her warm fur
And my wife called in a voice imperious with tears.
Though surrounded by love that would have upheld her, 15
Nevertheless she sank and, stiffening, disappeared.

Back home, we found that in the night her frame,
Drawing near to dissolution, had endured the shame
Of diarrhoea and had dragged across the floor
To a newspaper carelessly left there. *Good dog.* 20

Here's a simple question to get started with your own questions: What would its effect have been if Updike had titled the poem "Good Dog" instead of "Dog's Death"?

THE PLEASURE OF WORDS

What is special about poetry? What makes it valuable? Why should we read it? How is reading it different from reading prose? To begin with, poetry pervades our world in a variety of forms, ranging from advertising jingles to song lyrics. These may seem to be a long way from the chants heard around a primitive campfire, but they serve some of the same purposes. Like poems printed in a magazine or book, primitive chants, catchy jingles, and popular songs attempt to stir the imagination through the carefully measured use of words.

Although reading poetry usually makes more demands than does the kind of reading used to skim a magazine or newspaper, the appreciation of poetry comes naturally enough to anyone who enjoys playing with words. Play is an important element of poetry. Consider, for example, how the following words appeal to the children who gleefully chant them in playgrounds:

I scream, you scream
We all scream
For ice cream.

These lines are an exuberant evocation of the joy of ice cream. Indeed, chanting the words turns out to be as pleasurable as eating ice cream. In poetry, the expression of the idea is as important as the idea expressed.

But is "I scream . . ." poetry? Some poets and literary critics would say that it certainly is one kind of poem because the children who chant it experience some of the pleasures of poetry in its measured beat and repeated sounds. However, other poets and critics would define poetry more narrowly and insist, for a variety of reasons, that this isn't true poetry but merely **doggerel,** a term used for lines whose subject matter is trite and whose rhythm and sounds are monotonously heavy-handed.

Although probably no one would argue that "I scream . . ." is a great poem, it does contain some poetic elements that appeal, at the very least, to children. Does that make it poetry? The answer depends on one's definition, but poetry has a way of breaking loose from definitions. Because there are nearly as many definitions of poetry as there are poets, Edwin Arlington Robinson's succinct observations are useful: "poetry has two outstanding characteristics. One is that it is undefinable. The other is that it is eventually unmistakable."

This comment places more emphasis on how a poem affects a reader than on how a poem is defined. By characterizing poetry as "undefinable," Robinson acknowledges that it can include many different purposes, subjects, emotions, styles, and forms. What effect does the following poem have on you?

WILLIAM HATHAWAY (B. 1944)

Oh, Oh   *1982*

My girl and I amble a country lane,
moo cows chomping daisies, our own
sweet saliva green with grass stems.
"Look, look," she says at the crossing,
"the choo-choo's light is on." And sure   5
enough, right smack dab in the middle
of maple dappled summer sunlight
is the lit headlight — so funny.
An arm waves to us from the black window.
We wave gaily to the arm. "When I hear   10
trains at night I dream of being president,"
I say dreamily. "And me first lady," she
says loyally. So when the last boxcars,
named after wonderful, faraway places,
and the caboose chuckle by we look   15
eagerly to the road ahead. And there,
poised and growling, are fifty Hell's Angels.

Hathaway's poem serves as a convenient reminder that poetry can be full of surprises. Even on a first reading there is no mistaking the emotional reversal created by the last few words of this poem. With the exception of the final line, the poem's language conjures up an idyllic picture of a young couple taking a pleasant walk down a country lane. Contented as "moo cows," they taste the sweetness of the grass, hear peaceful country sounds, and are dazzled by "dappled summer sunlight." Their future together seems to be all optimism as they anticipate "wonderful, faraway places" and the "road ahead." Full of confidence, this couple, like the reader, is unprepared for the shock to come. When we see those "fifty Hell's Angels," we are confronted with something like a bucket of cold water in the face.

But even though our expectations are abruptly and powerfully reversed, we are finally invited to view the entire episode from a safe distance — the distance provided by the delightful humor in this poem. After all, how seriously can we take a poem that is titled "Oh, Oh"? The poet has his way with us, but we are brought in on the joke too. The terror takes on comic proportions as the innocent couple is confronted by no fewer than *fifty* Hell's Angels. This is the kind of raucous overkill that informs a short animated film produced some years ago titled *Bambi Meets Godzilla:* You might not have seen it, but you know how it ends. The poem's good humor comes through when we realize how pathetically inadequate the response of "Oh, Oh" is to the circumstances.

As you can see, reading a description of what happens in a poem is not the same as experiencing a poem. The exuberance of "I scream . . ." and the surprise of Hathaway's "Oh, Oh" are in the hearing or reading rather than in the retelling. A *paraphrase* is a prose restatement of the central ideas of a poem in your own language. Consider the difference between the following poem and the paraphrase that follows it. What is missing from the paraphrase?

ROBERT FRANCIS (1901–1987)

Catch   1950

Two boys uncoached are tossing a poem together,
Overhand, underhand, backhand, sleight of hand, every hand,
Teasing with attitudes, latitudes, interludes, altitudes,
High, make him fly off the ground for it, low, make him stoop,
Make him scoop it up, make him as-almost-as-possible miss it,   5
Fast, let him sting from it, now, now fool him slowly,
Anything, everything tricky, risky, nonchalant,
Anything under the sun to outwit the prosy,
Over the tree and the long sweet cadence down,
Over his head, make him scramble to pick up the meaning,   10
And now, like a posy, a pretty one plump in his hands.

Paraphrase: A poet's relationship to a reader is similar to a game of catch. The poem, like a ball, should be pitched in a variety of ways to challenge and create interest. Boredom and predictability must be avoided if the game is to be engaging and satisfying.

A paraphrase can help us achieve a clearer understanding of a poem, but, unlike a poem, it misses all the sport and fun. It is the poem that "outwit[s] the prosy" because the poem serves as an example of what it suggests poetry should be. Moreover, the two players — the poet and the reader — are "uncoached." They know how the game is played, but their expectations do not preclude spontaneity and creativity or their ability to surprise and be surprised. The solid pleasure of the workout — of reading poetry — is the satisfaction derived from exercising your imagination and intellect.

WOLE SOYINKA (B. 1934)

Telephone Conversation   *1960*

The price seemed reasonable, location
Indifferent. The landlady swore she lived
Off premises. Nothing remained
But self-confession. "Madam," I warned,
"I hate a wasted journey — I am African."   5
Silence. Silenced transmission of
Pressurized good-breeding. Voice, when it came,
Lipstick coated, long gold-rolled
Cigarette-holder pipped. Caught I was, foully.
"HOW DARK?" . . . I had not misheard . . . "ARE YOU LIGHT   10
OR VERY DARK?" Button B. Button A. Stench
Of rancid breath of public hide-and-speak.
Red booth. Red pillar-box. Red double-tiered
Omnibus squelching tar. It *was* real! Shamed
By ill-mannered silence, surrender   15
Pushed dumbfoundment to beg simplification.
Considerate she was, varying the emphasis —
"ARE YOU DARK? OR VERY LIGHT?" Revelation came.
"You mean — like plain or milk chocolate?"
Her assent was clinical, crushing in its light   20
Impersonality. Rapidly, wave-length adjusted,
I chose. "West African sepia" — and as afterthought,
"Down in my passport." Silence for spectroscopic
Flight of fancy, till truthfulness clanged her accent
Hard on the mouthpiece. "WHAT'S THAT?" conceding   25
"DON'T KNOW WHAT THAT IS." "Like brunette."
"THAT'S DARK, ISN'T IT?" "Not altogether.
Facially, I am brunette, but madam, you should see
The rest of me. Palm of my hand, soles of my feet
Are a peroxide blonde. Friction, caused —   30
Foolishly madam — by sitting down, has turned
My bottom raven black — One moment madam!" — sensing
Her receiver rearing on the thunderclap
About my ears — "Madam," I pleaded, "wouldn't you rather
See for yourself?"   35

The conversation that we hear in this traditional English telephone box evokes serious racial tensions as well as a humorous treatment of them; the benighted tradition represented by the landlady seems to be no match for the speaker's satiric wit. The **speaker** is the voice used by the author in the poem; like the narrator in a work of fiction, the speaker is often a created identity rather than the author's actual self. The two should not automatically be equated. Contrast the attitude toward life of the speaker in "Telephone Conversation" with that of the speaker in the following poem.

PHILIP LARKIN (1922–1985)

A Study of Reading Habits   1964

When getting my nose in a book
Cured most things short of school,
It was worth ruining my eyes
To know I could still keep cool,
And deal out the old right hook   5
To dirty dogs twice my size.

Later, with inch-thick specs,
Evil was just my lark:
Me and my cloak and fangs
Had ripping times in the dark.   10
The women I clubbed with sex!
I broke them up like meringues.

Don't read much now: the dude
Who lets the girl down before
The hero arrives, the chap   15
Who's yellow and keeps the store,
Seem far too familiar. Get stewed:
Books are a load of crap.

What the speaker records and describes in "Telephone Conversation" is close if not identical to Soyinka's own vision and voice. The satirical response to the landlady is clearly shared by the speaker and the poet, between whom there is little or no distance. In "A Study of Reading Habits," however, Larkin distances himself from a speaker whose sensibilities he does not wholly share. The poet — and many readers — might identify with the reading habits described by the speaker in the first twelve lines, but Larkin uses the last six lines to criticize the speaker's attitude toward life as well as reading. The speaker recalls in lines 1–6 how as a schoolboy he identified with the hero, whose virtuous strength always triumphed over "dirty dogs," and in lines 7–12 he recounts how his schoolboy fantasies were transformed by adolescence into a fascination with violence and sex. This description of early reading habits is pleasantly amusing, because many readers of popular fiction will probably recall having moved through similar stages, but at the end of the poem the speaker provides more information about himself than he intends to.

As an adult the speaker has lost interest in reading because it is no longer an escape from his own disappointed life. Instead of identifying with heroes or villains, he finds himself identifying with minor characters who are irresponsible and cowardly. Reading is now a reminder of his failures, so he turns to alcohol. His solution, to "Get stewed" because "Books are a load of crap," is obviously self-destructive. The speaker is ultimately exposed by Larkin as someone who never grew beyond fantasies. Getting drunk is consistent with the speaker's immature reading habits. Unlike the speaker, the poet understands that life is often distorted by escapist fantasies, whether through a steady diet of popular fiction or through alcohol. The speaker in this poem, then, is not Larkin but a created identity whose voice is filled with disillusionment and delusion.

Here is a poem that looks quite different from most *verse,* a term used for lines composed in a measured rhythmical pattern, which are often, but not necessarily, rhymed.

Robert Morgan (b. 1944)

Mountain Graveyard   1979

for the author of "Slow Owls"

Spore Prose

stone	notes
slate	tales
sacred	cedars
heart	earth
asleep	please
hated	death

Though unconventional in its appearance, this is unmistakably poetry because of its concentrated use of language. The poem demonstrates how serious play with words can lead to some remarkable discoveries. At first glance "Mountain Graveyard" may seem intimidating. What, after all, does this list of words add up to? How is it in any sense a poetic use of language? But if the words are examined closely, it is not difficult to see how they work. The wordplay here is literally in the form of a game. Morgan uses a series of *anagrams* (words made from the letters of other words, such as *read* and *dare*) to evoke feelings about death. "Mountain Graveyard" is one of several poems that Morgan has called "Spore Prose" (another anagram) because he finds in individual words the seeds of poetry. He wrote the poem in honor of the fiftieth birthday of another poet, Jonathan Williams, the author of "Slow Owls," whose title is also an anagram.

The title, "Mountain Graveyard," indicates the poem's setting, which is also the context in which the individual words in the poem interact to provide a larger meaning. Morgan's discovery of the words on the stones of a graveyard is more than just clever. The observations he makes among the silent graves go beyond the curious pleasure a reader experiences in finding the words *sacred cedars,* referring to evergreens common in cemeteries, to consist of the same letters. The surprise and delight of realizing the connection between heart and earth is tempered by the more sober recognition that everyone's story ultimately ends in the ground. The hope that the dead are merely asleep is expressed with a plea that is answered grimly by a hatred of death's finality.

Little is told in this poem. There is no way of knowing who is buried or who is looking at the graves, but the emotions of sadness, hope, and pain are unmistakable — and are conveyed in fewer than half the words of this sentence. Morgan takes words that initially appear to be a dead, prosaic list and energizes their meanings through imaginative juxtapositions.

The following poem also involves a startling discovery about words. With the peculiar title "l(a," the poem cannot be read aloud, so there is no sound, but is there sense, a *theme,* a central idea or meaning, in the poem?

E. E. CUMMINGS (1894–1962)

l(a   *1958*

l(a

le
af
fa

ll

s)
one
l

iness

CONSIDERATIONS FOR CRITICAL THINKING AND WRITING

1. FIRST RESPONSE. Discuss the connection between what appears inside and outside the parentheses in this poem.

2. What does Cummings draw attention to by breaking up the words? How do this strategy and the poem's overall shape contribute to its theme?

3. Which seems more important in this poem — what is expressed, or the way it is expressed?

Although "Mountain Graveyard" and "l(a" do not resemble the kind of verse that readers might recognize immediately as poetry on a page, both are actually a very common type of poem, called the *lyric,* usually a brief poem that expresses the personal emotions and thoughts of a single speaker. Lyrics are often written in the first person but sometimes — as in "Mountain Grave-yard" and "l(a" — no speaker is specified. Lyrics present a subjective mood, emotion, or idea. Very often they are about love or death, but almost any subject or experience that evokes some intense emotional response can be found in lyrics. In addition to brevity and emotional intensity, lyrics are also frequently characterized by their musical qualities. The word *lyric* derives from the Greek word *lyre,* meaning a musical instrument that originally accompanied the singing of a lyric. Lyric poems can be organized in a variety of ways, such as the sonnet, elegy, and ode, but it is enough to point out here that lyrics are an extremely popular kind of poetry with writers and readers.

The following anonymous lyric was found in a sixteenth-century manuscript.

ANONYMOUS

Western Wind
c. 1500

Western wind, when wilt thou blow,
The small rain down can rain?
Christ, if my love were in my arms,
And I in my bed again!

This speaker's intense longing for his lover is characteristic of lyric poetry. He impatiently addresses the western wind that brings spring to England and could make it possible for him to be reunited with the woman he loves. We do not know the details of these lovers' lives because this poem focuses on the speaker's emotion. We do not learn why the lovers are apart or if they will be together again. We don't even know if the speaker is a man. But those issues are not really important. The poetry gives us a feeling rather than a story.

A poem that tells a story is called a ***narrative poem.*** Narrative poetry may be short or very long. An ***epic,*** for example, is a long narrative poem on a serious subject chronicling heroic deeds and important events. Among the most famous epics are Homer's *Iliad* and *Odyssey,* the Old English *Beowulf,* Dante's *Divine Comedy,* and John Milton's *Paradise Lost.* More typically, however, narrative poems are considerably shorter, such as Hathaway's "Oh, Oh."

SUGGESTIONS FOR APPROACHING POETRY

1. Assume that it will be necessary to read a poem more than once. Give yourself a chance to become familiar with what the poem has to offer. Like a piece of music, a poem becomes more pleasurable with each encounter.

2. Pay attention to the title; it will often provide a helpful context for the poem and serve as an introduction to it. Larkin's "A Study of Reading Habits" is precisely what its title describes.

3. As you read the poem for the first time, avoid becoming entangled in words or lines that you don't understand. Instead, give yourself a chance to take in the entire poem before attempting to resolve problems encountered along the way.

4. On a second reading, identify any words or passages that you don't understand. Look up words you don't know; these might include names, places, historical and mythical references, or anything else that is unfamiliar to you.

5. Read the poem aloud (or perhaps have a friend read it to you). You'll probably discover that some puzzling passages suddenly fall into place when you hear them. You'll find that nothing helps, though, if the poem is read in an artificial, exaggerated manner. Read in as natural a voice as possible, with slight pauses at line breaks. Silent reading is preferable to imposing a te-tumpty-te-tum reading on a good poem.

6. Read the punctuation. Poems use punctuation marks — in addition to the space on the page — as signals for readers. Be especially careful not to assume that the end of a line marks the end of a sentence, unless it is concluded by punctuation. Consider, for example, the opening lines of Hathaway's "Oh, Oh":

> My girl and I amble a country lane,
> moo cows chomping daisies, our own
> sweet saliva green with grass stems.

Line 2 makes little or no sense if a reader stops after "own." Keeping track of the subjects and verbs will help you find your way among the sentences.

7. Paraphrase the poem to determine whether you understand what happens in it. As you work through each line of the poem, a paraphrase will help you to see which words or passages need further attention.

8. Try to get a sense of who is speaking and what the setting or situation is. Don't assume that the speaker is the author; often it is a created character.

9. Assume that each element in the poem has a purpose. Try to explain how the elements of the poem work together.

10. Be generous. Be willing to entertain perspectives, values, experiences, and subjects that you might not agree with or approve. Even if baseball bores you, you should be able to comprehend its imaginative use in Francis's "Catch."

11. Try developing a coherent approach to the poem that helps you to shape a discussion of the text. See Chapter 3, "Applying a Critical Strategy," to review formalist, biographical, historical, psychological, feminist, and other possible critical approaches.

12. Don't expect to produce a definitive reading. Many poems do not resolve all the ideas, issues, or tensions in them, and so it is not always possible to drive their meaning into an absolute corner. Your reading will explore rather than define the poem. Poems are not trophies to be stuffed and mounted. They're usually more elusive. And don't be afraid that a close reading will damage the poem. Poems aren't hurt when we analyze them; instead, they come alive as we experience them and put into words what we discover through them.

A list of more specific questions concerning the literary terms and concepts used in the discussions that follow begins on page 274. That list, like the suggestions just made, raises issues and questions that can help you to read just about any poem closely. These strategies should be a useful means for getting inside poems to understand how they work. Furthermore, because reading poetry inevitably increases sensitivity to language, you're likely to find yourself a better reader of words in any form — whether in a novel, a newspaper editorial, an advertisement, a political speech, or a conversation — after having studied poetry.

THE ELEMENTS

Diction

Like all good writers, poets are keenly aware of ***diction,*** their choice of words. Poets, however, choose words especially carefully because the words in poems call attention to themselves. Characters, actions, settings, and symbols may appear in a poem, but in the foreground, before all else, is the poem's language. Also, poems are usually briefer than other forms of writing. A few inappropriate words in a 200-page novel (which would have about 100,000 words) create fewer problems than they would in a 100-word poem. Functioning in a compressed atmosphere, the words in a poem must convey meanings gracefully and economically. Readers therefore have to be alert to the ways in which those meanings are released.

Although poetic language is often more intensely charged than ordinary speech, the words used in poetry are not necessarily different from everyday speech. Inexperienced readers may sometimes assume that language must be high-flown and out of date to be included in a poem: Instead of reading about a boy "enjoying a swim," they expect to read about a boy "disporting with pliant arm o'er a glassy wave." During the eighteenth century this kind of ***poetic diction*** — the use of elevated language over ordinary language — was highly valued in English poetry, but since the nineteenth century poets have generally overridden the distinctions that were once made between words used in everyday speech and those used in poetry. Today all levels of diction can be found in poetry.

A poet, like any writer, has several levels of diction from which to choose; they range from formal to middle to informal. ***Formal diction*** consists of a dignified, impersonal, and elevated use of language. Notice, for example, the formality of Thomas Hardy's description of the sunken luxury liner *Titanic* in this stanza from "The Convergence of the Twain" (the entire poem appears on p. 1164):

> In a solitude of the sea
> Deep from human vanity,
> And the Pride of Life that planned her, stilly couches she.

There is nothing casual or relaxed about these lines. Hardy's use of "stilly," meaning "quietly" or "calmly," is purely literary; the word rarely, if ever, turns up in everyday English.

The language used in Richard Wilbur's "A Late Aubade" (p. 843) represents a less formal level of diction; the speaker uses a ***middle diction*** spoken by most educated people. Consider how Wilbur's speaker tells his lover what she might be doing instead of being with him:

> You could be sitting now in a carrel
> Turning some liver-spotted page,
> Or rising in an elevator-cage
> Toward Ladies' Apparel.

The speaker elegantly enumerates his lover's unattractive alternatives to being with him — reading old books in a library or shopping in a department store — but the wit of his description lessens its formality.

Informal diction is evident in Larkin's "A Study of Reading Habits" (p. 220). The speaker's account of his early reading is presented ***colloquially,*** in a conversational manner that in this instance includes slang expressions not used by the culture at large:

> When getting my nose in a book
> Cured most things short of school,
> It was worth ruining my eyes
> To know I could still keep cool,
> And deal out the old right hook
> To dirty dogs twice my size.

This level of diction is clearly not that of Hardy's or Wilbur's speakers.

Poets may also draw on another form of informal diction, called ***dialect.*** Dialects are spoken by definable groups of people from a particular geographic region, economic group, or social class. New England dialects are often heard in Robert Frost's poems, for example. Langston Hughes employs a black dialect in "Rent-Party Shout: For a Lady Dancer" (p. 833) to characterize the speaker. Another form of diction related to particular groups is ***jargon,*** a category of language defined by a trade or profession. Sociologists, photographers, carpenters, baseball players, and dentists, for example, all use words that are specific to their fields. Alice Jones achieves powerful effects using medical jargon in "The Foot" (p. 1167).

Many levels of diction are available to poets. The variety of diction to be found in poetry is enormous, and that is how it should be. No language is foreign to poetry because it is possible to imagine any human voice as the speaker of a poem. When we say a poem is formal, informal, or somewhere in between, we are making a descriptive statement rather than an evaluative one. What matters in a poem is not only which words are used but how they are used.

Denotations and Connotations

One important way that the meaning of a word is communicated in a poem is through sound: snakes *hiss,* saws *buzz.* (This and other matters related to sound are discussed on pages 251–254.) Individual words also convey meanings through denotations and connotations. **Denotations** are the literal, dictionary meanings of a word. For example, *bird* denotes a feathered animal with wings (other denotations for the same word include a shuttlecock, an airplane, or an odd person), but in addition to its denotative meanings, *bird* also carries **connotations,** associations and implications that go beyond a word's literal meanings. Connotations derive from how the word has been used and the associations people make with it. Therefore, the connotations of *bird* might include fragility, vulnerability, altitude, the sky, or freedom, depending on the context in which the word is used. Consider also how different the connotations are for the following types of birds: hawk, dove, penguin, pigeon, chicken, peacock, duck, crow, turkey, gull, owl, goose, coot, and vulture. These words have long been used to refer to types of people as well as birds. They are rich in connotative meanings.

Connotative meanings are valuable because they allow poets to be economical and suggestive simultaneously. In this way emotions and attitudes are carefully woven into the texture of the poem's language. Read the following poem and pay close attention to the connotative meanings of its words.

RANDALL JARRELL (1914–1965)

The Death of the Ball Turret Gunner   1945

From my mother's sleep I fell into the State
And I hunched in its belly till my wet fur froze.
Six miles from earth, loosed from its dream of life,
I woke to black flak and the nightmare fighters.
When I died they washed me out of the turret with a hose.

The title of this poem establishes the setting and the speaker's situation. Like the setting of a short story, the setting of a poem is important when the time and place influence what happens. "The Death of the Ball Turret Gunner" is set in the midst of a war and, more specifically, in a ball turret—a Plexiglas sphere housing machine guns on the underside of a bomber. The speaker's situation obviously places him in extreme danger; indeed, his fate is announced in the title.

Although the poem is written in the first-person singular, its speaker is clearly not the poet. Jarrell uses a ***persona,*** a speaker created by the poet. In this poem the persona is a disembodied voice that makes the gunner's story all the more powerful. What is his story? A paraphrase might read something like this:

> After I was born, I grew up to find myself at war, cramped into the turret of a bomber's belly some 31,000 feet above the ground. Below me were exploding shells from antiaircraft guns and attacking fighter planes. I was killed, but the bomber returned to base, where my remains were cleaned out of the turret so the next man could take my place.

This paraphrase is accurate, but its language is much less suggestive than the poem's. The first line of the poem has the speaker emerge from his "mother's sleep," the anesthetized sleep of her giving birth. The phrase also suggests the comfort, warmth, and security he knew as a child. This safety was left behind when he "fell," a verb that evokes the danger and involuntary movement associated with his subsequent "State" (*fell* also echoes, perhaps, the fall from innocence to experience related in the Bible).

Several dictionary definitions appear for the noun *state;* it can denote a territorial unit, the power and authority of a government, a person's social status, or a person's emotional or physical condition. The context provided by the rest of the poem makes clear that "State" has several denotative meanings here: Because it is capitalized, it certainly refers to the violent world of a government at war, but it also refers to the gunner's vulnerable status as well as his physical and emotional condition. By having "State" carry more than one meaning, Jarrell has created an intentional ambiguity. ***Ambiguity*** allows for two or more simultaneous interpretations of a word, phrase, action, or situation, all of which can be supported by the context of a work. Through his ambiguous use of "State," Jarrell connects the horrors of war not just to bombers and gunners but to the governments that control them.

Related to this ambiguity is the connotative meaning of "State" in the poem. The context demands that the word be read with a negative charge. The word is not used with patriotic pride but to suggest an anonymous, impersonal "State" that kills rather than nurtures the life in its "belly." The state's "belly" is a bomber, and the gunner is "hunched" like a fetus in the cramped turret, where, in contrast to the warmth of his mother's womb, everything is frozen, even the "wet fur" of his flight jacket (newborn infants have wet fur too). The gunner is not just 31,000 feet from the ground but "Six miles from earth." *Six miles* has roughly the same denotative meaning as 31,000 feet, but Jarrell knew that the connotative meaning of *six miles* makes the speaker's position seem even more remote and frightening.

When the gunner is born into the violent world of war, he finds himself waking up to a "nightmare" that is all too real. The poem's final line is grimly understated, but it hits the reader with the force of an exploding shell: What the State-bomber-turret gives birth to is a gruesome death that is merely one of an endless series. It may be tempting to reduce the theme of this poem to the idea that "war is hell," but Jarrell's target is more specific. He implicates the "State," which routinely executes such violence, and he does so without preaching or hysterical denunciations. Instead, his use of language conveys his theme subtly and powerfully.

Word Order

Meanings in poems are conveyed not only by denotations and connotations but also by the poet's arrangement of words into phrases, clauses, and sentences to achieve particular effects. The ordering of words into meaningful verbal patterns is called **syntax.** A poet can manipulate the syntax of a line to place emphasis on a word; this is especially apparent when a poet varies normal word order. In Dickinson's "A narrow Fellow in the Grass" (p. 2), for example, the speaker says about the snake that "His notice sudden is." Ordinarily, that would be expressed as "his notice is sudden." By placing the verb *is* unexpectedly at the end of the line, Dickinson creates the sense of surprise we feel when we suddenly come upon a snake. Dickinson's inversion of the standard word order also makes the final sound of the line a hissing *is.*

Tone

Tone is the writer's attitude toward the subject, the mood created by all the elements in the poem. Writing, like speech, may be characterized as serious or light, sad or happy, private or public, angry or affectionate, bitter or nostalgic, or any other attitudes and feelings that human beings experience. In Jarrell's "The Death of the Ball Turret Gunner," the tone is clearly serious; the voice in the poem even sounds dead. Listen again to the persona's final words: "When I died they washed me out of the turret with a hose." The brutal, restrained matter-of-factness of this line is effective because the reader is called on to supply the appropriate anger and despair, a strategy that makes those emotions all the more convincing.

Consider how tone is used to convey meaning in the next poem.

MARTÍN ESPADA (B. 1957)

Latin Night at the Pawnshop   *1987*

Chelsea, Massachusetts
Christmas, 1987

The apparition of a salsa band
gleaming in the Liberty Loan
pawnshop window:

Golden trumpet,
silver trombone,
congas, maracas, tambourine,
all with price tags dangling
like the city morgue ticket
on a dead man's toe.

CONSIDERATIONS FOR CRITICAL THINKING AND WRITING

1. FIRST RESPONSE. What is "Latin" about this night at the pawnshop?
2. What kind of tone is created by the poet's word choice and by the rhythm of the poem?
3. Does it matter that this apparition occurs on Christmas night? Why or why not?
4. What do you think is the central point of this poem?

In the next poem a male speaker addresses a female urging that their love should not be delayed because time is running short. In Latin this is known as *carpe diem*, "seize the day." This theme is as familiar in poetry as it is in life.

ANDREW MARVELL (1621–1678)

To His Coy Mistress   *1681*

Had we but world enough, and time,
This coyness, lady, were no crime.
We would sit down, and think which way
To walk, and pass our long love's day.
Thou by the Indian Ganges'° side   5
Shouldst rubies find; I by the tide
Of Humber° would complain.° I would   *write love songs*
Love you ten years before the Flood,
And you should, if you please, refuse
Till the conversion of the Jews.   10
My vegetable love should grow°

---

5 *Ganges:* A river in India sacred to the Hindus.   7 *Humber:* A river that flows through Marvell's native town, Hull.   11 *My vegetable love ... grow:* A slow, unconscious growth.

Vaster than empires, and more slow;
An hundred years should go to praise
Thine eyes and on thy forehead gaze,
Two hundred to adore each breast,   15
But thirty thousand to the rest:
An age at least to every part,
And the last age should show your heart.
For, lady, you deserve this state,
Nor would I love at lower rate.   20
    But at my back I always hear
Time's wingèd chariot hurrying near;
And yonder all before us lie
Deserts of vast eternity.
Thy beauty shall no more be found,   25
Nor in thy marble vault shall sound
My echoing song; then worms shall try
That long preserved virginity,
And your quaint honor turn to dust,
And into ashes all my lust.   30
The grave's a fine and private place,
But none, I think, do there embrace.
    Now, therefore, while the youthful hue
Sits on thy skin like morning dew,
And while thy willing soul transpires°   *breathes forth* 35
At every pore with instant fires,
Now let us sport us while we may,
And now, like amorous birds of prey,
Rather at once our time devour
Than languish in his slow-chapped° power.   *slow-jawed* 40
Let us roll all our strength and all
Our sweetness up into one ball,
And tear our pleasures with rough strife
Thorough° the iron gates of life.   *through*
Thus, though we cannot make our sun   45
Stand still, yet we will make him run.

CONSIDERATIONS FOR CRITICAL THINKING AND WRITING

1. FIRST RESPONSE. Do you think this *carpe diem* poem is hopelessly dated or does it speak to our contemporary concerns?

2. This poem is divided into a three-part argument. Briefly summarize each section: if (lines 1–20), but (21–32), therefore (33–46).

3. What is the speaker's tone in lines 1–20? How much time would he spend adoring his mistress? Is he sincere? How does he expect his mistress to respond to these lines?

4. How does the speaker's tone change beginning with line 21? What is his view of time in lines 21–32? What does this description do to the lush and leisurely sense of time in lines 1–20? How do you think his mistress would react to lines 21–32?

5. What does Marvell's speaker urge in lines 33–46? How is the pace of these lines (notice the verbs) different from that of the first twenty lines of the poem?

6. This poem is sometimes read as a vigorous but simple celebration of flesh. Is there more to the theme than that?

Word Choice and Translations

Sometimes translation can inadvertently be a comic business. Consider, for example, the discovery made by John Steinbeck's wife, Elaine, when in a Yokohama bookstore she asked for a copy of her husband's famous novel *The Grapes of Wrath* and learned that it had been translated into Japanese as *Angry Raisins*. Close but no cigar (perhaps translated as: Nearby, yet no smoke). As amusing as that *Angry Raisins* title is, it teaches an important lesson about the significance of a poet's or a translator's choices when crafting a poem: A powerful piece moves us through diction and tone, both built word by careful word. Translations are frequently regarded as merely vehicular, a way to arrive at the original work. It is, of course, the original work — its spirit, style, and meaning — that most readers expect to find in a translation. Even so, it is important to understand that a translation is *by nature* different from the original — and that despite that difference, a fine translation can be an important part of the journey and become part of the literary landscape itself. Reading a translation of a poem is not the same as reading the original, but neither is watching two different performances of *Hamlet*. The translator provides a reading of the poem in much the same way that a director shapes the play. Each interprets the text from a unique perspective.

Basically, there are two distinct approaches to translation: literal translations and adaptations. A literal translation sets out to create a word-for-word equivalent that is absolutely faithful to the original. As simple and direct as this method may sound, literal translations are nearly impossible over extended passages because of the structural differences between languages. Moreover, the meaning of a single word in one language may not exist in another language, or it may require a phrase, clause, or entire sentence to capture its implications. Adaptations of works offer broader, more open-ended approaches to translation. Unlike a literal translation, an adaptation moves beyond denotative meanings in an attempt to capture the spirit of a work so that its idioms, dialects, slang, and other conventions are re-created in the language of the translation.

The question we ask of an adaptation should not be "Is this exactly how the original reads?" Instead, we ask "Is this an insightful, graceful rendering worth reading?" To translate poetry it is not enough to know the language of the original; it is also necessary that the translator be a poet. A translated poem is more than a collation of decisions based on dictionaries and grammars; it must also be poetry. However undefinable poetry may be, it is unmistakable in its intense use of language. Poems are not merely translated; they are savored.

Two Translations of Neruda's "Juventud"

Here are the original and two translations of "Juventud" written by the Chilean poet Pablo Neruda. Read through the Spanish version first even if you don't know Spanish so that you have a sense of what the translators worked through to create their poems. Pay particular attention to the way in which diction and word order help to create the tone in each of the translations.

PABLO NERUDA (1904–1973)

Juventud   *1942*

Un perfume como una ácida espada
de ciruelas en un camino,
los besos del azúcar en los dientes,
las gotas vitales resbalando en los dedos,
la dulce pulpa erótica,   5
las eras, los pajares, los incitantes
sitios secretos de las casas anchas,
los colchones dormidos en el pasado, el agrio valle verde
mirado desde arriba, desde el vidrio escondido:
toda la adolescencia mojándose y ardiendo   10
como una lámpara derribada en la lluvia.

Youth   *1942*

TRANSLATED BY ROBERT BLY (1971)

An odor like an acid sword made
of plum branches along the road,
the kisses like sugar in the teeth,
the drops of life slipping on the fingertips,
the sweet sexual fruit,   5
the yards, the haystacks, the inviting
rooms hidden in the deep houses,
the mattresses sleeping in the past, the savage green valley
seen from above, from the hidden window:
adolescence all sputtering and burning   10
like a lamp turned over in the rain.

Youth   *1942*

TRANSLATED BY JACK SCHMITT (1991)

A perfume like an acid plum
sword on a road,

sugary kisses on the teeth,
vital drops trickling down the fingers,
sweet erotic pulp,   5
threshing floors, haystacks, inciting
secret hideaways in spacious houses,
mattresses asleep in the past, the pungent green valley
seen from above, from the hidden window:
all adolescence becoming wet and burning   10
like a lantern tipped in the rain.

CONSIDERATIONS FOR CRITICAL THINKING AND WRITING

1. FIRST RESPONSE. How are the Bly and Schmitt translations similar in their
    treatment of youth?

2. Consult a Spanish dictionary and write a word-for-word translation of
    "Juventud" into English. Which lines are particularly difficult to translate?
    How does your translation compare with Bly's and Schmitt's? Explain why
    one of the two translations is closest to the original Spanish.

3. Compare the diction and images in the Bly and Schmitt translations and
    explain which you think is more effective. Explain why, for example,
    you find Bly's "sweet sexual fruit" or Schmitt's "sweet erotic pulp" more
    effective.

Images

A poet, to borrow a phrase from Henry James, is one of those on whom
nothing is lost. Poets take in the world and give us impressions of what
they experience through images. An *image* is language that addresses the
senses. The most common images in poetry are visual; they provide verbal
pictures of the poets' encounters — real or imagined — with the world. But
poets also create images that appeal to our other senses. Richard Wilbur
arouses several senses when he has the speaker in "A Late Aubade" gently
urge his lover to linger in bed with him instead of getting on with her daily
routines and obligations:

> Wait for a while, then slip downstairs
> And bring us up some chilled white wine,
> And some blue cheese, and crackers, and some fine
> Ruddy-skinned pears.

These images are simultaneously tempting and satisfying. We don't have to
literally touch that cold, clear glass of wine (or will it come in a green bottle
beaded with moisture?) or smell the cheese or taste the crackers to appreciate this vivid blend of colors, textures, tastes, and fragrances.

Images give us the physical world to experience in our imaginations.
Some poems, like the following one, are written to do just that; they make
no comment about what they describe.

WILLIAM CARLOS WILLIAMS (1883–1963)

Poem   1934

As the cat
climbed over
the top of

the jamcloset
first the right   5
forefoot

carefully
then the hind
stepped down

into the pit of   10
the empty
flowerpot

This poem defies paraphrase because it is all an image of agile movement. No statement is made about the movement; the title, "Poem"—
really no title—signals Williams's refusal to comment on the movements.
To impose a meaning on the poem, we'd probably have to knock over the
flowerpot.

We experience the image in Williams's "Poem" more clearly because of
how the sentence is organized into lines and groups of lines, or stanzas.
Consider how differently the sentence is read if it is arranged as prose:

As the cat climbed over the top of the jamcloset, first the right forefoot carefully then the hind stepped down into the pit of the empty flowerpot.

The poem's line and stanza division transforms what is essentially an awkward prose sentence into a rhythmic verbal picture. Especially when the
poem is read aloud, this line and stanza division allows us to feel the image
we see. Even the lack of a period at the end suggests that the cat is only
pausing.

Images frequently do more than offer only sensory impressions, however. They also convey emotions and moods, as in the following poem.

MATTHEW ARNOLD (1822–1888)

Dover Beach   1867

The sea is calm tonight.
The tide is full, the moon lies fair
Upon the straits;—on the French coast the light
Gleams and is gone; the cliffs of England stand,
Glimmering and vast, out in the tranquil bay.   5

Come to the window, sweet is the night-air!
Only, from the long line of spray
Where the sea meets the moon-blanched land,
Listen! you hear the grating roar
Of pebbles which the waves draw back, and fling,   10
At their return, up the high strand,
Begin, and cease, and then again begin,
With tremulous cadence slow, and bring
The eternal note of sadness in.

Sophocles long ago   15
Heard it on the Aegean, and it brought
Into his mind the turbid ebb and flow
Of human misery;° we
Find also in the sound a thought,
Hearing it by this distant northern sea.   20

The Sea of Faith
Was once, too, at the full, and round earth's shore
Lay like the folds of a bright girdle furled.
But now I only hear
Its melancholy, long, withdrawing roar,   25
Retreating, to the breath
Of the night-wind, down the vast edges drear
And naked shingles° of the world.   *pebble beaches*

Ah, love, let us be true
To one another! for the world, which seems 30
To lie before us like a land of dreams,
So various, so beautiful, so new,
Hath really neither joy, nor love, nor light,
Nor certitude, nor peace, nor help for pain;
And we are here as on a darkling plain   35
Swept with confused alarms of struggle and flight,
Where ignorant armies clash by night.

15–18 *Sophocles . . . misery:* In *Antigone* (lines 656–677), Sophocles likens the disasters that beset the house of Oedipus to a "mounting tide."

CONSIDERATIONS FOR CRITICAL THINKING AND WRITING

1. FIRST RESPONSE. Discuss what you consider to be this poem's central point. How do the speaker's descriptions of the ocean work toward making that point?

2. Contrast the images in lines 4–8 and 9–13. How do they reveal the speaker's mood? To whom is he speaking?

3. What is the cause of the "sadness" in line 14? What is the speaker's response to the ebbing "Sea of Faith"? Is there anything to replace his sense of loss?

4. What details of the beach seem related to the ideas in the poem? How is the sea used differently in lines 1–14 and lines 21–28?

5. Describe the differences in tone between lines 1–8 and 35–37. What has caused the change?

6. CRITICAL STRATEGIES. Read the section on mythological criticism (pp. 72–74) in Chapter 3, "Applying a Critical Strategy," and discuss how you think a mythological critic might make use of the allusion to Sophocles in this poem.

WILLIAM BLAKE (1757–1827)

London   *1794*

I wander through each chartered° street,	*defined by law*
Near where the chartered Thames does flow,	
And mark in every face I meet	
Marks of weakness, marks of woe.	

In every cry of every man,   5
In every Infant's cry of fear,
In every voice, in every ban,
The mind-forged manacles I hear.

How the Chimney-sweeper's cry
Every black'ning Church appalls;   10
And the hapless Soldier's sigh
Runs in blood down Palace walls.

But most through midnight streets I hear
How the youthful Harlot's curse
Blasts the new-born Infant's tear,   15
And blights with plagues the Marriage hearse.

CONSIDERATIONS FOR CRITICAL THINKING AND WRITING

1. FIRST RESPONSE. What feelings do the visual images in this poem suggest to you?
2. What is the predominant sound heard in the poem?
3. What is the meaning of line 8? What is the cause of the problems that the speaker sees and hears in London? Does the speaker suggest additional causes?
4. The image in lines 11 and 12 cannot be read literally. Comment on its effectiveness.
5. How does Blake's use of denotative and connotative language enrich this poem's meaning?
6. An earlier version of Blake's last stanza appeared this way:

> But most the midnight harlot's curse
> From every dismal street I hear,
> Weaves around the marriage hearse
> And blasts the new-born infant's tear.

Examine carefully the differences between the two versions. How do Blake's revisions affect his picture of London life? Which version do you think is more effective? Why?

Figures of Speech

Figures of speech are broadly defined as a way of saying one thing in terms of something else. An overeager funeral director might, for example, be described as a vulture. Although figures of speech are indirect, they are designed to clarify, not obscure, our understanding of what they describe. Poets frequently use them because, as Emily Dickinson said, the poet's work is to "Tell all the truth but tell it slant" to capture the reader's interest and imagination. But figures of speech are not limited to poetry. Hearing them, reading them, or using them is as natural as using language itself.

Suppose that in the middle of a class discussion concerning the economic causes of World War II your history instructor introduces a series of statistics by saying, "Let's get down to brass tacks." Would anyone be likely to expect a display of brass tacks for students to examine? Of course not. To interpret the statement literally would be to wholly misunderstand the instructor's point that the time has come for a close look at the economic circumstances leading to the war. A literal response transforms the statement into the sort of hilariously bizarre material often found in a sketch by Woody Allen.

Students do not look for brass tacks because, to put it in a nutshell, they understand that the instructor is speaking figuratively. They would understand, too, that in the preceding sentence "in a nutshell" refers to brevity and conciseness rather than to the covering of a kernel of a nut. Figurative language makes its way into our everyday speech and writing as well as into literature because it is a means of achieving color, vividness, and intensity.

Consider the difference, for example, between these two statements:

Literal: The diner strongly expressed anger at the waiter.
Figurative: The diner leaped from his table and roared at the waiter.

The second statement is more vivid because it creates a picture of ferocious anger by likening the diner to some kind of wild animal, such as a lion or tiger. By comparison, "strongly expressed anger" is neither especially strong nor especially expressive; it is flat. Not all figurative language avoids this kind of flatness, however. Figures of speech such as "getting down to brass tacks" and "in a nutshell" are clichés because they lack originality and freshness. Still, they suggest how these devices are commonly used to give language some color, even if that color is sometimes a bit faded.

There is nothing weak about William Shakespeare's use of figurative language in the following passage from *Macbeth*. Macbeth has just learned that his wife is dead, and he laments her loss as well as the course of his own life.

WILLIAM SHAKESPEARE (1564–1616)

From Macbeth *(Act V, Scene v)*   *1605–1606*

Tomorrow, and tomorrow, and tomorrow
Creeps in this petty pace from day to day
To the last syllable of recorded time;
And all our yesterdays have lighted fools
The way to dusty death. Out, out, brief candle!   5
Life's but a walking shadow, a poor player,
That struts and frets his hour upon the stage,
And then is heard no more. It is a tale
Told by an idiot, full of sound and fury,
Signifying nothing.   10

This passage might be summarized as "life has no meaning," but such a brief
paraphrase does not take into account the figurative language that reveals
the depth of Macbeth's despair and his view of the absolute meaninglessness
of life. By comparing life to a "brief candle," Macbeth emphasizes the darkness and death that surround human beings. The light of life is too brief and
unpredictable to be of any comfort. Indeed, life for Macbeth is a "walking
shadow," futilely playing a role that is more farcical than dramatic, because
life is, ultimately, a desperate story filled with pain and devoid of significance. What the figurative language provides, then, is the emotional force of
Macbeth's assertion; his comparisons are disturbing because they are so apt.

Simile and Metaphor

The two most common figures of speech are simile and metaphor.
Both compare things that are ordinarily considered unlike each other. A
simile makes an explicit comparison between two things by using words
such as *like, as, than, appears,* or *seems:* "A sip of Mrs. Cook's coffee is like a
punch in the stomach." The force of the simile is created by the differences
between the two things compared. There would be no simile if the comparison were stated this way: "Mrs. Cook's coffee is as strong as the cafeteria's
coffee." This is a literal comparison because Mrs. Cook's coffee is compared with something like it, another kind of coffee.

A *metaphor,* like a simile, makes a comparison between two unlike
things, but it does so implicitly, without words such as *like* or *as:* "Mrs.
Cook's coffee is a punch in the stomach." Metaphor asserts the identity of
dissimilar things. Macbeth tells us that life *is* a "brief candle," life *is* "a walking shadow," life *is* "a poor player," life *is* "a tale / Told by an idiot." Metaphor
transforms people, places, objects, and ideas into whatever the poet imagines
them to be, and if metaphors are effective, the reader's experience, understanding, and appreciation of what is described are enhanced. Metaphors
are frequently more demanding than similes because they are not signaled by
particular words. They are both subtle and powerful.

Here is a poem about presentiment, a foreboding that something terrible is about to happen.

Emily Dickinson (1830–1886)

Presentiment — is that long Shadow — on the lawn —   *c. 1863*

Presentiment — is that long Shadow — on the lawn —
Indicative that Suns go down —

The notice to the startled Grass
That Darkness — is about to pass —

The metaphors in this poem define the abstraction "Presentiment." The sense of foreboding that Dickinson expresses is identified with a particular moment, the moment when darkness is just about to envelop an otherwise tranquil ordinary scene. The speaker projects that fear onto the "startled Grass" so that it seems any life must be frightened by the approaching "Shadow" and "Darkness" — two richly connotative words associated with death. The metaphors obliquely tell us ("tell it slant" was Dickinson's motto, remember) that presentiment is related to a fear of death, and, more important, the metaphors convey the feelings that attend that idea.

Some metaphors are more subtle than others because their comparison of terms is less explicit. Notice the difference between the following two metaphors, both of which describe a shaggy derelict refusing to leave the warmth of a hotel lobby: "He was a mule standing his ground" is a quite explicit comparison. The man is a mule; X is Y. But this metaphor is much more covert: "He brayed his refusal to leave." This second version is an *implied metaphor* because it does not explicitly identify the man with a mule. Instead, it hints at or alludes to the mule. Braying is associated with mules and is especially appropriate in this context because of those animals' reputation for stubbornness. Implied metaphors can slip by readers, but they offer the alert reader the energy and resonance of carefully chosen, highly concentrated language.

Some poets write extended comparisons in which part or all of the poem consists of a series of related metaphors or similes. Extended metaphors are more common than extended similes. In "Catch" (p. 218), Francis creates an *extended metaphor* that compares poetry to a game of catch. The entire poem is organized around this comparison. Because these comparisons are at work throughout the entire poem, they are called *controlling metaphors*. Extended comparisons can serve as a poem's organizing principle; they are also a reminder that in good poems metaphor and simile are not merely decorative but inseparable from what is expressed.

Other Figures

Perhaps the humblest figure of speech — if not one of the most familiar — is the pun. A *pun* is a play on words that relies on a word having more than one meaning or sounding like another word. For example, "A fad is in one era and out the other" is the sort of pun that produces obligatory groans. But most of us find pleasant and interesting surprises in puns.

Puns can be used to achieve serious effects as well as humorous ones. Although we may have learned to underrate puns as figures of speech, it is a mistake to underestimate their power and the frequency with which they appear in poetry. A close examination, for example, of Robert Frost's "Design" (p. 1163), or almost any lengthy passage from a Shakespeare play will confirm the value of puns.

Synecdoche is a figure of speech in which part of something is used to signify the whole: A neighbor is a "wagging tongue" (a gossip); a criminal is placed "behind bars" (in prison). Less typically, synecdoche refers to the whole used to signify the part: "Germany invaded Poland"; "Princeton won the fencing match." Clearly, certain individuals participated in these activities, not all of Germany or Princeton. Another related figure of speech is **metonymy,** in which something closely associated with a subject is substituted for it: "She preferred the silver screen [motion pictures] to reading." "At precisely ten o'clock the paper shufflers [office workers] stopped for coffee."

Synecdoche and metonymy may overlap and are therefore sometimes difficult to distinguish. Consider this description of a disapproving minister entering a noisy tavern: "As those pursed lips came through the swinging door, the atmosphere was suddenly soured." The pursed lips signal the presence of the minister and are therefore a synecdoche, but they additionally suggest an inhibiting sense of sin and guilt that makes the bar patrons feel uncomfortable. Hence, the pursed lips are also a metonymy, since they are in this context so closely connected with religion. Although the distinction between synecdoche and metonymy can be useful, when a figure of speech overlaps categories, it is usually labeled a metonymy.

Knowing the precise term for a figure of speech is, finally, less important than responding to its use in a poem. Consider how metonymy and synecdoche convey the tone and meaning of the following poem.

DYLAN THOMAS (1914–1953)

The Hand That Signed the Paper   *1936*

The hand that signed the paper felled a city;
Five sovereign fingers taxed the breath,
Doubled the globe of dead and halved a country;
These five kings did a king to death.

The mighty hand leads to a sloping shoulder,   5
The finger joints are cramped with chalk;
A goose's quill has put an end to murder
That put an end to talk.

The hand that signed the treaty bred a fever,
And famine grew, and locusts came;   10
Great is the hand that holds dominion over
Man by a scribbled name.

The five kings count the dead but do not soften
The crusted wound nor stroke the brow;
A hand rules pity as a hand rules heaven;   15
Hands have no tears to flow.

    The "hand" in this poem is a synecdoche for a powerful ruler because it is a part of someone used to signify the entire person. The "goose's quill" is a metonymy that also refers to the power associated with the ruler's hand. By using these figures of speech, Thomas depersonalizes and ultimately dehumanizes the ruler. The final synecdoche tells us that "Hands have no tears to flow." It makes us see the political power behind the hand as remote and inhuman. How is the meaning of the poem enlarged when the speaker says, "A hand rules pity as a hand rules heaven"?

    One of the ways writers energize the abstractions, ideas, objects, and animals that constitute their created worlds is through *personification,* the attribution of human characteristics to nonhuman things: Temptation pursues the innocent; trees scream in the raging wind; mice conspire in the cupboard. We are not explicitly told that these things are people; instead, we are invited to see that they behave like people. Perhaps it is human vanity that makes personification a frequently used figure of speech. Whatever the reason, personification, a form of metaphor that connects the nonhuman with the human, makes the world understandable in human terms. Consider this concise example from William Blake's *The Marriage of Heaven and Hell,* a long poem that takes delight in attacking conventional morality: "Prudence is a rich ugly old maid courted by Incapacity." By personifying prudence, Blake transforms what is usually considered a virtue into a comic figure hardly worth emulating.

    Often related to personification is another rhetorical figure called *apostrophe,* an address either to someone who is absent and therefore cannot hear the speaker or to something nonhuman that cannot comprehend. Apostrophe provides an opportunity for the speaker of a poem to think aloud, and often the thoughts expressed are in a formal tone. John Keats, for example, begins "Ode on a Grecian Urn" this way: "Thou still unravished bride of quietness." Apostrophe is frequently accompanied by intense emotion that is signaled by phrasing such as "O Life." In the right hands — such as Keats's — apostrophe can provide an intense and immediate voice in a poem, but when it is overdone or extravagant it can be ludicrous. Modern poets are more wary of apostrophe than their predecessors because apostrophizing strikes many self-conscious twentieth-century sensibilities as too theatrical. Thus modern poets tend to avoid exaggerated situations in favor of less charged though equally meditative moments, as in this next poem, with its amusing, half-serious cosmic twist.

JANICE TOWNLEY MOORE (B. 1939)

To a Wasp   *1984*

You must have chortled
finding that tiny hole
in the kitchen screen. Right
into my cheese cake batter
you dived,   5
no chance to swim ashore,
no saving spoon,
the mixer whirring
your legs, wings, stinger,
churning you into such   10
delicious death.
Never mind the bright April day.
Did you not see
rising out of cumulus clouds
That fist aimed at both of us?   15

Moore's apostrophe "To a Wasp" is based on the simplest of domestic circumstances; there is almost nothing theatrical or exaggerated in the poem's tone until "That fist" in the last line, when exaggeration takes center stage. As a figure of speech exaggeration is known as **overstatement** or **hyperbole** and adds emphasis without intending to be literally true: "The teenage boy ate everything in the house." Notice how the speaker of Marvell's "To His Coy Mistress" (p. 230) exaggerates his devotion in the following overstatement:

> An hundred years should go to praise
> Thine eyes and on thy forehead gaze,
> Two hundred to adore each breast,
> But thirty thousand to the rest:

That comes to 30,500 years. What is expressed here is heightened emotion, not deception.

The speaker also uses the opposite figure of speech, **understatement,** which says less than is intended. In the next section he sums up why he cannot take 30,500 years to express his love:

> The grave's a fine and private place,
> But none, I think, do there embrace.

The speaker is correct, of course, but by deliberately understating — saying "I think" when he is actually certain — he makes his point, that death will overtake their love, all the more emphatic. Another powerful example of understatement appears in the final line of Randall Jarrell's "The Death of the Ball Turret Gunner" (p. 227), when the disembodied voice of the machine-gunner describes his death in a bomber: "When I died they washed me out of the turret with a hose."

Paradox is a statement that initially appears to be self-contradictory but that, on closer inspection, turns out to make sense: "The pen is mightier than the sword." In a fencing match, anyone would prefer the sword, but if the goal is to win the hearts and minds of people, the art of persuasion can be more compelling than swordplay. To resolve the paradox, it is necessary to discover the sense that underlies the statement. If we see that "pen" and "sword" are used as metonymies for writing and violence, then the paradox rings true. *Oxymoron* is a condensed form of paradox in which two contradictory words are used together. Combinations such as "sweet sorrow," "silent scream," "sad joy," and "cold fire" indicate the kinds of startling effects that oxymorons can produce. Paradox is useful in poetry because it arrests a reader's attention by its seemingly stubborn refusal to make sense, and once a reader has penetrated the paradox, it is difficult to resist a perception so well earned. Good paradoxes are knotty pleasures. Here is a simple but effective one.

J. Patrick Lewis (b. 1942)

The Unkindest Cut   *1993*

Knives can harm you, heaven forbid;
Axes may disarm you, kid;
Guillotines are painful, but
There's nothing like a paper cut!

This quatrain is a humorous version of "the pen is mightier than the sword." The wounds escalate to the paper cut, which paradoxically is more damaging than even the broad blade of a guillotine. "The unkindest cut" of all (an allusion to Shakespeare's *Julius Caesar,* III.ii.188) is produced by chilling words on a page rather than cold steel, but it is more painfully fatal nonetheless.

Symbol

A *symbol* is something that represents something else. An object, person, place, event, or action can suggest more than its literal meaning. A handshake between two world leaders might be simply a greeting, but if it is done ceremoniously before cameras, it could be a symbolic gesture signifying unity, issues resolved, and joint policies that will be followed. We live surrounded by symbols. When an $80,000 Mercedes-Benz comes roaring by in the fast lane, we get a quick glimpse of not only an expensive car but an entire life-style that suggests opulence, broad lawns, executive offices, and power. One of the reasons some buyers are willing to spend roughly the cost of five Chevrolets for a single Mercedes-Benz is that they are aware of the car's symbolic value. A symbol is a vehicle for two things at once: It functions as itself, and it implies meanings beyond itself.

The meanings suggested by a symbol are determined by the context in which they appear. The Mercedes could symbolize very different things depending on where it was parked. Would an American political candidate be likely to appear in a Detroit blue-collar neighborhood with such a car? Probably not. Although a candidate might be able to afford the car, it would be an inappropriate symbol for someone seeking votes from all the people. As a symbol, the German-built Mercedes would backfire if voters perceived it as representing an entity partially responsible for layoffs of automobile workers (despite its partnership with Chrysler) or, worse, as a sign of decadence and corruption. Similarly, a huge portrait of Mao Tse-tung conveys different meanings to residents of Beijing than it would to farmers in Prairie Center, Illinois. Because symbols depend on contexts for their meaning, literary artists provide those contexts so that the reader has enough information to determine the probable range of meanings suggested by a symbol.

In the following poem the speaker describes walking at night. How is the night used symbolically?

Robert Frost (1874–1963)

Acquainted with the Night   *1928*

I have been one acquainted with the night.
I have walked out in rain — and back in rain.
I have outwalked the furthest city light.

I have looked down the saddest city lane.
I have passed by the watchman on his beat   5
And dropped my eyes, unwilling to explain.

I have stood still and stopped the sound of feet
When far away an interrupted cry
Came over houses from another street,

But not to call me back or say good-by;   10
And further still at an unearthly height
One luminary clock against the sky

Proclaimed the time was neither wrong nor right.
I have been one acquainted with the night.

In approaching this or any poem, you should read for literal meanings first and then allow the elements of the poem to invite you to symbolic readings, if they are appropriate. Here the somber tone suggests that the lines have symbolic meaning too. The flat matter-of-factness created by the repetition of "I have" (lines 1–5, 7, 14) understates the symbolic subject matter of the poem, which is, finally, more about the "night" located in the speaker's mind or soul than it is about walking away from a city and back again. The speaker is "acquainted with the night." The importance of this phrase is emphasized by Frost's title and by the fact that he begins and ends the poem with it. Poets frequently use this kind of repetition to alert readers to details that carry more than literal meanings.

The speaker in this poem has personal knowledge of the night but does not indicate specifically what the night means. To arrive at the potential meanings of the night in this context, it is necessary to look closely at its connotations, along with the images provided in the poem. The connotative meanings of night suggest, for example, darkness, death, and grief. By drawing on these connotations, Frost uses a *conventional symbol,* something that is recognized by many people to represent certain ideas. Roses conventionally symbolize love or beauty; laurels, fame; spring, growth; the moon, romance. Poets often use conventional symbols to convey tone and meaning.

Frost uses the night as a conventional symbol, but he also develops it into a *literary* or *contextual symbol* that goes beyond traditional, public meanings. A literary symbol cannot be summarized in a word or two. It tends to be as elusive as experience itself. The night cannot be reduced to or equated with darkness or death or grief, but it evokes those associations and more. Frost took what perhaps initially appears to be an overworked, conventional symbol and prevented it from becoming a cliché by deepening and extending its meaning.

The images in "Acquainted with the Night" lead to the poem's symbolic meaning. Unwilling, and perhaps unable, to explain explicitly to the watchman (and to the reader) what the night means, the speaker nevertheless conveys feelings about it. The brief images of darkness, rain, sad city lanes, the necessity for guards, the eerie sound of a distressing cry coming over rooftops, and the "luminary clock against the sky" proclaiming "the time was neither wrong nor right" all help to create a sense of anxiety in this tight-lipped speaker. Although we cannot know what unnamed personal experiences have acquainted the speaker with the night, the images suggest that whatever the night means, it is somehow associated with insomnia, loneliness, isolation, coldness, darkness, death, fear, and a sense of alienation from humanity and even time. Daylight — ordinary daytime thoughts and life itself — seems remote and unavailable in this poem. The night is literally the period from sunset to sunrise, but, more important, it is an internal state of being felt by the speaker and revealed through the images.

Frost used symbols rather than an expository essay that would explain the conditions that cause these feelings because most readers can provide their own list of sorrows and terrors that evoke similar emotions. Through symbol, the speaker's experience is compressed and simultaneously expanded by the personal darkness that each reader brings to the poem. The suggestive nature of symbols makes them valuable for poets and evocative for readers.

Allegory

Unlike expansive, suggestive symbols, *allegory* is a narration or description usually restricted to a single meaning because its events, actions, characters, settings, and objects represent specific abstractions or ideas.

Although the elements in an allegory may be interesting in themselves, the emphasis tends to be on what they ultimately mean. Characters may be given names such as Hope, Pride, Youth, and Charity; they have few, if any, personal qualities beyond their abstract meanings. These personifications are a form of extended metaphor, but their meanings are severely restricted. They are not symbols because, for instance, the meaning of a character named Charity is precisely that virtue.

There is little or no room for broad speculation and exploration in allegories. If Frost had written "Acquainted with the Night" as an allegory, he might have named his speaker Loneliness and had him leave the City of Despair to walk the Streets of Emptiness, where Crime, Poverty, Fear, and other characters would define the nature of city life. The literal elements in an allegory tend to be de-emphasized in favor of the message. Symbols, however, function both literally and symbolically, so that "Acquainted with the Night" is about both a walk and a sense that something is terribly wrong.

Allegory especially lends itself to ***didactic poetry,*** which is designed to teach an ethical, moral, or religious lesson. Many stories, poems, and plays are concerned with values, but didactic literature is specifically created to convey a message. "Acquainted with the Night" does not impart advice or offer guidance. If the poem argued that city life is self-destructive or sinful, it would be didactic; instead, it is a lyric poem that expresses the emotions and thoughts of a single speaker.

Although allegory is often enlisted in didactic causes because it can so readily communicate abstract ideas through physical representations, not all allegories teach a lesson. Here is a poem describing a haunted palace while also establishing a consistent pattern that reveals another meaning.

Edgar Allan Poe (1809–1849)

The Haunted Palace   1839

I
In the greenest of our valleys,
  By good angels tenanted,
Once a fair and stately palace —
  Radiant palace — reared its head.
In the monarch Thought's dominion —   5
  It stood there!
Never seraph spread a pinion
  Over fabric half so fair.

II
Banners yellow, glorious, golden,
  On its roof did float and flow;   10
(This — all this — was in the olden
  Time long ago)
And every gentle air that dallied,

In that sweet day,
Along the ramparts plumed and pallid,   15
    A wingèd odor went away.

III
Wanderers in that happy valley
    Through two luminous windows saw
Spirits moving musically
    To a lute's well-tunèd law,   20
Round about a throne, where sitting
    (Porphyrogene!)°   *born to purple, royal*
In state his glory well befitting,
    The ruler of the realm was seen.

IV
And all with pearl and ruby glowing   25
    Was the fair palace door,
Through which came flowing, flowing, flowing
    And sparkling evermore,
A troop of Echoes whose sweet duty
    Was but to sing,   30
In voices of surpassing beauty,
    The wit and wisdom of their king.

V
But evil things, in robes of sorrow,
    Assailed the monarch's high estate;
(Ah, let us mourn, for never morrow   35
    Shall dawn upon him, desolate!)
And, round about his home, the glory
    That blushed and bloomed
Is but a dim-remembered story
    Of the old time entombed.   40

VI
And travelers now within that valley,
    Through the red-litten windows see
Vast forms that move fantastically
    To a discordant melody;
While, like a rapid ghastly river,   45
    Through the pale door,
A hideous throng rush out forever,
    And laugh—but smile no more.

   On one level this poem describes how a once happy palace is desolated
by "evil things" (line 33). If the reader pays close attention to the diction,
however, an allegorical meaning becomes apparent on a second reading. A
systematic pattern develops in the choice of words used to describe the
palace, so that it comes to stand for a human mind. The palace, banners,
windows, door, echoes, and throng are equated with a person's head, hair,
eyes, mouth, voice, and laughter. That mind, once harmoniously ordered,
is overthrown by evil, haunting thoughts that lead to the mad laughter in

the poem's final lines. Once the general pattern is seen, the rest of the details fall neatly into place to strengthen the parallels between the surface description of a palace and the allegorical representation of a disordered mind.

Modern writers generally prefer symbol over allegory because they tend to be more interested in opening up the potential meanings of an experience instead of transforming it into a closed pattern of meaning. Perhaps the major difference is that while allegory may delight a reader's imagination, symbol challenges and enriches it.

Irony

Another important resource writers use to take readers beyond literal meanings is *irony,* a technique that reveals a discrepancy between what appears to be and what is actually true. Here is a classic example in which appearances give way to the underlying reality.

EDWIN ARLINGTON ROBINSON (1869–1935)

Richard Cory   *1897*

Whenever Richard Cory went down town,
We people on the pavement looked at him:
He was a gentleman from sole to crown,
Clean favored, and imperially slim.

And he was always quietly arrayed,   5
And he was always human when he talked;
But still he fluttered pulses when he said,
"Good-morning," and he glittered when he walked.

And he was rich — yes, richer than a king —
And admirably schooled in every grace: 10
In fine, we thought that he was everything
To make us wish that we were in his place.

So on we worked, and waited for the light,
And went without the meat, and cursed the bread;
And Richard Cory, one calm summer night,   15
Went home and put a bullet through his head.

Richard Cory seems to have it all. Those less fortunate, the "people on the pavement," regard him as well-bred, handsome, tasteful, and richly endowed with both money and grace. Until the final line of the poem, the reader, like the speaker, is charmed by Cory's good fortune, so quietly expressed in his decent, easy manner. That final, shocking line, however, shatters the appearances of Cory's life and reveals him to have been a desperately unhappy man. While everyone else assumes that Cory represented "everything" to which they aspire, the reality is that he could escape his miserable life only as a suicide. This discrepancy between what appears to be true and what actually exists is known as **situational irony:** What happens is entirely different from what is expected. We are not told why Cory shoots himself; instead, the irony in the poem shocks us into the recognition that appearances do not always reflect realities.

Words are also sometimes intended to be taken at other than face value. **Verbal irony** is saying something different from what is meant. After reading "Richard Cory," to say "That rich gentleman sure was happy" is ironic. The tone of voice would indicate that just the opposite was meant; hence, verbal irony is usually easy to detect in spoken language. In literature, however, a reader can sometimes take literally what a writer intends ironically. The remedy for this kind of misreading is to pay close attention to the poem's context. There is no formula that can detect verbal irony, but contradictory actions and statements as well as the use of understatement and overstatement can often be signals that verbal irony is present.

Consider how verbal irony is used in this poem.

KENNETH FEARING (1902–1961)

AD   1938

Wanted: Men;
Millions of men are *wanted at once* in a big new field;
New, tremendous, thrilling, great.
If you've ever been a figure in the chamber of horrors,
If you've ever escaped from a psychiatric ward,   5
If you thrill at the thought of throwing poison into wells, have heavenly
    visions of people, by the thousands, dying in flames —

You are the very man we want
We mean business and our business is *you*
Wanted: A race of brand-new men.   10

Apply: Middle Europe;
No skill needed;
No ambition required; no brains wanted and no character allowed;

Take a permanent job in the coming profession
Wages: *Death.*   15

This poem was written as Nazi troops stormed across Europe at the start of World War II. The advertisement suggests on the surface that killing is just an ordinary job, but the speaker indicates through understatement that there is nothing ordinary about the "business" of this "*coming profession.*" Fearing uses verbal irony to indicate how casually and mindlessly people are prepared to accept the horrors of war.

"AD" is a **satire,** an example of the literary art of ridiculing a folly or vice in an effort to expose or correct it. The object of satire is usually some human frailty; people, institutions, ideas, and things are all fair game for satirists. Fearing satirizes the insanity of a world mobilizing itself for war: His irony reveals the speaker's knowledge that there is nothing *"New, tremendous, thrilling,* [or] *great"* about going off to kill and be killed. The implication of the poem is that no one should respond to advertisements for war. The poem serves as a satiric corrective to those who would troop off armed with unrealistic expectations; wage war and the wages consist of death.

Dramatic irony is used when a writer allows a reader to know more about a situation than a character does. This creates a discrepancy between what a character says or thinks and what the reader knows to be true. Dramatic irony is often used to reveal character.

Sounds: Listening to Poetry

Poems yearn to be read aloud. Much of their energy, charm, and beauty comes to life only when they are heard. Poets choose and arrange words for their sounds as well as for their meanings. Most poetry is best read with your lips, teeth, and tongue because they serve to articulate the effects that sound may have in a poem. When a voice is breathed into a good poem, there is pleasure in the reading, the saying, and the hearing.

The earliest poetry—before writing and painting—was chanted or sung. The rhythmic quality of such oral performances served two purposes: It helped the chanting bard remember the lines, and it entertained audiences with patterned sounds of language, which were sometimes accompanied by musical instruments. Poetry has always been closely related to music. Indeed, as the word suggests, lyric poetry evolved from songs. "Western Wind" (p. 223), an anonymous Middle English lyric, survived as song long before it was written down. Had Robert Frost lived in a nonliterate society, he probably would have sung some version—a very different version to be sure—of "Acquainted with the Night" (p. 245) instead of writing it down. Even though Frost creates a speaking rather than a singing voice, the speaker's anxious tone is distinctly heard in any careful reading of the poem.

Like lyrics, early narrative poems were originally part of an anonymous oral folk tradition. (A **ballad** such as "Bonny Barbara Allan" told a story that was sung from one generation to the next until it was finally transcribed.) Since the eighteenth century, this narrative form has sometimes been imitated by poets who write **literary ballads.** John Keats's "La Belle Dame sans Merci" (p. 834) is, for example, a more complex and sophisticated nineteenth-century reflection of the original ballad traditions that developed in the fifteenth century and earlier. In considering poetry as sound, we should not forget that poetry traces its beginnings to song.

Listen to the sound of this poem as you read it aloud. How do the words provide, in a sense, their own musical accompaniment?

JOHN UPDIKE (B. 1932)

Player Piano

1958

My stick fingers click with a snicker
And, chuckling, they knuckle the keys;
Light-footed, my steel feelers flicker
And pluck from these keys melodies.

My paper can caper; abandon   5
Is broadcast by dint of my din,
And no man or band has a hand in
The tones I turn on from within.

At times I'm a jumble of rumbles,
At others I'm light like the moon,   10
But never my numb plunker fumbles,
Misstrums me, or tries a new tune.

    The speaker in this poem is a piano that can play automatically by means of a mechanism that depresses keys in response to signals on a perforated roll. Notice how the speaker's voice approximates the sounds of a piano. In each stanza a predominant sound emerges from the carefully chosen words. How is the sound of each stanza tuned to its sense?

EMILY DICKINSON (1830–1886)

A Bird came down the Walk —

c. 1862

A Bird came down the Walk —
He did not know I saw —
He bit an Angleworm in halves
And ate the fellow, raw,

And then he drank a Dew   5
From a convenient Grass —
And then hopped sidewise to the Wall
To let a Beetle pass —

He glanced with rapid eyes
That hurried all around —   10
They looked like frightened Beads, I thought —
He stirred his Velvet Head

Like one in danger, Cautious,
I offered him a Crumb
And he unrolled his feathers   15
And rowed him softer home —

Than Oars divide the Ocean,
Too silver for a seam —
Or Butterflies, off Banks of Noon
Leap, plashless as they swim.   20

This description of a bird offers a close look at how differently a bird moves when it hops on the ground than when it flies in the air. On the ground the bird moves quickly, awkwardly, and irregularly as it plucks up a worm, washes it down with dew, and then hops aside to avoid a passing beetle. The speaker recounts the bird's rapid, abrupt actions from a somewhat superior, amused perspective. By describing the bird in human terms (as if, for example, it chose to eat the worm "raw"), the speaker is almost condescending. But when the attempt to offer a crumb fails and the frightened bird flies off, the speaker is left looking up instead of down at the bird.

With that shift in perspective the tone shifts from amusement to awe in response to the bird's graceful flight. The jerky movements of lines 1 to 13 give way to the smooth motion of lines 15 to 20. The pace of the first three stanzas is fast and discontinuous. We tend to pause at the end of each line, and this reinforces a sense of disconnected movements. In contrast, the final six lines are to be read as a single sentence in one flowing movement, lubricated by various sounds.

Read again the description of the bird flying away. Several *o*-sounds contribute to the image of the serene, expansive, confident flight, just as the *s*-sounds serve as smooth transitions from one line to the next. Notice how these sounds are grouped in the following vertical columns:

unrolled	softer	too	his	Ocean	Banks
rowed	Oars	Noon	feathers	silver	plashless
home	Or		softer	seam	as
Ocean	off		Oars	Butterflies	swim

This blending of sounds (notice how "Leap, plashless" brings together the *p*- and *l*-sounds without a ripple) helps convey the bird's smooth grace in the air. Like a feathered oar, the bird moves seamlessly in its element.

The repetition of sounds in poetry is similar to the function of the tones and melodies that are repeated, with variations, in music. Just as the patterned sounds in music unify a work, so do the words in poems, which have been carefully chosen for the combinations of sounds they create. These sounds are produced in a number of ways.

The most direct way in which the sound of a word suggests its meaning is through **onomatopoeia,** which is the use of a word that resembles the sound it denotes: *quack, buzz, rattle, bang, squeak, bowwow, burp, choo-choo, ding-a-ling, sizzle.* The sound and sense of these words are closely related, but they represent a very small percentage of the words available to us. Poets usually employ more subtle means for echoing meanings.

Onomatopoeia can consist of more than just single words. In its broadest meaning the term refers to lines or passages in which sounds help to convey meanings, as in these lines from Updike's "Player Piano":

My stick fingers click with a snicker
And, chuckling, they knuckle the keys.

The sharp, crisp sounds of these two lines approximate the sounds of a piano; the syllables seem to "click" against one another. Contrast Updike's rendition with the following lines:

> My long fingers play with abandon
> And, laughing, they cover the keys.

The original version is more interesting and alive because the sounds of the words are pleasurable and they reinforce the meaning through a careful blending of consonants and vowels.

Alliteration is the repetition of the same consonant sounds at the beginnings of nearby words: "*d*escending *d*ewdrops"; "*l*uscious *l*emons." Sometimes the term is also used to describe the consonant sounds within words: "tres*p*asser's re*p*roach"; "we*dd*ed la*d*y." Alliteration is based on sound rather than spelling. "*K*een" and "*c*ar" alliterate, but "*c*ar" does not alliterate with "*c*ite." Rarely is heavy-handed alliteration effective. Used too self-consciously, it can be distracting instead of strengthening meaning or emphasizing a relation between words. Consider the relentless *h*'s in this line: "Horrendous horrors haunted Helen's happiness." Those *h*'s certainly suggest that Helen is being pursued, but they have a more comic than serious effect because they are overdone.

Assonance is the repetition of the same vowel sound in nearby words: "asl*ee*p under a tr*ee*"; "t*i*me and t*i*de"; "h*au*nt" and "*aw*esome"; "*ea*ch *e*vening." Both alliteration and assonance help to establish relations among words in a line or a series of lines. Whether the effect is *euphony* (lines that are musically pleasant to the ear and smooth, like the final lines of Dickinson's "A Bird came down the Walk—") or the effect is *cacophony* (lines that are discordant and difficult to pronounce, like the claim that "never my numb plunker fumbles" in Updike's "Player Piano"), the sounds of words in poetry can be as significant as the words' denotative or connotative meanings.

Rhyme

Like alliteration and assonance, *rhyme* is a way of creating sound patterns. Rhyme, broadly defined, consists of two or more words or phrases that repeat the same sounds: *happy* and *snappy*. Rhyme words often have similar spellings, but that is not a requirement of rhyme; what matters is that the words sound alike: *vain* rhymes with *reign* as well as *rain*. Moreover, words may look alike but not rhyme at all. In *eye rhyme* the spellings are similar, but the pronunciations are not, as with *bough* and *cough*, or *brow* and *blow*.

Not all poems employ rhyme. Many great poems have no rhymes, and many weak verses use rhyme as a substitute for poetry. These are especially apparent in commercial messages and greeting-card lines. At its worst, rhyme is merely a distracting decoration that can lead to dullness and predictability. But used skillfully, rhyme creates lines that are memorable and musical.

Rhyme is used in the following poem to imitate the sound of cascading water.

ROBERT SOUTHEY (1774–1843)

From "The Cataract of Lodore"   *1820*

"How does the water
Come down at Lodore?"
· · · · · · · · · · · · · ·
From its sources which well
In the tarn on the fell;
From its fountains
In the mountains, 5
Its rills and its gills;
Through moss and through brake,
It runs and it creeps
For awhile, till it sleeps 10
In its own little lake.
And thence at departing,
Awakening and starting,
It runs through the reeds
And away it proceeds, 15
Through meadow and glade,
In sun and in shade,
And through the wood-shelter,
Among crags in its flurry,
Helter-skelter, 20
Hurry-scurry.
Here it comes sparkling,
And there it lies darkling;
Now smoking and frothing
Its tumult and wrath in, 25
Till in this rapid race
On which it is bent,
It reaches the place
Of its steep descent.

The cataract strong 30
Then plunges along,
Striking and raging
As if a war waging
Its caverns and rocks among:
Rising and leaping, 35
Sinking and creeping,
Swelling and sweeping,

Showering and springing,
    Flying and flinging,
      Writhing and ringing,   40
Eddying and whisking,
Spouting and frisking,
Turning and twisting,
    Around and around
    With endless rebound!   45
    Smiting and fighting,
      A sight to delight in;
    Confounding, astounding,
Dizzying and deafening the ear with its sound.
. . . .

Dividing and gliding and sliding,   50
And falling and brawling and spawling,
And driving and riving and striving,
And sprinkling and twinkling and wrinkling,
And sounding and bounding and rounding,
And bubbling and troubling and doubling,   55
And grumbling and rumbling and tumbling,
And clattering and battering and shattering;
Retreating and beating and meeting and sheeting,
Delaying and straying and playing and spraying,
Advancing and prancing and glancing and dancing,   60
Recoiling, turmoiling and toiling and boiling,
And gleaming and streaming and steaming and beaming,
And rushing and flushing and brushing and gushing,
And flapping and rapping and clapping and slapping,
And curling and whirling and purling and twirling,   65
And thumping and plumping and bumping and jumping,
And dashing and flashing and splashing and clashing;
And so never ending, but always descending,
Sounds and motions forever and ever are blending,
All at once and all o'er, with a mighty uproar;   70
And this way the water comes down at Lodore.

    This deluge of rhymes consists of "Sounds and motions forever and ever . . . blending" (line 69). The pace quickens as the water creeps from its mountain source and then descends in rushing cataracts. As the speed of the water increases, so do the number of rhymes, until they run in fours: "dashing and flashing and splashing and clashing" (line 67). Most rhymes meander through poems instead of flooding them; nevertheless, Southey's use of rhyme suggests how sounds can flow with meanings. "The Cataract of Lodore" has been criticized, however, for overusing onomatopoeia. Some readers find the poem silly; others regard it as a brilliant example of sound effects. What do you think?

    A variety of types of rhyme is available to poets. The most common form, ***end rhyme,*** comes at the ends of lines (lines 14–17).

> It runs through the reeds
>> And away it proceeds,
> Through meadow and glade,
>> In sun and in shade.

Internal rhyme places at least one of the rhymed words within the line, as in "Dividing and gliding and sliding" (line 50) or, more subtly, in the fourth and final words of "In mist or cloud, on mast or shroud."

The rhyming of single-syllable words such as *glade* and *shade* is known as ***masculine rhyme:***

> Loveliest of trees, the cherry now
> Is hung with bloom along the bough.
> —A. E. Housman

Rhymes using words of more than one syllable are also called masculine when the same sound occurs in a final stressed syllable, as in *defend, contend; betray, away.* A ***feminine rhyme*** consists of a rhymed stressed syllable followed by one or more rhymed unstressed syllables, as in *butter, clutter; gratitude, attitude; quivering, shivering:*

> Lord confound this surly sister,
> Blight her brow and blotch and blister.
> —John Millington Synge

All the examples so far have been ***exact rhymes*** because they share the same stressed vowel sounds as well as any sounds that follow the vowel. In ***near rhyme*** (also called ***off rhyme, slant rhyme,*** and ***approximate rhyme***), the sounds are almost but not exactly alike. There are several kinds of near rhyme. One of the most common is ***consonance,*** an identical consonant sound preceded by a different vowel sound: *home, same; worth, breath; trophy, daffy.* Near rhyme can also be achieved by using different vowel sounds with identical consonant sounds: *sound, sand; kind, conned; fellow, fallow.* The dissonance of *blade* and *blood* in the following lines helps to reinforce their grim tone:

> Let the boy try along this bayonet-blade
> How cold steel is, and keen with hunger of blood.
> —Wilfred Owen

Near rhymes greatly broaden the possibility for musical effects in English, a language that, compared with Spanish or Italian, contains few exact rhymes. Do not assume, however, that a near rhyme represents a failed attempt at exact rhyme. Near rhymes allow a musical subtlety and variety and can avoid the sometimes overpowering jingling effects that exact rhymes may create.

These basic terms hardly exhaust the ways in which the sounds in poems can be labeled and discussed, but the terms can help you to describe how poets manipulate sounds for effect. Read "God's Grandeur" (p. 258) aloud and try to determine how the sounds of the lines contribute to their sense.

Sound and Meaning

Gerard Manley Hopkins (1844–1889)

God's Grandeur   *1877*

The world is charged with the grandeur of God
    It will flame out, like shining from shook foil;°   *shaken gold foil*
    It gathers to a greatness, like the ooze of oil
Crushed.° Why do men then now not reck his rod?°
Generations have trod, have trod, have trod;   5
    And all is seared with trade; bleared, smeared with toil;
    And wears man's smudge and shares man's smell: the soil
Is bare now, nor can foot feel, being shod.
And for all this, nature is never spent;
    There lives the dearest freshness deep down things;   10
And though the last lights off the black West went
    Oh, morning, at the brown brink eastward, springs —
Because the Holy Ghost over the bent
    World broods with warm breast and with ah! bright wings.

The subject of this poem is announced in the title and the first line: "The world is charged with the grandeur of God." The poem is a celebration of the power and greatness of God's presence in the world, but the speaker is also perplexed and dismayed by people who refuse to recognize God's authority and grandeur as they are manifested in the creation. Instead of glorifying God, "men" have degraded the earth through meaningless toil and cut themselves off from the spiritual renewal inherent in the beauty of nature. The relentless demands of commerce and industry have blinded people to the earth's natural and spiritual resources. In spite of this abuse and insensitivity to God's grandeur, however, "nature is never spent"; the morning light that "springs" in the east redeems the "black West" of the night and is a sign that the spirit of the Holy Ghost is ever present in the world. This summary of the poem sketches some of the thematic significance of the lines, but it does not do justice to how they are organized around the use of sound. Hopkins's poem, unlike Southey's "The Cataract of Lodore," employs sounds in a subtle and complex way.

In the opening line Hopkins uses alliteration — a device apparent in almost every line of the poem — to connect "Go*d*" to the "worl*d*," which is "charge*d*" with his "gran*d*eur." These consonants unify the line as well. The alliteration in lines 2 and 3 suggests a harmony in the creation: The *f*'s in "*f*lame" and "*f*oil," the *sh*'s in "*sh*ining" and "*sh*ook," the *g*'s in "*g*athers" and "*g*reatness," and the visual (not alliterative) similarities of "*oo*ze of *oi*l" emphasize a world that is held together by God's will.

That harmony is abruptly interrupted by the speaker's angry question in line 4: "Why do men then now not reck his rod?" The question is as painful to the speaker as it is difficult to pronounce. The arrangement of

4 *Crushed:* Olives crushed in their oil;   *reck his rod:* Obey God.

the alliteration ("*now*," "*not*"; "*reck*," "*rod*"), the assonance ("n*o*t," "r*o*d"; "m*e*n," "th*e*n," "r*e*ck"), and the internal rhyme ("m*en*," "th*en*") contribute to the difficulty in saying the line, a difficulty associated with human behavior. That behavior is introduced in line 5 by the repetition of "have trod" to emphasize the repeated mistakes — sins — committed by human beings. The tone is dirgelike because humanity persists in its mistaken path rather than progressing. The speaker's horror at humanity is evident in the cacophonous sounds of lines 6 to 8. Here the alliteration of "*sm*eared," "*sm*udge," and "*sm*ell" along with the internal rhymes of "s*eared*," "bl*eared*," and "sm*eared*" echo the disgust with which the speaker views humanity's "toil" with the "soil," an end rhyme that calls attention to our mistaken equation of nature with production rather than with spirituality.

In contrast to this cacophony, the final six lines build toward the joyful recognition of the new possibilities that accompany the rising sun. This recognition leads to the euphonic description of the "H*o*ly Gh*o*st *o*ver" (notice the reassuring consistency of the assonance) the world. Traditionally represented as a dove, the Holy Ghost brings love and peace to the "*w*orld," and "*b*roods *w*ith *w*arm *b*reast and *w*ith ah! *b*right *w*ings." The effect of this alliteration is mellifluous: The sound bespeaks the harmony that prevails at the end of the poem resulting from the speaker's recognition that "nature is never spent" because God loves and protects the world.

The sounds of "God's Grandeur" enhance the poem's theme; more can be said about its sounds, but it is enough to point out here that for this poem the sound strongly echoes the theme in nearly every line.

Rhythm and Meter

The rhythms of everyday life surround us in regularly recurring movements and sounds. As you read these words, your heart pulsates while somewhere else a clock ticks, a cradle rocks, a drum beats, a dancer sways, a foghorn blasts, a wave recedes, or a child skips. We may tend to overlook rhythm since it is so tightly woven into the fabric of our experience, but it is there nonetheless, one of the conditions of life. Rhythm is also one of the conditions of speech because the voice alternately rises and falls as words are stressed or unstressed and as the pace quickens or slackens. In poetry **rhythm** refers to the recurrence of stressed and unstressed sounds. Depending on how the sounds are arranged, this can result in a pace that is fast or slow, choppy or smooth.

Poets use rhythm to create pleasurable sound patterns and to reinforce meanings. "Rhythm," Edith Sitwell once observed, "might be described as, to the world of sound, what light is to the world of sight. It shapes and gives new meaning." Prose can use rhythm effectively too, but prose that does so tends to be an exception. The following exceptional lines are from a speech by Winston Churchill to the House of Commons after Allied forces lost a great battle to German forces at Dunkirk during World War II:

We shall not flag or fail. We shall go on to the end. We shall fight in France, we shall fight on the seas and oceans, we shall fight with growing confidence and growing strength in the air, we shall defend our island, whatever the cost may be, we shall fight on the beaches, we shall fight on the landing grounds, we shall fight in the fields and in the streets, we shall fight in the hills; we shall never surrender.

The stressed repetition of "we shall" bespeaks the resolute singleness of purpose that Churchill had to convey to the British people if they were to win the war. Repetition is also one of the devices used in poetry to create rhythmic effects. In the following excerpt from "Song of the Open Road," Walt Whitman urges the pleasures of limitless freedom on his reader:

> Allons!° the road is before us!   *Let's go!*
> It is safe — I have tried it — my own feet have tried it well — be not detain'd!
> Let the paper remain on the desk unwritten, and the book on the
>   shelf unopen'd!
> Let the tools remain in the workshop! Let the money remain unearn'd!
> Let the school stand! mind not the cry of the teacher!   5
> Let the preacher preach in his pulpit! Let the lawyer plead in the
>   court, and the judge expound the law.
>
> Camerado,° I give you my hand!   *friend*
> I give you my love more precious than money,
> I give you myself before preaching or law;
> Will you give me yourself? will you come travel with me?   10
> Shall we stick by each other as long as we live?

These rhythmic lines quickly move away from conventional values to the open road of shared experiences. Their recurring sounds are not created by rhyme or alliteration and assonance but by the repetition of words and phrases.

Although the repetition of words and phrases can be an effective means of creating rhythm in poetry, the more typical method consists of patterns of accented or unaccented syllables. Words contain syllables that are either stressed or unstressed. A **stress** (or **accent**) places more emphasis on one syllable than on another. We say "*syl*lable" not "syl*lable*," "*em*phasis" not "em*pha*sis." We routinely stress syllables when we speak: "*Is* she con*tent* with the *con*tents of the *yel*low *pack*age?" To distinguish between two people we might say "Is *she* content . . . ?" In this way stress can be used to emphasize a particular word in a sentence. Poets often arrange words so that the desired meaning is suggested by the rhythm; hence, emphasis is controlled by the poet rather than left entirely to the reader.

When a rhythmic pattern of stresses recurs in a poem, the result is **meter**. Taken together, all the metrical elements in a poem make up what is called the poem's **prosody. Scansion** consists of measuring the stresses in a line to determine its metrical pattern. Several methods can be used to mark lines. One widely used system employs ´ for a stressed syllable and ˘ for an unstressed syllable. In a sense, the stress mark represents the equivalent of tapping one's foot to a beat:

Híckŏrў, díckŏrў, dóck,
Thĕ móuse răn úp thĕ clóck.
Thĕ clóck strŭck óne,
Ănd dówn hĕ rún,
Híckŏrў, díckŏrў, dóck.

In the first two lines and the final line of this familiar nursery rhyme we hear three stressed syllables. In lines 3 and 4, where the meter changes for variety, we hear just two stressed syllables. The combination of stresses provides the pleasure of the rhythm we hear.

To hear the rhythms of "Hickory, dickory, dock" does not require a formal study of meter. Nevertheless, an awareness of the basic kinds of meter that appear in English poetry can enhance your understanding of how a poem achieves its effects. Understanding the sound effects of a poem and having a vocabulary with which to discuss those effects can intensify your pleasure in poetry. Although the study of meter can be extremely technical, the terms used to describe the basic meters of English poetry are relatively easy to comprehend.

The *foot* is the metrical unit by which a line of poetry is measured. A foot usually consists of one stressed and one or two unstressed syllables. A vertical line is used to separate the feet: "Thĕ clóck | strŭck óne" consists of two feet. A foot of poetry can be arranged in a variety of patterns; here are five of the chief ones:

Foot	Pattern	Example
iamb	˘ ´	ăwáy
trochee	´ ˘	Lóvelў
anapest	˘ ˘ ´	ŭndĕrstánd
dactyl	´ ˘ ˘	déspĕrătĕ
spondee	´ ´	déad sét

The most common lines in English poetry contain meters based on iambic feet. However, even lines that are predominantly iambic will often include variations to create particular effects. Other important patterns include trochaic, anapestic, and dactylic feet. The spondee is not a sustained meter but occurs for variety or emphasis.

Iambic
Whăt képt | hĭs eýes | frŏm gív | ĭng báck | thĕ gáze

Trochaic
Hé wăs | lóudĕr | thán thĕ | préachĕr

Anapestic
Ĭ ăm cálled | tŏ thĕ frónt | ŏf thĕ róom

Dactylic
Síng ĭt áll | mérrĭlў

These meters have different rhythms and can create different effects. Iambic and anapestic are known as **rising meters** because they move from unstressed to stressed sounds, while trochaic and dactylic are known as *falling meters.* Anapests and dactyls tend to move more lightly and rapidly than iambs or trochees. Although no single kind of meter can be considered always better than another for a given subject, it is possible to determine whether the meter of a specific poem is appropriate for its subject. A serious poem about a tragic death would most likely not be well served by lilting rhythms. Keep in mind too that though one or another of these four basic meters might constitute the predominant rhythm of a poem, variations can occur within lines to change the pace or call attention to a particular word.

A *line* is measured by the number of feet it contains. Here, for example, is an iambic line with three feet: "If she | should write | a note." These are the names for line lengths:

monometer: one foot   pentameter: five feet

dimeter: two feet   hexameter: six feet

trimeter: three feet   heptameter: seven feet

tetrameter: four feet   octameter: eight feet

By combining the name of a line length with the name of a foot, we can describe the metrical qualities of a line concisely. Consider, for example, the pattern of feet and length of this line:

I didn't want the boy to hit the dog.

The iambic rhythm of this line falls into five feet; hence it is called *iambic pentameter.* Iambic is the most common pattern in English poetry because its rhythm appears so naturally in English speech and writing. Unrhymed iambic pentameter is called **blank verse;** Shakespeare's plays are built on such lines.

Less common than the iamb, trochee, anapest, or dactyl is the **spondee,** a two-syllable foot in which both syllables are stressed (´ ´). Note the effect of the spondaic foot at the beginning of this line:

Dead set | against | the plan | he went | away.

Spondees can slow a rhythm and provide variety and emphasis, particularly in iambic and trochaic lines. A line that ends with a stressed syllable is said to have a **masculine ending,** whereas a line that ends with an extra unstressed syllable is said to have a *feminine ending.* Consider, for example, these two lines from Timothy Steele's "Waiting for the Storm" (the entire poem appears on p. 264):

feminine: The sand | at my feet | grow cold | er,
masculine: The damp | air chill | and spread.

The effects of English meters are easily seen in the following lines by Samuel Taylor Coleridge, in which the rhythm of each line illustrates the meter described in it:

> Trochee trips from long to short;
> From long to long in solemn sort
> Slow Spondee stalks; strong foot yet ill able
> Ever to come up with Dactylic trisyllable.
> Iambics march from short to long —
> With a leap and a bound the swift Anapests throng.

The speed of a line is also affected by the number of pauses in it. A pause within a line is called a *caesura* and is indicated by a double vertical line (‖). A caesura can occur anywhere within a line and need not be indicated by punctuation:

> Camerado, ‖ I give you my hand!
> I give you my love ‖ more precious than money.

A slight pause occurs within each of these lines and at its end. Both kinds of pauses contribute to the lines' rhythm.

When a line has a pause at its end, it is called an ***end-stopped line.*** Such pauses reflect normal speech patterns and are often marked by punctuation. A line that ends without a pause and continues into the next line for its meaning is called a ***run-on line.*** Running over from one line to another is also called ***enjambment.*** The first and eighth lines of the following poem are run-on lines; the rest are end-stopped.

WILLIAM WORDSWORTH (1770–1850)

My Heart Leaps Up   1807

My heart leaps up when I behold
 A rainbow in the sky:
So was it when my life began;
So is it now I am a man;
So be it when I shall grow old,
 Or let me die!
The child is father of the Man;
And I could wish my days to be
Bound each to each by natural piety.

Run-on lines have a different rhythm from end-stopped lines. Lines 3 and 4 and lines 8 and 9 are iambic, but the effect of their two rhythms is very different when we read these lines aloud. The enjambment of lines 8 and 9 reinforces their meaning; just as the "days" are bound together, so are the lines.

The rhythm of a poem can be affected by several devices: the kind and number of stresses within lines, the length of lines, and the kinds of pauses that appear within lines or at their ends. In addition, as we saw in Chapter 20, the sound of a poem is affected by alliteration, assonance, rhyme, and consonance. These sounds help to create rhythms by controlling our pronunciations, as in the following lines by Alexander Pope:

> Soft is the strain when Zephyr gently blows,
> And the smooth stream in smoother numbers flows;
> But when loud surges lash the sounding shore,
> The hoarse, rough verse should like the torrent roar.

These lines are effective because their rhythm and sound work with their meaning.

Suggestions for Scanning a Poem

These suggestions should help you in talking about a poem's meter.

1. After reading the poem through, read it aloud and mark the stressed syllables in each line. Then mark the unstressed syllables.
2. From your markings, identify what kind of foot is dominant (iambic, trochaic, dactylic, or anapestic) and divide the lines into feet, keeping in mind that the vertical line marking a foot may come in the middle of a word as well as at its beginning or end.
3. Determine the number of feet in each line. Remember that there may be variations; some lines may be shorter or longer than the predominant meter. What is important is the overall pattern. Do not assume that variations represent the poet's inability to fulfill the overall pattern. Notice the effects of variations and whether they emphasize words and phrases or disrupt your expectation for some other purpose.
4. Listen for pauses within lines and mark the caesuras; many times there will be no punctuation to indicate them.
5. Recognize that scansion does not always yield a definitive measurement of a line. Even experienced readers may differ over the scansion of a given line. What is important is not a precise description of the line but an awareness of how a poem's rhythms contribute to its effects.

The following poem demonstrates how you can use an understanding of meter and rhythm to gain a greater appreciation for what a poem is saying.

TIMOTHY STEELE (B. 1948)

Waiting for the Storm   1986

Breeze sént | a wrínk | ling dárk | ness
Acróss | the bay. ‖ I knélt

Beneath | an up | turned boat,
And, mo | ment by mo | ment, felt

The sand | at my feet | grow cold | er,
The damp | air chill | and spread.
Then the | first rain | drops sound | ed
On the hull | above | my head.

The predominant meter of this poem is iambic trimeter, but there is plenty of variation as the storm rapidly approaches and finally begins to pelt the sheltered speaker. The emphatic spondee ("Breeze sent") pushes the darkness quickly across the bay while the caesura at the end of the sentence in line 2 creates a pause that sets up a feeling of suspense and expectation that is measured in the ticking rhythm of line 4, a run-on line that brings us into the chilly sand and air of the second stanza. Perhaps the most impressive sound effect used in the poem appears in the second syllable of "sounded" in line 7. That "ed" precedes the sound of the poem's final word "head" just as if it were the first drop of rain hitting the hull above the speaker. The visual, tactile, and auditory images make "Waiting for the Storm" an intense sensory experience.

SOME COMMON POETIC FORMS

Poems come in a variety of shapes. Although the best poems always have their own unique qualities, many of them also conform to traditional patterns. Frequently the *form* of a poem — its overall structure or shape — follows an already established design. A poem that can be categorized by the patterns of its lines, meter, rhymes, and stanzas is considered a *fixed form* because it follows a prescribed model such as a sonnet. However, poems written in a fixed form do not always fit models precisely; writers sometimes work variations on traditional forms to create innovative effects.

Not all poets are content with variations on traditional forms. Some prefer to create their own structures and shapes. Poems that do not conform to established patterns of meter, rhyme, and stanza are called *free verse* or *open form* poetry. This kind of poetry creates its own ordering principles through the careful arrangement of words and phrases in line lengths that embody rhythms appropriate to the meaning. Modern and contemporary poets in particular have learned to use the blank space on the page as a significant functional element (for a striking example, see Cummings's "l(a" on p. 222). Good poetry of this kind is structured in ways that can be as demanding, interesting, and satisfying as fixed forms. Open and fixed forms represent different poetic styles, but they are identical in the sense that both use language in concentrated ways to convey meanings, experiences, emotions, and effects.

A familiarity with some of the most frequently used fixed forms of poetry is useful because it allows for a better understanding of how a poem works. Classifying patterns allows us to talk about the effects of established rhythm and rhyme and recognize how significant variations from them affect the pace and meaning of the lines. An awareness of form also allows us to anticipate how a poem is likely to proceed. As we shall see, a sonnet creates a different set of expectations in a reader from those of, say, a limerick. A reader isn't likely to find in limericks the kind of serious themes that often make their way into sonnets. The discussion that follows identifies some of the important poetic forms frequently encountered in English poetry.

The shape of a fixed form poem is often determined by the way in which the lines are organized into stanzas. A *stanza* consists of a grouping of lines, set off by a space, that usually has a set pattern of meter and rhyme. This pattern is ordinarily repeated in other stanzas throughout the poem. What is usual is not obligatory, however; some poems may use a different pattern for each stanza, somewhat like paragraphs in prose.

Traditionally, though, stanzas do share a common **rhyme scheme,** the pattern of end rhymes. We can map out rhyme schemes by noting patterns of rhyme with lowercase letters: The first rhyme sound is designated *a,* the second becomes *b,* the third *c,* and so on.

Poets often create their own stanzaic patterns; hence there is an infinite number of kinds of stanzas. One way of talking about stanzaic forms is to describe a given stanza by how many lines it contains.

A *couplet* consists of two lines that usually rhyme and have the same meter; couplets are frequently not separated from each other by space on the page. A *heroic couplet* consists of rhymed iambic pentameter. Here is an example from Pope's "An Essay on Criticism":

One science only will one genius fit;	*a*
So vast is art, so narrow human wit:	*a*
Not only bounded to peculiar arts,	*b*
But oft in those confined to single parts.	*b*

A *tercet* is a three-line stanza. When all three lines rhyme they are called a *triplet.*

Terza rima consists of an interlocking three-line rhyme scheme: *aba, bcb, cdc, ded,* and so on. Dante's *The Divine Comedy* uses this pattern, as does Frost's "Acquainted with the Night" (p. 245).

A *quatrain,* or four-line stanza, is the most common stanzaic form in the English language and can have various meters and rhyme schemes (if any). The most common rhyme schemes are *aabb, abba, aaba,* and *abcb.* This last pattern is especially characteristic of the popular *ballad stanza,* which consists of alternating eight- and six-syllable lines. Samuel Taylor Coleridge adopted this pattern in "The Rime of the Ancient Mariner"; here is one representative stanza:

> All in a hot and copper sky
> The bloody Sun, at noon,
> Right up above the mast did stand,
> No bigger than the Moon.

There are a number of longer stanzaic forms and the list of types of stanzas could be extended considerably, but knowing these three most basic patterns should prove helpful to you in talking about the form of a great many poems. In addition to stanzaic forms, there are fixed forms that characterize entire poems. Lyric poems can be, for example, sonnets, villanelles, sestinas, or epigrams.

Sonnet

The **sonnet** has been a popular literary form in English since the sixteenth century, when it was adopted from the Italian *sonnetto,* meaning "little song." A sonnet consists of fourteen lines, usually written in iambic pentameter. Because the sonnet has been such a favorite form, writers have experimented with many variations on its essential structure. Nevertheless, there are two basic types of sonnets: the Italian and the English.

The **Italian sonnet** (also known as the **Petrarchan sonnet,** from the fourteenth-century Italian poet Petrarch) divides into two parts. The first eight lines (the **octave**) typically rhyme *abbaabba.* The final six lines (the **sestet**) may vary; common patterns are *cdecde, cdcdcd,* and *cdccdc.* Very often the octave presents a situation, attitude, or problem that the sestet comments upon or resolves, as in John Keats's "On First Looking into Chapman's Homer."

JOHN KEATS (1795–1821)

On First Looking into Chapman's Homer°   *1816*

> Much have I traveled in the realms of gold,
>   And many goodly states and kingdoms seen;
>   Round many western islands have I been
> Which bards in fealty to Apollo° hold.
> Oft of one wide expanse had I been told   5
>   That deep-browed Homer ruled as his demesne;
>   Yet did I never breathe its pure serene°   *atmosphere*
> Till I heard Chapman speak out loud and bold:
> Then felt I like some watcher of the skies
>   When a new planet swims into his ken;   10
> Or like stout Cortez° when with eagle eyes

Chapman's Homer: Before reading George Chapman's (c. 1560–1634) poetic Elizabethan translations of Homer's *Iliad* and *Odyssey,* Keats had known only stilted and pedestrian eighteenth-century translations.   4 *Apollo:* Greek god of poetry.   11 *Cortez:* Vasco Núñez de Balboa, not Hernando Cortés, was the first European to sight the Pacific from Darien, a peak in Panama.

He stared at the Pacific — and all his men
Looked at each other with a wild surmise —
Silent, upon a peak in Darien.

CONSIDERATIONS FOR CRITICAL THINKING AND WRITING

1. FIRST RESPONSE. How do the images shift from the octave to the sestet? How does the tone change? Does the meaning?
2. What is the controlling metaphor of this poem?
3. What is it that the speaker discovers?
4. How does the rhythm of the lines change between the octave and the sestet? How does that change reflect the tones of both the octave and the sestet?
5. Does Keats's mistake concerning Cortés and Balboa affect your reading of the poem? Explain why or why not.

The **English sonnet,** more commonly known as the **Shakespearean sonnet,** is organized into three quatrains and a couplet, which typically rhyme *abab cdcd efef gg.* This rhyme scheme is more suited to English poetry because English has fewer rhyming words than Italian. For an example of an English sonnet, see William Shakespeare's "My mistress' eyes are nothing like the sun" (p. 841).

Villanelle

The *villanelle* is a fixed form consisting of nineteen lines of any length divided into six stanzas: five tercets and a concluding quatrain. The first and third lines of the initial tercet rhyme; these rhymes are repeated in each subsequent tercet (*aba*) and in the final two lines of the quatrain (*abaa*). Moreover, line 1 appears in its entirety as lines 6, 12, and 18, while line 3 appears as lines 9, 15, and 19. This form may seem to risk monotony, but in competent hands a villanelle can create haunting echoes, as in Dylan Thomas's "Do not go gentle into that good night."

DYLAN THOMAS (1914–1953)

Do not go gentle into that good night   1952

Do not go gentle into that good night,
Old age should burn and rave at close of day;
Rage, rage against the dying of the light.

Though wise men at their end know dark is right,
Because their words had forked no lightning they   5
Do not go gentle into that good night.

Good men, the last wave by, crying how bright
Their frail deeds might have danced in a green bay,
Rage, rage against the dying of the light.

Wild men who caught and sang the sun in flight,   10
And learn, too late, they grieved it on its way,
Do not go gentle into that good night.

Grave men, near death, who see with blinding sight
Blind eyes could blaze like meteors and be gay,
Rage, rage against the dying of the light.   15

And you, my father, there on the sad height,
Curse, bless, me now with your fierce tears, I pray.
Do not go gentle into that good night.
Rage, rage against the dying of the light.

CONSIDERATIONS FOR CRITICAL THINKING AND WRITING

1. FIRST RESPONSE. How does Thomas vary the meanings of the poem's two refrains: "Do not go gentle into that good night," and "Rage, rage against the dying of the light"?

2. Thomas's father was close to death when this poem was written. How does the tone contribute to the poem's theme?

3. How is "good" used in line 1?

4. Characterize the men who are "wise" (line 4), "Good" (7), "Wild" (10), and "Grave" (13).

5. What do figures of speech contribute to this poem?

6. Discuss this villanelle's sound effects.

Open Form

Many poems, especially those written in the twentieth century, are composed of lines that cannot be scanned for a fixed or predominant meter. Moreover, very often these poems do not rhyme. Known as *free verse* (from the French, *vers libre*), such lines can derive their rhythmic qualities from the repetition of words, phrases, or grammatical structures; the arrangement of words on the printed page; or some other means. In recent years the term *open form* has been used in place of *free verse* to avoid the erroneous suggestion that this kind of poetry lacks all discipline and shape.

Although the following two poems do not use measurable meters, they do have rhythm.

E. E. CUMMINGS (1894–1962)

in Just-   *1923*

in Just-
spring   when the world is mud-
luscious the little
lame balloonman

whistles   far   and wee   5

and eddieandbill come
running from marbles and
piracies and it's
spring

when the world is puddle-wonderful   10

the queer
old balloonman whistles
far   and   wee
and bettyandisbel come dancing
from hop-scotch and jump-rope and   15

it's
spring
and

    the

        goat-footed   20

balloonMan   whistles
far
and
wee

CONSIDERATIONS FOR CRITICAL THINKING AND WRITING

1. FIRST RESPONSE. What is the effect of this poem's arrangement of words
   and use of space on the page? How would the effect differ if it was written
   out in prose?

2. What is the effect of Cummings's combining the names "eddieandbill" and
   "bettyandisbel"?

3. The allusion in line 20 refers to Pan, a Greek god associated with nature.
   How does this allusion add to the meaning of the poem?

WALT WHITMAN (1819–1892)

From "I Sing the Body Electric"   1855

O my body! I dare not desert the likes of you in other men and women,
    nor the likes of the parts of you,
I believe the likes of you are to stand or fall with the likes of the soul, (and
    that they are the soul,)
I believe the likes of you shall stand or fall with my poems, and that they
    are my poems.
Man's, woman's, child's, youth's, wife's, husband's, mother's, father's,
    young man's, young woman's poems.
Head, neck, hair, ears, drop and tympan of the ears.   5

Eyes, eye-fringes, iris of the eye, eyebrows, and the waking or sleeping of
    the lids,
Mouth, tongue, lips, teeth, roof of the mouth, jaws, and the jaw-hinges,
Nose, nostrils of the nose, and the partition,
Cheeks, temples, forehead, chin, throat, back of the neck, neck-slue,
Strong shoulders, manly beard, scapula, hind-shoulders, and the ample
    side-round of the chest,   10
Upper-arm, armpit, elbow-socket, lower-arm, arm-sinews, arm-bones,
Wrist and wrist-joints, hand, palm, knuckles, thumb, forefinger, finger-
    joints, finger-nails,
Broad breast-front, curling hair of the breast, breast-bone, breast-side,
Ribs, belly, backbone, joints of the backbone,
Hips, hip-sockets, hip-strength, inward and outward round, man-balls,
    man-root,   15
Strong set of thighs, well carrying the trunk above,
Leg-fibers, knee, knee-pan, upper-leg, under-leg,
Ankles, instep, foot-ball, toes, toe-joints, the heel;
All attitudes, all the shapeliness, all the belongings of my or your body or
    of any one's body, male or female,
The lung-sponges, the stomach-sac, the bowels sweet and clean,   20
The brain in its folds inside the skull-frame,
Sympathies, heart-valves, palate-valves, sexuality, maternity,
Womanhood, and all that is a woman, and the man that comes from woman,
The womb, the teats, nipples, breast-milk, tears, laughter, weeping, love-
    looks, love-perturbations and risings,
The voice, articulation, language, whispering, shouting aloud,   25
Food, drink, pulse, digestion, sweat, sleep, walking, swimming,
Poise on the hips, leaping, reclining, embracing, arm-curving and tightening,
The continual changes of the flex of the mouth, and around the eyes,
The skin, the sunburnt shade, freckles, hair,
The curious sympathy one feels when feeling with the hand the naked
    meat of the body,   30
The circling rivers the breath, and breathing it in and out,
The beauty of the waist, and thence of the hips, and thence downward
    toward the knees,
The thin red jellies within you or within me, the bones and the marrow
    in the bones,
The exquisite realization of health;
O I say these are not the parts and poems of the body only, but of the soul,   35
O I say now these are the soul!

CONSIDERATIONS FOR CRITICAL THINKING AND WRITING

1. FIRST RESPONSE. What informs this speaker's attitude toward the human
   body?

2. Read the poem aloud. Is it simply a tedious enumeration of body parts, or
   do the lines achieve some kind of rhythmic cadence?

3. CRITICAL STRATEGIES. Read the section on gender criticism (pp. 70–72) in
   Chapter 3, "Applying a Critical Strategy." Does this poem challenge or
   affirm traditional ideas about men and women?

Explication

This casebook shows you how one student, Rose Bostwick, moves through the stages from first response to informal outline to the final draft of an explication of a poem by John Donne, "Death Be Not Proud." Because explications require an intensive examination of a text—in this case a poem—line by line, Rose read the following poem several times, looked up both familiar and unfamiliar words, and took careful notes on the connotations of each word. She also reviewed the elements of poetry covered in this chapter and paid careful attention to figurative language, irony, symbol, rhythm, sound, and so on. Because her final paper is more concerned with the overall effect of the combination of the elements than with a line-by-line breakdown, her early notes are not included here. As you read and reread "Death Be Not Proud," however, keep notes on how you think the elements of this poem work together, and to what overall effect.

JOHN DONNE (1572–1631)

John Donne, now regarded as a major poet of the early seventeenth century, wrote love poems at the beginning of his career but shifted to religious themes after converting from Catholicism to Anglicanism in the early 1590s. Although trained in law, he was also ordained a priest and became dean of St. Paul's Cathedral in London in 1621. The following poem is from "Holy

John Donne (1573–1631), the English meta-physical poet and writer of sermons, as depicted in an engraving by W. Skelton Sculp.

Sonnets" and reflects both his religious faith and his ability to create elegant arguments in verse.

Death Be Not Proud

1611

Death be not proud, though some have callèd thee
Mighty and dreadful, for thou art not so;
For those whom thou think'st thou dost overthrow
Die not, poor Death, nor yet canst thou kill me.
From rest and sleep, which but thy pictures° be,　　　　　　*images*　5
Much pleasure; then from thee much more must flow,
And soonest our best men with thee do go,
Rest of their bones, and soul's delivery.°　　　　　　　　　*deliverance*
Thou art slave to Fate, Chance, kings, and desperate men,
And dost with Poison, War, and Sickness dwell;　　　　　　*10*
And poppy or charms can make us sleep as well,
And better than thy stroke; why swell'st° thou then?　　　*swell with pride*
One short sleep past, we wake eternally
And death shall be no more; Death, thou shalt die.

CONSIDERATIONS FOR THINKING AND WRITING

1. FIRST RESPONSE. Why doesn't the speaker fear death? Explain why you find the argument convincing or not.
2. How does the speaker compare death with rest and sleep in lines 5–8? What is the point of this comparison?
3. Discuss the poem's rhythm by examining the breaks and end-stopped lines. How does the poem's rhythm contribute to its meaning?
4. What are the signs that this poem is structured as a sonnet?

In addition to keeping careful notes on the poem, Rose used the following Questions for Writing about Poetry to sort out which elements are most important to sorting out the effects and meanings of "Death Be Not Proud." You can use these questions to help you think, talk, and write about each poem in Thinking and Writing about Literature; *before you do, though, be sure that you have read the poem several times without worrying actively about interpretation. With poetry, as with all literature, it's important to allow yourself the pleasure of enjoying whatever makes itself apparent to you. Then on subsequent readings, use the questions to understand and appreciate how the poem works; remember to keep in mind that not all questions will necessarily be relevant to a particular poem.*

QUESTIONS FOR WRITING ABOUT POETRY

1. Who is the speaker? Is it possible to determine the speaker's age, sex, sensibilities, level of awareness, and values?

2. Is the speaker addressing anyone in particular?

3. How do you respond to the speaker? Favorably? Negatively? What is the situation? Are there any special circumstances that inform what the speaker says?

4. Is there a specific setting of time and place?

5. Does reading the poem aloud help you to understand it?

6. Does a paraphrase reveal the basic purpose of the poem?

7. What does the title emphasize?

8. Is the theme presented directly or indirectly?

9. Do any allusions enrich the poem's meaning?

10. How does the diction reveal meaning? Are any words repeated? Do any carry evocative connotative meanings? Are there any puns or other forms of verbal wit?

11. Are figures of speech used? How does the figurative language contribute to the poem's vividness and meaning?

12. Do any objects, persons, places, events, or actions have allegorical or symbolic meanings? What other details in the poem support your interpretation?

13. Is irony used? Are there any examples of situational irony, verbal irony, or dramatic irony? Is understatement or paradox used?

14. What is the tone of the poem? Is the tone consistent?

15. Does the poem use onomatopoeia, assonance, consonance, or alliteration? How do these sounds affect you?

16. What sounds are repeated? If there are rhymes, what is their effect? Do they seem forced or natural? Is there a rhyme scheme? Do the rhymes contribute to the poem's meaning?

17. Do the lines have a regular meter? What is the predominant meter? Are there significant variations? Does the rhythm seem appropriate for the tone of the poem?

18. Does the poem's form — its overall structure — follow an established pattern? Do you think the form is a suitable vehicle for the poem's meaning and effects?

19. Is the language of the poem intense and concentrated? Do you think it warrants more than one or two close readings?

20. Did you enjoy the poem? What, specifically, pleased or displeased you about what was expressed and how it was expressed?

21. Is there a particular critical approach that seems especially appropriate for this poem? (See the discussion of "Applying a Critical Strategy" beginning on p. 56.)

22. How might biographical information about the author help to determine the central concerns of the poem?

23. How might historical information about the poem provide a useful context for interpretation?

24. To what extent do your own experiences, values, beliefs, and assumptions inform your interpretation?

25. What kinds of evidence from the poem are you focusing on to support your interpretation? Does your interpretation leave out any important elements that might undercut or qualify your interpretation?

26. Given that there are a variety of ways to interpret the poem, which one seems the most useful to you?

A Sample First Response

After Rose has carefully read the poem and has a sense of how it works, she takes the first step toward a formal explication by writing informally about how the poem works and addressing the question: *Why doesn't the speaker fear Death? Explain why you find the argument convincing or not.* Note that at this point, she is not so concerned with textual evidence and detail as she will need to be in her final paper.

I've read the poem "Death Be Not Proud" by John Donne a few times now, and I have a sense of how it works. The poem is a sonnet, and each of the three quatrains presents a piece of the argument that Death should not be proud, because it is not really all-powerful, and may even be a source of pleasure. As a reader, I resist this seeming paradox at first, but I know it must be a trick, a riddle of some sort that the poem will proceed to untangle. I think one of the reasons the poem comes off as such a powerful statement is that Donne at first seems to be playful and paradoxical in his characterizations of Death. He's almost teasing Death. But beneath the teasing tone you feel the strong foundation of the real reason Death should not be proud--Donne's faith in the immortality of the soul. The poem begins to feel more solemn as it progresses, as the hints at the idea of immortality become more clearly articulated.

Donne utilizes two literary conventions to increase the effect of this poem: he uses the convention of personifying Death, so that he can address it directly, and he uses the metaphor of death as a kind of sleep. These two things determine the tone and the progression from playful to solemn in the poem.

```
     The last clause of the poem (line 14) plays with the para-
doxical--seeming character of what he's been declaring. It
seems the only thing susceptible to death is death itself Or,
when death becomes powerless is when it only has power over
itself.
```

A Sample Informal Outline

Explications are difficult assignments; the simplest way to organize an explication is to do a line-by-line reading, but that can quickly become rote for writer and reader. Because you want to organize your paper in the way that serves your thesis, it may help to write an informal outline that charts how you think the argument moves. You may find, for example, that the argument is most persuasive if you start with the final lines and go back to the beginning of the poem or passage. Rose discovers, as you'll see in the following outline, that her argument works best if she begins at the beginning.

Thesis: From the very first word, addressing "Death" directly, Donne uses the literary conventions of personifying death and comparing it to sleep to begin an argument that Death should not be proud of its might or dreadfulness. But these two elements of his argument come to be seen as the superficial points when the true reason for death's powerlessness becomes clear. The Christian belief in the immortality of the soul is the reason for death's powerlessness and likeness to sleep.

Body of essay: Show how argument proceeds by quatrains from playful address to Death, and statement that Death is much like sleep, its "picture," to statement that Death is "slave" to other forces (and so should not be proud of being the mightiest), to the couplet, which articulates clearly the idea of immortality and gives the final paradox, "Death, thou shalt die."

Conclusion: Donne's faith in the immortality of the soul enables him to "prove" in this argument that Death is truly like its metaphorical representation, sleep. Faith allows him to derive a source for this conventional trope, and it allows him to state his truth in paradoxes. He relies on the conventional idea that death is an end, and a conqueror, and the only all-powerful force, to make the paradoxes that lend his argument the force of mystery — the mystery of faith.

A Sample Student Explication

In Rose's final draft of her explication, she focuses on the use of metaphor in "Death Be Not Proud." Her essay comments on every line of the poem and provides a coherent reading that relates each line to the speaker's intense awareness of death. Although the essay discusses each stanza in the order that it appears, the introductory paragraph provides a brief overview explaining how the poem's metaphors and arguments contribute to its total meaning. In addition, Rose does not hesitate to discuss a line out of sequence when it can be usefully connected to another phrase. She also works quotations into her sentences to support her points. When something is added to a quotation to clarify it, it is enclosed in brackets so her words will not be mistaken for the poet's, and a slash is used to indicate line divisions: "soonest . . . with thee do go, / [for] Rest of their bones, and soul's delivery." Finally, because the essay focuses on a short poem, it is not necessary to include line numbers, though they would be required in a study of a longer work. As you read through her final draft, remember that the word *explication* comes from the Latin *explicare,* "to unfold." How successful do you think Rose is at unfolding this poem to reveal how it works and what it signifies?

Rose Bostwick

English 101

Prof. Hart

February 14, 20--

The Use of Conventional Metaphors for Death
in John Donne's "Death Be Not Proud"

In the sonnet which begins, "Death be not proud . . ."
John Donne argues that death is not "mighty and dreadful," but is more like its metaphorical representation,
sleep, and is even a source of pleasure and rest. Donne
builds this argument on two foundations. One is made up
of the metaphors and literary conventions for death:
death is compared with sleep, and is often personified,
so that it can be addressed directly. The poem is an address to death that at first seems paradoxical and somewhat playful, but which then rises in all the emotion of
faith as it reveals the second foundation of the argu-
ment--the Christian belief in the immortality of the
soul. Seen against the backdrop of this belief, death
loses its powerful threat and comes to be seen as only a
metaphorical sleep, or rest.

The poem is an argument that proceeds according to
the structure of the sonnet form. Each quatrain contains
a new development or aspect of the argument, and the
final couplet serves as a conclusion. The metrical scheme
is mainly iambic pentameter, but in several places in
the poem, the stress pattern is altered for emphasis.
For example, the first foot of the poem is inverted, so
that "Death," the first word, receives the stress. This
announces to us right away that Death is being personified and addressed. This inversion also serves to begin
the poem energetically and forcefully. The second line
behaves in the same way. The first syllable of "Mighty"
receives the stress, emphasizing the meaning of the word
and its assumed relation to Death.

Bostwick 2

This first quatrain offers the first paradox and
sets up the argument that death has been conventionally
personified with the wrong attributes, might and dreadfulness. The poet tells death not to be proud, "though
some have called thee / Mighty and dreadful," because,
he says, death is not so. Donne will turn this conventional characterization of death on its head with
the paradox of the third and fourth lines: he says the
people overthrown by death (as if by a conqueror) "Die
not, poor death, nor yet canst thou kill me." These
lines establish the paradox of death not being able to
cause death.

The next quatrain will not begin to answer the
question of why this paradox is so, but will posit
another slight paradox--the idea of death as pleasurable.
In lines 5-8, Donne uses the literary convention of
describing death as a metaphorical sleep, or rest, to
construct the argument that death must give pleasure:
"From rest and sleep, which but thy pictures be, / Much
pleasure, then from thee much more must flow." At this
point, the argument seems almost playful, but is carefully hinting at the solemnity of the deeper foundation
of the belief in immortality. The metaphor of sleep for
death includes the idea of waking; one doesn't sleep forever. The next two lines put forth the idea that death
is pleasurable enough to be desired by "our best men"
who "soonest . . . with thee do go, / [for] Rest of their
bones, and soul's delivery." This last line comes closer
to announcing the true reason for death's powerlessness
and pleasure: it is the way to the "soul's delivery" from
the body and life on earth, and implicitly, into another,
better realm.

A new reason for death's powerlessness arises in the
next four lines. The poet says to death:

Thou art slave to Fate, Chance, kings,
   and desperate men,
And dost with Poison, War, and Sickness
   dwell;
And poppy or charms can make us sleep as
   well,
And better than thy stroke; why swell'st
   thou then?

Donne argues here that there are forces more powerful
than death that actually control it. Fate and chance
determine when death occurs, and to whom it comes. Kings,
with the powers of law and war, can summon death and
throw it on whom they wish. And desperate men, murderers
or suicides, can also summon death with the strength of
their emotions. In lines 11 and 12, Donne again uses the
metaphor of death as a kind of sleep, but says that drugs
or "charms" give one a better sleep than death. And he
asks playfully why death should be so proud, after all
these illustrations of its weakness have been given: "why
swell'st thou then?"

     Finally, with the last couplet, Donne reveals the
true, deeper reason behind his argument that death should
not be proud of its power. These lines also offer an
explanation of the metaphor for death of sleep, or rest:

One short sleep past, we wake eternally
And death shall be no more; Death, thou
   shalt die.

After death, the soul lives on, according to Christian
theology and belief. In the Christian heaven, where the
soul is immortal, death will no longer exist, and so this
last paradox, "Death, thou shalt die," becomes true.
Again in this line, a significant inversion of metrical

stress occurs. "Death," in the second clause, receives
the stress, recalling the first line, emphasizing that it
is an address and giving the clause a forceful sense of
finality. His belief in the immortality of the soul
enables Donne to "prove" in this argument that death is
in actuality like its metaphorical representation, sleep.
His faith allows him to derive a source for this conventional metaphor and to "disprove" the metaphor of death
as an all-powerful conqueror. His Christian beliefs also
allow him to state his truth in paradoxes, the mysteries
which are justified by the mystery of faith.

7

Reading and Writing about Drama

READING DRAMA RESPONSIVELY

The publication of a short story, novel, or poem represents for most writers the final step in a long creative process that might have begun with an idea, issue, emotion, or question that demanded expression. *Playwrights* — writers who make plays — may begin a work in the same way as other writers, but rarely are they satisfied with only its publication because most dramatic literature — what we call *plays* — is written to be performed by actors on a stage before an audience. Playwrights typically create a play keeping in mind not only readers but also actors, producers, directors, costumers, designers, technicians, and a theater full of other support staff who have a hand in presenting the play to a live audience.

Drama is literature equipped with arms, legs, tears, laughs, whispers, shouts, and gestures that are alive and immediate. Indeed, the word *drama* derives from the Greek word *dran*, meaning "to do" or "to perform." The text of many plays — the *script* — may come to life fully only when the written words are transformed into a performance. Although there are plays that do not invite production, they are relatively few. Such plays, written to be read rather than performed, are called *closet dramas.* In this kind of work (primarily associated with nineteenth-century English literature), literary art outweighs all other considerations. The majority of playwrights, however, view the written word as the beginning of a larger creation and hope that a producer will deem their scripts worthy of production.

Given that most playwrights intend their works to be performed, it might be argued that reading a play is a poor substitute for seeing it acted on a stage — perhaps something like reading a recipe without having access to the ingredients and a kitchen. This analogy is tempting, but it overlooks the literary dimensions of a script; the words we hear on a stage were written first. Read from a page, these words can feed an imagination in ways that a recipe cannot satisfy a hungry cook. We can fill in a play's missing faces, voices, actions, and settings in much the same way that we imagine these elements in a short story or novel. Like any play director, we are free to include as many ingredients as we have an appetite for.

This imaginative collaboration with the playwright creates a mental world that can be nearly as real and vivid as a live performance. Sometimes readers find that they prefer their own reading of a play to a director's interpretation. Shakespeare's Hamlet, for instance, has been presented as a whining son, but you may read him as a strong prince. Rich plays often accommodate a wide range of imaginative responses to their texts. Reading, then, is an excellent way to appreciate and evaluate a production of a play. Moreover, reading is valuable in its own right because it allows us to enter the playwright's created world even when a theatrical production is unavailable.

Reading a play, however, requires more creative imagining than sitting in an audience watching actors on a stage presenting lines and actions before you. As a reader you become the play's director; you construct an interpretation based on the playwright's use of language, development of character, arrangement of incidents, description of settings, and directions for staging. Keeping track of the playwright's handling of these elements will help you to organize your response to the play. You may experience suspense, fear, horror, sympathy, or humor, but whatever experience a play evokes, ask yourself why you respond to it as you do. You may discover that your assessment of Hamlet's character is different from someone else's, but whether you find him heroic, indecisive, neurotic, or a complex of competing qualities, you'll be better equipped to articulate your interpretation of him if you pay attention to your responses and ask yourself questions as you read. Consider, for example, how his reactions might be similar to or different from your own. How does his language reveal his character? Does his behavior seem justified? How would you play the role yourself? What actor do you think might best play the Hamlet that you have created in your imagination? Why would he or she (women have also played Hamlet onstage) fill the role best?

These kinds of questions (see Questions for Writing about Drama, p. 506) can help you to think and talk about your responses to a play. Happily, such questions needn't — and often can't — be fully answered as you read the play. Frequently you must experience the entire play before you can determine how its elements work together. That's why reading a play can be such a satisfying experience. You wouldn't think of asking a live actor onstage to repeat her lines because you didn't quite comprehend their significance, but you can certainly reread a page in a book. Rereading allows you to replay language, characters, and incidents carefully and thoroughly to your own satisfaction.

THE ELEMENTS

All plays share some basic elements, or conventions: they have settings, characters, plots, and themes. In addition, many modern plays share an emphasis on props, lighting, music, costume. Almost all plays take place within a defined time and place, often divided into parts. If the entire play takes place in a single location and unfolds in one continuous action, it is called a *one-act play;* *Trifles* (p. 496) is an example of a one-act play. The main divisions of a full-length play are typically acts; their ends are indicated by lowering a curtain or turning up the houselights. Playwrights frequently employ acts to accommodate changes in time, setting, characters on stage, or mood. In many full-length plays, such as Shakespeare's *Hamlet,* acts are further divided into *scenes;* according to tradition a scene changes when the location of the action changes or when a new character enters. Acts and scenes are *conventions* that are understood and accepted by audiences because they have come, through usage and time, to be recognized as familiar techniques.

Setting

The *setting* of a play is usually described at the very beginning; it establishes an atmosphere that will influence our judgment of the characters, plot, and theme. Setting refers to both the chronology and geography within which the action takes place and to the scenery, or physical surroundings of the characters. In *Hamlet,* the larger setting is established at the beginning with the information: "SCENE: *Denmark.*" As Act I, Scene I opens, we are further told that we are at the castle *"Elsinore. A platform before the castle."* Setting is often further developed through the use of *exposition,* a device that provides the necessary background information about the characters and their circumstances. As Bernardo and Francisco begin to speak at the beginning of *Hamlet,* we learn that it is a winter night (the clock is "now struck twelve," and "'tis bitter cold") and that the two men are guarding the castle and hoping not to encounter the ghost of the king. Often the descriptions of setting, especially for nineteenth- and twentieth-century plays, are more elaborate than those for *Hamlet,* explicitly suggesting what the symbolic value for a particular detail of the set might be.

Characterization

The playwright usually tells us at the beginning of the play who the characters are, and often gives us further information about their relationship to each other, as well as their personalities, dress, and position in life. Stage directions, or the playwright's instructions about how the actors are to move and behave, often give additional information about characterization. In *Trifles,* for example, directions tell the actress playing Mrs. Hale to respond "stiffly" to Mr. Henderson. *Characterization,* as in fiction, is the process through which a character is made real for the reader. A playwright can establish character by showing us what each character says and how he or she acts and by telling us additional information about the character (often conveyed through stage directions). Because we learn about characters through their own words and actions, they can be highly complex; and in fact in many plays the entire shape of the action derives from the characters, from their strengths and weaknesses. Most plays have an identifiable *protagonist,* or central character with whom we tend to identify; and an *antagonist,* a character who is in some kind of opposition to the central character. Another word to describe contrasting characters is *foil* — meaning a character whose behaviors and values clash with the protagonist's. The way characters interact with each other often embodies the major *conflict* presented in the play. In the hands of a skillful playwright, *exposition* presents necessary background information about the characters. In the same way, the *dialogue* — verbal exchanges between the characters — not only provides important information about characters but also moves the action forward.

Plot

As with fiction, *plot* in drama refers to the selection and arrangement of incidents to shape the action and suggest a particular focus. Discussions of plot include not just what happens but also how and why things happen the way they do. Many plays are plotted in what has come be called a *pyramidal pattern,* because the plot is divided into three essential parts. Such plays begin with a *rising action,* in which complication creates conflict for the protagonist. The resulting tension builds to the second major division, known as the *climax,* when the action reaches a final *crisis,* a turning point that has a powerful effect on the protagonist. The third part consists of *falling action;* here the tensions are diminished in the resolution of the plot's conflicts and complications (the *resolution* is also referred to as the *conclusion* or *dénouement,* a French word meaning "unknotting"). These divisions may occur at different times. There are many variations to this pattern. The terms are helpful for identifying various moments and movements within a given plot, but they are less useful if seen as a means of reducing dramatic art to a formula.

In the one-act play *Trifles* (p. 496), the basic elements of this pattern can be identified, though because of the length of the work the pyramidal pattern is less elaborately worked out. The rising action consists of Mrs. Hale, Mrs. Peters, and the men in the play confronting the aftermath of a man's murder: fruit jars, messy kitchen, and a badly sewn quilt. The complication consists mostly of Mrs. Hale's refusal to assign moral or legal guilt to Mrs. Wright's murder of her husband. The climax occurs when Mrs. Peters suddenly understands, along with Mrs. Hale, the motive for the killing, and the two women must decide to tell the men what they have discovered.

Plays often also include a ***subplot,*** a secondary action that reinforces or contrasts with the main plot. In *Trifles,* the actual murder investigation turns out to be the subplot; the main plot lies in the discussions between Mrs. Hale and Mrs. Peters and the tensions between the men and the women because they address the issues that Glaspell chooses to explore. Those issues are not about murder but about marriage and how men and women relate to each other.

Theme

Theme refers to the central meaning or dominant idea in a play, the unifying point around which the other elements are organized. Theme is not the same thing as the subject of the work necessarily—in *Hamlet,* for example, the subject is the title character but the themes include jealousy, revenge, and incest. Most plays, like most works of literature, have more than one theme, and often trying to choose just one leads us to oversimplify.

SOPHOCLES AND GREEK DRAMA

Sophocles lived a long, productive life (496?– 406 B.C.) in Athens. During his life Athens became a dominant political and cultural power after the Persian Wars, but before he died Sophocles witnessed the decline of Athens as a result of the Peloponnesian Wars and the city's subsequent surrender to Sparta. He saw Athenian culture reach remarkable heights as well as collapse under enormous pressures.

Sophocles embodied much of the best of Athenian culture; he enjoyed success as a statesman, general, treasurer, priest, and, of course, prize-winning dramatist. Although surviving fragments indicate that he wrote over 120 plays, only a handful remain intact. Those that survive consist of the three plays he wrote about Oedipus and his children— *Oedipus the King, Oedipus at Colonus,* and *Antigone*—and four additional tragedies: *Philoctetes, Ajax, Maidens of Trachis,* and *Electra.*

His plays won numerous prizes at festival competitions because of his careful, subtle plotting and the sense of inevitability with which their action is charged. Moreover, his development of character is richly complex. Instead of relying on the extreme situations and exaggerated actions

PHOTO: *Reprinted by permission of Corbis-Bettmann.*

that earlier tragedians used, Sophocles created powerfully motivated characters who even today fascinate audiences with their psychological depth.

In addition to crafting sophisticated tragedies for the Greek theater, Sophocles introduced several important innovations to the stage. Most important, he broke the tradition of using only two actors; adding a third resulted in more complicated relationships and intricate dialogue among characters. As individual actors took center stage more often, Sophocles reduced the role of the chorus (discussed on p. 288). This shift placed even more emphasis on the actors, although the chorus remained important as a means of commenting on the action and establishing its tone. Sophocles was also the first dramatist to write plays with specific actors in mind, a development that many later playwrights, including Shakespeare, exploited usefully. But without question Sophocles' greatest contribution to drama was *Oedipus the King,* which, it has been argued, is the most influential drama ever written.

Theatrical Conventions of Greek Drama

More than twenty-four hundred years have passed since 430 B.C., when Sophocles' *Oedipus the King* was probably first produced on a Greek stage. We inhabit a vastly different planet than Sophocles' audience did, yet concerns about what it means to be human in a world that frequently runs counter to our desires and aspirations have remained relatively constant. The ancient Greeks continue to speak to us. But inexperienced readers or viewers may have some initial difficulty understanding the theatrical conventions used in classical Greek tragedies such as *Oedipus the King.* If Sophocles were alive today, he would very likely need some sort of assistance with the conventions of an Arthur Miller play or a television production of *Seinfeld.*

Classical Greek drama developed from religious festivals that paid homage to Dionysus, the god of wine and fertility. Most of the details of these festivals have been lost, but we do know that they included dancing and singing that celebrated legends about Dionysus. From these choral songs developed stories of both Dionysus and mortal culture-heroes. These heroes became the subject of playwrights whose works were produced in contests at the festivals. The Dionysian festivals lasted more than five hundred years, but relatively few of their plays have survived. Among the works of the three great writers of tragedy, only seven plays each by Sophocles and Aeschylus (525?–456 B.C.) and nineteen plays by Euripides (480?–406 B.C.) survive.

Plays were such important events in Greek society that they were partially funded by the state. The Greeks associated drama with religious and community values as well as entertainment. In a sense, their plays celebrate their civilization; in approving the plays, audiences applauded their own culture. The enormous popularity of the plays is indicated by the size of surviving amphitheaters. Although information about these theaters is sketchy, we do know that most of them shared a common form. They were built into hillsides with rising rows of seats accommodating more than fourteen thousand people. These seats partially encircled an **orchestra** or "dancing place," where the **chorus** of a dozen or so men chanted lines and danced.

Tradition credits the Greek poet Thespis with adding an actor who was separate from the choral singing and dancing of early performances. A second actor was subsequently included by Aeschylus and a third, as noted earlier, by Sophocles. These additions made possible the conflicts and complicated relationships that evolved into the dramatic art we know today. The two or three male actors who played all the roles appeared behind the orchestra in front of the **skene,** a stage building that served as dressing rooms. As Greek theater evolved, a wall of the skene came to be painted to suggest a palace or some other setting, and the roof was employed to indicate, for instance, a mountain location. Sometimes gods were lowered from the roof by mechanical devices to set matters right among the mortals below. This method of rescuing characters from complications beyond their abilities to resolve was known in Latin as **deus ex machina** ("god from the machine"), a term now used to describe any improbable means by which an author provides a too-easy resolution for a story.

Inevitably, the conventions of the Greek theaters affected how plays were presented. Few if any scene changes occurred because the amphitheater stage was set primarily for one location. If an important event happened somewhere else, it was reported by a minor character, such as a messenger. The chorus also provided necessary background information. In *Oedipus the King,* the chorus, acting as townspeople, also assesses the characters' strengths and weaknesses, praising them for their virtues, chiding them for their rashness, and giving them advice. The reactions of the chorus provide a connection between the actors and audience because the chorus is at once a participant in and an observer of the action. In addition, the chorus helps structure the action by indicating changes in scene or mood. Thus the chorus could be used in a variety of ways to shape the audience's response to the play's action and characters.

Actors in classical Greek amphitheaters faced considerable challenges. An intimate relationship with the audience was impossible because many spectators would have been too far away to see a facial expression or subtle gesture. Indeed, some in the audience would have had difficulty even hearing the voices of individual actors. To compensate for these disadvantages, actors wore large masks that extravagantly expressed the major characters' emotions or identified the roles of minor characters. The masks also allowed the two or three actors in a performance to play all the characters without confusing the audience. Each mask was fitted so that the mouthpiece amplified the actor's voice. The actors were further equipped with padded costumes and elevated shoes (**cothurni** or **buskins**) that made them appear larger than life.

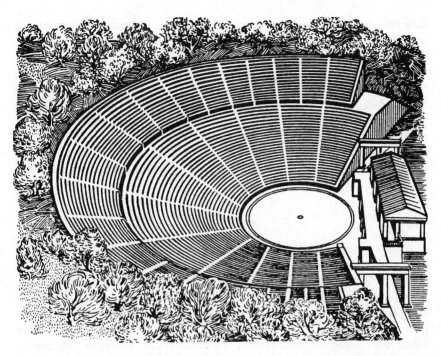

Based on scholarly sources, this drawing represents the features typical of classical Greek theater. (Drawing by Gerda Becker. From Kenneth Macgowan and William Melnitz, The Living Stage, © *1990 by Prentice Hall/A Division of Simon & Schuster.)*

As a result of these adaptive conventions, Greek plays tend to empha-size words — formal, impassioned speeches — more than physical action. We are invited to ponder actions and events rather than to see all of them enacted. Although the stark simplicity of Greek theater does not offer an audience realistic detail, the classical tragedies that have survived present characters in dramatic situations that transcend theatrical conventions. Tragedy, it seems, has always been compelling for human beings, regardless of the theatrical forms it has taken.

A Greek tragedy is typically divided into five parts: prologue, parodos, episodia, stasimon, and exodus. In some translations these terms appear as headings, but in more recent translations, such as the one by Robert Fagles included here, the headings do not appear. Still, understanding these terms provides a sense of the overall rhythm of a Greek play. The opening speech or dialogue is known as the *prologue* and usually gives the exposi-tion necessary to follow the subsequent action. In the *parodos* the chorus makes its first entrance and gives its perspective on what the audience has learned in the prologue. Several *episodia,* or episodes, follow, in which char-acters engage in dialogue that frequently consists of heated debates dra-matizing the play's conflicts. Following each episode is a choral ode or *stasimon,* in which the chorus responds to and interprets the preceding dialogue. The *exodus,* or last scene, follows the final episode and stasimon; in it the resolution occurs and the characters leave the stage.

The effect of alternating dialogues and choral odes has sometimes been likened to that of opera. Greek tragedies were written in verse, and the stasima were chanted or sung as the chorus moved rhythmically, so the plays have a strong musical element that is not always apparent on the printed page. If we remember their musical qualities we are less likely to forget that no matter how terrifying or horrific the conflicts they describe, these plays are stately, measured, and dignified works that reflect a classical Greek sense of order and proportion.

Tragedy

Newspapers are filled with daily reports of tragedies: A child is struck and crippled by a car; an airplane plunges into a suburban neighborhood; a volcano erupts and kills thousands. These unexpected instances of suffering are commonly and accurately described as tragic, but they are not tragedies in the literary sense of the term. A literary *tragedy* presents courageous individuals who confront powerful forces within or outside themselves with a dignity that reveals the breadth and depth of the human spirit in the face of failure, defeat, and even death.

Aristotle (384–322 B.C.), in his *Poetics,* defined *tragedy* on the basis of the plays contemporary to him. His definition has generated countless variations, qualifications, and interpretations, but we still derive our literary understanding of this term from Aristotle.

The protagonist of a Greek tragedy is someone regarded as extraordinary rather than typical: a great man or woman brought from happiness to agony. The character's stature is important because it makes his or her fall all the more terrifying. The protagonist also carries mythic significance for the audience. Oedipus and Antigone, for example, are not only human beings but legendary figures from a distant, revered past. Although the gods do not appear onstage in *Oedipus the King,* their power is ever present as the characters invoke their help or attempt to defy them. In addition, Greek tragedy tends to be public rather than private. The fate of the community—the state—is often linked with that of the protagonist, as when Thebes suffers a plague as a result of Oedipus's mistaken actions.

The protagonists of classical Greek tragedies (and of those of Shakespeare) are often rulers of noble birth who represent the monarchical values of their periods, but in modern tragedies the protagonists are more likely to reflect democratic values that make it possible for anyone to be a suitable subject. What is finally important is not so much the protagonist's social stature as a greatness of character that steadfastly confronts suffering, whether it comes from supernatural, social, or psychological forces. Although Greek tragic heroes were aristocrats, the nobility of their characters was more significant than their inherited titles and privileges.

The protagonist's eminence and determination to complete some task or goal make him or her admirable in Greek tragedy, but that does not free the protagonist from what Aristotle described as "some error or frailty" that brings about his or her misfortune. The term Aristotle used for this weakness is **hamartia**. This word has frequently been interpreted to mean that the protagonist's fall is the result of an internal **tragic flaw,** such as an excess of pride, ambition, passion, or some other character trait that leads directly to disaster.

Sometimes, however, misfortunes are not the result of a character flaw but of misunderstood events that overtake and thwart the protagonist's best intentions. Thus, virtue can lead to tragedy too. *Hamartia* has also been interpreted to mean "wrong act" — a mistake based not on a personal failure but on circumstances outside the protagonist's personality and control. Many readers find that a combination of these two interpretations sheds the most light on the causes of the tragic protagonist's fall. Both internal and external forces can lead to downfall because the protagonist's personality may determine crucial judgments that result in mistaken actions.

However the idea of tragic flaw is understood, it is best not to use it as a means of reducing the qualities of a complex character to an adjective or two that labels Oedipus as guilty of "overweening pride" (the Greek term for which is **hubris** or **hybris**). The protagonists of tragedies require more careful characterization than a simplistic label can provide.

Whatever the causes of the tragic protagonist's downfall, he or she accepts responsibility for it. Hence, even in his or her encounter with failure (and possibly death) the tragic protagonist displays greatness of character. Perhaps it is the witnessing of this greatness, which seems both to accept and to transcend human limitations, that makes audiences feel relief rather than hopelessness at the end of a tragedy. Aristotle described this response as a **catharsis,** or purgation of the emotions of "pity and fear." We are faced with the protagonist's misfortune, which often seems out of proportion to his or her actions, and so we are likely to feel compassionate pity. Simultaneously, we may experience fear because the failure of the protagonist, who is so great in stature and power, is a frightening reminder of our own vulnerabilities. Ultimately, however, both these negative emotions are purged because the tragic protagonist's suffering is an affirmation of human values — even if they are not always triumphant — rather than a despairing denial of them.

Nevertheless, tragedies are disturbing. Instead of coming away with the reassurance of a happy ending, we must take solace in the insight produced by the hero's suffering. And just as our expectations are changed, so are the protagonist's. Aristotle described the moment in the plot when this change occurs as a **reversal** (*peripeteia*), the point when the hero's fortunes turn in an unexpected direction. He more specifically defined this term as meaning an action performed by a character that has the opposite of its intended effect. An example cited by Aristotle is the messenger's attempts to relieve Oedipus's anxieties about his relationship to his father and mother. Instead, the messenger reveals previously unknown information that eventually results in a *recognition* (*anagnorisis*); Oedipus discovers the terrible truth that he has killed his father and married his mother.

Tragedy is typically filled with ironies because there are so many moments in the plot when what seems to be turns out to be radically different from what actually is. Because of this, a particular form of irony called *dramatic irony* is also known as *tragic irony*. In dramatic irony, the meaning of a character's words or actions is understood by the audience but not by the character. Audiences of Greek tragedy shared with the playwrights a knowledge of the stories on which many tragic plots were based. Consequently, they frequently were aware of what was going to happen before the characters were. When Oedipus declares that he will seek out the person responsible for the plague that ravishes his city, the audience already knows that the person Oedipus pursues is himself.

Oedipus the King

A familiarity with the Oedipus legend allows modern readers to appreciate the series of ironies that unfolds in Sophocles' *Oedipus the King*. In the opening scene, Oedipus appears with a "telltale limp." As an infant, he had been abandoned by his parents, Laius and Jocasta, the king and queen of Thebes, because a prophecy warned that their son would kill his father and marry his mother. They instructed a servant to leave him on a mountain to die. The infant's feet were pierced and pinned together, but he was not left on the mountain; instead the servant, out of pity, gave him to a shepherd, who in turn presented him to the king and queen of Corinth. They named him Oedipus (for "swollen foot") and raised him as their own son.

On reaching manhood, Oedipus learned from an oracle that he would kill his father and marry his mother; to avoid this horrendous fate, he left Corinth forever. In his travels, Oedipus found his way blocked by a chariot at a crossroads; in a fit of anger, he killed the servants and their passenger. That passenger, unknown to Oedipus, was his real father. In Thebes, Oedipus successfully answered the riddle of the Sphinx, a winged lion with a woman's head. The reward for defeating this dreaded monster was both the crown and the dead king's wife. Oedipus and Jocasta had four children and prospered. But when the play begins, Oedipus's rule is troubled by a plague that threatens to destroy Thebes, and he is determined to find the cause of the plague in order to save the city again.

Oedipus the King is widely recognized as the greatest of the surviving Greek tragedies. Numerous translations are available (Robert Fagles's recent highly regarded translation, the choice here, is especially accessible to modern readers). The play has absorbed readers for centuries because Oedipus's character — his intelligence, confidence, rashness, and suffering — represents powers and limitations that are both exhilarating and chastening. Although no reader or viewer is likely to identify with Oedipus's extreme circumstances, anyone can appreciate his heroic efforts to find the truth about himself. In that sense, he is one of us — at our best.

SOPHOCLES (496?–406 B.C.)

Oedipus the King

c. 430 B.C.

TRANSLATED BY ROBERT FAGLES

CHARACTERS

Oedipus, king of Thebes
A Priest of Zeus
Creon, brother of Jocasta
A Chorus of Theban citizens and their *Leader*
Tiresias, a blind prophet
Jocasta, the queen, wife of Oedipus
A Messenger from Corinth
A Shepherd
A Messenger from inside the palace
Antigone, Ismene, daughters of Oedipus and Jocasta
Guards and attendants
Priests of Thebes

TIME AND SCENE: *The royal house of Thebes. Double doors dominate the facade; a stone altar stands at the center of the stage.*

Many years have passed since Oedipus solved the riddle of the Sphinx and ascended the throne of Thebes, and now a plague has struck the city. A procession of priests enters; suppliants, broken and despondent, they carry branches wound in wool and lay them on the altar.

The doors open. Guards assemble. Oedipus comes forward, majestic but for a telltale limp, and slowly views the condition of his people.

Oedipus: Oh my children, the new blood of ancient Thebes,
why are you here? Huddling at my altar,
praying before me, your branches wound in wool.°
Our city reeks with the smoke of burning incense,
rings with cries for the Healer and wailing for the dead.   5
I thought it wrong, my children, to hear the truth
from others, messengers. Here I am myself —
you all know me, the world knows my fame:
I am Oedipus.

Helping a Priest to his feet.

                Speak up, old man. Your years,
your dignity — you should speak for the others.   10
Why here and kneeling, what preys upon you so?
Some sudden fear? some strong desire?

---

3 *wool:* Wool was used in offerings to Apollo, god of poetry, the sun, prophecy, and healing.

You can trust me; I am ready to help,
I'll do anything. I would be blind to misery
not to pity my people kneeling at my feet.   15
Priest: Oh Oedipus, king of the land, our greatest power!
You see us before you, men of all ages
clinging to your altars. Here are boys,
still too weak to fly from the nest,
and here the old, bowed down with the years,   20
the holy ones — a priest of Zeus° myself — and here
the picked, unmarried men, the young hope of Thebes.
And all the rest, your great family gathers now,
branches wreathed, massing in the squares,
kneeling before the two temples of queen Athena°   25
or the river-shrine where the embers glow and die
and Apollo sees the future in the ashes.
                              Our city —
look around you, see with your own eyes —
our ship pitches wildly, cannot lift her head
from the depths, the red waves of death . . .   30
Thebes is dying. A blight on the fresh crops
and the rich pastures, cattle sicken and die,
and the women die in labor, children stillborn,
and the plague, the fiery god of fever hurls down
on the city, his lightning slashing through us —   35
raging plague in all its vengeance, devastating
the house of Cadmus!° And Black Death luxuriates
in the raw, wailing miseries of Thebes.

Now we pray to you. You cannot equal the gods,
your children know that, bending at your altar.   40
But we do rate you first of men,
both in the common crises of our lives
and face-to-face encounters with the gods.
You freed us from the Sphinx; you came to Thebes
and cut us loose from the bloody tribute we had paid   45
that harsh, brutal singer. We taught you nothing,
no skill, no extra knowledge, still you triumphed.
A god was with you, so they say, and we believe it —
you lifted up our lives.
                              So now again,
Oedipus, king, we bend to you, your power —   50
we implore you, all of us on our knees:
find us strength, rescue! Perhaps you've heard
the voice of a god or something from other men,
Oedipus . . . what do you know?
The man of experience — you see it every day —   55

---

21 *Zeus:* The highest Olympian deity and father of Apollo.   25 *Athena:* Goddess of wisdom and protector of Greek cities.   37 *Cadmus:* The legendary founder of Thebes.

his plans will work in a crisis, his first of all.
Act now — we beg you, best of men, raise up our city!
Act, defend yourself, your former glory!
Your country calls you savior now
for your zeal, your action years ago.   60
Never let us remember of your reign:
you helped us stand, only to fall once more.
Oh raise up our city, set us on our feet.
The omens were good that day you brought us joy —
be the same man today!   65
Rule our land, you know you have the power,
but rule a land of the living, not a wasteland.
Ship and towered city are nothing, stripped of men
alive within it, living all as one.

Oedipus: My children,
I pity you. I see — how could I fail to see   70
what longings bring you here? Well I know
you are sick to death, all of you,
but sick as you are, not one is sick as I.
Your pain strikes each of you alone, each
in the confines of himself, no other. But my spirit   75
grieves for the city, for myself and all of you.
I wasn't asleep, dreaming. You haven't wakened me —
I've wept through the nights, you must know that,
groping, laboring over many paths of thought.
After a painful search I found one cure: 80
I acted at once. I sent Creon,
my wife's own brother, to Delphi° —
Apollo the Prophet's oracle — to learn
what I might do or say to save our city.

Today's the day. When I count the days gone by   85
it torments me . . . what is he doing?
Strange, he's late, he's gone too long.
But once he returns, then, then I'll be a traitor
if I do not do all the god makes clear.

Priest: Timely words. The men over there   90
are signaling — Creon's just arriving.
Oedipus:

Sighting Creon, then turning to the altar.

                                             Lord Apollo,
let him come with a lucky word of rescue,
shining like his eyes!
Priest: Welcome news, I think — he's crowned, look,
and the laurel wreath is bright with berries.   95
Oedipus: We'll soon see. He's close enough to hear —

---

82 *Delphi:* The shrine where the oracle of Apollo held forth.

Enter Creon from the side; his face is shaded with a wreath.

Creon, prince, my kinsman, what do you bring us?
What message from the god?
Creon: Good news.
   I tell you even the hardest things to bear,
   if they should turn out well, all would be well.   100
Oedipus: Of course, but what were the god's *words*? There's no hope
   and nothing to fear in what you've said so far.
Creon: If you want my report in the presence of these . . .

Pointing to the priests while drawing Oedipus toward the palace.

   I'm ready now, or we might go inside.
Oedipus: Speak out,
   speak to us all. I grieve for these, my people,   105
   far more than I fear for my own life.
Creon: Very well,
   I will tell you what I heard from the god.
   Apollo commands us — he was quite clear —
   "Drive the corruption from the land,
   don't harbor it any longer, past all cure,   110
   don't nurse it in your soil — root it out!"
Oedipus: How can we cleanse ourselves — what rites?
   What's the source of the trouble?
Creon: Banish the man, or pay back blood with blood.
   Murder sets the plague-storm on the city.
Oedipus: Whose murder?   115
   Whose fate does Apollo bring to light?
Creon: Our leader,
   my lord, was once a man named Laius,
   before you came and put us straight on course.
Oedipus: I know —
   or so I've heard. I never saw the man myself.
Creon: Well, he was killed, and Apollo commands us now —   120
   he could not be more clear,
   "Pay the killers back — whoever is responsible."
Oedipus: Where on earth are they? Where to find it now,
   the trail of the ancient guilt so hard to trace?
Creon: "Here in Thebes," he said.   125
   Whatever is sought for can be caught, you know,
   whatever is neglected slips away.
Oedipus: But where,
   in the palace, the fields or foreign soil,
   where did Laius meet his bloody death?
Creon: He went to consult an oracle, he said,   130
   and he set out and never came home again.
Oedipus: No messenger, no fellow-traveler saw what happened?
   Someone to cross-examine?
Creon: No,
   they were all killed but one. He escaped,
   terrified, he could tell us nothing clearly,   135

nothing of what he saw — just one thing.
Oedipus: What's that?
    One thing could hold the key to it all,
    a small beginning gives us grounds for hope.
Creon: He said thieves attacked them — a whole band,
    not single-handed, cut King Laius down.
Oedipus: A thief,   140
    so daring, wild, he'd kill a king? Impossible,
    unless conspirators paid him off in Thebes.
Creon: We suspected as much. But with Laius dead
    no leader appeared to help us in our troubles.
Oedipus: Trouble? Your *king* was murdered — royal blood!   145
    What stopped you from tracking down the killer
    then and there?
Creon: The singing, riddling Sphinx.
    She . . . persuaded us to let the mystery go
    and concentrate on what lay at our feet.
Oedipus: No,
    I'll start again — I'll bring it all to light myself!   150
    Apollo is right, and so are you, Creon,
    to turn our attention back to the murdered man.
    Now you have *me* to fight for you, you'll see:
    I am the land's avenger by all rights
    and Apollo's champion too.   155
    But not to assist some distant kinsman, no,
    for my own sake I'll rid us of this corruption.
    Whoever killed the king may decide to kill me too,
    with the same violent hand — by avenging Laius
    I defend myself.

To the priests.

    Quickly, my children.   160
    Up from the steps, take up your branches now.

To the guards.

    One of you summon the city here before us,
    tell them I'll do everything. God help us,
    we will see our triumph — or our fall.

Oedipus and Creon enter the palace, followed by the guards.

Priest: Rise, my sons. The kindness we came for   165
    Oedipus volunteers himself.
    Apollo has sent his word, his oracle —
    Come down, Apollo, save us, stop the plague.

The priests rise, remove their branches, and exit to the side. Enter a Chorus, the citizens of Thebes, who have not heard the news that Creon brings. They march around the altar, chanting.

Chorus: Zeus!
    Great welcome voice of Zeus, what do you bring?
    What word from the gold vaults of Delphi   170

comes to brilliant Thebes? I'm racked with terror—
        terror shakes my heart
and I cry your wild cries, Apollo, Healer of Delos°
I worship you in dread . . . what now, what is your price?
some new sacrifice? some ancient rite from the past   175
come round again each spring?—
      what will you bring to birth?
Tell me, child of golden Hope
    warm voice that never dies!

You are the first I call, daughter of Zeus   180
deathless Athena—I call your sister Artemis,°
heart of the market place enthroned in glory,
        guardian of our earth—
I call Apollo astride the thunderheads of heaven—
O triple shield against death, shine before me now!   185
If ever, once in the past, you stopped some ruin
launched against our walls
     you hurled the flame of pain
far, far from Thebes—you gods
    come now, come down once more!

              No, no   190
the miseries numberless, grief on grief, no end—
too much to bear, we are all dying
O my people . . .
   Thebes like a great army dying
and there is no sword of thought to save us, no   195
and the fruits of our famous earth, they will not ripen
no and the women cannot scream their pangs to birth—
screams for the Healer, children dead in the womb
     and life on life goes down
        you can watch them go   200
like seabirds winging west, outracing the day's fire
down the horizon, irresistibly
     streaking on to the shores of Evening
               Death
so many deaths, numberless deaths on deaths, no end—
Thebes is dying, look, her children   205
stripped of pity . . .
    generations strewn on the ground
unburied, unwept, the dead spreading death
and the young wives and gray-haired mothers with them
cling to the altars, trailing in from all over the city—   210
Thebes, city of death, one long cortege
     and the suffering rises
        wails for mercy rise
    and the wild hymn for the Healer blazes out

---

173 *Delos:* Apollo was born on this sacred island.   181 *Artemis:* Apollo's sister, goddess of hunting, the moon, and chastity.

clashing with our sobs our cries of mourning —   215
    O golden daughter of god, send rescue
    radiant as the kindness in your eyes!
Drive him back! — the fever, the god of death
              that raging god of war
not armored in bronze, not shielded now, he burns me,   220
battle cries in the onslaught burning on —
O rout him from our borders!
Sail him, blast him out to the Sea-queen's chamber
            the black Atlantic gulfs
    or the northern harbor, death to all   225
where the Thracian surf comes crashing.
Now what the night spares he comes by day and kills —
the god of death.

           O lord of the stormcloud,
you who twirl the lightning, Zeus, Father,
thunder Death to nothing!   230

Apollo, lord of the light, I beg you —
    whip your longbow's golden cord
showering arrows on our enemies — shafts of power
champions strong before us rushing on!

Artemis, Huntress,   235
torches flaring over the eastern ridges —
          ride Death down in pain!

God of the headdress gleaming gold, I cry to you —
your name and ours are one, Dionysus° —
    come with your face aflame with wine   240
        your raving women's cries°
    your army on the march! Come with the lightning
come with torches blazing, eyes ablaze with glory!
Burn that god of death that all gods hate!

Oedipus enters from the palace to address the Chorus, as if addressing the entire
city of Thebes.

Oedipus: You pray to the gods? Let me grant your prayers.   245
Come, listen to me — do what the plague demands:
you'll find relief and lift your head from the depths.

I will speak out now as a stranger to the story,
a stranger to the crime. If I'd been present then,
there would have been no mystery, no long hunt   250
without a clue in hand. So now, counted
a native Theban years after the murder,

---

239 *Dionysus:* God of fertility and wine.   241 *your . . . cries:* Dionysus was attended by
female celebrants.

to all of Thebes I make this proclamation:
if any one of you knows who murdered Laius,
the son of Labdacus, I order him to reveal   255
the whole truth to me. Nothing to fear,
even if he must denounce himself,
let him speak up
and so escape the brunt of the charge —
he will suffer no unbearable punishment,   260
nothing worse than exile, totally unharmed.

Oedipus pauses, waiting for a reply.

                                              Next,
if anyone knows the murderer is a stranger,
a man from alien soil, come, speak up.
I will give him a handsome reward, and lay up
gratitude in my heart for him besides.   265

Silence again, no reply.

But if you keep silent, if anyone panicking,
trying to shield himself or friend or kin,
rejects my offer, then hear what I will do.
I order you, every citizen of the state
where I hold throne and power: banish this man —   270
whoever he may be — never shelter him, never
speak a word to him, never make him partner
to your prayers, your victims burned to the gods.
Never let the holy water touch his hands.
Drive him out, each of you, from every home.   275
He is the plague, the heart of our corruption,
as Apollo's oracle has revealed to me
just now. So I honor my obligations:
I fight for the god and for the murdered man.

Now my curse on the murderer. Whoever he is,   280
a lone man unknown in his crime
or one among many, let that man drag out
his life in agony, step by painful step —
I curse myself as well . . . if by any chance
he proves to be an intimate of our house,   285
here at my hearth, with my full knowledge,
may the curse I just called down on him strike me!

These are your orders: perform them to the last.
I command you, for my sake, for Apollo's, for this country
blasted root and branch by the angry heavens.   290
Even if god had never urged you on to act,
how could you leave the crime uncleansed so long?
A man so noble — your king, brought down in blood —
you should have searched. But I am the king now,
I hold the throne that he held then, possess his bed   295

and a wife who shares our seed . . . why, our seed
might be the same, children born of the same mother
might have created blood-bonds between us
if his hope of offspring hadn't met disaster—
but fate swooped at his head and cut him short.   300
So I will fight for him as if he were my father,
stop at nothing, search the world
to lay my hands on the man who shed his blood,
the son of Labdacus descended of Polydorus,
Cadmus of old and Agenor, founder of the line: 305
their power and mine are one.
                              Oh dear gods,
my curse on those who disobey these orders!
Let no crops grow out of the earth for them—
shrivel their women, kill their sons,
burn them to nothing in this plague   310
that hits us now, or something even worse.
But you, loyal men of Thebes who approve my actions,
may our champion, Justice, may all the gods
be with us, fight beside us to the end!
Leader: In the grip of your curse, my king, I swear   315
  I'm not the murderer, cannot point him out.
  As for the search, Apollo pressed it on us—
  he should name the killer.
Oedipus: Quite right,
  but to force the gods to act against their will—
  no man has the power.
Leader: Then if I might mention   320
  the next best thing . . .
Oedipus: The third best too—
  don't hold back, say it.
Leader: I still believe . . .
  Lord Tiresias sees with the eyes of Lord Apollo.
  Anyone searching for the truth, my king,
  might learn it from the prophet, clear as day.   325
Oedipus: I've not been slow with that. On Creon's cue
  I sent the escorts, twice, within the hour.
  I'm surprised he isn't here.
Leader: We need him—
  without him we have nothing but old, useless rumors.
Oedipus: Which rumors? I'll search out every word.   330
Leader: Laius was killed, they say, by certain travelers.
Oedipus: I know—but no one can find the murderer.
Leader: If the man has a trace of fear in him
  he won't stay silent long,
  not with your curses ringing in his ears.   335
Oedipus: He didn't flinch at murder,
  he'll never flinch at words.

*Enter Tiresias, the blind prophet, led by a boy with escorts in attendance. He
remains at a distance.*

Leader: Here is the one who will convict him, look,
     they bring him on at last, the seer, the man of god.
     The truth lives inside him, him alone.
Oedipus: O Tiresias,   340
     master of all the mysteries of our life,
     all you teach and all you dare not tell,
     signs in the heavens, signs that walk the earth!
     Blind as you are, you can feel all the more
     what sickness haunts our city. You, my lord,   345
     are the one shield, the one savior we can find.

     We asked Apollo — perhaps the messengers
     haven't told you — he sent his answer back:
     "Relief from the plague can only come one way.
     Uncover the murderers of Laius,   350
     put them to death or drive them into exile."
     So I beg you, grudge us nothing now, no voice,
     no message plucked from the birds, the embers
     or the other mantic ways within your grasp.
     Rescue yourself, your city, rescue me —   355
     rescue everything infected by the dead.
     We are in your hands. For a man to help others
     with all his gifts and native strength:
     that is the noblest work.
Tiresias: How terrible — to see the truth
     when the truth is only pain to him who sees!   360
     I knew it well, but I put it from my mind,
     else I never would have come.
Oedipus: What's this? Why so grim, so dire?
Tiresias: Just send me home. You bear your burdens,
     I'll bear mine. It's better that way,   365
     please believe me.
Oedipus: Strange response — unlawful,
     unfriendly too to the state that bred and raised you;
     you're withholding the word of god.
Tiresias: I fail to see
     that your own words are so well-timed.
     I'd rather not have the same thing said of me . . .   370
Oedipus: For the love of god, don't turn away,
     not if you know something. We beg you,
     all of us on our knees.
Tiresias: None of you knows —
     and I will never reveal my dreadful secrets,
     not to say your own.   375
Oedipus: What? You know and you won't tell?
     You're bent on betraying us, destroying Thebes?
Tiresias: I'd rather not cause pain for you or me.
     So why this . . . useless interrogation?
     You'll get nothing from me.

Oedipus: Nothing! You,   380
    you scum of the earth, you'd enrage a heart of stone!
    You won't talk? Nothing moves you?
    Out with it, once and for all!
Tiresias: You criticize my temper . . . unaware
    of the one *you* live with, you revile me.   385
Oedipus: Who could restrain his anger hearing you?
    What outrage—you spurn the city!
Tiresias: What will come will come.
    Even if I shroud it all in silence.
Oedipus: What will come? You're bound to *tell* me that.   390
Tiresias: I'll say no more. Do as you like, build your anger
    to whatever pitch you please, rage your worst—
Oedipus: Oh I'll let loose, I have such fury in me—
    now I see it all. You helped hatch the plot,
    you did the work, yes, short of killing him   395
    with your own hands—and given eyes I'd say
    you did the killing single-handed!
Tiresias: Is that so!
    I charge you, then, submit to that decree
    you just laid down: from this day onward
    speak to no one, not these citizens, not myself.   400
    You are the curse, the corruption of the land!
Oedipus: You, shameless—
    aren't you appalled to start up such a story?
    You think you can get away with this?
Tiresias: I have already.
    The truth with all its power lives inside me.   405
Oedipus: Who primed you for this? Not your prophet's trade.
Tiresias: You did, you forced me, twisted it out of me.
Oedipus: What? Say it again—I'll understand it better.
Tiresias: Didn't you understand, just now?
    Or are you tempting me to talk?   410
Oedipus: No, I can't say I grasped your meaning.
    Out with it, again!
Tiresias: I say you are the murderer you hunt.
Oedipus: That obscenity, twice—by god, you'll pay.
Tiresias: Shall I say more, so you can really rage?   415
Oedipus: Much as you want. Your words are nothing—futile.
Tiresias: You cannot imagine . . . I tell you,
    you and your loved ones live together in infamy,
    you cannot see how far you've gone in guilt.
Oedipus: You think you can keep this up and never suffer? 420
Tiresias: Indeed, if the truth has any power.
Oedipus: It does
    but not for you, old man. You've lost your power,
    stone-blind, stone-deaf—senses, eyes blind as stone!
Tiresias: I pity you, flinging at me the very insults
    each man here will fling at you so soon.

Oedipus: Blind,   425
    lost in the night, endless night that nursed you!
    You can't hurt me or anyone else who sees the light —
    you can never touch me.
Tiresias: True, it is not your fate
    to fall at my hands. Apollo is quite enough,
    and he will take some pains to work this out.   430
Oedipus: Creon! Is this conspiracy his or yours?
Tiresias: Creon is not your downfall, no, you are your own.
Oedipus: O power —
    wealth and empire, skill outstripping skill
    in the heady rivalries of life,
    what envy lurks inside you! Just for this,   435
    the crown the city gave me — I never sought it,
    they laid it in my hands — for this alone, Creon,
    the soul of trust, my loyal friend from the start
    steals against me . . . so hungry to overthrow me
    he sets this wizard on me, this scheming quack,   440
    this fortune-teller peddling lies, eyes peeled
    for his own profit — seer blind in his craft!

    Come here, you pious fraud. Tell me,
    when did you ever prove yourself a prophet?
    When the Sphinx, that chanting Fury kept her deathwatch here,   445
    why silent then, not a word to set our people free?
    There was a riddle, not for some passer-by to solve —
    it cried out for a prophet. Where were you?
    Did you rise to the crisis? Not a word,
    you and your birds, your gods — nothing.   450
    No, but I came by, Oedipus the ignorant,
    I stopped the Sphinx! With no help from the birds,
    the flight of my own intelligence hit the mark.

    And this is the man you'd try to overthrow?
    You think you'll stand by Creon when he's king?   455
    You and the great mastermind —
    you'll pay in tears, I promise you, for this,
    this witch-hunt. If you didn't look so senile
    the lash would teach you what your scheming means!
Leader: I'd suggest his words were spoken in anger,   460
    Oedipus . . . yours too, and it isn't what we need.
    The best solution to the oracle, the riddle
    posed by god — we should look for that.
Tiresias: You are the king no doubt, but in one respect,
    at least, I am your equal: the right to reply.   465
    I claim that privilege too.
    I am not your slave. I serve Apollo.
    I don't need Creon to speak for me in public.
                                         So,
    you mock my blindness? Let me tell you this.

You with your precious eyes, 470
you're blind to the corruption of your life,
to the house you live in, those you live with —
who *are* your parents? Do you know? All unknowing
you are the scourge of your own flesh and blood,
the dead below the earth and the living here above, 475
and the double lash of your mother and your father's curse
will whip you from this land one day, their footfall
treading you down in terror, darkness shrouding
your eyes that now can see the light!
                              Soon, soon
you'll scream aloud — what haven won't reverberate? 480
What rock of Cithaeron° won't scream back in echo?
That day you learn the truth about your marriage,
the wedding-march that sang you into your halls,
the lusty voyage home to the fatal harbor!
And a load of other horrors you'd never dream 485
will level you with yourself and all your children.

There. Now smear us with insults — Creon, myself
and every word I've said. No man will ever
be rooted from the earth as brutally as you.
Oedipus: Enough! Such filth from him? Insufferable — 490
what, still alive? Get out —
faster, back where you came from — vanish!
Tiresias: I'd never have come if you hadn't called me here.
Oedipus: If I thought you'd blurt out such absurdities,
you'd have died waiting before I'd had you summoned. 495
Tiresias: Absurd, am I? To you, not to your parents:
the ones who bore you found me sane enough.
Oedipus: Parents — who? Wait . . . who is my father?
Tiresias: This day will bring your birth and your destruction.
Oedipus: Riddles — all you can say are riddles, murk and darkness. 500
Tiresias: Ah, but aren't you the best man alive at solving riddles?
Oedipus: Mock me for that, go on, and you'll reveal my greatness.
Tiresias: Your great good fortune, true, it was your ruin.
Oedipus: Not if I saved the city — what do I care?
Tiresias: Well then, I'll be going.

To his attendant.

                              Take me home, boy. 505
Oedipus: Yes, take him away. You're a nuisance here.
Out of the way, the irritation's gone.

Turning his back on Tiresias, moving toward the palace.

Tiresias: I will go,
once I have said what I came here to say.
I'll never shrink from the anger in your eyes —

---

481 *Cithaeron:* The mountains where Oedipus was abandoned as an infant.

you can't destroy me. Listen to me closely: 510
the man you've sought so long, proclaiming,
cursing up and down, the murderer of Laius —
he is here. A stranger,
you may think, who lives among you,
he soon will be revealed a native Theban   515
but he will take no joy in the revelation.
Blind who now has eyes, beggar who now is rich,
he will grope his way toward a foreign soil,
a stick tapping before him step by step.

Oedipus enters the palace.

Revealed at last, brother and father both   520
to the children he embraces, to his mother
son and husband both — he sowed the loins
his father sowed, he spilled his father's blood!

Go in and reflect on that, solve that.
And if you find I've lied   525
from this day onward call the prophet blind.

Tiresias and the boy exit to the side.

Chorus: Who —
who is the man the voice of god denounces
resounding out of the rocky gorge of Delphi?
    The horror too dark to tell,
whose ruthless bloody hands have done the work?   530
His time has come to fly
        to outrace the stallions of the storm
                    his feet a streak of speed —
Cased in armor, Apollo son of the Father
lunges on him, lightning-bolts afire!   535
And the grim unerring Furies°
        closing for the kill.
                              Look,
the word of god has just come blazing
flashing off Parnassus'° snowy heights!
    That man who left no trace —   540
after him, hunt him down with all our strength!
Now under bristling timber
        up through rocks and caves he stalks
                    like the wild mountain bull —
cut off from men, each step an agony, frenzied, racing blind   545
but he cannot outrace the dread voices of Delphi
ringing out of the heart of Earth,
        the dark wings beating around him shrieking doom
                    the doom that never dies, the terror —

536 *Furies:* Three spirits who avenged evildoers.   539 *Parnassus:* A mountain in Greece
associated with Apollo.

The skilled prophet scans the birds and shatters me with terror!   550
I can't accept him, can't deny him, don't know what to say,
I'm lost, and the wings of dark foreboding beating—
I cannot see what's come, what's still to come . . .
and what could breed a blood feud between
  Laius' house and the son of Polybus?°   555
I know of nothing, not in the past and not now,
no charge to bring against our king, no cause
to attack his fame that rings throughout Thebes—
  not without proof—not for the ghost of Laius,
  not to avenge a murder gone without a trace.   560

Zeus and Apollo know, they know, the great masters
  of all the dark and depth of human life.
But whether a mere man can know the truth,
whether a seer can fathom more than I—
there is no test, no certain proof   565
  though matching skill for skill
a man can outstrip a rival. No, not till I see
these charges proved will I side with his accusers.
We saw him then, when the she-hawk° swept against him,
saw with our own eyes his skill, his brilliant triumph—   570
  there was the test—he was the joy of Thebes!
  Never will I convict my king, never in my heart.

  Enter Creon from the side.

Creon: My fellow-citizens, I hear King Oedipus
  levels terrible charges at me. I had to come.
  I resent it deeply. If, in the present crisis,   575
  he thinks he suffers any abuse from me,
  anything I've done or said that offers him
  the slightest injury, why, I've no desire
  to linger out this life, my reputation a shambles.
  The damage I'd face from such an accusation   580
  is nothing simple. No, there's nothing worse:
  branded a traitor in the city, a traitor
  to all of you and my good friends.
Leader: True,
  but a slur might have been forced out of him,
  by anger perhaps, not any firm conviction.   585
Creon: The charge was made in public, wasn't it?
  I put the prophet up to spreading lies?
Leader: Such things were said . . .
  I don't know with what intent, if any.
Creon: Was his glance steady, his mind right   590
  when the charge was brought against me?

555 *Polybus:* The King of Corinth, who is thought to be Oedipus's father.   569 *she-hawk:* The Sphinx.

Leader: I really couldn't say. I never look
　　　to judge the ones in power.

　　The doors open. Oedipus enters.

　　　　　　　　　　　　　Wait,
　　here's Oedipus now.
Oedipus:　　　　　　　You — here? You have the gall
　　　to show your face before the palace gates?　　　　　　　595
　　　You, plotting to kill me, kill the king —
　　　I see it all, the marauding thief himself
　　　scheming to steal my crown and power!
　　　　　　　　　　　　Tell me,
　　　in god's name, what did you take me for,
　　　coward or fool, when you spun out your plot?　　　　　600
　　　Your treachery — you think I'd never detect it
　　　creeping against me in the dark? Or sensing it,
　　　not defend myself? Aren't you the fool,
　　　you and your high adventure. Lacking numbers,
　　　powerful friends, out for the big game of empire —　　605
　　　you need riches, armies to bring that quarry down!
Creon: Are you quite finished? It's your turn to listen
　　　for just as long as you've . . . instructed me.
　　　Hear me out, then judge me on the facts.
Oedipus: You've a wicked way with words, Creon,　　　610
　　　but I'll be slow to learn — from you.
　　　I find you a menace, a great burden to me.
Creon: Just one thing, hear me out in this.
Oedipus:　　　　　　　　　　　Just one thing,
　　　don't tell me you're not the enemy, the traitor.
Creon: Look, if you think crude, mindless stubbornness　　615
　　　such a gift, you've lost your sense of balance.
Oedipus: If you think you can abuse a kinsman,
　　　then escape the penalty, you're insane.
Creon: Fair enough, I grant you. But this injury
　　　you say I've done you, what is it?　　　　　　　620
Oedipus: Did you induce me, yes or no,
　　　to send for that sanctimonious prophet?
Creon: I did. And I'd do the same again.
Oedipus: All right then, tell me, how long is it now
　　　since Laius . . .
　　　　　　　Laius — what did *he* do?
Oedipus:　　　　　　　　Vanished,　　　　　　625
　　　swept from sight, murdered in his tracks.
Creon: The count of the years would run you far back . . .
Oedipus: And that far back, was the prophet at his trade?
Creon: Skilled as he is today, and just as honored.
Oedipus: Did he ever refer to me then, at that time?
Creon:　　　　　　　　　　　　No,　　　　　630
　　　never, at least, when I was in his presence.

Oedipus: But you did investigate the murder, didn't you?

Creon: We did our best, of course, discovered nothing.

Oedipus: But the great seer never accused me then — why not?

Creon: I don't know. And when I don't, *I* keep quiet.   635

Oedipus: You do know this, you'd tell it too —
   if you had a shred of decency.

Creon: What?
   If I know, I won't hold back.

Oedipus: Simply this:
   if the two of you had never put heads together,
   we'd never have heard about *my* killing Laius.   640

Creon: If that's what he says . . . well, you know best.
   But now I have a right to learn from you
   as you just learned from me.

Oedipus: Learn your fill,
   you never will convict me of the murder.

Creon: Tell me, you're married to my sister, aren't you?   645

Oedipus: A genuine discovery — there's no denying that.

Creon: And you rule the land with her, with equal power?

Oedipus: She receives from me whatever she desires.

Creon: And I am the third, all of us are equals?

Oedipus: Yes, and it's there you show your stripes —   650
   you betray a kinsman.

Creon: Not at all.
   Not if you see things calmly, rationally,
   as I do. Look at it this way first:
   who in his right mind would rather rule
   and live in anxiety than sleep in peace?   655
   Particularly if he enjoys the same authority.
   Not I, I'm not the man to yearn for kingship,
   not with a king's power in my hands. Who would?
   No one with any sense of self-control.
   Now, as it is, you offer me all I need,   660
   not a fear in the world. But if I wore the crown . . .
   there'd be many painful duties to perform,
   hardly to my taste.
                 How could kingship
   please me more than influence, power
   without a qualm? I'm not that deluded yet,   665
   to reach for anything but privilege outright,
   profit free and clear.
   Now all men sing my praises, all salute me,
   now all who request your favors curry mine.
   I'm their best hope: success rests in me.   670
   Why give up that, I ask you, and borrow trouble?
   A man of sense, someone who sees things clearly
   would never resort to treason.
   No, I've no lust for conspiracy in me,
   nor could I ever suffer one who does.   675

Do you want proof? Go to Delphi yourself,
examine the oracle and see if I've reported
the message word-for-word. This too:
if you detect that I and the clairvoyant
have plotted anything in common, arrest me,   680
execute me. Not on the strength of one vote,
two in this case, mine as well as yours.
But don't convict me on sheer unverified surmise.

How wrong it is to take the good for bad,
purely at random, or take the bad for good.   685
But reject a friend, a kinsman? I would as soon
tear out the life within us, priceless life itself.
You'll learn this well, without fail, in time.
Time alone can bring the just man to light;
the criminal you can spot in one short day.
Leader: Good advice,   690
my lord, for anyone who wants to avoid disaster.
Those who jump to conclusions may be wrong.
Oedipus: When my enemy moves against me quickly,
plots in secret, I move quickly too, I must,
I plot and pay him back. Relax my guard a moment,   695
waiting his next move — he wins his objective,
I lose mine.
Creon: What do you want?
You want me banished?
Oedipus: No, I want you dead.
Creon: Just to show how ugly a grudge can . . .
Oedipus: So,
still stubborn? you don't think I'm serious?   700
Creon: I think you're insane.
Oedipus: Quite sane — in my behalf.
Creon: Not just as much in mine?
Oedipus: You — my mortal enemy?
Creon: What if you're wholly wrong?
Oedipus: No matter — I must rule.
Creon: Not if you rule unjustly.
Oedipus: Hear him, Thebes, my city!
Creon: My city too, not yours alone!   705
Leader: Please, my lords.

  Enter Jocasta from the palace.

                          Look, Jocasta's coming,
and just in time too. With her help
you must put this fighting of yours to rest.
Jocasta: Have you no sense? Poor misguided men,
such shouting — why this public outburst?   710
Aren't you ashamed, with the land so sick,
to stir up private quarrels?

  To Oedipus.

Into the palace now. And Creon, you go home.
Why make such a furor over nothing?

Creon: My sister, it's dreadful . . . Oedipus, your husband,   715
he's bent on a choice of punishments for me,
banishment from the fatherland or death.

Oedipus: Precisely. I caught him in the act, Jocasta,
plotting, about to stab me in the back.

Creon: Never — curse me, let me die and be damned   720
if I've done you any wrong you charge me with.

Jocasta: Oh god, believe it, Oedipus,
honor the solemn oath he swears to heaven.
Do it for me, for the sake of all your people.

The Chorus begins to chant.

Chorus: Believe it, be sensible   725
           give way, my king, I beg you!

Oedipus: What do you want from me, concessions?

Chorus: Respect him — he's been no fool in the past
and now he's strong with the oath he swears to god.

Oedipus: You know what you're asking?

Chorus: I do.

Oedipus: Then out with it!   730

Chorus: The man's your friend, your kin, he's under oath —
don't cast him out, disgraced
branded with guilt on the strength of hearsay only.

Oedipus: Know full well, if that's what you want
you want me dead or banished from the land.

Chorus: Never —   735
no, by the blazing Sun, first god of the heavens!
      Stripped of the gods, stripped of loved ones,
let me die by inches if that ever crossed my mind.
But the heart inside me sickens, dies as the land dies
and now on top of the old griefs you pile this,   740
your fury — both of you!

Oedipus: Then let him go,
even if it does lead to my ruin, my death
or my disgrace, driven from Thebes for life.
It's you, not him I pity — your words move me.
He, wherever he goes, my hate goes with him.   745

Creon: Look at you, sullen in yielding, brutal in your rage —
you'll go too far. It's perfect justice:
natures like yours are hardest on themselves.

Oedipus: Then leave me alone — get out!

Creon: I'm going.
You're wrong, so wrong. These men know I'm right.   750

Exit to the side. The Chorus turns to Jocasta.

Chorus: Why do you hesitate, my lady
           why not help him in?

Jocasta: Tell me what's happened first.

There, you see?
Apollo brought neither thing to pass. My baby
no more murdered his father than Laius suffered — 795
his wildest fear — death at his own son's hands.
That's how the seers and their revelations
mapped out the future. Brush them from your mind.
Whatever the god needs and seeks
he'll bring to light himself, with ease.
Oedipus: Strange, 800
hearing you just now . . . my mind wandered,
my thoughts racing back and forth.
Jocasta: What do you mean? Why so anxious, startled?
Oedipus: I thought I heard you say that Laius
was cut down at a place where three roads meet. 805
Jocasta: That was the story. It hasn't died out yet.
Oedipus: Where did this thing happen? Be precise.
Jocasta: A place called Phocis, where two branching roads,
one from Daulia, one from Delphi,
come together — a crossroads. 810
Oedipus: When? How long ago?
Jocasta: The heralds no sooner reported Laius dead
than you appeared and they hailed you king of Thebes.
Oedipus: My god, my god — what have you planned to do to me?
Jocasta: What, Oedipus? What haunts you so?
Oedipus: Not yet. 815
Laius — how did he look? Describe him.
Had he reached his prime?
Jocasta: He was swarthy,
and the gray had just begun to streak his temples,
and his build . . . wasn't far from yours.
Oedipus: Oh no no,
I think I've just called down a dreadful curse 820
upon myself — I simply didn't know!
Jocasta: What are you saying? I shudder to look at you.
Oedipus: I have a terrible fear the blind seer can see.
I'll know in a moment. One thing more —
Jocasta: Anything,
afraid as I am — ask, I'll answer, all I can. 825
Oedipus: Did he go with a light or heavy escort,
several men-at-arms, like a lord, a king?
Jocasta: There were five in the party, a herald among them,
and a single wagon carrying Laius.
Oedipus: Ai —
now I can see it all, clear as day. 830
Who told you all this at the time, Jocasta?
Jocasta: A servant who reached home, the lone survivor.
Oedipus: So, could he still be in the palace — even now?
Jocasta: No indeed. Soon as he returned from the scene
and saw you on the throne with Laius dead and gone, 835
he knelt and clutched my hand, pleading with me

to send him into the hinterlands, to pasture,
far as possible, out of sight of Thebes.
I sent him away. Slave though he was,
he'd earned that favor—and much more.   840
Oedipus: Can we bring him back, quickly?
Jocasta: Easily. Why do you want him so?
Oedipus: I'm afraid,
Jocasta, I have said too much already.
That man—I've got to see him.
Jocasta: Then he'll come.
But even I have a right, I'd like to think,   845
to know what's torturing you, my lord.
Oedipus: And so you shall—I can hold nothing back from you,
now I've reached this pitch of dark foreboding.
Who means more to me than you? Tell me,
whom would I turn toward but you   850
as I go through all this?

My father was Polybus, king of Corinth.
My mother, a Dorian, Merope. And I was held
the prince of the realm among the people there,
till something struck me out of nowhere,   855
something strange . . . worth remarking perhaps,
hardly worth the anxiety I gave it.
Some man at a banquet who had drunk too much
shouted out—he was far gone, mind you—
that I am not my father's son. Fighting words!   860
I barely restrained myself that day
but early the next I went to mother and father,
questioned them closely, and they were enraged
at the accusation and the fool who let it fly.
So as for my parents I was satisfied,   865
but still this thing kept gnawing at me,
the slander spread—I had to make my move.
                                    And so,
unknown to mother and father I set out for Delphi,
and the god Apollo spurned me, sent me away
denied the facts I came for,   870
but first he flashed before my eyes a future
great with pain, terror, disaster—I can hear him cry,
"You are fated to couple with your mother, you will bring
a breed of children into the light no man can bear to see—
you will kill your father, the one who gave you life!"   875
I heard all that and ran. I abandoned Corinth,
from that day on I gauged its landfall only
by the stars, running, always running
toward some place where I would never see
the shame of all those oracles come true.   880
And as I fled I reached that very spot
where the great king, you say, met his death.

Now, Jocasta, I will tell you all.
Making my way toward this triple crossroad
I began to see a herald, then a brace of colts   885
drawing a wagon, and mounted on the bench . . . a man,
just as you've described him, coming face-to-face,
and the one in the lead and the old man himself
were about to thrust me off the road—brute force—
and the one shouldering me aside, the driver,   890
I strike him in anger!—and the old man, watching me
coming up along his wheels—he brings down
his prod, two prongs straight at my head!
I paid him back with interest!
Short work, by god—with one blow of the staff   895
in this right hand I knock him out of his high seat,
roll him out of the wagon, sprawling headlong—
I killed them all—every mother's son!

Oh, but if there is any blood-tie
between Laius and this stranger . . .   900
what man alive more miserable than I?
More hated by the gods? *I* am the man
no alien, no citizen welcomes to his house,
law forbids it—not a word to me in public,
driven out of every hearth and home.   905
And all these curses I—no one but I
brought down these piling curses on myself!
And you, his wife, I've touched your body with these,
the hands that killed your husband cover you with blood.

Wasn't I born for torment? Look me in the eyes!   910
I am abomination—heart and soul!
I must be exiled, and even in exile
never see my parents, never set foot
on native earth again. Else I'm doomed
to couple with my mother and cut my father down . . .   915
Polybus who reared me, gave me life.
                                    But why, why?
Wouldn't a man of judgment say—and wouldn't he be right—
some savage power has brought this down upon my head?

Oh no, not that, you pure and awesome gods,
never let me see that day! Let me slip   920
from the world of men, vanish without a trace
before I see myself stained with such corruption,
stained to the heart.
Leader: My lord, you fill our hearts with fear.
But at least until you question the witness,   925
do take hope.
Oedipus: Exactly. He is my last hope—
I'm waiting for the shepherd. He is crucial.

Jocasta: And once he appears, what then? Why so urgent?
Oedipus: I'll tell you. If it turns out that his story
    matches yours, I've escaped the worst.   930
Jocasta: What did I say? What struck you so?
Oedipus: You said *thieves* —
    he told you a whole band of them murdered Laius.
    So, if he still holds to the same number,
    I cannot be the killer. One can't equal many.
    But if he refers to one man, one alone,   935
    clearly the scales come down on me:
    I am guilty.
Jocasta: Impossible. Trust me,
    I told you precisely what he said,
    and he can't retract it now;
    the whole city heard it, not just I.   940
    And even if he should vary his first report
    by one man more or less, still, my lord,
    he could never make the murder of Laius
    truly fit the prophecy. Apollo was explicit:
    my son was doomed to kill my husband . . . my son,   945
    poor defenseless thing, he never had a chance
    to kill his father. They destroyed him first.

    So much for prophecy. It's neither here nor there.
    From this day on, I wouldn't look right or left.
Oedipus: True, true. Still, that shepherd,   950
    someone fetch him — now!
Jocasta: I'll send at once. But do let's go inside.
    I'd never displease you, least of all in this.

    Oedipus and Jocasta enter the palace.

Chorus: Destiny guide me always
    Destiny find me filled with reverence   955
           pure in word and deed.
    Great laws tower above us, reared on high
    born for the brilliant vault of heaven —
        Olympian sky their only father,
    nothing mortal, no man gave them birth,   960
    their memory deathless, never lost in sleep:
    within them lives a mighty god, the god does not grow old.

    Pride breeds the tyrant
    violent pride, gorging, crammed to bursting
        with all that is overripe and rich with ruin —   965
    clawing up to the heights, headlong pride
    crashes down the abyss — sheer doom!
        No footing helps, all foothold lost and gone,
    But the healthy strife that makes the city strong —
    I pray that god will never end that wrestling: 970
    god, my champion, I will never let you go.

But if any man comes striding, high and mighty
    in all he says and does,
no fear of justice, no reverence
for the temples of the gods —   975
    let a rough doom tear him down,
repay his pride, breakneck, ruinous pride!
If he cannot reap his profits fairly
    cannot restrain himself from outrage —
mad, laying hands on the holy things untouchable!   980

        Can such a man, so desperate, still boast
        he can save his life from the flashing bolts of god?
            If all such violence goes with honor now
                why join the sacred dance?

Never again will I go reverent to Delphi,   985
    the inviolate heart of Earth
or Apollo's ancient oracle at Abae
or Olympia of the fires —
    unless these prophecies all come true
for all mankind to point toward in wonder.   990
King of kings, if you deserve your titles
    Zeus, remember, never forget!
You and your deathless, everlasting reign.

        They are dying, the old oracles sent to Laius,
        now our masters strike them off the rolls.   995
            Nowhere Apollo's golden glory now —
                the gods, the gods go down.

Enter Jocasta from the palace, carrying a suppliant's branch wound in wool.

Jocasta: Lords of the realm, it occurred to me,
    just now, to visit the temples of the gods,
    so I have my branch in hand and incense too.   1000

Oedipus is beside himself. Racked with anguish,
no longer a man of sense, he won't admit
the latest prophecies are hollow as the old —
he's at the mercy of every passing voice
if the voice tells of terror.   1005
I urge him gently, nothing seems to help,
so I turn to you, Apollo, you are nearest.

Placing her branch on the altar, while an old herdsman enters from the side,
not the one just summoned by the king but an unexpected messenger from
Corinth.

I come with prayers and offerings . . . I beg you,
cleanse us, set us free of defilement!
Look at us, passengers in the grip of fear,   1010
watching the pilot of the vessel go to pieces.

Messenger:

> *Approaching Jocasta and the Chorus.*

> Strangers, please, I wonder if you could lead us
> to the palace of the king . . . I think it's Oedipus.
> Better, the man himself—you know where he is?

Leader: This is his palace, stranger. He's inside. 1015
> But here is his queen, his wife and mother
> of his children.

Messenger: Blessings on you, noble queen,
> queen of Oedipus crowned with all your family—
> blessings on you always!

Jocasta: And the same to you, stranger, you deserve it . . . 1020
> such a greeting. But what have you come for?
> Have you brought us news?

Messenger: Wonderful news—
> for the house, my lady, for your husband too.

Jocasta: Really, what? Who sent you?

Messenger: Corinth.
> I'll give you the message in a moment. 1025
> You'll be glad of it—how could you help it?—
> though it costs a little sorrow in the bargain.

Jocasta: What can it be, with such a double edge?

Messenger: The people there, they want to make your Oedipus
> king of Corinth, so they're saying now. 1030

Jocasta: Why? Isn't old Polybus still in power?

Messenger: No more. Death has got him in the tomb.

Jocasta: What are you saying? Polybus, dead?—dead?

Messenger: If not,
> if I'm not telling the truth, strike me dead too.

Jocasta:

> *To a servant.*

> Quickly, go to your master, tell him this! 1035

> You prophecies of the gods, where are you now?
> This is the man that Oedipus feared for years,
> he fled him, not to kill him—and now he's dead,
> quite by chance, a normal, natural death,
> not murdered by his son.

Oedipus:

> *Emerging from the palace.*

>   Dearest, 1040
> what now? Why call me from the palace?

Jocasta:

> *Bringing the Messenger closer.*

> Listen to *him,* see for yourself what all
> those awful prophecies of god have come to.

Oedipus: And who is he? What can he have for me?

Jocasta: He's from Corinth, he's come to tell you   1045
  your father is no more — Polybus — he's dead!
Oedipus:

Wheeling on the Messenger.

  What? Let me have it from your lips.
Messenger: Well,
  if that's what you want first, then here it is:
  make no mistake, Polybus is dead and gone.
Oedipus: How — murder? sickness? — what? what killed him?   1050
Messenger: A light tip of the scales can put old bones to rest.
Oedipus: Sickness then — poor man, it wore him down.
Messenger: That,
  and the long count of years he'd measured out.
Oedipus: So!
  Jocasta, why, why look to the Prophet's hearth,
  the fires of the future? Why scan the birds   1055
  that scream above our heads? They winged me on
  to the murder of my father, did they? That was my doom?
  Well look, he's dead and buried, hidden under the earth,
  and here I am in Thebes, I never put hand to sword —
  unless some longing for me wasted him away,   1060
  then in a sense you'd say I caused his death.
  But now, all those prophecies I feared — Polybus
  packs them off to sleep with him in hell!
  They're nothing, worthless.
Jocasta: There.
  Didn't I tell you from the start?   1065
Oedipus: So you did. I was lost in fear.
Jocasta: No more, sweep it from your mind forever.
Oedipus: But my mother's bed, surely I must fear —
Jocasta: Fear?
  What should a man fear? It's all chance,
  chance rules our lives. Not a man on earth   1070
  can see a day ahead, groping through the dark.
  Better to live at random, best we can.
  And as for this marriage with your mother —
  have no fear. Many a man before you,
  in his dreams, has shared his mother's bed.   1075
  Take such things for shadows, nothing at all —
  Live, Oedipus,
  as if there's no tomorrow!
Oedipus: Brave words,
  and you'd persuade me if mother weren't alive.
  But mother lives, so for all your reassurances   1080
  I live in fear, I must.
Jocasta: But your father's death,
  that, at least, is a great blessing, joy to the eyes!
Oedipus: Great, I know . . . but I fear *her* — she's still alive.
Messenger: Wait, who is this woman, makes you so afraid?

Oedipus: Merope, old man. The wife of Polybus.   1085
Messenger: The queen? What's there to fear in her?
Oedipus: A dreadful prophecy, stranger, sent by the gods.
Messenger: Tell me, could you? Unless it's forbidden
  other ears to hear.
Oedipus: Not at all.
  Apollo told me once — it is my fate —   1090
  I must make love with my own mother,
  shed my father's blood with my own hands.
  So for years I've given Corinth a wide berth,
  and it's been my good fortune too. But still,
  to see one's parents and look into their eyes   1095
  is the greatest joy I know.
Messenger: You're afraid of that?
  That kept you out of Corinth?
Oedipus: My *father,* old man —
  so I wouldn't kill my father.
Messenger: So that's it.
  Well then, seeing I came with such good will, my king,
  why don't I rid you of that old worry now?   1100
Oedipus: What a rich reward you'd have for that.
Messenger: What do you think I came for, majesty?
  So you'd come home and I'd be better off.
Oedipus: Never, I will never go near my parents.
Messenger: My boy, it's clear, you don't know what you're doing.   1105
Oedipus: What do you mean, old man? For god's sake, explain.
Messenger: If you ran from *them,* always dodging home . . .
Oedipus: Always, terrified Apollo's oracle might come true —
Messenger: And you'd be covered with guilt, from both your parents.
Oedipus: That's right, old man, that fear is always with me.   1110
Messenger: Don't you know? You've really nothing to fear.
Oedipus: But why? If I'm their son — Merope, Polybus?
Messenger: Polybus was nothing to you, that's why, not in blood.
Oedipus: What are you saying — Polybus was not my father?
Messenger: No more than I am. He and I are equals.
Oedipus: My father —   1115
  how can my father equal nothing? You're nothing to me!
Messenger: Neither was he, no more your father than I am.
Oedipus: Then why did he call me his son?
Messenger: You were a gift,
  years ago — know for a fact he took you
  from my hands.
Oedipus: No, from another's hands?   1120
  Then how could he love me so? He loved me, deeply . . .
Messenger: True, and his early years without a child
  made him love you all the more.
Oedipus: And you, did you . . .
  buy me? find me by accident?
Messenger: I stumbled on you,
  down the woody flanks of Mount Cithaeron.

Oedipus: So close,   1125
    what were you doing here, just passing through?
Messenger: Watching over my flocks, grazing them on the slopes.
Oedipus: A herdsman, were you? A vagabond, scraping for wages?
Messenger: Your savior too, my son, in your worst hour.
Oedipus: Oh—
    when you picked me up, was I in pain? What exactly?   1130
Messenger: Your ankles . . . they tell the story. Look at them.
Oedipus: Why remind me of that, that old affliction?
Messenger: Your ankles were pinned together; I set you free.
Oedipus: That dreadful mark—I've had it from the cradle.
Messenger: And you got your name from that misfortune too,   1135
    the name's still with you.
Oedipus: Dear god, who did it?—
    mother? father? Tell me.
Messenger: I don't know.
    The one who gave you to me, he'd know more.
Oedipus: What? You took me from someone else?
    You didn't find me yourself?
Messenger: No sir,   1140
    another shepherd passed you on to me.
Oedipus: Who? Do you know? Describe him.
Messenger: He called himself a servant of . . .
    if I remember rightly—Laius.

Jocasta turns sharply.

Oedipus: The king of the land who ruled here long ago?   1145
Messenger: That's the one. That herdsman was *his* man.
Oedipus: Is he still alive? Can I see him?
Messenger: They'd know best, the people of these parts.

Oedipus and the Messenger turn to the Chorus.

Oedipus: Does anyone know that herdsman,
    the one he mentioned? Anyone seen him   1150
    in the fields, in town? Out with it!
    The time has come to reveal this once for all.
Leader: I think he's the very shepherd you wanted to see,
    a moment ago. But the queen, Jocasta,
    she's the one to say.
Oedipus: Jocasta,   1155
    you remember the man we just sent for?
    Is *that* the one he means?
Jocasta: That man . . .
    why ask? Old shepherd, talk, empty nonsense,
    don't give it another thought, don't even think—
Oedipus: What—give up now, with a clue like this?   1160
    Fail to solve the mystery of my birth?
    Not for all the world!
Jocasta: Stop—in the name of god,
    if you love your own life, call off this search!

My suffering is enough.

Oedipus: Courage!
Even if my mother turns out to be a slave,   1165
and I a slave, three generations back,
you would not seem common.

Jocasta: Oh no,
listen to me, I beg you, don't do this.

Oedipus: Listen to you? No more. I must know it all,
see the truth at last.

Jocasta: No, please —   1170
for your sake — I want the best for you!

Oedipus: Your best is more than I can bear.

Jocasta: You're doomed —
may you never fathom who you are!

Oedipus:

To a servant.

Hurry, fetch me the herdsman, now!
Leave her to glory in her royal birth.   1175

Jocasta: Aieeeeee —
                    man of agony —
that is the only name I have for you,
that, no other — ever, ever, ever!

Flinging [herself] through the palace doors. A long, tense silence follows.

Leader: Where's she gone, Oedipus?
Rushing off, such wild grief . . .   1180
I'm afraid that from this silence
something monstrous may come bursting forth.

Oedipus: Let it burst! Whatever will, whatever must!
I must know my birth, no matter how common
it may be — must see my origins face-to-face.   1185
She perhaps, she with her woman's pride
may well be mortified by my birth,
but I, I count myself the son of Chance,
the great goddess, giver of all good things —
I'll never see myself disgraced. She is my mother!   1190
And the moons have marked me out, my blood-brothers,
one moon on the wane, the next moon great with power.
That is my blood, my nature — I will never betray it,
never fail to search and learn my birth!

Chorus: Yes — if I am a true prophet   1195
          if I can grasp the truth,
     by the boundless skies of Olympus,
at the full moon of tomorrow, Mount Cithaeron
you will know how Oedipus glories in you —
you, his birthplace, nurse, his mountain-mother!   1200
And we will sing you, dancing out your praise —
you lift our monarch's heart!
          Apollo, Apollo, god of the wild cry

may our dancing please you!

Oedipus —

son, dear child, who bore you?   1205
Who of the nymphs who seem to live forever
mated with Pan,° the mountain-striding Father?
Who was your mother? who, some bride of Apollo
the god who loves the pastures spreading toward the sun?
Or was it Hermes, king of the lightning ridges?   1210
Or Dionysus, lord of frenzy, lord of the barren peaks —
did he seize you in his hands, dearest of all his lucky finds? —
found by the nymphs, their warm eyes dancing, gift
to the lord who loves them dancing out his joy!

Oedipus strains to see a figure coming from the distance. Attended by palace
guards, an old Shepherd enters slowly, reluctant to approach the king.

Oedipus: I never met the man, my friends . . . still,   1215
if I had to guess, I'd say that's the shepherd,
the very one we've looked for all along.
Brothers in old age, two of a kind,
he and our guest here. At any rate
the ones who bring him in are my own men,   1220
I recognize them.

Turning to the Leader.

But you know more than I,
you should, you've seen the man before.
Leader: I know him, definitely. One of Laius' men,
a trusty shepherd, if there ever was one.
Oedipus: You, I ask you first, stranger,   1225
you from Corinth — is this the one you mean?
Messenger: You're looking at him. He's your man.
Oedipus:

To the Shepherd.

You, old man, come over here —
look at me. Answer all my questions.
Did you ever serve King Laius?
Shepherd: So I did . . .   1230
a slave, not bought on the block though,
born and reared in the palace.
Oedipus: Your duties, your kind of work?
Shepherd: Herding the flocks, the better part of my life.
Oedipus: Where, mostly? Where did you do your grazing?
Shepherd: Well,   1235
Cithaeron sometimes, or the foothills round about.
Oedipus: This man — you know him? ever see him there?
Shepherd:

Confused, glancing from the Messenger to the King.

1207 *Pan:* God of shepherds, who was, like Hermes and Dionysus, associated with the
wilderness.

Doing what — what man do you mean?
Oedipus:

> *Pointing to the Messenger.*

This one here — ever have dealings with him?
Shepherd: Not so I could say, but give me a chance,   1240
my memory's bad . . .
Messenger: No wonder he doesn't know me, master.
But let me refresh his memory for him.
I'm sure he recalls old times we had
on the slopes of Mount Cithaeron;   1245
he and I, grazing our flocks, he with two
and I with one — we both struck up together,
three whole seasons, six months at a stretch
from spring to the rising of Arcturus° in the fall,
then with winter coming on I'd drive my herds   1250
to my own pens, and back he'd go with his
to Laius' folds.

> *To the Shepherd.*

                    Now that's how it was,
wasn't it — yes or no?
Shepherd: Yes, I suppose . . .
it's all so long ago.
Messenger: Come, tell me,
you gave me a child back then, a boy, remember?   1255
A little fellow to rear, my very own.
Shepherd: What? Why rake up that again?
Messenger: Look, here he is, my fine old friend —
the same man who was just a baby then.
Shepherd: Damn you, shut your mouth — quiet!   1260
Oedipus: Don't lash out at him, old man —
you need lashing more than he does.
Shepherd: Why,
master, majesty — what have I done wrong?
Oedipus: You won't answer his question about the boy.
Shepherd: He's talking nonsense, wasting his breath.   1265
Oedipus: So, you won't talk willingly —
then you'll talk with pain.

> *The guards seize the Shepherd.*

Shepherd: No, dear god, don't torture an old man!
Oedipus: Twist his arms back, quickly!
Shepherd: God help us, why? —
what more do you need to know?   1270
Oedipus: Did you give him that child? He's asking.
Shepherd: I did . . . I wish to god I'd died that day.
Oedipus: You've got your wish if you don't tell the truth.

1249 *Arcturus:* A star whose rising marked the end of summer.

Shepherd: The more I tell, the worse the death I'll die.
Oedipus: Our friend here wants to stretch things out, does he?   1275

>*Motioning to his men for torture.*

Shepherd: No, no, I gave it to him—I just said so.
Oedipus: Where did you get it? Your house? Someone else's?
Shepherd: It wasn't mine, no, I got it from . . . someone.
Oedipus: Which one of them?

>*Looking at the citizens.*

Whose house?

Shepherd: No—
>god's sake, master, no more questions!   1280

Oedipus: You're a dead man if I have to ask again.
Shepherd: Then—the child came from the house . . .
>of Laius.

Oedipus: A slave? or born of his own blood?
Shepherd: Oh no,
>I'm right at the edge, the horrible truth—I've got to say it!

Oedipus: And I'm at the edge of hearing horrors, yes, but I must hear!   1285
Shepherd: All right! His son, they said it was—his son!
>But the one inside, your wife,
>she'd tell it best.

Oedipus: My wife—
>*she* gave it to you?   1290

Shepherd: Yes, yes, my king.
Oedipus: Why, what for?
Shepherd: To kill it.
Oedipus: Her own child,
>how could she?   1295

Shepherd: She was afraid—
>frightening prophecies.

Oedipus: What?
Shepherd: They said—
>he'd kill his parents.

Oedipus: But you gave him to this old man—why?   1300
Shepherd: I pitied the little baby, master,
>hoped he'd take him off to his own country,
>far away, but he saved him for this, this fate.
>If you are the man he says you are, believe me,
>you were born for pain.

Oedipus: O god—   1305
>all come true, all burst to light!
>O light—now let me look my last on you!
>I stand revealed at last—
>cursed in my birth, cursed in marriage,
>cursed in the lives I cut down with these hands!   1310

>*Rushing through the doors with a great cry. The Corinthian Messenger, the
>Shepherd, and attendants exit slowly to the side.*

Chorus: O the generations of men
  the dying generations — adding the total
  of all your lives I find they come to nothing . . .
     does there exist, is there a man on earth
  who seizes more joy than just a dream, a vision?   1315
  And the vision no sooner dawns than dies
  blazing into oblivion.

  You are my great example, you, your life,
  your destiny, Oedipus, man of misery —
  I count no man blest.

       You outranged all men!   1320
     Bending your bow to the breaking-point
  you captured priceless glory, O dear god,
  and the Sphinx came crashing down,
      the virgin, claws hooked
  like a bird of omen singing, shrieking death —   1325
  like a fortress reared in the face of death
  you rose and saved our land.

  From that day on we called you king
  we crowned you with honors, Oedipus, towering over all —
  mighty king of the seven gates of Thebes.   1330

  But now to hear your story — is there a man more agonized?
  More wed to pain and frenzy? Not a man on earth,
  the joy of your life ground down to nothing
  O Oedipus, name for the ages —
    one and the same wide harbor served you   1335
       son and father both
  son and father came to rest in the same bridal chamber.
  How, how could the furrows your father plowed
  bear you, your agony, harrowing on
  in silence O so long?
       But now for all your power   1340
  Time, all-seeing Time has dragged you to the light,
  judged your marriage monstrous from the start —
  the son and the father tangling, both one —
  O child of Laius, would to god
    I'd never seen you, never never!   1345
    Now I weep like a man who wails the dead
  and the dirge comes pouring forth with all my heart!
  I tell you the truth, you gave me life
  my breath leapt up in you
  and now you bring down night upon my eyes.   1350

Enter a Messenger from the palace.

Messenger: Men of Thebes, always the first in honor,
  what horrors you will hear, what you will see,

what a heavy weight of sorrow you will shoulder . . .
if you are true to your birth, if you still have
some feeling for the royal house of Thebes.   1355
I tell you neither the waters of the Danube
nor the Nile can wash this palace clean.
Such things it hides, it soon will bring to light—
terrible things, and none done blindly now,
all done with a will. The pains   1360
we inflict upon ourselves hurt most of all.
Leader: God knows we have pains enough already.
    What can you add to them?
Messenger: The queen is dead.
Leader: Poor lady—how?
Messenger: By her own hand. But you are spared the worst,   1365
    you never had to watch . . . I saw it all,
    and with all the memory that's in me
    you will learn what that poor woman suffered.

Once she'd broken in through the gates,
dashing past us, frantic, whipped to fury,   1370
ripping her hair out with both hands—
straight to her rooms she rushed, flinging herself
across the bridal-bed, doors slamming behind her—
once inside, she wailed for Laius, dead so long,
remembering how she bore his child long ago,   1375
the life that rose up to destroy him, leaving
its mother to mother living creatures
with the very son she'd borne.
Oh how she wept, mourning the marriage-bed
where she let loose that double brood—monsters—   1380
husband by her husband, children by her child.
                    And then—
but how she died is more than I can say. Suddenly
Oedipus burst in, screaming, he stunned us so
we couldn't watch her agony to the end,
our eyes were fixed on him. Circling   1385
like a maddened beast, stalking, here, there,
crying out to us—
           Give him a sword! His wife,
no wife, his mother, where can he find the mother earth
that cropped two crops at once, himself and all his children?
He was raging—one of the dark powers pointing the way,   1390
none of us mortals crowding around him, no,
with a great shattering cry—someone, something leading him on—
he hurled at the twin doors and bending the bolts back
out of their sockets, crashed through the chamber.
And there we saw the woman hanging by the neck,   1395
cradled high in a woven noose, spinning,
swinging back and forth. And when he saw her,
giving a low, wrenching sob that broke our hearts,

slipping the halter from her throat, he eased her down,
in a slow embrace he laid her down, poor thing . . .   1400
then, what came next, what horror we beheld!

He rips off her brooches, the long gold pins
holding her robes — and lifting them high,
looking straight up into the points,
he digs them down the sockets of his eyes, crying, "You,   1405
you'll see no more the pain I suffered, all the pain I caused!
Too long you looked on the ones you never should have seen,
blind to the ones you longed to see, to know! Blind
from this hour on! Blind in the darkness — blind!"
His voice like a dirge, rising, over and over   1410
raising the pins, raking them down his eyes.
And at each stroke blood spurts from the roots,
splashing his beard, a swirl of it, nerves and clots —
black hail of blood pulsing, gushing down.

These are the griefs that burst upon them both,   1415
coupling man and woman. The joy they had so lately,
the fortune of their old ancestral house
was deep joy indeed. Now, in this one day,
wailing, madness and doom, death, disgrace,
all the griefs in the world that you can name,   1420
all are theirs forever.
Leader: Oh poor man, the misery —
has he any rest from pain now?

A voice within, in torment.

Messenger: He's shouting,
"Loose the bolts, someone, show me to all of Thebes!
My father's murderer, my mother's — "
No, I can't repeat it, it's unholy.   1425
Now he'll tear himself from his native earth,
not linger, curse the house with his own curse.
But he needs strength, and a guide to lead him on.
This is sickness more than he can bear.

The palace doors open.

                                          Look,
he'll show you himself. The great doors are opening —   1430
you are about to see a sight, a horror
even his mortal enemy would pity.

Enter Oedipus, blinded, led by a boy. He stands at the palace steps, as if surveying
his people once again.

Chorus: O the terror —
the suffering, for all the world to see,
the worst terror that ever met my eyes.
What madness swept over you? What god,   1435
what dark power leapt beyond all bounds,

beyond belief, to crush your wretched life? —
godforsaken, cursed by the gods!
I pity you but I can't bear to look.
I've much to ask, so much to learn,   1440
so much fascinates my eyes,
but you . . . I shudder at the sight.
Oedipus: Oh, Ohhh —
the agony! I am agony —
where am I going? where on earth?
    where does all this agony hurl me?   1445
where's my voice? —
            winging, swept away on a dark tide —
My destiny, my dark power, what a leap you made!
Chorus: To the depths of terror, too dark to hear, to see.
Oedipus: Dark, horror of darkness   1450
my darkness, drowning, swirling around me
crashing wave on wave — unspeakable, irresistible
            headwind, fatal harbor! Oh again,
    the misery, all at once, over and over
    the stabbing daggers, stab of memory   1455
raking me insane.
Chorus: No wonder you suffer
twice over, the pain of your wounds,
    the lasting grief of pain.
Oedipus: Dear friend, still here?
    Standing by me, still with a care for me,
    the blind man? Such compassion,   1460
            loyal to the last. Oh it's you,
    I know you're here, dark as it is
    I'd know you anywhere, your voice —
it's yours, clearly yours.
Chorus: Dreadful, what you've done . . .
how could you bear it, gouging out your eyes?   1465
What superhuman power drove you on?
Oedipus: Apollo, friends, Apollo —
he ordained my agonies — these, my pains on pains!
    But the hand that struck my eyes was mine,
    mine alone — no one else —   1470
            I did it all myself!
    What good were eyes to me?
    Nothing I could see could bring me joy.
Chorus: No, no, exactly as you say.
Oedipus: What can I ever see?
    What love, what call of the heart   1475
can touch my ears with joy? Nothing, friends.
    Take me away, far, far from Thebes,
        quickly, cast me away, my friends —
this great murderous ruin, this man cursed to heaven,
    the man the deathless gods hate most of all!   1480
Chorus: Pitiful, you suffer so, you understand so much . . .

I wish you'd never known.
Oedipus: Die, die—
    whoever he was that day in the wilds
    who cut my ankles free of the ruthless pins,
        he pulled me clear of death, he saved my life   1485
    for this, this kindness—
                    Curse him, kill him!
    If I'd died then, I'd never have dragged myself,
        my loved ones through such hell.
Chorus: Oh if only . . . would to god.
Oedipus: I'd never have come to this,   1490
        my father's murderer—never been branded
    mother's husband, all men see me now! Now,
        loathed by the gods, son of the mother I defiled
            coupling in my father's bed, spawning lives in the loins
    that spawned my wretched life. What grief can crown this grief?   1495
            It's mine alone, my destiny—I am Oedipus!
Chorus: How can I say you've chosen for the best?
    Better to die than be alive and blind.
Oedipus: What I did was best—don't lecture me,
    no more advice. I, with *my* eyes,   1500
    how could I look my father in the eyes
    when I go down to death? Or mother, so abused . . .
    I've done such things to the two of them,
    crimes too huge for hanging.
                        Worse yet,
    the sight of my children, born as they were born,   1505
    how could I long to look into their eyes?
    No, not with these eyes of mine, never.
    Not this city either, her high towers,
    the sacred glittering images of her gods—
    I am misery! I, her best son, reared   1510
    as no other son of Thebes was ever reared,
    I've stripped myself, I gave the command myself.
    All men must cast away the great blasphemer,
    the curse now brought to light by the gods,
    the son of Laius—I, my father's son!   1515

    Now I've exposed my guilt, horrendous guilt,
    could I train a level glance on you, my countrymen?
    Impossible! No, if I could just block off my ears,
    the springs of hearing, I would stop at nothing—
    I'd wall up my loathsome body like a prison,   1520
    blind to the sound of life, not just the sight.
    Oblivion—what a blessing . . .
    for the mind to dwell a world away from pain.

    O Cithaeron, why did you give me shelter?
    Why didn't you take me, crush my life out on the spot?   1525
    I'd never have revealed my birth to all mankind.

O Polybus, Corinth, the old house of my fathers,
so I believed — what a handsome prince you raised —
under the skin, what sickness to the core.
Look at me! Born of outrage, outrage to the core.   1530

O triple roads — it all comes back, the secret,
dark ravine, and the oaks closing in
where the three roads join . . .
You drank my father's blood, my own blood
spilled by my own hands — you still remember me?   1535
What things you saw me do? Then I came here
and did them all once more!
               Marriages! O marriage,
you gave me birth, and once you brought me into the world
you brought my sperm rising back, springing to light
fathers, brothers, sons — one deadly breed —   1540
brides, wives, mothers. The blackest things
a man can do, I have done them all!
                    No more —
it's wrong to name what's wrong to do. Quickly,
for the love of god, hide me somewhere,
kill me, hurl me into the sea   1545
where you can never look on me again.

Beckoning to the Chorus as they shrink away.

                       Closer,
it's all right. Touch the man of sorrow.
Do. Don't be afraid. My troubles are mine
and I am the only man alive who can sustain them.

Enter Creon from the palace, attended by palace guards.

Leader: Put your requests to Creon. Here he is,   1550
    just when we need him. He'll have a plan, he'll act.
    Now that he's the sole defense of the country
    in your place.
Oedipus: Oh no, what can I say to him?
    How can I ever hope to win his trust?
    I wronged him so, just now, in every way.   1555
    You must see that — I was so wrong, so wrong.
Creon: I haven't come to mock you, Oedipus,
    or to criticize your former failings.

    Turning to the guards.

                  You there,
have you lost all respect for human feeling?
At least revere the Sun, the holy fire   1560
that keeps us all alive. Never expose a thing
of guilt and holy dread so great it appalls
the earth, the rain from heaven, the light of day!
Get him into the halls — quickly as you can.
Piety demands no less. Kindred alone   1565

should see a kinsman's shame. This is obscene.

Oedipus: Please, in god's name . . . you wipe my fears away,
    coming so generously to me, the worst of men.
    Do one thing more, for your sake, not mine.

Creon: What do you want? Why so insistent?   1570

Oedipus: Drive me out of the land at once, far from sight,
    where I can never hear a human voice.

Creon: I'd have done that already, I promise you.
    First I wanted the god to clarify my duties.

Oedipus: The god? His command was clear, every word: 1575
    death for the father-killer, the curse —
    he said destroy me!

Creon: So he did. Still, in such a crisis
    it's better to ask precisely what to do.

Oedipus: You'd ask the oracle about a man like me?   1580

Creon: By all means. And this time, I assume,
    even you will obey the god's decrees.

Oedipus: I will,
    I will. And you, I command you — I beg you . . .
    the woman inside, bury her as you see fit.
    It's the only decent thing,   1585
    to give your own the last rites. As for me,
    never condemn the city of my fathers
    to house my body, not while I'm alive, no,
    let me live on the mountains, on Cithaeron,
    my favorite haunt, I have made it famous.   1590
    Mother and father marked out that rock
    to be my everlasting tomb — buried alive.
    Let me die there, where they tried to kill me.
    Oh but this I know: no sickness can destroy me,
    nothing can. I would never have been saved   1595
    from death — I have been saved
    for something great and terrible, something strange.
    Well let my destiny come and take me on its way!

    About my children, Creon, the boys at least,
    don't burden yourself. They're men;   1600
    wherever they go, they'll find the means to live.
    But my two daughters, my poor helpless girls,
    clustering at our table, never without me
    hovering near them . . . whatever I touched,
    they always had their share. Take care of them,   1605
    I beg you. Wait, better — permit me, would you?
    Just to touch them with my hands and take
    our fill of tears. Please . . . my king.
    Grant it, with all your noble heart.
    If I could hold them, just once, I'd think   1610
    I had them with me, like the early days
    when I could see their eyes.

Antigone and Ismene, two small children, are led in from the palace by a nurse.

What's that?
O god! Do I really hear you sobbing? —
my two children. Creon, you've pitied me?
Sent me my darling girls, my own flesh and blood!   1615
Am I right?

Creon: Yes, it's my doing.
I know the joy they gave you all these years,
the joy you must feel now.

Oedipus: Bless you, Creon!
May god watch over you for this kindness,
better than he ever guarded me.

Children, where are you?   1620
Here, come quickly —

Groping for Antigone and Ismene, who approach their father cautiously, then embrace him.

Come to these hands of mine,
your brother's hands, your own father's hands
that served his once bright eyes so well —
that made them blind. Seeing nothing, children,
knowing nothing, I became your father,   1625
I fathered you in the soil that gave me life.

How I weep for you — I cannot see you now . . .
just thinking of all your days to come, the bitterness,
the life that rough mankind will thrust upon you.
Where are the public gatherings you can join,   1630
the banquets of the clans? Home you'll come,
in tears, cut off from the sight of it all,
the brilliant rites unfinished.
And when you reach perfection, ripe for marriage,
who will he be, my dear ones? Risking all   1635
to shoulder the curse that weighs down my parents,
yes and you too — that wounds us all together.
What more misery could you want?
Your father killed his father, sowed his mother,
one, one and the selfsame womb sprang you —   1640
he cropped the very roots of his existence.
Such disgrace, and you must bear it all!
Who will marry you then? Not a man on earth.
Your doom is clear: you'll wither away to nothing,
single, without a child.

Turning to Creon.

Oh Creon,   1645
you are the only father they have now . . .
we who brought them into the world
are gone, both gone at a stroke —

Don't let them go begging, abandoned,
women without men. Your own flesh and blood!   1650
Never bring them down to the level of my pains.
Pity them. Look at them, so young, so vulnerable,
shorn of everything—you're their only hope.
Promise me, noble Creon, touch my hand.

Reaching toward Creon, who draws back.

You, little ones, if you were old enough   1655
to understand, there is much I'd tell you.
Now, as it is, I'd have you say a prayer.
Pray for life, my children,
live where you are free to grow and season.
Pray god you find a better life than mine,   1660
the father who begot you.

Creon: Enough.
You've wept enough. Into the palace now.
Oedipus: I must, but I find it very hard.
Creon: Time is the great healer, you will see.
Oedipus: I am going—you know on what condition?   1665
Creon: Tell me. I'm listening.
Oedipus: Drive me out of Thebes, in exile.
Creon: Not I. Only the gods can give you that.
Oedipus: Surely the gods hate me so much—
Creon: You'll get your wish at once.
Oedipus: You consent?   1670
Creon: I try to say what I mean; it's my habit.
Oedipus: Then take me away. It's time.
Creon: Come along, let go of the children.
Oedipus: No—
don't take them away from me, not now! No no no!

Clutching his daughters as the guards wrench them loose and take them through the palace doors.

Creon: Still the king, the master of all things?   1675
No more: here your power ends.
None of your power follows you through life.

Exit Oedipus and Creon to the palace. The Chorus comes forward to address the audience directly.

Chorus: People of Thebes, my countrymen, look on Oedipus.
He solved the famous riddle with his brilliance,
he rose to power, a man beyond all power.   1680
Who could behold his greatness without envy?
Now what a black sea of terror has overwhelmed him.
Now as we keep our watch and wait the final day,
count no man happy till he dies, free of pain at last.

Exit in procession.

CONSIDERATIONS FOR CRITICAL THINKING AND WRITING

1. FIRST RESPONSE. Is it possible for a contemporary reader to identify with Oedipus's plight? What philosophic issues does he confront?

2. In the opening scene what does the priest's speech reveal about how Oedipus has been regarded as a ruler of Thebes?

3. What do Oedipus's confrontations with Tiresias and Creon indicate about his character?

4. Aristotle defined a tragic flaw as consisting of "error and frailties." What errors does Oedipus make? What are his frailties?

5. What causes Oedipus's downfall? Is he simply a pawn in a predetermined game played by the gods? Can he be regarded as responsible for the suffering and death in the play?

6. Locate instances of dramatic irony in the play. How do they serve as foreshadowings?

7. Describe the function of the Chorus. How does the Chorus's view of life and the gods differ from Jocasta's?

8. Trace the images of vision and blindness throughout the play. How are they related to the theme? Why does Oedipus blind himself instead of joining Jocasta in suicide?

9. What is your assessment of Oedipus at the end of the play? Was he foolish? Heroic? Fated? To what extent can your emotions concerning him be described as "pity and fear"?

10. CRITICAL STRATEGIES. Read the section on psychological criticism (pp. 64–66) in Chapter 3, "Applying a Critical Strategy." Given that the *Oedipus complex* is a well-known term used in psychoanalysis, what does it mean? Does the concept offer any insights into the conflicts dramatized in the play?

WILLIAM SHAKESPEARE AND ELIZABETHAN DRAMA

Although relatively little is known about William Shakespeare's life, his writings reveal him to have been an extraordinary man. His vitality, compassion, and insights are evident in his broad range of characters, who have fascinated generations of audiences, and his powerful use of the English

PHOTO: *Image of William Shakespeare included on the* First Folio, *a collected edition of Shakespeare plays published seven years after his death. Reprinted by permission of The Folger Shakespeare Library.*

language, which has been celebrated since his death nearly four centuries ago. Ben Jonson, his contemporary, rightly claimed that "he was not of an age, but for all time!" Shakespeare's plays have been produced so often and his writings read so widely that quotations from them have woven their way into our everyday conversations. If you have ever experienced "fear and trembling" because there was "something in the wind" or discovered that it was "a foregone conclusion" that you would "make a virtue of necessity," then it wouldn't be quite accurate for you to say that Shakespeare "was Greek to me" because these phrases come, respectively, from his plays *Much Ado about Nothing, Comedy of Errors, Othello, The Two Gentlemen of Verona,* and *Julius Caesar.* Many more examples could be cited, but it is enough to say that Shakespeare's art endures. His words may give us only an oblique glimpse of his life, but they continue to give us back the experience of our own lives.

Shakespeare was born in Stratford-on-Avon on or about April 23, 1564. His father, an important citizen who held several town offices, married a woman from a prominent family; however, when their son was only a teenager, the family's financial situation became precarious. Shakespeare probably attended the Stratford grammar school, but no records of either his schooling or his early youth exist. As limited as his education was, it is clear that he was for his time a learned man. At the age of eighteen, he struck out on his own and married the twenty-six-year-old Anne Hathaway, who bore him a daughter in 1583 and twins, a boy and a girl, in 1585. Before he was twenty-one, Shakespeare had a wife and three children to support.

What his life was like for the next seven years is not known, but there is firm evidence that by 1592 he was in London enjoying some success as both an actor and a playwright. By 1594 he had also established himself as a poet with two lengthy poems, *Venus and Adonis* and *The Rape of Lucrece.* But it was in the theater that he made his living and his strongest reputation. He was well connected with a successful troupe first known as the Lord Chamberlain's Men; they built the famous Globe Theatre in 1599. Later this company, because of the patronage of King James, came to be known as the King's Men. Writing plays for this company throughout his career, Shakespeare also became one of its principal shareholders, an arrangement that allowed him to prosper in London as well as in his native Stratford, where in 1597 he bought a fine house called New Place. About 1611 he retired there with his family, although he continued writing plays. He died on April 23, 1616, and was buried at Holy Trinity Church in Stratford.

The documented details of Shakespeare's life provide barely enough information for a newspaper obituary. But if his activities remain largely unknown, his writings — among them thirty-seven plays and 154 sonnets — more than compensate for that loss. Plenty of authors have produced more work, but no writer has created so much literature that has been so universally admired. Within twenty-five years Shakespeare's dramatic works included *Hamlet, Macbeth, King Lear, Othello, Julius Caesar, Richard III, 1 Henry IV, Romeo and Juliet, Love's Labour's Lost, A Midsummer Night's Dream,*

The Tempest, Twelfth Night, and *Measure for Measure.* These plays represent a broad range of characters and actions conveyed in poetic language that reveals human nature as well as the author's genius.

Shakespeare's Theater

Drama languished in Europe after the fall of Rome during the fifth and sixth centuries. From about A.D. 400 to 900 almost no record of dramatic productions exists except for those of minstrels and other entertainers, such as acrobats and jugglers, who traveled through the countryside. The Catholic church was instrumental in suppressing drama because the theater — represented by the excesses of Roman productions — was seen as subversive. No state-sponsored festivals brought people together in huge theaters the way they had in Greek and Roman times.

In the tenth century, however, the church helped revive theater by incorporating dialogues into the Mass as a means of dramatizing portions of the Gospels. These brief dialogues developed into more elaborate mystery plays, miracle plays, and morality plays, anonymous works that were created primarily to inculcate religious principles rather than to entertain. But these works also marked the reemergence of relatively large dramatic productions.

Mystery plays dramatize stories from the Bible, such as the Creation, the Fall of Adam and Eve, or the Crucifixion. The most highly regarded surviving example is *The Second Shepherd's Play* (c. 1400), which dramatizes Christ's nativity. **Miracle plays** are based on the lives of saints. An extant play of the late fifteenth century, for example, is titled *Saint Mary Magdalene.* **Morality plays** present allegorical stories in which virtues and vices are personified to teach humanity how to achieve salvation. *Everyman* (c. 1500), the most famous example, has as its central conflict every person's struggle to avoid the sins that lead to hell and practice the virtues that are rewarded in heaven.

The clergy who performed these plays gave way to trade guilds that presented them outside the church on stages featuring scenery and costumed characters. The plays' didactic content was gradually abandoned in favor of broad humor and worldly concerns. Thus by the sixteenth century religious drama had been replaced largely by secular drama.

Because theatrical productions were no longer sponsored and financed by the church or trade guilds during Shakespeare's lifetime, playwrights had to figure out ways to draw audiences willing to pay for entertainment. This necessitated some simple but important changes. Somehow, people had to be prevented from seeing a production unless they paid. Hence an enclosed space with controlled access was created. In addition, the plays had to change frequently enough to keep audiences returning, and this resulted in more experienced actors and playwrights sensitive to their audiences' tastes and interests. Plays compelling enough to attract audiences had to employ a powerful writing brought to life by convincing actors in entertaining productions. Shakespeare always wrote his dramas for the stage — for audiences who would see and hear the characters. The conventions of the theater for which he wrote are important, then, for appreciating and understanding his plays. Detailed information about Elizabethan theater (theater during the reign of Elizabeth I, from 1558 to 1603) is less than abundant, but historians have been able to piece together a good sense of what theaters were like from sources such as drawings, building contracts, and stage directions.

Early performances of various kinds took place in the courtyards of inns and taverns. These secular entertainments attracted people of all classes. To the dismay of London officials, such gatherings were also settings for the illegal activities of brawlers, thieves, and prostitutes. To avoid licensing regulations, some theaters were constructed outside the city's limits. The Globe, for instance, built by the Lord Chamberlain's Company, with which Shakespeare was closely associated, was located on the south bank of the Thames River. Regardless of the play, an Elizabethan theatergoer was likely to have an exciting time. Playwrights understood the varied nature of their audiences, so the plays appealed to a broad range of sensibilities and tastes. Philosophy and poetry rubbed shoulders with violence and sexual jokes, and somehow all were made compatible.

Physically, Elizabethan theaters resembled the courtyards where they originated, but the theaters could accommodate more people — perhaps as many as twenty-five hundred. The exterior of a theater building was many-sided or round and enclosed a yard that was only partially roofed over, to take advantage of natural light. The interior walls consisted of three galleries of seats looking onto a platform stage that extended from the rear wall. These seats were sheltered from the weather and more comfortable than the area in front of the stage, which was known as the *pit*. Here "groundlings" paid a penny to stand and watch the performance. Despite the large number of spectators, the theater created an intimate atmosphere because the audience closely surrounded the stage on three sides.

This arrangement produced two theatrical conventions: asides and soliloquies. An *aside* is a speech directed only to the audience. It makes the audience privy to a character's thoughts, allowing them to perceive ironies and intrigues that other characters know nothing about. In a large performing space, such as a Greek amphitheater, asides would be unconvincing because they would have to be declaimed loudly to be heard, but they were well suited to Elizabethan theaters. A *soliloquy* is a speech delivered while an actor is alone on the stage; like an aside, it reveals a character's state of mind. Hamlet's "To be or not to be" speech is the most famous example of a soliloquy.

The Elizabethan platform stage was large enough — approximately 25 feet deep and 40 feet wide — to allow a wide variety of actions, ranging from festive banquets to bloody battles. Sections of the floor could be opened or removed to create, for instance, the gravediggers' scene in *Hamlet* or to allow characters to exit through trapdoors. At the rear of the plat-

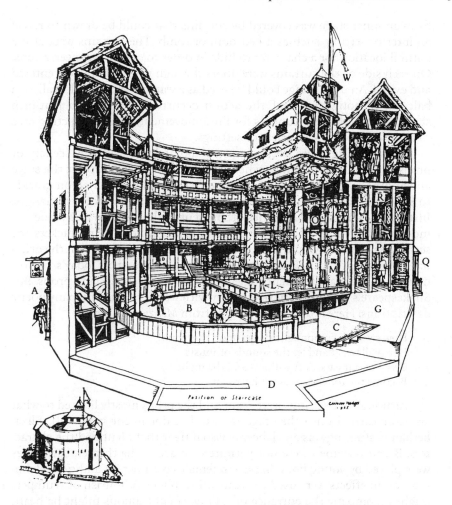

A   Main entrance
B   The yard
C   Entrances to lowest gallery
D   Position of entrances to staircase and upper galleries
E   Corridor serving the different sections of the middle gallery
F   Middle gallery ("Twopenny Rooms")
G   Position of "Gentlemen's Rooms" or "Lords' Rooms"
H   The stage
J   The hanging being put up round the stage
K   The "hell" under the stage

L   The stage trap leading down to the hell
M   Stage doors
N   Curtained "place behind the stage"
O   Gallery above the stage, used as required sometimes by musicians, sometimes by spectators, and often as part of the play
P   Backstage area (the tiring-house)
Q   Tiring-house door
R   Dressing-rooms
S   Wardrobe and storage
T   The hut housing the machine for lowering enthroned gods, etc., to the stage
U   The "heavens"
W   Hoisting the playhouse flag

A conjectural reconstruction of the Globe Theatre, 1599–1613. (Drawing by C. Walter Hodges from his The Globe Restored, *published by Oxford University Press. © 1968 C. Walter Hodges. Reprinted by permission of Oxford University Press.)*

form an inner stage was covered by curtains that could be drawn to reveal an interior setting, such as a bedroom or tomb. The curtains were also a natural location for a character to hide in order to overhear conversations. On each side of the curtains were doors through which characters entered and exited. An upper stage could be used as a watchtower, a castle wall, or a balcony. Although most of the action occurred on the main platform stage, there were opportunities for fluid movements from one acting area to another, providing a variety of settings.

These settings were not, however, elaborately indicated by scenery or props. A scene might change when one group of characters left the stage and another entered. A table and some chairs could be carried on quickly to suggest a tavern. But the action was not interrupted for set changes. Instead, the characters' speeches often identify the location of a scene. (In modern editions of Shakespeare's plays, editors indicate in brackets the scene breaks, settings, and movements of actors not identified in the original manuscripts to help readers keep track of things.) Today's performances of the plays frequently use more elaborate settings and props. But Shakespeare's need to paint his scenery with words resulted in many poetic descriptions. Here is one of moonlight from *Merchant of Venice*:

> How sweet the moonlight sleeps upon this bank!
> Here will we sit and let the sounds of music
> Creep in our ears. Soft stillness and the night
> Become the touches of sweet harmony.

Although the settings were scant and the props mostly limited to what an actor carried onto the stage (a sword, a document, a shovel), Elizabethan costuming was an elaborate visual treat that identified the characters. Because women were not permitted to act in the theater, their roles were played by young boys dressed in female costumes. In addition, elaborate sound effects were used to create atmosphere. A flourish of trumpets might accompany the entrance of a king; small cannons might be heard during a battle; thunder might punctuate a storm. In short, Elizabethan theater was alive with sights and sounds, but at the center of the stage was the playwright's language; that's where the magic began.

The Range of Shakespeare's Drama: History, Comedy, and Tragedy

Shakespeare's plays fall into three basic categories: histories, comedies, and tragedies. Broadly speaking, a history play is any drama based on historical materials. In this case, Shakespeare's *Antony and Cleopatra* and *Julius Caesar* would fit the definition, since they feature historical figures. More specifically, though, a **history play** is a British play based primarily on Raphael Holinshed's *Chronicles of England, Scotland, and Ireland* (1578). This account of British history was popular toward the end of the sixteenth century because of the patriotic pride that was produced by the British defeat of the Spanish Armada in 1588, and it was an important source for a series of plays Shakespeare wrote treating the reigns of British kings from Richard II to Henry VIII. The political subject matter of these plays both entertained audiences and instructed them in virtues and vices involved in England's past efforts to overcome civil war and disorder. Ambition, deception, and treason were of more than historical interest. Shakespeare's audiences saw these plays about the fifteenth century as ways of sorting through the meanings of both the calamities of the past and the uncertainties of the present.

Although Shakespeare used Holinshed's *Chronicles* as a source, he did not hesitate to make changes for dramatic purposes. In *1 Henry IV,* for example, he ages Henry IV to contrast him with the youthful Prince Hal, and he makes Hotspur younger than he actually was to have him serve as a foil to the prince. The serious theme of Hal's growth into the kind of man who would make an ideal king is counterweighted by Shakespeare's comic creation of Falstaff, that good-humored "huge hill of flesh" filled with delightful contradictions. Falstaff had historic antecedents, but the true source of his identity is the imagination of Shakespeare, a writer who was, after all, a dramatist first.

Comedy is a strong element in *1 Henry IV,* but the play's overall tone is serious. Falstaff's behavior ultimately gives way to the measured march of English history. While Shakespeare encourages us to laugh at some of the participants, we are not invited to laugh at the history of English monarchies. Comedy even appears in Shakespeare's tragedies, as in Hamlet's jests with the gravediggers or in Emilia's biting remarks in *Othello.* This use of comedy is called **comic relief,** a humorous scene or incident that alleviates tension in an otherwise serious work. In many instances these moments enhance the thematic significance of the story in addition to providing laughter. When Hamlet jokes with the gravediggers, we laugh, but something hauntingly serious about the humor also intensifies our more serious emotions.

A true comedy, however, lacks a tragedy's sense that some great disaster will finally descend on the protagonist. There are conflicts and obstacles that must be confronted, but in comedy the characters delight us by overcoming whatever initially thwarts them. We can laugh at their misfortunes because we are confident that everything will turn out fine in the end. Shakespearean comedy tends to follow this general principle; it begins with problems and ends with their resolution.

Shakespeare's comedies are called **romantic comedies** because they typically involve lovers whose hearts are set on each other but whose lives are complicated by disapproving parents, deceptions, jealousies, illusions, confused identities, disguises, or other misunderstandings. Conflicts are present, but they are more amusing than threatening. This lightness is apparent in some of the comedies' titles: The conflict in a play such as *A Midsummer Night's Dream* is, in a sense, *Much Ado about Nothing—As You Like*

It in a comedy. Shakespeare orchestrates the problems and confusion that typify the initial plotting of a romantic comedy into harmonious wedding arrangements in the final scenes. In these comedies life is a celebration, a feast that always satisfies, because the generosity of the humor leaves us with a revived appetite for life's surprising possibilities. Discord and misunderstanding give way to concord and love. Marriage symbolizes a pledge that life itself is renewable, so we are left with a sense of new beginnings.

Although a celebration of life, comedy is also frequently used as a vehicle for criticizing human affairs. *Satire* casts a critical eye on vices and follies by holding them up to ridicule — usually to point out an absurdity so that it can be avoided or corrected. In *Twelfth Night* Malvolio is satirized for his priggishness and pomposity. He thinks himself better than almost everyone around him, but Shakespeare reveals him to be comic as well as pathetic. We come to understand what Malvolio will apparently never comprehend: that no one can take him as seriously as he takes himself. Polonius is subjected to a similar kind of scrutiny in *Hamlet.*

Malvolio's ambitious efforts to attract Olivia's affections are rendered absurd by Shakespeare's use of both high and low comedy. **High comedy** consists of verbal wit, while **low comedy** is generally associated with physical action and is less intellectual. Through puns and witty exchanges, Shakespeare's high comedy displays Malvolio's inconsistencies of character. His self-importance is deflated by low comedy. We are treated to a *farce,* a form of humor based on exaggerated, improbable incongruities, when the staid Malvolio is tricked into wearing bizarre clothing and behaving like a fool to win Olivia. Our laughter is Malvolio's pain, but though he has been "notoriously abus'd" and he vows in the final scene to be "reveng'd on the whole pack" of laughing conspirators who have tricked him, the play ends on a light note. Indeed, it concludes with a song, the last line of which reminds us of the predominant tone of the play as well as the nature of comedy: "And we'll strive to please you every day."

Tragedy, in contrast, does not promise peace and contentment. The basic characteristics of tragedy have already been outlined in the context of Greek drama (see p. 290). Like Greek tragic heroes, Shakespeare's protagonists are exceptional human beings whose stature makes their misfortune all the more dramatic. These characters pay a high price for their actions. Oedipus's search for the killer of Laius, Antigone's and Creon's refusal to compromise their principles, Hamlet's agonized conviction that "The time is out of joint," and Othello's willingness to doubt his wife's fidelity all lead to irreversible results. Comic plots are largely free of this sense of inevitability. Instead of the festive mood that prevails once the characters in a comedy recognize their true connection to each other, tragedy gives us dark reflections that emanate from suffering. The laughter of comedy is a shared experience, a recognition of human likeness, but suffering estranges tragic heroes from the world around them.

Some of the wrenching differences between comedy and tragedy can be experienced in *Othello*. Although this play is a tragedy, Shakespeare includes in its plot many of the ingredients associated with comedy. For a time it seems possible that Othello and Desdemona will overcome the complications of a disapproving father, along with the seemingly minor deceptions, awkward misperceptions, and tender illusions that hover around them. But in *Othello* marriage is not a sign of concord displacing discord; instead, love and marriage mark the beginning of the tragic action.

Another important difference between tragedy and comedy is the way characters are presented. The tragic protagonist is portrayed as a remarkable individual whose unique qualities compel us with their power and complexity. Macbeth is not simply a murderer nor is Othello merely a jealous husband. But despite their extreme passions, behavior, and even crimes, we identify with tragic heroes in ways that we do not with comic characters. We can laugh at pretentious fools, smug hypocrites, clumsy oafs, and thwarted lovers because we see them from a distance. They are amusing precisely because their problems are not ours; we recognize them as types instead of as ourselves (or so we think). No reader of *Twelfth Night* worries about Sir Toby Belch's excessive drinking; he is a cheerful "sot" whose passion for ale is cause for celebration rather than concern. Shakespeare's comedy is sometimes disturbing—Malvolio's character certainly is—but it is never devastating. Tragic heroes do confront devastation; they command our respect and compassion because they act in spite of terrifying risks. Their triumph is not measured by the attainment of what they seek but by the wisdom that defeat imposes on them.

A Note on Reading Shakespeare

Readers who have had no previous experience with Shakespeare's language may find it initially daunting. They might well ask whether people ever talked the way, for example, Hamlet does in his most famous soliloquy:

> To be, or not to be: that is the question:
> Whether 'tis nobler in the mind to suffer
> The slings and arrows of outrageous fortune,
> Or to take arms against a sea of troubles,
> And by opposing end them?

People did not talk like this in Elizabethan times. Hamlet speaks poetry. Shakespeare might have had him say something like this: "The most important issue one must confront is whether the pain that life inevitably creates should be passively accepted or resisted." But Shakespeare chose poetry to reveal the depth and complexity of Hamlet's experience. This heightened language is used to clarify rather than obscure his characters' thoughts. Shakespeare has Hamlet, as well as many other characters, speak in prose too, but in general his plays are written in poetry. If you keep in mind that Shakespeare's dialogue is not typically intended to imitate everyday speech, it should be easier to understand that his language is more than simply a vehicle for expressing the action of the play.

Here are a few practical suggestions to enhance your understanding of and pleasure in reading Shakespeare's plays.

1. Keep track of the characters by referring to the *dramatis personae* (characters) listed and briefly described at the beginning of each play.
2. Remember that poetic language deserves to be read slowly and carefully. A difficult passage can sometimes be better understood if it's read aloud. Don't worry if every line isn't absolutely clear to you.
3. Pay attention to the annotations, which explain unfamiliar words, phrases, and allusions in the text. These can be distracting, but they are sometimes necessary to determine the basic meaning of a passage.
4. As you read each scene, try to imagine how it would be played on a stage.
5. If you find the reading especially difficult, try listening to a recording of the play. (Most college libraries have records and tapes of Shakespeare's plays.) Allowing professional actors to do the reading aloud for you can enrich your imaginative reconstruction of the action and characters. Hearing a play can help you with subsequent readings of it.
6. After reading the play, view a film or videocassette recording of a performance. It is important to view the performance *after* your reading, though, so that your own mental re-creation of the play is not short-circuited by a director's production.

And finally, to quote Hamlet, "Be not too tame . . . let your own discretion be your tutor." Read Shakespeare's work as best you can; it warrants such careful attention not because the language and characters are difficult to understand but because they offer so much to enjoy.

Hamlet, Prince of Denmark

Hamlet, the most famous play in English literature, continues to fascinate and challenge both readers and audiences. Interpretations of Hamlet's character and actions abound because the play has produced so many intense and varied responses. No small indication of the tragedy's power is that actors long to play its title role.

A brief summary can suggest the movement of the plot but not the depth of Hamlet's character. After learning of his father's death, Prince Hamlet returns to the Danish court from his university studies to find Claudius, the dead king's brother, ruling Denmark and married to Hamlet's mother, Gertrude. Her remarriage within two months of his father's death has left Hamlet disillusioned, confused, and suspicious of Claudius. When his father's ghost appears before Hamlet to reveal that Claudius murdered the king, Hamlet is confronted with having to avenge his father's death.

Hamlet's efforts to carry out this obligation would have been a familiar kind of plot to Elizabethan audiences. **Revenge tragedy** was a well-established type of drama that traced its antecedents to Greek and Roman plays, particularly through the Roman playwright Seneca (c. 3 B.C.–A.D. 65), whose plays were translated and produced in English in the late sixteenth century. Shakespeare's audiences knew its conventions, particularly from Thomas Kyd's popular *Spanish Tragedy* (c. 1587). Basically, this type of play consists of a murder that has to be avenged by a relative of the victim. Typically, the victim's ghost appears to demand revenge, and invariably madness of some sort is worked into subsequent events, which ultimately result in the deaths of the murderer, the avenger, and a number of other characters. Crime, madness, ghostly anguish, poison, overheard conversations, conspiracies, and a final scene littered with corpses: *Hamlet* subscribes to the basic ingredients of the formula, but it also transcends the conventions of revenge tragedy because Hamlet contemplates not merely revenge but suicide and the meaning of life itself.

Hamlet must face not only a diseased social order but also conflicts within himself when his indecisiveness becomes as agonizing as the corruption surrounding him. However, Hamlet is also a forceful and attractive character. His intelligence is repeatedly revealed in his penetrating use of language; through images and metaphors he creates a perspective on his world that is at once satiric and profoundly painful. His astonishing and sometimes shocking wit is leveled at his mother, his beloved Ophelia, and Claudius as well as himself. Nothing escapes his critical eye and divided imagination. Hamlet, no less than the people around him, is perplexed by his alienation from life.

Hamlet's limitations as well as his virtues make him one of Shakespeare's most complex characters. His keen self-awareness is both agonizing and liberating. Although he struggles throughout the play with painful issues ranging from family loyalties to matters of state, he retains his dignity as a tragic hero, whom generations of audiences have found compelling.

WILLIAM SHAKESPEARE (1564–1616)

Hamlet, Prince of Denmark

1600

[DRAMATIS PERSONAE

Claudius, King of Denmark
Hamlet, son to the late and nephew to the present king
Polonius, lord chamberlain
Horatio, friend to Hamlet
Laertes, son to Polonius
Voltimand
Cornelius
Rosencrantz   } courtiers
Guildenstern
Osric

A Gentleman
A Priest
Marcellus ⎫ officers
Bernardo ⎭
Francisco, a soldier
Reynaldo, servant to Polonius
Players
Two Clowns, grave-diggers
Fortinbras, Prince of Norway
A Captain
English Ambassadors
Gertrude, Queen of Denmark, and mother to Hamlet
Ophelia, daughter to Polonius
Lords, Ladies, Officers, Soldiers, Sailors, Messengers, and other Attendants
Ghost of Hamlet's Father

SCENE: *Denmark.*]

[A C T   I

SCENE I: *Elsinore. A platform° before the castle.*]

> *Enter Bernardo and Francisco, two sentinels.*

Bernardo: Who's there?
Francisco: Nay, answer me:° stand, and unfold yourself.
Bernardo: Long live the king!°
Francisco: Bernardo?
Bernardo: He.   5
Francisco: You come most carefully upon your hour.
Bernardo: 'Tis now struck twelve; get thee to bed, Francisco.
Francisco: For this relief much thanks: 'tis bitter cold,
> And I am sick at heart.
Bernardo: Have you had quiet guard?
Francisco: Not a mouse stirring.   10
Bernardo: Well, good night.
> If you do meet Horatio and Marcellus,
> The rivals° of my watch, bid them make haste.

> *Enter Horatio and Marcellus.*

Francisco: I think I hear them. Stand, ho! Who is there?
Horatio: Friends to this ground.
Marcellus: And liegemen to the Dane.   15

Act I, Scene I.   *platform:* A level space on the battlements of the royal castle at Elsinore, a
Danish seaport; now Helsingör.   2 *me:* This is emphatic, since Francisco is the sentry.
3 *Long live the king:* Either a password or greeting; Horatio and Marcellus use a different one
in line 15.   13 *rivals:* Partners.

Francisco: Give you° good night.
Marcellus: O, farewell, honest soldier:
    Who hath reliev'd you?
Francisco: Bernardo hath my place.
    Give you good night.   *Exit Francisco.*
Marcellus: Holla! Bernardo!
Bernardo: Say,
    What, is Horatio there?
Horatio: A piece of him.
Bernardo: Welcome, Horatio: welcome, good Marcellus.   20
Marcellus: What, has this thing appear'd again to-night?
Bernardo: I have seen nothing.
Marcellus: Horatio says 'tis but our fantasy,
    And will not let belief take hold of him
    Touching this dreaded sight, twice seen of us: 25
    Therefore I have entreated him along
    With us to watch the minutes of this night;
    That if again this apparition come,
    He may approve° our eyes and speak to it.
Horatio: Tush, tush, 'twill not appear.
Bernardo: Sit down awhile;   30
    And let us once again assail your ears,
    That are so fortified against our story
    What we have two nights seen.
Horatio: Well, sit we down,
    And let us hear Bernardo speak of this.
Bernardo: Last night of all,   35
    When yond same star that's westward from the pole°
    Had made his course t' illume that part of heaven
    Where now it burns, Marcellus and myself,
    The bell then beating one, —

    Enter Ghost.

Marcellus: Peace, break thee off; look, where it comes again!   40
Bernardo: In the same figure, like the king that's dead.
Marcellus: Thou art a scholar;° speak to it, Horatio.
Bernardo: Looks 'a not like the king? mark it, Horatio.
Horatio: Most like: it harrows° me with fear and wonder.
Bernardo: It would be spoke to.°
Marcellus: Speak to it, Horatio.   45
Horatio: What art thou that usurp'st this time of night,
    Together with that fair and warlike form
    In which the majesty of buried Denmark°
    Did sometimes march? by heaven I charge thee, speak!

---

16 *Give you:* God give you.   29 *approve:* Corroborate.   36 *pole:* Polestar.   42 *scholar:*
Exorcisms were performed in Latin, which Horatio as an educated man would be able to
speak.   44 *harrows:* Lacerates the feelings.   45 *It...to:* A ghost could not speak until
spoken to.   48 *buried Denmark:* The buried king of Denmark.

Marcellus: It is offended.
Bernardo: See it stalks away!   50
Horatio: Stay! speak, speak! I charge thee, speak!   *Exit Ghost.*
Marcellus: 'Tis gone, and will not answer.
Bernardo: How now, Horatio! you tremble and look pale:
    Is not this something more than fantasy?
    What think you on 't?   55
Horatio: Before my God, I might not this believe
    Without the sensible and true avouch
    Of mine own eyes.
Marcellus: Is it not like the king?
Horatio: As thou art to thyself:
    Such was the very armour he had on   60
    When he the ambitious Norway combated;
    So frown'd he once, when, in an angry parle,
    He smote° the sledded Polacks° on the ice.
    'Tis strange.
Marcellus: Thus twice before, and jump° at this dead hour,   65
    With martial stalk hath he gone by our watch.
Horatio: In what particular thought to work I know not;
    But in the gross and scope° of my opinion,
    This bodes some strange eruption to our state.
Marcellus: Good now,° sit down, and tell me, he that knows,   70
    Why this same strict and most observant watch
    So nightly toils° the subject° of the land,
    And why such daily cast° of brazen cannon,
    And foreign mart° for implements of war;
    Why such impress° of shipwrights, whose sore task   75
    Does not divide the Sunday from the week;
    What might be toward, that this sweaty haste
    Doth make the night joint-labourer with the day:
    Who is't that can inform me?
Horatio: That can I;
    At least, the whisper goes so. Our last king,   80
    Whose image even but now appear'd to us,
    Was, as you know, by Fortinbras of Norway,
    Thereto prick'd on° by a most emulate° pride,
    Dar'd to the combat; in which our valiant Hamlet—
    For so this side of our known world esteem'd him—   85
    Did slay this Fortinbras; who, by a seal'd compact,
    Well ratified by law and heraldry,°
    Did forfeit, with his life, all those his lands
    Which he stood seiz'd° of, to the conqueror:

---

63 *smote:* Defeated; *sledded Polacks:* Polanders using sledges. 65 *jump:* Exactly.
68 *gross and scope:* General drift.   70 *Good now:* An expression denoting entreaty or
expostulation.   72 *toils:* Causes or makes to toil; *subject:* People, subjects.   73 *cast:*
Casting, founding.   74 *mart:* Buying and selling, traffic.   75 *impress:* Impressment.
83 *prick'd on:* Incited; *emulate:* Rivaling.   87 *law and heraldry:* Heraldic law, governing
combat.   89 *seiz'd:* Possessed.

Against the which, a moiety competent°   90
Was gaged by our king; which had return'd
To the inheritance of Fortinbras,
Had he been vanquisher; as, by the same comart,°
And carriage° of the article design'd,
His fell to Hamlet. Now, sir, young Fortinbras,   95
Of unimproved° mettle hot and full,°
Hath in the skirts of Norway here and there
Shark'd up° a list of lawless resolutes,°
For food and diet,° to some enterprise
That hath a stomach in't; which is no other —   100
As it doth well appear unto our state —
But to recover of us, by strong hand
And terms compulsatory, those foresaid lands
So by his father lost: and this, I take it,
Is the main motive of our preparations,   105
The source of this our watch and the chief head
Of this post-haste and romage° in the land.
Bernardo: I think it be no other but e'en so:
     Well may it sort° that this portentous figure
     Comes armed through our watch; so like the king   110
     That was and is the question of these wars.
Horatio: A mote° it is to trouble the mind's eye.
     In the most high and palmy state° of Rome,
     A little ere the mightiest Julius fell,
     The graves stood tenantless and the sheeted dead   115
     Did squeak and gibber in the Roman streets:
     As stars with trains of fire° and dews of blood,
     Disasters° in the sun; and the moist star°
     Upon whose influence Neptune's empire° stands
     Was sick almost to doomsday with eclipse: 120
     And even the like precurse° of fear'd events,
     As harbingers preceding still the fates
     And prologue to the omen coming on,
     Have heaven and earth together demonstrated
     Unto our climatures and countrymen. —   125

     Enter Ghost.

     But soft, behold! lo, where it comes again!
     I'll cross° it, though it blast me. Stay, illusion!
     If thou hast any sound, or use of voice,

---

90 *moiety competent:* Adequate or sufficient portion.   93 *comart:* Joint bargain.   94 *carriage:* Import, bearing.   96 *unimproved:* Not turned to account; *hot and full:* Full of fight.
98 *Shark'd up:* Got together in haphazard fashion; *resolutes:* Desperadoes.   99 *food and diet:* No pay but their keep.   107 *romage:* Bustle, commotion.   109 *sort:* Suit.
112 *mote:* Speck of dust.   113 *palmy state:* Triumphant sovereignty.   117 *stars...fire:* I.e., comets.   118 *Disasters:* Unfavorable aspects; *moist star:* The moon, governing tides.
119 *Neptune's empire:* The sea.   121 *precurse:* Heralding.   127 *cross:* Meet, face, thus bringing down the evil influence on the person who crosses it.

Speak to me!   *It° spreads his arms.*
If there be any good thing to be done,   130
That may to thee do ease and grace to me,
Speak to me!
If thou art privy to thy country's fate,
Which, happily, foreknowing may avoid,
O, speak!   135
Or if thou hast uphoarded in thy life
Extorted treasure in the womb of earth,
For which, they say, you spirits oft walk in death,   *The cock crows.*
Speak of it:° stay, and speak! Stop it, Marcellus.
Marcellus: Shall I strike at it with my partisan?°   140
Horatio: Do, if it will not stand.
Bernardo: 'Tis here!
Horatio: 'Tis here!
     Marcellus: 'Tis gone!   *[Exit Ghost.]*
     We do it wrong, being so majestical,
     To offer it the show of violence;
     For it is, as the air, invulnerable,   145
     And our vain blows malicious mockery.
Bernardo: It was about to speak, when the cock crew.°
Horatio: And then it started like a guilty thing
     Upon a fearful summons. I have heard,
     The cock, that is the trumpet to the morn,   150
     Doth with his lofty and shrill-sounding throat
     Awake the god of day; and, at his warning,
     Whether in sea or fire, in earth or air,
     Th' extravagant and erring° spirit hies
     To his confine:° and of the truth herein   155
     This present object made probation.°
Marcellus: It faded on the crowing of the cock.
     Some say that ever 'gainst° that season comes
     Wherein our Saviour's birth is celebrated,
     The bird of dawning singeth all night long: 160
     And then, they say, no spirit dare stir abroad;
     The nights are wholesome; then no planets strike,°
     No fairy takes, nor witch hath power to charm,
     So hallow'd and so gracious° is that time.
Horatio: So have I heard and do in part believe it.   165
     But, look, the morn, in russet mantle clad,
     Walks o'er the dew of yon high eastward hill:
     Break we our watch up; and by my advice,
     Let us impart what we have seen to-night

---

129 *It:* The Ghost, or perhaps Horatio.   133–139 *If . . . it:* Horatio recites the traditional
reasons why ghosts might walk.   140 *partisan:* Long-handled spear with a blade having
lateral projections.   147 *cock crew:* According to traditional ghost lore, spirits returned to
their confines at cockcrow.   154 *extravagant and erring:* Wandering. Both words mean the
same thing.   155 *confine:* Place of confinement.   156 *probation:* Proof, trial.   158 *'gainst:*
Just before.   162 *planets strike:* It was thought that planets were malignant and might
strike travelers by night.   164 *gracious:* Full of goodness.

Unto young Hamlet; for, upon my life,   170
This spirit, dumb to us, will speak to him.
Do you consent we shall acquaint him with it,
As needful in our loves, fitting our duty?
Marcellus: Let's do 't, I pray; and I this morning know
Where we shall find him most conveniently.   *Exeunt.*   175

[SCENE II: *A room of state in the castle.*]

*Flourish. Enter Claudius, King of Denmark, Gertrude the Queen, Councilors,
Polonius and his Son Laertes, Hamlet, cum aliis° [including Voltimand and
Cornelius].*

King: Though yet of Hamlet our dear brother's death
The memory be green, and that it us befitted
To bear our hearts in grief and our whole kingdom
To be contracted in one brow of woe,
Yet so far hath discretion fought with nature   5
That we with wisest sorrow think on him,
Together with remembrance of ourselves.
Therefore our sometime sister, now our queen,
Th' imperial jointress° to this warlike state,
Have we, as 'twere with a defeated joy, —   10
With an auspicious and a dropping eye,
With mirth in funeral and with dirge in marriage,
In equal scale weighing delight and dole, —
Taken to wife: nor have we herein barr'd
Your better wisdoms, which have freely gone   15
With this affair along. For all, our thanks.
Now follows, that° you know, young Fortinbras,
Holding a weak supposal° of our worth,
Or thinking by our late dear brother's death
Our state to be disjoint° and out of frame,°   20
Colleagued° with this dream of his advantage,°
He hath not fail'd to pester us with message,
Importing° the surrender of those lands
Lost by his father, with all bands of law,
To our most valiant brother. So much for him.   25
Now for ourself and for this time of meeting:
Thus much the business is: we have here writ
To Norway, uncle of young Fortinbras, —
Who, impotent and bed-rid, scarcely hears
Of this his nephew's purpose, — to suppress   30
His further gait° herein; in that the levies,
The lists and full proportions, are all made

Scene II. *cum aliis:* With others.   9 *jointress:* Woman possessed of a jointure, or, joint
tenancy of an estate.   17 *that:* That which.   18 *weak supposal:* Low estimate.   20 *dis-
joint:* Distracted, out of joint; *frame:* Order.   21 *Colleagued:* Added to; *dream ... advantage:*
Visionary hope of success.   23 *Importing:* Purporting, pertaining to.   31 *gait:* Proceeding.

Out of his subject:° and we here dispatch
You, good Cornelius, and you, Voltimand,
For bearers of this greeting to old Norway;   35
Giving to you no further personal power
To business with the king, more than the scope
Of these delated° articles allow.
Farewell, and let your haste commend your duty.

Cornelius: }   In that and all things will we show our duty.   40
Voltimand:

King: We doubt it nothing: heartily farewell.

                                 [Exeunt Voltimand and Cornelius.]

And now, Laertes, what's the news with you?
You told us of some suit; what is't, Laertes?
You cannot speak of reason to the Dane,°
And lose your voice:° what wouldst thou beg, Laertes,   45
That shall not be my offer, not thy asking?
The head is not more native° to the heart,
The hand more instrumental° to the mouth,
Than is the throne of Denmark to thy father.
What wouldst thou have, Laertes?

Laertes: My dread lord,   50
Your leave and favour to return to France;
From whence though willingly I came to Denmark,
To show my duty in your coronation,
Yet now, I must confess, that duty done,
My thoughts and wishes bend again toward France   55
And bow them to your gracious leave and pardon.°

King: Have you your father's leave? What says Polonius?
Polonius: He hath, my lord, wrung from me my slow leave
By laboursome petition, and at last
Upon his will I seal'd my hard consent: 60
I do beseech you, give him leave to go.

King: Take thy fair hour, Laertes; time be thine,
And thy best graces spend it at thy will!
But now, my cousin° Hamlet, and my son, —

Hamlet [aside]: A little more than kin, and less than kind!°   65
King: How is it that the clouds still hang on you?
Hamlet: Not so, my lord; I am too much in the sun.°
Queen: Good Hamlet, cast thy nighted colour off,
And let thine eye look like a friend on Denmark.
Do not for ever with thy vailed lids   70

---

33 *Out of his subject:* At the expense of Norway's subjects (collectively).   38 *delated:* Expressly stated.   44 *the Dane:* Danish king.   45 *lose your voice:* Speak in vain. 47 *native:* Closely connected, related.   48 *instrumental:* Serviceable.   56 *leave and pardon:* Permission to depart.   64 *cousin:* Any kin not of the immediate family.   65 *A little . . . kind:* My relation to you has become more than kinship warrants; it has also become unnatural.   67 *I am . . . sun:* (1) I am too much out of doors, (2) I am too much in the sun of your grace (ironical), (3) I am too much of a son to you. Possibly an allusion to the proverb "Out of heaven's blessing into the warm sun"; i.e., Hamlet is out of house and home in being deprived of the kingship.

    Seek for thy noble father in the dust:
    Thou know'st 'tis common; all that lives must die,
        Passing through nature to eternity.
Hamlet: Ay, madam, it is common.°
Queen: If it be,
        Why seems it so particular with thee?   75
Hamlet: Seems, madam! nay, it is; I know not "seems."
        'Tis not alone my inky cloak, good mother,
        Nor customary suits° of solemn black,
        Nor windy suspiration° of forc'd breath,
        No, nor the fruitful river in the eye,   80
        Nor the dejected 'haviour of the visage,
        Together with all forms, moods, shapes of grief,
        That can denote me truly: these indeed seem,
        For they are actions that a man might play:
        But I have that within which passeth show;   85
        These but the trappings and the suits of woe.
King: 'Tis sweet and commendable in your nature, Hamlet,
        To give these mourning duties to your father:
        But, you must know, your father lost a father;
        That father lost, lost his, and the survivor bound   90
        In filial obligation for some term
        To do obsequious° sorrow: but to persever
        In obstinate condolement° is a course
        Of impious stubbornness; 'tis unmanly grief;
        It shows a will most incorrect° to heaven,   95
        A heart unfortified, a mind impatient,
        An understanding simple and unschool'd:
        For what we know must be and is as common
        As any the most vulgar thing° to sense,
        Why should we in our peevish opposition   100
        Take it to heart? Fie! 'tis a fault to heaven,
        A fault against the dead, a fault to nature,
        To reason most absurd; whose common theme
        Is death of fathers, and who still hath cried,
        From the first corse till he that died to-day,   105
        "This must be so." We pray you, throw to earth
        This unprevailing° woe, and think of us
        As of a father: for let the world take note,
        You are the most immediate° to our throne;
        And with no less nobility° of love   110
        Than that which dearest father bears his son,
        Do I impart° toward you. For your intent

---

74 *Ay... common:* It is common, but it hurts nevertheless; possibly a reference to the commonplace quality of the queen's remark.   78 *customary suits:* Suits prescribed by custom for mourning.   79 *windy suspiration:* Heavy sighing.   92 *obsequious:* Dutiful.   93 *condolement:* Sorrowing.   95 *incorrect:* Untrained, uncorrected.   99 *vulgar thing:* Common experience.   107 *unprevailing:* Unavailing.   109 *most immediate:* Next in succession.   110 *nobility:* High degree.   112 *impart:* The object is apparently *love* (l. 110).

In going back to school in Wittenberg,°
It is most retrograde° to our desire:
And we beseech you, bend you° to remain   115
Here, in the cheer and comfort of our eye,
Our chiefest courtier, cousin, and our son.
Queen: Let not thy mother lose her prayers, Hamlet:
I pray thee, stay with us; go not to Wittenberg.
Hamlet: I shall in all my best obey you, madam.   120
King: Why, 'tis a loving and a fair reply:
Be as ourself in Denmark. Madam, come;
This gentle and unforc'd accord of Hamlet
Sits smiling to my heart: in grace whereof,
No jocund health that Denmark drinks to-day,   125
But the great cannon to the clouds shall tell,
And the king's rouse° the heaven shall bruit again,°
Re-speaking earthly thunder. Come away.

                  Flourish. Exeunt all but Hamlet.

Hamlet: O, that this too too sullied flesh would melt,
Thaw and resolve itself into a dew!   130
Or that the Everlasting had not fix'd
His canon 'gainst self-slaughter! O God! God!
How weary, stale, flat and unprofitable,
Seem to me all the uses of this world!
Fie on't! ah fie! 'tis an unweeded garden,   135
That grows to seed; things rank and gross in nature
Possess it merely.° That it should come to this!
But two months dead: nay, not so much, not two:
So excellent a king; that was, to this,
Hyperion° to a satyr; so loving to my mother   140
That he might not beteem° the winds of heaven
Visit her face too roughly. Heaven and earth!
Must I remember? why, she would hang on him,
As if increase of appetite had grown
By what it fed on: and yet, within a month —   145
Let me not think on't — Frailty, thy name is woman! —
A little month, or ere those shoes were old
With which she followed my poor father's body,
Like Niobe,° all tears: — why she, even she —
O God! a beast, that wants discourse of reason,°   150
Would have mourn'd longer — married with my uncle,
My father's brother, but no more like my father
Than I to Hercules: within a month:
Ere yet the salt of most unrighteous tears

---

113 *Wittenberg:* Famous German university founded in 1502.   114 *retrograde:* Contrary.
115 *bend you:* Incline yourself; imperative.   127 *rouse:* Draft of liquor; *bruit again:* Echo.
137 *merely:* Completely, entirely.   140 *Hyperion:* God of the sun in the older regime of
ancient gods.   141 *beteem:* Allow.   149 *Niobe:* Tantalus's daughter, who boasted that
she had more sons and daughters than Leto; for this Apollo and Artemis slew her children.
She was turned into stone by Zeus on Mount Sipylus.   150 *discourse of reason:* Process or
faculty of reason.

Had left the flushing in her galled° eyes,   155
She married. O, most wicked speed, to post
With such dexterity° to incestuous sheets!
It is not nor it cannot come to good:
But break, my heart; for I must hold my tongue.

Enter Horatio, Marcellus, and Bernardo.

Horatio: Hail to your lordship!
Hamlet: I am glad to see you well: 160
    Horatio! — or I do forget myself.
Horatio: The same, my lord, and your poor servant ever.
Hamlet: Sir, my good friend; I'll change that name with you:°
    And what make you from Wittenberg, Horatio?
    Marcellus?   165
Marcellus: My good lord —
Hamlet: I am very glad to see you. Good even, sir.
    But what, in faith, make you from Wittenberg?
Horatio: A truant disposition, good my lord.
Hamlet: I would not hear your enemy say so,   170
    Nor shall you do my ear that violence,
    To make it truster of your own report
    Against yourself: I know you are no truant.
    But what is your affair in Elsinore?
    We'll teach you to drink deep ere you depart.   175
Horatio: My lord, I came to see your father's funeral.
Hamlet: I prithee, do not mock me, fellow-student;
    I think it was to see my mother's wedding.
Horatio: Indeed, my lord, it follow'd hard° upon.
Hamlet: Thrift, thrift, Horatio! the funeral bak'd meats°   180
    Did coldly furnish forth the marriage tables.
    Would I had met my dearest° foe in heaven
    Or ever I had seen that day, Horatio!
    My father! — methinks I see my father.
Horatio: Where, my lord!
Hamlet: In my mind's eye, Horatio.   185
Horatio: I saw him once; 'a° was a goodly king.
Hamlet: 'A was a man, take him for all in all,
    I shall not look upon his like again.
Horatio: My lord, I think I saw him yesternight.
Hamlet: Saw? who?
Horatio: My lord, the king your father.   190
Hamlet: The king my father!
Horatio: Season your admiration° for a while
    With an attent ear, till I may deliver,

---

155 *galled:* Irritated.   157 *dexterity:* Facility.   163 *I'll...you:* I'll be your servant, you
shall be my friend; also explained as "I'll exchange the name of friend with you."   179 *hard:*
Close.   180 *bak'd meats:* Meat pies.   182 *dearest:* Direst. The adjective *dear* in Shakespeare has two different origins: O.E. *deore,* "beloved," and O.E. *deor,* "fierce." *Dearest* is the
superlative of the second.   186 *'a:* He.   192 *Season your admiration:* Restrain your astonishment.

            Upon the witness of these gentlemen,
            This marvel to you.
Hamlet: For God's love, let me hear.   195
Horatio: Two nights together had these gentlemen,
            Marcellus and Bernardo, on their watch,
            In the dead waste and middle of the night,
            Been thus encount'red. A figure like your father,
            Armed at point exactly, cap-a-pe,°   200
            Appears before them, and with solemn march
            Goes slow and stately by them: thrice he walk'd
            By their oppress'd° and fear-surprised eyes,
            Within his truncheon's° length; whilst they, distill'd°
            Almost to jelly with the act° of fear,   205
            Stand dumb and speak not to him. This to me
            In dreadful secrecy impart they did;
            And I with them the third night kept the watch:
            Where, as they had deliver'd, both in time,
            Form of the thing, each word made true and good,   210
            The apparition comes: I knew your father;
            These hands are not more like.
Hamlet: But where was this?
Marcellus: My lord, upon the platform where we watch'd.
Hamlet: Did you not speak to it?
Horatio: My lord, I did;   215
            But answer made it none: yet once methought
            It lifted up it° head and did address
            Itself to motion, like as it would speak;
            But even then the morning cock crew loud,
            And at the sound it shrunk in haste away,
            And vanish'd from our sight.
Hamlet: 'Tis very strange.   220
Horatio: As I do live, my honour'd lord, 'tis true;
            And we did think it writ down in our duty
            To let you know of it.
Hamlet: Indeed, indeed, sirs, but this troubles me.
            Hold you the watch to-night?
Marcellus: ⎫   We do, my lord.   225
Bernardo: ⎭
Hamlet: Arm'd, say you?
Marcellus: ⎫   Arm'd, my lord.
Bernardo: ⎭
Hamlet: From top to toe?
Marcellus: ⎫   My lord, from head to foot.
Bernardo: ⎭
Hamlet: Then saw you not his face?
Horatio: O, yes, my lord; he wore his beaver° up.

---

200 *cap-a-pe:* From head to foot.   203 *oppress'd:* Distressed.   204 *truncheon:* Officer's
staff; *distill'd:* Softened, weakened.   205 *act:* Action.   216 *it:* Its.   229 *beaver:* Visor
on the helmet.

Hamlet: What, look'd he frowningly?
Horatio: A countenance more   230
   In sorrow than in anger.
Hamlet: Pale or red?
Horatio: Nay, very pale.
Hamlet: And fix'd his eyes upon you?
Horatio: Most constantly.
Hamlet: I would I had been there.
Horatio: It would have much amaz'd you.
Hamlet: Very like, very like. Stay'd it long?   235
Horatio: While one with moderate haste might tell a hundred.
Marcellus: ⎫
Bernardo: ⎭   Longer, longer.
Horatio: Not when I saw't.
Hamlet: His beard was grizzled,—no?
Horatio: It was, as I have seen it in his life,
   A sable° silver'd.
Hamlet: I will watch to-night;   240
   Perchance 'twill walk again.
Horatio: I warr'nt it will.
Hamlet: If it assume my noble father's person,
   I'll speak to it, though hell itself should gape
   And bid me hold my peace. I pray you all,
   If you have hitherto conceal'd this sight,   245
   Let it be tenable in your silence still;
   And whatsoever else shall hap to-night,
   Give it an understanding, but no tongue:
   I will requite your loves. So, fare you well:
   Upon the platform, 'twixt eleven and twelve,   250
   I'll visit you.
All: Our duty to your honour.
Hamlet: Your loves, as mine to you: farewell.   *Exeunt [all but Hamlet].*
   My father's spirit in arms! all is not well;
   I doubt° some foul play: would the night were come!
   Till then sit still, my soul: foul deeds will rise,   255
   Though all the earth o'erwhelm them, to men's eyes.   *Exit.*

[Scene III: *A room in Polonius's house.*]

   Enter Laertes and Ophelia, his Sister.

Laertes: My necessaries are embark'd: farewell:
   And, sister, as the winds give benefit
   And convoy is assistant,° do not sleep,
   But let me hear from you.
Ophelia: Do you doubt that?
Laertes: For Hamlet and the trifling of his favour,   5

---

240 *sable:* Black color.   254 *doubt:* Fear.   **Scene III.**   3 *convoy is assistant:* Means of
conveyance are available.

Hold it a fashion° and a toy in blood,°
A violet in the youth of primy° nature,
Forward,° not permanent, sweet, not lasting,
The perfume and suppliance of a minute;°
No more.
Ophelia: No more but so?
Laertes: Think it no more: 10
For nature, crescent,° does not grow alone
In thews° and bulk, but, as this temple° waxes,
The inward service of the mind and soul
Grows wide withal. Perhaps he loves you now,
And now no soil° nor cautel° doth besmirch   15
The virtue of his will: but you must fear,
His greatness weigh'd,° his will is not his own;
For he himself is subject to his birth:
He may not, as unvalued persons do,
Carve for himself; for on his choice depends   20
The safety and health of this whole state;
And therefore must his choice be circumscrib'd
Unto the voice and yielding° of that body
Whereof he is the head. Then if he says he loves you,
It fits your wisdom so far to believe it   25
As he in his particular act and place
May give his saying deed;° which is no further
Than the main voice of Denmark goes withal.
Then weigh what loss your honour may sustain,
If with too credent° ear you list his songs,   30
Or lose your heart, or your chaste treasure open
To his unmast'red° importunity.
Fear it, Ophelia, fear it, my dear sister,
And keep you in the rear of your affection,
Out of the shot and danger of desire.   35
The chariest° maid is prodigal enough,
If she unmask her beauty to the moon:
Virtue itself 'scapes not calumnious strokes:
The canker galls the infants of the spring,°
Too oft before their buttons° be disclos'd,°   40
And in the morn and liquid dew° of youth
Contagious blastments° are most imminent.
Be wary then; best safety lies in fear:
Youth to itself rebels, though none else near.

---

6 *fashion:* Custom, prevailing usage; *toy in blood:* Passing amorous fancy.   7 *primy:* In its prime.   8 *Forward:* Precocious.   9 *suppliance of a minute:* Diversion to fill up a minute. 11 *crescent:* Growing, waxing.   12 *thews:* Bodily strength; *temple:* Body.   15 *soil:* Blemish; *cautel:* Crafty device.   17 *greatness weigh'd:* High position considered.   23 *voice and yielding:* Assent, approval.   27 *deed:* Effect.   30 *credent:* Credulous.   32 *unmast'red:* Unrestrained.   36 *chariest:* Most scrupulously modest.   39 *The canker...spring:* The cankerworm destroys the young plants of spring.   40 *buttons:* Buds; *disclos'd:* Opened. 41 *liquid dew:* I.e., time when dew is fresh.   42 *blastments:* Blights.

Ophelia: I shall the effect of this good lesson keep,   45
    As watchman to my heart. But, good my brother,
    Do not, as some ungracious° pastors do,
    Show me the steep and thorny way to heaven;
    Whiles, like a puff'd° and reckless libertine,
    Himself the primrose path of dalliance treads,   50
    And recks° not his own rede.°

    Enter Polonius.

Laertes: O, fear me not.
    I stay too long: but here my father comes.
    A double° blessing is a double grace;
    Occasion° smiles upon a second leave.
Polonius: Yet here, Laertes? aboard, aboard, for shame!   55
    The wind sits in the shoulder of your sail,
    And you are stay'd for. There; my blessing with thee!
    And these few precepts° in thy memory
    Look thou character.° Give thy thoughts no tongue,
    Nor any unproportion'd° thought his act.   60
    Be thou familiar, but by no means vulgar.°
    Those friends thou hast, and their adoption tried,
    Grapple them to thy soul with hoops of steel;
    But do not dull thy palm with entertainment
    Of each new-hatch'd, unfledg'd° comrade. Beware   65
    Of entrance to a quarrel, but being in,
    Bear't that th' opposed may beware of thee.
    Give every man thy ear, but few thy voice;
    Take each man's censure, but reserve thy judgement.
    Costly thy habit as thy purse can buy,   70
    But not express'd in fancy;° rich, not gaudy;
    For the apparel oft proclaims the man,
    And they in France of the best rank and station
    Are of a most select and generous chief in that.°
    Neither a borrower nor a lender be;   75
    For loan oft loses both itself and friend,
    And borrowing dulleth edge of husbandry.°
    This above all: to thine own self be true,
    And it must follow, as the night the day,
    Thou canst not then be false to any man.   80
    Farewell: my blessing season° this in thee!
Laertes: Most humbly do I take my leave, my lord.
Polonius: The time invites you; go; your servants tend.

---

47 *ungracious:* Graceless.   49 *puff'd:* Bloated.   51 *recks:* Heeds; *rede:* Counsel.   53 *double:*
I.e., Laertes has already bade his father good-by.   54 *Occasion:* Opportunity.   58 *pre-*
cepts: Many parallels have been found to the series of maxims which follows, one of the
closer being that in Lyly's *Euphues.*   59 *character:* Inscribe.   60 *unproportion'd:* Inordinate.   61 *vulgar:* Common.   65 *unfledg'd:* Immature.   71 *express'd in fancy:* Fantastical in design.   74 *Are...that:* Chief is usually taken as a substantive meaning "head,"
"eminence."   77 *husbandry:* Thrift.   81 *season:* Mature.

Laertes: Farewell, Ophelia; and remember well
　　What I have said to you.
Ophelia: 　　　　　　　'Tis in my memory lock'd, 85
　　And you yourself shall keep the key of it.
Laertes: Farewell. 　　　　　　　　　　　　*Exit Laertes.*
Polonius: What is 't, Ophelia, he hath said to you?
Ophelia: So please you, something touching the Lord Hamlet.
Polonius: Marry, well bethought: 90
　　'Tis told me, he hath very oft of late
　　Given private time to you; and you yourself
　　Have of your audience been most free and bounteous:
　　If it be so, as so 't is put on° me,
　　And that in way of caution, I must tell you, 95
　　You do not understand yourself so clearly
　　As it behooves my daughter and your honour.
　　What is between you? give me up the truth.
Ophelia: He hath, my lord, of late made many tenders°
　　Of his affection to me. 100
Polonius: Affection! pooh! you speak like a green girl,
　　Unsifted° in such perilous circumstance.
　　Do you believe his tenders, as you call them?
Ophelia: I do not know, my lord, what I should think.
Polonius: Marry, I will teach you: think yourself a baby; 105
　　That you have ta'en these tenders° for true pay,
　　Which are not sterling.° Tender° yourself more dearly;
　　Or — not to crack the wind° of the poor phrase,
　　Running it thus — you'll tender me a fool.°
Ophelia: My lord, he hath importun'd me with love 110
　　In honourable fashion.
Polonius: Ay, fashion° you may call it; go to, go to.
Ophelia: And hath given countenance° to his speech, my lord,
　　With almost all the holy vows of heaven.
Polonius: Ay, springes° to catch woodcocks.° I do know, 115
　　When the blood burns, how prodigal the soul
　　Lends the tongue vows: these blazes, daughter,
　　Giving more light than heat, extinct in both,
　　Even in their promise, as it is a-making,
　　You must not take for fire. From this time 120
　　Be somewhat scanter of your maiden presence;
　　Set your entreatments° at a higher rate
　　Than a command to parley.° For Lord Hamlet,
　　Believe so much in him,° that he is young,
　　And with a larger tether may he walk 125

---

94 *put on:* Impressed on.　　99, 103 *tenders:* Offers.　　102 *Unsifted:* Untried.　　106 *tenders:* Promises to pay.　　107 *sterling:* Legal currency; *Tender:* Hold.　　108 *crack the wind:* I.e., run it until it is broken-winded.　　109 *tender . . . fool:* Show me a fool (for a daughter).　　112 *fashion:* Mere form, pretense.　　113 *countenance:* Credit, support.　　115 *springes:* Snares; *woodcocks:* Birds easily caught, type of stupidity.　　122 *entreatments:* Conversations, interviews.　　123 *command to parley:* Mere invitation to talk.　　124 *so . . . him:* This much concerning him.

Than may be given you: in few,° Ophelia,
Do not believe his vows; for they are brokers;°
Not of that dye° which their investments° show,
But mere implorators of° unholy suits,
Breathing° like sanctified and pious bawds,   130
The better to beguile. This is for all:
I would not, in plain terms, from this time forth,
Have you so slander° any moment leisure,
As to give words or talk with the Lord Hamlet.
Look to 't, I charge you: come your ways.   135
Ophelia: I shall obey, my lord.   *Exeunt.*

[SCENE IV: *The platform.*]

Enter Hamlet, Horatio, and Marcellus.

Hamlet: The air bites shrewdly; it is very cold.
Horatio: It is a nipping and an eager air.
Hamlet: What hour now?
Horatio: I think it lacks of twelve.
Marcellus: No, it is struck.
Horatio: Indeed? I heard it not: then it draws near the season   5
   Wherein the spirit held his wont to walk.

A flourish of trumpets, and two pieces go off.

   What does this mean, my lord?
Hamlet: The king doth wake° to-night and takes his rouse,°
   Keeps wassail,° and the swagg'ring up-spring° reels;°
   And, as he drains his draughts of Rhenish° down,   10
   The kettle-drum and trumpet thus bray out
   The triumph of his pledge.°
Horatio: Is it a custom?
Hamlet: Ay, marry, is 't:
   But to my mind, though I am native here
   And to the manner born,° it is a custom   15
   More honour'd in the breach than the observance.
   This heavy-headed revel east and west
   Makes us traduc'd and tax'd of other nations:
   They clepe° us drunkards, and with swinish phrase°
   Soil our addition;° and indeed it takes   20
   From our achievements, though perform'd at height,
   The pith and marrow of our attribute.°

---

126 *in few:* Briefly.   127 *brokers:* Go-betweens, procurers.   128 *dye:* Color or sort; *invest-*
ments: Clothes.   129 *implorators of:* Solicitors of.   130 *Breathing:* Speaking.   133 *slan-*
der: Bring disgrace or reproach upon.   **Scene IV.**   8 *wake:* Stay awake, hold revel; *rouse:*
Carouse, drinking bout.   9 *wassail:* Carousal; *up-spring:* Last and wildest dance at German
merry-makings; *reels:* Reels through.   10 *Rhenish:* Rhine wine.   12 *triumph...pledge:* His
glorious achievement as a drinker.   15 *to...born:* Destined by birth to be subject to the
custom in question.   19 *clepe:* Call; *with swinish phrase:* By calling us swine.   20 *addition:*
Reputation.   22 *attribute:* Reputation.

So, oft it chances in particular men,
That for some vicious mole of nature° in them,
As, in their birth—wherein they are not guilty,   25
Since nature cannot choose his origin—
By the o'ergrowth of some complexion,
Oft breaking down the pales° and forts of reason,
Or by some habit that too much o'er-leavens°
The form of plausive° manners, that these men,   30
Carrying, I say, the stamp of one defect,
Being nature's livery,° or fortune's star,°—
Their virtues else—be they as pure as grace,
As infinite as man may undergo—
Shall in the general censure take corruption   35
From that particular fault: the dram of eale°
Doth all the noble substance of a doubt
To his own scandal.°

Enter Ghost.

Horatio: Look, my lord, it comes!
Hamlet: Angels and ministers of grace° defend us!
Be thou a spirit of health or goblin damn'd,   40
Bring with thee airs from heaven or blasts from hell,
Be thy intents wicked or charitable,
Thou com'st in such a questionable° shape
That I will speak to thee: I'll call thee Hamlet,
King, father, royal Dane: O, answer me!   45
Let me not burst in ignorance; but tell
Why thy canoniz'd° bones, hearsed° in death,
Have burst their cerements;° why the sepulchre,
Wherein we saw thee quietly interr'd,
Hath op'd his ponderous and marble jaws,   50
To cast thee up again. What may this mean,
That thou, dead corse, again in complete steel
Revisits thus the glimpses of the moon,°
Making night hideous; and we fools of nature°
So horridly to shake our disposition   55
With thoughts beyond the reaches of our souls?
Say, why is this? wherefore? what should we do?

[Ghost] beckons [Hamlet].

24 *mole of nature:* Natural blemish in one's constitution.   28 *pales:* Palings (as of a fortifica-
tion).   29 *o'er-leavens:* Induces a change throughout (as yeast works in bread).   30 *plau-
sive:* Pleasing.   32 *nature's livery:* Endowment from nature; *fortune's star:* The position in
which one is placed by fortune, a reference to astrology. The two phrases are aspects of the
same thing.   36–38 *the dram . . . scandal:* A famous crux: *dram of eale* has had various interpretations, the preferred one being probably, "a dram of evil."   39 *ministers of grace:* Messengers of God.   43 *questionable:* Inviting question or conversation.   47 *canoniz'd:*
Buried according to the canons of the church; *hearsed:* Coffined.   48 *cerements:* Grave-
clothes.   53 *glimpses of the moon:* The earth by night.   54 *fools of nature:* Mere men, limited to natural knowledge.

Horatio: It beckons you to go away with it,
    As if it some impartment° did desire
    To you alone.
Marcellus: Look, with what courteous action   60
    It waves you to a more removed° ground:
    But do not go with it.
Horatio: No, by no means.
Hamlet: It will not speak; then I will follow it.
Horatio: Do not, my lord!
Hamlet: Why, what should be the fear?
    I do not set my life at a pin's fee;   65
    And for my soul, what can it do to that,
    Being a thing immortal as itself?
    It waves me forth again: I'll follow it.
Horatio: What if it tempt you toward the flood, my lord,
    Or to the dreadful summit of the cliff   70
    That beetles o'er° his base into the sea,
    And there assume some other horrible form,
    Which might deprive your sovereignty of reason°
    And draw you into madness? think of it:
    The very place puts toys of desperation,°   75
    Without more motive, into every brain
    That looks so many fathoms to the sea
    And hears it roar beneath.
Hamlet: It waves me still.
    Go on; I'll follow thee.
Marcellus: You shall not go, my lord.
Hamlet: Hold off your hands!   80
Horatio: Be rul'd; you shall not go.
Hamlet: My fate cries out,
    And makes each petty artere° in this body
    As hardy as the Nemean lion's° nerve.°
    Still am I call'd. Unhand me, gentlemen.
    By heaven, I'll make a ghost of him that lets° me!
    I say, away! Go on; I'll follow thee.   *Exeunt Ghost and Hamlet.* 85
Horatio: He waxes desperate with imagination.
Marcellus: Let's follow; 'tis not fit thus to obey him.
Horatio: Have after. To what issue° will this come?
Marcellus: Something is rotten in the state of Denmark.   90
Horatio: Heaven will direct it.°
Marcellus: Nay, let's follow him.   *Exeunt.*

---

59 *impartment:* Communication.   61 *removed:* Remote.   71 *beetles o'er:* Overhangs threat-eningly.   73 *deprive . . . reason:* Take away the sovereignty of your reason. It was thought that evil spirits would sometimes assume the form of departed spirits in order to work mad-ness in a human creature.   75 *toys of desperation:* Freakish notions of suicide.   82 *artere:* Artery.   83 *Nemean lion's:* The Nemean lion was one of the monsters slain by Hercules; *nerve:* Sinew, tendon. The point is that the arteries which were carrying the spirits out into the body were functioning and were as stiff and hard as the sinews of the lion.   85 *lets:* Hinders.   89 *issue:* Outcome.   91 *it:* I.e., the outcome.

[SCENE V: *Another part of the platform.*]

Enter Ghost and Hamlet.

Hamlet: Whither wilt thou lead me? speak; I'll go no further.
Ghost: Mark me.
Hamlet: I will.
Ghost: My hour is almost come,
     When I to sulphurous and tormenting flames
     Must render up myself.
Hamlet: Alas, poor ghost!
Ghost: Pity me not, but lend thy serious hearing   5
     To what I shall unfold.
Hamlet: Speak; I am bound to hear.
Ghost: So art thou to revenge, when thou shalt hear.
Hamlet: What?
Ghost: I am thy father's spirit,
     Doom'd for a certain term to walk the night,   10
     And for the day confin'd to fast° in fires,
     Till the foul crimes done in my days of nature
     Are burnt and purg'd away. But that I am forbid
     To tell the secrets of my prison-house,
     I could a tale unfold whose lightest word   15
     Would harrow up thy soul, freeze thy young blood,
     Make thy two eyes, like stars, start from their spheres,°
     Thy knotted° and combined° locks to part
     And each particular hair to stand an end,
     Like quills upon the fretful porpentine:°   20
     But this eternal blazon° must not be
     To ears of flesh and blood. List, list, O, list!
     If thou didst ever thy dear father love —
Hamlet: O God!
Ghost: Revenge his foul and most unnatural° murder.   25
Hamlet: Murder!
Ghost: Murder most foul, as in the best it is;
     But this most foul, strange and unnatural.
Hamlet: Haste me to know't, that I, with wings as swift
     As meditation or the thoughts of love,   30
     May sweep to my revenge.
Ghost: I find thee apt;
     And duller shouldst thou be than the fat weed°
     That roots itself in ease on Lethe wharf,°
     Wouldst thou not stir in this. Now, Hamlet, hear:

Scene V. 11 *fast:* Probably, do without food. It has been sometimes taken in the sense of doing general penance.   17 *spheres:* Orbits.   18 *knotted:* Perhaps intricately arranged; *combined:* Tied, bound.   20 *porpentine:* Porcupine.   21 *eternal blazon:* Promulgation or proclamation of eternity, revelation of the hereafter.   25 *unnatural:* I.e., pertaining to fratricide.   32 *fat weed:* Many suggestions have been offered as to the particular plant intended, including asphodel; probably a general figure for plants growing along rotting wharves and piles.   33 *Lethe wharf:* Bank of the river of forgetfulness in Hades.

'Tis given out that, sleeping in my orchard,   35
A serpent stung me; so the whole ear of Denmark
Is by a forged process of my death
Rankly abus'd: but know, thou noble youth,
The serpent that did sting thy father's life
Now wears his crown.

Hamlet: O my prophetic soul!   40
　　My uncle!
Ghost: Ay, that incestuous, that adulterate° beast,
　　With witchcraft of his wit, with traitorous gifts, —
　　O wicked wit and gifts, that have the power
　　So to seduce! — won to his shameful lust   45
　　The will of my most seeming-virtuous queen:
　　O Hamlet, what a falling-off was there!
　　From me, whose love was of that dignity
　　That it went hand in hand even with the vow
　　I made to her in marriage, and to decline   50
　　Upon a wretch whose natural gifts were poor
　　To those of mine!
　　But virtue, as it never will be moved,
　　Though lewdness court it in a shape of heaven,
　　So lust, though to a radiant angel link'd,   55
　　Will sate itself in a celestial bed,
　　And prey on garbage.
　　But, soft! methinks I scent the morning air;
　　Brief let me be. Sleeping within my orchard,
　　My custom always of the afternoon,   60
　　Upon my secure° hour thy uncle stole,
　　With juice of cursed hebona° in a vial,
　　And in the porches of my ears did pour
　　The leperous° distilment; whose effect
　　Holds such an enmity with blood of man   65
　　That swift as quicksilver it courses through
　　The natural gates and alleys of the body,
　　And with a sudden vigour it doth posset°
　　And curd, like eager° droppings into milk,
　　The thin and wholesome blood: so did it mine;   70
　　And a most instant tetter bark'd about,
　　Most lazar-like,° with vile and loathsome crust,
　　All my smooth body.
　　Thus was I, sleeping, by a brother's hand
　　Of life, of crown, of queen, at once dispatch'd:°   75
　　Cut off even in the blossoms of my sin,
　　Unhous'led,° disappointed,° unanel'd,°

---

42 *adulterate:* Adulterous.　61 *secure:* Confident,　unsuspicious.　62 *hebona:* Generally supposed to mean henbane, conjectured *hemlock; ebenus,* meaning "yew."　64 *leperous:* Causing leprosy.　68 *posset:* Coagulate, curdle.　69 *eager:* Sour, acid.　72 *lazar-like:* Leperlike.　75 *dispatch'd:* Suddenly bereft.　77 *Unhous'led:* Without having received the sacrament; *disappointed:* Unready, without equipment for the last journey; *unanel'd:* Without having received extreme unction.

No reck'ning made, but sent to my account
With all my imperfections on my head:
O, horrible! O, horrible! most horrible!°   80
If thou hast nature in thee, bear it not;
Let not the royal bed of Denmark be
A couch for luxury° and damned incest.
But, howsomever thou pursues this act,
Taint not thy mind,° nor let thy soul contrive   85
Against thy mother aught: leave her to heaven
And to those thorns that in her bosom lodge,
To prick and sting her. Fare thee well at once!
The glow-worm shows the matin° to be near,
And 'gins to pale his uneffectual fire:°   90
Adieu, adieu, adieu! remember me.   [*Exit.*]

Hamlet: O all you host of heaven! O earth! what else?
And shall I couple° hell? O, fie! Hold, hold, my heart;
And you, my sinews, grow not instant old,
But bear me stiffly up. Remember thee!   95
Ay, thou poor ghost, whiles memory holds a seat
In this distracted globe.° Remember thee!
Yea, from the table of my memory
I'll wipe away all trivial fond records,
All saws° of books, all forms, all pressures° past,   100
That youth and observation copied there;
And thy commandment all alone shall live
Within the book and volume of my brain,
Unmix'd with baser matter: yes, by heaven!
O most pernicious woman!   105
O villain, villain, smiling, damned villain!
My tables,° — meet it is I set it down,
That one may smile, and smile, and be a villain;
At least I am sure it may be so in Denmark: [*Writing.*]
So, uncle, there you are. Now to my word;°   110
It is "Adieu, adieu! remember me,"
I have sworn't.

Enter Horatio and Marcellus.

Horatio: My lord, my lord —
Marcellus: Lord Hamlet, —
Horatio: Heavens secure him!
Hamlet: So be it!
Marcellus: Hillo, ho, ho,° my lord!   115

---

80 *O . . . horrible:* Many editors give this line to Hamlet; Garrick and Sir Henry Irving spoke it
in that part.   83 *luxury:* Lechery.   85 *Taint . . . mind:* Probably, deprave not thy character,
do nothing except in the pursuit of a natural revenge.   89 *matin:* Morning.   90 *uneffectual fire:* Cold light.   93 *couple:* Add.   97 *distracted globe:* Confused head.   100 *saws:*
Wise sayings; *pressures:* Impressions stamped.   107 *tables:* Probably a small portable writing-
tablet carried at the belt.   110 *word:* Watchword.   115 *Hillo, ho, ho:* A falconer's call to a
hawk in air.

Hamlet: Hillo, ho, ho, boy! come, bird, come.
Marcellus: How is't, my noble lord?
Horatio: What news, my lord?
Hamlet: O, wonderful!
Horatio: Good my lord, tell it.
Hamlet: No; you will reveal it.
Horatio: Not I, my lord, by heaven.
Marcellus: Nor I, my lord.   120
Hamlet: How say you, then; would heart of man once think it?
     But you'll be secret?
Horatio: }
Marcellus: }   Ay, by heaven, my lord.
Hamlet: There's ne'er a villain dwelling in all Denmark
     But he's an arrant° knave.
Horatio: There needs no ghost, my lord, come from the grave   125
     To tell us this.
Hamlet: Why, right; you are in the right;
     And so, without more circumstance at all,
     I hold it fit that we shake hands and part:
     You, as your business and desire shall point you;
     For every man has business and desire,   130
     Such as it is; and for my own poor part,
     Look you, I'll go pray.
Horatio: These are but wild and whirling words, my lord.
Hamlet: I am sorry they offend you, heartily;
     Yes, 'faith, heartily.
Horatio: There's no offence, my lord.   135
Hamlet: Yes, by Saint Patrick,° but there is, Horatio,
     And much offence too. Touching this vision here,
     It is an honest° ghost, that let me tell you:
     For your desire to know what is between us,
     O'ermaster 't as you may. And now, good friends,   140
     As you are friends, scholars and soldiers,
     Give me one poor request.
Horatio: What is 't, my lord? we will.
Hamlet: Never make known what you have seen to-night.
Horatio: }
Marcellus: } My lord, we will not.
Hamlet: Nay, but swear 't.
Horatio: In faith,   145
     My lord, not I.
Marcellus: Nor I, my lord, in faith.
Hamlet: Upon my sword.°
Marcellus: We have sworn, my lord, already.

---

124 *arrant:* Thoroughgoing.   136 *Saint Patrick:* St. Patrick was keeper of Purgatory and patron saint of all blunders and confusion.   138 *honest:* I.e., a real ghost and not an evil spirit.   147 *sword:* I.e., the hilt in the form of a cross.

Hamlet: Indeed, upon my sword, indeed.   *Ghost cries under the stage.*
Ghost: Swear.
Hamlet: Ah, ha, boy! say'st thou so? art thou there, truepenny?°   150
    Come on—you hear this fellow in the cellarage—
    Consent to swear.
Horatio: Propose the oath, my lord.
Hamlet: Never to speak of this that you have seen,
    Swear by my sword.
Ghost [beneath]: Swear.   155
Hamlet: Hic et ubique?° then we'll shift our ground.
    Come hither, gentlemen,
    And lay your hands again upon my sword:
    Swear by my sword,
    Never to speak of this that you have heard.   160
Ghost [beneath]: Swear by his sword.
Hamlet: Well said, old mole! canst work i' th' earth so fast?
    A worthy pioner!° Once more remove, good friends.
Horatio: O day and night, but this is wondrous strange!
Hamlet: And therefore as a stranger give it welcome.   165
    There are more things in heaven and earth, Horatio,
    Than are dreamt of in your philosophy.
    But come;
    Here, as before, never, so help you mercy,
    How strange or odd soe'er I bear myself,   170
    As I perchance hereafter shall think meet
    To put an antic° disposition on,
    That you, at such times seeing me, never shall,
    With arms encumb'red° thus, or this head-shake,
    Or by pronouncing of some doubtful phrase,   175
    As "Well, well, we know," or "We could, an if we would,"
    Or "If we list to speak," or "There be, an if they might,"
    Or such ambiguous giving out,° to note°
    That you know aught of me: this not to do,
    So grace and mercy at your most need help you,   180
    Swear.
Ghost [beneath]: Swear.
Hamlet: Rest, rest, perturbed spirit! *[They swear.]* So, gentlemen,
    With all my love I do commend me to you:
    And what so poor a man as Hamlet is   185
    May do, t' express his love and friending° to you,
    God willing, shall not lack. Let us go in together;
    And still your fingers on your lips, I pray.
    The time is out of joint: O cursed spite,
    That ever I was born to set it right!   190
    Nay, come, let's go together.   *Exeunt.*

---

150 *truepenny:* Good old boy, or the like.   156 *Hic et ubique?:* Here and everywhere?
163 *pioner:* Digger, miner.   172 *antic:* Fantastic.   174 *encumb'red:* Folded or entwined.
178 *giving out:* Profession of knowledge; *to note:* To give a sign.   186 *friending:* Friendliness.

[ACT II

SCENE I: *A room in Polonius's house.*]

Enter old Polonius with his man [Reynaldo].

Polonius: Give him this money and these notes, Reynaldo.
Reynaldo: I will, my lord.
Polonius: You shall do marvellous wisely, good Reynaldo,
　　Before you visit him, to make inquire
　　Of his behaviour.
Reynaldo: 　　　　　My lord, I did intend it.　　　　　　5
Polonius: Marry, well said; very well said. Look you, sir,
　　Inquire me first what Danskers° are in Paris;
　　And how, and who, what means, and where they keep,°
　　What company, at what expense; and finding
　　By this encompassment° and drift° of question　　　10
　　That they do know my son, come you more nearer
　　Than your particular demands will touch it:°
　　Take° you as 'twere, some distant knowledge of him;
　　As thus, "I know his father and his friends,
　　And in part him": do you mark this, Reynaldo?　　　15
Reynaldo: Ay, very well, my lord.
Polonius: "And in part him; but" you may say "not well:
　　But, if 't be he I mean, he's very wild;
　　Addicted so and so": and there put on° him
　　What forgeries° you please; marry, none so rank　　　20
　　As may dishonour him; take heed of that;
　　But, sir, such wanton,° wild and usual slips
　　As are companions noted and most known
　　To youth and liberty.
Reynaldo: 　　　　　As gaming, my lord.
Polonius: Ay, or drinking, fencing,° swearing, quarrelling,　　25
　　Drabbing;° you may go so far.
Reynaldo: My lord, that would dishonour him.
Polonius: 'Faith, no; as you may season it in the charge.
　　You must not put another scandal on him,
　　That he is open to incontinency;°　　　　　　30
　　That's not my meaning: but breathe his faults so quaintly°
　　That they may seem the taints of liberty,°
　　The flash and outbreak of a fiery mind,

Act II, Scene I.　　7 *Danskers:* Danke was a common variant for "Denmark"; hence "Dane."
8 *keep:* Dwell.　　10 *encompassment:* Roundabout talking; *drift:* Gradual approach or
course.　　11–12 *come . . . it:* I.e., you will find out more this way than by asking pointed questions.　　13 *Take:* Assume, pretend.　　19 *put on:* Impute to.　　20 *forgeries:* Invented tales.
22 *wanton:* Sportive, unrestrained.　　25 *fencing:* Indicative of the ill repute of professional
fencers and fencing schools in Elizabethan times.　　26 *Drabbing:* Associating with
immoral women.　　30 *incontinency:* Habitual loose behavior.　　31 *quaintly:* Delicately,
ingeniously.　　32 *taints of liberty:* Blemishes due to freedom.

     A savageness in unreclaimed° blood,
     Of general assault.°
Reynaldo: But, my good lord, —   35
Polonius: Wherefore should you do this?
Reynaldo: Ay, my lord,
     I would know that.
Polonius: Marry, sir, here's my drift;
     And, I believe, it is a fetch of wit:°
     You laying these slight sullies on my son,
     As 'twere a thing a little soil'd i' th' working,   40
     Mark you,
     Your party in converse, him you would sound,
     Having ever° seen in the prenominate° crimes
     The youth you breathe of guilty, be assur'd
     He closes with you in this consequence;°   45
     "Good sir," or so, or "friend," or "gentleman,"
     According to the phrase or the addition
     Of man and country.
Reynaldo: Very good, my lord.
Polonius: And then, sir, does 'a this — 'a does — what was I about to say? By
     the mass, I was about to say something: where did I leave?   50
Reynaldo: At "closes in the consequence," at "friend or so," and "gentle-
     man."
Polonius: At "closes in the consequence," ay, marry;
     He closes thus: "I know the gentleman;
     I saw him yesterday, or t' other day,
     Or then, or then; with such, or such; and, as you say,   55
     There was 'a gaming; there o'ertook in 's rouse;°
     There falling out at tennis": or perchance,
     "I saw him enter such a house of sale,"
     Videlicet,° a brothel, or so forth.   60
     See you now;
     Your bait of falsehood takes this carp of truth:
     And thus do we of wisdom and of reach,°
     With windlasses° and with assays of bias,°
     By indirections° find directions° out: 65
     So by my former lecture° and advice,
     Shall you my son. You have me, have you not?
Reynaldo: My lord, I have.
Polonius: God bye ye;° fare ye well.
Reynaldo: Good my lord!
Polonius: Observe his inclination in yourself.°   70

---

34 *unreclaimed:* Untamed.   35 *general assault:* Tendency that assails all untrained youth.
38 *fetch of wit:* Clever trick.   43 *ever:* At any time; *prenominate:* Before-mentioned.
45 *closes . . . consequence:* Agrees with you in this conclusion.   57 *o'ertook in 's rouse:* Overcome by drink.   60 *Videlicet:* Namely.   63 *reach:* Capacity, ability.   64 *windlasses:* I.e.,
circuitous paths; *assays of bias:* Attempts that resemble the course of the bowl, which, being
weighted on one side, has a curving motion.   65 *indirections:* Devious courses; *directions:*
Straight courses, i.e., the truth.   66 *lecture:* Admonition.   68 *bye ye:* Be with you.
70 *Observe . . . yourself:* In your own person, not by spies; or conform your own conduct to
his inclination; or test him by studying yourself.

Reynaldo: I shall, my lord.
Polonius: And let him ply his music.°
Reynaldo: Well, my lord.
Polonius: Farewell!   *Exit Reynaldo.*

    Enter Ophelia.

              How now, Ophelia! what's the matter?
Ophelia: O, my lord, my lord, I have been so affrighted!
Polonius: With what, i' th' name of God?
Ophelia: My lord, as I was sewing in my closet,°   75
    Lord Hamlet, with his doublet° all unbrac'd;°
    No hat upon his head; his stockings foul'd,
    Ungart'red, and down-gyved° to his ankle;
    Pale as his shirt; his knees knocking each other;   80
    And with a look so piteous in purport
    As if he had been loosed out of hell
    To speak of horrors,—he comes before me.
Polonius: Mad for thy love?
Ophelia: My lord, I do not know;
    But truly, I do fear it.
Polonius: What said he?   85
Ophelia: He took me by the wrist and held me hard;
    Then goes he to the length of all his arm;
    And, with his other hand thus o'er his brow,
    He falls to such perusal of my face
    As 'a would draw it. Long stay'd he so;   90
    At last, a little shaking of mine arm
    And thrice his head thus waving up and down,
    He rais'd a sigh so piteous and profound
    As it did seem to shatter all his bulk°
    And end his being: that done, he lets me go: 95
    And, with his head over his shoulder turn'd,
    He seem'd to find his way without his eyes;
    For out o' doors he went without their helps,
    And, to the last, bended their light on me.
Polonius: Come, go with me: I will seek the king.   100
    This is the very ecstasy of love,
    Whose violent property° fordoes° itself
    And leads the will to desperate undertakings
    As oft as any passion under heaven
    That does afflict our natures. I am sorry.   105
    What, have you given him any hard words of late?
Ophelia: No, my good lord, but, as you did command,
    I did repel his letters and denied
    His access to me.
Polonius: That hath made him mad.
    I am sorry that with better heed and judgement   110

---

72 *ply his music:* Probably to be taken literally.   76 *closet:* Private chamber.   77 *doublet:*
Close-fitting coat; *unbrac'd:* Unfastened.   79 *down-gyved:* Fallen to the ankles (like gyves
or fetters).   94 *bulk:* Body.   102 *property:* Nature; *fordoes:* Destroys.

I had not quoted° him: I fear'd he did but trifle,
And meant to wrack thee; but, beshrew my jealousy!°
By heaven, it is as proper to our age
To cast beyond° ourselves in our opinions
As it is common for the younger sort   115
To lack discretion. Come, go we to the king:
This must be known; which, being kept close, might move
More grief to hide than hate to utter love.°
Come.   *Exeunt.*

[SCENE II: *A room in the castle.*]

Flourish. Enter King and Queen, Rosencrantz, and Guildenstern [with others].

King: Welcome, dear Rosencrantz and Guildenstern!
    Moreover that° we much did long to see you,
    The need we have to use you did provoke
    Our hasty sending. Something have you heard
    Of Hamlet's transformation; so call it,   5
    Sith° nor th' exterior nor the inward man
    Resembles that it was. What it should be,
    More than his father's death, that thus hath put him
    So much from th' understanding of himself,
    I cannot dream of: I entreat you both,   10
    That, being of so young days° brought up with him,
    And sith so neighbour'd to his youth and haviour,
    That you vouchsafe your rest° here in our court
    Some little time: so by your companies
    To draw him on to pleasures, and to gather,   15
    So much as from occasion you may glean,
    Whether aught, to us unknown, afflicts him thus,
    That, open'd, lies within our remedy.
Queen: Good gentlemen, he hath much talk'd of you;
    And sure I am two men there are not living   20
    To whom he more adheres. If it will please you
    To show us so much gentry° and good will
    As to expend your time with us awhile,
    For the supply and profit° of our hope,
    Your visitation shall receive such thanks   25
    As fits a king's remembrance.
Rosencrantz: Both your majesties
    Might, by the sovereign power you have of us,
    Put your dread pleasures more into command
    Than to entreaty.

---

111 *quoted:* Observed.   112 *beshrew my jealousy:* Curse my suspicions.   114 *cast beyond:*
Overshoot, miscalculate.   117–118 *might . . . love:* I.e., I might cause more grief to others by
hiding the knowledge of Hamlet's love to Ophelia than hatred to me and mine by telling of
it.   **Scene II.**   2 *Moreover that:* Besides the fact that.   6 *Sith:* Since.   11 *of . . . days:*
From such early youth.   13 *vouchsafe your rest:* Please to stay.   22 *gentry:* Courtesy.
24 *supply and profit:* Aid and successful outcome.

Guildenstern: But we both obey,
        And here give up ourselves, in the full bent°   30
        To lay our service freely at your feet,
        To be commanded.
King: Thanks, Rosencrantz and gentle Guildenstern.
Queen: Thanks, Guildenstern and gentle Rosencrantz:
        And I beseech you instantly to visit   35
        My too much changed son. Go, some of you,
        And bring these gentlemen where Hamlet is.
Guildenstern: Heavens make our presence and our practices
        Pleasant and helpful to him!
Queen: Ay, amen!
                Exeunt Rosencrantz and Guildenstern [with some Attendants].

        Enter Polonius.

Polonius: Th' ambassadors from Norway, my good lord,   40
        Are joyfully return'd.
King: Thou still hast been the father of good news.
Polonius: Have I, my lord? I assure my good liege,
        I hold my duty, as I hold my soul,
        Both to my God and to my gracious king: 45
        And I do think, or else this brain of mine
        Hunts not the trail of policy so sure
        As it hath us'd to do, that I have found
        The very cause of Hamlet's lunacy.
King: O, speak of that; that do I long to hear.   50
Polonius: Give first admittance to th' ambassadors;
        My news shall be the fruit to that great feast.
King: Thyself do grace to them, and bring them in.   *[Exit Polonius.]*
        He tells me, my dear Gertrude, he hath found
        The head and source of all your son's distemper.   55
Queen: I doubt° it is no other but the main;°
        His father's death, and our o'erhasty marriage.
King: Well, we shall sift him.

        Enter Ambassadors [Voltimand and Cornelius, with Polonius.]

                          Welcome, my good friends!
        Say, Voltimand, what from our brother Norway?
Voltimand: Most fair return of greetings and desires.   60
        Upon our first, he sent out to suppress
        His nephew's levies; which to him appear'd
        To be a preparation 'gainst the Polack;
        But, better look'd into, he truly found
        It was against your highness: whereat griev'd,   65
        That so his sickness, age and impotence
        Was falsely borne in hand,° sends out arrests
        On Fortinbras; which he, in brief, obeys;

---

30 *in . . . bent:* To the utmost degree of our mental capacity.   56 *doubt:* Fear; *main:* Chief
point, principal concern.   67 *borne in hand:* Deluded.

Receives rebuke from Norway, and in fine°
Makes vow before his uncle never more   70
To give th' assay° of arms against your majesty.
Whereon old Norway, overcome with joy,
Gives him three score thousand crowns in annual fee,
And his commission to employ those soldiers,
So levied as before, against the Polack: 75
With an entreaty, herein further shown,   *[Giving a paper.]*
That it might please you to give quiet pass
Through your dominions for this enterprise,
On such regards of safety and allowance°
As therein are set down.
King: It likes° us well;   80
And at our more consider'd° time we'll read,
Answer, and think upon this business.
Meantime we thank you for your well-took labour:
Go to your rest; at night we'll feast together:
Most welcome home!   *Exeunt Ambassadors.*
Polonius: This business is well ended.   85
My liege, and madam, to expostulate
What majesty should be, what duty is,
Why day is day, night night, and time is time,
Were nothing but to waste night, day and time.
Therefore, since brevity is the soul of wit,°   90
And tediousness the limbs and outward flourishes,°
I will be brief: your noble son is mad:
Mad call I it; for, to define true madness
What is 't but to be nothing else but mad?
But let that go.
Queen: More matter, with less art.   95
Polonius: Madam, I swear I use no art at all.
That he is mad, 'tis true: 'tis true 'tis pity;
And pity 'tis 'tis true: a foolish figure;°
But farewell it, for I will use no art.
Mad let us grant him, then: and now remains   100
That we find out the cause of this effect,
Or rather say, the cause of this defect,
For this effect defective comes by cause:
Thus it remains, and the remainder thus.
Perpend.°   105
I have a daughter — have while she is mine —
Who, in her duty and obedience, mark,
Hath given me this: now gather, and surmise. *[Reads the letter.]* "To the
celestial and my soul's idol,
the most beautified Ophelia," —   110

---

69 *in fine:* In the end.   71 *assay:* Assault, trial (of arms).   79 *safety and allowance:*
Pledges of safety to the country and terms of permission for the troops to pass.   80 *likes:*
Pleases.   81 *consider'd:* Suitable for deliberation.   90 *wit:* Sound sense or judgment.
91 *flourishes:* Ostentation, embellishments.   98 *figure:* Figure of speech.   105 *Perpend:*
Consider.

That's an ill phrase, a vile phrase; "beautified" is a vile phrase: but you
shall hear. Thus: *[Reads.]*
"In her excellent white bosom, these, & c."
Queen: Came this from Hamlet to her?
Polonius: Good madam, stay awhile; I will be faithful.   *[Reads.]* 115
           "Doubt thou the stars are fire;
               Doubt that the sun doth move;
               Doubt truth to be a liar;
               But never doubt I love.
"O dear Ophelia, I am ill at these numbers;° I have not art to reckon° 120
my groans: but that I love thee best, O most best, believe it. Adieu.
   "Thine evermore, most dear lady, whilst this machine° is to him,
                           HAMLET."
This, in obedience, hath my daughter shown me,
And more above,° hath his solicitings,   125
As they fell out° by time, by means° and place,
All given to mine ear.
King: But how hath she
Receiv'd his love?
Polonius: What do you think of me?
King: As of a man faithful and honourable.
Polonius: I would fain prove so. But what might you think,   130
When I had seen this hot love on the wing —
As I perceiv'd it, I must tell you that,
Before my daughter told me — what might you,
Or my dear majesty your queen here, think,
If I had play'd the desk or table-book,°   135
Or given my heart a winking,° mute and dumb,
Or look'd upon this love with idle sight;
What might you think? No, I went round to work,
And my young mistress thus I did bespeak:°
"Lord Hamlet is a prince, out of thy star;°   140
This must not be": and then I prescripts gave her,
That she should lock herself from his resort,
Admit no messengers, receive no tokens.
Which done, she took the fruits of my advice;
And he, repelled — a short tale to make —   145
Fell into a sadness, then into a fast,
Thence to a watch,° thence into a weakness,
Thence to a lightness,° and, by this declension,°
Into the madness wherein now he raves,
And all we mourn for.
King: Do you think 'tis this?
                                  150
Queen: It may be, very like.

---

120 *ill . . . numbers:* Unskilled at writing verses; *reckon:* Number metrically, scan.   122 *machine:* Bodily frame.   125 *more above:* Moreover.   126 *fell out:* Occurred; *means:* Opportunities (of access).   135 *play'd . . . table-book:* I.e., remained shut up, concealed this information.   136 *given . . . winking:* Given my heart a signal to keep silent.   139 *bespeak:* Address.   140 *out . . . star:* Above thee in position.   147 *watch:* State of sleeplessness.
148 *lightness:* Lightheadedness; *declension:* Decline, deterioration.

Polonius: Hath there been such a time — I would fain know that —
    That I have positively said " 'Tis so,"
    When it prov'd otherwise?
King: Not that I know.
Polonius [pointing to his head and shoulder]: Take this from this, if this be   155
    otherwise:
    If circumstances lead me, I will find
    Where truth is hid, though it were hid indeed
    Within the centre.°
King: How may we try it further?
Polonius: You know, sometimes he walks four hours together
    Here in the lobby.
Queen: So he does indeed.   160
Polonius: At such a time I'll loose my daughter to him:
    Be you and I behind an arras° then;
    Mark the encounter: if he love her not
    And be not from his reason fall'n thereon,°
    Let me be no assistant for a state,   165
    But keep a farm and carters.
King: We will try it.

    Enter Hamlet [reading on a book].

Queen: But, look, where sadly the poor wretch comes reading.
Polonius: Away, I do beseech you both, away:
                     Exeunt King and Queen [with Attendants].
    I'll board° him presently. O, give me leave.
    How does my good Lord Hamlet?   170
Hamlet: Well, God-a-mercy.
Polonius: Do you know me, my lord?
Hamlet: Excellent well; you are a fishmonger.°
Polonius: Not I, my lord.
Hamlet: Then I would you were so honest a man.   175
Polonius: Honest, my lord!
Hamlet: Ay, sir; to be honest, as this world goes, is to be one man picked
    out of ten thousand.
Polonius: That's very true, my lord.
Hamlet: For if the sun breed maggots in a dead dog, being a good kissing   180
    carrion,° — Have you a daughter?
Polonius: I have, my lord.
Hamlet: Let her not walk i' the sun:° conception° is a blessing: but as your
    daughter may conceive — Friend, look to 't.
Polonius [aside]: How say you by° that? Still harping on my daughter: yet   185
    he knew me not at first; 'a said I was a fishmonger: 'a is far gone, far

---

158 *centre:* Middle point of the earth.   162 *arras:* Hanging, tapestry.   164 *thereon:* On
that account.   169 *board:* Accost.   173 *fishmonger:* An opprobrious expression meaning
"bawd," "procurer."   180–181 *good kissing carrion:* I.e., a good piece of flesh for kissing (?).
183 *i' the sun:* In the sunshine of princely favors; *conception:* Quibble on "understanding"
and "pregnancy."   185 *by:* Concerning.

gone: and truly in my youth I suffered much extremity for love; very
near this. I'll speak to him again. What do you read, my lord?

Hamlet: Words, words, words.

Polonius: What is the matter,° my lord?   190

Hamlet: Between who?°

Polonius: I mean, the matter that you read, my lord.

Hamlet: Slanders, sir: for the satirical rogue says here that old men have
grey beards, that their faces are wrinkled, their eyes purging° thick
amber and plum-tree gum and that they have a plentiful lack of wit,   195
together with most weak hams: all which, sir, though I most powerfully and potently believe, yet I hold it not honesty° to have it thus set
down, for yourself, sir, should be old as I am, if like a crab you could
go backward.

Polonius [aside]: Though this be madness, yet there is method in 't.—Will   200
you walk out of the air, my lord?

Hamlet: Into my grave.

Polonius: Indeed, that's out of the air. *(Aside.)* How pregnant sometimes
his replies are! a happiness° that often madness hits on, which reason
and sanity could not so prosperously° be delivered of. I will leave   205
him, and suddenly contrive the means of meeting between him and
my daughter.—My honourable lord, I will most humbly take my
leave of you.

Hamlet: You cannot, sir, take from me any thing that I will more willingly
part withal: except my life, except my life, except my life.   210

Enter Guildenstern and Rosencrantz.

Polonius: Fare you well, my lord.

Hamlet: These tedious old fools!

Polonius: You go to seek the Lord Hamlet; there he is.

Rosencrantz [to Polonius]: God save you, sir!   *[Exit Polonius.]*

Guildenstern: My honoured lord!   215

Rosencrantz: My most dear lord!

Hamlet: My excellent good friends! How dost thou, Guildenstern? Ah,
Rosencrantz! Good lads, how do ye both?

Rosencrantz: As the indifferent° children of the earth.

Guildenstern: Happy, in that we are not over-happy;   220
On Fortune's cap we are not the very button.

Hamlet: Nor the soles of her shoe?

Rosencrantz: Neither, my lord.

Hamlet: Then you live about her waist, or in the middle of her favours?

Guildenstern: 'Faith, her privates° we.   225

Hamlet: In the secret parts of Fortune? O, most true; she is a strumpet.
What's the news?

Rosencrantz: None, my lord, but that the world's grown honest.

---

190 *matter:* Substance.   191 *Between who:* Hamlet deliberately takes *matter* as meaning
"basis of dispute."   194 *purging:* discharging.   197 *honesty:* Decency.   204 *happiness:*
Felicity   of   expression.   205 *prosperously:* Successfully.   219 *indifferent:* Ordinary.
225 *privates:* I.e., ordinary men (sexual pun on *private parts*).

Hamlet: Then is doomsday near: but your news is not true. Let me question more in particular: what have you, my good friends, deserved at 230
the hands of Fortune, that she sends you to prison hither?

Guildenstern: Prison, my lord!

Hamlet: Denmark's a prison.

Rosencrantz: Then is the world one.

Hamlet: A goodly one; in which there are many confines,° wards and 235
dungeons, Denmark being one o' the worst.

Rosencrantz: We think not so, my lord.

Hamlet: Why, then, 'tis none to you; for there is nothing either good or
bad, but thinking makes it so: to me it is a prison.

Rosencrantz: Why then, your ambition makes it one; 'tis too narrow for 240
your mind.

Hamlet: O God, I could be bounded in a nutshell and count myself a king
of infinite space, were it not that I have bad dreams.

Guildenstern: Which dreams indeed are ambition, for the very substance
of the ambitious° is merely the shadow of a dream.   245

Hamlet: A dream itself is but a shadow.

Rosencrantz: Truly, and I hold ambition of so airy and light a quality that
it is but a shadow's shadow.

Hamlet: Then are our beggars bodies, and our monarchs and outstretched heroes the beggars' shadows. Shall we to the court? for, by 250
my fay,° I cannot reason.°

Rosencrantz: ⎫
             ⎬ We'll wait upon° you.
Guildenstern: ⎭

Hamlet: No such matter: I will not sort° you with the rest of my servants,
for, to speak to you like an honest man, I am most dreadfully
attended.° But, in the beaten way of friendship,° what make you at 255
Elsinore?

Rosencrantz: To visit you, my lord: no other occasion.

Hamlet: Beggar that I am, I am ever poor in thanks; but I thank you: and
sure, dear friends, my thanks are too dear a° halfpenny. Were you not
sent for? Is it your own inclining? Is it a free visitation? Come, come, 260
deal justly with me: come, come; nay, speak.

Guildenstern: What should we say, my lord?

Hamlet: Why, any thing, but to the purpose. You were sent for; and there
is a kind of confession in your looks which your modesties have not
craft enough to colour: I know the good king and queen have sent for 265
you.

Rosencrantz: To what end, my lord?

Hamlet: That you must teach me. But let me conjure° you, by the rights of
our fellowship, by the consonancy of our youth,° by the obligation of
our ever-preserved love, and by what more dear a better proposer° 270

---

235 *confines:* Places of confinement.   244–245 *very . . . ambitious:* That seemingly most
substantial thing which the ambitious pursue.   251 *fay:* Faith; *reason:* Argue.   252 *wait
upon:* Accompany.   253 *sort:* Class.   254–255 *dreadfully attended:* Poorly provided with
servants.   255 *in the . . . friendship:* As a matter of course among friends.   259 *a:* I.e., at a.
268 *conjure:* Adjure, entreat.   269 *consonancy of our youth:* The fact that we are of the same
age.   270 *better proposer:* One more skillful in finding proposals.

could charge you withal, be even and direct with me, whether you
were sent for, or no?

Rosencrantz [aside to Guildenstern]: What say you?

Hamlet [aside]: Nay, then, I have an eye of you. — If you love me, hold not
off. 275

Guildenstern: My lord, we were sent for.

Hamlet: I will tell you why; so shall my anticipation prevent your discovery,° and your secrecy to the king and queen moult no feather. I have
of late — but wherefore I know not — lost all my mirth, forgone all custom of exercises; and indeed it goes so heavily with my disposition 280
that this goodly frame, the earth, seems to me a sterile promontory,
this most excellent canopy, the air, look you, this brave o'erhanging
firmament, this majestical roof fretted° with golden fire, why, it
appeareth nothing to me but a foul and pestilent congregation of
vapours. What a piece of work is a man! how noble in reason! how 285
infinite in faculties!° in form and moving how express° and admirable! in action how like an angel! in apprehension° how like a
god! the beauty of the world! the paragon of animals! And yet, to me,
what is this quintessence° of dust? man delights not me: no, nor
woman neither, though by your smiling you seem to say so. 290

Rosencrantz: My lord, there was no such stuff in my thoughts.

Hamlet: Why did you laugh then, when I said "man delights not me"?

Rosencrantz: To think, my lord, if you delight not in man, what lenten°
entertainment the players shall receive from you: we coted° them on
the way; and hither are they coming, to offer you service. 295

Hamlet: He that plays the king shall be welcome; his majesty shall have
tribute of me; the adventurous knight shall use his foil and target;°
the lover shall not sigh gratis; the humorous man° shall end his part
in peace; the clown shall make those laugh whose lungs are tickle o'
the sere;° and the lady shall say her mind freely, or the blank verse 300
shall halt for 't.° What players are they?

Rosencrantz: Even those you were wont to take delight in, the tragedians
of the city.

Hamlet: How chances it they travel? their residence,° both in reputation
and profit, was better both ways. 305

Rosencrantz: I think their inhibition° comes by the means of the late
innovation.°

Hamlet: Do they hold the same estimation they did when I was in the city?
are they so followed?

Rosencrantz: No, indeed, are they not. 310

277-278 *prevent your discovery:* Forestall your disclosure.   283 *fretted:* Adorned.   286 *faculties:* Capacity; *express:* Well-framed (?), exact (?).   287 *apprehension:* Understanding.
289 *quintessence:* The fifth essence of ancient philosophy, supposed to be the substance of the
heavenly bodies and to be latent in all things.   293 *lenten:* Meager.   294 *coted:* Overtook
and passed beyond.   297 *foil and target:* Sword and shield.   298 *humorous man:* Actor
who takes the part of the humor characters.   299-300 *tickle o' the sere:* Easy on the trigger.
300-301 *the lady . . . for 't:* The lady (fond of talking) shall have opportunity to talk, blank
verse or no blank verse.   304 *residence:* Remaining in one place.   306 *inhibition:* Formal
prohibition (from acting plays in the city or, possibly, at court).   307 *innovation:* The new
fashion in satirical plays performed by boy actors in the "private" theaters.

Hamlet: How° comes it? do they grow rusty?

Rosencrantz: Nay, their endeavour keeps in the wonted pace: but there is, sir, an aery° of children, little eyases,° that cry out on the top of question,° and are most tyrannically° clapped for 't: these are now the fashion, and so berattle° the common stages°—so they call them— 315 that many wearing rapiers° are afraid of goose-quills° and dare scarce come thither.

Hamlet: What, are they children? who maintains 'em? how are they escoted?° Will they pursue the quality° no longer than they can sing?° will they not say afterwards, if they should grow themselves to common° players—as it is most like, if their means are no better— their writers do them wrong, to make them exclaim against their own succession?°

Rosencrantz: 'Faith, there has been much to do on both sides; and the nation holds it no sin to tarre° them to controversy: there was, for a 325 while, no money bid for argument,° unless the poet and the player went to cuffs° in the question.°

Hamlet: Is't possible?

Guildenstern: O, there has been much throwing about of brains.

Hamlet: Do the boys carry it away?° 330

Rosencrantz: Ay, that they do, my lord; Hercules and his load° too.

Hamlet: It is not very strange; for my uncle is king of Denmark, and those that would make mows° at him while my father lived, give twenty, forty, fifty, a hundred ducats° a-piece for his picture in little.° 'Sblood, there is something in this more than natural, if philosophy could find 335 it out.   *A flourish [of trumpets within].*

Guildenstern: There are the players.

Hamlet: Gentlemen, you are welcome to Elsinore. Your hands, come then: the appurtenance of welcome is fashion and ceremony: let me comply° with you in this garb,° lest my extent° to the players, which, I tell 340 you, must show fairly outwards, should more appear like entertainment than yours. You are welcome: but my uncle-father and aunt-mother are deceived.

Guildenstern: In what, my dear lord?

311–331 *How...load:* The passage is the famous one dealing with the War of the Theatres (1599–1602); namely, the rivalry between the children's companies and the adult actors. 313 *aery:* Nest; *eyases:* Young hawks.   313–314 *cry...question:* Speak in a high key dominating conversation; clamor forth the height of controversy; probably "excel"; perhaps intended to decry leaders of the dramatic profession.   314 *tyrannically:* Outrageously. 315 *berattle:* Berate; *common stages:* Public theaters.   316 *many wearing rapiers:* Many men of fashion, who were afraid to patronize the common players for fear of being satirized by the poets who wrote for the children; *goose-quills:* I.e., pens of satirists.   318–319 *escoted:* Maintained.   319 *quality:* Acting profession; *no longer...sing:* I.e., until their voices change. 320–321 *common:* Regular, adult.   323 *succession:* Future careers.   325 *tarre:* Set on (as dogs).   326 *argument:* Probably, plot for a play.   327 *went to cuffs:* Came to blows; *question:* Controversy.   330 *carry it away:* Win the day.   331 *Hercules...load:* Regarded as an allusion to the sign of the Globe Theatre, which was Hercules bearing the world on his shoulder.   333 *mows:* Grimaces.   334 *ducats:* Gold coins worth 9s. 4d; *in little:* In miniature.   339–340 *comply:* Observe the formalities of courtesy.   340 *garb:* Manner; *extent:* Showing of kindness.

Hamlet: I am but mad north-north-west:° when the wind is southerly I   345
     know a hawk from a handsaw.°

     Enter Polonius.

Polonius: Well be with you, gentlemen!

Hamlet: Hark you, Guildenstern; and you too: at each ear a hearer: that
     great baby you see there is not yet out of his swaddling-clouts.°

Rosencrantz: Happily he is the second time come to them; for they say an   350
     old man is twice a child.

Hamlet: I will prophesy he comes to tell me of the players; mark it. — You
     say right, sir: o' Monday morning;° 'twas then indeed.

Polonius: My lord, I have news to tell you.

Hamlet: My lord, I have news to tell you. When Roscius° was an actor in   355
     Rome, —

Polonius: The actors are come hither, my lord.

Hamlet: Buz, buz!°

Polonius: Upon my honour, —

Hamlet: Then came each actor on his ass, —   360

Polonius: The best actors in the world, either for tragedy, comedy,
     history, pastoral, pastoral-comical, historical-pastoral, tragical-
     historical, tragical-comical-historical-pastoral, scene individable,° or
     poem unlimited:° Seneca° cannot be too heavy, nor Plautus° too light.
     For the law of writ and the liberty,° these are the only men.   365

Hamlet: O Jephthah, judge of Israel,° what a treasure hadst thou!

Polonius: What a treasure had he, my lord?

Hamlet: Why,
          "One fair daughter, and no more,
              The which he loved passing well."   370

Polonius [aside]: Still on my daughter.

Hamlet: Am I not i' the right, old Jephthah?

Polonius: If you call me Jephthah, my lord, I have a daughter that I love
     passing° well.

Hamlet: Nay, that follows not.   375

Polonius: What follows, then, my lord?

Hamlet: Why,
          "As by lot, God wot,"
     and then, you know,
          "It came to pass, as most like° it was," —   380

---

345 *I am ... north-north-west:* I am only partly mad, i.e., in only one point of the compass.
346 *handsaw:* A proposed reading of *hernshaw* would mean "heron"; *handsaw* may be an early
corruption of *hernshaw.* Another view regards *hawk* as the variant of *hack,* a tool of the pickax
type, and *handsaw* as a saw operated by hand.   349 *swaddling-clouts:* Cloths in which to
wrap a newborn baby.   353 *o' Monday morning:* Said to mislead Polonius.   355 *Roscius:*
A famous Roman actor.   358 *Buz, buz:* An interjection used at Oxford to denote stale
news.   363 *scene individable:* A play observing the unity of place.   364 *poem unlimited:* A
play disregarding the unities of time and place; *Seneca:* Writer of Latin tragedies, model of
early Elizabethan writers of tragedy; *Plautus:* Writer of Latin comedy.   365 *law ... liberty:*
Pieces written according to rules and without rules, i.e., "classical" and "romantic" dramas.
366 *Jephthah ... Israel:* Jephthah had to sacrifice his daughter; see Judges 11.   374 *passing:*
Surpassingly.   380 *like:* Probable.

the first row° of the pious chanson° will show you more; for look,
where my abridgement comes.°

Enter the Players.

You are welcome, masters; welcome, all. I am glad to see thee well. Welcome, good friends. O, old friend! why, thy face is valanced° since I
saw thee last: comest thou to beard me in Denmark? What, my   385
young lady and mistress! By'r lady, your ladyship is nearer to heaven
than when I saw you last, by the altitude of a chopine.° Pray God, your
voice, like a piece of uncurrent° gold, be not cracked within the ring.°
Masters, you are all welcome. We'll e'en to 't like French falconers, fly
at any thing we see: we'll have a speech straight: come, give us   390
a taste of your quality; come, a passionate speech.

First Player: What speech, my good lord?

Hamlet: I heard thee speak me a speech once, but it was never acted; or, if
it was, not above once; for the play, I remember, pleased not the million; 'twas caviary to the general:° but it was — as I received it, and   395
others, whose judgements in such matters cried in the top of°
mine — an excellent play, well digested in the scenes, set down with as
much modesty as cunning.° I remember, one said there were no sal-
lets° in the lines to make the matter savoury, nor no matter in the
phrase that might indict° the author of affectation; but called it an   400
honest method, as wholesome as sweet, and by very much more
handsome than fine.° One speech in 't I chiefly loved: 'twas Æneas'
tale to Dido;° and thereabout of it especially, where he speaks of
Priam's slaughter: if it live in your memory, begin at this line: let me
see, let me see —   405
"The rugged Pyrrhus,° like th' Hyrcanian beast,"° —
'tis not so: — it begins with Pyrrhus: —
"The rugged Pyrrhus, he whose sable arms,
Black as his purpose, did the night resemble
When he lay couched in the ominous horse,°   410
Hath now this dread and black complexion smear'd
With heraldry more dismal; head to foot
Now is he total gules;° horridly trick'd°
With blood of fathers, mothers, daughters, sons,
Bak'd and impasted° with the parching streets,   415

---

381 *row:* Stanza; *chanson:* Ballad.   382 *abridgement comes:* Opportunity comes for cutting
short the conversation.   384 *valanced:* Fringed (with a beard).   387 *chopine:* Kind of
shoe raised by the thickness of the heel; worn in Italy, particularly at Venice.   388 *un-
current:* Not passable as lawful coinage.   388 *cracked within the ring:* In the center of coins
were rings enclosing the sovereign's head; if the coin was cracked within this ring, it was
unfit for currency.   395 *caviary to the general:* Not relished by the multitude.   396 *cried
in the top of:* Spoke with greater authority than.   398 *cunning:* Skill.   398-399 *sallets:*
Salads: here, spicy improprieties.   400 *indict:* Convict.   401-402 *as wholesome . . . fine:* Its
beauty was not that of elaborate ornament, but that of order and proportion.   402-403
Æneas' tale to Dido: The lines recited by the player are imitated from Marlowe and Nashe's
Dido Queen of Carthage (II.i.214 ff.). They are written in such a way that the conventionality of
the play within a play is raised above that of ordinary drama.   406 *Pyrrhus:* A Greek hero
in the Trojan War; *Hyrcanian beast:* The tiger; see Virgil, *Aeneid,* IV.266.   410 *ominous horse:*
Trojan horse.   413 *gules:* Red, a heraldic term; *trick'd:* Spotted, smeared.   415 *impasted:*
Made into a paste.

    That lend a tyrannous and a damned light
    To their lord's murder: roasted in wrath and fire,
    And thus o'er-sized° with coagulate gore,
    With eyes like carbuncles, the hellish Pyrrhus
    Old grandsire Priam seeks."   420
    So, proceed you.
Polonius: 'Fore God, my lord, well spoken, with good accent and good
    discretion.
First Player: "Anon he finds him
    Striking too short at Greeks; his antique sword,   425
    Rebellious to his arm, lies where it falls,
    Repugnant° to command: unequal match'd,
    Pyrrhus at Priam drives; in rage strikes wide;
    But with the whiff and wind of his fell sword
    Th' unnerved father falls. Then senseless Ilium,°   430
    Seeming to feel this blow, with flaming top
    Stoops to his base, and with a hideous crash
    Takes prisoner Pyrrhus' ear: for, lo! his sword
    Which was declining on the milky head
    Of reverend Priam, seem'd i' th' air to stick: 435
    So, as a painted tyrant,° Pyrrhus stood,
    And like a neutral to his will and matter,°
    Did nothing.
    But, as we often see, against° some storm,
    A silence in the heavens, the rack° stand still,   440
    The bold winds speechless and the orb below
    As hush as death, anon the dreadful thunder
    Doth rend the region,° so, after Pyrrhus' pause,
    Aroused vengeance sets him new a-work;
    And never did the Cyclops' hammers fall   445
    On Mars's armour forg'd for proof eterne°
    With less remorse than Pyrrhus' bleeding sword
    Now falls on Priam.
    Out, out, thou strumpet, Fortune! All you gods,
    In general synod,° take away her power;   450
    Break all the spokes and fellies° from her wheel,
    And bowl the round nave° down the hill of heaven,
    As low as to the fiends!"
Polonius: This is too long.
Hamlet: It shall to the barber's, with your beard. Prithee, say on: he's for a   455
    jig° or a tale of bawdry,° or he sleeps: say on: come to Hecuba.°
First Player: "But who, ah woe! had seen the mobled° queen —"
Hamlet: "The mobled queen?"

---

418 *o'er-sized:* Covered as with size or glue.   427 *Repugnant:* Disobedient.   430 *Then senseless Ilium:* Insensate Troy.   436 *painted tyrant:* Tyrant in a picture.   437 *matter:* Task. 439 *against:* Before.   440 *rack:* Mass of clouds.   443 *region:* Assembly.   446 *proof eterne:* External resistance to assault.   450 *synod:* Assembly.   451 *fellies:* Pieces of wood forming the rim of a wheel.   452 *nave:* Hub.   456 *jig:* Comic performance given at the end or in an interval of a play; *bawdry:* Indecency; *Hecuba:* Wife of Priam, king of Troy. 457 *mobled:* Muffled.

Polonius: That's good; "mobled queen" is good.

First Player: "Run barefoot up and down, threat'ning the flames | 460
    With bisson rheum;° a clout° upon that head
    Where late the diadem stood, and for a robe,
    About her lank and all o'er-teemed° loins,
    A blanket, in the alarm of fear caught up;
    Who this had seen, with tongue in venom steep'd, | 465
    'Gainst Fortune's state would treason have pronounc'd:°
    But if the gods themselves did see her then
    When she saw Pyrrhus make malicious sport
    In mincing with his sword her husband's limbs,
    The instant burst of clamour that she made, | 470
    Unless things mortal move them not at all,
    Would have made milch° the burning eyes of heaven,
    And passion in the gods."

Polonius: Look, whe'r he has not turned° his colour and has tears in 's
    eyes. Prithee, no more. | 475

Hamlet: 'Tis well; I'll have thee speak out the rest soon. Good my lord, will
    you see the players well bestowed? Do you hear, let them be well used;
    for they are the abstract° and brief chronicles of the time: after your
    death you were better have a bad epitaph than their ill report
    while you live. | 480

Polonius: My lord, I will use them according to their desert.

Hamlet: God's bodykins,° man, much better: use every man after his
    desert, and who shall 'scape whipping? Use them after your own hon-
    our and dignity: the less they deserve, the more merit is in your
    bounty. Take them in. | 485

Polonius: Come, sirs.

Hamlet: Follow him, friends: we'll hear a play tomorrow. *[Aside to First
    Player.]* Dost thou hear me, old friend; can you play the Murder of
    Gonzago?

First Player: Ay, my lord. | 490

Hamlet: We'll ha 't to-morrow night. You could, for a need, study a speech
    of some dozen or sixteen lines,° which I would set down and insert
    in 't, could you not?

First Player: Ay, my lord.

Hamlet: Very well. Follow that lord; and look you mock him not.—My | 495
    good friends, I'll leave you till night: you are welcome to Elsinore.

                                       Exeunt Polonius and Players.

Rosencrantz: Good my lord!   *Exeunt [Rosencrantz and Guildenstern.]*

Hamlet: Ay, so, God bye to you.—Now I am alone.
    O, what a rogue and peasant° slave am I!
    Is it not monstrous that this player here, | 500
    But in a fiction, in a dream of passion,
    Could force his soul so to his own conceit

---

461 *bisson rheum:* Blinding tears; *clout:* Piece of cloth.   463 *o'er-teemed:* Worn out with bearing children.   466 *pronounc'd:* Proclaimed.   472 *milch:* Moist with tears.   474 *turned:*
Changed.   478 *abstract:* Summary account.   482 *bodykins:* Diminutive form of the oath
"by God's body."   492 *dozen or sixteen lines:* Critics have amused themselves by trying to
locate Hamlet's lines. Lucianus's speech III.ii.229–234 is the best guess.   499 *peasant:* Base.

That from her working all his visage wann'd,°
Tears in his eyes, distraction in 's aspect,
A broken voice, and his whole function suiting   505
With forms to his conceit?° and all for nothing!
For Hecuba!
What's Hecuba to him, or he to Hecuba,
That he should weep for her? What would he do,
Had he the motive and the cue for passion   510
That I have? He would drown the stage with tears
And cleave the general ear with horrid speech,
Make mad the guilty and appall the free,
Confound the ignorant, and amaze indeed
The very faculties of eyes and ears.   515
Yet I,
A dull and muddy-mettled° rascal, peak,°
Like John-a-dreams,° unpregnant of° my cause,
And can say nothing; no, not for a king.
Upon whose property° and most dear life   520
A damn'd defeat was made. Am I a coward?
Who calls me villain? breaks my pate across?
Plucks off my beard, and blows it in my face?
Tweaks me by the nose? gives me the lie i' th' throat,
As deep as to the lungs? who does me this?   525
Ha!
'Swounds, I should take it: for it cannot be
But I am pigeon-liver'd° and lack gall
To make oppression bitter, or ere this
I should have fatted all the region kites°   530
With this slave's offal: bloody, bawdy villain!
Remorseless, treacherous, lecherous, kindless° villain!
O, vengeance!
Why, what an ass am I! This is most brave,
That I, the son of a dear father murder'd,   535
Prompted to my revenge by heaven and hell,
Must, like a whore, unpack my heart with words,
And fall a-cursing, like a very drab,°
A stallion!°
Fie upon 't! foh! About,° my brains! Hum, I have heard   540
That guilty creatures sitting at a play
Have by the very cunning of the scene
Been struck so to the soul that presently
They have proclaim'd their malefactions;

---

503 *wann'd:* Grew pale.   505–506 *his whole...conceit:* His whole being responded with
forms to suit his thought.   517 *muddy-mettled:* Dull-spirited; *peak:* Mope, pine.   518 *John-a-dreams:* An expression occurring elsewhere in Elizabethan literature to indicate a dreamer; *unpregnant of:* Not quickened by.   520 *property:* Proprietorship (of crown and life).
528 *pigeon-liver'd:* The pigeon was supposed to secrete no gall; if Hamlet, so he says, had had
gall, he would have felt the bitterness of oppression, and avenged it.   530 *region kites:*
Kites of the air.   532 *kindless:* Unnatural.   538 *drab:* Prostitute.   539 *stallion:* Prostitute (male or female).   540 *About:* About it, or turn thou right about.

For murder, though it have no tongue, will speak   545
With most miraculous organ. I'll have these players
Play something like the murder of my father
Before mine uncle: I'll observe his looks:
I'll tent° him to the quick: if 'a do blench,°
I know my course. The spirit that I have seen   550
May be the devil:° and the devil hath power
T' assume a pleasing shape; yea, and perhaps
Out of my weakness and my melancholy,
As he is very potent with such spirits,°
Abuses me to damn me: I'll have grounds   555
More relative° than this:° the play's the thing
Wherein I'll catch the conscience of the king.   *Exit.*

[ACT III

SCENE I: *A room in the castle.*]

Enter King, Queen, Polonius, Ophelia, Rosencrantz, Guildenstern, Lords.

King: And can you, by no drift of conference,°
    Get from him why he puts on this confusion,
    Grating so harshly all his days of quiet
    With turbulent and dangerous lunacy?
Rosencrantz: He does confess he feels himself distracted;   5
    But from what cause 'a will by no means speak.
Guildenstern: Nor do we find him forward° to be sounded,
    But, with a crafty madness, keeps aloof,
    When we would bring him on to some confession
    Of his true state.
Queen: Did he receive you well?   10
Rosencrantz: Most like a gentleman.
Guildenstern: But with much forcing of his disposition.°
Rosencrantz: Niggard of question;° but, of our demands,
    Most free in his reply.
Queen: Did you assay° him
    To any pastime?   15
Rosencrantz: Madam, it so fell out, that certain players
    We o'er-raught° on the way: of these we told him;
    And there did seem in him a kind of joy
    To hear of it: they are here about the court,

---

549 *tent:* Probe; *blench:* Quail, flinch.   551 *May be the devil:* Hamlet's suspicion is properly grounded in the belief of the time.   554 *spirits:* Humors.   556 *relative:* Closely related, definite; *this:* I.e., the ghost's story.   **Act III, Scene I.**   1 *drift of conference:* Device of conversation.   7 *forward:* Willing.   12 *forcing of his disposition:* I.e., against his will.   13 *Niggard of question:* Sparing of conversation.   14 *assay:* Try to win.   17 *o'er-raught:* Overtook.

And, as I think, they have already order　　　　　　　　　　　　　20
This night to play before him.
Polonius:　　　　　　　　　　　　'Tis most true:
And he beseech'd me to entreat your majesties
To hear and see the matter.
King:　With all my heart; and it doth much content me
To hear him so inclin'd.　　　　　　　　　　　　　　　　　　25
Good gentlemen, give him a further edge,°
And drive his purpose into these delights.
Rosencrantz:　We shall, my lord.　　　　　　Exeunt Rosencrantz and Guildenstern.
King:　　　　　　　　　　　Sweet Gertrude, leave us too;
For we have closely° sent for Hamlet hither,
That he, as 'twere by accident, may here　　　　　　　　　　　30
Affront° Ophelia:
Her father and myself, lawful espials,°
Will so bestow ourselves that, seeing, unseen,
We may of their encounter frankly judge,
And gather by him, as he is behav'd,　　　　　　　　　　　35
If 't be th' affliction of his love or no
That thus he suffers for.
Queen:　　　　　　　　　I shall obey you.
And for your part, Ophelia, I do wish
That your good beauties be the happy cause
Of Hamlet's wildness:° so shall I hope your virtues　　　　　40
Will bring him to his wonted way again,
To both your honours.
Ophelia:　　　　　　　　Madam, I wish it may.　　　　　[Exit Queen.]
Polonius:　Ophelia, walk you here. Gracious,° so please you,
We will bestow ourselves. [To Ophelia.] Read on this book;
That show of such an exercise° may colour°　　　　　　　　45
Your loneliness. We are oft to blame in this, —
'Tis too much prov'd — that with devotion's visage
And pious action we do sugar o'er
The devil himself.
King:　　　　　　　　[aside] O, 'tis too true!
How smart a lash that speech doth give my conscience!　　　50
The harlot's cheek, beautied with plast'ring art,
Is not more ugly to° the thing° that helps it
Than is my deed to my most painted word:
O heavy burthen!
Polonius:　I hear him coming: let's withdraw, my lord.　　　　55
　　　　　　　　　　　　　　　[Exeunt King and Polonius.]

　　Enter Hamlet.

---

26 edge: Incitement.　　29 closely: Secretly.　　31 Affront: Confront.　　32 lawful espials:
Legitimate spies.　　40 wildness: Madness.　　43 Gracious: Your grace (addressed to the
king).　　45 exercise: Act of devotion (the book she reads is one of devotion); colour: Give a
plausible appearance to.　　52 to: Compared to; thing: I.e., the cosmetic.

Hamlet: To be, or not to be: that is the question:
    Whether 'tis nobler in the mind to suffer
    The slings and arrows of outrageous fortune,
    Or to take arms against a sea° of troubles,
    And by opposing end them? To die: to sleep;   60
    No more; and by a sleep to say we end
    The heart-ache and the thousand natural shocks
    That flesh is heir to, 'tis a consummation
    Devoutly to be wish'd. To die, to sleep;
    To sleep: perchance to dream: ay, there's the rub;   65
    For in that sleep of death what dreams may come
    When we have shuffled° off this mortal coil,°
    Must give us pause: there's the respect°
    That makes calamity of so long life;°
    For who would bear the whips and scorns of time,°   70
    Th' oppressor's wrong, the proud man's contumely,
    The pangs of despis'd° love, the law's delay,
    The insolence of office° and the spurns°
    That patient merit of th' unworthy takes,
    When he himself might his quietus° make   75
    With a bare bodkin?° who would fardels° bear,
    To grunt and sweat under a weary life,
    But that the dread of something after death,
    The undiscover'd country from whose bourn°
    No traveller returns, puzzles the will   80
    And makes us rather bear those ills we have
    Than fly to others that we know not of?
    Thus conscience° does make cowards of us all;
    And thus the native hue° of resolution
    Is sicklied o'er° with the pale cast° of thought,   85
    And enterprises of great pitch° and moment°
    With this regard° their currents° turn awry,
    And lose the name of action — Soft you now!
    The fair Ophelia! Nymph, in thy orisons°
    Be all my sins rememb'red.
Ophelia: Good my lord,   90
    How does your honour for this many a day?
Hamlet: I humbly thank you; well, well, well.
Ophelia: My lord, I have remembrances of yours,

---

59 *sea:* The mixed metaphor of this speech has often been commented on; a later emendation *siege* has sometimes been spoken on the stage.   67 *shuffled:* Sloughed, cast; *coil:* Usually means "turmoil"; here, possibly "body" (conceived of as wound about the soul like rope); *clay, soil, veil,* have been suggested as emendations.   68 *respect:* Consideration.   69 *of . . . life:* So long-lived.   70 *time:* The world.   72 *despis'd:* Rejected.   73 *office:* Officeholders; *spurns:* Insults.   75 *quietus:* Acquittance; here, death.   76 *bare bodkin:* Mere dagger; *bare* is sometimes understood as "unsheathed"; *fardels:* Burdens.   79 *bourn:* Boundary.   83 *conscience:* Probably, inhibition by the faculty of reason restraining the will from doing wrong.   84 *native hue:* Natural color; metaphor derived from the color of the face.   85 *sicklied o'er:* Given a sickly tinge; *cast:* Shade of color.   86 *pitch:* Height (as of a falcon's flight); *moment:* Importance.   87 *regard:* Respect, consideration; *currents:* Courses.   89 *orisons:* Prayers.

That I have longed long to re-deliver;
I pray you, now receive them.
Hamlet: No, not I;   95
I never gave you aught.
Ophelia: My honour'd lord, you know right well you did;
And, with them, words of so sweet breath compos'd
As made the things more rich: their perfume lost,
Take these again; for to the noble mind   100
Rich gifts wax poor when givers prove unkind.
There, my lord.
Hamlet: Ha, ha! are you honest?°
Ophelia: My lord?
Hamlet: Are you fair?   105
Ophelia: What means your lordship?
Hamlet: That if you be honest and fair, your honesty° should admit no
discourse to your beauty.°
Ophelia: Could beauty, my lord, have better commerce° than with honesty?
Hamlet: Ay, truly; for the power of beauty will sooner transform honesty   110
from what it is to a bawd than the force of honesty can trans-
late beauty into his likeness: this was sometime a paradox, but now
the time° gives it proof. I did love you once.
Ophelia: Indeed, my lord, you made me believe so.
Hamlet: You should not have believed me; for virtue cannot so inoculate°   115
our old stock but we shall relish of it:° I loved you not.
Ophelia: I was the more deceived.
Hamlet: Get thee to a nunnery: why wouldst thou be a breeder of sinners?
I am myself indifferent honest;° but yet I could accuse me of such
things that it were better my mother had not borne me: I am very   120
proud, revengeful, ambitious, with more offences at my beck° than I
have thoughts to put them in, imagination to give them shape, or
time to act them in. What should such fellows as I do crawling be-
tween earth and heaven? We are arrant knaves, all; believe none of us.
Go thy ways to a nunnery. Where's your father?   125
Ophelia: At home, my lord.
Hamlet: Let the doors be shut upon him, that he may play the fool no
where but in 's own house. Farewell.
Ophelia: O, help him, you sweet heavens!
Hamlet: If thou dost marry, I'll give thee this plague for thy dowry: be   130
thou as chaste as ice, as pure as snow, thou shalt not escape calumny.
Get thee to a nunnery, go: farewell. Or, if thou wilt needs marry,
marry a fool; for wise men know well enough what monsters° you
make of them. To a nunnery, go, and quickly too. Farewell.
Ophelia: O heavenly powers, restore him!   135

103–108 *are you honest . . . beauty: Honest* meaning "truthful" and "chaste" and *fair* meaning
"just, honorable" (line 105) and "beautiful" (line 107) are not mere quibbles; the speech has
the irony of a *double entendre.*   **107** *your honesty:* Your chastity.   **108** *discourse to:* Familiar
intercourse with.   **109** *commerce:* Intercourse.   **113** *the time:* The present age.   **115** *in-
oculate:* Graft (metaphorical).   **116** *but . . . it:* I.e., that we do not still have about us a taste
of the old stock; i.e., retain our sinfulness.   **119** *indifferent honest:* Moderately virtuous.
121 *beck:* Command.   **133** *monsters:* An allusion to the horns of a cuckold.

Hamlet: I have heard of your° paintings too, well enough; God hath given
you one face, and you make yourselves another: you jig,° you amble,
and you lisp; you nick-name God's creatures, and make your wanton-
ness your ignorance.° Go to, I'll no more on 't; it hath made me mad. I
say, we will have no moe marriage: those that are married already, all   140
but one,° shall live; the rest shall keep as they are. To a nunnery, go.
                                                                    Exit.

Ophelia: O, what a noble mind is here o'er-thrown!
The courtier's, soldier's, scholar's, eye, tongue, sword;
Th' expectancy and rose° of the fair state,
The glass of fashion and the mould of form,°   145
Th' observ'd of all observers,° quite, quite down!
And I, of ladies most deject and wretched,
That suck'd the honey of his music vows,
Now see that noble and most sovereign reason,
Like sweet bells jangled, out of time and harsh;   150
That unmatch'd form and feature of blown° youth
Blasted with ecstasy:° O, woe is me,
T' have seen what I have seen, see what I see!

Enter King and Polonius.

King: Love! his affections do not that way tend;
Nor what he spake, though it lack'd form a little,   155
Was not like madness. There's something in his soul,
O'er which his melancholy sits on brood;
And I do doubt° the hatch and the disclose°
Will be some danger: which for to prevent,
I have in quick determination   160
Thus set it down: he shall with speed to England,
For the demand of our neglected tribute:
Haply the seas and countries different
With variable° objects shall expel
This something-settled° matter in his heart,   165
Whereon his brains still beating puts him thus
From fashion of himself.° What think you on 't?

Polonius: It shall do well: but yet do I believe
The origin and commencement of his grief
Sprung from neglected love. How now, Ophelia!   170
You need not tell us what Lord Hamlet said;
We heard it all. My lord, do as you please;
But, if you hold it fit, after the play
Let his queen mother all alone entreat him

136 *your:* Indefinite use.   137 *jig:* Move with jerky motion; probably allusion to the *jig,* or
song and dance, of the current stage.   138–139 *make . . . ignorance:* I.e., excuse your wanton-
ness on the ground of your ignorance.   141 *one:* I.e., the king.   144 *expectancy and rose:*
Source of hope.   145 *The glass . . . form:* The mirror of fashion and the pattern of courtly
behavior.   146 *observ'd . . . observers:* I.e., the center of attention in the court.   151 *blown:*
Blooming.   152 *ecstasy:* Madness.   158 *doubt:* Fear; *disclose:* Disclosure or revelation (by
chipping of the shell).   164 *variable:* Various.   165 *something-settled:* Somewhat settled.
167 *From . . . himself:* Out of his natural manner.

To show his grief: let her be round° with him;　　　　　　175
And I'll be plac'd, so please you, in the ear
Of all their conference. If she find him not,
To England send him, or confine him where
Your wisdom best shall think.

King: It shall be so:　　　　　　　　　　　　　　　　180
Madness in great ones must not unwatch'd go.　　　　　*Exeunt.*

[SCENE II: *A hall in the castle.*]

Enter Hamlet and three of the Players.

Hamlet: Speak the speech, I pray you, as I pronounced it to you, trip-
pingly on the tongue: but if you mouth it, as many of your° players do, I had as lief the town-crier spoke my lines. Nor do not saw the
air too much with your hand, thus, but use all gently; for in the very
torrent, tempest, and, as I may say, whirlwind of your passion, you　　5
must acquire and beget a temperance that may give it smoothness.
O, it offends me to the soul to hear a robustious° periwig-pated° fellow tear a passion to tatters, to very rags, to split the ears of the
groundlings,° who for the most part are capable of° nothing but
inexplicable° dumb-shows and noise: I would have such a fellow　　10
whipped for o'er-doing Termagant;° it out-herods Herod:° pray you,
avoid it.

First Player: I warrant your honour.

Hamlet: Be not too tame neither, but let your own discretion be your
tutor: suit the action to the word, the word to the action; with this　　15
special observance, that you o'er-step not the modesty of nature: for
any thing so overdone is from the purpose of playing, whose end,
both at the first and now, was and is, to hold, as 't were, the mirror up
to nature; to show virtue her own feature, scorn her own image, and
the very age and body of the time his form and pressure.° Now this　　20
overdone, or come tardy off,° though it make the unskilful laugh,
cannot but make the judicious grieve; the censure of the which one°
must in your allowance o'erweigh a whole theatre of others. O, there
be players that I have seen play, and heard others praise, and that
highly, not to speak it profanely, that, neither having the accent of　　25
Christians nor the gait of Christian, pagan, nor man, have so strut-
ted and bellowed that I have thought some of nature's journeymen°
had made men and not made them well, they imitated humanity so
abominably.

---

175 *round:* Blunt.　　**Scene II.**　　2 *your:* Indefinite use.　　7 *robustious:* Violent, boisterous; *periwig-pated:* Wearing a wig.　　9 *groundlings:* Those who stood in the yard of the theater; *capable of:* Susceptible of being influenced by.　　10 *inexplicable:* Of no significance
worth explaining.　　11 *Termagant:* A god of the Saracens; a character in the St. Nicholas
play, where one of his worshipers, leaving him in charge of goods, returns to find them
stolen; whereupon he beats the god (or idol), which howls vociferously; *Herod:* Herod of
Jewry; a character in *The Slaughter of the Innocents* and other cycle plays. The part was played
with great noise and fury.　　20 *pressure:* Stamp, impressed character.　　21 *come tardy
off:* Inadequately done.　　22 *the censure... one:* The judgment of even one of whom.
27 *journeymen:* Laborers not yet masters in their trade.

First Player: I hope we have reformed that indifferently° with us, sir. 30
Hamlet: O, reform it altogether. And let those that play your clowns speak
no more than is set down for them; for there be of° them that will
themselves laugh, to set on some quantity of barren° spectators to
laugh too; though, in the mean time, some necessary question of the
play be then to be considered: that's villanous, and shows a most 35
pitiful ambition in the fool that uses it. Go, make you ready.

[Exeunt Players.]

Enter Polonius, Guildenstern, and Rosencrantz.

How now, my lord! will the king hear this piece of work?
Polonius: And the queen too, and that presently.
Hamlet: Bid the players make haste. *[Exit Polonius.]*
Will you two help to hasten them? 40

Rosencrantz: ⎫
Guildenstern: ⎭ We will, my lord. *Exeunt they two.*
Hamlet: What ho! Horatio!

Enter Horatio.

Horatio: Here, sweet lord, at your service.
Hamlet: Horatio, thou art e'en as just° a man
As e'er my conversation cop'd withal.
Horatio: O, my dear lord,—
Hamlet: Nay, do not think I flatter; 45
For what advancement may I hope from thee
That no revenue hast but thy good spirits,
To feed and clothe thee? Why should the poor be flatter'd?
No, let the candied tongue lick absurd pomp,
And crook the pregnant° hinges of the knee 50
Where thrift° may follow fawning. Dost thou hear?
Since my dear soul was mistress of her choice
And could of men distinguish her election,
S' hath seal'd thee for herself; for thou hast been
As one, in suff'ring all, that suffers nothing, 55
A man that fortune's buffets and rewards
Hast ta'en with equal thanks: and blest are those
Whose blood and judgement are so well commeddled,
That they are not a pipe for fortune's finger
To sound what stop° she please. Give me that man 60
That is not passion's slave, and I will wear him
In my heart's core, ay, in my heart of heart,
As I do thee.—Something too much of this.—
There is a play to-night before the king;
One scene of it comes near the circumstance 65
Which I have told thee of my father's death:
I prithee, when thou seest that act afoot,

---

30 *indifferently:* Fairly, tolerably. 32 *of:* I.e., some among them. 33 *barren:* I.e., of wit.
43 *just:* Honest, honorable. 50 *pregnant:* Pliant. 51 *thrift:* Profit. 60 *stop:* Hole in
a wind instrument for controlling the sound.

Even with the very comment of thy soul°
Observe my uncle: if his occulted° guilt
Do not itself unkennel in one speech,   70
It is a damned° ghost that we have seen,
And my imaginations are as foul
As Vulcan's stithy.° Give him heedful note;
For I mine eyes will rivet to his face,
And after we will both our judgements join   75
In censure of his seeming.°
Horatio: Well, my lord:
If 'a steal aught the whilst this play is playing,
And 'scape detecting, I will pay the theft.

Enter trumpets and kettledrums, King, Queen, Polonius, Ophelia,
[Rosencrantz, Guildenstern, and others].

Hamlet: They are coming to the play; I must be idle:° Get you a place.
King: How fares our cousin Hamlet?   80
Hamlet: Excellent, i' faith; of the chameleon's dish:° I eat the air, promise-
crammed: you cannot feed capons so.
King: I have nothing with° this answer, Hamlet; these words are not
mine.°
Hamlet: No, nor mine now. *[To Polonius.]* My lord, you played once i' the   85
university, you say?
Polonius: That did I, my lord; and was accounted a good actor.
Hamlet: What did you enact?
Polonius: I did enact Julius Cæsar: I was killed i' the Capitol; Brutus
killed me.   90
Hamlet: It was a brute part of him to kill so capital a calf there. Be the
players ready?
Rosencrantz: Ay, my lord; they stay upon your patience.
Queen: Come hither, my dear Hamlet, sit by me.
Hamlet: No, good mother, here's metal more attractive.   95
Polonius [to the king]: O, ho! do you mark that?
Hamlet: Lady, shall I lie in your lap?   *[Lying down at Ophelia's feet.]*
Ophelia: No, my lord.
Hamlet: I mean, my head upon your lap?
Ophelia: Ay, my lord.   100
Hamlet: Do you think I meant country° matters?
Ophelia: I think nothing, my lord.
Hamlet: That's a fair thought to lie between maids' legs.
Ophelia: What is, my lord?
Hamlet: Nothing.   105
Ophelia: You are merry, my lord.
Hamlet: Who, I?

---

68 *very . . . soul:* Inward and sagacious criticism.   69 *occulted:* Hidden.   71 *damned:* In
league with Satan.   73 *stithy:* Smithy, place of *stiths* (anvils).   76 *censure . . . seeming:*
Judgment of his appearance or behavior.   79 *idle:* Crazy, or not attending to anything
serious.   81 *chameleon's dish:* Chameleons were supposed to feed on air. (Hamlet deliberately misinterprets the king's "fares" as "feeds.")   83 *have . . . with:* Make nothing of.
83-84 *are not mine:* Do not respond to what I ask.   101 *country:* With a bawdy pun.

Ophelia: Ay, my lord.

Hamlet: O God, your only° jig-maker.° What should a man do but be merry? for, look you, how cheerfully my mother looks, and my father 110 died within's two hours.

Ophelia: Nay, 'tis twice two months, my lord.

Hamlet: So long? Nay then, let the devil wear black, for I'll have a suit of sables.° O heavens! die two months ago, and not forgotten yet? Then there's hope a great man's memory may outlive his life half a year: 115 but, by 'r lady, 'a must build churches, then; or else shall 'a suffer not thinking on,° with the hobbyhorse, whose epitaph is "For, O, for, O, the hobbyhorse is forgot."°

The trumpets sound. Dumb show follows.

    Enter a King and a Queen [very lovingly]; the Queen embracing him, and he her. [She kneels, and makes show of protestation unto him.] He takes her up, and declines his head upon her neck: he lies him down upon a bank of flowers: she, seeing him asleep, leaves him. Anon comes in another man, takes off his crown, kisses it, pours poison in the sleeper's ears, and leaves him. The Queen returns; finds the King dead, makes passionate action. The Poisoner, with some three or four come in again, seem to condole with her. The dead body is carried away. The Poisoner woos the Queen with gifts: she seems harsh awhile, but in the end accepts love. [Exeunt.]

Ophelia: What means this, my lord?

Hamlet: Marry, this is miching mallecho;° it means mischief. 120

Ophelia: Belike this show imports the argument of the play.

    Enter Prologue.

Hamlet: We shall know by this fellow: the players cannot keep counsel; they'll tell all.

Ophelia: Will 'a tell us what this show meant?

Hamlet: Ay, or any show that you'll show him: be not you ashamed to 125 show, he'll not shame to tell you what it means.

Ophelia: You are naught, you are naught:° I'll mark the play.

Prologue: For us, and for our tragedy,
    Here stooping° to your clemency,
    We beg your hearing patiently.   *[Exit.]* 130

Hamlet: Is this a prologue, or the posy° of a ring?

Ophelia: 'Tis brief, my lord.

Hamlet: As woman's love.

    Enter [two Players as] King and Queen.

Player King: Full thirty times hath Phoebus' cart gone round
    Neptune's salt wash° and Tellus'° orbed ground,   135
    And thirty dozen moons with borrowed° sheen

---

109 *your only:* Only your; *jig-maker:* Composer of jigs (song and dance).   113–114 *suit of sables:* Garments trimmed with the fur of the sable, with a quibble on *sable* meaning "black." 116–117 *suffer . . . on:* Undergo oblivion.   117–118 *"For . . . forgot":* Verse of a song occurring also in *Love's Labour's Lost,* III.i.30. The hobbyhorse was a character in the Morris Dance. 120 *miching mallecho:* Sneaking mischief.   127 *naught:* Indecent.   129 *stooping:* Bowing. 131 *posy:* Motto.   135 *salt wash:* The sea; *Tellus:* Goddess of the earth (*orbed ground*). 136 *borrowed:* I.e., reflected.

About the world have times twelve thirties been,
Since love our hearts and Hymen° did our hands
Unite commutual° in most sacred bands.
Player Queen: So many journeys may the sun and moon   140
Make us again count o'er ere love be done!
But, woe is me, you are so sick of late,
So far from cheer and from your former state,
That I distrust° you. Yet, though I distrust,
Discomfort you, my lord, it nothing must: 145
For women's fear and love holds quantity;°
In neither aught, or in extremity.
Now, what my love is, proof hath made you know;
And as my love is siz'd, my fear is so:
Where love is great, the littlest doubts are fear;   150
Where little fears grow great, great love grows there.
Player King: 'Faith, I must leave thee, love, and shortly too;
My operant° powers their functions leave° to do:
And thou shalt live in this fair world behind,
Honour'd, belov'd; and haply one as kind   155
For husband shalt thou—
Player Queen: O, confound the rest!
Such love must needs be treason in my breast:
In second husband let me be accurst!
None wed the second but who kill'd the first.
Hamlet (aside): Wormwood, wormwood.   160
Player Queen: The instances that second marriage move
Are base respects of thrift, but none of love:
A second time I kill my husband dead,
When second husband kisses me in bed.
Player King: I do believe you think what now you speak;   165
But what we do determine oft we break.
Purpose is but the slave to memory,
Of violent birth, but poor validity:
Which now, like fruit unripe, sticks on the tree;
But fall, unshaken, when they mellow be.   170
Most necessary 'tis that we forget
To pay ourselves what to ourselves is debt:
What to ourselves in passion we propose,
The passion ending, doth the purpose lose.
The violence of either grief or joy   175
Their own enactures° with themselves destroy:
Where joy most revels, grief doth most lament;
Grief joys, joy grieves, on slender accident.
This world is not for aye,° nor 'tis not strange
That even our loves should with our fortunes change;   180
For 'tis a question left us yet to prove,

---

138 *Hymen:* God of matrimony.   139 *commutual:* Mutually.   144 *distrust:* Am anxious about.   146 *holds quantity:* Keeps proportion between.   153 *operant:* Active; *leave:* Cease.   176 *enactures:* Fulfillments.   179 *aye:* Ever.

Whether love lead fortune, or else fortune love.
The great man down, you mark his favourite flies;
The poor advanc'd makes friends of enemies.
And hitherto doth love on fortune tend;   185
For who° not needs shall never lack a friend,
And who in want a hollow friend doth try,
Directly seasons° him his enemy.
But, orderly to end where I begun,
Our wills and fates do so contrary run   190
That our devices still are overthrown;
Our thoughts are ours, their ends° none of our own:
So think thou wilt no second husband wed;
But die thy thoughts when thy first lord is dead.
Player Queen: Nor earth to me give food, nor heaven light!   195
Sport and repose lock from me day and night!
To desperation turn my trust and hope!
An anchor's° cheer° in prison be my scope!
Each opposite° that blanks° the face of joy
Meet what I would have well and it destroy!   200
Both here and hence pursue me lasting strife,
If, once a widow, ever I be wife!
Hamlet: If she should break it now!
Player King: 'Tis deeply sworn. Sweet, leave me here awhile;
My spirits grow dull, and fain I would beguile   205
The tedious day with sleep.   *[Sleeps.]*
Player Queen: Sleep rock thy brain;
And never come mischance between us twain!   *Exit.*
Hamlet: Madam, how like you this play?
Queen: The lady doth protest too much, methinks.
Hamlet: O, but she'll keep her word.   210
King: Have you heard the argument? Is there no offence in 't?
Hamlet: No, no, they do but jest, poison in jest; no offence i' the world.
King: What do you call the play?
Hamlet: The Mouse-trap. Marry, how? Tropically.° This play is the image
of a murder done in Vienna: Gonzago° is the duke's name; his wife,   215
Baptista: you shall see anon; 't is a knavish piece of work: but what o'
that? your majesty and we that have free souls, it touches us not: let
the galled jade° winch,° our withers° are unwrung.°

Enter Lucianus.

This is one Lucianus, nephew to the king.
Ophelia: You are as good as a chorus,° my lord.   220

---

186 *who:* Whoever.   188 *seasons:* Matures, ripens.   192 *ends:* Results.   198 *An anchor's:*
An anchorite's; *cheer:* Fare; sometimes printed as *chair.*   199 *opposite:* Adverse thing;
blanks: Causes to blanch or grow pale.   214 *Tropically:* Figuratively, *trapically* suggests a pun
on *trap* in *Mouse-trap* (l. 214).   215 *Gonzago:* In 1538 Luigi Gonzago murdered the Duke of
Urbano by pouring poisoned lotion in his ears.   218 *galled jade:* Horse whose hide is
rubbed by saddle or harness; *winch:* Wince; *withers:* The part between the horse's shoulder
blades; *unwrung:* Not wrung or twisted.   220 *chorus:* In many Elizabethan plays the action
was explained by an actor known as the "chorus"; at a puppet show the actor who explained
the action was known as an "interpreter," as indicated by the lines following.

Hamlet: I could interpret between you and your love, if I could see the
    puppets dallying.°
Ophelia: You are keen, my lord, you are keen.
Hamlet: It would cost you a groaning to take off my edge.
Ophelia: Still better, and worse.°   225
Hamlet: So you mistake° your husbands. Begin, murderer; pox,° leave thy
    damnable faces, and begin. Come: the croaking raven doth bellow for
    revenge.
Lucianus: Thoughts black, hands apt, drugs fit, and time agreeing;
    Confederate° season, else no creature seeing;   230
    Thou mixture rank, of midnight weeds collected,
    With Hecate's° ban° thrice blasted, thrice infected,
    Thy natural magic and dire property,
    On wholesome life usurp immediately.
                              [Pours the poison into the sleeper's ears.]
Hamlet: 'A poisons him i' the garden for his estate. His name's Gonzago: 235
    the story is extant, and written in very choice Italian: you shall see
    anon how the murderer gets the love of Gonzago's wife.
Ophelia: The king rises.
Hamlet: What, frighted with false fire!°
Queen: How fares my lord?   240
Polonius: Give o'er the play.
King: Give me some light: away!
Polonius: Lights, lights, lights!   *Exeunt all but Hamlet and Horatio.*
Hamlet: Why, let the strucken deer go weep,
    The hart ungalled play;   245
    For some must watch, while some must sleep:
    Thus runs the world away.°
    Would not this,° sir, and a forest of feathers°—if the rest of my for-
    tunes turn Turk with° me—with two Provincial roses° on my razed°
    shoes, get me a fellowship in a cry° of players,° sir?   250
Horatio: Half a share.°
Hamlet: A whole one, I.
    For thou dost know, O Damon dear,
    This realm dismantled° was
    Of Jove himself; and now reigns here   255
    A very, very°—pajock.°

---

222 *dallying:* With sexual suggestion, continued in *keen* (sexually aroused), *groaning* (i.e., in
pregnancy), and *edge* (i.e., sexual desire or impetuosity).   225 *Still . . . worse:* More keen, less
decorous.   226 *mistake:* Err in taking; *pox:* An imprecation.   230 *Confederate:* Conspiring (to assist the murderer).   232 *Hecate:* The goddess of witchcraft; *ban:* Curse.
239 *false fire:* Fireworks, or a blank discharge.   244–247 *Why . . . away:* Probably from an
old ballad, with allusion to the popular belief that a wounded deer retires to weep and die. Cf.
As You Like It, II.i.66.   248 *this:* I.e., the play; *feathers:* Allusion to the plumes which Elizabethan actors were fond of wearing.   249 *turn Turk with:* Go back on; *two Provincial roses:*
Rosettes of ribbon like the roses of Provins near Paris, or else the roses of Provence; *razed:*
Cut, slashed (by way of ornament).   250 *cry:* Pack (as of hounds); *fellowship . . . players:*
Partnership in a theatrical company.   251 *Half a share:* Allusion to the custom in dramatic
companies of dividing the ownership into a number of shares among the householders.
254 *dismantled:* Stripped, divested.   253–256 *For . . . very:* Probably from an old ballad hav-
ing to do with Damon and Pythias.   256 *pajock:* Peacock (a bird with a bad reputation).
Possibly the word was *patchock,* diminutive of *patch,* clown.

Horatio: You might have rhymed.

Hamlet: O good Horatio, I'll take the ghost's word for a thousand pound.
     Didst perceive?

Horatio: Very well, my lord.   260

Hamlet: Upon the talk of the poisoning?

Horatio: I did very well note him.

Hamlet: Ah, ha! Come, some music! come, the recorders!°
     For if the king like not the comedy,
     Why then, belike, he likes it not, perdy.°   265
     Come, some music!

     Enter Rosencrantz and Guildenstern.

Guildenstern: Good my lord, vouchsafe me a word with you.

Hamlet: Sir, a whole history.

Guildenstern: The king, sir, —

Hamlet: Ay, sir, what of him?   270

Guildenstern: Is in his retirement marvellous distempered.

Hamlet: With drink, sir?

Guildenstern: No, my lord, rather with choler.°

Hamlet: Your wisdom should show itself more richer to signify this to
     his doctor; for, for me to put him to his purgation would perhaps   275
     plunge him into far more choler.

Guildenstern: Good my lord, put your discourse into some frame° and
     start not so wildly from my affair.

Hamlet: I am tame, sir: pronounce.

Guildenstern: The queen, your mother, in most great affliction of spirit,   280
     hath sent me to you.

Hamlet: You are welcome.

Guildenstern: Nay, good my lord, this courtesy is not of the right breed. If
     it shall please you to make me a wholesome° answer, I will do your
     mother's commandment; if not, your pardon and my return shall be   285
     the end of my business.

Hamlet: Sir, I cannot.

Guildenstern: What, my lord?

Hamlet: Make you a wholesome answer; my wit's diseased: but, sir, such
     answer as I can make, you shall command; or, rather, as you say, my   290
     mother: therefore no more, but to the matter:° my mother, you say, —

Rosencrantz: Then thus she says; your behaviour hath struck her into
     amazement and admiration.

Hamlet: O wonderful son, that can so 'stonish a mother! But is there no
     sequel at the heels of this mother's admiration? Impart.   295

Rosencrantz: She desires to speak with you in her closet, ere you go to bed.

Hamlet: We shall obey, were she ten times our mother. Have you any fur-
     ther trade with us?

Rosencrantz: My lord, you once did love me.

Hamlet: And do still, by these pickers and stealers.°   300

---

263 *recorders:* Wind instruments of the flute kind.   265 *perdy:* Corruption of *par dieu.*
273 *choler:* Bilious disorder, with quibble on the sense "anger."   277 *frame:* Order.
284 *wholesome:* Sensible.   291 *matter:* Matter in hand.   300 *pickers and stealers:* Hands,
so called from the catechism "to keep my hands from picking and stealing."

Rosencrantz: Good my lord, what is your cause of distemper? you do, surely, bar the door upon your own liberty, if you deny your griefs to your friend.

Hamlet: Sir, I lack advancement.

Rosencrantz: How can that be, when you have the voice° of the king him- 305
self for your succession in Denmark?

Hamlet: Ay, sir, but "While the grass grows,"° — the proverb is something musty.

Enter the Players with recorders.

O, the recorders! let me see one. To withdraw° with you: — why do you go about to recover the wind° of me, as if you would drive me 310 into a toil?°

Guildenstern: O, my lord, if my duty be too bold, my love is too unman-nerly.°

Hamlet: I do not well understand that. Will you play upon this pipe?

Guildenstern: My lord, I cannot.   315

Hamlet: I pray you.

Guildenstern: Believe me, I cannot.

Hamlet: I beseech you.

Guildenstern: I know no touch of it, my lord.

Hamlet: 'Tis as easy as lying: govern these ventages° with your fingers and 320 thumb, give it breath with your mouth, and it will discourse most eloquent music. Look you, these are the stops.

Guildenstern: But these cannot I command to any utterance of harmony; I have not the skill.

Hamlet: Why, look you now, how unworthy a thing you make of me! You 325 would play upon me; you would seem to know my stops; you would pluck out the heart of my mystery; you would sound me from my lowest note to the top of my compass:° and there is much music, excellent voice, in this little organ;° yet cannot you make it speak. 'Sblood, do you think I am easier to be played on than a pipe? Call me 330 what instrument you will, though you can fret° me, you cannot play upon me.

Enter Polonius.

God bless you, sir!

Polonius: My lord, the queen would speak with you, and presently.

Hamlet: Do you see yonder cloud that's almost in shape of a camel?   335

Polonius: By the mass, and 'tis like a camel, indeed.

Hamlet: Methinks it is like a weasel.

Polonius: It is backed like a weasel.

Hamlet: Or like a whale?

Polonius: Very like a whale.   340

---

305 *voice:* Support.   307 *"While...grows":* The rest of the proverb is "the silly horse starves." Hamlet may be destroyed while he is waiting for the succession to the kingdom. 309 *withdraw:* Speak in private.   310 *recover the wind:* Get to the windward side.   311 *toil:* Snare.   312–313 *if...unmannerly:* If I am using an unmannerly boldness, it is my love which occasions it.   320 *ventages:* Stops of the recorders.   328 *compass:* Range of voice. 329 *organ:* Musical instrument, i.e., the pipe.   331 *fret:* Quibble on meaning "irritate" and the piece of wood, gut, or metal which regulates the fingering.

Hamlet: Then I will come to my mother by and by. *[Aside.]* They fool me to
    the top of my bent.° — I will come by and by.°
Polonius: I will say so.   *[Exit.]*
Hamlet: By and by is easily said.
    Leave me, friends.   *[Exeunt all but Hamlet.]* 345
    'Tis now the very witching time° of night,
    When churchyards yawn and hell itself breathes out
    Contagion to this world: now could I drink hot blood,
    And do such bitter business as the day
    Would quake to look on. Soft! now to my mother.   350
    O heart, lose not thy nature; let not ever
    The soul of Nero° enter this firm bosom:
    Let me be cruel, not unnatural:
    I will speak daggers to her, but use none;
    My tongue and soul in this be hypocrites;   355
    How in my words somever she be shent,°
    To give them seals° never, my soul, consent!   *Exit.*

[SCENE III: *A room in the castle.*]

    Enter King, Rosencrantz, and Guildenstern.

King: I like him not, nor stands it safe with us
    To let his madness range. Therefore prepare you;
    I your commission will forthwith dispatch,°
    And he to England shall along with you:
    The terms° of our estate° may not endure   5
    Hazard so near us as doth hourly grow
    Out of his brows.°
Guildenstern: We will ourselves provide:
    Most holy and religious fear it is
    To keep those many many bodies safe
    That live and feed upon your majesty.   10
Rosencrantz: The single and peculiar° life is bound,
    With all the strength and armour of the mind,
    To keep itself from noyance;° but much more
    That spirit upon whose weal depend and rest
    The lives of many. The cess° of majesty   15
    Dies not alone; but, like a gulf,° doth draw
    What's near it with it: it is a massy wheel,
    Fix'd on the summit of the highest mount,
    To whose huge spokes ten thousand lesser things
    Are mortis'd and adjoin'd; which, when it falls,   20
    Each small annexment, petty consequence,

---

342 *top of my bent:* Limit of endurance, i.e., extent to which a bow may be bent; *by and by:*
Immediately.   346 *witching time:* I.e., time when spells are cast.   352 *Nero:* Murderer of
his mother, Agrippina.   356 *shent:* Rebuked.   357 *give them seals:* Confirm with deeds.
Scene III.   3 *dispatch:* Prepare.   5 *terms:* Condition, circumstances; *estate:* State.
7 *brows:* Effronteries.   11 *single and peculiar:* Individual and private.   13 *noyance:*
Harm.   15 *cess:* Decease.   16 *gulf:* Whirlpool.

Attends° the boist'rous ruin. Never alone
Did the king sigh, but with a general groan.

King: Arm° you, I pray you, to this speedy voyage;
    For we will fetters put about this fear,   25
    Which now goes too free-footed.

Rosencrantz: We will haste us.
           Exeunt Gentlemen [Rosencrantz and Guildenstern].

    Enter Polonius.

Polonius: My lord, he's going to his mother's closet:
    Behind the arras° I'll convey° myself,
    To hear the process;° I'll warrant she'll tax him home:°
    And, as you said, and wisely was it said,   30
    'Tis meet that some more audience than a mother,
    Since nature makes them partial, should o'erhear
    The speech, of vantage.° Fare you well, my liege:
    I'll call upon you ere you go to bed,
    And tell you what I know.

King: Thanks, dear my lord.   *Exit [Polonius].*   35
    O, my offence is rank, it smells to heaven;
    It hath the primal eldest curse° upon't,
    A brother's murder. Pray can I not,
    Though inclination be as sharp as will:°
    My stronger guilt defeats my strong intent;   40
    And, like a man to double business bound,
    I stand in pause where I shall first begin,
    And both neglect. What if this cursed hand
    Were thicker than itself with brother's blood,
    Is there not rain enough in the sweet heavens   45
    To wash it white as snow? Whereto serves mercy
    But to confront° the visage of offence?
    And what's in prayer but this two-fold force,
    To be forestalled° ere we come to fall,
    Or pardon'd being down? Then I'll look up;   50
    My fault is past. But, O, what form of prayer
    Can serve my turn? "Forgive me my foul murder"?
    That cannot be: since I am still possess'd
    Of those effects for which I did the murder,
    My crown, mine own ambition° and my queen.   55
    May one be pardon'd and retain th' offence?°
    In the corrupted currents° of this world
    Offence's gilded hand° may shove by justice,

---

22 *Attends:* Participates in.   24 *Arm:* Prepare.   28 *arras:* Screen of tapestry placed around the walls of household apartments; *convey:* Implication of secrecy, *convey* was often used to mean "steal."   29 *process:* Proceedings; *tax him home:* Reprove him severely.   33 *of vantage:* From an advantageous place.   37 *primal eldest curse:* The curse of Cain, the first to kill his brother.   39 *sharp as will:* I.e., his desire is as strong as his determination.   47 *confront:* Oppose directly.   49 *forestalled:* Prevented.   55 *ambition:* I.e., realization of ambition.   56 *offence:* Benefit accruing from offense.   57 *currents:* Courses.   58 *gilded hand:* Hand offering gold as a bribe.

And oft 'tis seen the wicked prize° itself
Buys out the law: but 'tis not so above;   60
There is no shuffling,° there the action lies°
In his true nature; and we ourselves compell'd,
Even to the teeth and forehead° of our faults,
To give in evidence. What then? what rests?°
Try what repentance can: what can it not?   65
Yet what can it when one can not repent?
O wretched state! O bosom black as death!
O limed° soul, that, struggling to be free,
Art more engag'd!° Help, angels! Make assay!°
Bow, stubborn knees; and, heart with strings of steel,   70
Be soft as sinews of the new-born babe!
All may be well.   *[He kneels.]*

Enter Hamlet.

Hamlet: Now might I do it pat,° now he is praying;
And now I'll do't. And so 'a goes to heaven;
And so am I reveng'd. That would be scann'd:°   75
A villain kills my father; and for that,
I, his sole son, do this same villain send
To heaven.
Why, this is hire and salary, not revenge.
'A took my father grossly, full of bread;°   80
With all his crimes broad blown,° as flush° as May;
And how his audit stands who knows save heaven?
But in our circumstance and course° of thought,
'Tis heavy with him: and am I then reveng'd,
To take him in the purging of his soul,   85
When he is fit and season'd for his passage?°
No!
Up, sword; and know thou a more horrid hent:°
When he is drunk asleep,° or in his rage,
Or in th' incestuous pleasure of his bed;   90
At game, a-swearing, or about some act
That has no relish of salvation in't;
Then trip him, that his heels may kick at heaven,
And that his soul may be as damn'd and black
As hell, whereto it goes. My mother stays: 95
This physic° but prolongs thy sickly days.   *Exit.*
King: *[Rising]* My words fly up, my thoughts remain below:
Words without thoughts never to heaven go.   *Exit.*

---

59 *wicked prize:* Prize won by wickedness. 61 *shuffling:* Escape by trickery; *lies:* Is sustainable. 63 *teeth and forehead:* Very face. 64 *rests:* Remains. 68 *limed:* Caught as with birdlime. 69 *engag'd:* Embedded; *assay:* Trial. 73 *pat:* Opportunely. 75 *would be scann'd:* Needs to be looked into. 80 *full of bread:* Enjoying his worldly pleasures (see Ezekiel 16:49). 81 *broad blown:* In full bloom; *flush:* Lusty. 83 *in . . . course:* As we see it in our mortal situation. 86 *fit . . . passage:* I.e., reconciled to heaven by forgiveness of his sins. 88 *hent:* Seizing; or more probably, occasion of seizure. 89 *drunk asleep:* In a drunken sleep. 96 *physic:* Purging (by prayer).

[SCENE IV: *The Queen's closet.*]

    Enter [Queen] Gertrude and Polonius.

Polonius: 'A will come straight. Look you lay° home to him:
    Tell him his pranks have been too broad° to bear with,
    And that your grace hath screen'd and stood between
    Much heat° and him. I'll sconce° me even here.
    Pray you, be round° with him.   5
Hamlet (within): Mother, mother, mother!
Queen: I'll warrant you,
    Fear me not: withdraw, I hear him coming.
                          [Polonius hides behind the arras.]

    Enter Hamlet.

Hamlet: Now, mother, what's the matter?
Queen: Hamlet, thou hast thy father much offended.
Hamlet: Mother, you have my father° much offended.   10
Queen: Come, come, you answer with an idle tongue.
Hamlet: Go, go, you question with a wicked tongue.
Queen: Why, how now, Hamlet!
Hamlet: What's the matter now?
Queen: Have you forgot me?
Hamlet: No, by the rood,° not so:
    You are the queen, your husband's brother's wife;   15
    And—would it were not so!—you are my mother.
Queen: Nay, then, I'll set those to you that can speak.
Hamlet: Come, come, and sit you down; you shall not budge;
    You go not till I set you up a glass
    Where you may see the inmost part of you.   20
Queen: What wilt thou do? thou wilt not murder me?
    Help, help, ho!
Polonius [behind]: What, ho! help, help; help!
Hamlet [drawing]: How now! a rat? Dead, for a ducat, dead!
                 [Makes a pass through the arras.]
Polonius [behind]: O, I am slain!   *[Falls and dies.]* 25
Queen: O me, what hast thou done?
Hamlet: Nay, I know not:
    Is it the king?
Queen: O, what a rash and bloody deed is this!
Hamlet: A bloody deed! almost as bad, good mother,
    As kill a king, and marry with his brother.   30
Queen: As kill a king!
Hamlet: Ay, lady, it was my word.
           [Lifts up the arras and discovers Polonius.]
    Thou wretched, rash, intruding fool, farewell!
    I took thee for thy better: take thy fortune;

Scene IV. 1 *lay:* Thrust.   2 *broad:* Unrestrained.   4 *Much heat:* I.e., the king's anger;
sconce: Hide.   5 *round:* Blunt.   9–10 *thy father, my father:* I.e., Claudius, the elder Hamlet.   14 *rood:* Cross.

Thou find'st to be too busy is some danger.
Leave wringing of your hands: peace! sit you down,   35
And let me wring your heart; for so I shall,
If it be made of penetrable stuff,
If damned custom have not braz'd° it so
That it be proof and bulwark against sense.
Queen: What have I done, that thou dar'st wag thy tongue   40
    In noise so rude against me?
Hamlet: Such an act
    That blurs the grace and blush of modesty,
    Calls virtue hypocrite, takes off the rose
    From the fair forehead of an innocent love
    And sets a blister° there, makes marriage-vows   45
    As false as dicers' oaths: O, such a deed
    As from the body of contraction° plucks
    The very soul, and sweet religion° makes
    A rhapsody° of words: heaven's face does glow
    O'er this solidity and compound mass   50
    With heated visage, as against the doom
    Is thought-sick at the act.°
Queen: Ay me, what act,
    That roars so loud, and thunders in the index?°
Hamlet: Look here, upon this picture, and on this.
    The counterfeit presentment° of two brothers.   55
    See, what a grace was seated on this brow;
    Hyperion's° curls; the front° of Jove himself;
    An eye like Mars, to threaten and command;
    A station° like the herald Mercury
    New-lighted on a heaven-kissing hill;   60
    A combination and a form indeed,
    Where every god did seem to set his seal,
    To give the world assurance° of a man:
    This was your husband. Look you now, what follows:
    Here is your husband; like a mildew'd ear,°   65
    Blasting his wholesome brother. Have you eyes?
    Could you on this fair mountain leave to feed,
    And batten° on this moor?° Ha! have you eyes?
    You cannot call it love; for at your age
    The hey-day° in the blood is tame, it's humble,   70
    And waits upon the judgement: and what judgement

---

38 *braz'd:* Brazened, hardened.   45 *sets a blister:* Brands as a harlot.   47 *contraction:* The marriage contract.   48 *religion:* Religious vows.   49 *rhapsody:* Senseless string. 49–52 *heaven's . . . act:* Heaven's face blushes to look down on this world, and Gertrude's marriage makes heaven feel as sick as though the day of doom were near.   53 *index:* Prelude or preface.   55 *counterfeit presentment:* Portrayed representation.   57 *Hyperion's:* The sun god's; *front:* Brow.   59 *station:* Manner of standing.   63 *assurance:* Pledge, guarantee.   65 *mildew'd ear:* See Genesis 41:5–7.   68 *batten:* Grow fat; *moor:* Barren upland.   70 *hey-day:* State of excitement.

Would step from this to this? Sense, sure, you have,
Else could you not have motion;° but sure, that sense
Is apoplex'd;° for madness would not err,
Nor sense to ecstasy was ne'er so thrall'd°   75
But it reserv'd some quantity of choice,°
To serve in such a difference. What devil was't
That thus hath cozen'd° you at hoodman-blind?°
Eyes without feeling, feeling without sight,
Ears without hands or eyes, smelling sans° all,   80
Or but a sickly part of one true sense
Could not so mope.°
O shame! where is thy blush? Rebellious hell,
If thou canst mutine° in a matron's bones,
To flaming youth let virtue be as wax,   85
And melt in her own fire: proclaim no shame
When the compulsive ardour gives the charge,°
Since frost itself as actively doth burn
And reason pandars will.°

Queen: O Hamlet, speak no more:
Thou turn'st mine eyes into my very soul;   90
And there I see such black and grained° spots
As will not leave their tinct.

Hamlet: Nay, but to live
In the rank sweat of an enseamed° bed,
Stew'd in corruption, honeying and making love
Over the nasty sty, —

Queen: O, speak to me no more;   95
These words, like daggers, enter in mine ears;
No more, sweet Hamlet!

Hamlet: A murderer and a villain;
A slave that is not twentieth part the tithe
Of your precedent lord;° a vice of kings;°
A cutpurse of the empire and the rule,   100
That from a shelf the precious diadem stole,
And put it in his pocket!

Queen: No more!

Enter Ghost.

72–73 *Sense . . . motion:* Sense and motion are functions of the middle or sensible soul, the possession of sense being the basis of motion.   74 *apoplex'd:* Paralyzed. Mental derangement was thus of three sorts: apoplexy, ecstasy, and diabolic possession.   75 *thrall'd:* Enslaved. 76 *quantity of choice:* Fragment of the power to choose.   78 *cozen'd:* Tricked, cheated; *hoodman-blind:* Blindman's buff.   80 *sans:* Without.   82 *mope:* Be in a depressed, spiritless state, act aimlessly.   84 *mutine:* Mutiny, rebel.   87 *gives the charge:* Delivers the attack. 89 *reason pandars will:* The normal and proper situation was one in which reason guided the will in the direction of good; here, reason is perverted and leads in the direction of evil. 91 *grained:* Dyed in grain.   93 *enseamed:* Loaded with grease, greased.   99 *precedent lord:* I.e., the elder Hamlet; *vice of kings:* Buffoon of kings; a reference to the Vice, or clown, of the morality plays and interludes.

Hamlet: A king of shreds and patches,° —
    Save me, and hover o'er me with your wings,
    You heavenly guards! What would your gracious figure?   105
Queen: Alas, he's mad!
Hamlet: Do you not come your tardy son to chide,
    That, laps'd in time and passion,° lets go by
    Th' important° acting of your dread command?
    O, say!   110
Ghost: Do not forget: this visitation
    Is but to whet thy almost blunted purpose.
    But, look, amazement° on thy mother sits:
    O, step between her and her fighting soul:
    Conceit in weakest bodies strongest works: 115
    Speak to her, Hamlet.
Hamlet: How is it with you, lady?
Queen: Alas, how is 't with you,
    That you do bend your eye on vacancy
    And with th' incorporal° air do hold discourse?
    Forth at your eyes your spirits wildly peep;   120
    And, as the sleeping soldiers in th' alarm,
    Your bedded° hair, like life in excrements,°
    Start up, and stand an° end. O gentle son,
    Upon the heat and flame of thy distemper
    Sprinkle cool patience. Whereon do you look?   125
Hamlet: On him, on him! Look you, how pale he glares!
    His form and cause conjoin'd,° preaching to stones,
    Would make them capable. — Do not look upon me;
    Lest with this piteous action you convert
    My stern effects:° then what I have to do   130
    Will want true colour;° tears perchance for blood.
Queen: To whom do you speak this?
Hamlet: Do you see nothing there?
Queen: Nothing at all; yet all that is I see.
Hamlet: Nor did you nothing hear?
Queen: No, nothing but ourselves.
Hamlet: Why, look you there! look, how it steals away!   135
    My father, in his habit as he liv'd!
    Look, where he goes, even now, out at the portal!   *Exit Ghost.*
Queen: This is the very coinage of your brain:
    This bodiless creation ecstasy
    Is very cunning in.

---

103 *shreds and patches:* I.e., motley, the traditional costume of the Vice.   108 *laps'd . . . passion:* Having suffered time to slip and passion to cool; also explained as "engrossed in casual events and lapsed into mere fruitless passion, so that he no longer entertains a rational purpose."   109 *important:* Urgent.   113 *amazement:* Frenzy, distraction.   119 *incorporal:* Immaterial.   122 *bedded:* Laid in smooth layers; *excrements:* The hair was considered an excrement or voided part of the body.   123 *an:* On.   127 *conjoin'd:* United.   129–130 *convert . . . effects:* Divert me from my stern duty. For *effects,* possibly *affects* (affections of the mind).   131 *want true colour:* Lack good reason so that (with a play on the normal sense of *colour*) I shall shed tears instead of blood.

Hamlet: Ecstasy!   140
  My pulse, as yours, doth temperately keep time,
  And makes as healthful music: it is not madness
  That I have utt'red: bring me to the test,
  And I the matter will re-word,° which madness
  Would gambol° from. Mother, for love of grace,   145
  Lay not that flattering unction° to your soul,
  That not your trespass, but my madness speaks:
  It will but skin and film the ulcerous place,
  Whiles rank corruption, mining° all within,
  Infects unseen. Confess yourself to heaven;   150
  Repent what's past; avoid what is to come;°
  And do not spread the compost° on the weeds,
  To make them ranker. Forgive me this my virtue;°
  For in the fatness° of these pursy° times
  Virtue itself of vice must pardon beg,   155
  Yea, curb° and woo for leave to do him good.
Queen: O Hamlet, thou hast cleft my heart in twain.
Hamlet: O, throw away the worser part of it,
  And live the purer with the other half.
  Good night: but go not to my uncle's bed;   160
  Assume a virtue, if you have it not.
  That monster, custom, who all sense doth eat,
  Of habits devil, is angel yet in this,
  That to the use of actions fair and good
  He likewise gives a frock or livery,   165
  That aptly is put on. Refrain to-night,
  And that shall lend a kind of easiness
  To the next abstinence: the next more easy;
  For use almost can change the stamp of nature,
  And either . . . the devil, or throw him out°   170
  With wondrous potency. Once more, good night:
  And when you are desirous to be bless'd,°
  I'll blessing beg of you. For this same lord,   *[Pointing to Polonius.]*
  I do repent: but heaven hath pleas'd it so,
  To punish me with this and this with me,   175
  That I must be their scourge and minister.
  I will bestow him, and will answer well
  The death I gave him. So, again, good night.
  I must be cruel, only to be kind:
  Thus bad begins and worse remains behind.   180
  One word more, good lady.

---

144 *re-word:* Repeat in words.   145 *gambol:* Skip away.   146 *unction:* Ointment used
medicinally or as a rite; suggestion that forgiveness for sin may not be so easily achieved.
149 *mining:* Working under the surface.   151 *what is to come:* I.e., the sins of the future.
152 *compost:* Manure.   153 *this my virtue:* My virtuous talk in reproving you.   154 *fatness:*
Grossness; *pursy:* Short-winded, corpulent.   156 *curb:* Bow, bend the knee.   170 Defective line usually emended by inserting *master* after *either.*   172 *be bless'd:* Become blessed,
i.e., repentant.

Queen: What shall I do?
Hamlet: Not this, by no means, that I bid you do:
    Let the bloat° king tempt you again to bed;
    Pinch wanton on your cheek; call you his mouse;
    And let him, for a pair of reechy° kisses,   185
    Or paddling in your neck with his damn'd fingers,
    Make you to ravel all this matter out,
    That I essentially° am not in madness,
    But mad in craft. 'Twere good you let him know;
    For who, that's but a queen, fair, sober, wise,   190
    Would from a paddock,° from a bat, a gib,°
    Such dear concernings° hide? who would do so?
    No, in despite of sense and secrecy,
    Unpeg the basket on the house's top,
    Let the birds fly, and, like the famous ape,°   195
    To try conclusions,° in the basket creep,
    And break your own neck down.
Queen: Be thou assur'd, if words be made of breath,
    And breath of life, I have no life to breathe
    What thou hast said to me.   200
Hamlet: I must to England; you know that?
Queen: Alack,
    I had forgot: 'tis so concluded on.
Hamlet: There's letters seal'd: and my two schoolfellows,
    Whom I will trust as I will adders fang'd,
    They bear the mandate; they must sweep my way,°   205
    And marshal me to knavery. Let it work;
    For 'tis the sport to have the enginer°
    Hoist° with his own petar:° and 't shall go hard
    But I will delve one yard below their mines,
    And blow them at the moon: O, 'tis most sweet,   210
    When in one line two crafts° directly meet.
    This man shall set me packing:°
    I'll lug the guts into the neighbour room.
    Mother, good night. Indeed this counsellor
    Is now most still, most secret and most grave,   215
    Who was in life a foolish prating knave.
    Come, sir, to draw° toward an end with you.
    Good night, mother.   *Exeunt [severally; Hamlet dragging in Polonius.]*

---

183 *bloat:* Bloated.   185 *reechy:* Dirty, filthy.   188 *essentially:* In my essential nature. 191 *paddock:* Toad; *gib:* Tomcat.   192 *dear concernings:* Important affairs.   195 *the famous ape:* A letter from Sir John Suckling seems to supply other details of the story, otherwise not identified: "It is the story of the jackanapes and the partridges; thou starest after a beauty till it be lost to thee, then let'st out another, and starest after that till it is gone too." 196 *conclusions:* Experiments.   205 *sweep my way:* Clear my path.   207 *enginer:* Constructor of military works, or possibly, artilleryman.   208 *Hoist:* Blown up; *petar:* Defined as a small engine of war used to blow in a door or make a breach, and as a case filled with explosive materials.   211 *two crafts:* Two acts of guile, with quibble on the sense of "two ships."   212 *set me packing:* Set me to making schemes, and set me to lugging (him), and, also, send me off in a hurry.   217 *draw:* Come, with quibble on literal sense.

[ACT IV

Scene I: *A room in the castle.*]

Enter King and Queen, with Rosencrantz and Guildenstern.

King: There's matter in these sighs, these profound heaves:
    You must translate: 'tis fit we understand them.
    Where is your son?
Queen: Bestow this place on us a little while.
                      [Exeunt Rosencrantz and Guildenstern.]
    Ah, mine own lord, what have I seen to-night!   5
King: What, Gertrude? How does Hamlet?
Queen: Mad as the sea and wind, when both contend
    Which is the mightier: in his lawless fit,
    Behind the arras hearing something stir,
    Whips out his rapier, cries, "A rat, a rat!"   10
    And, in this brainish° apprehension,° kills
    The unseen good old man.
King: O heavy deed!
    It had been so with us, had we been there:
    His liberty is full of threats to all;
    To you yourself, to us, to every one.   15
    Alas, how shall this bloody deed be answer'd?
    It will be laid to us, whose providence°
    Should have kept short,° restrain'd and out of haunt,°
    This mad young man: but so much was our love,
    We would not understand what was most fit;   20
    But, like the owner of a foul disease,
    To keep it from divulging,° let it feed
    Even on the pith of life. Where is he gone?
Queen: To draw apart the body he hath kill'd:
    O'er whom his very madness, like some ore   25
    Among a mineral° of metals base,
    Shows itself pure; 'a weeps for what is done.
King: O Gertrude, come away!
    The sun no sooner shall the mountains touch,
    But we will ship him hence: and this vile deed   30
    We must, with all our majesty and skill,
    Both countenance and excuse. Ho, Guildenstern!

Enter Rosencrantz and Guildenstern.

    Friends both, go join you with some further aid:
    Hamlet in madness hath Polonius slain,
    And from his mother's closet hath he dragg'd him: 35
    Go seek him out; speak fair, and bring the body
    Into the chapel. I pray you, haste in this.

Act IV, Scene I.   11 *brainish:* Headstrong, passionate; *apprehension:* Conception, imagination.   17 *providence:* Foresight.   18 *short:* I.e., on a short tether; *out of haunt:* Secluded.
22 *divulging:* Becoming evident.   26 *mineral:* Mine.

[Exeunt Rosencrantz and Guildenstern.]

Come, Gertrude, we'll call up our wisest friends;
And let them know, both what we mean to do,
And what's untimely done . . .°   40
Whose whisper o'er the world's diameter,°
As level° as the cannon to his blank,°
Transports his pois'ned shot, may miss our name,
And hit the woundless° air. O, come away!
My soul is full of discord and dismay.   *Exeunt.*   45

[SCENE II: *Another room in the castle.*]

Enter Hamlet.

Hamlet: Safely stowed.
Rosencrantz: ⎫ *(within)* Hamlet! Lord Hamlet!
Guildenstern: ⎭
Hamlet: But soft, what noise? who calls on Hamlet? O, here they come.

Enter Rosencrantz and Guildenstern.

Rosencrantz: What have you done, my lord, with the dead body?
Hamlet: Compounded it with dust, whereto 'tis kin.
Rosencrantz: Tell us where 'tis, that we may take it thence   5
    And bear it to the chapel.
Hamlet: Do not believe it.
Rosencrantz: Believe what?
Hamlet: That I can keep your counsel° and not mine own. Besides, to be
    demanded of a sponge! what replication° should be made by the son   10
    of a king?
Rosencrantz: Take you me for a sponge, my lord?
Hamlet: Ay, sir, that soaks up the king's countenance, his rewards, his
    authorities.° But such officers do the king best service in the end: he
    keeps them, like an ape an apple, in the corner of his jaw; first   15
    mouthed, to be last swallowed: when he needs what you have gleaned,
    it is but squeezing you, and, sponge, you shall be dry again.
Rosencrantz: I understand you not, my lord.
Hamlet: I am glad of it: a knavish speech sleeps in a foolish ear.
Rosencrantz: My lord, you must tell us where the body is, and go with us   20
    to the king.
Hamlet: The body is with the king, but the king is not with the body.° The
    king is a thing—
Guildenstern: A thing, my lord!
Hamlet: Of nothing: bring me to him. Hide fox, and all after.°   *Exeunt.*   25

---

40 Defective line; some editors add: *so, haply, slander;* others add: *for, haply, slander;* other con-
jectures.   41 *diameter:* Extent from side to side.   42 *level:* Straight; *blank:* white spot
in the center of a target.   44 *woundless:* Invulnerable.   **Scene II.**   9 *keep your counsel:*
Hamlet is aware of their treachery but says nothing about it.   10 *replication:* Reply.
14 *authorities:* Authoritative backing.   22 *The body . . . body:* There are many interpretations;
possibly, "The body lies in death with the king, my father; but my father walks disembodied"; or "Claudius has the bodily possession of kingship, but kingliness, or justice of inheritance, is not with him."   25 *Hide . . . after:* An old signal cry in the game of hide-and-seek.

[SCENE III: *Another room in the castle.*]

Enter King, and two or three.

King: I have sent to seek him, and to find the body.
How dangerous is it that this man goes loose!
Yet must not we put the strong law on him:
He's lov'd of the distracted° multitude,
Who like not in their judgement, but their eyes;   5
And where 'tis so, th' offender's scourge° is weigh'd,°
But never the offence. To bear all smooth and even,
This sudden sending him away must seem
Deliberate pause:° diseases desperate grown
By desperate appliance are reliev'd,   10
Or not at all.

Enter Rosencrantz, [Guildenstern,] and all the rest.

                    How now! what hath befall'n?
Rosencrantz: Where the dead body is bestow'd, my lord,
We cannot get from him.
King: But where is he?
Rosencrantz: Without, my lord; guarded, to know your pleasure.
King: Bring him before us.   15
Rosencrantz: Ho! bring in the lord.

They enter [with Hamlet].

King: Now, Hamlet, where's Polonius?
Hamlet: At supper.
King: At supper! where?
Hamlet: Not where he eats, but where 'a is eaten: a certain convocation of   20
politic° worms° are e'en at him. Your worm is your only emperor for
diet: we fat all creatures else to fat us, and we fat ourselves for mag-
gots: your fat king and your lean beggar is but variable service,° two
dishes, but to one table: that's the end.
King: Alas, alas!   25
Hamlet: A man may fish with the worm that hath eat of a king, and eat of
the fish that hath fed of that worm.
King: What dost thou mean by this?
Hamlet: Nothing but to show you how a king may go a progress° through
the guts of a beggar.   30
King: Where is Polonius?
Hamlet: In heaven; send thither to see: if your messenger find him not
there, seek him i' the other place yourself. But if indeed you find him
not within this month, you shall nose him as you go up the stairs
into the lobby.   35
King [to some Attendants]: Go seek him there.
    Hamlet: 'A will stay till you come.   *[Exeunt Attendants.]*
King: Hamlet, this deed, for thine especial safety, —

Scene III.   4 *distracted:* I.e., without power of forming logical judgments.   6 *scourge:*
Punishment; *weigh'd:* Taken into consideration.   9 *Deliberate pause:* Considered action.
20-21 *convocation . . . worms:* Allusion to the Diet of Worms (1521).   21 *politic:* Crafty.
23 *variable service:* A variety of dishes.   29 *progress:* Royal journey of state.

Which we do tender,° as we dearly grieve
For that which thou hast done, — must send thee hence   40
With fiery quickness: therefore prepare thyself;
The bark is ready, and the wind at help,
Th' associates tend, and everything is bent
For England.
Hamlet: For England!
King: Ay, Hamlet.
Hamlet: Good.
King: So is it, if thou knew'st our purposes.   45
Hamlet: I see a cherub° that sees them. But, come; for England! Farewell,
    dear mother.
King: Thy loving father, Hamlet.
Hamlet: My mother: father and mother is man and wife; man and wife is
    one flesh; and so, my mother. Come, for England!   *Exit.*   50
King: Follow him at foot;° tempt him with speed aboard;
    Delay it not; I'll have him hence to-night:
    Away! for every thing is seal'd and done
    That else leans on th' affair: pray you, make haste.
                               [Exeunt all but the King.]
    And, England, if my love thou hold'st at aught —   55
    As my great power thereof may give thee sense,
    Since yet thy cicatrice° looks raw and red
    After the Danish sword, and thy free awe°
    Pays homage to us — thou mayst not coldly set
    Our sovereign process; which imports at full,   60
    By letters congruing to that effect,
    The present death of Hamlet. Do it, England;
    For like the hectic° in my blood he rages,
    And thou must cure me: till I know 'tis done,
    Howe'er my haps,° my joys were ne'er begun.   *Exit.*   65

[SCENE IV: *A plain in Denmark.*]

    Enter Fortinbras with his Army over the stage.

Fortinbras: Go, captain, from me greet the Danish king;
    Tell him that, by his license,° Fortinbras
    Craves the conveyance° of a promis'd march
    Over his kingdom. You know the rendezvous.
    If that his majesty would aught with us,   5
    We shall express our duty in his eye;°
    And let him know so.
Captain: I will do't, my lord.
Fortinbras: Go softly° on.   *[Exeunt all but Captain.]*

---

39 *tender:* Regard, hold dear.   46 *cherub:* Cherubim are angels of knowledge.   51 *at foot:* Close behind, at heel.   57 *cicatrice:* Scar.   58 *free awe:* Voluntary show of respect. 63 *hectic:* Fever.   65 *haps:* Fortunes.   **Scene IV.**   2 *license:* Leave.   3 *conveyance:* Escort, convoy.   6 *in his eye:* In his presence.

Enter Hamlet, Rosencrantz, [Guildenstern,] &c.

Hamlet: Good sir, whose powers are these?
Captain: They are of Norway, sir.   10
Hamlet: How purpos'd, sir, I pray you?
Captain: Against some part of Poland.
Hamlet: Who commands them, sir?
Captain: The nephew to old Norway, Fortinbras.
Hamlet: Goes it against the main° of Poland, sir,   15
    Or for some frontier?
Captain: Truly to speak, and with no addition,
    We go to gain a little patch of ground
    That hath in it no profit but the name.
    To pay five ducats, five, I would not farm it;°   20
    Nor will it yield to Norway or the Pole
    A ranker rate, should it be sold in fee.°
Hamlet: Why, then the Polack never will defend it.
Captain: Yes, it is already garrison'd.
Hamlet: Two thousand souls and twenty thousand ducats   25
    Will not debate the question of this straw:°
    This is th' imposthume° of much wealth and peace,
    That inward breaks, and shows no cause without
    Why the man dies. I humbly thank you, sir.
Captain: God be wi' you, sir.   *[Exit.]*
Rosencrantz: Will 't please you go, my lord?   30
Hamlet: I'll be with you straight. Go a little before.
                         [Exeunt all except Hamlet.]
    How all occasions° do inform against° me,
    And spur my dull revenge! What is a man,
    If his chief good and market of his time°
    Be but to sleep and feed? a beast, no more.   35
    Sure, he that made us with such large discourse,
    Looking before and after, gave us not
    That capability and god-like reason
    To fust° in us unus'd. Now, whether it be
    Bestial oblivion, or some craven scruple   40
    Of thinking too precisely on th' event,
    A thought which, quarter'd, hath but one part wisdom
    And ever three parts coward, I do not know
    Why yet I live to say "This thing 's to do";
    Sith I have cause and will and strength and means   45
    To do 't. Examples gross as earth exhort me:
    Witness this army of such mass and charge
    Led by a delicate and tender prince,

---

8 *softly:* Slowly.   15 *main:* Country itself.   20 *farm it:* Take a lease of it.   22 *fee:* Fee simple.   26 *debate...straw:* Settle this trifling matter.   27 *imposthume:* Purulent abscess or swelling.   32 *occasions:* Incidents, events; *inform against:* Generally defined as "show," "betray" (i.e., his tardiness); more probably *inform* means "take shape," as in *Macbeth,* II.i.48.   34 *market of his time:* The best use he makes of his time, or, that for which he sells his time.   39 *fust:* Grow moldy.

Whose spirit with divine ambition puff'd
Makes mouths at the invisible event,   50
Exposing what is mortal and unsure
To all that fortune, death and danger dare,
Even for an egg-shell. Rightly to be great
Is not to stir without great argument,
But greatly to find quarrel in a straw   55
When honour's at the stake. How stand I then,
That have a father kill'd, a mother stain'd,
Excitements of° my reason and my blood,
And let all sleep? while, to my shame, I see
The imminent death of twenty thousand men,   60
That, for a fantasy and trick° of fame,
Go to their graves like beds, fight for a plot°
Whereon the numbers cannot try the cause,
Which is not tomb enough and continent
To hide the slain? O, from this time forth,   65
My thoughts be bloody, or be nothing worth!   *Exit.*

[SCENE V: *Elsinore. A room in the castle.*]

Enter Horatio, [Queen] Gertrude, and a Gentleman.

Queen: I will not speak with her.
Gentleman: She is importunate, indeed distract:
    Her mood will needs be pitied.
Queen: What would she have?
Gentleman: She speaks much of her father; says she hears
    There's tricks° i' th' world; and hems, and beats her heart;°   5
    Spurns enviously at straws;° speaks things in doubt,
    That carry but half sense: her speech is nothing,
    Yet the unshaped° use of it doth move
    The hearers to collection;° they yawn° at it,
    And botch° the words up fit to their own thoughts;   10
    Which, as her winks, and nods, and gestures yield° them,
    Indeed would make one think there might be thought,
    Though nothing sure, yet much unhappily.°
Horatio: 'Twere good she were spoken with: for she may strew
    Dangerous conjectures in ill-breeding minds.°   15
Queen: Let her come in.   [*Exit Gentleman.*]
    [*Aside.*] To my sick soul, as sin's true nature is,
    Each toy seems prologue to some great amiss:°
    So full of artless jealousy is guilt,

58 *Excitements of:* Incentives to.   61 *trick:* Toy, trifle.   62 *plot:* Piece of ground.
Scene V.   5 *tricks:* Deceptions; *heart:* I.e., breast.   6 *Spurns . . . straws:* Kicks spitefully at
small objects in her path.   8 *unshaped:* Unformed, artless.   9 *collection:* Inference, a
guess at some sort of meaning; *yawn:* Wonder.   10 *botch:* Patch.   11 *yield:* Deliver,
bring forth (her words).   13 *much unhappily:* Expressive of much unhappiness.   15 *ill-
breeding minds:* Minds bent on mischief.   18 *great amiss:* Calamity, disaster.

It spills itself in fearing to be spilt.°   20

Enter Ophelia [distracted].

Ophelia: Where is the beauteous majesty of Denmark?
Queen: How now, Ophelia!
Ophelia (she sings): How should I your true love know
    From another one?
  By his cockle hat° and staff,   25
    And his sandal shoon.°
Queen: Alas, sweet lady, what imports this song?
Ophelia: Say you? nay, pray you mark.
  (Song) He is dead and gone, lady,
    He is dead and gone;   30
  At his head a grass-green turf,
    At his heels a stone.
  O, ho!
Queen: Nay, but, Ophelia —
Ophelia: Pray you, mark   35
  [Sings.] White his shroud as the mountain snow, —

Enter King.

Queen: Alas, look here, my lord.
Ophelia (Song): Larded° all with flowers;
  Which bewept to the grave did not go
    With true-love showers.   40
King: How do you, pretty lady?
Ophelia: Well, God 'ild° you! They say the owl° was a baker's daughter.
  Lord, we know what we are, but know not what we may be. God be at
  your table!
King: Conceit upon her father.   45
Ophelia: Pray let's have no words of this; but when they ask you what it
  means, say you this:
  (Song) To-morrow is Saint Valentine's day,
    All in the morning betime,
  And I a maid at your window,   50
    To be your Valentine.°
  Then up he rose, and donn'd his clothes,
    And dupp'd° the chamber-door;
  Let in the maid, that out a maid
    Never departed more.   55
King: Pretty Ophelia!
Ophelia: Indeed, la, without an oath, I'll make an end on 't:

19-20 *So . . . spilt:* Guilt is so full of suspicion that it unskillfully betrays itself in fearing to be betrayed.   25 *cockle hat:* Hat with cockleshell stuck in it as a sign that the wearer has been a pilgrim to the shrine of St. James of Compostella. The pilgrim's garb was a conventional disguise for lovers.   26 *shoon:* Shoes.   38 *Larded:* Decorated.   42 *God 'ild:* God yield or reward; *owl:* Reference to a monkish legend that a baker's daughter was turned into an owl for refusing bread to the Savior.   51 *Valentine:* This song alludes to the belief that the first girl seen by a man on the morning of this day was his valentine or true love.
53 *dupp'd:* Opened.

[Sings.] By Gis° and by Saint Charity,
    Alack, and fie for shame!
Young men will do 't, if they come to 't;   60
    By cock,° they are to blame.
Quoth she, before you tumbled me,
    You promis'd me to wed.
So would I ha' done, by yonder sun,
    An thou hadst not come to my bed.   65
King: How long hath she been thus?
Ophelia: I hope all will be well. We must be patient: but I cannot choose
    but weep, to think they would lay him i' the cold ground. My brother
    shall know of it: and so I thank you for your good counsel. Come, my
    coach! Good night, ladies; good night, sweet ladies; good night, good   70
    night.   *[Exit.]*
King: Follow her close; give her good watch, I pray you.   *[Exit Horatio.]*
    O, this is the poison of deep grief; it springs
    All from her father's death. O Gertrude, Gertrude,
    When sorrows come, they come not single spies,   75
    But in battalions. First, her father slain:
    Next your son gone; and he most violent author
    Of his own just remove: the people muddied,
    Thick and unwholesome in their thoughts and whispers,
    For good Polonius' death; and we have done but greenly,°   80
    In hugger-mugger° to inter him: poor Ophelia
    Divided from herself and her fair judgement,
    Without the which we are pictures, or mere beasts:
    Last, and as much containing as all these,
    Her brother is in secret come from France;   85
    Feeds on his wonder, keeps himself in clouds,°
    And wants not buzzers° to infect his ear
    With pestilent speeches of his father's death;
    Wherein necessity, of matter beggar'd,°
    Will nothing stick° our person to arraign   90
    In ear and ear.° O my dear Gertrude, this,
    Like to a murd'ring-piece,° in many places
    Gives me superfluous death.   *A noise within.*
Queen: Alack, what noise is this?
King: Where are my Switzers?° Let them guard the door.

    Enter a Messenger.

    What is the matter?
Messenger: Save yourself, my lord: 95
    The ocean, overpeering° of his list,°
    Eats not the flats with more impiteous haste

---

58 *Gis:* Jesus.   61 *cock:* Perversion of "God" in oaths.   80 *greenly:* Foolishly.   81 *hugger-mugger:* Secret haste.   86 *in clouds:* Invisible.   87 *buzzers:* Gossipers.   89 *of matter beggar'd:* Unprovided with facts.   90 *nothing stick:* Not hesitate.   91 *In ear and ear:* In everybody's ears.   92 *murd'ring-piece:* Small cannon or mortar; suggestion of numerous missiles fired.   94 *Switzers:* Swiss guards, mercenaries.   96 *overpeering:* Overflowing; *list:* Shore.

Than young Laertes, in a riotous head,
O'erbears your officers. The rabble call him lord;
And, as the world were now but to begin,   100
Antiquity forgot, custom not known,
The ratifiers and props of every word,°
They cry "Choose we: Laertes shall be king":
Caps, hands, and tongues, applaud it to the clouds:
"Laertes shall be king, Laertes king!"   *A noise within.*   105
Queen: How cheerfully on the false trail they cry!
    O, this is counter,° you false Danish dogs!
King: The doors are broke.

    Enter Laertes with others.

Laertes: Where is this king? Sirs, stand you all without.
Danes: No, let's come in.
Laertes: I pray you, give me leave.   110
Danes: We will, we will.   *[They retire without the door.]*
Laertes: I thank you: keep the door. O thou vile king,
    Give me my father!
Queen: Calmly, good Laertes.
Laertes: That drop of blood that's calm proclaims me bastard,
    Cries cuckold to my father, brands the harlot   115
    Even here, between the chaste unsmirched brow
    Of my true mother.
King: What is the cause, Laertes,
    That thy rebellion looks so giant-like?
    Let him go, Gertrude; do not fear our person:
    There's such divinity doth hedge a king,   120
    That treason can but peep to° what it would,°
    Acts little of his will. Tell me, Laertes,
    Why thou art thus incens'd. Let him go, Gertrude.
    Speak, man.
Laertes: Where is my father?
King: Dead.
Queen: But not by him.   125
King: Let him demand his fill.
Laertes: How came he dead? I'll not be juggled with:
    To hell, allegiance! vows, to the blackest devil!
    Conscience and grace, to the profoundest pit!
    I dare damnation. To this point I stand,   130
    That both the worlds I give to negligence,°
    Let come what comes; only I'll be reveng'd
    Most throughly° for my father.
King: Who shall stay you?
Laertes: My will,° not all the world's:

---

102 *word:* Promise.   107 *counter:* A hunting term meaning to follow the trail in a direction opposite to that which the game has taken.   121 *peep to:* I.e., look at from afar off; *would:* Wishes to do.   131 *give to negligence:* He despises both the here and the hereafter. 133 *throughly:* Thoroughly.

And for my means, I'll husband them so well,   135
   They shall go far with little.

King: Good Laertes,
   If you desire to know the certainty
   Of your dear father, is 't writ in your revenge,
   That, swoopstake,° you will draw both friend and foe,
   Winner and loser?   140

Laertes: None but his enemies.

King: Will you know them then?

Laertes: To his good friends thus wide I'll ope my arms;
   And like the kind life-rend'ring pelican,°
   Repast° them with my blood.

King: Why, now you speak
   Like a good child and a true gentleman.   145
   That I am guiltless of your father's death,
   And am most sensibly in grief for it,
   It shall as level to your judgement 'pear
   As day does to your eye.   *A noise within: "Let her come in."*

Laertes: How now! what noise is that?   150

   Enter Ophelia.

   O heat,° dry up my brains! tears seven times salt,
   Burn out the sense and virtue of mine eye!
   By heaven, thy madness shall be paid with weight,
   Till our scale turn the beam. O rose of May!
   Dear maid, kind sister, sweet Ophelia!   155
   O heavens! is 't possible, a young maid's wits
   Should be as mortal as an old man's life?
   Nature is fine in love, and where 'tis fine,
   It sends some precious instance of itself
   After the thing it loves.   160

Ophelia (Song): They bore him barefac'd on the bier;
     Hey non nonny, nonny, hey nonny;
     And in his grave rain'd many a tear: —
     Fare you well, my dove!

Laertes: Hadst thou thy wits, and didst persuade revenge,   165
   It could not move thus.

Ophelia [sings]: You must sing a-down a-down,
     An you call him a-down-a.
O, how the wheel° becomes it! It is the false steward,° that stole his
   master's daughter.   170

Laertes: This nothing's more than matter.

---

134 *My will:* He will not be stopped except by his own will.   139 *swoopstake:* Literally, drawing the whole stake at once, i.e., indiscriminately.   143 *pelican:* Reference to the belief that the pelican feeds its young with its own blood.   144 *Repast:* Feed.   151 *heat:* Probably the heat generated by the passion of grief.   169 *wheel:* Spinning wheel as accompaniment to the song refrain; *false steward:* The story is unknown.

Ophelia: There's rosemary,° that's for remembrance; pray you, love,
 remember: and there is pansies,° that's for thoughts.
Laertes: A document° in madness, thoughts and remembrance fitted.
Ophelia: There's fennel° for you, and columbines:° there's rue° for you; 175
 and here's some for me: we may call it herb of grace° o' Sundays: O,
 you must wear your rue with a difference. There's a daisy:° I would
 give you some violets,° but they withered all when my father died:
 they say 'a made a good end, —
 [Sings.] For bonny sweet Robin is all my joy.° 180
Laertes: Thought° and affliction, passion, hell itself,
 She turns to favour and to prettiness.
Ophelia (Song): And will 'a not come again?°
  And will 'a not come again?
   No, no, he is dead: 185
    Go to thy death-bed:
  He never will come again.

  His beard was as white as snow,
  All flaxen was his poll:°
   He is gone, he is gone, 190
    And we cast away° moan:
  God ha' mercy on his soul!
  And of all Christian souls, I pray God. God be wi' you. *[Exit.]*
Laertes: Do you see this, O God?
King: Laertes, I must commune with your grief, 195
 Or you deny me right.° Go but apart,
 Make choice of whom your wisest friends you will,
 And they shall hear and judge 'twixt you and me:
 If by direct or by collateral° hand
 They find us touch'd,° we will our kingdom give, 200
 Our crown, our life, and all that we call ours,
 To you in satisfaction; but if not,
 Be you content to lend your patience to us,
 And we shall jointly labour with your soul
 To give it due content.
Laertes: Let this be so; 205
 His means of death, his obscure funeral —
 No trophy, sword, nor hatchment° o'er his bones,

---

172 *rosemary:* Used as a symbol of remembrance both at weddings and at funerals. 173
pansies: Emblems of love and courtship (from the French *pensée*). 174 *document:* Piece of
instruction or lesson. 175, 176 *fennel:* Emblem of flattery; *columbines:* Emblem of
unchastity (?) or ingratitude (?); *rue:* Emblem of repentance. It was usually mingled with
holy water and then known as *herb of grace*. Ophelia is probably playing on the two meanings of *rue*, "repentant" and "even for ruth (pity)"; the former signification is for
the queen, the latter for herself. 177 *daisy:* Emblem of dissembling, faithlessness.
178 *violets:* Emblems of faithfulness. 180 *For...joy:* Probably a line from a Robin
Hood ballad. 181 *Thought:* Melancholy thought. 183 *And...again:* This song appeared in the songbooks as "The Merry Milkmaids' Dumps." 189 *poll:* Head. 191 *cast
away:* Shipwrecked. 196 *right:* My rights. 199 *collateral:* Indirect. 200 *touch'd:* Im-
plicated. 207 *hatchment:* Tablet displaying the armorial bearings of a deceased person.

No noble rite nor formal ostentation —
Cry to be heard, as 'twere from heaven to earth,
That I must call 't in question.

King: So you shall;   210
And where th' offence is let the great axe fall.
I pray you, go with me.   *Exeunt.*

[SCENE VI: *Another room in the castle.*]

Enter Horatio and others.

Horatio: What are they that would speak with me?
Gentleman: Sea-faring men, sir: they say they have letters for you.
Horatio: Let them come in.   *[Exit Gentleman.]*
   I do not know from what part of the world
   I should be greeted, if not from lord Hamlet.   5

Enter Sailors.

First Sailor: God bless you, sir.
Horatio: Let him bless thee too.
First Sailor: 'A shall sir, an 't please him. There's a letter for you, sir; it
   comes from the ambassador that was bound for England; if your
   name be Horatio, as I am let to know it is.   10
Horatio [reads]: "Horatio, when thou shalt have overlooked this, give these
   fellows some means° to the king: they have letters for him. Ere we were
   two days old at sea, a pirate of very warlike appointment gave us
   chase. Finding ourselves too slow of sail, we put on a compelled val-
   our, and in the grapple I boarded them: on the instant they got clear   15
   of our ship; so I alone became their prisoner. They have dealt with me
   like thieves of mercy:° but they knew what they did; I am to do a good
   turn for them. Let the king have the letters I have sent; and repair
   thou to me with as much speed as thou wouldest fly death. I have
   words to speak in thine ear will make thee dumb; yet are they much   20
   too light for the bore° of the matter. These good fellows will bring
   thee where I am. Rosencrantz and Guildenstern hold their course for
   England: of them I have much to tell thee. Farewell.
                  "He that thou knowest thine, HAMLET."
   Come, I will give you way for these your letters;   25
   And do 't the speedier, that you may direct me
   To him from whom you brought them.   *Exeunt.*

[SCENE VII: *Another room in the castle.*]

Enter King and Laertes.

King: Now must your conscience° my acquittance seal,
   And you must put me in your heart for friend,

Scene VI.   12 *means:* Means of access.   17 *thieves of mercy:* Merciful thieves.   21 *bore:*
Caliber, importance.   **Scene VII.**   1 *conscience:* Knowledge that this is true.

Sith you have heard, and with a knowing ear,
That he which hath your noble father slain
Pursued my life.

Laertes: It well appears: but tell me   5
Why you proceeded not against these feats,
So criminal and so capital° in nature,
As by your safety, wisdom, all things else,
You mainly° were stirr'd up.

King: O, for two special reasons;
Which may to you, perhaps, seem much unsinew'd,°   10
But yet to me th' are strong. The queen his mother
Lives almost by his looks; and for myself—
My virtue or my plague, be it either which—
She's so conjunctive° to my life and soul,
That, as the star moves not but in his sphere,°   15
I could not but by her. The other motive,
Why to a public count° I might not go,
Is the great love the general gender° bear him;
Who, dipping all his faults in their affection,
Would, like the spring° that turneth wood to stone,   20
Convert his gyves° to graces; so that my arrows,
Too slightly timber'd° for so loud° a wind,
Would have reverted to my bow again,
And not where I had aim'd them.

Laertes: And so have I a noble father lost;   25
A sister driven into desp'rate terms,°
Whose worth, if praises may go back° again,
Stood challenger on mount° of all the age°
For her perfections: but my revenge will come.

King: Break not your sleeps for that: you must not think   30
That we are made of stuff so flat and dull
That we can let our beard be shook with danger
And think it pastime. You shortly shall hear more:
I lov'd your father, and we love ourself;
And that, I hope, will teach you to imagine—   35

Enter a Messenger with letters.

How now! what news?

Messenger: Letters, my lord, from Hamlet:
These to your majesty; this to the queen.°

King: From Hamlet! who brought them?

---

7 *capital:* Punishable by death.   9 *mainly:* Greatly.   10 *unsinew'd:* Weak.   14 *conjunctive:* Conformable (the next line suggesting planetary conjunction).   15 *sphere:* The hollow sphere in which, according to Ptolemaic astronomy, the planets were supposed to move. 17 *count:* Account, reckoning.   18 *general gender:* Common people.   20 *spring:* I.e., one heavily charged with lime.   21 *gyves:* Fetters; here, faults, or possibly, punishments inflicted (on him).   22 *slightly timber'd:* Light; *loud:* Strong.   26 *terms:* State, condition. 27 *go back:* Return to Ophelia's former virtues.   28 *on mount:* Set up on high, *mounted* (on horseback); *of all the age:* Qualifies *challenger* and not *mount.*   37 *to the queen:* One hears no more of the letter to the queen.

Messenger: Sailors, my lord, they say; I saw them not:
    They were given me by Claudio;° he receiv'd them   40
    Of him that brought them.
King: Laertes, you shall hear them.
    Leave us.   *[Exit Messenger.]*
[Reads.] "High and mighty, You shall know I am set naked° on your king-
    dom. To-morrow shall I beg leave to see your kingly eyes: when I shall,
    first asking your pardon thereunto, recount the occasion of my   45
    sudden and more strange return.   "HAMLET."
    What should this mean? Are all the rest come back?
    Or is it some abuse, and no such thing?
Laertes: Know you the hand?
King: 'Tis Hamlet's character. "Naked!"
    And in a postscript here, he says "alone."   50
    Can you devise° me?
Laertes: I'm lost in it, my lord. But let him come;
    It warms the very sickness in my heart,
    That I shall live and tell him to his teeth,
    "Thus didst thou."
King: If it be so, Laertes —   55
    As how should it be so? how otherwise?° —
    Will you be rul'd by me?
Laertes: Ay, my lord;
    So you will not o'errule me to a peace.
King: To thine own peace. If he be now return'd,
    As checking at° his voyage, and that he means   60
    No more to undertake it, I will work him
    To an exploit, now ripe in my device,
    Under the which he shall not choose but fall:
    And for his death no wind of blame shall breathe,
    But even his mother shall uncharge the practice°   65
    And call it accident.
Laertes: My lord, I will be rul'd;
    The rather, if you could devise it so
    That I might be the organ.°
King: It falls right.
    You have been talk'd of since your travel much,
    And that in Hamlet's hearing, for a quality   70
    Wherein, they say, you shine: your sum of parts
    Did not together pluck such envy from him
    As did that one, and that, in my regard,
    Of the unworthiest siege.°
Laertes: What part is that, my lord?

---

40 *Claudio:* This character does not appear in the play.   43 *naked:* Unprovided (with retinue).   51 *devise:* Explain to.   56 *As . . . otherwise?* How can this (Hamlet's return) be
true? (yet) how otherwise than true (since we have the evidence of his letter)? Some editors
read *How should it not be so*, etc., making the words refer to Laertes's desire to meet with Hamlet.   60 *checking at:* Used in falconry of a hawk's leaving the quarry to fly at a chance bird;
turn aside.   65 *uncharge the practice:* Acquit the stratagem of being a plot.   68 *organ:*
Agent, instrument.   74 *siege:* Rank.

King: A very riband in the cap of youth,   75
    Yet needful too; for youth no less becomes
    The light and careless livery that it wears
    Than settled age his sables° and his weeds,
    Importing health and graveness. Two months since,
    Here was a gentleman of Normandy: —   80
    I have seen myself, and serv'd against, the French,
    And they can well° on horseback: but this gallant
    Had witchcraft in 't; he grew unto his seat;
    And to such wondrous doing brought his horse,
    As had he been incorps'd and demi-natur'd°   85
    With the brave beast: so far he topp'd° my thought,
    That I, in forgery° of shapes and tricks,
    Come short of what he did.
Laertes: A Norman was 't?
King: A Norman.
Laertes: Upon my life, Lamord.°
King: The very same.   90
Laertes: I know him well: he is the brooch indeed
    And gem of all the nation.
King: He made confession° of you,
    And gave you such a masterly report
    For art and exercise° in your defence°   95
    And for your rapier most especial,
    That he cried out, 'twould be a sight indeed,
    If one could match you: the scrimers° of their nation,
    He swore, had neither motion, guard, nor eye,
    If you oppos'd them. Sir, this report of his   100
    Did Hamlet so envenom with his envy
    That he could nothing do but wish and beg
    Your sudden coming o'er, to play° with you.
    Now, out of this, —
Laertes: What out of this, my lord?
King: Laertes, was your father dear to you?   105
    Or are you like the painting of a sorrow,
    A face without a heart?
Laertes: Why ask you this?
King: Not that I think you did not love your father;
    But that I know love is begun by time;
    And that I see, in passages of proof,°   110
    Time qualifies the spark and fire of it.
    There lives within the very flame of love
    A kind of wick or snuff that will abate it;
    And nothing is at a like goodness still;

---

78 *sables:* Rich garments.   82 *can well:* Are skilled.   85 *incorps'd and demi-natur'd:* Of one body and nearly of one nature (like the centaur).   86 *topp'd:* Surpassed.   87 *forgery:* Invention.   90 *Lamord:* This refers possibly to Pietro Monte, instructor to Louis XII's master of the horse.   93 *confession:* Grudging admission of superiority.   95 *art and exercise:* Skillful exercise; *defence:* Science of defense in sword practice.   98 *scrimers:* Fencers.   103 *play:* Fence.   110 *passages of proof:* Proved instances.

For goodness, growing to a plurisy,°   115
Dies in his own too much:° that we would do,
We should do when we would; for this "would" changes
And hath abatements° and delays as many
As there are tongues, are hands, are accidents;°
And then this "should" is like a spendthrift° sigh,   120
That hurts by easing. But, to the quick o' th' ulcer:°—
Hamlet comes back: what would you undertake,
To show yourself your father's son in deed
More than in words?

Laertes: To cut his throat i' th' church.

King: No place, indeed, should murder sanctuarize;°   125
Revenge should have no bounds. But, good Laertes,
Will you do this, keep close within your chamber.
Hamlet return'd shall know you are come home:
We'll put on those shall praise your excellence
And set a double varnish on the fame   130
The Frenchman gave you, bring you in fine together
And wager on your heads: he, being remiss,
Most generous and free from all contriving,
Will not peruse the foils; so that, with ease,
Or with a little shuffling, you may choose   135
A sword unbated,° and in a pass of practice°
Requite him for your father.

Laertes: I will do 't:
And, for that purpose, I'll anoint my sword.
I bought an unction of a mountebank,°
So mortal that, but dip a knife in it,   140
Where it draws blood no cataplasm° so rare,
Collected from all simples° that have virtue
Under the moon,° can save the thing from death
That is but scratch'd withal: I'll touch my point
With this contagion, that, if I gall° him slightly,   145
It may be death.

King: Let's further think of this;
Weigh what convenience both of time and means
May fit us to our shape:° if this should fail,
And that our drift look through our bad performance,°
'Twere better not assay'd: therefore this project   150
Should have a back or second, that might hold,
If this should blast in proof.° Soft! let me see:

---

115 *plurisy:* Excess, plethora.   116 *in his own too much:* Of its own excess.   118 *abatements:*
Diminutions.   119 *accidents:* Occurrences, incidents.   120 *spendthrift:* An allusion to
the belief that each sigh cost the heart a drop of blood.   121 *quick o' th' ulcer:* Heart of the
difficulty.   125 *sanctuarize:* Protect from punishment; allusion to the right of sanctuary
with which certain religious places were invested.   136 *unbated:* Not blunted, having no
button; *pass of practice:* Treacherous thrust.   139 *mountebank:* Quack doctor.   141 *cata-
plasm:* Plaster or poultice.   142 *simples:* Herbs.   143 *Under the moon:* I.e., when collected
by moonlight to add to their medicinal value.   145 *gall:* Graze, wound.   148 *shape:* Part
we propose to act.   149 *drift . . . performance:* Intention be disclosed by our bungling.
152 *blast in proof:* Burst in the test (like a cannon).

We'll make a solemn wager on your cunnings:°
I ha 't:
When in your motion you are hot and dry—   155
As make your bouts more violent to that end—
And that he calls for drink, I'll have prepar'd him
A chalice° for the nonce, whereon but sipping,
If he by chance escape your venom'd stuck,°
Our purpose may hold there. But stay, what noise?   160

Enter Queen.

Queen: One woe doth tread upon another's heel,
    So fast they follow: your sister's drown'd, Laertes.
Laertes: Drown'd! O, where?
Queen: There is a willow° grows askant° the brook,
    That shows his hoar° leaves in the glassy stream;   165
    There with fantastic garlands did she make
    Of crow-flowers,° nettles, daisies, and long purples°
    That liberal° shepherds give a grosser name,
    But our cold maids do dead men's fingers call them:
    There, on the pendent boughs her crownet° weeds   170
    Clamb'ring to hang, an envious sliver° broke;
    When down her weedy° trophies and herself
    Fell in the weeping brook. Her clothes spread wide;
    And, mermaid-like, awhile they bore her up:
    Which time she chanted snatches of old lauds;°   175
    As one incapable° of her own distress,
    Or like a creature native and indued°
    Upon that element: but long it could not be
    Till that her garments, heavy with their drink,
    Pull'd the poor wretch from her melodious lay   180
    To muddy death.
Laertes: Alas, then, she is drown'd?
Queen: Drown'd, drown'd.
Laertes: Too much of water hast thou, poor Ophelia,
    And therefore I forbid my tears: but yet
    It is our trick;° nature her custom holds,   185
    Let shame say what it will: when these are gone,
    The woman will be out.° Adieu, my lord:
    I have a speech of fire, that fain would blaze,
    But that this folly drowns it.   *Exit.*
King: Let's follow, Gertrude:
    How much I had to do to calm his rage!   190
    Now fear I this will give it start again;
    Therefore let 's follow.   *Exeunt.*

153 *cunnings:* Skills.   158 *chalice:* Cup.   159 *stuck:* Thrust (from *stoccado*).   164 *willow:* For its significance of forsaken love; *askant:* Aslant.   165 *hoar:* White (i.e., on the underside).   167 *crow-flowers:* Buttercups; *long purples:* Early purple orchids.   168 *liberal:* Probably, free-spoken.   170 *crownet:* Coronet; made into a chaplet.   171 *sliver:* Branch.   172 *weedy:* I.e., of plants.   175 *lauds:* Hymns.   176 *incapable:* Lacking capacity to apprehend.   177 *indued:* Endowed with qualities fitting her for living in water.   185 *trick:* Way.   186–187 *when ... out:* When my tears are all shed, the woman in me will be satisfied.

[ACT V

SCENE I: *A churchyard.*]

Enter two Clowns° [with spades, &c.].

First Clown: Is she to be buried in Christian burial when she wilfully seeks
her own salvation?

Second Clown: I tell thee she is; therefore make her grave straight:° the
crowner° hath sat on her, and finds it Christian burial.

First Clown: How can that be, unless she drowned herself in her own   5
defence?

Second Clown: Why, 'tis found so.

First Clown: It must be "se offendendo";° it cannot be else. For here lies the
point: if I drown myself wittingly,° it argues an act: and an act hath
three branches;° it is, to act, to do, and to perform: argal,° she   10
drowned herself wittingly.

Second Clown: Nay, but hear you, goodman delver,° —

First Clown: Give me leave. Here lies the water; good: here stands the man;
good: if the man go to this water, and drown himself, it is, will he, nill
he, he goes, — mark you that; but if the water come to him and drown   15
him, he drowns not himself: argal, he that is not guilty of his
own death shortens not his own life.

Second Clown: But is this law?

First Clown: Ay, marry, is 't; crowner's quest° law.

Second Clown: Will you ha' the truth on 't? If this had not been a gentle-   20
woman, she should have been buried out o' Christian burial.

First Clown: Why, there thou say'st:° and the more pity that great folk
should have countenance° in this world to drown or hang themselves, more than their even° Christian. Come, my spade. There is
no ancient gentlemen but gardeners, ditchers, and grave-makers: they   25
hold up° Adam's profession.

Second Clown: Was he a gentleman?

First Clown: 'A was the first that ever bore arms.

Second Clown: Why, he had none.

First Clown: What, art a heathen? How dost thou understand the Scrip-   30
ture? The Scripture says "Adam digged": could he dig without arms?
I'll put another question to thee: if thou answerest me not to the purpose, confess thyself° —

Second Clown: Go to.°

First Clown: What is he that builds stronger than either the mason, the   35
shipwright, or the carpenter?

Act V, Scene I.   *Clowns:* The word *clown* was used to denote peasants as well as humorous
characters; here applied to the rustic type of clown.   3 *straight:* Straightway, immediately;
some interpret "from east to west in a direct line, parallel with the church."   4 *crowner:*
Coroner.   8 *"se offendendo":* For *se defendendo*, term used in verdicts of justifiable homi-
cide.   9 *wittingly:* Intentionally.   10 *three branches:* Parody of legal phraseology; *argal:*
Corruption of *ergo*, therefore.   12 *delver:* Digger.   19 *quest:* Inquest.   22 *there thou
say'st:* That's right.   23 *countenance:* Privilege.   24 *even:* Fellow.   26 *hold up:* Maintain, continue.   33 *confess thyself:* "And be hanged" completes the proverb.   34 *Go to:*
Perhaps, "begin," or some other form of concession.

Second Clown: The gallows-maker; for that frame outlives a thousand tenants.

First Clown: I like thy wit well, in good faith: the gallows does well; but
how does it well? it does well to those that do ill: now thou dost ill to   40
say the gallows is built stronger than the church: argal, the gallows
may do well to thee. To 't again, come.

Second Clown: "Who builds stronger than a mason, a shipwright, or a carpenter?"

First Clown: Ay, tell me that, and unyoke.°   45

Second Clown: Marry, now I can tell.

First Clown: To 't.

Second Clown: Mass,° I cannot tell.

>   *Enter Hamlet and Horatio [at a distance].*

First Clown: Cudgel thy brains no more about it, for your dull ass will not
mend his pace with beating; and, when you are asked this question   50
next, say "a grave-maker": the houses he makes lasts till doomsday.
Go, get thee in, and fetch me a stoup° of liquor.

>   *[Exit Second Clown.] Song. [He digs.]*

> In youth, when I did love, did love,
>   Methought it was very sweet,
> To contract — O — the time, for — a — my behove,°   55
>   O, methought, there — a — was nothing — a — meet.

Hamlet: Has this fellow no feeling of his business, that 'a sings at grave-
making?

Horatio: Custom hath made it in him a property of easiness.°

Hamlet: 'Tis e'en so: the hand of little employment hath the daintier   60
sense.

First Clown: (*Song.*) But age, with his stealing steps,
>   Hath claw'd me in his clutch,
> And hath shipped me into the land
>   As if I had never been such.   *[Throws up a skull.]*   65

Hamlet: That skull had a tongue in it, and could sing once: how the knave
jowls° it to the ground, as if 'twere Cain's jaw-bone,° that did the first
murder! This might be the pate of a politician,° which this ass now
o'er-reaches;° one that would circumvent God, might it not?

Horatio: It might, my lord.   70

Hamlet: Or of a courtier; which could say "Good morrow, sweet lord! How
dost thou, sweet lord?" This might be my lord such-a-one, that
praised my lord such-a-one's horse, when he meant to beg it; might
it not?

Horatio: Ay, my lord.   75

Hamlet: Why, e'en so: and now my Lady Worm's; chapless,° and knocked
about the mazzard° with a sexton's spade: here's fine revolution, an

---

45 *unyoke:* After this great effort you may unharness the team of your wits.   48 *Mass:* By
the Mass.   52 *stoup:* Two-quart measure.   55 *behove:* Benefit.   59 *property of easiness:* A
peculiarity that now is easy.   67 *jowls:* Dashes; *Cain's jaw-bone:* Allusion to the old tradition
that Cain slew Abel with the jawbone of an ass.   68 *politician:* Schemer, plotter.   69 *o'er-
reaches:* Quibble on the literal sense and the sense "circumvent."   76 *chapless:* Having no
lower jaw.   77 *mazzard:* Head.

we had the trick to see 't. Did these bones cost no more the breeding,
but to play at loggats° with 'em? mine ache to think on 't.

First Clown: (Song.) A pick-axe, and a spade, a spade,   80
    For and° a shrouding sheet:
    O, a pit of clay for to be made
    For such a guest is meet.   *[Throws up another skull.]*

Hamlet: There's another: why may not that be the skull of a lawyer?
Where be his quiddities° now, his quillities,° his cases, his tenures,°   85
and his tricks? why does he suffer this mad knave now to knock him
about the sconce° with a dirty shovel, and will not tell him of his
action of battery? Hum! This fellow might be in 's time a great buyer
of land, with his statutes, his recognizances,° his fines, his double
vouchers,° his recoveries:° is this the fine° of his fines, and the re-   90
covery of his recoveries, to have his fine pate full of fine dirt? will
his vouchers vouch him no more of his purchases, and double ones
too, than the length and breadth of a pair of indentures?° The very
conveyances of his lands will scarcely lie in this box; and must the
inheritor° himself have no more, ha?   95

Horatio: Not a jot more, my lord.

Hamlet: Is not parchment made of sheep-skins?

Horatio: Ay, my lord, and of calf-skins° too.

Hamlet: They are sheep and calves which seek out assurance in that.°
I will speak to this fellow. Whose grave's this, sirrah?   100

First Clown: Mine, sir.

    [Sings.] O, a pit of clay for to be made
    For such a guest is meet.

Hamlet: I think it be thine, indeed; for thou liest in 't.

First Clown: You lie out on 't, sir, and therefore 't is not yours: for my part,   105
I do not lie in 't, yet it is mine.

Hamlet: Thou dost lie in 't, to be in 't and say it is thine: 'tis for the dead,
not for the quick; therefore thou liest.

First Clown: 'Tis a quick lie, sir; 'twill away again, from me to you.

Hamlet: What man dost thou dig it for?   110

First Clown: For no man, sir.

Hamlet: What woman, then?

First Clown: For none, neither.

Hamlet: Who is to be buried in 't?

First Clown: One that was a woman, sir; but, rest her soul, she's dead.   115

Hamlet: How absolute° the knave is! we must speak by the card,° or
equivocation° will undo us. By the Lord, Horatio, these three years I

---

79 *loggats:* A game in which six sticks are thrown to lie as near as possible to a stake fixed in
the ground, or block of wood on a floor.   81 *For and:* And moreover.   85 *quiddities:*
Subtleties, quibbles; *quillities:* Verbal niceties, subtle distinctions; *tenures:* The holding of a
piece of property or office or the conditions or period of such holding.   87 *sconce:* Head.
89 *statutes, recognizances:* Legal terms connected with the transfer of land.   90 *vouchers:*
Persons called on to warrant a tenant's title; *recoveries:* Process for transfer of entailed estate;
fine: The four uses of this word are as follows: (1) end, (2) legal process, (3) elegant, (4) small.
93 *indentures:* Conveyances or contracts.   95 *inheritor:* Possessor, owner.   98 *calf-skins:*
Parchments.   99 *assurance in that:* Safety in legal parchments.   116 *absolute:* Positive,
decided; *by the card:* With precision, i.e., by the mariner's card on which the points of the
compass were marked.   117 *equivocation:* Ambiguity in the use of terms.

have taken note of it; the age is grown so picked° that the toe of the
peasant comes so near the heel of the courtier, he galls° his kibe.°
How long hast thou been a grave-maker?   120

First Clown: Of all the day i' the year, I came to 't that day that our last
king Hamlet overcame Fortinbras.

Hamlet: How long is that since?

First Clown: Cannot you tell that? every fool can tell that: it was the very
day that young Hamlet was born; he that is mad, and sent into   125
England.

Hamlet: Ay, marry, why was he sent into England?

First Clown: Why, because 'a was mad: 'a shall recover his wits there; or, if
'a do not, 'tis no great matter there.

Hamlet: Why?   130

First Clown: 'Twill not be seen in him there; there the men are as mad
as he.

Hamlet: How came he mad?

First Clown: Very strangely, they say.

Hamlet: How strangely?   135

First Clown: Faith, e'en with losing his wits.

Hamlet: Upon what ground?

First Clown: Why, here in Denmark: I have been sexton here, man and boy,
thirty years.°

Hamlet: How long will a man lie i' the earth ere he rot?   140

First Clown: Faith, if 'a be not rotten before 'a die—as we have many
pocky° corses now-a-days, that will scarce hold the laying in—'a will
last you some eight year or nine year: a tanner will last you nine year.

Hamlet: Why he more than another?

First Clown: Why, sir, his hide is so tanned with his trade, that 'a will keep 145
out water a great while; and your water is a sore decayer of your
whoreson dead body. Here's a skull now hath lain you i' th' earth
three and twenty years.

Hamlet: Whose was it?

First Clown: A whoreson mad fellow's it was: whose do you think it was?   150

Hamlet: Nay, I know not.

First Clown: A pestilence on him for a mad rogue! 'a poured a flagon of
Rhenish on my head once. This same skull, sir, was Yorick's skull, the
king's jester.

Hamlet: This?   155

First Clown: E'en that.

Hamlet: Let me see. *[Takes the skull.]* Alas, poor Yorick! I knew him, Horatio: a fellow of infinite jest, of most excellent fancy: he hath borne me
on his back a thousand times; and now, how abhorred in my imagination it is! my gorge rises at it. Here hung those lips that I have   160
kissed I know not how oft. Where be your gibes now? your gambols?
your songs? your flashes of merriment, that were wont to set the
table on a roar? Not one now, to mock your own grinning? quite

---

118 *picked:* Refined, fastidious.   119 *galls:* Chafes; *kibe:* Chilblain.   139 *thirty years:* This
statement with that in line 125 shows Hamlet's age to be thirty years.   142 *pocky:* Rotten,
diseased.

chap-fallen? Now get you to my lady's chamber, and tell her, let her
paint an inch thick, to this favour she must come; make her laugh at   165
that. Prithee, Horatio, tell me one thing.

Horatio: What's that, my lord?

Hamlet: Dost thou think Alexander looked o' this fashion i' the earth?

Horatio: E'en so.

Hamlet: And smelt so? pah!   *[Puts down the skull.]*   170

Horatio: E'en so, my lord.

Hamlet: To what base uses we may return, Horatio! Why may not imagination trace the noble dust of Alexander, till 'a find it stopping a
bung-hole?

Horatio: 'Twere to consider too curiously,° to consider so.   175

Hamlet: No, faith, not a jot; but to follow him thither with modesty
enough, and likelihood to lead it: as thus: Alexander died, Alexander
was buried, Alexander returneth into dust; the dust is earth; of earth
we make loam;° and why of that loam, whereto he was converted,
might they not stop a beer-barrel?   180

    Imperious° Cæsar, dead and turn'd to clay,
    Might stop a hole to keep the wind away:
    O, that that earth, which kept the world in awe,
    Should patch a wall t'expel the winter's flaw!°
But soft! but soft awhile! here comes the king,   185

*Enter King, Queen, Laertes, and the Corse of [Ophelia, in procession, with
Priest, Lords, etc.].*

The queen, the courtiers: who is this they follow?
And with such maimed rites? This doth betoken
The corse they follow did with desp'rate hand
Fordo° it° own life: 'twas of some estate.
Couch° we awhile, and mark.   *[Retiring with Horatio.]*   190

Laertes: What ceremony else?

Hamlet: That is Laertes,
    A very noble youth: mark.

Laertes: What ceremony else?

First Priest: Her obsequies have been as far enlarg'd°
    As we have warranty: her death was doubtful;   195
    And, but that great command o'ersways the order,
    She should in ground unsanctified have lodg'd
    Till the last trumpet; for charitable prayers,
    Shards,° flints and pebbles should be thrown on her:
    Yet here she is allow'd her virgin crants,°   200
    Her maiden strewments° and the bringing home
    Of bell and burial.°

---

175 *curiously:* Minutely.   179 *loam:* Clay paste for brickmaking.   181 *Imperious:* Imperial.   184 *flaw:* Gust of wind.   189 *Fordo:* Destroy; *it:* Its.   190 *Couch:* Hide, lurk.
194 *enlarg'd:* Extended, referring to the fact that suicides are not given full burial rites.
199 *Shards:* Broken bits of pottery.   200 *crants:* Garlands customarily hung upon the
biers of unmarried women.   201 *strewments:* Traditional strewing of flowers.
201–202 *bringing . . . burial:* The laying to rest of the body, to the sound of the bell.

Laertes: Must there no more be done?

First Priest: No more be done:
   We should profane the service of the dead
   To sing a requiem and such rest to her   205
   As to peace-parted° souls.

Laertes: Lay her i' th' earth:
   And from her fair and unpolluted flesh
   May violets spring! I tell thee, churlish priest,
   A minist'ring angel shall my sister be,
   When thou liest howling.°

Hamlet: What, the fair Ophelia!   210

Queen: Sweets to the sweet: farewell!   *[Scattering flowers.]*
   I hop'd thou shouldst have been my Hamlet's wife;
   I thought thy bride-bed to have deck'd, sweet maid,
   And not have strew'd thy grave.

Laertes: O, treble woe
   Fall ten times treble on that cursed head,   215
   Whose wicked deed thy most ingenious sense°
   Depriv'd thee of! Hold off the earth awhile,
   Till I have caught her once more in mine arms: *[Leaps into the grave.]*
   Now pile your dust upon the quick and dead,
   Till of this flat a mountain you have made,   220
   T' o'ertop old Pelion,° or the skyish head
   Of blue Olympus.

Hamlet: *[Advancing]* What is he whose grief
   Bears such an emphasis? whose phrase of sorrow
   Conjures the wand'ring stars,° and makes them stand
   Like wonder-wounded hearers? This is I,   225
   Hamlet the Dane.   *[Leaps into the grave.]*

Laertes: The devil take thy soul!   *[Grappling with him.]*

Hamlet: Thou pray'st not well.
   I prithee, take thy fingers from my throat;
   For, though I am not splenitive° and rash,
   Yet have I in me something dangerous,   230
   Which let thy wisdom fear: hold off thy hand.

King: Pluck them asunder.

Queen: Hamlet, Hamlet!

All: Gentlemen,—

Horatio: Good my lord, be quiet.

   [The Attendants part them, and they come out of the grave.]

Hamlet: Why, I will fight with him upon this theme
   Until my eyelids will no longer wag.°   235

Queen: O my son, what theme?

---

206 *peace-parted:* Allusion to the text "Lord, now lettest thou thy servant depart in peace."
210 *howling:* I.e., in hell.   216 *ingenious sense:* Mind endowed with finest qualities.
221 *Pelion:* Olympus, Pelion, and Ossa are mountains in the north of Thessaly.
224 *wand'ring stars:* Planets.   229 *splenitive:* Quick-tempered.   235 *wag:* Move (not used ludicrously).

Hamlet: I lov'd Ophelia: forty thousand brothers
        Could not, with all their quantity° of love,
        Make up my sum. What wilt thou do for her?
King: O, he is mad, Laertes.   240
Queen: For love of God, forbear° him.
Hamlet: 'Swounds,° show me what thou 'lt do:
        Woo 't° weep? woo 't fight? woo 't fast? woo 't tear thyself?
        Woo 't drink up eisel?° eat a crocodile?
        I'll do 't. Dost thou come here to whine?   245
        To outface me with leaping in her grave?
        Be buried quick with her, and so will I:
        And, if thou prate of mountains, let them throw
        Millions of acres on us, till our ground,
        Singeing his pate against the burning zone,°   250
        Make Ossa like a wart! Nay, an thou 'lt mouth,
        I'll rant as well as thou.
Queen: This is mere madness:
        And thus awhile the fit will work on him;
        Anon, as patient as the female dove.
        When that her golden couplets° are disclos'd,   255
        His silence will sit drooping.
Hamlet: Hear you, sir;
        What is the reason that you use me thus?
        I lov'd you ever: but it is no matter;
        Let Hercules himself do what he may,
        The cat will mew and dog will have his day.   260
King: I pray thee, good Horatio, wait upon him.   *Exit Hamlet and Horatio.*
        [To Laertes.] Strengthen your patience in° our last night's speech;
        We'll put the matter to the present push.°
        Good Gertrude, set some watch over your son.
        This grave shall have a living° monument: 265
        An hour of quiet shortly shall we see;
        Till then, in patience our proceeding be.   *Exeunt.*

[SCENE II: *A hall in the castle.*]

        Enter Hamlet and Horatio.

Hamlet: So much for this, sir: now shall you see the other;
        You do remember all the circumstance?
Horatio: Remember it, my lord!
Hamlet: Sir, in my heart there was a kind of fighting,
        That would not let me sleep: methought I lay   5

---

238 *quantity:* Some suggest that the word is used in a deprecatory sense (little bits, fragments).   241 *forbear:* Leave alone.   242 *'Swounds:* Oath, "God's wounds."   243 *Woo
't:* Wilt thou.   244 *eisel:* Vinegar. Some editors have taken this to be the name of a river,
such as the Yssel, the Weissel, and the Nile.   250 *burning zone:* Sun's orbit.   255 *golden
couplets:* The pigeon lays two eggs; the young when hatched are covered with golden down.
262 *in:* By recalling.   263 *present push:* Immediate test.   265 *living:* Lasting; also refers
(for Laerte's benefit) to the plot against Hamlet.

Worse than the mutines in the bilboes.° Rashly,°
And prais'd be rashness for it, let us know,
Our indiscretion sometime serves us well,
When our deep plots do pall:° and that should learn us
There's a divinity that shapes our ends,   10
Rough-hew° them how we will,—

Horatio: That is most certain.

Hamlet: Up from my cabin,
My sea-gown° scarf'd about me, in the dark
Grop'd I to find out them; had my desire,
Finger'd° their packet, and in fine° withdrew   15
To mine own room again; making so bold,
My fears forgetting manners, to unseal
Their grand commission; where I found, Horatio,—
O royal knavery!—an exact command,
Larded° with many several sorts of reasons   20
Importing Denmark's health and England's too,
With, ho! such bugs° and goblins in my life,°
That, on the supervise,° no leisure bated,°
No, not to stay the grinding of the axe,
My head should be struck off.

Horatio: Is 't possible?   25

Hamlet: Here's the commission: read it at more leisure.
But wilt thou hear me how I did proceed?

Horatio: I beseech you.

Hamlet: Being thus be-netted round with villanies,—
Ere I could make a prologue to my brains,   30
They had begun the play°—I sat me down,
Devis'd a new commission, wrote it fair:
I once did hold it, as our statists° do,
A baseness to write fair° and labour'd much
How to forget that learning, but, sir, now   35
It did me yeoman's° service: wilt thou know
Th' effect of what I wrote?

Horatio: Ay, good my lord.

Hamlet: An earnest conjuration from the king,
As England was his faithful tributary,
As love between them like the palm might flourish,   40
As peace should still her wheaten garland° wear
And stand a comma° 'tween their amities,

Scene II.   6 *mutines in the bilboes:* Mutineers in shackles; *Rashly:* Goes with line 12.   9 *pall:* Fail.   11 *Rough-hew:* Shape roughly; it may mean "bungle."   13 *sea-gown:* "A sea-gown, or a coarse, high-collered, and short-sleeved gowne, reaching down to the mid-leg, and used most by seamen and saylors" (Cotgrave, quoted by Singer).   15 *Finger'd:* Pilfered, filched; *in fine:* Finally.   20 *Larded:* Enriched.   22 *bugs:* Bugbears; *such...life:* Such imaginary dangers if I were allowed to live.   23 *supervise:* Perusal; *leisure bated:* Delay allowed.   30–31 *prologue...play:* I.e., before I could begin to think, my mind had made its decision.   33 *statists:* Statesmen.   34 *fair:* In a clear hand.   36 *yeoman's:* I.e., faithful. 41 *wheaten garland:* Symbol of peace.   42 *comma:* Smallest break or separation. Here *amity* begins and *amity* ends the period, and *peace* stands between like a dependent clause. The comma indicates continuity, link.

And many such-like 'As'es° of great charge,°
That, on the view and knowing of these contents,
Without debatement further, more or less,   45
He should the bearers put to sudden death,
Not shriving-time° allow'd.
Horatio: How was this seal'd?
Hamlet: Why, even in that was heaven ordinant.°
    I had my father's signet in my purse,
    Which was the model of that Danish seal;   50
    Folded the writ up in the form of th' other,
    Subscrib'd it, gave 't th' impression, plac'd it safely,
    The changeling never known. Now, the next day
    Was our sea-fight; and what to this was sequent°
    Thou know'st already.   55
Horatio: So Guildenstern and Rosencrantz go to 't.
Hamlet: Why, man, they did make love to this employment;
    They are not near my conscience; their defeat
    Does by their own insinuation° grow:
    'Tis dangerous when the baser nature comes   60
    Between the pass° and fell incensed° points
    Of mighty opposites.
Horatio: Why, what a king is this!
Hamlet: Does it not, think thee, stand° me now upon —
    He that hath kill'd my king and whor'd my mother,
    Popp'd in between th' election° and my hopes,   65
    Thrown out his angle° for my proper life,
    And with such coz'nage° — is 't not perfect conscience,
    To quit° him with this arm? and is 't not to be damn'd,
    To let this canker° of our nature come
    In further evil?   70
Horatio: It must be shortly known to him from England
    What is the issue of the business there.
Hamlet: It will be short: the interim is mine;
    And a man's life's no more than to say "One."
    But I am very sorry, good Horatio,   75
    That to Laertes I forgot myself;
    For, by the image of my cause, I see
    The portraiture of his: I'll court his favours:
    But, sure, the bravery° of his grief did put me
    Into a tow'ring passion.
Horatio: Peace! who comes here?   80

    Enter a Courtier [Osric].

---

43 *'As'es:* The "whereases" of a formal document, with play on the word *ass; charge:* Import, and burden.   47 *shriving-time:* Time for absolution.   48 *ordinant:* Directing.   54 *sequent:* Subsequent.   59 *insinuation:* Interference.   61 *pass:* Thrust;   *fell incensed:* Fiercely angered.   63 *stand:* Become incumbent.   65 *election:* The Danish throne was filled by election.   66 *angle:* Fishing line.   67 *coz'nage:* Trickery.   68 *quit:* Repay.   69 *canker:* Ulcer, or possibly the worm which destroys buds and leaves.   79 *bravery:* Bravado.

Osric: Your lordship is right welcome back to Denmark.

Hamlet: I humbly thank you, sir. *[To Horatio.]* Dost know this water-fly?°

Horatio: No, my good lord.

Hamlet: Thy state is the more gracious; for 'tis a vice to know him. He
　　hath much land, and fertile: let a beast be lord of beasts,° and his crib   85
　　shall stand at the king's mess:° 'tis a chough;° but, as I say, spacious
　　in the possession of dirt.

Osric: Sweet lord, if your lordship were at leisure, I should impart a thing
　　to you from his majesty.

Hamlet: I will receive it, sir, with all diligence of spirit. Put your bonnet to   90
　　his right use; 'tis for the head.

Osric: I thank you lordship, it is very hot.

Hamlet: No, believe me, 'tis very cold; the wind is northerly.

Osric: It is indifferent° cold, my lord, indeed.

Hamlet: But yet methinks it is very sultry and hot for my complexion.   95

Osric: Exceedingly, my lord; it is very sultry, — as 'twere, — I cannot tell
　　how. But, my lord, his majesty bade me signify to you that 'a has laid a
　　great wager on your head: sir, this is the matter, —

Hamlet: I beseech you, remember°—

　　　　　　　　　　　[Hamlet moves him to put on his hat.]

Osric: Nay, good my lord; for mine ease,° in good faith. Sir, here is newly   100
　　come to court Laertes; believe me, an absolute gentleman, full of most
　　excellent differences, of very soft° society and great showing:° indeed,
　　to speak feelingly° of him, he is the card° or calendar of gentry,°
　　for you shall find in him the continent of what part a gentleman
　　would see.   105

Hamlet: Sir, his definement° suffers no perdition° in you; though, I know,
　　to divide him inventorially° would dozy° the arithmetic of memory,
　　and yet but yaw° neither, in respect of his quick sail. But, in the verity
　　of extolment, I take him to be a soul of great article;° and his infu-
　　sion° of such dearth and rareness,° as, to make true diction of him,   110
　　his semblable° is his mirror; and who else would trace° him, his um-
　　brage,° nothing more.

Osric: Your lordship speaks most infallibly of him.

Hamlet: The concernancy,° sir? why do we wrap the gentleman in our
　　more rawer breath?°   115

Osric: Sir?

---

82 *water-fly:* Vain or busily idle person.   85 *lord of beasts:* See Genesis 1:26, 28.   85-86 *his
crib … mess:* He shall eat at the king's table and be one of the group of persons (usually
four) constituting a *mess* at a banquet.   86 *chough:* Probably, chattering jackdaw; also
explained as *chuff,* provincial boor or churl.   94 *indifferent:* Somewhat.   99 *remember:*
I.e., remember thy courtesy; conventional phrase for "Be covered."   100 *mine ease:* Conventional reply declining the invitation of "Remember thy courtesy."   102 *soft:* Gentle;
showing: Distinguished appearance.   103 *feelingly:* With just perception; *card:* Chart,
map; *gentry:* Good breeding.   106 *definement:* Definition; *perdition:* Loss, diminution.
107 *divide him inventorially:* I.e., enumerate his graces; *dozy:* Dizzy.   108 *yaw:* To move
unsteadily (of a ship).   109 *article:* Moment or importance.   109-110 *infusion:* Infused
temperament, character imparted by nature.   110 *dearth and rareness:* Rarity.   111 *sem-
blable:* True likeness; *trace:* Follow.   111-112 *umbrage:* Shadow.   114 *concernancy:* Import.
115 *breath:* Speech.

Horatio [aside to Hamlet]: Is 't not possible to understand in another
   tongue?° You will do 't, sir, really.

Hamlet: What imports the nomination° of this gentleman?

Osric: Of Laertes?   120

Horatio [aside to Hamlet]: His purse is empty already; all 's golden words are
   spent.

Hamlet: Of him, sir.

Osric: I know you are not ignorant —

Hamlet: I would you did, sir; yet, in faith, if you did, it would not much   125
   approve° me. Well, sir?

Osric: You are not ignorant of what excellence Laertes is —

Hamlet: I dare not confess that, lest I should compare with him in excellence; but, to know a man well, were to know himself.°

Osric: I mean, sir, for his weapon; but in the imputation° laid on him by   130
   them, in his meed° he's unfellowed.

Hamlet: What's his weapon?

Osric: Rapier and dagger.

Hamlet: That's two of his weapons: but, well.

Osric: The king, sir, hath wagered with him six Barbary horses: against the   135
   which he has impawned,° as I take it, six French rapiers and poniards,
   with their assigns, as girdle, hangers,° and so: three of the carriages,
   in faith, are very dear to fancy,° very responsive° to the hilts, most
   delicate° carriages, and of very liberal conceit.°

Hamlet: What call you the carriages?   140

Horatio [aside to Hamlet]: I knew you must be edified by the margent° ere
   you had done.

Osric: The carriages, sir, are the hangers.

Hamlet: The phrase would be more german° to the matter, if we could
   carry cannon by our sides: I would it might be hangers till then. But,   145
   on: six Barbary horses against six French swords, their assigns, and
   three liberal-conceited carriages; that's the French bet against the
   Danish. Why is this "impawned," as you call it?

Osric: The king, sir, hath laid, that in a dozen passes between yourself
   and him, he shall not exceed you three hits: he hath laid on twelve for   150
   nine; and it would come to immediate trial, if your lordship would
   vouchsafe the answer.

Hamlet: How if I answer "no"?

Osric: I mean, my lord, the opposition of your person in trial.

Hamlet: Sir, I will walk here in the hall: if it please his majesty, it is the   155
   breathing time° of day with me; let the foils be brought, the gentleman willing, and the king hold his purpose, I will win for him as I can;
   if not, I will gain nothing but my shame and the odd hits.

117–118 *Is 't... tongue?:* I.e., can one converse with Osric only in this outlandish jargon?
119 *nomination:* Naming.   126 *approve:* Command.   129 *but...himself:* But to know a
man as excellent were to know Laertes.   130 *imputation:* Reputation.   131 *meed:* Merit.
136 *he has impawned:* He has wagered.   137 *hangers:* Straps on the sword belt from which
the sword hung.   138 *dear to fancy:* Fancifully made; *responsive:* Probably, well balanced,
corresponding closely.   139 *delicate:* Fine in workmanship; *liberal conceit:* Elaborate
design.   141 *margent:* Margin of a book, place for explanatory notes.   144 *german:* Ger-
mane, appropriate.   156 *breathing time:* Exercise period.

Osric: Shall I re-deliver you e'en so?

Hamlet: To this effect, sir; after what flourish your nature will. 160

Osric: I commend my duty to your lordship.

Hamlet: Yours, yours. *[Exit Osric.]* He does well to commend it himself;
there are no tongues else for 's turn.

Horatio: This lapwing° runs away with the shell on his head.

Hamlet: 'A did comply, sir, with his dug,° before 'a sucked it. Thus has 165
hey—and many more of the same breed that I know the drossy° age
dotes on—only got the tune° of the time and out of an habit of
encounter;° a kind of yesty° collection, which carries them through
and through the most fann'd and winnowed° opinions; and do but
blow them to their trial, the bubbles are out.° 170

Enter a Lord.

Lord: My lord, his majesty commended him to you by young Osric, who
brings back to him, that you attend him in the hall: he sends to know
if your pleasure hold to play with Laertes, or that you will take longer
time.

Hamlet: I am constant to my purposes; they follow the king's pleasure: if 175
his fitness speaks, mine is ready; now or whensoever, provided I be so
able as now.

Lord: The king and queen and all are coming down.

Hamlet: In happy time.°

Lord: The queen desires you to use some gentle entertainment to Laertes 180
before you fall to play.

Hamlet: She well instructs me. 　　　　　　　　　　*[Exit Lord.]*

Horatio: You will lose this wager, my lord.

Hamlet: I do not think so; since he went into France, I have been in continual practice; I shall win at the odds. But thou wouldst not think 185
how ill all 's here about my heart: but it is no matter.

Horatio: Nay, good my lord,—

Hamlet: It is but foolery; but it is such a kind of gain-giving,° as would
perhaps trouble a woman.

Horatio: If your mind dislike any thing, obey it: I will forestall their repair 190
hither, and say you are not fit.

Hamlet: Not a whit, we defy augury: there's a special providence in the
fall of a sparrow. If it be now, 'tis not to come; if it be not to come,
it will be now; if it be not now, yet it will come: the readiness is all:°
since no man of aught he leaves knows, what is 't to leave betimes? 195
Let be.

*A table prepared. [Enter] Trumpets, Drums, and Officers with cushions; King,
Queen, [Osric,] and all the State; foils, daggers, [and wine borne in;] and Laertes.*

---

164 *lapwing:* Peewit; noted for its wiliness in drawing a visitor away from its nest and its supposed habit of running about when newly hatched with its head in the shell; possibly an
allusion to Osric's hat. 　　165 *did comply . . . dug:* Paid compliments to his mother's breast.
166 *drossy:* Frivolous. 　　167 *tune:* Temper, mood. 　　167–168 *habit of encounter:* Demeanor
of social intercourse. 　　168 *yesty:* Frothy. 　　169 *fann'd and winnowed:* Select and refined.
170 *blow . . . out:* I.e., put them to the test, and their ignorance is exposed. 　　179 *In happy
time:* A phrase of courtesy. 　　188 *gain-giving:* Misgiving. 　　194 *all:* All that matters.

King: Come, Hamlet, come, and take this hand from me.

[The King puts Laertes's hand into Hamlet's.]

Hamlet: Give me your pardon, sir: I have done you wrong;
But pardon 't as you are a gentleman.
This presence° knows, 200
And you must needs have heard, how I am punish'd
With a sore distraction. What I have done,
That might your nature, honour and exception°
Roughly awake, I here proclaim was madness.
Was 't Hamlet wrong'd Laertes? Never Hamlet: 205
If Hamlet from himself be ta'en away,
And when he's not himself does wrong Laertes,
Then Hamlet does it not, Hamlet denies it.
Who does it, then? His madness: if 't be so,
Hamlet is of the faction that is wrong'd; 210
His madness is poor Hamlet's enemy.
Sir, in this audience,
Let my disclaiming from a purpos'd evil
Free me so far in your most generous thoughts,
That I have shot mine arrow o'er the house, 215
And hurt my brother.
Laertes: I am satisfied in nature,°
Whose motive, in this case, should stir me most
To my revenge: but in my terms of honour
I stand aloof; and will no reconcilement,
Till by some elder masters, of known honour, 220
I have a voice° and precedent of peace,
To keep my name ungor'd. But till that time,
I do receive your offer'd love like love,
And will not wrong it.
Hamlet: I embrace it freely;
And will this brother's wager frankly play. 225
Give us the foils. Come on.
Laertes: Come, one for me.
Hamlet: I'll be your foil,° Laertes: in mine ignorance
Your skill shall, like a star i' th' darkest night,
Stick fiery off° indeed.
Laertes: You mock me, sir.
Hamlet: No, by this hand. 230
King: Give them the foils, young Osric. Cousin Hamlet,
You know the wager?
Hamlet: Very well, my lord;
Your grace has laid the odds o' th' weaker side.

---

200 *presence:* Royal assembly.   203 *exception:* Disapproval.   216 *nature:* I.e., he is personally satisfied, but his honor must be satisfied by the rules of the code of honor.   221 *voice:*
Authoritative pronouncement.   227 *foil:* Quibble on the two senses: "background which
sets something off," and "blunted rapier for fencing."   229 *Stick fiery off:* Stand out brilliantly.

King: I do not fear it; I have seen you both:
　　But since he is better'd, we have therefore odds.   235
Laertes: This is too heavy, let me see another.
Hamlet: This likes me well. These foils have all a length?

　　[They prepare to play.]

Osric: Ay, my good lord.
King: Set me the stoups of wine upon that table.
　　If Hamlet give the first or second hit,   240
　　Or quit in answer of the third exchange,
　　Let all the battlements their ordnance fire;
　　The king shall drink to Hamlet's better breath;
　　And in the cup an union° shall he throw,
　　Richer than that which four successive kings   245
　　In Denmark's crown have worn. Give me the cups;
　　And let the kettle° to the trumpet speak,
　　The trumpet to the cannoneer without,
　　The cannons to the heavens, the heavens to earth,
　　"Now the king drinks to Hamlet." Come begin:　　*Trumpets the while.* 250
　　And you, the judges, bear a wary eye.
Hamlet: Come on, sir.
Laertes:　　　　　　　　　　Come, my lord.　　　　　　　　*[They play.]*
Hamlet:　　　　　　　　　　　　　One.
Laertes:　　　　　　　　　　　　　　No.
Hamlet:　　　　　　　　　　　　　　　Judgement.
Osric: A hit, a very palpable hit.

　　Drum, trumpets, and shot. Flourish. A piece goes off.

Laertes:　　　　　　　　　　　Well; again.
King: Stay; give me drink. Hamlet, this pearl° is thine;
　　Here's to thy health. Give him the cup.   255
Hamlet: I'll play this bout first; set it by awhile.
　　Come. *[They play.]* Another hit; what say you?
Laertes: A touch, a touch, I do confess 't.
King: Our son shall win.
Queen:　　　　　　　　　　He's fat,° and scant of breath.
　　Here, Hamlet, take my napkin, rub thy brows: 260
　　The queen carouses° to thy fortune, Hamlet.
Hamlet: Good madam!
King:　　　　　　　　　　Gertrude, do not drink.
Queen: I will, my lord; I pray you, pardon me.　　　　　　*[Drinks.]*
King [aside]: It is the poison'd cup: it is too late.
Hamlet: I dare not drink yet, madam; by and by.   265
Queen: Come, let me wipe thy face.
Laertes: My lord, I'll hit him now.
King:　　　　　　　　　　　　I do not think 't.

---

244 *union:* Pearl.　　247 *kettle:* Kettledrum.　　254 *pearl:* I.e., the poison.　　259 *fat:* Not
physically fit, out of training. Some earlier editors speculated that the term applied to the
corpulence of Richard Burbage, who originally played the part, but the allusion now appears
unlikely. *Fat* may also suggest "sweaty."　　261 *carouses:* Drinks a toast.

Laertes [aside]: And yet 'tis almost 'gainst my conscience.
Hamlet: Come, for the third, Laertes: you but dally;
     I pray you, pass with your best violence;   270
     I am afeard you make a wanton° of me.
Laertes: Say you so? come on.   *[They play.]*
Osric: Nothing, neither way.
Laertes: Have at you now!

     [Laertes wounds Hamlet; then, in scuffling, they change rapiers,° and Hamlet wounds Laertes.]

King: Part them; they are incens'd.
Hamlet: Nay, come again.   *[The Queen falls.]*
Osric: Look to the queen there, ho!   275
Horatio: They bleed on both sides. How is it, my lord?
Osric: How is 't, Laertes?
Laertes: Why, as a woodcock° to mine own springe,° Osric;
     I am justly kill'd with mine own treachery.
Hamlet: How does the queen?
King: She swounds° to see them bleed.   280
Queen: No, no, the drink, the drink, — O my dear Hamlet, —
     The drink, the drink! I am poison'd.   *[Dies.]*
Hamlet: O villany! Ho! let the door be lock'd:
     Treachery! Seek it out.   *[Laertes falls.]*
Laertes: It is here, Hamlet: Hamlet, thou art slain;   285
     No med'cine in the world can do thee good;
     In thee there is not half an hour of life;
     The treacherous instrument is in thy hand,
     Unbated° and envenom'd: the foul practice
     Hath turn'd itself on me; lo, here I lie,   290
     Never to rise again: thy mother's poison'd:
     I can no more: the king, the king's to blame.
Hamlet: The point envenom'd too!
     Then, venom, to thy work.   *[Stabs the King.]*
All: Treason! treason!   295
King: O, yet defend me, friends; I am but hurt.
Hamlet: Here, thou incestuous, murd'rous, damned Dane,
     Drink off this potion. Is thy union here?
     Follow my mother.   *[King dies.]*
Laertes: He is justly serv'd;
     It is a poison temper'd° by himself.   300
     Exchange forgiveness with me, noble Hamlet:
     Mine and my father's death come not upon thee,
     Nor thine on me!   *[Dies.]*
Hamlet: Heaven make thee free of it! I follow thee.
     I am dead, Horatio. Wretched queen, adieu!   305
     You that look pale and tremble at this chance,

---

271 *wanton:* Spoiled child.   *in scuffling, they change rapiers:* According to a widespread stage tradition, Hamlet receives a scratch, realizes that Laertes's sword is unbated, and accordingly forces an exchange.   278 *woodcock:* As type of stupidity or as decoy; *springe:* Trap, snare. 280 *swounds:* Swoons.   289 *Unbated:* Not blunted with a button.   300 *temper'd:* Mixed.

That are but mutes° or audience to this act,
Had I but time — as this fell sergeant,° Death,
Is strict in his arrest — O, I could tell you —
But let it be. Horatio, I am dead;   310
Thou livest; report me and my cause aright
To the unsatisfied.

Horatio: Never believe it:
I am more an antique Roman° than a Dane:
Here 's yet some liquor left.

Hamlet: As th' art a man,
Give me the cup: let go, by heaven, I'll ha 't.   315
O God! Horatio, what a wounded name,
Things standing thus unknown, shall live behind me!
If thou didst ever hold me in thy heart,
Absent thee from felicity awhile,
And in this harsh world draw thy breath in pain,   320
To tell my story.   *A march afar off.*
                    What warlike noise is this?

Osric: Young Fortinbras, with conquest come from Poland,
To the ambassadors of England gives
This warlike volley.

Hamlet: O, I die, Horatio;
The potent poison quite o'er-crows° my spirit: 325
I cannot live to hear the news from England;
But I do prophesy th' election lights
On Fortinbras: he has my dying voice;
So tell him, with th' occurrents,° more and less,
Which have solicited.° The rest is silence.   *[Dies.]* 330

Horatio: Now cracks a noble heart. Good night, sweet prince;
And flights of angels sing thee to thy rest!
Why does the drum come hither?   *[March within.]*

Enter Fortinbras, with the [English] Ambassadors [and others].

Fortinbras: Where is this sight?

Horatio: What is it you would see?
If aught of woe or wonder, cease your search.   335

Fortinbras: This quarry° cries on havoc.° O proud Death,
What feast is toward in thine eternal cell,
That thou so many princes at a shot
So bloodily hast struck?

First Ambassador: The sight is dismal;
And our affairs from England come too late: 340
The ears are senseless that should give us hearing,
To tell him his commandment is fulfill'd,
That Rosencrantz and Guildenstern are dead:
Where should we have our thanks?

---

307 *mutes:* Performers in a play who speak no words.   308 *sergeant:* Sheriff's officer.
313 *Roman:* It was the Roman custom to follow masters in death.   325 *o'er-crows:* Triumphs
over.   329 *occurrents:* Events, incidents.   330 *solicited:* Moved, urged.   336 *quarry:*
Heap of dead; *cries on havoc:* Proclaims a general slaughter.

Horatio: Not from his mouth,°
     Had it th' ability of life to thank you: 345
     He never gave commandment for their death.
     But since, so jump° upon this bloody question,°
     You from the Polack wars, and you from England,
     Are here arriv'd, give order that these bodies
     High on a stage° be placed to the view;   350
     And let me speak to th' yet unknowing world
     How these things came about: so shall you hear
     Of carnal, bloody, and unnatural acts,
     Of accidental judgements, casual slaughters,
     Of deaths put on by cunning and forc'd cause,   355
     And, in this upshot, purposes mistook
     Fall'n on th' inventors' heads: all this can I
     Truly deliver.
Fortinbras: Let us haste to hear it,
     And call the noblest to the audience.
     For me, with sorrow I embrace my fortune: 360
     I have some rights of memory° in this kingdom,
     Which now to claim my vantage doth invite me.
Horatio: Of that I shall have also cause to speak,
     And from his mouth whose voice will draw on more:°
     But let this same be presently perform'd,   365
     Even while men's minds are wild; lest more mischance,
     On° plots and errors, happen.
Fortinbras: Let four captains
     Bear Hamlet, like a soldier, to the stage;
     For he was likely, had he been put on,
     To have prov'd most royal: and, for his passage,°   370
     The soldiers' music and the rites of war
     Speak loudly for him.
     Take up the bodies: such a sight as this
     Becomes the field,° but here shows much amiss.
     Go, bid the soldiers shoot.   375

*Exeunt [marching, bearing off the dead bodies; after which a peal of ordnance
is shot off].*

---

344 *his mouth:* I.e., the king's.   347 *jump:* Precisely; *question:* Dispute.   350 *stage:* Platform.   361 *of memory:* Traditional, remembered.   364 *voice . . . more:* Vote will influence still others.   367 *On:* On account of, or possibly, on top of, in addition to.   370 *passage:* Death.   374 *field:* I.e., of battle.

CONSIDERATIONS FOR CRITICAL THINKING AND WRITING

1. FIRST RESPONSE. Why does Hamlet find avenging his father's death so difficult? Why doesn't he take decisive action as soon as he seems convinced of Claudius's guilt?

2. Claudius urges Hamlet to leave behind his "obstinate condolement" and give up grieving for his dead father because it represents "impious stub-

bornness" (I.ii.93–94). Consider Claudius's advice in this speech (lines 87–117). Is it sensible? Why won't Hamlet heed this advice?

3. Are Polonius's admonitions to Laertes and Ophelia good advice (I.iii.55–81, 115–135)? What does his advice suggest about life at court, given that he is the chief counselor to the king?

4. When the ghost tells Hamlet that Claudius murdered him, Hamlet cries out, "O my prophetic soul!" (I.v.40). Why? What does the ghost demand of Hamlet?

5. What is known about the kind of person Hamlet was before his father's death? Does he have the stature of a tragic hero such as Oedipus? How does news of the murder and his mother's remarriage affect his behavior and view of life? Is he mad, as Polonius assumes, or is he pretending to be mad? Is there a "method in 't" (II.ii.200)? What do we learn from Hamlet's soliloquies?

6. What is the purpose of the play within the play? How does it provide a commentary on the action of the larger play?

7. Is Ophelia connected in any way with the crime Hamlet seeks to avenge? Why is he so brutal to Ophelia in Act III, Scene i? Why does she go mad?

8. Does Hamlet think Gertrude is as guilty as Claudius? Why is Hamlet so thoroughly disgusted by her in Act III, Scene iv?

9. Why doesn't Hamlet kill Claudius as he prays (III.iii)? Do you feel any sympathy for Claudius in this scene, or is he presented as a callous murderer?

10. If Hamlet had killed Claudius in Act III and the play had ended there, what would be missing in Hamlet's perceptions of himself and the world? How does his character develop in Acts IV and V? What softens our realization that Hamlet is in various degrees responsible for the deaths of Polonius, Ophelia, Laertes, Rosencrantz, Guildenstern, Claudius, and Gertrude?

11. What purpose does Fortinbras serve in the action? Would anything be lost if he were edited out of the play?

12. Despite its tragic dimensions, *Hamlet* includes humorous scenes and many witty lines delivered by the title character himself. Locate those scenes and lines, and then determine the tone and purpose of the play's humor.

13. CRITICAL STRATEGIES. Read the section on formalist criticism (pp. 60–62) in Chapter 3, "Applying a Critical Strategy." Choose a soliloquy by Hamlet and write an analysis of its images so that you reveal some significant portion of his character.

TENNESSEE WILLIAMS AND MODERN DRAMA

Thomas Lanier Williams, who kept his college nickname, Tennessee, was born in Columbus, Mississippi, the son of a traveling salesman. In 1918 the family moved to St. Louis, Missouri, where his father became the sales manager of a shoe company. Williams's mother, the daughter of an Episcopal clergyman, was withdrawn and genteel in contrast to his aggressive father, who contemptuously called him "Miss Nancy" as a way of mocking his weak physical condition and his literary pursuits. This family atmosphere of repression and anger makes its way into many of Williams's works through characterizations of domineering men and psychologically vulnerable women.

Williams began writing in high school and at the age of seventeen published his first short story in *Weird Tales*. His education at the University of Missouri was interrupted when he had to go to work in a shoe factory. This "living death," as he put it, led to a nervous breakdown, but he eventually resumed his studies at Washington University and finally graduated from the University of Iowa in 1938. During his college years, Williams wrote one-act plays; in 1940 his first full-length play, *Battle of Angels*, opened in Boston, but none of these early plays achieved commercial success. In 1945, however, *The Glass Menagerie* won large, enthusiastic audiences as well as the Drama Critics' Circle Award, which marked the beginning of a series of theatrical triumphs for Williams including *Streetcar Named Desire* (1947), *The Rose Tattoo* (1950), *Cat on a Hot Tin Roof* (1955), *Suddenly Last Summer* (1958), and *The Night of the Iguana* (1961).

Realism

Realism is a literary technique that attempts to create the appearance of life as it is actually experienced. Characters in modern realistic plays (written during and after the last quarter of the nineteenth century) speak dialogue that we might hear in our daily lives. These characters are not larger than life but representative of it; they seem to speak the way we do rather than in highly poetic language, formal declarations, asides, or soliloquies. It is impossible to imagine a heroic figure such as Oedipus inhabiting a comfortably furnished living room and chatting about his wife's household budget the way a character might in a modern drama. Realism brings into focus commonplace, everyday life rather than the extraordinary kinds of events that make up Sophocles' *Oedipus the King* or Shakespeare's *Hamlet.*

Realistic characters can certainly be heroic, but they find that their strength and courage are tested in the context of events ordinary people might experience. Work, love, marriage, children, and death are often the focus of realistic dramas. These subjects can also constitute much of the material in nonrealistic plays, but modern realistic dramas present such material in the realm of the probable. Conflicts in realistic plays are likely to reflect problems in our own lives. Hence, making ends meet takes precedence over saving a kingdom; middle- and lower-class individuals take center stage as primary characters in main plots rather than being secondary characters in subplots. Thus we can see why the nineteenth-century movement toward realism paralleled the rise of a middle class eagerly seeking representations of its concerns in the theater.

Before the end of the nineteenth century, however, few attempts were made in the theater to present life as it is actually lived. The chorus's role in Sophocles' *Oedipus the King*, the allegorical figures in morality plays, the remarkable mistaken identities in Shakespeare's comedies, or the rhymed couplets spoken in seventeenth-century plays such as Molière's *Tartuffe* represent theatrical conventions rather than life. Theatergoers have understood and appreciated these conventions for centuries — and still do — but in the nineteenth century social, political, and industrial revolutions helped create an atmosphere in which some playwrights found it necessary to create works that more directly reflected their audiences' lives.

Playwrights such as Henrik Ibsen and Anton Chekhov refused to join the ranks of their romantic contemporaries, who they felt falsely idealized life. The most popular plays immediately preceding the works of these realistic writers consisted primarily of love stories and action-packed plots. Such **melodramas** offer audiences thrills and chills as well as happy endings. They typically include a virtuous individual struggling under the tyranny of a wicked oppressor, who is defeated only at the last moment. Suspense is reinforced by a series of pursuits, captures, and escapes that move the plot quickly and de-emphasize character or theme. These representations of extreme conflicts enjoyed wide popularity in the nineteenth century — indeed, they still do — because their formula was varied enough to be entertaining yet their outcomes were always comforting to the audience's sense of justice. From the realists' perspective, melodramas were merely escape fantasies that distorted life by refusing to examine the real world closely and objectively.

Realists attempted to open their audiences' eyes; to their minds, the only genuine comfort was in knowing the truth. Many of their plays concern controversial issues of the day and focus on people who fall prey to indifferent societal institutions. English dramatist John Galsworthy (1867–1933) examined social values in *Strife* (1909) and *Justice* (1910), two plays whose titles broadly suggest the nature of his concerns. British playwright George Bernard Shaw (1856–1950) often used comedy and irony as means of awakening his audiences to contemporary problems: *Arms and the Man* (1894) satirizes romantic attitudes toward war, and *Mrs. Warren's Profession* (1898) indicts a social and economic system that drives a woman to prostitution. Chekhov's major plays are populated by characters frustrated by their social situations and their own sensibilities; they are ordinary people who long for happiness but become entangled in everyday circumstances that limit their lives. Ibsen also took a close look at his characters' daily lives. His plays attack social conventions and challenge popular attitudes toward marriage; he stunned audiences by dramatizing the suffering of a man dying of syphilis.

With these kinds of materials, Ibsen and his contemporaries popularized the **problem play,** a drama that represents a social issue in order to awaken the audience to it. These plays usually reject romantic plots in favor of holding up a mirror that reflects not simply what audiences want to see but what the playwright sees in them. Nineteenth-century realistic theater was no refuge from the social, economic, and psychological problems that melodrama ignored or sentimentalized.

Naturalism

Related to realism is another movement, called **naturalism.** Essentially more of a philosophical attitude than a literary technique, naturalism derives its name from the idea that human beings are part of nature and subject to its laws. According to naturalists, heredity and environment shape and control people's lives; their behavior is determined more by instinct than by reason. This deterministic view argues that human beings have no transcendent identity because there is no soul or spiritual world that ultimately distinguishes humanity from any other form of life. Characters in naturalistic plays are generally portrayed as victims overwhelmed by internal and external forces. Thus literary naturalism tends to include not only the commonplace but the sordid, destructive, and chaotic aspects of life. Naturalism, then, is an extreme form of realism.

The earliest and most articulate voice of naturalism was that of French author Émile Zola (1840–1902), who urged artists to draw their characters from life and present their histories as faithfully as scientists report laboratory findings. Zola's best-known naturalistic play, *Thérèse Raquin* (1873), is a dramatization of an earlier novel involving a woman whose passion causes her to take a lover and plot with him to kill her husband. In his preface to the novel, Zola explains that his purpose is to take "a strong man and unsatisfied woman," "throw them into a violent drama and note scrupulously the sensations and acts of these creatures." The diction of Zola's statement reveals his nearly clinical approach, which becomes even more explicit when Zola likens his method of revealing character to that of an autopsy: "I have simply done on two living bodies the work which surgeons do on corpses."

Although some naturalistic plays have been successfully produced and admired (notably Maxim Gorky's *The Lower Depths* [1902], set in a grim boardinghouse occupied by characters who suffer poverty, crime, betrayal, disease, and suicide), few important dramatists fully subscribed to naturalism's extreme methods and values. Nevertheless, the movement significantly influenced playwrights. Because of its insistence on the necessity of closely observing characters' environment, playwrights placed a new emphasis on detailed settings and natural acting. This verisimilitude became a significant feature of realistic drama.

Theatrical Conventions of Modern Drama

The picture-frame stage that is often used for realistic plays typically reproduces the setting of a room in some detail. Within the stage, framed by a proscenium arch (from which the curtain hangs), scenery and props are used to create an illusion of reality. Whether the "small bookcase with richly bound books" described in the opening scene of Ibsen's *A Doll House* is only painted scenery or an actual case with books, it will probably look real to the audience. Removing the fourth wall of a room so that an audience can look in fosters the illusion that the actions onstage are real events happening before unseen spectators. The texture of Nora's life is communicated by the set as well as by what she says and does. That doesn't happen in a play like Sophocles' *Oedipus the King*. Technical effects can make us believe there is wood burning in a fireplace or snow falling outside a window. Outdoor settings are made similarly realistic by props and painted sets. In one of Chekhov's full-length plays, for example, the second act opens in a meadow with the faint outline of a city on the horizon.

In addition to lifelike sets, a particular method of acting is used to create a realistic atmosphere. Actors address each other instead of directing formal speeches toward the audience; they act within the setting, not merely before it. At the beginning of the twentieth century Konstantin Stanislavsky (1863–1938), a Russian director, teacher, and actor, developed a system of acting that was an important influence in realistic theater. He trained actors to identify with the inner emotions of the characters they played. They were encouraged to recall from their own lives emotional responses similar to those they were portraying. The goal was to present a role truthfully by first feeling and then projecting the character's situation. Among Stanislavsky's early successes in this method were the plays of Chekhov.

There are, however, degrees of realism on the stage. Tennessee Williams's *The Glass Menagerie* (p. 448), for example, is a partially realistic portrayal of characters whose fragile lives are founded on illusions. Williams's dialogue rings true, and individual scenes resemble the kind of real-life action we would imagine such vulnerable characters engaging in, but other elements of the play are nonrealistic. For instance, Williams uses Tom as a major character in the play as well as a narrator and a stage manager. Here is part of Williams's stage directions: "The narrator is an undisguised convention of the play. He takes whatever license with dramatic convention as is convenient to his purposes." Although this play can be accurately described as including realistic elements, Williams, like many other contemporary playwrights, does not attempt an absolute fidelity to reality. He uses flashbacks—as does Arthur Miller in *Death of a Salesman* (p. 1007)—to present incidents that occurred before the opening scene because the past impinges so heavily on the present. Most playwrights don't attempt to duplicate reality, since that can now be done so well by motion pictures.

Realism needn't lock a playwright into a futile attempt to make everything appear as it is in life. There is no way to avoid theatrical conventions: Actors impersonate characters in a setting that is, after all, a stage. Indeed, even the dialogue in a realistic play is quite different from the pauses, sentence fragments, repetitions, silences, and incoherencies that characterize the way people usually speak. Realistic dialogue may seem like ordinary speech, but it, like Shakespeare's poetic language, is constructed. If we remember that realistic drama represents only the appearance of reality and that what we read on a page or see and hear onstage is the result of careful selecting, editing, and even distortion, then we are more likely to appreciate the playwright's art.

The Glass Menagerie

The Glass Menagerie reflects Williams's fascination with characters who face lonely struggles in emotionally and financially starved environments. Although Williams's use of colloquial southern speech is realistic, the play also employs nonrealistic techniques, such as shifts in time, projections on screens, music, and lighting effects, to express his characters' thoughts and inner lives. As much as these techniques are unconventional, Williams believed that they represented "a more penetrating and vivid expression of things as they are." The lasting popularity of *The Glass Menagerie* indicates that his assessment was correct.

TENNESSEE WILLIAMS (1911–1983)

The Glass Menagerie   *1945*

nobody, not even the rain, has such small hands
        —*E. E. Cummings*

LIST OF CHARACTERS

Amanda Wingfield, the mother. A little woman of great but confused vitality clinging frantically to another time and place. Her characterization must be carefully created, not copied from type. She is not paranoiac, but her life is paranoia. There is much to admire in Amanda, and as much to love and pity as there is to laugh at. Certainly she has endurance and a kind of heroism, and though her foolishness makes her unwittingly cruel at times, there is tenderness in her slight person.

Laura Wingfield, her daughter. Amanda, having failed to establish contact with reality, continues to live vitally in her illusions, but Laura's situation is even graver. A childhood illness has left her crippled, one leg slightly shorter than the other, and held in a brace. This defect need not be more than suggested on the stage. Stemming from this, Laura's separation increases till she is like a piece of her own glass collection, too exquisitely fragile to move from the shelf.

Tom Wingfield, her son. And the narrator of the play. A poet with a job in a warehouse. His nature is not remorseless, but to escape from a trap he has to act without pity.

Jim O'Connor, the gentleman caller. A nice, ordinary, young man.

SCENE: *An alley in St. Louis.*
PART I: *Preparation for a Gentleman Caller.*
PART II: *The Gentleman Calls.*
TIME: *Now and the Past.*

SCENE I

*The Wingfield apartment is in the rear of the building, one of those vast hivelike
conglomerations of cellular living-units that flower as warty growths in overcrowded urban centers of lower middle-class population and are symptomatic of
the impulse of this largest and fundamentally enslaved section of American society
to avoid fluidity and differentiation and to exist and function as one interfused
mass of automatism.*

*The apartment faces an alley and is entered by a fire-escape, a structure whose
name is a touch of accidental poetic truth, for all of these huge buildings are always
burning with the slow and implacable fires of human desperation. The fire-escape is
included in the set—that is, the landing of it and steps descending from it.*

*The scene is memory and is therefore nonrealistic. Memory takes a lot of
poetic license. It omits some details; others are exaggerated, according to the emotional value of the articles it touches, for memory is seated predominantly in the
heart. The interior is therefore rather dim and poetic.*

*At the rise of the curtain, the audience is faced with the dark, grim rear wall of
the Wingfield tenement. This building, which runs parallel to the footlights, is
flanked on both sides by dark, narrow alleys which run into murky canyons of
tangled clotheslines, garbage cans, and the sinister latticework of neighboring fire-
escapes. It is up and down these side alleys that exterior entrances and exits are
made, during the play. At the end of Tom's opening commentary, the dark tenement wall slowly reveals (by means of a transparency) the interior of the ground
floor Wingfield apartment.*

*Downstage is the living room, which also serves as a sleeping room for Laura,
the sofa unfolding to make her bed. Upstage, center, and divided by a wide arch or
second proscenium with transparent faded portieres (or second curtain), is the
dining room. In an old-fashioned what-not in the living room are seen scores of
transparent glass animals. A blown-up photograph of the father hangs on the wall
of the living room, facing the audience, to the left of the archway. It is the face of a
very handsome young man in a doughboy's First World War cap. He is gallantly
smiling, ineluctably smiling, as if to say, "I will be smiling forever."*

*The audience hears and sees the opening scene in the dining room through both
the transparent fourth wall of the building and the transparent gauze portieres of
the dining-room arch. It is during this revealing scene that the fourth wall slowly
ascends, out of sight. This transparent exterior wall is not brought down again until
the very end of the play, during Tom's final speech.*

*The narrator is an undisguised convention of the play. He takes whatever
license with dramatic convention as is convenient to his purposes.*

*Tom enters dressed as a merchant sailor from alley, stage left, and strolls
across the front of the stage to the fire-escape. There he stops and lights a cigarette.
He addresses the audience.*

Tom: Yes, I have tricks in my pocket, I have things up my sleeve. But I am the opposite of a stage magician. He gives you illusion that has the appearance of truth. I give you truth in the pleasant disguise of illusion. To begin with, I turn back time. I reverse it to that quaint period, the thirties, when the huge middle class of America was matriculating in a school for the blind. Their eyes had failed them, or they had failed their eyes, and so they were having their fingers pressed forcibly down on the fiery Braille alphabet of a dissolving economy. In Spain there was revolution. Here there was only shouting and confusion. In Spain there was Guernica.° Here there were disturbances of labor, sometimes pretty violent, in otherwise peaceful cities such as Chicago, Cleveland, Saint Louis. . . . This is the social background of the play.

(Music.)

The play is memory. Being a memory play, it is dimly lighted, it is sentimental, it is not realistic. In memory everything seems to happen to music. That explains the fiddle in the wings. I am the narrator of the play, and also a character in it. The other characters are my mother, Amanda, my sister, Laura, and a gentleman caller who appears in the final scenes. He is the most realistic character in the play, being an emissary from a world of reality that we were somehow set apart from. But since I have a poet's weakness for symbols, I am using this character also as a symbol; he is the long delayed but always expected something that we live for. There is a fifth character in the play who doesn't appear except in this larger-than-life photograph over the mantel. This is our father who left us a long time ago. He was a telephone man who fell in love with long distances; he gave up his job with the telephone company and skipped the light fantastic out of town. . . . The last we heard of him was a picture post-card from Mazatlán, on the Pacific coast of Mexico, containing a message of two words — "Hello — Good-bye!" and no address. I think the rest of the play will explain itself. . . .

Amanda's voice becomes audible through the portieres.

(Legend on screen: "Où sont les neiges."°)

   He divides the portieres and enters the upstage area.
   Amanda and Laura are seated at a drop-leaf table. Eating is indicated by gestures without food or utensils. Amanda faces the audience.
   Tom and Laura are seated in profile.
   The interior has lit up softly and through the scrim we see Amanda and Laura seated at the table in the upstage area.

Amanda (calling): Tom?
Tom: Yes, Mother.
Amanda: We can't say grace until you come to the table!
Tom: Coming, Mother. *(He bows slightly and withdraws, reappearing a few moments later in his place at the table.)*

Guernica: A town in northern Spain destroyed by German bombers in 1937 during the Spanish Civil War.   *Où sont les neiges:* Part of a line from a poem by the French medieval writer François Villon; the full line translates, "Where are the snows of yesteryear?"

Amanda (to her son): Honey, don't *push* with your *fingers.* If you have to push with something, the thing to push with is a crust of bread. And chew—chew! Animals have sections in their stomachs which enable them to digest food without mastication, but human beings are supposed to chew their food before they swallow it down. Eat food leisurely, son, and really enjoy it. A well-cooked meal has lots of delicate flavors that have to be held in the mouth for appreciation. So chew your food and give your salivary glands a chance to function!

Tom deliberately lays his imaginary fork down and pushes his chair back from the table.

Tom: I haven't enjoyed one bite of this dinner because of your constant directions on how to eat it. It's you that makes me rush through meals with your hawklike attention to every bite I take. Sickening—spoils my appetite—all this discussion of animals' secretion—salivary glands— mastication!

Amanda (lightly): Temperament like a Metropolitan star! *(He rises and crosses downstage.)* You're not excused from the table.

Tom: I am getting a cigarette.

Amanda: You smoke too much.

Laura rises.

Laura: I'll bring in the blanc mange.

He remains standing with his cigarette by the portieres during the following.

Amanda (rising): No, sister, no, sister—you be the lady this time and I'll be the darky.

Laura: I'm already up.

Amanda: Resume your seat, little sister—I want you to stay fresh and pretty— for gentlemen callers!

Laura: I'm not expecting any gentlemen callers.

Amanda (crossing out to kitchenette. Airily): Sometimes they come when they are least expected! Why, I remember one Sunday afternoon in Blue Mountain—*(Enters kitchenette.)*

Tom: I know what's coming!

Laura: Yes. But let her tell it.

Tom: Again?

Laura: She loves to tell it.

Amanda returns with bowl of dessert.

Amanda: One Sunday afternoon in Blue Mountain—your mother received— seventeen!—gentlemen callers! Why, sometimes there weren't chairs enough to accommodate them all. We had to send the nigger over to bring in folding chairs from the parish house.

Tom (remaining at portieres): How did you entertain those gentlemen callers?

Amanda: I understood the art of conversation!

Tom: I bet you could talk.

Amanda: Girls in those days *knew* how to talk, I can tell you.

Tom: Yes?

(Image: Amanda as a girl on a porch greeting callers.)

Amanda: They knew how to entertain their gentlemen callers. It wasn't enough for a girl to be possessed of a pretty face and a graceful figure — although I wasn't slighted in either respect. She also needed to have a nimble wit and a tongue to meet all occasions.

Tom: What did you talk about?

Amanda: Things of importance going on in the world! Never anything coarse or common or vulgar. (*She addresses Tom as though he were seated in the vacant chair at the table though he remains by portieres. He plays this scene as though he held the book.*) My callers were gentlemen — all! Among my callers were some of the most prominent young planters of the Mississippi Delta — planters and sons of planters!

> *Tom motions for music and a spot of light on Amanda.*
> *Her eyes lift, her face glows, her voice becomes rich and elegiac.*
> (*Screen legend: "Où sont les neiges."*)

There was young Champ Laughlin who later became vice-president of the Delta Planters Bank. Hadley Stevenson who was drowned in Moon Lake and left his widow one hundred and fifty thousand in Government bonds. There were the Cutrere brothers, Wesley and Bates. Bates was one of my bright particular beaux! He got in a quarrel with that wild Wainright boy. They shot it out on the floor of Moon Lake Casino. Bates was shot through the stomach. Died in the ambulance on his way to Memphis. His widow was also well-provided for, came into eight or ten thousand acres, that's all. She married him on the rebound — never loved her — carried my picture on him the night he died! And there was that boy that every girl in the Delta had set her cap for! That beautiful, brilliant young Fitzhugh boy from Green County!

Tom: What did he leave his widow?

Amanda: He never married! Gracious, you talk as though all of my old admirers had turned up their toes to the daisies!

Tom: Isn't this the first you mentioned that still survives?

Amanda: That Fitzhugh boy went North and made a fortune — came to be known as the Wolf of Wall Street! He had the Midas touch, whatever he touched turned to gold! And I could have been Mrs. Duncan J. Fitzhugh, mind you! But — I picked your *father!*

Laura (rising): Mother, let me clear the table.

Amanda: No dear, you go in front and study your typewriter chart. Or practice your shorthand a little. Stay fresh and pretty! — It's almost time for our gentlemen callers to start arriving. (*She flounces girlishly toward the kitchenette.*) How many do you suppose we're going to entertain this afternoon?

> *Tom throws down the paper and jumps up with a groan.*

Laura (alone in the dining room): I don't believe we're going to receive any, Mother.

Amanda (reappearing, airily): What? No one — not one? You must be joking! (*Laura nervously echoes her laugh. She slips in a fugitive manner through the half-open portieres and draws them gently behind her. A shaft of very clear light is thrown on her face against the faded tapestry of the curtains.*) (*Music: "The Glass Menagerie" under faintly.*) (*Lightly.*) Not one gentleman caller? It can't be true! There must be a flood, there must have been a tornado!

Laura: It isn't a flood, it's not a tornado, Mother. I'm just not popular like you were in Blue Mountain. . . . *(Tom utters another groan. Laura glances at him with a faint, apologetic smile. Her voice catching a little.)* Mother's afraid I'm going to be an old maid.

(The scene dims out with "Glass Menagerie" music.)

SCENE II

"Laura, Haven't You Ever Liked Some Boy?"

On the dark stage the screen is lighted with the image of blue roses.
    Gradually Laura's figure becomes apparent and the screen goes out.
    The music subsides.
    Laura is seated in the delicate ivory chair at the small clawfoot table.
    She wears a dress of soft violet material for a kimono — her hair tied back from her forehead with a ribbon.
    She is washing and polishing her collection of glass.
    Amanda appears on the fire-escape steps. At the sound of her ascent, Laura catches her breath, thrusts the bowl of ornaments away, and seats herself stiffly before the diagram of the typewriter keyboard as though it held her spellbound. Something has happened to Amanda. It is written in her face as she climbs to the landing: a look that is grim and hopeless and a little absurd.
    She has on one of those cheap or imitation velvety-looking cloth coats with imitation fur collar. Her hat is five or six years old, one of those dreadful cloche hats that were worn in the late twenties, and she is clasping an enormous black patent-leather pocketbook with nickel clasp and initials. This is her full-dress outfit, the one she usually wears to the D.A.R.°
    Before entering she looks through the door.
    She purses her lips, opens her eyes wide, rolls them upward, and shakes her head.
    Then she slowly lets herself in the door. Seeing her mother's expression Laura touches her lips with a nervous gesture.

Laura: Hello, Mother, I was — *(She makes a nervous gesture toward the chart on the wall. Amanda leans against the shut door and stares at Laura with a martyred look.)*

Amanda: Deception? Deception? *(She slowly removes her hat and gloves, continuing the swift suffering stare. She lets the hat and gloves fall on the floor — a bit of acting.)*

Laura (shakily): How was the D.A.R. meeting? *(Amanda slowly opens her purse and removes a dainty white handkerchief, which she shakes out delicately and delicately touches to her lips and nostrils.)* Didn't you go to the D.A.R. meeting, Mother?

Amanda (faintly, almost inaudibly): —No.—No. *(Then more forcibly.)* I did not have the strength — to go to the D.A.R. In fact, I did not have the courage! I wanted to find a hole in the ground and hide myself in it forever! *(She*

D.A.R.: Daughters of the American Revolution; members must document that they have ancestors who served the patriots' cause in the Revolutionary War.

crosses slowly to the wall and removes the diagram of the typewriter keyboard. She holds it in front of her for a second, staring at it sweetly and sorrowfully — then bites her lips and tears it in two pieces.)

Laura *(faintly)*: Why did you do that, Mother? *(Amanda repeats the same procedure with the chart of the Gregg Alphabet.°)* Why are you —

Amanda: Why? Why? How old are you, Laura?

Laura: Mother, you know my age.

Amanda: I thought that you were an adult; it seems that I was mistaken. *(She crosses slowly to the sofa and sinks down and stares at Laura.)*

Laura: Please don't stare at me, Mother.

Amanda closes her eyes and lowers her head. Count ten.

Amanda: What are we going to do, what is going to become of us, what is the future?

Count ten.

Laura: Has something happened, Mother? *(Amanda draws a long breath and takes out the handkerchief again. Dabbing process.)* Mother, has — something happened?

Amanda: I'll be all right in a minute. I'm just bewildered — *(count five)* — by life. . . .

Laura: Mother, I wish that you would tell me what's happened.

Amanda: As you know, I was supposed to be inducted into my office at the D.A.R. this afternoon. *(Image: A swarm of typewriters.)* But I stopped off at Rubicam's Business College to speak to your teachers about your having a cold and ask them what progress they thought you were making down there.

Laura: Oh. . . .

Amanda: I went to the typing instructor and introduced myself as your mother. She didn't know who you were. Wingfield, she said. We don't have any such student enrolled at the school! I assured her she did, that you had been going to classes since early in January. "I wonder," she said, "if you could be talking about that terribly shy little girl who dropped out of school after only a few days' attendance?" "No," I said, "Laura, my daughter, has been going to school every day for the past six weeks!" "Excuse me," she said. She took the attendance book out and there was your name, unmistakably printed, and all the dates you were absent until they decided that you had dropped out of school. I still said, "No, there must have been some mistake! There must have been some mix-up in the records!" And she said, "No — I remember her perfectly now. Her hand shook so that she couldn't hit the right keys! The first time we gave a speed-test, she broke down completely — was sick at the stomach and almost had to be carried into the wash-room! After that morning she never showed up any more. We phoned the house but never got any answer" — while I was working at Famous and Barr, I suppose, demonstrating those — Oh! I felt so weak I could barely keep on my feet. I had to sit down while they got me a glass of water! Fifty dollars' tuition, all of our plans — my hopes and ambitions for

---

Gregg Alphabet: System of shorthand symbols invented by John Robert Gregg.

you — just gone up the spout, just gone up the spout like that. *(Laura draws a long breath and gets awkwardly to her feet. She crosses to the Victrola, and winds it up.)* What are you doing?

Laura: Oh! *(She releases the handle and returns to her seat.)*

Amanda: Laura, where have you been going when you've gone out pretending that you were going to business college?

Laura: I've just been going out walking.

Amanda: That's not true.

Laura: It is. I just went walking.

Amanda: Walking? Walking? In winter? Deliberately courting pneumonia in that light coat? Where did you walk to, Laura?

Laura: It was the lesser of two evils, Mother. *(Image: Winter scene in park.)* I couldn't go back up. I — threw up — on the floor!

Amanda: From half past seven till after five every day you mean to tell me you walked around in the park, because you wanted to make me think that you were still going to Rubicam's Business College?

Laura: It wasn't as bad as it sounds. I went inside places to get warmed up.

Amanda: Inside where?

Laura: I went in the art museum and the bird-houses at the Zoo. I visited the penguins every day! Sometimes I did without lunch and went to the movies. Lately I've been spending most of my afternoons in the Jewel-box, that big glass house where they raise the tropical flowers.

Amanda: You did all this to deceive me, just for the deception? *(Laura looks down.)* Why?

Laura: Mother, when you're disappointed, you get that awful suffering look on your face, like the picture of Jesus' mother in the museum!

Amanda: Hush!

Laura: I couldn't face it.

> Pause. A whisper of strings.
> *(Legend: "The Crust of Humility.")*

Amanda (hopelessly fingering the huge pocketbook): So what are we going to do the rest of our lives? Stay home and watch the parades go by? Amuse ourselves with the glass menagerie, darling? Eternally play those worn-out phonograph records your father left as a painful reminder of him? We won't have a business career — we've given that up because it gave us nervous indigestion! *(Laughs wearily.)* What is there left but dependency all our lives? I know so well what becomes of unmarried women who aren't prepared to occupy a position. I've seen such pitiful cases in the South — barely tolerated spinsters living upon the grudging patronage of sister's husband or brother's wife! — stuck away in some little mousetrap of a room — encouraged by one in-law to visit another — little birdlike women without any nest — eating the crust of humility all their life! Is that the future that we've mapped out for ourselves? I swear it's the only alternative I can think of! It isn't a very pleasant alternative, is it? Of course — some girls *do* marry. *(Laura twists her hands nervously.)* Haven't you ever liked some boy?

Laura: Yes. I liked one once. *(Rises.)* I came across his picture a while ago.

Amanda (with some interest): He gave you his picture?

Laura: No, it's in the year-book.

Amanda (disappointed): Oh — a high-school boy.

(Screen image: Jim as a high-school hero bearing a silver cup.)

Laura: Yes. His name was Jim. *(Laura lifts the heavy annual from the clawfoot table.)* Here he is in *The Pirates of Penzance*.

Amanda (absently): The what?

Laura: The operetta the senior class put on. He had a wonderful voice and we sat across the aisle from each other Mondays, Wednesdays, and Fridays in the Aud. Here he is with the silver cup for debating! See his grin?

Amanda (absently): He must have had a jolly disposition.

Laura: He used to call me — Blue Roses.

(Image: Blue roses.)

Amanda: Why did he call you such a name as that?

Laura: When I had that attack of pleurosis — he asked me what was the matter when I came back. I said pleurosis — he thought that I said Blue Roses! So that's what he always called me after that. Whenever he saw me, he'd holler, "Hello, Blue Roses!" I didn't care for the girl that he went out with. Emily Meisenbach. Emily was the best-dressed girl at Soldan. She never struck me, though, as being sincere. . . . It says in the Personal Section — they're engaged. That's — six years ago! They must be married by now.

Amanda: Girls that aren't cut out for business careers usually wind up married to some nice man. *(Gets up with a spark of revival.)* Sister, that's what you'll do!

Laura utters a startled, doubtful laugh. She reaches quickly for a piece of glass.

Laura: But, Mother —

Amanda: Yes? *(Crossing to photograph.)*

Laura (in a tone of frightened apology): I'm — crippled!

(Image: Screen.)

Amanda: Nonsense! Laura, I've told you never, never to use that word. Why, you're not crippled, you just have a little defect — hardly noticeable, even! When people have some slight disadvantage like that, they cultivate other things to make up for it — develop charm — and vivacity — and — *charm!* That's all you have to do! *(She turns again to the photograph.)* One thing your father had *plenty of* — was *charm!*

Tom motions to the fiddle in the wings.
(The scene fades out with music.)

SCENE III

(Legend on the screen: "After the Fiasco —")
Tom speaks from the fire-escape landing.

Tom: After the fiasco at Rubicam's Business College, the idea of getting a gentleman caller for Laura began to play a more important part in Mother's calculations. It became an obsession. Like some archetype of the universal unconscious, the image of the gentleman caller haunted our small apartment. . . . *(Image: Young man at door with flowers.)* An evening at home rarely passed without some allusion to this image, this specter, this hope. . . . Even when he wasn't mentioned, his presence hung in Mother's preoccupied look and in my sister's frightened, apologetic manner — hung like a sentence passed upon the Wingfields! Mother was a woman of action as well as words. She began to take logical steps in the planned direction. Late that winter and in the early spring — realizing that extra money would be needed to properly feather the nest and plume the bird — she conducted a vigorous campaign on the telephone, roping in subscribers to one of those magazines for matrons called *The Home-maker's Companion,* the type of journal that features the serialized sublimations of ladies of letters who think in terms of delicate cuplike breasts, slim, tapering waists, rich, creamy thighs, eyes like wood-smoke in autumn, fingers that soothe and caress like strains of music, bodies as powerful as Etruscan sculpture.

(Screen image: Glamour magazine cover.)
   Amanda enters with phone on long extension cord. She is spotted in the dim stage.

Amanda: Ida Scott? This is Amanda Wingfield! We *missed* you at the D.A.R. last Monday! I said to myself: She's probably suffering with that sinus condition! How is that sinus condition? Horrors! Heaven have mercy! — You're a Christian martyr, yes, that's what you are, a Christian martyr! Well, I just now happened to notice that your subscription to the *Companion's* about to expire! Yes, it expires with the next issue, honey! — just when that wonderful new serial by Bessie Mae Hopper is getting off to such an exciting start. Oh, honey, it's something that you can't miss! You remember how *Gone with the Wind* took everybody by storm? You simply couldn't go out if you hadn't read it. All everybody *talked* was Scarlett O'Hara. Well, this is a book that critics already compare to *Gone with the Wind.* It's the *Gone with the Wind* of the post-World War generation! — What? — Burning? — Oh, honey, don't let them burn, go take a look in the oven and I'll hold the wire! Heavens — I think she's hung up!

(Dim out.)
   (Legend on screen: "You think I'm in love with Continental Shoemakers?")
   Before the stage is lighted, the violent voices of Tom and Amanda are heard. They are quarreling behind the portieres. In front of them stands Laura with clenched hands and panicky expression.
   A clear pool of light on her figure throughout this scene.

Tom: What in Christ's name am I —
Amanda (shrilly): Don't you use that —
Tom: Supposed to do!
Amanda: Expression! Not in my —
Tom: Ohhh!
Amanda: Presence! Have you gone out of your senses?
Tom: I have, that's true, *driven* out!
Amanda: What is the matter with you, you — big — big — IDIOT!
Tom: Look — I've got *no thing,* no single thing —
Amanda: Lower your voice!

Tom: In my life here that I can call my own! Everything is —

Amanda: Stop that shouting!

Tom: Yesterday you confiscated my books! You had the nerve to —

Amanda: I took that horrible novel back to the library — yes! That hideous book by that insane Mr. Lawrence.° *(Tom laughs wildly.)* I cannot control the output of diseased minds or people who cater to them — *(Tom laughs still more wildly.)* BUT I WON'T ALLOW SUCH FILTH BROUGHT INTO MY HOUSE! No, no, no, no, no!

Tom: House, house! Who pays rent on it, who makes a slave of himself to —

Amanda (fairly screeching): Don't you DARE to —

Tom: No, no, I mustn't say things! *I've* got to just —

Amanda: Let me tell you —

Tom: I don't want to hear any more! *(He tears the portieres open. The upstage area is lit with a turgid smoky red glow.)*

> *Amanda's hair is in metal curlers and she wears a very old bathrobe, much too large for her slight figure, a relic of the faithless Mr. Wingfield.*
> *An upright typewriter and a wild disarray of manuscripts are on the drop-leaf table. The quarrel was probably precipitated by Amanda's interruption of his creative labor. A chair lying overthrown on the floor.*
> *Their gesticulating shadows are cast on the ceiling by the fiery glow.*

Amanda: You *will* hear more, you —

Tom: No, I won't hear more, I'm going out!

Amanda: You come right back in —

Tom: Out, out, out! Because I'm —

Amanda: Come back here, Tom Wingfield! I'm not through talking to you!

Tom: Oh, go —

Laura (desperately): Tom!

Amanda: You're going to listen, and no more insolence from you! I'm at the end of my patience! *(He comes back toward her.)*

Tom: What do you think I'm at? Aren't I supposed to have any patience to reach the end of, Mother? I know, I know. It seems unimportant to you, what I'm *doing* — what I *want* to do — having a little *difference* between them! You don't think that —

Amanda: I think you've been doing things that you're ashamed of. That's why you act like this. I don't believe that you go every night to the movies. Nobody goes to the movies night after night. Nobody in their right minds goes to the movies as often as you pretend to. People don't go to the movies at nearly midnight, and movies don't let out at two A.M. Come in stumbling. Muttering to yourself like a maniac! You get three hours' sleep and then go to work. Oh, I can picture the way you're doing down there. Moping, doping, because you're in no condition.

Tom (wildly): No, I'm in no condition!

Amanda: What right have you got to jeopardize your job? Jeopardize the security of us all? How do you think we'd manage if you were —

Tom: Listen! You think I'm crazy *about* the *warehouse!* *(He bends fiercely toward her slight figure.)* You think I'm in love with the Continental Shoemakers?

Mr. Lawrence: D. H. Lawrence (1885–1930), English poet and novelist who advocated sexual freedom.

You think I want to spend fifty-five *years* down there in that — *celotex interior!* with — *fluorescent — tubes!* Look! I'd rather somebody picked up a crowbar and battered out my brains — than go back mornings! I *go!* Every time you come in yelling that God damn *"Rise and Shine!" "Rise and Shine!"* I say to myself "How *lucky dead* people are!" But I get up. I *go!* For sixty-five dollars a month I give up all that I dream of doing and being *ever!* And you say self — *self's* all I ever think of. Why, listen, if self is what I thought of, Mother, I'd be where he is — ! *(Pointing to father's picture.)* As far as the system of transportation reaches! *(He starts past her. She grabs his arm.)* Don't grab at me, Mother!

Amanda: Where are you going?

Tom: I'm going to the *movies!*

Amanda: I don't believe that lie!

Tom (crouching toward her, overtowering her tiny figure. She backs away, gasping): I'm going to opium dens! Yes, opium dens, dens of vice and criminals' hangouts, Mother. I've joined the Hogan gang, I'm a hired assassin, I carry a tommy-gun in a violin case! I run a string of cat-houses in the Valley! They call me Killer, Killer Wingfield, I'm leading a double-life, a simple, honest warehouse worker by day, by night a dynamic *czar* of the *underworld,* Mother. I go to gambling casinos, I spin away fortunes on the roulette table! I wear a patch over one eye and a false mustache, sometimes I put on green whiskers. On those occasions they call me — *El Diablo!°* Oh, I could tell you things to make you sleepless! My enemies plan to dynamite this place. They're going to blow us all sky-high some night! I'll be glad, very happy, and so will you! You'll go up, up on a broomstick, over Blue Mountain with seventeen gentlemen callers! You ugly — babbling old — *witch.* . . .

(He goes through a series of violent, clumsy movements, seizing his overcoat, lunging to the door, pulling it fiercely open. The women watch him, aghast. His arm catches in the sleeve of the coat as he struggles to pull it on. For a moment he is pinioned by the bulky garment. With an outraged groan he tears the coat off again, splitting the shoulders of it, and hurls it across the room. It strikes against the shelf of Laura's glass collection, there is a tinkle of shattering glass. Laura cries out as if wounded.)

(Music legend: "The Glass Menagerie.")

Laura (shrilly): My glass! — menagerie. . . . *(She covers her face and turns away.)*

But Amanda is still stunned and stupefied by the "ugly witch" so that she barely notices this occurrence. Now she recovers her speech.

Amanda (in an awful voice): I won't speak to you — until you apologize! *(She crosses through portieres and draws them together behind her. Tom is left with Laura. Laura clings weakly to the mantel with her face averted. Tom stares at her stupidly for a moment. Then he crosses to shelf. Drops awkwardly to his knees to collect the fallen glass, glancing at Laura as if he would speak but couldn't.)*

"The Glass Menagerie" steals in as
   (The scene dims out.)

El Diablo: The devil (Spanish).

SCENE IV

The interior is dark. Faint light in the alley.

A deep-voiced bell in a church is tolling the hour of five as the scene commences.

Tom appears at the top of the alley. After each solemn boom of the bell in the tower, he shakes a little noise-maker or rattle as if to express the tiny spasm of man in contrast to the sustained power and dignity of the Almighty. This and the unsteadiness of his advance make it evident that he has been drinking.

As he climbs the few steps to the fire-escape landing light steals up inside. Laura appears in night-dress, observing Tom's empty bed in the front room.

Tom fishes in his pockets for the door-key, removing a motley assortment of articles in the search, including a perfect shower of movie-ticket stubs and an empty bottle. At last he finds the key, but just as he is about to insert it, it slips from his fingers. He strikes a match and crouches below the door.

Tom (bitterly): One crack — and it falls through!

Laura opens the door.

Laura: Tom! Tom, what are you doing?

Tom: Looking for a door-key.

Laura: Where have you been all this time?

Tom: I have been to the movies.

Laura: All this time at the movies?

Tom: There was a very long program. There was a Garbo picture and a Mickey Mouse and a travelogue and a newsreel and a preview of coming attractions. And there was an organ solo and a collection for the milk-fund — simultaneously — which ended up in a terrible fight between a fat lady and an usher!

Laura (innocently): Did you have to stay through everything?

Tom: Of course! And, oh, I forgot! There was a big stage show! The headliner on this stage show was Malvolio the Magician. He performed wonderful tricks, many of them, such as pouring water back and forth between pitchers. First it turned to wine and then it turned to beer and then it turned to whiskey. I know it was whiskey it finally turned into because he needed somebody to come up out of the audience to help him, and I came up — both shows! It was Kentucky Straight Bourbon. A very generous fellow, he gave souvenirs. *(He pulls from his back pocket a shimmering rainbow-colored scarf.)* He gave me this. This is his magic scarf. You can have it, Laura. You wave it over a canary cage and you get a bowl of gold-fish. You wave it over the gold-fish bowl and they fly away canaries. . . . But the wonderfullest trick of all was the coffin trick. We nailed him into a coffin and he got out of the coffin without removing one nail. *(He has come inside.)* There is a trick that would come in handy for me — get me out of this 2 by 4 situation! *(Flops onto bed and starts removing shoes.)*

Laura: Tom — Shhh!

Tom: What you shushing me for?

Laura: You'll wake up Mother.

Tom: Goody, goody! Pay 'er back for all those "Rise an' Shines." *(Lies down, groaning.)* You know it don't take much intelligence to get yourself into a nailed-up coffin, Laura. But who in hell ever got himself out of one without removing one nail?

As if in answer, the father's grinning photograph lights up.
    (Scene dims out.)
        Immediately following: The church bell is heard striking six. At the sixth stroke the alarm clock goes off in Amanda's room, and after a few moments we hear her calling: "Rise and Shine! Rise and Shine! Laura, go tell your brother to rise and shine!"

Tom (sitting up slowly): I'll rise — but I won't shine.

The light increases.

Amanda: Laura, tell your brother his coffee is ready.

Laura slips into front room.

Laura: Tom! it's nearly seven. Don't make Mother nervous. *(He stares at her stupidly. Beseechingly.)* Tom, speak to Mother this morning. Make up with her, apologize, speak to her!

Tom: She won't to me. It's her that started not speaking.

Laura: If you just say you're sorry she'll start speaking.

Tom: Her not speaking — is that such a tragedy?

Laura: Please — please!

Amanda (calling from kitchenette): Laura, are you going to do what I asked you to do, or do I have to get dressed and go out myself?

Laura: Going, going — soon as I get on my coat! *(She pulls on a shapeless felt hat with nervous, jerky movement, pleadingly glancing at Tom. Rushes awkwardly for coat. The coat is one of Amanda's, inaccurately made-over, the sleeves too short for Laura.)* Butter and what else?

Amanda (entering upstage): Just butter. Tell them to charge it.

Laura: Mother, they make such faces when I do that.

Amanda: Sticks and stones may break my bones, but the expression on Mr. Garfinkel's face won't harm us! Tell your brother his coffee is getting cold.

Laura (at door): Do what I asked you, will you, will you, Tom?

He looks sullenly away.

Amanda: Laura, go now or just don't go at all!

Laura (rushing out): Going — going! *(A second later she cries out. Tom springs up and crosses to the door. Amanda rushes anxiously in. Tom opens the door.)*

Tom: Laura?

Laura: I'm all right. I slipped, but I'm all right.

Amanda (peering anxiously after her): If anyone breaks a leg on those fire-escape steps, the landlord ought to be sued for every cent he possesses! *(She shuts door. Remembers she isn't speaking and returns to other room.)*

As Tom enters listlessly for his coffee, she turns her back to him and stands rigidly facing the window on the gloomy gray vault of the areaway. Its light on her face with its aged but childish features is cruelly sharp, satirical as a Daumier° print.
    (Music under: "Ave Maria.")

Daumier: Honoré Daumier (1808–1879), French caricaturist, lithographer, and painter who mercilessly satirized bourgeois society.

Tom glances sheepishly but sullenly at her averted figure and slumps at the table. The coffee is scalding hot; he sips it and gasps and spits it back in the cup. At his gasp, Amanda catches her breath and half turns. Then catches herself and turns back to window.

Tom blows on his coffee, glancing sidewise at his mother. She clears her throat. Tom clears his. He starts to rise. Sinks back down again, scratches his head, clears his throat again. Amanda coughs. Tom raises his cup in both hands to blow on it, his eyes staring over the rim of it at his mother for several moments. Then he slowly sets the cup down and awkwardly and hesitantly rises from the chair.

Tom (hoarsely): Mother. I — I apologize. Mother. *(Amanda draws a quick, shuddering breath. Her face works grotesquely. She breaks into childlike tears.)* I'm sorry for what I said, for everything that I said, I didn't mean it.

Amanda (sobbingly): My devotion has made me a witch and so I make myself hateful to my children!

Tom: No, you *don't.*

Amanda: I worry so much, don't sleep, it makes me nervous!

Tom (gently): I understand that.

Amanda: I've had to put up a solitary battle all these years. But you're my right-hand bower! Don't fall down, don't fail!

Tom (gently): I try, Mother.

Amanda (with great enthusiasm): Try and you will SUCCEED! *(The notion makes her breathless.)* Why, you — you're just *full* of natural endowments! Both of my children — they're *unusual* children! Don't you think I know it? I'm so — proud! Happy and — feel I've — so much to be thankful for but — Promise me one thing, son!

Tom: What, Mother?

Amanda: Promise, son, you'll — never be a drunkard!

Tom (turns to her grinning): I will never be a drunkard, Mother.

Amanda: That's what frightened me so, that you'd be drinking! Eat a bowl of Purina!

Tom: Just coffee, Mother.

Amanda: Shredded wheat biscuit?

Tom: No. No, Mother, just coffee.

Amanda: You can't put in a day's work on an empty stomach. You've got ten minutes — don't gulp! Drinking too-hot liquids makes cancer of the stomach. . . . Put cream in.

Tom: No, thank you.

Amanda: To cool it.

Tom: No! No, thank you, I want it black.

Amanda: I know, but it's not good for you. We have to do all that we can to build ourselves up. In these trying times we live in, all that we have to cling to is — each other. . . . That's why it's so important to — Tom, I — I sent out your sister so I could discuss something with you. If you hadn't spoken I would have spoken to you. *(Sits down.)*

Tom (gently): What is it, Mother, that you want to discuss?

Amanda: Laura!

Tom puts his cup down slowly.
(Legend on screen: "Laura.")
(Music: "The Glass Menagerie.")

Tom: — Oh. — Laura . . .

Amanda (touching his sleeve): You know how Laura is. So quiet but — still water runs deep! She notices things and I think she — broods about them. *(Tom looks up.)* A few days ago I came in and she was crying.

Tom: What about?

Amanda: You.

Tom: Me?

Amanda: She has an idea that you're not happy here.

Tom: What gave her that idea?

Amanda: What gives her any idea? However, you do act strangely. I — I'm not criticizing, understand *that!* I know your ambitions do not lie in the warehouse, that like everybody in the whole wide world — you've had to — make sacrifices, but — Tom — Tom — life's not easy, it calls for — Spartan endurance! There's so many things in my heart that I cannot describe to you! I've never told you but I — *loved* your father. . . .

Tom (gently): I know that, Mother.

Amanda: And you — when I see you taking after his ways! Staying out late — and — well, you *had* been drinking the night you were in that — terrifying condition! Laura says that you hate the apartment and that you go out nights to get away from it! Is that true, Tom?

Tom: No. You say there's so much in your heart that you can't describe to me. That's true of me, too. There's so much in my heart that I can't describe to *you!* So let's respect each other's —

Amanda: But, why — *why,* Tom — are you always so *restless?* Where do you go to, nights?

Tom: I — go to the movies.

Amanda: Why do you go to the movies so much, Tom?

Tom: I go to the movies because — I like adventure. Adventure is something I don't have much of at work, so I go to the movies.

Amanda: But, Tom, you go to the movies *entirely too much!*

Tom: I like a lot of adventure.

> *Amanda looks baffled, then hurt. As the familiar inquisition resumes he becomes hard and impatient again. Amanda slips back into her querulous attitude toward him.*
> *(Image on screen: Sailing vessel with Jolly Roger.)*

Amanda: Most young men find adventure in their careers.

Tom: Then most young men are not employed in a warehouse.

Amanda: The world is full of young men employed in warehouses and offices and factories.

Tom: Do all of them find adventure in their careers?

Amanda: They do or they do without it! Not everybody has a craze for adventure.

Tom: Man is by instinct a lover, a hunter, a fighter, and none of those instincts are given much play at the warehouse!

Amanda: Man is by instinct! Don't quote instinct to me! Instinct is something that people have got away from! It belongs to animals! Christian adults don't want it!

Tom: What do Christian adults want, then, Mother?

Amanda: Superior things! Things of the mind and the spirit! Only animals have to satisfy instincts! Surely your aims are somewhat higher than theirs! Than monkeys — pigs —

Tom: I reckon they're not.

Amanda: You're joking. However, that isn't what I wanted to discuss.

Tom (rising): I haven't much time.

Amanda (pushing his shoulders): Sit down.

Tom: You want me to punch in red° at the warehouse, Mother?

Amanda: You have five minutes. I want to talk about Laura.

(Legend: "Plans and Provisions.")

Tom: All right! What about Laura?

Amanda: We have to be making plans and provisions for her. She's older than you, two years, and nothing has happened. She just drifts along doing nothing. It frightens me terribly how she just drifts along.

Tom: I guess she's the type that people call home girls.

Amanda: There's no such type, and if there is, it's a pity! That is unless the home is hers, with a husband!

Tom: What?

Amanda: Oh, I can see the handwriting on the wall as plain as I see the nose in front of my face! It's terrifying! More and more you remind me of your father! He was out all hours without explanation—Then *left! Good-bye!* And me with the bag to hold. I saw that letter you got from the Merchant Marine. I know what you're dreaming of. I'm not standing here blindfolded. Very well, then. Then *do* it! But not till there's somebody to take your place.

Tom: What do you mean?

Amanda: I mean that as soon as Laura has got somebody to take care of her, married, a home of her own, independent—why, then you'll be free to go wherever you please, on land, on sea, whichever way the wind blows! But until that time you've got to look out for your sister. I don't say me because I'm old and don't matter! I say for your sister because she's young and dependent. I put her in business college—a dismal failure! Frightened her so it made her sick to her stomach. I took her over to the Young People's League at the church. Another fiasco. She spoke to nobody, nobody spoke to her. Now all she does is fool with those pieces of glass and play those worn-out records. What kind of a life is that for a girl to lead!

Tom: What can I do about it?

Amanda: Overcome selfishness! Self, self, self is all that you ever think of! *(Tom springs up and crosses to get his coat. It is ugly and bulky. He pulls on a cap with earmuffs.)* Where is your muffler? Put your wool muffler on! *(He snatches it angrily from the closet and tosses it around his neck and pulls both ends tight.)* Tom! I haven't said what I had in mind to ask you.

Tom: I'm too late to—

Amanda (catching his arms—very importunately. Then shyly.): Down at the warehouse, aren't there some—nice young men?

Tom: No!

Amanda: There *must* be—*some.*

Tom: Mother—

Gesture.

---

punch in red: Be late for work.

Amanda: Find out one that's clean-living—doesn't drink and—ask him out
for sister!

Tom: What?

Amanda: For *sister!* To *meet!* Get *acquainted!*

Tom (stamping to door): Oh, my *go-osh!*

Amanda: Will you? *(He opens door. Imploringly.)* Will you? *(He starts down.)* Will
you? *Will* you, dear?

Tom (calling back): YES!

> Amanda closes the door hesitantly and with a troubled but faintly hopeful expres-
> sion.
>> *(Screen image:* Glamour *magazine cover.)*
>> *Spot Amanda at phone.*

Amanda: Ella Cartwright? This is Amanda Wingfield! How are you, honey?
How is that kidney condition? *(Count five.)* Horrors! *(Count five.)* You're a
Christian martyr, yes, honey, that's what you are, a Christian martyr! Well,
I just happened to notice in my little red book that your subscription to
the *Companion* has just run out! I knew that you wouldn't want to miss
out on the wonderful serial starting in this new issue. It's by Bessie Mae
Hopper, the first thing she's written since *Honeymoon for Three.* Wasn't
that a strange and interesting story? Well, this one is even lovelier, I
believe. It has a sophisticated society background. It's all about the horsey
set on Long Island!

(Fade out.)

SCENE V

> *(Legend on screen: "Annunciation.") Fade with music.*
> It is early dusk of a spring evening. Supper has just been finished in the Wing-
> field apartment. Amanda and Laura in light-colored dresses are removing dishes
> from the table, in the upstage area, which is shadowy, their movements formalized
> almost as a dance or ritual, their moving forms as pale and silent as moths.
> Tom, in white shirt and trousers, rises from the table and crosses toward the
> fire-escape.

Amanda (as he passes her): Son, will you do me a favor?

Tom: What?

Amanda: Comb your hair! You look so pretty when your hair is combed! *(Tom
slouches on sofa with evening paper. Enormous caption "Franco Triumphs."°)*
There is only one respect in which I would like you to emulate your father.

Tom: What respect is that?

Amanda: The care he always took of his appearance. He never allowed himself
to look untidy. *(He throws down the paper and crosses to fire-escape.)* Where are
you going?

Tom: I'm going out to smoke.

"Franco Triumphs": In January 1939 the Republican forces of Francisco Franco (1892–1975)
defeated the Loyalists, ending the Spanish Civil War.

Amanda: You smoke too much. A pack a day at fifteen cents a pack. How much would that amount to in a month? Thirty times fifteen is how much, Tom? Figure it out and you will be astounded at what you could save. Enough to give you a night-school course in accounting at Washington U! Just think what a wonderful thing that would be for you, son!

Tom is unmoved by the thought.

Tom: I'd rather smoke. (*He steps out on landing, letting the screen door slam.*)

Amanda (sharply): I know! That's the tragedy of it. . . . (*Alone, she turns to look at her husband's picture.*)

(*Dance music: "All the World Is Waiting for the Sunrise!"*)

Tom (to the audience): Across the alley from us was the Paradise Dance Hall. On evenings in spring the windows and doors were open and the music came outdoors. Sometimes the lights were turned out except for a large glass sphere that hung from the ceiling. It would turn slowly about and filter the dusk with delicate rainbow colors. Then the orchestra played a waltz or a tango, something that had a slow and sensuous rhythm. Couples would come outside, to the relative privacy of the alley. You could see them kissing behind ash-pits and telephone poles. This was the compensation for lives that passed like mine, without any change or adventure. Adventure and change were imminent in this year. They were waiting around the corner for all these kids. Suspended in the mist over the Berchtesgaden,° caught in the folds of Chamberlain's° umbrella—In Spain there was Guernica! But here there was only hot swing music and liquor, dance halls, bars, and movies, and sex that hung in the gloom like a chandelier and flooded the world with brief, deceptive rainbows. . . . All the world was waiting for bombardments!

Amanda turns from the picture and comes outside.

Amanda (sighing): A fire-escape landing's a poor excuse for a porch. (*She spreads a newspaper on a step and sits down, gracefully and demurely as if she were settling into a swing on a Mississippi veranda.*) What are you looking at?

Tom: The moon.

Amanda: Is there a moon this evening?

Tom: It's rising over Garfinkel's Delicatessen.

Amanda: So it is! A little silver slipper of a moon. Have you made a wish on it yet?

Tom: Um-hum.

Amanda: What did you wish for?

Tom: That's a secret.

Amanda: A secret, huh? Well, I won't tell mine either. I will be just as mysterious as you.

Tom: I bet I can guess what yours is.

Amanda: Is my head so transparent?

Tom: You're not a sphinx.

Berchtesgaden: A resort in the German Alps where Adolf Hitler had a heavily protected villa. *Chamberlain:* Neville Chamberlain (1869–1940), British prime minister who sought to avoid war with Hitler through a policy of appeasement.

Amanda: No, I don't have secrets. I'll tell you what I wished for on the moon. Success and happiness for my precious children! I wish for that whenever there's a moon, and when there isn't a moon, I wish for it, too.

Tom: I thought perhaps you wished for a gentleman caller.

Amanda: Why do you say that?

Tom: Don't you remember asking me to fetch one?

Amanda: I remember suggesting that it would be nice for your sister if you brought home some nice young man from the warehouse. I think I've made that suggestion more than once.

Tom: Yes, you have made it repeatedly.

Amanda: Well?

Tom: We are going to have one.

Amanda: What?

Tom: A gentleman caller!

> *(The Annunciation is celebrated with music.)*
>> Amanda rises.
>> *(Image on screen: Caller with bouquet.)*

Amanda: You mean you have asked some nice young man to come over?

Tom: Yep. I've asked him to dinner.

Amanda: You really did?

Tom: I did!

Amanda: You did, and did he — *accept?*

Tom: He did!

Amanda: Well, well — well, well! That's — lovely!

Tom: I thought that you would be pleased.

Amanda: It's definite, then?

Tom: Very definite.

Amanda: Soon?

Tom: Very soon.

Amanda: For heaven's sake, stop putting on and tell me some things, will you?

Tom: What things do you want me to tell you?

Amanda: Naturally I would like to know when he's *coming!*

Tom: He's coming tomorrow.

Amanda: *Tomorrow?*

Tom: Yep. Tomorrow.

Amanda: But, Tom!

Tom: Yes, Mother?

Amanda: Tomorrow gives me no time!

Tom: Time for what?

Amanda: Preparations! Why didn't you phone me at once, as soon as you asked him, the minute that he accepted? Then, don't you see, I could have been getting ready!

Tom: You don't have to make any fuss.

Amanda: Oh, Tom, Tom, Tom, of course I have to make a fuss! I want things nice, not sloppy! Not thrown together. I'll certainly have to do some fast thinking, won't I?

Tom: I don't see why you have to think at all.

Amanda: You just don't know. We can't have a gentleman caller in a pig-sty! All my wedding silver has to be polished, the monogrammed table linen ought to be laundered! The windows have to be washed and fresh curtains put up. And how about clothes? We have to *wear* something, don't we?

Tom: Mother, this boy is no one to make a fuss over!

Amanda: Do you realize he's the first young man we've introduced to your sister? It's terrible, dreadful, disgraceful that poor little sister has never received a single gentleman caller! Tom, come inside! *(She opens the screen door.)*

Tom: What for?

Amanda: I want to ask you some things.

Tom: If you're going to make such a fuss, I'll call it off, I'll tell him not to come.

Amanda: You certainly won't do anything of the kind. Nothing offends people worse than broken engagements. It simply means I'll have to work like a Turk! We won't be brilliant, but we'll pass inspection. Come on inside. *(Tom follows, groaning.)* Sit down.

Tom: Any particular place you would like me to sit?

Amanda: Thank heavens I've got that new sofa! I'm also making payments on a floor lamp I'll have sent out! And put the chintz covers on, they'll brighten things up! Of course I'd hoped to have these walls re-papered. . . . What is the young man's name?

Tom: His name is O'Connor.

Amanda: That, of course, means fish—tomorrow is Friday! I'll have that salmon loaf—with Durkee's dressing! What does he do? He works at the warehouse?

Tom: Of course! How else would I—

Amanda: Tom, he—doesn't drink?

Tom: Why do you ask me that?

Amanda: Your father *did!*

Tom: Don't get started on that!

Amanda: He *does* drink, then?

Tom: Not that I know of!

Amanda: Make sure, be certain! The last thing I want for my daughter's a boy who drinks!

Tom: Aren't you being a little premature? Mr. O'Connor has not yet appeared on the scene!

Amanda: But will tomorrow. To meet your sister, and what do I know about his character? Nothing! Old maids are better off than wives of drunkards!

Tom: Oh, my God!

Amanda: Be still!

Tom (leaning forward to whisper): Lots of fellows meet girls whom they don't marry!

Amanda: Oh, talk sensibly, Tom—and don't be sarcastic! *(She has gotten a hairbrush.)*

Tom: What are you doing?

Amanda: I'm brushing that cow-lick down! What is this young man's position at the warehouse?

Tom (submitting grimly to the brush and the interrogation): This young man's position is that of a shipping clerk, Mother.

Amanda: Sounds to me like a fairly responsible job, the sort of a job *you* would be in if you just had more *get-up*. What is his salary? Have you got any idea?

Tom: I would judge it to be approximately eighty-five dollars a month.

Amanda: Well — not princely, but —

Tom: Twenty more than I make.

Amanda: Yes, how well I know! But for a family man, eighty-five dollars a month is not much more than you can just get by on. . . .

Tom: Yes, but Mr. O'Connor is not a family man.

Amanda: He might be, mightn't he? Some time in the future?

Tom: I see. Plans and provisions.

Amanda: You are the only young man that I know of who ignores the fact that the future becomes the present, the present the past, and the past turns into everlasting regret if you don't plan for it!

Tom: I will think that over and see what I can make of it.

Amanda: Don't be supercilious with your mother! Tell me some more about this — what do you call him?

Tom: James D. O'Connor. The D. is for Delaney.

Amanda: Irish on *both* sides! *Gracious!* And doesn't drink?

Tom: Shall I call him up and ask him right this minute?

Amanda: The only way to find out about those things is to make discreet inquiries at the proper moment. When I was a girl in Blue Mountain and it was suspected that a young man drank, the girl whose attentions he had been receiving, if any girl *was,* would sometimes speak to the minister of his church, or rather her father would if her father was living, and sort of feel him out on the young man's character. That is the way such things are discreetly handled to keep a young woman from making a tragic mistake!

Tom: Then how did you happen to make a tragic mistake?

Amanda: That innocent look of your father's had everyone fooled! He *smiled —* the world was *enchanted!* No girl can do worse than put herself at the mercy of a handsome appearance! I hope that Mr. O'Connor is not too good-looking.

Tom: No, he's not too good-looking. He's covered with freckles and hasn't too much of a nose.

Amanda: He's not right-down homely, though?

Tom: Not right-down homely. Just medium homely, I'd say.

Amanda: Character's what to look for in a man.

Tom: That's what I've always said, Mother.

Amanda: You've never said anything of the kind and I suspect you would never give it a thought.

Tom: Don't be suspicious of me.

Amanda: At least I hope he's the type that's up and coming.

Tom: I think he really goes in for self-improvement.

Amanda: What reason have you to think so?

Tom: He goes to night school.

Amanda (beaming): Splendid! What does he do, I mean study?

Tom: Radio engineering and public speaking!

Amanda: Then he has visions of being advanced in the world! Any young man who studies public speaking is aiming to have an executive job some day! And radio engineering? A thing for the future! Both of these facts are very illuminating. Those are the sort of things that a mother should know concerning any young man who comes to call on her daughter. Seriously or — not.

Tom: One little warning. He doesn't know about Laura. I didn't let on that we had dark ulterior motives. I just said, why don't you come have dinner with us? He said okay and that was the whole conversation.

Amanda: I bet it was! You're eloquent as an oyster. However, he'll know about Laura when he gets here. When he sees how lovely and sweet and pretty she is, he'll thank his lucky stars he was asked to dinner.

Tom: Mother, you mustn't expect too much of Laura.

Amanda: What do you mean?

Tom: Laura seems all those things to you and me because she's ours and we love her. We don't even notice she's crippled any more.

Amanda: Don't say crippled! You know that I never allow that word to be used!

Tom: But face facts, Mother. She is and — that's not all —

Amanda: What do you mean "not all"?

Tom: Laura is very different from other girls.

Amanda: I think the difference is all to her advantage.

Tom: Not quite all — in the eyes of others — strangers — she's terribly shy and lives in a world of her own and those things make her seem a little peculiar to people outside the house.

Amanda: Don't say peculiar.

Tom: Face the facts. She is.

> (*The dance-hall music changes to a tango that has a minor and somewhat ominous tone.*)

Amanda: In what way is she peculiar — may I ask?

Tom (gently): She lives in a world of her own — a world of — little glass ornaments, Mother. . . . (*Gets up. Amanda remains holding brush, looking at him, troubled.*) She plays old phonograph records and — that's about all — (*He glances at himself in the mirror and crosses to door.*)

Amanda (sharply): Where are you going?

Tom: I'm going to the movies. (*Out screen door.*)

Amanda: Not to the movies, every night to the movies! (*Follows quickly to screen door.*) I don't believe you always go to the movies! (*He is gone. Amanda looks worriedly after him for a moment. Then vitality and optimism return and she turns from the door. Crossing to portieres.*) Laura! Laura! (*Laura answers from kitchenette.*)

Laura: Yes, Mother.

Amanda: Let those dishes go and come in front! (*Laura appears with dish towel. Gaily.*) Laura, come here and make a wish on the moon!

Laura (entering): Moon — moon?

Amanda: A little silver slipper of a moon. Look over your left shoulder, Laura, and make a wish! (*Laura looks faintly puzzled as if called out of sleep. Amanda seizes her shoulders and turns her at angle by the door.*) Now! Now, darling, *wish!*

Laura: What shall I wish for, Mother?

Amanda (her voice trembling and her eyes suddenly filling with tears): Happiness! Good Fortune!

> *The violin rises and the stage dims out.*

SCENE VI

(Image: High-school hero.)

Tom: And so the following evening I brought Jim home to dinner. I had known Jim slightly in high school. In high school Jim was a hero. He had tremendous Irish good nature and vitality with the scrubbed and polished look of white chinaware. He seemed to move in a continual spotlight. He was a star in basketball, captain of the debating club, president of the senior class and the glee club and he sang the male lead in the annual light operas. He was always running or bounding, never just walking. He seemed always at the point of defeating the law of gravity. He was shooting with such velocity through his adolescence that you would logically expect him to arrive at nothing short of the White House by the time he was thirty. But Jim apparently ran into more interference after his graduation from Soldan. His speed had definitely slowed. Six years after he left high school he was holding a job that wasn't much better than mine.

(Image: Clerk.)

He was the only one at the warehouse with whom I was on friendly terms. I was valuable to him as someone who could remember his former glory, who had seen him win basketball games and the silver cup in debating. He knew of my secret practice of retiring to a cabinet of the washroom to work on poems when business was slack in the warehouse. He called me Shakespeare. And while the other boys in the warehouse regarded me with suspicious hostility, Jim took a humorous attitude toward me. Gradually his attitude affected the others, their hostility wore off, and they also began to smile at me as people smile at an oddly fashioned dog who trots across their paths at some distance.

I knew that Jim and Laura had known each other at Soldan, and I had heard Laura speak admiringly of his voice. I didn't know if Jim remembered her or not. In high school Laura had been as unobtrusive as Jim had been astonishing. If he did remember Laura, it was not as my sister, for when I asked him to dinner, he grinned and said, "You know, Shakespeare, I never thought of you as having folks!"

He was about to discover that I did. . . .

(Light upstage.)

(Legend on screen: "The Accent of a Coming Foot.")

Friday evening. It is about five o'clock of a late spring evening which comes "scattering poems in the sky."

A delicate lemony light is in the Wingfield apartment.

Amanda has worked like a Turk in preparation for the gentleman caller. The results are astonishing. The new floor lamp with its rose-silk shade is in place, a colored paper lantern conceals the broken light fixture in the ceiling, new billowing white curtains are at the windows, chintz covers are on chairs and sofa, a pair of new sofa pillows make their initial appearance.

Open boxes and tissue paper are scattered on the floor.

Laura stands in the middle with lifted arms while Amanda crouches before her, adjusting the hem of the new dress, devout and ritualistic. The dress is colored and designed by memory. The arrangement of Laura's hair is changed; it is softer and more becoming. A fragile, unearthly prettiness has come out in Laura: she is like a piece of translucent glass touched by light, given a momentary radiance, not actual, not lasting.

Amanda (impatiently): Why are you trembling?

Laura: Mother, you've made me so nervous!

Amanda: How have I made you nervous?

Laura: By all this fuss! You make it seem so important!

Amanda: I don't understand you, Laura. You couldn't be satisfied with just sitting home, and yet whenever I try to arrange something for you, you seem to resist it. *(She gets up.)* Now take a look at yourself. No, wait! Wait just a moment—I have an idea!

Laura: What is it now?

Amanda produces two powder puffs which she wraps in handkerchiefs and stuffs in Laura's bosom.

Laura: Mother, what are you doing?

Amanda: They call them "Gay Deceivers"!

Laura: I won't wear them!

Amanda: You will!

Laura: Why should I?

Amanda: Because, to be painfully honest, your chest is flat.

Laura: You make it seem like we were setting a trap.

Amanda: All pretty girls are a trap, a pretty trap, and men expect them to be. *(Legend: "A Pretty Trap.")* Now look at yourself, young lady. This is the prettiest you will ever be! I've got to fix myself now! You're going to be surprised by your mother's appearance! *(She crosses through portieres, humming gaily.)*

Laura moves slowly to the long mirror and stares solemnly at herself.
  A wind blows the white curtains inward in a slow, graceful motion and with a faint, sorrowful sighing.

Amanda (off stage): It isn't dark enough yet. *(She turns slowly before the mirror with a troubled look).*

(Legend on screen: "This Is My Sister: Celebrate Her with Strings!" Music.)

Amanda (laughing, off): I'm going to show you something. I'm going to make a spectacular appearance!

Laura: What is it, Mother?

Amanda: Possess your soul in patience—you will see! Something I've resurrected from that old trunk! Styles haven't changed so terribly much after all. . . . *(She parts the portieres.)* Now just look at your mother! *(She wears a girlish frock of yellowed voile with a blue silk sash. She carries a bunch of jonquils—the legend of her youth is nearly revived. Feverishly.)* This is the dress in which I led the cotillion. Won the cakewalk twice at Sunset Hill, wore one spring to the Governor's ball in Jackson! See how I sashayed around the ballroom, Laura? *(She raises her skirt and does a mincing step around the room.)* I wore it on Sundays for my gentlemen callers! I had it on the day I met your father—I had malaria fever all that spring. The change of climate from East Tennessee to the Delta—weakened resistance—I had a little temperature all the time—not enough to be serious—just enough to make me restless and giddy! Invitations poured in — parties all over the Delta! — "Stay in bed," said Mother, "you have fever!" — but I just wouldn't. — I took quinine but kept on going, going! — Evenings, dances! — Afternoons, long, long rides! Picnics — lovely! — So lovely, that country in May. — All lacy with dogwood, literally flooded with jonquils! — That was the spring I had the craze for jonquils. Jonquils became an absolute obsession. Mother said, "Honey, there's no more room for jonquils." And still I kept bringing in more jonquils. Whenever, wherever I saw them, I'd say, "Stop! Stop! I see jonquils!" I made the young men help me gather the jonquils! It was a joke, Amanda and her jonquils! Finally there were no more vases to hold them, every available space was filled with jonquils. No vases to hold them? All right, I'll hold them myself! And then I — *(She stops in front of the picture.) (Music.)* met your father! Malaria fever and jonquils and then — this — boy. . . . *(She switches on the rose-colored lamp.)* I hope they get here before it starts to rain. *(She crosses upstage and places the jonquils in bowl on table.)* I gave your brother a little extra change so he and Mr. O'Connor could take the service car home.

Laura (with altered look): What did you say his name was?

Amanda: O'Connor.

Laura: What is his first name?

Amanda: I don't remember. Oh, yes, I do. It was — Jim!

Laura sways slightly and catches hold of a chair.
   (Legend on screen: "Not Jim!")

Laura (faintly): Not — Jim!

Amanda: Yes, that was it, it was Jim! I've never known a Jim that wasn't nice!

(Music: Ominous.)

Laura: Are you sure his name is Jim O'Connor?

Amanda: Yes. Why?

Laura: Is he the one that Tom used to know in high school?

Amanda: He didn't say so. I think he just got to know him at the warehouse.

Laura: There was a Jim O'Connor we both knew in high school — *(Then, with effort.)* If that is the one that Tom is bringing to dinner — you'll have to excuse me, I won't come to the table.

Amanda: What sort of nonsense is this?

Laura: You asked me once if I'd ever liked a boy. Don't you remember I showed you this boy's picture?

Amanda: You mean the boy you showed me in the year-book?

Laura: Yes, that boy.

Amanda: Laura, Laura, were you in love with that boy?

Laura: I don't know, Mother. All I know is I couldn't sit at the table if it was him!

Amanda: It won't be him! It isn't the least bit likely. But whether it is or not, you will come to the table. You will not be excused.

Laura: I'll have to be, Mother.

Amanda: I don't intend to humor your silliness, Laura. I've had too much from you and your brother, both! So just sit down and compose yourself till they come. Tom has forgotten his key so you'll have to let them in, when they arrive.

Laura (panicky): Oh, Mother — *you* answer the door!
Amanda (lightly): I'll be in the kitchen — busy!
Laura: Oh, Mother, please answer the door, don't make me do it!
Amanda (crossing into kitchenette): I've got to fix the dressing for the salmon.
    Fuss, fuss — silliness! — over a gentleman caller!

> *Door swings shut. Laura is left alone.*
>   (Legend: "Terror!")
>   *She utters a low moan and turns off the lamp — sits stiffly on the edge of the*
> *sofa, knotting her fingers together.*
>   (Legend on screen: "The Opening of a Door!")
>   *Tom and Jim appear on the fire-escape steps and climb to landing. Hearing*
> *their approach, Laura rises with a panicky gesture. She retreats to the portieres.*
> *The doorbell. Laura catches her breath and touches her throat. Low drums.*

Amanda (calling): Laura, sweetheart! The door!

> *Laura stares at it without moving.*

Jim: I think we just beat the rain.
Tom: Uh-huh. *(He rings again, nervously. Jim whistles and fishes for a cigarette.)*
Amanda (very, very gaily): Laura, that is your brother and Mr. O'Connor! Will
    you let them in, darling?

> *Laura crosses toward kitchenette door.*

Laura (breathlessly): Mother — you go to the door!

> *Amanda steps out of kitchenette and stares furiously at Laura. She points imperi-*
> *ously at the door.*

Laura: Please, please!
Amanda (in a fierce whisper): What is the matter with you, you silly thing?
Laura (desperately): Please, you answer it, *please!*
Amanda: I told you I wasn't going to humor you, Laura. Why have you chosen
    this moment to lose your mind?
Laura: Please, please, please, you go!
Amanda: You'll have to go to the door because I can't!
Laura (despairingly): I can't either!
Amanda: Why?
Laura: I'm *sick!*
Amanda: I'm sick, too — of your nonsense! Why can't you and your brother be
    normal people? Fantastic whims and behavior! *(Tom gives a long ring.)* Pre-
    posterous goings on! Can you give me one reason — *(Calls out lyrically.)*
    COMING! JUST ONE SECOND! — why should you be afraid to open a door?
    Now you answer it, Laura!
Laura: Oh, oh, oh . . . *(She returns through the portieres. Darts to the Victrola and*
    winds it frantically and turns it on.)
Amanda: Laura Wingfield, you march right to that door!
Laura: Yes — yes, Mother!

> *A faraway, scratchy rendition of "Dardanella" softens the air and gives her*
> *strength to move through it. She slips to the door and draws it cautiously open.*
> *Tom enters with the caller, Jim O'Connor.*

Tom: Laura, this is Jim. Jim, this is my sister, Laura.

Jim (stepping inside): I didn't know that Shakespeare had a sister!

Laura (retreating stiff and trembling from the door): How — how do you do?

Jim (heartily extending his hand): Okay!

> *Laura touches it hesitantly with hers.*

Jim: Your hand's *cold,* Laura!

Laura: Yes, well — I've been playing the Victrola . . .

Jim: Must have been playing classical music on it! You ought to play a little hot swing music to warm you up!

Laura: Excuse me — I haven't finished playing the Victrola . . .

> *She turns awkwardly and hurries into the front room. She pauses a second by the Victrola. Then catches her breath and darts through the portieres like a frightened deer.*

Jim (grinning): What was the matter?

Tom: Oh — with Laura? Laura is — terribly shy.

Jim: Shy, huh? It's unusual to meet a shy girl nowadays. I don't believe you ever mentioned you had a sister.

Tom: Well, now you know. I have one. Here is the *Post Dispatch.* You want a piece of it?

Jim: Uh-huh.

Tom: What piece? The comics?

Jim: Sports! *(Glances at it.)* Ole Dizzy Dean is on his bad behavior.

Tom (disinterest): Yeah? *(Lights cigarette and crosses back to fire-escape door.)*

Jim: Where are *you* going?

Tom: I'm going out on the terrace.

Jim (goes after him): You know, Shakespeare — I'm going to sell you a bill of goods!

Tom: What goods?

Jim: A course I'm taking.

Tom: Huh?

Jim: In public speaking! You and me, we're not the warehouse type.

Tom: Thanks — that's good news. But what has public speaking got to do with it?

Jim: It fits you for — executive positions!

Tom: Awww.

Jim: I tell you it's done a helluva lot for me.

> *(Image: Executive at desk.)*

Tom: In what respect?

Jim: In every! Ask yourself what is the difference between you an' me and men in the office down front? Brains? — No! — Ability? — No! Then what? Just one little thing —

Tom: What is that one little thing?

Jim: Primarily it amounts to — social poise! Being able to square up to people and hold your own on any social level!

Amanda (off stage): Tom?

Tom: Yes, Mother?

Amanda: Is that you and Mr. O'Connor?

Tom: Yes, Mother.

Amanda: Well, you just make yourselves comfortable in there.

Tom: Yes, Mother.

Amanda: Ask Mr. O'Connor if he would like to wash his hands.

Jim: Aw — no — no — thank you — I took care of that at the warehouse. Tom —

Tom: Yes?

Jim: Mr. Mendoza was speaking to me about you.

Tom: Favorably?

Jim: What do you think?

Tom: Well —

Jim: You're going to be out of a job if you don't wake up.

Tom: I am waking up —

Jim: You show no signs.

Tom: The signs are interior.

> *(Image on screen: The sailing vessel with Jolly Roger again.)*

Tom: I'm planning to change. *(He leans over the rail speaking with quiet exhilaration. The incandescent marquees and signs of the first-run movie houses light his face from across the alley. He looks like a voyager.)* I'm right at the point of committing myself to a future that doesn't include the warehouse and Mr. Mendoza or even a night-school course in public speaking.

Jim: What are you gassing about?

Tom: I'm tired of the movies.

Jim: Movies!

Tom: Yes, movies! Look at them — *(A wave toward the marvels of Grand Avenue.)* All of those glamorous people — having adventures — hogging it all, gobbling the whole thing up! You know what happens? People go to the *movies* instead of *moving!* Hollywood characters are supposed to have all the adventures for everybody in America, while everybody in America sits in a dark room and watches them have them! Yes, until there's a war. That's when adventure becomes available to the masses! *Everyone's* dish, not only Gable's! Then the people in the dark room come out of the dark room to have some adventures themselves — Goody, goody — It's our turn now, to go to the South Sea Island — to make a safari — to be exotic, far-off — But I'm not patient. I don't want to wait till then. I'm tired of the *movies* and I am *about* to *move!*

Jim (incredulously): Move?

Tom: Yes.

Jim: When?

Tom: Soon!

Jim: Where? Where?

> *(Theme three: Music seems to answer the question, while Tom thinks it over. He searches among his pockets.)*

Tom: I'm starting to boil inside. I know I seem dreamy, but inside — well, I'm boiling! Whenever I pick up a shoe, I shudder a little thinking how short life is and what I am doing! — Whatever that means. I know it doesn't mean shoes — except as something to wear on a traveler's feet! *(Finds paper.)* Look —

Jim: What?

Tom: I'm a member.

Jim (reading): The Union of Merchant Seamen.

Tom: I paid my dues this month, instead of the light bill.

Jim: You will regret it when they turn the lights off.

Tom: I won't be here.

Jim: How about your mother?

Tom: I'm like my father. The bastard son of a bastard! See how he grins? And he's been absent going on sixteen years!

Jim: You're just talking, you drip. How does your mother feel about it?

Tom: Shhh — Here comes Mother! Mother is not acquainted with my plans!

Amanda (enters portieres): Where are you all?

Tom: On the terrace, Mother.

> *They start inside. She advances to them. Tom is distinctly shocked at her appear-ance. Even Jim blinks a little. He is making his first contact with girlish Southern vivacity and in spite of the night-school course in public speaking is somewhat thrown off the beam by the unexpected outlay of social charm.*
>
> *Certain responses are attempted by Jim but are swept aside by Amanda's gay laughter and chatter. Tom is embarrassed but after the first shock Jim reacts very warmly. Grins and chuckles, is altogether won over.*
>
> *(Image: Amanda as a girl.)*

Amanda (coyly smiling, shaking her girlish ringlets): Well, well, well, so this is Mr. O'Connor. Introductions entirely unnecessary. I've heard so much about you from my boy. I finally said to him, Tom — good gracious! — why don't you bring this paragon to supper? I'd like to meet this nice young man at the warehouse! — Instead of just hearing him sing your praises so much! I don't know why my son is so stand-offish — that's not Southern behavior! Let's sit down and — I think we could stand a little more air in here! Tom, leave the door open. I felt a nice fresh breeze a moment ago. Where has it gone? Mmm, so warm already! And not quite summer, even. We're going to burn up when summer really gets started. However, we're having — we're having a very light supper. I think light things are better fo' this time of year. The same as light clothes are. Light clothes an' light food are what warm weather calls fo'. You know our blood gets so thick during th' winter — it takes a while fo' us to *adjust* ou'selves! — when the season changes. . . . It's come so quick this year. I wasn't prepared. All of a sudden — heavens! Already summer! — I ran to the trunk an' pulled out this light dress — Terribly old! Historical almost! But feels so good — so good an' co-ol, y'know. . . .

Tom: Mother —

Amanda: Yes, honey?

Tom: How about — supper?

Amanda: Honey, you go ask Sister if supper is ready! You know that Sister is in full charge of supper! Tell her you hungry boys are waiting for it. *(To Jim.)* Have you met Laura?

Jim: She —

Amanda: Let you in? Oh, good, you've met already! It's rare for a girl as sweet an' pretty as Laura to be domestic! But Laura is, thank heavens, not only pretty but also very domestic. I'm not at all. I never was a bit. I never could make a thing but angel-food cake. Well, in the South we had so many ser-vants. Gone, gone, gone. All vestiges of gracious living! Gone completely! I wasn't prepared for what the future brought me. All of my gentlemen callers were sons of planters and so of course I assumed that I would be married to one and raise my family on a large piece of land with plenty of servants. But man proposes — and woman accepts the proposal! — To vary that old, old saying a little bit — I married no planter! I married a man who worked for the telephone company! — that gallantly smiling gentleman over there! *(Points to the picture.)* A telephone man who — fell in love with long distance! — Now he travels and I don't even know where! — But what am I going on for about my — tribulations! Tell me yours — I hope you don't have any! Tom?

Tom (returning): Yes, Mother?

Amanda: Is supper nearly ready?

Tom: It looks to me like supper is on the table.

Amanda: Let me look — *(She rises prettily and looks through portieres.)* Oh, lovely — But where is Sister?

Tom: Laura is not feeling well and she says that she thinks she'd better not come to the table.

Amanda: What? — Nonsense! — Laura? Oh, Laura!

Laura (off stage, faintly): Yes, Mother.

Amanda: You really must come to the table. We won't be seated until you come to the table! Come in, Mr. O'Connor. You sit over there and I'll — Laura? Laura Wingfield! You're keeping us waiting, honey! We can't say grace until you come to the table!

> *The back door is pushed weakly open and Laura comes in. She is obviously quite faint, her lips trembling, her eyes wide and staring. She moves unsteadily toward the table.*
>
> *(Legend: "Terror!")*
>
> *Outside a summer storm is coming abruptly. The white curtains billow inward at the windows and there is a sorrowful murmur and deep blue dusk.*
>
> *Laura suddenly stumbles — She catches at a chair with a faint moan.*

Tom: Laura!

Amanda: Laura! *(There is a clap of thunder.)* *(Legend: "Ah!")* *(Despairingly.)* Why, Laura, you *are* sick, darling! Tom, help your sister into the living room, dear! Sit in the living room, Laura — rest on the sofa. Well! *(To the gentleman caller.)* Standing over the hot stove made her ill! — I told her that it was just too warm this evening, but — *(Tom comes back in. Laura is on the sofa.)* Is Laura all right now?

Tom: Yes.

Amanda: What *is* that? Rain? A nice cool rain has come up! *(She gives the gentleman caller a frightened look.)* I think we may — have grace — now . . . *(Tom looks at her stupidly.)* Tom, honey — you say grace!

Tom: Oh . . . "For these and all thy mercies —" *(They bow their heads, Amanda stealing a nervous glance at Jim. In the living room Laura, stretched on the sofa, clenches her hand to her lips, to hold back a shuddering sob.)* God's Holy Name be praised —

(The scene dims out.)

SCENE VII

A Souvenir

Half an hour later. Dinner is just being finished in the upstage area, which is concealed by the drawn portieres.

As the curtain rises Laura is still huddled upon the sofa, her feet drawn under her, her head resting on a pale blue pillow, her eyes wide and mysteriously watchful. The new floor lamp with its shade of rose-colored silk gives a soft, becoming light to her face, bringing out the fragile, unearthly prettiness which usually escapes attention. There is a steady murmur of rain, but it is slackening and stops soon after the scene begins; the air outside becomes pale and luminous as the moon breaks out.

A moment after the curtain rises, the lights in both rooms flicker and go out.

Jim: Hey, there, Mr. Light Bulb!

Amanda laughs nervously.
(Legend: "Suspension of a Public Service.")

Amanda: Where was Moses when the lights went out? Ha-ha. Do you know the answer to that one, Mr. O'Connor?
Jim: No, Ma'am, what's the answer?
Amanda: In the dark! *(Jim laughs appreciatively.)* Everybody sit still. I'll light the candles. Isn't it lucky we have them on the table? Where's a match? Which of you gentlemen can provide a match?
Jim: Here.
Amanda: Thank you, sir.
Jim: Not at all, Ma'am!
Amanda: I guess the fuse has burnt out. Mr. O'Connor, can you tell a burnt-out fuse? I know I can't and Tom is a total loss when it comes to mechanics. *(Sound: Getting up: Voices recede a little to kitchenette.)* Oh, be careful you don't bump into something. We don't want our gentleman caller to break his neck. Now wouldn't that be a fine howdy-do?
Jim: Ha-ha! Where is the fuse-box?
Amanda: Right here next to the stove. Can you see anything?
Jim: Just a minute.
Amanda: Isn't electricity a mysterious thing? Wasn't it Benjamin Franklin who tied a key to a kite? We live in such a mysterious universe, don't we? Some people say that science clears up all the mysteries for us. In my opinion it only creates more! Have you found it yet?
Jim: No, Ma'am. All these fuses look okay to me.
Amanda: Tom!
Tom: Yes, Mother?
Amanda: That light bill I gave you several days ago. The one I told you we got the notices about?
Tom: Oh. — Yeah.

(Legend: "Ha!")

Amanda: You didn't neglect to pay it by any chance?
Tom: Why, I —
Amanda: Didn't! I might have known it!
Jim: Shakespeare probably wrote a poem on that light bill, Mrs. Wingfield.

Amanda: I might have known better than to trust him with it! There's such a high price for negligence in this world!

Jim: Maybe the poem will win a ten-dollar prize.

Amanda: We'll just have to spend the remainder of the evening in the nineteenth century, before Mr. Edison made the Mazda lamp!

Jim: Candlelight is my favorite kind of light.

Amanda: That shows you're romantic! But that's no excuse for Tom. Well, we got through dinner. Very considerate of them to let us get through dinner before they plunged us into everlasting darkness, wasn't it, Mr. O'Connor?

Jim: Ha-ha!

Amanda: Tom, as a penalty for your carelessness you can help me with the dishes.

Jim: Let me give you a hand.

Amanda: Indeed you will not!

Jim: I ought to be good for something.

Amanda: Good for something? *(Her tone is rhapsodic.)* You? Why, Mr. O'Connor, nobody, nobody's given me this much entertainment in years—as you have!

Jim: Aw, now, Mrs. Wingfield!

Amanda: I'm not exaggerating, not one bit! But Sister is all by her lonesome. You go keep her company in the parlor! I'll give you this lovely old candelabrum that used to be on the altar at the church of the Heavenly Rest. It was melted a little out of shape when the church burnt down. Lightning struck it one spring. Gypsy Jones was holding a revival at the time and he intimated that the church was destroyed because the Episcopalians gave card parties.

Jim: Ha-ha.

Amanda: And how about coaxing Sister to drink a little wine? I think it would be good for her! Can you carry both at once?

Jim: Sure. I'm Superman!

Amanda: Now, Thomas, get into this apron!

> *The door of kitchenette swings closed on Amanda's gay laughter; the flickering light approaches the portieres.*
>
> *Laura sits up nervously as he enters. Her speech at first is low and breathless from the almost intolerable strain of being alone with a stranger.*
>
> *(Legend: "I Don't Suppose You Remember Me at All!")*
>
> *In her first speeches in this scene, before Jim's warmth overcomes her paralyzing shyness, Laura's voice is thin and breathless as though she has run up a steep flight of stairs.*
>
> *Jim's attitude is gently humorous. In playing this scene it should be stressed that while the incident is apparently unimportant, it is to Laura the climax of her secret life.*

Jim: Hello, there, Laura.

Laura (faintly): Hello. *(She clears her throat.)*

Jim: How are you feeling now? Better?

Laura: Yes. Yes, thank you.

Jim: This is for you. A little dandelion wine. *(He extends it toward her with extravagant gallantry.)*

Laura: Thank you.

Jim: Drink it — but don't get drunk! *(He laughs heartily. Laura takes the glass uncertainly; laughs shyly.)* Where shall I set the candles?

Laura: Oh — oh, anywhere . . .

Jim: How about here on the floor? Any objections?

Laura: No.

Jim: I'll spread a newspaper under to catch the drippings. I like to sit on the floor. Mind if I do?

Laura: Oh, no.

Jim: Give me a pillow?

Laura: What?

Jim: A pillow!

Laura: Oh . . . *(Hands him one quickly.)*

Jim: How about you? Don't you like to sit on the floor?

Laura: Oh — yes.

Jim: Why don't you, then?

Laura: I — will.

Jim: Take a pillow! *(Laura does. Sits on the other side of the candelabrum. Jim crosses his legs and smiles engagingly at her.)* I can't hardly see you sitting way over there.

Laura: I can — see you.

Jim: I know, but that's not fair, I'm in the limelight. *(Laura moves her pillow closer.)* Good! Now I can see you! Comfortable?

Laura: Yes.

Jim: So am I. Comfortable as a cow. Will you have some gum?

Laura: No, thank you.

Jim: I think that I will indulge, with your permission. *(Musingly unwraps it and holds it up.)* Think of the fortune made by the guy that invented the first piece of chewing gum. Amazing, huh? The Wrigley Building is one of the sights of Chicago. — I saw it summer before last when I went up to the Century of Progress. Did you take in the Century of Progress?

Laura: No, I didn't.

Jim: Well, it was quite a wonderful exposition. What impressed me most was the Hall of Science. Gives you an idea of what the future will be in America, even more wonderful than the present time is! *(Pause. Smiling at her.)* Your brother tells me you're shy. Is that right, Laura?

Laura: I — don't know.

Jim: I judge you to be an old-fashioned type of girl. Well, I think that's a pretty good type to be. Hope you don't think I'm being too personal — do you?

Laura (hastily, out of embarrassment): I believe I *will* take a piece of gum, if you — don't mind. *(Clearing her throat.)* Mr. O'Connor, have you — kept up with your singing?

Jim: Singing? Me?

Laura: Yes. I remember what a beautiful voice you had.

Jim: When did you hear me sing?

(Voice offstage in the pause.)

Voice (offstage):   O blow, ye winds, heigh-ho,
             A-roving I will go!
             I'm off to my love
             With a boxing glove —
             Ten thousand miles away!

Jim: You say you've heard me sing?

Laura: Oh, yes! Yes, very often . . . I—don't suppose you remember me—at all?

Jim (smiling doubtfully): You know I have an idea I've seen you before. I had that idea soon as you opened the door. It seemed almost like I was about to remember your name. But the name that I started to call you—wasn't a name! And so I stopped myself before I said it.

Laura: Wasn't it—Blue Roses?

Jim (springs up, grinning): Blue Roses! My gosh, yes—Blue Roses! That's what I had on my tongue when you opened the door! Isn't it funny what tricks your memory plays? I didn't connect you with the high school somehow or other. But that's where it was; it was high school. I didn't even know you were Shakespeare's sister! Gosh, I'm sorry.

Laura: I didn't expect you to. You—barely knew me!

Jim: But we did have a speaking acquaintance, huh?

Laura: Yes, we—spoke to each other.

Jim: When did you recognize me?

Laura: Oh, right away!

Jim: Soon as I came in the door?

Laura: When I heard your name I thought it was probably you. I knew that Tom used to know you a little in high school. So when you came in the door—Well, then I was—sure.

Jim: Why didn't you *say* something, then?

Laura (breathlessly): I didn't know what to say, I was—too surprised!

Jim: For goodness' sakes! You know, this sure is funny!

Laura: Yes! Yes, isn't it, though . . .

Jim: Didn't we have a class in something together?

Laura: Yes, we did.

Jim: What class was that?

Laura: It was—singing—Chorus!

Jim: Aw!

Laura: I sat across the aisle from you in the Aud.

Jim: Aw.

Laura: Mondays, Wednesdays, and Fridays.

Jim: Now I remember—you always came in late.

Laura: Yes, it was so hard for me, getting upstairs. I had that brace on my leg—it clumped so loud!

Jim: I never heard any clumping.

Laura (wincing in the recollection): To me it sounded like—thunder!

Jim: Well, well, well. I never even noticed.

Laura: And everybody was seated before I came in. I had to walk in front of all those people. My seat was in the back row. I had to go clumping all the way up the aisle with everyone watching!

Jim: You shouldn't have been self-conscious.

Laura: I know, but I was. It was always such a relief when the singing started.

Jim: Aw, yes, I've placed you now! I used to call you Blue Roses. How was it that I got started calling you that?

Laura: I was out of school a little while with pleurosis. When I came back you asked me what was the matter. I said I had pleurosis—you thought I said Blue Roses. That's what you always called me after that!

Jim: I hope you didn't mind.

Laura: Oh, no — I liked it. You see, I wasn't acquainted with many — people. . . .

Jim: As I remember you sort of stuck by yourself.

Laura: I — I — never had much luck at — making friends.

Jim: I don't see why you wouldn't.

Laura: Well, I — started out badly.

Jim: You mean being —

Laura: Yes, it sort of — stood between me —

Jim: You shouldn't have let it!

Laura: I know, but it did, and —

Jim: You were shy with people!

Laura: I tried not to be but never could —

Jim: Overcome it?

Laura: No, I — I never could!

Jim: I guess being shy is something you have to work out of kind of gradually.

Laura (sorrowfully): Yes — I guess it —

Jim: Takes time!

Laura: Yes —

Jim: People are not so dreadful when you know them. That's what you have to remember! And everybody has problems, not just you, but practically everybody has got some problems. You think of yourself as having the only problems, as being the only one who is disappointed. But just look around you and you will see lots of people as disappointed as you are. For instance, I hoped when I was going to high school that I would be further along at this time, six years later, than I am now — You remember that wonderful write-up I had in *The Torch?*

Laura: Yes! *(She rises and crosses to table.)*

Jim: It said I was bound to succeed in anything I went into! *(Laura returns with the annual.)* Holy Jeez! *The Torch! (He accepts it reverently. They smile across it with mutual wonder. Laura crouches beside him and they begin to turn through it. Laura's shyness is dissolving in his warmth.)*

Laura: Here you are in *Pirates of Penzance!*

Jim (wistfully): I sang the baritone lead in that operetta.

Laura (rapidly): So — *beautifully!*

Jim (protesting): Aw —

Laura: Yes, yes — beautifully — beautifully!

Jim: You heard me?

Laura: All three times!

Jim: No!

Laura: Yes!

Jim: All three performances?

Laura (looking down): Yes.

Jim: Why?

Laura: I — wanted to ask you to — autograph my program.

Jim: Why didn't you ask me to?

Laura: You were always surrounded by your own friends so much that I never had a chance to.

Jim: You should have just —

Laura: Well, I — thought you might think I was —

Jim: Thought I might think you was — what?

Laura: Oh —

Jim (with reflective relish): I was beleaguered by females in those days.

Laura: You were terribly popular!

Jim: Yeah —

Laura: You had such a — friendly way —

Jim: I was spoiled in high school.

Laura: Everybody — liked you!

Jim: Including you?

Laura: I — yes, I — I did, too — *(She gently closes the book in her lap.)*

Jim: Well, well, well! — Give me that program, Laura. *(She hands it to him. He signs it with a flourish.)* There you are — better late than never!

Laura: Oh, I — what a — surprise!

Jim: My signature isn't worth very much right now. But some day — maybe — it will increase in value! Being disappointed is one thing and being discouraged is something else. I am disappointed but I'm not discouraged. I'm twenty-three years old. How old are you?

Laura: I'll be twenty-four in June.

Jim: That's not old age.

Laura: No, but —

Jim: You finished high school?

Laura (with difficulty): I didn't go back.

Jim: You mean you dropped out?

Laura: I made bad grades in my final examinations. *(She rises and replaces the book and the program. Her voice strained.)* How is — Emily Meisenbach getting along?

Jim: Oh, that kraut-head!

Laura: Why do you call her that?

Jim: That's what she was.

Laura: You're not still — going with her?

Jim: I never see her.

Laura: It said in the Personal Section that you were — engaged!

Jim: I know, but I wasn't impressed by that — propaganda!

Laura: It wasn't — the truth?

Jim: Only in Emily's optimistic opinion!

Laura: Oh —

> *(Legend: "What Have You Done since High School?")*
>
> Jim lights a cigarette and leans indolently back on his elbows smiling at Laura with a warmth and charm which light her inwardly with altar candles. She remains by the table and turns in her hands a piece of glass to cover her tumult.

Jim (after several reflective puffs on a cigarette): What have you done since high school? *(She seems not to hear him.)* Huh? *(Laura looks up.)* I said what have you done since high school, Laura?

Laura: Nothing much.

Jim: You must have been doing something these six long years.

Laura: Yes.

Jim: Well, then, such as what?

Laura: I took a business course at business college —

Jim: How did that work out?

Laura: Well, not very — well — I had to drop out, it gave me — indigestion —

Jim laughs gently.

Jim: What are you doing now?

Laura: I don't do anything — much. Oh, please don't think I sit around doing nothing! My glass collection takes up a good deal of my time. Glass is something you have to take good care of.

Jim: What did you say — about glass?

Laura: Collection I said — I have one — *(She clears her throat and turns away again, acutely shy.)*

Jim (abruptly): You know what I judge to be the trouble with you? Inferiority complex! Know what that is? That's what they call it when someone low-rates himself! I understand it because I had it, too. Although my case was not so aggravated as yours seems to be. I had it until I took up public speaking, developed my voice, and learned that I had an aptitude for science. Before that time I never thought of myself as being outstanding in any way whatsoever! Now I've never made a regular study of it, but I have a friend who says I can analyze people better than doctors that make a profession of it. I don't claim that to be necessarily true, but I can sure guess a person's psychology, Laura! *(Takes out his gum.)* Excuse me, Laura. I always take it out when the flavor is gone. I'll use this scrap of paper to wrap it in. I know how it is to get it stuck on a shoe. Yep — that's what I judge to be your principal trouble. A lack of confidence in yourself as a person. You don't have the proper amount of faith in yourself. I'm basing that fact on a number of your remarks and also on certain observations I've made. For instance that clumping you thought was so awful in high school. You say that you even dreaded to walk into class. You see what you did? You dropped out of school, you gave up an education because of a clump, which as far as I know was practically nonexistent! A little physical defect is what you have. Hardly noticeable even! Magnified thousands of times by imagination! You know what my strong advice to you is? Think of yourself as *superior* in some way!

Laura: In what way would I think?

Jim: Why, man alive, Laura! Just look about you a little. What do you see? A world full of common people! All of 'em born and all of 'em going to die! Which of them has one-tenth of your good points! Or mine! Or anyone else's, as far as that goes — Gosh! Everybody excels in some one thing. Some in many! *(Unconsciously glances at himself in the mirror.)* All you've got to do is discover in *what!* Take me, for instance. *(He adjusts his tie at the mirror.)* My interest happened to lie in electrodynamics. I'm taking a course in radio engineering at night school, Laura, on top of a fairly responsible job at the warehouse. I'm taking that course and studying public speaking.

Laura: Ohhhh.

Jim: Because I believe in the future of television! *(Turning back to her.)* I wish to be ready to go up right along with it. Therefore I'm planning to get in on the ground floor. In fact, I've already made the right connections and all that remains is for the industry itself to get under way! Full steam — *(His eyes are starry.)* Knowledge — Zzzzzp! Money — Zzzzzzp! — Power! That's the cycle democracy is built on! *(His attitude is convincingly dynamic. Laura stares at him, even her shyness eclipsed in her absolute wonder. He suddenly grins.)* I guess you think I think a lot of myself!

Laura: No — o-o-o, I —

Jim: Now how about you? Isn't there something you take more interest in than anything else?

Laura: Well, I do — as I said — have my — glass collection —

A peal of girlish laughter from the kitchen.

Jim: I'm not right sure I know what you're talking about. What kind of glass is it?

Laura: Little articles of it, they're ornaments mostly! Most of them are little animals made out of glass, the tiniest little animals in the world. Mother calls them a glass menagerie! Here's an example of one, if you'd like to see it! This one is one of the oldest. It's nearly thirteen. *(He stretches out his hand.) (Music: "The Glass Menagerie.")* Oh, be careful — if you breathe, it breaks!

Jim: I'd better not take it. I'm pretty clumsy with things.

Laura: Go on, I trust you with him! *(Places it in his palm.)* There now — you're holding him gently! Hold him over the light, he loves the light! You see how the light shines through him?

Jim: It sure does shine!

Laura: I shouldn't be partial, but he is my favorite one.

Jim: What kind of thing is this one supposed to be?

Laura: Haven't you noticed the single horn on his forehead?

Jim: A unicorn, huh?

Laura: Mmm-hmmm!

Jim: Unicorns, aren't they extinct in the modern world?

Laura: I know!

Jim: Poor little fellow, he must feel sort of lonesome.

Laura (smiling): Well, if he does he doesn't complain about it. He stays on a shelf with some horses that don't have horns and all of them seem to get along nicely together.

Jim: How do you know?

Laura (lightly): I haven't heard any arguments among them!

Jim (grinning): No arguments, huh? Well, that's a pretty good sign! Where shall I set him?

Laura: Put him on the table. They all like a change of scenery once in a while!

Jim (stretching): Well, well, well, well — Look how big my shadow is when I stretch!

Laura: Oh, oh, yes — it stretches across the ceiling!

Jim (crossing to door): I think it's stopped raining. *(Opens fire-escape door.)* Where does the music come from?

Laura: From the Paradise Dance Hall across the alley.

Jim: How about cutting the rug a little, Miss Wingfield?

Laura: Oh, I —

Jim: Or is your program filled up? Let me have a look at it. *(Grasps imaginary card.)* Why, every dance is taken! I'll have to scratch some out. *(Waltz music: "La Golondrina.")* Ahhh, a waltz! *(He executes some sweeping turns by himself then holds his arms toward Laura.)*

Laura (breathlessly): I — can't dance!

Jim: There you go, that inferiority stuff!

Laura: I've never danced in my life!

Jim: Come on, try!

Laura: Oh, but I'd step on you!

Jim: I'm not made out of glass.

Laura: How — how — how do we start?

Jim: Just leave it to me. You hold your arms out a little.

Laura: Like this?

Jim: A little bit higher. Right. Now don't tighten up, that's the main thing about it — relax.

Laura (laughing breathlessly): It's hard not to.

Jim: Okay.

Laura: I'm afraid you can't budge me.

Jim: What do you bet I can't? *(He swings her into motion.)*

Laura: Goodness, yes, you can!

Jim: Let yourself go, now, Laura, just let yourself go.

Laura: I'm —

Jim: Come on!

Laura: Trying.

Jim: Not so stiff — Easy does it!

Laura: I know but I'm —

Jim: Loosen th' backbone! There now, that's a lot better.

Laura: Am I?

Jim: Lots, lots better! *(He moves her about the room in a clumsy waltz.)*

Laura: Oh, my!

Jim: Ha-ha!

Laura: Goodness, yes you can!

Jim: Ha-ha-ha! *(They suddenly bump into the table. Jim stops.)* What did we hit on?

Laura: Table.

Jim: Did something fall off it? I think —

Laura: Yes.

Jim: I hope it wasn't the little glass horse with the horn!

Laura: Yes.

Jim: Aw, aw, aw. Is it broken?

Laura: Now it is just like all the other horses.

Jim: It's lost its —

Laura: Horn! It doesn't matter. Maybe it's a blessing in disguise.

Jim: You'll never forgive me. I bet that that was your favorite piece of glass.

Laura: I don't have favorites much. It's no tragedy, Freckles. Glass breaks so easily. No matter how careful you are. The traffic jars the shelves and things fall off them.

Jim: Still I'm awfully sorry that I was the cause.

Laura (smiling): I'll just imagine he had an operation. The horn was removed to make him feel less — freakish! *(They both laugh.)* Now he will feel more at home with the other horses, the ones that don't have horns . . .

Jim: Ha-ha, that's very funny! *(Suddenly serious.)* I'm glad to see that you have a sense of humor. You know — you're — well — very different! Surprisingly different from anyone else I know! *(His voice becomes soft and hesitant with a genuine feeling.)* Do you mind me telling you that? *(Laura is abashed beyond speech.)* You make me feel sort of — I don't know how to put it! I'm usually pretty good at expressing things, but — This is something that I don't know how to say! *(Laura touches her throat and clears it — turns the broken unicorn in her hands.) (Even softer.)* Has anyone ever told you that you were pretty?

Pause: Music.

(Laura looks up slowly, with wonder, and shakes her head.) Well, you are! In a very different way from anyone else. And all the nicer because of the difference, too. *(His voice becomes low and husky. Laura turns away, nearly faint with the novelty of her emotions.)* I wish that you were my sister. I'd teach you to have some confidence in yourself. The different people are not like other people, but being different is nothing to be ashamed of. Because other people are not such wonderful people. They're one hundred times one thousand. You're one times one! They walk all over the earth. You just stay here. They're common as — weeds, but — you — well, you're — *Blue Roses!*

(Image on screen: Blue Roses.)
(Music changes.)

Laura: But blue is wrong for — roses . . .
Jim: It's right for you — You're — pretty!
Laura: In what respect am I pretty?
Jim: In all respects — believe me! Your eyes — your hair — are pretty! Your hands are pretty! *(He catches hold of her hand.)* You think I'm making this up because I'm invited to dinner and have to be nice. Oh, I could do that! I could put on an act for you, Laura, and say lots of things without being very sincere. But this time I am. I'm talking to you sincerely. I happened to notice you had this inferiority complex that keeps you from feeling comfortable with people. Somebody needs to build your confidence up and make you proud instead of shy and turning away and — blushing — Somebody ought to — ought to — *kiss* you, Laura! *(His hand slips slowly up her arm to her shoulder.) (Music swells tumultuously.) (He suddenly turns her about and kisses her on the lips. When he releases her Laura sinks on the sofa with a bright, dazed look. Jim backs away and fishes in his pocket for a cigarette.) (Legend on screen: "Souvenir.")* Stumble-john! *(He lights the cigarette, avoiding her look. There is a peal of girlish laughter from Amanda in the kitchen. Laura slowly raises and opens her hand. It still contains the little broken glass animal. She looks at it with a tender, bewildered expression.)* Stumble-john! I shouldn't have done that — That was way off the beam. You don't smoke, do you? *(She looks up, smiling, not hearing the question. He sits beside her a little gingerly. She looks at him speechlessly — waiting. He coughs decorously and moves a little farther aside as he considers the situation and senses her feelings, dimly, with perturbation. Gently.)* Would you — care for a — mint? *(She doesn't seem to hear him but her look grows brighter even.)* Peppermint — Life Saver? My pocket's a regular drug store — wherever I go . . . *(He pops a mint in his mouth. Then gulps and decides to make a clean breast of it. He speaks slowly and gingerly.)* Laura, you know, if I had a sister like you, I'd do the same thing as Tom. I'd bring out fellows — introduce her to them. The right type of boys of a type to — appreciate her. Only — well — he made a mistake about me. Maybe I've got no call to be saying this. That may not have been the idea in having me over. But what if it was? There's nothing wrong about that. The only trouble is that in my case — I'm not in a situation to — do the right thing. I can't take down your number and say I'll phone. I can't call up next week and — ask for a date. I

thought I had better explain the situation in case you misunderstood it and — hurt your feelings. . . . *(Pause. Slowly, very slowly, Laura's look changes, her eyes returning slowly from his to the ornament in her palm.)*

Amanda utters another gay laugh in the kitchen.

Laura (faintly): You — won't — call again?

Jim: No, Laura, I can't. *(He rises from the sofa.)* As I was just explaining, I've — got strings on me, Laura, I've — been going steady! I go out all the time with a girl named Betty. She's a home-girl like you, and Catholic, and Irish, and in a great many ways we — get along fine. I met her last summer on a moonlight boat trip up the river to Alton, on the *Majestic*. Well — right away from the start it was — love! *(Legend: Love!) (Laura sways slightly forward and grips the arm of the sofa. He fails to notice, now enrapt in his own comfortable being.)* Being in love has made a new man of me! *(Leaning stiffly forward, clutching the arm of the sofa, Laura struggles visibly with her storm. But Jim is oblivious, she is a long way off.)* The power of love is really pretty tremendous! Love is something that — changes the whole world, Laura! *(The storm abates a little and Laura leans back. He notices her again.)* It happened that Betty's aunt took sick, she got a wire and had to go to Centralia. So Tom — when he asked me to dinner — I naturally just accepted the invitation, not knowing that you — that he — that I — *(He stops awkwardly.)* Huh — I'm a stumble-john! *(He flops back on the sofa. The holy candles in the altar of Laura's face have been snuffed out! There is a look of almost infinite desolation. Jim glances at her uneasily.)* I wish that you would — say something. *(She bites her lip which was trembling and then bravely smiles. She opens her hand again on the broken glass ornament. Then she gently takes his hand and raises it level with her own. She carefully places the unicorn in the palm of his hand, then pushes his fingers closed upon it.)* What are you — doing that for? You want me to have him? — Laura? *(She nods.)* What for?

Laura: A — souvenir . . .

She rises unsteadily and crouches beside the Victrola to wind it up.
    (Legend on screen: "Things Have a Way of Turning Out So Badly.")
    (Or image: "Gentleman caller waving good-bye! — Gaily.")
    At this moment Amanda rushes brightly back in the front room. She bears a pitcher of fruit punch in an old-fashioned cut-glass pitcher and a plate of macaroons. The plate has a gold border and poppies painted on it.

Amanda: Well, well, well! Isn't the air delightful after the shower? I've made you children a little liquid refreshment. *(Turns gaily to the gentleman caller.)* Jim, do you know that song about lemonade?
"Lemonade, lemonade
Made in the shade and stirred with a spade —
Good enough for any old maid!"

Jim (uneasily): Ha-ha! No — I never heard it.

Amanda: Why, Laura! You look so serious!

Jim: We were having a serious conversation.

Amanda: Good! Now you're better acquainted!

Jim (uncertainly): Ha-ha! Yes.

Amanda: You modern young people are much more serious-minded than my generation. I was so gay as a girl!

Jim: You haven't changed, Mrs. Wingfield.

Amanda: Tonight I'm rejuvenated! The gaiety of the occasion, Mr. O'Connor! *(She tosses her head with a peal of laughter. Spills lemonade.)* Oooo! I'm baptizing myself!

Jim: Here — let me —

Amanda (setting the pitcher down): There now. I discovered we had some maraschino cherries. I dumped them in, juice and all!

Jim: You shouldn't have gone to that trouble, Mrs. Wingfield.

Amanda: Trouble, trouble? Why it was loads of fun! Didn't you hear me cutting up in the kitchen? I bet your ears were burning! I told Tom how outdone with him I was for keeping you to himself so long a time! He should have brought you over much, much sooner! Well, now that you've found your way, I want you to be a very frequent caller! Not just occasional but all the time. Oh, we're going to have a lot of gay times together! I see them coming! Mmm, just breathe that air! So fresh, and the moon's so pretty! I'll skip back out — I know where my place is when young folks are having a — serious conversation!

Jim: Oh, don't go out, Mrs. Wingfield. The fact of the matter is I've got to be going.

Amanda: Going, now? You're joking! Why, it's only the shank of the evening, Mr. O'Connor!

Jim: Well, you know how it is.

Amanda: You mean you're a young workingman and have to keep workingmen's hours. We'll let you off early tonight. But only on the condition that next time you stay later. What's the best night for you? Isn't Saturday night the best night for you workingmen?

Jim: I have a couple of time-clocks to punch, Mrs. Wingfield. One at morning, another one at night!

Amanda: My, but you *are* ambitious! You work at night, too?

Jim: No, Ma'am, not work but — Betty! *(He crosses deliberately to pick up his hat. The band at the Paradise Dance Hall goes into a tender waltz.)*

Amanda: Betty? Betty? Who's — Betty! *(There is an ominous cracking sound in the sky.)*

Jim: Oh, just a girl. The girl I go steady with! *(He smiles charmingly. The sky falls.)*

(Legend: "The Sky Falls.")

Amanda (a long-drawn exhalation): Ohhhh . . . Is it a serious romance, Mr. O'Connor?

Jim: We're going to be married the second Sunday in June.

Amanda: Ohhhh — how nice! Tom didn't mention that you were engaged to be married.

Jim: The cat's not out of the bag at the warehouse yet. You know how they are. They call you Romeo and stuff like that. *(He stops at the oval mirror to put on his hat. He carefully shapes the brim and the crown to give a discreetly dashing effect.)* It's been a wonderful evening, Mrs. Wingfield. I guess this is what they mean by Southern hospitality.

Amanda: It really wasn't anything at all.

Jim: I hope it don't seem like I'm rushing off. But I promised Betty I'd pick her up at the Wabash depot, an' by the time I get my jalopy down there her train'll be in. Some women are pretty upset if you keep 'em waiting.

Amanda: Yes, I know — The tyranny of women! *(Extends her hand.)* Good-bye, Mr. O'Connor. I wish you luck — and happiness — and success! All three of them, and so does Laura — Don't you, Laura?

Laura: Yes!

Jim (taking her hand): Good-bye, Laura. I'm certainly going to treasure that souvenir. And don't you forget the good advice I gave you. *(Raises his voice to a cheery shout.)* So long, Shakespeare! Thanks again, ladies — Good night!

> *He grins and ducks jauntily out.*
> *Still bravely grimacing, Amanda closes the door on the gentleman caller. Then she turns back to the room with a puzzled expression. She and Laura don't dare to face each other. Laura crouches beside the Victrola to wind it.*

Amanda (faintly): Things have a way of turning out so badly. I don't believe that I would play the Victrola. Well, well — well — Our gentleman caller was engaged to be married! Tom!

Tom (from back): Yes, Mother?

Amanda: Come in here a minute. I want to tell you something awfully funny.

Tom (enters with macaroon and a glass of the lemonade): Has the gentleman caller gotten away already?

Amanda: The gentleman caller has made an early departure. What a wonderful joke you played on us!

Tom: How do you mean?

Amanda: You didn't mention that he was engaged to be married.

Tom: Jim? Engaged?

Amanda: That's what he just informed us.

Tom: I'll be jiggered! I didn't know about that.

Amanda: That seems very peculiar.

Tom: What's peculiar about it?

Amanda: Didn't you call him your best friend down at the warehouse?

Tom: He is, but how did I know?

Amanda: It seems extremely peculiar that you wouldn't know your best friend was going to be married!

Tom: The warehouse is where I work, not where I know things about people!

Amanda: You don't know things anywhere! You live in a dream; you manufacture illusions! *(He crosses to door.)* Where are you going?

Tom: I'm going to the movies.

Amanda: That's right, now that you've had us make such fools of ourselves. The effort, the preparations, all the expense! The new floor lamp, the rug, the clothes for Laura! All for what? To entertain some other girl's fiancé! Go to the movies, go! Don't think about us, a mother deserted, an unmarried sister who's crippled and has no job! Don't let anything interfere with your selfish pleasure! Just go, go, go — to the movies!

Tom: All right, I will! The more you shout about my selfishness to me the quicker I'll go, and I won't go to the movies!

Amanda: Go, then! Then go to the moon — you selfish dreamer!

> *Tom smashes his glass on the floor. He plunges out on the fire-escape, slamming the door. Laura screams — cut by door.*
> *Dance-hall music up. Tom goes to the rail and grips it desperately, lifting his face in the chill white moonlight penetrating the narrow abyss of the alley.*
> *(Legend on screen: "And So Good-Bye . . .")*

Tom's closing speech is timed with the interior pantomime. The interior scene is played as though viewed through sound-proof glass. Amanda appears to be making a comforting speech to Laura who is huddled upon the sofa. Now that we cannot hear the mother's speech, her silliness is gone and she has dignity and tragic beauty. Laura's dark hair hides her face until at the end of the speech she lifts it to smile at her mother. Amanda's gestures are slow and graceful, almost dancelike, as she comforts the daughter. At the end of her speech she glances a moment at the father's picture — then withdraws through the portieres. At close of Tom's speech, Laura blows out the candles, ending the play.

Tom: I didn't go to the moon, I went much further — for time is the longest distance between two places — Not long after that I was fired for writing a poem on the lid of a shoe-box. I left Saint Louis. I descended the steps of this fire-escape for a last time and followed, from then on, in my father's footsteps, attempting to find in motion what was lost in space — I traveled around a great deal. The cities swept about me like dead leaves, leaves that were brightly colored but torn away from the branches. I would have stopped, but I was pursued by something. It always came upon me unawares, taking me altogether by surprise. Perhaps it was a familiar bit of music. Perhaps it was only a piece of transparent glass — Perhaps I am walking along a street at night, in some strange city, before I have found companions. I pass the lighted window of a shop where perfume is sold. The window is filled with pieces of colored glass, tiny transparent bottles in delicate colors, like bits of a shattered rainbow. Then all at once my sister touches my shoulder. I turn around and look into her eyes. . . . Oh, Laura, Laura, I tried to leave you behind me, but I am more faithful than I intended to be! I reach for a cigarette, I cross the street, I run into the movies or a bar, I buy a drink, I speak to the nearest stranger — anything that can blow your candles out! *(Laura bends over the candles)* — for nowadays the world is lit by lightning! Blow out your candles, Laura — and so good-bye . . .

She blows the candles out.
    (The Scene Dissolves.)

CONSIDERATIONS FOR CRITICAL THINKING AND WRITING

1. FIRST RESPONSE. Whose story is this? Explain why you think Amanda, Laura, or Tom is the play's protagonist.

2. Discuss Tom's role as the play's narrator. What is revealed about him in his role as narrator that is not by his role as a character in the story he tells?

3. Trace your emotional response to Laura. Explain why you find her a complicated character, sympathetic, or merely pathetic.

4. Describe the conflict in Tom's life. How does it compare with the conflicts experienced by his mother and sister?

5. What kind of mother is Amanda? Describe her relationship with Tom and Laura. What are her strengths and weaknesses?

6. Characterize Jim O'Connor. What does his role in the play reveal about Laura? Explain why you agree or disagree with Tom's assessment that Jim is "the most realistic character in the play."

7. Discuss the "fifth character." What is the function of the photograph of the father over the mantel?

8. Amanda is described as "having failed to establish contact with reality." To what extent do you think it is accurate or inaccurate to describe all of the play's characters this way?

9. Tom acknowledges that he has "a poet's weakness for symbols." Make a list of the symbols you find in the play and discuss the one that you think is the most significant.

10. Consider the social background of the play. How is the 1930s setting relevant to the characters' lives and the play's plot?

11. Describe the realistic and nonrealistic qualities of the play and explain why you think these elements work well together or not.

Character Analysis

This casebook shows you how one student, William Dean, develops a character analysis of Mrs. Hale, a character in Susan Glaspell's Trifles, *from first response through brainstorming and a final draft. Though brief,* Trifles *is a masterful representation of dramatic elements working together to keep both audiences and readers absorbed in its characters and situations. The action takes place right after a murder committed in a midwestern farmhouse, but the play goes beyond the kinds of questions raised by most whodunit stories. The murder is the occasion rather than the focus—the characters are the real focus of this play, the moral, social, and psychological aspects of the assumptions and perceptions of the men and women who search for the murderer's motive. Glaspell is finally more interested in the meaning of Mrs. Wright's life than in the details of Mr. Wright's death. As you read the play, keep track of the characters and note in the margin the moments when Glaspell reveals how men and women respond differently to the evidence before them. What do those moments suggest about the kinds of assumptions these men and women make about themselves and each other? How do their assumptions compare with your own? How do you respond to the character of Mrs. Hale?*

SUSAN GLASPELL (1882–1948)

In the following play, Susan Glaspell skillfully draws on many dramatic elements and creates an intense story that is as effective on the page as it is in the theater. Glaspell wrote *Trifles* in 1916 for the Provincetown Players on Cape Cod, in Massachusetts. Their performance of the work helped her develop a reputation as a writer sensitive to feminist issues. The year after *Trifles* was produced, Glaspell transformed the play into a short story titled "A Jury of Her Peers."

Susan Glaspell, a novelist and playwright whose best known work is Trifles, *also wrote many novels, short stories, and plays, including* Alison's House, *a play about Emily Dickinson's life, for which she won a Pulitzer Prize.*

Glaspell's life in the Midwest provided her with the setting for *Trifles.* Born and raised in Davenport, Iowa, she graduated from Drake University in 1899 and then worked for a short time as a reporter on the *Des Moines News,* until her short stories were accepted in magazines such as *Harper's* and *Ladies' Home Journal.* Glaspell moved to the Northeast when she was in her early thirties to continue writing fiction and drama. She published some twenty plays, novels, and more than forty short stories. *Alison's House,* based on Emily Dickinson's life, earned her a Pulitzer Prize for drama in 1931. *Trifles* and "A Jury of Her Peers" remain, however, Glaspell's best-known works.

Glaspell wrote *Trifles* to complete a bill that was to feature several one-act plays by Eugene O'Neill. In *The Road to the Temple* (1926) she recalls how the play came to her as she sat in the theater looking at a bare stage. First, "the stage became a kitchen. . . . Then the door at the back opened, and people all bundled up came in — two or three men. I wasn't sure which, but sure enough about the two women, who hung back, reluctant to enter that kitchen. When I was a newspaper reporter out in Iowa, I was sent downstate to do a murder trial, and I never forgot going to the kitchen of a woman who had been locked up in town."

Trifles

1916

CHARACTERS

George Henderson, county attorney
Henry Peters, sheriff
Lewis Hale, a neighboring farmer
Mrs. Peters
Mrs. Hale

SCENE: *The kitchen in the now abandoned farmhouse of John Wright, a gloomy kitchen, and left without having been put in order—unwashed pans under the sink, a loaf of bread outside the breadbox, a dish towel on the table—other signs of incompleted work. At the rear the outer door opens and the Sheriff comes in followed by the County Attorney and Hale. The Sheriff and Hale are men in middle life, the County Attorney is a young man; all are much bundled up and go at once to the stove. They are followed by the two women—the Sheriff's wife first; she is a slight wiry woman, a thin nervous face. Mrs. Hale is larger and would ordinarily be called more comfortable looking, but she is disturbed now and looks fearfully about as she enters. The women have come in slowly, and stand close together near the door.*

County Attorney (rubbing his hands): This feels good. Come up to the fire, ladies.
Mrs. Peters (after taking a step forward): I'm not—cold.
Sheriff (unbuttoning his overcoat and stepping away from the stove as if to mark the beginning of official business): Now, Mr. Hale, before we move things about, you explain to Mr. Henderson just what you saw when you came here yesterday morning.
County Attorney: By the way, has anything been moved? Are things just as you left them yesterday?
Sheriff (looking about): It's just about the same. When it dropped below zero last night I thought I'd better send Frank out this morning to make a fire for us—no use getting pneumonia with a big case on, but I told him not to touch anything except the stove—and you know Frank.
County Attorney: Somebody should have been left here yesterday.
Sheriff: Oh—yesterday. When I had to send Frank to Morris Center for that man who went crazy—I want you to know I had my hands full yesterday. I knew you could get back from Omaha by today and as long as I went over everything here myself—
County Attorney: Well, Mr. Hale, tell just what happened when you came here yesterday morning.
Hale: Harry and I had started to town with a load of potatoes. We came along the road from my place and as I got here I said, "I'm going to see if I can't get John Wright to go in with me on a party telephone." I spoke to Wright about it once before and he put me off, saying folks talked too much anyway, and all he asked was peace and quiet—I guess you know about how much he talked himself; but I thought maybe if I went to the house and talked about it before his wife, though I said to Harry that I didn't know as what his wife wanted made much difference to John—
County Attorney: Let's talk about that later, Mr. Hale. I do want to talk about that, but tell now just what happened when you got to the house.

Hale: I didn't hear or see anything; I knocked at the door, and still it was all quiet inside. I knew they must be up, it was past eight o'clock. So I knocked again, and I thought I heard somebody say, "Come in." I wasn't sure, I'm not sure yet, but I opened the door — this door *(indicating the door by which the two women are still standing)* and there in that rocker — *(pointing to it)* sat Mrs. Wright. *(They all look at the rocker.)*

County Attorney: What — was she doing?

Hale: She was rockin' back and forth. She had her apron in her hand and was kind of — pleating it.

County Attorney: And how did she — look?

Hale: Well, she looked queer.

County Attorney: How do you mean — queer?

Hale: Well, as if she didn't know what she was going to do next. And kind of done up.

County Attorney: How did she seem to feel about your coming?

Hale: Why, I don't think she minded — one way or other. She didn't pay much attention. I said, "How do, Mrs. Wright, it's cold, ain't it?" And she said, "Is it?" — and went on kind of pleating at her apron. Well, I was surprised; she didn't ask me to come up to the stove, or to set down, but just sat there, not even looking at me, so I said, "I want to see John." And then she — laughed. I guess you would call it a laugh. I thought of Harry and the team outside, so I said a little sharp: "Can't I see John?" "No," she says, kind o' dull like. "Ain't he home?" says I. "Yes," says she, "he's home." "Then why can't I see him?" I asked her, out of patience. " 'Cause he's dead," says she. *"Dead?"* says I. She just nodded her head, not getting a bit excited, but rockin' back and forth. "Why — where is he?" says I, not knowing what to say. She just pointed upstairs — like that *(himself pointing to the room above).* I started for the stairs, with the idea of going up there. I walked from there to here — then I says, "Why, what did he die of?" "He died of a rope round his neck," says she, and just went on pleatin' at her apron. Well, I went out and called Harry. I thought I might — need help. We went upstairs and there he was lyin' —

County Attorney: I think I'd rather have you go into that upstairs, where you can point it all out. Just go on now with the rest of the story.

Hale: Well, my first thought was to get that rope off. It looked . . . *(stops; his face twitches)* . . . but Harry, he went up to him, and he said, "No, he's dead all right, and we'd better not touch anything." So we went back downstairs. She was still sitting that same way. "Has anybody been notified?" I asked. "No," says she, unconcerned. "Who did this, Mrs. Wright?" said Harry. He said it businesslike — and she stopped pleatin' of her apron. "I don't know," she says. "You don't *know?*" says Harry. "No," says she. "Weren't you sleepin' in the bed with him?" says Harry. "Yes," says she, "but I was on the inside." "Somebody slipped a rope round his neck and strangled him and you didn't wake up?" says Harry. "I didn't wake up," she said after him. We must 'a' looked as if we didn't see how that could be, for after a minute she said, "I sleep sound." Harry was going to ask her more questions but I said maybe we ought to let her tell her story first to the coroner, or the sheriff, so Harry went fast as he could to Rivers' place, where there's a telephone.

County Attorney: And what did Mrs. Wright do when she knew that you had gone for the coroner?

Hale: She moved from the rocker to that chair over there *(pointing to a small chair in the corner)* and just sat there with her hands held together and looking down. I got a feeling that I ought to make some conversation, so I said I had come in to see if John wanted to put in a telephone, and at that she started to laugh, and then she stopped and looked at me — scared. *(The County Attorney, who has had his notebook out, makes a note.)* I dunno, maybe it wasn't scared. I wouldn't like to say it was. Soon Harry got back, and then Dr. Lloyd came and you, Mr. Peters, and so I guess that's all I know that you don't.

County Attorney (looking around): I guess we'll go upstairs first — and then out to the barn and around there. *(To the Sheriff.)* You're convinced that there was nothing important here — nothing that would point to any motive?

Sheriff: Nothing here but kitchen things. *(The County Attorney, after again looking around the kitchen, opens the door of a cupboard closet. He gets up on a chair and looks on a shelf. Pulls his hand away, sticky.)*

County Attorney: Here's a nice mess. *(The women draw nearer.)*

Mrs. Peters (to the other woman): Oh, her fruit; it did freeze. *(To the Lawyer.)* She worried about that when it turned so cold. She said the fire'd go out and her jars would break.

Sheriff: Well, can you beat the women! Held for murder and worryin' about her preserves.

County Attorney: I guess before we're through she may have something more serious than preserves to worry about.

Hale: Well, women are used to worrying over trifles. *(The two women move a little closer together.)*

County Attorney (with the gallantry of a young politician): And yet, for all their worries, what would we do without the ladies? *(The women do not unbend. He goes to the sink, takes a dipperful of water from the pail, and pouring it into a basin, washes his hands. Starts to wipe them on the roller towel, turns it for a cleaner place.)* Dirty towels! *(Kicks his foot against the pans under the sink.)* Not much of a housekeeper, would you say, ladies?

Mrs. Hale (stiffly): There's a great deal of work to be done on a farm.

County Attorney: To be sure. And yet *(with a little bow to her)* I know there are some Dickson county farmhouses which do not have such roller towels. *(He gives it a pull to expose its full length again.)*

Mrs. Hale: Those towels get dirty awful quick. Men's hands aren't always as clean as they might be.

County Attorney: Ah, loyal to your sex, I see. But you and Mrs. Wright were neighbors. I suppose you were friends, too.

Mrs. Hale (shaking her head): I've not seen much of her of late years. I've not been in this house — it's more than a year.

County Attorney: And why was that? You didn't like her?

Mrs. Hale: I liked her all well enough. Farmers' wives have their hands full, Mr. Henderson. And then —

County Attorney: Yes —?

Mrs. Hale (looking about): It never seemed a very cheerful place.

County Attorney: No — it's not cheerful. I shouldn't say she had the homemaking instinct.

Mrs. Hale: Well, I don't know as Wright had, either.

County Attorney: You mean that they didn't get on very well?

Mrs. Hale: No, I don't mean anything. But I don't think a place'd be any cheer-fuller for John Wright's being in it.

County Attorney: I'd like to talk more of that a little later. I want to get the lay of things upstairs now. *(He goes to the left where three steps lead to a stair door.)*

Sheriff: I suppose anything Mrs. Peters does'll be all right. She was to take in some clothes for her, you know, and a few little things. We left in such a hurry yesterday.

County Attorney: Yes, but I would like to see what you take, Mrs. Peters, and keep an eye out for anything that might be of use to us.

Mrs. Peters: Yes, Mr. Henderson. *(The women listen to the men's steps on the stairs, then look about the kitchen.)*

Mrs. Hale: I'd hate to have men coming into my kitchen, snooping around and criticizing. *(She arranges the pans under sink which the lawyer had shoved out of place.)*

Mrs. Peters: Of course it's no more than their duty.

Mrs. Hale: Duty's all right, but I guess that deputy sheriff that came out to make the fire might have got a little of this on. *(Gives the roller towel a pull.)* Wish I'd thought of that sooner. Seems mean to talk about her for not having things slicked up when she had to come away in such a hurry.

Mrs. Peters (who has gone to a small table in the left rear corner of the room, and lifted one end of a towel that covers a pan): She had bread set. *(Stands still.)*

Mrs. Hale (eyes fixed on a loaf of bread beside the breadbox, which is on a low shelf at the other side of the room. Moves slowly toward it.): She was going to put this in there. *(Picks up loaf, then abruptly drops it. In a manner of returning to famil-iar things.)* It's a shame about her fruit. I wonder if it's all gone. *(Gets up on the chair and looks.)* I think there's some here that's all right, Mrs. Peters. Yes — here; *(holding it toward the window)* this is cherries, too. *(Looking again.)* I declare I believe that's the only one. *(Gets down, bottle in her hand. Goes to the sink and wipes it off on the outside.)* She'll feel awful bad after all her hard work in the hot weather. I remember the afternoon I put up my cherries last summer. *(She puts the bottle on the big kitchen table, center of the room. With a sigh, is about to sit down in the rocking-chair. Before she is seated realizes what chair it is; with a slow look at it, steps back. The chair which she has touched rocks back and forth.)*

Mrs. Peters: Well, I must get those things from the front room closet. *(She goes to the door at the right, but after looking into the other room, steps back.)* You com-ing with me, Mrs. Hale? You could help me carry them. *(They go in the other room; reappear, Mrs. Peters carrying a dress and skirt, Mrs. Hale following with a pair of shoes.)* My, it's cold in there. *(She puts the clothes on the big table, and hurries to the stove.)*

Mrs. Hale (examining the skirt): Wright was close. I think maybe that's why she kept so much to herself. She didn't even belong to the Ladies' Aid. I sup-pose she felt she couldn't do her part, and then you don't enjoy things when you feel shabby. I heard she used to wear pretty clothes and be lively, when she was Minnie Foster, one of the town girls singing in the choir. But that — oh, that was thirty years ago. This all you want to take in?

Mrs. Peters: She said she wanted an apron. Funny thing to want, for there isn't much to get you dirty in jail, goodness knows. But I suppose just to make her feel more natural. She said they was in the top drawer in this cupboard. Yes, here. And then her little shawl that always hung behind the door. *(Opens stair door and looks.)* Yes, here it is. *(Quickly shuts door leading upstairs.)*

Mrs. Hale *(abruptly moving toward her)*: Mrs. Peters?

Mrs. Peters: Yes, Mrs. Hale?

Mrs. Hale: Do you think she did it?

Mrs. Peters *(in a frightened voice)*: Oh, I don't know.

Mrs. Hale: Well, I don't think she did. Asking for an apron and her little shawl. Worrying about her fruit.

Mrs. Peters *(starts to speak, glances up, where footsteps are heard in the room above. In a low voice.)*: Mr. Peters says it looks bad for her. Mr. Henderson is awful sarcastic in a speech and he'll make fun of her sayin' she didn't wake up.

Mrs. Hale: Well, I guess John Wright didn't wake when they was slipping that rope under his neck.

Mrs. Peters: No, it's strange. It must have been done awful crafty and still. They say it was such a — funny way to kill a man, rigging it all up like that.

Mrs. Hale: That's just what Mr. Hale said. There was a gun in the house. He says that's what he can't understand.

Mrs. Peters: Mr. Henderson said coming out that what was needed for the case was a motive; something to show anger, or — sudden feeling.

Mrs. Hale *(who is standing by the table)*: Well, I don't see any signs of anger around here. *(She puts her hand on the dish towel which lies on the table, stands looking down at table, one half of which is clean, the other half messy.)* It's wiped to here. *(Makes a move as if to finish work, then turns and looks at loaf of bread outside the breadbox. Drops towel. In that voice of coming back to familiar things.)* Wonder how they are finding things upstairs. I hope she had it a little more red-up up there. You know, it seems kind of *sneaking*. Locking her up in town and then coming out here and trying to get her own house to turn against her!

Mrs. Peters: But, Mrs. Hale, the law is the law.

Mrs. Hale: I s'pose 'tis. *(Unbuttoning her coat.)* Better loosen up your things, Mrs. Peters. You won't feel them when you go out. *(Mrs. Peters takes off her fur tippet, goes to hang it on hook at back of room, stands looking at the under part of the small corner table.)*

Mrs. Peters: She was piecing a quilt. *(She brings the large sewing basket and they look at the bright pieces.)*

Mrs. Hale: It's a log cabin pattern. Pretty, isn't it? I wonder if she was goin' to quilt it or just knot it? *(Footsteps have been heard coming down the stairs. The Sheriff enters followed by Hale and the County Attorney.)*

Sheriff: They wonder if she was going to quilt it or just knot it! *(The men laugh, the women look abashed.)*

County Attorney *(rubbing his hands over the stove)*: Frank's fire didn't do much up there, did it? Well, let's go out to the barn and get that cleared up. *(The men go outside.)*

Mrs. Hale *(resentfully)*: I don't know as there's anything so strange, our takin' up our time with little things while we're waiting for them to get the evidence. *(She sits down at the big table smoothing out a block with decision.)* I don't see as it's anything to laugh about.

Mrs. Peters (apologetically): Of course they've got awful important things on their minds. *(Pulls up a chair and joins Mrs. Hale at the table.)*

Mrs. Hale (examining another block): Mrs. Peters, look at this one. Here, this is the one she was working on, and look at the sewing! All the rest of it has been so nice and even. And look at this! It's all over the place! Why, it looks as if she didn't know what she was about! *(After she has said this they look at each other, then start to glance back at the door. After an instant Mrs. Hale has pulled at a knot and ripped the sewing.)*

Mrs. Peters: Oh, what are you doing, Mrs. Hale?

Mrs. Hale (mildly): Just pulling out a stitch or two that's not sewed very good. *(Threading a needle.)* Bad sewing always made me fidgety.

Mrs. Peters (nervously): I don't think we ought to touch things.

Mrs. Hale: I'll just finish up this end. *(Suddenly stopping and leaning forward.)* Mrs. Peters?

Mrs. Peters: Yes, Mrs. Hale?

Mrs. Hale: What do you suppose she was so nervous about?

Mrs. Peters: Oh—I don't know. I don't know as she was nervous. I sometimes sew awful queer when I'm just tired. *(Mrs. Hale starts to say something, looks at Mrs. Peters, then goes on sewing.)* Well, I must get these things wrapped up. They may be through sooner than we think. *(Putting apron and other things together.)* I wonder where I can find a piece of paper, and string. *(Rises.)*

Mrs. Hale: In that cupboard, maybe.

Mrs. Peters (looking in cupboard): Why, here's a bird-cage. *(Holds it up.)* Did she have a bird, Mrs. Hale?

Mrs. Hale: Why, I don't know whether she did or not—I've not been here for so long. There was a man around last year selling canaries cheap, but I don't know as she took one; maybe she did. She used to sing real pretty herself.

Mrs. Peters (glancing around): Seems funny to think of a bird here. But she must have had one, or why would she have a cage? I wonder what happened to it?

Mrs. Hale: I s'pose maybe the cat got it.

Mrs. Peters: No, she didn't have a cat. She's got that feeling some people have about cats—being afraid of them. My cat got in her room and she was real upset and asked me to take it out.

Mrs. Hale: My sister Bessie was like that. Queer, ain't it?

Mrs. Peters (examining the cage): Why, look at this door. It's broke. One hinge is pulled apart.

Mrs. Hale (looking too): Looks as if someone must have been rough with it.

Mrs. Peters: Why, yes. *(She brings the cage forward and puts it on the table.)*

Mrs. Hale: I wish if they're going to find any evidence they'd be about it. I don't like this place.

Mrs. Peters: But I'm awful glad you came with me, Mrs. Hale. It would be lonesome for me sitting here alone.

Mrs. Hale: It would, wouldn't it? *(Dropping her sewing.)* But I tell you what I do wish, Mrs. Peters. I wish I had come over sometimes when *she* was here. I—*(looking around the room)*—wish I had.

Mrs. Peters: But of course you were awful busy, Mrs. Hale—your house and your children.

Mrs. Hale: I could've come. I stayed away because it weren't cheerful—and that's why I ought to have come. I—I've never liked this place. Maybe because it's down in a hollow and you don't see the road. I dunno what it is, but it's a lonesome place and always was. I wish I had come over to see Minnie Foster sometimes. I can see now— *(Shakes her head.)*

Mrs. Peters: Well, you mustn't reproach yourself, Mrs. Hale. Somehow we just don't see how it is with other folks until—something turns up.

Mrs. Hale: Not having children makes less work—but it makes a quiet house, and Wright out to work all day, and no company when he did come in. Did you know John Wright, Mrs. Peters?

Mrs. Peters: Not to know him; I've seen him in town. They say he was a good man.

Mrs. Hale: Yes—good; he didn't drink, and kept his word as well as most, I guess, and paid his debts. But he was a hard man, Mrs. Peters. Just to pass the time of day with him— *(Shivers.)* Like a raw wind that gets to the bone. *(Pauses, her eye falling on the cage.)* I should think she would 'a' wanted a bird. But what do you suppose went with it?

Mrs. Peters: I don't know, unless it got sick and died. *(She reaches over and swings the broken door, swings it again, both women watch it.)*

Mrs. Hale: You weren't raised round here, were you? *(Mrs. Peters shakes her head.)* You didn't know—her?

Mrs. Peters: Not till they brought her yesterday.

Mrs. Hale: She—come to think of it, she was kind of like a bird herself—real sweet and pretty, but kind of timid and—fluttery. How—she—did—change. *(Silence: then as if struck by a happy thought and relieved to get back to everyday things.)* Tell you what, Mrs. Peters, why don't you take the quilt in with you? It might take up her mind.

Mrs. Peters: Why, I think that's a real nice idea, Mrs. Hale. There couldn't possibly be any objection to it could there? Now, just what would I take? I wonder if her patches are in here—and her things. *(They look in the sewing basket.)*

Mrs. Hale: Here's some red. I expect this has got sewing things in it. *(Brings out a fancy box.)* What a pretty box. Looks like something somebody would give you. Maybe her scissors are in here. *(Opens box. Suddenly puts her hand to her nose.)* Why— *(Mrs. Peters bends nearer, then turns her face away.)* There's something wrapped up in this piece of silk.

Mrs. Peters: Why, this isn't her scissors.

Mrs. Hale (lifting the silk): Oh, Mrs. Peters—it's— *(Mrs. Peters bends closer.)*

Mrs. Peters: It's the bird.

Mrs. Hale (jumping up): But, Mrs. Peters—look at it! Its neck! Look at its neck! It's all—other side *to*.

Mrs. Peters: Somebody—wrung—its—neck. *(Their eyes meet. A look of growing comprehension, of horror. Steps are heard outside. Mrs. Hale slips box under quilt pieces, and sinks into her chair. Enter Sheriff and County Attorney. Mrs. Peters rises.)*

County Attorney (as one turning from serious things to little pleasantries): Well, ladies, have you decided whether she was going to quilt it or knot it?

Mrs. Peters: We think she was going to—knot it.

County Attorney: Well, that's interesting, I'm sure. *(Seeing the bird-cage.)* Has the bird flown?

Mrs. Hale (putting more quilt pieces over the box): We think the—cat got it.

County Attorney (preoccupied): Is there a cat? *(Mrs. Hale glances in a quick covert way at Mrs. Peters.)*

Mrs. Peters: Well, not *now.* They're superstitious, you know. They leave.

County Attorney (to Sheriff Peters, continuing an interrupted conversation): No sign at all of anyone having come from the outside. Their own rope. Now let's go up again and go over it piece by piece. *(They start upstairs.)* It would have to have been someone who knew just the—*(Mrs. Peters sits down. The two women sit there not looking at one another, but as if peering into something and at the same time holding back. When they talk now it is in the manner of feeling their way over strange ground, as if afraid of what they are saying, but as if they cannot help saying it.)*

Mrs. Hale: She liked the bird. She was going to bury it in that pretty box.

Mrs. Peters (in a whisper): When I was a girl—my kitten—there was a boy took a hatchet, and before my eyes—and before I could get there—*(Covers her face an instant.)* If they hadn't held me back I would have—*(catches herself, looks upstairs where steps are heard, falters weakly)*—hurt him.

Mrs. Hale (with a slow look around her): I wonder how it would seem never to have had any children around. *(Pause.)* No, Wright wouldn't like the bird— a thing that sang. She used to sing. He killed that, too.

Mrs. Peters (moving uneasily): We don't know who killed the bird.

Mrs. Hale: I knew John Wright.

Mrs. Peters: It was an awful thing was done in this house that night, Mrs. Hale. Killing a man while he slept, slipping a rope around his neck that choked the life out of him.

Mrs. Hale: His neck. Choked the life out of him. *(Her hand goes out and rests on the bird-cage.)*

Mrs. Peters (with rising voice): We don't know who killed him. We don't *know.*

Mrs. Hale (her own feeling not interrupted): If there'd been years and years of nothing, then a bird to sing to you, it would be awful—still, after the bird was still.

Mrs. Peters (something within her speaking): I know what stillness is. When we homesteaded in Dakota, and my first baby died—after he was two years old, and me with no other then—

Mrs. Hale (moving): How soon do you suppose they'll be through looking for the evidence?

Mrs. Peters: I know what stillness is. *(Pulling herself back.)* The law has got to punish crime, Mrs. Hale.

Mrs. Hale (not as if answering that): I wish you'd seen Minnie Foster when she wore a white dress with blue ribbons and stood up there in the choir and sang. *(A look around the room.)* Oh, I *wish* I'd come over here once in a while! That was a crime! That was a crime! Who's going to punish that?

Mrs. Peters (looking upstairs): We mustn't—take on.

Mrs. Hale: I might have known she needed help! I know how things can be— for women. I tell you, it's queer, Mrs. Peters. We live close together and we live far apart. We all go through the same things—it's all just a different kind of the same thing. *(Brushes her eyes, noticing the bottle of fruit, reaches out for it.)* If I was you I wouldn't tell her her fruit was gone. Tell her it *ain't.* Tell her it's all right. Take this in to prove it to her. She—she may never know whether it was broke or not.

*Mrs. Peters (takes the bottle, looks about for something to wrap it in; takes petticoat from
the clothes brought from the other room, very nervously begins winding this around
the bottle. In a false voice.):* My, it's a good thing the men couldn't hear us.
Wouldn't they just laugh! Getting all stirred up over a little thing like a —
dead canary. As if that could have anything to do with — with — wouldn't
they *laugh! (The men are heard coming down stairs.)*

Mrs. Hale (under her breath): Maybe they would — maybe they wouldn't.

County Attorney: No, Peters, it's all perfectly clear except a reason for doing it.
But you know juries when it comes to women. If there was some definite
thing. Something to show — something to make a story about — a thing
that would connect up with this strange way of doing it — *(The women's
eyes meet for an instant. Enter Hale from outer door.)*

Hale: Well, I've got the team around. Pretty cold out there.

County Attorney: I'm going to stay here a while by myself. *(To the Sheriff.)* You
can send Frank out for me, can't you? I want to go over everything. I'm not
satisfied that we can't do better.

Sheriff: Do you want to see what Mrs. Peters is going to take in? *(The Lawyer
goes to the table, picks up the apron, laughs.)*

County Attorney: Oh, I guess they're not very dangerous things the ladies have
picked out. *(Moves a few things about, disturbing the quilt pieces which cover
the box. Steps back.)* No, Mrs. Peters doesn't need supervising. For that matter a sheriff's wife is married to the law. Ever think of it that way, Mrs.
Peters?

Mrs. Peters: Not — just that way.

Sheriff (chuckling): Married to the law. *(Moves toward the other room.)* I just want
you to come in here a minute, George. We ought to take a look at these
windows.

County Attorney (scoffingly): Oh, windows!

Sheriff: We'll be right out, Mr. Hale. *(Hale goes outside. The Sheriff follows the
County Attorney into the other room. Then Mrs. Hale rises, hands tight together,
looking intensely at Mrs. Peters, whose eyes make a slow turn, finally meeting Mrs.
Hale's. A moment Mrs. Hale holds her, then her own eyes point the way to where the
box is concealed. Suddenly Mrs. Peters throws back quilt pieces and tries to put the
box in the bag she is wearing. It is too big. She opens box, starts to take bird out, cannot touch it, goes to pieces, stands there helpless. Sound of a knob turning in the
other room. Mrs. Hale snatches the box and puts it in the pocket of her big coat.
Enter County Attorney and Sheriff.)*

County Attorney (facetiously): Well, Henry, at least we found out that she was
not going to quilt it. She was going to — what is it you call it, ladies?

Mrs. Hale (her hand against her pocket): We call it — knot it, Mr. Henderson.

> *Curtain.*

CONSIDERATIONS FOR CRITICAL THINKING AND WRITING

1. FIRST RESPONSE. Describe the setting of this play. What kind of atmosphere is established by the details in the opening scene? Does the atmosphere change through the course of the play?

2. Where are Mrs. Hale and Mrs. Peters while Mr. Hale explains to the county attorney how the murder was discovered? How does their location suggest the relationship between the men and the women in the play?

3. What kind of person was Minnie Foster before she married? How do you think her marriage affected her?

4. Characterize John Wright. Why did his wife kill him?

5. Why do the men fail to see the clues that Mrs. Hale and Mrs. Peters discover?

6. What is the significance of the birdcage and the dead bird? Why do Mrs. Hale and Mrs. Peters respond so strongly to them? How do you respond?

7. Why don't Mrs. Hale and Mrs. Peters reveal the evidence they have uncovered? What would you have done?

8. How do the men's conversations and actions reveal their attitudes toward women?

9. Why do you think Glaspell allows us only to hear about Mr. and Mrs. Wright? What is the effect of their never appearing on stage?

10. Does your impression of Mrs. Wright change during the course of the play? If so, what changes it?

11. What is the significance of the play's last line, spoken by Mrs. Hale: "We call it — knot it, Mr. Henderson"? Explain what you think the tone of Mrs. Hale's voice is when she says this line. What is she feeling? What are you feeling?

12. Explain the significance of the play's title. Do you think *Trifles* or "A Jury of Her Peers," Glaspell's title for the short story version of the play, is more appropriate? Can you think of other titles that capture the play's central concerns?

13. If possible, find a copy of "A Jury of Her Peers" in the library (reprinted in *The Best Short Stories of 1917*, ed. E. J. O'Brien [Boston: Small, Maynard, 1918], pp. 256–282), and write an essay that explores the differences between the play and the short story.

14. CRITICAL STRATEGIES. Read the section on formalist criticism (pp. 60–62) in Chapter 3, "Applying a Critical Strategy." Several times the characters say things that they don't mean, and this creates a discrepancy between what appears to be and what is actually true. Point to instances of irony in the play and explain how they contribute to its effects and meanings. (For discussions of irony elsewhere in this book, see the Index of Terms.)

After reading Trifles *carefully and taking notes on the characters, William uses the following "Questions for Writing" to further think about the elements of the play. These same questions can help you consider important elements that reveal any play's effects and meanings. These questions are general and will not, therefore, always be relevant to a particular play. Many of them, however, should prove to be useful for thinking, talking, and writing about drama. If you are uncertain about the meaning of a term used in a question, consult the Glossary of Literary Terms beginning on page 1381.*

QUESTIONS FOR WRITING ABOUT DRAMA

1. Did you enjoy the play? What, specifically, pleased or displeased you about what was expressed and how it was expressed?

2. What is the significance of the play's title? How does it suggest the author's overall emphasis?

3. What information do the stage directions provide about the characters, action, and setting? Are these directions primarily descriptive, or are they also interpretive?

4. How is the exposition presented? What does it reveal? How does the playwright's choice *not* to dramatize certain events on stage help to determine what the focus of the play is?

5. In what ways is the setting important? Would the play be altered significantly if the setting were changed?

6. Are foreshadowings used to suggest what is to come? Are flashbacks used to dramatize what has already happened?

7. What is the major conflict the protagonist faces? What complications constitute the rising action? Where is the climax? Is the conflict resolved?

8. Are one or more subplots used to qualify or complicate the main plot? Is the plot unified so that each incident somehow has a function that relates it to some other element in the play?

9. Does the author purposely avoid a pyramidal plot structure of rising action, climax, and falling action? Is the plot experimental? Is the plot logically and chronologically organized, or is it fantastical or absurd? What effects are produced by the plot? How does it reflect the author's view of life?

10. Who is the protagonist? Who (or what) is the antagonist?

11. By what means does the playwright reveal character? What do the characters' names, physical qualities, actions, and words convey about them? What do the characters reveal about each other?

12. What is the purpose of the minor characters? Are they individualized, or do they primarily represent ideas or attitudes? Are any character foils used?

13. Do the characters all use the same kind of language, or is their speech differentiated? Is it formal or informal? How do the characters' diction and manner of speaking serve to characterize them?

14. Does your response to the characters change in the course of the play? What causes the change?

15. Are words and images repeated in the play so that they take on special meanings? Which speeches seem particularly important? Why?

16. How does the playwright's use of language contribute to the tone of the play? Is the dialogue, for example, predominantly light, humorous, relaxed, sentimental, sad, angry, intense, or violent?

17. Are any symbols used in the play? Which actions, characters, settings, objects, or words convey more than their literal meanings?

18. Are any unfamiliar theatrical conventions used that present problems in understanding the play? How does knowing more about the nature of the theater from which the play originated help to resolve these problems?

19. Is the theme stated directly, or is it developed implicitly through the plot, characters, or some other element? Does the theme confirm or challenge most people's values?

20. How does the play reflect the values of the society in which it is set and in which it was written?

21. How does the play reflect or challenge your own values?

22. Is there a recording, film, or videocassette of the play available in your library or media center? How does this version compare with your own reading?

23. How would you produce the play on a stage? Consider scenery, costumes, casting, and characterizations. What would you emphasize most in your production?

24. Is there a particular critical approach that seems especially appropriate for this play? (See Chapter 3, "Applying a Critical Strategy," which begins on p. 56.)

25. How might biographical information about the author help the reader to grasp the central concerns of the play?

26. How might historical information about the play provide a useful context for interpretation?

27. To what extent do your own experiences, values, beliefs, and assumptions inform your interpretation?

28. What kinds of evidence from the play are you focusing on to support your interpretation? Does your interpretation leave out any important elements that might undercut or qualify your interpretation?

29. Given that there are a variety of ways to interpret the play, which one seems the most useful to you?

A Sample First Response

William has been asked to write a character analysis. In his following informal response to the character of Mrs. Hale, he focuses particularly on those Questions for Writing about Drama that focus on character (questions 11–15). Note that in thinking about her character, he moves to thinking about Mrs. Hale's larger function in *Trifles* and larger thematic issues as well.

```
        Reading Susan Glaspell's Trifles, I was impressed by the
character of Mrs. Hale. It seemed to me that she moved all the
play's action along, made all of the most vital discoveries
about the murder. The men in the play ignored what they thought
to be "trifles," but these very trifles were crucial clues.
Mrs. Hale, however, didn't just have an eye for detail. I want
to show in my paper how her insights into emotional motivations
and into unfair gender roles allow her to act justly by not
```

revealing evidence. I want to show how these character traits
of Mrs. Hale's give the play its depth.

A Sample of Brainstorming

After his first response, William brainstorms about the connection
between what Mrs. Hale *does* in the play (her actions) and the character
traits that are subsequently revealed. As you'll see, these notes will shape
the argument he makes in his final draft.

Mrs. Hale's Actions in the Play	Character Traits Revealed
dishtowel argument	Mrs. Hale knows what it takes to do the hard work Mrs. Wright would have been doing. She is not prejudiced against women and therefore makes a valid conjecture about the possibility of the deputy soiling the towel.
rope knots matching quilting knots	Mrs. Hale doesn't consider women's work to be "trifles." Therefore, she finds vital clues on the quilt.
the strangled canary	Mrs. Hale discovers it and links it to a motive.
emotional motivations considered	Mrs. Hale is the only character who considers Mr. and Mrs. Wright's personalities and sees the unfair gender roles in their relationship.

A Sample Student Character Analysis

In William's final paper, he describes Mrs. Hale's function in the play
and how her character points to the play's thematic significance. As you
read through his argument, pay attention to the evidence he uses and the
conclusions he draws. Do you agree with William's assessment of the
importance of Mrs. Hale's character traits to the play's action? Would you
use different examples or draw different conclusions from his?

William Dean
Professor McConathy
English 114
April 15, 20--

               The Centrality of Mrs. Hale to Trifles

     Susan Glaspell's one-act play Trifles takes place
during the county attorney George Henderson's investigation into the murder of the farmer John Wright. The
play's protaganist, however, is Wright's neighbor, Mrs.
Hale. While Henderson leads an investigation based merely
on assumptions, Mrs. Hale conducts her own inquiry. Her
discovery of Mrs. Wright's guilt and her subsequent decision not to reveal incriminating evidence form the play's
central action. As this action advances and concludes,
Mrs. Hale's character traits, in particular her eye for
crucial details and her understanding of emotional motivations, give the story its depth.

     As he considers Mrs. Wright's kitchen, Mr. Hale
says, "women are used to worrying over trifles," but his
own wife's careful consideration of evidence is anything
but trifling. After the men have assumed that the dirty
dishtowel is a sign of Mrs. Wright's messiness, Mrs. Hale
correctly suggests to Mrs. Peters that the towel might
have been dirtied by the deputy sheriff. The men laugh
dismissively at Mrs. Hale's and Mrs. Peters' discussion
of the quilt. Mrs. Hale notices, however, that the knots
used on the quilt match those on the rope used for the
murder. She also connects the strangled canary to the
crime. Presuming that Mr. Wright strangled the canary
because its singing annoyed him, Mrs. Hale remembers that
before Mrs. Wright married she sang in a choir. Mrs. Hale
remarks, "She used to sing. He killed that, too." Just as
Glaspell makes her play's main plot out of what might
seem a subplot to the murder, so Mrs. Hale makes vital
connections from what might seem peripheral, even

trifling details. Her speech itself reflects this attention to detail. At the end of the play when Mr. Henderson facetiously asks whether Mrs. Wright was going to quilt or knot, Mrs. Hale gives him a clue with the very words "knot it." Mrs. Hale knows that Mr. Henderson will not pick up this clue, because women's work is to him mere trifling.

Not only does Mrs. Hale observe these important physical clues more clearly than the other characters, she also understands emotional motivations more deeply. In addition to remembering Mrs. Wright's long-gone happiness as an unmarried chorister, she evocatively remembers Mr. Wright as being "[l]ike a raw wind that gets to the bone." These insights allow Mrs. Hale to understand, before the other characters, the emotionally oppressive situation that led to the murder. Mrs. Hale is the only character who sees this situation as inequity between men and women. Even Mrs. Peters defends the men's callous views when she says, "they've got awful important things on their minds." Mrs. Hale, however, isn't swayed by her society's version of men's and women's respective roles. This unprejudiced understanding leads Mrs. Hale to withhold the evidence that would condemn Mrs. Wright, the very evidence Mrs. Hale herself uncovered.

By having Mrs. Hale and Mrs. Peters keep their knowledge to themselves, Glaspell asks the play's audience to consider how justice may exist outside the justice system. Near the beginning of the play, when the county attorney pretends to concede to the women's "trifles," Mrs. Hale sees through what Glaspell's stage directions call "the gallantry of a young politician." By the play's end, Mrs. Hale's ability to see vital details and to understand emotional motivation gives her the opportunity to act justly in a way the young politician never could.

8

Reading and Writing
about the Essay

READING ESSAYS RESPONSIVELY

Although essays are generally nonfictional compositions that examine
and explore actual events and people, most good essays — the memorable
ones — are as imaginative and inventive as stories, poems, or plays. You'll
find many of the same kinds of literary elements used in essays that you're
already familiar with in fiction, poetry, and drama. An awareness, for example, of tone, character, setting, theme, diction, images, figures of speech,
symbol, irony, dialogue, and narration can be just as useful and significant
in reading essays responsively as they are for other kinds of literature. A
sensitivity to these matters can greatly enhance your understanding and
reading pleasure. Whether you applaud or growl at an essayist's observations, you can still learn to appreciate the techniques and strategies used to
convey the writer's ideas.

Like any other kind of literature, essays can be about anything: topics
range from scientific descriptions of insects to philosophic arguments
about the existence of God, or from information about how to build a
stone wall to narratives recounting some critical moment in a person's life.
Essays can be short or long, formal or informal, serious or hilarious, tight
or rambling, precise or anecdotal. They can be — and have been — whatever
a writer has made of this elastic and enduring literary form.

The term *essay* has its origin in the French verb *essayer*, meaning "to
try" or "to attempt." The French writer Michel de Montaigne (1533–1592)
used the word *essai* to describe a 1580 collection of informal compositions
on such general topics as sadness and ancient customs that were offered to
readers as a series of exploratory ruminations or reflections rather than as
definitive statements. This term appeared for the first time in English
when Francis Bacon (1561–1626) used it as the title of his of his *Essays* in

1597. The origins of the word serve to emphasize that essays are not necessarily systematic elucidations of a topic that proceed with the kind of precision you might find in a laboratory report. Instead, essays often try out ideas on an informed but not always expert audience. Owing to the broad scope of essay writing — from the scientific findings of an article on gallstones in the *AMA Archives of Internal Medicine* to a freewheeling tour of San Francisco Bay area rock groups in *Rolling Stone* magazine — definitions of types of essays must be as flexible as the literary form itself. Even so, there are some broad distinctions that are useful enough to make the attempt worthwhile.

TYPES OF ESSAYS

There are many potential ways of classifying essays, but four particularly useful categories for thinking about essays are *narration, description, exposition,* and *argumentation.* These types of essays sometimes overlap and are often combined with a motive for writing: to inform, to persuade, or to move the reader to action. The terms are helpful primarily as a means of providing a convenient vocabulary to consider the overall purpose of an essay.

A *narrative essay* typically tells a story by recounting an event or series of events in some kind of chronological order. These events are often autobiographical, as in Frederick Douglass's account of his growing up a slave (pp. 748–752). The retrospective and simultaneously immediate story that Douglass tells focuses on a crucial moment when, as a boy, he is introduced to the cruelties of slavery as he witnesses his Aunt Hester suffering a beating by her master. This vivid recounting of how slavery impressed itself on Douglass also includes an implicit argument against slavery that is designed to move his white readers into the ranks of antislavery abolitionists. What is significant about Douglass's narrative strategy is that he doesn't argue that slavery is evil; instead, he allows the details of his story to make argument for him.

Related to the narrative essay is the *descriptive essay.* Details are at the heart of description and represent the heart's blood of just about any effective essay. Without details, the essay frequently becomes abstract and vague; but with vivid details — the kind that allow you to see, hear, touch, smell, and taste — the essay can provide pleasure as well as information. Consider, for example, E. B. White's description of early mornings in "Once More to the Lake" (pp. 532–536):

> I guess I remembered clearest of all the early mornings, when the lake was cool and motionless, remembered how the bedroom smelled of the lumber it was made of and of the wet woods whose scent entered through the screen. The partitions in the camp were thin and did not extend clear to the top of the rooms, and as I was always the first up I would dress softly so as not to wake

the others, and sneak out into the sweet outdoors and start out in the canoe, keeping close along the shore in the long shadows of the pines. I remembered being very careful never to rub my paddle against the gunwale for fear of disturbing the stillness of the cathedral.

Compare White's description with this summary statement stripped of details:

> I remember best the early mornings when I would get up before everyone else so that I could canoe by myself on the lake.

Of course, what gets lost in this objective paraphrase are White's delicious details and the subjective emotional content of the passage. Sometimes objective, detailed information is all you need — when, for example, you want clear, unembellished information from plans for building a canoe. Similarly, emotions have no place in a scientific description of a chemical reaction. In White's description of the lake, however, those details are what finally convince us that the lake is not simply a topographical location but, as White concludes, a "cathedral."

If we wanted only an objective topographical description of the lake, we would look to an *expository essay* to do the job, an essay that mostly provides information in a clear, straightforward manner. The purpose of most expository essays is to explain something. This can be accomplished in a variety of ways including defining, comparing, analyzing, or showing how a cause leads to a particular effect. In "Calculated Risks" (pp. 538–544), for example, K. C. Cole explains why and how people misjudge real as well as imagined risks in their lives. Cole deftly presents a wide array of examples to support her analysis. This careful examination prompts readers to evaluate their own anxieties and blind spots concerning risk-taking. Although expository essays are largely informational, they are not always devoid of efforts to persuade readers to think a particular way or to take a specific course of action, even though exposition is primarily to inform rather than to argue.

An *argumentative essay*, however, typically presents a writer's point of view in a clear and forceful manner. Such essays are organized to persuade readers, to win them over to the writer's perspective, by presenting evidence to support a particular position or to take some kind of action. In order to be persuasive, it is usually necessary to have a specific thesis and to demonstrate sound, logical reasoning. The supporting evidence can take many forms ranging from statistics, facts, examples, narrative, and personal anecdotes to emotional appeals. In making their case, argumentative essays also frequently present opposing arguments in order to demonstrate that they are weak, faulty, or fatally wrong. No one who reads Linda Chavez's "Demystifying Multiculturalism" (pp. 546–550) will miss her attack on the multicultural movement in the United States. Writing for the conservative *National Review*, Chavez makes absolutely clear to readers her argument that multiculturalism exacerbates racial issues in the United States rather than reducing them. Her argumentative essay is not simply an observation but a firmly held position.

It's worth emphasizing again that these four types of essays — narrative, descriptive, expository, and argumentative — neither exhaust the possible forms that essays can take nor are mutually exclusive. Most writers typically use whatever strategies they find helpful in conveying the information, ideas, and perspectives that they bring to a topic. As you read the essays in this chapter and throughout the book, you'll discover how writers blend a variety of approaches to reach their readers.

THE ELEMENTS

If you read enough essays you're likely to encounter just about all the literary elements you'd find in fiction, poetry, and drama. Essay writers don't read only nonfiction, and there are no hard and fast rules to prevent writers from drawing on other genres to communicate with their audiences. There are, however, several elements used in essays that warrant special attention because focused awareness of them serves to make essays more accessible for both your reading and your writing.

Voice and Tone

As you begin reading an essay, the narrator's *voice* will gradually make itself apparent to you; the process of establishing this familiarity is similar to being introduced to someone. First you determine the sort of person you are speaking with — largely based on what is said and how it is said. Pretty soon you determine whether a person's voice is rude or polite, angry or genial, upset or calm. Reading an essay doesn't provide you with the additional kinds of clues ordinarily found in conversation — dress, age, accent, and so on — but if you know something about an author or even the date and source of the essay's publication, you can place the voice more completely. To know, for instance, that Frederick Douglass was an American black slave who escaped from bondage as a young man, provides a powerful and significant context for the voice that emerges from the first three sentences of his 1845 *Narrative:*

> I was born in Tuckahoe, near Hillsborough, and about twelve miles from Easton, in Talbot County, Maryland. I have no accurate knowledge of my age, never having any authentic record containing it. By far the larger part of the slaves know as little of their ages as horses know of theirs, and it is the wish of most masters within my knowledge to keep their slaves thus ignorant.

Douglass's voice is restrained and matter-of-fact. He does not express rage against the master who deprived him of his freedom and the most basic knowledge about himself; instead, his voice is calm, deliberate, and factual. He allows the reader to reflect on the meaning of his slave experience, and by avoiding accusations, anger, and indignant outrage, he allows the reader

to supply the emotion, making his description of slavery all the more powerful and persuasive. The reader is invited to contemplate what it means
not to know one's own birthdate, and therefore the reader identifies with
Douglass's plight all the more.

Douglass's *tone* — his attitude toward what he is writing about and the
mood created by his use of language — encourages a sympathetic and
empathetic reader response. He achieves that mood by carefully choosing
his words, pacing his sentences, and avoiding imposing his emotions on
the reader. Compare the tone of his writing to that of William Lloyd Garrison, a white abolitionist leader who wrote a preface for the *Narrative* when
it was first published:

> Reader! are you with the man-stealers in sympathy and purpose, or on the side
> of their down-trodden victims? If with the former, then you are the foe of
> God and man. . . . Be faithful, be vigilant, be untiring in your efforts to break
> every yoke, and let the oppressed go free. Come what may — cost what it may —
> inscribe on the banner which you unfurl to the breeze, as your religious and
> political motto — "NO COMPROMISE WITH SLAVERY! NO UNION WITH
> SLAVE HOLDERS!"

Garrison's voice comes from delivering antislavery lectures; it's at a shout,
and his tone demands commitment and action from the reader. On the
page even the exclamation points and capital letters are loud. Clearly, the
writer's persona, the personality that emerges from each sample, is quite
different in Douglass and Garrison. Which piece of writing do you find
more effective? The choice is yours, but whichever you prefer, your decision
will be based on an assessment of the voice and tone of each passage.

Probably one of literature's most famous voices is that of Jonathan
Swift, whose gift for writing **satire** remains arguably unmatched after two
hundred years. Swift's career was spent variously in the service of politics and
religion, and most of his writing can be linked to a specific cause and message — from the fictional *Gulliver's Travels* to the essay reprinted here, "A Modest Proposal." Swift called good style nothing more than "proper words in
proper places," which every writer knows is more complicated than it looks.
As you read "A Modest Proposal," pay particular attention to Swift's use of
irony to develop his points. Note how he carefully constructs his argument so
that we are almost unaware of what he is "modestly" proposing — a horrifying elaboration of the metaphor "The English are devouring the Irish."

JONATHAN SWIFT (1667–1745)

Although Jonathan Swift was the son of English parents, he was born
in Ireland, where he grew up and studied at Trinity College, Dublin. He
moved to London in 1689 and steeped himself in literary and political
issues from a Tory perspective. In 1713 he was appointed — to his dismay —
dean of St. Patrick's Cathedral in Dublin, but he remained in charge of

that church for the rest of his life, supporting Irish interests against the English government and thereby earning the respect of the Irish people. Swift's satires are generally regarded as among the best in English literature; they include *A Tale of a Tub* (1704), *The Battle of the Books* (1704), "A Modest Proposal" (1729), and his best-known book, a satiric novel concerning the nature of humanity, *Gulliver's Travels* (1726).

A Modest Proposal   1729

For Preventing the Children of Poor People in Ireland
from Being a Burden to Their Parents or Country,
and for Making Them Beneficial to the Public

It is a melancholy object to those who walk through this great town° or travel in the country, when they see the streets, the roads, and cabin doors, crowded with beggars of the female sex, followed by three, four, or six children, all in rags and importuning every passenger for an alms. These mothers instead of being able to work for their honest livelihood, are forced to employ all their time in strolling to beg sustenance for their helpless infants: who as they grow up either turn thieves for want of work, or leave their dear native country to fight for the pretender in Spain,° or sell themselves to the Barbadoes.°

I think it is agreed by all parties that this prodigious number of children in the arms, or on the backs, or at the heels of their mothers, and frequently of their fathers, is in the present deplorable state of the kingdom a very great additional grievance; and, therefore, whoever could find out a fair, cheap, and easy method of making these children sound, useful members of the commonwealth, would deserve so well of the public as to have his statute set up for a preserver of the nation.

But my intention is very far from being confined to provide only for the children of professed beggars; it is of a much greater extent, and shall take in the whole number of infants at a certain age who are born of parents in effect as little able to support them as those who demand our charity in the streets.

As to my own part, having turned my thoughts for many years upon this important subject, and maturely weighed the several schemes of our projectors,° I have always found them grossly mistaken in their computation. It is true, a child just dropped from its dam may be supported by her milk for a solar year, with little other nourishment; at most not above the value of two shillings, which the mother may certainly get, or the value in scraps, by her lawful occupation of begging; and it is exactly at one year old that I propose to provide for them in such a manner as instead of being a charge upon their parents or the parish, or wanting food and raiment for the rest of their lives, they shall on the contrary contribute to the feeding, and partly to the clothing, of many thousands.

---

great town: Dublin.   *pretender in Spain:* James Stuart (1688–1766); exiled in Spain and claimant to the English crown was supported by many Irishmen who sought to restore him to the throne.   *Barbadoes:* A British colony in the Caribbean where Irish immigrants worked as indentured servants to pay for their passage over.   *projectors:* Planners.

There is likewise another great advantage in my scheme, that it will pre- 5
vent those voluntary abortions, and that horrid practice of women murdering
their bastard children, alas! too frequent among us! sacrificing the poor innocent babes I doubt more to avoid the expense than the shame, which would
move tears and pity in the most savage and inhuman breast.

The number of souls in this kingdom being usually reckoned one million
and a half, of these I calculate there may be about 200,000 couple whose wives
are breeders; from which number I subtract 30,000 couple who are able to
maintain their own children (although I apprehend there cannot be so many,
under the present distress of the kingdom); but this being granted, there will
remain 170,000 breeders. I again subtract 50,000 for those women who mis-
carry, or whose children die by accident or disease within the year. There only
remain 120,000 children of poor parents annually born. The question therefore is, how this number shall be reared and provided for? which, as I have
already said, under the present situation of affairs, is utterly impossible by all
the methods hitherto proposed. For we can neither employ them in handicraft
of agriculture; we neither build houses (I mean in the country) nor cultivate
land; they can very seldom pick up a livelihood by stealing, till they arrive at six
years old, except where they are of towardly parts;° although I confess they
learn the rudiments much earlier; during which time they can, however, be
properly looked upon only as probationers; as I have been informed by a principal gentleman in the county of Cavan, who protested to me that he never
knew above one or two instances under the age of six, even in a part of the
kingdom so renowned for the quickest proficiency in that art.

I am assured by our merchants, that a boy or a girl before twelve years old
is no salable commodity; and even when they come to this age they will not
yield above 3£. or 3£. 2s. 6d. at most on the exchange; which cannot turn to
account either to the parents or kingdom, the charge of nutriment and rags
having been at least four times that value.

I shall now therefore humbly propose my own thoughts, which I hope will
not be liable to the least objection.

I have been assured by a very knowing American of my acquaintance in
London, that a young healthy child well nursed is at a year old a most delicious, nourishing, and wholesome food, whether stewed, roasted, baked, or
broiled; and I make no doubt that it will equally serve in a fricassee or a
ragout.°

I do therefore humbly offer it to public consideration that of the 120,000 10
children already computed, 20,000 may be reserved for breed, whereof only one-
fourth part to be males; which is more than we allow to sheep, black cattle, or
swine; and my reason is, that these children are seldom the fruits of marriage, a
circumstance not much regarded by our savages; therefore one male will be sufficient to serve four females. That the remaining 100,000 may, at a year old, be
offered in sale to the persons of quality and fortune through the kingdom;
always advising the mother to let them suck plentifully in the last month, so as
to render them plump and fat for a good table. A child will make two dishes at
an entertainment for friends; and when the family dines alone, the fore and
hind quarter will make a reasonable dish, and seasoned with a little pepper or
salt will be very good boiled on the fourth day, especially in winter.

---

towardly parts: Innate abilities.   *ragout:* Stew.

I have reckoned upon a medium that a child just born will weigh 12 pounds, and in a solar year, if tolerably nursed, will increase to 28 pounds.

I grant this food will be somewhat dear, and therefore very proper for landlords, who, as they have already devoured most of the parents, seem to have the best title to the children.

Infants' flesh will be in season throughout the year, but more plentiful in March, and a little before and after: for we are told by a grave author, an eminent French physician,° that fish being a prolific diet, there are more children born in Roman Catholic countries about nine months after Lent than at any other season; therefore, reckoning a year after Lent, the markets will be more glutted than usual, because the number of popish infants is at least three to one in this kingdom: and therefore it will have one other collateral advantage, by lessening the number of papists among us.

I have already computed the charge of nursing a beggar's child (in which list I reckon all cottagers, laborers, and four-fifths of the farmers) to be about 2s. per annum, rags included; and I believe no gentleman would repine to give 10s. for the carcass of a good fat child, which, as I have said, will make four dishes of excellent nutritive meat, when he has only some particular friend or his own family to dine with him. Thus the squire will learn to be a good landlord, and grow popular among the tenants; the mother will have 8s. net profit, and be fit for work till she produces another child.

Those who are more thrifty (as I must confess the times require) may flay the carcass; the skin of which artificially° dressed will make admirable gloves for ladies, and summer boots for fine gentlemen. 15

As to our city of Dublin, shambles° may be appointed for this purpose in the most convenient parts of it, and butchers we may be assured will not be wanting: although I rather recommend buying the children alive, and dressing them hot from the knife as we do roasting pigs.

A very worthy person, a true lover of his country, and whose virtues I highly esteem, was lately pleased in discoursing on this matter to offer a refinement upon my scheme. He said that many gentlemen of this kingdom, having of late destroyed their deer, he conceived that the want of venison might be well supplied by the bodies of young lads and maidens, not exceeding fourteen years of age nor under twelve; so great a number of both sexes in every country being now ready to starve for want of work and service; and these to be disposed of by their parents, if alive, or otherwise by their nearest relations. But with due deference to so excellent a friend and so deserving a patriot, I cannot be altogether in his sentiments; for as to the males, my American acquaintance assured me from frequent experience that their flesh was generally tough and lean, like that of our schoolboys by continual exercise, and their taste disagreeable; and to fatten them would not answer the charge. Then as to the females, it would, I think, with humble submission be a loss to the public, because they soon would become breeders themselves: and besides, it is not improbable that some scrupulous people might be apt to censure such a practice (although indeed very unjustly), as a little bordering upon cruelty; which, I confess, has always been with me the strongest objection against any project, how well soever intended.

French physician: François Rabelais (c. 1494–1553), Renaissance author of the comic *Gargantua and Pantagruel.*   *artificially:* Skillfully.   *shambles:* Slaughterhouses.

But in order to justify my friend, he confessed that this expedient was put into his head by the famous Psalmanazar° a native of the island Formosa, who came from thence to London about twenty years ago: and in conversation told my friend, that in his country when any young person happened to be put to death, the executioner sold the carcass to persons of quality as a prime dainty; and that in his time the body of a plump girl of fifteen, who was crucified for an attempt to poison the emperor, was sold to his imperial majesty's prime minister of state, and other great mandarins of the court, in joints from the gibbet, at 400 crowns. Neither indeed can I deny, that if the same use were made of several plump young girls in this town, who without one single groat to their fortunes cannot stir abroad without a chair,° and appear at the playhouse and assemblies in foreign fineries which they never will pay for, the kingdom would not be the worse.

Some persons of a desponding spirit are in great concern about the vast number of poor people, who are aged, diseased, or maimed, and I have been desired to employ my thoughts what course may be taken to ease the nation of so grievous an encumbrance. But I am not in the least pain upon that matter, because it is very well known that they are every day dying and rotting by cold and famine, and filth and vermin, as fast as can be reasonably expected. And as to the young laborers, they are now in as hopeful a condition: They cannot get work, and consequently pine away for want of nourishment, to a degree that if at any time they are accidentally hired to common labor, they have not strength to perform it; and thus the country and themselves are happily delivered from the evils to come.

I have too long digressed, and therefore shall return to my subject. I think 20 the advantages by the proposal which I have made are obvious and many, as well as of the highest importance.

For first, as I have already observed, it would greatly lessen the number of papists, with whom we are yearly overrun, being the principal breeders of the nation as well as our most dangerous enemies; and who stay at home on purpose to deliver the kingdom to the Pretender, hoping to take their advantage by the absence of so many good Protestants, who have chosen rather to leave their country than stay at home and pay tithes against their conscience to an Episcopal curate.

Secondly, The poor tenants will have something valuable of their own, which by law may be made liable to distress° and help to pay their landlord's rent, their corn and cattle being already seized, and money a thing unknown.

Thirdly, Whereas the maintenance of 100,000 children from two years old and upward, cannot be computed at less than 10s. a-piece per annum, the nation's stock will be thereby increased £50,000 per annum, beside the profit of a new dish introduced to the tables of all gentlemen of fortune in the kingdom who have any refinement in taste. And the money will circulate among ourselves, the goods being entirely of our own growth and manufacture.

Fourthly, The constant breeders beside the gain of 8s. sterling per annum by the sale of their children, will be rid of the charge of maintaining them after the first year.

Psalmanazar: George Psalmanazar (c. 1679-1763), Frenchman who fooled the gullible of London into believing he was from Formosa (now Taiwan).   *a chair:* A sedan chair.   *distress:* Confiscation for payment of debt.

Fifthly, This food would likewise bring great custom to taverns, where the   25
vintners will certainly be so prudent as to procure the best receipts for dressing
it to perfection, and consequently have their houses frequented by all the fine
gentlemen, who justly value themselves upon their knowledge in good eating;
and a skilful cook who understands how to oblige his guests, will contrive to
make it as expensive as they please.

Sixthly, This would be a great inducement to marriage, which all wise
nations have either encouraged by rewards or enforced by laws and penalties. It
would increase the care and tenderness of mothers toward their children,
when they were sure of a settlement for life to the poor babes, provided in
some sort by the public, to their annual profit instead of expense. We should
see an honest emulation among the married women, which of them would
bring the fattest child to the market. Men would become as fond of their wives
during the time of their pregnancy as they are now of their mares in foal, their
cows in calf, their sows when they are ready to farrow; nor offer to beat or kick
them (as is too frequent a practice) for fear of a miscarriage.

Many other advantages might be enumerated. For instance, the addition
of some thousand carcasses in our exportation of barreled beef, the propaga-
tion of swine's flesh, and improvement in the art of making good bacon, so
much wanted among us by the great destruction of pigs, too frequent at our
table; which are no way comparable in taste or magnificence to a well-grown,
fat, yearling child, which roasted whole will make a considerable figure at a
lord mayor's feast or any other public entertainment. But this and many others I omit, being studious of brevity.

Supposing that 1,000 families in this city would be constant customers for
infants' flesh, besides others who might have it at merry-meetings, particularly
at weddings and christenings, I compute that Dublin would take off annually
about 20,000 carcasses; and the rest of the kingdom (where probably they will
be sold somewhat cheaper) the remaining 80,000.

I can think of no one objection that will possibly be raised against this
proposal unless it should be urged that the number of people will be thereby
much lessened in the kingdom. This I freely own, and it was indeed one principal design in offering it to the world. I desire the reader will observe, that I calculate my remedy for this one individual kingdom of Ireland and for no other
that ever was, is, or I think ever can be upon earth. Therefore let no man talk to
me of other expedients: of taxing our absentees at 5s. a pound: of using neither clothes nor household furniture except what is of our own growth and
manufacture: of utterly rejecting the materials and instruments that promote
foreign luxury: of curing the expensiveness of pride, vanity, idleness, and gaming in our women: of introducing a vein of parsimony, prudence, and temperance: of learning to love our country, in the want of which we differ even from
Laplanders and the inhabitants of Topinamboo:° of quitting our animosities
and factions, nor acting any longer like the Jews, who were murdering one
another at the very moment their city was taken:° of being a little cautious not
to sell our country and conscience for nothing: of teaching landlords to have
at least one degree of mercy toward their tenants: lastly, of putting a spirit of
honesty, industry, and skill into our shopkeepers; who, if a resolution could
now be taken to buy only our native goods, would immediately unite to cheat

Topinamboo: An area in Brazil.   *was taken:* A reference to the siege of Jerusalem by
Romans (A.D. 70).

and exact upon us in the price the measure, and the goodness, nor could ever yet be brought to make one fair proposal of just dealing, though often and earnestly invited to it.

Therefore I repeat, let no man talk to me of these and the like expedients, 30 till he has at least some glimpse of hope that there will be ever some hearty and sincere attempt to put them in practice.

But as to myself, having been wearied out for many years with offering vain, idle, visionary thoughts, and at length utterly despairing of success, I fortunately fell upon this proposal; which, as it is wholly new, so it has something solid and real, of no expense and little trouble, full in our own power, and whereby we can incur no danger in disobliging England. For this kind of commodity will not bear exportation, the flesh being of too tender a consistence to admit a long continuance in salt, although perhaps I could name a country which would be glad to eat up our whole nation without it.

After all, I am not so violently bent upon my own opinion as to reject any offer proposed by wise men, which shall be found equally innocent, cheap, easy, and effectual. But before something of that kind shall be advanced in contradiction to my scheme, and offering a better, I desire the author or authors will be pleased maturely to consider two points. First, as things now stand, how they will be able to find food and raiment for 100,000 useless mouths and backs. And secondly, there being a round million of creatures in human figure throughout this kingdom, whose subsistence put into a common stock would leave them in debt 2,000,000£. sterling, adding those who are beggars by profession to the bulk of farmers, cottagers, and laborers, with the wives and children who are beggars in effect; I desire those politicians who dislike my overture, and may perhaps be so bold as to attempt an answer, that they will first ask the parents of these mortals, whether they would not at this day think it a great happiness to have been sold for food at a year old in the manner I prescribe, and thereby have avoided such a perpetual scene of misfortunes as they have since gone through by the oppression of landlords, the impossibility of paying rent without money or trade, the want of common sustenance, with neither house nor clothes to cover them from the inclemencies of the weather, and the most inevitable prospect of entailing the like or greater miseries upon their breed for ever.

I profess, in the sincerity of my heart, that I have not the least personal interest in endeavoring to promote this necessary work, having no other motive than the public good of my country, by advancing our trade, providing for infants, relieving the poor, and giving some pleasure to the rich. I have no children by which I can propose to get a single penny; the youngest being nine years old, and my wife past childbearing.

CONSIDERATIONS FOR CRITICAL THINKING AND WRITING

1. FIRST RESPONSE. Why do you suppose Swift withholds the nature of his proposal until paragraph nine? What effect did that paragraph have on you? How did it change your reading of the essay?

2. Describe Swift's use of irony. How does his irony serve to convey his argument?

3. Given that Swift is clearly not in favor of eating poor children, what is he in favor of in this essay? What serious proposals does he make, and how does he present them to the reader?

4. How is the speaker — the persona who advances the modest proposal — different from Swift? Why would it be inaccurate to describe the speaker's beliefs and attitudes as identical to Swift's?

5. What are the advantages of Swift's ironic strategy? What is gained by presenting the issue ironically rather than straightforwardly arguing for a set of proposals to alleviate the problems of a starving population?

Style

The way in which an author arranges individual words, sentences, paragraphs, and the entire structure of a work is known as the writer's *style.* Whatever literary devices a writer uses to convey the subject matter of a work constitutes its style. An awareness of literary style is no more foreign to you than is your understanding that wearing an elegant tuxedo is more formal than slipping into shorts and a T-shirt. There are different styles of just about anything, including furniture, business, music, hair, laughing, speaking, and of course, writing. Style creates variety, stimulates interest, and offers pleasure; it can be fascinating, irritating, or puzzling. Indeed, the possibilities of style are endless because it is the very texture of our lives.

As omnipresent as style is, a useful starting point for talking about the style of essays is to make a distinction between formal and informal writing. *Formal* essays are characterized by a serious, impersonal tone and include diction drawn from written discourse that results in an elevated use of the language. *Informal* essays tend to be more personal, colloquial, and subjective. Read the following passage from Ralph Waldo Emerson's *Nature* (1836) and consider its style:

> Our age is retrospective. It builds the sepulchres of the fathers. It writes biographies, histories, and criticism. The foregoing generations beheld God and nature face to face; we, through their eyes. Why should not we also enjoy an original relation to the universe? Why should not we have a poetry and philosophy of insight and not of tradition, and a religion by revelation to us, and not the history of theirs? Embosomed for a season in nature, whose floods of life stream around and through us, and invite us by the powers they supply, to action proportioned to nature, why should we grope among the dry bones of the past, or put the living generation into masquerade out of its faded wardrobe? The sun shines to-day also. There is more wool and flax in the fields. There are new lands, new men, new thoughts. Let us demand our own works and laws and worship.

Notice that Emerson's style is formal and dignified. He presents his complaint that Americans are too tied to the past and not centered in their own present moment by using formal diction that emphasizes his serious purpose. Which words strike you as especially formal? Emerson also uses repetition, rhythm, and word order to create a solemn tone. Try reading the passage aloud to determine how he achieves this tone. The next passage, published in 1996, is from an essay by Regina Barreca titled "Envy" (The entire essay is reprinted in Chapter 11, pp. 1073–1076):

"Envy," said a friend on a cold night over a glass of red wine, "is the one vice everybody has experienced. There are people who aren't gluttons, who aren't greedy, and even some who aren't particularly proud. But everybody," he leaned over the table and lowered his voice to emphasize the point, "everybody has been envious at some time in their life." I knew what he meant, given that the very day on which we were speaking was full of envy for me. Hell, I envied him as he spoke to me, what with his good job and happy family. Then I remembered that I also had a pretty good job and a pretty happy family. Why, when everything is going fairly well, do we still spend time envying others?

The tone of this paragraph is much lighter and informal than Emerson's. Barreca intentionally uses a gossipy anecdotal style to bring the reader into a seemingly private conversation in which feelings of envy are acknowledged on both sides. The simple language includes a mild profanity, the sentence patterns are conversational, and the quoted friend is even ungrammatical when he uses a plural pronoun to refer to a singular antecedent. This casual and intimate style signals that what is to follow is not a treatise on the immorality of envy but rather a more tolerant and exploratory treatment of a very human emotion. You might contrast Emerson's and Barreca's passages further by attempting to rewrite each of their paragraphs in the other's style.

The following essay by Bernard Cooper is also characterized by an informal style. As you read "A Clack of Tiny Sparks," pay attention to how Cooper uses detail. What kinds of detail does he include? How much? What is the effect of this usage on his overall style?

BERNARD COOPER (b. 1951)

Born in Los Angeles, Bernard Cooper has spent his life in California. He has taught expository and creative writing at a variety of institutions and has published widely, both fiction and nonfiction: a novel, *A Year of Rhymes* (1993); two collections of essays, *Maps to Anywhere* (1990) and *Truth Serum: Memoirs* (1996); and a collection of short stories, *Guess Again* (forthcoming). "A Clack of Tiny Sparks: Remembrances of a Gay Boyhood" first appeared in *Harper's* magazine in January 1991.

A Clack of Tiny Sparks: Remembrances of a Gay Boyhood   *1991*

Theresa Sanchez sat behind me in ninth-grade algebra. When Mr. Hubbley faced the blackboard, I'd turn around to see what she was reading; each week a new book was wedged inside her copy of *Today's Equations*. The deception worked; from Mr. Hubbley's point of view, Theresa was engrossed in the value of *X*, but I knew otherwise. One week she perused *The Wisdom of the Orient*, and I could tell from Theresa's contemplative expression that the book contained exotic thoughts, guidelines handed down from high. Another week it was a paperback novel whose title, *Let Me Live My Life,* appeared in bold print atop every page, and whose cover, a gauzy photograph of a woman biting a strand of pearls, head thrown back in an attitude of ecstasy, confirmed my suspicion that Theresa Sanchez was mature beyond her years. She was the tallest girl in school. Her bouffant hairdo, streaked with blond, was higher than the flaccid bouffants of other girls. Her smooth skin, plucked eyebrows, and painted fingernails suggested hours of pampering, a worldly and sensual vanity that placed her within the domain of adults. Smiling dimly, steeped in daydreams, Theresa moved through the crowded halls with a languid, self-satisfied indifference to those around her. "You are merely children," her posture seemed to say. "I can't be bothered." The week Theresa hid *101 Ways to Cook Hamburger* behind her algebra book, I could stand it no longer and, after the bell rang, ventured a question.

"Because I'm having a dinner party," said Theresa. "Just a couple of intimate friends."

No fourteen-year-old I knew had ever given a dinner party, let alone used the word "intimate" in conversation. "Don't you have a mother?" I asked.

Theresa sighed a weary sigh, suffered my strange inquiry. "Don't be so naive," she said. "Everyone has a mother." She waved her hand to indicate the brick school buildings outside the window. "A higher education should have taught you that." Theresa draped an angora sweater over her shoulders, scooped her books from the graffiti-covered desk, and just as she was about to walk away, she turned and asked me, "Are you a fag?"

There wasn't the slightest hint of rancor or condescension in her voice. 5 The tone was direct, casual. Still I was stunned, giving a sidelong glance to make sure no one had heard. "No," I said. Blurted really, with too much defensiveness, too much transparent fear in my response. Octaves lower than usual, I tried a "Why?"

Theresa shrugged. "Oh, I don't know. I have lots of friends who are fags. You remind me of them." Seeing me bristle, Theresa added, "It was just a guess." I watched her erect, angora back as she sauntered out the classroom door.

She had made an incisive and timely guess. Only days before, I'd invited Grady Rogers to my house after school to go swimming. The instant Grady shot from the pool, shaking water from his orange hair, freckled shoulders shining, my attraction to members of my own sex became a matter I could no longer suppress or rationalize. Sturdy and boisterous and gap-toothed, Grady was an inveterate backslapper, a formidable arm wrestler, a wizard at basketball. Grady was a boy at home in his body.

My body was a marvel I hadn't gotten used to; my arms and legs would sometimes act of their own accord, knocking over a glass at dinner or flinching at an oncoming pitch. I was never singled out as a sissy, but I could have been just as easily as Bobby Keagan, a gentle, intelligent, and introverted boy reviled by my classmates. And although I had always been aware of a tacit rapport with Bobby, a suspicion that I might find with him a rich friendship, I stayed away. Instead, I emulated Grady in the belief that being seen with him, being like him, would somehow vanquish my self-doubt, would make me normal by association.

Apart from his athletic prowess, Grady had been gifted with all the trappings of what I imagined to be a charmed life: a fastidious, aproned mother who radiated calm, maternal concern; a ruddy, stoic father with a knack for home repairs. Even the Rogerses' small suburban house in Hollywood, with its spindly Colonial furniture and chintz curtains, was a testament to normalcy.

Grady and his family bore little resemblance to my clan of Eastern Euro- 10 pean Jews, a dark and vociferous people who ate with abandon — matzo and halvah and gefilte fish; foods the goyim couldn't pronounce — who cajoled one another during endless games of canasta, making the simplest remark about the weather into a lengthy philosophical discourse on the sun and the seasons and the passage of time. My mother was a chain-smoker, a dervish in a frowsy housedress. She showed her love in the most peculiar and obsessive ways, like spending hours extracting every seed from a watermelon before she served it in perfectly bite-sized, geometric pieces. Preoccupied and perpetually frantic, my mother succumbed to bouts of absentmindedness so profound she'd forget what she was saying midsentence, smile and blush and walk away. A divorce attorney, my father wore roomy, iridescent suits, and the intricacies, the deceits inherent in his profession, had the effect of making him forever tense and vigilant. He was "all wound up," as my mother put it. But when he relaxed, his laughter was explosive, his disposition prankish: "Walk this way," a wait-ress would say, leading us to our table, and my father would mimic the way she walked, arms akimbo, hips liquid, while my mother and I were wracked with laughter. Buoyant or brooding, my parents' moods were unpredictable, and in a household fraught with extravagant emotion it was odd and awful to keep my longing secret.

One day I made the mistake of asking my mother what a "fag" was. I knew exactly what Theresa had meant but hoped against hope it was not what I thought; maybe "fag" was some French word, a harmless term like "naive." My mother turned from the stove, flew at me, and grabbed me by the shoulders. "Did someone call you that?" she cried.

"Not me," I said. "Bobby Keagan."

"Oh," she said, loosening her grip. She was visibly relieved. And didn't answer. The answer was unthinkable.

For weeks after, I shook with the reverberations from that afternoon in the kitchen with my mother, pained by the memory of her shocked expression and, most of all, her silence. My longing was wrong in the eyes of my mother, whose hazel eyes were the eyes of the world, and if that longing continued unchecked, the unwieldy shape of my fate would be cast, and I'd be subjected to a lifetime of scorn.

During the remainder of the semester, I became the scientist of my own 15 desire, plotting ways to change my yearning for boys into a yearning for girls. I had enough evidence to believe that any habit, regardless of how compulsive, how deeply ingrained, could be broken once and for all: The plastic cigarette my mother purchased at the Thrifty pharmacy — one end was red to approxi-mate an ember, the other tan like a filtered tip — was designed to wean her from the real thing. To change a behavior required self-analysis, cold resolve, and the substitution of one thing for another: plastic, say, for tobacco. Could I also find a substitute for Grady? What I needed to do, I figured, was kiss a girl and learn to like it.

This conclusion was affirmed one Sunday morning when my father, see-ing me wrinkle my nose at the pink slabs of lox he layered on a bagel, tried to convince me of its salty appeal. "You should try some," he said. "You don't know what you're missing."

"It's loaded with protein," added my mother, slapping a platter of sliced onions onto the dinette table. She hovered above us, cinching her housedress, eyes wet from onion fumes, the mock cigarette dangling from her lips.

My father sat there chomping with gusto, emitting a couple of hearty grunts to dramatize his satisfaction. And still I was not convinced. After a loud and labored swallow, he told me I may not be fond of lox today, but sooner or later I'd learn to like it. One's tastes, he assured me, are destined to change.

"Live," shouted my mother over the rumble of the Mixmaster. "Expand your horizons. Try new things." And the room grew fragrant with the batter of a spice cake.

The opportunity to put their advice into practice, and try out my plan to   20 adapt to girls, came the following week when Debbie Coburn, a member of Mr. Hubbley's algebra class, invited me to a party. She cornered me in the hall, furtive as a spy, telling me her parents would be gone for the evening and slipping into my palm a wrinkled sheet of notebook paper. On it were her address and telephone number, the lavender ink in a tidy cursive. "Wear cologne," she advised, wary eyes darting back and forth. "It's a make-out party. Anything can happen."

The Santa Ana wind blew relentlessly the night of Debbie's party, careening down the slopes of the Hollywood hills, shaking the road signs and stoplights in its path. As I walked down Beachwood Avenue, trees thrashed, surrendered their leaves, and carob pods bombarded the pavement. The sky was a deep but luminous blue, the air hot, abrasive, electric. I had to squint in order to check the number of the Coburns' apartment, a three-story building with glitter embedded in its stucco walls. Above the honeycombed balconies was a sign that read BEACHWOOD TERRACE in lavender script resembling Debbie's.

From down the hall, I could hear the plaintive strains of Little Anthony's "I Think I'm Going Out of My Head." Debbie answered the door bedecked in an Empire dress, the bodice blue and orange polka dots, the rest a sheath of black and white stripes. "Op art," proclaimed Debbie. She turned in a circle, then proudly announced that she'd rolled her hair in orange juice cans. She patted the huge unmoving curls and dragged me inside. Reflections from the swimming pool in the courtyard, its surface ruffled by wind, shuddered over the ceiling and walls. A dozen of my classmates were seated on the sofa or huddled together in corners, their whispers full of excited imminence, their bodies barely discernible in the dim light. Drapes flanking the sliding glass doors bowed out with every gust of wind, and it seemed that the room might lurch from its foundations and sail with its cargo of silhouettes into the hot October night.

Grady was the last to arrive. He tossed a six-pack of beer into Debbie's arms, barreled toward me, and slapped my back. His hair was slicked back with Vitalis, lacquered furrows left by the comb. The wind hadn't shifted a single hair. "Ya ready?" he asked, flashing the gap between his front teeth and leering into the darkened room. "You bet," I lied.

Once the beers had been passed around, Debbie provoked everyone's attention by flicking on the overhead light. "Okay," she called. "Find a partner." This was the blunt command of a hostess determined to have her guests aroused in an orderly fashion. Everyone blinked, shuffled about, and grabbed a member of the opposite sex. Sheila Garabedian landed beside me — entirely at random, though I wanted to believe she was driven by passion — her timid smile giving way to plain fear as the light went out. Nothing for a moment but the heave of the wind and the distant banter of dogs. I caught a whiff of Sheila's perfume, tangy and sweet as Hawaiian Punch. I probed her face with my own, grazing the small scallop of an ear, a velvety temple, and though Sheila's trembling made me want to stop, I persisted with my mission until I found her lips, tightly sealed as a private letter. I held my mouth over hers and gathered her shoulders closer, resigned to the possibility that, no matter how long we stood there, Sheila would be too scared to kiss me back. Still, she exhaled through her nose, and I listened to the squeak of every breath as though it were a sigh of inordinate pleasure. Diving within myself, I monitored my heartbeat and respiration, trying to will stimulation into being, and all the while an image intruded, an image of Grady erupting from our pool, rivulets of water sliding down his chest. "Change," shouted Debbie, switching on the light. Sheila thanked me, pulled away, and continued her routine of gracious terror with every boy throughout the evening. It didn't matter whom I held — Margaret Sims, Betty Vernon, Elizabeth Lee — my experiment was a failure; I continued to picture Grady's wet chest, and Debbie would bellow "change" with such fervor, it could have been my own voice, my own incessant reprimand.

Our hostess commandeered the light switch for nearly half an hour. Whenever the light came on, I watched Grady pivot his head toward the newest prospect, his eyebrows arched in expectation, his neck blooming with hickeys, his hair, at last, in disarray. All that shuffling across the carpet charged everyone's arms and lips with static, and eventually, between low moans and soft osculations, I could hear the clack of tiny sparks and see them flare here and there in the dark like meager, short-lived stars.

I saw Theresa, sultry and aloof as ever, read three more books — *North American Reptiles, Bonjour Tristesse,* and *MGM: A Pictorial History* — before she vanished early in December. Rumors of her fate abounded. Debbie Coburn swore that Theresa had been "knocked up" by an older man, a traffic cop, she thought, or a grocer. Nearly quivering with relish, Debbie told me and Grady about the home for unwed mothers in the San Fernando Valley, a compound teeming with pregnant girls who had nothing to do but touch their stomachs and contemplate their mistake. Even Bobby Keagan, who took Theresa's place behind me in algebra, had a theory regarding her disappearance colored by his own wish for escape; he imagined that Theresa, disillusioned with society, booked passage to a tropical island, there to live out the rest of her days without restrictions or ridicule. "No wonder she flunked out of school," I overheard Mr. Hubbley tell a fellow teacher one afternoon. "Her head was always in a book."

Along with Theresa went my secret, or at least the dread that she might divulge it, and I felt, for a while, exempt from suspicion. I was, however, to run across Theresa one last time. It happened during a period of torrential rain that, according to reports on the six o'clock news, washed houses from the hillsides and flooded the downtown streets. The halls of Joseph Le Conte Junior High were festooned with Christmas decorations: crepe-paper garlands, wreaths studded with plastic berries, and one requisite Star of David twirling above the attendance desk. In Arts and Crafts, our teacher, Gerald (he was the only teacher who allowed us — *required* us — to call him by his first name), handed out blocks of balsa wood and instructed us to carve them into bugs. We would paint eyes and antennae with tempera and hang them on a Christmas tree he'd made the previous night. "Voilà," he crooned, unveiling his creation from a burlap sack. Before us sat a tortured scrub, a wardrobe-worth of wire hangers that were bent like branches and soldered together. Gerald credited his inspiration to a Charles Addams cartoon he's seen in which Morticia, grimly preparing for the holidays, hangs vampire bats on a withered pine. "All that red and green," said Gerald. "So predictable. So *boring.*"

As I chiseled a beetle and listened to rain pummel the earth, Gerald handed me an envelope and asked me to take it to Mr. Kendrick, the drama teacher. I would have thought nothing of his request if I hadn't seen Theresa on my way down the hall. She was cleaning out her locker, blithely dropping the sum of its contents — pens and textbooks and mimeographs — into a trash can. "Have a nice life," she sang as I passed. I mustered the courage to ask her what had happened. We stood alone in the silent hall, the reflections of wreaths and garlands submerged in brown linoleum.

"I transferred to another school. They don't have grades or bells, and you get to study whatever you want." Theresa was quick to sense my incredulity. "Honest," she said. "The school is progressive." She gazed into a glass cabinet that held the trophies of track meets and intramural spelling bees. "God," she sighed, "this place is so . . . barbaric." I was still trying to decide whether or not to believe her story when she asked me where I was headed. "Dear," she said, her exclamation pooling in the silence, "that's no ordinary note, if you catch my drift." The envelope was blank and white; I looked up at Theresa, baffled. "Don't be so naive," she muttered, tossing an empty bottle of nail polish into the trash can. It struck bottom with a resolute thud. "Well," she said, closing her locker and breathing deeply, "bon voyage." Theresa swept through the double doors and in seconds her figure was obscured by rain.

As I walked toward Mr. Kendrick's room, I could feel Theresa's insinuation burrow in. I stood for a moment and watched Mr. Kendrick through the pane in the door. He paced intently in front of the class, handsome in his shirt and tie, reading from a thick book. Chalked on the blackboard behind him was THE ODYSSEY BY HOMER. I have no recollection of how Mr. Kendrick reacted to the note, whether he accepted it with pleasure or embarrassment, slipped it into his desk drawer or the pocket of his shirt. I have scavenged that day in retrospect, trying to see Mr. Kendrick's expression, wondering if he acknowledged me in any way as his liaison. All I recall is the sight of his mime through a pane of glass, a lone man mouthing an epic, his gestures ardent in empty air.

Had I delivered a declaration of love? I was haunted by the need to know. In fantasy, a kettle shot steam, the glue released its grip, and I read the letter with impunity. But how would such a letter begin? Did the common endearments apply? This was a message between two men, a message for which I had no precedent, and when I tried to envision the contents, apart from a hasty, impassioned scrawl, my imagination faltered.

Once or twice I witnessed Gerald and Mr. Kendrick walk together into the faculty lounge or say hello at the water fountain, but there was nothing especially clandestine or flirtatious in their manner. Besides, no matter how acute my scrutiny, I wasn't sure, short of a kiss, exactly what to look for—what sema-phore of gesture, what encoded word. I suspected there were signs, covert signs that would give them away, just as I'd unwittingly given myself away to Theresa.

In the school library, a *Webster's* unabridged dictionary lay on a wooden podium, and I padded toward it with apprehension; along with clues to the bond between my teachers, I risked discovering information that might incriminate me as well. I had decided to consult the dictionary during lunch period, when most of the students would be on the playground. I clutched my notebook, moving in such a way as to appear both studious and nonchalant, actually believing that, unless I took precautions, someone would see me and guess what I was up to. The closer I came to the podium, the more obvious, I thought, was my endeavor; I felt like the model of The Visible Man in our sci-ence class, my heart's undulations, my overwrought nerves legible through transparent skin. A couple of kids riffled through the card catalogue. The librarian, a skinny woman whose perpetual whisper and rubber-soled shoes caused her to drift through the room like a phantom, didn't seem to register my presence. Though I'd looked up dozens of words before, the pages felt strange beneath my fingers. *Homer* was the first word I saw. *Hominid. Homogenize.* I feigned interest and skirted other words before I found the word I was after. Under the heading HO • MO • SEX • U • AL was the terse definition: *adj. Pertaining to, characteristic of, or exhibiting homosexuality.*—*n. A homosexual person.* I read the definition again and again, hoping the words would yield more than they could. I shut the dictionary, swallowed hard, and, none the wiser, hurried away.

As for Gerald and Mr. Kendrick, I never discovered evidence to prove or dispute Theresa's claim. By the following summer, however, I had overheard from my peers a confounding amount about homosexuals: They wore green on Thursday, couldn't whistle, hypnotized boys with a piercing glance. To this lore, Grady added a surefire test to ferret them out.

"A test?" I said.

"You ask a guy to look at his fingernails, and if he looks at them like this"—Grady closed his fingers into a fist and examined his nails with manly detachment—"then he's okay. But if he does this"—he held out his hands at arm's length, splayed his fingers, and coyly cocked his head—"you'd better watch out." Once he'd completed his demonstration, Grady peeled off his shirt and plunged into our pool. I dove in after. It was early June, the sky immense, glassy, placid. My father was cooking spareribs on the barbecue, an artist with a basting brush. His apron bore the caricature of a frazzled French chef. Mother curled on a chaise lounge, plumes of smoke wafting from her nostrils. In a stupor of contentment she took another drag, closed her eyes, and arched her face toward the sun.

Grady dog-paddled through the deep end, spouting a fountain of chlori-nated water. Despite shame and confusion, my longing for him hadn't dimin-ished; it continued to thrive without air and light, like a luminous fish in the dregs of the sea. In the name of play, I swam up behind him, encircled his shoulders, astonished by his taut flesh. The two of us flailed, pretended to drown. Beneath the heavy press of water, Grady's orange hair wavered, a flame that couldn't be doused.

35

I've lived with a man for seven years. Some nights, when I'm half-asleep and the room is suffused with blue light, I reach out to touch the expanse of his back, and it seems as if my fingers sink into his skin, and I feel the pleasure a diver feels the instant he enters a body of water.

I have few regrets. But one is that I hadn't said to Theresa, "Of course I'm a fag." Maybe I'd have met her friends. Or become friends with her. Imagine the meals we might have concocted: hamburger Stroganoff, Swedish meatballs in a sweet translucent sauce, steaming slabs of Salisbury steak.

Considerations for Critical Thinking and Writing

1. FIRST RESPONSE. Notice the details that Cooper uses in his first paragraph to create a character sketch of Theresa Sanchez. Try writing a substantial one-paragraph description of a fellow student whom you remember from high school or earlier. Use details that will make a definite impression on the reader concerning your subject's character.

2. Comment on the significance of Theresa's response to the possibility of the narrator being gay compared to that of his mother.

3. Although the narrator's memory of his boyhood focuses on his growing realization that he is gay, do you think his experience as a ninth-grader is radically different from that of most fourteen-year olds — gay or not? Explain why or why not.

4. Discuss the meaning of the title. Can you think of an additional revealing title?

5. What is the effect of the final two paragraphs? Consider whether this is an abrupt ending to the essay or an appropriate resolution.

Structure

The way in which the material of an essay is arranged is called its *structure*. You may have been trained always to begin an essay with an introductory paragraph that clearly states your thesis, followed by a series of paragraphs that each begin with a topic sentence and develop that topic using several examples. That's certainly not bad advice, but it's not the only way to structure an essay. If all essays were written in such a formulaic pattern, reading essays would not be the pleasure it so often is. Imagine, for example, if the plot of every short story you read were restricted to only a pyramidal pattern consisting of a complication leading to a climax followed by a falling action. Many excellent stories closely follow this structure, but there are also plenty of powerful stories that don't (see, for example, Andre Dubus's short story "Killings," pp. 565–578). Essays, like stories, poems, and plays, come in a variety of structures.

The major types of essays already discussed in this chapter — narration, description, exposition, and argumentation — represent ways of classifying essays, but they do not follow prescribed patterns to achieve their effects. Essayists mostly rely on their instincts and creativity rather than rules to shape what they want to say. E. B. White once described his writing this way: "A great deal of writing is not 'plotted' — most of my essays have no plot structure, they are a ramble in the woods, or a ramble in the basement of my mind." That's not to say that White's writing contains no structure. Instead, he seems to be acknowledging that like most writers, he discovers the optimum structure for his ideas as he goes along.

George Orwell's "Shooting an Elephant" (p. 1358) is also a highly descriptive narrative essay, but unlike White's "ramble," it is more firmly organized by a chronological account of how and why the narrator was forced to shoot an elephant when he served as a British police officer in Burma during the 1920s. Though Orwell clearly structures the essay chronologically, he frames the account with the narrator's commentary and reflections at the beginning, middle, and end (paragraphs 1-2, 7, 14). In these passages the narrator thinks about how "in a roundabout way [the incident] was enlightening" because it offered "a better glimpse than I had before of the real nature of imperialism." The political significance of his shooting the elephant is provided by the narrator's comments, but what the shooting reveals about the narrator himself is only implied. The structure of the essay allows Orwell to make interesting and complex connections between one's private and public identity as well as one's personal and political values.

Probably the majority of the essays you read will have their own unique structure. Some will be more apparent than others, but you can assume that an awareness of an essay's particular structure and how the parts relate to the whole will allow you to understand more clearly the essay's effects and how those effects are achieved. What perhaps starts as a ramble for the writer eventually emerges as the completed structure of the essay. You can be sure that White's rambling in "Once More to the Lake" includes detours leading to revisions. The carefully chosen details he uses to describe his return visit to the lake with his son take on considerably more meaning when you read the last sentence of the last paragraph so that, like the essay's narrator, we look back on his reflections about experience with a new — chilling — perspective, a perspective emphasized by the placement and structure of the final paragraph.

E. B. White (1899–1985)

Born in Mount Vernon, New York, Elwyn Brooks White graduated from Cornell University and began writing for the *New Yorker* in 1927, only two years after the magazine was founded. Over the next sixty years White's essays, poems, and editing talent helped to establish the sophisticated tone and style of the *New Yorker*. Many of his articles are collected in *Essays* (1977), but he is even more well known for three of his children's books, *Stuart Little* (1945), *Charlotte's Web* (1952), and *The Trumpet of the Swan* (1970). "Once More to the Lake" is from his collection of essays titled *One Man's Meat* (1941).

Once More to the Lake 1941

One summer, along about 1904, my father rented a camp on a lake in Maine and took us all there for the month of August. We all got ringworm from some kittens and had to rub Pond's Extract on our arms and legs night and morning, and my father rolled over in a canoe with all his clothes on; but outside of that the vacation was a success and from then on none of us ever thought there was any place in the world like that lake in Maine. We returned summer after summer — always on August 1st for one month. I have since become a salt-water man, but sometimes in summer there are days when the restlessness of the tides and the fearful cold of the sea water and the incessant wind that blows across the afternoon and into the evening make me wish for the placidity of a lake in the woods. A few weeks ago this feeling got so strong I bought myself a couple of bass hooks and a spinner and returned to the lake where we used to go, for a week's fishing and to revisit old haunts.

I took along my son, who had never had any fresh water up his nose and who had seen lily pads only from train windows. On the journey over to the lake I began to wonder what it would be like. I wondered how time would have marred this unique, this holy spot — the coves and streams, the hills that the sun set behind, the camps and the paths behind the camps. I was sure that the tarred road would have found it out and I wondered in what other ways it would be desolated. It is strange how much you can remember about places like that once you allow your mind to return into the grooves that lead back. You remember one thing, and that suddenly reminds you of another thing. I guess I remembered clearest of all the early mornings, when the lake was cool and motionless, remembered how the bedroom smelled of the lumber it was made of and the wet woods whose scent entered through the screen. The partitions in the camp were thin and did not extend clear to the top of the rooms, and as I was always the first up I would dress softly so as not to wake the others, and sneak out into the sweet outdoors and start out in the canoe, keeping close along the shore in the long shadows of the pines. I remembered being very careful never to rub my paddle against the gunwale for fear of disturbing the stillness of the cathedral.

The lake had never been what you would call a wild lake. There were cottages sprinkled about the shores, and it was in farming country although the shores of the lake were quite heavily wooded. Some of the cottages were owned by nearby farmers, and you would live at the shore and eat your meals at the farmhouse. That's what our family did. But although it wasn't wild, it was a fairly large and undisturbed lake and there were places in it which, to a child at least, seemed infinitely remote and primeval.

I was right about the tar: It led to within half a mile of the shore. But when I got back there, with my boy, and we settled into a camp near a farmhouse and into the kind of summertime I had known, I could tell that it was going to be pretty much the same as it had been before — I knew it, lying in bed the first morning, smelling the bedroom, and hearing the boy sneak quietly out and go off along the shore in a boat. I began to sustain the illusion that he was I, and therefore, by simple transposition, that I was my father. This sensation persisted, kept cropping up all the time we were there. It was not an entirely new feeling, but in this setting it grew much stronger. I seemed to be living a dual existence. I would be in the middle of some simple act, I would be picking up a bait box or laying down a table fork, or I would be saying something, and suddenly it would be not I but my father who was saying the words or making the gesture. It gave me a creepy sensation.

We went fishing the first morning. I felt the same damp moss covering the worms in the bait can, and saw the dragonfly alight on the tip of my rod as it hovered a few inches from the surface of the water. It was the arrival of this fly that convinced me beyond any doubt that everything was as it always had been, that the years were a mirage and there had been no years. The small waves were the same, chucking the rowboat under the chin as we fished at anchor, and the boat was the same boat, the same color green and the ribs broken in the same places, and under the floor-boards the same fresh-water leavings and debris — the dead hellgrammite, the wisps of moss, the rusty discarded fishhook, the dried blood from yesterday's catch. We stared silently at the tips of our rods, at the dragonflies that came and went. I lowered the tip of mine into the water, tentatively, pensively dislodging the fly, which darted two feet away, poised, darted two feet back, and came to rest again a little farther up the rod. There had been no years between the ducking of this dragonfly and the other one — the one that was part of memory. I looked at the boy, who was silently watching his fly, and it was my hands that held his rod, my eyes watching. I felt dizzy and didn't know which rod I was at the end of.

We caught two bass, hauling them in briskly as though they were mackerel, pulling them over the side of the boat in a businesslike manner without any landing net, and stunning them with a blow on the back of the head. When we got back for a swim before lunch, the lake was exactly where we had left it, the same number of inches from the dock, and there was only the merest suggestion of a breeze. This seemed an utterly enchanted sea, this lake you could leave to its own devices for a few hours and come back to, and find that it had not stirred, this constant and trustworthy body of water. In the shallows, the dark, watersoaked sticks and twigs, smooth and old, were undulating in clusters on the bottom against the clean ribbed sand, and the track of the mussel was plain. A school of minnows swam by, each minnow with its small individual shadow, doubling the attendance, so clear and sharp in the sunlight. Some of the other campers were in swimming, along the shore, one of them with a cake of soap, and the water felt thin and clear and unsubstantial. Over the years there had been this person with the cake of soap, this cultist, and here he was. There had been no years.

Up to the farmhouse to dinner through the teeming, dusty field, the road under our sneakers was only a two-track road. The middle track was missing, the one with the marks of the hooves and splotches of dried, flaky manure. There had always been three tracks to choose from in choosing which track to walk in; now the choice was narrowed down to two. For a moment I missed terribly the middle alternative. But the way led past the tennis court, and something about the way it lay there in the sun reassured me; the tape had loosened along the backline, the alleys were green with plantains and other weeds, and the net (installed in June and removed in September) sagged in the dry noon, and the whole place steamed with midday heat and hunger and emptiness. There was a choice of pie for dessert, and one was blueberry and one was apple, and the waitresses were the same country girls, there having been no passage of time, only the illusion of it as in a dropped curtain — the waitresses were still fifteen; their hair had been washed, that was the only difference — they had been to the movies and seen the pretty girls with the clean hair.

Summertime, oh summertime, pattern of life indelible, the fade-proof lake, the woods unshatterable, the pasture with the sweetfern and the juniper forever and ever, summer without end; this was the background, and the life along the shore was the design, the cottages with their innocent and tranquil design, their tiny docks with the flagpole and the American flag floating against the white clouds in the blue sky, the little paths over the roots of the trees leading from camp to camp and the paths leading back to the outhouses and the can of lime for sprinkling, and at the souvenir counters at the store the miniature birch-bark canoes and the post cards that showed things looking a little better than they looked. This was the American family at play, escaping the city heat, wondering whether the newcomers in the camp at the head of the cove were "common" or "nice," wondering whether it was true that the people who drove up for Sunday dinner at the farmhouse were turned away because there wasn't enough chicken.

It seemed to me, as I kept remembering all this, that those times and those summers had been infinitely precious and worth saving. There had been jollity and peace and goodness. The arriving (at the beginning of August) had been so big a business in itself, at the railway station the farm wagon drawn up, the first smell of the pine-laden air, the first glimpse of the smiling farmer, and the great importance of the trunks and your father's enormous authority in such matters, and the feel of the wagon under you for the long ten-mile haul, and at the top of the last long hill catching the first view of the lake after eleven months of not seeing this cherished body of water. The shouts and cries of the other campers when they saw you, and the trunks to be unpacked, to give up their rich burden. (Arriving was less exciting nowadays, when you sneaked up in your car and parked it under a tree near the camp and took out the bags and in five minutes it was all over, no fuss, no loud wonderful fuss about trunks).

Peace and goodness and jollity. The only thing that was wrong now, really, 10 was the sound of the place, an unfamiliar nervous sound of the outboard motors. This was the note that jarred, the one thing that would sometimes break the illusion and set the years moving. In those other summertimes all motors were inboard; and when they were at a little distance, the noise they made was a sedative, an ingredient of summer sleep. They were one-cylinder and two-cylinder engines, and some were make-and-break and some were jump-spark, but they all made a sleepy sound across the lake. The one-lungers throbbed and fluttered, and the twin-cylinder ones purred and purred, and that was a quiet sound too. But now the campers all had outboards. In the daytime, in the hot mornings, these motors made a petulant, irritable sound; at night, in the still evening when the afterglow lit the water, they whined about one's ears like mosquitoes. My boy loved our rented outboard, and his great desire was to achieve singlehanded mastery over it, and authority, and he soon learned the trick of choking it a little (but not too much), and the adjustment of the needle valve. Watching him I would remember the things you could do with the old one-cylinder engines with the heavy flywheel, how you could have it eating out of your hand if you got really close to it spiritually. Motor boats in those days didn't have clutches, and you would make a landing by shutting off the motor at the proper time and coasting in with a dead rudder. But there was a way of reversing them, if you learned the trick, by cutting the switch and putting it on again exactly on the final dying revolution of the flywheel, so that it would kick back against compression and begin reversing. Approaching a dock in a strong following breeze, it was difficult to slow up sufficiently by the ordinary coasting method, and if a boy felt he had complete mastery over his motor, he was tempted to keep it running beyond its time and then reverse it a few feet from the dock. It took a cool nerve, because if you threw the switch a twentieth of a second too soon you could catch the flywheel when it still had speed enough to go up past center, and the boat would leap ahead, charging bull-fashion at the dock.

We had a good week at the camp. The bass were biting well and the sun shone endlessly, day after day. We would be tired at night and lie down in the accumulated heat of the little bedrooms after the long hot day and the breeze would stir almost imperceptibly outside and the smell of the swamp drift in through the rusty screens. Sleep would come easily and in the morning the red squirrel would be on the roof, tapping out his gay routine. I kept remembering everything, lying in bed in the mornings — the small steamboat that had a long rounded stern like the lip of a Ubangi, and how quietly she ran on the moonlight sails, when the older boys played their mandolins and the girls sang and we ate doughnuts dipped in sugar, and how sweet the music was on the water in the shining night, and what it had felt like to think about girls then. After breakfast we would go up to the store and the things were in the same place — the minnows in a bottle, the plugs and spinners disarranged and pawed over by the youngsters from the boys' camp, the Fig Newtons and the Beeman's gum. Outside, the road was tarred and cars stood in front of the store. Inside, all was just as it had always been, except there was more Coca-Cola and not so much Moxie and root beer and birch beer and sarsaparilla. We would walk out with a bottle of pop apiece and sometimes the pop would backfire up our noses and hurt. We explored the streams, quietly, where the turtles slid off the sunny logs and dug their way into the soft bottom; and we lay on the town wharf and fed worms to the tame bass. Everywhere we went I had trouble making out which was I, the one walking at my side, the one walking in my pants.

One afternoon while we were there at that lake a thunderstorm came up. It was like the revival of an old melodrama that I had seen long ago with childish awe. The second-act climax of the drama of the electrical disturbance over a lake in America had not changed in any important respect. This was the big scene, still the big scene. The whole thing was so familiar, the first feeling of oppression and heat and a general air around camp of not wanting to go very far away. In midafternoon (it was all the same) a curious darkening of the sky, and a lull in everything that had made life tick; and then the way the boats suddenly swung the other way at their moorings with the coming of a breeze out of the new quarter, and the premonitory rumble. Then the kettle drum, then the snare, then the bass drum and cymbals, then crackling light against the dark, and the gods grinning and licking their chops in the hills. Afterward the calm, the rain steadily rustling in the calm lake, the return of light and hope and spirits, and the campers running out in joy and relief to go swimming in the rain, their bright cries perpetuating the deathless joke about how they were getting simply drenched, and the children screaming with delight at the new sensation of bathing in the rain, and the joke about getting drenched linking the generations in a strong indestructible chain. And the comedian who waded in carrying an umbrella.

When the others went swimming my son said he was going in too. He pulled his dripping trunks from the line where they had hung all through the shower, and wrung them out. Languidly, and with no thought of going in, I watched him, his hard little body, skinny and bare, saw him wince slightly as he pulled up around his vitals the small, soggy, icy garment. As he buckled the swollen belt suddenly my groin felt the chill of death.

Considerations for Critical Thinking and Writing

1. FIRST RESPONSE. When you read the final sentence of this essay, were you surprised? How did it make you feel? What do you think is the overall purpose of this essay?

2. Describe the speaker's tone. What feelings are created in you by the details he gives about the lake?

3. Choose any single paragraph and analyze how it functions in the essay by describing its purpose and style.

4. Compare the speaker's perspective on the lake when he was a boy with that of his current view as a returning father. What impact, if any, has the passage of time had on the speaker's response to the lake?

5. What do you think is the significance of the son's role in this essay? Why do you think White includes him in this meditative remembrance of the lake?

Theme

The ***theme*** is the central meaning or dominant idea behind an essay. Another word often used to refer to the central idea of an essay is *thesis*, particularly if the essay attempts to prove an argument about some topic. *Theme* is the term used in this discussion, however, because it can more readily apply to short stories, poems, and plays as well as essays. To describe, for example, a lyric poem that captures the solitary beauty of a single flower growing in a field of hay as having a thesis seems like a stretch. Though the term *thesis* is certainly useful for describing argumentative essays, *theme* is better for the purposes of this discussion because not all essays are argumentative. Some simply make interesting observations and are reflective. *Theme*, therefore, is a more inclusive and useful term.

The theme is not simply the subject matter of an essay. Instead, the theme makes some kind of point about the subject. A possible theme about the subject of long-distance learning might look like this: "Long-distance learning is an effective way to deliver high-quality courses to low-income students living in remote locations." Notice that this complete sentence is reasonably specific and avoids vague generalities such as "long-distance learning is a good thing."

In general, themes are expressed more directly in essays than they are in stories, poems, or plays. Essayists tend to state their central points explicitly in order to make their ideas and positions clear. K. C. Cole makes explicit in the second paragraph of "Calculated Risks" (p. 538) her theme that "most people are quite properly confused about risk," because they don't know how to assess what is risky behavior and what isn't. Cole's method is straightforward and direct; the rest of her essay expands on this theme by further explaining and providing examples of how people perceive risks in their lives. Explicit statements are not, however, the only means by which themes are offered in essays. E. B. White's "Once More to the Lake" consists of a series of descriptions and reflections of his visit with his son to the lake he used to frequent as a boy. The narrator, now much older, talks about summer life on the lake, fishing, the sound of outboard motors, and the small changes that were barely noticeable over the years. At no point in the essay does White explicitly indicate a theme. Instead, he indirectly moves beyond the nostalgic tone created by his descriptions when he concludes the essay with a jarring image of his feeling deeply within himself "the chill of death," an image that becomes implicitly the theme of the essay and toward which all the description and reflection has been moving.

Essays that make an argument — like Cole's — typically include explicit themes, but essays that are narrative descriptions characterized by reflection rather than argumentation — like White's — usually require the reader to discover and determine the theme of the piece. Neither an explicit nor an implicit strategy is inherently better or worse than the other, but, depending on the type of essay, one can be more appropriate than the other. The difference in strategy can be accounted for by White's attempt to re-create a felt experience in the reader, in contrast to Cole's efforts to provide a persuasive argument.

When you determine the theme(s) of a work, don't be surprised if your reacting isn't identical to that of the reader sitting beside you in class. There is no absolutely correct way to talk about an essay's theme. Different readers are likely to emphasize different aspects of an essay just as they do when reading other forms of literature. Indeed, reader-response critics (see pp. 74–76) emphasize how individual readers construct the text based on their own experiences, expectations, and assumptions. Reading can, in this sense, be regarded as a highly individual act, because there is no single definitive interpretation of the theme. Anyone, for example, who has survived a plane crash before reading Cole's essay on how we mistakenly assess risks in our lives is likely to respond quite differently to Cole's point that driving a car is more risky than flying. That does not mean, however, that such a reader would be correct in describing Cole's central point as an argument for staying home and avoiding all potential risks in life. Finally, the text — what is written and how it is written — sets limits on how we can accurately describe the theme of a work.

Clarifying and articulating what you take to be the theme of an essay is a valuable and useful process, because it requires that you consider all the literary elements of a work along with its explicit or implied argument (if it has one). This process allows you to see how the various parts of the essay contribute to the theme and how its effects and meanings are achieved. As you read "Calculated Risks" pay careful attention to how Cole first establishes and then develops her themes. How many different threads can you identify?

K. C. COLE (b. 1946)

K. C. Cole, born in Detroit, is known for her engaging essays on topics in science and women's issues. She was working for a science museum in San Francisco when she discovered her vocation as a science and health writer, a career she has excelled at ever since. With accessible, interesting descriptions of complicated mathematical and scientific concepts that are unfamiliar to the "average guy," she explains in her collection of essays, *The Universe and the Teacup: The Mathematics of Truth and Beauty* (1998), such topics as the risks of smoking, the effects of changing our scale of vision, and whether or not our votes count. Cole was awarded the American Institute of Physics Award for Best Science Writer in 1995.

Calculated Risks   *1998*

Newsweek magazine plunged American women into a state of near panic some years ago when it announced that the chance of a college-educated thirty-five-year-old woman finding a husband was less than her chance of being killed by a terrorist. Although Susan Faludi made mincemeat of this so-called statistic in her book *Backlash,* the notion that we can precisely quantify risk has a strong hold on the Western psyche. Scientists, statisticians, and policy makers attach numbers to the risk of getting breast cancer or AIDS, to flying and food additives, to getting hit by lightning or falling in the bathtub.

Yet despite (or perhaps because of) all the numbers floating around, most people are quite properly confused about risk. I know people who live happily on the San Andreas Fault and yet are afraid to ride the New York subways (and vice versa). I've known smokers who can't stand to be in the same room with a fatty steak, and women afraid of the side effects of birth control pills who have unprotected sex with strangers. Risk assessment is rarely based on purely rational considerations — even if people could agree on what those considerations were. We worry about negligible quantities of Alar in apples, yet shrug off the much higher probability of dying from smoking. We worry about flying, but not driving. We worry about getting brain cancer from cellular phones, although the link is quite tenuous. In fact, it's easy to make a statistical argument — albeit a fallacious one — that cellular phones prevent cancer, because the proportion of people with brain tumors is smaller among cell phone users than among the general population.[1]

---

[1] John Allen Paulos was the first person I know of to make this calculation; it is probably related to the fact that people who use cellular phones are on average richer, and therefore healthier, than people who don't.

Even simple pleasures such as eating and breathing have become suspect. Love has always been risky, and AIDS has made intimacy more perilous than ever. On the other hand, not having relationships may be riskier still. According to at least one study, the average male faces three times the threat of early death associated with not being married as he does from cancer.

Of course, risk isn't all bad. Without knowingly taking risks, no one would ever walk out the door, much less go to school, drive a car, have a baby, submit a proposal for a research grant, fall in love, or swim in the ocean. It's hard to have any fun, accomplish anything productive, or experience life without taking on risks—sometimes substantial ones. Life, after all, is a fatal disease, and the mortality rate for humans, at the end of the day, is 100 percent.

Yet, people are notoriously bad at risk assessment. I couldn't get over this 5 feeling watching the aftermath of the crash of TWA Flight 800 and the horror it spread about flying, with the long lines at airports, the increased security measures, the stories about grieving families day after day in the newspaper, the ongoing attempt to figure out why and who and what could be done to prevent such a tragedy from happening again.

Meanwhile, tens of thousands of children die every day around the world from common causes such as malnutrition and disease. That's roughly the same as a hundred exploding jumbo jets full of children every single day. People who care more about the victims of Flight 800 aren't callous or ignorant. It's just the way our minds work. Certain kinds of tragedies make an impact; others don't. Our perceptual apparatus is geared toward threats that are exotic, personal, erratic, and dramatic. This doesn't mean we're ignorant; just human.

This skewed perception of risk has serious social consequences, however. We aim our resources at phantoms, while real hazards are ignored. Parents, for example, tend to rate drug abuse and abduction by strangers as the greatest threats to their children. Yet hundreds of times more children die each year from choking, burns, falls, drowning, and other accidents that public safety efforts generally ignore.

We spend millions to fight international terrorism and wear combat fatigues for a morning walk to protect against Lyme disease. At the same time, "we see several very major problems that have received relatively little attention," write Bernard Cohen and I-Sing Lee in *Health Physics.* The physicists suggest— not entirely tongue in cheek—that resources might be far more efficiently spent on programs such as government-organized computer dating services. "Favorable publicity on the advantages of marriage might be encouraged."

It's as if we incarcerated every petty criminal with zeal, while inviting mass murderers into our bedrooms. If we wanted to put the money on the real killers, we'd go after suicide, not asbestos.

Even in terms of simple dollars, our policies don't make any sense. It's well 10 known, for example, that prenatal care for pregnant women saves enormous amounts of money—in terms of care infants need in the first year of life—and costs a pittance. Yet millions of low-income women don't get it.

Numbers are clearly not enough to make sense of risk assessment. Context counts, too. Take cancer statistics. It's always frightening to hear that cancer is on the rise. However, at least one reason for the increase is simply that people are living longer—long enough to get the disease.

Certain conclusions we draw from statistics are downright silly. Physicist Hal Lewis writes in *Technological Risk* that per mile traveled a person is more likely to be killed by a car as a pedestrian than as a driver or passenger. Should we conclude that driving is safer than walking and therefore that all pedestrians should be forced into cars?

Charles Dickens made a point about the absurdity of misunderstanding numbers associated with risk by refusing to ride the train. One day late in December, the story goes, Dickens announced that he couldn't travel by train any more that year, "on the grounds that the average annual quota of railroad accidents in Britain had not been filled and therefore further disasters were obviously imminent."

Purely numerical comparisons also may be socially unacceptable. When the state of Oregon decided to rank its medical services according to benefit-cost ratios, some results had to be thrown out—despite their statistical validity. Treatment for thumb sucking, crooked teeth, and headaches, for example, came out on the priorities list ahead of therapy for cystic fibrosis and AIDS.

What you consider risky, after all, depends somewhat on the circum- 15 stances of your life and lifestyle. People who don't have enough to eat don't worry about apples contaminated with Alar. People who face daily violence at their front door don't worry about hijackings on flights to the Bahamas. Attitudes toward risk evolve in cultural contexts and are influenced by everything from psychology to ethics to beliefs about personal responsibility.

In addition to context, another factor needed to see through the maze of conflicting messages about risk is human psychology. For example, imminent risks strike much more fear in our hearts than distant ones; it's much harder to get a teenager than an older person to take long-term dangers like smoking seriously.

Smoking is also a habit people believe they can control, which makes the risk far more acceptable. (People seem to get more upset about the effects of passive smoking than smoking itself—at least in part because smokers get to choose, and breathers don't.)

As a general principle, people tend to grossly exaggerate the risk of any danger perceived to be beyond their control, while shrugging off risks they think they can manage. Thus, we go skiing and skydiving, but fear asbestos. We resent and fear the idea that anonymous chemical companies are putting additives into our food; yet the additives we load onto our own food—salt, sugar, butter—are millions of times more dangerous.

This is one reason that airline accidents seem so unacceptable—because strapped into our seats in the cabin, what happens is completely beyond our control. In a poll taken soon after the TWA Flight 800 crash, an overwhelming majority of people said they'd be willing to pay up to fifty dollars more for a round-trip ticket if it increased airline safety. Yet the same people resist moves to improve automobile safety, for example, especially if it costs money.

The idea that we can control what happens also influences who we blame 20 when things go wrong. Most people don't like to pay the costs for treating people injured by cigarettes or riding motorcycles because we think they brought these things on themselves. Some people also hold these attitudes toward victims of AIDS, or mental illness, because they think the illness results from lack of character or personal morals.

In another curious perceptual twist, risks associated with losing something and gaining something appear to be calculated in our minds according to quite different scales. In a now-classic series of studies, Stanford psychologist Amos Tversky and colleague Daniel Kahneman concluded that most people will bend over backward to avoid small risks, even if that means sacrificing great potential rewards. "The threat of a loss has a greater impact on a decision than the possibility of an equivalent gain," they concluded.

In one of their tests, Tversky and Kahneman asked physicians to choose between two strategies for combating a rare disease, expected to kill 600 people. Strategy A promised to save 200 people (the rest would die), while Strategy B offered a one-third probability that everyone would be saved, and a two-thirds probability that no one would be saved. Betting on a sure thing, the physicians choose A. But presented with the identical choice, stated differently, they choose B. The difference in language was simply this: Instead of stating that Strategy A would guarantee 200 out of 600 saved lives, it stated that Strategy A would mean 400 sure deaths.

People will risk a lot to prevent a loss, in other words, but risk very little for possible gain. Running into a burning house to save a pet or fighting back when a mugger asks for your wallet are both high-risk gambles that people take repeatedly in order to hang on to something they care about. The same people might not risk the hassle of, say, fastening a seat belt in a car even though the potential gain might be much higher.

The bird in the hand always seems more attractive than the two in the bush. Even if holding on to the one in your hand comes at a higher risk and the two in the bush are gold-plated.

The reverse situation comes into play when we judge risks of commission versus risks of omission. A risk that you assume by actually doing something seems far more risky than a risk you take by not doing something, even though the risk of doing nothing may be greater. 25

Death from natural causes, like cancer, are more readily acceptable than deaths from accidents or murder. That's probably one reason it's so much easier to accept thousands of starving children than the death of one in a drive-by shooting. The former is an act of omission — a failure to step in and help, send food or medicine. The latter is the commission of a crime — somebody pulled the trigger.

In the same way, the Food and Drug Administration is far more likely to withhold a drug that might help a great number of people if it threatens to harm a few; better to hurt a lot of people by failing to do something than act with the deliberate knowledge that some people will be hurt. Or as the doctors' credo puts it: First do no harm.

For obvious reasons, dramatic or exotic risks seem far more dangerous than more familiar ones. Plane crashes and AIDS are risks associated with ambulances and flashing lights, sex and drugs. While red dye #2 strikes terror in our hearts, that great glob of butter melting into our baked potato is accepted as an old friend. "A woman drives down the street with her child romping around in the front seat," says John Allen Paulos. "Then they arrive at the shopping mall, and she grabs the child's hand so hard it hurts, because she's afraid he'll be kidnapped."

Children who are kidnapped are far more likely to be whisked away by relatives than strangers, just as most people are murdered by people they know.

Familiar risks creep up on us like age and are often difficult to see until it's 30 too late to take action. Mathematician Sam C. Saunders of Washington State University reminds us that a frog placed in hot water will struggle to escape, but the same frog placed in cool water that's slowly warmed up will sit peacefully until it's cooked. "One cannot anticipate what one does not perceive," he says, which is why gradual accumulations of risk due to lifestyle choices (like smoking or eating) are so often ignored. We're in hot water, but it's gotten hot so slowly that no one notices.

To bring home his point, Saunders asks us to imagine that cigarettes are not harmful — with the exception of an occasional one that has been packed with explosives instead of tobacco. These dynamite-stuffed cigarettes look just like normal ones. There's only one hidden away in every 18,250 packs — not a grave risk, you might say. The only catch is, if you smoke one of those explosive cigarettes, it might blow your head off.

The mathematician speculates, I think correctly, that given such a situation, cigarettes would surely be banned outright. After all, if 30 million packs of cigarettes are sold each day, an average of 1,600 people a day would die in gruesome explosions. Yet the number of deaths is the same to be expected from normal smoking. "The total expected loss of life or health to smokers using dynamite-loaded (but otherwise harmless) cigarettes over forty years would not be as great as with ordinary filtered cigarettes," says Saunders.

We can accept getting cooked like a frog, in other words, but not getting blown up like a firecracker.

It won't come as a great surprise to anyone that ego also plays a role in the way we assess risks. Psychological self-protection leads us to draw consistently wrong conclusions. In general, we overestimate the risks of bad things happening to others, while vastly underrating the possibility that they will happen to ourselves. Indeed, the lengths people go to minimize their own perceived risks can be downright "ingenious," according to Rutgers psychologist Neil Weinstein. For example, people asked about the risk of finding radon in their houses always rate their risk as "low" or "average," never "high." "If you ask them why," says Weinstein, "they take anything and twist it around in a way that reassures them. Some say their risk is low because the house is new; others, because the house is old. Some will say their risk is low because their house is at the top of a hill; others, because it's at the bottom of a hill."

Whatever the evidence to the contrary, we think: "It won't happen to me." 35 Weinstein and others speculate that this has something to do with preservation of self-esteem. We don't like to see ourselves as vulnerable. We like to think we've got some magical edge over the others. Ego gets involved especially in cases where being vulnerable to risk implies personal failure — for example, the risk of depression, suicide, alcoholism, drug addiction. "If you admit you're at risk," says Weinstein, "you're admitting that you can't handle stress. You're not as strong as the next person."

Average people, studies have shown, believe that they will enjoy longer lives, healthier lives, and longer marriages than the "average" person. Despite the obvious fact that they themselves are, well, average people, too. According to a recent poll, 3 out of 4 baby boomers (those born between 1946 and 1964) think they look younger than their peers, and 4 out of 5 say they have fewer wrinkles than other people their age — a statistical impossibility.

Kahneman and Tversky studied this phenomenon as well and found that people think they'll beat the odds because they're special. This is no doubt a necessary psychological defense mechanism, or no one would ever get married again without thinking seriously about the potential for divorce. A clear view of personal vulnerability, however, could go a long way toward preventing activities like drunken driving. But then again, most people think they are better than average drivers — even when intoxicated.

We also seem to believe it won't happen to us if it hasn't happened yet. That is, we extrapolate from the past to the future. "I've been taking that highway at eighty miles per hour for ten years and I haven't crashed yet," we tell ourselves. This is rather like reasoning that flipping a coin ten times that comes up heads guarantees that heads will continue to come up indefinitely.

Curiously, one advertising campaign against drunken driving that was quite successful featured the faces of children killed by drunken drivers. These children looked real to us. We could identify with them. In the same way as we could identify with the people on TWA Flight 800. It's much easier to empathize with someone who has a name and a face than a statistic.

That explains in part why we go to great expense to rescue children who 40 fall down mine shafts, but not children dying from preventable diseases. Economists call this the "rule of rescue." If you know that someone is in danger and you know that you can help, you have a moral obligation to do so. If you don't know about it, however, you have no obligation. Columnist Roger Simon speculates that's one reason the National Rifle Association lobbied successfully to eliminate the program at the Centers for Disease Control that keeps track of gun deaths. If we don't have to face what's happening, we won't feel obligated to do anything about it.

Even without the complication of all these psychological factors, however, calculating risks can be tricky because not everything is known about every situation. "We have to concede that a single neglected or unrecognized risk can invalidate all the reliability calculations, which are based on known risk," writes Ivar Ekeland. There is always a risk, in other words, that the risk assessment itself is wrong.

Genetic screening, like tests for HIV infection, has a certain probability of being wrong. If your results come back positive, how much should you worry? If they come back negative, how safe should you feel?

The more factors involved, the more complicated the risk assessment becomes. When you get to truly complex systems like nationwide telephone networks and power grids, worldwide computer networks and hugely complex machines like space shuttles, the risk of disaster becomes infinitely harder to pin down. No one knows when a minor glitch will set off a chain reaction of events that will culminate in disaster. . . .

Needless to say, the way a society assesses risk is very different from the way an individual views the same choices. Whether or not you wish to ride a motorcycle is your own business. Whether society pays the bills for the thousands of people maimed by cycle accidents, however, is everybody's business. Any one of us might view our own survival on a transatlantic flight as more important than the needs of the nation's children. Governments, one presumes, ought to have a somewhat different agenda.

But how far does society want to go in strictly numerical accounting? It certainly hasn't helped much in the all-important issue of health care, where an ounce of prevention has been proven again and again to be worth many pounds of cures. Most experts agree that we should be spending much more money preventing common diseases and accidents, especially in children. But no one wants to take health dollars away from precarious newborns or the elderly—where most of it goes. These are decisions that ultimately will not be made by numbers alone. Calculating risk only helps us to see more clearly what exactly is going on.

According to anthropologist Melvin Konner, author of *Why the Reckless Survive*, our poor judgment about potential risks may well be the legacy of evolution. Early peoples lived at constant risk from predators, disease, accidents. They died young. And in evolutionary terms, "winning" means not longevity, but merely sticking around long enough to pass on your genes to the next generation. Taking risk was therefore a "winning" strategy, especially if it meant a chance to mate before dying. Besides, decisions had to be made quickly. If going for a meal of ripe berries meant risking an attack from a saber-toothed tiger, you dove for the berries. For a half-starved cave dweller, this was a relatively simple choice. Perhaps our brains are simply not wired, speculates Konner, for the careful calculations presented by the risks of modern life.

Indeed, some of our optimistic biases toward personal risk may still serve important psychological purposes. In times of stress and danger, they help us to put one foot in front of the other; they help us to get on with our lives, and out the door.

In the end, Konner, the cautious professor, ruminates somewhat wistfully about his risk-taking friends—who smoke, and ride motorcycles, and drive with their seat belts fastened behind them. Beside them, he feels "safe and virtuous," yet somehow uneasy. "I sometimes think," he muses, "that the more reckless among us may have something to teach the careful about the sort of immortality that comes from living fully every day."

CONSIDERATIONS FOR CRITICAL THINKING AND WRITING

1. FIRST RESPONSE. What kinds of risks do you take in your own life? Consider your own behavior; do you agree with Cole that "Risk assessment is rarely based on purely rational considerations" (paragraph 2)?

2. What examples does Cole use to support the assertion that "We aim our resources at phantoms, while real hazards are ignored"? Explain why or why not you find these examples persuasive.

3. Describe the tone of the following sentence: "Life, after all, is a fatal disease, and the mortality rate for humans, at the end of the day, is 100 percent" (paragraph 4). Discuss whether or not the tone of this sentence is representative of Cole's entire essay.

4. What do you think is Cole's central thesis? Choose a paragraph that most succinctly expresses the thesis and explain how it does so.

5. Comment on Cole's use of statistics. Do you think that including more statistics would make this essay more convincing? Explain why or why not.

Argument

This casebook shows you how one student, April Bovet, developed an argument that qualifies yet also supports the main points in an essay by Linda Chavez, "Demystifying Multiculturalism," moving through first response through brainstorming to final draft. Because making an argument effectively requires understanding the complexities of an issue, April first read Chavez's article several times to be sure she could identify clearly what is at stake, find where she thinks Chavez positions herself politically, and find the implicit as well as the explicit assumptions that are being made in the essay. Try to do the same as you read and reread "Demystifying Multiculturalism"; you may find that you agree or disagree with April Bovet's response to this controversial essay, but the more you think about it the more uncertain you may find yourself. Finally, what do you think about the multicultural movement?

LINDA CHAVEZ (b. 1947)

Born in Albuquerque, New Mexico, Linda Chavez grew up in a Spanish American family. After earning a bachelor's degree at the University of Colorado (1970), she attended the University of California, Los Angeles, and the University of Maryland for graduate study. Chavez's work is primarily concerned with issues related to affirmative action, voting rights, immigration, and bilingual education. Her conservative perspectives have been widely published in newspapers and magazines, and she has appeared on national television and radio programs. From 1977 to 1983 she served as editor of *American Educator* for the American Federation of Teachers, and from 1983 to 1985 she was director of the United States Commission on Civil Rights. She also served as director of the White House Office of Public Liaison in 1985 and as a member of the United Nations Subcommission on Human Rights from 1992 to 1996. She has published two books, *Out of the Barrio: Toward a New Politics of Hispanic Assimilation* (1991) and *From Sugar Daddies to Uncle Sam* (1999).

Linda Chavez (1986), whose work focuses on the political and cultural issues Hispanic Americans face, announcing her campaign for the Republican nomination for the U.S. Senate.

Demystifying Multiculturalism   1994

Multiculturalism is on the advance, everywhere from President Clinton's cabinet to corporate boardrooms to public-school classrooms. If you believe the multiculturalists' progaganda, whites are on the verge of becoming a minority in the United States. The multiculturalists predict that this demographic shift will fundamentally change American culture—indeed destroy the very idea that America *has* a single, unified culture. They aren't taking any chances, however. They have enlisted the help of government, corporate leaders, the media, and the education establishment in waging a cultural revolution. But has America truly become a multicultural nation? And if not, will those who capitulate to these demands create a self-fulfilling prophecy?

At the heart of the argument is the assumption that the white population is rapidly declining in relation to the nonwhite population. A 1987 Hudson Institute report helped catapult this claim to national prominence. The study, *Workforce 2000*, estimated that by the turn of the century only 15 percent of new workers would be white males. The figure was widely interpreted to mean that whites were about to become a minority in the workplace—and in the country.

In fact, white males will still constitute about 45 percent—a plurality—of the workforce in the year 2000. The proportion of white men in the workforce *is* declining—it was nearly 51 percent in 1980—but primarily because the proportion of white women is growing. They will make up 39 percent of the workforce within ten years, according to government projections, up from 36 percent in 1980. Together, white men and women will account for 84 percent of all workers by 2000—hardly a minority share.

But the business world is behaving as if a demographic tidal wave is about to hit. A whole new industry of "diversity professionals" has emerged to help managers cope with the expected deluge of nonwhite workers. These consultants are paid as much as $10,000 a day to train managers to "value diversity," a term so ubiquitous that it has appeared in more than seven hundred articles in major newspapers in the last three years. According to Heather MacDonald in *The New Republic*, about half of *Fortune* 500 corporations now employ someone responsible for "diversity."

What precisely does valuing diversity mean? The underlying assumptions 5 seem to be that nonwhites are so different from whites that employers must make major changes to accommodate them, and that white workers will be naturally resistant to including nonwhites in their ranks. Public-opinion polls don't bear out the latter. They show that support among whites for equal job opportunity for blacks is extraordinarily high, exceeding 90 percent as early as 1975. As for accommodating different cultures, the problem is not culture — or race, or ethnicity — but education. Many young people, in particular, are poorly prepared for work, and the problem is most severe among those who attended inner-city schools, most of them blacks and Hispanics.

Nevertheless, multiculturalists insist on treating race and ethnicity as if they were synonymous with culture. They presume that skin color and national origin, which are immutable traits, determine values, mores, language, and other cultural attributes, which, of course, are learned. In the multiculturalists' world view, African-Americans, Puerto Ricans, or Chinese-Americans living in New York City have more in common with persons of their ancestral group living in Lagos or San Juan or Hong Kong than they do with other New Yorkers who are white. Culture becomes a fixed entity, transmitted, as it were, in the genes, rather than through experience. Thus, "Afrocentricity," a variant of multiculturalism, is "a way of being," its exponents claim. According to a leader of the Afrocentric education movement, Molefi Kete Asante, there is "one African Cultural System manifested in diversities," whether one speaks of Afro-Brazilians, Cubans, or Nigerians (or, presumably, African-Americans). Exactly how this differs from the traditional racist notion that all blacks (Jews, Mexicans, Chinese, etc.) think alike is unclear. What is clear is that the multiculturalists have abandoned the ideal that all persons should be judged by the content of their character, not the color of their skin. Indeed, the multiculturalists seem to believe that a person's character is *determined* by the color of his skin and by his ancestry.

Such convictions lead multiculturalists to conclude that, again in the words of Asante, "[T]here is no common American culture." The logic is simple, but wrong-headed: Since Americans (or more often, their forebears) hail from many different places, each of which has its own specific culture, the argument goes, America must be multicultural. And it is becoming more so every day as new immigrants bring their cultures with them.

Indeed, multiculturalists hope to ride the immigrant wave to greater power and influence. They have certainly done so in education. Some 2.3 million children who cannot speak English well now attend public school, an increase of 1 million in the last seven years. Multicultural advocates cite the presence of such children to demand bilingual education and other multicultural services. The Los Angeles Unified School District alone currently offers instruction in Spanish, Armenian, Korean, Cantonese, Tagalog, Russian, and Japanese. Federal and state governments now spend literally billions of dollars on these programs.

Ironically, the multiculturalists' emphasis on education undercuts their argument that culture is inextricable from race or national origin. They are acutely aware just how fragile cultural identification is; why else are they so adamant about reinforcing it? Multiculturalists insist on teaching immigrant children in their native language, instructing them in the history and customs of their native land and imbuing them with reverence for their ancestral heroes, lest these youngsters be seduced by American culture. Far from losing faith in the power of assimilation, they seem to believe that without a heavy dose of multicultural indoctrination, immigrants won't be able to resist it. And they're right, though it remains to be seen whether anything, including the multiculturalists' crude methods, will ultimately detour immigrants from the assimilation path.

The urge to assimilate has traditionally been overpowering in the United 10
States, especially among the children of immigrants. Only groups that maintain strict rules against intermarriage with persons outside the group, such as Orthodox Jews and the Amish, have ever succeeded in preserving distinct, full-blown cultures within American society. (It is interesting to note that religion seems to be a more effective deterrent to full assimilation than the secular elements of culture, including language.) Although many Americans worry that Hispanic immigrants, for example, are not learning English and will therefore fail to assimilate into the American mainstream, little evidence supports the case. By the third generation in the United States, a majority of Hispanics, like other ethnic groups, speak only English and are closer to other Americans on most measures of social and economic status than they are to Hispanic immigrants. On one of the most rigorous gauges of assimilation — intermarriage — Hispanics rank high. About one-third of young third-generation Hispanics marry non-Hispanic whites, a pattern similar to that of young Asians. Even for blacks, exogamy rates, which have been quite low historically, are going up; about 3 percent of blacks now marry outside their group.

The impetus for multiculturalism is not coming from immigrants, but from their more affluent and assimilated native-born counterparts. The proponents are most often the elite — the best educated and most successful members of their respective racial and ethnic groups. College campuses, where the most radical displays of multiculturalism take place, are fertile recruiting grounds. Last May, for example, a group of Mexican-American students at UCLA, frustrated that the university would not elevate the school's 23-year-old Chicano-studies program to full department status, stormed the faculty center, breaking windows and furniture and causing half a million dollars in damage. The same month, a group of Asian-American students at UC Irvine went on a hunger strike to pressure administrators into hiring more professors of Asian-American studies. These were not immigrants, or even, by and large, disadvantaged students, but middle-class beneficiaries of their parents' or grandparents' successful assimilation to the American mainstream.

The protestors' quest had almost nothing to do with any effort to maintain their ethnic identity. For the most part, such students probably never thought of themselves as anything but American before they entered college. A recent study of minority students at the University of California at Berkeley found that most Hispanic and Asian students "discovered" their ethnic identity after they arrived on campus — when they also discovered that they were victims of systematic discrimination. As one Mexican-American freshman summed it up, she was "unaware of the things that have been going on with our people, all the injustice we've suffered, how the world really is. I thought racism didn't exist and here, you know, it just comes to light." The researchers added that "students of color" had difficulty pinpointing exactly what constituted this "subtle form of the new racism. . . . There was much talk about certain facial expressions, or the way people look, and how white students 'take over the class' and speak past you."

Whatever their new-found victim status, these students look amazingly like other Americans on most indices. For example, the median family income of Mexican-American students at Berkeley in 1989 was $32,500, slightly above the national median for all Americans that year, $32,191; and 17 percent of those students came from families that earned more than $75,000 a year, even though they were admitted to the university under affirmative-action programs (presumably because they suffered some educational disadvantage attributed to their ethnicity).

Affirmative-action programs make less and less sense as discrimination diminishes in this society — which it indisputably has — and as minorities improve their economic status. Racial and ethnic identity, too, might wane if there weren't such aggressive efforts to ensure that this not happen. The multiculturalists know they risk losing their constituency if young blacks, Hispanics, Asians, and others don't maintain strong racial and ethnic affiliations. Young generations must be *trained* to think of themselves as members of oppressed minority groups entitled to special treatment. And the government provides both the incentives and the money to ensure that this happens. Meanwhile, the main beneficiaries are the multicultural professionals, who often earn exorbitant incomes peddling identity.

One particularly egregious example occurred in the District of Columbia 15 last fall. The school system paid $250,000 to a husband-and-wife consultant team to produce an Afrocentric study guide to be used in a single public elementary school. Controversy erupted after the two spent three years and produced only a five-page outline. Although the husband had previously taught at Howard University, the wife's chief credential was a master's degree from an unaccredited "university" which she and her husband had founded. When the *Washington Post* criticized the school superintendent for his handling of the affair, he called a press conference to defend the couple, who promptly claimed they were the victims of a racist vendetta.

D.C. students rank lowest in the nation in math and fourth-lowest in verbal achievement; one can only wonder what $250,000 in tutoring at one school might have done. Instead, the students were treated to bulletin boards in the classrooms proclaiming on their behalf: "We are the sons and daughters of The Most High. We are the princes and princesses of African kings and queens. We are the descendants of our black ancestors. We are black and we are proud." This incident is not unique. Thousands of consultants with little or no real expertise sell feel-good programs to school systems across the nation.

Multiculturalism is not a grassroots movement. It was created, nurtured, and expanded through government policy. Without the expenditure of vast sums of public money, it would wither away and die. That is not to say that ethnic communities would disappear from the American scene or that groups would not retain some attachment to their ancestral roots. American assimilation has always entailed some give and take, and American culture has been enriched by what individual groups brought to it. The distinguishing characteristic of American culture is its ability to incorporate so many disparate groups, creating a new whole from the many parts. What could be more American, for example, than jazz and film, two distinctive art forms created, respectively, by blacks and immigrant Jews but which all Americans think of as their own? But in the past, government — especially public schools — saw it as a duty to try to bring newcomers into the fold by teaching them English, by introducing them to the great American heroes as their own, by instilling respect for American institutions. Lately, we have nearly reversed course, treating each group, new and old, as if what is most important is to preserve its separate identity and space.

It is easy to blame the ideologues and radicals who are pushing the disuniting of America, to use Arthur Schlesinger's phrase, but the real culprits are those who provide multiculturalists the money and the access to press their cause. Without the acquiescence of policymakers and ordinary citizens, multiculturalism would be no threat. Unfortunately, most major institutions have little stomach for resisting the multicultural impulse — and many seem eager to comply with whatever demands the muliculturalists make. Americans should have learned by now that policy matters. We have only to look at the failure of our welfare and crime policies to know that providing perverse incentives can change the way individuals behave — for the worse. Who is to say that if we pour enough money into dividing Americans we won't succeed?

CONSIDERATIONS FOR CRITICAL THINKING AND WRITING

1. FIRST RESPONSE. In what sense is Chavez "demystifying" issues concerning multiculturalism in America?

2. What is Chavez's main argument? Explain why you agree or disagree.

3. How do your own experiences with race and ethnicity inform your responses to Chavez's views on multiculturalism?

4. What conflicts does Chavez describe between assimilationist and multiculturalist ideas? Explain why you think these competing ideas are mutually exclusive or not.

5. Discuss the intended audience for this essay. For what audience do you think Chavez is writing? What kind of response do you think she hopes to evoke from her audience?

April used the following questions to be sure she identified the important elements in Chavez's essay. These same questions can help you to consider important elements that reveal the effects and meanings of any of the essays in Thinking and

Writing about Literature. These questions are general, so not all of them will nec-
essarily be relevant to a particular essay. Many of them, however, should prove to
be useful for thinking, talking, and writing about an essay. If you are uncertain
about the meaning of a term used in a question, consult the Glossary of Literary
Terms beginning on p. 1381.

QUESTIONS FOR WRITING ABOUT THE ESSAY

1. What does the title of the essay reveal about the author's subject, purpose, and approach?

2. What is your response to a first reading of the essay? Is it positive or negative? Are you interested or disengaged? Do you agree or disagree? Do you feel and think the same way after subsequent readings?

3. Have you consulted a dictionary or other appropriate reference source for any unfamiliar words or allusions in the essay?

4. Have you reread difficult passages that escaped your understanding on first reading?

5. What do you think is the overall purpose of the essay?

6. Is the essay's theme presented implicitly or explicitly? If explicitly, specifically where in the essay is the theme most clearly articulated?

7. What do you know about the author that might be relevant to your understanding of the essay?

8. What occasion or motivation do you think has prompted the author to write the essay?

9. How might knowledge of the historical context of the essay provide useful information for interpreting the essay?

10. To whom do you think the essay is addressed? Is the author aiming at a general or a specific audience?

11. Can the essay be categorized primarily as narrative, descriptive, expository, or argumentative? Is it best described as a combination of types?

12. How do you characterize the essay's voice? Is the voice a created persona or is it clearly the author speaking? If the voice is that of a persona, how would you describe it as different from the author's?

13. What is the author's point of view? Would changing the point of view from first person to third person or vice versa make a significant difference in the essay's effects?

14. Is the style formal or informal? Which words and phrases help to reveal the style most directly?

15. What sort of tone is created in the essay? Specifically, what can you point to in the essay that helps to achieve this attitude and mood?

16. How do various elements of the essay such as diction, image, figures of speech, irony, and symbolism serve to contribute to its meaning and effects?

17. How is the essay structured? How does the structure contribute to the essay's effects?

18. What beliefs, values, and positions are advanced in the essay? To what extent do you wish to agree with, disagree with, or qualify the author's views?

19. If the essay is an argument, does the author present fairly opposing points of view?

20. Does the author's biographical background (sex, age, class, ethnicity, and so on) suggest any possible biases, assumptions, or hidden agendas?

21. Does the author present the argument with or without emotion? Is emotionally charged language used to reduce complex issues to slogans or epithets?

22. Does the author use sound logical reasoning or fall into logical fallacies such as making personal attacks on an opponent rather than addressing the issue?

23. Does the author use circular arguments by beginning with a premise that is identical to its conclusion?

24. Do you need more information about the topic to agree or disagree with the author's argument?

25. Are you able to evaluate the quality of the author's evidence? Does the evidence seem reliable, up-to-date, and consistent with your own knowledge and experience?

26. Is there a particular critical approach that seems especially appropriate for this essay? (See "Applying a Critical Strategy," beginning on p. 56.)

27. Did you enjoy the essay? What, in particular, pleased or displeased you about what was expressed and how it was expressed?

A Sample First Response

April was asked to write informally in answer to the question, *What is Chavez's main argument? Explain why you agree or disagree.* Note that she hasn't fully worked through all the nuances of her own response yet — she's more involved with thinking through what works for her in Chavez's argument and what seems unsatisfying.

Chavez's essay is meant as a challenge: she attacks multiculturalism, an idea that most people I know think of in a positive light. I have never heard someone criticize multiculturalism as vehemently as Chavez does. At first, I thought she was way off the mark, but her argument is convincing and makes sense the more I think about it. One very effective point is her comparison of multiculturalist assumptions with traditional racist beliefs. She criticizes both because

they operate on the unfair belief that value judgments should
be based on race.

Chavez makes an interesting point about how the drive for
multiculturalism is not coming from recent immigrants, but
mostly from the more assimilated second- and third-generation
minority groups. Also, it generally shows itself at the university level, where minority students seem to embrace their ethnic and racial identities because they come into increased
contact with discrimination. Although I have never experienced
this kind of discrimination, I know that other people in my
school have. However, she is not refuting the fact that discrimination exists; she is saying that this new drive for
multiculturalism will increase the differences between all
Americans and lead to more race-related clashes.

Although I believe that Chavez has some very important
points to make, I don't know if the majority of the population
would agree with her. She points her finger at policies that
favor multiculturalist professionals who are making a lot of
money from this movement. It may be true that some people take
advantage of the popularity of multiculturalism, but I also
think that there have been positive results of an increased
awareness of race and ethnicity. Personally, I appreciate the
variety of events on my school campus that reflect the diversity of the student population. While I do sometimes think that
this increased awareness also increases differences between us,
there are undoubtedly more positive aspects to the multiculturalist movement than Chavez admits in her essay.

A Sample of Brainstorming

After writing informally, April was asked to develop her first response
into a formal essay that argues either for or against multiculturalism,
using Chavez's essay to back up her points. Because organization and
structure are so important to an argumentative essay — you need to build a
compelling case to win people to your point of view — she spends some
time brainstorming to make sure the parallelism is clear in her mind
before she starts to write her essay. You'll see below how April lined up the
"traditional" viewpoint against Chavez's.

Multiculturalism

Traditional views	Chavez's views
— Based on assumption that white population is declining in numbers	— Believes whites will still be a majority in future
— Race and ethnicity determine culture	— Culture transmitted through experience
— Culture is a fixed entity	— Culture is continually changing
— Affirmative action is necessary to counteract years of oppression	— Affirmative action is becoming less and less necessary
— Multiculturalism is a movement supported by all minority groups	— Multiculturalism is a political tool used by the middle class, third-generation minorities and funded by government
— It is most important to preserve each group's uniting separate identity and space	— Americans should focus on themselves and embrace a give-and-take culture

A Sample Student Argument

In April's final argument, she focused first on spelling out what Chavez's argument is, noting along the way the points of divergence from her own perspective. It is not until her conclusion that she established her own position. How compelling do you find April's essay? Do you agree or disagree with her point of view? How would *you* structure a paper in response to Chavez?

April Bovet

English 101

Professor Hill

12/6/20--

                    Embrace Multiculturalism or Assimilate:

                              A Fair Distinction?

    Culture is a dynamic, complex entity that is con-
stantly influenced by innumerable forces. Where one
lives, what language one speaks, and the food that one
eats can all be part of one's culture. In her essay
"Demystifying Multiculturalism," Linda Chavez makes a
point of distinguishing learned aspects of culture from
given traits such as race and national origin. According
to Chavez, the main flaw in multiculturalist doctrine is
the tendency to equate race with culture. She also argues
that the multiculturalists' belief that cultural identity
is a fixed entity inherently contradicts their efforts to
instill this identity in order to deter assimilation. She
emphasizes that multiculturalists "presume that skin
color and national origin, which are immutable traits,
determine values, mores, language, and other cultural
attributes, which, of course, are learned" (6). She notes
the similarity between this and traditional racist
notions. The comparison is very effective at highlighting
the negative aspects of multiculturalism. Although Chavez
occasionally goes too far in criticizing the entire multiculturalist movement, she succeeds in demonstrating the
validity of her main point: that the multiculturalist
movement is increasing racial tensions, which are harming
rather than bettering American culture.

    Chavez believes that some of the main reasons for
this increase in destructive racial tensions are the government policies which spend billions of dollars on the
multicultural issue, and, in turn, encourage certain
self-proclaimed multiculturalist professionals to charge

exorbitant amounts for nominal work. There are an increasing number of these "specialists" who are hired by
school systems and private businesses in order to promote
awareness. Their effectiveness has yet to be proven and,
in some cases, it certainly seems like a waste of money.
Chavez believes that these efforts are not only a waste
of time and money but are actively destructive. They will
divide Americans into separate racial and ethnic groups
and prevent us from uniting as a whole. Chavez points out
this negative result of multiculturalist policies and
convinces us that it deserves to be given more attention
and debate in the public arena. Her argument may seem
extreme to some, especially when she claims that bilingual education isn't necessary and is basically a vehicle
for multiculturalists to gain power and influence. However, Chavez isn't objecting to the mingling of languages
and cultures in the classroom, but merely to huge expenditures of public money that basically convince immigrants to preserve an isolated, separate identity.
Specifically, she objects that multiculturalism "was
created, nurtured, and expanded through government
policy" (17).

Chavez notes an interesting phenomenon that she
believes is a result of these unnecessary government
policies. Exploring the roots of the multiculturalist
movement, Chavez points out that it is most strongly
visible on college campuses. In fact, this is probably
where many people, minorities as well as whites, come
into contact with the movement for the first time. Campuses are now filled with groups embracing every conceivable race and ethnicity, and new departments and classes
are cropping up everywhere. These are generally viewed as
positive advances that promote tolerance and knowledge.
For the most part, they are; however, the very measures

that are taken to ensure support for minority groups can often turn into barriers between people of all races. This is the most important part of Chavez's argument, a point that is often overlooked or avoided by people who are afraid to criticize the politically correct multiculturalist movement.

Chavez is highly suspicious of the sudden ethnic "discovery" that many college students of color have while at school. She points out that these students have trouble citing examples of blatant discriminatory action, and that most of them come from affluent, assimilated families. This may be true, but I have trouble following Chavez's logic that this must mean that the students are actively being "trained" to think of themselves as victims. There may be other explanations for this trend, some of them no more complicated than that it is natural for many young adults of all colors to experiment with their own personal identities and that the environment of college may give them the first opportunity to do this.

But she keeps her argument focused on a specific identity discovery to make her bold point. Her willingness to talk about an issue that has no easy answers and may even offend many people is as admirable as it is risky. Her argument against multiculturalism has valid points that should be given more attention and discussion in the public forum, such as the tendency for multiculturalism to fragment American culture instead of uniting and enriching it. Undoubtedly, some of her more radical points, such as her emphasis on the government's role in consciously promoting racial and ethnic divisions, will be met with skepticism and even outrage. However, her main point that the multiculturalist movement may be increasing the differences between Americans and leading to unnecessary racial conflict is well-argued and

understandable. This conflict is a persistent problem in
contemporary society that does not currently have a perfect answer. Although we have not yet arrived at a viable
solution to the difficult issue of racial and ethnic
identity, only by engaging in a continuing dialogue will
such a solution be found.

PART THREE

Literature and Life

9

Home and Family

THE THEMES OF LITERATURE

The four chapters that make up Part One of *Thinking and Writing* focus on the writing process; the four chapters in Part Two focus on the elements of fiction, poetry, drama, and the essay. The next five chapters ask you to put all that you've learned together as you sample from within a rich anthology of stories, poems, plays, and essays organized by **theme.** Every genre includes *theme* as one of its elements; every literary text has one or more themes. Theme is the central idea, the focal point around which a story winds, a poem turns, a play moves, or an essay revolves. Ultimately, what a text suggests about its main theme is what we respond to—or fail to respond to. All other elements are there to support theme, ultimately, whether or not that theme is explicitly stated. Reading thematically means extending what you have learned about the analysis of individual genres to make connections, both between different kinds of texts and between the text and the world we inhabit. Reading thematically gives you something to write about.

The five chapters in this part of the book are organized around universal themes—Home and Family, Love and Its Complications, Lessons from Life, the Natural and Unnatural, and Culture and Identity. As a whole, the stories, poems, plays, and essays in these chapters have much to say about human experience—experience that is contradictory, confusing, complicated, and absolutely fascinating. You'll find diverse perspectives in each chapter, from different historical, cultural, generational, and political moments in time. You'll discover writers who aim to entertain, to describe, to convince, to complain. And, we hope, you'll come away, after reading, with a better and richer understanding of these themes and how they play out in your own life—your experience with family, with love, with learning, with the explained and the unexplainable, and with how you define and position yourself.

HOME AND FAMILY

Each story, poem, play, and essay in this chapter deals with the concept of home and family, though very rarely of the Dick and Jane variety. In John Cheever's "Reunion," a young boy describes his last strained meeting with his father; in Tobias Wolff's "Powder," a son describes a wild drive in the snow with his estranged father. Sylvia Plath explores her relationship with her dead father in "Daddy"; Margaret Atwood does the same in "Bored." And Henrik Ibsen's play *A Doll House* and Barbara Kingsolver's essay "Stone Soup" each suggest a redefinition of what makes a family truly a family, though written in a far different time and place and for a different purpose. As you read, remember that the formal elements of each of these selections are working together to support a theme—and remember to think about how they do so because that work will help you when you sit down to write. And finally, remember that the selections in this chapter have all been chosen because they share a focus on home and family—but that does not mean that there are not other themes worth exploring in the material you're about to encounter. The more connections and discoveries you make about literature, the more you'll take away from the reading experience.

FICTION

John Cheever (1912–1982)

Born in Quincy, Massachusetts, John Cheever was raised in a prosperous family until the stock market crash of 1929, after which his father left the family. Cheever's formal education ended when he was expelled from Thayer Academy for majoring in trouble and being what he described as "a lousy student." Though he had no more formal schooling, he taught himself to write and published his first story, "Expelled," in *The New Republic* in 1930—before his eighteenth birthday. He became a disciplined writer of short stories—many of which appeared in *The New Yorker*—and published several collections of them over four decades, culminating in *The Stories of John Cheever* (1978), which won both the Pulitzer Prize and the National Book Critics' Circle Award. Cheever also wrote four novels; his best known, *The Wapshot Chronicles*, won the National Book Award in 1957. Nearly all of his writing focuses on affluent urban and suburban characters whose morality and manners complicate their lives.

Reunion   1962

The last time I saw my father was in Grand Central Station. I was going from my grandmother's in the Adirondacks to a cottage on the Cape that my mother had rented, and I wrote my father that I would be in New York between trains for an hour and a half and asked if we could have lunch together. His secretary wrote to say that he would meet me at the information booth at noon, and at twelve o'clock sharp I saw him coming through the crowd. He was a stranger to me—my mother divorced him three years ago, and I hadn't been with him since—but as soon as I saw him I felt that he was my father, my flesh and blood, my future and my doom. I knew that when I was grown I would be something like him; I would have to plan my campaigns within his limitations. He was a big, good-looking man, and I was terribly happy to see him again. He struck me on the back and shook my hand. "Hi, Charlie," he said. "Hi, boy. I'd like to take you up to my club, but it's in the Sixties, and if you have to catch an early train I guess we'd better get something to eat around here." He put his arm around me, and I smelled my father the way my mother sniffs a rose. It was a rich compound of whiskey, after-shave lotion, shoe polish, woolens, and the rankness of a mature male. I hoped that someone would see us together. I wished that we could be photographed. I wanted some record of our having been together.

We went out of the station and up a side street to a restaurant. It was still early, and the place was empty. The bartender was quarreling with a delivery boy, and there was one very old waiter in a red coat down by the kitchen door. We sat down, and my father hailed the waiter in a loud voice. *"Kellner!"* he shouted. *"Garçon! Cameriere!°* You!" His boisterousness in the empty restaurant seemed out of place. "Could we have a little service here!" he shouted. "Chop-chop." Then he clapped his hands. This caught the waiter's attention, and he shuffled over to our table.

"Were you clapping your hands at me?" he asked.

"Calm down, calm down, *sommelier,"°* my father said. "If it isn't too much to ask of you—if it wouldn't be too much above and beyond the call of duty, we would like a couple of Beefeater Gibsons."

"I don't like to be clapped at," the waiter said.   5

"I should have brought my whistle," my father said. "I have a whistle that is audible only to the ears of old waiters. Now, take out your little pad and your little pencil and see if you can get this straight: two Beefeater Gibsons. Repeat after me: two Beefeater Gibsons."

"I think you'd better go somewhere else," the waiter said quietly.

"That," said my father, "is one of the most brilliant suggestions I have ever heard. Come on, Charlie, let's get the hell out of here."

I followed my father out of that restaurant into another. He was not so boisterous this time. Our drinks came, and he cross-questioned me about the baseball season. He then struck the edge of his empty glass with his knife and began shouting again. *"Garçon! Kellner! You!* Could we trouble you to bring us two more of the same."

Kellner! . . . Garçon! Cameriere!: German, French, and Italian respectively for "Waiter!"
sommelier: Wine waiter (French).

"How old is the boy?" the waiter asked.   10

"That," my father said, "is none of your goddamned business."

"I'm sorry, sir," the waiter said, "but I won't serve the boy another drink."

"Well, I have some news for you," my father said. "I have some very inter-esting news for you. This doesn't happen to be the only restaurant in New York. They've opened another on the corner. Come on, Charlie."

He paid the bill, and I followed him out of that restaurant into another. Here the waiters wore pink jackets like hunting coats, and there was a lot of horse tack on the walls. We sat down, and my father began to shout again. "Master of the hounds! Tallyhoo and all that sort of thing. We'd like a little something in the way of a stirrup cup. Namely, two Bibson Greefeaters."

"Two Bibson Greefeaters?" the waiter asked, smiling.   15

"You know damned well what I want," my father said angrily. "I want two Beefeater Gibsons, and make it snappy. Things have changed in jolly old Eng-land. So my friend the duke tells me. Let's see what England can produce in the way of a cocktail."

"This isn't England," the waiter said.

"Don't argue with me," my father said. "Just do as you're told."

"I just thought you might like to know where you are," the waiter said.

"If there is one thing I cannot tolerate," my father said, "it is an impudent   20 domestic. Come on, Charlie."

The fourth place we went to was Italian. *"Buon giorno,"* my father said *"Per favore, possiamo avere due cocktail americani, forti, forti. Molto gin, poco, vermut."*°

"I don't understand Italian," the waiter said.

"Oh, come off it," my father said. "You understand Italian, and you know damned well you do. *Vogliamo due cocktail americani. Subito."*°

The waiter left us and spoke with the captain, who came over to our table and said, "I'm sorry, sir, but this table is reserved."

"All right," my father said. "Get us another table."   25

"All the tables are reserved," the captain said.

"I get it," my father said. "You don't desire our patronage. Is that it? Well, the hell with you. *Vada all'inferno.*° Let's go, Charlie."

"I have to get my train," I said.

"I'm sorry, sonny," my father said. "I'm terribly sorry." He put his arm around me and pressed me against him. "I'll walk you back to the station. If there had only been time to go up to my club."

"That's all right, Daddy," I said.   30

"I'll get you a paper," he said. "I'll get you a paper to read on the train."

Then he went up to a newsstand and said, "Kind sir, will you be good enough to favor me with one of your goddamned, no-good, ten-cent after-noon papers?" The clerk turned away from him and stared at a magazine cover. "Is it asking too much, kind sir," my father said, "is it asking too much for you to sell me one of your disgusting specimens of yellow journalism?"

Buon giorno . . . Per favore . . . : "Good morning . . . Please, may we have two American cock-tails, strong ones. Much gin, little vermouth" (Italian).
Vogliamo due cocktail . . . : "We want two American cocktails. Immediately" (Italian).
Vada all'inferno: "Go to hell" (Italian).

"I have to go, Daddy," I said. "It's late."

"Now, just wait a second, sonny," he said. "Just wait a second. I want to get a rise out of this chap."

"Goodbye, Daddy," I said, and I went down the stairs and got my train, 35 and that was the last time I saw my father.

CONSIDERATIONS FOR CRITICAL THINKING AND WRITING

1. FIRST RESPONSE. Characterize Charlie's father as he is described in the first paragraph. How does Charlie feel about him?

2. What does the encounter with the waiter in paragraphs 2–8 reveal about the father? What do you think Charlie is feeling during this episode?

3. How does the tone of the story change as Charlie and his father move from bar to bar?

4. Trace your response to the father during the course of the story. What emotion does his behavior evoke in you?

5. Are there any differences between the father's encounters with the newsstand clerk and with the bar waiters? How is the father further revealed in the final episode?

6. What kind of life do you imagine for this family prior to the parents' divorce "three years ago"?

7. Do you think Charlie is justified in never seeing his father again? Why or why not?

8. CRITICAL STRATEGIES. Read the section on reader-response criticism (pp. 74–76) in Chapter 3, "Applying a Critical Strategy." How does your own experience with family life influence your response to "Reunion"?

ANDRE DUBUS (1936–1999)

Though a native of Louisiana, where he attended the Christian Brothers School and McNeese State College, Andre Dubus lived much of his life in Massachusetts; many of his stories are set in the Merrimack Valley north of Boston. After college Dubus served as an officer for five years in the Marine Corps. He then took an M.F.A. at the University of Iowa in 1966 and began teaching at Bradford College in Massachusetts. His fiction earned him numerous awards, and he was both a Guggenheim and a MacArthur Fellow. Among his collections of fiction are *Separate Flights* (1975); *Adultery and Other Choices* (1977); *Finding a Girl in America* (1980), from which "Killings" is taken; *The Last Worthless Evening* (1986); *Collected Stories* (1988); and *Dancing after Hours* (1996). In 1991 he published *Broken Vessels*, a collection of autobiographical essays. His fictions are often tense with violence, anger, tenderness, and guilt; they are populated by characters who struggle to understand and survive their experiences, painful with failure and the weight of imperfect relationships. In "Killings" Dubus offers a powerful blend of intimate domestic life and shocking violence.

Killings

On the August morning when Matt Fowler buried his youngest son, Frank, who had lived for twenty-one years, eight months, and four days, Matt's older son, Steve, turned to him as the family left the grave and walked between their friends, and said: "I should kill him." He was twenty-eight, his brown hair starting to thin in front where he used to have a cowlick. He bit his lower lip, wiped his eyes, then said it again. Ruth's arm, linked with Matt's, tightened; he looked at her. Beneath her eyes there was swelling from the three days she had suffered. At the limousine Matt stopped and looked back at the grave, the casket, and the Congregationalist minister who he thought had probably had a difficult job with the eulogy though he hadn't seemed to, and the old funeral director who was saying something to the six young pallbearers. The grave was on a hill and overlooked the Merrimack, which he could not see from where he stood; he looked at the opposite bank, at the apple orchard with its symmetrically planted trees going up a hill.

Next day Steve drove with his wife back to Baltimore where he managed the branch office of a bank, and Cathleen, the middle child, drove with her husband back to Syracuse. They had left the grandchildren with friends. A month after the funeral Matt played poker at Willis Trottier's because Ruth, who knew this was the second time he had been invited, told him to go, he couldn't sit home with her for the rest of her life, she was all right. After the game Willis went outside to tell everyone good night and, when the others had driven away, he walked with Matt to his car. Willis was a short, silver-haired man who had opened a diner after World War II, his trade then mostly very early breakfast, which he cooked, and then lunch for the men who worked at the leather and shoe factories. He now owned a large restaurant.

"He walks the Goddamn streets," Matt said.

"I know. He was in my place last night, at the bar. With a girl."

"I don't see him. I'm in the store all the time. Ruth sees him. She sees him too much. She was at Sunnyhurst today getting cigarettes and aspirin, and there he was. She can't even go out for cigarettes and aspirin. It's killing her."

"Come back in for a drink."

Matt looked at his watch. Ruth would be asleep. He walked with Willis back into the house, pausing at the steps to look at the starlit sky. It was a cool summer night; he thought vaguely of the Red Sox, did not even know if they were at home tonight; since it happened he had not been able to think about any of the small pleasures he believed he had earned, as he had earned also what was shattered now forever: the quietly harried and quietly pleasurable days of fatherhood. They went inside. Willis's wife, Martha, had gone to bed hours ago, in the rear of the large house which was rigged with burglar and fire alarms. They went downstairs to the game room: the television set suspended from the ceiling, the pool table, the poker table with beer cans, cards, chips, filled ashtrays, and the six chairs where Matt and his friends had sat, the friends picking up the old banter as though he had only been away on vacation; but he could see the affection and courtesy in their eyes. Willis went behind the bar and mixed them each a Scotch and soda; he stayed behind the bar and looked at Matt sitting on the stool.

"How often have you thought about it?" Willis said.

"Every day since he got out. I didn't think about bail. I thought I wouldn't have to worry about him for years. She sees him all the time. It makes her cry."

"He was in my place a long time last night. He'll be back."   10

"Maybe he won't."

"The band. He likes the band."

"What's he doing now?"

"He's tending bar up to Hampton Beach. For a friend. Ever notice even the worst bastard always has friends? He couldn't get work in town. It's just tourists and kids up to Hampton. Nobody knows him. If they do, they don't care. They drink what he mixes."

"Nobody tells me about him."   15

"I hate him, Matt. My boys went to school with him. He was the same then. Know what he'll do? Five at the most. Remember that woman about seven years ago? Shot her husband and dropped him off the bridge in the Merrimack with a hundred-pound sack of cement and said all the way through it that nobody helped her. Know where she is now? She's in Lawrence now, a secretary. And whoever helped her, where the hell is he?"

"I've got a .38 I've had for years, I take it to the store now. I tell Ruth it's for the night deposits. I tell her things have changed: we got junkies here now too. Lots of people without jobs. She knows though."

"What does she know?"

"She knows I started carrying it after the first time she saw him in town. She knows it's in case I see him, and there's some kind of a situation —"

He stopped, looked at Willis, and finished his drink. Willis mixed him   20 another.

"What kind of situation?"

"Where he did something to me. Where I could get away with it."

"How does Ruth feel about that?"

"She doesn't know."

"You said she does, she's got it figured out."   25

He thought of her that afternoon: when she went into Sunnyhurst, Strout was waiting at the counter while the clerk bagged the things he had bought; she turned down an aisle and looked at soup cans until he left.

"Ruth would shoot him herself, if she thought she could hit him."

"You got a permit?"

"No."

"I do. You could get a year for that."   30

"Maybe I'll get one. Or maybe I won't. Maybe I'll just stop bringing it to the store."

Richard Strout was twenty-six years old, a high school athlete, football scholarship to the University of Massachusetts where he lasted for almost two semesters before quitting in advance of the final grades that would have forced him not to return. People then said: Dickie can do the work; he just doesn't want to. He came home and did construction work for his father but refused his father's offer to learn the business; his two older brothers had learned it, so that Strout and Sons trucks going about town, and signs on construction sites, now slashed wounds into Matt Fowler's life. Then Richard married a young girl and became a bartender, his salary and tips augmented and perhaps sometimes matched by his father, who also posted his bond. So his friends, his enemies (he had those: fist fights or, more often, boys and then young men who had not fought him when they thought they should have), and those who simply knew him by face and name, had a series of images of him which they recalled when they heard of the killing: the high school running back, the young drunk in bars, the oblivious hard-hatted young man eating lunch at a counter, the bartender who could perhaps be called courteous but not more than that: as he tended bar, his dark eyes and dark, wide-jawed face appeared less sullen, near blank.

One night he beat Frank. Frank was living at home and waiting for September, for graduate school in economics, and working as a lifeguard at Salisbury Beach, where he met Mary Ann Strout, in her first month of separation. She spent most days at the beach with her two sons. Before ten o'clock one night Frank came home; he had driven to the hospital first, and he walked into the living room with stitches over his right eye and both lips bright and swollen.

"I'm all right," he said, when Matt and Ruth stood up, and Matt turned off the television, letting Ruth get to him first: the tall, muscled but slender suntanned boy. Frank tried to smile at them but couldn't because of his lips.

"It was her husband, wasn't it?" Ruth said. 35

"Ex," Frank said. "He dropped in."

Matt gently held Frank's jaw and turned his face to the light, looked at the stitches, the blood under the white of the eye, the bruised flesh.

"Press charges," Matt said.

"No."

"What's to stop him from doing it again? Did you hit him at all? Enough 40 so he won't want to next time?"

"I don't think I touched him."

"So what are you going to do?"

"Take karate," Frank said, and tried again to smile.

"That's not the problem," Ruth said.

"You know you like her," Frank said. 45

"I like a lot of people. What about the boys? Did they see it?"

"They were asleep."

"Did you leave her alone with him?"

"He left first. She was yelling at him. I believe she had a skillet in her hand."

"Oh for God's sake," Ruth said. 50

Matt had been dealing with that too: at the dinner table on evenings when Frank wasn't home, was eating with Mary Ann; or, on the other nights—and Frank was with her every night—he talked with Ruth while they watched television, or lay in bed with the windows open and he smelled the night air and imagined, with both pride and muted sorrow, Frank in Mary Ann's arms. Ruth didn't like it because Mary Ann was in the process of divorce, because she had two children, because she was four years older than Frank, and finally—she told this in bed, where she had during all of their marriage told him of her deepest feelings: of love, of passion, of fears about one of the children, of pain Matt had caused her or she had caused him—she was against it because of what she had heard: that the marriage had gone bad early, and for most of it Richard and Mary Ann had both played around.

"That can't be true," Matt said. "Strout wouldn't have stood for it."

"Maybe he loves her."

"He's too hot-tempered. He couldn't have taken that."

But Matt knew Strout had taken it, for he had heard the stories too. He wondered who had told them to Ruth; and he felt vaguely annoyed and isolated: living with her for thirty-one years and still not knowing what she talked about with her friends. On these summer nights he did not so much argue with her as try to comfort her, but finally there was no difference between the two: she had concrete objections, which he tried to overcome. And in his attempt to do this, he neglected his own objections, which were the same as hers, so that as he spoke to her he felt as disembodied as he sometimes did in the store when he helped a man choose a blouse or dress or piece of costume jewelry for his wife.

"The divorce doesn't mean anything," he said. "She was young and maybe she liked his looks and then after a while she realized she was living with a bastard. I see it as a positive thing."

"She's not divorced yet."

"It's the same thing. Massachusetts has crazy laws, that's all. Her age is no problem. What's it matter when she was born? And that other business: even if it's true, which it probably isn't, it's got nothing to do with Frank, and it's in the past. And the kids are no problem. She's been married six years; she ought to have kids. Frank likes them. He plays with them. And he's not going to marry her anyway, so it's not a problem of money."

"Then what's he doing with her?"

"She probably loves him, Ruth. Girls always have. Why can't we just leave it at that?"

"He got home at six o'clock Tuesday morning."

"I didn't know you knew. I've already talked to him about it."

Which he had: since he believed almost nothing he told Ruth, he went to Frank with what he believed. The night before, he had followed Frank to the car after dinner.

"You wouldn't make much of a burglar," he said.

"How's that?"

Matt was looking up at him; Frank was six feet tall, an inch and a half taller than Matt, who had been proud when Frank at seventeen outgrew him; he had only felt uncomfortable when he had to reprimand or caution him. He touched Frank's bicep, thought of the young taut passionate body, believed he could sense the desire, and again he felt the pride and sorrow and envy too, not knowing whether he was envious of Frank or Mary Ann.

"When you came in yesterday morning, I woke up. One of these mornings your mother will. And I'm the one who'll have to talk to her. She won't interfere with you. Okay? I know it means—" But he stopped, thinking: I know it means getting up and leaving that suntanned girl and going sleepy to the car, I know—

"Okay," Frank said, and touched Matt's shoulder and got into the car.

There had been other talks, but the only long one was their first one: a night driving to Fenway Park, Matt having ordered the tickets so they could talk, and knowing when Frank said yes, he would go, that he knew the talk was coming too. It took them forty minutes to get to Boston, and they talked about Mary Ann until they joined the city traffic along the Charles River, blue in the late sun. Frank told him all the things that Matt would later pretend to believe when he told them to Ruth.

"It seems like a lot for a young guy to take on," Matt finally said.   70

"Sometimes it is. But she's worth it."

"Are you thinking about getting married?"

"We haven't talked about it. She can't for over a year. I've got school."

"I *do* like her," Matt said.

He did. Some evenings, when the long summer sun was still low in the sky,   75
Frank brought her home; they came into the house smelling of suntan lotion
and the sea, and Matt gave them gin and tonics and started the charcoal in the
backyard, and looked at Mary Ann in the lawn chair: long and very light brown
hair (Matt thinking that twenty years ago she would have dyed it blonde), and
the long brown legs he loved to look at; her face was pretty; she had probably
never in her adult life gone unnoticed into a public place. It was in her wide
brown eyes that she looked older than Frank; after a few drinks Matt thought
what he saw in her eyes was something erotic, testament to the rumors about
her; but he knew it wasn't that, or all that: she had, very young, been through a
sort of pain that his children, and he and Ruth, had been spared. In the
moments of his recognizing that pain, he wanted to tenderly touch her hair,
wanted with some gesture to give her solace and hope. And he would glance at
Frank, and hope they would love each other, hope Frank would soothe that
pain in her heart, take it from her eyes; and her divorce, her age, and her children did not matter at all. On the first two evenings she did not bring her boys,
and then Ruth asked her to bring them the next time. In bed that night Ruth
said, "She hasn't brought them because she's embarrassed. She shouldn't feel
embarrassed."

Richard Strout shot Frank in front of the boys. They were sitting on the
living room floor watching television, Frank sitting on the couch, and Mary
Ann just returning from the kitchen with a tray of sandwiches. Strout came in
the front door and shot Frank twice in the chest and once in the face with a
9 mm automatic. Then he looked at the boys and Mary Ann, and went home to
wait for the police.

It seemed to Matt that from the time Mary Ann called weeping to tell him
until now, a Saturday night in September, sitting in the car with Willis, parked
beside Strout's car, waiting for the bar to close, that he had not so much
moved through his life as wandered through it, his spirits like a dazed body
bumping into furniture and corners. He had always been a fearful father: when
his children were young, at the start of each summer he thought of them
drowning in a pond or the sea, and he was relieved when he came home in the
evenings and they were there; usually that relief was his only acknowledgment
of his fear, which he never spoke of, and which he controlled within his heart.
As he had when they were very young and all of them in turn, Cathleen too,
were drawn to the high oak in the backyard, and had to climb it. Smiling, he
watched them, imagining the fall: and he was poised to catch the small body
before it hit the earth. Or his legs were poised; his hands were in his pockets or
his arms were folded and, for the child looking down, he appeared relaxed and
confident while his heart beat with the two words he wanted to call out but did
not: *Don't fall.* In winter he was less afraid: he made sure the ice would hold him
before they skated, and he brought or sent them to places where they could
sled without ending in the street. So he and his children had survived their
childhood, and he only worried about them when he knew they were driving a

long distance, and then he lost Frank in a way no father expected to lose his son, and he felt that all the fears he had borne while they were growing up, and all the grief he had been afraid of, had backed up like a huge wave and struck him on the beach and swept him out to sea. Each day he felt the same and when he was able to forget how he felt, when he was able to force himself not to feel that way, the eyes of his clerks and customers defeated him. He wished those eyes were oblivious, even cold; he felt he was withering in their tenderness. And beneath his listless wandering, every day in his soul he shot Richard Strout in the face; while Ruth, going about town on errands, kept seeing him. And at nights in bed she would hold Matt and cry, or sometimes she was silent and Matt would touch her tightening arm, her clenched fist.

As his own right fist was now, squeezing the butt of the revolver, the last of the drinkers having left the bar, talking to each other, going to their separate cars which were in the lot in front of the bar, out of Matt's vision. He heard their voices, their cars, and then the ocean again, across the street. The tide was in and sometimes it smacked the sea wall. Through the windshield he looked at the dark red side wall of the bar, and then to his left, past Willis, at Strout's car, and through its windows he could see the now-emptied parking lot, the road, the sea wall. He could smell the sea.

The front door of the bar opened and closed again and Willis looked at Matt then at the corner of the building; when Strout came around it alone Matt got out of the car, giving up the hope he had kept all night (and for the past week) that Strout would come out with friends, and Willis would simply drive away; thinking: *All right then. All right;* and he went around the front of Willis's car, and at Strout's he stopped and aimed over the hood at Strout's blue shirt ten feet away. Willis was aiming too, crouched on Matt's left, his elbow resting on the hood.

"Mr. Fowler," Strout said. He looked at each of them, and at the guns. 80 "Mr. Trottier."

Then Matt, watching the parking lot and the road, walked quickly between the car and the building and stood behind Strout. He took one leather glove from his pocket and put it on his left hand.

"Don't talk. Unlock the front and back and get in."

Strout unlocked the front door, reached in and unlocked the back, then got in, and Matt slid into the back seat, closed the door with his gloved hand, and touched Strout's head once with the muzzle.

"It's cocked. Drive to your house."

When Strout looked over his shoulder to back the car, Matt aimed at his 85 temple and did not look at his eyes.

"Drive slowly," he said. "Don't try to get stopped."

They drove across the empty front lot and onto the road, Willis's headlights shining into the car; then back through town, the sea wall on the left hiding the beach, though far out Matt could see the ocean; he uncocked the revolver; on the right were the places, most with their neon signs off, that did so much business in summer: the lounges and cafés and pizza houses, the street itself empty of traffic, the way he and Willis had known it would be when they decided to take Strout at the bar rather than knock on his door at two o'clock one morning and risk that one insomniac neighbor. Matt had not told Willis he was afraid he could not be alone with Strout for very long, smell his smells, feel the presence of his flesh, hear his voice, and then shoot him.

They left the beach town and then were on the high bridge over the channel: to the left the smacking curling white at the breakwater and beyond that the dark sea and the full moon, and down to his right the small fishing boats bobbing at anchor in the cove. When they left the bridge, the sea was blocked by abandoned beach cottages, and Matt's left hand was sweating in the glove. Out here in the dark in the car he believed Ruth knew. Willis had come to his house at eleven and asked if he wanted a nightcap; Matt went to the bedroom for his wallet, put the gloves in one trouser pocket and the .38 in the other and went back to the living room, his hand in his pocket covering the bulge of the cool cylinder pressed against his fingers, the butt against his palm. When Ruth said good night she looked at his face, and he felt she could see in his eyes the gun, and the night he was going to. But he knew he couldn't trust what he saw. Willis's wife had taken her sleeping pill, which gave her eight hours — the reason, Willis had told Matt, he had the alarms installed, for nights when he was late at the restaurant — and when it was all done and Willis got home he would leave ice and a trace of Scotch and soda in two glasses in the game room and tell Martha in the morning that he had left the restaurant early and brought Matt home for a drink.

"He was making it with my wife." Strout's voice was careful, not pleading.

Matt pressed the muzzle against Strout's head, pressed it harder than he wanted to, feeling through the gun Strout's head flinching and moving forward; then he lowered the gun to his lap.

"Don't talk," he said.

Strout did not speak again. They turned west, drove past the Dairy Queen closed until spring, and the two lobster restaurants that faced each other and were crowded all summer and were now also closed, onto the short bridge crossing the tidal stream, and over the engine Matt could hear through his open window the water rushing inland under the bridge; looking to his left he saw its swift moonlit current going back into the marsh which, leaving the bridge, they entered: the salt marsh stretching out on both sides, the grass tall in patches but mostly low and leaning earthward as though windblown, a large dark rock sitting as though it rested on nothing but itself, and shallow pools reflecting the bright moon.

Beyond the marsh they drove through woods, Matt thinking now of the hole he and Willis had dug last Sunday afternoon after telling their wives they were going to Fenway Park. They listened to the game on a transistor radio, but heard none of it as they dug into the soft earth on the knoll they had chosen because elms and maples sheltered it. Already some leaves had fallen. When the hole was deep enough they covered it and the piled earth with dead branches, then cleaned their shoes and pants and went to a restaurant farther up in New Hampshire where they ate sandwiches and drank beer and watched the rest of the game on television. Looking at the back of Strout's head he thought of Frank's grave; he had not been back to it; but he would go before winter, and its second burial of snow.

He thought of Frank sitting on the couch and perhaps talking to the children as they watched television, imagined him feeling young and strong, still warmed from the sun at the beach, and feeling loved, hearing Mary Ann moving about in the kitchen, hearing her walking into the living room; maybe he looked up at her and maybe she said something, looking at him over the tray of sandwiches, smiling at him, saying something the way women do when they

90

offer food as a gift, then the front door opening and this son of a bitch coming in and Frank seeing that he meant the gun in his hand, this son of a bitch and his gun the last person and thing Frank saw on earth.

When they drove into town the streets were nearly empty: a few slow cars, a policeman walking his beat past the darkened fronts of stores. Strout and Matt both glanced at him as they drove by. They were on the main street, and all the stoplights were blinking yellow. Willis and Matt had talked about that too: the lights changed at midnight, so there would be no place Strout had to stop and where he might try to run. Strout turned down the block where he lived and Willis's headlights were no longer with Matt in the back seat. They had planned that too, had decided it was best for just the one car to go to the house, and again Matt had said nothing about his fear of being alone with Strout, especially in his house: a duplex, dark as all the houses on the street were, the street itself lit at the corner of each block. As Strout turned into the driveway Matt thought of the one insomniac neighbor, thought of some man or woman sitting alone in the dark living room, watching the all-night channel from Boston. When Strout stopped the car near the front of the house, Matt said: "Drive it to the back."

He touched Strout's head with the muzzle.   95

"You wouldn't have it cocked, would you? For when I put on the brakes."

Matt cocked it, and said: "It is now."

Strout waited a moment; then he eased the car forward, the engine doing little more than idling, and as they approached the garage he gently braked. Matt opened the door, then took off the glove and put it in his pocket. He stepped out and shut the door with his hip and said: "All right."

Strout looked at the gun, then got out, and Matt followed him across the grass, and as Strout unlocked the door Matt looked quickly at the row of small backyards on either side, and scattered tall trees, some evergreens, others not, and he thought of the red and yellow leaves on the trees over the hole, saw them falling soon, probably in two weeks, dropping slowly, covering. Strout stepped into the kitchen.

"Turn on the light."   100

Strout reached to the wall switch, and in the light Matt looked at his wide back, the dark blue shirt, the white belt, the red plaid pants.

"Where's your suitcase?"

"My suitcase?"

"Where is it?"

"In the bedroom closet."   105

"That's where we're going then. When we get to a door you stop and turn on the light."

They crossed the kitchen, Matt glancing at the sink and stove and refrigerator: no dishes in the sink or even the dish rack beside it, no grease splashings on the stove, the refrigerator door clean and white. He did not want to look at any more but he looked quickly at all he could see: in the living room magazines and newspapers in a wicker basket, clean ashtrays, a record player, the records shelved next to it, then down the hall where, near the bedroom door, hung a color photograph of Mary Ann and the two boys sitting on a lawn — there was no house in the picture — Mary Ann smiling at the camera or Strout or whoever held the camera, smiling as she had on Matt's lawn this summer while he waited for the charcoal and they all talked and he looked at her brown legs and at Frank touching her arm, her shoulder, her hair; he moved down the hall with her smile in his mind, wondering: was that when they were both playing around and she was smiling like that at him and they were happy, even sometimes, making it worth it? He recalled her eyes, the pain in them, and he was conscious of the circles of love he was touching with the hand that held the revolver so tightly now as Strout stopped at the door at the end of the hall.

"There's no wall switch."

"Where's the light?"

"By the bed." 110

"Let's go."

Matt stayed a pace behind, then Strout leaned over and the room was lighted: The bed, a double one, was neatly made; the ashtray on the bedside table clean, the bureau top dustless, and no photographs; probably so the girl—who *was* she?—would not have to see Mary Ann in the bedroom she believed was theirs. But because Matt was a father and a husband, though never an ex-husband, he knew (and did not want to know) that this bedroom had never been theirs alone. Strout turned around; Matt looked at his lips, his wide jaw, and thought of Frank's doomed and fearful eyes looking up from the couch.

"Where's Mr. Trottier?"

"He's waiting. Pack clothes for warm weather."

"What's going on?" 115

"You're jumping bail."

"Mr. Fowler—"

He pointed the cocked revolver at Strout's face. The barrel trembled but not much, not as much as he had expected. Strout went to the closet and got the suitcase from the floor and opened it on the bed. As he went to the bureau, he said: "He was making it with my wife. I'd go pick up my kids and he'd be there. Sometimes he spent the night. My boys told me."

He did not look at Matt as he spoke. He opened the top drawer and Matt stepped closer so he could see Strout's hands: underwear and socks, the socks rolled, the underwear folded and stacked. He took them back to the bed, arranged them neatly in the suitcase, then from the closet he was taking shirts and trousers and a jacket; he laid them on the bed and Matt followed him to the bathroom and watched from the door while he packed those things a person accumulated and that became part of him so that at times in the store Matt felt he was selling more than clothes.

"I wanted to try to get together with her again." He was bent over the suit- 120 case. "I couldn't even talk to her. He was always with her. I'm going to jail for it; if I ever get out I'll be an old man. Isn't that enough?"

"You're not going to jail."

Strout closed the suitcase and faced Matt, looking at the gun. Matt went to his rear, so Strout was between him and the lighted hall; then using his handkerchief he turned off the lamp and said: "Let's go."

They went down the hall, Matt looking again at the photograph, and through the living room and kitchen, Matt turning off the lights and talking, frightened that he was talking, that he was telling this lie he had not planned: "It's the trial. We can't go through that, my wife and me. So you're leaving. We've got you a ticket, and a job. A friend of Mr. Trottier's. Out west. My wife keeps seeing you. We can't have that anymore."

Matt turned out the kitchen light and put the handkerchief in his pocket, and they went down the two brick steps and across the lawn. Strout put the suitcase on the floor of the back seat, then got into the front seat and Matt got in the back and put on his glove and shut the door.

"They'll catch me. They'll check passenger lists." 125

"We didn't use your name."

"They'll figure that out too. You think I wouldn't have done it myself if it was that easy?"

He backed into the street, Matt looking down the gun barrel but not at the profiled face beyond it.

"You were alone," Matt said. "We've got it worked out."

"There's no planes this time of night, Mr. Fowler." 130

"Go back through town. Then north on 125."

They came to the corner and turned, and now Willis's headlights were in the car with Matt.

"Why north, Mr. Fowler?"

"Somebody's going to keep you for a while. They'll take you to the airport." He uncocked the hammer and lowered the revolver to his lap and said wearily: "No more talking."

As they drove back through town, Matt's body sagged, going limp with his 135
spirit and its new and false bond with Strout, the hope his lie had given Strout. He had grown up in this town whose streets had become places of apprehension and pain for Ruth as she drove and walked, doing what she had to do; and for him too, if only in his mind as he worked and chatted six days a week in his store; he wondered now if his lie would have worked, if sending Strout away would have been enough; but then he knew that just thinking of Strout in Montana or whatever place lay at the end of the lie he had told, thinking of him walking the streets there, loving a girl there (who *was* she?) would be enough to slowly rot the rest of his days. And Ruth's. Again he was certain that she knew, that she was waiting for him.

They were in New Hampshire now, on the narrow highway, passing the shopping center at the state line, and then houses and small stores and sandwich shops. There were few cars on the road. After ten minutes he raised his trembling hand, touched Strout's neck with the gun, and said: "Turn in up here. At the dirt road."

Strout flicked on the indicator and slowed.

"Mr. Fowler?"

"They're waiting here."

Strout turned very slowly, easing his neck away from the gun. In the moon- 140
light the road was light brown, lighter and yellowed where the headlights shone; weeds and a few trees grew on either side of it, and ahead of them were the woods.

"There's nothing back here, Mr. Fowler."

"It's for your car. You don't think we'd leave it at the airport, do you?"

He watched Strout's large, big-knuckled hands tighten on the wheel, saw Frank's face that night: not the stitches and bruised eye and swollen lips, but his own hand gently touching Frank's jaw, turning his wounds to the light. They rounded a bend in the road and were out of sight of the highway: tall trees all around them now, hiding the moon. When they reached the abandoned gravel pit on the left, the bare flat earth and steep pale embankment behind it, and the black crowns of trees at its top, Matt said: "Stop here."

Strout stopped but did not turn off the engine. Matt pressed the gun hard against his neck, and he straightened in the seat and looked in the rearview mirror, Matt's eyes meeting his in the glass for an instant before looking at the hair at the end of the gun barrel.

"Turn it off."   145

Strout did, then held the wheel with two hands, and looked in the mirror.

"I'll do twenty years, Mr. Fowler; at least. I'll be forty-six years old."

"That's nine years younger than I am," Matt said, and got out and took off the glove and kicked the door shut. He aimed at Strout's ear and pulled back the hammer. Willis's headlights were off and Matt heard him walking on the soft thin layer of dust, the hard earth beneath it. Strout opened the door, sat for a moment in the interior light, then stepped out onto the road. Now his face was pleading. Matt did not look at his eyes, but he could see it in the lips.

"Just get the suitcase. They're right up the road."

Willis was beside him now, to his left. Strout looked at both guns. Then he   150
opened the back door, leaned in, and with a jerk brought the suitcase out. He was turning to face them when Matt said: "Just walk up the road. Just ahead."

Strout turned to walk, the suitcase in his right hand, and Matt and Willis followed; as Strout cleared the front of his car he dropped the suitcase and, ducking, took one step that was the beginning of a sprint to his right. The gun kicked in Matt's hand, and the explosion of the shot surrounded him, isolated him in a nimbus of sound that cut him off from all his time, all his history, isolated him standing absolutely still on the dirt road with the gun in his hand, looking down at Richard Strout squirming on his belly, kicking one leg behind him, pushing himself forward, toward the woods. Then Matt went to him and shot him once in the back of the head.

Driving south to Boston, wearing both gloves now, staying in the middle lane and looking often in the rearview mirror at Willis's headlights, he relived the suitcase dropping, the quick dip and turn of Strout's back, and the kick of the gun, the sound of the shot. When he walked to Strout, he still existed within the first shot, still trembled and breathed with it. The second shot and the burial seemed to be happening to someone else, someone he was watching. He and Willis each held an arm and pulled Strout face-down off the road and into the woods, his bouncing sliding belt white under the trees where it was so dark that when they stopped at the top of the knoll, panting and sweating, Matt could not see where Strout's blue shirt ended and the earth began. They pulled off the branches then dragged Strout to the edge of the hole and went behind him and lifted his legs and pushed him in. They stood still for a moment. The woods were quiet save for their breathing, and Matt remembered hearing the movements of birds and small animals after the first shot. Or maybe he had not heard them. Willis went down to the road. Matt could see him clearly out on the tan dirt, could see the glint of Strout's car and, beyond the road, the gravel pit. Willis came back up the knoll with the suitcase. He dropped it in the hole and took off his gloves and they went down to his car for the spades. They worked quietly. Sometimes they paused to listen to the woods. When they were finished Willis turned on his flashlight and they covered the earth with leaves and branches and then went down to the spot in front of the car, and while Matt held the light Willis crouched and sprinkled dust on the blood, backing up till he reached the grass and leaves, then he used leaves until they had worked up to the grave again. They did not stop. They walked around the grave and through the woods, using the light on the ground, looking up through the trees to where they ended at the lake. Neither of them spoke above the sounds of their heavy and clumsy strides through low brush and over fallen branches. Then they reached it: wide and dark, lapping softly at the bank, pine needles smooth under Matt's feet, moonlight on the lake, a small island near its middle, with black, tall evergreens. He took out the gun and threw for the island: taking two steps back on the pine needles, striding with the throw and going to one knee as he followed through, looking up to see the dark shapeless object arcing downward, splashing.

They left Strout's car in Boston, in front of an apartment building on Commonwealth Avenue. When they got back to town Willis drove slowly over the bridge and Matt threw the keys into the Merrimack. The sky was turning light. Willis let him out a block from his house, and walking home he listened for sounds from the houses he passed. They were quiet. A light was on in his living room. He turned it off and undressed in there, and went softly toward the bedroom; in the hall he smelled the smoke, and he stood in the bedroom doorway and looked at the orange of her cigarette in the dark. The curtains were closed. He went to the closet and put his shoes on the floor and felt for a hanger.

"Did you do it?" she said.

He went down the hall to the bathroom and in the dark he washed his 155 hands and face. Then he went to her, lay on his back, and pulled the sheet up to his throat.

"Are you all right?" she said.

"I think so."

Now she touched him, lying on her side, her hand on his belly, his thigh.

"Tell me," she said.

He started from the beginning, in the parking lot at the bar; but soon with 160 his eyes closed and Ruth petting him, he spoke of Strout's house: the order, the woman presence, the picture on the wall.

"The way she was smiling," he said.

"What about it?"

"I don't know. Did you ever see Strout's girl? When you saw him in town?"

"No."

"I wonder who she was." 165

Then he thought: *not was: is. Sleeping now she is his girl.* He opened his eyes, then closed them again. There was more light beyond the curtains. With Ruth now he left Strout's house and told again his lie to Strout, gave him again that hope that Strout must have for a while believed, else he would have to believe only the gun pointed at him for the last two hours of his life. And with Ruth he saw again the dropping suitcase, the darting move to the right: and he told of the first shot, feeling her hand on him but his heart isolated still, beating on the road still in that explosion like thunder. He told her the rest, but the words had no images for him, he did not see himself doing what the words said he had done; he only saw himself on that road.

"We can't tell the other kids," she said. "It'll hurt them, thinking he got away. But we mustn't."

"No."

She was holding him, wanting him, and he wished he could make love with her but he could not. He saw Frank and Mary Ann making love in her bed, their eyes closed, their bodies brown and smelling of the sea; the other girl was faceless, bodiless, but he felt her sleeping now; and he saw Frank and Strout, their faces alive; he saw red and yellow leaves falling on the earth, then snow: falling and freezing and falling; and holding Ruth, his cheek touching her breast, he shuddered with a sob that he kept silent in his heart.

CONSIDERATIONS FOR CRITICAL THINKING AND WRITING

1. FIRST RESPONSE. How do you feel about Matt's act of revenge? Trace the emotions his character produces in you as the plot unfolds.

2. Discuss the significance of the title. Why is "Killings" a more appropriate title than "Killers"?

3. What are the effects of Dubus's ordering of events in the story? How would the effects be different if the story were told in a chronological order?

4. Describe the Fowler family before Frank's murder. How does the murder affect Matt?

5. What is learned about Richard from the flashback in paragraphs 32 through 75? How does this information affect your attitude toward him?

6. What is the effect of the description of Richard shooting Frank in paragraph 76?

7. How well planned is Matt's revenge? Why does he lie to Richard about sending him out west?

8. Describe Matt at the end of the story when he tells his wife about the killing. How do you think this revenge killing will affect the Fowler family?

9. How might "Killings" be considered a love story as well as a murder story?

10. CRITICAL STRATEGIES. Read the section on psychological criticism (pp. 64-66) in Chapter 3, "Applying a Critical Strategy." How do the details of the killing and the disposal of Richard's body reveal Matt's emotions? What is he thinking and feeling as he performs these actions? How did you feel as you read about them?

ERNEST HEMINGWAY (1899-1961)

In 1918, a year after graduating from high school in Oak Park, Illinois, Ernest Hemingway volunteered as an ambulance driver in World War I. At the Italian front, he was seriously wounded. This experience haunted him and many of the characters in his short stories and novels. *In Our Time* (1925) is a collection of short stories, including "Soldier's Home," that reflect some of Hemingway's own attempts to readjust to life back home after the war. *The Sun Also Rises* (1926), *A Farewell to Arms* (1929), and *For Whom the Bell Tolls* (1940) are also about war and its impact on people's lives. Hemingway courted violence all his life in war, the bullring, the boxing ring, and big-game hunting. When he was sixty-two years old and terminally ill with cancer, he committed suicide by shooting himself with a shotgun. "Soldier's Home" takes place in a small town in Oklahoma; the war, however, is never distant from the protagonist's mind as he struggles to come home again.

Soldier's Home   *1925*

Krebs went to the war from a Methodist college in Kansas. There is a picture which shows him among his fraternity brothers, all of them wearing exactly the same height and style collar. He enlisted in the Marines in 1917 and did not return to the United States until the second division returned from the Rhine in the summer of 1919.

There is a picture which shows him on the Rhine with two German girls and another corporal. Krebs and the corporal look too big for their uniforms. The German girls are not beautiful. The Rhine does not show in the picture.

By the time Krebs returned to his home town in Oklahoma the greeting of heroes was over. He came back much too late. The men from the town who had been drafted had all been welcomed elaborately on their return. There had been a great deal of hysteria. Now the reaction had set in. People seemed to think it was rather ridiculous for Krebs to be getting back so late, years after the war was over.

At first Krebs, who had been at Belleau Wood, Soissons, the Champagne, St. Mihiel, and in the Argonne° did not want to talk about the war at all. Later he felt the need to talk but no one wanted to hear about it. His town had heard too many atrocity stories to be thrilled by actualities. Krebs found that to be listened to at all he had to lie, and after he had done this twice he, too, had a reaction against the war and against talking about it. A distaste for everything that had happened to him in the war set in because of the lies he had told. All of the times that had been able to make him feel cool and clear inside himself when he thought of them; the times so long back when he had done the one thing, the only thing for a man to do, easily and naturally, when he might have done something else, now lost their cool, valuable quality and then were lost themselves.

His lies were quite unimportant lies and consisted in attributing to himself   5 things other men had seen, done, or heard of, and stating as facts certain apocryphal incidents familiar to all soldiers. Even his lies were not sensational at the pool room. His acquaintances, who had heard detailed accounts of German women found chained to machine guns in the Argonne forest and who could not comprehend, or were barred by their patriotism from interest in, any German machine gunners who were not chained, were not thrilled by his stories.

Krebs acquired the nausea in regard to experience that is the result of untruth or exaggeration, and when he occasionally met another man who had really been a soldier and they talked a few minutes in the dressing room at a dance he fell into the easy pose of the old soldier among other soldiers: that he had been badly, sickeningly frightened all the time. In this way he lost everything.

Belleau Wood . . . Argonne: Sites of battles in World War I in which American troops were instrumental in pushing back the Germans.

During this time, it was late summer, he was sleeping late in bed, getting up to walk down town to the library to get a book, eating lunch at home, reading on the front porch until he became bored, and then walking down through the town to spend the hottest hours of the day in the cool dark of the pool room. He loved to play pool.

In the evening he practiced on his clarinet, strolled down town, read, and went to bed. He was still a hero to his two young sisters. His mother would have given him breakfast in bed if he had wanted it. She often came in when he was in bed and asked him to tell her about the war, but her attention always wandered. His father was noncommittal.

Before Krebs went away to the war he had never been allowed to drive the family motor car. His father was in the real estate business and always wanted the car to be at his command when he required it to take clients out into the country to show them a piece of farm property. The car always stood outside the First National Bank building where his father had an office on the second floor. Now, after the war, it was still the same car.

Nothing was changed in the town except that the young girls had grown 10 up. But they lived in such a complicated world of already defined alliances and shifting feuds that Krebs did not feel the energy or the courage to break into it. He liked to look at them, though. There were so many good-looking young girls. Most of them had their hair cut short. When he went away only little girls wore their hair like that or girls that were fast. They all wore sweaters and shirt waists with round Dutch collars. It was a pattern. He liked to look at them from the front porch as they walked on the other side of the street. He liked to watch them walking under the shade of the trees. He liked the round Dutch collars above their sweaters. He liked their silk stockings and flat shoes. He liked their bobbed hair and the way they walked.

When he was in town their appeal to him was not very strong. He did not like them when he saw them in the Greek's ice cream parlor. He did not want them themselves really. They were too complicated. There was something else. Vaguely he wanted a girl but he did not want to have to work to get her. He would have liked to have a girl but he did not want to have to spend a long time getting her. He did not want to get into the intrigue and the politics. He did not want to have to do any courting. He did not want to tell any more lies. It wasn't worth it.

He did not want any consequences. He did not want any consequences ever again. He wanted to live along without consequences. Besides he did not really need a girl. The army had taught him that. It was all right to pose as though you had to have a girl. Nearly everybody did that. But it wasn't true. You did not need a girl. That was the funny thing. First a fellow boasted how girls mean nothing to him, that he never thought of them, that they could not touch him. Then a fellow boasted that he could not get along without girls, that he had to have them all the time, that he could not go to sleep without them.

That was all a lie. It was all a lie both ways. You did not need a girl unless you thought about them. He learned that in the army. Then sooner or later you always got one. When you were really ripe for a girl you always got one. You did not have to think about it. Sooner or later it would come. He had learned that in the army.

Now he would have liked a girl if she had come to him and not wanted to talk. But here at home it was all too complicated. He knew he could never get through it all again. It was not worth the trouble. That was the thing about French girls and German girls. There was not all this talking. You couldn't talk much and you did not need to talk. It was simple and you were friends. He thought about France and then he began to think about Germany. On the whole he had liked Germany better. He did not want to leave Germany. He did not want to come home. Still, he had come home. He sat on the front porch.

He liked the girls that were walking along the other side of the street. He 15 liked the look of them much better than the French girls or the German girls. But the world they were in was not the world he was in. He would like to have one of them. But it was not worth it. They were such a nice pattern. He liked the pattern. It was exciting. But he would not go through all the talking. He did not want one badly enough. He liked to look at them all, though. It was not worth it. Not now when things were getting good again.

He sat there on the porch reading a book on the war. It was a history and he was reading about all the engagements he had been in. It was the most interesting reading he had ever done. He wished there were more maps. He looked forward with a good feeling to reading all the really good histories when they would come out with good detail maps. Now he was really learning about the war. He had been a good soldier. That made a difference.

One morning after he had been home about a month his mother came into his bedroom and sat on the bed. She smoothed her apron.

"I had a talk with your father last night, Harold," she said, "and he is willing for you to take the car out in the evenings."

"Yeah?" said Krebs, who was not fully awake. "Take the car out? Yeah?"

"Yes. Your father has felt for some time that you should be able to take the 20 car out in the evenings whenever you wished but we only talked it over last night."

"I'll bet you made him," Krebs said.

"No. It was your father's suggestion that we talk the matter over."

"Yeah. I'll bet you made him," Krebs sat up in bed.

"Will you come down to breakfast, Harold?" his mother said.

"As soon as I get my clothes on," Krebs said.   25

His mother went out of the room and he could hear her frying something downstairs while he washed, shaved, and dressed to go down into the dining-room for breakfast. While he was eating breakfast his sister brought in the mail.

"Well, Hare," she said. "You old sleepyhead. What do you ever get up for?"

Krebs looked at her. He liked her. She was his best sister.

"Have you got the paper?" he asked.

She handed him the Kansas City *Star* and he shucked off its brown wrap- 30 per and opened it to the sporting page. He folded the *Star* open and propped it against the water pitcher with his cereal dish to steady it, so he could read while he ate.

"Harold," his mother stood in the kitchen doorway, "Harold, please don't muss up the paper. Your father can't read his *Star* if it's been mussed."

"I won't muss it," Krebs said.

His sister sat down at the table and watched him while he read.

"We're playing indoor over at school this afternoon," she said. "I'm going to pitch."

"Good," said Krebs. "How's the old wing?"   35

"I can pitch better than lots of the boys. I tell them all you taught me. The other girls aren't much good."

"Yeah?" said Krebs.

"I tell them all you're my beau. Aren't you my beau, Hare?"

"You bet."

"Couldn't your brother really be your beau just because he's your brother?" 40

"I don't know."

"Sure you know. Couldn't you be my beau, Hare, if I was old enough and if you wanted to?"

"Sure. You're my girl now."

"Am I really your girl?"

"Sure."   45

"Do you love me?"

"Uh, huh."

"Will you love me always?"

"Sure."

"Will you come over and watch me play indoor?"   50

"Maybe."

"Aw, Hare, you don't love me. If you loved me, you'd want to come over and watch me play indoor."

Krebs's mother came into the dining-room from the kitchen. She carried a plate with two fried eggs and some crisp bacon on it and a plate of buckwheat cakes.

"You run along, Helen," she said. "I want to talk to Harold."

She put the eggs and bacon down in front of him and brought in a jug of 55 maple syrup for the buckwheat cakes. Then she sat down across the table from Krebs.

"I wish you'd put down the paper a minute, Harold," she said.

Krebs took down the paper and folded it.

"Have you decided what you are going to do yet, Harold?" his mother said, taking off her glasses.

"No," said Krebs.

"Don't you think it's about time?" His mother did not say this in a mean 60 way. She seemed worried.

"I hadn't thought about it," Krebs said.

"God has some work for everyone to do," his mother said. "There can be no idle hands in His Kingdom."

"I'm not in His Kingdom," Krebs said.

"We are all of us in His Kingdom."

Krebs felt embarrassed and resentful as always.   65

"I've worried about you so much, Harold," his mother went on. "I know the temptations you must have been exposed to. I know how weak men are. I know what your own dear grandfather, my own father, told us about the Civil War and I have prayed for you. I pray for you all day long, Harold."

Krebs looked at the bacon fat hardening on his plate.

"Your father is worried, too," his mother went on. "He thinks you have lost your ambition, that you haven't got a definite aim in life. Charley Simmons, who is just your age, has a good job and is going to be married. The boys are all settling down; they're all determined to get somewhere; you can see that boys like Charley Simmons are on their way to being really a credit to the community."

Krebs said nothing.

"Don't look that way, Harold," his mother said. "You know we love you and 70 I want to tell you for your own good how matters stand. Your father does not want to hamper your freedom. He thinks you should be allowed to drive the car. If you want to take some of the nice girls out riding with you, we are only too pleased. We want you to enjoy yourself. But you are going to have to settle down to work, Harold. Your father doesn't care what you start in at. All work is honorable as he says. But you've got to make a start at something. He asked me to speak to you this morning and then you can stop in and see him at his office."

"Is that all?" Krebs said.

"Yes. Don't you love your mother, dear boy?"

"No," Krebs said.

His mother looked at him across the table. Her eyes were shiny. She started crying.

"I don't love anybody," Krebs said. 75

It wasn't any good. He couldn't tell her, he couldn't make her see it. It was silly to have said it. He had only hurt her. He went over and took hold of her arm. She was crying with her head in her hands.

"I didn't mean it," he said. "I was just angry at something. I didn't mean I didn't love you."

His mother went on crying. Krebs put his arm on her shoulder.

"Can't you believe me, mother?"

His mother shook her head. 80

"Please, please, mother. Please believe me."

"All right," his mother said chokily. She looked up at him. "I believe you, Harold."

Krebs kissed her hair. She put her face up to him.

"I'm your mother," she said. "I held you next to my heart when you were a tiny baby."

Krebs felt sick and vaguely nauseated. 85

"I know, Mummy," he said. "I'll try and be a good boy for you."

"Would you kneel and pray with me, Harold?" his mother asked.

They knelt down beside the dining-room table and Krebs's mother prayed.

"Now, you pray, Harold," she said.

"I can't," Krebs said. 90

"Try, Harold."

"I can't."

"Do you want me to pray for you?"

"Yes."

So his mother prayed for him and then they stood up and Krebs kissed his 95 mother and went out of the house. He had tried so to keep his life from being complicated. Still, none of it had touched him. He had felt sorry for his mother and she had made him lie. He would go to Kansas City and get a job and she would feel all right about it. There would be one more scene maybe before he got away. He would not go down to his father's office. He would miss that one. He wanted his life to go smoothly. It had just gotten going that way. Well, that was all over now, anyway. He would go over to the schoolyard and watch Helen play indoor baseball.

CONSIDERATIONS FOR CRITICAL THINKING AND WRITING

1. FIRST RESPONSE. The title, "Soldier's Home," focuses on the setting. Do you have a clear picture of Krebs's home? Describe it, filling in missing details from your associations of home, Krebs's routine, or anything else you can use.

2. What does the photograph of Krebs, the corporal, and the German girls reveal?

3. Belleau Wood, Soissons, the Champagne, St. Mihiel, and the Argonne were the sites of fierce and bloody fighting. What effect have these battles had on Krebs? Why do you think he won't talk about them to the people at home?

4. Why does Krebs avoid complications and consequences? How has the war changed his attitudes toward work and women? How is his hometown different from Germany and France? What is the conflict in the story?

5. Why do you think Hemingway refers to the protagonist as Krebs rather than Harold? What is the significance of his sister calling him "Hare"?

6. How does Krebs's mother embody the community's values? What does Krebs think of those values?

7. Why can't Krebs pray with his mother?

8. What is the resolution to Krebs's conflict?

9. Comment on the appropriateness of the story's title.

10. Explain how Krebs's war experiences are present throughout the story even though we get no details about them.

11. CRITICAL STRATEGIES. Read the section on reader-response criticism (pp. 74–76) in Chapter 3, "Applying a Critical Strategy," and consider the following: Perhaps, after having been away from home for a time, you have returned to find yourself alienated from your family or friends. Describe your experience. What caused the change? How does this experience affect your understanding of Krebs? Alternately, if alienation hasn't been your experience, how does that difference affect your reading of Krebs?

BHARATI MUKHERJEE (B. 1940)

Born in Calcutta, India, Bharati Mukherjee lived in London as a young girl but returned to India at the age of eleven, where she was subsequently educated at the universities of Calcutta and Baroda. After winning a scholarship to the University of Iowa Writers' Workshop, she moved to the United States and married novelist Clark Blaise in the early sixties. Though she lived in Canada for a decade and returned to India for a year, she now lives in the United States, where she teaches and writes. Mukherjee's fiction includes five novels — *The Tiger's Daughter* (1971), *Wife* (1972), *Jasmine* (1989), *The Holder of the World* (1993), and *Leave It To Me* (1997) — and two collections of short stories, *Darkness* (1985) and *The Middleman and Other Stories* (1988). Much of her work examines the stress and confusion immigrants experience as they struggle to secure identities and find a place in foreign cultures that tend to render them invisible or cast them as ethnic stereotypes. In "A Father," taken from *Darkness*, Mukherjee explores the painful relationship between a father and his daughter.

A Father   *1985*

One Wednesday morning in mid-May Mr. Bhowmick woke up as he usually did at 5:43 A.M., checked his Rolex against the alarm clock's digital readout, punched down the alarm (set for 5:45), then nudged his wife awake. She worked as a claims investigator for an insurance company that had an office in a nearby shopping mall. She didn't really have to leave the house until 8:30, but she liked to get up early and cook him a big breakfast. Mr. Bhowmick had to drive a long way to work. He was a naturally dutiful, cautious man, and he set the alarm clock early enough to accommodate a margin for accidents.

While his wife, in a pink nylon negligee she had paid for with her own MasterCard card, made him a new version of French toast from a clipping ("Eggs-cellent Recipes!") Scotchtaped to the inside of a kitchen cupboard, Mr. Bhowmick brushed his teeth. He brushed, he gurgled with the loud, hawking noises that he and his brother had been taught as children to make in order to flush clean not merely teeth but also tongue and palate.

After that he showered, then, back in the bedroom again, he recited prayers in Sanskrit to Kali, the patron goddess of his family, the goddess of wrath and vengeance. In the pokey flat of his childhood in Ranchi, Bihar, his mother had given over a whole bedroom to her collection of gods and goddesses. Mr. Bhowmick couldn't be that extravagant in Detroit. His daughter, twenty-six and an electrical engineer, slept in the other of the two bedrooms in his apartment. But he had done his best. He had taken Woodworking I and II at a nearby recreation center and built a grotto for the goddess. Kali-Mata was eight inches tall, made of metal and painted a glistening black so that the metal glowed like the oiled, black skin of a peasant woman. And though Kali-Mata was totally nude except for a tiny gilt crown and a garland strung together from sinners' chopped off heads, she looked warm, cozy, *pleased*, in her makeshift wooden shrine in Detroit. Mr. Bhowmick had gathered quite a crowd of admiring, fellow woodworkers in those final weeks of decoration.

"Hurry it up with the prayers," his wife shouted from the kitchen. She was an agnostic, a believer in ambition, not grace. She frequently complained that his prayers had gotten so long that soon he wouldn't have time to go to work, play duplicate bridge with the Ghosals, or play the tabla in the Bengali Association's one Sunday per month musical soirees. Lately she'd begun to drain him in a wholly new way. He wasn't praying, she nagged; he was shutting her out of his life. There'd be no peace in the house until she hid Kali-Mata in a suitcase.

She nagged, and he threatened to beat her with his shoe as his father had   5
threatened his mother: it was the thrust and volley of marriage. There was no question of actually taking off a shoe and applying it to his wife's body. She was bigger than he was. And, secretly, he admired her for having the nerve, the agnosticism, which as a college boy in backward Bihar he too had claimed.

"I have time," he shot at her. He was still wrapped in a damp terry towel.

"You have time for everything but domestic life."

It was the fault of the shopping mall that his wife had started to buy pop psychology paperbacks. These paperbacks preached that for couples who could sit down and talk about their "relationship," life would be sweet again. His engineer daughter was on his wife's side. She accused him of holding things in.

"Face it, Dad," she said. "You have an affect deficit."

But surely everyone had feelings they didn't want to talk about or talk 10 over. He definitely did not want to blurt out anything about the sick-in-the-guts sensations that came over him most mornings and that he couldn't bubble down with Alka-Seltzer or smother with Gas-X. The women in his family were smarter than him. They were cheerful, outgoing, more American somehow.

How could he tell these bright, mocking women that in the 5:43 A.M. darkness, he sensed invisible presences: gods and snakes frolicked in the master bedroom, little white sparks of cosmic static crackled up the legs of his pajamas. Something was out there in the dark, something that could invent accidents and coincidences to remind mortals that even in Detroit they were no more than mortal. His wife would label this paranoia and dismiss it. Paranoia, premonition: whatever it was, it had begun to undermine his composure.

Take this morning. Mr. Bhowmick had woken up from a pleasant dream about a man taking a Club Med vacation, and the postdream satisfaction had lasted through the shower, but when he'd come back to the shrine in the bedroom, he'd noticed all at once how scarlet and saucy was the tongue that Kali-Mata stuck out at the world. Surely he had not lavished such alarming detail, such admonitory colors on that flap of flesh.

Watch out, ambulatory sinners. Be careful out there, the goddess warned him, and not with the affection of Sergeant Esterhaus,° either.

"French toast must be eaten hot-hot," his wife nagged. "Otherwise they'll taste like rubber."

Mr. Bhowmick laid the trousers of a two-trouser suit he had bought on 15 sale that winter against his favorite tweed jacket. The navy stripes in the trousers and the small, navy tweed flecks in the jacket looked quite good together. So what if the Chief Engineer had already started wearing summer cottons?

"I am coming, I am coming," he shouted back. "You want me to eat hot-hot, you start the frying only when I am sitting down. You didn't learn anything from Mother in Ranchi?"

"Mother cooked French toast from fancy recipes? I mean French Sandwich Toast with complicated filling?"

He came into the room to give her his testiest look. "You don't know the meaning of complicated cookery. And mother had to get the coal fire of the *chula* going first."

His daughter was already at the table. "Why don't you break down and buy her a microwave oven? That's what I mean about sitting down and talking things out." She had finished her orange juice. She took a plastic measure of

Sergeant Esterhaus: A character from *Hill Street Blues*, a popular television program in the 1980s that began each episode with Esterhaus urging his officers, "Be careful out there."

Slim-Fast out of its can and poured the powder into a glass of skim milk. "It's ridiculous."

Babli was not the child he would have chosen as his only heir. She was 20 brighter certainly than the sons and daughters of the other Bengalis he knew in Detroit, and she had been the only female student in most of her classes at Georgia Tech, but as she sat there in her beige linen business suit, her thick chin dropping into a polka-dotted cravat, he regretted again that she was not the child of his dreams. Babli would be able to help him out moneywise if something happened to him, something so bad that even his pension plans and his insurance policies and his money market schemes wouldn't be enough. But Babli could never comfort him. She wasn't womanly or tender the way that unmarried girls had been in the wistful days of his adolescence. She could sing Hindi film songs, mimicking exactly the high, artificial voice of Lata Mungeshkar, and she had taken two years of dance lessons at Sona Devi's Dance Academy in Southfield, but these accomplishments didn't add up to real femininity. Not the kind that had given him palpitations in Ranchi.

Mr. Bhowmick did his best with his wife's French toast. In spite of its filling of marshmallows, apricot jam and maple syrup, it tasted rubbery. He drank two cups of Darjeeling tea, said, "Well, I'm off," and took off.

All might have gone well if Mr. Bhowmick hadn't fussed longer than usual about putting his briefcase and his trenchcoat in the backseat. He got in behind the wheel of his Oldsmobile, fixed his seatbelt and was just about to turn the key in the ignition when his neighbor, Al Stazniak, who was starting up his Buick Skylark, sneezed. A sneeze at the start of a journey brings bad luck. Al Stazniak's sneeze was fierce, made up of five short bursts, too loud to be ignored.

Be careful out there! Mr. Bhowmick could see the goddess's scarlet little tongue tip wagging at him.

He was a modern man, an intelligent man. Otherwise he couldn't have had the options in life that he did have. He couldn't have given up a good job with perks in Bombay and found a better job with General Motors in Detroit. But Mr. Bhowmick was also a prudent enough man to know that some abiding truth lies bunkered within each wanton Hindu superstition. A sneeze was more than a sneeze. The heedless are carried off in ambulances. He had choices to make. He could ignore the sneeze, and so challenge the world unseen by men. Perhaps Al Stazniak had hay fever. For a sneeze to be a potent omen, surely it had to be unprovoked and terrifying, a thunderclap cleaving the summer skies. Or he could admit the smallness of mortals, undo the fate of the universe by starting over, and go back inside the apartment, sit for a second on the sofa, then re-start his trip.

Al Stazniak rolled down his window. "Everything okay?"   25

Mr. Bhowmick nodded shyly. They weren't really friends in the way neighbors can sometimes be. They talked as they parked or pulled out of their adjacent parking stalls. For all Mr. Bhowmick knew, Al Stazniak had no legs. He had never seen the man out of his Skylark.

He let the Buick back out first. Everything was okay, yes, please. All the same he undid his seatbelt. Compromise, adaptability, call it what you will. A dozen times a day he made these small trade-offs between new-world reasonableness and old-world beliefs.

While he was sitting in his parked car, his wife's ride came by. For fifty dollars a month, she was picked up and dropped off by a hard up, newly divorced woman who worked at a florist's shop in the same mall. His wife came out the front door in brown K-Mart pants and a burgundy windbreaker. She waved to him, then slipped into the passenger seat of the florist's rusty Japanese car.

He was a metallurgist. He knew about rust and ways of preventing it, secret ways, thus far unknown to the Japanese.

Babli's fiery red Mitsubishi was still in the lot. She wouldn't leave for work 30 for another eight minutes. He didn't want her to know he'd been undone by a sneeze. Babli wasn't tolerant of superstitions. She played New Wave music in her tapedeck. If asked about Hinduism, all she'd ever said to her American friends was that "it's neat." Mr. Bhowmick had heard her on the phone years before. The cosmos balanced on the head of a snake was like a beachball balanced on the snout of a circus seal. "This Hindu myth stuff," he'd heard her say, "is like a series of super graphics."

He'd forgiven her. He could probably forgive her anything. It was her way of surviving high school in a city that was both native to her, and alien.

There was no question of going back where he'd come from. He hated Ranchi. Ranchi was no place for dreamers. All through his teenage years, Mr. Bhowmick had dreamed of success abroad. What form that success would take he had left vague. Success had meant to him escape from the constant plotting and bitterness that wore out India's middle class.

Babli should have come out of the apartment and driven off to work by now. Mr. Bhowmick decided to take a risk, to dash inside and pretend he'd left his briefcase on the coffee table.

When he entered the living room, he noticed Babli's spring coat and large vinyl pocketbook on the sofa. She was probably sorting through the junk jewelry on her dresser to give her business suit a lift. She read hints about dressing in women's magazines and applied them to her person with seriousness. If his luck held, he could sit on the sofa, say a quick prayer and get back to the car without her catching on.

It surprised him that she didn't shout out from her bedroom, "Who's 35 there?" What if he had been a rapist?

Then he heard Babli in the bathroom. He heard unladylike squawking noises. She was throwing up. A squawk, a spitting, then the horrible gurgle of a waterfall.

A revelation came to Mr. Bhowmick. A woman vomiting in the privacy of the bathroom could mean many things. She was coming down with the flu. She was nervous about a meeting. But Mr. Bhowmick knew at once that his daughter, his untender, unloving daughter whom he couldn't love and hadn't tried to love, was not, in the larger world of Detroit, unloved. Sinners are everywhere, even in the bosom of an upright, unambitious family like the Bhowmicks. It was the goddess sticking out her tongue at him.

The father sat heavily on the sofa, shrinking from contact with her coat and pocketbook. His brisk, bright engineer daughter was pregnant. Someone had taken time to make love to her. Someone had thought her tender, feminine. Someone even now was perhaps mooning over her. The idea excited him. It was so grotesque and wondrous. At twenty-six Babli had found the man of her dreams; whereas at twenty-six Mr. Bhowmick had given up on truth, beauty and poetry and exchanged them for two years at Carnegie Tech.

Mr. Bhowmick's tweed-jacketed body sagged against the sofa cushions. Babli would abort, of course. He knew his Babli. It was the only possible option if she didn't want to bring shame to the Bhowmick family. All the same, he could see a chubby baby boy on the rug, crawling to his granddaddy. Shame like that was easier to hide in Ranchi. There was always a barren womb sanctified by marriage that could claim sudden fructifying by the goddess Parvati. Babli would do what she wanted. She was headstrong and independent and he was afraid of her.

Babli staggered out of the bathroom. Damp stains ruined her linen suit. It 40 was the first time he had seen his daughter look ridiculous, quite unprofessional. She didn't come into the living room to investigate the noises he'd made. He glimpsed her shoeless stockinged feet flip-flop on collapsed arches down the hall to her bedroom.

"Are you all right?" Mr. Bhowmick asked, standing in the hall. "Do you need Sinutab?"

She wheeled around. "What're you doing here?"

He was the one who should be angry. "I'm feeling poorly too," he said. "I'm taking the day off."

"I feel fine," Babli said.

Within fifteen minutes Babli had changed her clothes and left. Mr. 45 Bhowmick had the apartment to himself all day. All day for praising or cursing the life that had brought him along with its other surprises an illegitimate grandchild.

It was his wife that he blamed. Coming to America to live had been his wife's idea. After the wedding, the young Bhowmicks had spent two years in Pittsburgh on his student visa, then gone back home to Ranchi for nine years. Nine crushing years. Then the job in Bombay had come through. All during those nine years his wife had screamed and wept. She was a woman of wild, progressive ideas — she'd called them her "American" ideas — and she'd been martyred by her neighbors for them. American *memsahib. Markin mem, Markin mem.* In bazaars the beggar boys had trailed her and hooted. She'd done provocative things. She'd hired a *chamar* woman who by caste rules was forbidden to cook for higher caste families, especially for widowed mothers of decent men. This had caused a blowup in the neighborhood. She'd made other, lesser errors. While other wives shopped and cooked every day, his wife had cooked the whole week's menu on weekends.

"What's the point of having a refrigerator, then?" She'd been scornful of the Ranchi women.

His mother, an old-fashioned widow, had accused her of trying to kill her by poisoning. "You are in such a hurry? You want to get rid of me quick-quick so you can go back to the States?"

Family life had been turbulent.

He had kept aloof, inwardly siding with his mother. He did not love his 50 wife now, and he had not loved her then. In any case, he had not defended her. He felt some affection, and he felt guilty for having shunned her during those unhappy years. But he had thought of it then as revenge. He had wanted to marry a beautiful woman. Not being a young man of means, only a young man with prospects, he had had no right to yearn for pure beauty. He cursed his fate and after a while, settled for a barrister's daughter, a plain girl with a wide, flat plank of a body and myopic eyes. The barrister had sweetened the deal by throwing in an all-expenses-paid two years' study at Carnegie Tech to which Mr. Bhowmick had been admitted. Those two years had changed his wife from pliant girl to ambitious woman. She wanted America, nothing less.

It was his wife who had forced him to apply for permanent resident status in the U.S. even though he had a good job in Ranchi as a government engineer. The putting together of documents for the immigrant visa had been a long and humbling process. He had had to explain to a chilly clerk in the Embassy that, like most Indians of his generation, he had no birth certificate. He had to swear out affidavits, suffer through police checks, bribe orderlies whose job it was to move his dossier from desk to desk. The decision, the clerk had advised him, would take months, maybe years. He hadn't dared hope that merit might be rewarded. Merit could collapse under bad luck. It was for grace that he prayed.

While the immigration papers were being processed, he had found the job in Bombay. So he'd moved his mother in with his younger brother's family, and left his hometown for good. Life in Bombay had been lighthearted, almost fulfilling. His wife had thrown herself into charity work with the same energy that had offended the Ranchi women. He was happy to be in a big city at last. Bombay was the Rio de Janeiro of the East; he'd read that in a travel brochure. He drove out to Nariman Point at least once a week to admire the necklace of municipal lights, toss coconut shells into the dark ocean, drink beer at the Oberoi-Sheraton where overseas Indian girls in designer jeans beckoned him in sly ways. His nights were full. He played duplicate bridge, went to the movies, took his wife to Bingo nights at his club. In Detroit he was a lonelier man.

Then the green card had come through. For him, for his wife, and for the daughter who had been born to them in Bombay. He sold what he could sell, and put in his brother's informal trust what he couldn't to save on taxes. Then he had left for America, and one more start.

All through the week, Mr. Bhowmick watched his daughter. He kept furtive notes on how many times she rushed to the bathroom and made hawking, wrenching noises, how many times she stayed late at the office, calling her mother to say she'd be taking in a movie and pizza afterwards with friends.

He had to tell her that he knew. And he probably didn't have much time.   55
She shouldn't be on Slim-Fast in her condition. He had to talk things over with her. But what would he say to her? What position could he take? He had to choose between public shame for the family, and murder.

For three more weeks he watched her and kept his silence. Babli wore shifts to the office instead of business suits, and he liked her better in those garments. Perhaps she was dressing for her young man, not from necessity. Her skin was pale and blotchy by turn. At breakfast her fingers looked stiff, and she had trouble with silverware.

Two Saturdays running, he lost badly at duplicate bridge. His wife scolded him. He had made silly mistakes. When was Babli meeting this man? Where? He must be American; Mr. Bhowmick prayed only that he was white. He pictured his grandson crawling to him, and the grandson was always fat and brown and buttery-skinned, like the infant Krishna. An American son-in-law was a terrifying notion. Why was she not mentioning men, at least, preparing the way for the major announcement? He listened sharply for men's names, rehearsed little lines like, "Hello, Bob, I'm Babli's old man," with a cracked little laugh. Bob, Jack, Jimmy, Tom. But no names surfaced. When she went out for pizza and a movie it was with the familiar set of Indian girls and their strange, unpopular, American friends, all without men. Mr. Bhowmick tried to be reasonable. Maybe she had already gotten married and was keeping it secret. "Well, Bob, you and Babli sure had Mrs. Bhowmick and me going there, heh-heh," he mumbled one night with the Sahas and Ghosals, over cards. "Pardon?" asked Pronob Saha. Mr. Bhowmick dropped two tricks, and his wife glared. "Such stupid blunders," she fumed on the drive back. A new truth was dawning; there would be no marriage for Babli. Her young man probably was not so young and not so available. He must be already married. She must have yielded to passion or been raped in the office. His wife seemed to have noticed nothing. Was he a murderer, or a conspirator? He kept his secret from his wife; his daughter kept her decision to herself.

Nights, Mr. Bhowmick pretended to sleep, but as soon as his wife began her snoring — not real snores so much as loud, gaspy gulpings for breath — he turned on his side and prayed to Kali-Mata.

In July, when Babli's belly had begun to push up against the waistless dresses she'd bought herself, Mr. Bhowmick came out of the shower one week-day morning and found the two women screaming at each other. His wife had a rolling pin in one hand. His daughter held up a *National Geographic* as a shield for her head. The crazy look that had been in his wife's eyes when she'd shooed away beggar kids was in her eyes again.

"Stop it!" His own boldness overwhelmed him. "Shut up! Babli's preg-   60 nant, so what? It's your fault, you made us come to the States."

Girls like Babli were caught between rules, that's the point he wished to make. They were too smart, too impulsive for a backward place like Ranchi, but not tough nor smart enough for sex-crazy places like Detroit.

"My fault?" his wife cried. "I told her to do hanky-panky with boys? I told her to shame us like this?"

She got in one blow with the rolling pin. The second glanced off Babli's shoulder and fell on his arm which he had stuck out for his grandson's sake.

"I'm calling the police," Babli shouted. She was out of the rolling pin's range. "This is brutality. You can't do this to me."

"Shut up! Shut your mouth, foolish woman." He wrenched the weapon from   65 his wife's fist. He made a show of taking off his shoe to beat his wife on the face.

"What do you know? You don't know anything." She let herself down slowly on a dining chair. Her hair, curled overnight, stood in wild whorls around her head. "Nothing."

"And you do!" He laughed. He remembered her tormentors, and laughed again. He had begun to enjoy himself. Now *he* was the one with the crazy, progressive ideas.

"Your daughter is pregnant, yes," she said, "any fool knows that. But ask her the name of the father. Go, ask."

He stared at his daughter who gazed straight ahead, eyes burning with hate, jaw clenched with fury.

"Babli?"   70

"Who needs a man?" she hissed. "The father of my baby is a bottle and a syringe. Men louse up your lives. I just want a baby. Oh, don't worry — he's a certified fit donor. No diseases, college graduate, above average, and he made the easiest twenty-five dollars of his life—"

"Like animals," his wife said. For the first time he heard horror in her voice. His daughter grinned at him. He saw her tongue, thick and red, squirming behind her row of perfect teeth.

"Yes, yes, yes," she screamed, "like livestock. Just like animals. You should be happy—that's what marriage is all about, isn't it? Matching bloodlines, matching horoscopes, matching castes, matching, matching, matching . . ." and it was difficult to know if she was laughing or singing, or mocking and like a madwoman.

Mr. Bhowmick lifted the rolling pin high above his head and brought it down hard on the dome of Babli's stomach. In the end, it was his wife who called the police.

CONSIDERATIONS FOR CRITICAL THINKING AND WRITING

1. FIRST RESPONSE. What do we learn from the story's exposition that helps us to understand the father's character? How does his behavior in the first few pages of the story reveal his character?

2. Do you think the father is a superstitious or a religious man? How does this affect his behavior?

3. Why did the father marry his wife? What sort of relationship does he have with her?

4. How does the father regard his daughter Babli? What is his initial response to her pregnancy?

5. Why does the father believe he "had to choose between public shame for the family, and murder" (para. 55)? Are those his only alternatives at this point in the story?

6. How does life for the family in the United States differ from their life in India?

7. Why do you think Babli chooses artificial insemination as a means of getting pregnant? What do you think it reveals about her character? What do her parents think of her decision?

8. Discuss the effect of the final paragraph. How does it affect your response to the father?

9. Who do you think is the central character of the story? Explain your choice.

10. What is the significance of the title? To whom does the title refer?

11. CRITICAL STRATEGIES. Read the section on cultural criticism (pp. 69–70) in Chapter 3, "Applying a Critical Strategy." To what extent do the characters' cultural backgrounds and experiences determine their behavior?

ALICE MUNRO (B. 1931)

Alice Munro began writing in her teens in the small rural town of Wingham, Ontario, Canada, where she was born. She published her first story in 1950 while a student at the University of Western Ontario, but she left school to marry and moved to British Columbia, where she had three children and helped her husband establish a bookstore. This marriage broke up in 1972 when she returned to Ontario, and she remarried in 1976. Her first collection of stories, *Dance of the Happy Shades*, was not published until 1968, but it was highly acclaimed and won that year's Governor General's Award, Canada's highest literary prize. This success was followed by *Lives of Girls and Women* (1971), a collection of interlinked stories that was published as a novel and won the Canadian Booksellers Association International Book Year Award. Her remaining eight books are all short story collections, two of which also won the Governor General's Award in 1978 and 1986: *Something I've Been Meaning to Tell You* (1974); *Who Do You Think You Are?* (1978, titled *The Beggar Maid* in English and American editions); *The Moons of Jupiter* (1982); *The Progress of Love* (1986); *Friend of My Youth* (1990); *Open Secrets* (1994); *Selected Stories* (1996); and *The Love of a Good Woman* (1998). In addition, her stories are regularly printed in such publications as *The New Yorker*, the *Atlantic Monthly*, *Grand Street*, *Mademoiselle*, and *The Paris Review*. Her accessible and moving stories offer immediate pleasures while simultaneously exploring human complexities in what appear to be effortless anecdotal re-creations of everyday life.

An Ounce of Cure   1968

My parents didn't drink. They weren't rabid about it, and in fact I remember that when I signed the pledge in grade seven, with the rest of that superbly if impermanently indoctrinated class, my mother said, "It's just nonsense and fanaticism, children of that age." My father would drink a beer on a hot day, but my mother did not join him, and — whether accidentally or symbolically — this drink was always consumed *outside* the house. Most of the people we knew were the same way, in the small town where we lived. I ought not to say that it was this which got me into difficulties, because the difficulties I got into were a faithful expression of my own incommodious nature — the same nature that caused my mother to look at me, on any occasion which traditionally calls for feelings of pride and maternal accomplishment (my departure for my first formal dance, I mean, or my hellbent preparations for a descent on college) with an expression of brooding and fascinated despair, as if she could not possibly expect, did not ask, that it should go with me as it did with other girls; the dreamed-of spoils of daughters — orchids, nice boys, diamond rings — would be borne home in due course by the daughters of her friends, but not by me; all she could do was hope for a lesser rather than a greater disaster — an elopement, say, with a boy who could never earn his living, rather than an abduction into the White Slave trade.

But ignorance, my mother said, ignorance, or innocence if you like, is not always such a fine thing as people think and I am not sure it may not be dangerous for a girl like you; then she emphasized her point, as she had a habit of doing, with some quotation which had an innocent pomposity and odor of mothballs. I didn't even wince at it, knowing full well how it must have worked wonders with Mr. Berryman.

The evening I baby-sat for the Berrymans must have been in April. I had been in love all year, or at least since the first week in September, when a boy named Martin Collingwood had given me a surprised, appreciative, and rather ominously complacent smile in the school assembly. I never knew what surprised him; I was not looking like anybody but me; I had an old blouse on and my home-permanent had turned out badly. A few weeks after that he took me out for the first time, and kissed me on the dark side of the porch — also, I ought to say, on the mouth; I am sure it was the first time anybody had ever kissed me effectively, and I know that I did not wash my face that night or the next morning, in order to keep the imprint of those kisses intact. (I showed the most painful banality in the conduct of this whole affair, as you will see.) Two months, and a few amatory stages later, he dropped me. He had fallen for the girl who played opposite him in the Christmas production of *Pride and Prejudice*.

I said I was not going to have anything to do with that play, and I got another girl to work on Makeup in my place, but of course I went to it after all, and sat down in front with my girl friend Joyce, who pressed my hand when I was overcome with pain and delight at the sight of Mr. Darcy° in white breeches, silk waistcoat, and sideburns. It was surely seeing Martin as Darcy that did it for me; every girl is in love with Darcy anyway, and the part gave Martin an arrogance and male splendor in my eyes which made it impossible to remember that he was simply a high-school senior, passably good-looking and of medium intelligence (and with a reputation slightly tainted, at that, by such preferences as the Drama Club and the Cadet *Band*) who happened to be the first boy, the first really presentable boy, to take an interest in me. In the last act they gave him a chance to embrace Elizabeth (Mary Bishop, with a sallow complexion and no figure, but big vivacious eyes) and during this realistic encounter I dug my nails bitterly into Joyce's sympathetic palm.

That night was the beginning of months of real, if more or less self-inflicted, misery for me. Why is it a temptation to refer to this sort of thing lightly, with irony, with amazement even, at finding oneself involved with such preposterous emotions in the unaccountable past? That is what we are apt to do, speaking of love; with adolescent love, of course, it's practically obligatory; you would think we sat around, dull afternoons, amusing ourselves with these tidbit recollections of pain. But it really doesn't make me feel very gay — worse still, it doesn't really surprise me — to remember all the stupid, sad, half-ashamed things I did, that people in love always do. I hung around the places where he might be seen, and then pretended not to see him; I made absurdly roundabout approaches, in conversation, to the bitter pleasure of casually mentioning his name. I daydreamed endlessly; in fact if you want to put it mathematically, I spent perhaps ten times as many hours thinking about Martin Collingwood — yes, pining and weeping for him — as I ever spent with him; the idea of him dominated my mind relentlessly and, after a while, against my will. For if at first I had dramatized my feelings, the time came when I would have been glad to escape them; my well-worn daydreams had become depressing and not even temporarily consoling. As I worked my math problems I would torture myself, quite mechanically and helplessly, with an exact recollection of Martin kissing my throat. I had an exact recollection of *everything*. One

---

Darcy: The hero of Jane Austen's (1775–1817) *Pride and Prejudice*.

night I had an impulse to swallow all the aspirins in the bathroom cabinet, but stopped after I had taken six.

My mother noticed that something was wrong and got me some iron pills. She said, "Are you sure everything is going all right at school?" *School!* When I told her that Martin and I had broken up all she said was, "Well so much the better for that. I never saw a boy so stuck on himself." "Martin has enough conceit to sink a battleship," I said morosely and went upstairs and cried.

The night I went to the Berrymans was a Saturday night. I baby-sat for them quite often on Saturday nights because they liked to drive over to Baileyville, a much bigger, livelier town about twenty miles away, and perhaps have supper and go to a show. They had been living in our town only two or three years—Mr. Berryman had been brought in as plant manager of the new door-factory—and they remained, I suppose by choice, on the fringes of its society; most of their friends were youngish couples like themselves, born in other places, who lived in new ranch-style houses on a hill outside town where we used to go tobogganing. This Saturday night they had two other couples in for drinks before they all drove over to Baileyville for the opening of a new supper-club; they were all rather festive. I sat in the kitchen and pretended to do Latin. Last night had been the Spring Dance at the high school. I had not gone, since the only boy who had asked me was Millerd Crompton, who asked so many girls that he was suspected of working his way through the whole class alphabetically. But the dance was held in the Armories, which was only half a block away from our house; I had been able to see the boys in dark suits, the girls in long pale formals under their coats, passing gravely under the street-lights, stepping around the last patches of snow. I could even hear the music and I have not forgotten to this day that they played "Ballerina," and—oh, song of my aching heart—"Slow Boat to China." Joyce had phoned me up this morning and told me in her hushed way (we might have been discussing an incurable disease I had) that yes, M.C. *had* been there with M.B., and she had on a formal that must have been made out of somebody's old lace tablecloth, it just *hung*.

When the Berrymans and their friends had gone I went into the living room and read a magazine. I was mortally depressed. The big softly lit room, with its green and leaf-brown colors, made an uncluttered setting for the development of the emotions, such as you would get on a stage. At home the life of the emotions went on all right, but it always seemed to get buried under the piles of mending to be done, the ironing, the children's jigsaw puzzles and rock collections. It was the sort of house where people were always colliding with one another on the stairs and listening to hockey games and Superman on the radio.

I got up and found the Berrymans' "Danse Macabre" and put it on the record player and turned out the living-room lights. The curtains were only partly drawn. A street light shone obliquely on the windowpane, making a rectangle of thin dusty gold, in which the shadows of bare branches moved, caught in the huge sweet winds of spring. It was a mild black night when the last snow was melting. A year ago all this—the music, the wind and darkness, the shadows of the branches—would have given me tremendous happiness; when they did not do so now, but only called up tediously familiar, somehow humiliatingly personal thoughts, I gave up my soul for dead and walked into the kitchen and decided to get drunk.

No, it was not like that. I walked into the kitchen to look for a coke or 10
something in the refrigerator, and there on the front of the counter were three
tall beautiful bottles, all about half full of gold. But even after I had looked at
them and lifted them to feel their weight I had not decided to get drunk; I had
decided to have a drink.

Now here is where my ignorance, my disastrous innocence, comes in. It is
true that I had seen the Berrymans and their friends drinking their highballs
as casually as I would drink a coke, but I did not apply this attitude to myself.
No; I thought of hard liquor as something to be taken in extremities, and
relied upon for extravagant results, one way or another. My approach could
not have been less casual if I had been the Little Mermaid drinking the witch's
crystal potion. Gravely, with a glance at my set face in the black window above
the sink, I poured a little whisky from each of the bottles (I think now there
were two brands of rye and an expensive Scotch) until I had my glass full. For I
had never in my life seen anyone pour a drink and I had no idea that people
frequently diluted their liquor with water, soda, et cetera, and I had seen that
the glasses the Berrymans' guests were holding when I came through the living
room were nearly full.

I drank it off as quickly as possible. I set the glass down and stood looking
at my face in the window, half expecting to see it altered. My throat was burning, but I felt nothing else. It was very disappointing, when I had worked
myself up to it. But I was not going to let it go at that. I poured another full
glass, then filled each of the bottles with water to approximately the level I had
seen when I came in. I drank the second glass only a little more slowly than the
first. I put the empty glass down on the counter with care, perhaps feeling in
my head a rustle of things to come, and went and sat down on a chair in the
living room. I reached up and turned on a floor lamp beside the chair, and the
room jumped on me.

When I say I was expecting extravagant results I do not mean that I was
expecting this. I had thought of some sweeping emotional change, an upsurge
of gaiety and irresponsibility, a feeling of lawlessness and escape, accompanied
by a little dizziness and perhaps a tendency to giggle out loud. I did not have in
mind the ceiling spinning like a great plate somebody had thrown at me, nor
the pale green blobs of the chairs swelling, converging, disintegrating, playing
with me a game full of enormous senseless inanimate malice. My head sank
back; I closed my eyes. And at once opened them, opened them wide, threw
myself out of the chair and down the hall and reached — thank God, thank
God! — the Berrymans' bathroom, where I was sick everywhere, everywhere,
and dropped like a stone.

From this point on I have no continuous picture of what happened; my
memories of the next hour or two are split into vivid and improbable seg-
ments, with nothing but murk and uncertainty between. I do remember lying
on the bathroom floor looking sideways at the little six-sided white tiles, which
lay together in such an admirable and logical pattern, seeing them with the
brief broken gratitude and sanity of one who has just been torn to pieces with
vomiting. Then I remember sitting on the stool in front of the hall phone, asking weakly for Joyce's number. Joyce was not home. I was told by her mother (a
rather rattlebrained woman, who didn't seem to notice a thing the matter —
for which I felt weakly, mechanically grateful) that she was at Kay Stringer's

house. I didn't know Kay's number so I just asked the operator; I felt I couldn't risk looking down at the telephone book.

Kay Stringer was not a friend of mine but a new friend of Joyce's. She had 15 a vague reputation for wildness and a long switch of hair, very oddly, though naturally, colored — from soap-yellow to caramel-brown. She knew a lot of boys more exciting than Martin Collingwood, boys who had quit school or been imported into town to play on the hockey team. She and Joyce rode around in these boys' cars, and sometimes went with them — having lied of course to their mothers — to the Gay-la dance hall on the highway north of town.

I got Joyce on the phone. She was very keyed-up, as she always was with boys around, and she hardly seemed to hear what I was saying.

"Oh, I can't tonight," she said. "Some kids are here. We're going to play cards. You know Bill Kline? He's here. Ross Armour —"

"I'm *sick*," I said trying to speak distinctly; it came out an inhuman croak. "I'm *drunk*. Joyce!" Then I fell off the stool and the receiver dropped out of my hand and banged for a while dismally against the wall.

I had not told Joyce where I was, so after thinking about it for a moment she phoned my mother, and using the elaborate and unnecessary subterfuge that young girls delight in, she found out. She and Kay and the boys — there were three of them — told some story about where they were going to Kay's mother, and got into the car and drove out. They found me still lying on the broadloom carpet in the hall; I had been sick again, and this time I had not made it to the bathroom.

It turned out that Kay Stringer, who arrived on this scene only by acci- 20 dent, was exactly the person I needed. She loved a crisis, particularly one like this, which had a shady and scandalous aspect and which must be kept secret from the adult world. She became excited, aggressive, efficient; that energy which was termed wildness was simply the overflow of a great female instinct to manage, comfort, and control. I could hear her voice coming at me from all directions, telling me not to worry, telling Joyce to find the biggest coffeepot they had and make it full of coffee (*strong* coffee, she said), telling the boys to pick me up and carry me to the sofa. Later, in the fog beyond my reach, she was calling for a scrub-brush.

Then I was lying on the sofa, covered with some kind of crocheted throw they had found in the bedroom. I didn't want to lift my head. The house was full of the smell of coffee. Joyce came in, looking very pale; she said that the Berryman kids had wakened up but she had given them a cookie and told them to go back to bed, it was all right; she hadn't let them out of their room and she didn't believe they'd remember. She said that she and Kay had cleaned up the bathroom and the hall though she was afraid there was still a spot on the rug. The coffee was ready. I didn't understand anything very well. The boys had turned on the radio and were going through the Berrymans' record collection; they had it out on the floor. I felt there was something odd about this but I could not think what it was.

Kay brought me a huge breakfast mug full of coffee.

"I don't know if I can," I said. "Thanks."

"Sit up," she said briskly, as if dealing with drunks was an everyday business for her, I had no need to feel myself important. (I met, and recognized, that tone of voice years later, in the maternity ward.) "Now drink," she said. I drank and at the same time realized that I was wearing only my slip. Joyce and Kay had taken off my blouse and skirt. They had brushed off the skirt and washed out the blouse, since it was nylon; it was hanging in the bathroom. I pulled the throw up under my arms and Kay laughed. She got everybody coffee. Joyce brought in the coffeepot and on Kay's instruction she kept filling my cup whenever I drank from it. Somebody said to me with interest. "You must have really wanted to tie one on."

"No," I said rather sulkily, obediently drinking my coffee. "I only had two 25 drinks."

Kay laughed, "Well it certainly gets to you, I'll say that. What time do you expect *they'll* be back?" she said.

"Late. After one I think."

"You should be all right by that time. Have some more coffee."

Kay and one of the boys began dancing to the radio. Kay danced very sexily, but her face had the gently superior and indulgent, rather cold look it had when she was lifting me up to drink the coffee. The boy was whispering to her and she was smiling, shaking her head. Joyce said she was hungry, and she went out to the kitchen to see what there was—potato chips or crackers, or something like that, that you could eat without making too noticeable a dint. Bill Kline came over and sat on the sofa beside me and patted my legs through the crocheted throw. He didn't say anything to me, just patted my legs and looked at me with what seemed to me a very stupid, half-sick, absurd, and alarming expression. I felt very uncomfortable; I wondered how it had ever got around that Bill Kline was so good-looking, with an expression like that. I moved my legs nervously and he gave me a look of contempt, not ceasing to pat me. Then I scrambled off the sofa, pulling the throw around me, with the idea of going to the bathroom to see if my blouse was dry. I lurched a little when I started to walk, and for some reason—probably to show Bill Kline that he had not panicked me—I immediately exaggerated this, and calling out, "Watch me walk a straight line!" I lurched and stumbled, to the accompaniment of everyone's laughter, towards the hall. I was standing in the archway between the hall and the living room when the knob of the front door turned with a small matter-of-fact click and everything became silent behind me except the radio of course and the crocheted throw inspired by some delicate malice of its own slithered down around my feet and there—oh, delicious moment in a well-organized farce!—there stood the Berrymans, Mr. and Mrs., with expressions on their faces as appropriate to the occasion as any old-fashioned director of farces could wish. They must have been preparing those expressions, of course; they could not have produced them in the first moment of shock; with the noise we were making, they had no doubt heard us as soon as they got out of the car; for the same reason, we had not heard them. I don't think I ever knew what brought them home so early—a headache, an argument—and I was not really in a position to ask.

Mr. Berryman drove me home. I don't remember how I got into that car, 30 or how I found my clothes and put them on, or what kind of a good-night, if any, I said to Mrs. Berryman. I don't remember what happened to my friends, though I imagine they gathered up their coats and fled, covering up the ignominy of their departure with a mechanical roar of defiance. I remember

Joyce with a box of crackers in her hand, saying that I had become terribly sick from eating—I think she said *sauerkraut*—for supper, and that I had called them for help. (When I asked her later what they made of this she said, "It wasn't any use. You *reeked*.") I remember also her saying, "Oh, no, Mr. Berryman I beg of you, my mother is a terribly nervous person I don't know what the shock might do to her. I will go down on my knees to you if you like but *you must not phone my mother*." I have no picture of her down on her knees—and she would have done it in a minute—so it seems this threat was not carried out.

Mr. Berryman said to me, "Well I guess you know your behavior tonight is a pretty serious thing." He made it sound as if I might be charged with criminal negligence or something worse. "It would be very wrong of me to overlook it," he said. I suppose that besides being angry and disgusted with *me*, he was worried about taking me home in this condition to my strait-laced parents, who could always say I got the liquor in his house. Plenty of Temperance people would think that enough to hold him responsible, and the town was full of Temperance people. Good relations with the town were very important to him from a business point of view.

"I have an idea it wasn't the first time," he said. "If it was the first time, would a girl be smart enough to fill three bottles up with water? No. Well in this case, she *was* smart enough, but not smart enough to know I could spot it. What do you say to that?" I opened my mouth to answer and although I was feeling quite sober the only sound that came out was a loud, desolate-sounding giggle. He stopped in front of our house. "Light's on," he said. "Now go in and tell your parents the straight truth. And if you don't, remember I will." He did not mention paying me for my baby-sitting services of the evening and the subject did not occur to me either.

I went into the house and tried to go straight upstairs but my mother called to me. She came into the front hall, where I had not turned on the light, and she must have smelled me at once for she ran forward with a cry of pure amazement, as if she had seen somebody falling, and caught me by the shoulders, as I did indeed fall down against the banister, overwhelmed by my fantastic lucklessness, and I told her everything from the start, not omitting even the name of Martin Collingwood and my flirtation with the aspirin bottle, which was a mistake.

On Monday morning my mother took the bus over to Baileyville and found the liquor store and bought a bottle of Scotch whisky. Then she had to wait for a bus back, and she met some people she knew and she was not quite able to hide the bottle in her bag; she was furious with herself for not bringing a proper shopping-bag. As soon as she got back she walked out to the Berrymans'; she had not even had lunch. Mr. Berryman had not gone back to the factory. My mother went in and had a talk with both of them and made an excellent impression and then Mr. Berryman drove her home. She talked to them in the forthright and unemotional way she had, which was always agreeably surprising to people prepared to deal with a mother, and she told them that although I seemed to do well enough at school I was extremely backward—or perhaps eccentric—in my emotional development. I imagine that this analysis of my behavior was especially effective with Mrs. Berryman, a great reader of Child Guidance books. Relations between them warmed to the point where my mother brought up a specific instance of my difficulties, and disarmingly related the whole story of Martin Collingwood.

Within a few days it was all over town and the school that I had tried to ₃₅ commit suicide over Martin Collingwood. But it was already all over school and the town that the Berrymans had come home on Saturday night to find me drunk, staggering, wearing nothing but my slip, in a room with three boys, one of whom was Bill Kline. My mother had said that I was to pay for the bottle she had taken the Berrymans out of my baby-sitting earnings, but my clients melted away like the last April snow, and it would not be paid for yet if newcomers to town had not moved in across the street in July, and needed a baby sitter before they talked to any of their neighbors.

My mother also said that it had been a great mistake to let me go out with boys and that I would not be going out again until well after my sixteenth birthday, if then. This did not prove to be a concrete hardship at all, because it was at least that long before anybody asked me. If you think that news of the Berrymans' adventure would put me in demand for whatever gambols and orgies were going on in and around that town, you could not be more mistaken. The extraordinary publicity which attended my first debauch may have made me seem marked for a special kind of ill luck, like the girl whose illegitimate baby turns out to be triplets: nobody wants to have anything to do with her. At any rate I had at the same time one of the most silent telephones and positively the most sinful reputation in the whole high school. I had to put up with this until the next fall, when a fat blonde girl in grade ten ran away with a married man and was picked up two months later, living in sin — though not with the same man — in the city of Saulte Ste. Marie. Then everybody forgot about me.

But there was a positive, a splendidly unexpected, result of this affair: I got completely over Martin Collingwood. It was not only that he at once said, publicly, that he had always thought I was a nut; where he was concerned I had no pride, and my tender fancy could have found a way around that, a month, a week, before. What was it that brought me back into the world again? It was the terrible and fascinating reality of my disaster; it was *the way things happened.* Not that I enjoyed it; I was a self-conscious girl and I suffered a good deal from all this exposure. But the development of events on that Saturday night — that fascinated me; I felt that I had had a glimpse of the shameless, marvelous, shattering absurdity with which the plots of life, though not of fiction, are improvised. I could not take my eyes off it.

And of course Martin Collingwood wrote his Senior Matric that June, and went away to the city to take a course at a school for Morticians, as I think it is called, and when he came back he went into his uncle's undertaking business. We lived in the same town and we would hear most things that happened to each other but I do not think we met face to face or saw one another, except at a distance, for years. I went to a shower for the girl he married, but then everybody went to everybody else's showers. No, I do not think I really saw him again until I came home after I had been married several years, to attend a relative's funeral. Then I saw him; not quite Mr. Darcy but still very nice-looking in those black clothes. And I saw him looking over at me with an expression as close to a reminiscent smile as the occasion would permit, and I knew that he had been surprised by a memory either of my devotion or my little buried catastrophe. I gave him a gentle, uncomprehending look in return. I am a grown-up woman now; let him unbury his own catastrophes.

CONSIDERATIONS FOR CRITICAL THINKING AND WRITING

1. FIRST RESPONSE. Would you call the protagonist a typical teenager? What details make her unique?

2. Does the narrator's mother seem to be fairly typical in her concerns? Explain why or why not.

3. How important is the setting for this story? Describe the values the narrator associates with "the small town where we lived" (para. 1).

4. Discuss the narrator's sense of humor. How does her humor affect your attitude toward her?

5. Describe the differences in perspective and sensibilities between the teenager who experiences the events in the story and the adult who recounts them.

6. How does the narrator's drunken baby-sitting episode affect her reputation? What does this reveal about her and the town?

7. Why is the narrator "fascinated" by the "events on that Saturday night" (para. 37)? Why is the episode she recounts important to her?

8. How convincing are the narrator's descriptions of the effects of alcohol on her? Cite specific passages to illustrate your points.

9. How would you describe the conflict in the story? How is it resolved?

10. How do you think this story would be different if the protagonist/narrator were male rather than female?

11. Discuss the significance of the title.

FAE MYENNE NG (B. 1957)

The daughter of a seamstress and a laborer, Fae Myenne Ng (her last name is pronounced "Ing") was born in San Francisco. She attended the University of California-Berkeley, and received her M.F.A. at Columbia University. Ng has supported herself by working as a waitress and at other temporary jobs. *Bone* (1993), her first novel, is a story about a Chinese American family. Her short stories have appeared in the *American Voice, Calyx, City Lights Review, Crescent Review, Harper's,* and in a number of anthologies. She was awarded a grant by the National Endowment for the Arts. She currently lives in New York City.

A Red Sweater 1987

I chose red for my sister. Fierce, dark red. Made in Hong Kong. Hand Wash Only because it's got that skin of fuzz. She'll look happy. That's good. Everything's perfect, for a minute. That seems enough.

Red. For Good Luck. Of course. This fire-red sweater is swollen with good cheer. Wear it, I will tell her. You'll look lucky.

We're a family of three girls. By Chinese standards, that's not lucky. "Too bad," outsiders whisper, ". . . nothing but daughters. A failed family."

First, Middle, and End girl. Our order of birth marked us. That came to tell more than our given names.

My eldest sister, Lisa, lives at home. She quit San Francisco State, one semester short of a psychology degree. One day she said, "Forget about it, I'm tired." She's working full time at Pacific Bell now. Nine hundred a month with benefits. Mah and Deh think it's a great deal. They tell everybody, "Yes, our Number One makes good pay, but that's not even counting the discount. If we call Hong Kong, China even, there's forty percent off!" As if anyone in their part of China had a telephone.

Number Two, the in-between, jumped off the "M" floor three years ago. Not true! What happened? Why? Too sad! All we say about that is, "It was her choice."

We sent Mah to Hong Kong. When she left Hong Kong thirty years ago, she was the envy of all: "Lucky girl! You'll never have to work." To marry a sojourner was to have a future. Thirty years in the land of gold and good fortune, and then she returned to tell the story: three daughters, one dead, one unmarried, another who-cares-where, the thirty years in sweatshops, and the prince of the Golden Mountain turned into a toad. I'm glad I didn't have to go with her. I felt her shame and regret. To return, seeking solace and comfort, instead of offering banquets and stories of the good life.

I'm the youngest. I started flying with American the year Mah returned to Hong Kong, so I got her a good discount. She thought I was good for something then. But when she returned, I was pregnant.

"Get an abortion," she said. "Drop the baby," she screamed.

"No."

"Then get married."

"No. I don't want to."

I was going to get an abortion all along. I just didn't like the way they talked about the whole thing. They made me feel like dirt, that I was a disgrace. Now I can see how I used it as an opportunity. Sometimes I wonder if there wasn't another way. Everything about those years was so steamy and angry. There didn't seem to be any answers.

"I have no eyes for you," Mah said.

"Don't call us," Deh said.

They wouldn't talk to me. They ranted idioms to each other for days. The apartment was filled with images and curses I couldn't perceive. I got the general idea: I was a rotten, no-good, dead thing. I would die in a gutter without rice in my belly. My spirit — if I had one — wouldn't be fed. I wouldn't see good days in this life or the next.

My parents always had a special way of saying things.

Now I'm based in Honolulu. When our middle sister jumped, she kind of closed the world. The family just sort of fell apart. I left. Now, I try to make up for it; the folks still won't see me, but I try to keep in touch with them through Lisa. Flying cuts up your life, hits hardest during the holidays. I'm always sensitive then. I feel like I'm missing something, that people are doing something really important while I'm up in the sky, flying through time zones.

So I like to see Lisa around the beginning of the year. January, New Year's, and February, New Year's again, double luckiness with our birthdays in between. With so much going on, there's always something to talk about.

"You pick the place this year," I tell her.

"Around here?"

"No," I say. "Around here" means the food is good and the living hard. You eat a steaming rice plate, and then you feel like rushing home to sew garments or assemble radio parts or something. We eat together only once a year, so I feel we should splurge. Besides, at the Chinatown places, you have nothing to talk about except the bare issues. In American restaurants, the atmosphere helps you along. I want nice light and a view and handsome waiters.

"Let's go somewhere with a view," I say.

We decide to go to Following Sea, a new place on the Pier 39 track. We're early, the restaurant isn't crowded. It's been clear all day, so I think the sunset will be nice. I ask for a window table. I turn to talk to my sister, but she's already talking to a waiter. He's got that dark island tone that she likes. He's looking her up and down. My sister does not blink at it. She holds his look and orders two Johnny Walkers. I pick up a fork, turn it around in my hand. I seldom use chopsticks now. At home, I eat my rice in a plate, with a fork. The only chopsticks I own, I wear in my hair. For a moment, I feel strange sitting here at this unfamiliar table. I don't know this tablecloth, this linen, these candles. Everything seems foreign. It feels like we should be different people. But each time I look up, she's the same. I know this person. She's my sister. We sat together with chopsticks, mismatched bowls, braids, and braces, across the formica tabletop.

"I like three-pronged forks," I say, pressing my thumb against the sharp points.

My sister rolls her eyes. She lights a cigarette.

I ask for one.

I finally say, "So, what's new?"

"Not much." Her voice is sullen. She doesn't look at me. Once a year, I come in, asking questions. She's got the answers, but she hates them. For me, I think she's got the peace of heart, knowing that she's done her share for Mah and Deh. She thinks I have the peace, not caring. Her life is full of questions, too, but I have no answers.

I look around the restaurant. The sunset is not spectacular, and we don't comment on it. The waiters are lighting candles. Ours is bringing the drinks. He stops very close to my sister, seems to breathe her in. She raises her face toward him. "Ready?" he asks. My sister orders for us. The waiter struts off.

"Tight ass," I say.

"The best," she says.

My scotch tastes good. It reminds me of Deh. Johnny Walker or Seagrams 7, that's what they served at Chinese banquets. Nine courses and a bottle. No ice. We learned to drink it Chinese style, in teacups. Deh drank from his rice bowl, sipping it like hot soup. By the end of the meal, he took it like cool tea, in bold mouthfuls. We sat watching, our teacups in our laps, his three giggly girls.

Relaxed, I'm thinking there's a connection. Johnny Walker then and Johnny Walker now. I ask for another cigarette and this one I enjoy. Now my Johnny Walker pops with ice. I twirl the glass to make the ice tinkle.

We clink glasses. Three times for good luck. She giggles. I feel better.   35
"Nice sweater," I say.

"Michael Owyang," she says. She laughs. The light from the candle makes her eyes shimmer. She's got Mah's eyes. Eyes that make you want to talk. Lisa is reed-thin and tall. She's got a body that clothes look good on. My sister slips something on, and it wraps her like skin. Fabric has pulse on her.

"Happy birthday, soon," I say.

"Thanks, and to yours too, just as soon."

"Here's to Johnny Walker in shark's fin soup," I say.   40

"And squab dinners."

"'I Love Lucy,'" I say.

We laugh. It makes us feel like children again. We remember how to be sisters. I raise my glass, "To 'I Love Lucy,' squab dinners, and brown bags."

"To bones," she says.   45

"Bones," I repeat. This is a funny story that gets sad, and knowing it, I keep laughing. I am surprised how much memory there is in one word. Pigeons. Only recently did I learn they're called squab. Our word for them was pigeon — on a plate or flying over Portsmouth Square. A good meal at forty cents a bird. In line by dawn, we waited at the butcher's listening for the slow churning motor of the trucks. We watched the live fish flushing out of the tanks into the garbage pails. We smelled the honey-crushed cha sui bows baking. When the white laundry truck turned into Wentworth, there was a puffing trail of feathers following it. A stench filled the alley. The crowd squeezed in around the truck. Old ladies reached into the crates, squeezing and tugging for the plumpest pigeons.

My sister and I picked the white ones, those with the most expressive eyes. Dove birds, we called them. We fed them leftover rice in water, and as long as they stayed plump, they were our pets, our baby dove birds. And then one day we'd come home from school and find them cooked. They were a special, nutritious treat. Mah let us fill our bowls high with little pigeon parts: legs, breasts, and wings, and take them out to the front room to watch "I Love Lucy." We took brown bags for the bones. We balanced our bowls on our laps and laughed at Lucy. We leaned forward, our chopsticks crossed in mid-air, and called out, "Mah! Mah! Come watch! Watch Lucy cry!"

But she always sat alone in the kitchen sucking out the sweetness of the lesser parts: necks, backs, and the head. "Bones are sweeter than you know," she always said. She came out to check the bags. "Clean bones," she said, shaking the bags. "No waste," she said.

Our dinners come with a warning. "Plate's hot. Don't touch." My sister orders a carafe of house white. "Enjoy," he says, smiling at my sister. She doesn't look up.

I can't remember how to say scallops in Chinese. I ask my sister, she doesn't   50
know either. The food isn't great. Or maybe we just don't have the taste buds in us to go crazy over it. Sometimes I get very hungry for Chinese flavors: black beans, garlic and ginger, shrimp paste and sesame oil. These are tastes we grew up with, still dream about. Crave. Run around town after. Duck liver sausage, bean curd, jook, salted fish, and fried dace with black beans. Western flavors don't stand out, the surroundings do. Three pronged forks. Pink tablecloths. Fresh flowers. Cute waiters. An odd difference.

"Maybe we should have gone to Sun Hung Heung. At least the vegetables are real," I say.

"Hung toh-yee-foo-won-tun!" she says.

"Yeah, yum!" I say.

I remember Deh teaching us how to pick bok choy, his favorite vegetable. "Stick your fingernail into the stem. Juicy and firm, good. Limp and tough, no good." The three of us followed Deh, punching our thumbnails into every stem of bok choy we saw.

"Deh still eating bok choy?" 55

"Breakfast, lunch, and dinner." My sister throws her head back, and laughs. It is Deh's motion. She recites in a mimic tone. "Your Deh, all he needs is a good hot bowl of rice and a plate full of greens. A good monk."

There was always bok choy. Even though it was nonstop for Mah — rushing to the sweatshop in the morning, out to shop on break, and then home to cook by evening — she did this for him. A plate of bok choy, steaming with the taste of ginger and garlic. He said she made good rice. Timed full-fire until the first boil, medium until the grains formed a crust along the sides of the pot, and then low-flamed to let the rice steam. Firm, that's how Deh liked his rice.

The waiter brings the wine, asks if everything is all right.

"Everything," my sister says.

There's something else about this meeting. I can hear it in the edge of her 60 voice. She doesn't say anything and I don't ask. Her lips make a contorting line; her face looks sour. She lets out a breath. It sounds like she's been holding it in too long.

"Another fight. The bank line," she says. "He waited four times in the bank line. Mah ran around outside shopping. He was doing her a favor. She was doing him a favor. Mah wouldn't stop yelling. 'Get out and go die! Useless Thing! Stinking Corpse!'"

I know he answered. His voice must have had that fortune teller's tone to it. You listened because you knew it was a warning.

He always threatened to disappear, jump off the Golden Gate. His thousand-year-old threat. I've heard it all before. "I will go. Even when dead, I won't be far enough away. Curse the good will that blinded me into taking you as wife!"

I give Lisa some of my scallops. "Eat," I tell her.

She keeps talking. "Of course, you know how Mah thinks, that nobody 65 should complain because she's been the one working all these years."

I nod. I start eating, hoping she'll follow.

One bite and she's talking again. "You know what shopping with Mah is like, either you stand outside with the bags like a servant, or inside like a marker, holding a place in line. You know how she gets into being frugal — saving time because it's the one free thing in her life. Well, they're at the bank and she had him hold her place in line while she runs up and down Stockton doing her quick shopping maneuvers. So he's in line, and it's his turn, but she's not back. So he has to start all over at the back again. Then it's his turn but she's still not back. When she finally comes in, she's got bags in both hands, and he's going through the line for the fourth time. Of course she doesn't say sorry or anything."

I interrupt. "How do you know all this?" I tell myself not to come back next year. I tell myself to apply for another transfer, to the East Coast.

"She told me. Word for word." Lisa spears a scallop, puts it in her mouth. I know it's cold by now. "Word for word," she repeats. She cuts a piece of chicken. "Try," she says.

I think about how we're sisters. We eat slowly, chewing carefully like old people. A way to make things last, to fool the stomach. 70

Mah and Deh both worked too hard; it's as if their marriage was a marriage of toil — of toiling together. The idea is that the next generation can marry for love.

In the old country, matches were made, strangers were wedded, and that was fate. Those days, sojourners like Deh were considered princes. To become the wife to such a man was to be saved from the war-torn villages.

Saved to work. After dinner, with the rice still in between her teeth, Mah sat down at her Singer. When we pulled out the wall-bed, she was still there, sewing. The street noises stopped long before she did. The hot lamp made all the stitches blur together. And in the mornings, long before any of us awoke, she was already there, sewing again.

His work was hard, too. He ran a laundry on Polk Street. He sailed with the American President Lines. Things started to look up when he owned the take-out place in Vallejo, and then his partner ran off. So he went to Alaska and worked the canneries.

She was good to him, too. We remember. How else would we have known 75 him all those years he worked in Guam, in the Fiji Islands, in Alaska? Mah always gave him majestic welcomes home. It was her excitement that made us remember him.

I look around. The restaurant is full. The waiters move quickly.

I know Deh. His words are ugly. I've heard him. I've listened. And I've always wished for the street noises, as if in the traffic of sound, I believe I can escape. I know the hard color of his eyes and the tightness of his jaw. I can almost hear his teeth grind. I know this. Years of it.

Their lives weren't easy. So is their discontent without reason?

What about the first one? You didn't even think to come to the hospital. The first one, I say! Son or daughter, dead or alive, you didn't even come!

What about living or dying? Which did you want for me that time you pushed me 80 *back to work before my back brace was off?*

Money! Money! Money to eat with, to buy clothes with, to pass this life with!

Don't start that again! Everything I make at that dead place I hand . . .

How come . . .
What about . . .
So . . . 85

It was obvious. The stories themselves mean little. It was how hot and furious they could become.

Is there no end to it? What makes their ugliness so alive, so thick and impossible to let go of?

"I don't want to think about it anymore." The way she says it surprises me. This time I listen. I imagine what it would be like to take her place. It will be my turn one day.

"Ron," she says, wiggling her fingers above the candle. "A fun thing."

The opal flickers above the flame. I tell her that I want to get her something special for her birthday, ". . . next trip I get abroad." She looks up at me, smiles. 90

For a minute, my sister seems happy. But she won't be able to hold onto it. She grabs at things out of despair, out of fear. Gifts grow old for her. Emotions never ripen, they sour. Everything slips away from her. Nothing sustains her. Her beauty has made her fragile.

We should have eaten in Chinatown. We could have gone for coffee in North Beach, then for jook at Sam Wo's.

"No work, it's been like that for months, just odd jobs," she says.

I'm thinking, it's not like I haven't done my share. I was a kid once, I did things because I felt I should. I helped fill out forms at the Chinatown employment agencies. I went with him to the Seaman's Union. I waited too, listening and hoping for those calls: "Busboy! Presser! Prep Man!" His bags were packed, he was always ready to go. "On standby," he said.

Every week. All the same. Quitting and looking to start all over again. In 95 the end, it was like never having gone anywhere. It was like the bank line, waiting for nothing.

How many times did my sister and I have to hold them apart? The flat *ting!* sound as the blade slapped onto the linoleum floor, the wooden handle of the knife slamming into the corner. Was it she or I who screamed, repeating all of their ugliest words? Who shook them? Who made them stop?

The waiter comes to take the plates. He stands by my sister for a moment. I raise my glass to the waiter.

"You two Chinese?" he asks.

"No," I say, finishing off my wine. I roll my eyes. I wish I had another Johnny Walker. Suddenly I don't care.

"We're two sisters," I say. I laugh. I ask for the check, leave a good tip. I see 100 him slip my sister a box of matches.

Outside, the air is cool and brisk. My sister links her arm into mine. We walk up Bay onto Chestnut. We pass Galileo High School and then turn down Van Ness to head toward the pier. The bay is black. The foghorns sound far away. We walk the whole length of the pier without talking.

The water is white where it slaps against the wooden stakes.

For a long time Lisa's wanted out. She can stay at that point of endurance forever. Desire that becomes old feels too good, it's seductive. I know how hard it is to go.

The heart never travels. You have to be heartless. My sister holds that heart, too close and for too long. This is her weakness, and I like to think, used to be mine. Lisa endures too much.

We're lucky, not like the bondmaids growing up in service, or the newborn 105 daughters whose mouths were stuffed with ashes. Courtesans with the three-inch feet, beardless, soft-shouldered eunuchs, and the frightened child-brides, they're all stories to us. We're the lucky generation. Our parents forced themselves to live through the humiliation in this country so that we could have it better. We know so little of the old country. We repeat names of Grandfathers and Uncles, but they will always be strangers to us. Family exists only because somebody has a story, and knowing the story connects us to a history. To us, the deformed man is oddly compelling, the forgotten man is a good story. A beautiful woman suffers.

I want her beauty to buy her out.

The sweater cost two weeks' pay. Like the forty-cent birds that are now a delicacy, this is a special treat. The money doesn't mean anything. It is, if anything, time. Time is what I would like to give her.

A red sweater. One hundred percent angora. The skin of fuzz will be a fierce rouge on her naked breasts.

Red. Lucky. Wear it. Find that man. The new one. Wrap yourself around him. Feel the pulsing between you. Fuck him and think about it. One hundred percent. Hand Wash Only. Worn Once.

Considerations for Critical Thinking and Writing

1. FIRST RESPONSE. How do you read this story's final paragraph? What emotions is the narrator revealing? Does it change the way you've thought of her up to the end?

2. Describe the narrator. What details of her personal life reveal her values and sensibilities?

3. Why is the narrator concerned about the quality of her older sister's life? Why does Lisa live with her parents?

4. How does knowing that the middle sister committed suicide affect your understanding of the family?

5. How is Chinese immigrant life portrayed in the story? How do Mah and Deh cope with their everyday lives?

6. Toward the end of the story, the narrator says, "Family exists only because somebody has a story, and knowing the story connects us to a history" (para. 105). Is this idea true of this family?

7. How does the memory of her family life affect the narrator's present life? How does she feel about her sister?

8. Which of the narrator's stories about family life seem to have significant symbolic value? Choose one to analyze in detail.

9. The red sweater frames the story. How does it function as a symbol? Does its meaning evolve over the course of the narration?

TOBIAS WOLFF (B. 1945)

Born in Alabama, Tobias Wolff grew up in the state of Washington. After quitting high school, he worked on a ship and for a carnival. In the army he served four years as a paratrooper, after which he studied to pass the entrance exams for Oxford University, from which he graduated with honors. He has published two memoirs — *This Boy's Life* (1989) and *In Pharoah's Army: Memories of the Lost War* (1994). His fiction includes a novel, *The Barracks Thief* (1984), and three collections of stories — *In the Garden of North American Martyrs* (1981), *Back in the World* (1985), and *The Night in Question* (1996). "Powder" was included in *The Best American Short Stories* for 1997.

Powder   1996

Just before Christmas my father took me skiing at Mount Baker. He'd had to fight for the privilege of my company, because my mother was still angry with him for sneaking me into a night-club during our last visit, to see Thelonious Monk.

He wouldn't give up. He promised, hand on heart, to take good care of me and have me home for dinner on Christmas Eve, and she relented. But as we were checking out of the lodge that morning it began to snow, and in this snow he observed some quality that made it necessary for us to get in one last run. We got in several last runs. He was indifferent to my fretting. Snow whirled around us in bitter, blinding squalls, hissing like sand, and still we skied. As the lift bore us to the peak yet again, my father looked at his watch and said, "Criminey. This'll have to be a fast one."

By now I couldn't see the trail. There was no point in trying. I stuck to him like white on rice and did what he did and somehow made it to the bottom without sailing off a cliff. We returned our skis and my father put chains on the Austin-Healy while I swayed from foot to foot, clapping my mittens and wishing I were home. I could see everything. The green tablecloth, the plates with the holly pattern, the red candles waiting to be lit.

We passed a diner on our way out. "You want some soup?" my father asked. I shook my head. "Buck up," he said. "I'll get you there. Right, doctor?"

I was supposed to say, "Right, doctor," but I didn't say anything.   5

A state trooper waved us down outside the resort. A pair of sawhorses were blocking the road. The trooper came up to our car and bent down to my father's window. His face was bleached by the cold. Snowflakes clung to his eyebrows and to the fur trim of his jacket and cap.

"Don't tell me," my father said.

The trooper told him. The road was closed. It might get cleared, it might not. Storm took everyone by surprise. So much, so fast. Hard to get people moving. Christmas Eve. What can you do?

My father said, "Look. We're talking about four, five inches. I've taken this car through worse than that."

The trooper straightened up, boots creaking. His face was out of sight but   10
I could hear him. "The road is closed."

My father sat with both hands on the wheel, rubbing the wood with his thumbs. He looked at the barricade for a long time. He seemed to be trying to master the idea of it. Then he thanked the trooper, and with a weird, old-maidy show of caution turned the car around. "Your mother will never forgive me for this," he said.

"We should have left before," I said. "Doctor."

He didn't speak to me again until we were both in a booth at the diner, waiting for our burgers. "She won't forgive me," he said. "Do you understand? Never."

"I guess," I said, but no guesswork was required; she wouldn't forgive him.

"I can't let that happen." He bent toward me. "I'll tell you what I want. I 15 want us to be together again. Is that what you want?"

I wasn't sure, but I said, "Yes, sir."

He bumped my chin with his knuckles. "That's all I needed to hear."

When we finished eating he went to the pay phone in the back of the diner, then joined me in the booth again. I figured he'd called my mother, but he didn't give a report. He sipped at his coffee and stared out the window at the empty road. "Come on!" When the trooper's car went past, lights flashing, he got up and dropped some money on the check. "Okay. *Vamanos.*"

The wind had died. The snow was falling straight down, less of it now; lighter. We drove away from the resort, right up to the barricade. "Move it," my father told me. When I looked at him he said, "What are you waiting for?" I got out and dragged one of the sawhorses aside, then pushed it back after he drove through. When I got inside the car he said, "Now you're an accomplice. We go down together." He put the car in gear and looked at me. "Joke, doctor."

"Funny, doctor."   20

Down the first long stretch I watched the road behind us, to see if the trooper was on our tail. The barricade vanished. Then there was nothing but snow: snow on the road, snow kicking up from the chains, snow on the trees, snow in the sky; and our trail in the snow. I faced around and had a shock. The lie of the road behind us had been marked by our own tracks, but there were no tracks ahead of us. My father was breaking virgin snow between a line of tall trees. He was humming "Stars Fell on Alabama." I felt snow brush along the floorboards under my feet. To keep my hands from shaking I clamped them between my knees.

My father grunted in a thoughtful way and said, "Don't ever try this yourself."

"I won't."

"That's what you say now, but someday you'll get your license and then you'll think you can do anything. Only you won't be able to do this. You need, I don't know—a certain instinct."

"Maybe I have it."   25

"You don't. You have your strong points, but not . . . you know. I only mention it because I don't want you to get the idea this is something just anybody can do. I'm a great driver. That's not a virtue, okay? It's just a fact, and one you should be aware of. Of course you have to give the old heap some credit, too—there aren't many cars I'd try this with. Listen!"

I listened. I heard the slap of the chains, the stiff, jerky rasp of the wipers, the purr of the engine. It really did purr. The car was almost new. My father couldn't afford it, and kept promising to sell it, but here it was.

I said, "Where do you think that policeman went to?"

"Are you warm enough?" He reached over and cranked up the blower. Then he turned off the wipers. We didn't need them. The clouds had brightened. A few sparse, feathery flakes drifted into our slipstream and were swept away. We left the trees and entered a broad field of snow that ran level for a while and then tilted sharply downward. Orange stakes had been planted at intervals in two parallel lines and my father ran a course between them, though they were far enough apart to leave considerable doubt in my mind as to where exactly the road lay. He was humming again, doing little scat riffs around the melody.

"Okay, then. What are my strong points?"   30

"Don't get me started," he said. "It'd take all day."

"Oh, right. Name one."

"Easy. You always think ahead."

True. I always thought ahead. I was a boy who kept his clothes on numbered hangers to ensure proper rotation. I bothered my teachers for homework assignments far ahead of their due dates so I could make up schedules. I thought ahead, and that was why I knew that there would be other troopers waiting for us at the end of our ride, if we got there. What I did not know was that my father would wheedle and plead his way past them — he didn't sing "O Tannenbaum" but just about — and get me home for dinner, buying a little more time before my mother decided to make the split final. I knew we'd get caught; I was resigned to it. And maybe for this reason I stopped moping and began to enjoy myself.

Why not? This was one for the books. Like being in a speedboat, only bet- 35
ter. You can't go downhill in a boat. And it was all ours. And it kept coming, the laden trees, the unbroken surface of snow, the sudden white vistas. Here and there I saw hints of the road, ditches, fences, stakes, but not so many that I could have found my way. But then I didn't have to. My father in his forty-eighth year, rumpled, kind, bankrupt of honor, flushed with certainty. He was a great driver. All persuasion, no coercion. Such subtlety at the wheel, such tactful pedalwork. I actually trusted him. And the best was yet to come — switchbacks and hairpins impossible to describe. Except maybe to say this: if you haven't driven fresh powder, you haven't driven.

CONSIDERATIONS FOR CRITICAL THINKING AND WRITING

1. FIRST RESPONSE. Does your response to the narrator's father change over the course of the story? Explain why or why not.

2. Though the mother does not actually appear in "Powder," her presence is felt. What role does she play in the story?

3. How does the father's response to the state trooper reveal the way the father handles conflict?

4. How is the son's personality different from his father's? How do you think those differences can be accounted for in this family?

5. What do you think is the son's attitude toward his father at the end of the story?

6. Comment on the significance of the story's title.

7. CRITICAL STRATEGIES. Read the section on formalist criticism (pp. 60–62) in Chapter 3, "Applying a Critical Strategy" and comment on how the father's driving can be read symbolically and as a means of determining the story's potential themes.

POETRY

Elizabeth Alexander (b. 1962)

Harlem Birthday Party   1996

When my grandfather turned ninety we had a party
in a restaurant in Harlem called Copeland's.
Harlem restaurants are always dim to dark and this
was no exception. Daddy would have gone downtown
but Baba, as we called him, wanted to stay   5
in the neighborhood, and this place was "swanky."
We picked him up in his house on Hamilton Terrace.
His wife, "poor Minnette," had Alzheimer's disease
and thought Hordgie, who was not dead, was dead. She kept
cluck-clucking, "Poor Hordgie," and filling with tears.   10
They had organized a block watch on Hamilton
Terrace, which I was glad of; I worried always
about old people getting mugged; I was afraid
of getting old myself and knocked down in the street;
I was afraid it would happen to my grandfather.   15

My father moves fast always but in Harlem
something clicks into his walk which I love watching.
We argued about taking a car, about parking;
in the end some walked, some drove, and the restaurant
parked the car for us. They treated my grandfather   20
like a Pope or like Duke Ellington. We ate salad,
fried chicken, mashed potatoes, broccoli, chocolate
cake, and Gustavo, who was then my boyfriend, cut Minnette's
meat for her and that became one of the things I would cite
forever when people asked me, How did you know   25
you wanted to marry him? I remember looking
at all the people at the party I had never seen,
and thinking, My grandfather has a whole life
we know nothing about, like at his funeral,
two years later, when a dreadlocked man about my age   30
went on and on about coming to Harlem
from Jamaica, they all said, talk to Mister Alexander, and they talked, and my grandfather scolded,
advised, and today the young brother owns a patty stand
in Brooklyn. Who ever knew this young man, or all the rest?   35

The star appearance at Copeland's, besides my father, was
my grandfather's wife's cousin, Jane Tillman Irving,
who broadcast on WCBS all-news radio.
What is a Harlem birthday party without a star?
What is a black family without someone   40
who's related to someone else who is a little
bit famous, if only to other black people?

And then goodbye, and then goodbye, and back
to New Haven, Washington, and Philadelphia,
where I lived with Gustavo. We walked downtown   45
after the party to Macy's to get feather pillows
on sale, and then we took Amtrak home. I cannot think
about this party without thinking how glad I am
we had it, that he lived long and healthy, that two years
later he was gone. He was born in Jamaica,   50
West Indies, and he died in Harlem, New York.

Considerations for Critical Thinking and Writing

1. FIRST RESPONSE. How do the details provided in this poem suggest the rich texture of family life?

2. What kind of man was the grandfather? How does the narrator feel about him?

3. Why do you suppose this description of the birthday party is written in verse rather than as a prose narrative?

Margaret Atwood (B. 1939)

Bored   *1995*

All those times I was bored
out of my mind. Holding the log
while he sawed it. Holding
the string while he measured, boards,
distances between things, or pounded   5
stakes into the ground for rows and rows
of lettuces and beets, which I then (bored)
weeded. Or sat in the back
of the car, or sat still in boats,
sat, sat, while at the prow, stern, wheel   10
he drove, steered, paddled. It
wasn't even boredom, it was looking,
looking hard and up close at the small
details. Myopia. The worn gunwales,
the intricate twill of the seat   15
cover. The acid crumbs of loam, the granular
pink rock, its igneous veins, the sea-fans
of dry moss, the blackish and then the greying
bristles on the back of his neck.
Sometimes he would whistle, sometimes   20
I would. The boring rhythm of doing
things over and over, carrying
the wood, drying
the dishes. Such minutiae. It's what
the animals spend most of their time at,   25

ferrying the sand, grain by grain, from their tunnels,
shuffling the leaves in their burrows. He pointed
such things out, and I would look
at the whorled texture of his square finger, earth under
the nail. Why do I remember it as sunnier   30
all the time then, although it more often
rained, and more birdsong?
I could hardly wait to get
the hell out of there to
anywhere else. Perhaps though   35
boredom is happier. It is for dogs or
groundhogs. Now I wouldn't be bored.
Now I would know too much.
Now I would know.

CONSIDERATIONS FOR CRITICAL THINKING AND WRITING

1. FIRST RESPONSE. Atwood has described this poem as one of several about
   her father and his death. Is it possible to determine that "he" is the
   speaker's father from the details of the poem? Explain whether or not you
   think it matters who "he" is.

2. Play with the possible meanings of the word "bored" and its variations in
   the poem. What function does the repetition of the word serve?

3. What does the speaker "know" at the end of the poem that she didn't
   before?

REGINA BARRECA (B. 1957)

Nighttime Fires   1986

When I was five in Louisville
we drove to see nighttime fires. Piled seven of us,
all pajamas and running noses, into the Olds,
drove fast toward smoke. It was after my father
lost his job, so not getting up in the morning   5
gave him time: awake past midnight, he read old newspapers
with no news, tried crosswords until he split the pencil
between his teeth, mad. When he heard
the wolf whine of the siren, he woke my mother,
and she pushed and shoved   10
us all into waking. Once roused we longed for burnt wood
and a smell of flames high into the pines. My old man liked
driving to rich neighborhoods best, swearing in a good mood
as he followed fire engines that snaked like dragons
and split the silent streets. It was festival, carnival.   15

If there were a Cadillac or any car
in a curved driveway, my father smiled a smile
from a secret, brittle heart.

His face lit up in the heat given off by destruction
like something was being made, or was being set right.   20
I bent my head back to see where sparks
ate up the sky. My father who never held us
would take my hand and point to falling cinders that
covered the ground like snow, or, excited, show us
the swollen collapse of a staircase. My mother   25
watched my father, not the house. She was happy
only when we were ready to go, when it was finally over
and nothing else could burn.
Driving home, she would sleep in the front seat
as we huddled behind. I could see his quiet face in the   30
rearview mirror, eyes like hallways filled with smoke.

CONSIDERATIONS FOR CRITICAL THINKING AND WRITING

1. FIRST RESPONSE. Why do you think the father takes such pleasure in watching fire consume other people's property? Why is it important to have his family with him at these times?

2. How do you think the narrator regards her father? What do you think of him?

3. Examine the images used to describe the father. What do they reveal about his state of mind?

ROBERT BLY (B. 1927)

The Man Who Didn't Know What Was His   1988

Suppose a man can't find what is his.
Suppose as a boy he imagined that some demon
Forced him to live in "his room,"
And sit on "his chair" and be a child of "his parents."

That would happen each time he sat down to dinner.   5
His own birthday party belonged to someone else.
And — was it sweet potatoes that he liked? —
He should resist them. Whose plate is this?

That man would be like a lean-to attached
To a house. It doesn't have a foundation.   10
He would be helpful and hostile at the same time.
Such a person leans toward you and leans away.

Do you feel me leaning?

CONSIDERATIONS FOR CRITICAL THINKING AND WRITING

1. FIRST RESPONSE. Do you feel the speaker leaning toward you or away from you? Explain your response.

2. What kind of "demon" is described in line 2?

3. How do the boy's experiences with his family serve to shape the man, according to the speaker?

4. Discuss the symbolic values associated with "dinner" in this poem.

GWENDOLYN BROOKS (B. 1917)

The Mother   *1945*

Abortions will not let you forget.
You remember the children you got that you did not get,
The damp small pulps with a little or with no hair,
The singers and workers that never handled the air.
You will never neglect or beat   5
Them, or silence or buy with a sweet.
You will never wind up the sucking-thumb
Or scuttle off ghosts that come.
You will never leave them, controlling your luscious sigh,
Return for a snack of them, with gobbling mother-eye.   10

I have heard in the voices of the wind the voices of my dim
          killed children
I have contracted. I have eased
My dim dears at the breasts they could never suck.
I have said, Sweets, if I sinned, if I seized
Your luck   15
And your lives from your unfinished reach,
If I stole your births and your names,
Your straight baby tears and your games,
Your stilted or lovely loves, your tumults, your marriages, aches,
          and your deaths,
If I poisoned the beginnings of your breaths,   20
Believe that even in my deliberateness I was not deliberate.
Though why should I whine,
Whine that the crime was other than mine? —
Since anyhow you are dead.
Or rather, or instead,   25
You were never made.

But that too, I am afraid,
Is faulty: oh, what shall I say, how is the truth to be said?
You were born, you had body, you died.
It is just that you never giggled or planned or cried.   30

Believe me, I loved you all.
Believe me, I knew you, though faintly, and I loved, I loved you
All.

CONSIDERATIONS FOR CRITICAL THINKING AND WRITING

1. FIRST RESPONSE. Why is the title ironic? How is it related to the contradictions expressed in the poem?

2. What is the effect of the narrator shifting from "You" in the first stanza to "I" in the second stanza?

3. Compare the rhyme scheme in the first stanza and the second stanza. How does this help to reflect the meanings of these stanzas?

4. CRITICAL STRATEGIES. Read the section on reader-response criticism (pp. 74–76) in Chapter 3, "Applying a Critical Strategy." How does your own attitude toward abortion affect your response to "The Mother"?

EMILY DICKINSON (1830–1886)

The Bustle in a House   *c. 1866*

The Bustle in a House
The Morning after Death
Is solemnest of industries
Enacted upon Earth —

The Sweeping up the Heart
And putting Love away
We shall not want to use again
Until Eternity.

CONSIDERATIONS FOR CRITICAL THINKING AND WRITING

1. FIRST RESPONSE. What is the relationship between love and death in this poem?

2. Why do you think mourning (notice the pun in line 2) is described as an industry?

3. Discuss the tone of the ending of the poem. Consider whether you think it is hopeful, sad, resigned, or some other mood.

4. How does ritualized mourning help families to cope with such losses?

ROBERT FROST (1874–1963)

Home Burial   *1914*

He saw her from the bottom of the stairs
Before she saw him. She was starting down,
Looking back over her shoulder at some fear.
She took a doubtful step and then undid it
To raise herself and look again. He spoke   5
Advancing toward her: "What is it you see
From up there always — for I want to know."
She turned and sank upon her skirts at that,
And her face changed from terrified to dull.

He said to gain time: "What is it you see,"   10
Mounting until she cowered under him.
"I will find out now—you must tell me, dear."
She, in her place, refused him any help
With the least stiffening of her neck and silence.
She let him look, sure that he wouldn't see,   15
Blind creature; and awhile he didn't see.
But at last he murmured, "Oh," and again, "Oh."

"What is it—what?" she said.

                    "Just that I see."

"You don't," she challenged. "Tell me what it is."   20

"The wonder is I didn't see at once.
I never noticed it from here before.
I must be wonted° to it—that's the reason.
The little graveyard where my people are!
So small the window frames the whole of it.   25
Not so much larger than a bedroom, is it?
There are three stones of slate and one of marble,
Broad-shouldered little slabs there in the sunlight
On the sidehill. We haven't to mind *those*.
But I understand: it is not the stones,   30
But the child's mound—"

                    "Don't, don't, don't, don't," she cried.

She withdrew, shrinking from beneath his arm
That rested on the banister, and slid downstairs;
And turned on him with such a daunting look,   35
He said twice over before he knew himself:
"Can't a man speak of his own child he's lost?"

"Not you!—Oh, where's my hat? Oh, I don't need it!
I must get out of here. I must get air.
I don't know rightly whether any man can."   40

"Amy! Don't go to someone else this time.
Listen to me. I won't come down the stairs."
He sat and fixed his chin between his fists.
"There's something I should like to ask you, dear."

"You don't know how to ask it."   45

                    "Help me, then."
Her fingers moved the latch for all reply.

"My words are nearly always an offense.
I don't know how to speak of anything
So as to please you. But I might be taught,   50
I should suppose. I can't say I see how.
A man must partly give up being a man
With women-folk. We could have some arrangement

23 *wonted:* Accustomed.

By which I'd bind myself to keep hands off
Anything special you're a-mind to name.   55
Though I don't like such things 'twixt those that love.
Two that don't love can't live together without them.
But two that do can't live together with them."
She moved the latch a little. "Don't — don't go.
Don't carry it to someone else this time.   60
Tell me about it if it's something human.
Let me into your grief. I'm not so much
Unlike other folks as your standing there
Apart would make me out. Give me my chance.
I do think, though, you overdo it a little.   65
What was it brought you up to think it the thing
To take your mother-loss of a first child
So inconsolably — in the face of love.
You'd think his memory might be satisfied —"

"There you go sneering now!"   70

            "I'm not, I'm not!

You make me angry. I'll come down to you.
God, what a woman! And it's come to this,
A man can't speak of his own child that's dead."

"You can't because you don't know how to speak.   75
If you had any feelings, you that dug
With your own hand — how could you? — his little grave;
I saw you from that very window there,
Making the gravel leap and leap in air,
Leap up, like that, like that, and land so lightly   80
And roll back down the mound beside the hole.
I thought, Who is that man? I didn't know you.
And I crept down the stairs and up the stairs
To look again, and still your spade kept lifting.
Then you came in. I heard your rumbling voice   85
Out in the kitchen, and I don't know why,
But I went near to see with my own eyes.
You could sit there with the stains on your shoes
Of the fresh earth from your own baby's grave
And talk about your everyday concerns.   90
You had stood the spade up against the wall
Outside there in the entry, for I saw it."

"I shall laugh the worst laugh I ever laughed.
I'm cursed. God, if I don't believe I'm cursed."

"I can repeat the very words you were saying.   95
'Three foggy mornings and one rainy day
Will rot the best birch fence a man can build.'
Think of it, talk like that at such a time!
What had how long it takes a birch to rot
To do with what was in the darkened parlor   100
You *couldn't* care! The nearest friends can go

With anyone to death, comes so far short
They might as well not try to go at all.
No, from the time when one is sick to death,
One is alone, and he dies more alone.   105
Friends make pretense of following to the grave.
But before one is in it, their minds are turned
And making the best of their way back to life
And living people, and things they understand.
But the world's evil. I won't have grief so   110
If I can change it. Oh, I won't, I won't!"

"There, you have said it all and you feel better.
You won't go now. You're crying. Close the door.
The heart's gone out of it: why keep it up.
Amy! There's someone coming down the road!"   115

"*You* — oh, you think the talk is all. I must go —
Somewhere out of this house. How can I make you —"

"If — you — do!" She was opening the door wider.
"Where do you mean to go? First tell me that.
I'll follow and bring you back by force. I *will!* —"   120

CONSIDERATIONS FOR CRITICAL THINKING AND WRITING

1. FIRST RESPONSE. This poem tells a story of a relationship. Is the husband insensitive and indifferent to his wife's grief? Characterize the wife. Has Frost invited us to sympathize with one character more than with the other?

2. How has the burial of the child within sight of the stairway window affected the relationship of the couple in this poem? Is the child's grave a symptom or a cause of the conflict between them?

3. What is the effect of splitting the iambic pentameter pattern in lines 18 and 19, 31 and 32, 45 and 46, and 70 and 71?

4. Is the conflict resolved at the conclusion of the poem? Do you think the husband and wife will overcome their differences?

RACHEL HADAS (B. 1948)

The Red Hat   *1995*

It started before Christmas. Now our son
officially walks to school alone.
Semi-alone, it's accurate to say:
I or his father track him on the way.
He walks up on the east side of West End,   5
we on the west side. Glances can extend
(and do) across the street; not eye contact.
Already ties are feeling and not fact.
Straus Park is where these parallel paths part;
he goes alone from there. The watcher's heart   10
stretches, elastic in its love and fear,

toward him as we see him disappear,
striding briskly. Where two weeks ago,
holding a hand, he'd dawdle, dreamy, slow,
he now is hustled forward by the pull   15
of something far more powerful than school.

The mornings we turn back to are no more
than forty minutes longer than before,
but they feel vastly different — flimsy, strange,
wavering in the eddies of this change,   20
empty, unanchored, perilously light
since the red hat vanished from our sight.

CONSIDERATIONS FOR CRITICAL THINKING AND WRITING

1. FIRST RESPONSE. What emotions do the parents experience throughout the poem? How do you think the boy feels? Does the metrical pattern affect your understanding of the parents or the boy?

2. What prevents the rhymed couplets in this poem from sounding sing-songy? What is the predominant meter?

3. What is it that "pull[s]" the boy along in lines 15–16?

4. Why do you think Hadas titled the poem "The Red Hat" rather than, for example, "Paths Part" (line 9)?

5. CRITICAL STRATEGIES. Read the section on psychological criticism (pp. 64–66) in Chapter 3, "Applying a Critical Strategy." How does the speaker reveal her personal psychology in this poem?

DONALD HALL (B. 1928)

Letter with No Address   1996

Your daffodils rose up
and collapsed in their yellow
bodies on the hillside
garden above the bricks
you laid out in sand, squatting   5
with pants pegged and face
masked like a beekeeper's
against the black flies.
Buttercups circle the planks
of the old wellhead   10
this May while your silken
gardener's body withers or moulds
in the Proctor graveyard.
I drive and talk to you crying
and come back to this house   15
to talk to your photographs.

There's news to tell you:
Maggie Fisher's pregnant.
I carried myself like an egg

at Abigail's birthday party   20
a week after you died,
as three-year-olds bounced
uproarious on a mattress.
Joyce and I met for lunch
at the mall and strolled weepily   25
through Sears and B. Dalton.

Today it's four weeks
since you lay on our painted bed
and I closed your eyes.
Yesterday I cut irises to set   30
in a pitcher on your grave;
today I brought a carafe
to fill it with fresh water.
I remember the bone pain,
vomiting, and delirium. I remember   35
the pond afternoons.

                  My routine
is established: coffee;
the *Globe;* breakfast;
writing you this letter   40
at my desk. When I go to bed
to sleep after baseball,
Gus follows me into the bedroom
as he used to follow us.
Most of the time he flops   45
down in the parlor
with his head on his paws.

Once a week I drive to Tilton
to see Dick and Nan.
Nan doesn't understand much   50
but she knows you're dead;
I feel her fretting. The tune
of Dick and me talking
seems to console her.

                  You know now   55
whether the soul survives death.
Or you don't. When you were dying
you said you didn't fear
punishment. We never dared
to speak of Paradise.   60

At five A.M., when I walk outside,
mist lies thick on hayfields.
By eight, the air is clear,
cool, sunny with the pale yellow
light of mid-May. Kearsarge   65
rises huge and distinct,
each birch and balsam visible.
To the west the waters

of Eagle Pond waver
and flash through popples just   70
leafing out.

        Always the weather,
writing its book of the world,
returns you to me.
Ordinary days were best,   75
when we worked over poems
in our separate rooms.
I remember watching you gaze
out the January window
into the garden of snow   80
and ice, your face rapt
as you imagined burgundy lilies.

Your presence in this house
is almost as enormous
and painful as your absence.   85
Driving home from Tilton,
I remember how you cherished
that vista with its center
the red door of a farmhouse
against green fields.   90
Are you past pity?
If you have consciousness now,
if something I can call
"you" has something
like "consciousness," I doubt   95
you remember the last days.
I play them over and over:
I lift your wasted body
onto the commode, your arms
looped around my neck, aiming   100
your bony bottom so that
it will not bruise on a rail.
Faintly you repeat,
"Momma, Momma."

        You lay   105
astonishing in the long box
while Alice Ling prayed
and sang "Amazing Grace"
a capella. Three times today
I drove to your grave.   110
Sometimes, coming back home
to our circular driveway,
I imagine you've returned
before me, bags of groceries upright
in the back of the Saab,   115
its trunklid delicately raised
as if proposing an encounter,
dog-fashion, with the Honda.

CONSIDERATIONS FOR CRITICAL THINKING AND WRITING

1. FIRST RESPONSE. Describe the tone of this poem. What prevents it from being sentimental?

2. Which details most effectively describe for you the nature of this couple's relationship?

3. Consider the final image in lines 111–18 and contrast it with the opening image in lines 1–8. What is the effect of the speaker beginning and ending with these images?

ANDREW HUDGINS (B. 1951)

Elegy for My Father, Who Is Not Dead 1991

One day I'll lift the telephone
and be told my father's dead. He's ready.
In the sureness of his faith, he talks
about the world beyond this world
as though his reservations have   5
been made. I think he wants to go,
a little bit — a new desire
to travel building up, an itch
to see fresh worlds. Or older ones.
He thinks that when I follow him   10
he'll wrap me in his arms and laugh,
the way he did when I arrived
on earth. I do not think he's right.
He's ready. I am not. I can't
just say good-bye as cheerfully   15
as if he were embarking on a trip
to make my later trip go well.
I see myself on deck, convinced
his ship's gone down, while he's convinced
I'll see him standing on the dock   20
and waving, shouting, Welcome back.

CONSIDERATIONS FOR CRITICAL THINKING AND WRITING

1. FIRST RESPONSE. Why does this speaker elegize his father if the father "is not dead"?

2. How does the speaker's view of immortality differ from his father's?

3. Explain why you think this is an optimistic or pessimistic poem — or explain why these two categories fail to describe the poem.

4. In what sense can this poem be regarded as an elegy?

LANGSTON HUGHES (1902–1967)

doorknobs 　　*1961*

The simple silly terror
of a doorknob on a door
that turns to let in life
on two feet standing,
walking, talking, 　　5
wearing dress or trousers,
maybe drunk or maybe sober,
maybe smiling, laughing, happy,
maybe tangled in the terror
of a yesterday past grandpa 　　10
when the door from out there opened
into here where I, antenna,
recipient of your coming,
received the talking image
of the simple silly terror 　　15
of a door that opens
at the turning of a knob
to let in life
walking, talking, standing
wearing dress or trousers, 　　20
drunk or maybe sober,
smiling, laughing, happy,
or tangled in the terror
of a yesterday past grandpa
not of our own doing. 　　25

CONSIDERATIONS FOR CRITICAL THINKING AND WRITING

1. FIRST RESPONSE. Why is the doorknob associated with "terror"? Does it have any symbolic value or should it be read literally?

2. The final eight lines repeat much of the first part of the poem. What is repeated and what is changed? What is the effect of this repetition?

3. How does knowing that Hughes was a black American writer affect your understanding of lines 10 and 24–25?

GALWAY KINNELL (B. 1927)

After Making Love We Hear Footsteps 　　*1980*

For I can snore like a bullhorn
or play loud music
or sit up talking with any reasonably sober Irishman
and Fergus will only sink deeper
into his dreamless sleep, which goes by all in one flash, 　　5
but let there be that heavy breathing

or a stifled come-cry anywhere in the house
and he will wrench himself awake
and make for it on the run — as now, we lie together,
after making love, quiet, touching along the length of our bodies,   10
familiar touch of the long-married,
and he appears — in his baseball pajamas, it happens,
the neck opening so small
he has to screw them on, which one day may make him wonder
about the mental capacity of baseball players —   15
and says, "Are you loving and snuggling? May I join?"
He flops down between us and hugs us and snuggles himself to sleep,
his face gleaming with satisfaction at being this very child.

In the half darkness we look at each other
and smile   20
and touch arms across his little, startlingly muscled body —
this one whom habit of memory propels to the ground of his making,
sleeper only the mortal sounds can sing awake,
this blessing love gives again into our arms.

CONSIDERATIONS FOR CRITICAL THINKING AND WRITING

1. FIRST RESPONSE. Explore Kinnell's line endings. Why does he break the lines where he does?

2. How does the speaker's language reveal his character?

3. Describe the shift in tone between lines 18 and 19 with the shift in focus from child to adult. How does the use of space here emphasize this shift?

4. Do you think this poem is sentimental? Explain why or why not.

PHILIP LARKIN (1922–1985)

This Be the Verse   1974

They fuck you up, your mum and dad.
   They may not mean to, but they do.
They fill you with the faults they had
   And add some extras, just for you.

But they were fucked up in their turn   5
   By fools in old-style hats and coats,
Who half the time were soppy-stern
   And half at one another's throats.

Man hands on misery to man.
   It deepens like a coastal shelf.   10
Get out as early as you can,
   And don't have any kids yourself.

1. FIRST RESPONSE. Do you think there is a serious point to this humorous poem? Explain why or why not.
2. What is the effect of the speaker's use of obscenity?
3. Discuss the speaker's diction. Is the tone consistent?
4. What do you make of the poem's title?

SHARON OLDS (B. 1942)

Rite of Passage
1983

As the guests arrive at my son's party
they gather in the living room —
short men, men in first grade
with smooth jaws and chins.
Hands in pockets, they stand around   5
jostling, jockeying for place, small fights
breaking out and calming. One says to another
How old are you? Six. I'm seven. So?
They eye each other, seeing themselves
tiny in the other's pupils. They clear their   10
throats a lot, a room of small bankers,
they fold their arms and frown. *I could beat you
up*, a seven says to a six,
the dark cake, round and heavy as a
turret, behind them on the table. My son,   15
freckles like specks of nutmeg on his cheeks,
chest narrow as the balsa keel of a
model boat, long hands
cool and thin as the day they guided him
out of me, speaks up as a host   20
for the sake of the group.
We could easily kill a two-year-old,
he says in his clear voice. The other
men agree, they clear their throats
like Generals, they relax and get down to   25
playing war, celebrating my son's life.

1. FIRST RESPONSE. In what sense is this birthday party a "Rite of Passage"?
2. How does the speaker transform these six- and seven-year-old boys into men? What is the point of doing so?
3. Comment on the appropriateness of the image of the cake in lines 14–15.
4. Why does the son's claim that "We could easily kill a two-year-old" (line 22) come as such a shock at that point in the poem?

Sylvia Plath (1932–1963)

Daddy   *1962*

You do not do, you do not do
Any more, black shoe
In which I have lived like a foot
For thirty years, poor and white,
Barely daring to breathe or Achoo.   5

Daddy, I have had to kill you.
You died before I had time —
Marble-heavy, a bag full of God,
Ghastly statue with one gray toe
Big as a Frisco seal   10

And a head in the freakish Atlantic
Where it pours bean green over blue
In the waters off beautiful Nauset.°   *Cape Cod inlet*
I used to pray to recover you.
Ach, du.°   *Oh, you*   15

In the German tongue, in the Polish Town°
Scraped flat by the roller
Of wars, wars, wars.
But the name of the town is common.
My Polack friend   20

Says there are a dozen or two.
So I never could tell where you
Put your foot, your root,
I never could talk to you.
The tongue stuck in my jaw.   25

It stuck in a barb wire snare.
Ich, ich, ich, ich,°   *I, I, I, I,*
I could hardly speak.
I thought every German was you.
And the language obscene   30

An engine, an engine
Chuffing me off like a Jew.
A Jew to Dachau, Auschwitz, Belsen.°
I began to talk like a Jew.
I think I may well be a Jew.   35

The snows of the Tyrol, the clear beer of Vienna
Are not very pure or true.
With my gypsy-ancestress and my weird luck

---

16 *Polish Town:* Refers to Otto Plath's birthplace, Granbow.   33 *Dachau . . . Belsen:* Nazi death camps in World War II.

And my Taroc° pack and my Taroc pack
I may be a bit of a Jew.   40

I have always been scared of *you*,
With your Luftwaffe,° your gobbledygoo.
And your neat mustache
And your Aryan eye, bright blue.
Panzer-man, panzer-man,° O You —   45

Not God but a swastika
So black no sky could squeak through.
Every woman adores a Fascist,
The boot in the face, the brute
Brute heart of a brute like you.   50

You stand at the blackboard, daddy,
In the picture I have of you,
A cleft in your chin instead of your foot
But no less a devil for that, no not
Any less the black man who   55

Bit my pretty red heart in two.
I was ten when they buried you.
At twenty I tried to die
And get back, back, back to you.
I thought even the bones would do   60

But they pulled me out of the sack,
And they stuck me together with glue.
And then I knew what to do.
I made a model of you,
A man in black with a Meinkampf° look   65

And a love of the rack and the screw.
And I said I do, I do.
So daddy, I'm finally through.
The black telephone's off at the root,
The voices just can't worm through.   70

If I've killed one man, I've killed two —
The vampire who said he was you
And drank my blood for a year,
Seven years, if you want to know.
Daddy, you can lie back now.   75

There's a stake in your fat black heart
And the villagers never liked you.
They are dancing and stamping on you.
They always *knew* it was you.
Daddy, daddy, you bastard, I'm through.   80

39 *Taroc:* Or *Tarot,* a pack of cards used to tell fortunes. It is said to have originated among the early Jewish Cabalists and to have been transmitted to European Gypsies during the Middle Ages.   42 *Luftwaffe:* World War II German air force.   45 *panzer-man:* A member of the panzer division of the German army in World War II, which used armored vehicles and was organized for rapid attack.   65 *Meinkampf:* An allusion to Hitler's autobiography (*My Struggle*).

CONSIDERATIONS FOR CRITICAL THINKING AND WRITING

1. FIRST RESPONSE. What do you think is the speaker's purpose in describing her father in such a fiercely negative manner?

2. Discuss the effect of the similes and metaphors used to describe the father.

3. What, if anything, has the speaker achieved in the poem's final stanza?

4. CRITICAL STRATEGIES. Read the section on biographical criticism (pp. 62–64) in Chapter 3, "Applying a Critical Strategy," and research Plath's relationship with her own father. How does this information enhance your understanding of "Daddy"?

THEODORE ROETHKE (1908–1963)

My Papa's Waltz   *1948*

The whiskey on your breath
Could make a small boy dizzy;
But I hung on like death:
Such waltzing was not easy.

We romped until the pans   5
Slid from the kitchen shelf;
My mother's countenance
Could not unfrown itself.

The hand that held my wrist
Was battered on one knuckle;   10
At every step you missed
My right ear scraped a buckle.

You beat time on my head
With a palm caked hard by dirt,
Then waltzed me off to bed   15
Still clinging to your shirt.

CONSIDERATIONS FOR CRITICAL THINKING AND WRITING

1. FIRST RESPONSE. What details characterize the father in this poem? How does the speaker's choice of words reveal his feeling about his father? Is the remembering speaker still a boy?

2. Characterize the rhythm of the poem. Does it move "like death," or is it more like a waltz? Is the rhythm regular throughout the poem? What is its effect?

3. Comment on the appropriateness of the title. Why do you suppose Roethke didn't use "My Father's Waltz"?

INDIRA SANT (B. 1914)

Household Fires   *1989*

TRANSLATED BY VINAY DHARWADKER

The daughter's job: without a murmur
to do the chores piling up around the house
until she leaves for work,
to pay her younger brother's fees,
to buy her sister ribbons,   5
to get her father's spectacles changed.
To take the others to the movies on holidays,
to keep back a little and hand over the rest
on payday.

The son's job: fresh savory snacks   10
for the whole household to eat:
to bring back the clothes from the washerman,
to clean and put away the bicycle,
to sing out of key while packing his father's lunch
at the stroke of the hour,   15
to open the door sulkily
whenever someone comes home from the movies,
to wrinkle his brow
when he puts out his hand for money
and is asked instead, "How much? For what?"   20

The younger daughter's job:
to savor the joys of shyness,
to shrink back minute by minute.
The younger son's job:
to choke all the while, grow up slowly   25
in states of wet and dry.

Four children learning in her fold,
her body drained by hardship,
what's left of her? A mass of tatters,
five tongues of flame   30
licking and licking at her on every side,
fanning and fanning the fire in her eyes
till her mind boils over,
gets burned.

CONSIDERATIONS FOR CRITICAL THINKING AND WRITING

1. FIRST RESPONSE. How does the delineation of the family members' roles
   serve to characterize the household?
2. How might the poem's title be regarded as ironic?
3. Which family member is the focus of the poem? With whom do you sympathize the most?

CATHY SONG (B. 1955)

The Youngest Daughter   *1983*

The sky has been dark
for many years.
My skin has become as damp
and pale as rice paper
and feels the way   5
mother's used to before the drying sun
parched it out there in the fields.

    Lately, when I touch myself,
My hands react as if
I had just touched something   10
hot enough to burn.
My skin, aspirin-colored,
tingles with migraine. Mother
has been massaging the left side of my face
especially in the evenings   15
when it flares up.

This morning
her breathing was graveled,
her voice gruff with affection
when I took her into the bath.   20
She was in a good humor,
making jokes about her great breasts,
floating in the milky water
like two walruses,
flaccid and whiskered around the nipples.   25
I scrubbed them with a sour taste
in my mouth, thinking:
six children and an old man
have sucked from these brown nipples.

I was almost tender   30
when I came to the blue bruises
that freckle her body,
places where she has been injecting insulin
for thirty years, ever since
I can remember. I soaped her slowly,   35
she sighed deeply, her eyes closed.

In the afternoons
when she has rested,
she prepares our ritual of tea and rice,
garnished with a shred of gingered fish,   40
a slice of pickled turnip,
a token for my white body.
We eat in the familiar silence.
She knows I am not to be trusted,

even now planning my escape.   45
As I toast to her health
with the tea she has poured,
a thousand cranes curtain the window,
fly up in a sudden breeze.

CONSIDERATIONS FOR CRITICAL THINKING AND WRITING

1. FIRST RESPONSE. Though the speaker is the youngest daughter in the family, how old do you think she is, based on the description of her in the poem?
2. "She knows I am not to be trusted, / even now planning my escape." How do these lines (44–45) reveal the nature of the relationship between mother and daughter?
3. Interpret the final four lines of the poem. Why do you think it ends with this image?

GARY SOTO (B. 1952)

Behind Grandma's House   *1985*

At ten I wanted fame. I had a comb
And two Coke bottles, a tube of Bryl-creem.
I borrowed a dog, one with
Mismatched eyes and a happy tongue,
And wanted to prove I was tough   5
In the alley, kicking over trash cans,
A dull chime of tuna cans falling.
I hurled light bulbs like grenades
And men teachers held their heads,
Fingers of blood lengthening   10
On the ground. I flicked rocks at cats,
Their goofy faces spurred with foxtails.
I kicked fences. I shooed pigeons.
I broke a branch from a flowering peach
And frightened ants with a stream of spit.   15
I said "*Chale*," "In your face," and "No way
Daddy-O" to an imaginary priest
Until grandma came into the alley,
Her apron flapping in a breeze,
Her hair mussed, and said, "Let me help you,"   20
And punched me between the eyes.

CONSIDERATIONS FOR CRITICAL THINKING AND WRITING

1. FIRST RESPONSE. What is the central irony of this poem?
2. How does the speaker characterize himself at ten?

3. Though the "grandma" appears only briefly, she seems, in a sense, fully characterized. How would you describe her? Why do you think she says, "Let me help you"?

4. In spite of the punch, would you consider this a happy family? Explain why or why not.

Mitsuye Yamada (b. 1923)

A Bedtime Story   *1976*

Once upon a time,
an old Japanese legend
goes as told
by Papa,
an old woman traveled through   5
many small villages
seeking refuge
for the night.
Each door opened
a sliver   10
in answer to her knock
then closed.
Unable to walk
any further
she wearily climbed a hill   15
found a clearing
and there lay down to rest
a few moments to catch
her breath.

The village town below   20
lay asleep except
for a few starlike lights.
Suddenly the clouds opened
and a full moon came into view
over the town.   25

The old woman sat up
turned toward
the village town
and in supplication
called out   30
Thank you people
of the village,
If it had not been for your
kindness
in refusing me a bed   35
for the night
these humble eyes would never
have seen this
memorable sight.

Papa paused, I waited.   40
In the comfort of our
hilltop home in Seattle
overlooking the valley,
I shouted
"That's the *end?*"   45

CONSIDERATIONS FOR CRITICAL THINKING AND WRITING

1. FIRST RESPONSE. What is it that the speaker doesn't understand about her father's story?
2. Why is the final stanza especially ironic?
3. Contrast the attitudes and expectations of the speaker and the father. To what extent do cultural and age differences explain the gap between them?

DRAMA

LORRAINE HANSBERRY (1930–1965)

Lorraine Hansberry, the youngest of four children raised by African American parents who migrated from the South, was born in Chicago, Illinois. After graduating from the segregated public schools of Chicago, Hansberry studied at the University of Wisconsin for two years but in 1950 moved to New York City. There she attended classes at the New School for Social Research and wrote for *Freedom,* a radical Harlem periodical published by Paul Robeson. During the course of her brief career, ended by cancer when she was only thirty-four years old, Hansberry remained a committed civil rights activist. She began writing *A Raisin in the Sun* in 1956. It was produced on Broadway in 1959, bringing her international recognition. At the age of twenty-eight, Hansberry was the first black female playwright to be produced on Broadway, and the play was awarded the New York Drama Critics' Circle Award for Best Play of the Year in competition with such successful dramatists as Eugene O'Neill and Tennessee Williams. *A Raisin in the Sun* has been translated into more than thirty languages and produced around the world. Among Hansberry's other writings are *The Movement: Documentary of a Struggle for Equality* (1964); *The Sign in Sidney Brustein's Window* (1965), a play in production at the time of her death; *To Be Young, Gifted and Black* (1969), a play published posthumously; and *Lorraine Hansberry: The Collected Last Plays* (1983).

In *A Raisin in the Sun,* Hansberry does not flinch from the tough realities that confronted African Americans contemporary to her. The following poem by Langston Hughes (1902–1967) is the source for the play's title and serves as a fitting introduction to many of the issues dramatized in *A Raisin in the Sun.*

Harlem (A Dream Deferred)

What happens to a dream deferred?

Does it dry up
Like a raisin in the sun?
Or fester like a sore —
And then run?
Does it stink like rotten meat?   5
Or crust and sugar over —
Like a syrupy sweet?

Maybe it just sags
Like a heavy load.

Or does it explode?   10

— Langston Hughes

A Raisin in the Sun   *1959*

CHARACTERS (IN ORDER OF APPEARANCE)

Ruth Younger
Travis Younger
Walter Lee Younger, brother
Beneatha Younger
Lena Younger, Mama
Joseph Asagai
George Murchison
Mrs. Johnson
Karl Lindner
Bobo
Moving Men

The action of the play is set in Chicago's Southside, sometime between World War II and the present.

ACT I

SCENE I. *[Friday morning.]*

The Younger living room would be a comfortable and well-ordered room if it were not for a number of indestructible contradictions to this state of being. Its furnishings are typical and undistinguished and their primary feature now is that they have clearly had to accommodate the living of too many people for too many years — and they are tired. Still, we can see that at some time, a time probably no *longer remembered by the family (except perhaps for Mama), the furnishings of this room were actually selected with care and love and even hope—and brought to this apartment and arranged with taste and pride.*

That was a long time ago. Now the once loved pattern of the couch upholstery has to fight to show itself from under acres of crocheted doilies and couch covers which have themselves finally come to be more important than the upholstery. And here a table or a chair has been moved to disguise the worn places in the carpet; but the carpet has fought back by showing its weariness, with depressing uniformity, elsewhere on its surface.

Weariness has, in fact, won in this room. Everything has been polished, washed, sat on, used, scrubbed too often. All pretenses but living itself have long since vanished from the very atmosphere of this room.

Moreover, a section of this room, for it is not really a room unto itself, though the landlord's lease would make it seem so, slopes backward to provide a small kitchen area, where the family prepares the meals that are eaten in the living room proper, which must also serve as dining room. The single window that has been provided for these "two" rooms is located in this kitchen area. The sole natural light the family may enjoy in the course of a day is only that which fights its way through this little window.

At left, a door leads to a bedroom which is shared by Mama and her daughter, Beneatha. At right, opposite, is a second room (which in the beginning of the life of this apartment was probably a breakfast room) which serves as a bedroom for Walter and his wife, Ruth.

Time: Sometime between World War II and the present.

Place: Chicago's Southside.

At Rise: It is morning dark in the living room. Travis is asleep on the make-down bed at center. An alarm clock sounds from within the bedroom at right, and presently Ruth enters from that room and closes the door behind her. She crosses sleepily toward the window. As she passes her sleeping son she reaches down and shakes him a little. At the window she raises the shade and a dusky Southside morning light comes in feebly. She fills a pot with water and puts it on to boil. She calls to the boy, between yawns, in a slightly muffled voice.

Ruth is about thirty. We can see that she was a pretty girl, even exceptionally so, but now it is apparent that life has been little that she expected, and disappointment has already begun to hang in her face. In a few years, before thirty-five even, she will be known among her people as a "settled woman."

She crosses to her son and gives him a good, final, rousing shake.

Ruth: Come on now, boy, it's seven thirty! *(Her son sits up at last, in a stupor of sleepiness.)* I say hurry up, Travis! You ain't the only person in the world got to use a bathroom! *(The child, a sturdy, handsome little boy of ten or eleven, drags himself out of the bed and almost blindly takes his towels and "today's clothes" from drawers and a closet and goes out to the bathroom, which is in an outside hall and which is shared by another family or families on the same floor. Ruth crosses to the bedroom door at right and opens it and calls in to her husband.)* Walter Lee! . . . It's after seven thirty! Lemme see you do some waking up in there now! *(She waits.)* You better get up from there, man! It's after seven thirty I tell you. *(She waits again.)* All right, you just go ahead and lay there and next thing you know Travis be finished and Mr. Johnson'll be in there and you'll be fussing and cussing round here like a madman! And be late too! *(She waits, at the end of patience.)* Walter Lee — it's time for you to GET UP!

She waits another second and then starts to go into the bedroom, but is apparently satisfied that her husband has begun to get up. She stops, pulls the door to, and returns to the kitchen area. She wipes her face with a moist cloth and runs her fingers through her sleep-disheveled hair in a vain effort and ties an apron around her housecoat. The bedroom door at right opens and her husband stands in the doorway in his pajamas, which are rumpled and mismated. He is a lean, intense young man in his middle thirties, inclined to quick nervous movements and erratic speech habits — and always in his voice there is a quality of indictment.

Walter: Is he out yet?

Ruth: What you mean *out?* He ain't hardly got in there good yet.

Walter (wandering in, still more oriented to sleep than to a new day): Well, what was you doing all that yelling for if I can't even get in there yet? *(Stopping and thinking.)* Check coming today?

Ruth: They *said* Saturday and this is just Friday and I hopes to God you ain't going to get up here first thing this morning and start talking to me 'bout no money — 'cause I 'bout don't want to hear it.

Walter: Something the matter with you this morning?

Ruth: No — I'm just sleepy as the devil. What kind of eggs you want?

Walter: Not scrambled. *(Ruth starts to scramble eggs.)* Paper come? *(Ruth points impatiently to the rolled up* Tribune *on the table, and he gets it and spreads it out and vaguely reads the front page.)* Set off another bomb yesterday.

Ruth (maximum indifference): Did they?

Walter (looking up): What's the matter with you?

Ruth: Ain't nothing the matter with me. And don't keep asking me that this morning.

Walter: Ain't nobody bothering you. *(Reading the news of the day absently again.)* Say Colonel McCormick is sick.

Ruth (affecting tea-party interest): Is he now? Poor thing.

Walter (sighing and looking at his watch): Oh, me. *(He waits.)* Now what is that boy doing in that bathroom all this time? He just going to have to start getting up earlier. I can't be being late to work on account of him fooling around in there.

Ruth (turning on him): Oh, no he ain't going to be getting up no earlier no such thing! It ain't his fault that he can't get to bed no earlier nights 'cause he got a bunch of crazy good-for-nothing clowns sitting up running their mouths in what is supposed to be his bedroom after ten o'clock at night . . .

Walter: That's what you mad about, ain't it? The things I want to talk about with my friends just couldn't be important in your mind, could they?

He rises and finds a cigarette in her handbag on the table and crosses to the little window and looks out, smoking and deeply enjoying this first one.

Ruth (almost matter of factly, a complaint too automatic to deserve emphasis): Why you always got to smoke before you eat in the morning?

Walter (at the window): Just look at 'em down there . . . Running and racing to work . . . *(He turns and faces his wife and watches her a moment at the stove, and then, suddenly.)* You look young this morning, baby.

Ruth (indifferently): Yeah?

Walter: Just for a second—stirring them eggs. Just for a second it was—you looked real young again. (He reaches for her; she crosses away. Then, drily.) It's gone now—you look like yourself again!

Ruth: Man, if you don't shut up and leave me alone.

Walter (looking out to the street again): First thing a man ought to learn in life is not to make love to no colored woman first thing in the morning. You all some eeeevil people at eight o'clock in the morning.

Travis appears in the hall doorway, almost fully dressed and quite wide awake now, his towels and pajamas across his shoulders. He opens the door and signals for his father to make the bathroom in a hurry.

Travis (watching the bathroom): Daddy, come on!

Walter gets his bathroom utensils and flies out to the bathroom.

Ruth: Sit down and have your breakfast, Travis.

Travis: Mama, this is Friday. (Gleefully.) Check coming tomorrow, huh?

Ruth: You get your mind off money and eat your breakfast.

Travis (eating): This is the morning we supposed to bring the fifty cents to school.

Ruth: Well, I ain't got no fifty cents this morning.

Travis: Teacher say we have to.

Ruth: I don't care what teacher say. I ain't got it. Eat your breakfast, Travis.

Travis: I *am* eating.

Ruth: Hush up now and just eat!

The boy gives her an exasperated look for her lack of understanding, and eats grudgingly.

Travis: You think Grandmama would have it?

Ruth: No! And I want you to stop asking your grandmother for money, you hear me?

Travis (outraged): Gaaaleee! I don't ask her, she just gimme it sometimes!

Ruth: Travis Willard Younger—I got too much on me this morning to be—

Travis: Maybe Daddy—

Ruth: Travis!

The boy hushes abruptly. They are both quiet and tense for several seconds.

Travis (presently): Could I maybe go carry some groceries in front of the super-market for a little while after school then?

Ruth: Just hush, I said. (Travis jabs his spoon into his cereal bowl viciously, and rests his head in anger upon his fists.) If you through eating, you can get over there and make up your bed.

The boy obeys stiffly and crosses the room, almost mechanically, to the bed and more or less folds the bedding into a heap, then angrily gets his books and cap.

Travis (sulking and standing apart from her unnaturally): I'm gone.

Ruth (looking up from the stove to inspect him automatically): Come here. (He crosses to her and she studies his head.) If you don't take this comb and fix this here head, you better! (Travis puts down his books with a great sigh of oppression, and crosses to the mirror. His mother mutters under her breath about his "slubborn-ness.") 'Bout to march out of here with that head looking just like chickens slept in it! I just don't know where you get your slubborn ways . . . And get your jacket, too. Looks chilly out this morning.

Travis (with conspicuously brushed hair and jacket): I'm gone.

Ruth: Get carfare and milk money — *(Waving one finger.)* — and not a single penny for no caps, you hear me?

Travis (with sullen politeness): Yes'm.

He turns in outrage to leave. His mother watches after him as in his frustration he approaches the door almost comically. When she speaks to him, her voice has become a very gentle tease.

Ruth (mocking; as she thinks he would say it): Oh, Mama makes me so mad sometimes, I don't know what to do! *(She waits and continues to his back as he stands stock-still in front of the door.)* I wouldn't kiss that woman good-bye for nothing in this world this morning! *(The boy finally turns around and rolls his eyes at her, knowing the mood has changed and he is vindicated; he does not, however, move toward her yet.)* Not for nothing in this world! *(She finally laughs aloud at him and holds out her arms to him and we see that it is a way between them, very old and practiced. He crosses to her and allows her to embrace him warmly but keeps his face fixed with masculine rigidity. She holds him back from her presently and looks at him and runs her fingers over the features of his face. With utter gentleness —.)* Now — whose little old angry man are you?

Travis (the masculinity and gruffness start to fade at last): Aw gaalee — Mama . . .

Ruth (mimicking): Aw — gaaaaalleeeee, Mama! *(She pushes him, with rough playfulness and finality, toward the door.)* Get on out of here or you going to be late.

Travis (in the face of love, new aggressiveness): Mama, could I *please* go carry groceries?

Ruth: Honey, it's starting to get so cold evenings.

Walter (coming in from the bathroom and drawing a make-believe gun from a make-believe holster and shooting at his son): What is it he wants to do?

Ruth: Go carry groceries after school at the supermarket.

Walter: Well, let him go . . .

Travis (quickly, to the ally): I have to — she won't gimme the fifty cents . . .

Walter (to his wife only): Why not?

Ruth (simply, and with flavor): 'Cause we don't have it.

Walter (to Ruth only): What you tell the boy things like that for? *(Reaching down into his pants with a rather important gesture.)* Here, son —

He hands the boy the coin, but his eyes are directed to his wife's. Travis takes the money happily.

Travis: Thanks, Daddy.

He starts out. Ruth watches both of them with murder in her eyes. Walter stands and stares back at her with defiance, and suddenly reaches into his pocket again on an afterthought.

Walter (without even looking at his son, still staring hard at his wife): In fact, here's another fifty cents . . . Buy yourself some fruit today — or take a taxicab to school or something!

Travis: Whoopee —

He leaps up and clasps his father around the middle with his legs, and they face each other in mutual appreciation; slowly Walter Lee peeks around the boy to catch the violent rays from his wife's eyes and draws his head back as if shot.

Walter: You better get down now — and get to school, man.

Travis (at the door): O.K. Good-bye.

>   He exits.

Walter (after him, pointing with pride): That's *my* boy. *(She looks at him in disgust and turns back to her work.)* You know what I was thinking 'bout in the bathroom this morning?

Ruth: No.

Walter: How come you always try to be so pleasant!

Ruth: What is there to be pleasant 'bout!

Walter: You want to know what I was thinking 'bout in the bathroom or not!

Ruth: I know what you thinking 'bout.

Walter (ignoring her): 'Bout what me and Willy Harris was talking about last night.

Ruth (immediately — a refrain): Willy Harris is a good-for-nothing loudmouth.

Walter: Anybody who talks to me has got to be a good-for-nothing loudmouth, ain't he? And what you know about who is just a good-for-nothing loud-mouth? Charlie Atkins was just a "good-for-nothing loudmouth" too, wasn't he! When he wanted me to go in the dry-cleaning business with him. And now — he's grossing a hundred thousand a year. A hundred thousand dollars a year! You still call *him* a loudmouth!

Ruth (bitterly): Oh, Walter Lee . . .

>   She folds her head on her arms over the table.

Walter (rising and coming to her and standing over her): You tired, ain't you? Tired of everything. Me, the boy, the way we live — this beat-up hole — every-thing. Ain't you? *(She doesn't look up, doesn't answer.)* So tired — moaning and groaning all the time, but you wouldn't do nothing to help, would you? You couldn't be on my side that long for nothing, could you?

Ruth: Walter, please leave me alone.

Walter: A man needs for a woman to back him up . . .

Ruth: Walter —

Walter: Mama would listen to you. You know she listen to you more than she do me and Bennie. She think more of you. All you have to do is just sit down with her when you drinking your coffee one morning and talking 'bout things like you do and — *(He sits down beside her and demonstrates graph-ically what he thinks her methods and tone should be.)* — you just sip your coffee, see, and say easy like that you been thinking 'bout that deal Walter Lee is so interested in, 'bout the store and all, and sip some more coffee, like what you saying ain't really that important to you — And the next thing you know, she be listening good and asking you questions and when I come home — I can tell her the details. This ain't no fly-by-night proposi-tion, baby. I mean we figured it out, me and Willy and Bobo.

Ruth (with a frown): Bobo?

Walter: Yeah. You see, this little liquor store we got in mind cost seventy-five thousand and we figured the initial investment on the place be 'bout thirty thousand, see. That be ten thousand each. Course, there's a couple of hundred you got to pay so's you don't spend your life just waiting for them clowns to let your license get approved —

Ruth: You mean graft?

Walter (frowning impatiently): Don't call it that. See there, that just goes to show you what women understand about the world. Baby, don't *nothing* happen for you in the world 'less you pay *somebody* off!

Ruth: Walter, leave me alone! *(She raises her head and stares at him vigorously — then says, more quietly.)* Eat your eggs, they gonna be cold.

Walter (straightening up from her and looking off): That's it. There you are. Man say to his woman: I got me a dream. His woman say: Eat your eggs. *(Sadly, but gaining in power.)* Man say: I got to take hold of this here world, baby! And a woman will say: Eat your eggs and go to work. *(Passionately now.)* Man say: I got to change my life, I'm choking to death, baby! And his woman say — *(In utter anguish as he brings his fists down on his thighs.)* — Your eggs is getting cold!

Ruth (softly): Walter, that ain't none of our money.

Walter (not listening at all or even looking at her): This morning, I was lookin' in the mirror and thinking about it . . . I'm thirty-five years old; I been married eleven years and I got a boy who sleeps in the living room — *(Very, very quietly.)* — and all I got to give him is stories about how rich white people live . . .

Ruth: Eat your eggs, Walter.

Walter (slams the table and jumps up): — DAMN MY EGGS — DAMN ALL THE EGGS THAT EVER WAS!

Ruth: Then go to work.

Walter (looking up at her): See — I'm trying to talk to you 'bout myself — *(Shaking his head with the repetition.)* — and all you can say is eat them eggs and go to work.

Ruth (wearily): Honey, you never say nothing new. I listen to you every day, every night and every morning, and you never say nothing new. *(Shrugging.)* So you would rather *be* Mr. Arnold than be his chauffeur. So — I would *rather* be living in Buckingham Palace.

Walter: That is just what is wrong with the colored woman in this world . . . Don't understand about building their men up and making 'em feel like they somebody. Like they can do something.

Ruth (drily, but to hurt): There *are* colored men who do things.

Walter: No thanks to the colored woman.

Ruth: Well, being a colored woman, I guess I can't help myself none.

She rises and gets the ironing board and sets it up and attacks a huge pile of rough-dried clothes, sprinkling them in preparation for the ironing and then rolling them into tight fat balls.

Walter (mumbling): We one group of men tied to a race of women with small minds!

His sister Beneatha enters. She is about twenty, as slim and intense as her brother. She is not as pretty as her sister-in-law, but her lean, almost intellectual face has a handsomeness of its own. She wears a bright-red flannel nightie, and her thick hair stands wildly about her head. Her speech is a mixture of many things; it is different from the rest of the family's insofar as education has permeated her sense of English — and perhaps the Midwest rather than the South has finally — at last — won out in her inflection; but not altogether, because over all of it is a soft slurring and transformed use of vowels which is the decided influence of the Southside. She passes through the room without looking at either Ruth or Walter and goes to the outside door and looks, a little blindly, out to the bathroom. She sees that it has been lost to the Johnsons. She closes the door with a sleepy vengeance and crosses to the table and sits down a little defeated.

Beneatha: I am going to start timing those people.

Walter: You should get up earlier.

Beneatha (her face in her hands. She is still fighting the urge to go back to bed): Really—would you suggest dawn? Where's the paper?

Walter (pushing the paper across the table to her as he studies her almost clinically, as though he has never seen her before): You a horrible-looking chick at this hour.

Beneatha (drily): Good morning, everybody.

Walter (senselessly): How is school coming?

Beneatha (in the same spirit): Lovely. Lovely. And you know, biology is the greatest. *(Looking up at him.)* I dissected something that looked just like you yesterday.

Walter: I just wondered if you've made up your mind and everything.

Beneatha (gaining in sharpness and impatience): And what did I answer yesterday morning—and the day before that?

Ruth (from the ironing board, like someone disinterested and old): Don't be so nasty, Bennie.

Beneatha (still to her brother): And the day before that and the day before that!

Walter (defensively): I'm interested in you. Something wrong with that? Ain't many girls who decide—

Walter and Beneatha (in unison): —"to be a doctor."

Silence.

Walter: Have we figured out yet just exactly how much medical school is going to cost?

Ruth: Walter Lee, why don't you leave that girl alone and get out of here to work?

Beneatha (exits to the bathroom and bangs on the door): Come on out of there, please!

She comes back into the room.

Walter (looking at his sister intently): You know the check is coming tomorrow.

Beneatha (turning on him with a sharpness all her own): That money belongs to Mama, Walter, and it's for her to decide how she wants to use it. I don't care if she wants to buy a house or a rocket ship or just nail it up somewhere and look at it. It's hers. Not ours—*hers.*

Walter (bitterly): Now ain't that fine! You just got your mother's interest at heart, ain't you, girl? You such a nice girl—but if Mama got that money she can always take a few thousand and help you through school too—can't she?

Beneatha: I have never asked anyone around here to do anything for me!

Walter: No! And the line between asking and just accepting when the time comes is big and wide—ain't it!

Beneatha (with fury): What do you want from me, Brother—that I quit school or just drop dead, which!

Walter: I don't want nothing but for you to stop acting holy 'round here. Me and Ruth done made some sacrifices for you—why can't you do something for the family?

Ruth: Walter, don't be dragging me in it.

Walter: You are in it—Don't you get up and go work in somebody's kitchen for the last three years to help put clothes on her back?

Ruth: Oh, Walter—that's not fair . . .

Walter: It ain't that nobody expects you to get on your knees and say thank you, Brother; thank you, Ruth; thank you, Mama—and thank you, Travis, for wearing the same pair of shoes for two semesters—

Beneatha (dropping to her knees): Well—I *do*—all right?—thank everybody! And forgive me for ever wanting to be anything at all! *(Pursuing him on her knees across the floor.)* FORGIVE ME, FORGIVE ME, FORGIVE ME!

Ruth: Please stop it! Your mama'll hear you.

Walter: Who the hell told you you had to be a doctor? If you so crazy 'bout messing 'round with sick people—then go be a nurse like other women—or just get married and be quiet . . .

Beneatha: Well—you finally got it said . . . It took you three years but you finally got it said. Walter, give up; leave me alone—it's Mama's money.

Walter: He was my father, too!

Beneatha: So what? He was mine, too—and Travis' grandfather—but the insurance money belongs to Mama. Picking on me is not going to make her give it to you to invest in any liquor stores—*(Under breath, dropping into a chair.)*—and I for one say, God bless Mama for that!

Walter (to Ruth): See—did you hear? Did you hear!

Ruth: Honey, please go to work.

Walter: Nobody in this house is ever going to understand me.

Beneatha: Because you're a nut.

Walter: Who's a nut?

Beneatha: You—you are a nut. Thee is mad, boy.

Walter (looking at his wife and his sister from the door, very sadly): The world's most backward race of people, and that's a fact.

Beneatha (turning slowly in her chair): And then there are all those prophets who would lead us out of the wilderness—*(Walter slams out of the house.)*—into the swamps!

Ruth: Bennie, why you always gotta be pickin' on your brother? Can't you be a little sweeter sometimes? *(Door opens. Walter walks in. He fumbles with his cap, starts to speak, clears throat, looks everywhere but at Ruth. Finally:)*

Walter (to Ruth): I need some money for carfare.

Ruth (looks at him, then warms; teasing, but tenderly): Fifty cents? *(She goes to her bag and gets money.)* Here—take a taxi!

Walter exits. Mama enters. She is a woman in her early sixties, full-bodied and strong. She is one of those women of a certain grace and beauty who wear it so unobtrusively that it takes a while to notice. Her dark-brown face is surrounded by the total whiteness of her hair, and, being a woman who has adjusted to many things in life and overcome many more, her face is full of strength. She has, we can see, wit and faith of a kind that keep her eyes lit and full of interest and expectancy. She is, in a word, a beautiful woman. Her bearing is perhaps most like the noble bearing of the women of the Hereros of Southwest Africa—rather as if she imagines that as she walks she still bears a basket or a vessel upon her head. Her speech, on the other hand, is as careless as her carriage is precise — she is inclined to slur every- thing — but her voice is perhaps not so much quiet as simply soft.

Mama: Who that 'round here slamming doors at this hour?

> *She crosses through the room, goes to the window, opens it, and brings in a feeble little plant growing doggedly in a small pot on the window sill. She feels the dirt and puts it back out.*

Ruth: That was Walter Lee. He and Bennie was at it again.

Mama: My children and they tempers. Lord, if this little old plant don't get more sun than it's been getting it ain't never going to see spring again. *(She turns from the window.)* What's the matter with you this morning, Ruth? You looks right peaked. You aiming to iron all them things? Leave some for me. I'll get to 'em this afternoon. Bennie honey, it's too drafty for you to be sitting 'round half dressed. Where's your robe?

Beneatha: In the cleaners.

Mama: Well, go get mine and put it on.

Beneatha: I'm not cold, Mama, honest.

Mama: I know — but you so thin . . .

Beneatha (irritably): Mama, I'm not cold.

Mama (seeing the make-down bed as Travis has left it): Lord have mercy, look at that poor bed. Bless his heart — he tries, don't he?

> *She moves to the bed Travis has sloppily made up.*

Ruth: No — he don't half try at all 'cause he knows you going to come along behind him and fix everything. That's just how come he don't know how to do nothing right now — you done spoiled that boy so.

Mama (folding bedding): Well — he's a little boy. Ain't supposed to know 'bout housekeeping. My baby, that's what he is. What you fix for his breakfast this morning?

Ruth (angrily): I feed my son, Lena!

Mama: I ain't meddling — *(Under breath; busy-bodyish.)* I just noticed all last week he had cold cereal, and when it starts getting this chilly in the fall a child ought to have some hot grits or something when he goes out in the cold —

Ruth (furious): I gave him hot oats — is that all right!

Mama: I ain't meddling. *(Pause.)* Put a lot of nice butter on it? *(Ruth shoots her an angry look and does not reply.)* He likes lots of butter.

Ruth (exasperated): Lena —

Mama (to Beneatha. Mama is inclined to wander conversationally sometimes): What was you and your brother fussing 'bout this morning?

Beneatha: It's not important, Mama.

> *She gets up and goes to look out at the bathroom, which is apparently free, and she picks up her towels and rushes out.*

Mama: What was they fighting about?

Ruth: Now you know as well as I do.

Mama (shaking her head): Brother still worrying hisself sick about that money?

Ruth: You know he is.

Mama: You had breakfast?

Ruth: Some coffee.

Mama: Girl, you better start eating and looking after yourself better. You almost thin as Travis.

Ruth: Lena —

Mama: Un-hunh?

Ruth: What are you going to do with it?

Mama: Now don't you start, child. It's too early in the morning to be talking about money. It ain't Christian.

Ruth: It's just that he got his heart set on that store —

Mama: You mean that liquor store that Willy Harris want him to invest in?

Ruth: Yes —

Mama: We ain't no business people, Ruth. We just plain working folks.

Ruth: Ain't nobody business people till they go into business. Walter Lee say colored people ain't never going to start getting ahead till they start gambling on some different kinds of things in the world — investments and things.

Mama: What done got into you, girl? Walter Lee done finally sold you on investing.

Ruth: No. Mama, something is happening between Walter and me. I don't know what it is — but he needs something — something I can't give him any more. He needs this chance, Lena.

Mama (frowning deeply): But liquor, honey —

Ruth: Well — like Walter say — I spec people going to always be drinking themselves some liquor.

Mama: Well — whether they drinks it or not ain't none of my business. But whether I go into business selling it to 'em *is,* and I don't want that on my ledger this late in life. *(Stopping suddenly and studying her daughter-in-law.)* Ruth Younger, what's the matter with you today? You look like you could fall over right there.

Ruth: I'm tired.

Mama: Then you better stay home from work today.

Ruth: I can't stay home. She'd be calling up the agency and screaming at them, "My girl didn't come in today — send me somebody! My girl didn't come in!" Oh, she just have a fit . . .

Mama: Well, let her have it. I'll just call her up and say you got the flu —

Ruth (laughing): Why the flu?

Mama: 'Cause it sounds respectable to 'em. Something white people get, too. They know 'bout the flu. Otherwise they think you been cut up or something when you tell 'em you sick.

Ruth: I got to go in. We need the money.

Mama: Somebody would of thought my children done all but starved to death the way they talk about money here late. Child, we got a great big old check coming tomorrow.

Ruth (sincerely, but also self-righteously): Now that's your money. It ain't got nothing to do with me. We all feel like that — Walter and Bennie and me — even Travis.

Mama (thoughtfully, and suddenly very far away): Ten thousand dollars —

Ruth: Sure is wonderful.

Mama: Ten thousand dollars.

Ruth: You know what you should do, Miss Lena? You should take yourself a trip somewhere. To Europe or South America or someplace —

Mama (throwing up her hands at the thought): Oh, child!

Ruth: I'm serious. Just pack up and leave! Go on away and enjoy yourself some. Forget about the family and have yourself a ball for once in your life —

Mama (drily): You sound like I'm just about ready to die. Who'd go with me? What I look like wandering 'round Europe by myself?

Ruth: Shoot — these here rich white women do it all the time. They don't think nothing of packing up they suitcases and piling on one of them big steamships and — swoosh! — they gone, child.

Mama: Something always told me I wasn't no rich white woman.

Ruth: Well — what are you going to do with it then?

Mama: I ain't rightly decided. *(Thinking. She speaks now with emphasis.)* Some of it got to be put away for Beneatha and her schoolin' — and ain't nothing going to touch that part of it. Nothing. *(She waits several seconds, trying to make up her mind about something, and looks at Ruth a little tentatively before going on.)* Been thinking that we maybe could meet the notes on a little old two-story somewhere, with a yard where Travis could play in the summertime, if we use part of the insurance for a down payment and everybody kind of pitch in. I could maybe take on a little day work again, few days a week —

Ruth (studying her mother-in-law furtively and concentrating on her ironing, anxious to encourage without seeming to): Well, Lord knows, we've put enough rent into this here rat trap to pay for four houses by now . . .

Mama (looking up at the words "rat trap" and then looking around and leaning back and sighing — in a suddenly reflective mood —): "Rat trap" — yes, that's all it is. *(Smiling.)* I remember just as well the day me and Big Walter moved in here. Hadn't been married but two weeks and wasn't planning on living here no more than a year. *(She shakes her head at the dissolved dream.)* We was going to set away, little by little, don't you know, and buy a little place out in Morgan Park. We had even picked out the house. *(Chuckling a little.)* Looks right dumpy today. But Lord, child, you should know all the dreams I had 'bout buying that house and fixing it up and making me a little garden in the back — *(She waits and stops smiling.)* And didn't none of it happen.

Dropping her hands in a futile gesture.

Ruth (keeps her head down, ironing): Yes, life can be a barrel of disappointments, sometimes.

Mama: Honey, Big Walter would come in here some nights back then and slump down on that couch there and just look at the rug, and look at me and look at the rug and then back at me — and I'd know he was down then . . . really down. *(After a second very long and thoughtful pause; she is seeing back to times that only she can see.)* And then, Lord, when I lost that baby — little Claude — I almost thought I was going to lose Big Walter too. Oh, that man grieved hisself! He was one man to love his children.

Ruth: Ain't nothin' can tear at you like losin' your baby.

Mama: I guess that's how come that man finally worked hisself to death like he done. Like he was fighting his own war with this here world that took his baby from him.

Ruth: He sure was a fine man, all right. I always liked Mr. Younger.

Mama: Crazy 'bout his children! God knows there was plenty wrong with Walter Younger — hard-headed, mean, kind of wild with women — plenty wrong with him. But he sure loved his children. Always wanted them to have something—be something. That's where Brother gets all these notions, I reckon. Big Walter used to say, he'd get right wet in the eyes sometimes, lean his head back with the water standing in his eyes and say, "Seem like God didn't see fit to give the black man nothing but dreams—but He did give us children to make them dreams seem worthwhile." *(She smiles.)* He could talk like that, don't you know.

Ruth: Yes, he sure could. He was a good man, Mr. Younger.

Mama: Yes, a fine man—just couldn't never catch up with his dreams, that's all.

Beneatha comes in, brushing her hair and looking up to the ceiling, where the sound of a vacuum cleaner has started up.

Beneatha: What could be so dirty on that woman's rugs that she has to vacuum them every single day?

Ruth: I wish certain young women 'round here who I could name would take inspiration about certain rugs in a certain apartment I could also mention.

Beneatha (shrugging): How much cleaning can a house need, for Christ's sakes.

Mama (not liking the Lord's name used thus): Bennie!

Ruth: Just listen to her—just listen!

Beneatha: Oh, God!

Mama: If you use the Lord's name just one more time—

Beneatha (a bit of a whine): Oh, Mama—

Ruth: Fresh—just fresh as salt, this girl!

Beneatha (drily): Well—if the salt loses its savor—

Mama: Now that will do. I just ain't going to have you 'round here reciting the scriptures in vain—you hear me?

Beneatha: How did I manage to get on everybody's wrong side by just walking into a room?

Ruth: If you weren't so fresh—

Beneatha: Ruth, I'm twenty years old.

Mama: What time you be home from school today?

Beneatha: Kind of late. *(With enthusiasm.)* Madeline is going to start my guitar lessons today.

Mama and Ruth look up with the same expression.

Mama: Your *what* kind of lessons?

Beneatha: Guitar.

Ruth: Oh, Father!

Mama: How come you done taken it in your mind to learn to play the guitar?

Beneatha: I just want to, that's all.

Mama (smiling): Lord, child, don't you know what to do with yourself? How long it going to be before you get tired of this now—like you got tired of that little play-acting group you joined last year? *(Looking at Ruth.)* And what was it the year before that?

Ruth: The horseback-riding club for which she bought that fifty-five-dollar riding habit that's been hanging in the closet ever since!

Mama (to Beneatha): Why you got to flit so from one thing to another, baby?

Beneatha (sharply): I just want to learn to play the guitar. Is there anything wrong with that?

Mama: Ain't nobody trying to stop you. I just wonders sometimes why you has to flit so from one thing to another all the time. You ain't never done nothing with all that camera equipment you brought home —

Beneatha: I don't flit! I — I experiment with different forms of expression —

Ruth: Like riding a horse?

Beneatha: — People have to express themselves one way or another.

Mama: What is it you want to express?

Beneatha (angrily): Me! *(Mama and Ruth look at each other and burst into raucous laughter.)* Don't worry — I don't expect you to understand.

Mama (to change the subject): Who you going out with tomorrow night?

Beneatha (with displeasure): George Murchison again.

Mama (pleased): Oh — you getting a little sweet on him?

Ruth: You ask me, this child ain't sweet on nobody but herself — *(Under breath.)* Express herself!

> They laugh.

Beneatha: Oh — I like George all right, Mama. I mean I like him enough to go out with him and stuff, but —

Ruth (for devilment): What does *and stuff* mean?

Beneatha: Mind your own business.

Mama: Stop picking at her now, Ruth. *(She chuckles — then a suspicious sudden look at her daughter as she turns in her chair for emphasis.)* What DOES it mean?

Beneatha (wearily): Oh, I just mean I couldn't ever really be serious about George. He's — he's so shallow.

Ruth: Shallow — what do you mean he's shallow? He's *rich!*

Mama: Hush, Ruth.

Beneatha: I know he's rich. He knows he's rich, too.

Ruth: Well — what other qualities a man got to have to satisfy you, little girl?

Beneatha: You wouldn't even begin to understand. Anybody who married Walter could not possibly understand.

Mama (outraged): What kind of way is that to talk about your brother?

Beneatha: Brother is a flip — let's face it.

Mama (to Ruth, helplessly): What's a flip?

Ruth (glad to add kindling): She's saying he's crazy.

Beneatha: Not crazy. Brother isn't really crazy yet — he — he's an elaborate neurotic.

Mama: Hush your mouth!

Beneatha: As for George. Well. George looks good — he's got a beautiful car and he takes me to nice places and, as my sister-in-law says, he is probably the richest boy I will ever get to know and I even like him sometimes — but if the Youngers are sitting around waiting to see if their little Bennie is going to tie up the family with the Murchisons, they are wasting their time.

Ruth: You mean you wouldn't marry George Murchison if he asked you someday? That pretty, rich thing? Honey, I knew you was odd —

Beneatha: No I would not marry him if all I felt for him was what I feel now. Besides, George's family wouldn't really like it.

Mama: Why not?

Beneatha: Oh, Mama — The Murchisons are honest-to-God-real-*live*-rich colored people, and the only people in the world who are more snobbish than

rich white people are rich colored people. I thought everybody knew that.
I've met Mrs. Murchison. She's a scene!

Mama: You must not dislike people 'cause they well off, honey.

Beneatha: Why not? It makes just as much sense as disliking people 'cause they
are poor, and lots of people do that.

Ruth (a wisdom-of-the-ages manner. To Mama): Well, she'll get over some of this—

Beneatha: Get over it? What are you talking about, Ruth? Listen, I'm going to
be a doctor. I'm not worried about who I'm going to marry yet—if I ever
get married.

Mama and Ruth: If!

Mama: Now, Bennie—

Beneatha: Oh, I probably will . . . but first I'm going to be a doctor, and George,
for one, still thinks that's pretty funny. I couldn't be bothered with that. I
am going to be a doctor and everybody around here better understand
that!

Mama (kindly): 'Course you going to be a doctor, honey, God willing.

Beneatha (drily): God hasn't got a thing to do with it.

Mama: Beneatha—that just wasn't necessary.

Beneatha: Well—neither is God. I get sick of hearing about God.

Mama: Beneatha!

Beneatha: I mean it! I'm just tired of hearing about God all the time. What has
He got to do with anything? Does He pay tuition?

Mama: You 'bout to get your fresh little jaw slapped!

Ruth: That's just what she needs, all right!

Beneatha: Why? Why can't I say what I want to around here, like everybody else?

Mama: It don't sound nice for a young girl to say things like that—you wasn't
brought up that way. Me and your father went to trouble to get you and
Brother to church every Sunday.

Beneatha: Mama, you don't understand. It's all a matter of ideas, and God is
just one idea I don't accept. It's not important. I am not going out and
be immoral or commit crimes because I don't believe in God. I don't
even think about it. It's just that I get tired of Him getting credit for all
the things the human race achieves through its own stubborn effort.
There simply is no blasted God—there is only man and it is *He* who makes
miracles!

*Mama absorbs this speech, studies her daughter, and rises slowly and crosses to
Beneatha and slaps her powerfully across the face. After, there is only silence and
the daughter drops her eyes from her mother's face, and Mama is very tall before
her.*

Mama: Now—you say after me, in my mother's house there is still God.
*(There is a long pause and Beneatha stares at the floor wordlessly. Mama repeats
the phrase with precision and cool emotion.)* In my mother's house there is still
God.

Beneatha: In my mother's house there is still God.

A long pause.

*Mama (walking away from Beneatha, too disturbed for triumphant posture. Stopping
and turning back to her daughter):* There are some ideas we ain't going to
have in this house. Not long as I am at the head of this family.

Beneatha: Yes, ma'am.

   Mama walks out of the room.

Ruth (almost gently, with profound understanding): You think you a woman, Bennie—but you still a little girl. What you did was childish—so you got treated like a child.

Beneatha: I see. *(Quietly.)* I also see that everybody thinks it's all right for Mama to be a tyrant. But all the tyranny in the world will never put a God in the heavens!

   She picks up her books and goes out. Pause.

Ruth (goes to Mama's door): She said she was sorry.

Mama (coming out, going to her plant): They frightens me, Ruth. My children.

Ruth: You got good children, Lena. They just a little off sometimes—but they're good.

Mama: No—there's something come down between me and them that don't let us understand each other and I don't know what it is. One done almost lost his mind thinking 'bout money all the time and the other done commence to talk about things I can't seem to understand in no form or fashion. What is it that's changing, Ruth.

Ruth (soothingly, older than her years): Now . . . you taking it all too seriously. You just got strong-willed children and it takes a strong woman like you to keep 'em in hand.

Mama (looking at her plant and sprinkling a little water on it): They spirited all right, my children. Got to admit they got spirit—Bennie and Walter. Like this little old plant that ain't never had enough sunshine or nothing—and look at it . . .

   She has her back to Ruth, who has had to stop ironing and lean against something and put the back of her hand to her forehead.

Ruth (trying to keep Mama from noticing): You . . . sure . . . loves that little old thing, don't you? . . .

Mama: Well, I always wanted me a garden like I used to see sometimes at the back of the houses down home. This plant is close as I ever got to having one. *(She looks out of the window as she replaces the plant.)* Lord, ain't nothing as dreary as the view from this window on a dreary day, is there? Why ain't you singing this morning, Ruth? Sing that "No Ways Tired." That song always lifts me up so— *(She turns at last to see that Ruth has slipped quietly to the floor, in a state of semiconsciousness.)* Ruth! Ruth honey—what's the matter with you . . . Ruth!

   Curtain.

SCENE II. *[The following morning.]*

   It is the following morning; a Saturday morning, and house cleaning is in progress at the Youngers'. Furniture has been shoved hither and yon and Mama is giving the kitchen-area walls a washing down. Beneatha, in dungarees, with a handkerchief tied around her face, is spraying insecticide into the cracks in the walls. As they work, the radio is on and a Southside disk-jockey program is inappropriately filling the house with a rather exotic saxophone blues. Travis, the sole idle one, is leaning on his arms, looking out of the window.

Travis: Grandmama, that stuff Bennie is using smells awful. Can I go downstairs, please?

Mama: Did you get all them chores done already? I ain't seen you doing much.

Travis: Yes'm — finished early. Where did Mama go this morning?

Mama (looking at Beneatha): She had to go on a little errand.

> *The phone rings. Beneatha runs to answer it and reaches it before Walter, who has
> entered from bedroom.*

Travis: Where?

Mama: To tend to her business.

Beneatha: Haylo . . . *(Disappointed.)* Yes, he is. *(She tosses the phone to Walter, who
barely catches it.)* It's Willie Harris again.

Walter (as privately as possible under Mama's gaze): Hello, Willie. Did you get the
papers from the lawyer? . . . No, not yet. I told you the mailman doesn't
get here till ten-thirty . . . No, I'll come there . . . Yeah! Right away. *(He
hangs up and goes for his coat.)*

Beneatha: Brother, where did Ruth go?

Walter (as he exits): How should I know!

Travis: Aw come on, Grandma. Can I go outside?

Mama: Oh, I guess so. You stay right in front of the house, though, and keep a
good lookout for the postman.

Travis: Yes'm. *(He darts into bedroom for stickball and bat, reenters, and sees Beneatha
on her knees spraying under sofa with behind upraised. He edges closer to the target,
takes aim, and lets her have it. She screams.)* Leave them poor little cockroaches alone, they ain't bothering you none! *(He runs as she swings the
spraygun at him viciously and playfully.)* Grandma! Grandma!

Mama: Look out there, girl, before you be spilling some of that stuff on that
child!

Travis (safely behind the bastion of Mama): That's right — look out, now! *(He exits.)*

Beneatha (drily): I can't imagine that it would hurt him — it has never hurt the
roaches.

Mama: Well, little boys' hides ain't as tough as Southside roaches. You better
get over there behind the bureau. I seen one marching out of there like
Napoleon yesterday.

Beneatha: There's really only one way to get rid of them, Mama —

Mama: How?

Beneatha: Set fire to this building! Mama, where did Ruth go?

Mama (looking at her with meaning): To the doctor, I think.

Beneatha: The doctor? What's the matter? *(They exchange glances.)* You don't
think —

Mama (with her sense of drama): Now I ain't saying what I think. But I ain't never
been wrong 'bout a woman neither.

> *The phone rings.*

Beneatha (at the phone): Hay-lo . . . *(Pause, and a moment of recognition.)* Well —
when did you get back! . . . And how was it? . . . Of course I've missed
you — in my way . . . This morning? No . . . house cleaning and all that
and Mama hates it if I let people come over when the house is like
this . . . You *have?* Well, that's different . . . What is it — Oh, what the hell,
come on over . . . Right, see you then. *Arrividerci.*

She hangs up.

Mama (who has listened vigorously, as is her habit): Who is that you inviting over here with this house looking like this? You ain't got the pride you was born with!

Beneatha: Asagai doesn't care how houses look, Mama — he's an intellectual.

Mama: Who?

Beneatha: Asagai — Joseph Asagai. He's an African boy I met on campus. He's been studying in Canada all summer.

Mama: What's his name?

Beneatha: Asagai, Joseph. Ah-sah-guy . . . He's from Nigeria.

Mama: Oh, that's the little country that was founded by slaves way back . . .

Beneatha: No, Mama — that's Liberia.

Mama: I don't think I never met no African before.

Beneatha: Well, do me a favor and don't ask him a whole lot of ignorant questions about Africans. I mean, do they wear clothes and all that —

Mama: Well, now, I guess if you think we so ignorant 'round here maybe you shouldn't bring your friends here —

Beneatha: It's just that people ask such crazy things. All anyone seems to know about when it comes to Africa is Tarzan —

Mama (indignantly): Why should I know anything about Africa?

Beneatha: Why do you give money at church for the missionary work?

Mama: Well, that's to help save people.

Beneatha: You mean save them from *heathenism* —

Mama (innocently): Yes.

Beneatha: I'm afraid they need more salvation from the British and the French.

Ruth comes in forlornly and pulls off her coat with dejection. They both turn to look at her.

Ruth (dispiritedly): Well, I guess from all the happy faces — everybody knows.

Beneatha: You pregnant?

Mama: Lord have mercy, I sure hope it's a little old girl. Travis ought to have a sister.

Beneatha and Ruth give her a hopeless look for this grandmotherly enthusiasm.

Beneatha: How far along are you?

Ruth: Two months.

Beneatha: Did you mean to? I mean did you plan it or was it an accident?

Mama: What do you know about planning or not planning?

Beneatha: Oh, Mama.

Ruth (wearily): She's twenty years old, Lena.

Beneatha: Did you plan it, Ruth?

Ruth: Mind your own business.

Beneatha: It is my business — where is he going to live, on the *roof*? *(There is silence following the remark as the three women react to the sense of it.)* Gee — I didn't mean that, Ruth, honest. Gee, I don't feel like that at all. I — I think it is wonderful.

Ruth (dully): Wonderful.

Beneatha: Yes — really.

Mama (looking at Ruth, worried): Doctor say everything going to be all right?

Ruth (far away): Yes — she says everything is going to be fine . . .

Mama (immediately suspicious): "She" — What doctor you went to?

> *Ruth folds over, near hysteria.*

Mama (worriedly hovering over Ruth): Ruth honey — what's the matter with you — you sick?

> *Ruth has her fists clenched on her thighs and is fighting hard to suppress a scream that seems to be rising in her.*

Beneatha: What's the matter with her, Mama?

Mama (working her fingers in Ruth's shoulders to relax her): She be all right. Women gets right depressed sometimes when they get her way. *(Speaking softly, expertly, rapidly.)* Now you just relax. That's right . . . just lean back, don't think 'bout nothing at all . . . nothing at all —

Ruth: I'm all right . . .

> *The glassy-eyed look melts and then she collapses into a fit of heavy sobbing. The bell rings.*

Beneatha: Oh, my God — that must be Asagai.

Mama (to Ruth): Come on now, honey. You need to lie down and rest awhile . . . then have some nice hot food.

> *They exit, Ruth's weight on her mother-in-law. Beneatha, herself profoundly disturbed, opens the door to admit a rather dramatic-looking young man with a large package.*

Asagai: Hello, Alaiyo —

Beneatha (holding the door open and regarding him with pleasure): Hello . . . *(Long pause.)* Well — come in. And please excuse everything. My mother was very upset about my letting anyone come here with the place like this.

Asagai (coming into the room): You look disturbed too . . . Is something wrong?

Beneatha (still at the door, absently): Yes . . . we've all got acute ghetto-itus. *(She smiles and comes toward him, finding a cigarette and sitting.)* So — sit down! No! Wait! *(She whips the spraygun off sofa where she had left it and puts the cushions back. At last perches on arm of sofa. He sits.)* So, how was Canada?

Asagai (a sophisticate): Canadian.

Beneatha (looking at him): Asagai, I'm very glad you are back.

Asagai (looking back at her in turn): Are you really?

Beneatha: Yes — very.

Asagai: Why? — you were quite glad when I went away. What happened?

Beneatha: You went away.

Asagai: Ahhhhhhhh.

Beneatha: Before — you wanted to be so serious before there was time.

Asagai: How much time must there be before one knows what one feels?

Beneatha (stalling this particular conversation. Her hands pressed together, in a deliberately childish gesture): What did you bring me?

Asagai (handing her the package): Open it and see.

Beneatha (eagerly opening the package and drawing out some records and the colorful robes of a Nigerian woman): Oh Asagai! . . . You got them for me! . . . How beautiful . . . and the records too! *(She lifts out the robes and runs to the mirror with them and holds the drapery up in front of herself.)*

Asagai (coming to her at the mirror): I shall have to teach you how to drape it properly. *(He flings the material about her for the moment and stands back to look at her.)* Ah — *Oh-pay-gay-day, oh-gbah-mu-shay. (A Yoruba exclamation for admiration.)* You wear it well . . . very well . . . mutilated hair and all.

Beneatha (turning suddenly): My hair — what's wrong with my hair?

Asagai (shrugging): Were you born with it like that?

Beneatha (reaching up to touch it): No . . . of course not.

She looks back to the mirror, disturbed.

Asagai (smiling): How then?

Beneatha: You know perfectly well how . . . as crinkly as yours . . . that's how.

Asagai: And it is ugly to you that way?

Beneatha (quickly): Oh, no — not ugly . . . *(More slowly, apologetically.)* But it's so hard to manage when it's, well — raw.

Asagai: And so to accommodate that — you mutilate it every week?

Beneatha: It's not mutilation!

Asagai (laughing aloud at her seriousness): Oh . . . please! I am only teasing you because you are so very serious about these things. *(He stands back from her and folds his arms across his chest as he watches her pulling at her hair and frowning in the mirror.)* Do you remember the first time you met me at school? . . . *(He laughs.)* You came up to me and you said — and I thought you were the most serious little thing I had ever seen — you said: *(He imitates her.)* "Mr. Asagai — I want very much to talk with you. About Africa. You see, Mr. Asagai, I am looking for my *identity!*"

He laughs.

Beneatha (turning to him, not laughing): Yes —

Her face is quizzical, profoundly disturbed.

Asagai (still teasing and reaching out and taking her face in his hands and turning her profile to him): Well . . . it is true that this is not so much a profile of a Hollywood queen as perhaps a queen of the Nile — *(A mock dismissal of the importance of the question.)* But what does it matter? Assimilationism is so popular in your country.

Beneatha (wheeling, passionately, sharply): I am not an assimilationist!

Asagai (the protest hangs in the room for a moment and Asagai studies her, his laughter fading): Such a serious one. *(There is a pause.)* So — you like the robes? You must take excellent care of them — they are from my sister's personal wardrobe.

Beneatha (with incredulity): You — you sent all the way home — for me?

Asagai (with charm): For you — I would do much more . . . Well, that is what I came for. I must go.

Beneatha: Will you call me Monday?

Asagai: Yes . . . We have a great deal to talk about. I mean about identity and time and all that.

Beneatha: Time?

Asagai: Yes. About how much time one needs to know what one feels.

Beneatha: You see! You never understood that there is more than one kind of feeling which can exist between a man and a woman — or, at least, there should be.

Asagai (shaking his head negatively but gently): No. Between a man and a woman there need be only one kind of feeling. I have that for you . . . Now even . . . right this moment . . .

Beneatha: I know — and by itself — it won't do. I can find that anywhere.

Asagai: For a woman it should be enough.

Beneatha: I know — because that's what it says in all the novels that men write. But it isn't. Go ahead and laugh — but I'm not interested in being someone's little episode in America or — *(With feminine vengeance.)* — one of them! *(Asagai has burst into laughter again.)* That's funny as hell, huh!

Asagai: It's just that every American girl I have known has said that to me. White — black — in this you are all the same. And the same speech, too!

Beneatha (angrily): Yuk, yuk, yuk!

Asagai: It's how you can be sure that the world's most liberated women are not liberated at all. You all talk about it too much!

Mama enters and is immediately all social charm because of the presence of a guest.

Beneatha: Oh — Mama — this is Mr. Asagai.

Mama: How do you do?

Asagai (total politeness to an elder): How do you do, Mrs. Younger. Please forgive me for coming at such an outrageous hour on a Saturday.

Mama: Well, you are quite welcome. I just hope you understand that our house don't always look like this. *(Chatterish.)* You must come again. I would love to hear all about — *(Not sure of the name.)* — your country. I think it's so sad the way our American Negroes don't know nothing about Africa 'cept Tarzan and all that. And all that money they pour into these churches when they ought to be helping you people over there drive out them French and Englishmen done taken away your land.

The mother flashes a slightly superior look at her daughter upon completion of the recitation.

Asagai (taken aback by this sudden and acutely unrelated expression of sympathy): Yes . . . yes . . .

Mama (smiling at him suddenly and relaxing and looking him over): How many miles is it from here to where you come from?

Asagai: Many thousands.

Mama (looking at him as she would Walter): I bet you don't half look after yourself, being away from your mama either. I spec you better come 'round here from time to time to get yourself some decent homecooked meals . . .

Asagai (moved): Thank you. Thank you very much. *(They are all quiet, then —)* Well . . . I must go. I will call you Monday, Alaiyo.

Mama: What's that he call you?

Asagai: Oh — "Alaiyo." I hope you don't mind. It is what you would call a nickname, I think. It is a Yoruba word. I am a Yoruba.

Mama (looking at Beneatha): I — I thought he was from — *(Uncertain.)*

Asagai (understanding): Nigeria is my country. Yoruba is my tribal origin —

Beneatha: You didn't tell us what Alaiyo means . . . for all I know, you might be calling me Little Idiot or something . . .

Asagai: Well . . . let me see . . . I do not know how just to explain it . . . The sense of a thing can be so different when it changes languages.

Beneatha: You're evading.

Asagai: No — really it is difficult . . . *(Thinking.)* It means . . . it means One for Whom Bread — Food — Is Not Enough. *(He looks at her.)* Is that all right?

Beneatha (understanding, softly): Thank you.

Mama (looking from one to the other and not understanding any of it): Well . . . that's nice . . . You must come see us again — Mr. —
Asagai: Ah-sah-guy . . .
Mama: Yes . . . Do come again.
Asagai: Good-bye.

> *He exits.*

Mama (after him): Lord, that's a pretty thing just went out here! *(Insinuatingly, to her daughter.)* Yes, I guess I see why we done commence to get so interested in Africa 'round here. Missionaries my aunt Jenny!

> *She exits.*

Beneatha: Oh, Mama! . . .

> *She picks up the Nigerian dress and holds it up to her in front of the mirror again. She sets the headdress on haphazardly and then notices her hair again and clutches at it and then replaces the headdress and frowns at herself. Then she starts to wriggle in front of the mirror as she thinks a Nigerian woman might. Travis enters and stands regarding her.*

Travis: What's the matter, girl, you cracking up?
Beneatha: Shut up.

> *She pulls the headdress off and looks at herself in the mirror and clutches at her hair again and squinches her eyes as if trying to imagine something. Then, suddenly, she gets her raincoat and kerchief and hurriedly prepares for going out.*

Mama (coming back into the room): She's resting now. Travis, baby, run next door and ask Miss Johnson to please let me have a little kitchen cleanser. This here can is empty as Jacob's kettle.
Travis: I just came in.
Mama: Do as you told. *(He exits and she looks at her daughter.)* Where you going?
Beneatha (halting at the door): To become a queen of the Nile!

> *She exits in a breathless blaze of glory. Ruth appears in the bedroom doorway.*

Mama: Who told you to get up?
Ruth: Ain't nothing wrong with me to be lying in no bed for. Where did Bennie go?
Mama (drumming her fingers): Far as I could make out — to Egypt. *(Ruth just looks at her.)* What time is it getting to?
Ruth: Ten twenty. And the mailman going to ring that bell this morning just like he done every morning for the last umpteen years.

> *Travis comes in with the cleanser can.*

Travis: She say to tell you that she don't have much.
Mama (angrily): Lord, some people I could name sure is tight-fisted! *(Directing her grandson.)* Mark two cans of cleanser on the list there. If she that hard up for kitchen cleanser, I sure don't want to forget to get her none!
Ruth: Lena — maybe the woman is just short on cleanser —
Mama (not listening): — Much baking powder as she done borrowed from me all these years, she could of done gone into the baking business!

> *The bell sounds suddenly and sharply and all three are stunned — serious and silent — midspeech. In spite of all the other conversations and distractions of the*

morning, this is what they have been waiting for, even Travis, who looks helplessly from his mother to his grandmother. Ruth is the first to come to life again.

Ruth (to Travis): *Get down them steps, boy!*

Travis snaps to life and flies out to get the mail.

Mama (her eyes wide, her hand to her breast): You mean it done really come?

Ruth (excited): Oh, Miss Lena!

Mama (collecting herself): Well . . . I don't know what we all so excited about 'round here for. We known it was coming for months.

Ruth: That's a whole lot different from having it come and being able to hold it in your hands . . . a piece of paper worth ten thousand dollars . . . (*Travis bursts back into the room. He holds the envelope high above his head, like a little dancer, his face is radiant and he is breathless. He moves to his grandmother with sudden slow ceremony and puts the envelope into her hands. She accepts it, and then merely holds it and looks at it.*) Come on! Open it . . . Lord have mercy, I wish Walter Lee was here!

Travis: Open it, Grandmama!

Mama (staring at it): Now you all be quiet. It's just a check.

Ruth: Open it . . .

Mama (still staring at it): Now don't act silly . . . We ain't never been no people to act silly 'bout no money—

Ruth (swiftly): We ain't never had none before—OPEN IT!

Mama finally makes a good strong tear and pulls out the thin blue slice of paper and inspects it closely. The boy and his mother study it raptly over Mama's shoulders.

Mama: Travis! (*She is counting off with doubt.*) Is that the right number of zeros?

Travis: Yes'm . . . ten thousand dollars. Gaalee, grandmama, you rich.

Mama (She holds the check away from her, still looking at it. Slowly her face sobers into a mask of unhappiness): Ten thousand dollars. (*She hands it to Ruth.*) Put it away somewhere, Ruth. (*She does not look at Ruth; her eyes seem to be seeing something somewhere very far off.*) Ten thousand dollars they give you. Ten thousand dollars.

Travis (to his mother, sincerely): What's the matter with Grandmama—don't she want to be rich?

Ruth (distractedly): You go on out and play now, baby. (*Travis exits. Mama starts wiping dishes absently, humming intently to herself. Ruth turns to her, with kind exasperation.*) You've gone and got yourself upset.

Mama (not looking at her): I spec if it wasn't for you all . . . I would just put that money away or give it to the church or something.

Ruth: Now what kind of talk is that. Mr. Younger would just be plain mad if he could hear you talking foolish like that.

Mama (stopping and staring off): Yes . . . he sure would. (*Sighing.*) We got enough to do with that money, all right. (*She halts then, and turns and looks at her daughter-in-law hard; Ruth avoids her eyes and Mama wipes her hands with finality and starts to speak firmly to Ruth.*) Where did you go today, girl?

Ruth: To the doctor.

Mama (impatiently): Now, Ruth . . . you know better than that. Old Doctor Jones is strange enough in his way but there ain't nothing 'bout him make somebody slip and call him "she"—like you done this morning.

Ruth: Well, that's what happened — my tongue slipped.

Mama: You went to see that woman, didn't you?

Ruth (defensively, giving herself away): What woman you talking about?

Mama (angrily): That woman who —

Walter enters in great excitement.

Walter: Did it come?

Mama (quietly): Can't you give people a Christian greeting before you start asking about money?

Walter (to Ruth): Did it come? *(Ruth unfolds the check and lays it quietly before him, watching him intently with thoughts of her own. Walter sits down and grasps it close and counts off the zeros.)* Ten thousand dollars — *(He turns suddenly, frantically to his mother and draws some papers out of his breast pocket.)* Mama — look. Old Willy Harris put everything on paper —

Mama: Son — I think you ought to talk to your wife . . . I'll go on out and leave you alone if you want —

Walter: I can talk to her later — Mama, look —

Mama: Son —

Walter: WILL SOMEBODY PLEASE LISTEN TO ME TODAY!

Mama (quietly): I don't 'low no yellin' in this house, Walter Lee, and you know it — *(Walter stares at them in frustration and starts to speak several times.)* And there ain't going to be no investing in no liquor stores.

Walter: But, Mama, you ain't even looked at it.

Mama: I don't aim to have to speak on that again.

A long pause.

Walter: You ain't looked at it and you don't aim to have to speak on that again? You ain't even looked at it and *you* have decided — *(Crumpling his papers.)* Well, *you* tell that to my boy tonight when you put him to sleep on the living-room couch . . . *(Turning to Mama and speaking directly to her.)* Yeah — and tell it to my wife, Mama, tomorrow when she has to go out of here to look after somebody else's kids. And tell it to *me*, Mama, every time we need a new pair of curtains and I have to watch *you* go out and work in somebody's kitchen. Yeah, you tell me then!

Walter starts out.

Ruth: Where you going?

Walter: I'm going out!

Ruth: Where?

Walter: Just out of this house somewhere —

Ruth (getting her coat): I'll come too.

Walter: I don't want you to come!

Ruth: I got something to talk to you about, Walter.

Walter: That's too bad.

Mama (still quietly): Walter Lee — *(She waits and he finally turns and looks at her.)* Sit down.

Walter: I'm a grown man, Mama.

Mama: Ain't nobody said you wasn't grown. But you still in my house and my presence. And as long as you are — you'll talk to your wife civil. Now sit down.

Ruth (suddenly): Oh, let him go on out and drink himself to death! He makes me sick to my stomach! *(She flings her coat against him and exits to bedroom.)*

Walter (violently flinging the coat after her): And you turn mine too, baby! *(The door slams behind her.)* That was my biggest mistake—

Mama (still quietly): Walter, what is the matter with you?

Walter: Matter with me? Ain't nothing the matter with *me!*

Mama: Yes there is. Something eating you up like a crazy man. Something more than me not giving you this money. The past few years I been watching it happen to you. You get all nervous acting and kind of wild in the eyes—*(Walter jumps up impatiently at her words.)* I said sit there now, I'm talking to you!

Walter: Mama—I don't need no nagging at me today.

Mama: Seem like you getting to a place where you always tied up in some kind of knot about something. But if anybody ask you 'bout it you just yell at 'em and bust out the house and go out and drink somewheres. Walter Lee, people can't live with that. Ruth's a good, patient girl in her way—but you getting to be too much. Boy, don't make the mistake of driving that girl away from you.

Walter: Why—what she do for me?

Mama: She loves you.

Walter: Mama—I'm going out. I want to go off somewhere and be by myself for a while.

Mama: I'm sorry 'bout your liquor store, son. It just wasn't the thing for us to do. That's what I want to tell you about—

Walter: I got to go out, Mama—

    He rises.

Mama: It's dangerous, son.

Walter: What's dangerous?

Mama: When a man goes outside his home to look for peace.

Walter (beseechingly): Then why can't there never be no peace in this house then?

Mama: You done found it in some other house?

Walter: No—there ain't no woman! Why do women always think there's a woman somewhere when a man gets restless. *(Picks up the check.)* Do you know what this money means to me? Do you know what this money can do for us? *(Puts it back.)* Mama—Mama—I want so many things . . .

Mama: Yes, son—

Walter: I want so many things that they are driving me kind of crazy . . . Mama—look at me.

Mama: I'm looking at you. You a good-looking boy. You got a job, a nice wife, a fine boy, and—

Walter: A job. *(Looks at her.)* Mama, a job? I open and close car doors all day long. I drive a man around in his limousine and I say, "Yes, sir; no, sir; very good, sir; shall I take the Drive, sir?" Mama, that ain't no kind of job . . . that ain't nothing at all. *(Very quietly.)* Mama, I don't know if I can make you understand.

Mama: Understand what, baby?

Walter (quietly): Sometimes it's like I can see the future stretched out in front of me—just plain as day. The future, Mama. Hanging over there at the edge of my days. Just waiting for me—a big, looming blank space—full of *nothing.* Just waiting for *me.* But it don't have to be. *(Pause. Kneeling beside her chair.)* Mama—sometimes when I'm downtown and I pass them cool, quiet-looking restaurants where them white boys are sitting back and talking 'bout things . . . sitting there turning deals worth millions of dollars . . . sometimes I see guys don't look much older than me—

Mama: Son—how come you talk so much 'bout money?

Walter (with immense passion): Because it is life, Mama!

Mama (quietly): Oh—*(Very quietly.)* So now it's life. Money is life. Once upon a time freedom used to be life—now it's money. I guess the world really do change . . .

Walter: No—it was always money, Mama. We just didn't know about it.

Mama: No . . . something has changed. *(She looks at him.)* You something new, boy. In my time we was worried about not being lynched and getting to the North if we could and how to stay alive and still have a pinch of dignity too . . . Now here come you and Beneatha—talking 'bout things we ain't never even thought about hardly, me and your daddy. You ain't satisfied or proud of nothing we done. I mean that you had a home; that we kept you out of trouble till you was grown; that you don't have to ride to work on the back of nobody's streetcar—You my children—but how different we done become.

Walter (a long beat. He pats her hand and gets up): You just don't understand, Mama, you just don't understand.

Mama: Son—do you know your wife is expecting another baby? *(Walter stands, stunned, and absorbs what his mother has said.)* That's what she wanted to talk to you about. *(Walter sinks down into a chair.)* This ain't for me to be telling—but you ought to know. *(She waits.)* I think Ruth is thinking 'bout getting rid of that child.

Walter (slowly understanding): —No—no—Ruth wouldn't do that.

Mama: When the world gets ugly enough—a woman will do anything for her family. *The part that's already living.*

Walter: You don't know Ruth, Mama, if you think she would do that.

Ruth opens the bedroom door and stands there a little limp.

Ruth (beaten): Yes I would too, Walter. *(Pause.)* I gave her a five-dollar down payment.

There is total silence as the man stares at his wife and the mother stares at her son.

Mama (presently): Well—*(Tightly.)* Well—son, I'm waiting to hear you say something . . . *(She waits.)* I'm waiting to hear how you be your father's son. Be the man he was . . . *(Pause. The silence shouts.)* Your wife say she going to destroy your child. And I'm waiting to hear you talk like him and say we a people who give children life, not who destroys them—*(She rises.)* I'm waiting to see you stand up and look like your daddy and say we done give up one baby to poverty and that we ain't going to give up nary another one . . . I'm waiting.

Walter: Ruth—*(He can say nothing.)*

Mama: If you a son of mine, tell her! *(Walter picks up his keys and his coat and walks out. She continues, bitterly.)* You . . . you are a disgrace to your father's memory. Somebody get me my hat!

Curtain.

ACT II

Scene I

TIME: *Later the same day.*
> *At rise: Ruth is ironing again. She has the radio going. Presently Beneatha's bedroom door opens and Ruth's mouth falls and she puts down the iron in fascination.*

Ruth: What have we got on tonight!

Beneatha (emerging grandly from the doorway so that we can see her thoroughly robed in the costume Asagai brought): You are looking at what a well-dressed Nigerian woman wears — *(She parades for Ruth, her hair completely hidden by the head-dress; she is coquettishly fanning herself with an ornate oriental fan, mistakenly more like Butterfly than any Nigerian that ever was.)* Isn't it beautiful? *(She promenades to the radio and, with an arrogant flourish, turns off the good loud blues that is playing.)* Enough of this assimilationist junk! *(Ruth follows her with her eyes as she goes to the phonograph and puts on a record and turns and waits ceremoniously for the music to come up. Then, with a shout—)* OCOMOGOSIAY!

> *Ruth jumps. The music comes up, a lovely Nigerian melody. Beneatha listens, enraptured, her eyes far way — "back to the past." She begins to dance. Ruth is dumfounded.*

Ruth: What kind of dance is that?
Beneatha: A folk dance.
Ruth (Pearl Bailey): What kind of folks do that, honey?
Beneatha: It's from Nigeria. It's a dance of welcome.
Ruth: Who you welcoming?
Beneatha: The men back to the village.
Ruth: Where they been?
Beneatha: How should I know — out hunting or something. Anyway, they are coming back now . . .
Ruth: Well, that's good.
Beneatha (with the record):

> *Alundi, alundi*
> *Alundi alunya*
> *Jop pu a jeepua*
> *Ang gu soooooooooo*
> *Ai yai yae . . .*
> *Ayehaye — alundi . . .*

> *Walter comes in during this performance; he has obviously been drinking. He leans against the door heavily and watches his sister, at first with distaste. Then his eyes look off— "back to the past"—as he lifts both his fists to the roof, screaming.*

Walter: YEAH . . . AND ETHIOPIA STRETCH FORTH HER HANDS AGAIN! . . .
Ruth (drily, looking at him): Yes — and Africa sure is claiming her own tonight. *(She gives them both up and starts ironing again.)*
Walter (all in a drunken, dramatic shout): Shut up! . . . I'm diggin them drums . . . them drums move me! . . . *(He makes his weaving way to his wife's face and*

leans in close to her.) In my *heart of hearts* — (He thumps his chest.) — I am much warrior!

Ruth (without even looking up): In your heart of hearts you are much drunkard.

Walter (coming away from her and starting to wander around the room, shouting): Me and Jomo . . . (Intently, in his sister's face. She has stopped dancing to watch him in this unknown mood.) That's my man, Kenyatta. (Shouting and thumping his chest.) FLAMING SPEAR! HOT DAMN! (He is suddenly in possession of an imaginary spear and actively spearing enemies all over the room.) OCO-MOGOSIAY . . .

Beneatha (to encourage Walter, thoroughly caught up with this side of him): OCO-MOGOSIAY, FLAMING SPEAR!

Walter: THE LION IS WAKING . . . OWIMOWEH!

He pulls his shirt open and leaps up on the table and gestures with his spear.

Beneatha: OWIMOWEH!

Walter (on the table, very far gone, his eyes pure glass sheets. He sees what we cannot, that he is a leader of his people, a great chief, a descendant of Chaka, and that the hour to march has come): Listen, my black brothers —

Beneatha: OCOMOGOSIAY!

Walter: — Do you hear the waters rushing against the shores of the coast-lands —

Beneatha: OCOMOGOSIAY!

Walter: — Do you hear the screeching of the cocks in yonder hills beyond where the chiefs meet in council for the coming of the mighty war —

Beneatha: OCOMOGOSIAY!

And now the lighting shifts subtly to suggest the world of Walter's imagination, and the mood shifts from pure comedy. It is the inner Walter speaking: the Southside chauffeur has assumed an unexpected majesty.

Walter: — Do you hear the beating of the wings of the birds flying low over the mountains and the low places of our land —

Beneatha: OCOMOGOSIAY!

Walter: — Do you hear the singing of the women, singing the war songs of our fathers to the babies in the great houses? Singing the sweet war songs! (The doorbell rings.) OH, DO YOU HEAR, MY *BLACK* BROTHERS!

Beneatha (completely gone): We hear you, Flaming Spear —

Ruth shuts off the phonograph and opens the door. George Murchison enters.

Walter: Telling us to prepare for the GREATNESS OF THE TIME! (Lights back to normal. He turns and sees George.) Black Brother!

He extends his hand for the fraternal clasp.

George: Black Brother, hell!

Ruth (having had enough, and embarrassed for the family): Beneatha, you got company — what's the matter with you? Walter Lee Younger, get down off that table and stop acting like a fool . . .

Walter comes down off the table suddenly and makes a quick exit to the bathroom.

Ruth: He's had a little to drink . . . I don't know what her excuse is.

George (to Beneatha): Look honey, we're going to the theater — we're not going to be *in* it . . . so go change, huh?

Beneatha looks at him and slowly, ceremoniously, lifts her hands and pulls off the headdress. Her hair is close-cropped and unstraightened. George freezes mid-sentence and Ruth's eyes all but fall out of her head.

George: What in the name of—

Ruth *(touching Beneatha's hair):* Girl, you done lost your natural mind? Look at your head!

George: What have you done to your head—I mean your hair!

Beneatha: Nothing—except cut it off.

Ruth: Now that's the truth—it's what ain't been done to it! You expect this boy to go out with you with your head all nappy like that?

Beneatha *(looking at George):* That's up to George. If he's ashamed of his heritage—

George: Oh, don't be so proud of yourself, Bennie—just because you look eccentric.

Beneatha: How can something that's natural be eccentric?

George: That's what being eccentric means—being natural. Get dressed.

Beneatha: I don't like that, George.

Ruth: Why must you and your brother make an argument out of everything people say?

Beneatha: Because I hate assimilationist Negroes!

Ruth: Will somebody please tell me what assimila-whoever means!

George: Oh, it's just a college girl's way of calling people Uncle Toms—but that isn't what it means at all.

Ruth: Well, what does it mean?

Beneatha *(cutting George off and staring at him as she replies to Ruth):* It means someone who is willing to give up his own culture and submerge himself completely in the dominant, and in this case *oppressive* culture!

George: Oh, dear, dear, dear! Here we go! A lecture on the African past! On our Great West African Heritage! In one second we will hear all about the great Ashanti empires; the great Songhay civilizations; and the great sculpture of Bénin—and then some poetry in the Bantu—and the whole monologue will end with the word *heritage!* *(Nastily.)* Let's face it, baby, your heritage is nothing but a bunch of raggedy-assed spirituals and some grass huts!

Beneatha: GRASS HUTS! *(Ruth crosses to her and forcibly pushes her toward the bedroom.)* See there . . . you are standing there in your splendid ignorance talking about people who were the first to smelt iron on the face of the earth! *(Ruth is pushing her through the door.)* The Ashanti were performing surgical operations when the English— *(Ruth pulls the door to, with Beneatha on the other side, and smiles graciously at George. Beneatha opens the door and shouts the end of the sentence defiantly at George.)* —were still tattooing themselves with blue dragons! *(She goes back inside.)*

Ruth: Have a seat, George. *(They both sit. Ruth folds her hands rather primly on her lap, determined to demonstrate the civilization of the family.)* Warm, ain't it? I mean for September. *(Pause.)* Just like they always say about Chicago weather: if it's too hot or cold for you, just wait a minute and it'll change. *(She smiles happily at this cliché of clichés.)* Everybody say it's got to do with them bombs and things they keep setting off. *(Pause.)* Would you like a nice cold beer?

George: No, thank you. I don't care for beer. *(He looks at his watch.)* I hope she hurries up.

Ruth: What time is the show?

George: It's an eight-thirty curtain. That's just Chicago, though. In New York standard curtain time is eight forty.

He is rather proud of this knowledge.

Ruth (properly appreciating it): You get to New York a lot?

George (offhand): Few times a year.

Ruth: Oh — that's nice. I've never been to New York.

Walter enters. We feel he has relieved himself, but the edge of unreality is still with him.

Walter: New York ain't got nothing Chicago ain't. Just a bunch of hustling people all squeezed up together — being "Eastern."

He turns his face into a screw of displeasure.

George: Oh — you've been?

Walter: Plenty of times.

Ruth (shocked at the lie): Walter Lee Younger!

Walter (staring her down): Plenty! *(Pause.)* What we got to drink in this house? Why don't you offer this man some refreshment. *(To George.)* They don't know how to entertain people in this house, man.

George: Thank you — I don't really care for anything.

Walter (feeling his head; sobriety coming): Where's Mama?

Ruth: She ain't come back yet.

Walter (looking Murchison over from head to toe, scrutinizing his carefully casual tweed sports jacket over cashmere V-neck sweater over soft eyelet shirt and tie, and soft slacks, finished off with white buckskin shoes): Why all you college boys wear them faggoty-looking white shoes?

Ruth: Walter Lee!

George Murchison ignores the remark.

Walter (to Ruth): Well, they look crazy as hell — white shoes, cold as it is.

Ruth (crushed): You have to excuse him —

Walter: No he don't! Excuse me for what? What you always excusing me for! I'll excuse myself when I needs to be excused! *(A pause.)* They look as funny as them black knee socks Beneatha wears out of here all the time.

Ruth: It's the college *style*, Walter.

Walter: Style, hell. She looks like she got burnt legs or something!

Ruth: Oh, Walter —

Walter (an irritable mimic): Oh, Walter! Oh, Walter! *(To Murchison.)* How's your old man making out? I understand you all going to buy that big hotel on the Drive? *(He finds a beer in the refrigerator, wanders over to Murchison, sipping and wiping his lips with the back of his hand, and straddling a chair backwards to talk to the other man.)* Shrewd move. Your old man is all right, man. *(Tapping his head and half winking for emphasis.)* I mean he knows how to operate. I mean he thinks *big*, you know what I mean, I mean for a *home*, you know? But I think he's kind of running out of ideas now. I'd like to talk to him. Listen, man, I got some plans that could turn this city upside down. I mean think like he does. *Big.* Invest big, gamble big, hell, lose *big* if you have to, you know what I mean. It's hard to find a man on this whole Southside who understands my kind of thinking—you dig? *(He scrutinizes Murchison again, drinks his beer, squints his eyes and leans in close, confidential, man to man.)* Me and you ought to sit down and talk sometimes, man. Man, I got me some ideas . . .

Murchison (with boredom): Yeah—sometimes we'll have to do that, Walter.

Walter (understanding the indifference, and offended): Yeah—well, when you get the time, man. I know you a busy little boy.

Ruth: Walter, please—

Walter (bitterly, hurt): I know ain't nothing in this world as busy as you colored college boys with your fraternity pins and white shoes . . .

Ruth (covering her face with humiliation): Oh, Walter Lee—

Walter: I see you all all the time—with the books tucked under your arms— going to your *(British A—a mimic.)* "clahsses." And for what! What the hell you learning over there? Filling up your heads—*(Counting off on his fingers.)*—with the sociology and the psychology—but they teaching you how to be a man? How to take over and run the world? They teaching you how to run a rubber plantation or a steel mill? Naw—just to talk proper and read books and wear them faggoty-looking white shoes . . .

George (looking at him with distaste, a little above it all): You're all wacked up with bitterness, man.

Walter (intently, almost quietly, between the teeth, glaring at the boy): And you—ain't you bitter, man? Ain't you just about had it yet? Don't you see no stars gleaming that you can't reach out and grab? You happy?—You contented son-of-a-bitch—you happy? You got it made? Bitter? Man, I'm a volcano. Bitter? Here I am a giant—surrounded by ants! Ants who can't even understand what it is the giant is talking about.

Ruth (passionately and suddenly): Oh, Walter—ain't you with nobody!

Walter (violently): No! 'Cause ain't nobody with me! Not even my own mother!

Ruth: Walter, that's a terrible thing to say!

Beneatha enters, dressed for the evening in a cocktail dress and earrings, hair natural.

George: Well—hey—*(Crosses to Beneatha; thoughtful, with emphasis, since this is a reversal.)* You look great!

Walter (seeing his sister's hair for the first time): What's the matter with your head?

Beneatha (tired of the jokes now): I cut it off, Brother.

Walter (coming close to inspect it and walking around her): Well, I'll be damned. So that's what they mean by the African bush . . .

Beneatha: Ha ha. Let's go, George.

George (looking at her): You know something? I like it. It's sharp. I mean it really is. *(Helps her into her wrap.)*

Ruth: Yes—I think so, too. *(She goes to the mirror and starts to clutch at her hair.)*

Walter: Oh no! You leave yours alone, baby. You might turn out to have a pin-shaped head or something!

Beneatha: See you all later.

Ruth: Have a nice time.

George: Thanks. Good night. *(Half out the door, he reopens it. To Walter.)* Good night, Prometheus!

Beneatha and George exit.

Walter (to Ruth): Who is Prometheus?

Ruth: I don't know. Don't worry about it.

Walter (in fury, pointing after George): See there — they get to a point where they can't insult you man to man — they got to go talk about something ain't nobody never heard of!

Ruth: How do you know it was an insult? *(To humor him.)* Maybe Prometheus is a nice fellow.

Walter: Prometheus! I bet there ain't even no such thing! I bet that simple-minded clown —

Ruth: Walter —

> *She stops what she is doing and looks at him.*

Walter (yelling): Don't start!

Ruth: Start what?

Walter: Your nagging! Where was I? Who was I with? How much money did I spend?

Ruth (plaintively): Walter Lee — why don't we just try to talk about it . . .

Walter (not listening): I been out talking with people who understand me. People who care about the things I got on my mind.

Ruth (wearily): I guess that means people like Willy Harris.

Walter: Yes, people like Willy Harris.

Ruth (with a sudden flash of impatience): Why don't you all just hurry up and go into the banking business and stop talking about it!

Walter: Why? You want to know why? 'Cause we all tied up in a race of people that don't know how to do nothing but moan, pray and have babies!

> *The line is too bitter even for him and he looks at her and sits down.*

Ruth: Oh, Walter . . . *(Softly.)* Honey, why can't you stop fighting me?

Walter (without thinking): Who's fighting you? Who even cares about you?

> *This line begins the retardation of his mood.*

Ruth: Well — *(She waits a long time, and then with resignation starts to put away her things.)* I guess I might as well go on to bed . . . *(More or less to herself.)* I don't know where we lost it . . . but we have . . . *(Then, to him.)* I — I'm sorry about this new baby, Walter. I guess maybe I better go on and do what I started . . . I guess I just didn't realize how bad things was with us . . . I guess I just didn't really realize — *(She starts out to the bedroom and stops.)* You want some hot milk?

Walter: Hot milk?

Ruth: Yes — hot milk.

Walter: Why hot milk?

Ruth: 'Cause after all that liquor you come home with you ought to have something hot in your stomach.

Walter: I don't want no milk.

Ruth: You want some coffee then?

Walter: No, I don't want no coffee. I don't want nothing hot to drink. *(Almost plaintively.)* Why you always trying to give me something to eat?

Ruth (standing and looking at him helplessly): What *else* can I give you, Walter Lee Younger?

She stands and looks at him and presently turns to go out again. He lifts his head and watches her going away from him in a new mood which began to emerge when he asked her "Who cares about you?"

Walter: It's been rough, ain't it, baby? *(She hears and stops but does not turn around and he continues to her back.)* I guess between two people there ain't never as much understood as folks generally thinks there is. I mean like between me and you — *(She turns to face him.)* How we gets to the place where we scared to talk softness to each other. *(He waits, thinking hard himself.)* Why you think it got to be like that? *(He is thoughtful, almost as a child would be.)* Ruth, what is it gets into people ought to be close?

Ruth: I don't know, honey. I think about it a lot.

Walter: On account of you and me, you mean? The way things are with us. The way something done come down between us.

Ruth: There ain't so much between us, Walter . . . Not when you come to me and try to talk to me. Try to be with me . . . a little even.

Walter (total honesty): Sometimes . . . sometimes . . . I don't even know how to try.

Ruth: Walter —

Walter: Yes?

Ruth (coming to him, gently and with misgiving, but coming to him): Honey . . . life don't have to be like this. I mean sometimes people can do things so that things are better . . . You remember how we used to talk when Travis was born . . . about the way we were going to live . . . the kind of house . . . *(She is stroking his head.)* Well, it's all starting to slip away from us . . .

He turns her to him and they look at each other and kiss, tenderly and hungrily. The door opens and Mama enters — Walter breaks away and jumps up. A beat.

Walter: Mama, where have you been?

Mama: My — them steps is longer than they used to be. Whew! *(She sits down and ignores him.)* How you feeling this evening, Ruth?

Ruth shrugs, disturbed at having been interrupted and watching her husband knowingly.

Walter: Mama, where have you been all day?

Mama (still ignoring him and leaning on the table and changing to more comfortable shoes): Where's Travis?

Ruth: I let him go out earlier and he ain't come back yet. Boy, is he going to get it!

Walter: Mama!

Mama (as if she has heard him for the first time): Yes, son?

Walter: Where did you go this afternoon?

Mama: I went downtown to tend to some business that I had to tend to.

Walter: What kind of business?

Mama: You know better than to question me like a child, Brother.

Walter (rising and bending over the table): Where were you, Mama? *(Bringing his fists down and shouting.)* Mama, you didn't go do something with that insurance money, something crazy?

The front door opens slowly, interrupting him, and Travis peeks his head in, less than hopefully.

Travis (to his mother): Mama, I—

Ruth: "Mama I" nothing! You're going to get it, boy! Get on in that bedroom and get yourself ready!

Travis: But I—

Mama: Why don't you all never let the child explain hisself.

Ruth: Keep out of it now, Lena.

Mama clamps her lips together, and Ruth advances toward her son menacingly.

Ruth: A thousand times I have told you not to go off like that—

Mama (holding out her arms to her grandson): Well—at least let me tell him something. I want him to be the first one to hear . . . Come here, Travis. *(The boy obeys, gladly.)* Travis—*(She takes him by the shoulder and looks into his face.)*—you know that money we got in the mail this morning?

Travis: Yes'm—

Mama: Well—what you think your grandmama gone and done with that money?

Travis: I don't know, Grandmama.

Mama (putting her finger on his nose for emphasis): She went out and she bought you a house! *(The explosion comes from Walter at the end of the revelation and he jumps up and turns away from all of them in a fury. Mama continues, to Travis.)* You glad about the house? It's going to be yours when you get to be a man.

Travis: Yeah—I always wanted to live in a house.

Mama: All right, gimme some sugar then—*(Travis puts his arms around her neck as she watches her son over the boy's shoulder. Then, to Travis, after the embrace.)* Now when you say your prayers tonight, you thank God and your grandfather—'cause it was him who give you the house—in his way.

Ruth (taking the boy from Mama and pushing him toward the bedroom): Now you get out of here and get ready for your beating.

Travis: Aw, Mama—

Ruth: Get on in there—*(Closing the door behind him and turning radiantly to her mother-in-law.)* So you went and did it!

Mama (quietly, looking at her son with pain): Yes, I did.

Ruth (raising both arms classically): PRAISE GOD! *(Looks at Walter a moment, who says nothing. She crosses rapidly to her husband.)* Please, honey—let me be glad . . . you be glad too. *(She has laid her hands on his shoulders, but he shakes himself free of her roughly, without turning to face her.)* Oh, Walter . . . a home . . . a home. *(She comes back to Mama.)* Well—where is it? How big is it? How much it going to cost?

Mama: Well—

Ruth: When we moving?

Mama (smiling at her): First of the month.

Ruth (throwing back her head with jubilance): Praise God!

Mama (tentatively, still looking at her son's back turned against her and Ruth): It's—it's a nice house too . . . *(She cannot help speaking directly to him. An imploring quality in her voice, her manner, makes her almost like a girl now.)* Three bedrooms—nice big one for you and Ruth . . . Me and Beneatha still have to share our room, but Travis have one of his own—and *(With difficulty.)* I figure if the—new baby—is a boy, we could get one of them double-decker outfits . . . And there's a yard with a little patch of dirt where I could maybe get to grow me a few flowers . . . And a nice big basement . . .

Ruth: Walter honey, be glad—

Mama (still to his back, fingering things on the table): 'Course I don't want to make it sound fancier than it is . . . It's just a plain little old house—but it's made good and solid—and it will be *ours*. Walter Lee—it makes a difference in a man when he can walk on floors that belong to *him* . . .

Ruth: Where is it?

Mama (frightened at this telling): Well—well—it's out there in Clybourne Park—

> *Ruth's radiance fades abruptly, and Walter finally turns slowly to face his mother with incredulity and hostility.*

Ruth: Where?

Mama (matter-of-factly): Four o six Clybourne Street, Clybourne Park.

Ruth: Clybourne Park? Mama, there ain't no colored people living in Clybourne Park.

Mama (almost idiotically): Well, I guess there's going to be some now.

Walter (bitterly): So that's the peace and comfort you went out and bought for us today!

Mama (raising her eyes to meet his finally): Son—I just tried to find the nicest place for the least amount of money for my family.

Ruth (trying to recover from the shock): Well—well—'course I ain't one never been 'fraid of no crackers, mind you—but—well, wasn't there no other houses nowhere?

Mama: Them houses they put up for colored in them areas way out all seem to cost twice as much as other houses. I did the best I could.

Ruth (struck senseless with the news, in its various degrees of goodness and trouble, she sits a moment, her fists propping her chin in thought, and then she starts to rise, bringing her fists down with vigor, the radiance spreading from cheek to cheek again): Well—well—All I can say is—if this is my time in life—MY TIME—to say good-bye—*(And she builds with momentum as she starts to circle the room with an exuberant, almost tearfully happy release.)*—to these God-damned cracking walls!—*(She pounds the walls.)*—and these marching roaches!—*(She wipes at an imaginary army of marching roaches.)*—and this cramped little closet which ain't now or never was no kitchen! . . . then I say it loud and good, HALLELUJAH! AND GOOD-BYE MISERY . . . I DON'T NEVER WANT TO SEE YOUR UGLY FACE AGAIN! *(She laughs joyously, having practically destroyed the apartment, and flings her arms up and lets them come down happily, slowly, reflectively, over her abdomen, aware for the first time perhaps that the life therein pulses with happiness and not despair.)* Lena?

Mama (moved, watching her happiness): Yes, honey?

Ruth (looking off): Is there—is there a whole lot of sunlight?

Mama (understanding): Yes, child, there's a whole lot of sunlight.

> *Long pause.*

Ruth (collecting herself and going to the door of the room Travis is in): Well—I guess I better see 'bout Travis. *(To Mama.)* Lord, I sure don't feel like whipping nobody today!

> *She exits.*

Mama (the mother and son are left alone now and the mother waits a long time, considering deeply, before she speaks): Son—you—you understand what I done, don't you? *(Walter is silent and sullen.)* I—I just seen my family falling apart today . . . just falling to pieces in front of my eyes . . . We couldn't of gone on like we was today. We was going backwards 'stead of forwards — talking 'bout killing babies and wishing each other was dead . . . When it gets like that in life — you just got to do something different, push on out and do something bigger . . . *(She waits.)* I wish you say something, son . . . I wish you'd say how deep inside you you think I done the right thing —

Walter (crossing slowly to his bedroom door and finally turning there and speaking measuredly): What you need me to say you done right for? *You* the head of this family. You run our lives like you want to. It was your money and you did what you wanted with it. So what you need for me to say it was all right for? *(Bitterly, to hurt her as deeply as he knows is possible.)* So you butchered up a dream of mine — you — who always talking 'bout your children's dreams . . .

Mama: Walter Lee —

He just closes the door behind him. Mama sits alone, thinking heavily.

Curtain.

SCENE II

TIME: *Friday night, a few weeks later.*
    At rise: Packing crates mark the intention of the family to move. Beneatha and George come in, presumably from an evening out again.

George: O.K. . . . O.K., whatever you say . . . *(They both sit on the couch. He tries to kiss her. She moves away.)* Look, we've had a nice evening; let's not spoil it, huh? . . .

He again turns her head and tries to nuzzle in and she turns away from him, not with distaste but with momentary lack of interest; in a mood to pursue what they were talking about.

Beneatha: I'm *trying* to talk to you.

George: We always talk.

Beneatha: Yes — and I love to talk.

George (exasperated; rising): I know it and I don't mind it sometimes . . . I want you to cut it out, see — The moody stuff, I mean. I don't like it. You're a nice-looking girl . . . all over. That's all you need, honey, forget the atmosphere. Guys aren't going to go for the atmosphere — they're going to go for what they see. Be glad for that. Drop the Garbo routine. It doesn't go with you. As for myself, I want a nice — *(Groping.)* — simple *(Thoughtfully.)* — sophisticated girl . . . not a poet — O.K.?

He starts to kiss her, she rebuffs him again and he jumps up.

Beneatha: Why are you angry, George?

George: Because this is stupid! I don't go out with you to discuss the nature of "quiet desperation" or to hear all about your thoughts — because the world will go on thinking what it thinks regardless —

Beneatha: Then why read books? Why go to school?

George (with artificial patience, counting on his fingers): It's simple. You read books — to learn facts — to get grades — to pass the course — to get a degree. That's all — it has nothing to do with thoughts.

A long pause.

Beneatha: I see. *(He starts to sit.)* Good night, George.

> *George looks at her a little oddly, and starts to exit. He meets Mama coming in.*

George: Oh — hello, Mrs. Younger.

Mama: Hello, George, how you feeling?

George: Fine — fine, how are you?

Mama: Oh, a little tired. You know them steps can get you after a day's work. You all have a nice time tonight?

George: Yes — a fine time. A fine time.

Mama: Well, good night.

George: Good night. *(He exits. Mama closes the door behind her.)* Hello, honey. What you sitting like that for?

Beneatha: I'm just sitting.

Mama: Didn't you have a nice time?

Beneatha: No.

Mama: No? What's the matter?

Beneatha: Mama, George is a fool — honest. *(She rises.)*

Mama (hustling around unloading the packages she has entered with. She stops): Is he, baby?

Beneatha: Yes.

> *Beneatha makes up Travis's bed as she talks.*

Mama: You sure?

Beneatha: Yes.

Mama: Well — I guess you better not waste your time with no fools.

> *Beneatha looks up at her mother, watching her put groceries in the refrigerator. Finally she gathers up her things and starts into the bedroom. At the door she stops and looks back at her mother.*

Beneatha: Mama —

Mama: Yes, baby —

Beneatha: Thank you.

Mama: For what?

Beneatha: For understanding me this time.

> *She exits quickly and the mother stands, smiling a little, looking at the place where Beneatha just stood. Ruth enters.*

Ruth: Now don't you fool with any of this stuff, Lena —

Mama: Oh, I just thought I'd sort a few things out. Is Brother here?

Ruth: Yes.

Mama (with concern): Is he —

Ruth (reading her eyes): Yes.

> *Mama is silent and someone knocks on the door. Mama and Ruth exchange weary and knowing glances and Ruth opens it to admit the neighbor, Mrs. Johnson,[1] who is a rather squeaky wide-eyed lady of no particular age, with a newspaper under her arm.*

Mama (changing her expression to acute delight and a ringing cheerful greeting): Oh — hello there, Johnson.

---

[1] This character and the scene of her visit were cut from the original production and early editions of the play.

Johnson (this is a woman who decided long ago to be enthusiastic about EVERYTHING in life and she is inclined to wave her wrist vigorously at the height of her exclamatory comments): Hello there, yourself! H'you this evening, Ruth?

Ruth (not much of a deceptive type): Fine, Mis' Johnson, h'you?

Johnson: Fine. *(Reaching out quickly, playfully, and patting Ruth's stomach.)* Ain't you starting to poke out none yet! *(She mugs with delight at the over familiar remark and her eyes dart around looking at the crates and packing preparation; Mama's face is a cold sheet of endurance.)* Oh, ain't we getting ready round here, though! Yessir! Lookathere! I'm telling you the Youngers is really getting ready to "move on up a little higher!" — Bless God!

Mama (a little drily, doubting the total sincerity of the Blesser): Bless God.

Johnson: He's good, ain't He?

Mama: Oh yes, He's good.

Johnson: I mean sometimes He works in mysterious ways . . . but He works, don't He!

Mama (the same): Yes, he does.

Johnson: I'm just soooooo happy for y'all. And this here child — *(About Ruth.)* looks like she could just pop open with happiness, don't she. Where's all the rest of the family?

Mama: Bennie's gone to bed —

Johnson: Ain't no . . . *(The implication is pregnancy.)* sickness done hit you — I hope . . . ?

Mama: No — she just tired. She was out this evening.

Johnson (all is a coo, an emphatic coo): Aw — ain't that lovely. She still going out with the little Murchison boy?

Mama (drily): Ummmm huh.

Johnson: That's lovely. You sure got lovely children, Younger. Me and Isaiah talks all the time 'bout what fine children you was blessed with. We sure do.

Mama: Ruth, give Mis' Johnson a piece of sweet potato pie and some milk.

Johnson: Oh honey, I can't stay hardly a minute — I just dropped in to see if there was anything I could do. *(Accepting the food easily.)* I guess y'all seen the news what's all over the colored paper this week . . .

Mama: No — didn't get mine yet this week.

Johnson (lifting her head and blinking with the spirit of catastrophe): You mean you ain't read 'bout them colored people that was bombed out their place out there?

Ruth straightens with concern and takes the paper and reads it. Johnson notices her and feeds commentary.

Johnson: Ain't it something how bad these here white folks is getting here in Chicago! Lord, getting so you think you right down in Mississippi! *(With a tremendous and rather insincere sense of melodrama.)* 'Course I thinks it's wonderful how our folk keeps on pushing out. You hear some of these Negroes round here talking 'bout how they don't go where they ain't wanted and all that — but not me, honey! *(This is a lie.)* Wilhemenia Othella Johnson goes anywhere, any time she feels like it! *(With head movement for emphasis.)* Yes I do! Why if we left it up to these here crackers, the poor niggers wouldn't have nothing — *(She clasps her hand over her mouth.)* Oh, I always forgets you don't 'low that word in your house.

Mama (quietly, looking at her): No—I don't 'low it.

Johnson (vigorously again): Me neither! I was just telling Isaiah yesterday when he come using it in front of me—I said, "Isaiah, it's just like Mis' Younger says all the time—"

Mama: Don't you want some more pie?

Johnson: No—no thank you; this was lovely. I got to get on over home and have my midnight coffee. I hear some people say it don't let them sleep but I finds I can't close my eyes right lessen I done had that laaaast cup of coffee . . . *(She waits. A beat. Undaunted.)* My Goodnight coffee, I calls it!

Mama (with much eye-rolling and communication between herself and Ruth): Ruth, why don't you give Mis' Johnson some coffee.

Ruth gives Mama an unpleasant look for her kindness.

Johnson (accepting the coffee): Where's Brother tonight?

Mama: He's lying down.

Johnson: MMmmmmm, he sure gets his beauty rest, don't he? Good-looking man. Sure is a good-looking man! *(Reaching out to pat Ruth's stomach again.)* I guess that's how come we keep on having babies around here. *(She winks at Mama.)* One thing 'bout Brother, he always know how to have a *good* time. And soooooo ambitious! I bet it was his idea y'all moving out to Clybourne Park. Lord—I bet this time next month y'all's names will have been in the papers plenty— *(Holding up her hands to mark off each word of the headline she can see in front of her.)* "NEGROES INVADE CLYBOURNE PARK—BOMBED!"

Mama (she and Ruth look at the woman in amazement): We ain't exactly moving out there to get bombed.

Johnson: Oh honey—you know I'm praying to God every day that don't nothing like that happen! But you have to think of life like it is—and these here Chicago peckerwoods is some baaaad peckerwoods.

Mama (wearily): We done thought about all that Mis' Johnson.

Beneatha comes out of the bedroom in her robe and passes through to the bathroom. Mrs. Johnson turns.

Johnson: Hello there, Bennie!

Beneatha (crisply): Hello, Mrs. Johnson.

Johnson: How is school?

Beneatha (crisply): Fine, thank you. *(She goes out.)*

Johnson (insulted): Getting so she don't have much to say to nobody.

Mama: The child was on her way to the bathroom.

Johnson: I know—but sometimes she act like she ain't got time to pass the time of day with nobody ain't been to college. Oh—I ain't criticizing her none. It's just—you know how some of our young people gets when they get a little education. *(Mama and Ruth say nothing, just look at her.)* Yes—well. Well, I guess I better get on home. *(Unmoving.)* 'Course I can understand how she must be proud and everything—being the only one in the family to make something of herself. I know just being a chauffeur ain't never satisfied Brother none. He shouldn't feel like that, though. Ain't nothing wrong with being a chauffeur.

Mama: There's plenty wrong with it.

Johnson: What?

Mama: Plenty. My husband always said being any kind of a servant wasn't a fit thing for a man to have to be. He always said a man's hands was made to make things, or to turn the earth with — not to drive nobody's car for 'em — or — *(She looks at her own hands.)* carry they slop jars. And my boy is just like him — he wasn't meant to wait on nobody.

Johnson (rising, somewhat offended): Mmmmmmmmmm. The Youngers is too much for me! *(She looks around.)* You sure one proud-acting bunch of colored folks. Well — I always thinks like Booker T. Washington said that time — "Education has spoiled many a good plow hand" —

Mama: Is that what old Booker T. said?

Johnson: He sure did.

Mama: Well, it sounds just like him. The fool.

Johnson (indignantly): Well — he was one of our great men.

Mama: Who said so?

Johnson (nonplussed): You know, me and you ain't never agreed about some things, Lena Younger. I guess I better be going —

Ruth (quickly): Good night.

Johnson: Good night. Oh — *(Thrusting it at her.)* You can keep the paper! *(With a trill.)* 'Night.

Mama: Good night, Mis' Johnson.

Mrs. Johnson exits.

Ruth: If ignorance was gold . . .

Mama: Shush. Don't talk about folks behind their backs.

Ruth: You do.

Mama: I'm old and corrupted. *(Beneatha enters.)* You was rude to Mis' Johnson, Beneatha, and I don't like it at all.

Beneatha (at her door): Mama, if there are two things we, as a people, have got to overcome, one is the Klu Klux Klan — and the other is Mrs. Johnson. *(She exits.)*

Mama: Smart aleck.

The phone rings.

Ruth: I'll get it.

Mama: Lord, ain't this a popular place tonight.

Ruth (at the phone): Hello — Just a minute. *(Goes to door.)* Walter, it's Mrs. Arnold. *(Waits. Goes back to the phone. Tense.)* Hello. Yes, this is his wife speaking . . . He's lying down now. Yes . . . well, he'll be in tomorrow. He's been very sick. Yes — I know we should have called, but we were so sure he'd be able to come in today. Yes — yes, I'm very sorry. Yes . . . Thank you very much. *(She hangs up. Walter is standing in the doorway of the bedroom behind her.)* That was Mrs. Arnold.

Walter (indifferently): Was it?

Ruth: She said if you don't come in tomorrow that they are getting a new man . . .

Walter: Ain't that sad — ain't that crying sad.

Ruth: She said Mr. Arnold has had to take a cab for three days . . . Walter, you ain't been to work for three days! *(This is a revelation to her.)* Where you been, Walter Lee Younger? *(Walter looks at her and starts to laugh.)* You're going to lose your job.

Walter: That's right . . . *(He turns on the radio.)*
Ruth: Oh, Walter, and with your mother working like a dog every day —

> *A steamy, deep blues pours into the room.*

Walter: That's sad too — Everything is sad.
Mama: What you been doing for these three days, son?
Walter: Mama — you don't know all the things a man what got leisure can find
     to do in this city . . . What's this — Friday night? Well — Wednesday I bor-
     rowed Willy Harris' car and I went for a drive . . . just me and myself and I
     drove and drove . . . Way out . . . way past South Chicago, and I parked the
     car and I sat and looked at the steel mills all day long. I just sat in the car
     and looked at them big black chimneys for hours. Then I drove back and I
     went to the Green Hat. *(Pause.)* And Thursday — Thursday I borrowed the
     car again and I got in it and I pointed it the other way and I drove
     the other way — for hours — way, way up to Wisconsin, and I looked at the
     farms. I just drove and looked at the farms. Then I drove back and I went
     to the Green Hat. *(Pause.)* And today — today I didn't get the car. Today I
     just walked. All over the Southside. And I looked at the Negroes and they
     looked at me and finally I just sat down on the curb at Thirty-ninth and
     South Parkway and I just sat there and watched the Negroes go by. And
     then I went to the Green Hat. You all sad? You all depressed? And you
     know where I am going right now —

> *Ruth goes out quietly.*

Mama: Oh, Big Walter, is this the harvest of our days?
Walter: You know what I like about the Green Hat? I like this little cat they got
     there who blows a sax . . . He blows. He talks to me. He ain't but 'bout five
     feet tall and he's got a conked head and his eyes is always closed and he's
     all music —
Mama (rising and getting some papers out of her handbag): Walter —
Walter: And there's this other guy who plays the piano . . . and they got a
     sound. I mean they can work on some music . . . They got the best little
     combo in the world in the Green Hat . . . You can just sit there and drink
     and listen to them three men play and you realize that don't nothing mat-
     ter worth a damn, but just being there —
Mama: I've helped do it to you, haven't I, son? Walter I been wrong.
Walter: Naw — you ain't never been wrong about nothing, Mama.
Mama: Listen to me, now. I say I been wrong, son. That I been doing to you what
     the rest of the world been doing to you. *(She turns off the radio.)* Walter — *(She
     stops and he looks up slowly at her and she meets his eyes pleadingly.)* What you
     ain't never understood is that I ain't got nothing, don't own nothing, ain't
     never really wanted nothing that wasn't for you. There ain't nothing as pre-
     cious to me . . . There ain't nothing worth holding on to, money, dreams,
     nothing else — if it means — if it means it's going to destroy my boy. *(She
     takes an envelope out of her handbag and puts it in front of him and he watches her
     without speaking or moving.)* I paid the man thirty-five hundred dollars down
     on the house. That leaves sixty-five hundred dollars. Monday morning I
     want you to take this money and take three thousand dollars and put it in
     a savings account for Beneatha's medical schooling. The rest you put in a
     checking account — with your name on it. And from now on any penny that

come out of it or that go in it is for you to look after. For you to decide. *(She drops her hands a little helplessly.)* It ain't much, but it's all I got in the world and I'm putting it in your hands. I'm telling you to be the head of this family from now on like you supposed to be.

Walter (stares at the money): You trust me like that, Mama?

Mama: I ain't never stop trusting you. Like I ain't never stop loving you.

She goes out, and Walter sits looking at the money on the table. Finally, in a decisive gesture, he gets up, and, in mingled joy and desperation, picks up the money. At the same moment, Travis enters for bed.

Travis: What's the matter, Daddy? You drunk?

Walter (sweetly, more sweetly than we have ever known him): No, Daddy ain't drunk. Daddy ain't going to never be drunk again . . .

Travis: Well, good night, Daddy.

The father has come from behind the couch and leans over, embracing his son.

Walter: Son, I feel like talking to you tonight.

Travis: About what?

Walter: Oh, about a lot of things. About you and what kind of man you going to be when you grow up . . . Son—son, what do you want to be when you grow up?

Travis: A bus driver.

Walter (laughing a little): A what? Man, that ain't nothing to want to be!

Travis: Why not?

Walter: 'Cause, man—it ain't big enough—you know what I mean.

Travis: I don't know then. I can't make up my mind. Sometimes Mama asks me that too. And sometimes when I tell her I just want to be like you—she says she don't want me to be like that and sometimes she says she does. . . .

Walter (gathering him up in his arms): You know what, Travis? In seven years you going to be seventeen years old. And things is going to be very different with us in seven years, Travis. . . . One day when you are seventeen I'll come home—home from my office downtown somewhere—

Travis: You don't work in no office, Daddy.

Walter: No—but after tonight. After what your daddy gonna do tonight, there's going to be offices—a whole lot of offices. . . .

Travis: What you gonna do tonight, Daddy?

Walter: You wouldn't understand yet, son, but your daddy's gonna make a transaction . . . a business transaction that's going to change our lives. . . . That's how come one day when you 'bout seventeen years old I'll come home and I'll be pretty tired, you know what I mean, after a day of conferences and secretaries getting things wrong the way they do . . . 'cause an executive's life is hell, man—*(The more he talks the farther away he gets.)* And I'll pull the car up on the driveway . . . just a plain black Chrysler, I think, with white walls—no—black tires. More elegant. Rich people don't have to be flashy . . . though I'll have to get something a little sportier for Ruth—maybe a Cadillac convertible to do her shopping in. . . . And I'll come up the steps to the house and the gardener will be clipping away at the hedges and he'll say, "Good evening, Mr. Younger." And I'll say, "Hello, Jefferson, how are you this evening?" And I'll go inside and Ruth will come downstairs and meet me at the door and we'll kiss each other and she'll take my arm and we'll go up to your room to see you sitting on the floor with the catalogues of all the great schools in America around you. . . . All the great schools in the world! And — and I'll say, all right son — it's your seventeenth birthday, what is it you've decided? . . . Just tell me where you want to go to school and you'll *go*. Just tell me, what it is you want to be — and you'll *be* it. . . . Whatever you want to be — Yessir! *(He holds his arms open for Travis.)* You just name it, son . . . *(Travis leaps into them.)* and I hand you the world!

Walter's voice has risen in pitch and hysterical promise and on the last line he lifts Travis high.

Blackout.

SCENE III

TIME: *Saturday, moving day, one week later.*

    Before the curtain rises, Ruth's voice, a strident, dramatic church alto, cuts through the silence.

    It is, in the darkness, a triumphant surge, a penetrating statement of expectation: "Oh, Lord, I don't feel no ways tired! Children, oh, glory hallelujah!"

    As the curtain rises we see that Ruth is alone in the living room, finishing up the family's packing. It is moving day. She is nailing crates and tying cartons. Beneatha enters, carrying a guitar case, and watches her exuberant sister-in-law.

Ruth: Hey!

Beneatha (putting away the case): Hi.

Ruth (pointing at a package): Honey — look in that package there and see what I found on sale this morning at the South Center. *(Ruth gets up and moves to the package and draws out some curtains.)* Lookahere — hand-turned hems!

Beneatha: How do you know the window size out there?

Ruth (who hadn't thought of that): Oh — Well, they bound to fit something in the whole house. Anyhow, they was too good a bargain to pass up. *(Ruth slaps her head, suddenly remembering something.)* Oh, Bennie — I meant to put a special note on that carton over there. That's your mama's good china and she wants 'em to be very careful with it.

Beneatha: I'll do it.

Beneatha finds a piece of paper and starts to draw large letters on it.

Ruth: You know what I'm going to do soon as I get in that new house?

Beneatha: What?

Ruth: Honey — I'm going to run me a tub of water up to here . . . *(With her fingers practically up to her nostrils.)* And I'm going to get in it — and I am going to sit . . . and sit . . . and sit in that hot water and the first person who knocks to tell *me* to hurry up and come out —

Beneatha: Gets shot at sunrise.

Ruth (laughing happily): You said it, sister! *(Noticing how large Beneatha is absent-mindedly making the note):* Honey, they ain't going to read that from no airplane.

Beneatha (laughing herself): I guess I always think things have more emphasis if they are big, somehow.

Ruth (looking up at her and smiling): You and your brother seem to have that as a philosophy of life. Lord, that man — done changed so 'round here. You know — you know what we did last night? Me and Walter Lee?

Beneatha: What?

Ruth (smiling to herself): We went to the movies. *(Looking at Beneatha to see if she understands.)* We went to the movies. You know the last time me and Walter went to the movies together?

Beneatha: No.

Ruth: Me neither. That's how long it been. *(Smiling again.)* But we went last night. The picture wasn't much good, but that didn't seem to matter. We went — and we held hands.

Beneatha: Oh, Lord!

Ruth: We held hands — and you know what?

Beneatha: What?

Ruth: When we come out of the show it was late and dark and all the stores and things was closed up . . . and it was kind of chilly and there wasn't many people on the streets . . . and we was still holding hands, me and Walter.

Beneatha: You're killing me.

Walter enters with a large package. His happiness is deep in him; he cannot keep still with his newfound exuberance. He is singing and wiggling and snapping his fingers. He puts his package in a corner and puts a phonograph record, which he has brought in with him, on the record player. As the music, soulful and sensuous, comes up he dances over to Ruth and tries to get her to dance with him. She gives in at last to his raunchiness and in a fit of giggling allows herself to be drawn into his mood. They dip and she melts into his arms in a classic, body-melting "slow drag."

Beneatha (regarding them a long time as they dance, then drawing in her breath for a deeply exaggerated comment which she does not particularly mean): Talk about — olddddddddddd-fashionedddddddd — Negroes!

Walter (stopping momentarily): What kind of Negroes?

He says this in fun. He is not angry with her today, nor with anyone. He starts to dance with his wife again.

Beneatha: Old-fashioned.

Walter (as he dances with Ruth): You know, when these *New Negroes* have their convention — *(Pointing at his sister.)* — that is going to be the chairman of the Committee on Unending Agitation. *(He goes on dancing, then stops.)* Race, race, race! . . . Girl, I do believe you are the first person in the history of the entire human race to successfully brainwash yourself. *(Beneatha breaks up and he goes on dancing. He stops again, enjoying his tease.)* Damn, even the N double A C P takes a holiday sometimes! *(Beneatha and Ruth laugh. He dances with Ruth some more and starts to laugh and stops and pantomimes someone over an operating table.)* I can just see that chick someday looking down at some poor cat on an operating table and before she starts to slice him, she says . . . *(Pulling his sleeves back maliciously.)* "By the way, what are your views on civil rights down there? . . ."

He laughs at her again and starts to dance happily. The bell sounds.

Beneatha: Sticks and stones may break my bones but . . . words will never hurt me!

Beneatha goes to the door and opens it as Walter and Ruth go on with the clowning. Beneatha is somewhat surprised to see a quiet-looking middle-aged white man in a business suit holding his hat and a briefcase in his hand and consulting a small piece of paper.

Man: Uh — how do you do, miss. I am looking for a Mrs. — *(He looks at the slip of paper.)* Mrs. Lena Younger? *(He stops short, struck dumb at the sight of the oblivious Walter and Ruth.)*

Beneatha (smoothing her hair with slight embarrassment): Oh — yes, that's my mother. Excuse me. *(She closes the door and turns to quiet the other two.)* Ruth! Brother! *(Enunciating precisely but soundlessly: "There's a white man at the door!" They stop dancing, Ruth cuts off the phonograph, Beneatha opens the door. The man casts a curious quick glance at all of them.)* Uh — come in please.

Man (coming in): Thank you.

Beneatha: My mother isn't here just now. Is it business?

Man: Yes . . . well, of a sort.

Walter (freely, the Man of the House): Have a seat. I'm Mrs. Younger's son. I look after most of her business matters.

Ruth and Beneatha exchange amused glances.

Man (regarding Walter, and sitting): Well — My name is Karl Lindner . . .

Walter (stretching out his hand): Walter Younger. This is my wife — *(Ruth nods politely.)* — and my sister.

Lindner: How do you do.

Walter (amiably, as he sits himself easily on a chair, leaning forward on his knees with interest and looking expectantly into the newcomer's face): What can we do for you, Mr. Lindner!

Lindner (some minor shuffling of the hat and briefcase on his knees): Well — I am a representative of the Clybourne Park Improvement Association —

Walter (pointing): Why don't you sit your things on the floor?

Lindner: Oh — yes. Thank you. *(He slides the briefcase and hat under the chair.)* And as I was saying — I am from the Clybourne Park Improvement Association and we have had it brought to our attention at the last meeting that you people — or at least your mother — has bought a piece of residential property at — *(He digs for the slip of paper again.)* — four o six Clybourne Street . . .

Walter: That's right. Care for something to drink? Ruth, get Mr. Lindner a beer.

Lindner (upset for some reason): Oh — no, really. I mean thank you very much, but no thank you.

Ruth (innocently): Some coffee?

Lindner: Thank you, nothing at all.

Beneatha is watching the man carefully.

Lindner: Well, I don't know how much you folks know about our organization. *(He is a gentle man; thoughtful and somewhat labored in his manner.)* It is one of these community organizations set up to look after — oh, you know, things like block upkeep and special projects and we also have what we call our New Neighbors Orientation Committee . . .

Beneatha (drily): Yes—and what do they do?

Lindner (turning a little to her and then returning the main force to Walter): Well—it's what you might call a sort of welcoming committee, I guess. I mean they, we—I'm the chairman of the committee—go around and see the new people who move into the neighborhood and sort of give them the lowdown on the way we do things out in Clybourne Park.

Beneatha (with appreciation of the two meanings, which escape Ruth and Walter): Un-huh.

Lindner: And we also have the category of what the association calls—*(He looks elsewhere.)*—uh—special community problems . . .

Beneatha: Yes—and what are some of those?

Walter: Girl, let the man talk.

Lindner (with understated relief): Thank you. I would sort of like to explain this thing in my own way. I mean I want to explain to you in a certain way.

Walter: Go ahead.

Lindner: Yes. Well. I'm going to try to get right to the point. I'm sure we'll all appreciate that in the long run.

Beneatha: Yes.

Walter: Be still now!

Lindner: Well—

Ruth (still innocently): Would you like another chair—you don't look comfortable.

Lindner (more frustrated than annoyed): No, thank you very much. Please. Well—to get right to the point, I—*(A great breath, and he is off at last.)* I am sure you people must be aware of some of the incidents which have happened in various parts of the city when colored people have moved into certain areas—*(Beneatha exhales heavily and starts tossing a piece of fruit up and down in the air.)* Well—because we have what I think is going to be a unique type of organization in American community life—not only do we deplore that kind of thing—but we are trying to do something about it. *(Beneatha stops tossing and turns with a new and quizzical interest to the man.)* We feel—*(gaining confidence in his mission because of the interest in the faces of the people he is talking to)*—we feel that most of the trouble in this world, when you come right down to it—*(He hits his knee for emphasis.)*—most of the trouble exists because people just don't sit down and talk to each other.

Ruth (nodding as she might in church, pleased with the remark): You can say that again, mister.

Lindner (more encouraged by such affirmation): That we don't try hard enough in this world to understand the other fellow's problem. The other guy's point of view.

Ruth: Now that's right.

Beneatha and Walter merely watch and listen with genuine interest.

Lindner: Yes—that's the way we feel out in Clybourne Park. And that's why I was elected to come here this afternoon and talk to you people. Friendly like, you know, the way people should talk to each other and see if we couldn't find some way to work this thing out. As I say, the whole business is a matter of *caring* about the other fellow. Anybody can see that you are a nice family of folks, hard working and honest I'm sure. *(Beneatha frowns slightly, quizzically, her head tilted regarding him.)* Today everybody knows what it means to be on the outside of *something*. And of course, there is always somebody who is out to take advantage of people who don't always understand.

Walter: What do you mean?

Lindner: Well—you see our community is made up of people who've worked hard as the dickens for years to build up that little community. They're not rich and fancy people; just hard-working, honest people who don't really have much but those little homes and a dream of the kind of community they want to raise their children in. Now, I don't say we are perfect and there is a lot wrong in some of the things they want. But you've got to admit that a man, right or wrong, has the right to want to have the neighborhood he lives in a certain kind of way. And at the moment the overwhelming majority of our people out there feel that people get along better, take more of a common interest in the life of the community, when they share a common background. I want you to believe me when I tell you that race prejudice simply doesn't enter into it. It is a matter of the people of Clybourne Park believing, rightly or wrongly, as I say, that for the happiness of all concerned that our Negro families are happier when they live in their *own* communities.

Beneatha (with a grand and bitter gesture): This, friends, is the Welcoming Committee!

Walter (dumfounded, looking at Lindner): Is this what you came marching all the way over here to tell us?

Lindner: Well, now we've been having a fine conversation. I hope you'll hear me all the way through.

Walter (tightly): Go ahead, man.

Lindner: You see—in the face of all the things I have said, we are prepared to make your family a very generous offer . . .

Beneatha: Thirty pieces and not a coin less!

Walter: Yeah?

Lindner (putting on his glasses and drawing a form out of the briefcase): Our association is prepared, through the collective effort of our people, to buy the house from you at a financial gain to your family.

Ruth: Lord have mercy, ain't this the living gall!

Walter: All right, you through?

Lindner: Well, I want to give you the exact terms of the financial arrangement—

Walter: We don't want to hear no exact terms of no arrangements. I want to know if you got any more to tell us 'bout getting together?

Lindner (taking off his glasses): Well—I don't suppose that you feel . . .

Walter: Never mind how I feel—you got any more to say 'bout how people ought to sit down and talk to each other? . . . Get out of my house, man.

He turns his back and walks to the door.

Lindner (looking around at the hostile faces and reaching and assembling his hat and briefcase): Well—I don't understand why you people are reacting this way. What do you think you are going to gain by moving into a neighborhood where you just aren't wanted and where some elements—well—people can get awful worked up when they feel that their whole way of life and everything they've ever worked for is threatened.

Walter: Get out.

Lindner (at the door, holding a small card): Well—I'm sorry it went like this.

Walter: Get out.

Lindner (almost sadly regarding Walter): You just can't force people to change their hearts, son.

He turns and puts his card on a table and exits. Walter pushes the door to with stinging hatred, and stands looking at it. Ruth just sits and Beneatha just stands. They say nothing. Mama and Travis enter.

Mama: Well—this all the packing got done since I left out of here this morning. I testify before God that my children got all the energy of the *dead!* What time the moving men due?

Beneatha: Four o'clock. You had a caller, Mama.

She is smiling, teasingly.

Mama: Sure enough—who?

Beneatha (her arms folded saucily): The Welcoming Committee.

Walter and Ruth giggle.

Mama (innocently): Who?

Beneatha: The Welcoming Committee. They said they're sure going to be glad to see you when you get there.

Walter (devilishly): Yeah, they said they can't hardly wait to see your face.

Laughter.

Mama (sensing their facetiousness): What's the matter with you all?

Walter: Ain't nothing the matter with us. We just telling you 'bout the gentleman who came to see you this afternoon. From the Clybourne Park Improvement Association.

Mama: What he want?

Ruth (in the same mood as Beneatha and Walter): To welcome you, honey.

Walter: He said they can't hardly wait. He said the one thing they don't have, that they just *dying* to have out there is a fine family of fine colored people! *(To Ruth and Beneatha.)* Ain't that right!

Ruth (mockingly): Yeah! He left his card—

Beneatha (handing card to Mama): In case.

Mama reads and throws it on the floor—understanding and looking off as she draws her chair up to the table on which she has put her plant and some sticks and some cord.

Mama: Father, give us strength. *(Knowingly—and without fun.)* Did he threaten us?

Beneatha: Oh—Mama—they don't do it like that any more. He talked Brotherhood. He said everybody ought to learn how to sit down and hate each other with good Christian fellowship.

She and Walter shake hands to ridicule the remark.

Mama (sadly): Lord, protect us . . .

Ruth: You should hear the money those folks raised to buy the house from us. All we paid and then some.

Beneatha: What they think we going to do—eat 'em?

Ruth: No, honey, marry 'em.

Mama (shaking her head): Lord, Lord, Lord . . .

Ruth: Well — that's the way the crackers crumble. *(A beat.)* Joke.

Beneatha (laughingly noticing what her mother is doing): Mama, what are you doing?

Mama: Fixing my plant so it won't get hurt none on the way . . .

Beneatha: Mama, you going to take *that* to the new house?

Mama: Un-huh —

Beneatha: That raggedy-looking old thing?

Mama (stopping and looking at her): It expresses ME!

Ruth (with delight, to Beneatha): So there, Miss Thing!

> *Walter comes to Mama suddenly and bends down behind her and squeezes her in his arms with all his strength. She is overwhelmed by the suddenness of it and, though delighted, her manner is like that of Ruth and Travis.*

Mama: Look out now, boy! You make me mess up my thing here!

Walter (his face lit, he slips down on his knees beside her, his arms still about her): Mama . . . you know what it means to climb up in the chariot?

Mama (gruffly, very happy): Get on away from me now . . .

Ruth (near the gift-wrapped package, trying to catch Walter's eye): Psst —

Walter: What the old song say, Mama . . .

Ruth: Walter — Now?

> *She is pointing at the package.*

Walter (speaking the lines, sweetly, playfully, in his mother's face):
I got wings . . . you got wings . . .
All God's Children got wings . . .

Mama: Boy — get out of my face and do some work . . .

Walter:
When I get to heaven gonna put on my wings,
Gonna fly all over God's heaven . . .

Beneatha (teasingly, from across the room): Everybody talking 'bout heaven ain't going there!

Walter (to Ruth, who is carrying the box across to them): I don't know, you think we ought to give her that . . . Seems to me she ain't been very appreciative around here.

Mama (eying the box, which is obviously a gift): What is that?

Walter (taking it from Ruth and putting it on the table in front of Mama): Well — what you all think? Should we give it to her?

Ruth: Oh — she was pretty good today.

Mama: I'll good you —

> *She turns her eyes to the box again.*

Beneatha: Open it, Mama.

> *She stands up, looks at it, turns and looks at all of them, and then presses her hands together and does not open the package.*

Walter (sweetly): Open it, Mama. It's for you. *(Mama looks in his eyes. It is the first present in her life without its being Christmas. Slowly she opens her package and lifts out, one by one, a brand-new sparkling set of gardening tools. Walter continues, prodding.)* Ruth made up the note — read it . . .

Mama (picking up the card and adjusting her glasses): "To our own Mrs. Miniver —
    Love from Brother, Ruth, and Beneatha." Ain't that lovely . . .
Travis (tugging at his father's sleeve): Daddy, can I give her mine now?
Walter: All right, son. *(Travis flies to get his gift.)*
Mama: Now I don't have to use my knives and forks no more . . .
Walter: Travis didn't want to go in with the rest of us, Mama. He got his own.
    (Somewhat amused.) We don't know what it is . . .
*Travis (racing back in the room with a large hatbox and putting it in front of his grand-
    mother):* Here!
Mama: Lord have mercy, baby. You done gone and bought your grandmother
    a hat?
Travis (very proud): Open it!

>   She does and lifts out an elaborate, but very elaborate, wide gardening hat, and all
>   the adults break up at the sight of it.

Ruth: Travis, honey, what is that?
Travis (who thinks it is beautiful and appropriate): It's a gardening hat! Like the
    ladies always have on in the magazines when they work in their gardens.
Beneatha (giggling fiercely): Travis — we were trying to make Mama Mrs. Miniver —
    not Scarlett O'Hara!
Mama (indignantly): What's the matter with you all! This here is a beautiful
    hat! *(Absurdly.)* I always wanted me one just like it!

>   She pops it on her head to prove it to her grandson, and the hat is ludicrous and
>   considerably oversized.

Ruth: Hot dog! Go, Mama!
Walter (doubled over with laughter): I'm sorry, Mama — but you look like you
    ready to go out and chop you some cotton sure enough!

>   They all laugh except Mama, out of deference to Travis's feelings.

Mama (gathering the boy up to her): Bless your heart — this is the prettiest hat I
    ever owned — *(Walter, Ruth, and Beneatha chime in — noisily, festively, and insin-
    cerely congratulating Travis on his gift.)* What are we all standing around here
    for? We ain't finished packin' yet. Bennie, you ain't packed one book.

>   The bell rings.

Beneatha: That couldn't be the movers . . . it's not hardly two good yet —

>   Beneatha goes into her room. Mama starts for door.

Walter (turning, stiffening): Wait — wait — I'll get it.

>   He stands and looks at the door.

Mama: You expecting company, son?
Walter (just looking at the door): Yeah — yeah . . .

>   Mama looks at Ruth, and they exchange innocent and unfrightened glances.

Mama (not understanding): Well, let them in, son.
Beneatha (from her room): We need some more string.
Mama: Travis — you run to the hardware and get me some string cord.

>   Mama goes out and Walter turns and looks at Ruth. Travis goes to a dish for
>   money.

Ruth: Why don't you answer the door, man?

Walter (suddenly bounding across the floor to embrace her): 'Cause sometimes it hard to let the future begin! *(Stooping down in her face.)*
> I got wings! You got wings!
> All God's children got wings!

He crosses to the door and throws it open. Standing there is a very slight little man in a not-too-prosperous business suit and with haunted frightened eyes and a hat pulled down tightly, brim up, around his forehead. Travis passes between the men and exits. Walter leans deep in the man's face, still in his jubilance.

> When I get to heaven gonna put on my wings,
> Gonna fly all over God's heaven . . .

The little man just stares at him.

> Heaven—

Suddenly he stops and looks past the little man into the empty hallway.

Where's Willy, man?

Bobo: He ain't with me.

Walter (not disturbed): Oh—come on in. You know my wife.

Bobo (dumbly, taking off his hat): Yes—h'you, Miss Ruth.

Ruth (quietly, a mood apart from her husband already, seeing Bobo): Hello, Bobo.

Walter: You right on time today . . . Right on time. That's the way! *(He slaps Bobo on his back.)* Sit down . . . lemme hear.

Ruth stands stiffly and quietly in back of them, as though somehow she senses death, her eyes fixed on her husband.

Bobo (his frightened eyes on the floor, his hat in his hands): Could I please get a drink of water, before I tell you about it, Walter Lee?

Walter does not take his eyes off the man. Ruth goes blindly to the tap and gets a glass of water and brings it to Bobo.

Walter: There ain't nothing wrong, is there?

Bobo: Lemme tell you—

Walter: Man—didn't nothing go wrong?

Bobo: Lemme tell you—Walter Lee. *(Looking at Ruth and talking to her more than to Walter.)* You know how it was. I got to tell you how it was. I mean first I got to tell you how it was all the way . . . I mean about the money I put in, Walter Lee . . .

Walter (with taut agitation now): What about the money you put in?

Bobo: Well—it wasn't much as we told you—me and Willy—*(He stops.)* I'm sorry, Walter. I got a bad feeling about it. I got a real bad feeling about it . . .

Walter: Man, what you telling me about all this for? . . . Tell me what happened in Springfield . . .

Bobo: Springfield.

Ruth (like a dead woman): What was supposed to happen in Springfield?

Bobo (to her): This deal that me and Walter went into with Willy—Me and Willy was going to go down to Springfield and spread some money 'round so's we wouldn't have to wait so long for the liquor license . . . That's what we were going to do. Everybody said that was the way you had to do, you understand, Miss Ruth?

Walter: Man — what happened down there?

Bobo (a pitiful man, near tears): I'm trying to tell you, Walter.

Walter (screaming at him suddenly): THEN TELL ME, GODDAMMIT . . . WHAT'S THE MATTER WITH YOU?

Bobo: Man . . . I didn't go to no Springfield, yesterday.

Walter (halted, life hanging in the moment): Why not?

Bobo (the long way, the hard way to tell): 'Cause I didn't have no reasons to . . .

Walter: Man, what are you talking about!

Bobo: I'm talking about the fact that when I got to the train station yesterday morning — eight o'clock like we planned . . . Man — *Willy didn't never show up.*

Walter: Why . . . where was he . . . where is he?

Bobo: That's what I'm trying to tell you . . . I don't know . . . I waited six hours . . . I called his house . . . and I waited . . . six hours . . . I waited in that train station six hours . . . *(Breaking into tears.)* That was all the extra money I had in the world . . . *(Looking up at Walter with the tears running down his face.)* Man, *Willy is gone.*

Walter: Gone, what you mean Willy is gone? Gone where? You mean he went by himself. You mean he went off to Springfield by himself — to take care of getting the license — *(Turns and looks anxiously at Ruth.)* You mean maybe he didn't want too many people in on the business down there? *(Looks to Ruth again, as before.)* You know Willy got his own ways. *(Looks back to Bobo.)* Maybe you was late yesterday and he just went on down there without you. Maybe — maybe — he's been callin' you at home tryin' to tell you what happened or something. Maybe — maybe — he just got sick. He's somewhere — he's got to be somewhere. We just got to find him — me and you got to find him. *(Grabs Bobo senselessly by the collar and starts to shake him.)* We got to!

Bobo (in sudden angry, frightened agony): What's the matter with you, Walter! *When a cat take off with your money he don't leave you no road maps!*

Walter (turning madly, as though he is looking for Willy in the very room): Willy! . . . Willy . . . don't do it . . . Please don't do it . . . Man, not with that money . . . Man, please, not with that money . . . Oh, God . . . Don't let it be true . . . *(He is wandering around, crying out for Willy and looking for him or perhaps for help from God.)* Man . . . I trusted you . . . Man, I put my life in your hands . . . *(He starts to crumple down on the floor as Ruth just covers her face in horror. Mama opens the door and comes into the room, with Beneatha behind her.)* Man . . . *(He starts to pound the floor with his fists, sobbing wildly.)* THAT MONEY IS MADE OUT OF MY FATHER'S FLESH —

Bobo (standing over him helplessly): I'm sorry, Walter . . . *(only Walter's sobs reply. Bobo puts on his hat.)* I had my life staked on this deal, too . . .

He exits.

Mama (to Walter): Son — *(She goes to him, bends down to him, talks to his bent head.)* Son . . . Is it gone? Son, I gave you sixty-five hundred dollars. Is it gone? All of it? Beneatha's money too?

Walter (lifting his head slowly): Mama . . . I never . . . went to the bank at all . . .

Mama (not wanting to believe him): You mean . . . your sister's school money . . . you used that too . . . Walter? . . .

Walter: Yessss! All of it . . . It's all gone . . .

> *There is total silence. Ruth stands with her face covered with her hands; Beneatha leans forlornly against a wall, fingering a piece of red ribbon from the mother's gift. Mama stops and looks at her son without recognition and then, quite without thinking about it, starts to beat him senselessly in the face. Beneatha goes to them and stops it.*

Beneatha: Mama!

> *Mama stops and looks at both of her children and rises slowly and wanders vaguely, aimlessly away from them.*

Mama: I seen . . . him . . . night after night . . . come in . . . and look at that rug . . . and then look at me . . . the red showing in his eyes . . . the veins moving in his head . . . I seen him grow thin and old before he was forty . . . working and working and working like somebody's old horse . . . killing himself . . . and you—you give it all away in a day— *(She raises her arms to strike him again.)*

Beneatha: Mama—

Mama: Oh, God . . . *(She looks up to Him.)* Look down here—and show me the strength.

Beneatha: Mama—

Mama (folding over): Strength . . .

Beneatha (plaintively): Mama . . .

Mama: Strength!

> *Curtain.*

ACT III

TIME: *An hour later.*

> At curtain, there is a sullen light of gloom in the living room, gray light not unlike that which began the first scene of Act I. At left we can see Walter within his room, alone with himself. He is stretched out on the bed, his shirt out and open, his arms under his head. He does not smoke, he does not cry out, he merely lies there, looking up at the ceiling, much as if he were alone in the world.
>
> In the living room Beneatha sits at the table, still surrounded by the now almost ominous packing crates. She sits looking off. We feel that this is a mood struck perhaps an hour before, and it lingers now, full of the empty sound of profound disappointment. We see on a line from her brother's bedroom the sameness of their attitudes. Presently the bell rings and Beneatha rises without ambition or interest in answering. It is Asagai, smiling broadly, striding into the room with energy and happy expectation and conversation.

Asagai: I came over . . . I had some free time. I thought I might help with the packing. Ah, I like the look of packing crates! A household in preparation for a journey! It depresses some people . . . but for me . . . it is another feeling. Something full of the flow of life, do you understand? Movement, progress . . . It makes me think of Africa.

Beneatha: Africa!

Asagai: What kind of a mood is this? Have I told you how deeply you move me?

Beneatha: He gave away the money, Asagai . . .

Asagai: Who gave away what money?

Beneatha: The insurance money. My brother gave it away.

Asagai: Gave it away?

Beneatha: He made an investment! With a man even Travis wouldn't have trusted with his most worn-out marbles.

Asagai: And it's gone?

Beneatha: Gone!

Asagai: I'm very sorry . . . And you, now?

Beneatha: Me? . . . Me? . . . Me, I'm nothing . . . Me. When I was very small . . . we used to take our sleds out in the wintertime and the only hills we had were the ice-covered stone steps of some houses down the street. And we used to fill them in with snow and make them smooth and slide down them all day . . . and it was very dangerous, you know . . . far too steep . . . and sure enough one day a kid named Rufus came down too fast and hit the sidewalk and we saw his face just split open right there in front of us . . . And I remember standing there looking at his bloody open face thinking that was the end of Rufus. But the ambulance came and they took him to the hospital and they fixed the broken bones and they sewed it all up . . . and the next time I saw Rufus he just had a little line down the middle of his face . . . I never got over that . . .

Asagai: What?

Beneatha: That that was what one person could do for another, fix him up — sew up the problem, make him all right again. That was the most marvelous thing in the world . . . I wanted to do that. I always thought it was the one concrete thing in the world that a human being could do. Fix up the sick, you know — and make them whole again. This was truly being God . . .

Asagai: You wanted to be God?

Beneatha: No — I wanted to cure. It used to be so important to me. I wanted to cure. It used to matter. I used to care. I mean about people and how their bodies hurt . . .

Asagai: And you've stopped caring?

Beneatha: Yes — I think so.

Asagai: Why?

Beneatha (bitterly): Because it doesn't seem deep enough, close enough to what ails mankind! It was a child's way of seeing things — or an idealist's.

Asagai: Children see things very well sometimes — and idealists even better.

Beneatha: I know that's what you think. Because you are still where I left off. You with all your talk and dreams about Africa! You still think you can patch up the world. Cure the Great Sore of Colonialism — *(Loftily, mocking it.)* with the Penicillin of Independence — !

Asagai: Yes!

Beneatha: Independence *and then what?* What about all the crooks and thieves and just plain idiots who will come into power and steal and plunder the same as before — only now they will be black and do it in the name of the new Independence — WHAT ABOUT THEM?!

Asagai: That will be the problem for another time. First we must get there.

Beneatha: And where does it end?

Asagai: End? Who even spoke of an end? To life? To living?

Beneatha: An end to misery! To stupidity! Don't you see there isn't any real progress, Asagai, there is only one large circle that we march in, around and around, each of us with our own little picture in front of us — our own little mirage that we think is the future.

Asagai: That is the mistake.

Beneatha: What?

Asagai: What you just said — about the circle. It isn't a circle — it is simply a long line — as in geometry, you know, one that reaches into infinity. And because we cannot see the end — we also cannot see how it changes. And it is very odd but those who see the changes — who dream, who will not give up — are called idealists . . . and those who see only the circle — we call *them* the "realists"!

Beneatha: Asagai, while I was sleeping in that bed in there, people went out and took the future right out of my hands! And nobody asked me, nobody consulted me — they just went out and changed my life!

Asagai: Was it your money?

Beneatha: What?

Asagai: Was it your money he gave away?

Beneatha: It belonged to all of us.

Asagai: But did you earn it? Would you have had it at all if your father had not died?

Beneatha: No.

Asagai: Then isn't there something wrong in a house — in a world — where all dreams, good or bad, must depend on the death of a man? I never thought to see *you* like this, Alaiyo. You! Your brother made a mistake and you are grateful to him so that now you can give up the ailing human race on account of it! You talk about what good is struggle, what good is anything! Where are we all going and why are we bothering!

Beneatha: AND YOU CANNOT ANSWER IT!

Asagai (shouting over her): I LIVE THE ANSWER! (*Pause.*) In my village at home it is the exceptional man who can even read a newspaper . . . or who ever sees a book at all. I will go home and much of what I will have to say will seem strange to the people of my village. But I will teach and work and things will happen, slowly and swiftly. At times it will seem that nothing changes at all . . . and then again the sudden dramatic events which make history leap into the future. And then quiet again. Retrogression even. Guns, murder, revolution. And I even will have moments when I wonder if the quiet was not better than all that death and hatred. But I will look about my village at the illiteracy and disease and ignorance and I will not wonder long. And perhaps . . . perhaps I will be a great man . . . I mean perhaps I will hold on to the substance of truth and find my way always with the right course . . . and perhaps for it I will be butchered in my bed some night by the servants of empire . . .

Beneatha: The martyr!

Asagai (he smiles): . . . or perhaps I shall live to be a very old man, respected and esteemed in my new nation . . . And perhaps I shall hold office and this is what I'm trying to tell you, Alaiyo: perhaps the things I believe now for my country will be wrong and outmoded, and I will not understand and do terrible things to have things my way or merely to keep my power. Don't you see that there will be young men and women — not British soldiers then, but my own black countrymen — to step out of the shadows some evening and slit my then useless throat? Don't you see they have always been there . . . that they always will be. And that such a thing as my own death will be an advance? They who might kill me even . . . actually replenish all that I was.

Beneatha: Oh, Asagai, I know all that.

Asagai: Good! Then stop moaning and groaning and tell me what you plan to do.

Beneatha: Do?

Asagai: I have a bit of a suggestion.

Beneatha: What?

Asagai (rather quietly for him): That when it is all over — that you come home with me —

Beneatha (staring at him and crossing away with exasperation): Oh — Asagai — at this moment you decide to be romantic!

Asagai (quickly understanding the misunderstanding): My dear, young creature of the New World — I do not mean across the city — I mean across the ocean: home — to Africa.

Beneatha (slowly understanding and turning to him with murmured amazement): To Africa?

Asagai: Yes! . . . *(smiling and lifting his arms playfully.)* Three hundred years later the African Prince rose up out of the seas and swept the maiden back across the middle passage over which her ancestors had come —

Beneatha (unable to play): To — to Nigeria?

Asagai: Nigeria. Home. *(Coming to her with genuine romantic flippancy.)* I will show you our mountains and our stars; and give you cool drinks from gourds and teach you the old songs and the ways of our people — and, in time, we will pretend that — *(Very softly.)* — you have only been away for a day. Say that you'll come — *(He swings her around and takes her full in his arms in a kiss which proceeds to passion.)*

Beneatha (pulling away suddenly): You're getting me all mixed up —

Asagai: Why?

Beneatha: Too many things — too many things have happened today. I must sit down and think. I don't know what I feel about anything right this minute.

She promptly sits down and props her chin on her fist.

Asagai (charmed): All right, I shall leave you. No — don't get up. *(Touching her, gently, sweetly.)* Just sit awhile and think . . . Never be afraid to sit awhile and think. *(He goes to door and looks at her.)* How often I have looked at you and said, "Ah — so this is what the New World hath finally wrought . . ."

He exits. Beneatha sits on alone. Presently Walter enters from his room and starts to rummage through things, feverishly looking for something. She looks up and turns in her seat.

Beneatha (hissingly): Yes — just look at what the New World hath wrought! . . . Just look! *(She gestures with bitter disgust.)* There he is! *Monsieur le petit bourgeois noir°*—himself! There he is—Symbol of a Rising Class! Entrepreneur! Titan of the system! *(Walter ignores her completely and continues frantically and destructively looking for something and hurling things to floor and tearing things out of their place in his search. Beneatha ignores the eccentricity of his actions and goes on with the monologue of insult.)* Did you dream of yachts on Lake Michigan, Brother? Did you see yourself on that Great Day sitting down at the Conference Table, surrounded by all the mighty bald-headed men in America? All halted, waiting, breathless, waiting for your pronouncements on industry? Waiting for you—Chairman of the Board! *(Walter finds what he is looking for—a small piece of white paper—and pushes it in his pocket and puts on his coat and rushes out without ever having looked at her. She shouts after him.)* I look at you and I see the final triumph of stupidity in the world!

The door slams and she returns to just sitting again. Ruth comes quickly out of Mama's room.

Ruth: Who was that?

Beneatha: Your husband.

Ruth: Where did he go?

Beneatha: Who knows—maybe he has an appointment at U.S. Steel.

Ruth (anxiously, with frightened eyes): You didn't say nothing bad to him, did you?

Beneatha: Bad? Say anything bad to him? No—I told him he was a sweet boy and full of dreams and everything is strictly peachy keen, as the ofay kids say!

Mama enters from her bedroom. She is lost, vague, trying to catch hold, to make some sense of her former command of the world, but it still eludes her. A sense of waste overwhelms her gait; a measure of apology rides on her shoulders. She goes to her plant, which has remained on the table, looks at it, picks it up and takes it to the window sill and sits it outside, and she stands and looks at it a long moment. Then she closes the window, straightens her body with effort and turns around to her children.

Mama: Well—ain't it a mess in here, though? *(A false cheerfulness, a beginning of something.)* I guess we all better stop moping around and get some work done. All this unpacking and everything we got to do. *(Ruth raises her head slowly in response to the sense of the line; and Beneatha in similar manner turns very slowly to look at her mother.)* One of you all better call the moving people and tell 'em not to come.

Ruth: Tell 'em not to come?

Mama: Of course, baby. Ain't no need in 'em coming all the way here and having to go back. They charges for that too. *(She sits down, fingers to her brow, thinking.)* Lord, ever since I was a little girl, I always remembers people saying, "Lena—Lena Eggleston, you aims too high all the time. You needs to slow down and see life a little more like it is. Just slow down some." That's what they always used to say down home—"Lord, that Lena Eggleston is a high-minded thing. She'll get her due one day!"

Monsieur le petit bourgeois noir: Mr. Black Bourgeoisie (French).

Ruth: No, Lena . . .

Mama: Me and Big Walter just didn't never learn right.

Ruth: Lena, no! We gotta go. Bennie — tell her . . .

She rises and crosses to Beneatha with her arms outstretched. Beneatha doesn't respond.

Tell her we can still move . . . the notes ain't but a hundred and twenty-five a month. We got four grown people in this house — we can work . . .

Mama (to herself): Just aimed too high all the time —

Ruth (turning and going to Mama fast — the words pouring out with urgency and desperation): Lena — I'll work . . . I'll work twenty hours a day in all the kitchens in Chicago . . . I'll strap my baby on my back if I have to and scrub all the floors in America and wash all the sheets in America if I have to — but we got to MOVE! We got to get OUT OF HERE!!

Mama reaches out absently and pats Ruth's hand.

Mama: No — I sees things differently now. Been thinking 'bout some of the things we could do to fix this place up some. I seen a second-hand bureau over on Maxwell Street just the other day that could fit right there. *(She points to where the new furniture might go. Ruth wanders away from her.)* Would need some new handles on it and then a little varnish and it look like something brand-new. And — we can put up them new curtains in the kitchen . . . Why this place be looking fine. Cheer us all up so that we forget trouble ever come . . . *(To Ruth.)* And you could get some nice screens to put up in your room round the baby's bassinet . . . *(She looks at both of them pleadingly.)* Sometimes you just got to know when to give up some things . . . and hold on to what you got . . .

Walter enters from the outside, looking spent and leaning against the door, his coat hanging from him.

Mama: Where you been, son?

Walter (breathing hard): Made a call.

Mama: To who, son?

Walter: To The Man. *(He heads for his room.)*

Mama: What man, baby?

Walter (stops in the door): The Man, Mama. Don't you know who The Man is?

Ruth: Walter Lee?

Walter: The Man. Like the guys in the streets say — The Man. Captain Boss — Mistuh Charley . . . Old Cap'n Please Mr. Bossman . . .

Beneatha (suddenly): Lindner!

Walter: That's right! That's good. I told him to come right over.

Beneatha (fiercely, understanding): For what? What do you want to see him for!

Walter (looking at his sister): We going to do business with him.

Mama: What you talking 'bout, son?

Walter: Talking 'bout life, Mama. You all always telling me to see life like it is. Well — I laid in there on my back today . . . and I figured it out. Life just like it is. Who gets and who don't get. *(He sits down with his coat on and laughs.)* Mama, you know it's all divided up. Life is. Sure enough. Between the takers and the "tooken." *(He laughs.)* I've figured it out finally. *(He looks around at them.)* Yeah. Some of us always getting "tooken." *(He laughs.)*

People like Willy Harris, they don't never get "tooken." And you know why the rest of us do? 'Cause we all mixed up. Mixed up bad. We get to looking 'round for the right and the wrong; and we worry about it and cry about it and stay up nights trying to figure out 'bout the wrong and the right of things all the time . . . And all the time, man, them takers is out there operating, just taking and taking. Willy Harris? Shoot—Willy Harris don't even count. He don't even count in the big scheme of things. But I'll say one thing for old Willy Harris . . . he's taught me something. He's taught me to keep my eye on what counts in this world. Yeah—(*Shouting out a little.*) Thanks, Willy!

Ruth: What did you call that man for, Walter Lee?

Walter: Called him to tell him to come on over to the show. Gonna put on a show for the man. Just what he wants to see. You see, Mama, the man came here today and he told us that them people out there where you want us to move—well they so upset they willing to pay us *not* to move! (*He laughs again.*) And—and oh, Mama—you would of been proud of the way me and Ruth and Bennie acted. We told him to get out . . . Lord have mercy! We told the man to get out! Oh, we was some proud folks this afternoon, yeah. (*He lights a cigarette.*) We were still full of that old-time stuff . . .

Ruth (coming toward him slowly): You talking 'bout taking them people's money to keep us from moving in that house?

Walter: I ain't just talking 'bout it, baby—I'm telling you that's what's going to happen!

Beneatha: Oh, God! Where is the bottom! Where is the real honest-to-God bottom so he can't go any farther!

Walter: See—that's the old stuff. You and that boy that was here today. You all want everybody to carry a flag and a spear and sing some marching songs, huh? You wanna spend your life looking into things and trying to find the right and the wrong part, huh? Yeah. You know what's going to happen to that boy someday—he'll find himself sitting in a dungeon, locked in forever—and the takers will have the key! Forget it, baby! There ain't no causes—there ain't nothing but taking in this world, and he who takes most is smartest—and it don't make a damn bit of difference *how.*

Mama: You making something inside me cry, son. Some awful pain inside me.

Walter: Don't cry, Mama. Understand. That white man is going to walk in that door able to write checks for more money than we ever had. It's important to him and I'm going to help him . . . I'm going to put on the show, Mama.

Mama: Son—I come from five generations of people who was slaves and sharecroppers—but ain't nobody in my family never let nobody pay 'em no money that was a way of telling us we wasn't fit to walk the earth. We ain't never been that poor. (*Raising her eyes and looking at him.*) We ain't never been that—dead inside.

Beneatha: Well—we are dead now. All the talk about dreams and sunlight that goes on in this house. It's all dead now.

Walter: What's the matter with you all! I didn't make this world! It was give to me this way! Hell, yes, I want me some yachts someday! Yes, I want to hang some real pearls 'round my wife's neck. Ain't she supposed to wear no pearls? Somebody tell me — tell me, who decides which women is suppose to wear pearls in this world. I tell you I am a *man* — and I think my wife should wear some pearls in this world!

This last line hangs a good while and Walter begins to move about the room. The word "Man" has penetrated his consciousness; he mumbles it to himself repeatedly between strange agitated pauses as he moves about.

Mama: Baby, how you going to feel on the inside?

Walter: Fine! . . . Going to feel fine . . . a man . . .

Mama: You won't have nothing left then, Walter Lee.

Walter (coming to her): I'm going to feel fine, Mama. I'm going to look that son-of-a-bitch in the eyes and say — *(He falters.)* — and say, "All right, Mr. Lindner — *(He falters even more.)* — that's *your* neighborhood out there! You got the right to keep it like you want! You got the right to have it like you want! Just write the check and — the house is yours." And — and I am going to say — *(His voice almost breaks.)* "And you — you people just put the money in my hand and you won't have to live next to this bunch of stinking niggers! . . ." *(He straightens up and moves away from his mother, walking around the room.)* And maybe — maybe I'll just get down on my black knees . . . *(He does so; Ruth and Bennie and Mama watch him in frozen horror.)* "Captain, Mistuh, Bossman — *(Groveling and grinning and wringing his hands in profoundly anguished imitation of the slow-witted movie stereotype.)* A-hee-hee-hee! Oh, yassuh boss! Yasssssuh! Great white — *(Voice breaking, he forces himself to go on.)* — Father, just gi' ussen de money, fo' God's sake, and we's — we's ain't gwine come out deh and dirty up yo' white folks neighborhood . . ." *(He breaks down completely.)* And I'll feel fine! Fine! FINE! *(He gets up and goes into the bedroom.)*

Beneatha: That is not a man. That is nothing but a toothless rat.

Mama: Yes — death done come in this here house. *(She is nodding, slowly, reflectively.)* Done come walking in my house on the lips of my children. You what supposed to be my beginning again. You — what supposed to be my harvest. *(To Beneatha.)* You — you mourning your brother?

Beneatha: He's no brother of mine.

Mama: What you say?

Beneatha: I said that that individual in that room is no brother of mine.

Mama: That's what I thought you said. You feeling like you better than he is today? *(Beneatha does not answer.)* Yes? What you tell him a minute ago? That he wasn't a man? Yes? You give him up for me? You done wrote his epitaph too — like the rest of the world? Well, who give you the privilege?

Beneatha: Be on my side for once! You saw what he just did, Mama! You saw him — down on his knees. Wasn't it you who taught me to despise any man who would do that? Do what he's going to do?

Mama: Yes — I taught you that. Me and your daddy. But I thought I taught you something else too . . . I thought I taught you to love him.

Beneatha: Love him? There is nothing left to love.

Mama: There is *always* something left to love. And if you ain't learned that, you ain't learned nothing. *(Looking at her.)* Have you cried for that boy today? I don't mean for yourself and for the family 'cause we lost the money. I mean for him: what he been through and what it done to him. Child, when do you think is the time to love somebody the most? When they done good and made things easy for everybody? Well then, you ain't through learning — because that ain't the time at all. It's when he's at his lowest and can't believe in hisself 'cause the world done whipped him so! When you starts measuring somebody, measure him right, child, measure him right. Make sure you done taken into account what hills and valleys he come through before he got to wherever he is.

Travis bursts into the room at the end of the speech, leaving the door open.

Travis: Grandmama — the moving men are downstairs! The truck just pulled up.

Mama (turning and looking at him): Are they, baby? They downstairs?

She sighs and sits. Lindner appears in the doorway. He peers in and knocks lightly, to gain attention, and comes in. All turn to look at him.

Lindner (hat and briefcase in hand): Uh — hello . . .

Ruth crosses mechanically to the bedroom door and opens it and lets it swing open freely and slowly as the lights come up on Walter within, still in his coat, sitting at the far corner of the room. He looks up and out through the room to Lindner.

Ruth: He's here.

A long minute passes and Walter slowly gets up.

Lindner (coming to the table with efficiency, putting his briefcase on the table and starting to unfold papers and unscrew fountain pens): Well, I certainly was glad to hear from you people. *(Walter has begun the trek out of the room, slowly and awkwardly, rather like a small boy, passing the back of his sleeve across his mouth from time to time.)* Life can really be so much simpler than people let it be most of the time. Well — with whom do I negotiate? You, Mrs. Younger, or your son here? *(Mama sits with her hands folded on her lap and her eyes closed as Walter advances. Travis goes closer to Lindner and looks at the papers curiously.)* Just some official papers, sonny.

Ruth: Travis, you go downstairs —

Mama (opening her eyes and looking into Walter's): No. Travis, you stay right here. And you make him understand what you doing, Walter Lee. You teach him good. Like Willy Harris taught you. You show where our five generations done come to. *(Walter looks from her to the boy, who grins at him innocently.)* Go ahead, son — *(She folds her hands and closes her eyes.)* Go ahead.

Walter (at last crosses to Lindner, who is reviewing the contract): Well, Mr. Lindner. *(Beneatha turns away.)* We called you — *(There is a profound, simple groping quality in his speech.)* — because, well, me and my family *(He looks around and shifts from one foot to the other.)* Well — we are very plain people . . .

Lindner: Yes —

Walter: I mean — I have worked as a chauffeur most of my life — and my wife here, she does domestic work in people's kitchens. So does my mother. I mean — we are plain people . . .

Lindner: Yes, Mr. Younger —

Walter (really like a small boy, looking down at his shoes and then up at the man): And — uh — well, my father, well, he was a laborer most of his life. . . .

Lindner (absolutely confused): Uh, yes — yes, I understand. *(He turns back to the contract.)*

Walter (a beat; staring at him): And my father — *(With sudden intensity.)* My father almost *beat a man to death* once because this man called him a bad name or something, you know what I mean?

Lindner (looking up, frozen): No, no, I'm afraid I don't —

Walter (a beat. The tension hangs; then Walter steps back from it): Yeah. Well — what I mean is that we come from people who had a lot of *pride.* I mean — we are very proud people. And that's my sister over there and she's going to be a doctor — and we are very proud —

Lindner: Well — I am sure that is very nice, but —

Walter: What I am telling you is that we called you over here to tell you that we are very proud and that this — *(Signaling to Travis.)* Travis, come here. *(Travis crosses and Walter draws him before him facing the man.)* This is my son, and he makes the sixth generation our family in this country. And we have all thought about your offer —

Lindner: Well, good . . . good —

Walter: And we have decided to move into our house because my father — my father — he earned it for us brick by brick. *(Mama has her eyes closed and is rocking back and forth as though she were in church, with her head nodding the Amen yes.)* We don't want to make no trouble for nobody or fight no causes, and we will try to be good neighbors. And that's *all* we got to say about that. *(He looks the man absolutely in the eyes.)* We don't want your money. *(He turns and walks away.)*

Lindner (looking around at all of them): I take it then — that you have decided to occupy . . .

Beneatha: That's what the man said.

Lindner (to Mama in her reverie): Then I would like to appeal to you, Mrs. Younger. You are older and wiser and understand things better I am sure . . .

Mama: I am afraid you don't understand. My son said we was going to move and there ain't nothing left for me to say. *(Briskly.)* You know how these young folks is nowadays, mister. Can't do a thing with 'em! *(As he opens his mouth, she rises.)* Good-bye.

Lindner (folding up his materials): Well — if you are that final about it . . . there is nothing left for me to say. *(He finishes, almost ignored by the family, who are concentrating on Walter Lee. At the door Lindner halts and looks around.)* I sure hope you people know what you're getting into.

He shakes his head and exits.

Ruth (looking around and coming to life): Well, for God's sake — if the moving men are here — LET'S GET THE HELL OUT OF HERE!

Mama (into action): Ain't it the truth! Look at all this here mess. Ruth, put Travis' good jacket on him . . . Walter Lee, fix your tie and tuck your shirt in, you look like somebody's hoodlum! Lord have mercy, where is my plant? *(She flies to get it amid the general bustling of the family, who are deliberately trying to ignore the nobility of the past moment.)* You all start on down . . . Travis child, don't go empty-handed . . . Ruth, where did I put that box with my skillets in it? I want to be in charge of it my- self . . . I'm going to make us the biggest dinner we ever ate tonight . . . Be- neatha, what's the matter with them stockings? Pull them things up, girl . . .

The family starts to file out as two moving men appear and begin to carry out the heavier pieces of furniture, bumping into the family as they move about.

Beneatha: Mama, Asagai asked me to marry him today and go to Africa—

Mama (in the middle of her getting-ready activity): He did? You ain't old enough to marry nobody—*(Seeing the moving men lifting one of her chairs precariously.)* Darling, that ain't no bale of cotton, please handle it so we can sit in it again! I had that chair twenty-five years . . .

The movers sigh with exasperation and go on with their work.

Beneatha (girlishly and unreasonably trying to pursue the conversation): To go to Africa, Mama—be a doctor in Africa . . .

Mama (distracted): Yes, baby—

Walter: Africa! What he want you to go to Africa for?

Beneatha: To practice there . . .

Walter: Girl, if you don't get all them silly ideas out your head! You better marry yourself a man with some loot . . .

Beneatha (angrily, precisely as in the first scene of the play): What have you got to do with who I marry!

Walter: Plenty. Now I think George Murchison—

Beneatha: George Murchison! I wouldn't marry him if he was Adam and I was Eve!

Walter and Beneatha go out yelling at each other vigorously and the anger is loud and real till their voices diminish. Ruth stands at the door and turns to Mama and smiles knowingly.

Mama (fixing her hat at last): Yeah—they something all right, my children . . .

Ruth: Yeah—they're something. Let's go, Lena.

Mama (stalling, starting to look around at the house): Yes—I'm coming. Ruth—

Ruth: Yes?

Mama (quietly, woman to woman): He finally come into his manhood today, didn't he? Kind of like a rainbow after the rain . . .

Ruth (biting her lip lest her own pride explode in front of Mama): Yes, Lena.

Walter's voice calls for them raucously.

Walter (off stage): Y'all come on! These people charges by the hour, you know!

Mama (waving Ruth out vaguely): All right, honey—go on down. I be down directly.

Ruth hesitates, then exits. Mama stands, at last alone in the living room, her plant on the table before her as the lights start to come down. She looks around at all the walls and ceilings and suddenly, despite herself, while the children call below, a great heaving thing rises in her and she puts her fist to her mouth to stifle it, takes a final desperate look, pulls her coat about her, pats her hat, and goes out. The lights dim down. The door opens and she comes back in, grabs her plant, and goes out for the last time.

Curtain.

CONSIDERATIONS FOR CRITICAL THINKING AND WRITING

1. FIRST RESPONSE. The play's title is a line from the Langston Hughes poem that introduces the play (p. 636). Consider how the context of the entire poem helps to explain the play's title and its major concerns.

2. Comment on the significance of the play's setting in an apartment in Chicago's Southside after World War II.

3. Consider Lena Younger's role as a mother in the play. Explain why you think she is nurturing or overbearing.

4. How does the Younger's family history affect the family's present?

5. What are the causes of Walter's anger and resistance? To what extent do you empathize with him?

6. Do any of the characters seem stereotyped or sentimental to you? Why or why not?

7. What do you think are the dramatic purposes of Karl Lindner, Joseph Asagai, and George Murchison?

8. How do the stage directions affect your response to the characters? Explain whether or not you think these character descriptions are necessary in the play.

9. What kind of picture of black-white relations does the play draw? How are prejudice and segregation handled by the playwright?

10. How are conflicts between men and women related to other issues raised by the play?

11. How do you read the ending? Is it optimistic, pessimistic, or something else? What do you think the play suggests about the future of the family, of African Americans, and of America in general?

12. CRITICAL STRATEGIES. Read the section on literary history criticism (pp. 67–68) in Chapter 3, "Applying a Critical Strategy," and discuss how the social and economic pressures the Youngers confront contribute to the conflicts the characters experience.

HENRIK IBSEN (1828–1906)

Henrik Ibsen was born in Skien, Norway, to wealthy parents who lost their money while he was a young boy. His early experiences with small-town life and genteel poverty sensitized him to the problems that he subsequently dramatized in a number of his plays. Ibsen's earliest dramatic works were historical and romantic plays, some in verse. His first truly realistic work was *The Pillars of Society* (1877), whose title ironically hints at the corruption and hypocrisy exposed in it. The realistic social-problem plays for which he is best known followed. These dramas at once fascinated and shocked international audiences. Among his most produced and admired works are *A Doll House* (1879), *Ghosts* (1881), *An Enemy of the People* (1882), *The Wild Duck* (1884), and *Hedda Gabler* (1890). *A Doll House* dramatizes the tensions of a nineteenth-century middle-class marriage in which a wife struggles to step beyond the limited identity imposed on her by her husband and society. Several critical approaches to the play can be found in the casebook (pp. 762–68).

A Doll House 1879

TRANSLATED BY ROLF FJELDE

THE CHARACTERS

Torvald Helmer, a lawyer
Nora, his wife
Dr. Rank
Mrs. Linde
Nils Krogstad, a bank clerk
The Helmers' three small children
Anne-Marie, their nurse
Helene, a maid
A Delivery Boy

SCENE: *The action takes place in Helmer's residence.*

ACT I

A comfortable room, tastefully but not expensively furnished. A door to the right in the back wall leads to the entryway; another to the left leads to Helmer's study. Between these doors, a piano. Midway in the left-hand wall a door, and further back a window. Near the window a round table with an armchair and a small sofa. In the right-hand wall, toward the rear, a door, and nearer the foreground a porcelain stove with two armchairs and a rocking chair beside it. Between the stove and the side door, a small table. Engravings on the walls. An étagère with china figures and other small art objects; a small bookcase with richly bound books; the floor carpeted; a fire burning in the stove. It is a winter day.

A bell rings in the entryway; shortly after we hear the door being unlocked. Nora comes into the room, humming happily to herself; she is wearing street clothes and carries an armload of packages, which she puts down on the table to the right. She has left the hall door open; and through it a Delivery Boy is seen, holding a Christmas tree and a basket, which he gives to the Maid who let them in.

Nora: Hide the tree well, Helene. The children mustn't get a glimpse of it till this evening, after it's trimmed. *(To the Delivery Boy, taking out her purse.)* How much?

Delivery Boy: Fifty, ma'am.

Nora: There's a crown. No, keep the change. *(The Boy thanks her and leaves. Nora shuts the door. She laughs softly to herself while taking off her street things. Drawing a bag of macaroons from her pocket, she eats a couple, then steals over and listens at her husband's study door.)* Yes, he's home. *(Hums again as she moves to the table right.)*

Helmer (from the study): Is that my little lark twittering out there?

Nora (busy opening some packages): Yes, it is.

Helmer: Is that my squirrel rummaging around?

Nora: Yes!

Helmer: When did my squirrel get in?

Nora: Just now. *(Putting the macaroon bag in her pocket and wiping her mouth.)* Do come in, Torvald, and see what I've bought.

Helmer: Can't be disturbed. *(After a moment he opens the door and peers in, pen in hand.)* Bought, you say? All that there? Has the little spendthrift been out throwing money around again?

Nora: Oh, but Torvald, this year we really should let ourselves go a bit. It's the first Christmas we haven't had to economize.

Helmer: But you know we can't go squandering.

Nora: Oh yes, Torvald, we can squander a little now. Can't we? Just a tiny, wee bit. Now that you've got a big salary and are going to make piles and piles of money.

Helmer: Yes — starting New Year's. But then it's a full three months till the raise comes through.

Nora: Pooh! We can borrow that long.

Helmer: Nora! *(Goes over and playfully takes her by the ear.)* Are your scatter-brains off again? What if today I borrowed a thousand crowns, and you squandered them over Christmas week, and then on New Year's Eve a roof tile fell on my head and I lay there —

Nora (putting her hand on his mouth): Oh! Don't say such things!

Helmer: Yes, but what if it happened — then what?

Nora: If anything so awful happened, then it just wouldn't matter if I had debts or not.

Helmer: Well, but the people I'd borrowed from?

Nora: Them? Who cares about them! They're strangers.

Helmer: Nora, Nora, how like a woman! No, but seriously, Nora, you know what I think about that. No debts! Never borrow! Something of freedom's lost — and something of beauty, too — from a home that's founded on borrowing and debt. We've made a brave stand up to now, the two of us; and we'll go right on like that the little while we have to.

Nora (going toward the stove): Yes, whatever you say, Torvald.

Helmer (following her): Now, now, the little lark's wings mustn't droop. Come on, don't be a sulky squirrel. *(Taking out his wallet.)* Nora, guess what I have here.

Nora (turning quickly): Money!

Helmer: There, see. *(Hands her some notes.)* Good grief, I know how costs go up in a house at Christmastime.

Nora: Ten — twenty — thirty — forty. Oh, thank you, Torvald; I can manage no end on this.

Helmer: You really will have to.

Nora: Oh yes, I promise I will! But come here so I can show you everything I bought. And so cheap! Look, new clothes for Ivar here — and a sword. Here a horse and a trumpet for Bob. And a doll and a doll's bed here for Emmy; they're nothing much, but she'll tear them to bits in no time anyway. And here I have dress material and handkerchiefs for the maids. Old Anne-Marie really deserves something more.

Helmer: And what's in that package there?

Nora (with a cry): Torvald, no! You can't see that till tonight!

Helmer: I see. But tell me now, you little prodigal, what have you thought of for yourself?

Nora: For myself? Oh, I don't want anything at all.

Helmer: Of course you do. Tell me just what — within reason — you'd most like to have.

Nora: I honestly don't know. Oh, listen, Torvald —

Helmer: Well?

Nora (fumbling at his coat buttons, without looking at him): If you want to give me something, then maybe you could — you could —

Helmer: Come on, out with it.

Nora (hurriedly): You could give me money, Torvald. No more than you think you can spare; then one of these days I'll buy something with it.

Helmer: But Nora —

Nora: Oh please, Torvald darling, do that! I beg you, please. Then I could hang the bills in pretty gilt paper on the Christmas tree. Wouldn't that be fun?

Helmer: What are those little birds called that always fly through their fortunes?

Nora: Oh yes, spendthrifts: I know all that. But let's do as I say, Torvald; then I'll have time to decide what I really need most. That's very sensible, isn't it?

Helmer (smiling): Yes, very — that is, if you actually hung onto the money I give you, and you actually used it to buy yourself something. But it goes for the house and for all sorts of foolish things, and then I only have to lay out some more.

Nora: Oh, but Torvald —

Helmer: Don't deny it, my dear little Nora. *(Putting his arm around her waist.)* Spendthrifts are sweet, but they use up a frightful amount of money. It's incredible what it costs a man to feed such birds.

Nora: Oh, how can you say that! Really, I save everything I can.

Helmer (laughing): Yes, that's the truth. Everything you can. But that's nothing at all.

Nora (humming, with a smile of quiet satisfaction): Hm, if you only knew what expenses we larks and squirrels have, Torvald.

Helmer: You're an odd little one. Exactly the way your father was. You're never at a loss for scaring up money; but the moment you have it, it runs right out through your fingers; you never know what you've done with it. Well, one takes you as you are. It's deep in your blood. Yes, these things are hereditary, Nora.

Nora: Ah, I could wish I'd inherited many of Papa's qualities.

Helmer: And I couldn't wish you anything but just what you are, my sweet little lark. But wait; it seems to me you have a very — what should I call it? — a very suspicious look today —

Nora: I do?

Helmer: You certainly do. Look me straight in the eye.

Nora (looking at him): Well?

Helmer (shaking an admonitory finger): Surely my sweet tooth hasn't been running riot in town today, has she?

Nora: No. Why do you imagine that?

Helmer: My sweet tooth really didn't make a little detour through the confectioner's?

Nora: No, I assure you, Torvald —

Helmer: Hasn't nibbled some pastry?

Nora: No, not at all.

Helmer: Not even munched a macaroon or two?

Nora: No, Torvald, I assure you, really —

Helmer: There, there now. Of course I'm only joking.

Nora (going to the table, right): You know I could never think of going against you.

Helmer: No, I understand that; and you *have* given me your word. *(Going over to her.)* Well, you keep your little Christmas secrets to yourself, Nora darling. I expect they'll come to light this evening, when the tree is lit.

Nora: Did you remember to ask Dr. Rank?

Helmer: No. But there's no need for that: it's assumed he'll be dining with us. All the same, I'll ask him when he stops by here this morning. I've ordered some fine wine. Nora, you can't imagine how I'm looking forward to this evening.

Nora: So am I. And what fun for the children, Torvald!

Helmer: Ah, it's so gratifying to know that one's gotten a safe, secure job, and with a comfortable salary. It's a great satisfaction, isn't it?

Nora: Oh, it's wonderful!

Helmer: Remember last Christmas? Three whole weeks before, you shut yourself in every evening till long after midnight, making flowers for the Christmas tree, and all the other decorations to surprise us. Ugh, that was the dullest time I've ever lived through.

Nora: It wasn't at all dull for me.

Helmer (smiling): But the outcome *was* pretty sorry, Nora.

Nora: Oh, don't tease me with that again. How could I help it that the cat came in and tore everything to shreds.

Helmer: No, poor thing, you certainly couldn't. You wanted so much to please us all, and that's what counts. But it's just as well that the hard times are past.

Nora: Yes, it's really wonderful.

Helmer: Now I don't have to sit here alone, boring myself, and you don't have to tire your precious eyes and your fair little delicate hands —

Nora (clapping her hands): No, is it really true, Torvald, I don't have to? Oh, how wonderfully lovely to hear! *(Taking his arm.)* Now I'll tell you just how I've thought we should plan things. Right after Christmas — *(The doorbell rings.)* Oh, the bell. *(Straightening the room up a bit.)* Somebody would have to come. What a bore!

Helmer: I'm not home to visitors, don't forget.

Maid (from the hall doorway): Ma'am, a lady to see you —

Nora: All right, let her come in.

Maid (to Helmer): And the doctor's just come too.

Helmer: Did he go right to my study?

Maid: Yes, he did.

Helmer goes into his room. The Maid shows in Mrs. Linde, dressed in traveling clothes, and shuts the door after her.

Mrs. Linde (in a dispirited and somewhat hesitant voice): Hello, Nora.

Nora (uncertain): Hello —

Mrs. Linde: You don't recognize me.

Nora: No, I don't know — but wait, I think — *(Exclaiming.)* What! Kristine! Is it really you?

Mrs. Linde: Yes, it's me.

Nora: Kristine! To think I didn't recognize you. But then, how could I? *(More quietly.)* How you've changed, Kristine!

Mrs. Linde: Yes, no doubt I have. In nine — ten long years.

Nora: Is it so long since we met! Yes, it's all of that. Oh, these last eight years have been a happy time, believe me. And so now you've come in to town, too. Made the long trip in the winter. That took courage.

Mrs. Linde: I just got here by ship this morning.

Nora: To enjoy yourself over Christmas, of course. Oh, how lovely! Yes, enjoy ourselves, we'll do that. But take your coat off. You're not still cold? *(Helping her.)* There now, let's get cozy here by the stove. No, the easy chair there! I'll take the rocker here. *(Seizing her hands.)* Yes, now you have your old look again; it was only in that first moment. You're a bit more pale, Kristine — and maybe a bit thinner.

Mrs. Linde: And much, much older, Nora.

Nora: Yes, perhaps a bit older: a tiny, tiny bit; not much at all. *(Stopping short; suddenly serious.)* Oh, but thoughtless me, to sit here, chattering away. Sweet, good Kristine, can you forgive me?

Mrs. Linde: What do you mean, Nora?

Nora (softly): Poor Kristine, you've become a widow.

Mrs. Linde: Yes, three years ago.

Nora: Oh, I knew it, of course: I read it in the papers. Oh, Kristine, you must believe me; I often thought of writing you then, but I kept postponing it, and something always interfered.

Mrs. Linde: Nora dear, I understand completely.

Nora: No, it was awful of me, Kristine. You poor thing, how much you must have gone through. And he left you nothing?

Mrs. Linde: No.

Nora: And no children?

Mrs. Linde: No.

Nora: Nothing at all, then?

Mrs. Linde: Not even a sense of loss to feed on.

Nora (looking incredulously at her): But Kristine, how could that be?

Mrs. Linde (smiling wearily and smoothing her hair): Oh, sometimes it happens, Nora.

Nora: So completely alone. How terribly hard that must be for you. I have three lovely children. You can't see them now; they're out with the maid. But now you must tell me everything —

Mrs. Linde: No, no, no, tell me about yourself.

Nora: No, you begin. Today I don't want to be selfish. I want to think only of you today. But there *is* something I must tell you. Did you hear of the wonderful luck we had recently?

Mrs. Linde: No, what's that?

Nora: My husband's been made manager in the bank, just think!

Mrs. Linde: Your husband? How marvelous!

Nora: Isn't it? Being a lawyer is such an uncertain living, you know, especially if one won't touch any cases that aren't clean and decent. And of course Torvald would never do that, and I'm with him completely there. Oh, we're simply delighted, believe me! He'll join the bank right after New Year's and start getting a huge salary and lots of commissions. From now on we can live quite differently — just as we want. Oh, Kristine, I feel so light and happy! Won't it be lovely to have stacks of money and not a care in the world?

Mrs. Linde: Well, anyway, it would be lovely to have enough for necessities.

Nora: No, not just for necessities, but stacks and stacks of money!

Mrs. Linde (smiling): Nora, Nora, aren't you sensible yet? Back in school you were such a free spender.

Nora (with a quiet laugh): Yes, that's what Torvald still says. *(Shaking her finger.)* But "Nora, Nora" isn't as silly as you all think. Really, we've been in no position for me to go squandering. We've had to work, both of us.

Mrs. Linde: You too?

Nora: Yes, at odd jobs — needlework, crocheting, embroidery, and such — *(Casually.)* and other things too. You remember that Torvald left the department when we were married? There was no chance of promotion in his office, and of course he needed to earn more money. But that first year he drove himself terribly. He took on all kinds of extra work that kept him going morning and night. It wore him down, and then he fell deathly ill. The doctors said it was essential for him to travel south.

Mrs. Linde: Yes, didn't you spend a whole year in Italy?

Nora: That's right. It wasn't easy to get away, you know. Ivar had just been born. But of course we had to go. Oh, that was a beautiful trip, and it saved Torvald's life. But it cost a frightful sum, Kristine.

Mrs. Linde: I can well imagine.

Nora: Four thousand, eight hundred crowns it cost. That's really a lot of money.

Mrs. Linde: But it's lucky you had it when you needed it.

Nora: Well, as it was, we got it from Papa.

Mrs. Linde: I see. It was just about the time your father died.

Nora: Yes, just about then. And, you know, I couldn't make that trip out to nurse him. I had to stay here, expecting Ivar any moment, and with my poor sick Torvald to care for. Dearest Papa, I never saw him again, Kristine. Oh, that was the worst time I've known in all my marriage.

Mrs. Linde: I know how you loved him. And then you went off to Italy?

Nora: Yes. We had the means now, and the doctors urged us. So we left a month after.

Mrs. Linde: And your husband came back completely cured?

Nora: Sound as a drum!

Mrs. Linde: But — the doctor?

Nora: Who?

Mrs. Linde: I thought the maid said he was a doctor, the man who came in with me.

Nora: Yes, that was Dr. Rank — but he's not making a sick call. He's our closest friend, and he stops by at least once a day. No, Torvald hasn't had a sick moment since, and the children are fit and strong, and I am, too. *(Jumping up and clapping her hands.)* Oh, dear God, Kristine, what a lovely thing to live and be happy! But how disgusting of me — I'm talking of nothing but my own affairs. *(Sits on a stool close by Kristine, arms resting across her knees.)* Oh, don't be angry with me! Tell me, is it really true that you weren't in love with your husband? Why did you marry him, then?

Mrs. Linde: My mother was still alive, but bedridden and helpless — and I had my two younger brothers to look after. In all conscience, I didn't think I could turn him down.

Nora: No, you were right there. But was he rich at the time?

Mrs. Linde: He was very well off, I'd say. But the business was shaky, Nora. When he died, it all fell apart, and nothing was left.

Nora: And then — ?

Mrs. Linde: Yes, so I had to scrape up a living with a little shop and a little teaching and whatever else I could find. The last three years have been like one endless workday without a rest for me. Now it's over, Nora. My poor mother doesn't need me, for she's passed on. Nor the boys, either; they're working now and can take care of themselves.

Nora: How free you must feel —

Mrs. Linde: No — only unspeakably empty. Nothing to live for now. *(Standing up anxiously.)* That's why I couldn't take it any longer out in that desolate hole. Maybe here it'll be easier to find something to do and keep my mind occupied. If I could only be lucky enough to get a steady job, some office work —

Nora: Oh, but Kristine, that's so dreadfully tiring, and you already look so tired. It would be much better for you if you could go off to a bathing resort.

Mrs. Linde (going toward the window): I have no father to give me travel money, Nora.

Nora (rising): Oh, don't be angry with me.

Mrs. Linde (going to her): Nora dear, don't you be angry with me. The worst of my kind of situation is all the bitterness that's stored away. No one to work for, and yet you're always having to snap up your opportunities. You have to live; and so you grow selfish. When you told me the happy change in your lot, do you know I was delighted less for your sakes than for mine?

Nora: How so? Oh, I see. You think maybe Torvald could do something for you.

Mrs. Linde: Yes, that's what I thought.

Nora: And he will, Kristine! Just leave it to me; I'll bring it up so delicately — find something attractive to humor him with. Oh, I'm so eager to help you.

Mrs. Linde: How very kind of you, Nora, to be so concerned over me — doubly kind, considering you really know so little of life's burdens yourself.

Nora: I — ? I know so little — ?

Mrs. Linde (smiling): Well, my heavens — a little needlework and such — Nora, you're just a child.

Nora (tossing her head and pacing the floor): You don't have to act so superior.

Mrs. Linde: Oh?

Nora: You're just like the others. You all think I'm incapable of anything serious —

Mrs. Linde: Come now —

Nora: That I've never had to face the raw world.

Mrs. Linde: Nora dear, you've just been telling me all your troubles.

Nora: Hm! Trivia! *(Quietly.)* I haven't told you the big thing.

Mrs. Linde: Big thing? What do you mean?

Nora: You look down on me so, Kristine, but you shouldn't. You're proud that you worked so long and hard for your mother.

Mrs. Linde: I don't look down on a soul. But it *is* true: I'm proud — and happy, too — to think it was given to me to make my mother's last days almost free of care.

Nora: And you're also proud thinking of what you've done for your brothers.

Mrs. Linde: I feel I've a right to be.

Nora: I agree. But listen to this, Kristine — I've also got something to be proud and happy for.

Mrs. Linde: I don't doubt it. But whatever do you mean?

Nora: Not so loud. What if Torvald heard! He mustn't, not for anything in the world. Nobody must know, Kristine. No one but you.

Mrs. Linde: But what is it, then?

Nora: Come here. *(Drawing her down beside her on the sofa.)* It's true — I've also got something to be proud and happy for. I'm the one who saved Torvald's life.

Mrs. Linde: Saved — ? Saved how?

Nora: I told you about the trip to Italy. Torvald never would have lived if he hadn't gone south —

Mrs. Linde: Of course; your father gave you the means —

Nora (smiling): That's what Torvald and all the rest think, but —

Mrs. Linde: But — ?

Nora: Papa didn't give us a pin. I was the one who raised the money.

Mrs. Linde: You? That whole amount?

Nora: Four thousand, eight hundred crowns. What do you say to that?

Mrs. Linde: But Nora, how was it possible? Did you win the lottery?

Nora (disdainfully): The lottery? Pooh! No art to that.

Mrs. Linde: But where did you get it from then?

Nora (humming, with a mysterious smile): Hmm, tra-la-la-la.

Mrs. Linde: Because you couldn't have borrowed it.

Nora: No? Why not?

Mrs. Linde: A wife can't borrow without her husband's consent.

Nora (tossing her head): Oh, but a wife with a little business sense, a wife who knows how to manage —

Mrs. Linde: Nora, I simply don't understand —

Nora: You don't have to. Whoever said I *borrowed* the money? I could have gotten it other ways. *(Throwing herself back on the sofa.)* I could have gotten it from some admirer or other. After all, a girl with my ravishing appeal —

Mrs. Linde: You lunatic.

Nora: I'll bet you're eaten up with curiosity, Kristine.

Mrs. Linde: Now listen here, Nora — you haven't done something indiscreet?

Nora (sitting up again): Is it indiscreet to save your husband's life?

Mrs. Linde: I think it's indiscreet that without his knowledge you —

Nora: But that's the point: he mustn't know! My Lord, can't you understand? He mustn't ever know the close call he had. It was to *me* the doctors came to say his life was in danger — that nothing could save him but a stay in the south. Didn't I try strategy then! I began talking about how lovely it would be for me to travel abroad like other young wives; I begged and I cried; I told him please to remember my condition, to be kind and indulge me; and then I dropped a hint that he could easily take out a loan. But at that, Kristine, he nearly exploded. He said I was frivolous, and it was his duty as man of the house not to indulge me in whims and fancies — as I think he called them. Aha, I thought, now you'll just have to be saved — and that's when I saw my chance.

Mrs. Linde: And your father never told Torvald the money wasn't from him?

Nora: No, never. Papa died right about then. I'd considered bringing him into my secret and begging him never to tell. But he was too sick at the time — and then, sadly, it didn't matter.

Mrs. Linde: And you've never confided in your husband since?

Nora: For heaven's sake, no! Are you serious? He's so strict on that subject. Besides — Torvald, with all his masculine pride — how painfully humiliating for him if he ever found out he was in debt to me. That would just ruin our relationship. Our beautiful, happy home would never be the same.

Mrs. Linde: Won't you ever tell him?

Nora (thoughtfully, half smiling): Yes — maybe sometime, years from now, when I'm no longer so attractive. Don't laugh! I only mean when Torvald loves me less than now, when he stops enjoying my dancing and dressing up and reciting for him. Then it might be wise to have something in reserve — *(Breaking off.)* How ridiculous! That'll never happen — Well, Kristine, what do you think of my big secret? I'm capable of something too, hm? You can imagine, of course, how this thing hangs over me. It really hasn't been easy meeting the payments on time. In the business world there's what they call quarterly interest and what they call amortization, and these are always so terribly hard to manage. I've had to skimp a little here and there, wherever I could, you know. I could hardly spare anything from my house allowance, because Torvald has to live well. I couldn't let the children go poorly dressed; whatever I got for them, I felt I had to use up completely — the darlings!

Mrs. Linde: Poor Nora, so it had to come out of your own budget, then?

Nora: Yes, of course. But I was the one most responsible, too. Every time Torvald gave me money for new clothes and such, I never used more than half; always bought the simplest, cheapest outfits. It was a godsend that everything looks so well on me that Torvald never noticed. But it did weigh me down at times, Kristine. It *is* such a joy to wear fine things. You understand.

Mrs. Linde: Oh, of course.

Nora: And then I found other ways of making money. Last winter I was lucky enough to get a lot of copying to do. I locked myself in and sat writing every evening till late in the night. Ah, I was tired so often, dead tired. But still it was wonderful fun, sitting and working like that, earning money. It was almost like being a man.

Mrs. Linde: But how much have you paid off this way so far?

Nora: That's hard to say, exactly. These accounts, you know, aren't easy to figure. I only know that I've paid out all I could scrape together. Time and again I haven't known where to turn. *(Smiling.)* Then I'd sit here dreaming of a rich old gentleman who had fallen in love with me —

Mrs. Linde: What! Who is he?

Nora: Oh, really! And that he'd died, and when his will was opened, there in big letters it said, "All my fortune shall be paid over in cash, immediately, to that enchanting Mrs. Nora Helmer."

Mrs. Linde: But Nora dear — who *was* this gentleman?

Nora: Good grief, can't you understand? The old man never existed; that was only something I'd dream up time and again whenever I was at my wits' end for money. But it makes no difference now; the old fossil can go where he pleases for all I care; I don't need him or his will — because now I'm free. *(Jumping up.)* Oh, how lovely to think of that, Kristine! Carefree! To know you're carefree, utterly carefree; to be able to romp and play with the children, and to keep up a beautiful, charming home — everything just the way Torvald likes it! And think, spring is coming, with big blue skies. Maybe we can travel a little then. Maybe I'll see the ocean again. Oh yes, it *is* so marvelous to live and be happy!

    The front doorbell rings.

Mrs. Linde (rising): There's the bell. It's probably best that I go.

Nora: No, stay. No one's expected. It must be for Torvald.

Maid (from the hall doorway): Excuse me, ma'am — there's a gentleman here to see Mr. Helmer, but I didn't know — since the doctor's with him —

Nora: Who is the gentleman?

Krogstad (from the doorway): It's me, Mrs. Helmer.

    Mrs. Linde starts and turns away toward the window.

Nora (stepping toward him, tense, her voice a whisper): You? What is it? Why do you want to speak to my husband?

Krogstad: Bank business — after a fashion. I have a small job in the investment bank, and I hear now your husband is going to be our chief —

Nora: In other words, it's —

Krogstad: Just dry business, Mrs. Helmer. Nothing but that.

Nora: Yes, then please be good enough to step into the study. *(She nods indifferently as she sees him out by the hall door, then returns and begins stirring up the stove.)*

Mrs. Linde: Nora — who was that man?

Nora: That was a Mr. Krogstad — a lawyer.

Mrs. Linde: Then it really was him.

Nora: Do you know that person?

Mrs. Linde: I did once — many years ago. For a time he was a law clerk in our town.

Nora: Yes, he's been that.

Mrs. Linde: How he's changed.

Nora: I understand he had a very unhappy marriage.

Mrs. Linde: He's a widower now.

Nora: With a number of children. There now, it's burning. *(She closes the stove door and moves the rocker a bit to one side.)*

Mrs. Linde: They say he has a hand in all kinds of business.

Nora: Oh? That may be true; I wouldn't know. But let's not think about business. It's so dull.

    Dr. Rank enters from Helmer's study.

Rank (still in the doorway): No, no really — I don't want to intrude, I'd just as soon talk a little while with your wife. *(Shuts the door, then notices Mrs. Linde.)* Oh, beg pardon. I'm intruding here too.

Nora: No, not at all. *(Introducing him.)* Dr. Rank, Mrs. Linde.

Rank: Well now, that's a name much heard in this house. I believe I passed the lady on the stairs as I came.

Mrs. Linde: Yes, I take the stairs very slowly. They're rather hard on me.

Rank: Uh-hm, some touch of internal weakness?

Mrs. Linde: More overexertion, I'd say.

Rank: Nothing else? Then you're probably here in town to rest up in a round of parties?

Mrs. Linde: I'm here to look for work.

Rank: Is that the best cure for overexertion?

Mrs. Linde: One has to live, Doctor.

Rank: Yes, there's a common prejudice to that effect.

Nora: Oh, come on, Dr. Rank—you really do want to live yourself.

Rank: Yes, I really do. Wretched as I am, I'll gladly prolong my torment indefinitely. All my patients feel like that. And it's quite the same, too, with the morally sick. Right at this moment there's one of those moral invalids in there with Helmer—

Mrs. Linde (softly): Ah!

Nora: Who do you mean?

Rank: Oh, it's a lawyer, Krogstad, a type you wouldn't know. His character is rotten to the root—but even he began chattering all-importantly about how he had to *live.*

Nora: Oh? What did he want to talk to Torvald about?

Rank: I really don't know. I only heard something about the bank.

Nora: I didn't know that Krog—that this man Krogstad had anything to do with the bank.

Rank: Yes, he's gotten some kind of berth down there. *(To Mrs. Linde.)* I don't know if you also have, in your neck of the woods, a type of person who scuttles about breathlessly, sniffing out hints of moral corruption, and then maneuvers his victim into some sort of key position where he can keep an eye on him. It's the healthy these days that are out in the cold.

Mrs. Linde: All the same, it's the sick who most need to be taken in.

Rank (with a shrug): Yes, there we have it. That's the concept that's turning society into a sanatorium.

Nora, lost in her thoughts, breaks out into quiet laughter and claps her hands.

Rank: Why do you laugh at that? Do you have any real idea of what society is?

Nora: What do I care about dreary old society? I was laughing at something quite different—something terribly funny. Tell me, Doctor—is everyone who works in the bank dependent now on Torvald?

Rank: Is that what you find so terribly funny?

Nora (smiling and humming): Never mind, never mind! *(Pacing the floor.)* Yes, that's really immensely amusing: that we—that Torvald has so much power now over all those people. *(Taking the bag out of her pocket.)* Dr. Rank, a little macaroon on that?

Rank: See here, macaroons! I thought they were contraband here.

Nora: Yes, but these are some that Kristine gave me.

Mrs. Linde: What? I—?

Nora: Now, now, don't be afraid. You couldn't possibly know that Torvald had forbidden them. You see, he's worried they'll ruin my teeth. But hmp! Just this once! Isn't that so, Dr. Rank? Help yourself! *(Puts a macaroon in his mouth.)* And you too, Kristine. And I'll also have one, only a little one—or two, at the most. *(Walking about again.)* Now I'm really tremendously happy. Now there's just one last thing in the world that I have an enormous desire to do.

Rank: Well! And what's that?

Nora: It's something I have such a consuming desire to say so Torvald could hear.

Rank: And why can't you say it?

Nora: I don't dare. It's quite shocking.

Mrs. Linde: Shocking?

Rank: Well, then it isn't advisable. But in front of us you certainly can. What do you have such a desire to say so Torvald could hear?

Nora: I have such a huge desire to say — to hell and be damned!

Rank: Are you crazy?

Mrs. Linde: My goodness, Nora!

Rank: Go on, say it. Here he is.

Nora (hiding the macaroon bag): Shh, shh, shh!

Helmer comes in from his study, hat in hand, overcoat over his arm.

Nora (going toward him): Well, Torvald dear, are you through with him?

Helmer: Yes, he just left.

Nora: Let me introduce you — this is Kristine, who's arrived here in town.

Helmer: Kristine — ? I'm sorry, but I don't know —

Nora: Mrs. Linde, Torvald dear. Mrs. Kristine Linde.

Helmer: Of course. A childhood friend of my wife's, no doubt?

Mrs. Linde: Yes, we knew each other in those days.

Nora: And just think, she made the long trip down here in order to talk with you.

Helmer: What's this?

Mrs. Linde: Well, not exactly —

Nora: You see, Kristine is remarkably clever in office work, and so she's terribly eager to come under a capable man's supervision and add more to what she already knows —

Helmer: Very wise, Mrs. Linde.

Nora: And then when she heard that you'd become a bank manager — the story was wired out to the papers — then she came in as fast as she could and — Really, Torvald, for my sake you can do a little something for Kristine, can't you?

Helmer: Yes, it's not at all impossible. Mrs. Linde, I suppose you're a widow?

Mrs. Linde: Yes.

Helmer: Any experience in office work?

Mrs. Linde: Yes, a good deal.

Helmer: Well, it's quite likely that I can make an opening for you —

Nora (clapping her hands): You see, you see!

Helmer: You've come at a lucky moment, Mrs. Linde.

Mrs. Linde: Oh, how can I thank you?

Helmer: Not necessary. *(Putting his overcoat on.)* But today you'll have to excuse me —

Rank: Wait, I'll go with you. *(He fetches his coat from the hall and warms it at the stove.)*

Nora: Don't stay out long, dear.

Helmer: An hour; no more.

Nora: Are you going too, Kristine?

Mrs. Linde (putting on her winter garments): Yes, I have to see about a room now.

Helmer: Then perhaps we can all walk together.

Nora (helping her): What a shame we're so cramped here, but it's quite impossible for us to —

Mrs. Linde: Oh, don't even think of it! Good-bye, Nora dear, and thanks for everything.

Nora: Good-bye for now. Of course you'll be back this evening. And you too, Dr. Rank. What? If you're well enough? Oh, you've got to be! Wrap up tight now.

In a ripple of small talk the company moves out into the hall; children's voices are heard outside on the steps.

Nora: There they are! There they are! *(She runs to open the door. The children come in with their nurse, Anne-Marie.)* Come in, come in! *(Bends down and kisses them.)* Oh, you darlings — ! Look at them, Kristine. Aren't they lovely!

Rank: No loitering in the draft here.

Helmer: Come, Mrs. Linde — this place is unbearable now for anyone but mothers.

Dr. Rank, Helmer, and Mrs. Linde go down the stairs. Anne-Marie goes into the living room with the children. Nora follows, after closing the hall door.

Nora: How fresh and strong you look. Oh, such red cheeks you have! Like apples and roses. *(The children interrupt her throughout the following.)* And it was so much fun? That's wonderful. Really? You pulled both Emmy and Bob on the sled? Imagine, all together! Yes, you're a clever boy, Ivar. Oh, let me hold her a bit, Anne-Marie. My sweet little doll baby! *(Takes the smallest from the nurse and dances with her.)* Yes, yes, Mama will dance with Bob as well. What? Did you throw snowballs? Oh, if I'd only been there! No, don't bother, Anne-Marie — I'll undress them myself. Oh yes, let me. It's such fun. Go in and rest; you look half frozen. There's hot coffee waiting for you on the stove. *(The nurse goes into the room to the left. Nora takes the children's winter things off, throwing them about, while the children talk to her all at once.)* Is that so? A big dog chased you? But it didn't bite? No, dogs never bite little, lovely doll babies. Don't peek in the packages, Ivar! What is it? Yes, wouldn't you like to know. No, no, it's an ugly something. Well? Shall we play? What shall we play? Hide-and-seek? Yes, let's play hide-and-seek. Bob must hide first. I must? Yes, let me hide first. *(Laughing and shouting, she and the children play in and out of the living room and the adjoining room to the right. At last Nora hides under the table. The children come storming in, search, but cannot find her, then hear her muffled laughter, dash over to the table, lift the cloth up and find her. Wild shouting. She creeps forward as if to scare them. More shouts. Meanwhile, a knock at the hall door; no one has noticed it. Now the door half opens, and Krogstad appears. He waits a moment; the game goes on.)*

Krogstad: Beg pardon, Mrs. Helmer —

Nora (with a strangled cry, turning and scrambling to her knees): Oh! What do you want?

Krogstad: Excuse me. The outer door was ajar; it must be someone forgot to shut it —

Nora (rising): My husband isn't home, Mr. Krogstad.

Krogstad: I know that.

Nora: Yes — then what do you want here?

Krogstad: A word with you.

Nora: With — ? *(To the children, quietly.)* Go in to Anne-Marie. What? No, the strange man won't hurt Mama. When he's gone, we'll play some more. *(She leads the children into the room to the left and shuts the door after them. Then, tense and nervous:)* You want to speak to me?

Krogstad: Yes, I want to.

Nora: Today? But it's not yet the first of the month —

Krogstad: No, it's Christmas Eve. It's going to be up to you how merry a Christmas you have.

Nora: What is it you want? Today I absolutely can't —

Krogstad: We won't talk about that till later. This is something else. You do have a moment to spare, I suppose?

Nora: Oh yes, of course — I do, except —

Krogstad: Good. I was sitting over at Olsen's Restaurant when I saw your husband go down the street —

Nora: Yes?

Krogstad: With a lady.

Nora: Yes. So?

Krogstad: If you'll pardon my asking: wasn't that lady a Mrs. Linde?

Nora: Yes.

Krogstad: Just now come into town?

Nora: Yes, today.

Krogstad: She's a good friend of yours?

Nora: Yes, she is. But I don't see —

Krogstad: I also knew her once.

Nora: I'm aware of that.

Krogstad: Oh? You know all about it. I thought so. Well, then let me ask you short and sweet: is Mrs. Linde getting a job in the bank?

Nora: What makes you think you can cross-examine me, Mr. Krogstad — you, one of my husband's employees? But since you ask, you might as well know — yes, Mrs. Linde's going to be taken on at the bank. And I'm the one who spoke for her, Mr. Krogstad. Now you know.

Krogstad: So I guessed right.

Nora (pacing up and down): Oh, one does have a tiny bit of influence, I should hope. Just because I am a woman, don't think it means that — When one has a subordinate position, Mr. Krogstad, one really ought to be careful about pushing somebody who — hm —

Krogstad: Who has influence?

Nora: That's right.

Krogstad (in a different tone): Mrs. Helmer, would you be good enough to use your influence on my behalf?

Nora: What? What do you mean?

Krogstad: Would you please make sure that I keep my subordinate position in the bank?

Nora: What does that mean? Who's thinking of taking away your position?

Krogstad: Oh, don't play the innocent with me. I'm quite aware that your friend would hardly relish the chance of running into me again; and I'm also aware now whom I can thank for being turned out.

Nora: But I promise you—

Krogstad: Yes, yes, yes, to the point: there's still time, and I'm advising you to use your influence to prevent it.

Nora: But Mr. Krogstad, I have absolutely no influence.

Krogstad: You haven't? I thought you were just saying—

Nora: You shouldn't take me so literally. I! How can you believe that I have any such influence over my husband?

Krogstad: Oh, I've known your husband from our student days. I don't think the great bank manager's more steadfast than any other married man.

Nora: You speak insolently about my husband, and I'll show you the door.

Krogstad: The lady has spirit.

Nora: I'm not afraid of you any longer. After New Year's, I'll soon be done with the whole business.

Krogstad (restraining himself): Now listen to me, Mrs. Helmer. If necessary, I'll fight for my little job in the bank as if it were life itself.

Nora: Yes, so it seems.

Krogstad: It's not just a matter of income; that's the least of it. It's something else—All right, out with it! Look, this is the thing. You know, just like all the others, of course, that once, a good many years ago, I did something rather rash.

Nora: I've heard rumors to that effect.

Krogstad: The case never got into court; but all the same, every door was closed in my face from then on. So I took up those various activities you know about. I had to grab hold somewhere; and I dare say I haven't been among the worst. But now I want to drop all that. My boys are growing up. For their sakes, I'll have to win back as much respect as possible here in town. That job in the bank was like the first rung in my ladder. And now your husband wants to kick me right back down in the mud again.

Nora: But for heaven's sake, Mr. Krogstad, it's simply not in my power to help you.

Krogstad: That's because you haven't the will to—but I have the means to make you.

Nora: You certainly won't tell my husband that I owe you money?

Krogstad: Hm—what if I told him that?

Nora: That would be shameful of you. *(Nearly in tears.)* This secret—my joy and my pride—that he should learn it in such a crude and disgusting way—learn it from you. You'd expose me to the most horrible unpleasantness—

Krogstad: Only unpleasantness?

Nora (vehemently): But go on and try. It'll turn out the worse for you, because then my husband will really see what a crook you are, and then you'll *never* be able to hold your job.

Krogstad: I asked if it was just domestic unpleasantness you were afraid of?

Nora: If my husband finds out, then of course he'll pay what I owe at once, and then we'd be through with you for good.

Krogstad (a step closer): Listen, Mrs. Helmer—you've either got a very bad memory, or else no head at all for business. I'd better put you a little more in touch with the facts.

Nora: What do you mean?

Krogstad: When your husband was sick, you came to me for a loan of four thousand, eight hundred crowns.

Nora: Where else could I go?

Krogstad: I promised to get you that sum —

Nora: And you got it.

Krogstad: I promised to get you that sum, on certain conditions. You were so involved in your husband's illness, and so eager to finance your trip, that I guess you didn't think out all the details. It might just be a good idea to remind you. I promised you the money on the strength of a note I drew up.

Nora: Yes, and that I signed.

Krogstad: Right. But at the bottom I added some lines for your father to guarantee the loan. He was supposed to sign down there.

Nora: Supposed to? He did sign.

Krogstad: I left the date blank. In other words, your father would have dated his signature himself. Do you remember that?

Nora: Yes, I think —

Krogstad: Then I gave you the note for you to mail to your father. Isn't that so?

Nora: Yes.

Krogstad: And naturally you sent it at once — because only some five, six days later you brought me the note, properly signed. And with that, the money was yours.

Nora: Well, then; I've made my payments regularly, haven't I?

Krogstad: More or less. But — getting back to the point — those were hard times for you then, Mrs. Helmer.

Nora: Yes, they were.

Krogstad: Your father was very ill, I believe.

Nora: He was near the end.

Krogstad: He died soon after?

Nora: Yes.

Krogstad: Tell me, Mrs. Helmer, do you happen to recall the date of your father's death? The day of the month, I mean.

Nora: Papa died the twenty-ninth of September.

Krogstad: That's quite correct; I've already looked into that. And now we come to a curious thing — *(Taking out a paper.)* which I simply cannot comprehend.

Nora: Curious thing? I don't know —

Krogstad: This is the curious thing: that your father co-signed the note for your loan three days after his death.

Nora: How — ? I don't understand.

Krogstad: Your father died the twenty-ninth of September. But look. Here your father dated his signature October second. Isn't that curious, Mrs. Helmer? *(Nora is silent.)* Can you explain it to me? *(Nora remains silent.)* It's also remarkable that the words "October second" and the year aren't written in your father's hand, but rather in one that I think I know. Well, it's easy to understand. Your father forgot perhaps to date his signature, and then someone or other added it, a bit sloppily, before anyone knew of his death. There's nothing wrong in that. It all comes down to the signature. And there's no question about *that*, Mrs. Helmer. It really *was* your father who signed his own name here, wasn't it?

Nora (after a short silence, throwing her head back and looking squarely at him): No, it wasn't. I signed Papa's name.

Krogstad: Wait, now — are you fully aware that this is a dangerous confession?

Nora: Why? You'll soon get your money.

Krogstad: Let me ask you a question — why didn't you send the paper to your father?

Nora: That was impossible. Papa was so sick. If I'd asked him for his signature, I also would have had to tell him what the money was for. But I couldn't tell him, sick as he was, that my husband's life was in danger. That was just impossible.

Krogstad: Then it would have been better if you'd given up the trip abroad.

Nora: I couldn't possibly. The trip was to save my husband's life. I couldn't give that up.

Krogstad: But didn't you ever consider that this was a fraud against me?

Nora: I couldn't let myself be bothered by that. You weren't any concern of mine. I couldn't stand you, with all those cold complications you made, even though you knew how badly off my husband was.

Krogstad: Mrs. Helmer, obviously you haven't the vaguest idea of what you've involved yourself in. But I can tell you this: it was nothing more and nothing worse that I once did — and it wrecked my whole reputation.

Nora: You? Do you expect me to believe that you ever acted bravely to save your wife's life?

Krogstad: Laws don't inquire into motives.

Nora: Then they must be very poor laws.

Krogstad: Poor or not — if I introduce this paper in court, you'll be judged according to law.

Nora: This I refuse to believe. A daughter hasn't a right to protect her dying father from anxiety and care? A wife hasn't a right to save her husband's life? I don't know much about laws, but I'm sure that somewhere in the books these things are allowed. And you don't know anything about it — you who practice the law? You must be an awful lawyer, Mr. Krogstad.

Krogstad: Could be. But business — the kind of business we two are mixed up in — don't you think I know about that? All right. Do what you want now. But I'm telling you *this:* if I get shoved down a second time, you're going to keep me company. *(He bows and goes out through the hall.)*

Nora (pensive for a moment, then tossing her head): Oh, really! Trying to frighten me! I'm not so silly as all that. *(Begins gathering up the children's clothes, but soon stops.)* But — ? No, but that's impossible! I did it out of love.

The Children (in the doorway, left): Mama, that strange man's gone out the door.

Nora: Yes, yes, I know it. But don't tell anyone about the strange man. Do you hear? Not even Papa!

The Children: No, Mama. But now will you play again?

Nora: No, not now.

The Children: Oh, but Mama, you promised.

Nora: Yes, but I can't now. Go inside; I have too much to do. Go in, go in, my sweet darlings. *(She herds them gently back in the room and shuts the door after them. Settling on the sofa, she takes up a piece of embroidery and makes some stitches, but soon stops abruptly.)* No! *(Throws the work aside, rises, goes to the hall door and calls out.)* Helene! Let me have the tree in here. *(Goes to the table, left, opens the table drawer, and stops again.)* No, but that's utterly impossible!

Maid (with the Christmas tree): Where should I put it, ma'am?
Nora: There. The middle of the floor.
Maid: Should I bring anything else?
Nora: No, thanks. I have what I need.

> *The Maid, who has set the tree down, goes out.*

Nora (absorbed in trimming the tree): Candles here — and flowers here. That terrible creature! Talk, talk, talk! There's nothing to it at all. The tree's going to be lovely. I'll do anything to please you, Torvald. I'll sing for you, dance for you —

> *Helmer comes in from the hall, with a sheaf of papers under his arm.*

Nora: Oh! You're back so soon?
Helmer: Yes. Has anyone been here?
Nora: Here? No.
Helmer: That's odd. I saw Krogstad leaving the front door.
Nora: So? Oh yes, that's true. Krogstad was here a moment.
Helmer: Nora, I can see by your face that he's been here, begging you to put in a good word for him.
Nora: Yes.
Helmer: And it was supposed to seem like your own idea? You were to hide it from me that he'd been here. He asked you that, too, didn't he?
Nora: Yes, Torvald, but —
Helmer: Nora, Nora, and you could fall for that? Talk with that sort of person and promise him anything? And then in the bargain, tell me an untruth.
Nora: An untruth — ?
Helmer: Didn't you say that no one had been here? *(Wagging his finger.)* My little songbird must never do that again. A songbird needs a clean beak to warble with. No false notes. *(Putting his arm about her waist.)* That's the way it should be, isn't it? Yes, I'm sure of it. *(Releasing her.)* And so, enough of that. *(Sitting by the stove.)* Ah, how snug and cozy it is here. *(Leafing among his papers.)*
Nora (busy with the tree, after a short pause): Torvald!
Helmer: Yes.
Nora: I'm so much looking forward to the Stenborgs' costume party, day after tomorrow.
Helmer: And I can't wait to see what you'll surprise me with.
Nora: Oh, that stupid business!
Helmer: What?
Nora: I can't find anything that's right. Everything seems so ridiculous, so inane.
Helmer: So my little Nora's come to *that* recognition?
Nora (going behind his chair, her arms resting on its back): Are you very busy, Torvald?
Helmer: Oh —
Nora: What papers are those?
Helmer: Bank matters.
Nora: Already?
Helmer: I've gotten full authority from the retiring management to make all necessary changes in personnel and procedure. I'll need Christmas week for that. I want to have everything in order by New Year's.

Nora: So that was the reason this poor Krogstad —

Helmer: Hm.

Nora (still leaning on the chair and slowly stroking the nape of his neck): If you weren't so very busy, I would have asked you an enormous favor, Torvald.

Helmer: Let's hear. What is it?

Nora: You know, there isn't anyone who has your good taste — and I want so much to look well at the costume party. Torvald, couldn't you take over and decide what I should be and plan my costume?

Helmer: Ah, is my stubborn little creature calling for a lifeguard?

Nora: Yes, Torvald, I can't get anywhere without your help.

Helmer: All right — I'll think it over. We'll hit on something.

Nora: Oh, how sweet of you. *(Goes to the tree again. Pause.)* Aren't the red flowers pretty —? But tell me, was it really such a crime that this Krogstad committed?

Helmer: Forgery. Do you have any idea what that means?

Nora: Couldn't he have done it out of need?

Helmer: Yes, or thoughtlessness, like so many others. I'm not so heartless that I'd condemn a man categorically for just one mistake.

Nora: No, of course not, Torvald!

Helmer: Plenty of men have redeemed themselves by openly confessing their crimes and taking their punishment.

Nora: Punishment —?

Helmer: But now Krogstad didn't go that way. He got himself out by sharp practices, and that's the real cause of his moral breakdown.

Nora: Do you really think that would —?

Helmer: Just imagine how a man with that sort of guilt in him has to lie and cheat and deceive on all sides, has to wear a mask even with the nearest and dearest he has, even with his own wife and children. And with the children, Nora — that's where it's most horrible.

Nora: Why?

Helmer: Because that kind of atmosphere of lies infects the whole life of a home. Every breath the children take in is filled with the germs of something degenerate.

Nora (coming closer behind him): Are you sure of that?

Helmer: Oh, I've seen it often enough as a lawyer. Almost everyone who goes bad early in life has a mother who's a chronic liar.

Nora: Why just — the mother?

Helmer: It's usually the mother's influence that's dominant, but the father's works in the same way, of course. Every lawyer is quite familiar with it. And still this Krogstad's been going home year in, year out, poisoning his own children with lies and pretense; that's why I call him morally lost. *(Reaching his hands out toward her.)* So my sweet little Nora must promise me never to plead his cause. Your hand on it. Come, come, what's this? Give me your hand. There, now. All settled. I can tell you it'd be impossible for me to work alongside of him. I literally feel physically revolted when I'm anywhere near such a person.

Nora (withdraws her hand and goes to the other side of the Christmas tree): How hot it is here! And I've got so much to do.

Helmer (getting up and gathering his papers): Yes, and I have to think about getting some of these read through before dinner. I'll think about your costume, too. And something to hang on the tree in gilt paper, I may even see about that. *(Putting his hand on her head.)* Oh you, my darling little songbird. *(He goes into his study and closes the door after him.)*

Nora (softly, after a silence): Oh, really! It isn't so. It's impossible. It must be impossible.

Anne-Marie (in the doorway, left): The children are begging so hard to come in to Mama.

Nora: No, no, no, don't let them in to me! You stay with them, Anne-Marie.

Anne-Marie: Of course, ma'am. *(Closes the door.)*

Nora (pale with terror): Hurt my children—! Poison my home? *(A moment's pause; then she tosses her head.)* That's not true. Never. Never in all the world.

ACT II

Same room. Beside the piano the Christmas tree now stands stripped of ornament, burned-down candle stubs on its ragged branches. Nora's street clothes lie on the sofa. Nora, alone in the room, moves restlessly about; at last she stops at the sofa and picks up her coat.

Nora (dropping the coat again): Someone's coming! *(Goes toward the door, listens.)* No—there's no one. Of course—nobody's coming today, Christmas Day—or tomorrow, either. But maybe— *(Opens the door and looks out.)* No, nothing in the mailbox. Quite empty. *(Coming forward.)* What nonsense! He won't do anything serious. Nothing terrible could happen. It's impossible. Why, I have three small children.

Anne-Marie, with a large carton, comes in from the room to the left.

Anne-Marie: Well, at last I found the box with the masquerade clothes.

Nora: Thanks. Put it on the table.

Anne-Marie (does so): But they're all pretty much of a mess.

Nora: Ahh! I'd love to rip them in a million pieces!

Anne-Marie: Oh, mercy, they can be fixed right up. Just a little patience.

Nora: Yes, I'll go get Mrs. Linde to help me.

Anne-Marie: Out again now? In this nasty weather? Miss Nora will catch cold—get sick.

Nora: Oh, worse things could happen. How are the children?

Anne-Marie: The poor mites are playing with their Christmas presents, but—

Nora: Do they ask for me much?

Anne-Marie: They're so used to having Mama around, you know.

Nora: Yes, but Anne-Marie, I *can't* be together with them as much as I was.

Anne-Marie: Well, small children get used to anything.

Nora: You think so? Do you think they'd forget their mother if she was gone for good?

Anne-Marie: Oh, mercy—gone for good!

Nora: Wait, tell me, Anne-Marie—I've wondered so often—how could you ever have the heart to give your child over to strangers?

Anne-Marie: But I had to, you know, to become little Nora's nurse.

Nora: Yes, but how could you *do* it?

Anne-Marie: When I could get such a good place? A girl who's poor and who's gotten in trouble is glad enough for that. Because that slippery fish, he didn't do a thing for me, you know.

Nora: But your daughter's surely forgotten you.

Anne-Marie: Oh, she certainly has not. She's written to me, both when she was confirmed and when she was married.

Nora (clasping her about the neck): You old Anne-Marie, you were a good mother for me when I was little.

Anne-Marie: Poor little Nora, with no other mother but me.

Nora: And if the babies didn't have one, then I know that you'd — What silly talk! *(Opening the carton.)* Go in to them. Now I'll have to — Tomorrow you can see how lovely I'll look.

Anne-Marie: Oh, there won't be anyone at the party as lovely as Miss Nora. *(She goes off into the room, left.)*

Nora (begins unpacking the box, but soon throws it aside): Oh, if I dared to go out. If only nobody would come. If only nothing would happen here while I'm out. What craziness — nobody's coming. Just don't think. This muff — needs a brushing. Beautiful gloves, beautiful gloves. Let it go. Let it go! One, two, three, four, five, six — *(With a cry.)* Oh, there they are! *(Poises to move toward the door, but remains irresolutely standing. Mrs. Linde enters from the hall, where she has removed her street clothes.)*

Nora: Oh, it's you, Kristine. There's no one else out there? How good that you've come.

Mrs. Linde: I hear you were up asking for me.

Nora: Yes, I just stopped by. There's something you really can help me with. Let's get settled on the sofa. Look, there's going to be a costume party tomorrow evening at the Stenborgs' right above us, and now Torvald wants me to go as a Neapolitan peasant girl and dance the tarantella that I learned in Capri.

Mrs. Linde: Really, are you giving a whole performance?

Nora: Torvald says yes, I should. See, here's the dress. Torvald had it made for me down there; but now it's all so tattered that I just don't know —

Mrs. Linde: Oh, we'll fix that up in no time. It's nothing more than the trimmings — they're a bit loose here and there. Needle and thread? Good, now we have what we need.

Nora: Oh, how sweet of you!

Mrs. Linde (sewing): So you'll be in disguise tomorrow, Nora. You know what? I'll stop by then for a moment and have a look at you all dressed up. But listen, I've absolutely forgotten to thank you for that pleasant evening yesterday.

Nora (getting up and walking about): I don't think it was as pleasant as usual yesterday. You should have come to town a bit sooner, Kristine — Yes, Torvald really knows how to give a home elegance and charm.

Mrs. Linde: And you do, too, if you ask me. You're not your father's daughter for nothing. But tell me, is Dr. Rank always so down in the mouth as yesterday?

Nora: No, that was quite an exception. But he goes around critically ill all the time — tuberculosis of the spine, poor man. You know, his father was a disgusting thing who kept mistresses and so on — and that's why the son's been sickly from birth.

Mrs. Linde (lets her sewing fall to her lap): But my dearest Nora, how do you know about such things?

Nora (walking more jauntily): Hmp! When you've had three children, then you've had a few visits from — from women who know something of medicine, and they tell you this and that.

Mrs. Linde (resumes sewing; a short pause): Does Dr. Rank come here every day?

Nora: Every blessed day. He's Torvald's best friend from childhood, and *my* good friend, too. Dr. Rank almost belongs to this house.

Mrs. Linde: But tell me — is he quite sincere? I mean, doesn't he rather enjoy flattering people?

Nora: Just the opposite. Why do you think that?

Mrs. Linde: When you introduced us yesterday, he was proclaiming that he'd often heard my name in this house; but later I noticed that your husband hadn't the slightest idea who I really was. So how could Dr. Rank —?

Nora: But it's all true, Kristine. You see, Torvald loves me beyond words, and, as he puts it, he'd like to keep me all to himself. For a long time he'd almost be jealous if I even mentioned any of my old friends back home. So of course I dropped that. But with Dr. Rank I talk a lot about such things, because he likes hearing about them.

Mrs. Linde: Now listen, Nora; in many ways you're still like a child. I'm a good deal older than you, with a little more experience. I'll tell you something: you ought to put an end to all this with Dr. Rank.

Nora: What should I put an end to?

Mrs. Linde: Both parts of it, I think. Yesterday you said something about a rich admirer who'd provide you with money —

Nora: Yes, one who doesn't exist — worse luck. So?

Mrs. Linde: Is Dr. Rank well off?

Nora: Yes, he is.

Mrs. Linde: With no dependents?

Nora: No, no one. But —

Mrs. Linde: And he's over here every day?

Nora: Yes, I told you that.

Mrs. Linde: How can a man of such refinement be so grasping?

Nora: I don't follow you at all.

Mrs. Linde: Now don't try to hide it, Nora. You think I can't guess who loaned you the forty-eight hundred crowns?

Nora: Are you out of your mind? How could you think such a thing! A friend of ours, who comes here every single day. What an intolerable situation that would have been!

Mrs. Linde: Then it really wasn't him.

Nora: No, absolutely not. It never even crossed my mind for a moment — And he had nothing to lend in those days; his inheritance came later.

Mrs. Linde: Well, I think that was a stroke of luck for you, Nora dear.

Nora: No, it never would have occurred to me to ask Dr. Rank — Still, I'm quite sure that if I had asked him —

Mrs. Linde: Which you won't, of course.

Nora: No, of course not. I can't see that I'd ever need to. But I'm quite positive that if I talked to Dr. Rank —

Mrs. Linde: Behind your husband's back?

Nora: I've got to clear up this other thing; *that's* also behind his back. I've *got* to clear it all up.

Mrs. Linde: Yes, I was saying that yesterday, but—

Nora (pacing up and down): A man handles these problems so much better than a woman—

Mrs. Linde: One's husband does, yes.

Nora: Nonsense. *(Stopping.)* When you pay everything you owe, then you get your note back, right?

Mrs. Linde: Yes, naturally.

Nora: And can rip it into a million pieces and burn it up—that filthy scrap of paper!

Mrs. Linde (looking hard at her, laying her sewing aside, and rising slowly): Nora, you're hiding something from me.

Nora: You can see it in my face?

Mrs. Linde: Something's happened to you since yesterday morning. Nora, what is it?

Nora (hurrying toward her): Kristine! *(Listening.)* Shh! Torvald's home. Look, go in with the children a while. Torvald can't bear all this snipping and stitching. Let Anne-Marie help you.

Mrs. Linde (gathering up some of the things): All right, but I'm not leaving here until we've talked this out. *(She disappears into the room, left, as Torvald enters from the hall.)*

Nora: Oh, how I've been waiting for you, Torvald dear.

Helmer: Was that the dressmaker?

Nora: No, that was Kristine. She's helping me fix up my costume. You know, it's going to be quite attractive.

Helmer: Yes, wasn't that a bright idea I had?

Nora: Brilliant! But then wasn't I good as well to give in to you?

Helmer: Good—because you give in to your husband's judgment? All right, you little goose, I know you didn't mean it like that. But I won't disturb you. You'll want to have a fitting, I suppose.

Nora: And you'll be working?

Helmer: Yes. *(Indicating a bundle of papers.)* See. I've been down to the bank. *(Starts toward his study.)*

Nora: Torvald.

Helmer (stops): Yes.

Nora: If your little squirrel begged you, with all her heart and soul, for something—?

Helmer: What's that?

Nora: Then would you do it?

Helmer: First, naturally, I'd have to know what it was.

Nora: Your squirrel would scamper about and do tricks, if you'd only be sweet and give in.

Helmer: Out with it.

Nora: Your lark would be singing high and low in every room—

Helmer: Come on, she does that anyway.

Nora: I'd be a wood nymph and dance for you in the moonlight.

Helmer: Nora—don't tell me it's that same business from this morning?

Nora (coming closer): Yes, Torvald, I beg you, please!

Helmer: And you actually have the nerve to drag that up again?

Nora: Yes, yes, you've got to give in to me; you *have* to let Krogstad keep his job in the bank.

Helmer: My dear Nora, I've slated his job for Mrs. Linde.

Nora: That's awfully kind of you. But you could just fire another clerk instead of Krogstad.

Helmer: This is the most incredible stubbornness! Because you go and give an impulsive promise to speak up for him, I'm expected to —

Nora: That's not the reason, Torvald. It's for your own sake. That man does writing for the worst papers; you said it yourself. He could do you any amount of harm. I'm scared to death of him —

Helmer: Ah, I understand. It's the old memories haunting you.

Nora: What do you mean by that?

Helmer: Of course, you're thinking about your father.

Nora: Yes, all right. Just remember how those nasty gossips wrote in the papers about Papa and slandered him so cruelly. I think they'd have had him dismissed if the department hadn't sent you up to investigate, and if you hadn't been so kind and open-minded toward him.

Helmer: My dear Nora, there's a notable difference between your father and me. Your father's official career was hardly above reproach. But mine is; and I hope it'll stay that way as long as I hold my position.

Nora: Oh, who can ever tell what vicious minds can invent? We could be so snug and happy now in our quiet, carefree home — you and I and the children, Torvald! That's why I'm pleading with you so —

Helmer: And just by pleading for him you make it impossible for me to keep him on. It's already known at the bank that I'm firing Krogstad. What if it's rumored around now that the new bank manager was vetoed by his wife —

Nora: Yes, what then — ?

Helmer: Oh yes — as long as our little bundle of stubbornness gets her way — ! I should go and make myself ridiculous in front of the whole office — give people the idea I can be swayed by all kinds of outside pressure. Oh, you can bet I'd feel the effects of that soon enough! Besides — there's something that rules Krogstad right out at the bank as long as I'm the manager.

Nora: What's that?

Helmer: His moral failings I could maybe overlook if I had to —

Nora: Yes, Torvald, why not?

Helmer: And I hear he's quite efficient on the job. But he was a crony of mine back in my teens — one of those rash friendships that crop up again and again to embarrass you later in life. Well, I might as well say it straight out: we're on a first-name basis. And that tactless fool makes no effort at all to hide it in front of others. Quite the contrary — he thinks that entitles him to take a familiar air around me, and so every other second he comes booming out with his "Yes, Torvald!" and "Sure thing, Torvald!" I tell you, it's been excruciating for me. He's out to make my place in the bank unbearable.

Nora: Torvald, you can't be serious about all this.

Helmer: Oh no? Why not?

Nora: Because these are such petty considerations.

Helmer: What are you saying? Petty? You think I'm petty!

Nora: No, just the opposite, Torvald dear. That's exactly why —

Helmer: Never mind. You call my motives petty; then I might as well be just that. Petty! All right! We'll put a stop to this for good. *(Goes to the hall door and calls.)* Helene!

Nora: What do you want?

Helmer (searching among his papers): A decision. *(The maid comes in.)* Look here; take this letter; go out with it at once. Get hold of a messenger and have him deliver it. Quick now. It's already addressed. Wait, here's some money.

Maid: Yes, sir. *(She leaves with the letter.)*

Helmer (straightening his papers): There, now, little Miss Willful.

Nora (breathlessly): Torvald, what was that letter?

Helmer: Krogstad's notice.

Nora: Call it back, Torvald! There's still time. Oh, Torvald, call it back! Do it for my sake — for your sake, for the children's sake! Do you hear, Torvald; do it! You don't know how this can harm us.

Helmer: Too late.

Nora: Yes, too late.

Helmer: Nora dear, I can forgive you this panic, even though basically you're insulting me. Yes, you are! Or isn't it an insult to think that I should be afraid of a courtroom hack's revenge? But I forgive you anyway, because this shows so beautifully how much you love me. *(Takes her in his arms.)* This is the way it should be, my darling Nora. Whatever comes, you'll see; when it really counts, I have strength and courage enough as a man to take on the whole weight myself.

Nora (terrified): What do you mean by that?

Helmer: The whole weight, I said.

Nora (resolutely): No, never in all the world.

Helmer: Good. So we'll share it, Nora, as man and wife. That's as it should be. *(Fondling her.)* Are you happy now? There, there, there — not these frightened dove's eyes. It's nothing at all but empty fantasies — Now you should run through your tarantella and practice your tambourine. I'll go to the inner office and shut both doors, so I won't hear a thing; you can make all the noise you like. *(Turning in the doorway.)* And when Rank comes, just tell him where he can find me. *(He nods to her and goes with his papers into the study, closing the door.)*

Nora (standing as though rooted, dazed with fright, in a whisper): He really could do it. He will do it. He'll do it in spite of everything. No, not that, never, never! Anything but that! Escape! A way out — *(The doorbell rings.)* Dr. Rank! Anything but that! *Anything*, whatever it is! *(Her hands pass over her face, smoothing it; she pulls herself together, goes over and opens the hall door. Dr. Rank stands outside, hanging his fur coat up. During the following scene, it begins getting dark.)*

Nora: Hello, Dr. Rank. I recognized your ring. But you mustn't go in to Torvald yet; I believe he's working.

Rank: And you?

Nora: For you, I always have an hour to spare — you know that. *(He has entered, and she shuts the door after him.)*

Rank: Many thanks. I'll make use of these hours while I can.

Nora: What do you mean by that? While you can?

Rank: Does that disturb you?

Nora: Well, it's such an odd phrase. Is anything going to happen?

Rank: What's going to happen is what I've been expecting so long — but I honestly didn't think it would come so soon.

Nora (gripping his arm): What is it you've found out? Dr. Rank, you have to tell me!

Rank (sitting by the stove): It's all over for me. There's nothing to be done about it.

Nora (breathing easier): Is it you — then — ?

Rank: Who else? There's no point in lying to one's self. I'm the most miserable of all my patients, Mrs. Helmer. These past few days I've been auditing my internal accounts. Bankrupt! Within a month I'll probably be laid out and rotting in the churchyard.

Nora: Oh, what a horrible thing to say.

Rank: The thing itself is horrible. But the worst of it is all the other horror before it's over. There's only one final examination left; when I'm finished with that, I'll know about when my disintegration will begin. There's something I want to say. Helmer with his sensitivity has such a sharp distaste for anything ugly. I don't want him near my sickroom.

Nora: Oh, but Dr. Rank —

Rank: I won't have him in there. Under no condition. I'll lock my door to him — As soon as I'm completely sure of the worst, I'll send you my calling card marked with a black cross, and you'll know then the wreck has started to come apart.

Nora: No, today you're completely unreasonable. And I wanted you so much to be in a really good humor.

Rank: With death up my sleeve? And then to suffer this way for somebody else's sins. Is there any justice in that? And in every single family, in some way or another, this inevitable retribution of nature goes on —

Nora (her hands pressed over her ears): Oh, stuff! Cheer up! Please — be gay!

Rank: Yes, I'd just as soon laugh at it all. My poor, innocent spine, serving time for my father's gay army days.

Nora (by the table, left): He was so infatuated with asparagus tips and pâté de foie gras, wasn't that it?

Rank: Yes — and with truffles.

Nora: Truffles, yes. And then with oysters, I suppose?

Rank: Yes, tons of oysters, naturally.

Nora: And then the port and champagne to go with it. It's so sad that all these delectable things have to strike at our bones.

Rank: Especially when they strike at the unhappy bones that never shared in the fun.

Nora: Ah, that's the saddest of all.

Rank (looks searchingly at her): Hm.

Nora (after a moment): Why did you smile?

Rank: No, it was you who laughed.

Nora: No, it was you who smiled, Dr. Rank!

Rank (getting up): You're even a bigger tease than I'd thought.

Nora: I'm full of wild ideas today.

Rank: That's obvious.

Nora (putting both hands on his shoulders): Dear, dear Dr. Rank, you'll never die for Torvald and me.

Rank: Oh, that loss you'll easily get over. Those who go away are soon forgotten.

Nora (looks fearfully at him): You believe that?

Rank: One makes new connections, and then —

Nora: Who makes new connections?

Rank: Both you and Torvald will when I'm gone. I'd say you're well under way already. What was that Mrs. Linde doing here last evening?

Nora: Oh, come — you can't be jealous of poor Kristine?

Rank: Oh yes, I am. She'll be my successor here in the house. When I'm down under, that woman will probably —

Nora: Shh! Not so loud. She's right in there.

Rank: Today as well. So you see.

Nora: Only to sew on my dress. Good gracious, how unreasonable you are. *(Sitting on the sofa.)* Be nice now, Dr. Rank. Tomorrow you'll see how beautifully I'll dance; and you can imagine then that I'm dancing only for you — yes, and of course for Torvald, too — that's understood. *(Takes various items out of the carton.)* Dr. Rank, sit over here and I'll show you something.

Rank (sitting): What's that?

Nora: Look here. Look.

Rank: Silk stockings.

Nora: Flesh-colored. Aren't they lovely? Now it's so dark here, but tomorrow — No, no, no, just look at the feet. Oh well, you might as well look at the rest.

Rank: Hm —

Nora: Why do you look so critical? Don't you believe they'll fit?

Rank: I've never had any chance to form an opinion on that.

Nora (glancing at him a moment): Shame on you. *(Hits him lightly on the ear with the stockings.)* That's for you. *(Puts them away again.)*

Rank: And what other splendors am I going to see now?

Nora: Not the least bit more, because you've been naughty. *(She hums a little and rummages among her things.)*

Rank (after a short silence): When I sit here together with you like this, completely easy and open, then I don't know — I simply can't imagine — whatever would have become of me if I'd never come into this house.

Nora (smiling): Yes, I really think you feel completely at ease with us.

Rank (more quietly, staring straight ahead): And then to have to go away from it all —

Nora: Nonsense, you're not going away.

Rank (his voice unchanged): — and not even be able to leave some poor show of gratitude behind, scarcely a fleeting regret — no more than a vacant place that anyone can fill.

Nora: And if I asked you now for — ? No —

Rank: For what?

Nora: For a great proof of your friendship —

Rank: Yes, yes?

Nora: No, I mean — for an exceptionally big favor —

Rank: Would you really, for once, make me so happy?

Nora: Oh, you haven't the vaguest idea what it is.

Rank: All right, then tell me.

Nora: No, but I can't, Dr. Rank — it's all out of reason. It's advice and help, too — and a favor —

Rank: So much the better. I can't fathom what you're hinting at. Just speak out. Don't you trust me?

Nora: Of course. More than anyone else. You're my best and truest friend, I'm sure. That's why I want to talk to you. All right, then, Dr. Rank: there's something you can help me prevent. You know how deeply, how inexpressibly dearly Torvald loves me; he'd never hesitate a second to give up his life for me.

Rank (leaning close to her): Nora — do you think he's the only one —

Nora (with a slight start): Who — ?

Rank: Who'd gladly give up his life for you.

Nora (heavily): I see.

Rank: I swore to myself you should know this before I'm gone. I'll never find a better chance. Yes, Nora, now you know. And also you know now that you can trust me beyond anyone else.

Nora (rising, natural and calm): Let me by.

Rank (making room for her, but still sitting): Nora —

Nora (in the hall doorway): Helene, bring the lamp in. *(Goes over to the stove.)* Ah, dear Dr. Rank, that was really mean of you.

Rank (getting up): That I've loved you just as deeply as somebody else? Was *that* mean?

Nora: No, but that you came out and told me. That was quite unnecessary —

Rank: What do you mean? Have you known — ?

The Maid comes in with the lamp, sets it on the table, and goes out again.

Rank: Nora — Mrs. Helmer — I'm asking you: have you known about it?

Nora: Oh, how can I tell what I know or don't know? Really, I don't know what to say — Why did you have to be so clumsy, Dr. Rank! Everything was so good.

Rank: Well, in any case, you now have the knowledge that my body and soul are at your command. So won't you speak out?

Nora (looking at him): After that?

Rank: Please, just let me know what it is.

Nora: You can't know anything now.

Rank: I have to. You mustn't punish me like this. Give me the chance to do whatever is humanly possible for you.

Nora: Now there's nothing you can do for me. Besides, actually, I don't need any help. You'll see — it's only my fantasies. That's what it is. Of course! *(Sits in the rocker, looks at him, and smiles.)* What a nice one you are, Dr. Rank. Aren't you a little bit ashamed, now that the lamp is here?

Rank: No, not exactly. But perhaps I'd better go — for good?

Nora: No, you certainly can't do that. You must come here just as you always have. You know Torvald can't do without you.

Rank: Yes, but *you?*

Nora: You know how much I enjoy it when you're here.

Rank: That's precisely what threw me off. You're a mystery to me. So many times I've felt you'd almost rather be with me than with Helmer.

Nora: Yes — you see, there are some people that one loves most and other people that one would almost prefer being with.

Rank: Yes, there's something to that.

Nora: When I was back home, of course I loved Papa most. But I always thought it was so much fun when I could sneak down to the maids' quarters, because they never tried to improve me, and it was always so amusing, the way they talked to each other.

Rank: Aha, so it's *their* place that I've filled.

Nora (jumping up and going to him): Oh, dear, sweet Dr. Rank, that's not what I meant at all. But you can understand that with Torvald it's just the same as with Papa —

The Maid enters from the hall.

Maid: Ma'am — please! *(She whispers to Nora and hands her a calling card.)*

Nora (glancing at the card): Ah! *(Slips it into her pocket.)*

Rank: Anything wrong?

Nora: No, no, not at all. It's only some — it's my new dress —

Rank: Really? But — there's your dress.

Nora: Oh, that. But this is another one — I ordered it — Torvald mustn't know —

Rank: Ah, now we have the big secret.

Nora: That's right. Just go in with him — he's back in the inner study. Keep him there as long as —

Rank: Don't worry. He won't get away. *(Goes into the study.)*

Nora (to the Maid): And he's standing waiting in the kitchen?

Maid: Yes, he came up by the back stairs.

Nora: But didn't you tell him somebody was here?

Maid: Yes, but that didn't do any good.

Nora: He won't leave?

Maid: No, he won't go till he's talked with you, ma'am.

Nora: Let him come in, then — but quietly. Helene, don't breathe a word about this. It's a surprise for my husband.

Maid: Yes, yes, I understand — *(Goes out.)*

Nora: This horror — it's going to happen. No, no, no, it can't happen, it mustn't. *(She goes and bolts Helmer's door. The Maid opens the hall door for Krogstad and shuts it behind him. He is dressed for travel in a fur coat, boots, and a fur cap.)*

Nora (going toward him): Talk softly. My husband's home.

Krogstad: Well, good for him.

Nora: What do you want?

Krogstad: Some information.

Nora: Hurry up, then. What is it?

Krogstad: You know, of course, that I got my notice.

Nora: I couldn't prevent it, Mr. Krogstad. I fought for you to the bitter end, but nothing worked.

Krogstad: Does your husband's love for you run so thin? He knows everything I can expose you to, and all the same he dares to —

Nora: How can you imagine he knows anything about this?

Krogstad: Ah, no — I can't imagine it either, now. It's not at all like my fine Torvald Helmer to have so much guts —

Nora: Mr. Krogstad, I demand respect for my husband!

Krogstad: Why, of course — all due respect. But since the lady's keeping it so carefully hidden, may I presume to ask if you're also a bit better informed than yesterday about what you've actually done?

Nora: More than you could ever teach me.

Krogstad: Yes, I *am* such an awful lawyer.

Nora: What is it you want from me?

Krogstad: Just a glimpse of how you are, Mrs. Helmer. I've been thinking about you all day long. A cashier, a night-court scribbler, a — well, a type like me also has a little of what they call a heart, you know.

Nora: Then show it. Think of my children.

Krogstad: Did you or your husband ever think of mine? But never mind. I simply wanted to tell you that you don't need to take this thing too seriously. For the present, I'm not proceeding with any action.

Nora: Oh no, really! Well — I knew that.

Krogstad: Everything can be settled in a friendly spirit. It doesn't have to get around town at all; it can stay just among us three.

Nora: My husband must never know anything of this.

Krogstad: How can you manage that? Perhaps you can pay me the balance?

Nora: No, not right now.

Krogstad: Or you know some way of raising the money in a day or two?

Nora: No way that I'm willing to use.

Krogstad: Well, it wouldn't have done you any good, anyway. If you stood in front of me with a fistful of bills, you still couldn't buy your signature back.

Nora: Then tell me what you're going to do with it.

Krogstad: I'll just hold onto it — keep it on file. There's no outsider who'll even get wind of it. So if you've been thinking of taking some desperate step —

Nora: I have.

Krogstad: Been thinking of running away from home —

Nora: I have!

Krogstad: Or even of something worse —

Nora: How could you guess that?

Krogstad: You can drop those thoughts.

Nora: How could you guess I was thinking of *that*?

Krogstad: Most of us think about *that* at first. I thought about it too, but I discovered I hadn't the courage —

Nora (lifelessly): I don't either.

Krogstad (relieved): That's true, you haven't the courage? You too?

Nora: I don't have it — I don't have it.

Krogstad: It would be terribly stupid, anyway. After that first storm at home blows out, why, then — I have here in my pocket a letter for your husband —

Nora: Telling everything?

Krogstad: As charitably as possible.

Nora (quickly): He mustn't ever get that letter. Tear it up. I'll find some way to get money.

Krogstad: Beg pardon, Mrs. Helmer, but I think I just told you —

Nora: Oh, I don't mean the money I owe you. Let me know how much you want from my husband, and I'll manage it.

Krogstad: I don't want money from your husband.

Nora: What do you want, then?

Krogstad: I'll tell you what. I want to recoup, Mrs. Helmer; I want to get on in the world — and there's where your husband can help me. For a year and a half I've kept myself clean of anything disreputable — all that time struggling with the worst conditions; but I was satisfied, working my way up step by step. Now I've been written right off, and I'm just not in the mood to come crawling back. I tell you, I want to move on. I want to get back in the bank — in a better position. Your husband can set up a job for me —

Nora: He'll never do that!

Krogstad: He'll do it. I know him. He won't dare breathe a word of protest. And once I'm in there together with him, you just wait and see! Inside of a year, I'll be the manager's right-hand man. It'll be Nils Krogstad, not Torvald Helmer, who runs the bank.

Nora: You'll never see the day!

Krogstad: Maybe you think you can —

Nora: I have the courage now — for *that.*

Krogstad: Oh, you don't scare me. A smart, spoiled lady like you —

Nora: You'll see; you'll see!

Krogstad: Under the ice, maybe? Down in the freezing coal-black water? There, till you float up in the spring, ugly, unrecognizable, with your hair falling out —

Nora: You don't frighten me.

Krogstad: Nor do you frighten me. One doesn't do these things, Mrs. Helmer. Besides, what good would it be? I'd still have him safe in my pocket.

Nora: Afterwards? When I'm no longer — ?

Krogstad: Are you forgetting that *I'll* be in control then over your final reputation? *(Nora stands speechless, staring at him.)* Good; now I've warned you. Don't do anything stupid. When Helmer's read my letter, I'll be waiting for his reply. And bear in mind that it's your husband himself who's forced me back to my old ways. I'll never forgive him for that. Good-bye, Mrs. Helmer. *(He goes out through the hall.)*

Nora (goes to the hall door, opens it a crack, and listens): He's gone. Didn't leave the letter. Oh no, no, that's impossible too! *(Opening the door more and more.)* What's that? He's standing outside — not going downstairs. He's thinking it over? Maybe he'll — ? *(A letter falls in the mailbox; then Krogstad's footsteps are heard, dying away down a flight of stairs. Nora gives a muffled cry and runs over toward the sofa table. A short pause.)* In the mailbox. *(Slips warily over to the hall door.)* It's lying there. Torvald, Torvald — now we're lost!

Mrs. Linde (entering with costume from the room, left): There now, I can't see anything else to mend. Perhaps you'd like to try —

Nora (in a hoarse whisper): Kristine, come here.

Mrs. Linde (tossing the dress on the sofa): What's wrong? You look upset.

Nora: Come here. See that letter? *There!* Look — through the glass in the mailbox.

Mrs. Linde: Yes, yes, I see it.

Nora: That letter's from Krogstad —

Mrs. Linde: Nora — it's Krogstad who loaned you the money!

Nora: Yes, and now Torvald will find out everything.

Mrs. Linde: Believe me, Nora, it's best for both of you.

Nora: There's more you don't know. I forged a name.

Mrs. Linde: But for heaven's sake — ?

Nora: I only want to tell you that, Kristine, so that you can be my witness.

Mrs. Linde: Witness? Why should I — ?

Nora: If I should go out of my mind — it could easily happen —

Mrs. Linde: Nora!

Nora: Or anything else occurred — so I couldn't be present here —

Mrs. Linde: Nora, Nora, you aren't yourself at all!

Nora: And someone should try to take on the whole weight, all of the guilt, you follow me—

Mrs. Linde: Yes, of course, but why do you think—?

Nora: Then you're the witness that it isn't true, Kristine. I'm very much myself; my mind right now is perfectly clear; and I'm telling you: nobody else has known about this; I alone did everything. Remember that.

Mrs. Linde: I will. But I don't understand all this.

Nora: Oh, how could you ever understand it? It's the miracle now that's going to take place.

Mrs. Linde: The miracle?

Nora: Yes, the miracle. But it's so awful, Kristine. It mustn't take place, not for anything in the world.

Mrs. Linde: I'm going right over and talk with Krogstad.

Nora: Don't go near him; he'll do you some terrible harm!

Mrs. Linde: There was a time once when he'd gladly have done anything for me.

Nora: He?

Mrs. Linde: Where does he live?

Nora: Oh, how do I know? Yes. *(Searches in her pocket.)* Here's his card. But the letter, the letter—!

Helmer (from the study, knocking on the door): Nora!

Nora (with a cry of fear): Oh! What is it? What do you want?

Helmer: Now, now, don't be so frightened. We're not coming in. You locked the door—are you trying on the dress?

Nora: Yes, I'm trying it. I'll look just beautiful, Torvald.

Mrs. Linde (who has read the card): He's living right around the corner.

Nora: Yes, but what's the use? We're lost. The letter's in the box.

Mrs. Linde: And your husband has the key?

Nora: Yes, always.

Mrs. Linde: Krogstad can ask for his letter back unread; he can find some excuse—

Nora: But it's just this time that Torvald usually—

Mrs. Linde: Stall him. Keep him in there. I'll be back as quick as I can. *(She hurries out through the hall entrance.)*

Nora (goes to Helmer's door, opens it, and peers in): Torvald!

Helmer (from the inner study): Well—does one dare set foot in one's own living room at last? Come on, Rank, now we'll get a look— *(In the doorway.)* But what's this?

Nora: What, Torvald dear?

Helmer: Rank had me expecting some grand masquerade.

Rank (in the doorway): That was my impression, but I must have been wrong.

Nora: No one can admire me in my splendor—not till tomorrow.

Helmer: But Nora dear, you look so exhausted. Have you practiced too hard?

Nora: No, I haven't practiced at all yet.

Helmer: You know, it's necessary—

Nora: Oh, it's absolutely necessary, Torvald. But I can't get anywhere without your help. I've forgotten the whole thing completely.

Helmer: Ah, we'll soon take care of that.

Nora: Yes, take care of me, Torvald, please! Promise me that? Oh, I'm so nervous. That big party—You must give up everything this evening for me. No business—don't even touch your pen. Yes? Dear Torvald, promise?

Helmer: It's a promise. Tonight I'm totally at your service — you little helpless thing. Hm — but first there's one thing I want to — *(Goes toward the hall door.)*

Nora: What are you looking for?

Helmer: Just to see if there's any mail.

Nora: No, no, don't do that, Torvald!

Helmer: Now what?

Nora: Torvald, please. There isn't any.

Helmer: Let me look, though. *(Starts out. Nora, at the piano, strikes the first notes of the tarantella. Helmer, at the door, stops.)* Aha!

Nora: I can't dance tomorrow if I don't practice with you.

Helmer (going over to her): Nora dear, are you really so frightened?

Nora: Yes, so terribly frightened. Let me practice right now; there's still time before dinner. Oh, sit down and play for me, Torvald. Direct me. Teach me, the way you always have.

Helmer: Gladly, if it's what you want. *(Sits at the piano.)*

Nora (snatches the tambourine up from the box, then a long, varicolored shawl, which she throws around herself, whereupon she springs forward and cries out): Play for me now! Now I'll dance!

Helmer plays and Nora dances. Rank stands behind Helmer at the piano and looks on.

Helmer (as he plays): Slower. Slow down.

Nora: Can't change it.

Helmer: Not so violent, Nora!

Nora: Has to be just like this.

Helmer (stopping): No, no, that won't do at all.

Nora (laughing and swinging her tambourine): Isn't that what I told you?

Rank: Let me play for her.

Helmer (getting up): Yes, go on. I can teach her more easily then.

Rank sits at the piano and plays; Nora dances more and more wildly. Helmer has stationed himself by the stove and repeatedly gives her directions; she seems not to hear them; her hair loosens and falls over her shoulders; she does not notice, but goes on dancing. Mrs. Linde enters.

Mrs. Linde (standing dumbfounded at the door): Ah — !

Nora (still dancing): See what fun, Kristine!

Helmer: But Nora darling, you dance as if your life were at stake.

Nora: And it is.

Helmer: Rank, stop! This is pure madness. Stop it, I say!

Rank breaks off playing, and Nora halts abruptly.

Helmer (going over to her): I never would have believed it. You've forgotten everything I taught you.

Nora (throwing away the tambourine): You see for yourself.

Helmer: Well, there's certainly room for instruction here.

Nora: Yes, you see how important it is. You've got to teach me to the very last minute. Promise me that, Torvald?

Helmer: You can bet on it.

Nora: You mustn't, either today or tomorrow, think about anything else but me; you mustn't open any letters — or the mailbox —

Helmer: Ah, it's still the fear of that man —

Nora: Oh yes, yes, that too.

Helmer: Nora, it's written all over you — there's already a letter from him out there.

Nora: I don't know. I guess so. But you mustn't read such things now; there mustn't be anything ugly between us before it's all over.

Rank (quietly to Helmer): You shouldn't deny her.

Helmer (putting his arms around her): The child can have her way. But tomorrow night, after you've danced —

Nora: Then you'll be free.

Maid (in the doorway, right): Ma'am, dinner is served.

Nora: We'll be wanting champagne, Helene.

Maid: Very good, ma'am. *(Goes out.)*

Helmer: So — a regular banquet, hm?

Nora: Yes, a banquet — champagne till daybreak! *(Calling out.)* And some macaroons, Helene. Heaps of them — just this once.

Helmer (taking her hands): Now, now, now — no hysterics. Be my own little lark again.

Nora: Oh, I will soon enough. But go on in — and you, Dr. Rank. Kristine, help me put up my hair.

Rank (whispering, as they go): There's nothing wrong — really wrong, is there?

Helmer: Oh, of course not. It's nothing more than this childish anxiety I was telling you about. *(They go out, right.)*

Nora: Well?

Mrs. Linde: Left town.

Nora: I could see by your face.

Mrs. Linde: He'll be home tomorrow evening. I wrote him a note.

Nora: You shouldn't have. Don't try to stop anything now. After all, it's a wonderful joy, this waiting here for the miracle.

Mrs. Linde: What is it you're waiting for?

Nora: Oh, you can't understand that. Go in to them; I'll be along in a moment.

Mrs. Linde goes into the dining room. Nora stands a short while as if composing herself; then she looks at her watch.

Nora: Five. Seven hours to midnight. Twenty-four hours to the midnight after, and then the tarantella's done. Seven and twenty-four? Thirty-one hours to live.

Helmer (in the doorway, right): What's become of the little lark?

Nora (going toward him with open arms): Here's your lark!

ACT III

Same scene. The table, with chairs around it, has been moved to the center of the room. A lamp on the table is lit. The hall door stands open. Dance music drifts down from the floor above. Mrs. Linde sits at the table, absently paging through a book, trying to read, but apparently unable to focus her thoughts. Once or twice she pauses, tensely listening for a sound at the outer entrance.

Mrs. Linde (glancing at her watch): Not yet — and there's hardly any time left. If only he's not — *(Listening again.)* Ah, there he is. *(She goes out in the hall and cautiously opens the outer door. Quiet footsteps are heard on the stairs. She whispers:)* Come in. Nobody's here.

Krogstad (in the doorway): I found a note from you at home. What's back of all this?

Mrs. Linde: I just *had* to talk to you.

Krogstad: Oh? And it just *had* to be here in this house?

Mrs. Linde: At my place it was impossible; my room hasn't a private entrance. Come in; we're all alone. The maid's asleep, and the Helmers are at the dance upstairs.

Krogstad (entering the room): Well, well, the Helmers are dancing tonight? Really?

Mrs. Linde: Yes, why not?

Krogstad: How true — why not?

Mrs. Linde: All right, Krogstad, let's talk.

Krogstad: Do we two have anything more to talk about?

Mrs. Linde: We have a great deal to talk about.

Krogstad: I wouldn't have thought so.

Mrs. Linde: No, because you've never understood me, really.

Krogstad: Was there anything more to understand — except what's all too common in life? A calculating woman throws over a man the moment a better catch comes by.

Mrs. Linde: You think I'm so thoroughly calculating? You think I broke it off lightly?

Krogstad: Didn't you?

Mrs. Linde: Nils — is that what you really thought?

Krogstad: If you cared, then why did you write me the way you did?

Mrs. Linde: What else could I do? If I had to break off with you, then it was my job as well to root out everything you felt for me.

Krogstad (wringing his hands): So that was it. And this — all this, simply for money!

Mrs. Linde: Don't forget I had a helpless mother and two small brothers. We couldn't wait for you, Nils; you had such a long road ahead of you then.

Krogstad: That may be; but you still hadn't the right to abandon me for somebody else's sake.

Mrs. Linde: Yes — I don't know. So many, many times I've asked myself if I did have that right.

Krogstad (more softly): When I lost you, it was as if all the solid ground dissolved from under my feet. Look at me; I'm a half-drowned man now, hanging onto a wreck.

Mrs. Linde: Help may be near.

Krogstad: It was near — but then you came and blocked it off.

Mrs. Linde: Without my knowing it, Nils. Today for the first time I learned that it's you I'm replacing at the bank.

Krogstad: All right — I believe you. But now that you know, will you step aside?

Mrs. Linde: No, because that wouldn't benefit you in the slightest.

Krogstad: Not "benefit" me, hm! I'd step aside anyway.

Mrs. Linde: I've learned to be realistic. Life and hard, bitter necessity have taught me that.

Krogstad: And life's taught me never to trust fine phrases.

Mrs. Linde: Then life's taught you a very sound thing. But you do have to trust in actions, don't you?

Krogstad: What does that mean?

Mrs. Linde: You said you were hanging on like a half-drowned man to a wreck.

Krogstad: I've good reason to say that.

Mrs. Linde: I'm also like a half-drowned woman on a wreck. No one to suffer with; no one to care for.

Krogstad: You made your choice.

Mrs. Linde: There wasn't any choice then.

Krogstad: So—what of it?

Mrs. Linde: Nils, if only we two shipwrecked people could reach across to each other.

Krogstad: What are you saying?

Mrs. Linde: Two on one wreck are at least better off than each on his own.

Krogstad: Kristine!

Mrs. Linde: Why do you think I came into town?

Krogstad: Did you really have some thought of me?

Mrs. Linde: I have to work to go on living. All my born days, as long as I can remember, I've worked, and it's been my best and my only joy. But now I'm completely alone in the world; it frightens me to be so empty and lost. To work for yourself—there's no joy in that. Nils, give me something—someone to work for.

Krogstad: I don't believe all this. It's just some hysterical feminine urge to go out and make a noble sacrifice.

Mrs. Linde: Have you ever found me to be hysterical?

Krogstad: Can you honestly mean this? Tell me—do you know everything about my past?

Mrs. Linde: Yes.

Krogstad: And you know what they think I'm worth around here.

Mrs. Linde: From what you were saying before, it would seem that with me you could have been another person.

Krogstad: I'm positive of that.

Mrs. Linde: Couldn't it happen still?

Krogstad: Kristine—you're saying this in all seriousness? Yes, you are! I can see it in you. And do you really have the courage, then—?

Mrs. Linde: I need to have someone to care for; and your children need a mother. We both need each other. Nils, I have faith that you're good at heart—I'll risk everything together with you.

Krogstad (gripping her hands): Kristine, thank you, thank you—Now I know I can win back a place in their eyes. Yes—but I forgot—

Mrs. Linde (listening): Shh! The tarantella. Go now! Go on!

Krogstad: Why? What is it?

Mrs. Linde: Hear the dance up there? When that's over, they'll be coming down.

Krogstad: Oh, then I'll go. But—it's all pointless. Of course, you don't know the move I made against the Helmers.

Mrs. Linde: Yes, Nils, I know.

Krogstad: And all the same, you have the courage to—?

Mrs. Linde: I know how far despair can drive a man like you.

Krogstad: Oh, if I only could take it all back.

Mrs. Linde: You easily could—your letter's still lying in the mailbox.

Krogstad: Are you sure of that?

Mrs. Linde: Positive. But—

Krogstad (looks at her searchingly): Is that the meaning of it, then? You'll save your friend at any price. Tell me straight out. Is that it?

Mrs. Linde: Nils—anyone who's sold herself for somebody else once isn't going to do it again.

Krogstad: I'll demand my letter back.

Mrs. Linde: No, no.

Krogstad: Yes, of course. I'll stay here till Helmer comes down; I'll tell him to give me my letter again—that it only involves my dismissal—that he shouldn't read it—

Mrs. Linde: No, Nils, don't call the letter back.

Krogstad: But wasn't that exactly why you wrote me to come here?

Mrs. Linde: Yes, in that first panic. But it's been a whole day and night since then, and in that time I've seen such incredible things in this house. Helmer's got to learn everything; this dreadful secret has to be aired; those two have to come to a full understanding; all these lies and evasions can't go on.

Krogstad: Well, then, if you want to chance it. But at least there's one thing I can do, and do right away—

Mrs. Linde (listening): Go now, go quick! The dance is over. We're not safe another second.

Krogstad: I'll wait for you downstairs.

Mrs. Linde: Yes, please do; take me home.

Krogstad: I can't believe it; I've never been so happy. *(He leaves by way of the outer door; the door between the room and the hall stays open.)*

Mrs. Linde (straightening up a bit and getting together her street clothes): How different now! How different! Someone to work for, to live for—a home to build. Well, it is worth the try! Oh, if they'd only come! *(Listening.)* Ah, there they are. Bundle up. *(She picks up her hat and coat. Nora's and Helmer's voices can be heard outside; a key turns in the lock, and Helmer brings Nora into the hall almost by force. She is wearing the Italian costume with a large black shawl about her; he is on evening dress, with a black domino open over it.)*

Nora (struggling in the doorway): No, no, no, not inside! I'm going up again. I don't want to leave so soon.

Helmer: But Nora dear—

Nora: Oh, I beg you, please, Torvald. From the bottom of my heart, *please*—only an hour more!

Helmer: Not a single minute, Nora darling. You know our agreement. Come on, in we go; you'll catch cold out here. *(In spite of her resistance, he gently draws her into the room.)*

Mrs. Linde: Good evening.

Nora: Kristine!

Helmer: Why, Mrs. Linde—are you here so late?

Mrs. Linde: Yes, I'm sorry, but I did want to see Nora in costume.

Nora: Have you been sitting here, waiting for me?

Mrs. Linde: Yes. I didn't come early enough; you were all upstairs; and then I thought I really couldn't leave without seeing you.

Helmer (removing Nora's shawl): Yes, take a good look. She's worth looking at, I can tell you that, Mrs. Linde. Isn't she lovely?

Mrs. Linde: Yes, I should say —

Helmer: A dream of loveliness, isn't she? That's what everyone thought at the party, too. But she's horribly stubborn — this sweet little thing. What's to be done with her? Can you imagine, I almost had to use force to pry her away.

Nora: Oh, Torvald, you're going to regret you didn't indulge me, even for just a half hour more.

Helmer: There, you see. She danced her tarantella and got a tumultuous hand — which was well earned, although the performance may have been a bit too naturalistic — I mean it rather overstepped the proprieties of art. But never mind — what's important is, she made a success, an overwhelming success. You think I could let her stay on after that and spoil the effect? Oh no; I took my lovely little Capri girl — my capricious little Capri girl, I should say — took her under my arm; one quick tour of the ballroom, a curtsy to every side, and then — as they say in novels — the beautiful vision disappeared. An exit should always be effective, Mrs. Linde, but that's what I can't get Nora to grasp. Phew, it's hot in here. *(Flings the domino on a chair and opens the door to his room.)* Why's it dark in here? Oh yes, of course. Excuse me. *(He goes in and lights a couple of candles.)*

Nora (in a sharp, breathless whisper): So?

Mrs. Linde (quietly): I talked with him.

Nora: And — ?

Mrs. Linde: Nora — you must tell your husband everything.

Nora (dully): I knew it.

Mrs. Linde: You've got nothing to fear from Krogstad, but you have to speak out.

Nora: I won't tell.

Mrs. Linde: Then the letter will.

Nora: Thanks, Kristine. I know now what's to be done. Shh!

Helmer (reentering): Well, then, Mrs. Linde — have you admired her?

Mrs. Linde: Yes, and now I'll say good night.

Helmer: Oh, come, so soon? Is this yours, this knitting?

Mrs. Linde: Yes, thanks. I nearly forgot it.

Helmer: Do you knit, then?

Mrs. Linde: Oh yes.

Helmer: You know what? You should embroider instead.

Mrs. Linde: Really? Why?

Helmer: Yes, because it's a lot prettier. See here, one holds the embroidery so, in the left hand, and then one guides the needle with the right — so — in an easy, sweeping curve — right?

Mrs. Linde: Yes, I guess that's —

Helmer: But, on the other hand, knitting — it can never be anything but ugly. Look, see here, the arms tucked in, the knitting needles going up and down — there's something Chinese about it. Ah, that was really a glorious champagne they served.

Mrs. Linde: Yes, good night, Nora, and don't be stubborn anymore.

Helmer: Well put, Mrs. Linde!

Mrs. Linde: Good night, Mr. Helmer.

Helmer (accompanying her to the door): Good night, good night. I hope you get home all right. I'd be very happy to — but you don't have far to go. Good night, good night. (*She leaves. He shuts the door after her and returns.*) There, now, at last we got her out the door. She's a deadly bore, that creature.

Nora: Aren't you pretty tired, Torvald?

Helmer: No, not a bit.

Nora: You're not sleepy?

Helmer: Not at all. On the contrary, I'm feeling quite exhilarated. But you? Yes, you really look tired and sleepy.

Nora: Yes, I'm very tired. Soon now I'll sleep.

Helmer: See! You see! I was right all along that we shouldn't stay longer.

Nora: Whatever you do is always right.

Helmer (kissing her brow): Now my little lark talks sense. Say, did you notice what a time Rank was having tonight?

Nora: Oh, was he? I didn't get to speak with him.

Helmer: I scarcely did either, but it's a long time since I've seen him in such high spirits. (*Gazes at her a moment, then comes nearer her.*) Hm—it's marvelous, though, to be back home again—to be completely alone with you. Oh, you bewitchingly lovely young woman!

Nora: Torvald, don't look at me like that!

Helmer: Can't I look at my richest treasure? At all that beauty that's mine, mine alone—completely and utterly.

Nora (moving around to the other side of the table): You mustn't talk to me that way tonight.

Helmer (following her): The tarantella is still in your blood, I can see—and it makes you even more enticing. Listen. The guests are beginning to go. (*Dropping his voice.*) Nora—it'll soon be quiet through this whole house.

Nora: Yes, I hope so.

Helmer: You do, don't you, my love? Do you realize—when I'm out at a party like this with you—do you know why I talk to you so little, and keep such a distance away; just send you a stolen look now and then—you know why I do it? It's because I'm imagining then that you're my secret darling, my secret bride-to-be, and that no one suspects there's anything between us.

Nora: Yes, yes; oh, yes, I know you're always thinking of me.

Helmer: And then when we leave and I place the shawl over those fine young rounded shoulders—over that wonderful curving neck—then I pretend that you're my young bride, that we're just coming from the wedding, that for the first time I'm bringing you into my house—that for the first time I'm alone with you—completely alone with you, your trembling young beauty! All this evening I've longed for nothing but you. When I saw you turn and sway in the tarantella—my blood was pounding till I couldn't stand it—that's why I brought you down here so early—

Nora: Go away, Torvald! Leave me alone. I don't want all this.

Helmer: What do you mean? Nora, you're teasing me. You will, won't you? Aren't I your husband—?

A knock at the outside door.

Nora (startled): What's that?

Helmer (going toward the hall): Who is it?

Rank (outside): It's me. May I come in a moment?

Helmer (with quiet irritation): Oh, what does he want now? (*Aloud.*) Hold on. (*Goes and opens the door.*) Oh, how nice that you didn't just pass us by!

Rank: I thought I heard your voice, and then I wanted so badly to have a look in. (*Lightly glancing about.*) Ah, me, these old familiar haunts. You have it snug and cozy in here, you two.

Helmer: You seemed to be having it pretty cozy upstairs, too.

Rank: Absolutely. Why shouldn't I? Why not take in everything in life? As much as you can, anyway, and as long as you can. The wine was superb—

Helmer: The champagne especially.

Rank: You noticed that too? It's amazing how much I could guzzle down.

Nora: Torvald also drank a lot of champagne this evening.

Rank: Oh?

Nora: Yes, and that always makes him so entertaining.

Rank: Well, why shouldn't one have a pleasant evening after a well-spent day?

Helmer: Well spent? I'm afraid I can't claim that.

Rank (slapping him on the back): But I can, you see!

Nora: Dr. Rank, you must have done some scientific research today.

Rank: Quite so.

Helmer: Come now—little Nora talking about scientific research!

Nora: And can I congratulate you on the results?

Rank: Indeed you may.

Nora: Then they were good?

Rank: The best possible for both doctor and patient—certainty.

Nora (quickly and searchingly): Certainty?

Rank: Complete certainty. So don't I owe myself a gay evening afterwards?

Nora: Yes, you're right, Dr. Rank.

Helmer: I'm with you—just so long as you don't have to suffer for it in the morning.

Rank: Well, one never gets something for nothing in life.

Nora: Dr. Rank—are you very fond of masquerade parties?

Rank: Yes, if there's a good array of odd disguises—

Nora: Tell me, what should we two go as at the next masquerade?

Helmer: You little featherhead—already thinking of the next!

Rank: We two? I'll tell you what: you must go as Charmed Life—

Helmer: Yes, but find a costume for *that!*

Rank: Your wife can appear just as she looks every day.

Helmer: That was nicely put. But don't you know what you're going to be?

Rank: Yes, Helmer, I've made up my mind.

Helmer: Well?

Rank: At the next masquerade I'm going to be invisible.

Helmer: That's a funny idea.

Rank: They say there's a hat—black, huge—have you never heard of the hat that makes you invisible? You put it on, and then no one on earth can see you.

Helmer (suppressing a smile): Ah, of course.

Rank: But I'm quite forgetting what I came for. Helmer, give me a cigar, one of the dark Havanas.

Helmer: With the greatest pleasure. (*Holds out his case.*)

Rank: Thanks. (*Takes one and cuts off the tip.*)

Nora (striking a match): Let me give you a light.

Rank: Thank you. (*She holds the match for him; he lights the cigar.*) And now good-bye.

Helmer: Good-bye, good-bye, old friend.

Nora: Sleep well, Doctor.

Rank: Thanks for that wish.

Nora: Wish me the same.

Rank: You? All right, if you like — Sleep well. And thanks for the light. (*He nods to them both and leaves.*)

Helmer (his voice subdued): He's been drinking heavily.

Nora (absently): Could be. (*Helmer takes his keys from his pocket and goes out in the hall.*) Torvald — what are you after?

Helmer: Got to empty the mailbox; it's nearly full. There won't be room for the morning papers.

Nora: Are you working tonight?

Helmer: You know I'm not. Why — what's this? Someone's been at the lock.

Nora: At the lock — ?

Helmer: Yes, I'm positive. What do you suppose — ? I can't imagine one of the maids — ? Here's a broken hairpin. Nora, it's yours —

Nora (quickly): Then it must be the children —

Helmer: You'd better break them of that. Hm, hm — well, opened it after all. (*Takes the contents out and calls into the kitchen.*) Helene! Helene, would you put out the lamp in the hall. (*He returns to the room shutting the hall door, then displays the handful of mail.*) Look how it's piled up. (*Sorting through them.*) Now what's this?

Nora (at the window): The letter! Oh, Torvald, no!

Helmer: Two calling cards — from Rank.

Nora: From Dr. Rank?

Helmer (examining them): "Dr. Rank, Consulting Physician." They were on top. He must have dropped them in as he left.

Nora: Is there anything on them?

Helmer: There's a black cross over the name. See? That's a gruesome notion. He could almost be announcing his own death.

Nora: That's just what he's doing.

Helmer: What! You've heard something? Something he's told you?

Nora: Yes. That when those cards came, he'd be taking his leave of us. He'll shut himself in now and die.

Helmer: Ah, my poor friend! Of course I knew he wouldn't be here much longer. But so soon — And then to hide himself away like a wounded animal.

Nora: If it has to happen, then it's best it happens in silence — don't you think so, Torvald?

Helmer (pacing up and down): He'd grown right into our lives. I simply can't imagine him gone. He with his suffering and loneliness — like a dark cloud setting off our sunlit happiness. Well, maybe it's best this way. For him, at least. (*Standing still.*) And maybe for us too, Nora. Now we're thrown back on each other, completely. (*Embracing her.*) Oh you, my darling wife, how can I hold you close enough? You know what, Nora — time and again I've wished you were in some terrible danger, just so I could stake my life and soul and everything, for your sake.

Nora (tearing herself away, her voice firm and decisive): Now you must read your mail, Torvald.

Helmer: No, no, not tonight. I want to stay with you, dearest.

Nora: With a dying friend on your mind?

Helmer: You're right. We've both had a shock. There's ugliness between us—these thoughts of death and corruption. We'll have to get free of them first. Until then—we'll stay apart.

Nora (clinging about his neck): Torvald—good night! Good night!

Helmer (kissing her on the cheek): Good night, little songbird. Sleep well, Nora. I'll be reading my mail now. *(He takes the letters into his room and shuts the door after him.)*

Nora (with bewildered glances, groping about, seizing Helmer's domino, throwing it around her, and speaking in short, hoarse, broken whispers): Never see him again. Never, never. *(Putting her shawl over her head.)* Never see the children either—them, too. Never, never. Oh, the freezing black water! The depths—down—Oh, I wish it were over—He has it now; he's reading it—now. Oh no, no, not yet. Torvald, good-bye, you and the children— *(She starts for the hall; as she does, Helmer throws open his door and stands with an open letter in his hand.)*

Helmer: Nora!

Nora (screams): Oh—!

Helmer: What is this? You know what's in this letter?

Nora: Yes, I know. Let me go! Let me out!

Helmer (holding her back): Where are you going?

Nora (struggling to break loose): You can't save me, Torvald!

Helmer (slumping back): True! Then it's true what he writes? How horrible! No, no, it's impossible—it can't be true.

Nora: It *is* true. I've loved you more than all this world.

Helmer: Ah, none of your slippery tricks.

Nora (taking one step toward him): Torvald—!

Helmer: What *is* this you've blundered into!

Nora: Just let me loose. You're not going to suffer for my sake. You're not going to take on my guilt.

Helmer: No more play-acting. *(Locks the hall door.)* You stay right here and give me a reckoning. You understand what you've done? Answer! You understand?

Nora (looking squarely at him, her face hardening): Yes. I'm beginning to understand everything now.

Helmer (striding about): Oh, what an awful awakening! In all these eight years—she who was my pride and joy—a hypocrite, a liar—worse, worse—a criminal! How infinitely disgusting it all is! The shame! *(Nora says nothing and goes on looking straight at him. He stops in front of her.)* I should have suspected something of the kind. I should have known. All your father's flimsy values—Be still! All your father's flimsy values have come out in you. No religion, no morals, no sense of duty—Oh, how I'm punished for letting him off! I did it for your sake, and you repay me like this.

Nora: Yes, like this.

Helmer: Now you've wrecked all my happiness—ruined my whole future. Oh, it's awful to think of. I'm in a cheap little grafter's hands; he can do anything he wants with me, ask for anything, play with me like a puppet—and I can't breathe a word. I'll be swept down miserably into the depths on account of a featherbrained woman.

Nora: When I'm gone from this world, you'll be free.

Helmer: Oh, quit posing. Your father had a mess of those speeches too. What good would that ever do me if you were gone from this world, as you say? Not the slightest. He can still make the whole thing known; and if he does, I could be falsely suspected as your accomplice. They might even think that I was behind it — that I put you up to it. And all that I can thank you for — you that I've coddled the whole of our marriage. Can you see now what you've done to me?

Nora (icily calm): Yes.

Helmer: It's so incredible, I just can't grasp it. But we'll have to patch up whatever we can. Take off the shawl. I said, take if off! I've got to appease him some-how or other. The thing has to be hushed up at any cost. And as for you and me, it's got to seem like everything between us is just as it was — to the out-side world, that is. You'll go right on living in this house, of course. But you can't be allowed to bring up the children; I don't dare trust you with them — Oh, to have to say this to someone I've loved so much! Well, that's done with. From now on happiness doesn't matter; all that matters is saving the bits and pieces, the appearance — *(The doorbell rings. Helmer starts.)* What's that? And so late. Maybe the worst —? You think he'd —? Hide, Nora! Say you're sick. *(Nora remains standing motionless. Helmer goes and opens the door.)*

Maid (half dressed, in the hall): A letter for Mrs. Helmer.

Helmer: I'll take it. *(Snatches the letter and shuts the door.)* Yes, it's from him. You don't get it; I'm reading it myself.

Nora: Then read it.

Helmer (by the lamp): I hardly dare. We may be ruined, you and I. But — I've got to know. *(Rips open the letter, skims through a few lines, glances at an enclosure, then cries out joyfully.)* Nora! *(Nora looks inquiringly at him.)* Nora! Wait — bet-ter check it again — Yes, yes, it's true. I'm saved. Nora, I'm saved!

Nora: And I?

Helmer: You too, of course. We're both saved, both of us. Look. He's sent back your note. He says he's sorry and ashamed — that a happy development in his life — oh, who cares what he says! Nora, we're saved! No one can hurt you. Oh, Nora, Nora — but first, this ugliness all has to go. Let me see — *(Takes a look at the note.)* No, I don't want to see it; I want the whole thing to fade like a dream. *(Tears the note and both letters to pieces, throws them into the stove and watches them burn.)* There — now there's nothing left — He wrote that since Christmas Eve you — Oh, they must have been three terrible days for you, Nora.

Nora: I fought a hard fight.

Helmer: And suffered pain and saw no escape but — No, we're not going to dwell on anything unpleasant. We'll just be grateful and keep on repeat-ing: it's over now, it's over! You hear me, Nora? You don't seem to realize — it's over. What's it mean — that frozen look? Oh, poor little Nora, I under-stand. You can't believe I've forgiven you. But I have, Nora; I swear I have. I know that what you did, you did out of love for me.

Nora: That's true.

Helmer: You loved me the way a wife ought to love her husband. It's simply the means that you couldn't judge. But you think I love you any the less for not knowing how to handle your affairs? No, no — just lean on me; I'll guide you and teach you. I wouldn't be a man if this feminine helplessness didn't make you twice as attractive to me. You mustn't mind those sharp words I said — that was all in the first confusion of thinking my world had collapsed. I've forgiven you, Nora; I swear I've forgiven you.

Nora: My thanks for your forgiveness. *(She goes out through the door, right.)*

Helmer: No, wait — *(Peers in.)* What are you doing in there?

Nora (inside): Getting out of my costume.

Helmer (by the open door): Yes, do that. Try to calm yourself and collect your thoughts again, my frightened little songbird. You can rest easy now; I've got wide wings to shelter you with. *(Walking about close by the door.)* How snug and nice our home is, Nora. You're safe here; I'll keep you like a hunted dove I've rescued out of a hawk's claws. I'll bring peace to your poor, shuddering heart. Gradually it'll happen, Nora; you'll see. Tomorrow all this will look different to you; then everything will be as it was. I won't have to go on repeating I forgive you; you'll feel it for yourself. How can you imagine I'd ever conceivably want to disown you — or even blame you in any way? Ah, you don't know a man's heart, Nora. For a man there's something indescribably sweet and satisfying in knowing he's forgiven his wife — and forgiven her out of a full and open heart. It's as if she belongs to him in two ways now: in a sense he's given her fresh into the world again, and she's become his wife and his child as well. From now on that's what you'll be to me — you little, bewildered, helpless thing. Don't be afraid of anything, Nora; just open your heart to me, and I'll be conscience and will to you both — *(Nora enters in her regular clothes.)* What's this? Not in bed? You've changed your dress?

Nora: Yes, Torvald, I've changed my dress.

Helmer: But why now, so late?

Nora: Tonight I'm not sleeping.

Helmer: But Nora dear —

Nora (looking at her watch): It's still not so very late. Sit down, Torvald; we have a lot to talk over. *(She sits at one side of the table.)*

Helmer: Nora — what is this? That hard expression —

Nora: Sit down. This'll take some time. I have a lot to say.

Helmer (sitting at the table directly opposite her): You worry me, Nora. And I don't understand you.

Nora: No, that's exactly it. You don't understand me. And I've never understood you either — until tonight. No, don't interrupt. You can just listen to what I say. We're closing out accounts, Torvald.

Helmer: How do you mean that?

Nora (after a short pause): Doesn't anything strike you about our sitting here like this?

Helmer: What's that?

Nora: We've been married now eight years. Doesn't it occur to you that this is the first time we two, you and I, man and wife, have ever talked seriously together?

Helmer: What do you mean — seriously?

Nora: In eight whole years — longer even — right from our first acquaintance, we've never exchanged a serious word on any serious thing.

Helmer: You mean I should constantly go and involve you in problems you couldn't possibly help me with?

Nora: I'm not talking of problems. I'm saying that we've never sat down seriously together and tried to get to the bottom of anything.

Helmer: But dearest, what good would that ever do you?

Nora: That's the point right there: you've never understood me. I've been wronged greatly, Torvald — first by Papa, and then by you.

Helmer: What! By us — the two people who've loved you more than anyone else?

Nora (shaking her head): You never loved me. You've thought it fun to be in love with me, that's all.

Helmer: Nora, what a thing to say!

Nora: Yes, it's true now, Torvald. When I lived at home with Papa, he told me all his opinions, so I had the same ones too; or if they were different I hid them, since he wouldn't have cared for that. He used to call me his doll-child, and he played with me the way I played with my dolls. Then I came into your house —

Helmer: How can you speak of our marriage like that?

Nora (unperturbed): I mean, then I went from Papa's hands into yours. You arranged everything to your own taste, and so I got the same taste as you — or I pretended to; I can't remember. I guess a little of both, first one, then the other. Now when I look back, it seems as if I'd lived here like a beggar — just from hand to mouth. I've lived by doing tricks for you, Torvald. But that's the way you wanted it. It's a great sin what you and Papa did to me. You're to blame that nothing's become of me.

Helmer: Nora, how unfair and ungrateful you are! Haven't you been happy here?

Nora: No, never. I thought so — but I never have.

Helmer: Not — not happy!

Nora: No, only lighthearted. And you've always been so kind to me. But our home's been nothing but a playpen. I've been your doll-wife here, just as at home I was Papa's doll-child. And in turn the children have been my dolls. I thought it was fun when you played with me, just as they thought it fun when I played with them. That's been our marriage, Torvald.

Helmer: There's some truth in what you're saying — under all the raving exaggeration. But it'll all be different after this. Playtime's over; now for the schooling.

Nora: Whose schooling — mine or the children's?

Helmer: Both yours and the children's, dearest.

Nora: Oh, Torvald, you're not the man to teach me to be a good wife to you.

Helmer: And you can say that?

Nora: And I — how am I equipped to bring up children?

Helmer: Nora!

Nora: Didn't you say a moment ago that that was no job to trust me with?

Helmer: In a flare of temper! Why fasten on that?

Nora: Yes, but you were so very right. I'm not up to the job. There's another job I have to do first. I have to try to educate myself. You can't help me with that. I've got to do it alone. And that's why I'm leaving you now.

Helmer (jumping up): What's that?

Nora: I have to stand completely alone, if I'm ever going to discover myself and the world out there. So I can't go on living with you.

Helmer: Nora, Nora!

Nora: I want to leave right away. Kristine should put me up for the night —

Helmer: You're insane! You've no right! I forbid you!

Nora: From here on, there's no use forbidding me anything. I'll take with me whatever is mine. I don't want a thing from you, either now or later.

Helmer: What kind of madness is this!

Nora: Tomorrow I'm going home—I mean, home where I came from. It'll be easier up there to find something to do.

Helmer: Oh, you blind, incompetent child!

Nora: I must learn to be competent, Torvald.

Helmer: Abandon your home, your husband, your children! And you're not even thinking what people will say.

Nora: I can't be concerned about that. I only know how essential this is.

Helmer: Oh, it's outrageous. So you'll run out like this on your most sacred vows.

Nora: What do you think are my most sacred vows?

Helmer: And I have to tell you that! Aren't they your duties to your husband and children?

Nora: I have other duties equally sacred.

Helmer: That isn't true. What duties are they?

Nora: Duties to myself.

Helmer: Before all else, you're a wife and mother.

Nora: I don't believe in that anymore. I believe that, before all else, I'm a human being, no less than you—or anyway, I ought to try to become one. I know the majority thinks you're right, Torvald, and plenty of books agree with you, too. But I can't go on believing what the majority says, or what's written in books. I have to think over these things myself and try to understand them.

Helmer: Why can't you understand your place in your own home? On a point like that, isn't there one everlasting guide you can turn to? Where's your religion?

Nora: Oh, Torvald, I'm really not sure what religion is.

Helmer: What—?

Nora: I only know what the minister said when I was confirmed. He told me religion was this thing and that. When I get clear and away by myself, I'll go into that problem too. I'll see if what the minister said was right, or, in any case, if it's right for me.

Helmer: A young woman your age shouldn't talk like that. If religion can't move you, I can try to rouse your conscience. You do have some moral feeling? Or, tell me—has that gone too?

Nora: It's not easy to answer that, Torvald. I simply don't know. I'm all confused about these things. I just know I see them so differently from you. I find out, for one thing, that the law's not at all what I'd thought—but I can't get it through my head that the law is fair. A woman hasn't a right to protect her dying father or save her husband's life! I can't believe that.

Helmer: You talk like a child. You don't know anything of the world you live in.

Nora: No, I don't. But now I'll begin to learn for myself. I'll try to discover who's right, the world or I.

Helmer: Nora, you're sick; you've got a fever. I almost think you're out of your head.

Nora: I've never felt more clearheaded and sure in my life.

Helmer: And—clearheaded and sure—you're leaving your husband and children?

Nora: Yes.

Helmer: Then there's only one possible reason.

Nora: What?

Helmer: You no longer love me.

Nora: No. That's exactly it.

Helmer: Nora! You can't be serious!

Nora: Oh, this is so hard, Torvald — you've been so kind to me always. But I can't help it. I don't love you anymore.

Helmer (struggling for composure): Are you also clearheaded and sure about that?

Nora: Yes, completely. That's why I can't go on staying here.

Helmer: Can you tell me what I did to lose your love?

Nora: Yes, I can tell you. It was this evening when the miraculous thing didn't come — then I knew you weren't the man I'd imagined.

Helmer: Be more explicit; I don't follow you.

Nora: I've waited now so patiently eight long years — for, my Lord, I know miracles don't come every day. Then this crisis broke over me, and such a certainty filled me: *now* the miraculous event would occur. While Krogstad's letter was lying out there, I never for an instant dreamed that you could give in to his terms. I was so utterly sure you'd say to him: go on, tell your tale to the whole wide world. And when he'd done that —

Helmer: Yes, what then? When I'd delivered my own wife into shame and disgrace —

Nora: When he'd done that, I was so utterly sure that you'd step forward, take the blame on yourself and say: I am the guilty one.

Helmer: Nora — !

Nora: You're thinking I'd never accept such a sacrifice from you? No, of course not. But what good would my protests be against you? That was the miracle I was waiting for, in terror and hope. And to stave that off, I would have taken my life.

Helmer: I'd gladly work for you day and night, Nora — and take on pain and deprivation. But there's no one who gives up honor for love.

Nora: Millions of women have done just that.

Helmer: Oh, you think and talk like a silly child.

Nora: Perhaps. But you neither think nor talk like the man I could join myself to. When your big fright was over — and it wasn't from any threat against me, only for what might damage you — when all the danger was past, for you it was just as if nothing had happened. I was exactly the same, your little lark, your doll, that you'd have to handle with double care now that I'd turned out so brittle and frail. *(Gets up.)* Torvald — in that instant it dawned on me that for eight years I've been living here with a stranger, and that I've even conceived three children — oh, I can't stand the thought of it! I could tear myself to bits.

Helmer (heavily): I see. There's a gulf that's opened between us — that's clear. Oh, but Nora, can't we bridge it somehow?

Nora: The way I am now, I'm no wife for you.

Helmer: I have the strength to make myself over.

Nora: Maybe — if your doll gets taken away.

Helmer: But to part! To part from you! No, Nora no — I can't imagine it.

Nora (going out, right): All the more reason why it has to be. *(She reenters with her coat and a small overnight bag, which she puts on a chair by the table.)*

Helmer: Nora, Nora, not now! Wait till tomorrow.

Nora: I can't spend the night in a strange man's room.

Helmer: But couldn't we live here like brother and sister—

Nora: You know very well how long that would last. *(Throws her shawl about her.)* Good-bye, Torvald. I won't look in on the children. I know they're in better hands than mine. The way I am now, I'm no use to them.

Helmer: But someday, Nora—someday—?

Nora: How can I tell? I haven't the least idea what'll become of me.

Helmer: But you're my wife, now and wherever you go.

Nora: Listen, Torvald—I've heard that when a wife deserts her husband's house just as I'm doing, then the law frees him from all responsibility. In any case, I'm freeing you from being responsible. Don't feel yourself bound, any more than I will. There has to be absolute freedom for us both. Here, take your ring back. Give me mine.

Helmer: That too?

Nora: That too.

Helmer: There it is.

Nora: Good. Well, now it's all over. I'm putting the keys here. The maids know all about keeping up the house—better than I do. Tomorrow, after I've left town, Kristine will stop by to pack up everything that's mine from home. I'd like those things shipped up to me.

Helmer: Over! All over! Nora, won't you ever think about me?

Nora: I'm sure I'll think of you often, and about the children and the house here.

Helmer: May I write you?

Nora: No—never. You're not to do that.

Helmer: Oh, but let me send you—

Nora: Nothing. Nothing.

Helmer: Or help you if you need it.

Nora: No. I accept nothing from strangers.

Helmer: Nora—can I never be more than a stranger to you?

Nora (picking up her overnight bag): Ah, Torvald—it would take the greatest miracle of all—

Helmer: Tell me the greatest miracle!

Nora: You and I both would have to transform ourselves to the point that— Oh, Torvald, I've stopped believing in miracles.

Helmer: But I'll believe. Tell me! Transform ourselves to the point that—?

Nora: That our living together could be a true marriage. *(She goes out down the hall.)*

Helmer (sinks down on a chair by the door, face buried in his hands): Nora! Nora! *(Looking about and rising.)* Empty. She's gone. *(A sudden hope leaps in him.)* The greatest miracle—?

From below, the sound of a door slamming shut.

Considerations for Critical Thinking and Writing

1. FIRST RESPONSE. What is the significance of the play's title in relation to the nature of the Helmers' family life?

2. Nora lies several times during the play. What kinds of lies are they? Do her lies indicate that she is not to be trusted, or are they a sign of something else about her personality?

3. What kind of wife does Helmer want Nora to be? He affectionately calls her names such as "lark" and "squirrel." What does this reveal about his attitude toward her?

4. Why is Nora "pale with terror" at the end of Act I? What is the significance of the description of the Christmas tree now "stripped of ornament, [with] burned-down candle stubs on its ragged branches" that opens Act II? What other symbols are used in the play?

5. What is Dr. Rank's purpose in the play?

6. How does the relationship between Krogstad and Mrs. Linde serve to emphasize certain qualities in the Helmers' marriage?

7. Is Krogstad's decision not to expose Nora's secret convincing? Does his shift from villainy to generosity seem adequately motivated?

8. Why does Nora reject Helmer's efforts to smooth things over between them and start again? Do you have any sympathy for Helmer?

9. Would you describe the ending as essentially happy or unhappy? Is the play more like a comedy or a tragedy?

10. Ibsen believed that a "dramatist's business is not to answer questions, but only to ask them." What questions are raised in the play? Does Ibsen propose any specific answers?

11. What makes this play a work of realism? Are there any elements that seem not to be realistic?

12. CRITICAL STRATEGIES. Read the section on new historicist criticism (pp. 68–69) in Chapter 3, "Applying a Critical Strategy," and consider the following: Ibsen once wrote a different ending for the play to head off producers who might have been tempted to change the final scene to placate the public's sense of morality. In the second conclusion, Helmer forces Nora to look in on their sleeping children. This causes her to realize that she cannot leave her family even though it means sacrificing herself. Ibsen called this version of the ending a "barbaric outrage" and didn't use it. How do you think the play reflects or refutes social values contemporary to it?

ESSAYS

FREDERICK DOUGLASS (1818–1895)

Born into slavery in Maryland, Frederick Douglass taught himself to read and write in spite of his master's vehement objections and escaped to Massachusetts at the age of twenty-one. From the lectures he gave for the Massachusetts Anti-Slavery Society (and after he purchased his freedom), Douglass put together his *Narrative of the Life of Frederick Douglass, an American Slave, Written by Himself* (1845). This autobiography was revised and updated twice: *My Bondage and My Freedom* (1855) was followed by *The Life and Times of Frederick Douglass* (1881), which he revised in 1893. These later autobiographies chronicled his careers as a writer, lecturer, newspaper publisher, and government official in Washington, D.C., and his appointment as United States Minister and Consul General to Haiti. The following excerpt consists of the entire first chapter of the 1845 *Narrative*. The title is supplied by the editor.

A Slave's Family Life   1845

I was born in Tuckahoe, near Hillsborough, and about twelve miles from Easton, in Talbot county, Maryland. I have no accurate knowledge of my age, never having seen any authentic record containing it. By far the larger part of the slaves know as little of their age as horses know of theirs, and it is the wish of most masters within my knowledge to keep their slaves thus ignorant. I do not remember to have ever met a slave who could tell of his birthday. They seldom come nearer to it than planting-time, harvest-time, cherry-time, spring-time, or fall-time. A want of information concerning my own was a source of unhappiness to me even during childhood. The white children could tell their ages. I could not tell why I ought to be deprived of the same privilege. I was not allowed to make any inquiries of my master concerning it. He deemed all such inquiries on the part of a slave improper and impertinent, and evidence of a restless spirit. The nearest estimate I can give makes me now between twenty-seven and twenty-eight years of age. I come to this, from hearing my master say, some time during 1835, I was about seventeen years old.

My mother was named Harriet Bailey. She was the daughter of Isaac and Betsey Bailey, both colored, and quite dark. My mother was of a darker complexion than either my grandmother or grandfather.

My father was a white man. He was admitted to be such by all I ever heard speak of my parentage. The opinion was also whispered that my master was my father; but of the correctness of this opinion, I know nothing; the means of knowing was withheld from me. My mother and I were separated when I was but an infant — before I knew her as my mother. It is a common custom, in the part of Maryland from which I ran away, to part children from their mothers at a very early age. Frequently, before the child has reached its twelfth month, its mother is taken from it, and hired out on some farm a considerable distance off, and the child is placed under the care of an old woman, too old for field labor. For what this separation is done, I do not know, unless it be to hinder the development of the child's affection toward its mother, and to blunt and destroy the natural affection of the mother for the child. This is the inevitable result.

I never saw my mother, to know her as such, more than four or five times in my life; and each of these times was very short in duration, and at night. She was hired by a Mr. Stewart, who lived about twelve miles from my home. She made her journeys to see me in the night, travelling the whole distance on foot, after the performance of her day's work. She was a field hand, and a whipping is the penalty of not being in the field at sunrise, unless a slave has special permission from his or her master to the contrary — a permission which they seldom get, and one that gives to him that gives it the proud name of being a kind master. I do not recollect of ever seeing my mother by the light of day. She was with me in the night. She would lie down with me, and get me to sleep, but long before I waked she was gone. Very little communication ever took place between us. Death soon ended what little we could have while she lived, and with it her hardships and suffering. She died when I was about seven years old, on one of my master's farms, near Lee's Mill. I was not allowed to be present during her illness, at her death, or burial. She was gone long before I knew any thing about it. Never having enjoyed, to any considerable extent, her soothing presence, her tender and watchful care, I received the tidings of her death with much the same emotions I should have probably felt at the death of a stranger.

Called thus suddenly away, she left me without the slightest intimation of who my father was. The whisper that my master was my father, may or may not be true; and, true or false, it is of but little consequence to my purpose whilst the fact remains, in all its glaring odiousness, that slaveholders have ordained, and by law established, that the children of slave women shall in all cases follow the condition of their mothers; and this is done too obviously to administer to their own lusts, and make a gratification of their wicked desires profitable as well as pleasurable; for by this cunning arrangement, the slaveholder, in cases not a few, sustains to his slaves the double relation of master and father. 5

I know of such cases; and it is worthy of remark that such slaves invariably suffer greater hardships, and have more to contend with, than others. They are, in the first place, a constant offence to their mistress. She is ever disposed to find fault with them; they can seldom do any thing to please her; she is never better pleased than when she sees them under the lash, especially when she suspects her husband of showing to his mulatto children favors which he withholds from his black slaves. The master is frequently compelled to sell this class of his slaves, out of deference to the feelings of his white wife; and, cruel as the deed may strike any one to be, for a man to sell his own children to human flesh-mongers, it is often the dictate of humanity for him to do so; for, unless he does this, he must not only whip them himself, but must stand by and see one white son tie up his brother, of but few shades darker complexion than himself, and ply the gory lash to his naked back; and if he lisp one word of disapproval, it is set down to his parental partiality, and only makes a bad matter worse, both for himself and the slave whom he would protect and defend.

Every year brings with it multitudes of this class of slaves. It was doubtless in consequence of a knowledge of this fact, that one great statesman of the south predicted the downfall of slavery by the inevitable laws of population. Whether this prophecy is ever fulfilled or not, it is nevertheless plain that a very different-looking class of people are springing up at the south, and are now held in slavery, from those originally brought to this country from Africa; and if their increase will do no other good, it will do away the force of the argument, that God cursed Ham, and therefore American slavery is right. If the lineal descendants of Ham are alone to be scripturally enslaved, it is certain that slavery at the south must soon become unscriptural; for thousands are ushered into the world, annually, who, like myself, owe their existence to white fathers, and those fathers most frequently their own masters.

I have had two masters. My first master's name was Anthony. I do not remember his first name. He was generally called Captain Anthony—a title which, I presume, he acquired by sailing a craft on the Chesapeake Bay. He was not considered a rich slaveholder. He owned two or three farms, and about thirty slaves. His farms and slaves were under the care of an overseer. The overseer's name was Plummer. Mr. Plummer was a miserable drunkard, a profane swearer, and a savage monster. He always went armed with a cowskin and a heavy cudgel. I have known him to cut and slash the women's heads so horribly, that even master would be enraged at his cruelty, and would threaten to whip him if he did not mind himself. Master, however, was not a humane slaveholder. It required extraordinary barbarity on the part of an overseer to affect him. He was a cruel man, hardened by a long life of slaveholding. He would at times seem to take great pleasure in whipping a slave. I have often been awakened at the dawn of day by the most heart-rending shrieks of an own aunt of mine, whom he used to tie up to a joist, and whip upon her naked back till she was literally covered with blood. No words, no tears, no prayers, from his gory victim, seemed to move his iron heart from its bloody purpose. The louder she screamed, the harder he whipped; and where the blood ran fastest, there he whipped longest. He would whip her to make her scream, and whip her to make her hush; and not until overcome by fatigue, would he cease to swing the blood-clotted cowskin. I remember the first time I ever witnessed this horrible exhibition. I was quite a child, but I well remember it. I never shall forget it whilst I remember any thing. It was the first of a long series of such outrages, of which I was doomed to be a witness and a participant. It struck me with awful force. It was the blood-stained gate, the entrance to the hell of slavery, through which I was about to pass. It was a most terrible spectacle. I wish I could commit to paper the feelings with which I beheld it.

This occurrence took place very soon after I went to live with my old master, and under the following circumstances. Aunt Hester went out one night, — where or for what I do not know, — and happened to be absent when my master desired her presence. He had ordered her not to go out evenings, and warned her that she must never let him catch her in company with a young man, who was paying attention to her belonging to Colonel Lloyd. The young man's name was Ned Roberts, generally called Lloyd's Ned. Why master was so careful of her, may be safely left to conjecture. She was a woman of noble form, and of graceful proportions, having very few equals, and fewer superiors, in personal appearance, among the colored or white women of our neighborhood.

Aunt Hester had not only disobeyed his orders in going out, but had been found in company with Lloyd's Ned; which circumstance, I found, from what he said while whipping her, was the chief offence. Had he been a man of pure morals himself, he might have been thought interested in protecting the innocence of my aunt; but those who knew him will not suspect him of any such virtue. Before he commenced whipping Aunt Hester, he took her into the kitchen, and stripped her from neck to waist, leaving her neck, shoulders, and back, entirely naked. He then told her to cross her hands, calling her at the same time a d—d b—h. After crossing her hands, he tied them with a strong rope, and led her to a stool under a large hook in the joist, put in for the purpose. He made her get upon the stool, and tied her hands to the hook. She now stood fair for his infernal purpose. Her arms were stretched up at their full length, so that she stood upon the ends of her toes. He then said to her, "Now, you d—d b—h, I'll learn you how to disobey my orders!" and after rolling up his sleeves, he commenced to lay on the heavy cowskin, and soon the warm, red blood (amid heart-rending shrieks from her, and horrid oaths from him) came dripping to the floor. I was so terrified and horror-stricken at the sight, that I hid myself in a closet, and dared not venture out till long after the bloody transaction was over. I expected it would be my turn next. It was all new to me. I had never seen any thing like it before. I had always lived with my grandmother on the outskirts of the plantation, where she was put to raise the children of the younger women. I had therefore been, until now, out of the way of the bloody scenes that often occurred on the plantation.

CONSIDERATIONS FOR CRITICAL THINKING AND WRITING

1. FIRST RESPONSE. Describe the tone of the opening paragraph. What is the effect of Douglass's use of details?
2. How do you think you would feel if you did not know your birth date? Why do you think Douglass presents this as an important fact in his life?
3. Describe Douglass's relationship with his parents. Why do you think he includes this information?
4. How does Douglass respond to Aunt Hester's being whipped? What is your reaction?
5. What is the implicit argument made in this autobiographical account of a young slave's family life?

BARBARA KINGSOLVER (B. 1955)

Born in Annapolis, Maryland, Barbara Kingsolver was raised in Kentucky and earned science degrees at DePauw University (B.A., 1977) and the University of Arizona (M.S., 1981). After working in a variety of jobs ranging from housecleaning to archaeology, she became a full-time writer in the mid-eighties. Among her books are a poetry collection, *Another America* (1990); a short story collection, *Homeland and Other Stories* (1989); and four novels: *The Bean Trees* (1988), *Animal Dreams* (1990), *Pigs in Heaven* (1993), and *The Poisonwood Bible* (1998). "Stone Soup" appeared in an essay collection, *High Tide in Tucson* (1995).

Stone Soup   *1995*

In the catalog of family values, where do we rank an occasion like this? A curly-haired boy who wanted to run before he walked, age seven now, a soccer player scoring a winning goal. He turns to the bleachers with his fists in the air and a smile wide as a gap-toothed galaxy. His own cheering section of grown-ups and kids all leap to their feet and hug each other, delirious with love for this boy. He's Andy, my best friend's son. The cheering section includes his mother and her friends, his brother, his father and stepmother, a stepbrother and stepsister, and a grandparent. Lucky is the child with this many relatives on hand to hail a proud accomplishment. I'm there too, witnessing a family fortune. But in spite of myself, defensive words take shape in my head. I am thinking: I dare *anybody* to call this a broken home.

Families change, and remain the same. Why are our names for home so slow to catch up to the truth of where we live?

When I was a child, I had two parents who loved me without cease. One of them attended every excuse for attention I ever contrived, and the other made it to the ones with higher production values, like piano recitals and appendicitis. So I was a lucky child too. I played with a set of paper dolls called "The Family of Dolls," four in number, who came with the factory-assigned names of Dad, Mom, Sis, and Junior. I think you know what they looked like, at least before I loved them to death and their heads fell off.

Now I've replaced the dolls with a life. I knit my days around my daughter's survival and happiness, and am proud to say her head is still on. But we aren't the Family of Dolls. Maybe you're not, either. And if not, even though you are statistically no oddity, it's probably been suggested to you in a hundred ways that yours isn't exactly a real family, but an impostor family, a harbinger of cultural ruin, a slapdash substitute — something like counterfeit money. Here at the tail end of our century, most of us are up to our ears in the noisy business of trying to support and love a thing called family. But there's a current in the air with ferocious moral force that finds its way even into political campaigns, claiming there is only one right way to do it, the Way It Has Always Been.

In the face of a thriving, particolored world, this narrow view is so pickled   5 and absurd I'm astonished that it gets airplay. And I'm astonished that it still stings.

Every parent has endured the arrogance of a child-unfriendly grump sitting in judgment, explaining what those kids of ours really need (for example, "a good licking"). If we're polite, we move our crew to another bench in the park. If we're forthright (as I am in my mind, only, for the rest of the day), we fix them with a sweet imperious stare and say, "Come back and let's talk about it after you've changed a thousand diapers."

But it's harder somehow to shrug off the Family-of-Dolls Family Values crew when they judge (from their safe distance) that divorced people, blended families, gay families, and single parents are failures. That our children are at risk, and the whole arrangement is messy and embarrassing. A marriage that ends is not called "finished," it's called *failed*. The children of this family may have been born to a happy union, but now they are called *the children of divorce*.

I had no idea how thoroughly these assumptions overlaid my culture until I went through divorce myself. I wrote to a friend: "This might be worse than being widowed. Overnight I've suffered the same losses — companionship, financial and practical support, my identity as a wife and partner, the future I'd taken for granted. I am lonely, grieving, and hard-pressed to take care of my household alone. But instead of bringing casseroles, people are acting like I had a fit and broke up the family china."

Once upon a time I held these beliefs about divorce: That everyone who does it could have chosen not to do it. That it's a lazy way out of marital problems. That it selfishly puts personal happiness ahead of family integrity. Now I tremble for my ignorance. It's easy, in fortunate times, to forget about the ambush that could leave your head reeling: serious mental or physical illness, death in the family, abandonment, financial calamity, humiliation, violence, despair.

I started out like any child, intent on being the Family of Dolls. I set upon   10 young womanhood believing in most of the doctrines of my generation: I wore my skirts four inches above the knee. I had that Barbie with her zebra-striped swimsuit and a figure unlike anything found in nature. And I understood the Prince Charming Theory of Marriage, a quest for Mr. Right that ends smack dab where you find him. I did not completely understand that another whole story *begins* there, and no fairy tale prepared me for the combination of bad luck and persistent hope that would interrupt my dream and lead me to other arrangements. Like a cancer diagnosis, a dying marriage is a thing to fight, to deny, and finally, when there's no choice left, to dig in and survive. Casseroles would help. Likewise, I imagine it must be a painful reckoning in adolescence (or later on) to realize one's own true love will never look like the soft-focus fragrance ads because Prince Charming (surprise!) is a princess. Or vice versa. Or has skin the color your parents didn't want you messing with, except in the Crayola box.

It's awfully easy to hold in contempt the straw broken home, and that mythical category of persons who toss away nuclear family for the sheer fun of it. Even the legal terms we use have a suggestion of caprice. I resent the phrase "irreconcilable differences," which suggest a stubborn refusal to accept a spouse's little quirks. This is specious. Every happily married couple I know has loads of irreconcilable differences. Negotiating where to set the thermostat is not the point. A nonfunctioning marriage is a slow asphyxiation. It is waking up despised each morning, listening to the pulse of your own loneliness before the radio begins to blare its raucous gospel that you're nothing if you aren't loved. It is sharing your airless house with the threat of suicide or other kinds of violence, while the ghost that whispers, "Leave here and destroy your children," has passed over every door and nailed it shut. Disassembling a marriage in these circumstances is as much *fun* as amputating your own gangrenous leg. You do it, if you can, to save a life — or two, or more.

I know of no one who really went looking to hoe the harder row, especially the daunting one of single parenthood. Yet it seems to be the most American of customs to blame the burdened for their destiny. We'd like so desperately to believe in freedom and justice for all, we can hardly name that rogue bad luck, even when he's a close enough snake to bite us. In the wake of my divorce, some friends (even a few close ones) chose to vanish, rather than linger within striking distance of misfortune.

But most stuck around, bless their hearts, and if I'm any the wiser for my trials, it's from having learned the worth of steadfast friendship. And also, what not to say. The least helpful question is: "Did you want the divorce, or didn't you?" Did I want to keep that gangrenous leg, or not? How to explain, in a culture that venerates choice: Two terrifying options are much worse than none at all. Give me any day the quick hand of cruel fate that will leave me scarred but blameless. As it was, I kept thinking of that wicked third-grade joke in which some boy comes up behind you and grabs your ear, starts in with a prolonged tug, and asks, "Do you want this ear any longer?"

Still, the friend who holds your hand and says the wrong thing is made of dearer stuff than the one who stays away. And generally, through all of it, you live. My favorite fictional character, Kate Vaiden (in the novel by Reynolds Price), advises: "Strength just comes in one brand — you stand up at sunrise and meet what they send you and keep your hair combed."

Once you've weathered the straits, you get to cross the tricky juncture 15 from casualty to survivor. If you're on your feet at the end of a year or two, and have begun putting together a happy new existence, those friends who were kind enough to feel sorry for you when you needed it must now accept you back to the ranks of the living. If you're truly blessed, they will dance at your second wedding. Everybody else, for heaven's sake, should stop throwing stones.

Arguing about whether nontraditional families deserve pity or tolerance is a little like the medieval debate about left-handedness as a mark of the devil. Divorce, remarriage, single parenthood, gay parents, and blended families simply are. They're facts of our time. Some of the reasons listed by sociologists for these family reconstructions are: the idea of marriage as a romantic partnership rather than a pragmatic one; a shift in women's expectations, from servility to self-respect and independence; and longevity (prior to antibiotics no marriage was expected to last many decades — in Colonial days the average couple lived to be married less than twelve years). Add to all this our growing sense of entitlement to happiness and safety from abuse. Most would agree these are all good things. Yet their result — a culture in which serial monogamy and the consequent reshaping of families are the norm — gets diagnosed as "failing."

For many of us, once we have put ourselves Humpty-Dumpty-wise back together again, the main problem with our reorganized family is that other people think we have a problem. My daughter tells me the only time she's uncomfortable about being the child of divorced parents is when her friends say they feel sorry for her. It's a bizarre sympathy, given that half the kids in her school and nation are in the same boat, pursuing childish happiness with the same energy as their married-parent peers. When anyone asks how *she* feels about it, she spontaneously lists the benefits: Our house is in the country and we have a dog, but she can go to her dad's neighborhood for the urban thrills of a pool and sidewalks for roller-skating. What's more, she has three sets of grandparents!

Why is it surprising that a child would revel in a widened family and the right to feel at home in more than one house? Isn't it the opposite that should worry us — a child with no home at all, or too few resources to feel safe? The child at risk is the one whose parents are too immature themselves to guide wisely; too diminished by poverty to nurture; too far from opportunity to offer hope. The number of children in the U.S. living in poverty at this moment is almost unfathomably large: 20 percent. There are families among us that need help all right, and by no means are they new on the landscape. The rate at which teenage girls had babies in 1957 (ninety-six per thousand) was twice what it is now. That remarkable statistic is ignored by the religious right — probably because the teen birth rate was cut in half mainly by legalized abortion. In fact, the policy gatekeepers who coined the phrase "family values" have steadfastly ignored the desperation of too-small families, and since 1979 have steadily reduced the amount of financial support available to a single parent. But this camp's most outspoken attacks seem aimed at the notion of families getting too complex, with add-ons and extras such as a gay parent's partner, or a remarried mother's new husband and his children.

To judge a family's value by its tidy symmetry is to purchase a book for its cover. There's no moral authority there. The famous family comprised of Dad, Mom, Sis, and Junior living as an isolated economic unit is not built on historical bedrock. In *The Way We Never Were,* Stephanie Coontz writes, "Whenever people propose that we go back to the traditional family, I always suggest that they pick a ballpark date for the family they have in mind." Colonial families were tidily disciplined, but their members (meaning everyone but infants) labored incessantly and died young. Then the Victorian family adopted a new division of labor, in which women's role was domestic and children were allowed time for study and play, but this was an upper-class construct supported by myriad slaves. Coontz writes, "For every nineteenth-century middle-class family that protected its wife and child within the family circle, there was an Irish or German girl scrubbing floors . . . a Welsh boy mining coal to keep the home-baked goodies warm, a black girl doing the family laundry, a black mother and child picking cotton to be made into clothes for the family, and a Jewish or an Italian daughter in a sweatshop making 'ladies' dresses or artificial flowers for the family to purchase."

The abolition of slavery brought slightly more democratic arrangements, 20 in which extended families were harnessed together in cottage industries; at the turn of the century came a steep rise in child labor in mines and sweatshops. Twenty percent of American children lived in orphanages at the time; their parents were not necessarily dead, but couldn't afford to keep them.

During the Depression and up to the end of World War II, many millions of U.S. households were more multigenerational than nuclear. Women my grandmother's age were likely to live with a fluid assortment of elderly relatives, in-laws, siblings, and children. In many cases they spent virtually every waking hour working in the company of other women — a companionable scenario in which it would be easier, I imagine, to tolerate an estranged or difficult spouse. I'm reluctant to idealize a life of so much hard work and so little spousal intimacy, but its advantage may have been resilience. A family so large and varied would not easily be brought down by a single blow: It could absorb a death, long illness, an abandonment here or there, and any number of irreconcilable differences.

The Family of Dolls came along midcentury as a great American experiment. A booming economy required a mobile labor force and demanded that women surrender jobs to returning soldiers. Families came to be defined by a single breadwinner. They struck out for single-family homes at an earlier age than ever before, and in unprecedented numbers they raised children in suburban isolation. The nuclear family was launched to sink or swim.

More than a few sank. Social historians corroborate that the suburban family of the postwar economic boom, which we have recently selected as our definition of "traditional," was no panacea. Twenty-five percent of Americans were poor in the mid-1950s, and as yet there were no food stamps. Sixty percent of the elderly lived on less than $1,000 a year, and most had no medical insurance. In the sequestered suburbs, alcoholism and sexual abuse of children were far more widespread than anyone imagined.

Expectations soared, and the economy sagged. It's hard to depend on one other adult for everything, come what may. In the last three decades, that amorphous, adaptable structure we call "family" has been reshaped once more by economic tides. Compared with fifties families, mothers are far more likely now to be employed. We are statistically more likely to divorce, and to live in blended families or other extranuclear arrangements. We are also more likely to plan and space our children, and to rate our marriages as "happy." We are less likely to suffer abuse without recourse, or to stare out at our lives through a glaze of prescription tranquilizers. Our aged parents are less likely to be destitute, and we're half as likely to have a teenage daughter turn up a mother herself. All in all, I would say that if "intact" in modern family-values jargon means living quietly desperate in the bell jar,° then hip-hip-hooray for "broken." A neat family model constructed to service the Baby Boom economy seems to be returning gradually to a grand, lumpy shape that human families apparently have tended toward since they first took root in the Olduvai Gorge.° We're social animals, deeply fond of companionship, and children love best to run in packs. If there is a *normal* for humans, at all, I expect it looks like two or three Families of Dolls, connected variously by kinship and passion, shuffled like cards and strewn over several shoeboxes.

The sooner we can let go the fairy tale of families functioning perfectly in   25
isolation, the better we might embrace the relief of community. Even the admirable parents who've stayed married through thick and thin are very likely, at present, to incorporate other adults into their families — household help and baby-sitters if they can afford them, or neighbors and grandparents if they can't. For single parents, this support is the rock-bottom definition of family. And most parents who have split apart, however painfully, still manage to maintain family continuity for their children, creating in many cases a boisterous phenomenon that Constance Ahrons in her book *The Good Divorce* calls the "binuclear family." Call it what you will — when ex-spouses beat swords into plowshares and jump up and down at a soccer game together, it makes for happy kids.

Cinderella, look, who needs her? All those evil stepsisters? That story always seemed like too much cotton-picking fuss over clothes. A childhood tale that fascinated me more was the one called "Stone Soup," and the gist of it is this: Once upon a time, a pair of beleagured soldiers straggled home to a village empty-handed, in a land ruined by war. They were famished, but the villagers had so little they shouted evil words and slammed their doors. So the soldiers dragged out a big kettle, filled it with water, and put it on a fire to boil. They rolled a clean round stone into the pot, while the villagers peered through their curtains in amazement.

"What kind of soup is that?" they hooted.

"Stone soup," the soldiers replied. "Everybody can have some when it's done."

"Well, thanks," one matron grumbled, coming out with a shriveled carrot. "But it'd be better if you threw this in."

And so on, of course, a vegetable at a time, until the whole suspicious vil-   30
lage managed to feed itself grandly.

Any family is a big empty pot, save for what gets thrown in. Each stew turns out different. Generosity, a resolve to turn bad luck into good, and respect for variety — these things will nourish a nation of children. Name-calling and suspicion will not. My soup contains a rock or two of hard times, and maybe yours does too. I expect it's a heck of a bouillabaisse.

---

bell jar: A glass shaped like a bell that protects a fragile object.
Olduvai Gorge: A location in Tanzania, Africa, where the remains of very early human ancestors were found.

Considerations for Critical Thinking and Writing

1. How does Kingsolver's descriptions of the "Family of Dolls" in paragraphs 3, 10, and 22 explain her perspective on traditional family values?

2. Describe how Kingsolver's own definition of what constitutes a family differs from what she describes as the traditional family.

3. Do you think this essay is an attack on traditional family life? Explain why or why not.

4. What purpose is served by the story about stone soup in the essay's final paragraph?

5. To what extent does Kingsolver's perspective on family life reflect your own experiences and perceptions?

Feminist Analysis

This casebook shows how one student, Kathy Atner, uses several critical approaches to Henrik Ibsen's A Doll House *(p. 700) to develop her paper, a feminist response to the play. Critics have employed numerous approaches to this play because it raises so many issues relating to matters such as relationships between men and women, history, and biography as well as imagery, symbolism, and irony. The critical excerpts in this casebook offer a small, partial sample of the biographical, historical, mythological, psychological, and other perspectives critics have used in their attempts to shed light on the play (see Chapter 3, "Applying a Critical Strategy," for a discussion of a variety of critical methods). After Kathy has read the play several times, focusing on the theme of home and family in* A Doll House, *she reads these critical excerpts and takes notes, asking herself whether the ideas in each excerpt change her reading of the play or complicate how she had been thinking about the theme. Because Kathy's final paper concerns applying a critical strategy, her early notes are not included here. As you read and reread the following critical perspectives, however, keep notes on how useful you think each one is and what moments and elements in the play each highlights.*

HISTORICAL DOCUMENT

The following letter offers a revealing vignette of the historical contexts for *A Doll House*. Professor Richard Panofsky of the University of Massachusetts–Dartmouth has provided the letter and this background information: "The translated letter was written in 1844 by Marcus (1807–1865) to his wife Ulrike (1816–1888), after six children had been born. This upper-middle-class Jewish

family lived in Hamburg, Germany, where Marcus was a doctor. As the letter implies, Ulrike had left home and children: the letter establishes conditions for her to return. A woman in upper-class society of the time had few choices in an unhappy marriage. Divorce or separation meant ostracism; as Marcus writes, 'your husband, children, and the entire city threaten indifference or even contempt.' And she could not take a job, as she would have no profession to step into. In any case, Ulrike did return home. Between 1846 and 1857 the marriage produced eight more children. Beyond what the letter shows, we do not know the reasons for the separation or what the later marriage relationship was like."

A Nineteenth-Century Husband's Letter to His Wife   1844

Dear Wife,   June 23, 1844

You have sinned greatly—and maybe I too; but this much is certain: Adam sinned after Eve had already sinned. So it is with us; you, alone, carry the guilt of all the misfortune which, however, I helped to enlarge later by my behavior. Listen now, since I still believe certain things to be necessary in order that we may have a peaceful life. If we want not only to be content for a day but forever, you will have to follow my wishes. So examine yourself and determine if you are strong enough to conquer your false ambitions and your stubbornness to submit to all the conditions, the fulfillment of which I cannot ignore. Every sensible person will tell you that all I ask of you is what is easily understood. If you insist on remaining stubborn, then do not return to my house, for you will never be happy with me; your husband, children, and the entire city threaten indifference or even contempt.

But if you decide to act *sensibly* and *correctly*, that is *justly* and *kindly*, then be certain that many in the world will envy you.

I am including here the paper which I read to you in front of the rabbi; ask anyone in your residence if the wishes expressed by me are not quite reasonable, and are of a kind to which every wife can agree for the welfare of domestic happiness. In any case, act in a way you think best.

When you decide to return, write to tell me on which day and hour you depart from Berlin and give me your itinerary whether by way of Kuestrin and Pinne or by way of Wollstein. I will then meet you at Wollstein or Pinne. I expect you will bring Solomon with you.

Don't travel unprepared. If you need money, ask your father.

May God enlighten your heart and mind

                    I remain your so far unhappy,   [Marcus]

Greetings to my parents, brothers, and sisters; also your brother. Show them what you wish, this letter, the enclosure, whatever you want. The children are fortunately healthy.

If you want to return with joy and peace, write me by return mail. In that case, I would rather send you a carriage. Maybe Madam Fraenkel will come along. . . .

[*Enclosure*]

My wife promises—for which every wife is obligated to her husband—to follow my wishes in everything and to strictly obey my orders. It is already self-evident that our marital relations have often been disturbed by the fact that my wife does not follow my wishes but believes herself to be entitled to act on her own, even if this is totally against my orders. In order not to have to remind my wife every second what my wishes are regarding homemaking and public conduct—wishes which I have often expressed—I want to make here a few rules which shall serve as a code of conduct. A home is best run if the work for each hour is planned ahead of time, if possible.

Servants get up no later than 5:00 A.M. in summer and 6:00 A.M. in winter, the children an hour later. The cook prepares breakfast. The nursemaid puts out clothes for every child, prepares water and sponge, cleans the combs, etc. The cook should stay in the kitchen unless there is time to clean the rooms. At least once a week the rooms should be cleaned whenever possible, but not all on the same day.

Every Wednesday, the people in the house should do a laundry. Every last Wednesday in the month, there shall be a large laundry with an outside washer-woman. At least every Monday, the seamstress shall come into the house to fix what is necessary.

Every Thursday or Friday, bread is baked for the week; I think it is best to buy grain and have it ground, but to knead it at home.

Every Friday special bread (Barches) should be bought for the evening meal.

The kitchen list will be prepared and discussed every Thursday evening, jointly, by me and my wife; but my wish is to be decisive.

After this, provisions are to be bought every Friday at the market. For this purpose, my wife, herself, will go to the market on Fridays, accompanied by a servant; she can substitute a special woman who does errands (*Faktorfrau*) if she wishes, but not a servant.

All expenditures have to be written down daily and punctually.

The children receive a bath every Thursday evening. The children's clothes must be kept in a specially appointed chest, with a separate compartment for each child with the child's name upon it. The boys' suits and girls' dresses are to be kept separately. To keep used laundry, there must be a hamper easily accessible. Equally important is the food storage box in which provisions are kept in order, locked and safe from vermin.

The kitchen should be kept in order. Once a week all woodwork and copper must be scoured. The lights and lamps have to be cleaned daily. Toward servants, one has to be strict and just. Therefore, one should not call them names which aren't suitable for a decent wife. One should give them enough nourishing food. Disobedience and obstinacy are to be referred to me.

My wife will never make visits in my absence. However, she should visit the synagogue every Saturday—at least once a month; also she should go for a walk with the children at least once a week.

CONSIDERATIONS FOR CRITICAL THINKING AND WRITING

1. Describe the tone of Marcus's letter to his wife. To what extent does he accept responsibility for their separation? What significant similarities and differences do you find between Marcus and Torvald Helmer?

2. Read the discussion on historical criticism in Chapter 3, "Applying a Critical Strategy" (pp. 66–67). How do you think a new historicist would use this letter to shed light on *A Doll House*?

3. Write a response to the letter from what you imagine to be the wife's point of view.

4. No information is available about this couple's marriage after Ulrike returned home. In an essay, speculate on what you think their relationship was like later in their marriage.

BARRY WITHAM (b. 1939) AND
JOHN LUTTERBIE (b. 1948)

Witham and Lutterbie describe how they use a Marxist approach to teach *A Doll House* in their drama class, in which they teach plays from a variety of critical perspectives.

A Marxist Approach to A Doll House   *1985*

A principal tenet of Marxist criticism is that human consciousness is a product of social conditions and that human relationships are often subverted by and through economic considerations. Mrs. Linde has sacrificed a genuine love to provide for her brothers, and Krogstad has committed a crime to support his children. Anne-Marie, the maid, has also been the victim of her economic background. Because she's "a girl who's poor and gotten in trouble," her relationship with her child has been interrupted and virtually destroyed. In each instance the need for money is linked with the ability to exist. But while the characters accept the social realities of their misfortunes, they do not appear to question how their human attitudes have been thoroughly shaped by socioeconomic considerations.

Once students begin to perceive how consciousness is affected by economics, a Marxist reading of Ibsen's play can illuminate a number of areas. Krogstad, for example, becomes less of a traditional villain when we realize that he is fighting for his job at the bank "as if it were life itself." And his realization of the senselessness of their lives is poignantly revealed when he reflects on Mrs. Linde's past, "all this simply for money." Even Dr. Rank speaks about his failing health and imminent death in entirely financial terms. "These past few days I've been auditing my internal accounts. Bankrupt! Within a month I'll probably be laid out and rotting in the churchyard."

All these characters, however, serve as foils for the central struggle between Nora and Torvald and highlight the pilgrimage that Nora makes in the play. At the outset two things are clear: (1) Nora is enslaved by Torvald in economic terms, and (2) she equates personal freedom with the acquisition of wealth. The play begins joyfully not only because it is the holiday season but also because

Torvald's promotion to bank manager will ensure "a safe, secure job with a comfortable salary." Nora is happy because she sees the future in wholly economic terms. "Won't it be lovely to have stacks of money and not a care in the world?"

What she learns, however, is that financial enslavement is symptomatic of other forms of enslavement — master-slave, male-female, sexual objectification, all of which characterize her relationship with Torvald — and that money is no guarantee of happiness. At the end of the play she renounces not only her marital vows but also her financial dependence because she has discovered that personal and human freedom are not measured in economic terms.

This discovery also prompts her to reexamine the society of which she is a part and leads us into a consideration of the ideology in the play. In what sense has Nora committed a criminal offense in forging her father's name? Is it indeed just that she should be punished for an altruistic act, one that cost her dearly both in terms of self-denial and the destruction of her family? Ibsen's defense of Nora is clear, of course, and his implicit indictment of a society that encourages this kind of injustice stimulates a discussion of the assumptions that created the law.

One of the striking things about *A Doll House* is how Anne-Marie accepts her alienation from her child as if it were natural, given the circumstances of class and money. It does not occur to her that laws were framed by other people and thus are capable of imperfection and susceptible to change. Nora broke a law that not only tries to stop thievery (the appropriation of capital) by outlawing forgery but also discriminates against anyone deemed a bad risk. Question leads to question as the class investigates why women were bad risks and why they had difficulty finding employment. It becomes obvious that the function of women in this society was not "natural" but artificial, a role created by their relationship to the family and by their subservience to men. In the marketplace they were a labor force expecting subsistence wages and providing an income to supplement that earned by their husbands or fathers.

An even clearer picture of Nora's society emerges when the Marxist critic examines those features or elements that are not in the play. These "absences" become valuable clues in understanding the ideology in the text. In the words of Fredric Jameson, absences are

> terms or nodal points implicit in the ideological system which have, however, remained unrealized in surface of the text, which have failed to become manifest in the logic of the narrative, and which we can therefore read as what the text represses.[1]

The notion of absences is particularly intriguing for students, who learn quickly to apply it to such popular media as films and television (what can we learn about the experience of urban black Americans from sitcoms like *Julia* and *The Jeffersons*?). Absent from *A Doll House* is Nora's mother, an omission that ties her more firmly to a male-dominated world and the bank owners who promoted Torvald. These absences shape our view because they form a layer of reality that is repressed in the play. And an examination of this "repressed" material leads us to our final topic of discussion: What is the relation between this play and the society in which it was created and produced?

Most Marxist critics believe that there are only three possible answers: the play supports the status quo, argues for reforms in an essentially sound system,

---

[1]Frederic Jameson, *The Political Unconscious: Narrative as a Socially Symbolic Act* (Ithaca: Cornell UP, 1981), p. 48.

or advocates a radical restructuring. Though these options are seemingly reductive, discussion reveals the complexities of reaching any unanimous agreement, and students frequently disagree about Ibsen's intentions regarding reform or revolution. Nora's leaving is obviously a call for change, but many students are not sure whether this leave-taking is a way forward or a cul-de-sac for a system that is thoroughly controlled by the prevailing power structure. . . .

Viewing the play through the lens of Marxist atheists does make one thing clear. Nora's departure had ramifications for her society that went beyond the marriage bed. By studying the play within the context of its socio-economic structure, we can see how the ideology in the text affects the characters and how they perpetuate the ideology. The conclusion of *A Doll House* was a challenge to the economic superstructures that had controlled and excluded the Noras of the world by manipulating their economic status and, by extension, their conscious estimation of themselves and their place in society.

From "A Marxist Approach to *A Doll House*"
in *Approaches to Teaching Ibsen's* A Doll House

CONSIDERATIONS FOR CRITICAL THINKING AND WRITING

1. To what extent do you agree or disagree with the Marxist "tenet" (para. 1) that "consciousness is affected by economics" (para. 2)?

2. Do you think that Nora's "leave-taking is a way forward or a cul-de-sac for a system that is thoroughly controlled by the prevailing power structure" (para. 8)? Explain your response.

3. Consider whether "A Nineteenth-Century Husband's Letter to His Wife" (p. 760) supports or challenges Witham and Lutterbie's Marxist reading of *A Doll House*.

CAROL STRONGIN TUFTS (b. 1947)

A Psychoanalytic Reading of Nora   *1986*

I am not a member of the Women's Rights League. Whatever I have written has been without any conscious thought of making propaganda. I have been more the poet and less the social philosopher than people generally seem inclined to believe. . . . To me it has seemed a problem of mankind in general. And if you read my books carefully you will understand this. . . . My task has been the *description of humanity*. To be sure, whenever such a description is felt to be reasonably true, the reader will read his own feelings and sentiments into the work of the poet. These are then attributed to the poet; but incorrectly so. Every reader remolds the work beautifully and neatly, each according to his own personality. Not only those who write but also those who read are poets. They are collaborators.[1]

To look again at Ibsen's famous and often-quoted words—his assertion that *A Doll House* was not intended as propaganda to promote the cause of women's rights—is to realize the sarcasm aimed by the playwright at those

---

[1]Speech delivered at the Banquet of the Norwegian League for Women's Rights, Christiana, 26 May 1898, in Ibsen, *Letters and Speeches,* ed. Evert Sprinchorn (New York: Hill, 1964), 337.

nineteenth-century "collaborators" who insisted on viewing his play as a treatise and Nora, his heroine, as the romantic standard-bearer for the feminist
cause. Yet there is also a certain irony implicit in such a realization, for directors,
actors, audiences, and critics turning to this play a little over one hundred years
after its first performance bring with them the historical, cultural, and psychological experience which itself places them in the role of Ibsen's collaborators.
Because it is a theatrical inevitability that each dramatic work which survives its
time and place of first performance does so to be recast in productions
mounted in succeeding times and different places, *A Doll House* can never so
much be simply reproduced as it must always be re-envisioned. And if the spectacle of a woman walking out on her husband and children in order to fulfill
her "duties to (her)self" is no longer the shock for us today that it was for audiences at the end of the nineteenth century, a production of *A Doll House* which
resonates with as much immediacy and power for us as it did for its first audiences may do so through the discovery within Ibsen's text of something of our
own time and place. For in *A Doll House,* as Rolf Fjelde has written, "(i)t is the
entire house . . . which is on trial, the total complex of relationships, including
husband, wife, children, servants, upstairs and downstairs, that is tested by the
visitors that come and go, embodying aspects of the inescapable reality outside."[2] And a production which approaches that reality through the experience
of Western culture in the last quarter of the twentieth century may not only discover how uneasy was Ibsen's relationship to certain aspects of the forces of
Romanticism at work in his own society, but, in so doing, may also come to
fashion *A Doll House* which shifts emphasis away from the celebration of the
Romantic belief in the sovereignty of the individual to the revelation of an iso-
lating narcissism — a narcissism that has become all too familiar to us today.[3]

The characters of *A Doll House* are, to be sure, not alone in dramatic literature in being self-preoccupied, for self-preoccupation is a quality shared by
characters from Oedipus to Hamlet and on into modern drama. Yet if a contemporary production is to suggest the narcissistic self-absorption of Ibsen's
characters, it must do so in such a way as to imply motivations for their actions
and delineate their relationships with one another. Thus it is important to
establish a conceptual framework which will provide a degree of precision for
the use of the term "narcissism" in this discussion so as to distinguish it from
the kind of self-absorption which is an inherent quality necessarily shared by
all dramatic characters. For that purpose, it is useful to turn to the criteria
established by the Task Force on Nomenclature and Statistics of the American
Psychiatric Association for diagnosing the narcissistic personality:

A. Grandiose sense of self-importance and uniqueness, e.g., exaggerates
   achievements and talents, focuses on how special one's problems are.
B. Preoccupation with fantasies of unlimited success, power, brilliance,
   beauty, or ideal love.

[2]Rolf Fjelde, Introduction to *A Doll House,* in Henrik Ibsen, *The Complete Major Prose Plays*
(New York: Farrar, Straus, Giroux, 1978), p. 121.
[3]For studies of the prevalence of the narcissistic personality disorder in contemporary psy-
choanalytic literature, see Otto F. Kernberg, *Borderline Conditions and Pathological Narcissism*
(New York: J. Aronson, 1975); Heinz Kohut, *The Analysis of the Self* (New York: International
Universities Press, 1971); and Peter L. Giovachinni, *Psychoanalysis of Character Disorders* (New
York: J. Aronson, 1975). See also Christopher Lasch, *The Culture of Narcissism* (New York: Nor-
ton, 1979), for a discussion of narcissism as the defining characteristic of contemporary
American society.

C. Exhibitionistic: requires constant attention and admiration.
D. Responds to criticism, indifference of others, or defeat with either cool indifference, or with marked feelings of rage, inferiority, shame, humiliation, or emptiness.
E. At least two of the following are characteristics of disturbances in interpersonal relationships:
    1. Lack of empathy: inability to recognize how others feel, e.g., unable to appreciate the distress of someone who is seriously ill.
    2. Entitlement: expectation of special favors without assuming reciprocal responsibilities, e.g., surprise and anger that people won't do what he wants.
    3. Interpersonal exploitiveness: takes advantage of others to indulge own desires for self-aggrandizement, with disregard for the personal integrity and rights of others.
    4. Relationships characteristically vacillate between the extremes of over-idealization and devaluation.[4]

These criteria, as they provide a background against which to consider Nora's relationship with both Kristine Linde and Dr. Rank, will serve to illuminate not only those relationships themselves, but also the relationship of Nora and her husband which is at the center of the play. Moreover, if these criteria are viewed as outlines for characterization — but not as reductive psychoanalytic constructs leading to "case studies" — it becomes possible to discover a Nora of greater complexity than the totally sympathetic victim turned romantic heroine who has inhabited most productions of the play. And, most important of all, as Nora and her relationships within the walls of her "doll house" come to imply a paradigm of the dilemma of all human relationships in the greater society outside, the famous sound of the slamming door may come to resonate even more loudly for us than it did for the audiences of the nineteenth century with a profound and immediate sense of irony and ambiguity, an irony and ambiguity which could not have escaped Ibsen himself.

From "Recasting *A Doll House:* Narcissism as Character Motivation
in Ibsen's Play," *Comparative Drama,* Summer 1986

[4]Task Force on Nomenclature and Statistics, American Psychiatric Association, *DSM-III: Diagnostic Criteria Draft* (New York, 1978), pp. 103–04.

Considerations for Critical Thinking and Writing

1. What is Tufts's purpose in arguing that Nora be seen as narcissistic?
2. Using the criteria of the American Psychiatric Association, consider Nora's personality. Write an essay either refuting the assertion that she has a narcissistic personality or supporting it.
3. How does Tufts's reading compare with Joan Templeton's feminist reading of Nora in the perspective that follows? Which do you find more convincing? Why?

JOAN TEMPLETON (b. 1940)

This feminist perspective summarizes the arguments against reading the play as dramatization of a feminist heroine.

Is A Doll House *a Feminist Text?*   *1989*

A Doll House *is no more about women's rights than Shakespeare's* Richard II *is about the divine right of kings, or* Ghosts *about syphilis. . . . Its theme is the need of every individual to find out the kind of person he or she is and to strive to become that person.*[1]

Ibsen has been resoundingly saved from feminism, or, as it was called in his day, "the woman question." His rescuers customarily cite a statement the dramatist made on 26 May 1898 at a seventieth-birthday banquet given in his honor by the Norwegian Women's Rights League:

> I thank you for the toast, but must disclaim the honor of having consciously worked for the women's rights movement. . . . True enough, it is desirable to solve the woman problem, along with all the others; but that has not been the whole purpose. My task has been the description of humanity.[2]

Ibsen's champions like to take this disavowal as a precise reference to his purpose in writing *A Doll House* twenty years earlier, his "original intention," according to Maurice Valency.[3] Ibsen's biographer Michael Meyer urges all reviewers of *Doll House* revivals to learn Ibsen's speech by heart,[4] and James McFarlane, editor of *The Oxford Ibsen,* includes it in his explanatory material on *A Doll House,* under "Some Pronouncements of the Author," as though Ibsen had been speaking of the play.[5] Whatever propaganda feminists may have made of *A Doll House,* Ibsen, it is argued, never meant to write a play about the highly topical subject of women's rights; Nora's conflict represents something other than, or something more than, woman's. In an article commemorating the half century of Ibsen's death, R. M. Adams explains, "*A Doll House* represents a woman imbued with the idea of becoming a person, but it proposes nothing categorical about women becoming people; in fact, its real theme has nothing to do with the sexes."[6] Over twenty years later, after feminism had resurfaced as an international movement, Einar Haugen, the doyen of American Scandinavian studies, insisted that "Ibsen's Nora is not just a woman arguing for female liberation; she is much more. She embodies the comedy as well as the tragedy of modern life."[7] In the Modern Language Association's *Approaches to Teaching Ibsen's* A Doll House, the editor speaks disparagingly of "reductionist views of *(A Doll House)* as a feminist drama." Summarizing a "major theme" in the volume as "the need for a broad view of the play and a condemnation of a static approach," she warns that discussions of the play's "connection with feminism" have value only if they are monitored, "properly channeled and kept firmly linked to Ibsen's text."[8]

Removing the woman question from *A Doll House* is presented as part of a corrective effort to free Ibsen from his erroneous reputation as a writer of thesis plays, a wrongheaded notion usually blamed on Shaw, who, it is claimed,

---

[1]Michael Meyer, *Ibsen* (Garden City: Doubleday, 1971), 457. [This is not the Michael Meyer who is editor of *Thinking and Writing about Literature.*]

[2]Henrik Ibsen, *Letter and Speeches,* ed. and trans. Evert Sprinchorn (New York: Hill, 1964), 337.

[3]Maurice Valency, *The Flower and the Castle: An Introduction to Modern Drama* (New York: Schocken, 1982), 151.

[4]Meyer, 774.

[5]James McFarlane, *"A Doll's House:* Commentary" in *The Oxford Ibsen,* ed. McFarlane (Oxford UP, 1961), V, 456.

[6]R. M. Adams, "The Fifty-First Anniversary," *Hudson Review* 10 (1957), 416.

[7]Einar Haugen, *Ibsen's Drama: Author to Audience* (Minneapolis: U of Minnesota P, 1979), vii.

[8]Yvonne Shafer, ed., *Approaches to Teaching Ibsen's* A Doll House (New York: MLA, 1985), 32.

mistakenly saw Ibsen as the nineteenth century's greatest iconoclast and offered that misreading to the public as *The Quintessence of Ibsenism*. Ibsen, it is now de rigueur to explain, did not stoop to "issues." He was a poet of the truth of the human soul. That Nora's exit from her dollhouse has long been the principal international symbol for women's issues, including many that far exceed the confines of her small world, is irrelevant to the essential meaning of *A Doll House*, a play, in Richard Gilman's phrase, "pitched beyond sexual difference."[9] Ibsen, explains Robert Brustein, "was completely indifferent to (the woman question) except as a metaphor for individual freedom."[10] Discussing the relation of *A Doll House* to feminism, Halvdan Koht, author of the definitive Norwegian Ibsen life, says in summary, "Little by little the topical controversy died away; what remained was the work of art, with its demand for truth in every human relation."[11]

Thus, it turns out, the *Uncle Tom's Cabin* of the women's rights movement is not really about women at all. "Fiddle-faddle," pronounced R. M. Adams, dismissing feminist claims for the play.[12] Like angels, Nora has no sex. Ibsen meant her to be Everyman.

From "The *Doll House* Backlash: Criticism, Feminism, and Ibsen,"
PMLA, January 1989

[9]Richard Gilman, *The Making of Modern Drama* (New York: Farrar, 1972), 65.
[10]Robert Brustein, *The Theatre of Revolt* (New York: Little, 1962), 105.
[11]Halvdan Koht, *Life of Ibsen* (New York: Blom, 1971), 323.
[12]Adams, 416.

CONSIDERATIONS FOR CRITICAL THINKING AND WRITING

1. According to Templeton, what kinds of arguments are used to reject *A Doll House* as a feminist text?

2. From the tone of the summaries provided, what would you say is Templeton's attitude toward these arguments?

3. Read the section on feminist criticism in Chapter 3, "Applying a Critical Strategy" (pp. 71–72), and write an essay addressing the summarized arguments as you think a feminist critic might respond.

A Sample First Response

After Kathy has read through all the critical perspectives, she takes the first step toward formal writing through informal writing. Her instructor told her to record her initial response to the play and to extend that response into a more formal approach. Kathy also reads through the Questions for Writing: Applying a Critical Analysis in Chapter 3 (p. 97) to make sure that she can identify exactly which critical lens she wants to use.

```
While I was reading this play, what struck me again
and again was the theme of fictions, in the marriage, and in
Nora's behaviors, which are conventionally feminine, until she
realizes that these are not authentic. The Helmers' marriage
```

depends so much on maintaining all of the fictions--of feelings, behaviors, and knowledge. Although Torvald thinks of
Nora as naive and unsensible, she is ironically the one who
does the most to maintain the fictions. But this doesn't mean
she's entirely aware of how her position compromises herself.
She conceals from her husband the fact that she saved his life
by borrowing money to protect him from the shame he would
feel if he knew he wasn't the main manager of the household.
She also, for much of the play, conceals from herself the
feelings she might have if her secret were out in the open
between them. But as the plot develops she begins to see that
if one fiction in their marriage dissolves, all of them will.
I think that these fictions aren't particular to the Helmers.
They are, generally, the fictions of gender roles and expectations. I think Joan Templeton's summary of the feminist
readings of this play is closest to how I read the play--
it's <u>obviously</u> about women's rights! The 19th-century letter
was pretty wild though--it makes me realize that women's
rights didn't exist in the same way a hundred years ago.
I wonder if I can combine a feminist and a historical perspective?

A Sample Student Historical Feminist Analysis

The following sample paper focuses on the magnitude of Nora
Helmer's decision to leave her husband in *A Doll House*. Kathy Atner uses
a new historicist perspective to show just how difficult Nora's decision would have been in the context of nineteenth-century attitudes
toward marriage and women. The paper develops an argument primarily
from evidence supplied by "A Nineteenth-Century Husband's Letter to
His Wife" (p. 760). By drawing on a source that ordinarily might have
been ignored by literary critics, Kathy is able to suggest how difficult
Nora's life would have been after abandoning her husband and family.
This historical strategy is combined with a feminist perspective that
gives the modern reader a greater understanding of the issues Nora must
inevitably confront once she slams the door shut on her conventional and
accepted life as devoted wife and mother. By using both new historicist
and feminist perspectives, Kathy suggests that contemporary readers
should be sensitive to the tragic as well as the heroic dimension of Nora's
life.

Kathy Atner
Professor Porter
English 216
April 8, 20--

On the Other Side of the Slammed Door

in A Doll House

   Nora Helmer's decision to leave her family in Henrik
Ibsen's 1879 play A Doll House reflects the dilemma faced
by many nineteenth-century women who were forced either
to conform to highly restrictive gender roles or to abandon these roles in order to realize their value as individuals. Although Ibsen brings his audience to the moment
that Nora chooses to disregard her social role and opt
for her "freedom," his play does not clearly reveal the
true fate of women who followed Nora's path in the nineteenth century. Historically, most women who chose not to
acquiesce to the socially prescribed roles of marriage
were treated as unnatural creatures and shunned by the
respectable public. An actual letter, written in 1844 by
Marcus to his estranged wife, Ulrike, reveals the effects
of this severe social condemnation (760). His letter
implies the desperate fate that inevitably befalls women
who reject their prescribed duties as wives and mothers.
Through Marcus's letter to his wife, the painful ramifications of Nora's decision to accommodate her own personal desires instead of those of her family become even
more poignant, courageous, and tragic.

   In the nineteenth century, women had few alternatives to marriage, and women who "failed" at marriage
were thought to have failed in their most important duty.
In his letter, Marcus articulates society's deep disgust
for women who reject what it believes is the sacred female role of homemaker. His letter, while on one level
an angry condemnation of his wife's "stubbornness" (760)

and a cruelly condescending list of conditions to be met
on her return, is on another level a plea for her to accept again the role that society has assigned her. He is
clearly shaken by his wife's abandonment and interprets
it as a betrayal of a social "law" or tradition, which,
to Marcus's mind, ought to be carved in stone. He responds
to this betrayal by demanding complete obedience from his
wife in the form of a promise "to follow my wishes in
everything and to strictly obey my orders" (761). Only
when she acquiesces to his conditions and returns to her
role as docile and obedient wife will Marcus in turn be
able to resume the comfortably familiar, socially sanc-
tioned role of dominant, morally superior husband.

   Like Ulrike, Nora decides to leave the security and
comfort of her restrictive domestic life to try to become
a human being. Ibsen neglects, however, to show his audience the actual result of that decision. At the conclusion of A Doll House, Nora slams the door on her past
life, hoping to begin a new life that will somehow be
more satisfying. Yet the modern audience has no genuine
sense of what she may have found beyond that door, and
perhaps neither did Nora. Through Ulrike's story, however, the reader understands the historical truth that
the world awaiting Nora was hostile and unsympathetic.
Marcus warns his wife that "your husband, your children,
and the entire city threaten indifference or even contempt" (760) if she refuses to return immediately to her
socially acceptable domestic role. This pressure to conform, combined with the bleak prospects of a single
woman, results in Ulrike's ultimate choice to keep up
"appearances" rather than further subject herself to a
contemptuous world that neither wants nor understands
her. Although we cannot know Nora's fate after she leaves
Torvald, we may assume that her future would be as bleak

as Ulrike's and that the pressure to return to her domestic life would be equally strong.

When A Doll House was first produced in 1879, audiences had no more sympathy for Nora's predicament than
they did for the real-life stories of women such as
Ulrike. As Errol Durbach points out, in the nineteenth
century, Ibsen's play "did not precipitate heated debate about feminism, women's rights, or male domination.
The sound and the fury were addressed to the very question . . . What credible wife and mother would ever walk
out this way on her family?" (14). A great many readers
and audience members tended to side with Torvald, who
seemed, to them, the innocent victim of Nora's consuming selfishness. The audience's repulsion toward Nora's
apparently "unnatural" action of abandoning her family
mirrors the responses of Marcus and Torvald Helmer,
the bereft, perplexed, and angry husbands. Nora and
Ulrike radically disrupt their husbands' perceptions
of family relationships by walking out of their lives,
preferring to recognize their own needs before any
others. These women suggest that Torvald's claim that
"before all else, you're a wife and mother" (745) may
not necessarily be true for all women, but their brave
rejections of domestic life cannot force society to
condone their behavior.

Ibsen maintains that A Doll House is not about
women's rights specifically but encompasses a more universal "description of humanity" (Letters 337). In showing a human being trying to create a new identity for
herself, however, Ibsen reveals the extent to which
people are trapped in societal norms and expectations.
Nora's acknowledgment that she "can't go on believing
what the majority says, or what's written in books"
(745) suggests a profound social upheaval that has the

Atner 4

potential to subvert long-established gender roles. If
Nora and Ulrike relinquish the role of the subservient
and helpless wife, then Torvald and Marcus can no longer
play the role of the dominating, protective husband.
Without this role, the men are as helpless as they want
their wives to be, and the traditional gender expectations are no longer beyond question. Yet the historical
reality is that in spite of Nora's daring escape from her
oppressive family, the world was not ready to accommodate
women who rejected their feminine duties. Ulrike was
thwarted in her attempt to free herself from her family;
history suggests that Nora may have met a similar fate.

Modern audiences tend to see Nora as a strong,
admirable woman who is courageous enough to sacrifice
everything in order to fulfill her own needs as an individual and as a woman. She shatters gender stereotypes
through her defiant disregard for all that society demands of her. Yet, taken in the context of nineteenth-
century life, perhaps Nora's story is more tragic than we
might initially like to believe. Ulrike's story, told
through her husband's letter, suggests that in a time of
turbulent social upheaval, what was interpreted as a collapse of what we now call "family values" was shocking,
scandalous, and deeply frightening to many. In the nineteenth century, Nora was not the sympathetic character
that she is today; instead, she symbolized many negative
attributes -- what Marcus calls "false ambitions" and
"stubbornness" (760) that were often ascribed to women.
Ulrike's forced return to her role as dutiful wife and
mother suggests that society was quick to punish disobedient women and that the slamming door at the end of A
Doll House was not necessarily the sound of freedom for
Nora.

                                                           Atner 5
                              Works Cited

Durbach, Errol. <u>A Doll's House: Ibsen's Myth of Transfor-</u>
    <u>mation</u>. Boston: Twayne, 1991.

Ibsen, Henrik. <u>A Doll House</u>. Trans. Rolf Fjelde. Meyer
    700-47.

---. <u>Letters and Speeches</u>. Ed. and trans. Evert Sprin-
    chorn. New York: Hill, 1964. 337.

Meyer, Michael, ed. <u>Thinking and Writing about</u>
    <u>Literature</u>. 2nd ed. Boston: Bedford/St. Martin's,
    2001.

"A Nineteenth-Century Husband's Letter to His Wife."
    Meyer 760-61.

Love and Its Complications

As everyone who has been in a relationship can attest, the path of love is rarely without its rocky patches—and sometimes complications are all that remain after love is gone. Each story, poem, play, and essay in this chapter deals with one of the faces of love. The speakers in Katerina Angheláki-Rooke's "Jealousy" and Robert Browning's "My Last Duchess" convey complicated passions that go well beyond love; the lover in John Donne's "The Flea" speaks persuasively on living for the moment, while Sharon Olds's "Sex without Love" questions how two people engage in such activity. Susan Minot's story "Lust" is a litany of chance physical encounters. David Ives's one-act play *Sure Thing* is a series of failed conversational hookups, until the boy and girl finally figure out how to say what the other wants to hear, a subject that Deborah Tannen treats seriously in her essay "Sex, Lies, and Conversation." Love is indeed an engaging theme—but as you read, don't forget to pay attention to the formal elements of each of these selections and how they work together. Also, don't read just for the presence of love; many other themes can be found in these works, and many other connections can be made to the literature elsewhere in this anthology.

FICTION

ANTON CHEKHOV (1860–1904)

Born in a small town in Russia, Anton Chekhov gave up the career his medical degree prepared him for in order to devote himself to writing. His concentration on realistic detail in the hundreds of short stories he published has had an important influence on fiction writing. Modern drama has also been strengthened by his plays, among them these classics: *The Seagull* (1896), *Uncle Vanya* (1899), *The Three Sisters* (1901), and *The Cherry Orchard* (1904). Chekhov was a close observer of people in ordinary situations who struggle to live their lives as best they can. They are not very often completely successful. Chekhov's compassion, however, makes their failures less significant than their humanity. In "The Lady with the Pet Dog," love is at the heart of a struggle that begins in Yalta, a resort town on the Black Sea.

The Lady with the Pet Dog   *1899*

TRANSLATED BY AVRAHM YARMOLINSKY (1947)

I

A new person, it was said, had appeared on the esplanade: a lady with a pet dog. Dmitry Dmitrich Gurov, who had spent a fortnight at Yalta and had got used to the place, had also begun to take an interest in new arrivals. As he sat in Vernet's confectionery shop, he saw, walking on the esplanade, a fair-haired young woman of medium height, wearing a beret; a white Pomeranian was trotting behind her.

And afterwards he met her in the public garden and in the square several times a day. She walked alone, always wearing the same beret and always with the white dog; no one knew who she was and everyone called her simply "the lady with the pet dog."

"If she is here alone without husband or friends," Gurov reflected, "it wouldn't be a bad thing to make her acquaintance."

He was under forty, but he already had a daughter twelve years old, and two sons at school. They had found a wife for him when he was very young, a student in his second year, and by now she seemed half as old again as he. She was a tall, erect woman with dark eyebrows, stately and dignified and, as she said of herself, intellectual. She read a great deal, used simplified spelling in her letters, called her husband, not Dmitry, but Dimitry, while he privately considered her of limited intelligence, narrow-minded, dowdy, was afraid of her, and did not like to be at home. He had begun being unfaithful to her long ago — had been unfaithful to her often and, probably for that reason, almost always spoke ill of women, and when they were talked of in his presence used to call them "the inferior race."

It seemed to him that he had been sufficiently tutored by bitter experience to call them what he pleased, and yet he could not have lived without "the inferior race" for two days together. In the company of men he was bored and ill at ease, he was chilly and uncommunicative with them; but when he was among women he felt free, and knew what to speak to them about and how to comport himself; and even to be silent with them was no strain on him. In his appearance, in his character, in his whole makeup there was something attractive and elusive that disposed women in his favor and allured them. He knew that, and some force seemed to draw him to them, too.

Oft-repeated and really bitter experience had taught him long ago that with decent people — particularly Moscow people — who are irresolute and slow to move, every affair which at first seems a light and charming adventure inevitably grows into a whole problem of extreme complexity, and in the end a painful situation is created. But at every new meeting with an interesting woman this lesson of experience seemed to slip from his memory, and he was eager for life, and everything seemed so simple and diverting.

One evening while he was dining in the public garden the lady in the beret walked up without haste to take the next table. Her expression, her gait, her dress, and the way she did her hair told him that she belonged to the upper class, that she was married, that she was in Yalta for the first time and alone, and that she was bored there. The stories told of the immorality in Yalta are to a great extent untrue; he despised them, and knew that such stories were made up for the most part by persons who would have been glad to sin themselves if they had had the chance; but when the lady sat down at the next table three paces from him, he recalled these stories of easy conquests, of trips to the mountains, and the tempting thought of swift, fleeting liaison, a romance with an unknown woman of whose very name he was ignorant suddenly took hold of him.

He beckoned invitingly to the Pomeranian, and when the dog approached him, shook his finger at it. The Pomeranian growled; Gurov threatened it again.

The lady glanced at him and at once dropped her eyes.

"He doesn't bite," she said and blushed.   10

"May I give him a bone?" he asked; and when she nodded he inquired affably, "Have you been in Yalta long?"

"About five days."

"And I am dragging out the second week here."

There was a short silence.

"Time passes quickly, and yet it is so dull here!" she said, not looking at him.   15

"It's only the fashion to say it's dull here. A provincial will live in Belyov or Zhizdra and not be bored, but when he comes here it's 'Oh, the dullness! Oh, the dust!' One would think he came from Granada."

She laughed. Then both continued eating in silence, like strangers, but after dinner they walked together and there sprang up between them the light banter of people who are free and contented, to whom it does not matter where they go or what they talk about. They walked and talked of the strange light on the sea: the water was a soft, warm, lilac color, and there was a golden band of moonlight upon it. They talked of how sultry it was after a hot day. Gurov told her that he was a native of Moscow, that he had studied languages and literature at the university, but had a post in a bank; that at one time he had trained to become an opera singer but had given it up, that he owned two houses in Moscow. And he learned from her that she had grown up in Petersburg, but had lived in S—— since her marriage two years previously, that she was going to stay in Yalta for about another month, and that her husband, who needed a rest, too, might perhaps come to fetch her. She was not certain whether her husband was a member of a Government Board or served on a Zemstvo Council,° and this amused her. And Gurov learned too that her name was Anna Sergeyevna.

Afterwards in his room at the hotel he thought about her—and was certain that he would meet her the next day. It was bound to happen. Getting into bed he recalled that she had been a schoolgirl only recently, doing lessons like

---

Zemstvo Council: A district council.

his own daughter; he thought how much timidity and angularity there was still in her laugh and her manner of talking with a stranger. It must have been the first time in her life that she was alone in a setting in which she was followed, looked at, and spoken to for one secret purpose alone, which she could hardly fail to guess. He thought of her slim, delicate throat, her lovely gray eyes.

"There's something pathetic about her, though," he thought, and dropped off.

II

A week had passed since they had struck up an acquaintance. It was a holiday. It was close indoors, while in the street the wind whirled the dust about and blew people's hats off. One was thirsty all day, and Gurov often went into the restaurant and offered Anna Sergeyevna a soft drink or ice cream. One did not know what to do with oneself.

In the evening when the wind had abated they went out on the pier to watch the steamer come in. There were a great many people walking about the dock; they had come to welcome someone and they were carrying bunches of flowers. And two peculiarities of a festive Yalta crowd stood out: the elderly ladies were dressed like young ones and there were many generals.

Owing to the choppy sea, the steamer arrived late, after sunset, and it was a long time tacking about before it put in at the pier. Anna Sergeyevna peered at the steamer and the passengers through her lorgnette as though looking for acquaintances, and whenever she turned to Gurov her eyes were shining. She talked a great deal and asked questions jerkily, forgetting the next moment what she had asked; then she lost her lorgnette in the crush.

The festive crowd began to disperse; it was now too dark to see people's faces; there was no wind any more, but Gurov and Anna Sergeyevna still stood as though waiting to see someone else come off the steamer. Anna Sergeyevna was silent now, and sniffed her flowers without looking at Gurov.

"The weather has improved this evening," he said. "Where shall we go now? Shall we drive somewhere?"

She did not reply.

Then he looked at her intently, and suddenly embraced her and kissed her on the lips, and the moist fragrance of her flowers enveloped him; and at once he looked round him anxiously, wondering if anyone had seen them.

"Let us go to your place," he said softly. And they walked off together rapidly.

The air in her room was close and there was the smell of the perfume she had bought at the Japanese shop. Looking at her, Gurov thought: "What encounters life offers!" From the past he preserved the memory of carefree, good-natured women whom love made gay and who were grateful to him for the happiness he gave them, however brief it might be; and of women like his wife who loved without sincerity, with too many words, affectedly, hysterically, with an expression that it was not love or passion that engaged them but something more significant; and of two or three others, very beautiful, frigid women, across whose faces would suddenly flit a rapacious expression—an obstinate desire to take from life more than it could give, and these were women no longer young, capricious, unreflecting, domineering, unintelligent, and when Gurov grew cold to them their beauty aroused his hatred, and the lace on their lingerie seemed to him to resemble scales.

But here there was the timidity, the angularity of inexperienced youth, a feeling of awkwardness; and there was a sense of embarrassment, as though someone had suddenly knocked at the door. Anna Sergeyevna, "the lady with the pet dog," treated what had happened in a peculiar way, very seriously, as though it were her fall — so it seemed, and this was odd and inappropriate. Her features drooped and faded, and her long hair hung down sadly on either side of her face; she grew pensive and her dejected pose was that of a Magdalene in a picture by an old master.

"It's not right," she said. "You don't respect me now, you first of all." 30

There was a watermelon on the table. Gurov cut himself a slice and began eating it without haste. They were silent for at least half an hour.

There was something touching about Anna Sergeyevna; she had the purity of a well-bred, naive woman who has seen little of life. The single candle burning on the table barely illumined her face, yet it was clear that she was unhappy.

"Why should I stop respecting you, darling?" asked Gurov. "You don't know what you're saying."

"God forgive me," she said, and her eyes filled with tears. "It's terrible."

"It's as though you were trying to exonerate yourself." 35

"How can I exonerate myself? No. I am a bad, low woman; I despise myself and I have no thought of exonerating myself. It's not my husband but myself I have deceived. And not only just now; I have been deceiving myself for a long time. My husband may be a good, honest man, but he is a flunkey! I don't know what he does, what his work is, but I know he is a flunkey! I was twenty when I married him. I was tormented by curiosity; I wanted something better. 'There must be a different sort of life,' I said to myself. I wanted to live! To live, to live! Curiosity kept eating at me — you don't understand it, but I swear to God I could no longer control myself; something was going on in me: I could not be held back. I told my husband I was ill, and came here. And here I have been walking about as though in a daze, as though I were mad; and now I have become a vulgar, vile woman whom anyone may despise."

Gurov was already bored with her; he was irritated by her naive tone, by her repentance, so unexpected and so out of place; but for the tears in her eyes he might have thought she was joking or play-acting.

"I don't understand, my dear," he said softly. "What do you want?"

She hid her face on his breast and pressed close to him.

"Believe me, believe me, I beg you," she said, "I love honesty and purity, 40 and sin is loathsome to me; I don't know what I'm doing. Simple people say, 'The Evil One has led me astray.' And I may say of myself now that the Evil One has led me astray."

"Quiet, quiet," he murmured.

He looked into her fixed, frightened eyes, kissed her, spoke to her softly and affectionately, and by degrees she calmed down, and her gaiety returned; both began laughing.

Afterwards when they went out there was not a soul on the esplanade. The town with its cypresses looked quite dead, but the sea was still sounding as it broke upon the beach; a single launch was rocking on the waves and on it a lantern was blinking sleepily.

They found a cab and drove to Oreanda.

"I found out your surname in the hall just now: it was written on the 45
board—von Dideritz," said Gurov. "Is your husband German?"

"No; I believe his grandfather was German, but he is Greek Orthodox himself."

At Oreanda they sat on a bench not far from the church, looked down at
the sea, and were silent. Yalta was barely visible through the morning mist;
white clouds rested motionlessly on the mountaintops. The leaves did not stir
on the trees, cicadas twanged, and the monotonous muffled sound of the sea
that rose from below spoke of the peace, the eternal sleep awaiting us. So it
rumbled below when there was no Yalta, no Oreanda here; so it rumbles now,
and it will rumble as indifferently and as hollowly when we are no more. And
in this constancy, in this complete indifference to the life and death of each of
us, there lies, perhaps, a pledge of our eternal salvation, of the unceasing
advance of life upon earth, of unceasing movement towards perfection. Sitting beside a young woman who in the dawn seemed so lovely, Gurov, soothed
and spellbound by these magical surroundings—the sea, the mountains, the
clouds, the wide sky—thought how everything is really beautiful in this world
when one reflects: everything except what we think or do ourselves when we
forget the higher aims of life and our own human dignity.

A man strolled up to them—probably a guard—looked at them and
walked away. And this detail, too, seemed so mysterious and beautiful. They saw
a steamer arrive from Feodosia, its lights extinguished in the glow of dawn.

"There is dew on the grass," said Anna Sergeyevna, after a silence.

"Yes, it's time to go home." 50

They returned to the city.

Then they met every day at twelve o'clock on the esplanade, lunched and
dined together, took walks, admired the sea. She complained that she slept
badly, that she had palpitations, asked the same questions, troubled now by
jealousy and now by the fear that he did not respect her sufficiently. And often
in the square or the public garden, when there was no one near them, he suddenly drew her to him and kissed her passionately. Complete idleness, these
kisses in broad daylight exchanged furtively in dread of someone's seeing
them, the heat, the smell of the sea, and the continual flitting before his eyes of
idle, well-dressed, well-fed people, worked a complete change in him; he kept
telling Anna Sergeyevna how beautiful she was, how seductive, was urgently
passionate; he would not move a step away from her, while she was often pensive and continually pressed him to confess that he did not respect her, did not
love her in the least, and saw in her nothing but a common woman. Almost
every evening rather late they drove somewhere out of town, to Oreanda or to
the waterfall; and the excursion was always a success, the scenery invariably
impressed them as beautiful and magnificent.

They were expecting her husband, but a letter came from him saying that
he had eye-trouble, and begging his wife to return home as soon as possible.
Anna Sergeyevna made haste to go.

"It's a good thing I am leaving," she said to Gurov. "It's the hand of Fate!"

She took a carriage to the railway station, and he went with her. They were 55
driving the whole day. When she had taken her place in the express, and when
the second bell had rung, she said, "Let me look at you once more—let me look
at you again. Like this."

She was not crying but was so sad that she seemed ill, and her face was quivering.

"I shall be thinking of you—remembering you," she said. "God bless you; be happy. Don't remember evil against me. We are parting forever—it has to be, for we ought never to have met. Well, God bless you."

The train moved off rapidly, its lights soon vanished, and a minute later there was no sound of it, as though everything had conspired to end as quickly as possible that sweet trance, that madness. Left alone on the platform, and gazing into the dark distance, Gurov listened to the twang of the grasshoppers and the hum of the telegraph wires, feeling as though he had just waked up. And he reflected, musing, that there had now been another episode or adventure in his life, and it, too, was at an end, and nothing was left of it but a memory. He was moved, sad, and slightly remorseful: this young woman whom he would never meet again had not been happy with him; he had been warm and affectionate with her, but yet in his manner, his tone, and his caresses there had been a shade of light irony, the slightly coarse arrogance of a happy male who was, besides, almost twice her age. She had constantly called him kind, exceptional, high-minded; obviously he had seemed to her different from what he really was, so he had involuntarily deceived her.

Here at the station there was already a scent of autumn in the air; it was a chilly evening.

"It is time for me to go north, too," thought Gurov as he left the platform. 60
"High time!"

III

At home in Moscow the winter routine was already established: the stoves were heated, and in the morning it was still dark when the children were having breakfast and getting ready for school, and the nurse would light the lamp for a short time. There were frosts already. When the first snow falls, on the first day the sleighs are out, it is pleasant to see the white earth, the white roofs; one draws easy, delicious breaths, and the season brings back the days of one's youth. The old limes and birches, white with hoar-frost, have a good-natured look; they are closer to one's heart than cypresses and palms, and near them one no longer wants to think of mountains and the sea.

Gurov, a native of Moscow, arrived there on a fine frosty day, and when he put on his fur coat and warm gloves and took a walk along Petrovka, and when on Saturday night he heard the bells ringing, his recent trip and the places he had visited lost all charm for him. Little by little he became immersed in Moscow life, greedily read three newspapers a day, and declared that he did not read the Moscow papers on principle. He already felt a longing for restaurants, clubs, formal dinners, anniversary celebrations, and it flattered him to entertain distinguished lawyers and actors, and to play cards with a professor at the physicians' club. He could eat a whole portion of meat stewed with pickled cabbage and served in a pan, Moscow style.

A month or so would pass and the image of Anna Sergeyevna, it seemed to him, would become misty in his memory, and only from time to time he would dream of her with her touching smile as he dreamed of others. But more than a month went by, winter came into its own, and everything was still clear in his memory as though he had parted from Anna Sergeyevna only yesterday. And his memories glowed more and more vividly. When in the evening stillness the voices of his children preparing their lessons reached his study, or when he listened to a song or to an organ playing in a restaurant, or when the storm howled in the chimney, suddenly everything would rise up in his memory: what had happened on the pier and the early morning with the mist on the mountains, and the steamer coming from Feodosia, and the kisses. He would pace about his room a long time, remembering and smiling; then his memories passed into reveries, and in his imagination the past would mingle with what was to come. He did not dream of Anna Sergeyevna, but she followed him about everywhere and watched him. When he shut his eyes he saw her before him as though she were there in the flesh; and she seemed to him lovelier, younger, tenderer than she had been, and he imagined himself a finer man than he had been in Yalta. Of evenings she peered out at him from the bookcase, from the fireplace, from the corner — he heard her breathing, the caressing rustle of her clothes. In the street he followed the women with his eyes, looking for someone who resembled her.

Already he was tormented by a strong desire to share his memories with someone. But in his home it was impossible to talk of his love, and he had no one to talk to outside; certainly he could not confide in his tenants or in anyone at the bank. And what was there to talk about? He hadn't loved her then, had he? Had there been anything beautiful, poetical, edifying, or simply interesting in his relations with Anna Sergeyevna? And he was forced to talk vaguely of love, of women, and no one guessed what he meant; only his wife would twitch her black eyebrows and say, "The part of a philanderer does not suit you at all, Dimitry."

One evening, coming out of the physicians' club with an official with 65 whom he had been playing cards, he could not resist saying:

"If you only knew what a fascinating woman I became acquainted with at Yalta!"

The official got into his sledge and was driving away, but turned suddenly and shouted: "Dmitry Dmitrich!"

"What is it?"

"You were right this evening: the sturgeon was a bit high."

These words, so commonplace, for some reason moved Gurov to indigna- 70 tion, and struck him as degrading and unclean. What savage manners, what mugs! What stupid nights, what dull, humdrum days! Frenzied gambling, gluttony, drunkenness, continual talk always about the same things! Futile pursuits and conversations always about the same topics take up the better part of one's time, the better part of one's strength, and in the end there is left a life clipped and wingless, an absurd mess, and there is no escaping or getting away from it — just as though one were in a madhouse or a prison.

Gurov, boiling with indignation, did not sleep all night. And he had a headache all the next day. And the following nights too he slept badly; he sat up in bed, thinking, or paced up and down his room. He was fed up with his children, fed up with the bank; he had no desire to go anywhere or to talk of anything.

In December during the holidays he prepared to take a trip and told his wife he was going to Petersburg to do what he could for a young friend — and he set off for S——. What for? He did not know, himself. He wanted to see Anna Sergeyevna and talk with her, to arrange a rendezvous if possible.

He arrived at S—— in the morning, and at the hotel took the best room, in which the floor was covered with gray army cloth, and on the table there was an inkstand, gray with dust and topped by a figure on horseback, its hat in its raised hand and its head broken off. The porter gave him the necessary information: von Dideritz lived in a house of his own on Staro-Goncharnaya Street, not far from the hotel: he was rich and lived well and kept his own horses; everyone in the town knew him. The porter pronounced the name: "Dridiritz."

Without haste Gurov made his way to Staro-Goncharnaya Street and found the house. Directly opposite the house stretched a long gray fence studded with nails.

"A fence like that would make one run away," thought Gurov, looking now 75 at the fence, now at the windows of the house.

He reflected: this was a holiday, and the husband was apt to be at home. And in any case, it would be tactless to go into the house and disturb her. If he were to send her a note, it might fall into her husband's hands, and that might spoil everything. The best thing was to rely on chance. And he kept walking up and down the street and along the fence, waiting for the chance. He saw a beggar go in at the gate and heard the dogs attack him; then an hour later he heard a piano, and the sound came to him faintly and indistinctly. Probably it was Anna Sergeyevna playing. The front door opened suddenly, and an old woman came out, followed by the familiar white Pomeranian. Gurov was on the point of calling to the dog, but his heart began beating violently, and in his excitement he could not remember the Pomeranian's name.

He kept walking up and down, and hated the gray fence more and more, and by now he thought irritably that Anna Sergeyevna had forgotten him, and was perhaps already diverting herself with another man, and that that was very natural in a young woman who from morning till night had to look at that damn fence. He went back to his hotel room and sat on the couch for a long while, not knowing what to do, then he had dinner and a long nap.

"How stupid and annoying all this is!" he thought when he woke and looked at the dark windows: it was already evening. "Here I've had a good sleep for some reason. What am I going to do at night?"

He sat on the bed, which was covered with a cheap gray blanket of the kind seen in hospitals, and he twitted himself in his vexation:

"So there's your lady with the pet dog. There's your adventure. A nice 80 place to cool your heels in."

That morning at the station a playbill in large letters had caught his eye. *The Geisha* was to be given for the first time. He thought of this and drove to the theater.

"It's quite possible that she goes to first nights," he thought.

The theater was full. As in all provincial theaters, there was a haze above the chandelier, the gallery was noisy and restless; in the front row, before the beginning of the performance the local dandies were standing with their hands clasped behind their backs; in the Governor's box the Governor's daughter, wearing a boa, occupied the front seat, while the Governor himself hid modestly behind the portiere and only his hands were visible; the curtain swayed; the orchestra was a long time tuning up. While the audience were coming in and taking their seats, Gurov scanned the faces eagerly.

Anna Sergeyevna, too, came in. She sat down in the third row, and when Gurov looked at her his heart contracted, and he understood clearly that in the whole world there was no human being so near, so precious, and so important to him; she, this little, undistinguished woman, lost in a provincial crowd, with a vulgar lorgnette in her hand, filled his whole life now, was his sorrow and his joy, the only happiness that he now desired for himself, and to the sounds of the bad orchestra, of the miserable local violins, he thought how lovely she was. He thought and dreamed.

A young man with small side-whiskers, very tall and stooped, came in with 85 Anna Sergeyevna and sat down beside her; he nodded his head at every step and seemed to be bowing continually. Probably this was the husband whom at Yalta, in an excess of bitter feeling, she had called a flunkey. And there really was in his lanky figure, his side-whiskers, his small bald patch, something of a flunkey's retiring manner; his smile was mawkish, and in his buttonhole there was an academic badge like a waiter's number.

During the first intermission the husband went out to have a smoke; she remained in her seat. Gurov, who was also sitting in the orchestra, went up to her and said in a shaky voice, with a forced smile:

"Good evening!"

She glanced at him and turned pale, then looked at him again in horror, unable to believe her eyes, and gripped the fan and the lorgnette tightly together in her hands, evidently trying to keep herself from fainting. Both were silent. She was sitting, he was standing, frightened by her distress and not daring to take a seat beside her. The violins and the flute that were being tuned up sang out. He suddenly felt frightened: it seemed as if all the people in the boxes were looking at them. She got up and went hurriedly to the exit; he followed her, and both of them walked blindly along the corridors and up and down stairs, and figures in the uniforms prescribed for magistrates, teachers, and officials of the Department of Crown Lands, all wearing badges, flitted before their eyes, as did also ladies, and fur coats on hangers; they were conscious of drafts and the smell of stale tobacco. And Gurov, whose heart was beating violently, thought:

"Oh, Lord! Why are these people here and this orchestra!"

And at that instant he suddenly recalled how when he had seen Anna 90 Sergeyevna off at the station he had said to himself that all was over between them and that they would never meet again. But how distant the end still was!

On the narrow, gloomy staircase over which it said "To the Amphitheatre," she stopped.

"How you frightened me!" she said, breathing hard, still pale and stunned. "Oh, how you frightened me! I am barely alive. Why did you come? Why?"

"But do understand, Anna, do understand —" he said hurriedly, under his breath. "I implore you, do understand —"

She looked at him with fear, with entreaty, with love; she looked at him intently, to keep his features more distinctly in her memory.

"I suffer so," she went on, not listening to him. "All this time I have been 95 thinking of nothing but you; I live only by the thought of you. And I wanted to forget, to forget; but why, oh, why have you come?"

On the landing above them two high school boys were looking down and smoking, but it was all the same to Gurov; he drew Anna Sergeyevna to him and began kissing her face and her hands.

"What are you doing, what are you doing!" she was saying in horror, pushing him away. "We have lost our senses. Go away today; go away at once — I conjure you by all that is sacred, I implore you — People are coming this way!"

Someone was walking up the stairs.

"You must leave," Anna Sergeyevna went on in a whisper. "Do you hear, Dmitry Dmitrich? I will come and see you in Moscow. I have never been happy; I am unhappy now, and I never, never shall be happy, never! So don't make me suffer still more! I swear I'll come to Moscow. But now let us part. My dear, good, precious one, let us part!"

She pressed his hand and walked rapidly downstairs, turning to look 100 round at him, and from her eyes he could see that she really was unhappy. Gurov stood for a while, listening, then when all grew quiet, he found his coat and left the theater.

IV

And Anna Sergeyevna began coming to see him in Moscow. Once every two or three months she left S——, telling her husband that she was going to consult a doctor about a woman's ailment from which she was suffering—and her husband did and did not believe her. When she arrived in Moscow she would stop at the Slavyansky Bazar Hotel, and at once send a man in a red cap to Gurov. Gurov came to see her, and no one in Moscow knew of it.

Once he was going to see her in this way on a winter morning (the messenger had come the evening before and not found him in). With him walked his daughter, whom he wanted to take to school: it was on the way. Snow was coming down in big wet flakes.

"It's three degrees above zero,° and yet it's snowing," Gurov was saying to his daughter. "But this temperature prevails only on the surface of the earth; in the upper layers of the atmosphere there is quite a different temperature."

"And why doesn't it thunder in winter, papa?"

He explained that, too. He talked, thinking all the while that he was on his 105 way to a rendezvous, and no living soul knew of it, and probably no one would ever know. He had two lives: an open one, seen and known by all who needed to know it, full of conventional truth and conventional falsehood, exactly like the lives of his friends and acquaintances; and another life that went on in secret. And through some strange, perhaps accidental, combination of circumstances, everything that was of interest and importance to him, everything that was essential to him, everything about which he felt sincerely and did not deceive himself, everything that constituted the core of his life, was going on concealed from others; while all that was false, the shell in which he hid to cover the truth—his work at the bank, for instance, his discussions at the club, his references to the "inferior race," his appearances at anniversary celebrations with his wife—all that went on in the open. Judging others by himself, he did not believe what he saw, and always fancied that every man led his real, most interesting life under cover of secrecy as under cover of night. The personal life of every individual is based on secrecy, and perhaps it is partly for that reason that civilized man is so nervously anxious that personal privacy should be respected.

Having taken his daughter to school, Gurov went on to the Slavyansky Bazar Hotel. He took off his fur coat in the lobby, went upstairs, and knocked gently at the door. Anna Sergeyevna, wearing his favorite gray dress, exhausted

___

three degrees above zero: On the Celsius scale; about thirty-eight degrees Fahrenheit.

by the journey and by waiting, had been expecting him since the previous evening. She was pale, and looked at him without a smile, and he had hardly entered when she flung herself on his breast. Their kiss was a long, lingering one, as though they had not seen one another for two years.

"Well, darling, how are you getting on there?" he asked. "What news?"

"Wait; I'll tell you in a moment — I can't speak."

She could not speak; she was crying. She turned away from him, and pressed her handkerchief to her eyes.

"Let her have her cry; meanwhile I'll sit down," he thought, and he seated himself in an armchair.

Then he rang and ordered tea, and while he was having his tea she remained standing at the window with her back to him. She was crying out of sheer agitation, in the sorrowful consciousness that their life was so sad; that they could only see each other in secret and had to hide from people like thieves! Was it not a broken life?

"Come, stop now, dear!" he said.

It was plain to him that this love of theirs would not be over soon, that the end of it was not in sight. Anna Sergeyevna was growing more and more attached to him. She adored him, and it was unthinkable to tell her that their love was bound to come to an end some day; besides, she would not have believed it!

He went up to her and took her by the shoulders, to fondle her and say something diverting, and at that moment he caught sight of himself in the mirror.

His hair was already beginning to turn gray. And it seemed odd to him that he had grown so much older in the last few years, and lost his looks. The shoulders on which his hands rested were warm and heaving. He felt compassion for this life, still so warm and lovely, but probably already about to begin to fade and wither like his own. Why did she love him so much? He always seemed to women different from what he was, and they loved in him not himself, but the man whom their imagination created and whom they had been eagerly seeking all their lives; and afterwards, when they saw their mistake, they loved him nevertheless. And not one of them had been happy with him. In the past he had met women, come together with them, parted from them, but he had never once loved; it was anything you please, but not love. And only now when his head was gray he had fallen in love, really, truly — for the first time in his life.

Anna Sergeyevna and he loved each other as people do who are very close and intimate, like man and wife, like tender friends; it seemed to them that Fate itself had meant them for one another, and they could not understand why he had a wife and she a husband; and it was as though they were a pair of migratory birds, male and female, caught and forced to live in different cages. They forgave each other what they were ashamed of in their past, they forgave everything in the present, and felt that this love of theirs had altered them both.

Formerly in moments of sadness he had soothed himself with whatever logical arguments came into his head, but now he no longer cared for logic; he felt profound compassion, he wanted to be sincere and tender.

"Give it up now, my darling," he said. "You've had your cry; that's enough. Let us have a talk now, we'll think up something."

Then they spent a long time taking counsel together, they talked of how to avoid the necessity for secrecy, for deception, for living in different cities, and not seeing one another for long stretches of time. How could they free themselves from these intolerable fetters?

"How? How?" he asked, clutching his head. "How?"   120

And it seemed as though in a little while the solution would be found, and then a new and glorious life would begin; and it was clear to both of them that the end was still far off, and that what was to be most complicated and difficult for them was only just beginning.

CONSIDERATIONS FOR CRITICAL THINKING AND WRITING

1. FIRST RESPONSE. Consider the following assessment of the story: "No excuses can be made for the lovers' adulterous affair. They behave selfishly and irresponsibly. They are immoral — and so is the story." Explain what you think Chekhov's response to this view would be, given his treatment of the lovers. How does this compare with your own views?

2. Why is it significant that the setting of this story is a resort town? How does the vacation atmosphere affect the action?

3. What does Gurov's view of women reveal about him? Why does he regard them as an "inferior race"?

4. What do we learn about Gurov's wife and Anna's husband? Why do you think Chekhov includes this exposition? How does it affect our view of the lovers?

5. When and why do Gurov's feelings about Anna begin to change? Is he really in love with her?

6. Who or what is the antagonist in this story? What is the nature of the conflict?

7. What is the effect of having Gurov as the central consciousness? How would the story be different if it were told from Anna's perspective?

8. Why do you think Chekhov does not report what ultimately becomes of the lovers? Is there a resolution to the conflict? Is the ending of the story effective?

9. Discuss the validity of Gurov's belief that people lead their real lives in private rather than in public: "The personal life of every individual is based on secrecy, and perhaps it is partly for that reason that civilized man is so nervously anxious that personal privacy should be respected."

10. Describe your response to Gurov in Parts I and II, and discuss how your judgment of him changes in the last two parts of the story.

11. Based on your understanding of the characterizations of Gurov and Anna, consider the final paragraph of the story and summarize what you think will happen to them.

LOUISE ERDRICH (B. 1954)

Louise Erdrich is of Chippewa Indian and German heritage. Born in 1954 in Little Falls, Minnesota, she grew up as part of the Turtle Mountain Band of Chippewa in Wahpeton, North Dakota. After graduating from

Dartmouth College (where her poetry and fiction won several awards, including the American Academy of Poets Prize), she moved back to North Dakota to teach in the Poetry in the Schools Program. Her first novel, *Love Medicine,* winner of the 1984 National Book Critics' Circle Award, is part of an interlocking series of novels concerning Native American life in North Dakota. She has also published *The Beet Queen* (1986), *Tracks* (1988), and *Antelope Wife* (1998). She had a very close professional relationship with her husband, Michael Dorris, now deceased. The two worked together on Dorris's *The Broken Cord: A Family's Ongoing Struggle with Fetal Alcohol Syndrome* (1989) and on a novel called *The Crown of Columbus* (1991), which concerns a Native American woman who discovers Christopher Columbus. In the following story a girlfriend's Christmas present leads to the narrator's desperate tumbling life.

I'm a Mad Dog Biting Myself for Sympathy   *1990*

Who I am is just the habit of what I always was, and who I'll be is the result. This comes clear to me at the wrong time. I am standing in a line, almost rehabilitated. Walgreens is the store in downtown Fargo. I have my purchase in my arms, and I am listening to canned carols on the loudspeaker. I plan to buy this huge stuffed parrot with purple wings and a yellow beak. Really, it is a toucan, I get told this later in the tank.

You think you know everything about yourself—how much money it would take, for instance, to make you take it. How you would react when caught. But then you find yourself walking out the door with a stuffed toucan, just to see if shit happens, if do-do occurs. And it does, though no one stops me right at first.

My motive is my girlfriend's Christmas present. And it is strange because I do have the money to pay for a present, though nothing very big or elaborate. I think of Dawn the minute I see the bird, and wish I'd won it for her at a county fair, though we never went to a fair. I see myself throwing a half-dozen softballs and hitting every wooden milk jug, or maybe tossing rings. But those things are weighted or loaded wrong and that's another reason. I never could have won this toucan for Dawn, because the whole thing's a cheat in general. So what the hell, I think, and lift the bird.

Outside in the street it is one of my favorite kind of days, right there in the drag middle of winter when the snow is a few hard gray clumps and a dusty grass shows on the boulevards. I like the smell in the air, the dry dirt, the patches of water shrinking and the threat of snow, too, in the gloom of the sky.

The usual rubber-neck turns to look at me. This bird is really huge and   5 furry, with green underneath its floppy wings and fat stuffed orange feet. I don't know why they'd have a strange thing like this in Walgreens. Maybe a big promotion, maybe some kind of come-on for the holiday season. And then the manager yells at me from the door. I am half-way down the street when I hear him. "Come back here!" Probably pointing at me, too, though there is no reason, as I stick out plenty and still more when I run.

First I put the bird underneath my arm. But it throws off my balance. So I clutch it to my chest; that is no better. Thinking back now I should have ditched it, and slipped off through the alleys and disappeared. Of course, I didn't—otherwise none of all that happened would have happened. I sit the bird on my shoulders and hold the lumpy feet under my chin and then I bear down, like going for the distance or the gold, let my legs churn beneath me. I leap curbs, dodge among old men in long gray coats and babies in strollers, shoot up and over car hoods until I come to the railroad depot and, like it is some sort of destination, though it isn't, I slip in the door and look out the window.

A gathering crowd follows with the manager. There is a policewoman, a few local mall-sitters, passers-by. They are stumbling and talking together and making big circles of their arms, to illustrate the toucan, and closing in.

That's when my stroke of luck, good or bad is no telling, occurs. The car drives into the parking lot, a solid plastic luggage rack strapped on its roof. A man and a woman jump out, late for a connection, and they leave the car running in neutral. I walk out of the depot and stand before the car. At that moment, it seems as though events are taking me somewhere. I open up the hinges on the plastic rack, stuff in the bird. No one seems to notice me. Encouraged, I get in. I put my hands on the wheel. I take the car out of neutral and we start to roll, back out of the lot. I change gears, then turn at the crossroads, and look both ways.

I don't know what you'd do in this situation. I'll ask you. There you are in a car. It isn't yours but for the time being that doesn't matter. You look up the street one way. It's clear. You look down the other, and a clump of people still are arguing and trying to describe you with their hands, Either way, the road will take you straight out of town. The clear way is north, where you don't know anyone. South, what's there?

I let the car idle. 10

My parents. It's not like I hate them or anything. I just can't see them. I can close my eyes and form my sister's face behind my eyelids, but not my parents' faces. Where their eyes should meet mine, nothing. That's all. I shouldn't show up at the farm, not with the toucan. Much less the car. I think a few seconds longer. The bird on the roof. It is for Dawn. You could say she got me into this, so Dawn should get me out. But she doesn't live in Fargo anymore, she lives south. She lives in Colorado, which complicates everything later for it means crossing state lines and all just to bring her that bird, and then another complexity, although at the time I don't realize, occurs when the woman at the depot, the one who has left the car, appears very suddenly in the rearview mirror.

I have just started moving south when I hear a thump from behind. It is so surprising. Just imagine. She is there on the trunk, hanging on as though by magnetics. She reaches up and grabs the hitches on the roof-top luggage rack, gets a better grip, and sprawls across the back window. She is a little woman. Through the side-view, I see her blue heels in the air, the edge of a black coat. I hear her shrieking in an inhuman desperate way that horrifies me so much I floor the gas.

We must go by everyone fast, but the effect is dreamlike, so slow. I see the faces of the clump of people, their mouths failing open, arms stretching and grasping as I turn the corner and the woman rolls over and over like a seal in water. Then she flies off the trunk and bowls them before in her rush so they heap on the ground. She is in their arms. They put her down as though she is a live torpedo and keep running after me.

"Scandinavians," I think, because my grandmother's one, "they don't give up the ghost." I just want to yell out, tell them. "OK, so it's stolen. It's gone! It's a cheap stuffed bird anyhow and I will *park* the car. I promise."

I start talking to myself "I'll check the oil in Sioux Falls. No sweat." Then the worst thing comes about, and all of a sudden I understand the woman with her eyes rearing back in her skull, her little heels pointed in the air. I understand the faces of the people in the group, their blurting voices, "b . . . b . . . baby." 15

As from the back seat, it wails.

I have my first reaction, disbelief. I have taken the scenic route at a fast clip, but I know the view anyway. I am down near the river and have decided from there I will take 30 and avoid the interstate, always so well patrolled. I park and turn around in a frantic whirl. I revolve twice in my seat. And I still can't see the baby. I am behind on the new equipment. He sits in something round and firm, shaped like a big football, strapped down the chest and over the waist, held tight by a padded cushion. Above his face there is a little diamond attachment made of plastic, a bunch of keys and plastic balls that dangle out of reach.

I have never seen a child this little before, so small that it is not a child yet. Its face is tiny and dark, almost reddish, or copper, and its fingers, splayed out against its cheeks, are the feet of a sparrow. There is a bottle of milk in a bag beside it. I put the end in its mouth and it sucks. But it will not hold the bottle. I keep putting the end in its hand, and it won't grasp.

"Oh screw it," I finally say, and gun right out of there. Its cry begins again and I wish I knew how to stop it. I have to slow down to get through some traffic. Sirens rush ahead on their way to the Interstate, passing in a squeal which surprises me. This car, this pack on top, I am so obvious. I think I'll maybe park at the old King Leo's, get out, and run. But then I pass it. I think it will be better if I get down south around the South Dakota border, or in the sandhills, where I can hide out in cow shelters. So I do go south. Over me the sky is bearing down and bearing down, so I think now maybe snow will fall. A White Christmas like the music in the drugstore. I know how to drive in snow and this car has decent tires, I can feel them. They never lose grip or plane above the road. They just keep rolling, humming, below me, all four in this unified direction, so dull that after some time it all seems right again.

The baby drops off, stops crying. It shouldn't have been there, should it. I have to realize the situation. There is no use in thinking back, in saying to myself, well you shouldn't have stole the damn bird in the first place, because I did do that and then, well as you see, it is like I went along with the arrangement of things as they happened. 20

Of course, around halfway down there is a smokey waiting, which I knew would happen, but not whether it would be before or behind me. So now my answer comes. The officer's car turns off a dirt road and starts flashing, starts coming at me from the rear. I take it up to eighty and we move, *move*, so the frozen water standing in the fields flashes by like scarves and the silver snow whirls out of nowhere, to either side of us, and what rushes up before us is a heat of road and earth.

I am not all that afraid. I never am and that's my problem. I feel sure they will not use their weapons. I keep driving and then, as we take a turn, as we come to a railroad crossing, I hear the plastic roof rack snap open. I look through the rearview by reflex, and see the bird as it dives out of the sky, big and plush, a purple blur that plunges its yellow beak through the windshield and throws the state police off course so that they skid, roll over once, come back with such force the car rights itself. They sit there in shock.

I keep on going. The pack blows off and I reason that now the car is less obvious. I should have thought about that in the first place, but then the bird would not have hatched out and demolished the police car. Just about this time, however, being as the toucan is gone, I begin to feel perhaps there is no reason to go on traveling this way. I begin to think I will just stop at the nearest farm, leave the car and the baby, and keep hitching south. I begin to think if I show up at Dawn's, even with nothing, on a Christmas Eve, she will not throw me out. She will have to take me, let me stay there, on the couch. She lives with someone now, a guy ten years older than me, five years older than her. By now he has probably taken her places, shown her restaurants and zoos, gone camping in the wilderness, skied. She will know things and I will still be the same person that I was the year before. And I am glad about the toucan, then, which would have made me look ridiculous. Showing up there like a kid in junior high school with a stuffed animal, when her tastes have broadened. I should have sent her chocolates, a little red and green box. I was wishing I had. And then I look past the road in front of me and realize it is snowing.

It isn't just like ordinary snow even from the first. It is like that rhyme or story in the second grade, the sky falling and let's go and tell the king. It comes down. I think to myself, *well, let it come down.* And I keep driving. I know you'll say it, you'll wonder, you'll think what about the child in back of him, that baby, only three weeks old, little Mason Joseph Andrews? Because he does have a name and all, but what could I know of that?

I talk to it. I am good at driving in the snow but I need to talk while I'm   25 driving. I'll tell this now, it doesn't matter. I say, "You little bastard you, what are you doing here!" It is my state of mind. I put the window open. Snow whites out the windshield and I can't see the road in front of us. I watch the margin, try to follow the yellow line which is obscured by a twisting blanket. I am good at this though I need my concentration, which vanishes when he bawls. My ears are full. He roars and I hear the sound as wind, as sounds that came out of its mother. I hit the plastic egg and feel the straps give, feel the car give on the road. I swerve into another car's ruts, weave along the dotted yellow, and then under me is snow and still I keep going at a steady pace although the ground feels all hollow and uncertain. The tracks narrow into one, and then widen, so I suddenly realize this: I have followed a snowmobile trail and now I am somewhere off the road. Immediately, just like in a cartoon, like Dumbo flying and he realizes that he isn't supposed to be up in the air, I panic and get stuck.

So now I am in awful shape, out there in a field, in a storm that could go on for three more minutes or three more days. I sit there thinking until the baby gets discouraged and falls asleep. And get this. It is a white car. Harder to see than ever. And not a bit of this did I ever think or plan for. I can't remember what they say in the papers every fall, the advice about what to do when a blizzard hits. Whether to stay on the road, with the car, or set out walking for help. There is the baby. It is helpless, but does not seem so helpless. I know now that I should have left the car run, the heater, but at the time I don't think. Except I do rip that dangle of toys off its seat and tie it on the aerial when I go out, and I do leave its blankets in there, never take any. I just wrap my arms around my chest and start walking south.

By not stopping for a minute I live through the storm, though I am easy to catch after it lets up, and I freeze an ear. All right, you know that baby wasn't hurt anyway. You heard. Cold, yes, but it lived. They ask me in court why I didn't take it along with me, bundled in my jacket, and I say, well it lived, didn't it? Proving I did right. But I know better sometimes, now that I've spent time alone here in Mandan, more time running than I knew I had available.

I think about that boy. He'll grow up, but already I am more to him than his own father because I taught him what I know about the cold. It sinks in, there to stay, doesn't it? And people. They will leave you, no matter what you say there's no return. There's just the emptiness all around, and you in it, like singing up from the bottom of a well, like nothing else, until you harm yourself, until you are a mad dog just biting yourself for sympathy, because there is no relenting, and there is no hand that falls, and there is no woman come home to take you in her arms.

I know I taught that boy something in those hours I was walking south. I know I'll always be inside him, cold and black, about the size of a coin, maybe, something he touches against and skids. And he'll say, *what is this,* and the thing is he won't know it is a piece of thin ice I have put there, the same as I have in me.

CONSIDERATIONS FOR CRITICAL THINKING AND WRITING

1. FIRST RESPONSE. Consider the first sentence of the story as a statement that summarizes the narrator's life. How accurate is this self-assessment of his character?

2. What do you learn about his past? How much control does he have over his life?

3. Why is it significant that the narrator's name is never mentioned?

4. Why does the narrator steal the toucan instead of paying for it? How does this reveal his attitude toward life?

5. Describe the various settings that the narrator moves through. Do they have any qualities in common?

6. Consider the significance of some of the story's details. Why, for example, do you think the story begins in Fargo at a Walgreens? What is the significance of the present for Dawn being a toucan rather than just a stuffed parrot? Why do you think Erdrich named the girlfriend "Dawn"?

7. When the narrator finds the car idling at the railroad depot, he calls it a "stroke of luck." What role does "luck" play in the plot? Would "luck" or "fate" be a more accurate term to describe how and why events occur?

8. Explain why you do or don't sympathize with the narrator.

9. Try to recall your first reading of the story. Before reading the final three paragraphs, how did you think the story would end when you reached the end of paragraph 26?

10. Discuss the significance of the title.

11. What has the narrator taught the baby boy he inadvertently kidnapped and abandoned in the car? Why do you think the story ends with this information?

DAGOBERTO GILB (B. 1950)

Born in Los Angeles, Dagoberto Gilb is a journeyman carpenter who considers both Los Angeles and El Paso to be home. He has been a visiting writer at the University of Texas and the University of Arizona. Among his literary prizes are the James D. Phelan Award in literature and the Whiting Award; he has also won a National Endowment for the Arts Creative Writing Fellowship. Gilb's fiction has been published in a variety of journals including the *Threepenny Review, ZYZZYVA,* and *American Short Fiction.* His stories, collected in *The Magic of Blood* (1993), from which "Love in L.A." is taken, often reflect his experiences as a worker moving between Los Angeles and El Paso. In 1994 he published his first novel, *The Last Known Residence of Mickey Acuna.*

Love in L.A.   *1993*

Jake slouched in a clot of near motionless traffic, in the peculiar gray of concrete, smog, and early morning beneath the overpass of the Hollywood Freeway on Alvarado Street. He didn't really mind because he knew how much worse it could be trying to make a left onto the onramp. He certainly didn't do that every day of his life, and he'd assure anyone who'd ask that he never would either. A steady occupation had its advantages and he couldn't deny thinking about that too. He needed an FM radio in something better than this '58 Buick he drove. It would have crushed velvet interior with electric controls for the L.A. summer, a nice warm heater and defroster for the winter drives at the beach, a cruise control for those longer trips, mellow speakers front and rear of course, windows that hum closed, snuffing out that nasty exterior noise of freeways. The fact was that he'd probably have to change his whole style. Exotic colognes, plush, dark nightclubs, maitais and daiquiris, necklaced ladies in satin gowns, misty and sexy like in a tequila ad. Jake could imagine lots of possibilities when he let himself, but none that ended up with him pressed onto a stalled freeway.

Jake was thinking about this freedom of his so much that when he glimpsed its green light he just went ahead and stared bye bye to the steadily employed. When he turned his head the same direction his windshield faced, it was maybe one second too late. He pounced the brake pedal and steered the front wheels away from the tiny brakelights but the smack was unavoidable. Just one second sooner and it would only have been close. One second more and he'd be crawling up the Toyota's trunk. As it was, it seemed like only a harmless smack, much less solid than the one against his back bumper.

Jake considered driving past the Toyota but was afraid the traffic ahead would make it too difficult. As he pulled up against the curb a few carlengths ahead, it occurred to him that the traffic might have helped him get away too. He slammed the car door twice to make sure it was closed fully and to give himself another second more, then toured front and rear of his Buick for damage on or near the bumpers. Not an impressionable scratch even in the chrome. He perked up. Though the car's beauty was secondary to its ability to start and move, the body and paint were clean except for a few minor dings. This stood out as one of his few clearcut accomplishments over the years.

Before he spoke to the driver of the Toyota, whose looks he could see might present him with an added complication, he signaled to the driver of the car that hit him, still in his car and stopped behind the Toyota, and waved his hands and shook his head to let the man know there was no problem as far as he was concerned. The driver waved back and started his engine.

"It didn't even scratch my paint," Jake told her in that way of his. "So how 5 you doin? Any damage to the car? I'm kinda hoping so, just so it takes a little more time and we can talk some. Or else you can give me your phone number now and I won't have to lay my regular b.s. on you to get it later."

He took her smile as a good sign and relaxed. He inhaled her scent like it was clean air and straightened out his less than new but not unhip clothes.

"You've got Florida plates. You look like you must be Cuban."

"My parents are from Venezuela."

"My name's Jake." He held out his hand.

"Mariana."   10

They shook hands like she'd never done it before in her life.

"I really am sorry about hitting you like that." He sounded genuine. He fondled the wide dimple near the cracked taillight. "It's amazing how easy it is to put a dent in these new cars. They're so soft they might replace waterbeds soon." Jake was confused about how to proceed with this. So much seemed so unlikely, but there was always possibility. "So maybe we should go out to breakfast somewhere and talk it over."

"I don't eat breakfast."

"Some coffee then."

"Thanks, but I really can't."   15

"You're not married, are you? Not that that would matter that much to me. I'm an openminded kinda guy."

She was smiling. "I have to get to work."

"That sounds boring."

"I better get your driver's license," she said.

Jake nodded, disappointed. "One little problem," he said. "I didn't bring 20 it. I just forgot it this morning. I'm a musician," he exaggerated greatly, "and, well, I dunno, I left my wallet in the pants I was wearing last night. If you have some paper and a pen I'll give you my address and all that."

He followed her to the glove compartment side of her car.

"What if we don't report it to the insurance companies? I'll just get it fixed for you."

"I don't think my dad would let me do that."

"Your dad? It's not your car?"

"He bought it for me. And I live at home."   25

"Right." She was slipping away from him. He went back around to the back of her new Toyota and looked over the damage again. There was the trunk lid, the bumper, a rear panel, a taillight.

"You do have insurance?" she asked, suspicious, as she came around the back of the car.

"Oh yeah," he lied.

"I guess you better write the name of that down too."

He made up a last name and address and wrote down the name of an 30 insurance company an old girlfriend once belonged to. He considered giving a real phone number but went against that idea and made one up.

"I act too," he lied to enhance the effect more. "Been in a couple of movies."

She smiled like a fan.

"So how about your phone number?" He was rebounding maturely.

She gave it to him.

"Mariana, you are beautiful," he said in his most sincere voice. 35

"Call me," she said timidly.

Jake beamed. "We'll see you, Mariana," he said holding out his hand. Her hand felt so warm and soft he felt like he'd been kissed.

Back in his car he took a moment or two to feel both proud and sad about his performance. Then he watched the rear view mirror as Mariana pulled up behind him. She was writing down the license plate numbers on his Buick, ones that he'd taken off a junk because the ones that belonged to his had expired so long ago. He turned the ignition key and revved the big engine and clicked into drive. His sense of freedom swelled as he drove into the now moving street traffic, though he couldn't stop the thought about that FM stereo radio and crushed velvet interior and the new car smell that would even make it better.

CONSIDERATIONS FOR CRITICAL THINKING AND WRITING

1. FIRST RESPONSE. Is "Love in L.A." a love story? Try to argue that it is. (If the story ended with paragraph 37, how would your interpretation of the story be affected?)

2. What is the effect of setting the story's action in a Los Angeles traffic jam on the Hollywood Freeway?

3. Characterize Jake. What do his thoughts in the first two paragraphs reveal about him? About how old do you think he is?

4. There is little physical description of Jake in the story, but given what you learn about him, how would you describe his physical features and the way he dresses?

5. What causes Jake to smack into the back of Mariana's car? What is revealed about his character by the manner in which he has the accident?

6. Describe how Jake responds to Mariana when he introduces himself to her, especially in paragraph 12. What does his behavior reveal about his character?

7. How does Mariana respond to Jake? Explain whether you think she is a round or flat character.

8. Explain how their respective cars serve to characterize Jake and Mariana.

9. What does the final paragraph reveal about each character?

10. In a sentence or two write down what you think the story's theme is. How does the title contribute to that theme?

SUSAN MINOT (B. 1956)

Born and raised in Massachusetts, Susan Minot earned a B.A. at Brown University and an M.F.A. at Columbia University. Before devoting herself full-time to writing, Minot worked as an assistant editor at *Grand Street* magazine. Her stories have appeared in the *Atlantic Monthly, Harper's, The New Yorker, Mademoiselle,* and *Paris Review.* Her short stories have been collected in *Lust and Other Stories* (1989), and she has published three novels — *Monkeys* (1986), *Folly* (1992), and *Evening* (1998).

Lust   *1984*

Leo was from a long time ago, the first one I ever saw nude. In the spring before the Hellmans filled their pool, we'd go down there in the deep end, with baby oil, and like that. I met him the first month away at boarding school. He had a halo from the campus light behind him. I flipped.

Roger was fast. In his illegal car, we drove to the reservoir, the radio blaring, talking fast, fast, fast. He was always going for my zipper. He got kicked out sophomore year.

By the time the band got around to playing "Wild Horses," I had tasted Bruce's tongue. We were clicking in the shadows on the other side of the amplifier, out of Mrs. Donovan's line of vision. It tasted like salt, with my neck bent back, because we had been dancing so hard before.

Tim's line: "I'd like to see you in a bathing suit." I knew it was his line when he said the exact same thing to Annie Hines.

You'd go on walks to get off campus. It was raining like hell, my sweater as sopped as a wet sheep. Tim pinned me to a tree, the woods light brown and dark brown, a white house half hidden with the lights already on. The water was as loud as a crowd hissing. He made certain comments about my forehead, about my cheeks.

We started off sitting at one end of the couch and then our feet were squished against the armrest and then he went over to turn off the TV and came back after he had taken off his shirt and then we slid onto the floor and he got up again to close the door, then came back to me, a body waiting on the rug.

You'd try to wipe off the table or to do the dishes and Willie would untuck your shirt and get his hands up under in front, standing behind you, making puffy noises in your ear.

He likes it when I wash my hair. He covers his face with it and if I start to say something, he goes, "Shush."

For a long time, I had Philip on the brain. The less they noticed you, the more you got them on the brain.

My parents had no idea. Parents never really know what's going on, espe- 10 cially when you're away at school most of the time. If she met them, my mother might say, "Oliver seems nice" or "I like that one" without much of an opinion. If she didn't like them, "He's a funny fellow, isn't he?" or "Johnny's perfectly nice but a drink of water." My father was too shy to talk to them at all unless they played sports and he'd ask them about that.

The sand was almost cold underneath because the sun was long gone. Eben piled a mound over my feet, patting around my ankles, the ghostly surf rumbling behind him in the dark. He was the first person I ever knew who died, later that summer, in a car crash. I thought about it for a long time.

"Come here," he says on the porch.
I go over to the hammock and he takes my wrist with two fingers.
"What?"
He kisses my palm then directs my hand to his fly. 15

Songs went with whichever boy it was. "Sugar Magnolia" was Tim, with the line "Rolling in the rushes/down by the riverside." With "Darkness Darkness," I'd picture Philip with his long hair. Hearing "Under My Thumb" there'd be the smell of Jamie's suede jacket.

We hid in the listening rooms during study hall. With a record cover over the door's window, the teacher on duty couldn't look in. I came out flushed and heady and back at the dorm was surprised how red my lips were in the mirror.

One weekend at Simon's brother's, we stayed inside all day with the shades down, in bed, then went out to Store 24 to get some ice cream. He stood at the magazine rack and read through *MAD* while I got butterscotch sauce, craving something sweet.

I could do some things well. Some things I was good at, like math or painting or even sports, but the second a boy put his arm around me, I forgot about wanting to do anything else, which felt like a relief at first until it became like sinking into a muck.

It was different for a girl. 20

When we were little, the brothers next door tied up our ankles. They held the door of the goat house and wouldn't let us out till we showed them our underpants. Then they'd forget about being after us and when we played whiffle ball, I'd be just as good as they were.

Then it got to be different. Just because you have on a short skirt, they yell from the cars, slowing down for a while, and if you don't look, they screech off and call you a bitch.

"What's the matter with me?" they say, point-blank.

Or else, "Why won't you go out with me? I'm not asking you to get married," about to get mad.

Or it'd be, trying to be reasonable, in a regular voice, "Listen, I just want to have a good time."

So I'd go because I couldn't think of something to say back that wouldn't be obvious, and if you go out with them, you sort of have to do something.

I sat between Mack and Eddie in the front seat of the pickup. They were having a fight about something. I've a feeling about me.

Certain nights you'd feel a certain surrender, maybe if you'd had wine. The surrender would be forgetting yourself and you'd put your nose to his neck and feel like a squirrel, safe, at rest, in a restful dream. But then you'd start to slip from that and the dark would come in and there'd be a cave. You make out the dim shape of the windows and feel yourself become a cave, filled absolutely with air, or with a sadness that wouldn't stop.

Teenage years. You know just what you're doing and don't see the things that start to get in the way.

Lots of boys, but never two at the same time. One was plenty to keep you in a state. You'd start to see a boy and something would rush over you like a fast storm cloud and you couldn't possibly think of anyone else. Boys took it differently. Their eyes perked up at any little number that walked by. You'd act like you weren't noticing.

The joke was that the school doctor gave out the pill like aspirin. He didn't ask you anything. I was fifteen. We had a picture of him in assembly, holding up an IUD shaped like a T. Most girls were on the pill, if anything, because they couldn't handle a diaphragm. I kept the dial in my top drawer like my mother and thought of her each time I tipped out the yellow tablets in the morning before chapel.

If they were too shy, I'd be more so. Andrew was nervous. We stayed up with his family album, sharing a pack of Old Golds. Before it got light, we turned on the TV. A man was explaining how to plant seedlings. His mouth jerked to the side in a tic. Andrew thought it was a riot and kept imitating him. I laughed to be polite. When we finally dozed off, he dared to put his arm around me, but that was it.

You wait till they come to you. With half fright, half swagger, they stand one step down. They dare to touch the button on your coat then lose their nerve and quickly drop their hand so you—you'd do anything for them. You touch their cheek.

The girls sit around in the common room and talk about boys, smoking their heads off.

"What are you complaining about?" says Jill to me when we talk about 35 problems.

"Yeah," says Giddy. "You always have a boyfriend."

I look at them and think, As if.

I thought the worst thing anyone could call you was a cock-teaser. So, if you flirted, you had to be prepared to go through with it. Sleeping with someone was perfectly normal once you had done it. You didn't really worry about it. But there were other problems. The problems had to do with something else entirely.

Mack was during the hottest summer ever recorded. We were renting a house on an island with all sorts of other people. No one slept during the heat wave, walking around the house with nothing on which we were used to because of the nude beach. In the living room, Eddie lay on top of a coffee table to cool off. Mack and I, with the bedroom door open for air, sweated and sweated all night.

"I can't take this," he said at three A.M. "I'm going for a swim." He and 40 some guys down the hall went to the beach. The heat put me on edge. I sat on a cracked chest by the open window and smoked and smoked till I felt even worse, waiting for something — I guess for him to get back.

One was on a camping trip in Colorado. We zipped our sleeping bags together, the coyotes' hysterical chatter far away. Other couples murmured in other tents. Paul was up before sunrise, starting a fire for breakfast. He wasn't much of a talker in the daytime. At night, his hand leafed about in the hair at my neck.

There'd be times when you overdid it. You'd get carried away. All the next day, you'd be in a total fog, delirious, absent-minded, crossing the street and nearly getting run over.

The more girls a boy has, the better. He has a bright look, having reaped fruits, blooming. He stalks around, sure-shouldered, and you have the feeling he's got more in him, a fatter heart, more stories to tell. For a girl, with each boy it's as though a petal gets plucked each time.

Then you start to get tired. You begin to feel diluted, like watered-down stew.

Oliver came skiing with us. We lolled by the fire after everyone had gone to 45 bed. Each creak you'd think was someone coming downstairs. The silver loop bracelet he gave me had been a present from his girlfriend before.

On vacations, we went skiing, or you'd go south if someone invited you. Some people had apartments in New York that their families hardly ever used. Or summer houses, or older sisters. We always managed to find someplace to go.

We made the plan at coffee hour. Simon snuck out and met me at Main Gate after lights-out. We crept to the chapel and spent the night in the balcony. He tasted like onions from a submarine sandwich.

The boys are one of two ways: either they can't sit still or they don't move. In front of the TV, they won't budge. On weekends they play touch football while we sit on the sidelines, picking blades of grass to chew on, and watch. We're always watching them run around. We shiver in the stands, knocking our boots together to keep our toes warm, and they whizz across the ice, chopping their sticks around the puck. When they're in the rink, they refuse to look at you, only eyeing each other beneath low helmets. You cheer for them but they don't look up, even if it's a face-off when nothing's happening, even if they're doing drills before any game has started at all.

Dancing under the pink tent, he bent down and whispered in my ear. We slipped away to the lawn on the other side of the hedge. Much later, as he was leaving the buffet with two plates of eggs and sausage, I saw the grass stains on the knees of his white pants.

Tim's was shaped like a banana, with a graceful curve to it. They're all different. Willie's like a bunch of walnuts when nothing was happening, another's as thin as a thin hot dog. But it's like faces; you're never really surprised. 50

Still, you're not sure what to expect.

I look into his face and he looks back. I look into his eyes and they look back at mine. Then they look down at my mouth so I look at his mouth, then back to his eyes then, backing up, at his whole face. I think, Who? Who are you? His head tilts to one side.
I say, "Who are you?"
"What do you mean?"
"Nothing." 55
I look at his eyes again, deeper. Can't tell who he is, what he thinks.
"What?" he says. I look at his mouth.
"I'm just wondering," I say and go wandering across his face. Study the chin line. It's shaped like a persimmon.
"Who are you? What are you thinking?"
He says, "What the hell are you talking about?" 60

Then they get mad after, when you say enough is enough. After, when it's easier to explain that you don't want to. You wouldn't dream of saying that maybe you weren't really ready to in the first place.

Gentle Eddie. We waded into the sea, the waves round and plowing in, buffalo-headed, slapping our thighs. I put my arms around his freckled shoulders and he held me up, buoyed by the water, and rocked me like a sea shell.

I had no idea whose party it was, the apartment jam-packed, stepping over people in the hallway. The room with the music was practically empty, the bare floor, me in red shoes. This fellow slides onto one knee and takes me around the waist and we rock to jazzy tunes, with my toes pointing heavenward, and waltz and spin and dip to "Smoke Gets in Your Eyes" or "I'll Love You Just for Now." He puts his head to my chest, runs a sweeping hand down my inside thigh and we go loose-limbed and sultry and as smooth as silk and I stamp my red heels and he takes me into a swoon. I never saw him again after that but I thought, I could have loved that one.

You wonder how long you can keep it up. You begin to feel as if you're showing through, like a bathroom window that only lets in grey light, the kind you can't see out of.

They keep coming around. Johnny drives up at Easter vacation from Balti- 65 more and I let him in the kitchen with everyone sound asleep. He has friends waiting in the car.

"What are you, crazy? It's pouring out there," I say.

"It's okay," he says. "They understand."

So he gets some long kisses from me, against the refrigerator, before he goes because I hate those girls who push away a boy's face as if she were made out of Ivory soap, as if she's that much greater than he is.

The note on my cubby told me to see the headmaster. I had no idea for what. He had received complaints about my amorous displays on the town green. It was Willie that spring. The headmaster told me he didn't care what I did but that Casey Academy had a reputation to uphold in the town. He lowered his glasses on his nose. "We've got twenty acres of woods on this campus," he said. "If you want to smooch with your boyfriend, there are twenty acres for you to do it out of the public eye. You read me?"

Everybody'd get weekend permissions for different places, then we'd all go 70 to someone's house whose parents were away. Usually there'd be more boys than girls. We raided the liquor closet and smoked pot at the kitchen table and you'd never know who would end up where, or with whom. There were always disasters. Ceci got bombed and cracked her head open on the banister and needed stitches. Then there was the time Wendel Blair walked through the picture window at the Lowes' and got slashed to ribbons.

He scared me. In bed, I didn't dare look at him. I lay back with my eyes closed, luxuriating because he knew all sorts of expert angles, his hands never fumbling, going over my whole body, pressing the hair up and off the back of my head, giving an extra hip shove, as if to say *There*. I parted my eyes slightly, keeping the screen of my lashes low because it was too much to look at him, his mouth loose and pink and parted, his eyes looking through my forehead, or kneeling up, looking through my throat. I was ashamed but couldn't look him in the eye.

You wonder about things feeling a little off-kilter. You begin to feel like a piece of pounded veal.

At boarding school, everyone gets depressed. We go in and see the housemother, Mrs. Gunther. She got married when she was eighteen. Mr. Gunther was her high school sweetheart, the only boyfriend she ever had.

"And you knew you wanted to marry him right off?" we ask her.

She smiles and says, "Yes."

75

"They always want something from you," says Jill, complaining about her boyfriend.

"Yeah," says Giddy. "You always feel like you have to deliver something."

"You do," says Mrs. Gunther. "Babies."

After sex, you curl up like a shrimp, something deep inside you ruined, slammed in a place that sickens at slamming, and slowly you fill up with an overwhelming sadness, an elusive gaping worry. You don't try to explain it, filled with the knowledge that it's nothing after all, everything filling up finally and absolutely with death. After the briskness of loving, loving stops. And you roll over with death stretched out alongside you like a feather boa, or a snake, light as air, and you . . . you don't even ask for anything or try to say something to him because it's obviously your own damn fault. You haven't been able to — to what? To open your heart. You open your legs but can't, or don't dare anymore, to open your heart.

It starts this way: 80

You stare into their eyes. They flash like all the stars are out. They look at you seriously, their eyes at a low burn and their hands no matter what starting off shy and with such a gentle touch that the only thing you can do is take that tenderness and let yourself be swept away. When, with one attentive finger they tuck the hair behind your ear, you —

You do everything they want.

Then comes after. After when they don't look at you. They scratch their balls, stare at the ceiling. Or if they do turn, their gaze is altogether changed. They are surprised. They turn casually to look at you, distracted, and get a mild distracted surprise. You're gone. Their blank look tells you that the girl they were fucking is not there anymore. You seem to have disappeared.

CONSIDERATIONS FOR CRITICAL THINKING AND WRITING

1. FIRST RESPONSE. What do you think of the narrator? Why? Do you agree with the definition the story offers for *lust*?

2. Do you think that the narrator's depiction of male and female responses to sex are accurate? Explain why or why not.

3. How effective is the narrator's description of teenage sex? What do you think she means when she says "You know just what you're doing and don't see the things that start to get in the way" (para. 29)?

4. What is the story's conflict? Explain whether you think the conflict is resolved.

5. Discuss the story's tone. Is it what you expected from the title?

6. What do you think is the theme of "Lust"? Does its style carry its theme?

7. What is the primary setting for the story? What does it reveal about the nature of the narrator's economic and social class?

8. In a *Publisher's Weekly* interview (November 6, 1992), Minot observed, "There's more fictional material in unhappiness and disappointment and frustration than there is in happiness. Who was it said, 'Happiness is like a blank page'?" What do you think of this observation?

FLANNERY O'CONNOR (1925–1964)

Born in Savannah, Georgia, Flannery O'Connor earned a bachelor's degree at Georgia State College and an M.F.A. degree at the Writers Workshop of the University of Iowa. When she died of lupus before her fortieth birthday, her work was cruelly cut short. Nevertheless, she had completed two novels, *Wise Blood* (1952) and *The Violent Bear It Away* (1960) as well as thirty-one short stories. Despite her short life and relatively modest output, her work is regarded as among the most distinguished American fiction of the mid-twentieth century. Her two collections of stories, *A Good Man Is Hard to Find* (1955) and *Everything That Rises Must Converge* (1965), were included in *The Complete Stories of Flannery O'Connor* (1971), which won the National Book Award.

Good Country People   *1955*

Besides the neutral expression that she wore when she was alone, Mrs. Freeman had two others, forward and reverse, that she used for all her human dealings. Her forward expression was steady and driving like the advance of a heavy truck. Her eyes never swerved to left or right but turned as the story turned as if they followed a yellow line down the center of it. She seldom used the other expression because it was not often necessary for her to retract a statement, but when she did, her face came to a complete stop, there was an almost imperceptible movement of her black eyes, during which they seemed to be receding, and then the observer would see that Mrs. Freeman, though she might stand there as real as several grain sacks thrown on top of each other, was no longer there in spirit. As for getting anything across to her when this was the case, Mrs. Hopewell had given it up. She might talk her head off. Mrs. Freeman could never be brought to admit herself wrong on any point. She would stand there and if she could be brought to say anything, it was something like, "Well, I wouldn't of said it was and I wouldn't of said it wasn't," or letting her gaze range over the top kitchen shelf where there was an assortment of dusty bottles, she might remark, "I see you ain't ate many of them figs you put up last summer."

They carried on their most important business in the kitchen at breakfast. Every morning Mrs. Hopewell got up at seven o'clock and lit her gas heater and Joy's. Joy was her daughter, a large blonde girl who had an artificial leg. Mrs. Hopewell thought of her as a child though she was thirty-two years old and highly educated. Joy would get up while her mother was eating and lumber into the bathroom and slam the door, and before long, Mrs. Freeman would arrive at the back door. Joy would hear her mother call, "Come on in," and then they would talk for a while in low voices that were indistinguishable in the bathroom. By the time Joy came in, they had usually finished the weather report and were on one or the other of Mrs. Freeman's daughters, Glynese or Carramae, Joy called them Glycerin and Caramel. Glynese, a redhead, was eighteen and had many admirers; Carramae, a blonde, was only fifteen but already married and pregnant. She could not keep anything in her stomach. Every morning Mrs. Freeman told Mrs. Hopewell how many times she had vomited since the last report.

Mrs. Hopewell liked to tell people that Glynese and Carramae were two of the finest girls she knew and that Mrs. Freeman was a *lady* and that she was never ashamed to take her anywhere or introduce her to anybody they might meet. Then she would tell how she had happened to hire the Freemans in the first place and how they were a godsend to her and how she had had them four years. The reason for her keeping them so long was that they were not trash. They were good country people. She had telephoned the man whose name they had given as a reference and he had told her that Mr. Freeman was a good farmer but that his wife was the nosiest woman ever to walk the earth. "She's got to be into everything," the man said. "If she don't get there before the dust settles, you can bet she's dead, that's all. She'll want to know all your business. I can stand him real good," he had said, "but me nor my wife neither could have stood that woman one more minute on this place." That had put Mrs. Hopewell off for a few days.

She had hired them in the end because there were no other applicants but she had made up her mind beforehand exactly how she would handle the woman. Since she was the type who had to be into everything, then, Mrs. Hopewell decided, she would not only let her be into everything, she would *see to it* that she was into everything—she would give her the responsibility of everything, she would put her in charge. Mrs. Hopewell had no bad qualities of her own but she was able to use other people's in such a constructive way that she never felt the lack. She had hired the Freemans and she had kept them four years.

Nothing is perfect. This was one of Mrs. Hopewell's favorite sayings. 5
Another was: that is life! And still another, the most important, was: well, other people have their opinions too. She would make these statements, usually at the table, in a tone of gentle insistence as if no one held them but her, and the large hulking Joy, whose constant outrage had obliterated every expression from her face, would stare just a little to the side of her, her eyes icy blue, with the look of someone who has achieved blindness by an act of will and means to keep it.

When Mrs. Hopewell said to Mrs. Freeman that life was like that, Mrs. Freeman would say, "I always said so myself." Nothing had been arrived at by anyone that had not first been arrived at by her. She was quicker than Mr. Freeman. When Mrs. Hopewell said to her after they had been on the place a while, "You know, you're the wheel behind the wheel," and winked, Mrs. Freeman had said, "I know it. I've always been quick. It's some that are quicker than others."

"Everybody is different," Mrs. Hopewell said.

"Yes, most people is," Mrs. Freeman said.

"It takes all kinds to make the world."

"I always said it did myself." 10

The girl was used to this kind of dialogue for breakfast and more of it for dinner; sometimes they had it for supper too. When they had no guest they ate in the kitchen because that was easier. Mrs. Freeman always managed to arrive at some point during the meal and to watch them finish it. She would stand in the doorway if it were summer but in the winter she would stand with one elbow on top of the refrigerator and look down on them, or she would stand by the gas heater, lifting the back of her skirt slightly. Occasionally she would stand against the wall and roll her head from side to side. At no time was she in any hurry to leave. All this was very trying on Mrs. Hopewell but she was a woman of great patience. She realized that nothing is perfect and that in the Freemans she had good country people and that if, in this day and age, you get good country people, you had better hang onto them.

She had had plenty of experience with trash. Before the Freemans she had averaged one tenant family a year. The wives of these farmers were not the kind you would want to be around you for very long. Mrs. Hopewell, who had divorced her husband long ago, needed someone to walk over the fields with her; and when Joy had to be impressed for these services, her remarks were usually so ugly and her face so glum that Mrs. Hopewell would say, "If you can't come pleasantly, I don't want you at all," to which the girl, standing square and rigid-shouldered with her neck thrust slightly forward, would reply, "If you want me, here I am — LIKE I AM."

Mrs. Hopewell excused this attitude because of the leg (which had been shot off in a hunting accident when Joy was ten). It was hard for Mrs. Hopewell to realize that her child was thirty-two now and that for more than twenty years she had had only one leg. She thought of her still as a child because it tore her heart to think instead of the poor stout girl in her thirties who had never danced a step or had any *normal* good times. Her name was really Joy but as soon as she was twenty-one and away from home, she had had it legally changed. Mrs. Hopewell was certain that she had thought and thought until she had hit upon the ugliest name in any language. Then she had gone and had the beautiful name, Joy, changed without telling her mother until after she had done it. Her legal name was Hulga.

When Mrs. Hopewell thought the name, Hulga, she thought of the broad blank hull of a battleship. She would not use it. She continued to call her Joy to which the girl responded but in a purely mechanical way.

Hulga had learned to tolerate Mrs. Freeman who saved her from taking 15 walks with her mother. Even Glynese and Carramae were useful when they occupied attention that might otherwise have been directed at her. At first she had thought she could not stand Mrs. Freeman for she had found that it was not possible to be rude to her. Mrs. Freeman would take on strange resentments and for days together she would be sullen but the source of her displeasure was always obscure; a direct attack, a positive leer, blatant ugliness to her face — these never touched her. And without warning one day, she began calling her Hulga.

She did not call her that in front of Mrs. Hopewell who would have been incensed but when she and the girl happened to be out of the house together, she would say something and add the name Hulga to the end of it, and the big spectacled Joy-Hulga would scowl and redden as if her privacy had been intruded upon. She considered the name her personal affair. She had arrived at it first purely on the basis of its ugly sound and then the full genius of its fitness had struck her. She had a vision of the name working like the ugly sweating Vulcan° who stayed in the furnace and to whom, presumably, the goddess had to come when called. She saw it as the name of her highest creative act.

Vulcan: Roman god of fire.

One of her major triumphs was that her mother had not been able to turn her dust into Joy, but the greater one was that she had been able to turn it herself into Hulga. However, Mrs. Freeman's relish for using the name only irritated her. It was as if Mrs. Freeman's beady steel-pointed eyes had penetrated far enough behind her face to reach some secret fact. Something about her seemed to fascinate Mrs. Freeman and then one day Hulga realized that it was the artificial leg. Mrs. Freeman had a special fondness for the details of secret infections, hidden deformities, assaults upon children. Of diseases, she preferred the lingering or incurable. Hulga had heard Mrs. Hopewell give her the details of the hunting accident, how the leg had been literally blasted off, how she had never lost consciousness. Mrs. Freeman could listen to it any time as if it had happened an hour ago.

When Hulga stumped into the kitchen in the morning (she could walk without making the awful noise but she made it—Mrs. Hopewell was certain—because it was ugly-sounding), she glanced at them and did not speak. Mrs. Hopewell would be in her red kimono with her hair tied around her head in rags. She would be sitting at the table, finishing her breakfast and Mrs. Freeman would be hanging by her elbow outward from the refrigerator, looking down at the table. Hulga always put her eggs on the stove to boil and then stood over them with her arms folded, and Mrs. Hopewell would look at her—a kind of indirect gaze divided between her and Mrs. Freeman—and would think that if she would only keep herself up a little, she wouldn't be so bad looking. There was nothing wrong with her face that a pleasant expression wouldn't help. Mrs. Hopewell said that people who looked on the bright side of things would be beautiful even if they were not.

Whenever she looked at Joy this way, she could not help but feel that it would have been better if the child had not taken the Ph.D. It had certainly not brought her out any and now that she had it, there was no more excuse for her to go to school again. Mrs. Hopewell thought it was nice for girls to go to school to have a good time but Joy had "gone through." Anyhow, she would not have been strong enough to go again. The doctors had told Mrs. Hopewell that with the best of care, Joy might see forty-five. She had a weak heart. Joy had made it plain that if it had not been for this condition, she would be far from these red hills and good country people. She would be in a university lecturing to people who knew what she was talking about. And Mrs. Hopewell could very well picture her there, looking like a scarecrow and lecturing to more of the same. Here she went about all day in a six-year-old skirt and a yellow sweat shirt with a faded cowboy on a horse embossed on it. She thought this was funny; Mrs. Hopewell thought it was idiotic and showed simply that she was still a child. She was brilliant but she didn't have a grain of sense. It seemed to Mrs. Hopewell that every year she grew less like other people and more like herself—bloated, rude, and squint-eyed. And she said such strange things! To her own mother she had said—without warning, without excuse, standing up in the middle of a meal with her face purple and her mouth half full—"Woman! do you ever look inside? Do you ever look inside and see what you are *not*? God!" she had cried sinking down again and staring at her plate, "Malebranche° was right: we are not our own light. We are not our own light!" Mrs. Hopewell had no idea to this day what brought that on. She had

---

Malebranche: Nicolas Malebranche (1638–1715), a French philosopher.

only made the remark, hoping Joy would take it in, that a smile never hurt anyone.

The girl had taken the Ph.D. in philosophy and this left Mrs. Hopewell at a complete loss. You could say, "My daughter is a nurse," or "My daughter is a schoolteacher," or even, "My daughter is a chemical engineer." You could not say, "My daughter is a philosopher." That was something that had ended with the Greeks and Romans. All day Joy sat on her neck in a deep chair, reading. Sometimes she went for walks but she didn't like dogs or cats or birds or flowers or nature or nice young men. She looked at nice young men as if she could smell their stupidity.

One day Mrs. Hopewell had picked up one of the books the girl had just 20 put down and opening it at random, she read, "Science, on the other hand, has to assert its soberness and seriousness afresh and declare that it is concerned solely with what-is. Nothing — how can it be for science anything but a horror and a phantasm? If science is right, then one thing stands firm: science wishes to know nothing of nothing. Such is after all the strictly scientific approach to Nothing. We know it by wishing to know nothing of Nothing." These words had been underlined with a blue pencil and they worked on Mrs. Hopewell like some evil incantation in gibberish. She shut the book quickly and went out of the room as if she were having a chill.

This morning when the girl came in, Mrs. Freeman was on Carramae. "She thrown up four times after supper," she said, "and was up twict in the night after three o'clock. Yesterday she didn't do nothing but ramble in the bureau drawer. All she did. Stand up there and see what she could run up on."

"She's got to eat," Mrs. Hopewell muttered, sipping her coffee, while she watched Joy's back at the stove. She was wondering what the child had said to the Bible salesman. She could not imagine what kind of a conversation she could possibly have had with him.

He was a tall gaunt hatless youth who had called yesterday to sell them a Bible. He had appeared at the door, carrying a large black suitcase that weighted him so heavily on one side that he had to brace himself against the door facing. He seemed on the point of collapse but he said in a cheerful voice, "Good morning, Mrs. Cedars!" and set the suitcase down on the mat. He was not a bad-looking young man though he had on a bright blue suit and yellow socks that were not pulled up far enough. He had prominent face bones and a streak of sticky-looking brown hair falling across his forehead.

"I'm Mrs. Hopewell," she said.

"Oh!" he said, pretending to look puzzled but with his eyes sparkling, "I 25 saw it said 'The Cedars' on the mailbox so I thought you was Mrs. Cedars!" and he burst out in a pleasant laugh. He picked up the satchel and under cover of a pant, he fell forward into her hall. It was rather as if the suitcase had moved first, jerking him after it. "Mrs. Hopewell!" he said and grabbed her hand. "I hope you are well!" and he laughed again and then all at once his face sobered completely. He paused and gave her a straight earnest look and said, "Lady, I've come to speak of serious things."

"Well, come in," she muttered, none too pleased because her dinner was almost ready. He came into the parlor and sat down on the edge of a straight chair and put the suitcase between his feet and glanced around the room as if he were sizing her up by it. Her silver gleamed on the two sideboards; she decided he had never been in a room as elegant as this.

"Mrs. Hopewell," he began, using her name in a way that sounded almost intimate, "I know you believe in Chrustian service."

"Well yes," she murmured.

"I know," he said and paused, looking very wise with his head cocked on one side, "that you're a good woman. Friends have told me."

Mrs. Hopewell never liked to be taken for a fool. "What are you selling?" 30 she asked.

"Bibles," the young man said and his eye raced around the room before he added, "I see you have no family Bible in your parlor, I see that is the one lack you got!"

Mrs. Hopewell could not say, "My daughter is an atheist and won't let me keep the Bible in the parlor." She said, stiffening slightly, "I keep my Bible by my bedside." This was not the truth. It was in the attic somewhere.

"Lady," he said, "the word of God ought to be in the parlor."

"Well, I think that's a matter of taste," she began. "I think . . ."

"Lady," he said, "for a Chrustian, the word of God ought to be in every 35 room in the house besides in his heart. I know you're a Chrustian because I can see it in every line of your face."

She stood up and said, "Well, young man, I don't want to buy a Bible and I smell my dinner burning."

He didn't get up. He began to twist his hands and looking down at them, he said softly, "Well lady, I'll tell you the truth — not many people want to buy one nowadays and besides, I know I'm real simple. I don't know how to say a thing but to say it. I'm just a country boy." He glanced up into her unfriendly face. "People like you don't like to fool with country people like me!"

"Why!" she cried, "good country people are the salt of the earth! Besides, we all have different ways of doing, it takes all kinds to make the world go 'round. That's life!"

"You said a mouthful," he said.

"Why, I think there aren't enough good people in the world!" she said, 40 stirred. "I think that's what's wrong with it!"

His face had brightened. "I didn't introduce myself," he said. "I'm Manley Pointer from out in the country around Willohobie, not even from a place, just from near a place."

"You wait a minute," she said. "I have to see about my dinner." She went out to the kitchen and found Joy standing near the door where she had been listening.

"Get rid of the salt of the earth," she said, "and let's eat."

Mrs. Hopewell gave her a pained look and turned the heat down under the vegetables. "*I* can't be rude to anybody," she murmured and went back into the parlor.

He had opened the suitcase and was sitting with a Bible on each knee. 45

"You might as well put those up," she told him. "I don't want one."

"I appreciate your honesty," he said. "You don't see any more real honest people unless you go way out in the country."

"I know," she said, "real genuine folks!" Through the crack in the door she heard a groan.

"I guess a lot of boys come telling you they're working their way through college," he said, "but I'm not going to tell you that. Somehow," he said, "I don't want to go to college. I want to devote my life to Chrustian service. See," he said, lowering his voice, "I got this heart condition. I may not live long. When you know it's something wrong with you and you may not live long, well then, lady . . ." He paused, with his mouth open, and stared at her.

He and Joy had the same condition! She knew that her eyes were filling with tears but she collected herself quickly and murmured, "Won't you stay for dinner? We'd love to have you!" and was sorry the instant she heard herself say it. 50

"Yes mam," he said in an abashed voice, "I would sher love to do that!"

Joy had given him one look on being introduced to him and then throughout the meal had not glanced at him again. He had addressed several remarks to her, which she had pretended not to hear. Mrs. Hopewell could not understand deliberate rudeness, although she lived with it, and she felt she had always to overflow with hospitality to make up for Joy's lack of courtesy. She urged him to talk about himself and he did. He said he was the seventh child of twelve and that his father had been crushed under a tree when he himself was eight years old. He had been crushed very badly, in fact, almost cut in two and was practically not recognizable. His mother had got along the best she could by hard working and she had always seen that her children went to Sunday School and that they read the Bible every evening. He was now nineteen years old and he had been selling Bibles for four months. In that time he had sold seventy-seven Bibles and had the promise of two more sales. He wanted to become a missionary because he thought that was the way you could do most for people. "He who losest his life shall find it," he said simply and he was so sincere, so genuine and earnest that Mrs. Hopewell would not for the world have smiled. He prevented his peas from sliding onto the table by blocking them with a piece of bread which he later cleaned his plate with. She could see Joy observing sidewise how he handled his knife and fork and she saw too that every few minutes, the boy would dart a keen appraising glance at the girl as if he were trying to attract her attention.

After dinner Joy cleared the dishes off the table and disappeared and Mrs. Hopewell was left to talk with him. He told her again about his childhood and his father's accident and about various things that had happened to him. Every five minutes or so she would stifle a yawn. He sat for two hours until finally she told him she must go because she had an appointment in town. He packed his Bibles and thanked her and prepared to leave, but in the doorway he stopped and wrung her hand and said that not on any of his trips had he met a lady as nice as her and he asked if he could come again. She had said she would always be happy to see him.

Joy had been standing in the road, apparently looking at something in the distance, when he came down the steps toward her, bent to the side with his heavy valise. He stopped where she was standing and confronted her directly. Mrs. Hopewell could not hear what he said but she trembled to think what Joy would say to him. She could see that after a minute Joy said something and that then the boy began to speak again, making an excited gesture with his free hand. After a minute Joy said something else at which the boy began to speak once more. Then to her amazement, Mrs. Hopewell saw the two of them walk off together, toward the gate. Joy had walked all the way to the gate with him and Mrs. Hopewell could not imagine what they had said to each other, and she had not yet dared to ask.

Mrs. Freeman was insisting upon her attention. She had moved from the refrigerator to the heater so that Mrs. Hopewell had to turn and face her in 55 order to seem to be listening. "Glynese gone out with Harvey Hill again last night," she said. "She had this sty."

"Hill," Mrs. Hopewell said absently, "is the one who works in the garage?"

"Nome, he's the one that goes to chiropracter school," Mrs. Freeman said. "She had this sty. Been had it two days. So she says when he brought her in the other night he says, 'Lemme get rid of that sty for you,' and she says, 'How?' and he says, 'You just lay yourself down acrost the seat of that car and I'll show you.' So she done it and he popped her neck. Kept on a-popping it several times until she made him quit. This morning," Mrs. Freeman said, "she ain't got no sty. She ain't got no traces of a sty."

"I never heard of that before," Mrs. Hopewell said.

"He ast her to marry him before the Ordinary,"° Mrs. Freeman went on, "and she told him she wasn't going to be married in no *office.*"

"Well, Glynese is a fine girl," Mrs. Hopewell said. "Glynese and Carramae are both fine girls." 60

"Carramae said when her and Lyman was married Lyman said it sure felt sacred to him. She said he said he wouldn't take five hundred dollars for being married by a preacher."

"How much would he take?" the girl asked from the stove.

"He said he wouldn't take five hundred dollars," Mrs. Freeman repeated.

"Well we all have work to do," Mrs. Hopewell said.

"Lyman said it just felt more sacred to him," Mrs. Freeman said. "The doc- 65 tor wants Carramae to eat prunes. Says instead of medicine. Says them cramps is coming from pressure. You know where I think it is?"

"She'll be better in a few weeks," Mrs. Hopewell said.

"In the tube," Mrs. Freeman said. "Else she wouldn't be as sick as she is."

Hulga had cracked her two eggs into a saucer and was bringing them to the table along with a cup of coffee that she had filled too full. She sat down carefully and began to eat, meaning to keep Mrs. Freeman there by questions if for any reason she showed an inclination to leave. She could perceive her mother's eye on her. The first round-about question would be about the Bible salesman and she did not wish to bring it on. "How did he pop her neck?" she asked.

Mrs. Freeman went into a description of how he had popped her neck. She said he owned a '55 Mercury but that Glynese said she would rather marry a man with only a '36 Plymouth who would be married by a preacher. The girl asked what if he had a '32 Plymouth and Mrs. Freeman said what Glynese had said was a '36 Plymouth.

Mrs. Hopewell said there were not many girls with Glynese's common 70 sense. She said what she admired in those girls was their common sense. She said that reminded her that they had had a nice visitor yesterday, a young man selling Bibles. "Lord," she said, "he bored me to death but he was so sincere and genuine I couldn't be rude to him. He was just good country people, you know," she said, " — just the salt of the earth."

"I seen him walk up," Mrs. Freeman said, "and then later — I seen him walk off," and Hulga could feel the slight shift in her voice, the slight insinuation, that he had not walked off alone, had he? Her face remained expressionless but the color rose into her neck and she seemed to swallow it down with the

Ordinary: Justice of the peace.

next spoonful of egg. Mrs. Freeman was looking at her as if they had a secret together.

"Well, it takes all kinds of people to make the world go 'round," Mrs. Hopewell said. "It's very good we aren't all alike."

"Some people are more alike than others," Mrs. Freeman said.

Hulga got up and stumped, with about twice the noise that was necessary, into her room and locked the door. She was to meet the Bible salesman at ten o'clock at the gate. She had thought about it half the night. She had started thinking of it as a great joke and then she had begun to see profound implications in it. She had lain in bed imagining dialogues for them that were insane on the surface but that reached below to depths that no Bible salesman would be aware of. Their conversation yesterday had been of this kind.

He had stopped in front of her and had simply stood there. His face was 75 bony and sweaty and bright, with a little pointed nose in the center of it, and his look was different from what it had been at the dinner table. He was gazing at her with open curiosity, with fascination, like a child watching a new fantastic animal at the zoo, and he was breathing as if he had run a great distance to reach her. His gaze seemed somehow familiar but she could not think where she had been regarded with it before. For almost a minute he didn't say anything. Then on what seemed an insuck of breath, he whispered, "You ever ate a chicken that was two days old?"

The girl looked at him stonily. He might have just put this question up for consideration at the meeting of a philosophical association. "Yes," she presently replied as if she had considered it from all angles.

"It must have been mighty small!" he said triumphantly and shook all over with little nervous giggles, getting very red in the face, and subsiding finally into his gaze of complete admiration, while the girl's expression remained exactly the same.

"How old are you?" he asked softly.

She waited some time before she answered. Then in a flat voice she said, "Seventeen."

His smiles came in succession like waves breaking on the surface of a little 80 lake. "I see you got a wooden leg," he said. "I think you're brave. I think you're real sweet."

The girl stood blank and solid and silent.

"Walk to the gate with me," he said. "You're a brave sweet little thing and I liked you the minute I seen you walk in the door."

Hulga began to move forward.

"What's your name?" he asked, smiling down on the top of her head.

"Hulga," she said.   85

"Hulga," he murmured, "Hulga. Hulga. I never heard of anybody name Hulga before. You're shy, aren't you, Hulga?" he asked.

She nodded, watching his large red hand on the handle of the giant valise.

"I like girls that wear glasses," he said. "I think a lot. I'm not like these people that a serious thought don't ever enter their heads. It's because I may die."

"I may die too," she said suddenly and looked up at him. His eyes were very small and brown, glittering feverishly.

"Listen," he said, "don't you think some people was meant to meet on 90 account of what all they got in common and all? Like they both think serious thoughts and all?" He shifted the valise to his other hand so that the hand nearest her was free. He caught hold of her elbow and shook it a little. "I don't work on Saturday," he said. "I like to walk in the woods and see what Mother Nature is wearing. O'er the hills and far away. Pic-nics and things. Couldn't we go on a pic-nic tomorrow? Say yes, Hulga," he said and gave her a dying look as if he felt his insides about to drop out of him. He had even seemed to sway slightly toward her.

During the night she had imagined that she seduced him. She imagined that the two of them walked on the place until they came to the storage barn beyond the two back fields and there, she imagined, that things came to such a pass that she very easily seduced him and that then, of course, she had to reckon with his remorse. True genius can get an idea across even to an inferior mind. She imagined that she took his remorse in hand and changed it into a deeper understanding of life. She took all his shame away and turned it into something useful.

She set off for the gate at exactly ten o'clock, escaping without drawing Mrs. Hopewell's attention. She didn't take anything to eat, forgetting that food is usually taken on a picnic. She wore a pair of slacks and a dirty white shirt, and as an afterthought, she had put some Vapex° on the collar of it since she did not own any perfume. When she reached the gate no one was there.

She looked up and down the empty highway and had the furious feeling that she had been tricked, that he had only meant to make her walk to the gate after the idea of him. Then suddenly he stood up, very tall, from behind a bush on the opposite embankment. Smiling, he lifted his hat which was new and wide-brimmed. He had not worn it yesterday and she wondered if he had bought it for the occasion. It was toast-colored with a red and white band around it and was slightly too large for him. He stepped from behind the bush still carrying the black valise. He had on the same suit and the same yellow socks sucked down in his shoes from walking. He crossed the highway and said, "I knew you'd come!"

The girl wondered acidly how he had known this. She pointed to the valise and asked, "Why did you bring your Bibles?"

He took her elbow, smiling down on her as if he could not stop. "You can never tell when you'll need the word of God, Hulga," he said. She had a moment in which she doubted that this was actually happening and then they began to climb the embankment. They went down into the pasture toward the woods. The boy walked lightly by her side, bouncing on his toes. The valise did not seem to be heavy today; he even swung it. They crossed half the pasture without saying anything and then, putting his hand easily on the small of her back, he asked softly, "Where does your wooden leg join on?"

She turned an ugly red and glared at him and for an instant the boy looked abashed. "I didn't mean you no harm," he said. "I only meant you're so brave and all. I guess God takes care of you."

"No," she said, looking forward and walking fast, "I don't even believe in God."

At this he stopped and whistled. "No!" he exclaimed as if he were too astonished to say anything else.

She walked on and in a second he was bouncing at her side, fanning with his hat. "That's very unusual for a girl," he remarked, watching her out of the

95

Vapex: Trade name for a nasal spray.

corner of his eye. When they reached the edge of the wood, he put his hand on her back again and drew her against him without a word and kissed her heavily.

The kiss, which had more pressure than feeling behind it, produced that 100 extra surge of adrenaline in the girl that enables one to carry a packed trunk out of a burning house, but in her, the power went at once to the brain. Even before he released her, her mind, clear and detached and ironic anyway, was regarding him from a great distance, with amusement but with pity. She had never been kissed before and she was pleased to discover that it was an unexceptional experience and all a matter of the mind's control. Some people might enjoy drain water if they were told it was vodka. When the boy, looking expectant but uncertain, pushed her gently away, she turned and walked on, saying nothing as if such business, for her, were common enough.

He came along panting at her side, trying to help her when he saw a root that she might trip over. He caught and held back the long swaying blades of thorn vine until she had passed beyond them. She led the way and he came breathing heavily behind her. Then they came out on a sunlit hillside, sloping softly into another one a little smaller. Beyond, they could see the rusted top of the old barn where the extra hay was stored.

The hill was sprinkled with small pink weeds. "Then you ain't saved?" he asked suddenly, stopping.

The girl smiled. It was the first time she had smiled at him at all. "In my economy," she said, "I'm saved and you are damned but I told you I didn't believe in God."

Nothing seemed to destroy the boy's look of admiration. He gazed at her now as if the fantastic animal at the zoo had put its paw through the bars and given him a loving poke. She thought he looked as if he wanted to kiss her again and she walked on before he had the chance.

"Ain't there somewheres we can sit down sometime?" he murmured, his 105 voice softening toward the end of the sentence.

"In that barn," she said.

They made for it rapidly as if it might slide away like a train. It was a large two-story barn, cool and dark inside. The boy pointed up the ladder that led into the loft and said, "It's too bad we can't go up there."

"Why can't we?" she asked.

"Yer leg," he said reverently.

The girl gave him a contemptuous look and putting both hands on the 110 ladder, she climbed it while he stood below, apparently awestruck. She pulled herself expertly through the opening and then looked down at him and said, "Well, come on if you're coming," and he began to climb the ladder, awkwardly bringing the suitcase with him.

"We won't need the Bible," she observed.

"You never can tell," he said, panting. After he had got into the loft, he was a few seconds catching his breath. She had sat down in a pile of straw. A wide sheath of sunlight, filled with dust particles, slanted over her. She lay back against a bale, her face turned away, looking out the front opening of the barn where hay was thrown from a wagon into the loft. The two pink-speckled hillsides lay back against a dark ridge of woods. The sky was cloudless and cold blue. The boy dropped down by her side and put one arm under her and the other over her and began methodically kissing her face, making little noises like a fish. He did not remove his hat but it was pushed far enough back not to interfere. When her glasses got in his way, he took them off of her and slipped them into his pocket.

The girl at first did not return any of the kisses but presently she began to and after she had put several on his cheek, she reached his lips and remained there, kissing him again and again as if she were trying to draw all the breath out of him. His breath was clear and sweet like a child's and the kisses were sticky like a child's. He mumbled about loving her and about knowing when he first seen her that he loved her, but the mumbling was like the sleepy fretting of a child being put to sleep by his mother. Her mind, throughout this, never stopped or lost itself for a second to her feelings. "You ain't said you loved me none," he whispered finally, pulling back from her. "You got to say that."

She looked away from him off into the hollow sky and then down at a black ridge and then down farther into what appeared to be two green swelling lakes. She didn't realize he had taken her glasses but this landscape could not seem exceptional to her for she seldom paid any close attention to her surroundings.

"You got to say it," he repeated. "You got to say you love me."   115

She was always careful how she committed herself. "In a sense," she began, "if you use the word loosely, you might say that. But it's not a word I use. I don't have illusions. I'm one of those people who see *through* to nothing."

The boy was frowning. "You got to say it. I said it and you got to say it," he said.

The girl looked at him almost tenderly. "You poor baby," she murmured. "It's just as well you don't understand," and she pulled him by the neck, face-down, against her. "We are all damned," she said, "but some of us have taken off our blindfolds and see that there's nothing to see. It's a kind of salvation."

The boy's astonished eyes looked blankly through the ends of her hair. "Okay," he almost whined, "but do you love me or don'tcher?"

"Yes," she said and added, "in a sense. But I must tell you something.   120 There mustn't be anything dishonest between us." She lifted his head and looked him in the eye. "I am thirty years old," she said. "I have a number of degrees."

The boy's look was irritated but dogged. "I don't care," he said. "I don't care a thing about what all you done. I just want to know if you love me or don'tcher?" and he caught her to him and wildly planted her face with kisses until she said, "Yes, yes."

"Okay then," he said, letting her go. "Prove it."

She smiled, looking dreamily out on the shifty landscape. She had seduced him without even making up her mind to try. "How?" she asked, feeling that he should be delayed a little.

He leaned over and put his lips to her ear. "Show me where your wooden leg joins on," he whispered.

The girl uttered a sharp little cry and her face instantly drained of color.   125 The obscenity of the suggestion was not what shocked her. As a child she had sometimes been subject to feelings of shame but education had removed the last traces of that as a good surgeon scrapes for cancer; she would no more have felt it over what he was asking than she would have believed in his Bible. But she was as sensitive about the artificial leg as a peacock about his tail. No one ever touched it but her. She took care of it as someone else would his soul, in private and almost with her own eyes turned away. "No," she said.

"I known it," he muttered, sitting up. "You're just playing me for a sucker."

"Oh no no!" she cried. "It joins on at the knee. Only at the knee. Why do you want to see it?"

The boy gave her a long penetrating look. "Because," he said, "it's what makes you different. You ain't like anybody else."

She sat staring at him. There was nothing about her face or her round freezing-blue eyes to indicate that this had moved her; but she felt as if her heart had stopped and left her mind to pump her blood. She decided that for the first time in her life she was face to face with real innocence. This boy, with an instinct that came from beyond wisdom, had touched the truth about her. When after a minute, she said in a hoarse high voice, "All right," it was like surrendering to him completely. It was like losing her own life and finding it again, miraculously, in his.

Very gently he began to roll the slack leg up. The artificial limb, in a white sock and brown flat shoe, was bound in a heavy material like canvas and ended in an ugly jointure where it was attached to the stump. The boy's face and his voice were entirely reverent as he uncovered it and said, "Now show me how to take it off and on." 130

She took it off for him and put it back on again and then he took it off himself, handling it as tenderly as if it were a real one. "See!" he said with a delighted child's face. "Now I can do it myself!"

"Put it back on," she said. She was thinking that she would run away with him and that every night he would take the leg off and every morning put it back on again. "Put it back on," she said.

"Not yet," he murmured, setting it on its foot out of her reach. "Leave it off for a while. You got me instead."

She gave a little cry of alarm but he pushed her down and began to kiss her again. Without the leg she felt entirely dependent on him. Her brain seemed to have stopped thinking altogether and to be about some other function that it was not very good at. Different expressions raced back and forth over her face. Every now and then the boy, his eyes like two steel spikes, would glance behind him where the leg stood. Finally she pushed him off and said, "Put it back on me now."

"Wait," he said. He leaned the other way and pulled the valise toward him and opened it. It had a pale blue spotted lining and there were only two Bibles in it. He took one of these out and opened the cover of it. It was hollow and contained a pocket flask of whiskey, a pack of cards, and a small blue box with printing on it. He laid these out in front of her one at a time in an evenly-spaced row, like one presenting offerings at the shrine of a goddess. He put the blue box in her hand. THIS PRODUCT TO BE USED ONLY FOR THE PREVENTION OF DISEASE, she read, and dropped it. The boy was unscrewing the top of the flask. He stopped and pointed, with a smile, to the deck of cards. It was not an ordinary deck but one with an obscene picture on the back of each card. "Take a swig," he said, offering her the bottle first. He held it in front of her, but like one mesmerized, she did not move. 135

Her voice when she spoke had an almost pleading sound. "Aren't you," she murmured, "aren't you just good country people?"

The boy cocked his head. He looked as if he were just beginning to understand that she might be trying to insult him. "Yeah," he said, curling his lip slightly, "but it ain't held me back none. I'm as good as you any day in the week."

"Give me my leg," she said.

He pushed it farther away with his foot. "Come on now, let's begin to have us a good time," he said coaxingly. "We ain't got to know one another good yet."

"Give me my leg!" she screamed and tried to lunge for it but he pushed her 140 down easily.

"What's the matter with you all of a sudden?" he asked, frowning as he screwed the top on the flask and put it quickly back inside the Bible. "You just a while ago said you didn't believe in nothing. I thought you was some girl!"

Her face was almost purple. "You're a Christian!" she hissed. "You're a fine Christian! You're just like them all — say one thing and do another. You're a perfect Christian, you're . . ."

The boy's mouth was set angrily. "I hope you don't think," he said in a lofty indignant tone, "that I believe in that crap! I may sell Bibles but I know which end is up and I wasn't born yesterday and I know where I'm going!"

"Give me my leg!" she screeched. He jumped up so quickly that she barely saw him sweep the cards and the blue box into the Bible and throw the Bible into his valise. She saw him grab the leg and then she saw it for an instant slanted forlornly across the inside of the suitcase with a Bible at either side of its opposite ends. He slammed the lid shut and snatched up the valise and swung it down the hole and then stepped through himself.

When all of him had passed but his head, he turned and regarded her with 145 a look that no longer had any admiration in it. "I've gotten a lot of interesting things," he said. "One time I got a woman's glass eye this way. And you needn't to think you'll catch me because Pointer ain't really my name. I use a different name at every house I call at and don't stay nowhere long. And I'll tell you another thing, Hulga," he said, using the name as if he didn't think much of it, "you ain't so smart. I been believing in nothing ever since I was born!" and then the toast-colored hat disappeared down the hole and the girl was left, sitting on the straw in the dusty sunlight. When she turned her churning face toward the opening, she saw his blue figure struggling successfully over the green speckled lake.

Mrs. Hopewell and Mrs. Freeman, who were in the back pasture, digging up onions, saw him emerge a little later from the woods and head across the meadow toward the highway. "Why, that looks like that nice dull young man that tried to sell me a Bible yesterday," Mrs. Hopewell said, squinting. "He must have been selling them to the Negroes back in there. He was so simple," she said, "but I guess the world would be better off if we were all that simple."

Mrs. Freeman's gaze drove forward and just touched him before he disappeared under the hill. Then she returned her attention to the evil-smelling onion shoot she was lifting from the ground. "Some can't be that simple," she said. "I know I never could."

CONSIDERATIONS FOR CRITICAL THINKING AND WRITING

1. FIRST RESPONSE. What do you think of Hulga's conviction that intelligence and education are incompatible with religious faith?

2. Why is it significant that Mrs. Hopewell's daughter has two names? How do the other characters' names serve to characterize them?

3. Why do you think Mrs. Freeman and Mrs. Hopewell are introduced before Hulga? What do they contribute to Hulga's story?

4. Identify the conflict in this story. How is it resolved?

5. Hulga and the Bible salesman play a series of jokes on each other. How are these deceptions related to the theme?

6. What is the effect of O'Connor's use of the phrase "good country people" throughout the story? Why is it an appropriate title?

7. The Bible salesman's final words to Hulga are "You ain't so smart. I been believing in nothing ever since I was born!" What religious values are expressed in the story?

8. After the Bible salesman leaves Hulga at the end of the story, O'Connor adds two more paragraphs concerning Mrs. Hopewell and Mrs. Freeman. What is the purpose of these final paragraphs?

9. Hulga's perspective on life is ironic, but she is also the subject of O'Connor's irony. Explain how O'Connor uses irony to reveal Hulga's character.

10. This story would be different if told from Hulga's point of view. Describe how the use of a limited omniscient narrator contributes to the story's effects.

FAY WELDON (B. 1933)

Born in England and raised in New Zealand, Fay Weldon graduated from St. Andrew's University in Scotland. She wrote advertising copy for various companies and was a propaganda writer for the British Foreign Office before turning to fiction. She has written novels, short stories, plays, and radio scripts. In 1971 her script for an episode of "Upstairs, Downstairs" won an award from the Society of Film and Television Arts. She has written more than a score of novels, including *The Fat Woman's Joke* (1967), *Down among the Women* (1971), *Praxis* (1978), *The Life and Loves of a She-Devil* (1983), *Life Force* (1991), and *Big Women* (1998), and an equal number of plays and scripts. Her collections of short stories include *Moon over Minneapolis* (1992), *Wicked Women* (American edition, 1997), and *A Hard Time to Be a Father* (1998). Weldon often uses ironic humor to portray carefully drawn female characters coming to terms with the facts of their lives.

IND AFF   *1988*
or Out of Love in Sarajevo

This is a sad story. It has to be. It rained in Sarajevo, and we had expected fine weather.

The rain filled up Sarajevo's pride, two footprints set into a pavement which mark the spot where the young assassin Princip stood to shoot the Archduke Franz Ferdinand and his wife. (Don't forget his wife: everyone forgets his wife, the archduchess.) That was in the summer of 1914. Sarajevo is a pretty town, Balkan style, mountain-rimmed. A broad, swift, shallow river runs through its center, carrying the mountain snow away, arched by many bridges. The one nearest the two footprints has been named the Princip Bridge. The young man is a hero in these parts. Not only does he bring in the tourists — look, look, the spot, the very spot! — but by his action, as everyone knows, he lit a spark which fired the timber which caused World War I which crumbled the Austro-Hungarian Empire, the crumbling of which made modern Yugoslavia possible. Forty million dead (or was it thirty?) but who cares? So long as he loved his country.

The river, they say, can run so shallow in the summer it's known derisively as "the wet road." Today, from what I could see through the sheets of falling rain, it seemed full enough. Yugoslavian streets are always busy — no one stays home if they can help it (thus can an indecent shortage of housing space create a sociable nation) and it seemed as if by common consent a shield of bobbing umbrellas had been erected two meters high to keep the rain off the streets. It just hadn't worked around Princip's corner.

"Come all this way," said Peter, who was a professor of classical history, "and you can't even see the footprints properly, just two undistinguished puddles." Ah, but I loved him. I shivered for his disappointment. He was supervising my thesis on varying concepts of morality and duty in the early Greek States as evidenced in their poetry and drama. I was dependent upon him for my academic future. He said I had a good mind but not a first-class mind and somehow I didn't take it as an insult. I had a feeling first-class minds weren't all that good in bed.

Sarajevo is in Bosnia, in the center of Yugoslavia, that grouping of 5 unlikely states, that distillation of languages into the phonetic reasonableness of Serbo-Croatian. We'd sheltered from the rain in an ancient mosque in Serbian Belgrade; done the same in a monastery in Croatia; now we spent a wet couple of days in Sarajevo beneath other people's umbrellas. We planned to go on to Montenegro, on the coast, where the fish and the artists come from, to swim and lie in the sun, and recover from the exhaustion caused by the sexual and moral torments of the last year. It couldn't possibly go on raining forever. Could it? Satellite pictures showed black clouds swishing gently all over Europe, over the Balkans, into Asia — practically all the way from Moscow to London, in fact. It wasn't that Peter and myself were being singled out. No. It was raining on his wife, too, back in Cambridge.

Peter was trying to decide, as he had been for the past year, between his wife and myself as his permanent life partner. To this end we had gone away, off the beaten track, for a holiday; if not with his wife's blessing, at least with her knowledge. Were we really, truly suited? We had to be sure, you see, that this was more than just any old professor-student romance; that it was the Real Thing, because the longer the indecision went on the longer Mrs. Piper would be left dangling in uncertainty and distress. They had been married for twenty-four years; they had stopped loving each other a long time ago, of course — but there would be a fearful personal and practical upheaval entailed if he decided to leave permanently and shack up, as he put it, with me. Which I certainly wanted him to do. I loved him. And so far I was winning hands down. It didn't seem much of a contest at all, in fact. I'd been cool and thin and informed on the seat next to him in a Zagreb theater (Mrs. Piper was sweaty and only liked telly); was now eager and anxious for social and political instruction in Sarajevo (Mrs. Piper spat in the face of knowledge, he'd once told me); and planned to be lissome (and I thought topless but I hadn't quite decided: this might be the area where the age difference showed) while I splashed and shrieked like a bathing belle in the shallows of the Montenegrin coast. (Mrs. Piper was a swimming coach: I imagined she smelt permanently of chlorine.)

In fact so far as I could see, it was no contest at all between his wife and myself. But Peter liked to luxuriate in guilt and indecision. And I loved him with an inordinate affection.

Princip's prints are a meter apart, placed as a modern cop on a training shoot-out would place his feet — the left in front at a slight outward angle, the right behind, facing forward. There seemed great energy focused here. Both hands on the gun, run, stop, plant the feet, aim, fire! I could see the footprints well enough, in spite of Peter's complaint. They were clear enough to me.

We went to a restaurant for lunch, since it was too wet to do what we loved to do: that is, buy bread, cheese, sausage, wine, and go off somewhere in our hired car, into the woods or the hills, and picnic and make love. It was a private restaurant — Yugoslavia went over to a mixed capitalist-communist economy years back, so you get either the best or worst of both systems, depending on your mood — that is to say, we knew we would pay more but be given a choice. We chose the wild boar.

"Probably ordinary pork soaked in red cabbage water to darken it," said ₁₀ Peter. He was not in a good mood.

Cucumber salad was served first.

"Everything in this country comes with cucumber salad," complained Peter. I noticed I had become used to his complaining. I supposed that when you had been married a little you simply wouldn't hear it. He was forty-six and I was twenty-five.

"They grow a lot of cucumber," I said.

"If they can grow cucumbers," Peter then asked, "why can't they grow *mange-tout?*"° It seemed a why-can't-they-eat-cake sort of argument to me, but not knowing enough about horticulture not to be outflanked if I debated the point, I moved the subject on to safer ground.

"I suppose Princip's action couldn't really have started World War I," I ₁₅ remarked. "Otherwise, what a thing to have on your conscience! One little shot and the deaths of thirty million."

"Forty," he corrected me. Though how they reckon these things and get them right I can't imagine. "Of course he didn't start the war. That's just a simple tale to keep the children quiet. It takes more than an assassination to start a war. What happened was that the buildup of political and economic tensions in the Balkans was such that it had to find some release."

"So it was merely the shot that lit the spark that fired the timber that started the war, et cetera?"

"Quite," he said. "World War I would have had to have started sooner or later."

"A bit later or a bit sooner," I said, "might have made the difference of a million or so; if it was you on the battlefield in the mud and the rain you'd

---

mange-tout: A sugar pea or bean (French).

notice; exactly when they fired the starting-pistol; exactly when they blew the final whistle. Is that what they do when a war ends; blow a whistle? So that everyone just comes in from the trenches."

But he wasn't listening. He was parting the flesh of the soft collapsed orangey-red pepper which sat in the middle of his cucumber salad; he was carefully extracting the pips. His nan had once told him they could never be digested, would stick inside and do terrible damage. I loved him for his dexterity and patience with his knife and fork. I'd finished my salad yonks ago, pips and all. I was hungry. I wanted my wild boar.

Peter might be forty-six, but he was six foot two and grizzled and muscled with it, in a dark-eyed, intelligent, broad-jawed kind of way. I adored him. I loved to be seen with him. "Muscular academic, not weedy academic" as my younger sister Clare once said. "Muscular academic is just a generally superior human being: everything works well from the brain to the toes. Weedy academic is when there isn't enough vital energy in the person, and the brain drains all the strength from the other parts." Well, Clare should know. Clare is only twenty-three, but of the superior human variety kind herself, vividly pretty, bright and competent — somewhere behind a heavy curtain of vibrant red hair, which she only parts for effect. She had her first degree at twenty. Now she's married to a Harvard professor of economics seconded to the United Nations. She can even cook. I gave up competing yonks ago. Though she too is capable of self-deception. I would say her husband was definitely of the weedy academic rather than the muscular academic type. And they have to live in Brussels.

The archduke's chauffeur had lost his way, and was parked on the corner trying to recover his nerve when Princip came running out of a café, planted his feet, aimed, and fired. Princip was nineteen — too young to hang. But they sent him to prison for life and, since he had TB to begin with, he only lasted three years. He died in 1918, in an Austrian prison. Or perhaps it was more than TB: perhaps they gave him a hard time, not learning till later, when the Austro-Hungarian Empire collapsed, that he was a hero. Poor Princip, too young to die — like so many other millions. Dying for love of a country.

"I love you," I said to Peter, my living man, progenitor already of three children by his chlorinated, swimming-coach wife.

"How much do you love me?"

"Inordinately! I love you with inordinate affection." It was a joke between us. Ind Aff!

"Inordinate affection is a sin," he'd told me. "According to the Wesleyans. John Wesley° himself worried about it to such a degree he ended up abbreviating it in his diaries, Ind Aff. He maintained that what he felt for young Sophy, the eighteen-year-old in his congregation, was not Ind Aff, which bears the spirit away from God towards the flesh: he insisted that what he felt was a pure and spiritual, if passionate, concern for her soul."

Peter said now, as we waited for our wild boar, and he picked over his pepper, "Your Ind Aff is my wife's sorrow, that's the trouble." He wanted, I knew, one of the long half-wrangles, half soul-sharings that we could keep going for hours, and led to piercing pains in the heart which could only be made better in bed. But our bedroom at the Hotel Europa was small and dark and looked out into the well of the building — a punishment room if ever there was one.

John Wesley (1703-1791): English religious leader and founder of Methodism.

(Reception staff did sometimes take against us.) When Peter had tried to change it in his quasi-Serbo-Croatian, they'd shrugged their Bosnian shoulders and pretended not to understand, so we'd decided to put up with it. I did not fancy pushing hard single beds together—it seemed easier not to have the pain in the heart in the first place. "Look," I said, "this holiday is supposed to be just the two of us, not Mrs. Piper as well. Shall we talk about something else?"

Do not think that the archduke's chauffeur was merely careless, an inefficient chauffeur, when he took the wrong turning. He was, I imagine, in a state of shock, fright, and confusion. There had been two previous attempts on the archduke's life since the cavalcade had entered town. The first was a bomb which got the car in front and killed its driver. The second was a shot fired by none other than young Princip, which had missed. Princip had vanished into the crowd and gone to sit down in a corner café and ordered coffee to calm his nerves. I expect his hand trembled at the best of times—he did have TB. (Not the best choice of assassin, but no doubt those who arrange these things have to make do with what they can get.) The archduke's chauffeur panicked, took the wrong road, realized what he'd done, and stopped to await rescue and instructions just outside the café where Princip sat drinking his coffee.

"What shall we talk about?" asked Peter, in even less of a good mood.

"The collapse of the Austro-Hungarian Empire?" I suggested. "How does 30 an empire collapse? Is there no money to pay the military or the police, so everyone goes home? Or what?" He liked to be asked questions.

"The Hungro-Austrarian Empire," said Peter to me, "didn't so much collapse as fail to exist any more. War destroys social organizations. The same thing happened after World War II. There being no organized bodies left between Moscow and London—and for London read Washington, then as now—it was left to these two to put in their own puppet governments. Yalta, 1944. It's taken the best part of forty-five years for nations of West and East Europe to remember who they are."

"Austro-Hungarian," I said, "not Hungro-Austrarian."

"I didn't say Hungro-Austrarian," he said.

"You did," I said.

"Didn't," he said. "What the hell are they doing about our wild boar? Are 35 they out in the hills shooting it?"

My sister Clare had been surprisingly understanding about Peter. When I worried about him being older, she pooh-poohed it; when I worried about him being married, she said, "Just go for it, sister. If you can unhinge a marriage, it's ripe for unhinging, it would happen sooner or later, it might as well be you. See a catch, go ahead and catch! Go for it!"

Princip saw the archduke's car parked outside, and went for it. Second chances are rare in life: they must be responded to. Except perhaps his second chance was missing in the first place? Should he have taken his cue from fate, and just sat and finished his coffee, and gone home to his mother? But what's a man to do when he loves his country? Fate delivered the archduke into his hands: how could he resist it? A parked car, a uniformed and medaled chest, the persecutor of his country—how could Princip not, believing God to be on his side, but see this as His intervention, push his coffee aside and leap to his feet?

Two waiters stood idly by and watched us waiting for our wild boar. One was young and handsome in a mountainous Bosnian way—flashing eyes, hooked nose, luxuriant black hair, sensuous mouth. He was about my age. He smiled. His teeth were even and white. I smiled back, and instead of the pain in the heart I'd become accustomed to as an erotic sensation, now felt, quite violently, an associated yet different pang which got my lower stomach. The true, the real pain of Ind Aff!

"Fancy him?" asked Peter.

"No," I said. "I just thought if I smiled the wild boar might come quicker." 40

The other waiter was older and gentler: his eyes were soft and kind. I thought he looked at me reproachfully. I could see why. In a world which for once, after centuries of savagery, was finally full of young men, unslaughtered, what was I doing with this man with thinning hair?

"What are you thinking of?" Professor Piper asked me. He liked to be in my head.

"How much I love you," I said automatically, and was finally aware how much I lied. "And about the archduke's assassination," I went on, to cover the kind of tremble in my head as I came to my senses, "and let's not forget his wife, she died too—how can you say World War I would have happened anyway. If Princip hadn't shot the archduke, something else, some undisclosed, unsuspected variable, might have come along and defused the whole political/military situation, and neither World War I nor II ever happened. We'll just never know, will we?"

I had my passport and my travelers' checks with me. (Peter felt it was less confusing if we each paid our own way.) I stood up, and took my raincoat from the peg.

"Where are you going?" he asked, startled.

"Home," I said. I kissed the top of his head, where it was balding. It smelt gently of chlorine, which may have come from thinking about his wife so much, 45 but might merely have been that he'd taken a shower that morning. ("The water all over Yugoslavia, though safe to drink, is unusually chlorinated": Guide Book.) As I left to catch a taxi to the airport the younger of the two waiters emerged from the kitchen with two piled plates of roasted wild boar, potatoes duchesse, and stewed peppers. ("Yugoslavian diet is unusually rich in proteins and fats": Guide Book.) I could tell from the glisten of oil that the food was no longer hot, and I was not tempted to stay, hungry though I was. Thus fate—or was it Bosnian willfulness?—confirmed the wisdom of my intent.

And that was how I fell out of love with my professor, in Sarajevo, a city to which I am grateful to this day, though I never got to see very much of it, because of the rain.

It was a silly sad thing to do, in the first place, to confuse mere passing academic ambition with love: to try and outdo my sister Clare. (Professor Piper was spiteful, as it happened, and did his best to have my thesis refused, but I went to appeal, which he never thought I'd dare, and won. I had a first-class mind after all.) A silly sad episode, which I regret. As silly and sad as Princip, poor young man, with his feverish mind, his bright tubercular cheeks, and his inordinate affection for his country, pushing aside his cup of coffee, leaping to his feet, taking his gun in both hands, planting his feet, aiming, and firing—one, two, three shots—and starting World War I. The first one missed, the second got the wife (never forget the wife), and the third got the archduke and a whole generation, and their children, and their children's children, and on and on forever. If he'd just hung on a bit, there in Sarajevo, that June day, he might have come to his senses. People do, sometimes quite quickly.

Considerations for Critical Thinking and Writing

1. FIRST RESPONSE. Do you agree with Weldon's first line, "This is a sad story"? Explain why or why not.

2. How does the rain establish the mood for the story in the first five paragraphs?

3. Characterize Peter. What details concerning him reveal his personality?

4. Describe the narrator's relationship with Peter. How do you think he regards her? Why is she attracted to him?

5. Why is Sarajevo important for the story's setting? What is the effect of having the story of Princip's assassination of the Archduke Franz Ferdinand and his wife woven through the plot?

6. Describe Mrs. Piper. Though she doesn't appear in the story, she does have an important role. What do you think her role is?

7. What is "Ind Aff"? Why is it an important element of this story?

8. What is the significance of the two waiters (paras. 38–40)? How do they affect the narrator?

9. Why does the narrator decide to go home (para. 46)? Do you think she makes a reasoned or an impulsive decision? Explain why you think so.

10. Discuss the relationship between the personal history and the public history recounted in the story. How are the two interconnected? Explain whether you think it is necessary to be familiar with the assassinations in Sarajevo before reading the story.

11. CRITICAL STRATEGIES. Read the section on cultural criticism (pp. 69–70) in Chapter 3, "Applying a Critical Strategy." How do you think a cultural critic might describe the nature of the narrator's relationship with her professor given the current attitudes on college campuses concerning teacher-student affairs?

POETRY

DIANE ACKERMAN (B. 1948)

A Fine, a Private Place   1983

He took her one day
under the blue horizon
where long sea fingers
parted like beads
hitched in the doorway   5
of an opium den,
and canyons mazed the deep
reef with hollows,
cul-de-sacs, and narrow boudoirs,
and had to ask twice   10
before she understood
his stroking her arm

with a marine feather
slobbery as aloe pulp
was wooing, or saw the octopus   15
in his swimsuit
stretch one tentacle
and ripple its silky bag.

While bubbles rose
like globs of mercury,   20
they made love
mask to mask, floating
with oceans of air between them,
she his sea-geisha
in an orange kimono   25
of belts and vests,
her lacquered hair waving,
as Indigo Hamlets
tattooed the vista,
and sunlight   30
cut through the water,
twisting its knives
into corridors of light.

His sandy hair
and sea-blue eyes,   35
his kelp-thin waist
and chest ribbed wider
than a sandbar
where muscles domed
clear and taut as shells   40
(freckled cowries,
flat, brawny scallops
the color of dawn),
his sea-battered hands
gripping her thighs   45
like tawny starfish
and drawing her close
as a pirate vessel
to let her board:
who was this she loved?   50

Overhead, sponges
sweating raw color
jutted from a coral arch,
Clown Wrasses°   *brightly colored tropical fish*
hovered like fireworks,   55
and somewhere an abalone opened
its silver wings.
Part of a lusty dream
under aspic, her hips rolled
like a Spanish galleon,   60

her eyes swam
and chest began to heave.
Gasps melted on the tide.
Knowing she would soon be
breathless as her tank, 65
he pumped his brine
deep within her,
letting sea water drive it
through petals
delicate as anemone veils 70
to the dark purpose
of a conch-shaped womb.
An ear to her loins
would have heard the sea roar.

When panting ebbed, 75
and he signaled *Okay?*
as lovers have asked,
land or waterbound
since time heaved ho,
he led her to safety: 80
shallower realms,
heading back toward
the boat's even keel,
though ocean still petted her
cell by cell, murmuring 85
along her legs and neck,
caressing her
with pale, endless arms.

Later, she thought often
of that blue boudoir, 90
pillow-soft and filled
with cascading light,
where together
they'd made a bell
that dumbly clanged 95
beneath the waves
and minutes lurched
like mountain goats.
She could still see
the quilted mosaics 100
that were fish
twitching spangles overhead,
still feel the ocean
inside and out, turning her
evolution around. 105

She thought of it miles
and fathoms away, often,
at odd moments: watching

the minnow snowflakes
dip against the windowframe,   110
holding a sponge
idly under tap-gush,
sinking her teeth
into the cleft
of a voluptuous peach.   115

CONSIDERATIONS FOR CRITICAL THINKING AND WRITING

1. FIRST RESPONSE. How is your response to this poem affected by the fact
   that the speaker is female?

2. Read Marvell's "To His Coy Mistress" (p. 230). To what in Marvell's poem
   does Ackerman's title allude? Explain how the allusion to Marvell is crucial
   to understanding Ackerman's poem.

3. Comment on the descriptive passages of "A Fine, a Private Place." Which
   images seem especially vivid to you? How do they contribute to the poem's
   meanings?

4. What are the speaker's reflections on her experience in lines 106–115? What
   echoes of Marvell do you hear in these lines?

KATERINA ANGHELÁKI-ROOKE (B. 1939)

Jealousy   *1990*

TRANSLATED BY RAE DALVEN

On Sundays he goes out with that woman
together they enjoy the rural
landscapes in ruins.
Here they are now, passing in front of the farms;
two dead pigs against the fence   5
stretch their hoofs in the afternoon;
light frost covers the mud
the snows have melted
but the earth is still mute
and alone before it becomes a butterfly.   10
Is their love peace,
is it tyranny?
The sun is a lemon color.
Who is she?
What is her face like?   15
Her breast?
The countryside gluts itself slowly with night
this geography has nothing
exotic; and he
holds the woman with so much passion   20
and they slip as one body into the room.

He removes his shirt
his tormented breast
smells of sweat and fresh air
little by little the dry branches retreat   25
in memory
and the landscape starts anew within them
in full spring.

CONSIDERATIONS FOR CRITICAL THINKING AND WRITING

1. FIRST RESPONSE. Comment on the significance of the poem's title. Would you read the poem any differently if it were untitled?
2. Describe the speaker. Is she a sympathetic figure? Why or why not?
3. What do the images of the landscape contribute to the poem's meanings?
4. Explain whether or not you think this poem is more about love or hatred.

ROBERT BROWNING (1812–1889)
My Last Duchess   *1842*

Ferrara°

That's my last Duchess painted on the wall,
Looking as if she were alive. I call
That piece a wonder, now: Frà Pandolf's° hands
Worked busily a day, and there she stands.
Will't please you sit and look at her? I said   5
"Frà Pandolf" by design, for never read
Strangers like you that pictured countenance,
The depth and passion of its earnest glance,
But to myself they turned (since none puts by
The curtain I have drawn for you, but I)   10
And seemed as they would ask me, if they durst,
How such a glance came there; so, not the first
Are you to turn and ask thus. Sir, 'twas not
Her husband's presence only, called that spot
Of joy into the Duchess' cheek: perhaps   15
Frà Pandolf chanced to say "Her mantle laps
Over my lady's wrist too much," or "Paint
Must never hope to reproduce the faint
Half-flush that dies along her throat": such stuff
Was courtesy, she thought, and cause enough   20

Ferrara: In the sixteenth century, the duke of this Italian city arranged to marry a second time after the mysterious death of his very young first wife.   3 *Frà Pandolf:* A fictitious artist.

For calling up that spot of joy. She had
A heart—how shall I say?—too soon made glad,
Too easily impressed; she liked whate'er
She looked on, and her looks went everywhere.
Sir, 'twas all one! My favor at her breast,   25
The dropping of the daylight in the West,
The bough of cherries some officious fool
Broke in the orchard for her, the white mule
She rode with round the terrace—all and each
Would draw from her alike the approving speech,   30
Or blush, at least. She thanked men,—good! but thanked
Somehow—I know not how—as if she ranked
My gift of a nine-hundred-years-old name
With anybody's gift. Who'd stoop to blame
This sort of trifling? Even had you skill   35
In speech—which I have not—to make your will
Quite clear to such an one, and say, "Just this
Or that in you disgusts me; here you miss,
Or there exceed the mark"—and if she let
Herself be lessoned so, nor plainly set   40
Her wits to yours, forsooth, and made excuse,
—E'en then would be some stooping; and I choose
Never to stoop. Oh sir, she smiled, no doubt,
Whene'er I passed her; but who passed without
Much the same smile? This grew; I gave commands;   45
Then all smiles stopped together. There she stands
As if alive. Will't please you rise? We'll meet
The company below, then. I repeat,
The Count your master's known munificence
Is ample warrant that no just pretense   50
Of mine for dowry will be disallowed;
Though his fair daughter's self, as I avowed
At starting, is my object. Nay, we'll go
Together down, sir. Notice Neptune, though,
Taming a sea-horse, thought a rarity,   55
Which Claus of Innsbruck° cast in bronze for me!

Claus of Innsbruck: Also a fictitious artist.

CONSIDERATIONS FOR CRITICAL THINKING AND WRITING

1. FIRST RESPONSE. What do you think happened to the duchess?

2. To whom is the duke addressing his remarks about the duchess in this poem? What is ironic about the situation?

3. Why was the duke unhappy with his first wife? What does this reveal about the duke? What does the poem's title suggest about his attitude toward women in general?

4. What seems to be the visitor's response (lines 53–54) to the duke's account of his first wife?

SALLY CROFT (B. 1935)
Home-Baked Bread

1981

Nothing gives a household a greater sense of stability and common comfort than the aroma of cooling bread. Begin, if you like, with a loaf of whole wheat, which requires neither sifting nor kneading, and go on from there to more cunning triumphs.

— The Joy of Cooking

What is it she is not saying?
Cunning triumphs. It rings
of insinuation. Step into my kitchen,
I have prepared a cunning triumph
for you. Spices and herbs   5
sealed in this porcelain jar,

a treasure of my great-aunt
who sat up past midnight
in her Massachusetts bedroom
when the moon was dark. Come,   10
rest your feet. I'll make
you tea with honey and slices

of warm bread spread with peach butter.
I picked the fruit this morning
still fresh with dew. The fragrance   15
is seductive? I hoped you would say that.
See how the heat rises
when the bread opens. Come,

we'll eat together, the small flakes
have scarcely any flavor. What cunning   20
triumphs we can discover in my upstairs room
where peach trees breathe their sweetness
beside the open window and
sun lies like honey on the floor.

CONSIDERATIONS FOR CRITICAL THINKING AND WRITING

1. FIRST RESPONSE. Why does the speaker in this poem seize on the phrase "cunning triumphs" from the *Joy of Cooking* excerpt?
2. Distinguish between the voice we hear in lines 1–3 and the second voice in lines 3–24. Who is the "you" in the poem?
3. Why is "insinuation" an especially appropriate word choice in line 3?
4. How do the images in lines 20–24 bring together all the senses evoked in the preceding lines?
5. Write a paragraph that describes the sensuous (and perhaps sensual) qualities of a food you enjoy.

E. E. Cummings (1894–1962)

since feeling is first 1926

since feeling is first
who pays any attention
to the syntax of things
will never wholly kiss you;

wholly to be a fool   5
while Spring is in the world

my blood approves,
and kisses are a better fate
than wisdom
lady i swear by all flowers. Don't cry   10
— the best gesture of my brain is less than
your eyelids' flutter which says

we are for each other: then
laugh, leaning back in my arms
for life's not a paragraph   15

And death i think is no parenthesis

Considerations for Critical Thinking and Writing

1. **first response.** Why does the speaker prefer feeling to rational thought?

2. Why do you suppose line 10 reads "i swear by all flowers" rather than "i swear to God"?

3. How might this poem, though unconventional in style, be read as a conventional *carpe diem* poem?

Emily Dickinson (1830–1886)

Wild Nights — Wild Nights! c. 1861

Wild Nights — Wild Nights!
Were I with thee
Wild Nights should be
Our luxury!

Futile — the Winds —   5

To a Heart in port —
Done with the Compass —
Done with the Chart!

Rowing in Eden —
Ah, the Sea!   10
Might I but moor — Tonight —
In Thee!

CONSIDERATIONS FOR CRITICAL THINKING AND WRITING

1. FIRST RESPONSE. Thomas Wentworth Higginson, Dickinson's mentor, once said he was afraid that some "malignant" readers might "read into [a poem like this] more than that virgin recluse ever dreamed of putting there." What do you think?

2. Look up the meaning of "luxury" in a dictionary. Why does this word work especially well here?

3. Given the imagery of the final stanza, do you think the speaker is a man or a woman? Explain why.

4. CRITICAL STRATEGIES. Read the section on psychological criticism (pp. 64–66) in Chapter 3, "Applying a Critical Strategy." What do you think this poem reveals about the author's personal psychology?

JOHN DONNE (1572–1631)

The Flea   *1633*

Mark but this flea, and mark in this°
How little that which thou deny'st me is;
It sucked me first, and now sucks thee,
And in this flea our two bloods mingled be;
Thou know'st that this cannot be said   5
A sin, nor shame, nor loss of maidenhead,
　　Yet this enjoys before it woo,
　　And pampered swells with one blood made of two,
　　And this, alas, is more than we would do.°

Oh stay, three lives in one flea spare,   10
Where we almost, yea more than, married are.
This flea is you and I, and this
Our marriage bed, and marriage temple is;
Though parents grudge, and you, we're met
And cloistered in these living walls of jet.   15
　　Though use° make you apt to kill me,   *habit*
　　Let not to that, self-murder added be,
　　And sacrilege, three sins in killing three.

Cruel and sudden, hast thou since
Purpled thy nail in blood of innocence?   20
Wherein could this flea guilty be,
Except in that drop which it sucked from thee?
Yet thou triumph'st, and say'st that thou
Find'st not thyself, nor me, the weaker now;
'Tis true; then learn how false, fears be;   25
　　Just so much honor, when thou yield'st to me,
　　Will waste, as this flea's death took life from thee.

1 *mark in this:* Take note of the moral lesson in this object.   9 *more than we would do:* That is, if we do not join our blood in conceiving a child.

CONSIDERATIONS FOR CRITICAL THINKING AND WRITING

1. FIRST RESPONSE. Paraphrase the poem. What's going on here?

2. What is the speaker's argument? How is it related to a *carpe diem* tradition?

3. Explain what you think might be the silent listener's response to the speaker.

ROBERT HASS (B. 1941)

A Story About the Body   1989

The young composer, working that summer at an artists' colony, had watched her for a week. She was Japanese, a painter, almost sixty, and he thought he was in love with her. He loved her work, and her work was like the way she moved her body, used her hands, looked at him directly when she made amused and considered answers to his questions. One night, walking back from a concert, they came to her door and she turned to him and said, "I think you would like to have me. I would like that too, but I must tell you that I have had a double mastectomy," and when he didn't understand, "I've lost both my breasts." The radiance that he had carried around in his belly and chest cavity — like music — withered very quickly, and he made himself look at her when he said, "I'm sorry. I don't think I could." He walked back to his own cabin through the pines, and in the morning he found a small blue bowl on the porch outside his door. It looked to be full of rose petals, but he found when he picked it up that the rose petals were on top; the rest of the bowl — she must have swept them from the corners of her studio — was full of dead bees.

CONSIDERATIONS FOR CRITICAL THINKING AND WRITING

1. FIRST RESPONSE. How might this prose poem also be described as a remarkable short story?

2. What is it that the young composer loves about the Japanese woman?

3. Comment on the significance of the bowl the woman leaves for the young man. How does this affect the tone of the poem?

ROBERT HERRICK (1591–1674)

To the Virgins, to Make Much of Time   1648

Gather ye rose-buds while ye may,
  Old Time is still a-flying;
And this same flower that smiles today,
  Tomorrow will be dying.

The glorious lamp of heaven, the sun,   5
  The higher he's a-getting,
The sooner will his race be run,
  And nearer he's to setting.

That age is best which is the first,
    When youth and blood are warmer; 10
But being spent, the worse, and worst
    Times still succeed the former.

Then be not coy, but use your time,
    And while ye may, go marry;
For having lost but once your prime, 15
    You may for ever tarry.

CONSIDERATIONS FOR CRITICAL THINKING AND WRITING

1. FIRST RESPONSE. Would there be any change in meaning if the title of this poem were "To Young Women, to Make Much of Time"? Do you think the poem can apply to young men too?

2. What do the virgins have in common with the flowers (lines 1–4) and the course of the day (5–8)?

3. How does the speaker develop his argument? What will happen to the virgins if they don't "marry"? Paraphrase the poem.

4. What is the tone of the speaker's advice?

LANGSTON HUGHES

Rent-Party° Shout: For a Lady Dancer   *1930*

Whip it to a jelly!
Too bad Jim!
Mamie's got ma man —
An' I can't find him.
Shake that thing! O! 5
Shake it slow!
That man I love is
Mean an' low.
Pistol an' razor!
Razor an' gun! 10
If I sees ma man he'd
Better run —
For I'll shoot him in de shoulder,
Else I'll cut him down,
Cause I knows I can find him 15
When he's in de ground —
Then can't no other women
Have him layin' round.
So play it, Mr. Nappy!
Yo' music's fine! 20
I'm gonna kill that
Man o' mine!

Rent-Party: In Harlem during the 1920s, parties were given that charged admission to raise money for rent.

CONSIDERATIONS FOR CRITICAL THINKING AND WRITING

1. FIRST RESPONSE. Describe the type of music you think might be played at this party today.

2. In what sense is this poem a kind of "Shout"?

3. How is the speaker's personality characterized by her use of language?

4. How does Hughes's use of short lines affect your reading of the poem?

JOHN KEATS (1795–1821)

La Belle Dame sans Merci° 1819

O what can ail thee, knight-at-arms,
    Alone and palely loitering?
The sedge has withered from the lake,
    And no birds sing.

O what can ail thee, knight-at-arms, 5
    So haggard and so woe-begone?
The squirrel's granary is full,
    And the harvest's done.

I see a lily on thy brow,
    With anguish moist and fever dew, 10
And on thy cheeks a fading rose
    Fast withereth too.

I met a lady in the meads,
    Full beautiful—a faery's child,
Her hair was long, her foot was light, 15
    And her eyes were wild.

I made a garland for her head,
    And bracelets too, and fragrant zone;° *belt*
She looked at me as she did love,
    And made sweet moan. 20

I set her on my pacing steed,
    And nothing else saw all day long,
For sidelong would she bend, and sing
    A faery's song.

She found me roots of relish sweet, 25
    And honey wild, and manna dew,
And sure in language strange she said,
    "I love thee true."

La Belle Dame sans Merci: This title is borrowed from a medieval poem and means "The Beautiful Lady without Mercy."

She took me to her elfin grot,
    And there she wept, and sighed full sore,   30
And there I shut her wild wild eyes
    With kisses four.

And there she lullèd me asleep,
    And there I dreamed — Ah! woe betide!
The latest° dream I ever dreamed   *last* 35
    On the cold hill side.

I saw pale kings and princes too,
    Pale warriors, death-pale were they all;
They cried — "La Belle Dame sans Merci
    Hath thee in thrall!"   40

I saw their starved lips in the gloam,
    With horrid warning gapèd wide,
And I awoke and found me here,
    On the cold hill's side.

And this is why I sojourn here,   45
    Alone and palely loitering,
Though the sedge has withered from the lake,
    And no birds sing.

CONSIDERATIONS FOR CRITICAL THINKING AND WRITING

1. FIRST RESPONSE. The lady is a familiar character in literature, a "femme fatale." Characterize her. Have you encountered other versions of her in literature or film?

2. How do the first three stanzas of this ballad serve to characterize the knight who describes his experience with the lady?

3. What is the effect of the shortened line in each stanza of this ballad?

JANE KENYON (1947–1995)

Surprise   *1996*

He suggests pancakes at the local diner,
followed by a walk in search of mayflowers,
while friends convene at the house
bearing casseroles and a cake, their cars
pulled close along the sandy shoulders   5
of the road, where tender ferns unfurl
in the ditches, and this year's budding leaves
push last year's spectral leaves from the tips
of the twigs of the ash trees. The gathering
itself is not what astounds her, but the casual   10
accomplishment with which he has lied.

CONSIDERATIONS FOR CRITICAL THINKING AND WRITING

1. FIRST RESPONSE. Does it matter that this poem is set in the spring?

2. Consider the connotative meaning of "ash trees." Why are they particularly appropriate?

3. Why do you suppose Kenyon uses "astounds" rather than "surprises" in line 10? Use a dictionary to help you determine the possible reasons for this choice.

4. Discuss the irony in the poem.

CHRISTOPHER MARLOWE (1564–1593)

The Passionate Shepherd to His Love   *1599?*

Come live with me and be my love,
And we will all the pleasure prove
That valleys, groves, hills, and fields,
Woods, or steepy mountain yields.

And we will sit upon the rocks,   5
Seeing the shepherds feed their flocks,
By shallow rivers to whose falls
Melodious birds sing madrigals.

And I will make thee beds of roses
And a thousand fragrant posies,   10
A cap of flowers, and a kirtle°
Embroidered all with leaves of myrtle;

A gown made of the finest wool
Which from our pretty lambs we pull;
Fair lined slippers for the cold,   15
With buckles of the purest gold;

A belt of straw and ivy buds,
With coral clasps and amber studs:
And if these pleasures may thee move,
Come live with me, and be my love.   20

The shepherd swains shall dance and sing
For thy delight each May morning:
If these delights thy mind may move,
Then live with me and be my love.

11 *kirtle:* Dress or skirt.

CONSIDERATIONS FOR CRITICAL THINKING AND WRITING

1. FIRST RESPONSE. Do you find the speaker appealing? Why or why not?

2. Why do you suppose the poem is set in May? How is the time of year related to the speaker's plea?

3. Discuss the poem's tone. What images serve to establish the tone?

JOAN MURRAY (B. 1945)
Play-By-Play   *1997*

Yaddo°

Would it surprise the young men
playing softball on the hill to hear the women
on the terrace admiring their bodies:
the slim waist of the pitcher, the strength
of the runner's legs, the torso of the catcher   5
rising off his knees to toss the ball back to the mound?
Would it embarrass them
to hear two women, sitting together after dinner,
praising even their futile motions:
the flex of a batter's hips   10
before his missed swing, the wide-spread stride
of a man picked off his base, the intensity
on the new man's face
as he waits on deck and fans the air?

Would it annoy them, the way some women   15
take offense when men caress them with their eyes?
And why should it surprise me that these women,
well past sixty, haven't put aside desire
but sit at ease and in pleasure,
watching the young men move above the rose garden   20
where the marble Naiads
pose and yawn in their fountain?
Who better than these women, with their sweaters
draped across their shoulders, their perspectives
honed from years of lovers, to recognize   25
the beauty that would otherwise
go unnoticed on this hill?
And will it compromise their pleasure
if I sit down at their table to listen
to the play-by-play and see it through their eyes?   30

Would it distract the young men if they realized
that three women laughing softly on the terrace
above closed books and half-filled wineglasses
are moving beside them on the field?
Would they want to know how they've been   35
held to the light till some motion or expression
showed the unsuspected loveliness
in a common shape or face?
Wouldn't they have liked to see how they looked
down there, as they stood for a moment at the plate,   40
bathed in the light of perfect expectation,

Yaddo: An artists' colony in Saratoga Springs, New York.

before their shadows lengthened, before they
walked together up the darkened hill,
so beautiful they would not have
recognized themselves?   45

CONSIDERATIONS FOR CRITICAL THINKING AND WRITING

1. FIRST RESPONSE. What effect does this poem have on you? What do you
   think of older women admiring the bodies of young men?

2. What do you make of the setting — an artists' colony? How is the setting
   relevant to the poem's theme?

3. Try answering each question raised by the speaker. Is your response at all
   affected by your being male or female?

SHARON OLDS (B. 1942)

Sex without Love   1984

How do they do it, the ones who make love
without love? Beautiful as dancers,
gliding over each other like ice skaters
over the ice, fingers hooked
inside each other's bodies, faces   5
red as steak, wine, wet as the
children at birth whose mothers are going to
give them away. How do they come to the
come to the   come to the   God   come to the
still waters, and not love   10
the one who came there with them, light
rising slowly as steam off their joined
skin? These are the true religious,
the purists, the pros, the ones who will not
accept a false Messiah, love the   15
priest instead of the God. They do not
mistake the lover for their own pleasure,
they are like great runners: they know they are alone
with the road surface, the cold, the wind,
the fit of their shoes, their over-all cardio-   20
vascular health — just factors, like the partner
in the bed, and not the truth, which is the
single body alone in the universe
against its own best time.

CONSIDERATIONS FOR CRITICAL THINKING AND WRITING

1. FIRST RESPONSE. What is the nature of the question asked by the speaker in
   the poem's first two lines? What is being asked here?

2. What is the effect of describing the lovers as athletes? How do these
   descriptions and phrases reveal the speaker's tone toward the lovers?

3. To what extent does the title suggest the central meaning of this poem? Try
   to create some alternative titles that are equally descriptive.

BARBARA REBECCA (B. 1957)

Junior Year Abroad   2000

We were amateurs, that winter in Paris.

The summer before we agreed:
he would come over to keep me company at Christmas.
But the shelf life of my promise expired
before the date on his airline ticket.   5
So there we were, together under the muslin winter sky.
I was alone, inside dark hair, inside foreign blankets, against white
    sheets
swirled like a cocoon, covering my bare skin,
keeping me apart
The invited man snored beside me not knowing   10
I didn't love him anymore.

On the first night I tried,
pert and perky as a circus pony, waiting at the airport gate,
to be again as I once had been.
But betrayal, the snake under the evergreen,   15
threw me into dreams of floods and nightmares of dying birds.

You see, a new boy just last week
had raised my shy hand to his warm mouth
and kissed the inside of my palm as I thought "this is impossible."
Too close to Christmas, too soon, too dangerous.   20

Deceiving this man stirring in his sleep
is even more dangerous.
See him opening his eyes, looking at my face,
dropping his eyes to my breasts and smiling
as if he were seeing two old friends? Dangerous.   25
When I move away and hold the sheet against
myself, he, sensing what this means,
refuses, adamantly polite, to traffic in the currency of my rejection.
He made a journey. I offered a welcome.
Why should he give me up?   30

CONSIDERATIONS FOR CRITICAL THINKING AND WRITING

1. FIRST RESPONSE. This poem is about strength and dominance as much as it
   is about love and attraction. Discuss the ways in which the two characters
   are vying for control.

2. Why is the setting important? How might the sense of the poem be different if this were happening during a typical school year as opposed to
   "Junior Year Abroad"?

3. Do you think the girl has the right to reject her old boyfriend under these
   circumstances? Does the old boyfriend have the right to expect a "welcome" since he was invited to visit?

4. The girl is wrapped in sheets that are like a "cocoon." What does it suggest
   about the changes she is experiencing during this encounter?

ALBERTO RÍOS (B. 1952)

Seniors 1985

William cut a hole in his Levi's pocket
so he could flop himself out in class
behind the girls so the other guys
could see and shit what guts we all said.
All Konga wanted to do over and over   5
was the rubber band trick, but he showed
everyone how, so nobody wanted to see
anymore and one day he cried, just cried
until his parents took him away forever.
Maya had a Hotpoint refrigerator standing   10
in his living room, just for his family to show
anybody who came that they could afford it.

Me, I got a French kiss, finally, in the catholic
darkness, my tongue's farthest half vacationing
loudly in another mouth like a man in Bermudas,   15
and my body jumped against a flagstone wall,
I could feel it through her thin, almost
nonexistent body: I had, at that moment, that moment,
a hot girl on a summer night, the best of all
the things we tried to do. Well, she   20
let me kiss her, anyway, all over.

Or it was just a flagstone wall
with a flaw in the stone, an understanding cavity
for burning young men with smooth dreams —
the true circumstance is gone, the true   25
circumstances about us all then
are gone. But when I kissed her, all water,
she would close her eyes, and they into somewhere
would disappear. Whether she was there
or not, I remember her, clearly, and she moves   30
around the room, sometimes, until I sleep.

I have lain on the desert in watch
low in the back of a pick-up truck
for nothing in particular, for stars, for
the things behind stars, and nothing comes   35
more than the moment: always now, here in a truck,
the moment again to dream of making love and sweat,
this time to a woman, or even to all of them
in some allowable way, to those boys, then,
who couldn't cry, to the girls before they were   40
women, to friends, me on my back, the sky over me
pressing its simple weight into her body
on me, into the bodies of them all, on me.

CONSIDERATIONS FOR CRITICAL THINKING AND WRITING

1. FIRST RESPONSE. Comment on the use of slang in the poem. Does it surprise you? How does it characterize the speaker?

2. How does the language of the final stanza differ from that of the first stanza? To what purpose?

3. Write an essay that discusses the speaker's attitudes toward sex and life. How are they related?

WILLIAM SHAKESPEARE (1564–1616)

My mistress' eyes are nothing like the sun   *1609*

My mistress' eyes are nothing like the sun;
Coral is far more red than her lips' red;
If snow be white, why then her breasts are dun;
If hairs be wires, black wires grow on her head.
I have seen roses damasked red and white,   5
But no such roses see I in her cheeks;
And in some perfumes is there more delight
Than in the breath that from my mistress reeks.
I love to hear her speak, yet well I know
That music hath a far more pleasing sound;   10
I grant I never saw a goddess go:
My mistress, when she walks, treads on the ground.
   And yet, by heaven, I think my love as rare
   As any she,° belied with false compare.   *lady*

CONSIDERATIONS FOR CRITICAL THINKING AND WRITING

1. FIRST RESPONSE. What does "mistress" mean in this sonnet? Write a description of this particular mistress based on the images used in the sonnet.

2. What sort of person is the speaker? Does he truly love the woman he describes?

3. In what sense is this sonnet about poetry as well as love?

CATHY SONG (B. 1955)

The White Porch   *1983*

I wrap the blue towel
after washing,
around the damp
weight of hair, bulky
as a sleeping cat,   5
and sit out on the porch.

Still dripping water,
it'll be dry by supper,
by the time the dust
settles off your shoes,   10
though it's only five
past noon. Think
of the luxury: how to use
the afternoon like the stretch
of lawn spread before me.   15
There's the laundry,
sun-warm clothes at twilight,
and the mountain of beans
in my lap. Each one,
I'll break and snap   20
thoughtfully in half.

But there is this slow arousal.
The small buttons
of my cotton blouse
are pulling away from my body.   25
I feel the strain of threads,
the swollen magnolias
heavy as a flock of birds
in the tree. Already,
the orange sponge cake   30
is rising in the oven.
I know you'll say it makes
your mouth dry
and I'll watch you
drench your slice of it   35
in canned peaches
and lick the plate clean.

So much hair, my mother
used to say, grabbing
the thick braided rope   40
in her hands while we washed
the breakfast dishes, discussing
dresses and pastries.
My mind often elsewhere
as we did the morning chores together.   45
Sometimes, a few strands
would catch in her gold ring.
I worked hard then,
anticipating the hour
when I would let the rope down   50
at night, strips of sheets,
knotted and tied,
while she slept in tight blankets.
My hair, freshly washed
like a measure of wealth,   55

like a bridal veil.
Crouching in the grass,
you would wait for the signal,
for the movement of curtains
before releasing yourself   60
from the shadow of moths.
Cloth, hair and hands,
smuggling you in.

CONSIDERATIONS FOR CRITICAL THINKING AND WRITING

1. FIRST RESPONSE. How is hair made erotic in this poem? Discuss the images
   that you deem especially effective.
2. Who is the "you" that the speaker refers to in each stanza?
3. What role does the mother play in this poem about desire?
4. Why do you think the poem is titled "The White Porch"?

RICHARD WILBUR (B. 1921)

A Late Aubade   *1968*

You could be sitting now in a carrel
Turning some liver-spotted page,
Or rising in an elevator-cage
Toward Ladies' Apparel.
You could be planting a raucous bed   5
Of salvia, in rubber gloves,
Or lunching through a screed of someone's loves
With pitying head,

Or making some unhappy setter
Heel, or listening to a bleak   10
Lecture on Schoenberg's serial technique.
Isn't this better?

Think of all the time you are not
Wasting, and would not care to waste,
Such things, thank God, not being to your taste.   15
Think what a lot

Of time, by woman's reckoning,
You've saved, and so may spend on this,
You who had rather lie in bed and kiss
Than anything.   20

It's almost noon, you say? If so,
Time flies, and I need not rehearse
The rosebuds-theme of centuries of verse.
If you *must* go,

Wait for a while, then slip downstairs   25
And bring us up some chilled white wine,
And some blue cheese, and crackers, and some fine
Ruddy-skinned pears.

CONSIDERATIONS FOR CRITICAL THINKING AND WRITING

1. FIRST RESPONSE. Explain whether or not you find the speaker appealing.

2. An *aubade* is a song about lovers parting at dawn, but in this "late aubade," "It's almost noon." Is there another way of reading the adjective *late* in the title?

3. How does the speaker's diction characterize both him and his lover? What sort of lives do they live? What does the casual allusion to Herrick's poem (line 23) reveal about them?

4. What is the effect of using "liver-spotted page," "elevator-cage," "raucous bed," "screed," "unhappy setter," and "bleak / Lecture" to describe the woman's activities?

DRAMA

DAVID IVES (B. 1950)

Born in Chicago and educated at Northwestern University and the Yale Drama School, David Ives writes for television, film, and opera and has created a number of one-act plays for the annual comedy festival of Manhattan Punch Line, where *Sure Thing* was first produced in 1988. *All in the Timing* (1993), a series of one-act plays that includes *Sure Thing,* was awarded the Outer Critics' Circle Award for playwriting. His other plays include *Don Juan in Chicago* (1995) and *Ancient History* (1995).

Sure Thing   *1988*

CHARACTERS

Bill and *Betty,* both in their late twenties

SETTING: *A café table, with a couple of chairs*

   Betty, reading at the table. An empty chair opposite her. Bill enters.

Bill: Excuse me. Is this chair taken?
Betty: Excuse me?
Bill: Is this taken?
Betty: Yes it is.
Bill: Oh. Sorry.

Betty: Sure thing. *(A bell rings softly.)*
Bill: Excuse me. Is this chair taken?
Betty: Excuse me?
Bill: Is this taken?
Betty: No, but I'm expecting somebody in a minute.
Bill: Oh. Thanks anyway.
Betty: Sure thing. *(A bell rings softly.)*
Bill: Excuse me. Is this chair taken?
Betty: No, but I'm expecting somebody very shortly.
Bill: Would you mind if I sit here till he or she or it comes?
Betty (glances at her watch): They seem to be pretty late. . . .
Bill: You never know who you might be turning down.
Betty: Sorry. Nice try, though.
Bill: Sure thing. *(Bell.)* Is this seat taken?
Betty: No it's not.
Bill: Would you mind if I sit here?
Betty: Yes I would.
Bill: Oh. *(Bell.)* Is this chair taken?
Betty: No it's not.
Bill: Would you mind if I sit here?
Betty: No. Go ahead.
Bill: Thanks. *(He sits. She continues reading.)* Everyplace else seems to be taken.
Betty: Mm-hm.
Bill: Great place.
Betty: Mm-hm.
Bill: What's the book?
Betty: I just wanted to read in quiet, if you don't mind.
Bill: No. Sure thing. *(Bell.)*
Bill: Everyplace else seems to be taken.
Betty: Mm-hm.
Bill: Great place for reading.
Betty: Yes, I like it.
Bill: What's the book?
Betty: *The Sound and the Fury.*
Bill: Oh. Hemingway. *(Bell.)* What's the book?
Betty: *The Sound and the Fury.*
Bill: Oh. Faulkner.
Betty: Have you read it?
Bill: Not . . . actually. I've sure read *about* . . . it, though. It's supposed to be great.
Betty: It is great.
Bill: I hear it's great. *(Small pause.)* Waiter? *(Bell.)* What's the book?
Betty: *The Sound and the Fury.*
Bill: Oh. Faulkner.
Betty: Have you read it?
Bill: I'm a Mets fan, myself. *(Bell.)*
Betty: Have you read it?
Bill: Yeah, I read it in college.
Betty: Where was college?
Bill: I went to Oral Roberts University. *(Bell.)*

Betty: Where was college?

Bill: I was lying. I never really went to college. I just like to party. *(Bell.)*

Betty: Where was college?

Bill: Harvard.

Betty: Do you like Faulkner?

Bill: I love Faulkner. I spent a whole winter reading him once.

Betty: I've just started.

Bill: I was so excited after ten pages that I went out and bought everything else he wrote. One of the greatest reading experiences of my life. I mean, all that incredible psychological understanding. Page after page of gorgeous prose. His profound grasp of the mystery of time and human existence. The smells of the earth . . . What do you think?

Betty: I think it's pretty boring. *(Bell.)*

Bill: What's the book?

Betty: *The Sound and the Fury.*

Bill: Oh! Faulkner!

Betty: Do you like Faulkner?

Bill: I love Faulkner.

Betty: He's incredible.

Bill: I spent a whole winter reading him once.

Betty: I was so excited after ten pages that I went out and bought everything else he wrote.

Bill: All that incredible psychological understanding.

Betty: And the prose is so gorgeous.

Bill: And the way he's grasped the mystery of time —

Betty: — and human existence. I can't believe I've waited this long to read him.

Bill: You never know. You might not have liked him before.

Betty: That's true.

Bill: You might not have been ready for him. You have to hit these things at the right moment or it's no good.

Betty: That's happening to me.

Bill: It's all in the timing. *(Small pause.)* My name's Bill, by the way.

Betty: I'm Betty.

Bill: Hi.

Betty: Hi. *(Small pause.)*

Bill: Yes I thought reading Faulkner was . . . a great experience.

Betty: Yes. *(Small pause.)*

Bill: *The Sound and the Fury* . . . *(Another small pause.)*

Betty: Well. Onwards and upwards. *(She goes back to her book.)*

Bill: Waiter —? *(Bell.)* You have to hit these things at the right moment or it's no good.

Betty: That's happened to me.

Bill: It's all in the timing. My name's Bill, by the way.

Betty: I'm Betty.

Bill: Hi.

Betty: Hi.

Bill: Do you come in here a lot?

Betty: Actually I'm just in town for two days from Pakistan.

Bill: Oh. Pakistan. *(Bell.)* My name's Bill, by the way.

Betty: I'm Betty.

Bill: Hi.

Betty: Hi.

Bill: Do you come here a lot?

Betty: Every once in a while. Do you?

Bill: Not much anymore. Not as much as I used to. Before my nervous break-down. *(Bell.)* Do you come in here a lot?

Betty: Why are you asking?

Bill: Just interested.

Betty: Are you really interested, or do you just want to pick me up?

Bill: No, I'm really interested.

Betty: Why would you be interested in whether I come in here a lot?

Bill: Just . . . getting acquainted.

Betty: Maybe you're only interested for the sake of making small talk long enough to ask me back to your place to listen to some music, or because you've just rented some great tape for your VCR, or because you've got some terrific unknown Django Reinhardt record, only all you'll really want to do is fuck — which you won't do very well — after which you'll go into the bathroom and pee very loudly, then pad into the kitchen and get yourself a beer from the refrigerator without asking me whether I'd like anything, and then you'll proceed to lie back down beside me and confess that you've got a girlfriend named Stephanie who's away at medical school in Belgium for a year, and that you've been involved with her — *off and on* — in what you'll call a very "intricate" relationship, for about *seven YEARS.* None of which *interests* me, mister!

Bill: Okay. *(Bell.)* Do you come in here a lot?

Betty: Every other day, I think.

Bill: I come in here quite a lot and I don't remember seeing you.

Betty: I guess we must be on different schedules.

Bill: Missed connections.

Betty: Yes. Different time zones.

Bill: Amazing how you can live right next door to somebody in this town and never even know it.

Betty: I know.

Bill: City life.

Betty: It's crazy.

Bill: We probably pass each other in the street every day. Right in front of this place, probably.

Betty: Yep.

Bill (looks around): Well, the waiters here sure seem to be in some different time zone. I can't seem to locate one anywhere . . . Waiter! *(He looks back.)* So what do you — *(He sees that she's gone back to her book.)*

Betty: I beg pardon?

Bill: Nothing. Sorry. *(Bell.)*

Betty: I guess we must be on different schedules.

Bill: Missed connections.

Betty: Yes. Different time zones.

Bill: Amazing how you can live right next door to somebody in this town and never even know it.

Betty: I know.

Bill: City life.

Betty: It's crazy.

Bill: You weren't waiting for somebody when I came in, were you?

Betty: Actually, I was.

Bill: Oh. Boyfriend?

Betty: Sort of.

Bill: What's a sort-of boyfriend?

Betty: My husband.

Bill: Ah-ha. *(Bell.)* You weren't waiting for somebody when I came in, were you?

Betty: Actually I was.

Bill: Oh. Boyfriend?

Betty: Sort of.

Bill: What's a sort-of boyfriend?

Betty: We were meeting here to break up.

Bill: Mm-hm . . . *(Bell.)* What's a sort-of boyfriend?

Betty: My lover. Here she comes right now! *(Bell.)*

Bill: You weren't waiting for somebody when I came in, were you?

Betty: No, just reading.

Bill: Sort of a sad occupation for a Friday night, isn't it? Reading here, all by yourself?

Betty: Do you think so?

Bill: Well sure. I mean, what's a good-looking woman like you doing out alone on a Friday night?

Betty: Trying to keep away from lines like that.

Bill: No, listen — *(Bell.)* You weren't waiting for somebody when I came in, were you?

Betty: No, just reading.

Bill: Sort of a sad occupation for a Friday night, isn't it? Reading here all by yourself?

Betty: I guess it is, in a way.

Bill: What's a good-looking woman like you doing out alone on a Friday night anyway? No offense, but . . .

Betty: I'm out alone on a Friday night for the first time in a very long time.

Bill: Oh.

Betty: You see, I just recently ended a relationship.

Bill: Oh.

Betty: Of rather long standing.

Bill: I'm sorry. *(Small pause.)* Well listen, since reading by yourself *is* such a sad occupation for a Friday night, would you like to go elsewhere?

Betty: No . . .

Bill: Do something else?

Betty: No thanks.

Bill: I was headed out to the movies in a while anyway.

Betty: I don't think so.

Bill: Big chance to let Faulkner catch his breath. All those long sentences get him pretty tired.

Betty: Thanks anyway.

Bill: Okay.

Betty: I appreciate the invitation.

Bill: Sure thing. *(Bell.)* You weren't waiting for somebody when I came in, were you?

Betty: No, just reading.

Bill: Sort of a sad occupation for a Friday night, isn't it? Reading here all by yourself?

Betty: I guess I was trying to think of it as existentially romantic. You know — cappuccino, great literature, rainy night . . .

Bill: That only works in Paris. We *could* hop the late plane to Paris. Get on a Concorde. Find a café . . .

Betty: I'm a little short on plane fare tonight.

Bill: Darn it, so am I.

Betty: To tell you the truth, I was headed to the movies after I finished this section. Would you like to come along? Since you can't locate a waiter?

Bill: That's a very nice offer, but . . .

Betty: Uh-huh. Girlfriend?

Bill: Two, actually. One of them's pregnant, and Stephanie — *(Bell.)*

Betty: Girlfriend?

Bill: No, I don't have a girlfriend. Not if you mean the castrating bitch I dumped last night. *(Bell.)*

Betty: Girlfriend?

Bill: Sort of. Sort of.

Betty: What's a sort-of girlfriend?

Bill: My mother. *(Bell.)* I just ended a relationship, actually.

Betty: Oh.

Bill: Of rather long standing.

Betty: I'm sorry to hear it.

Bill: This is my first night out alone in a long time. I feel a little bit at sea, to tell you the truth.

Betty: So you didn't stop to talk because you're a Moonie, or you have some weird political affiliation —?

Bill: Nope. Straight-down-the-ticket Republican. *(Bell.)* Straight-down-the-ticket Democrat. *(Bell.)* Can I tell you something about politics? *(Bell.)* I like to think of myself as a citizen of the universe. *(Bell.)* I'm unaffiliated.

Betty: That's a relief. So am I.

Bill: I vote my beliefs.

Betty: Labels are not important.

Bill: Labels are not important, exactly. Like me, for example. I mean, what does it matter if I had a two-point at — *(bell)* — three-point at *(bell)* — four-point at college, or if I did come from Pittsburgh — *(bell)* — Cleveland — *(bell)* — Westchester County?

Betty: Sure.

Bill: I believe that a man is what he is. *(Bell.)* A person is what he is. *(Bell.)* A person is . . . what they are.

Betty: I think so too.

Bill: So what if I admire Trotsky? *(Bell.)* So what if I once had a total-body liposuction? *(Bell.)* So what if I don't have a penis? *(Bell.)* So what if I once spent a year in the Peace Corps? I was acting on my convictions.

Betty: Sure.

Bill: You can't just hang a sign on a person.

Betty: Absolutely. I'll bet you're a Scorpio. *(Many bells ring.)* Listen, I was headed to the movies after I finished this section. Would you like to come along?

Bill: That sounds like fun. What's playing?

Betty: A couple of the really early Woody Allen movies.
Bill: Oh.
Betty: Don't you like Woody Allen?
Bill: Sure. I like Woody Allen.
Betty: But you're not crazy about Woody Allen.
Bill: Those early ones kind of get on my nerves.
Betty: Uh-huh. *(Bell.)*
Bill: Y'know I was   — *(simultaneously)* —   *Betty:* I was thinking
  headed to the —   about —
Bill: I'm sorry.
Betty: No, go ahead.
Bill: I was going to say that I was headed to the movies in a little while, and . . .
Betty: So was I.
Bill: The Woody Allen festival?
Betty: Just up the street.
Bill: Do you like the early ones?
Betty: I think anybody who doesn't ought to be run off the planet.
Bill: How many times have you seen *Bananas*?
Betty: Eight times.
Bill: Twelve. So are you still interested? *(Long pause.)*
Betty: Do you like Entenmann's crumb cake . . . ?
Bill: Last night I went out at two in the morning to get one. *(Small pause.)* Did
  you have an Etch-a-Sketch as a child?
Betty: Yes! And do you like Brussels sprouts? *(Small pause.)*
Bill: I think they're gross.
Betty: They *are* gross!
Bill: Do you still believe in marriage in spite of current sentiments against it?
Betty: Yes.
Bill: And children?
Betty: Three of them.
Bill: Two girls and a boy.
Betty: Harvard, Vassar, and Brown.
Bill: And will you love me?
Betty: Yes.
Bill: And cherish me forever?
Betty: Yes.
Bill: Do you still want to go to the movies?
Betty: Sure thing.
Bill and Betty (together): Waiter!

   (Blackout.)

CONSIDERATIONS FOR CRITICAL THINKING AND WRITING

1. FIRST RESPONSE. Very little information is provided about the play's setting. How do you envision the café? What does the setting suggest to you
   about the characters?
2. What is the purpose of the ringing bell?
3. Which character would you describe as the antagonist? What do you think
   is the play's central conflict?

4. How is the formulaic plot of "boy meets girl" complicated and made suspenseful in this play? Where would you say that the climax occurs? What is the plot's resolution?

5. How would you describe the play's theme?

6. Discuss the significance of the title. How is it related to your understanding of the play's theme?

7. At one point Bill says, "You have to hit these things at the right moment or it's no good" (p. 846). How might this line be used to describe Ives's strategy for writing this play?

8. Try your hand at writing another scene between Betty and Bill that takes place after they come out of the movies. Write a comic scene the way you think Ives might create it.

WILLIAM SHAKESPEARE (1564–1616)

A biographical note for William Shakespeare appears in Chapter 7, page 335.

A Midsummer Night's Dream

A Midsummer Night's Dream, one of Shakespeare's most popular plays with readers and audiences, is a romantic comedy about the complex nature of love and marriage. Though some serious points about law and social order are made along the way, the action is propelled by the powers of youth, romance, love, passion, and the hilarious pursuits of characters turned about by fairies, illusions, and their own misunderstandings.

Shakespeare uses several sets of couples to dramatize love's tribulations and triumphs. The play opens with Theseus, Duke of Athens, making arrangements to wed Hippolyta, queen of the Amazons. Once enemies, they now seek love and peace in the harmony of marriage. Their union represents the happy necessity of order in the state and suggests a model of behavior that the other characters struggle to achieve.

In contrast to the serene plans for the royal wedding is the conflict produced by four Athenian youths who are thwarted in love: Helena loves Demetrius, but Demetrius loves Hermia, who wants to marry Lysander. This collision of passions is further complicated by Hermia's father, who insists in the Duke's presence that if she doesn't marry Demetrius, she must die or spend her life in a nunnery. Much of the play's conflict concerns how these two young couples align their love for one another so that each desires and is desired by the right person. When Hermia defies her father and refuses to marry Demetrius, she flees to the woods, followed by Lysander and Demetrius as well as Helena, who is in pursuit of Demetrius.

Once in the woods, the lovers find themselves in a supernatural world, the unpredictable kingdom of Oberon and Titania, the king and queen of the fairies. The fourth couple creates even more confusion through Oberon's impatience with Titania. Their quarrel results in Oberon ordering his servant, Puck, to cast magical spells on the lovers as well as on Titania. This gives Puck the license to reveal their foolishness while eventually saving them from their own confused passions. Their reconciliations and reunions are not achieved, however, until Puck puts them through a series of comic encounters based on their illusions and vulnerabilities.

The final act includes the play within the play, "the most lamentable comedy" of two more lovers, Pyramus and Thisbe, who misunderstand one another. This travesty of a tragedy is put on by Athenian craftsmen — who are clearly better laborers than they are actors — at the Duke's request for a wedding entertainment. This play within the play reinforces the larger play's concerns about the nature of love and, indeed, of reality itself, because it raises questions about the fluid, complex relationship between art and reality. Ultimately, however, questions, issues, and conflicts give way to a generous sense of everything working out for the best as the play ends with Puck's warm assurances to the audience and his gentle urging to "Give me your hands."

WILLIAM SHAKESPEARE (1564–1616)

A Midsummer Night's Dream

c. 1595

[DRAMATIS PERSONAE

Theseus, Duke of Athens
Hippolyta, Queen of the Amazons, betrothed to Theseus
Philostrate, Master of the Revels
Egeus, father of Hermia

Hermia, daughter of Egeus, in love with Lysander
Lysander, in love with Hermia
Demetrius, in love with Hermia and favored by Egeus
Helena, in love with Demetrius

Oberon, King of the Fairies
Titania, Queen of the Fairies
Puck, or *Robin Goodfellow*
Peaseblossom,
Cobweb, } fairies attending Titania
Mote,
Mustardseed,
Other Fairies attending

Peter Quince, a carpenter, ⎫   Prologue
Nick Bottom, a weaver,   ⎪   Pyramus
Francis Flute, a bellows mender, ⎬ representing   Thisbe
Tom Snout, a tinker,   ⎪   Wall
Snug, a joiner,   ⎪   Lion
Robin Starveling, a tailor, ⎭   Moonshine
Lords and Attendants on Theseus and Hippolyta

SCENE: *Athens, and a wood near it.*]

[ACT I

SCENE I: *Athens. Theseus' court.*]

 Enter Theseus, Hippolyta, [and Philostrate,] with others.

Theseus: Now, fair Hippolyta, our nuptial hour
 Draws on apace. Four happy days bring in
 Another moon; but, O, methinks, how slow
 This old moon wanes! She lingers° my desires,
 Like to a stepdame° or a dowager°   5
 Long withering out° a young man's revenue.
Hippolyta: Four days will quickly steep themselves° in night;
 Four nights will quickly dream away the time;
 And then the moon, like to a silver bow
 New bent in heaven, shall behold the night   10
 Of our solemnities.°
Theseus: Go Philostrate,
 Stir up the Athenian youth to merriments.
 Awake the pert and nimble spirit of mirth.
 Turn melancholy forth to funerals;
 The pale companion° is not for our pomp.°   *[Exit Philostrate.]* 15
 Hippolyta, I wooed thee with my sword°
 And won thy love doing thee injuries;
 But I will wed thee in another key,
 With pomp, with triumph,° and with reveling.

 Enter Egeus and his daughter Hermia, and Lysander, and Demetrius.

Egeus: Happy be Theseus, our renownèd duke!   20
Theseus: Thanks, good Egeus. What's the news with thee?
Egeus: Full of vexation come I, with complaint
 Against my child, my daughter Hermia. —
 Stand forth, Demetrius. — My noble lord,

Act I, Scene I. 4 *lingers:* Postpones, delays the fulfillment of. 5 *stepdame:* Stepmother;
a dowager: I.e., a widow (whose right of inheritance from her dead husband is eating into her
son's estate). 6 *withering out:* Causing to dwindle. 7 *steep themselves:* Saturate themselves, to be absorbed in. 11 *solemnities:* Festive ceremonies of marriage. 15 *companion:*
Fellow; *pomp:* Ceremonial magnificence. 16 *with my sword:* In a military engagement
against the Amazons, when Hippolyta was taken captive. 19 *triumph:* Public festivity.

    This man hath my consent to marry her. —   25
    Stand forth, Lysander. — And, my gracious Duke,
    This man hath bewitched the bosom of my child.
    Thou, thou Lysander, thou hast given her rhymes
    And interchanged love tokens with my child.
    Thou hast by moonlight at her window sung   30
    With feigning° voice verses of feigning° love,
    And stol'n the impression of her fantasy°
    With bracelets of thy hair, rings, gauds,° conceits,°
    Knacks,° trifles, nosegays, sweetmeats — messengers
    Of strong prevailment in° unhardened youth.   35
    With cunning hast thou filched my daughter's heart,
    Turned her obedience, which is due to me,
    To stubborn harshness. And, my gracious Duke,
    Be it so° she will not here before Your Grace
    Consent to marry with Demetrius,   40
    I beg the ancient privilege of Athens:
    As she is mine, I may dispose of her,
    Which shall be either to this gentleman
    Or to her death, according to our law
    Immediately° provided in that case.   45
Theseus: What say you, Hermia? Be advised, fair maid.
    To you your father should be as a god —
    One that composed your beauties, yea, and one
    To whom you are but as a form in wax
    By him imprinted, and within his power   50
    To leave° the figure or disfigure° it.
    Demetrius is a worthy gentleman.
Hermia: So is Lysander.
Theseus: In himself he is;
    But in this kind,° wanting° your father's voice,°
    The other must be held the worthier.   55
Hermia: I would my father looked but with my eyes.
Theseus: Rather your eyes must with his judgment look.
Hermia: I do entreat Your Grace to pardon me.
    I know not by what power I am made bold,
    Nor how it may concern° my modesty   60
    In such a presence here to plead my thoughts;
    But I beseech Your Grace that I may know
    The worst that may befall me in this case
    If I refuse to wed Demetrius.
Theseus: Either to die the death° or to abjure   65
    Forever the society of men.
    Therefore, fair Hermia, question your desires,

---

31 *feigning:* (1) Counterfeiting (2) faining, desirous.   32 *And ... fantasy:* And made her fall in love with you (imprinting your image on her imagination) by stealthy and dishonest means. 33 *gauds:* Playthings; *conceits:* Fanciful trifles.   34 *Knacks:* Knickknacks.   35 *prevailment in:* Influence on.   39 *Be it so:* If.   45 *Immediately:* Directly, with nothing intervening. 51 *leave:* Leave unaltered; *disfigure:* Obliterate.   54 *kind:* Respect; *wanting:* Lacking; *voice:* Approval.   65 *die the death:* Be executed by legal process.

Know of your youth, examine well your blood,°
Whether, if you yield not to your father's choice,
You can endure the livery° of a nun,   70
For aye° to be in shady cloister mewed,°
To live a barren sister all your life,
Chanting faint hymns to the cold fruitless moon.
Thrice blessèd they that master so their blood
To undergo such maiden pilgrimage;   75
But earthlier happy° is the rose distilled°
Than that which, withering on the virgin thorn,
Grows, lives, and dies in single blessedness.

Hermia: So will I grow, so live, so die, my lord,
Ere I will yield my virgin patent° up   80
Unto his lordship, whose unwishèd yoke
My soul consents not to give sovereignty.

Theseus: Take time to pause, and by the next new moon —
The sealing day betwixt my love and me
For everlasting bond of fellowship —   85
Upon that day either prepare to die
For disobedience to your father's will,
Or° else to wed Demetrius, as he would,
Or on Diana's altar to protest°
For aye austerity and single life.   90

Demetrius: Relent, sweet Hermia, and, Lysander, yield
Thy crazèd° title to my certain right.

Lysander: You have her father's love, Demetrius;
Let me have Hermia's. Do you marry him.

Egeus: Scornful Lysander! True, he hath my love,   95
And what is mine my love shall render him.
And she is mine, and all my right of her
I do estate unto° Demetrius.

Lysander: I am, my lord, as well derived° as he,
As well possessed;° my love is more than his;   100
My fortunes every way as fairly° ranked,
If not with vantage,° as Demetrius';
And, which is more than all these boasts can be,
I am beloved of beauteous Hermia.
Why should not I then prosecute my right?   105
Demetrius, I'll avouch it to his head,°
Made love to Nedar's daughter, Helena,
And won her soul; and she, sweet lady, dotes,
Devoutly dotes, dotes in idolatry
Upon this spotted° and inconstant man.   110

---

68 *blood:* Passions.   70 *livery:* Habit, costume.   71 *aye:* Ever; *mewed:* Shut in (said of a hawk, poultry, etc.).   76 *earthlier happy:* Happier as respects this world; *distilled:* Separated to make perfume.   80 *patent:* Privilege.   88 *Or:* Either.   89 *protest:* Vow.   92 *crazèd:* Cracked, unsound.   98 *estate unto:* Settle or bestow upon.   99 *as well derived:* As well born and descended.   100 *possessed:* Endowed with wealth.   101 *fairly:* Handsomely.   102 *vantage:* Superiority.   106 *head:* I.e., face.   110 *spotted:* I.e., morally stained.

Theseus: I must confess that I have heard so much,
    And with Demetrius thought to have spoke thereof;
    But, being overfull of self-affairs,°
    My mind did lose it. But, Demetrius, come,
    And come, Egeus, you shall go with me;   115
    I have some private schooling° for you both.
    For you, fair Hermia, look you arm° yourself
    To fit your fancies° to your father's will,
    Or else the law of Athens yields you up—
    Which by no means we may extenuate°—   120
    To death or to a vow of single life.
    Come, my Hippolyta. What cheer, my love?
    Demetrius and Egeus, go° along.
    I must employ you in some business
    Against° our nuptial, and confer with you   125
    Of something nearly that° concerns yourselves.
Egeus: With duty and desire we follow you.
                  Exeunt [all but Lysander and Hermia].
Lysander: How now, my love, why is your cheek so pale?
    How chance the roses there do fade so fast?
Hermia: Belike° for want of rain, which I could well   130
    Beteem° them from the tempest of my eyes.
Lysander: Ay me! For aught that I could ever read,
    Could ever hear by tale or history,
    The course of true love never did run smooth;
    But either it was different in blood°—   135
Hermia: O cross!° Too high to be enthralled to low.
Lysander: Or else misgrafted° in respect of years—
Hermia: O spite! Too old to be engaged to young.
Lysander: Or else it stood upon the choice of friends°—
Hermia: O hell, to choose love by another's eyes!   140
Lysander: Or if there were a sympathy° in choice,
    War, death, or sickness did lay siege to it,
    Making it momentany° as a sound,
    Swift as a shadow, short as any dream,
    Brief as the lightning in the collied° night   145
    That in a spleen° unfolds° both heaven and earth,
    And ere a man hath power to say "Behold!"
    The jaws of darkness do devour it up.
    So quick° bright things come to confusion.°
Hermia: If then true lovers have been ever crossed,°   150

---

113 *self-affairs:* My own concerns.   116 *schooling:* Admonition.   117 *look you arm:* Take care you prepare.   118 *fancies:* Likings, thoughts of love.   120 *extenuate:* Mitigate, relax.   123 *go:* I.e., come.   125 *Against:* In preparation for.   126 *nearly that:* That closely.   130 *Belike:* Very likely.   131 *Beteem:* Grant, afford.   135 *blood:* Hereditary station.   136 *cross:* Vexation.   137 *misgrafted:* Ill-grafted, badly matched.   139 *friends:* Relatives.   141 *sympathy:* Agreement.   143 *momentany:* Lasting but a moment.   145 *collied:* Blackened (as with coal dust), darkened.   146 *in a spleen:* In a swift impulse, in a violent flash; *unfolds:* Reveals.   149 *quick:* Quickly; also, living, alive; *confusion:* Ruin. 150 *ever crossed:* Always thwarted.

It stands as an edict in destiny.
Then let us teach our trial patience,°
Because it is a customary cross,
As due to love as thoughts, and dreams, and sighs,
Wishes, and tears, poor fancy's° followers.   155
Lysander: A good persuasion.° Therefore, hear me, Hermia:
I have a widow aunt, a dowager
Of great revenue, and she hath no child.
From Athens is her house remote seven leagues;
And she respects° me as her only son.   160
There, gentle Hermia, may I marry thee,
And to that place the sharp Athenian law
Cannot pursue us. If thou lovest me, then,
Steal forth thy father's house tomorrow night;
And in the wood, a league without° the town,   165
Where I did meet thee once with Helena
To do observance to a morn of May,°
There will I stay for thee.
Hermia: My good Lysander!
I swear to thee, by Cupid's strongest bow,
By his best arrow° with the golden head,   170
By the simplicity° of Venus' doves,°
By that which knitteth souls and prospers loves,
And by that fire which burned the Carthage queen°
When the false Trojan° under sail was seen,
By all the vows that ever men have broke,   175
In number more than ever women spoke,
In that same place thou hast appointed me
Tomorrow truly will I meet with thee.
Lysander: Keep promise, love. Look, here comes Helena.

Enter Helena.

Hermia: God speed, fair° Helena! Whither away?   180
Helena: Call you me fair? That "fair" again unsay.
Demetrius loves your fair.° O happy fair!°
Your eyes are lodestars,° and your tongue's sweet air°
More tunable° than lark to shepherd's ear
When wheat is green, when hawthorn buds appear.   185
Sickness is catching. O, were favor° so,
Yours would I catch, fair Hermia, ere I go;

---

152 *teach...patience:* I.e., teach ourselves patience in this trial.   155 *fancy's:* Amorous passion's.
156 *persuasion:* Doctrine.   160 *respects:* Regards.   165 *without:* Outside.   167 *do...*
May: Perform the ceremonies of May Day.   170 *best arrow:* Cupid's best gold-pointed arrows
were supposed to induce love; his blunt leaden arrows, aversion.   171 *simplicity:* Innocence;
Venus' doves: Doves that drew Venus's chariot.   173, 174 *Carthage queen, false Trojan:* (Dido,
Queen of Carthage, immolated herself on a funeral pyre after having been deserted by the Trojan hero Aeneas.)   180 *fair:* Fair-complexioned (generally regarded by the Elizabethans as
more beautiful than a dark complexion).   182 *your fair:* Your beauty (even though Hermia is
dark-complexioned); *happy fair:* Lucky fair one.   183 *lodestars:* Guiding stars; *air:* Music.
184 *tunable:* Tuneful, melodious.   186 *favor:* Appearance, looks.

My ear should catch your voice, my eye your eye,
My tongue should catch your tongue's sweet melody.
Were the world mine, Demetrius being bated,°   190
The rest I'd give to be to you translated.°
O, teach me how you look and with what art
You sway the motion° of Demetrius' heart.

Hermia: I frown upon him, yet he loves me still.
Helena: O, that your frowns would teach my smiles such skill!   195
Hermia: I give him curses, yet he gives me love.
Helena: O, that my prayers could such affection° move!°
Hermia: The more I hate, the more he follows me.
Helena: The more I love, the more he hateth me.
Hermia: His folly, Helena, is no fault of mine.   200
Helena: None, but your beauty. Would that fault were mine!
Hermia: Take comfort. He no more shall see my face.
  Lysander and myself will fly this place.
  Before the time I did Lysander see
  Seemed Athens as a paradise to me.°   205
  O, then, what graces in my love do dwell,
  That he hath turned a heaven unto a hell?
Lysander: Helen, to you our minds we will unfold.
  Tomorrow night, when Phoebe° doth behold
  Her silver visage in the watery glass,°   210
  Decking with liquid pearl the bladed grass,
  A time that lovers' flights doth still° conceal,
  Through Athens' gates have we devised to steal.
Hermia: And in the wood, where often you and I
  Upon faint° primrose beds were wont to lie,   215
  Emptying our bosoms of their counsel° sweet,
  There my Lysander and myself shall meet,
  And thence from Athens turn away our eyes
  To seek new friends and stranger companies.°
  Farewell, sweet playfellow. Pray thou for us,   220
  And good luck grant thee thy Demetrius!
  Keep word, Lysander. We must starve our sight
  From lovers' food till morrow deep midnight.
Lysander: I will, my Hermia. *(Exit Hermia.)* Helena, adieu.
  As you on him, Demetrius dote on you!   *Exit Lysander.* 225
Helena: How happy some o'er other some can be!°
  Through Athens I am thought as fair as she.
  But what of that? Demetrius thinks not so;
  He will not know what all but he do know.
  And as he errs, doting on Hermia's eyes,   230

---

190 *bated:* Excepted.   191 *translated:* Transformed.   193 *sway the motion:* Control the
impulse.   197 *affection:* Passion; *move:* Arouse.   204–205 *Before...to me:* (Hermia
seemingly means that love has led to complications and jealousies, making Athens hell for
her.)   209 *Phoebe:* Diana, the moon.   210 *glass:* Mirror.   212 *still:* Always.   215 *faint:*
Pale.   216 *counsel:* Secret thought.   219 *stranger companies:* The company of strangers.
226 *o'er...can be:* Can be in comparison to some others.

So I, admiring of° his qualities.
Things base and vile, holding no quantity,°
Love can transpose to form and dignity.
Love looks not with the eyes, but with the mind,
And therefore is winged Cupid painted blind.   235
Nor hath Love's mind of any judgment taste;°
Wings and no eyes figure° unheedy haste.
And therefore is Love said to be a child,
Because in choice° he is so oft beguiled.°
As waggish° boys in game° themselves forswear,   240
So the boy Love is perjured everywhere.
For ere Demetrius looked on Hermia's eyne,°
He hailed down oaths that he was only mine;
And when this hail some heat from Hermia felt,
So he dissolved, and showers of oaths did melt.   245
I will go tell him of fair Hermia's flight.
Then to the wood will he tomorrow night
Pursue her; and for this intelligence°
If I have thanks, it is a dear° expense.°
But herein mean I to enrich my pain,   250
To have his sight thither and back again.   *Exit.*

[SCENE II: *Athens.*]

*Enter Quince the carpenter, and Snug the joiner, and Bottom the weaver, and Flute
the bellows mender, and Snout the tinker, and Starveling the tailor.*

Quince: Is all our company here?
Bottom: You were best to call them generally,° man by man, according to
  the scrip.°
Quince: Here is the scroll of every man's name which is thought fit,
  through all Athens, to play in our interlude° before the Duke and the   5
  Duchess on his wedding day at night.
Bottom: First, good Peter Quince, say what the play treats on, then read
  the names of the actors, and so grow to° a point.
Quince: Marry,° our play is "The most lamentable comedy and most cruel
  death of Pyramus and Thisbe."   10
Bottom: A very good piece of work, I assure you, and a merry. Now, good
  Peter Quince, call forth your actors by the scroll. Masters, spread
  yourselves.
Quince: Answer as I call you. Nick Bottom,° the weaver.

---

231 *admiring of:* Wondering at.   232 *holding no quantity:* I.e., unsubstantial, unshapely.
236 *Nor . . . taste:* I.e., nor has Love, which dwells in the fancy or imagination, any *taste* or
least bit of judgment or reason.   237 *figure:* Are a symbol of.   239 *in choice:* In choosing;
beguiled: Self-deluded, making unaccountable choices.   240 *waggish:* Playful, mischievous; *game:* Sport, jest.   242 *eyne:* Eyes (old form of plural).   248 *intelligence:* Information.   249 *a dear expense:* I.e., a trouble worth taking on my part, or a begrudging effort
on his part; *dear:* Costly.   **Scene II.**   2 *generally:* (Bottom's blunder for "individually.")
3 *scrip:* Scrap (Bottom's error for "script").   5 *interlude:* Play.   8 *grow to:* Come to.
9 *Marry:* (A mild oath; originally the name of the Virgin Mary.)   14 *Bottom:* Object
around which weavers wound thread.

Bottom: Ready. Name what part I am for, and proceed.   15

Quince: You, Nick Bottom, are set down for Pyramus.

Bottom: What is Pyramus? A lover or a tyrant?

Quince: A lover, that kills himself most gallant for love.

Bottom: That will ask some tears in the true performing of it. If I do it, let
the audience look to their eyes. I will move storms; I will condole° in   20
some measure. To the rest—yet my chief humor° is for a tyrant. I
could play Ercles° rarely, or a part to tear a cat° in, to make all split.°

> "The raging rocks
> And shivering shocks
> Shall break the locks   25
>   Of prison gates;
> And Phibbus' car°
> Shall shine from far
> And make and mar
>   The foolish Fates."   30

This was lofty! Now name the rest of the players. This is Ercles' vein, a
tyrant's vein. A lover is more condoling.

Quince: Francis Flute, the bellows mender.

Flute: Here, Peter Quince.

Quince: Flute, you must take Thisbe on you.   35

Flute: What is Thisbe? A wandering knight?

Quince: It is the lady that Pyramus must love.

Flute: Nay, faith, let not me play a woman. I have a beard coming.

Quince: That's all one.° You shall play it in a mask, and you may speak as
small° as you will.   40

Bottom: An° I may hide my face, let me play Thisbe too. I'll speak in a monstrous little voice: "Thisne, Thisne!" "Ah, Pyramus, my lover dear! Thy
Thisbe dear, and lady dear!"

Quince: No, no, you must play Pyramus, and Flute, you Thisbe.

Bottom: Well, proceed.   45

Quince: Robin Starveling, the tailor.

Starveling: Here, Peter Quince.

Quince: Robin Starveling, you must play Thisbe's mother. Tom Snout, the
tinker.

Snout: Here, Peter Quince.   50

Quince: You, Pyramus' father; myself, Thisbe's father; Snug, the joiner,
you, the lion's part; and I hope here is a play fitted.

Snug: Have you the lion's part written? Pray you, if it be, give it me, for I
am slow of study.

Quince: You may do it extempore, for it is nothing but roaring.   55

Bottom: Let me play the lion too. I will roar that I will do any man's heart
good to hear me. I will roar that I will make the Duke say, "Let him
roar again, let him roar again."

Quince: An you should do it too terribly, you would fright the Duchess

---

20 *condole:* Lament, arouse pity.   21 *humor:* Inclination, whim.   22 *Ercles:* Hercules (the
tradition of ranting came from Seneca's *Hercules Furens*); *tear a cat:* I.e., rant; *make all split:*
I.e., cause a stir, bring the house down.   27 *Phibbus' car:* Phoebus', the sun god's, chariot.
39 *That's all one:* It makes no difference.   40 *small:* High-pitched.   41 *An:* If (also at
line 59).

and the ladies, that they would shriek; and that were enough to hang   60
us all.

All: That would hang us, every mother's son.

Bottom: I grant you, friends, if you should fright the ladies out of their
wits, they would have no more discretion but to hang us; but I will
aggravate° my voice so that I will roar you° as gently as any sucking   65
dove;° I will roar you an 'twere° any nightingale.

Quince: You can play no part but Pyramus; for Pyramus is a sweet-faced
man, a proper° man as one shall see in a summer's day, a most lovely
gentlemanlike man. Therefore you must needs play Pyramus.

Bottom: Well, I will undertake it. What beard were I best to play it in?   70

Quince: Why, what you will.

Bottom: I will discharge° it in either your° straw-color beard, your orange-
tawny beard, your purple-in-grain° beard, or your French-crown-
color° beard, your perfect yellow.

Quince: Some of your French crowns° have no hair at all, and then you   75
will play barefaced. But, masters, here are your parts. *[He distributes
parts.]* And I am to entreat you, request you, and desire you to con°
them by tomorrow night, and meet me in the palace wood, a mile
without the town, by moonlight. There will we rehearse; for if we meet
in the city, we shall be dogged with company, and our devices°   80
known. In the meantime I will draw a bill° of properties, such as our
play wants. I pray you, fail me not.

Bottom: We will meet, and there we may rehearse most obscenely° and
courageously. Take pains, be perfect.° Adieu.

Quince: At the Duke's oak we meet.   85

Bottom: Enough. Hold, or cut bowstrings.°   *Exeunt.*

[ACT II

SCENE I: *A wood near Athens.]*

    Enter a Fairy at one door, and Robin Goodfellow [Puck] at another.

Puck: How now, spirit, whither wander you?

Fairy: Over hill, over dale,
      Thorough° bush, thorough brier,
      Over park, over pale,°

---

65 *aggravate:* (Bottom's blunder for "moderate."); *roar you:* I.e., roar for you.   65–66 *sucking
dove:* (Bottom conflates *sitting dove* and *sucking lamb,* two proverbial images of innocence.).
66 *an 'twere:* As if it were.   68 *proper:* Handsome.   72 *discharge:* Perform; *your:* I.e., you
know the kind I mean.   73 *purple-in-grain:* Dyed a very deep red (from *grain,* the name
applied to the dried insect used to make the dye).   73–74 *French-crown-color:* I.e., color of a
French crown, a gold coin.   75 *crowns:* Heads bald from syphilis, the "French disease."
77 *con:* Learn by heart.   80 *devices:* Plans.   81 *draw a bill:* Draw up a list.   83 *ob-
scenely:* (An unintentionally funny blunder, whatever Bottom meant to say.)   84 *perfect:*
I.e., letter-perfect in memorizing your parts.   86 *Hold . . . bowstrings:* (An archer's expression, not definitely explained, but probably meaning here "keep your promises, or give up
the play.")   **Act II, Scene I.**   3 *Thorough:* Through.   4 *pale:* Enclosure.

   Thorough flood, thorough fire,   5
  I do wander everywhere,
  Swifter than the moon's sphere;°
  And I serve the Fairy Queen,
  To dew° her orbs° upon the green.
  The cowslips tall her pensioners° be.   10
  In their gold coats spots you see;
  Those be rubies, fairy favors;°
  In those freckles live their savors.°
  I must go seek some dewdrops here
  And hang a pearl in every cowslip's ear.   15
  Farewell, thou lob° of spirits; I'll be gone.
  Our Queen and all her elves come here anon.°
Puck: The King doth keep his revels here tonight.
  Take heed the Queen come not within his sight.
  For Oberon is passing fell° and wrath,°   20
  Because that she as her attendant hath
  A lovely boy, stolen from an Indian king;
  She ne'er had so sweet a changeling.°
  And jealous Oberon would have the child
  Knight of his train, to trace° the forests wild.   25
  But she perforce° withholds the lovèd boy,
  Crowns him with flowers, and makes him all her joy.
  And now they never meet in grove or green,
  By fountain° clear, or spangled starlight sheen,°
  But they do square,° that all their elves for fear   30
  Creep into acorn cups and hide them there.
Fairy: Either I mistake your shape and making quite,
  Or else you are that shrewd° and knavish sprite°
  Called Robin Goodfellow. Are not you he
  That frights the maidens of the villagery,°   35
  Skim milk,° and sometimes labor in the quern,°
  And bootless° make the breathless huswife° churn,
  And sometimes make the drink to bear no barm,°
  Mislead night wanderers,° laughing at their harm?
  Those that "Hobgoblin" call you, and "Sweet Puck,"° 40
  You do their work, and they shall have good luck.
  Are you not he?

---

7 *sphere:* Orbit. 9 *dew:* Sprinkle with dew; *orbs:* Circles, i.e., fairy rings (circular bands of grass, darker than the surrounding area, caused by fungi enriching the soil). 10 *pensioners:* Retainers, members of the royal bodyguard. 12 *favors:* Love tokens. 13 *savors:* Sweet smells. 16 *lob:* Country bumpkin. 17 *anon:* At once. 20 *passing fell:* Exceedingly angry; *wrath:* Wrathful. 23 *changeling:* Child exchanged for another by the fairies. 25 *trace:* Range through. 26 *perforce:* Forcibly. 29 *fountain:* Spring; *starlight sheen:* Shining starlight. 30 *square:* Quarrel. 33 *shrewd:* Mischievous; *sprite:* Spirit. 35 *villagery:* Village population. 36 *Skim milk:* I.e., steal the cream; *quern:* Hand mill (where Puck presumably hampers the grinding of grain). 37 *bootless:* In vain (Puck prevents the cream from turning to butter); *huswife:* Housewife. 38 *barm:* Head on the ale (Puck prevents the barm or yeast from producing fermentation). 39 *Mislead night wanderers:* I.e., mislead with false fire those who walk abroad at night (hence earning Puck his other names of Jack o' Lantern and Will o' the Wisp). 40 *Those . . . Puck:* I.e., those who call you by the names you favor rather than those denoting the mischief you do.

Puck: Thou speakest aright;
   I am that merry wanderer of the night.
   I jest to Oberon and make him smile
   When I a fat and bean-fed° horse beguile,   45
   Neighing in likeness of a filly foal;
   And sometimes lurk I in a gossip's° bowl
   In very likeness of a roasted crab,°
   And when she drinks, against her lips I bob
   And on her withered dewlap° pour the ale.   50
   The wisest aunt,° telling the saddest° tale,
   Sometimes for three-foot stool mistaketh me;
   Then slip I from her bum, down topples she,
   And "Tailor"° cries, and falls into a cough;
   And then the whole choir° hold their hips and laugh,   55
   And waxen° in their mirth, and neeze,° and swear
   A merrier hour was never wasted° there.
   But, room,° fairy! Here comes Oberon.
Fairy: And here my mistress. Would that he were gone!

*Enter [Oberon] the King of Fairies at one door, with his train, and [Titania] the
Queen at another, with hers.*

Oberon: Ill met by moonlight, proud Titania.   60
Titania: What, jealous Oberon? Fairies, skip hence.
   I have forsworn his bed and company.
Oberon: Tarry, rash wanton.° Am not I thy lord?
Titania: Then I must be thy lady; but I know
   When thou hast stolen away from Fairyland   65
   And in the shape of Corin° sat all day,
   Playing on the pipes of corn° and versing love
   To amorous Phillida.° Why art thou here
   Come from the farthest step° of India,
   But that, forsooth, the bouncing Amazon,   70
   Your buskined° mistress and your warrior love,
   To Theseus must be wedded, and you come
   To give their bed joy and prosperity.
Oberon: How canst thou thus for shame, Titania,
   Glance at my credit with Hippolyta,°   75
   Knowing I know thy love to Theseus?
   Didst not thou lead him through the glimmering night
   From Perigenia,° whom he ravishèd?

---

45 *bean-fed:* Well fed on field beans.   47 *gossip's:* Old woman's.   48 *crab:* Crab apple.
50 *dewlap:* Loose skin on neck.   51 *aunt:* Old woman; *saddest:* Most serious.   54 *Tailor:*
(Possibly because she ends up sitting cross-legged on the floor, looking like a tailor, or else
referring to the *tail* or buttocks.)   55 *choir:* Company.   56 *waxen:* Increase; *neeze:* Sneeze.
57 *wasted:* Spent.   58 *room:* Stand aside, make room.   63 *wanton:* Headstrong creature.
66, 68 *Corin, Phillida:* (Conventional names of pastoral lovers.)   67 *corn:* (Here, oat
stalks.)   69 *step:* Farthest limit of travel, or, perhaps, *steep,* "mountain range."   71 *busk-
ined:* Wearing half-boots called buskins.   75 *Glance . . . Hippolyta:* Make insinuations
about my favored relationship with Hippolyta.   78 *Perigenia:* I.e., Perigouna, one of Theseus' conquests. (This and the following women are named in Thomas North's translation
of Plutarch's "Life of Theseus.")

And make him with fair Aegles° break his faith,
With Ariadne° and Antiopa?°   80
Titania: These are the forgeries of jealousy;
And never, since the middle summer's spring,°
Met we on hill, in dale, forest, or mead,°
By pavèd° fountain or by rushy° brook,
Or in° the beachèd margent° of the sea,   85
To dance our ringlets to° the whistling wind,
But with thy brawls thou hast disturbed our sport.
Therefore the winds, piping to us in vain,
As in revenge, have sucked up from the sea
Contagious° fogs which, falling in the land,   90
Hath every pelting° river made so proud
That they have overborne their continents.°
The ox hath therefore stretched his yoke° in vain,
The plowman lost his sweat, and the green corn°
Hath rotted ere his youth attained a beard;   95
The fold° stands empty in the drownèd field,
And crows are fatted with the murrain° flock;
The nine-men's morris° is filled up with mud,
And the quaint mazes° in the wanton° green
For lack of tread are indistinguishable.   100
The human mortals want° their winter° here;
No night is now with hymn or carol blessed.
Therefore° the moon, the governess of floods,
Pale in her anger, washes° all the air,
That rheumatic diseases° do abound.   105
And thorough this distemperature° we see
The seasons alter: hoary-headed frosts
Fall in the fresh lap of the crimson rose,
And on old Hiems'° thin and icy crown
An odorous chaplet of sweet summer buds   110
Is, as in mockery, set. The spring, the summer,
The childing° autumn, angry winter, change

---

79 *Aegles:* I.e., Aegle, for whom Theseus deserted Ariadne according to some accounts.
80 *Ariadne:* The daughter of Minos, King of Crete, who helped Theseus to escape the
labyrinth after killing the Minotaur; later she was abandoned by Theseus; *Antiopa:* Queen of
the Amazons and wife of Theseus, elsewhere identified with Hippolyta, but here thought of
as a separate woman.   82 *middle summer's spring:* Beginning of midsummer.   83 *mead:*
Meadow.   84 *pavèd:* With pebbled bottom; *rushy:* Bordered with rushes.   85 *in:* On;
margent: Edge, border.   86 *ringlets to:* Dances in a ring (see *orbs* in II.i.9) to the sound of.
90 *Contagious:* Noxious.   91 *pelting:* Paltry.   92 *continents:* Banks that contain them.
93 *stretched his yoke:* I.e., pulled at his yoke in plowing.   94 *corn:* Grain of any kind.
96 *fold:* Pen for sheep or cattle.   97 *murrain:* Having died of the plague.   98 *nine-men's
morris:* I.e., portion of the village green marked out in a square for a game played with nine
pebbles or pegs.   99 *quaint mazes:* I.e., intricate paths marked out on the village green to be
followed rapidly on foot as a kind of contest; *wanton:* Luxuriant.   101 *want:* Lack; *winter:*
I.e., regular winter season; or, proper observances of winter, such as the *hymn* or *carol* in the
next line (?).   103 *Therefore:* I.e., as a result of our quarrel.   104 *washes:* Saturates with
moisture.   105 *rheumatic diseases:* Colds, flu, and other respiratory infections.   106 *dis-
temperature:* Disturbance in nature.   109 *Hiems':* The winter god's.   112 *childing:* Fruit-
ful, pregnant.

Their wonted liveries,° and the mazèd° world
By their increase° now knows not which is which.
And this same progeny of evils comes   115
From our debate,° from our dissension.
We are their parents and original.°
Oberon: Do you amend it, then. It lies in you.
Why should Titania cross her Oberon?
I do but beg a little changeling boy   120
To be my henchman.°
Titania: Set your heart at rest.
The fairy land buys not the child of me.
His mother was a vot'ress of my order,°
And in the spicèd Indian air by night
Full often hath she gossiped by my side   125
And sat with me on Neptune's yellow sands,
Marking th' embarkèd traders° on the flood,°
When we have laughed to see the sails conceive
And grow big-bellied with the wanton° wind;
Which she, with pretty and with swimming° gait,   130
Following — her womb then rich with my young squire —
Would imitate, and sail upon the land
To fetch me trifles, and return again
As from a voyage, rich with merchandise.
But she, being mortal, of that boy did die;   135
And for her sake do I rear up her boy,
And for her sake I will not part with him.
Oberon: How long within this wood intend you stay?
Titania: Perchance till after Theseus' wedding day.
If you will patiently dance in our round°   140
And see our moonlight revels, go with us;
If not, shun me, and I will spare° your haunts.
Oberon: Give me that boy, and I will go with thee.
Titania: Not for thy fairy kingdom. Fairies, away!
We shall chide downright, if I longer stay.   145
                              Exeunt [Titania with her train].
Oberon: Well, go thy way. Thou shalt not from° this grove
Till I torment thee for this injury.
My gentle Puck, come hither. Thou rememb'rest
Since° once I sat upon a promontory,
And heard a mermaid on a dolphin's back   150
Uttering such dulcet° and harmonious breath°
That the rude° sea grew civil at her song,

---

113 *wonted liveries:* Usual apparel; *mazèd:* Bewildered.   114 *their increase:* Their yield,
what they produce.   116 *debate:* Quarrel.   117 *original:* Origin.   121 *henchman:* Attendant, page.   123 *was...order:* Had taken a vow to serve me.   127 *traders:* Trading vessels;
flood: Flood tide.   129 *wanton:* (1) Playful (2) amorous.   130 *swimming:* Smooth, gliding.
140 *round:* Circular dance.   142 *spare:* Shun.   146 *from:* Go from.   149 *Since:* When.
151 *dulcet:* Sweet; *breath:* Voice, song.   152 *rude:* Rough.

                And certain stars shot madly from their spheres
                To hear the sea-maid's music?
Puck: I remember.
Oberon: That very time I saw, but thou couldst not,   155
                Flying between the cold moon and the earth
                Cupid, all° armed. A certain° aim he took
                At a fair vestal° thronèd by° the west,
                And loosed° his love shaft smartly from his bow
                As° it should pierce a hundred thousand hearts;   160
                But I might° see young Cupid's fiery shaft
                Quenched in the chaste beams of the watery moon,
                And the imperial vot'ress passèd on,
                In maiden meditation, fancy-free.°
                Yet marked I where the bolt° of Cupid fell: 165
                It fell upon a little western flower,
                Before milk-white, now purple with love's wound,
                And maidens call it love-in-idleness.°
                Fetch me that flower; the herb I showed thee once.
                The juice of it on sleeping eyelids laid   170
                Will make or man or° woman madly dote
                Upon the next live creature that it sees.
                Fetch me this herb, and be thou here again
                Ere the leviathan° can swim a league.
Puck: I'll put a girdle round about the earth   175
                In forty° minutes.   *[Exit.]*
Oberon: Having once this juice,
                I'll watch Titania when she is asleep
                And drop the liquor of it in her eyes.
                The next thing then she waking looks upon,
                Be it on lion, bear, or wolf, or bull,   180
                On meddling monkey, or on busy ape,
                She shall pursue it with the soul of love.
                And ere I take this charm from off her sight,
                As I can take it with another herb,
                I'll make her render up her page to me.   185
                But who comes here? I am invisible,
                And I will overhear their conference.

                Enter Demetrius, Helena following him.

Demetrius: I love thee not; therefore pursue me not.
                Where is Lysander and fair Hermia?
                The one I'll slay; the other slayeth me.
                Thou toldst me they were stol'n unto this wood;   190

---

157 *all:* Fully; *certain:* Sure.   158 *vestal:* Vestal virgin (contains a complimentary allusion to
Queen Elizabeth as a votaress of Diana and probably refers to an actual entertainment in her
honor at Elvetham in 1591); *by:* In the region of.   159 *loosed:* Released.   160 *As:* As if.
161 *might:* Could.   164 *fancy-free:* Free of love's spell.   165 *bolt:* Arrow.   168 *love-in-
idleness:* Pansy, heartsease.   171 *or . . . or:* Either . . . or.   174 *leviathan:* Sea monster, whale.
176 *forty:* (Used indefinitely.)

And here am I, and wood° within this wood
Because I cannot meet my Hermia.
Hence, get thee gone, and follow me no more.

Helena: You draw me, you hardhearted adamant!°   195
But yet you draw not iron, for my heart
Is true as steel. Leave you° your power to draw,
And I shall have no power to follow you.

Demetrius: Do I entice you? Do I speak you fair?°
Or rather do I not in plainest truth   200
Tell you I do not nor I cannot love you?

Helena: And even for that do I love you the more.
I am your spaniel; and, Demetrius,
The more you beat me I will fawn on you.
Use me but as your spaniel, spurn me, strike me,   205
Neglect me, lose me; only give me leave,
Unworthy as I am, to follow you.
What worser place can I beg in your love—
And yet a place of high respect with me—
Than to be usèd as you use your dog?   210

Demetrius: Tempt not too much the hatred of my spirit,
For I am sick when I do look on thee.

Helena: And I am sick when I look not on you.

Demetrius: You do impeach° your modesty too much
To leave° the city and commit yourself   215
Into the hands of one that loves you not,
To trust the opportunity of night
And the ill counsel of a desert° place
With the rich worth of your virginity.

Helena: Your virtue° is my privilege.° For that°   220
It is not night when I do see your face,
Therefore I think I am not in the night;
Nor doth this wood lack worlds of company,
For you, in my respect,° are all the world.
Then how can it be said I am alone   225
When all the world is here to look on me?

Demetrius: I'll run from thee and hide me in the brakes,°
And leave thee to the mercy of wild beasts.

Helena: The wildest hath not such a heart as you.
Run when you will. The story shall be changed: 230
Apollo flies and Daphne holds the chase,°

---

192 *and wood:* And mad, frantic (with an obvious wordplay on *wood,* meaning "woods").
195 *adamant:* Lodestone, magnet (with pun on *hardhearted,* since adamant was also thought
to be the hardest of all stones and was confused with the diamond).   197 *Leave you:* Give
up.   199 *speak you fair:* Speak courteously to you.   214 *impeach:* Call into question.
215 *To leave:* By leaving.   218 *desert:* Deserted.   220 *virtue:* Goodness or power to
attract; *privilege:* Safeguard, warrant; *For that:* Because.   224 *in my respect:* As far as I am
concerned, in my esteem.   227 *brakes:* Thickets.   231 *Apollo ... chase:* (In the ancient
myth, Daphne fled from Apollo and was saved from rape by being transformed into a laurel
tree; here it is the female who *holds the chase,* or pursues, instead of the male.)

The dove pursues the griffin,° the mild hind°
Makes speed to catch the tiger — bootless° speed,
When cowardice pursues and valor flies!
Demetrius: I will not stay thy questions.° Let me go!   235
Or if thou follow me, do not believe
But I shall do thee mischief in the wood.
Helena: Ay, in the temple, in the town, the field,
You do me mischief. Fie, Demetrius!
Your wrongs do set a scandal on my sex.°   240
We cannot fight for love, as men may do;
We should be wooed and were not made to woo.   *[Exit Demetrius.]*
I'll follow thee and make a heaven of hell,
To die upon° the hand I love so well.   *[Exit.]*
Oberon: Fare thee well, nymph. Ere he do leave this grove   245
Thou shalt fly him, and he shall seek thy love.

Enter Puck.

Has thou the flower there? Welcome, wanderer.
Puck: Aye, there it is.   *[He offers the flower.]*
Oberon: I pray thee, give it to me.
I know a bank where the wild thyme blows,°
Where oxlips° and the nodding violet grows,   250
Quite overcanopied with luscious woodbine,°
With sweet muskroses° and with eglantine.°
There sleeps Titania sometime of° the night,
Lulled in these flowers with dances and delight;
And there the snake throws° her enameled skin,   255
Weed° wide enough to wrap a fairy in.
And with the juice of this I'll streak° her eyes
And make her full of hateful fantasies.
Take thou some of it, and seek through this grove.
                              [He gives some love juice.]
A sweet Athenian lady is in love   260
With a disdainful youth. Anoint his eyes,
But do it when the next thing he espies
May be the lady. Thou shalt know the man
By the Athenian garments he hath on.
Effect it with some care, that he may prove   265
More fond on° her than she upon her love;
And look thou meet me ere the first cock crow.
Puck: Fear not, my lord, your servant shall do so.   *Exeunt [separately].*

---

232 *griffin:* A fabulous monster with the head and wings of an eagle and the body of a lion;
hind: Female deer.   233 *bootless:* Fruitless.   235 *stay thy questions:* Wait for or put up with
your talk or argument.   240 *Your . . . sex:* I.e., the wrongs that you do me cause me to act in
a manner that disgraces my sex.   244 *upon:* By.   249 *blows:* Blooms.   250 *oxlips:*
Flowers resembling cowslip and primrose.   251 *woodbine:* Honeysuckle.   252 *muskroses:*
A kind of large, sweet-scented rose; *eglantine:* Sweetbrier, another kind of rose.   253 *sometime of:* For part of.   255 *throws:* Sloughs off, sheds.   256 *Weed:* Garment.   257 *streak:*
Anoint, touch gently.   266 *fond on:* Doting on.

[SCENE II: *The wood.*]

Enter Titania, Queen of Fairies, with her train.

Titania: Come, now a roundel° and a fairy song;
  Then, for the third part of a minute,° hence —
  Some to kill cankers° in the muskrose buds,
  Some war with reremice° for their leathern wings
  To make my small elves coats, and some keep back   5
  The clamorous owl, that nightly hoots and wonders
  At our quaint° spirits. Sing me now asleep.
  Then to your offices, and let me rest.

Fairies sing.

First Fairy: You spotted snakes with double° tongue,
    Thorny hedgehogs, be not seen;   10
  Newts° and blindworms, do no wrong;
    Come not near our Fairy Queen.
Chorus [dancing]: Philomel,° with melody
    Sing in our sweet lullaby;
  Lulla, lulla, lullaby, lulla, lulla, lullaby.   15
    Never harm
    Nor spell nor charm
  Come our lovely lady nigh.
  So good night, with lullaby.
First Fairy: Weaving spiders, come not here;   20
    Hence, you long-legged spinners, hence!
  Beetles black, approach not near;
    Worm nor snail, do no offense.°
Chorus [dancing]: Philomel, with melody
    Sing in our sweet lullaby;   25
  Lulla, lulla, lullaby, lulla, lulla, lullaby.
    Never harm
    Nor spell nor charm
  Come our lovely lady nigh.
  So good night, with lullaby.   *[Titania sleeps.]*   30
Second Fairy: Hence, away! Now all is well.
  One aloof stand sentinel.°   *[Exeunt Fairies, leaving one sentinel.]*

Enter Oberon [and squeezes the flower on Titania's eyelids].

Oberon: What thou seest when thou dost wake,
  Do it for thy true love take;
  Love and languish for his sake.   35
  Be it ounce,° or cat, or bear,

Scene II.   1 *roundel:* Dance in a ring.   2 *the third . . . minute:* (Indicative of the fairies'
quickness.)   3 *cankers:* Cankerworms (i.e., caterpillars or grubs).   4 *reremice:* Bats.
7 *quaint:* Dainty.   9 *double:* Forked.   11 *Newts:* Water lizards (considered poisonous,
as were *blindworms* — small snakes with tiny eyes — and spiders).   13 *Philomel:* The nightingale. (Philomela, daughter of King Pandion, was transformed into a nightingale, according
to Ovid's *Metamorphoses* 6, after she had been raped by her sister Procne's husband, Tereus.)
23 *offense:* Harm.   32 *sentinel:* (Presumably Oberon is able to outwit or intimidate this
guard.)   36 *ounce:* Lynx.

Pard,° or boar with bristled hair,
In thy eye that shall appear
When thou wak'st, it is thy dear.
Wake when some vile thing is near.   *[Exit.]* 40

Enter Lysander and Hermia.

Lysander: Fair love, you faint with wandering in the wood;
    And to speak truth, I have forgot our way.
We'll rest us, Hermia, if you think it good,
    And tarry for the comfort of the day.
Hermia: Be it so, Lysander. Find you out a bed,   45
For I upon this bank will rest my head.
Lysander: One turf shall serve as pillow for us both;
One heart, one bed, two bosoms, and one troth.°
Hermia: Nay, good Lysander, for my sake, my dear,
Lie further off yet. Do not lie so near.   50
Lysander: O, take the sense, sweet, of my innocence!°
Love takes the meaning in love's conference.°
I mean that my heart unto yours is knit,
So that but one heart we can make of it;
Two bosoms interchainèd with an oath —   55
So then two bosoms and a single troth.
Then by your side no bed-room me deny,
For lying so, Hermia, I do not lie.°
Hermia: Lysander riddles very prettily.
Now much beshrew° my manners and my pride   60
If Hermia meant to say Lysander lied.
But, gentle friend, for love and courtesy
Lie further off, in human° modesty.
Such separation as may well be said
Becomes a virtuous bachelor and a maid,   65
So far be distant; and, good night, sweet friend.
Thy love ne'er alter till thy sweet life end!
Lysander: Amen, amen, to that fair prayer, say I,
And then end life when I end loyalty!
Here is my bed. Sleep give thee all his rest!   70
Hermia: With half that wish the wisher's eyes be pressed!°

[They sleep, separated by a short distance.]

Enter Puck.

Puck: Through the forest have I gone,
    But Athenian found I none
    On whose eyes I might approve°
    This flower's force in stirring love.   75
    Night and silence. — Who is here?

---

37 *Pard:* Leopard.   48 *troth:* Faith, trothplight.   51 *take . . . innocence:* I.e., interpret my intention as innocent.   52 *Love . . . conference:* I.e., when lovers confer, love teaches each lover to interpret the other's meaning lovingly.   58 *lie:* Tell a falsehood (with a riddling pun on *lie,* "recline").   60 *beshrew:* Curse (but mildly meant).   63 *human:* Courteous (and perhaps suggesting "humane").   71 *With . . . pressed:* I.e., may we share your wish, so that your eyes too are *pressed,* closed, in sleep.   74 *approve:* Test.

Weeds of Athens he doth wear.
This is he, my master said,
Despisèd the Athenian maid;
And here the maiden, sleeping sound,   80
On the dank and dirty ground.
Pretty soul, she durst not lie
Near this lack-love, this kill-courtesy.
Churl, upon thy eyes I throw
All the power this charm doth owe.°   *[He applies the love juice.]*   85
When thou wak'st, let love forbid
Sleep his seat on thy eyelid.
So awake when I am gone,
For I must now to Oberon.   *Exit.*

Enter Demetrius and Helena, running.

Helena: Stay, though thou kill me, sweet Demetrius!   90
Demetrius: I charge thee, hence, and do not haunt me thus.
Helena: O, wilt thou darkling° leave me? Do not so.
Demetrius: Stay, on thy peril!° I alone will go.   *[Exit.]*
Helena: O, I am out of breath in this fond° chase!
The more my prayer, the lesser is my grace.°   95
Happy is Hermia, wheresoe'er she lies,°
For she hath blessèd and attractive eyes.
How came her eyes so bright? Not with salt tears;
If so, my eyes are oftener washed than hers.
No, no, I am as ugly as a bear,   100
For beasts that meet me run away for fear.
Therefore no marvel though Demetrius
Do, as a monster, fly my presence thus.°
What wicked and dissembling glass of mine
Made me compare° with Hermia's sphery eyne?°   105
But who is here? Lysander, on the ground?
Dead, or asleep? I see no blood, no wound.
Lysander, if you live, good sir, awake.
Lysander [awaking]: And run through fire I will for thy sweet sake.
Transparent° Helena! Nature shows art,°   110
That through thy bosom makes me see thy heart.
Where is Demetrius? O, how fit a word
Is that vile name to perish on my sword!
Helena: Do not say so, Lysander; say not so.
What though he love your Hermia? Lord, what though?   115
Yet Hermia still loves you. Then be content.
Lysander: Content with Hermia? No! I do repent
The tedious minutes I with her have spent.
Not Hermia but Helena I love.

85 *owe:* Own.   92 *darkling:* In the dark.   93 *on thy peril:* I.e., on pain of danger to you if
you don't obey me and stay.   94 *fond:* Doting.   95 *my grace:* The favor I obtain.   96 *lies:*
Dwells.   102–103 *no marvel . . . thus:* I.e., no wonder that Demetrius flies from me as
from a monster.   105 *compare:* Vie; *sphery eyne:* Eyes as bright as stars in their spheres.
110 *Transparent:* (1) Radiant (2) able to be seen through, lacking in deceit; *art:* Skill, magic
power.

Who will not change a raven for a dove?　　　　　　　　　　120
The will° of man is by his reason swayed,
And reason says you are the worthier maid.
Things growing are not ripe until their season;
So I, being young, till now ripe not° to reason.
And, touching° now the point° of human skill,°　　　　　125
Reason becomes the marshal to my will
And leads me to your eyes, where I o'erlook°
Love's stories written in love's richest book.

Helena: Wherefore° was I to this keen mockery born?
When at your hands did I deserve this scorn?　　　　　　130
Is't not enough, is't not enough, young man,
That I did never — no, nor never can —
Deserve a sweet look from Demetrius' eye,
But you must flout my insufficiency?
Good troth,° you do me wrong, good sooth,° you do,　　　135
In such disdainful manner me to woo.
But fare you well. Perforce I must confess
I thought you lord of° more true gentleness.°
O, that a lady, of° one man refused,
Should of another therefore be abused!°　　　　*Exit.*　140

Lysander: She sees not Hermia. Hermia, sleep thou there,
And never mayst thou come Lysander near!
For as a surfeit of the sweetest things
The deepest loathing to the stomach brings,
Or as the heresies that men do leave　　　　　　　　　145
Are hated most of those they did deceive,°
So thou, my surfeit and my heresy,
Of all be hated, but the most of° me!
And, all my powers, address° your love and might
To honor Helen and to be her knight!　　　　*Exit.*　150

Hermia [awaking]: Help me, Lysander, help me! Do thy best
To pluck this crawling serpent from my breast!
Ay me, for pity! What a dream was here!
Lysander, look how I do quake with fear.
Methought a serpent ate my heart away,　　　　　　155
And you sat smiling at his cruel prey.°
Lysander! What, removed? Lysander! Lord!
What, out of hearing? Gone? No sound, no word?
Alack, where are you? Speak, an if° you hear;
Speak, of all loves!° I swoon almost with fear.　　　160
No? Then I well perceive you are not nigh.
Either death, or you, I'll find immediately.
　　　　　　　　　Exit. [The sleeping Titania remains.]

---

121 *will:* Desire.　　124 *ripe not:* (Am) not ripened.　　125 *touching:* Reaching; *point:* Summit; *skill:* Judgment.　　127 *o'erlook:* Read.　　129 *Wherefore:* Why.　　135 *Good troth, good sooth:* I.e., indeed, truly.　　138 *lord of:* I.e., possessor of; *gentleness:* Courtesy.　　139 *of:* By.　　140 *abused:* Ill-treated.　　145-146 *as . . . deceive:* As renounced heresies are hated most by those persons who formerly were deceived by them.　　148 *Of . . . of:* By . . . by.　　149 *address:* Direct, apply.　　156 *prey:* Act of preying.　　159 *an if:* If.　　160 *of all loves:* For love's sake.

[ACT III

SCENE I: *The wood.*]

Enter the clowns°[Quince, Snug, Bottom, Flute, Snout, and Starveling].

Bottom: Are we all met?

Quince: Pat, pat,° and here's a marvelous convenient place for our
rehearsal. This green plot shall be our stage, this hawthorn brake° our
tiring-house,° and we will do it in action as we will do it before
the Duke.   5

Bottom: Peter Quince?

Quince: What sayest thou, bully° Bottom?

Bottom: There are things in this comedy of Pyramus and Thisbe that will
never please. First, Pyramus must draw a sword to kill himself, which
the ladies cannot abide. How answer you that?   10

Snout: By 'r lakin,° a parlous° fear.

Starveling: I believe we must leave the killing out, when all is done.°

Bottom: Not a whit. I have a device to make all well. Write me° a prologue,
and let the prologue seem to say, we will do no harm with our swords,
and that Pyramus is not killed indeed; and for the more better assur-   15
ance, tell them that I, Pyramus, am not Pyramus but Bottom the
weaver. This will put them out of fear.

Quince: Well, we will have such a prologue, and it shall be written in eight
and six.°

Bottom: No, make it two more: let it be written in eight and eight.   20

Snout: Will not the ladies be afeard of the lion?

Starveling: I fear it, I promise you.

Bottom: Masters, you ought to consider with yourself, to bring in—God
shield us!—a lion among ladies° is a most dreadful thing. For there is
not a more fearful° wildfowl than your lion living, and we ought to   25
look to 't.

Snout: Therefore another prologue must tell he is not a lion.

Bottom: Nay, you must name his name, and half his face must be seen
through the lion's neck, and he himself must speak through, saying
thus or to the same defect:° "Ladies," or "Fair ladies, I would wish   30
you," or "I would request you," or "I would entreat you, not to fear,
not to tremble; my life for yours.° If you think I come hither as a lion,
it were pity of my life.° No, I am no such thing; I am a man as other
men are." And there indeed let him name his name, and tell them
plainly he is Snug the joiner.   35

Act III, Scene I.   *clowns:* Rustics.   2 *Pat:* On the dot, punctually.   3 *brake:* Thicket.
4 *tiring-house:* Attiring area, hence backstage.   7 *bully:* I.e., worthy, jolly, fine fellow.   11 *By
'r lakin:* By our ladykin, i.e., the Virgin Mary; *parlous:* Perilous, alarming.   12 *when all is
done:* I.e., when all is said and done.   13 *Write me:* I.e., write at my suggestion (*me* is used
colloquially).   18–19 *eight and six:* Alternate lines of eight and six syllables, a common ballad
measure.   24 *lion among ladies:* (A contemporary pamphlet tells how, at the christening in
1594 of Prince Henry, eldest son of King James VI of Scotland, later James I of England, a
"blackamoor" instead of a lion drew the triumphal chariot, since the lion's presence might
have "brought some fear to the nearest.")   25 *fearful:* Fear-inspiring.   30 *defect:* (Bottom's blunder for "effect.")   32 *my life for yours:* I.e., I pledge my life to make your lives safe.
33 *it were . . . life:* I.e., I should be sorry, by my life; or, my life would be endangered.

Quince: Well, it shall be so. But there is two hard things: that is, to bring
the moonlight into a chamber; for, you know, Pyramus and Thisbe
meet by moonlight.

Snout: Doth the moon shine that night we play our play?

Bottom: A calendar, a calendar! Look in the almanac. Find out moon-   40
shine, find out moonshine.   *[They consult an almanac.]*

Quince: Yes, it doth shine that night.

Bottom: Why then may you leave a casement of the great chamber window where we play open, and the moon may shine in at the casement.   45

Quince: Ay; or else one must come in with a bush of thorns° and a lantern
and say he comes to disfigure,° or to present,° the person of Moonshine. Then there is another thing: we must have a wall in the great
chamber; for Pyramus and Thisbe, says the story, did talk through
the chink of a wall.   50

Snout: You can never bring in a wall. What say you, Bottom?

Bottom: Some man or other must present Wall. And let him have some
plaster, or some loam, or some roughcast° about him, to signify wall;
or let him hold his fingers thus, and through that cranny shall
Pyramus and Thisbe whisper.   55

Quince: If that may be, then all is well. Come, sit down, every mother's
son, and rehearse your parts. Pyramus, you begin. When you have spoken your speech, enter into that brake, and so everyone according to
his cue.

Enter Robin [Puck].

Puck [aside]: What hempen homespuns° have we swaggering here   60
So near the cradle° of the Fairy Queen?
What, a play toward?° I'll be an auditor;
An actor, too, perhaps, if I see cause.

Quince: Speak, Pyramus. Thisbe, stand forth.

Bottom [as Pyramus]: "Thisbe, the flowers of odious savors sweet—"   65

Quince: Odors, odors.

Bottom: "—Odors savors sweet;
So hath thy breath, my dearest Thisbe dear.
But hark, a voice! Stay thou but here awhile,
And by and by I will to thee appear."   *Exit.*   70

Puck: A stranger Pyramus than e'er played here.°   *[Exit.]*

Flute: Must I speak now?

Quince: Ay, marry, must you; for you must understand he goes but to see a
noise that he heard, and is to come again.

Flute [as Thisbe]: "Most radiant Pyramus, most lily-white of hue,   75
Of color like the red rose on triumphant° brier,

46 *bush of thorns:* Bundle of thornbush fagots (part of the accoutrements of the man in the
moon, according to the popular notions of the time, along with his lantern and his dog).
47 *disfigure:* (Quince's blunder for "figure"); *present:* Represent.   53 *roughcast:* A mixture
of lime and gravel used to plaster the outside of buildings.   60 *hempen homespuns:* I.e.,
rustics dressed in clothes woven of coarse, homespun fabric made from hemp.   61 *cradle:*
I.e., Titania's bower.   62 *toward:* About to take place.   71 *A stranger...here:* (Either
Puck refers to an earlier dramatic version played in the same theater, or he has conceived of a
plan to present a "stranger" Pyramus than ever seen before.)   76 *triumphant:* Magnificent.

Most brisky juvenal° and eke° most lovely Jew,°
  As true as truest horse that yet would never tire.
I'll meet thee, Pyramus, at Ninny's tomb."

Quince: "Ninus'° tomb," man. Why, you must not speak that yet. That you   80
answer to Pyramus. You speak all your part° at once, cues and all.
Pyramus, enter. Your cue is past; it is "never tire."

Flute: O — "As true as truest horse, that yet would never tire."

[Enter Puck, and Bottom as Pyramus with the ass head.°]

Bottom: "If I were fair,° Thisbe, I were° only thine."

Quince: O, monstrous! O, strange! We are haunted. Pray, masters! Fly,   85
masters! Help!   *[Exeunt Quince, Snug, Flute, Snout, and Starveling.]*

Puck: I'll follow you, I'll lead you about a round,°
  Thorough bog, thorough bush, thorough brake, thorough brier.
Sometimes a horse I'll be, sometimes a hound,
  A hog, a headless bear, sometimes a fire;°   90
And neigh, and bark, and grunt, and roar, and burn,
Like horse, hound, hog, bear, fire, at every turn.   *Exit.*

Bottom: Why do they run away? This is a knavery of them to make me
afeard.

  Enter Snout.

Snout: O Bottom, thou art changed! What do I see on thee?   95

Bottom: What do you see? You see an ass head of your own, do you?
                                         [Exit Snout.]

  Enter Quince.

Quince: Bless thee, Bottom, bless thee! Thou art translated.°   *Exit.*

Bottom: I see their knavery. This is to make an ass of me, to fright me, if
they could. But I will not stir from this place, do what they can. I will
walk up and down here, and will sing, that they shall hear I am not   100
afraid.   *[He sings.]*
  The ouzel cock° so black of hue,
    With orange-tawny bill,
  The throstle° with his note so true,
    The wren with little quill°—   105

Titania [awaking]: What angel wakes me from my flowery bed?

Bottom [sings]:
  The finch, the sparrow, and the lark,
    The plainsong° cuckoo gray,
  Whose note full many a man doth mark,

---

77 *brisky juvenal:* Lively youth; *eke:* Also; *Jew:* (An absurd repetition of the first syllable of
juvenal and an indication of how desperately Quince searches for his rhymes.)   80 *Ninus':*
Mythical founder of Nineveh (whose wife, Semiramis, was supposed to have built the walls
of Babylon where the story of Pyramus and Thisbe takes place).   81 *part:* (An actor's *part*
was a script consisting only of his speeches and their cues.)   *with the ass head:* (This stage
direction presumably refers to a standard stage property.)   84 *fair:* Handsome; *were:*
Would be.   87 *about a round:* Roundabout.   90 *fire:* Will-o'-the-wisp.   97 *translated:*
Transformed.   102 *ouzel cock:* Male blackbird.   104 *throstle:* Song thrush.   105 *quill:*
(Literally, a reed pipe; hence, the bird's piping song.)   108 *plainsong:* Singing a melody
without variations.

> And dares not answer nay°—   110
> For indeed, who would set his wit to° so foolish a bird? Who would
> give a bird the lie,° though he cry "cuckoo" never so?°

Titania: I pray thee, gentle mortal, sing again.
> Mine ear is much enamored of thy note;
> So is mine eye enthrallèd to thy shape;   115
> And thy fair virtue's force° perforce doth move me
> On the first view to say, to swear, I love thee.

Bottom: Methinks, mistress, you should have little reason for that. And
> yet, to say the truth, reason and love keep little company together
> nowadays—the more the pity that some honest neighbors will not   120
> make them friends. Nay, I can gleek° upon occasion.

Titania: Thou art as wise as thou art beautiful.

Bottom: Not so, neither. But if I had wit enough to get out of this wood, I
> have enough to serve mine own turn.°

Titania: Out of this wood do not desire to go.   125
> Thou shalt remain here, whether thou wilt or no.
> I am a spirit of no common rate.°
> The summer still doth tend upon my state,°
> And I do love thee. Therefore, go with me.
> I'll give thee fairies to attend on thee,   130
> And they shall fetch thee jewels from the deep,
> And sing while thou on pressèd flowers dost sleep.
> And I will purge thy mortal grossness° so
> That thou shalt like an airy spirit go.
> Peaseblossom, Cobweb, Mote,° and Mustardseed!   135

Enter four Fairies [Peaseblossom, Cobweb, Mote, and Mustardseed].

Peaseblossom: Ready.
Cobweb: And I.
Mote: And I.
Mustardseed: And I.
All: Where shall we go?
Titania: Be kind and courteous to this gentleman.
> Hop in his walks and gambol in his eyes;°
> Feed him with apricots and dewberries,°   140
> With purple grapes, green figs, and mulberries;
> The honey bags steal from the humble-bees,
> And for night tapers crop their waxen thighs
> And light them at the fiery glowworms' eyes,
> To have my love to bed and to arise;   145
> And pluck the wings from painted butterflies

110 *dares . . . nay:* I.e., cannot deny that he is a cuckold.   111 *set his wit to:* Employ his intelligence to answer.   112 *give . . . lie:* Call the bird a liar; *never so:* Ever so much.   116 *thy . . .*
force: The power of your unblemished excellence.   121 *gleek:* Jest.   124 *serve . . . turn:*
Answer my purpose.   127 *rate:* Rank, value.   128 *still . . . state:* Always waits upon me as
a part of my royal retinue.   133 *mortal grossness:* Materiality (i.e., the corporeal nature of a
mortal being).   135 *Mote:* I.e., speck. (The two words *moth* and *mote* were pronounced
alike, and both meanings may be present.)   139 *in his eyes:* In his sight (i.e., before him).
140 *dewberries:* Blackberries.

To fan the moonbeams from his sleeping eyes.
Nod to him, elves, and do him courtesies.
Peaseblossom: Hail, mortal!
Cobweb: Hail!   150
Mote: Hail!
Mustardseed: Hail!
Bottom: I cry your worships mercy,° heartily. I beseech your worship's name.
Cobweb: Cobweb.
Bottom: I shall desire you of more acquaintance,° good Master Cobweb. If   155
   I cut my finger, I shall make bold with you.°—Your name, honest
   gentleman?
Peaseblossom: Peaseblossom.
Bottom: I pray you, commend me to Mistress Squash,° your mother, and
   to Master Peascod,° your father. Good Master Peaseblossom, I shall   160
   desire you of more acquaintance too.—Your name, I beseech you, sir?
Mustardseed: Mustardseed.
Bottom: Good Master Mustardseed, I know your patience° well. That same
   cowardly, giantlike ox-beef hath devoured many a gentleman of your
   house. I promise you, your kindred hath made my eyes water° ere now.   165
   I desire you of more acquaintance, good Master Mustardseed.
Titania: Come wait upon him; lead him to my bower. The moon methinks
      looks with a watery eye;
And when she weeps,° weeps every little flower,
      Lamenting some enforcèd° chastity.   170
   Tie up my lover's tongue;° bring him silently.   *Exeunt.*

[Scene II: *The wood.*]

      Enter [Oberon,] King of Fairies.

Oberon: I wonder if Titania be awaked;
      Then, what it was that next came in her eye,
      Which she must dote on in extremity.

   [Enter] Robin Goodfellow [Puck].

      Here comes my messenger. How now, mad spirit?
      What night-rule° now about this haunted° grove?   5
Puck: My mistress with a monster is in love.
      Near to her close° and consecrated bower,
      While she was in her dull° and sleeping hour,

---

153 *I cry . . . mercy:* I beg pardon of your worships (for presuming to ask a question).   155 *I . . .
acquaintance:* I crave to be better acquainted with you.   155–156 *If . . . you:* (Cobwebs were used
to stanch bleeding.)   159 *Squash:* Unripe pea pod.   160 *Peascod:* Ripe pea pod.   163 *your
patience:* What you have endured (mustard is eaten with beef).   165 *water:* (1) Weep for sympathy (2) smart, sting.   169 *she weeps:* I.e., she causes dew.   170 *enforcèd:* Forced, violated;
or, possibly, constrained (since Titania at this moment is hardly concerned about chastity).
171 *Tie . . . tongue:* (Presumably Bottom is braying like an ass.)   **Scene II.**   5 *night-
rule:* Diversion or misrule for the night; *haunted:* Much frequented.   7 *close:* Secret, private.
8 *dull:* Drowsy.

A crew of patches,° rude mechanicals,°
That work for bread upon Athenian stalls,°   10
Were met together to rehearse a play
Intended for great Theseus' nuptial day.
The shallowest thickskin of that barren sort,°
Who Pyramus presented,° in their sport
Forsook his scene° and entered in a brake.   15
When I did him at this advantage take,
An ass's noll° I fixèd on his head.
Anon his Thisbe must be answerèd,
And forth my mimic° comes. When they him spy,
As wild geese that the creeping fowler° eye,   20
Or russet-pated choughs,° many in sort,°
Rising and cawing at the gun's report,
Sever° themselves and madly sweep the sky,
So, at his sight, away his fellows fly;
And, at our stamp, here o'er and o'er one falls;   25
He "Murder!" cries and help from Athens calls.
Their sense thus weak, lost with their fears thus strong,
Made senseless things begin to do them wrong,
For briers and thorns at their apparel snatch;
Some, sleeves — some, hats; from yielders all things catch.°   30
I led them on in this distracted fear
And left sweet Pyramus translated there,
When in that moment, so it came to pass,
Titania waked and straightway loved an ass.

Oberon: This falls out better than I could devise.   35
But hast thou yet latched° the Athenian's eyes
With the love juice, as I did bid thee do?

Puck: I took him sleeping — that is finished too —
And the Athenian woman by his side,
That, when he waked, of force° she must be eyed.   40

     Enter Demetrius and Hermia.

Oberon: Stand close. This is the same Athenian.
Puck: This is the woman, but not this the man.   *[They stand aside.]*
Demetrius: O, why rebuke you him that loves you so?
     Lay breath so bitter on your bitter foe.
Hermia: Now I but chide; but I should use thee worse,   45
     For thou, I fear, hast given me cause to curse.
     If thou hast slain Lysander in his sleep,
     Being o'er shoes° in blood, plunge in the deep,
     And kill me too.
     The sun was not so true unto the day   50

---

9 *patches:* Clowns, fools; *rude mechanicals:* Ignorant artisans.   10 *stalls:* Market booths.
13 *barren sort:* Stupid company or crew.   14 *presented:* Acted.   15 *scene:* Playing area.
17 *noll:* Noddle, head.   19 *mimic:* Burlesque actor.   20 *fowler:* Hunter of game birds.
21 *russet-pated choughs:* Reddish brown or gray-headed jackdaws; *in sort:* In a flock.   23 *Sever:*
I.e., scatter.   30 *from . . . catch:* I.e., everything preys on those who yield to fear.   36 *latched:*
Fastened, snared.   40 *of force:* Perforce.   48 *Being o'er shoes:* Having waded in so far.

As he to me. Would he have stolen away
From sleeping Hermia? I'll believe as soon
This whole° earth may be bored, and that the moon
May through the center creep, and so displease
Her brother's° noontide with th' Antipodes.°   55
It cannot be but thou hast murdered him;
So should a murderer look, so dead,° so grim.
Demetrius: So should the murdered look, and so should I,
Pierced through the heart with your stern cruelty.
Yet you, the murderer, look as bright, as clear   60
As yonder Venus in her glimmering sphere.
Hermia: What's this to° my Lysander? Where is he?
Ah, good Demetrius, wilt thou give him me?
Demetrius: I had rather give his carcass to my hounds.
Hermia: Out, dog! Out, cur! Thou driv'st me past the bounds   65
Of maiden's patience. Hast thou slain him, then?
Henceforth be never numbered among men.
O, once° tell true, tell true, even for my sake:
Durst thou have looked upon him being awake?
And hast thou killed him sleeping? O brave touch!°   70
Could not a worm,° an adder, do so much?
An adder did it; for with doubler° tongue
Than thine, thou serpent, never adder stung.
Demetrius: You spend your passion° on a misprised mood.°
I am not guilty of Lysander's blood,   75
Nor is he dead, for aught that I can tell.
Hermia: I pray thee, tell me then that he is well.
Demetrius: And if I could, what should I get therefor?°
Hermia: A privilege never to see me more.
And from thy hated presence part I so.   80
See me no more, whether he be dead or no.   *Exit.*
Demetrius: There is no following her in this fierce vein.
Here therefore for a while I will remain.
So sorrow's heaviness doth heavier° grow
For debt that bankrupt° sleep doth sorrow owe,   85
Which now in some slight measure it will pay,
If for his tender here I make some stay.°   *[He] lie[s] down [and sleeps].*
Oberon: What hast thou done? Thou hast mistaken quite
And laid the love juice on some true love's sight.
Of thy misprision° must perforce ensue   90
Some true love turned, and not a false turned true.

---

53 *whole:* Solid.   55 *Her brother's:* I.e., the sun's; *th' Antipodes:* The people on the opposite
side of the earth (where the moon is imagined bringing night to noontime).   57 *dead:*
Deadly, or deathly pale.   62 *to:* To do with.   68 *once:* Once and for all.   70 *brave
touch!:* Fine stroke! (said ironically).   71 *worm:* Serpent.   72 *doubler:* (1) More forked
(2) more deceitful.   74 *passion:* Violent feelings; *misprised mood:* Anger based on misconception.   78 *therefor:* In return for that.   84 *heavier:* (1) Harder to bear (2) more drowsy.
85 *bankrupt:* (Demetrius is saying that his sleepiness adds to the weariness caused by sorrow.)   86–87 *Which . . . stay:* I.e., to a small extent, I will be able to "pay back" and hence
find some relief from sorrow, if I pause here awhile (*make some stay*) while sleep "tenders" or
offers itself by way of paying the debt owed to sorrow.   90 *misprision:* Mistake.

Puck: Then fate o'errules, that, one man holding troth,°
    A million fail, confounding oath on oath.°
Oberon: About the wood go swifter than the wind,
    And Helena of Athens look° thou find.   95
    All fancy-sick° she is and pale of cheer°
    With sighs of love, that cost the fresh blood° dear.
    By some illusion see thou bring her here.
    I'll charm his eyes against she do appear.°
Puck: I go, I go, look how I go,   100
    Swifter than arrow from the Tartar's bow.°   *[Exit.]*
Oberon [applying love juice to Demetrius' eyes]: Flower of this purple dye,
        Hit with Cupid's archery,
        Sink in apple° of his eye.
        When his love he doth espy,   105
        Let her shine as gloriously
        As the Venus of the sky.
        When thou wak'st, if she be by,
        Beg of her for remedy.

    Enter Puck.

Puck: Captain of our fairy band,   110
    Helena is here at hand,
    And the youth, mistook by me,
    Pleading for a lover's fee.°
    Shall we their fond pageant° see?
    Lord, what fools these mortals be!   115
Oberon: Stand aside. The noise they make
    Will cause Demetrius to awake.
Puck: Then will two at once woo one;
    That must needs be sport alone.°
    And those things do best please me   120
    That befall preposterously.°   *[They stand aside.]*

    Enter Lysander and Helena.

Lysander: Why should you think that I should woo in scorn?
    Scorn and derision never come in tears.
    Look when° I vow, I weep; and vows so born,
        In their nativity all truth appears.°   125
    How can these things in me seem scorn to you,
    Bearing the badge° of faith to prove them true?
Helena: You do advance° your cunning more and more.

---

92 *that . . . troth:* In that, for each man keeping true faith in love.   93 *confounding . . . oath:* I.e., breaking oath after oath.   95 *look:* I.e., be sure.   96 *fancy-sick:* Lovesick; *cheer:* Face. 97 *sighs . . . blood:* (An allusion to the physiological theory that each sigh costs the heart a drop of blood.)   99 *against . . . appear:* In anticipation of her coming.   101 *Tartar's bow:* (Tartars were famed for their skill with the bow.)   104 *apple:* Pupil.   113 *fee:* Privilege, reward.   114 *fond pageant:* Foolish spectacle.   119 *alone:* Unequaled.   121 *preposterously:* Out of the natural order.   124 *Look when:* Whenever.   124–125 *vows . . . appears:* I.e., vows made by one who is weeping give evidence thereby of their sincerity.   127 *badge:* Identifying device such as that worn on the servants' livery (here, his tears).   128 *advance:* Carry forward, display.

When truth kills truth,° O, devilish-holy fray!
These vows are Hermia's. Will you give her o'er?   130
   Weigh oath with oath, and you will nothing weigh.
Your vows to her and me, put in two scales,
Will even weigh, and both as light as tales.°

Lysander: I had no judgment when to her I swore.
Helena: Nor none, in my mind, now you give her o'er.   135
Lysander: Demetrius loves her, and he loves not you.
Demetrius [awaking]: O Helen, goddess, nymph, perfect, divine!
   To what, my love, shall I compare thine eyne?
   Crystal is muddy. O, how ripe in show°
   Thy lips, those kissing cherries, tempting grow!   140
   That pure congealèd white, high Taurus'° snow,
   Fanned with the eastern wind, turns to a crow°
   When thou hold'st up thy hand. O, let me kiss
   This princess of pure white, this seal° of bliss!
Helena: O spite! O hell! I see you all are bent   145
   To set against° me for your merriment.
   If you were civil and knew courtesy,
   You would not do me thus much injury.
   Can you not hate me, as I know you do,
   But you must join in souls° to mock me too?   150
   If you were men, as men you are in show,
   You would not use a gentle lady so —
   To vow, and swear, and superpraise° my parts,°
   When I am sure you hate me with your hearts.
   You both are rivals, and love Hermia,   155
   And now both rivals to mock Helena.
   A trim° exploit, a manly enterprise,
   To conjure tears up in a poor maid's eyes
   With your derision! None of noble sort°
   Would so offend a virgin and extort°   160
   A poor soul's patience, all to make you sport.
Lysander: You are unkind, Demetrius. Be not so.
   For you love Hermia; this you know I know.
   And here, with all good will, with all my heart,
   In Hermia's love I yield you up my part;   165
   And yours of Helena to me bequeath,
   Whom I do love, and will do till my death.
Helena: Never did mockers waste more idle breath.
Demetrius: Lysander, keep thy Hermia; I will none.°
   If e'er I loved her, all that love is gone.   170
   My heart to her but as guestwise sojourned,°

---

129 *truth kills truth:* I.e., one of Lysander's vows must invalidate the other.   133 *tales:* Lies.
139 *show:* Appearance.   141 *Taurus:* A lofty mountain range in Asia Minor.   142 *turns to a crow:* I.e., seems black by contrast.   144 *seal:* Pledge.   146 *set against:* Attack.   150 *in souls:* I.e., heart and soul.   153 *superpraise:* Overpraise; *parts:* Qualities.   157 *trim:* Pretty, fine (said ironically).   159 *sort:* Character, quality.   160 *extort:* Twist, torture.   169 *will none:* I.e., want no part of her.   171 *to . . . sojourned:* Only visited with her.

And now to Helen is it home returned,
  There to remain.
Lysander: Helen, it is not so.
Demetrius: Disparage not the faith thou dost not know,
  Lest, to thy peril, thou aby° it dear.   175
  Look where thy love comes; yonder is thy dear.

    Enter Hermia.

Hermia: Dark night, that from the eye his° function takes,
  The ear more quick of apprehension makes;
  Wherein it doth impair the seeing sense,
  It pays the hearing double recompense.   180
  Thou art not by mine eye, Lysander, found;
  Mine ear, I thank it, brought me to thy sound.
  But why unkindly didst thou leave me so?
Lysander: Why should he stay, whom love doth press to go?
Hermia: What love could press Lysander from my side?   185
Lysander: Lysander's love, that would not let him bide —
  Fair Helena, who more engilds° the night
  Than all yon fiery oes° and eyes of light.
  Why seek'st thou me? Could not this make thee know
  The hate I bear thee made me leave thee so?   190
Hermia: You speak not as you think. It cannot be.
Helena: Lo, she is one of this confederacy!
  Now I perceive they have conjoined all three
  To fashion this false sport, in spite of me.°
  Injurious Hermia, most ungrateful maid!   195
  Have you conspired, have you with these contrived°
  To bait° me with this foul derision?
  Is all the counsel° that we two have shared —
  The sisters' vows, the hours that we have spent
  When we have chid the hasty-footed time   200
  For parting us — O, is all forgot?
  All schooldays' friendship, childhood innocence?
  We, Hermia, like two artificial° gods
  Have with our needles created both one flower,
  Both on one sampler, sitting on one cushion,   205
  Both warbling of one song, both in one key,
  As if our hands, our sides, voices, and minds
  Had been incorporate.° So we grew together,
  Like to a double cherry, seeming parted,
  But yet an union in partition,   210
  Two lovely° berries molded on one stem;
  So, with two seeming bodies but one heart,
  Two of the first, like coats in heraldry,

---

175 *aby:* Pay for.   177 *his:* Its.   187 *engilds:* Gilds, brightens with a golden light.   188 *oes:* Spangles (here, stars).   194 *in spite of me:* To vex me.   196 *contrived:* Plotted.   197 *bait:* Torment, as one sets on dogs to bait a bear.   198 *counsel:* Confidential talk.   203 *artificial:* Skilled in art or creation.   208 *incorporate:* Of one body.   211 *lovely:* Loving.

Due but to one and crownèd with one crest.°
And will you rend our ancient love asunder,   215
To join with men in scorning your poor friend?
It is not friendly, 'tis not maidenly.
Our sex, as well as I, may chide you for it,
Though I alone do feel the injury.

Hermia: I am amazèd at your passionate words.   220
I scorn you not. It seems that you scorn me.

Helena: Have you not set Lysander, as in scorn,
To follow me and praise my eyes and face?
And made your other love, Demetrius,
Who even but now did spurn me with his foot,   225
To call me goddess, nymph, divine, and rare,
Precious, celestial? Wherefore speaks he this
To her he hates? And wherefore doth Lysander
Deny your love, so rich within his soul,
And tender° me, forsooth, affection,   230
But by your setting on, by your consent?
What though I be not so in grace° as you,
So hung upon with love, so fortunate,
But miserable most, to love unloved?
This you should pity rather than despise.   235

Hermia: I understand not what you mean by this.

Helena: Ay, do! Persever, counterfeit sad° looks,
Make mouths° upon° me when I turn my back,
Wink each at other, hold the sweet jest up.°
This sport, well carried,° shall be chronicled.   240
If you have any pity, grace, or manners,
You would not make me such an argument.°
But fare ye well. 'Tis partly my own fault,
Which death, or absence, soon shall remedy.

Lysander: Stay, gentle Helena; hear my excuse,   245
My love, my life, my soul, fair Helena!

Helena: O excellent!

Hermia [to Lysander]: Sweet, do not scorn her so.

Demetrius [to Lysander]: If she cannot entreat,° I can compel.

Lysander: Thou canst compel no more than she entreat.   250
Thy threats have no more strength than her weak prayers.
Helen, I love thee, by my life, I do!
I swear by that which I will lose for thee,
To prove him false that says I love thee not.

Demetrius [to Helena]: I say I love thee more than he can do.   255

Lysander: If thou say so, withdraw, and prove it too.°

213–214 *Two . . . crest:* I.e., we have two separate bodies, just as a coat of arms in heraldry can
be represented twice on a shield but surmounted by a single crest.   230 *tender:* Offer.
232 *grace:* Favor.   237 *sad:* Grave, serious.   238 *mouths:* I.e., mows, faces, grimaces;
upon: At.   239 *hold . . . up:* Keep up the joke.   240 *carried:* Managed.   242 *argument:*
Subject for a jest.   249 *entreat:* I.e., succeed by entreaty.   256 *withdraw . . . too:* I.e., withdraw with me and prove your claim in a duel (the two gentlemen are armed).

Demetrius: Quick, come!

Hermia: Lysander, whereto tends all this?

Lysander: Away, you Ethiope!°   *[He tries to break away from Hermia.]*

Demetrius: No, no; he'll

    Seem to break loose; take on as° you would follow,

    But yet come not. You are a tame man. Go!   260

Lysander [to Hermia]: Hang off,° thou cat, thou burr! Vile thing, let loose,

    Or I will shake thee from me like a serpent!

Hermia: Why are you grown so rude? What change is this,

    Sweet love?

Lysander: Thy love? Out, tawny Tartar, out!

    Out, loathèd med'cine!° O hated potion, hence!   265

Hermia: Do you not jest?

Helena: Yes, sooth,° and so do you.

Lysander: Demetrius, I will keep my word with thee.

Demetrius: I would I had your bond, for I perceive

    A weak bond° holds you. I'll not trust your word.

Lysander: What, should I hurt her, strike her, kill her dead?   270

    Although I hate her, I'll not harm her so.

Hermia: What, can you do me greater harm than hate?

    Hate me? Wherefore? O me, what news,° my love?

    Am not I Hermia? Are not you Lysander?

    I am as fair now as I was erewhile.°   275

    Since night you loved me; yet since night you left me.

    Why, then you left me — O, the gods forbid! —

    In earnest, shall I say?

Lysander: Ay, by my life!

    And never did desire to see thee more.

    Therefore be out of hope, of question, of doubt;   280

    Be certain, nothing truer. 'Tis no jest

    That I do hate thee and love Helena.

Hermia [to Helena]: O me! You juggler! You cankerblossom!°

    You thief of love! What, have you come by night

    And stol'n my love's heart from him?

Helena: Fine, i' faith!   285

    Have you no modesty, no maiden shame,

    No touch of bashfulness? What, will you tear

    Impatient answers from my gentle tongue?

    Fie, fie! You counterfeit, you puppet,° you!

Hermia: "Puppet"? Why, so!° Ay, that way goes the game.   290

    Now I perceive that she hath made compare

    Between our statures; she hath urged her height,

---

258 *Ethiope:* (Referring to Hermia's relatively dark hair and complexion; see also *tawny Tartar* six lines later.)   259 *take on as:* Act as if, make a fuss as if.   261 *Hang off:* Let go. 265 *med'cine:* I.e., poison.   266 *sooth:* Truly.   269 *weak bond:* I.e., Hermia's arm (with a pun on *bond,* "oath," in the previous line).   273 *what news:* What is the matter. 275 *erewhile:* Just now.   283 *cankerblossom:* Worm that destroys the flower bud, or wild rose.   289 *puppet:* (1) Counterfeit (2) dwarfish woman (in reference to Hermia's smaller stature).   290 *Why, so:* I.e., Oh, so that's how it is.

And with her personage, her tall personage,
Her height, forsooth, she hath prevailed with him.
And are you grown so high in his esteem   295
Because I am so dwarfish and so low?
How low am I, thou painted maypole? Speak!
How low am I? I am not yet so low
But that my nails can reach unto thine eyes.

      [She flails at Helena but is restrained.]

Helena: I pray you, though you mock me, gentlemen,   300
 Let her not hurt me. I was never curst;°
 I have no gift at all in shrewishness;
 I am a right° maid for my cowardice.
 Let her not strike me. You perhaps may think,
 Because she is something° lower than myself,   305
 That I can match her.
Hermia: Lower? Hark, again!
Helena: Good Hermia, do not be so bitter with me.
 I evermore did love you, Hermia,
 Did ever keep your counsels, never wronged you,
 Save that, in love unto Demetrius,   310
 I told him of your stealth° unto this wood.
 He followed you; for love I followed him.
 But he hath chid me hence° and threatened me
 To strike me, spurn me, nay, to kill me too.
 And now, so° you will let me quiet go,   315
 To Athens will I bear my folly back
 And follow you no further. Let me go.
 You see how simple and how fond° I am.
Hermia: Why, get you gone. Who is't that hinders you?
Helena: A foolish heart, that I leave here behind.   320
Hermia: What, with Lysander?
Helena: With Demetrius.
Lysander: Be not afraid; she shall not harm thee, Helena.
Demetrius: No, sir, she shall not, though you take her part.
Helena: O, when she is angry, she is keen° and shrewd.°
 She was a vixen when she went to school;   325
 And though she be but little, she is fierce.
Hermia: "Little" again? Nothing but "low" and "little"?
 Why will you suffer her to flout me thus?
 Let me come to her.
Lysander: Get you gone, you dwarf!
 You minimus,° of hindering knotgrass° made!   330
 You bead, you acorn!
Demetrius: You are too officious
 In her behalf that scorns your services.
 Let her alone. Speak not of Helena;

---

301 *curst:* Shrewish. 303 *right:* True. 305 *something:* Somewhat. 311 *stealth:* Stealing away. 313 *chid me hence:* Driven me away with his scolding. 315 *so:* If only.
318 *fond:* Foolish. 324 *keen:* Fierce, cruel; *shrewd:* Shrewish. 330 *minimus:* Diminutive creature; *knotgrass:* A weed, an infusion of which was thought to stunt the growth.

Take not her part. For, if thou dost intend°
Never so little show of love to her,   335
Thou shalt aby° it.
Lysander: Now she holds me not.
Now follow, if thou dar'st, to try whose right,
Of thine or mine, is most in Helena.   *[Exit.]*
Demetrius: Follow? Nay, I'll go with thee, cheek by jowl.°
                                            [Exit, following Lysander.]
Hermia: You, mistress, all this coil° is 'long of° you.   340
Nay, go not back.°
Helena: I will not trust you, I,
Nor longer stay in your curst company.
Your hands than mine are quicker for a fray;
My legs are longer, though, to run away.   *[Exit.]*
Hermia: I am amazed and know not what to say.   *Exit.* 345

[Oberon and Puck come forward.]

Oberon: This is thy negligence. Still thou mistak'st,
Or else committ'st thy knaveries willfully.
Puck: Believe me, king of shadows, I mistook.
Did not you tell me I should know the man
By the Athenian garments he had on?   350
And so far blameless proves my enterprise
That I have 'nointed an Athenian's eyes;
And so far° am I glad it so did sort,°
As° this their jangling I esteem a sport.
Oberon: Thou seest these lovers seek a place to fight.   355
Hie° therefore, Robin, overcast the night;
The starry welkin° cover thou anon
With drooping fog as black as Acheron,°
And lead these testy rivals so astray
As° one come not within another's way.   360
Like to Lysander sometimes frame thy tongue,
Then stir Demetrius up with bitter wrong;°
And sometimes rail thou like Demetrius.
And from each other look thou lead them thus,
Till o'er their brows death-counterfeiting sleep   365
With leaden legs and batty° wings doth creep.
Then crush this herb° into Lysander's eye,   *[giving herb]*
Whose liquor hath this virtuous° property,
To take from thence all error with his° might
And make his eyeballs roll with wonted° sight.   370
When they next wake, all this derision°
Shall seem a dream and fruitless vision,

---

334 *intend:* Give sign of.   336 *aby:* Pay for.   339 *cheek by jowl:* I.e., side by side.   340 *coil:* Turmoil, dissension; *'long of:* On account of.   341 *go not back:* I.e., don't retreat (Hermia is again proposing a flight).   353 *so far:* At least to this extent; *sort:* Turn out.   354 *As:* In that.   356 *Hie:* Hasten.   357 *welkin:* Sky.   358 *Acheron:* River of Hades (here representing Hades itself).   360 *As:* That.   362 *wrong:* Insults.   366 *batty:* Batlike.   367 *this herb:* I.e., the antidote (mentioned in II.i.184) to love-in-idleness.   368 *virtuous:* Efficacious.   369 *his:* Its.   370 *wonted:* Accustomed.   371 *derision:* Laughable business.

And back to Athens shall the lovers wend
With league whose date° till death shall never end.
Whiles I in this affair do thee employ,   375
I'll to my queen and beg her Indian boy;
And then I will her charmèd eye release
From monster's view, and all things shall be peace.

Puck: My fairy lord, this must be done with haste,
For night's swift dragons° cut the clouds full fast,   380
And yonder shines Aurora's harbinger,°
At whose approach ghosts, wand'ring here and there,
Troop home to churchyards. Damnèd spirits all,
That in crossways and floods have burial,°
Already to their wormy beds are gone.   385
For fear lest day should look their shames upon,
They willfully themselves exile from light
And must for aye° consort with black-browed night.

Oberon: But we are spirits of another sort.
I with the Morning's love° have oft made sport,   390
And, like a forester,° the groves may tread
Even till the eastern gate, all fiery red,
Opening on Neptune with fair blessèd beams,
Turns into yellow gold his salt green streams.
But notwithstanding, haste, make no delay.   395
We may effect this business yet ere day.   *[Exit.]*

Puck: Up and down, up and down,
    I will lead them up and down.
    I am feared in field and town.
    Goblin,° lead them up and down.   400
Here comes one.

    Enter Lysander.

Lysander: Where art thou, proud Demetrius? Speak thou now.
Puck [mimicking Demetrius]: Here, villain, drawn° and ready. Where art thou?
Lysander: I will be with thee straight.°
Puck: Follow me, then,
    To plainer° ground.   *[Lysander wanders about,° following the voice.]*

    Enter Demetrius.

Demetrius: Lysander! Speak again!   405
    Thou runaway, thou coward, art thou fled?
    Speak! In some bush? Where dost thou hide thy head?

---

374 *date:* Term of existence.   380 *dragons:* (Supposed by Shakespeare to be yoked to the car
of the goddess of night or the moon.)   381 *Aurora's harbinger:* The morning star, precursor
of dawn.   384 *crossways . . . burial:* (Those who had committed suicide were buried at crossways, with a stake driven through them; those who intentionally or accidentally drowned [in
floods or deep water] would be condemned to wander disconsolately for lack of burial rights.)
388 *for aye:* Forever.   390 *the Morning's love:* Cephalus, a beautiful youth beloved by Aurora;
or perhaps the goddess of the dawn herself.   391 *forester:* Keeper of a royal forest.   400 *Goblin:* Hobgoblin (Puck refers to himself).   403 *drawn:* With drawn sword.   404 *straight:*
Immediately.   405 *plainer:* More open.   *Lysander wanders about:* (Lysander may exit here,
but perhaps not; neither exit nor reentrance is indicated in the early texts.)

Puck [mimicking Lysander]: Thou coward, art thou bragging to the stars,
  Telling the bushes that thou look'st for wars,
  And wilt not come? Come, recreant;° come, thou child,   410
  I'll whip thee with a rod. He is defiled
  That draws a sword on thee.
Demetrius: Yea, art thou there?
Puck: Follow my voice. We'll try° no manhood here.   *Exeunt.*

  [Lysander returns.]

Lysander: He goes before me and still dares me on.
  When I come where he calls, then he is gone.   415
  The villain is much lighter-heeled than I.
  I followed fast, but faster he did fly,
  That fallen am I in dark uneven way,
  And here will rest me. *[He lies down.]* Come, thou gentle day!
  For if but once thou show me thy gray light,   420
  I'll find Demetrius and revenge this spite. *[He sleeps.]*

  [Enter] Robin [Puck] and Demetrius.

Puck: Ho, ho, ho! Coward, why com'st thou not?
Demetrius: Abide° me, if thou dar'st; for well I wot°
  Thou runn'st before me, shifting every place,
  And dar'st not stand nor look me in the face.   425
  Where art thou now?
Puck: Come hither. I am here.
Demetrius: Nay, then, thou mock'st me. Thou shalt buy° this dear,°
  If ever I thy face by daylight see.
  Now go thy way. Faintness constraineth me
  To measure out my length on this cold bed.   430
  By day's approach look to be visited.   *[He lies down and sleeps.]*

  Enter Helena.

Helena: O weary night, O long and tedious night,
  Abate° thy hours! Shine comforts from the east,
  That I may back to Athens by daylight
  From these that my poor company detest;   435
  And sleep, that sometimes shuts up sorrow's eye,
  Steal me awhile from mine own company.   *[She lies down and] sleep[s].*
Puck: Yet but three? Come one more;
  Two of both kinds makes up four.
  Here she comes, curst° and sad.   440
  Cupid is a knavish lad,
  Thus to make poor females mad.

  [Enter Hermia.]

Hermia: Never so weary, never so in woe,
  Bedabbled with the dew and torn with briers,
  I can no further crawl, no further go;   445
  My legs can keep no pace with my desires.

---

410 *recreant:* Cowardly wretch.   413 *try:* Test.   423 *Abide:* Confront, face; *wot:* know.
427 *buy:* Aby, pay for; *dear:* Dearly.   433 *Abate:* Lessen, shorten.   440 *curst:* Ill-tempered.

Here will I rest me till the break of day.
Heavens shield Lysander, if they mean a fray! *[She lies down and sleeps.]*
Puck: On the ground
   Sleep sound.   450
   I'll apply
   To your eye,
   Gentle lover, remedy.   *[He squeezes the juice on Lysander's eyes.]*
   When thou wak'st,
   Thou tak'st   455
   True delight
   In the sight
Of thy former lady's eye;
And the country proverb known,
That every man should take his own,   460
In your waking shall be shown:
   Jack shall have Jill;°
   Naught shall go ill;
The man shall have his mare again, and all shall be well.
             [Exit. The four sleeping lovers remain.]

[ACT IV

SCENE I: *The wood. The lovers are still asleep onstage.*]

*Enter [Titania,] Queen of Fairies, and [Bottom the] clown, and Fairies; and
[Oberon,] the King, behind them.*

Titania: Come, sit thee down upon this flowery bed,
   While I thy amiable° cheeks do coy,°
And stick muskroses in thy sleek smooth head,
   And kiss thy fair large ears, my gentle joy.   *[They recline.]*
Bottom: Where's Peaseblossom?   5
Peaseblossom: Ready.
Bottom: Scratch my head, Peaseblossom. Where's Monsieur Cobweb?
Cobweb: Ready.
Bottom: Monsieur Cobweb, good monsieur, get you your weapons in your
hand, and kill me a red-lipped humble-bee on the top of a thistle; and,   10
good monsieur, bring me the honey bag. Do not fret yourself too
much in the action, monsieur; and, good monsieur, have a care the
honey bag break not. I would be loath to have you overflown with a
honey bag, signor. *[Exit Cobweb.]* Where's Monsieur Mustardseed?
Mustardseed: Ready.   15
Bottom: Give me your neaf,° Monsieur Mustardseed. Pray you, leave your
   courtesy,° good monsieur.
Mustardseed: What's your will?

---

462 *Jack shall have Jill:* (Proverbial for "boy gets girl.")   **Act IV, Scene I.**   2 *amiable:*
Lovely; *coy:* Caress.   16 *neaf:* Fist.   16–17 *leave your courtesy:* I.e., stop bowing, or put on
your hat.

Bottom: Nothing, good monsieur, but to help Cavalery° Cobweb° to
    scratch. I must to the barber's, monsieur, for methinks I am mar-   20
    velous hairy about the face; and I am such a tender ass, if my hair do
    but tickle me I must scratch.
Titania: What, wilt thou hear some music, my sweet love?
Bottom: I have a reasonable good ear in music. Let's have the tongs and
    the bones.°   *[Music: tongs, rural music.°]*   25
Titania: Or say, sweet love, what thou desirest to eat.
Bottom: Truly, a peck of provender.° I could munch your good dry oats.
    Methinks I have a great desire to a bottle° of hay. Good hay, sweet hay,
    hath no fellow.°
Titania: I have a venturous fairy that shall seek   30
    The squirrel's hoard, and fetch thee new nuts.
Bottom: I had rather have a handful or two of dried peas. But, I pray you,
    let none of your people stir° me. I have an exposition of° sleep come
    upon me.
Titania: Sleep thou, and I will wind thee in my arms.   35
    Fairies, begone, and be all ways° away.   *[Exeunt Fairies.]*
    So doth the woodbine° the sweet honeysuckle
    Gently entwist; the female ivy so
    Enrings the barky fingers of the elm.
    O, how I love thee! How I dote on thee!   *[They sleep.]*   40

    Enter Robin Goodfellow [Puck].

Oberon [coming forward]: Welcome, good Robin. Seest thou this sweet sight?
    Her dotage now I do begin to pity.
    For, meeting her of late behind the wood
    Seeking sweet favors° for this hateful fool,
    I did upbraid her and fall out with her.   45
    For she his hairy temples then had rounded
    With coronet of fresh and fragrant flowers;
    And that same dew, which sometime° on the buds
    Was wont to swell like round and orient pearls,°
    Stood now within the pretty flowerets' eyes   50
    Like tears that did their own disgrace bewail.
    When I had at my pleasure taunted her,
    And she in mild terms begged my patience,
    I then did ask of her her changeling child,
    Which straight she gave me, and her fairy sent   55
    To bear him to my bower in Fairyland.
    And, now I have the boy, I will undo

---

19 *Cavalery:* Cavalier (form of address for a gentleman); *Cobweb:* (Seemingly an error, since
Cobweb has been sent to bring honey, while Peaseblossom has been asked to scratch.)
24–25 *tongs...bones:* Instruments for rustic music (the tongs were played like a triangle,
whereas the bones were held between the fingers and used as clappers).   *Music...music:*
(This stage direction is added from the Folio.)   27 *peck of provender:* One-quarter bushel
of grain.   28 *bottle:* Bundle.   29 *fellow:* Equal.   33 *stir:* Disturb; *exposition of:* (Bottom's phrase for "disposition to.")   36 *all ways:* In all directions.   37 *woodbine:*
Bindweed, a climbing plant that twines in the opposite direction from that of honeysuckle.
44 *favors:* I.e., gifts of flowers.   48 *sometime:* Formerly.   49 *orient pearls:* I.e., the most
beautiful of all pearls, those coming from the Orient.

This hateful imperfection of her eyes.
And, gentle Puck, take this transformèd scalp
From off the head of this Athenian swain,   60
That he, awaking when the other° do,
May all to Athens back again repair,°
And think no more of this night's accidents
But as the fierce vexation of a dream.
But first I will release the Fairy Queen.   65

                              [He squeezes an herb on her eyes.]

      Be as thou wast wont to be;
      See as thou wast wont to see.
      Dian's bud° o'er Cupid's flower
      Hath such force and blessèd power.
Now, my Titania, wake you, my sweet queen.   70
Titania [awaking]: My Oberon! What visions have I seen!
      Methought I was enamored of an ass.
Oberon: There lies your love.
Titania: How came these things to pass?
      O, how mine eyes do loathe his visage now!
Oberon: Silence awhile. Robin, take off this head.   75
      Titania, music call, and strike more dead
      Than common sleep of all these five° the sense.
Titania: Music, ho! Music, such as charmeth° sleep!   *[Music.]*
Puck [removing the ass head]: Now, when thou wak'st, with thine own fool's
      eyes peep.
Oberon: Sound, music! Come, my queen, take hands with me,   80
And rock the ground whereon these sleepers be.   *[They dance.]*
      Now thou and I are new in amity,
      And will tomorrow midnight solemnly°
      Dance in Duke Theseus' house triumphantly,
      And bless it to all fair prosperity.   85
      There shall the pairs of faithful lovers be
      Wedded, with Theseus, all in jollity.
Puck: Fairy King, attend, and mark:
      I do hear the morning lark.
Oberon: Then, my queen, in silence sad,°   90
      Trip we after night's shade.
      We the globe can compass soon,
      Swifter than the wandering moon.
Titania: Come, my lord, and in our flight
      Tell me how it came this night   95
      That I sleeping here was found
      With these mortals on the ground.
            Exeunt [Oberon, Titania, and Puck]. Wind horn [within].

---

61 *other:* Others.   62 *repair:* Return.   68 *Dian's bud:* (Perhaps the flower of the *agnus castus* or chaste-tree, supposed to preserve chastity; or perhaps referring simply to Oberon's herb by which he can undo the effects of "Cupid's flower," the love-in-idleness of II.i.166–168.)   77 *these five:* I.e., the four lovers and Bottom.   78 *charmeth:* Brings about, as though by a charm.   83 *solemnly:* Ceremoniously.   90 *sad:* Sober.

Enter Theseus and all his train; [Hippolyta, Egeus].

Theseus: Go, one of you, find out the forester,
  For now our observation° is performed;
  And since we have the vaward° of the day,   100
  My love shall hear the music of my hounds.
  Uncouple° in the western valley; let them go.
  Dispatch, I say, and find the forester.   *[Exit an Attendant.]*
  We will, fair queen, up to the mountain's top
  And mark the musical confusion   105
  Of hounds and echo in conjunction.
Hippolyta: I was with Hercules and Cadmus° once
  When in a wood of Crete they bayed° the bear
  With hounds of Sparta.° Never did I hear
  Such gallant chiding;° for, besides the groves,   110
  The skies, the fountains, every region near
  Seemed all one mutual cry. I never heard
  So musical a discord, such sweet thunder.
Theseus: My hounds are bred out of the Spartan kind,°
  So flewed,° so sanded,° and their heads are hung   115
  With ears that sweep away the morning dew;
  Crook-kneed, and dewlapped° like Thessalian bulls;
  Slow in pursuit, but matched in mouth like bells,
  Each under each.° A cry° more tunable°
  Was never holloed to nor cheered° with horn   120
  In Crete, in Sparta, nor in Thessaly.
Judge when you hear. *[He sees the sleepers.]* But soft!° What nymphs
  are these?
Egeus: My lord, this is my daughter here asleep,
  And this Lysander; this Demetrius is;
  This Helena, old Nedar's Helena.   125
  I wonder of° their being here together.
Theseus: No doubt they rose up early to observe
  The rite of May, and hearing our intent,
  Came here in grace of our solemnity.°
  But speak, Egeus. Is not this the day   130
  That Hermia should give answer of her choice?
Egeus: It is, my lord.
Theseus: Go bid the huntsmen wake them with their horns.
                               [Exit an Attendant.]

  Shout within. Wind horns. They all start up.

---

99 *observation:* I.e., observance to a morn of May (I.i.167).   100 *vaward:* Vanguard, i.e., earliest part.   102 *Uncouple:* Set free for the hunt.   107 *Cadmus:* Mythical founder of Thebes. (This story about him is unknown.)   108 *bayed:* Brought to bay.   109 *hounds of Sparta:* (A breed famous in antiquity for their hunting skill.)   110 *chiding:* I.e., yelping. 114 *kind:* Strain, breed.   115 *So flewed:* Similarly having large hanging chaps or fleshy covering of the jaw; *sanded:* Of sandy color.   117 *dewlapped:* Having pendulous folds of skin under the neck.   118–119 *matched . . . each:* I.e., harmoniously matched in their various cries like a set of bells, from treble down to bass.   119 *cry:* Pack of hounds; *tunable:* Well tuned, melodious.   120 *cheered:* Encouraged.   122 *soft:* I.e., gently, wait a minute. 126 *wonder of:* Wonder at.   129 *in . . . solemnity:* In honor of our wedding ceremony.

Good morrow, friends. Saint Valentine° is past.
Begin these woodbirds but to couple now?   135
Lysander: Pardon, my lord.   *[They kneel.]*
Theseus: I pray you all, stand up.   *[They stand.]*
    I know you two are rival enemies;
    How comes this gentle concord in the world,
    That hatred is so far from jealousy°
    To sleep by hate and fear no enmity?   140
Lysander: My lord, I shall reply amazedly,
    Half sleep, half waking; but as yet, I swear,
    I cannot truly say how I came here.
    But, as I think — for truly would I speak,
    And now I do bethink me, so it is —   145
    I came with Hermia hither. Our intent
    Was to be gone from Athens, where° we might,
    Without° the peril of the Athenian law —
Egeus: Enough, enough, my lord; you have enough.
    I beg the law, the law, upon his head.   150
    They would have stol'n away; they would, Demetrius,
    Thereby to have defeated° you and me,
    You of your wife and me of my consent,
    Of my consent that she should be your wife.
Demetrius: My lord, fair Helen told me of their stealth,   155
    Of this their purpose hither° to this wood,
    And I in fury hither followed them,
    Fair Helena in fancy° following me.
    But, my good lord, I wot not by what power —
    But by some power it is — my love to Hermia,   160
    Melted as the snow, seems to me now
    As the remembrance of an idle gaud°
    Which in my childhood I did dote upon;
    And all the faith, the virtue of my heart,
    The object and the pleasure of mine eye,   165
    Is only Helena. To her, my lord,
    Was I betrothed ere I saw Hermia,
    But like a sickness did I loathe this food;
    But, as in health, come to my natural taste,
    Now I do wish it, love it, long for it,   170
    And will forevermore be true to it.
Theseus: Fair lovers, you are fortunately met.
    Of this discourse we more will hear anon.
    Egeus, I will overbear your will;
    For in the temple, by and by, with us   175
    These couples shall eternally be knit.
    And, for° the morning now is something° worn,
    Our purposed hunting shall be set aside.

---

134 *Saint Valentine:* (Birds were supposed to choose their mates on Saint Valentine's Day.)
139 *jealousy:* Suspicion.   147 *where:* Wherever; or, to where.   148 *Without:* Outside of,
beyond.   152 *defeated:* Defrauded.   156 *hither:* In coming hither.   158 *in fancy:* Driven
by love.   162 *idle gaud:* Worthless trinket.   177 *for:* Since; *something:* Somewhat.

Away with us to Athens. Three and three,
We'll hold a feast in great solemnity.°   180
Come Hippolyta.   *[Exeunt Theseus, Hippolyta, Egeus, and train.]*
Demetrius: These things seem small and undistinguishable,
Like far-off mountains turnèd into clouds.
Hermia: Methinks I see these things with parted° eye,
When everything seems double.
Helena: So methinks;   185
And I have found Demetrius like a jewel,
Mine own, and not mine own.°
Demetrius: Are you sure
That we are awake? It seems to me
That yet we sleep, we dream. Do not you think
The Duke was here, and bid us follow him?   190
Hermia: Yea, and my father.
Helena: And Hippolyta.
Lysander: And he did bid us follow to the temple.
Demetrius: Why, then, we are awake. Let's follow him,
And by the way let us recount our dreams.   *[Exeunt the lovers.]*
Bottom [awaking]: When my cue comes, call me, and I will answer. My next   195
is "Most fair Pyramus." Heigh-ho! Peter Quince! Flute, the bellows
mender! Snout, the tinker! Starveling! God's° my life, stolen hence
and left me asleep! I have had a most rare vision. I have had a dream,
past the wit of man to say what dream it was. Man is but an ass if he
go about° to expound this dream. Methought I was — there is no man   200
can tell what. Methought I was — and methought I had — but man is
but a patched° fool if he will offer° to say what methought I had. The
eye of man hath not heard, the ear of man hath not seen, man's hand
is not able to taste, his tongue to conceive, nor his heart to report°
what my dream was. I will get Peter Quince to write a ballad° of this   205
dream. It shall be called "Bottom's Dream," because it hath no
bottom;° and I will sing it in the latter end of a play, before the Duke.
Peradventure, to make it the more gracious, I shall sing it at her°
death.   *[Exit.]*

[SCENE II: *Athens.]*

Enter Quince, Flute, [Snout, and Starveling].

Quince: Have you sent to Bottom's house? Is he come home yet?
Starveling: He cannot be heard of. Out of doubt he is transported.°
Flute: If he come not, then the play is marred. It goes not forward. Doth it?

---

180 *in great solemnity:* With great ceremony.   184 *parted:* I.e., improperly focused.   186–
187 *like . . . mine own:* I.e., like a jewel that one finds by chance and therefore possesses but
cannot certainly consider one's own property.   197 *God's:* May God save.   200 *go about:*
Attempt.   202 *patched:* Wearing motley, i.e., a dress of various colors; *offer:* Venture.
202–204 *The eye . . . report:* (Bottom garbles the terms of 1 Corinthians 2:9.)   205 *ballad:*
(The proper medium for relating sensational stories and preposterous events.)
206–207 *hath no bottom:* Is unfathomable.   208 *her:* Thisbe's (?).   **Scene II.**   2 *transported:* Carried off by fairies; or, possibly, transformed.

Quince: It is not possible. You have not a man in all Athens able to dis-
charge° Pyramus but he.   5

Flute: No, he hath simply the best wit° of any handicraft man in Athens.

Quince: Yea, and the best person° too, and he is a very paramour for a sweet
voice.

Flute: You must say "paragon." A paramour is, God bless us, a thing of
naught.°   10

    Enter Snug the joiner.

Snug: Masters, the Duke is coming from the temple, and there is two or
three lords and ladies more married. If our sport had gone forward,
we had all been made men.°

Flute: O sweet bully Bottom! Thus hath he lost sixpence a day° during his
life; he could not have scaped sixpence a day. An the Duke had not   15
given him sixpence a day for playing Pyramus, I'll be hanged. He
would have deserved it. Sixpence a day in Pyramus, or nothing.

    Enter Bottom.

Bottom: Where are these lads? Where are these hearts?°

Quince: Bottom! O most courageous day! O most happy hour!

Bottom: Masters, I am to discourse wonders.° But ask me not what; for if I   20
tell you, I am no true Athenian. I will tell you everything, right as it fell
out.

Quince: Let us hear, sweet Bottom.

Bottom: Not a word of° me. All that I will tell you is that the Duke hath
dined. Get your apparel together, good strings° to your beards, new   25
ribbons to your pumps;° meet presently° at the palace; every man
look o'er his part; for the short and the long is, our play is preferred.°
In any case, let Thisbe have clean linen; and let not him that plays the
lion pare his nails, for they shall hang out for the lion's claws. And,
most dear actors, eat no onions nor garlic, for we are to utter sweet   30
breath; and I do not doubt but to hear them say it is a sweet comedy.
No more words. Away! Go, away!   *[Exeunt.]*

[ACT V

SCENE I: *Athens. The palace of Theseus.*]

    Enter Theseus, Hippolyta, and Philostrate, [lords, and attendants].

Hippolyta: 'Tis strange, my Theseus, that° these lovers speak of.

Theseus: More strange than true. I never may° believe
    These antique° fables nor these fairy toys.°

4–5 *discharge:* Perform.   6 *wit:* Intellect.   7 *person:* Appearance.   9–10 *a . . . naught:*
A shameful thing.   13 *we . . . men:* I.e., we would have had our fortunes made.   14 *sixpence a day:* I.e., as a royal pension.   18 *hearts:* Good fellows.   20 *am . . . wonders:* Have
wonders to relate.   24 *of:* Out of.   25 *strings:* (To attach the beards.)   26 *pumps:*
Light shoes or slippers; *presently:* Immediately.   27 *preferred:* Selected for consideration.
Act V, Scene I.   1 *that:* That which.   2 *may:* Can.   3 *antique:* Old-fashioned (pun-
ning, too, on *antic,* "strange," "grotesque"); *fairy toys:* Trifling stories about fairies.

Lovers and madmen have such seething brains,
Such shaping fantasies,° that apprehend°   5
More than cool reason ever comprehends.°
The lunatic, the lover, and the poet
Are of imagination all compact.°
One sees more devils than vast hell can hold;
That is the madman. The lover, all as frantic,   10
Sees Helen's° beauty in a brow of Egypt.°
The poet's eye, in a fine frenzy rolling,
Doth glance from heaven to earth, from earth to heaven;
And as imagination bodies forth
The forms of things unknown, the poet's pen   15
Turns them to shapes and gives to airy nothing
A local habitation and a name.
Such tricks hath strong imagination
That, if it would but apprehend some joy,
It comprehends some bringer° of that joy;   20
Or in the night, imagining some fear,°
How easy is a bush supposed a bear!

Hippolyta: But all the story of the night told over,
And all their minds transfigured so together,
More witnesseth than fancy's images°   25
And grows to something of great constancy;°
But, howsoever,° strange and admirable.°

Enter lovers: Lysander, Demetrius, Hermia, and Helena.

Theseus: Here come the lovers, full of joy and mirth.
Joy, gentle friends! Joy and fresh days of love
Accompany your hearts!
Lysander: More than to us   30
Wait in your royal walks, your board, your bed!
Theseus: Come now, what masques,° what dances shall we have,
To wear away this long age of three hours
Between our after-supper and bedtime?
Where is our usual manager of mirth?   35
What revels are in hand? Is there no play
To ease the anguish of a torturing hour?
Call Philostrate.
Philostrate: Here, mighty Theseus.
Theseus: Say, what abridgment° have you for this evening?
What masque? What music? How shall we beguile   40
The lazy time, if not with some delight?
Philostrate [giving him a paper]: There is a brief° how many sports are ripe.

---

5 *fantasies:* Imaginations; *apprehend:* Conceive, imagine.   6 *comprehends:* Understands.
8 *compact:* Formed, composed.   11 *Helen's:* I.e., of Helen of Troy, pattern of beauty; *brow of Egypt:* I.e., face of a gypsy.   20 *bringer:* I.e., source.   21 *fear:* Object of fear.
25 *More... images:* Testifies to something more substantial than mere imaginings.
26 *constancy:* Certainty.   27 *howsoever:* In any case; *admirable:* A source of wonder.
32 *masques:* Courtly entertainments.   39 *abridgment:* Pastime (to abridge or shorten the evening).   42 *brief:* Short written statement, summary.

Make choice of which Your Highness will see first.
Theseus [reads.]: "The battle with the Centaurs,° to be sung
    By an Athenian eunuch to the harp"?   45
    We'll none of that. That have I told my love,
    In glory of my kinsman° Hercules.
    [He reads.] "The riot of the tipsy Bacchanals,
    Tearing the Thracian singer in their rage"?°
    That is an old device;° and it was played   50
    When I from Thebes came last a conqueror.
    [He reads.] "The thrice three Muses mourning for the death
    Of Learning, late deceased in beggary"?°
    That is some satire, keen and critical,
    Not sorting with° a nuptial ceremony.   55
    [He reads.] "A tedious brief scene of young Pyramus
    And his love Thisbe; very tragical mirth"?
    Merry and tragical? Tedious and brief?
    That is, hot ice and wondrous strange° snow.
    How shall we find the concord of this discord?   60
Philostrate: A play there is, my lord, some ten words long,
    Which is as brief as I have known a play;
    But by ten words, my lord, it is too long,
    Which makes it tedious. For in all the play
    There is not one word apt, one player fitted.   65
    And tragical, my noble lord, it is,
    For Pyramus therein doth kill himself.
    Which, when I saw rehearsed, I must confess,
    Made mine eyes water; but more merry tears
    The passion of loud laughter never shed.   70
Theseus: What are they that do play it?
Philostrate: Hardhanded men that work in Athens here,
    Which never labored in their minds till now,
    And now have toiled° their unbreathed° memories
    With this same play, against° your nuptial.   75
Theseus: And we will hear it.
Philostrate: No, my noble lord,
    It is not for you. I have heard it over,
    And it is nothing, nothing in the world;
    Unless you can find sport in their intents,
    Extremely stretched° and conned° with cruel pain   80

---

44 *battle . . . Centaurs:* (Probably refers to the battle of the Centaurs and the Lapithae, when
the Centaurs attempted to carry off Hippodamia, bride of Theseus' friend Pirothous. The
story is told in Ovid's *Metamorphoses* 12.)   47 *kinsman:* (Plutarch's "Life of Theseus" states
that Hercules and Theseus were near kinsmen. Theseus is referring to a version of the battle
of the Centaurs in which Hercules was said to be present.)   48–49 *The riot . . . rage:* (This
was the story of the death of Orpheus, as told in *Metamorphoses* 11.)   50 *device:* Show, performance.   52–53 *The thrice . . . beggary:* (Possibly an allusion to Spenser's *Teares of the Muses*,
1591, though "satires" deploring the neglect of learning and the creative arts were commonplace.)   55 *sorting with:* Befitting.   59 *strange:* (Sometimes emended to an adjective that
would contrast with *snow,* just as *hot* contrasts with *ice.*)   74 *toiled:* Taxed; *unbreathed:* Unex-
ercised.   75 *against:* In preparation for.   80 *stretched:* Strained; *conned:* Memorized.

    To do you service.
Theseus: I will hear that play;
    For never anything can be amiss
    When simpleness° and duty tender it.
    Go, bring them in; and take your places, ladies.
                  [Philostrate goes to summon the players.]
Hippolyta: I love not to see wretchedness o'ercharged,°   85
    And duty in his service° perishing.
Theseus: Why, gentle sweet, you shall see no such thing.
Hippolyta: He says they can do nothing in this kind.°
Theseus: The kinder we, to give them thanks for nothing.
    Our sport shall be to take what they mistake;   90
    And what poor duty cannot do, noble respect°
    Takes it in might, not merit.°
    Where I have come, great clerks° have purposèd
    To greet me with premeditated welcomes;
    Where I have seen them shiver and look pale,   95
    Make periods in the midst of sentences,
    Throttle their practiced accent° in their fears,
    And in conclusion dumbly have broke off,
    Not paying me a welcome. Trust me, sweet,
    Out of this silence yet I picked a welcome;   100
    And in the modesty of fearful duty
    I read as much as from the rattling tongue
    Of saucy and audacious eloquence.
    Love, therefore, and tongue-tied simplicity
    In least° speak most, to my capacity.°   105

    [Philostrate returns.]

Philostrate: So please Your Grace, the Prologue° is addressed.°
Theseus: Let him approach.   *[A flourish of trumpets.]*

    Enter the Prologue [Quince].

Prologue: If we offend, it is with our good will.
    That you should think, we come not to offend,
    But with good will. To show our simple skill,   110
    That is the true beginning of our end.
    Consider, then, we come but in despite.
    We do not come, as minding° to content you,
    Our true intent is. All for your delight
    We are not here. That you should here repent you,   115
    The actors are at hand; and, by their show,
    You shall know all that you are like to know.

---

83 *simpleness:* Simplicity.   85 *wretchedness o'ercharged:* Social or economic inferiors overburdened.   86 *his service:* Its attempt to serve.   88 *kind:* Kind of thing.   91 *respect:* Evaluation, consideration.   92 *Takes . . . merit:* Values it for the effort made rather than for the excellence achieved.   93 *clerks:* Learned men.   97 *practiced accent:* I.e., rehearsed speech; or, usual way of speaking.   105 *least:* I.e., saying least; *to my capacity:* In my judgment and understanding.   106 *Prologue:* Speaker of the prologue; *addressed:* Ready.   113 *minding:* Intending.

Theseus: This fellow doth not stand upon points.°

Lysander: He hath rid° his prologue like a rough° colt; he knows not the
     stop.° A good moral, my lord: it is not enough to speak, but to speak   120
     true.

Hippolyta: Indeed, he hath played on his prologue like a child on a
     recorder:° a sound, but not in government.°

Theseus: His speech was like a tangled chain: nothing° impaired, but all
     disordered. Who is next?   125

*Enter Pyramus [Bottom], and Thisbe [Flute], and Wall [Snout], and Moonshine
[Starveling], and Lion [Snug].*

Prologue: Gentles, perchance you wonder at this show;
          But wonder on, till truth make all things plain.
     This man is Pyramus, if you would know;
          This beauteous lady Thisbe is, certain.
     This man with lime and roughcast doth present   130
          Wall, that vile wall which did these lovers sunder;
     And through Wall's chink, poor souls, they are content
          To whisper. At the which let no man wonder.
     This man, with lantern, dog, and bush of thorn,
          Presenteth Moonshine; for, if you will know,   135
     By moonshine did these lovers think no scorn°
          To meet at Ninus' tomb, there, there to woo.
     This grisly beast, which Lion hight° by name,
          The trusty Thisbe coming first by night
     Did scare away, or rather did affright;   140
     And as she fled, her mantle she did fall,°
          Which Lion vile with bloody mouth did stain.
     Anon comes Pyramus, sweet youth and tall,°
          And finds his trusty Thisbe's mantle slain;
     Whereat, with blade, with bloody, blameful blade,   145
          He bravely broached° his boiling bloody breast.
     And Thisbe, tarrying in mulberry shade,
          His dagger drew, and died. For all the rest,
     Let Lion, Moonshine, Wall, and lovers twain
     At large° discourse, while here they do remain.   150
                              Exeunt Lion, Thisbe, and Moonshine.

Theseus: I wonder if the lion be to speak.

Demetrius: No wonder, my lord. One lion may, when many asses do.

Wall: In this same interlude° it doth befall
          That I, one Snout by name, present a wall;
     And such a wall as I would have you think   155
          That had in it a crannied hole or chink,

---

118 *stand upon points:* (1) Heed niceties or small points (2) pay attention to punctuation in his
reading. (The humor of Quince's speech is in the blunders of its punctuation.)   119 *rid:*
Ridden; *rough:* unbroken.   120 *stop:* (1) Stopping of a colt by reining it in (2) punctuation
mark.   123 *recorder:* Wind instrument like a flute; *government:* Control.   124 *nothing:*
Not at all.   136 *think no scorn:* Think it no disgraceful matter.   138 *hight:* Is called.
141 *fall:* Let fall.   143 *tall:* Courageous.   146 *broached:* Stabbed.   150 *At large:* In full,
at length.   153 *interlude:* Play.

Through which the lovers, Pyramus and Thisbe,
Did whisper often, very secretly.
This loam, this roughcast, and this stone doth show
That I am that same wall; the truth is so.   160
And this the cranny is, right and sinister,°
Through which the fearful lovers are to whisper.
Theseus: Would you desire lime and hair to speak better?
Demetrius: It is the wittiest partition° that ever I heard discourse, my lord.

   [Pyramus comes forward.]

Theseus: Pyramus draws near the wall. Silence!   165
Pyramus: O grim-looked° night! O night with hue so black!
   O night, which ever art when day is not!
O night, O night! Alack, alack, alack,
   I fear my Thisbe's promise is forgot.
And thou, O wall, O sweet, O lovely wall,   170
   That stand'st between her father's ground and mine,
Thou wall, O wall, O sweet and lovely wall,
   Show me thy chink, to blink through with mine eyne.
Thanks, courteous wall. Jove shield thee well for this.
   But what see I? No Thisbe do I see.   175
O wicked wall, through whom I see no bliss!
   Cursed be thy stones for thus deceiving me!
Theseus: The wall, methinks, being sensible,° should curse again.°
Pyramus: No, in truth, sir, he should not. "Deceiving me" is Thisbe's cue:
she is to enter now, and I am to spy her through the wall. You shall see,   180
it will fall pat° as I told you. Yonder she comes.

   Enter Thisbe.

Thisbe: O wall, full often hast thou heard my moans
   For parting my fair Pyramus and me.
My cherry lips have often kissed thy stones,
   Thy stones with lime and hair knit up in thee.   185
Pyramus: I see a voice. Now will I to the chink,
   To spy an° I can hear my Thisbe's face.
   Thisbe!
Thisbe: My love! Thou art my love, I think.
Pyramus: Think what thou wilt, I am thy lover's grace,°   190
   And like Limander° am I trusty still.
Thisbe: And I like Helen,° till the Fates me kill.
Pyramus: Not Shafalus to Procrus° was so true.
Thisbe: As Shafalus to Procrus, I to you.
Pyramus: O, kiss me through the hole of this vile wall!   195
Thisbe: I kiss the wall's hole, not your lips at all.

---

161 *right and sinister:* I.e., the right side of it and the left; or, running from right to left, hori-
zontally.   164 *partition:* (1) Wall (2) section of a learned treatise or oration.   166 *grim-
looked:* Grim-looking.   178 *sensible:* Capable of feeling; *again:* In return.   181 *pat:*
Exactly.   187 *an:* If.   190 *lover's grace:* I.e., gracious lover.   191, 192 *Limander, Helen:*
(Blunders for "Leander" and "Hero.")   193 *Shafalus, Procrus:* (Blunders for "Cephalus" and
"Procris," also famous lovers.)

Pyramus: Wilt thou at Ninny's tomb meet me straightway?

Thisbe: 'Tide life, 'tide° death, I come without delay.

   [Exeunt Pyramus and Thisbe.]

Wall: Thus have I, Wall, my part dischargèd so;

   And, being done, thus Wall away doth go.   *[Exit.]* 200

Theseus: Now is the mural down between the two neighbors.

Demetrius: No remedy, my lord, when walls are so willful° to hear without
   warning.°

Hippolyta: This is the silliest stuff that ever I heard.

Theseus: The best in this kind° are but shadows,° and the worst are no 205
   worse, if imagination amend them.

Hippolyta: It must be your imagination then, and not theirs.

Theseus: If we imagine no worse of them than they of themselves, they
   may pass for excellent men. Here come two noble beasts in, a man
   and a lion.   210

   Enter Lion and Moonshine.

Lion: You, ladies, you, whose gentle hearts do fear

   The smallest monstrous mouse that creeps on floor,

  May now perchance both quake and tremble here,

   When lion rough in wildest rage doth roar.

  Then know that I, as Snug the joiner, am   215

  A lion fell,° nor else no lion's dam;

  For, if I should as lion come in strife

  Into this place, 'twere pity on my life.

Theseus: A very gentle beast, and of a good conscience.

Demetrius: The very best at a beast, my lord, that e'er I saw.   220

Lysander: This lion is a very fox for his valor.°

Theseus: True; and a goose for his discretion.°

Demetrius: Not so, my lord, for his valor cannot carry his discretion, and the
   fox carries the goose.

Theseus: His discretion, I am sure, cannot carry his valor; for the goose car- 225
   ries not the fox. It is well. Leave it to his discretion, and let us listen
   to the moon.

Moon: This lanthorn° doth the hornèd moon present—

Demetrius: He should have worn the horns on his head.°

Theseus: He is no crescent,° and his horns are invisible within the cir- 230
   cumference.

Moon: This lanthorn doth the hornèd moon present;

   Myself the man i' the moon do seem to be.

---

198 *'tide:* Betide, come.   202 *willful:* Willing.   202–203 *without warning:* I.e., without
warning the parents. (Demetrius makes a joke on the proverb "Walls have ears.")   205 *in
this kind:* Of this sort; *shadows:* Likenesses, representations.   216 *lion fell:* Fierce lion (with
a play on the idea of "lion skin").   221 *is . . . valor:* I.e., his valor consists of craftiness and
discretion.   222 *a goose . . . discretion:* I.e., as discreet as a goose, that is, more foolish than
discreet.   228 *lanthorn:* (This original spelling, *lanthorn,* may suggest a play on the *horn* of
which lanterns were made and also on a cuckold's horns; however, the spelling *lanthorn* is not
used consistently for comic effect in this play or elsewhere. At Act V, Scene I, line 134, for
example, the word is *lantern* in the original.)   229 *on his head:* (As a sign of cuckoldry.)
230 *crescent:* A waxing moon.

Theseus: This is the greatest error of all the rest. The man should be put
into the lanthorn. How is it else the man i' the moon?   235
Demetrius: He dares not come there for° the candle, for you see it is already
in snuff.°
Hippolyta: I am weary of this moon. Would he would change!
Theseus: It appears, by his small light of discretion, that he is in the wane;
but yet, in courtesy, in all reason, we must stay the time.   240
Lysander: Proceed, Moon.
Moon: All that I have to say is to tell you that the lanthorn is the moon, I,
the man i' the moon, this thornbush my thornbush, and this dog my
dog.
Demetrius: Why, all these should be in the lanthorn, for all these are in   245
the moon. But silence! Here comes Thisbe.

    Enter Thisbe.

Thisbe: This is old Ninny's tomb. Where is my love?
Lion [roaring]: O!
Demetrius: Well roared, Lion.   *[Thisbe runs off, dropping her mantle.]*
Theseus: Well run, Thisbe.   250
Hippolyta: Well shone, Moon. Truly, the moon shines with a good grace.
                            [The Lion worries Thisbe's mantle.]
Theseus: Well moused,° Lion.

    [Enter Pyramus; exit Lion.]

Demetrius: And then came Pyramus.
Lysander: And so the Lion vanished.
Pyramus: Sweet Moon, I thank thee for thy sunny beams;   255
    I thank thee, Moon, for shining now so bright;
For, by thy gracious, golden, glittering gleams,
    I trust to take of truest Thisbe sight.
        But stay, O spite!
        But mark, poor knight,   260
    What dreadful dole° is here?
        Eyes, do you see?
        How can it be?
    O dainty duck! O dear!
        Thy mantle good,   265
        What, stained with blood?
    Approach, ye Furies° fell!°
        O Fates,° come, come,
        Cut thread and thrum;°
    Quail,° crush, conclude, and quell!°   270

---

236 *for:* Because of, for fear of.   237 *in snuff:* (1) Offended (2) in need of snuffing or
trimming.   252 *moused:* Shaken, torn, bitten.   261 *dole:* Grievous event.   267 *Furies:*
Avenging goddesses of Greek myth; *fell:* Fierce.   268 *Fates:* The three goddesses (Clotho,
Lachesis, Atropos) of Greek myth who spun, drew, and cut the thread of human life.
269 *thread and thrum:* I.e., everything — the good and bad alike; literally, the warp in weaving
and the loose end of the warp.   270 *Quail:* Overpower; *quell:* Kill, destroy.

Theseus: This passion, and the death of a dear friend, would go near to make a man look sad.°

Hippolyta: Beshrew my heart, but I pity the man.

Pyramus: O, wherefore, Nature, didst thou lions frame?
    Since lion vile hath here deflowered my dear,   275
    Which is — no, no, which was — the fairest dame
    That lived, that loved, that liked, that looked with cheer.°
        Come, tears, confound,
        Out, sword, and wound
    The pap° of Pyramus;   280
        Ay, that left pap,
        Where heart doth hop.   *[He stabs himself.]*
    Thus die I, thus, thus, thus.
        Now am I dead,
        Now am I fled;   285
    My soul is in the sky.
        Tongue, lose thy light;
        Moon, take thy flight.   *[Exit Moonshine.]*
    Now die, die, die, die, die.   *[Pyramus dies.]*

Demetrius: No die, but an ace,° for him; for he is but one.°   290

Lysander: Less than an ace, man; for he is dead, he is nothing.

Theseus: With the help of a surgeon he might yet recover, and yet prove an ass.°

Hippolyta: How chance Moonshine is gone before Thisbe comes back and finds her lover?   295

Theseus: She will find him by starlight.

    [Enter Thisbe.]

    Here she comes; and her passion ends the play.

Hippolyta: Methinks she should not use a long one for such a Pyramus. I hope she will be brief.

Demetrius: A mote° will turn the balance, which Pyramus, which° Thisbe,   300
is the better: he for a man, God warrant us; she for a woman, God bless us.

Lysander: She hath spied him already with those sweet eyes.

Demetrius: And thus she means,° videlicet:°

Thisbe: Asleep, my love?   305
      What, dead, my dove?
    O Pyramus, arise!
      Speak, speak. Quite dumb?
      Dead, dead? A tomb
    Must cover thy sweet eyes.   310

271–272 *This . . . sad:* I.e., if one had other reason to grieve, one might be sad, but not from this absurd portrayal of passion.   277 *cheer:* Countenance.   280 *pap:* Breast.   290 *ace:* The side of the die featuring the single pip, or spot (the pun is on *die* as a singular of *dice;* Bottom's performance is not worth a whole *die* but rather one single face of it, one small portion); *one:* (1) An individual person (2) unique.   293 *ass:* (With a pun on *ace.*)   300 *mote:* Small particle; *which . . . which:* Whether . . . or.   304 *means:* Moans, laments (with a pun on the meaning "lodge a formal complaint"); *videlicet:* To wit.

These lily lips,
This cherry nose,
These yellow cowslip cheeks,
Are gone, are gone!
Lovers, make moan.   315
His eyes were green as leeks.
O Sisters Three,°
Come, come to me,
With hands as pale as milk;
Lay them in gore,   320
Since you have shore°
With shears his thread of silk.
Tongue, not a word.
Come, trusty sword,

Come, blade, my breast imbrue!°   *[She stabs herself.]* 325

And farewell, friends.
Thus Thisbe ends.

Adieu, adieu, adieu.   *[She dies.]*

Theseus: Moonshine and Lion are left to bury the dead.

Demetrius: Ay, and Wall too.   330

Bottom [starting up, as Flute does also]: No, I assure you, the wall is down that parted their fathers. Will it please you to see the epilogue, or to hear a Bergomask dance° between two of our company?

[The other players enter.]

Theseus: No epilogue, I pray you; for your play needs no excuse. Never excuse; for when the players are all dead, there need none to be   335 blamed. Marry, if he that writ it had played Pyramus and hanged himself in Thisbe's garter, it would have been a fine tragedy; and so it is, truly, and very notably discharged. But, come, your Bergomask. Let your epilogue alone.   *[A dance.]*

The iron tongue° of midnight hath told° twelve.   340
Lovers, to bed, 'tis almost fairy time.
I fear we shall outsleep the coming morn
As much as we this night have overwatched.°
This palpable-gross° play hath well beguiled
The heavy° gait of night. Sweet friends, to bed.   345
A fortnight hold we this solemnity,
In nightly revels and new jollity.   *Exeunt.*

Enter Puck [carrying a broom].

Puck: Now the hungry lion roars,
And the wolf behowls the moon,
Whilst the heavy° plowman snores,   350
All with weary task fordone.°

---

317 *Sisters Three:* The Fates.   321 *shore:* Shorn.   325 *imbrue:* Stain with blood.   333 *Bergomask dance:* A rustic dance named from Bergamo, a province in the state of Venice.   340 *iron tongue:* Clapper of a bell; *told:* Counted, struck ("tolled").   343 *overwatched:* Stayed up too late.   344 *palpable-gross:* Palpably gross, obviously crude.   345 *heavy:* Drowsy, dull.   350 *heavy:* Tired.   351 *fordone:* Exhausted.

Now the wasted brands° do glow,
    Whilst the screech owl, screeching loud,
Puts the wretch that lies in woe
    In remembrance of a shroud.   355
Now it is the time of night
    That the graves, all gaping wide,
Every one lets forth his sprite,°
    In the church-way paths to glide.
And we fairies, that do run   360
    By the triple Hecate's° team
From the presence of the sun,
    Following darkness like a dream,
Now are frolic.° Not a mouse
    Shall disturb this hallowed house.   365
I am sent with broom before,
To sweep the dust behind° the door.

Enter [Oberon and Titania,] King and Queen of Fairies, with all their train.

Oberon: Through the house give glimmering light,
    By the dead and drowsy fire;
Every elf and fairy sprite   370
    Hop as light as bird from brier;
And this ditty, after me,
    Sing, and dance it trippingly.
Titania: First, rehearse° your song by rote,
    To each word a warbling note.   375
Hand in hand, with fairy grace,
Will we sing, and bless this place.   *[Song and dance.]*
Oberon: Now, until the break of day,
    Through this house each fairy stray.
To the best bride-bed will we,   380
    Which by us shall blessèd be;
And the issue there create°
    Ever shall be fortunate.
So shall all the couples three
    Ever true in loving be;   385
And the blots of Nature's hand
    Shall not in their issue stand;
Never mole, harelip, nor scar,
    Nor mark prodigious,° such as are
Despisèd in nativity,   390
    Shall upon their children be.
With this field dew consecrate,°

---

352 *wasted brands:* Burned-out logs.   358 *Every . . . sprite:* Every grave lets forth its ghost.
361 *triple Hecate's:* (Hecate ruled in three capacities: as Luna or Cynthia in heaven, as Diana
on earth, and as Proserpina in hell.)   364 *frolic:* Merry.   367 *behind:* From behind,
or else like sweeping the dirt under the carpet (Robin Goodfellow was a household
spirit who helped good housemaids and punished lazy ones, but he could, of course, be mischievous).   374 *rehearse:* Recite.   382 *create:* Created.   389 *prodigious:* Monstrous,
unnatural.   392 *consecrate:* Consecrated.

Every fairy take his gait,°
And each several° chamber bless,
Through this palace, with sweet peace;   395
And the owner of it blest
Ever shall in safety rest.
Trip away; make no stay;
Meet me all by break of day.   *Exeunt [Oberon, Titania, and train].*
Puck [to the audience]: If we shadows have offended,   400
Think but this, and all is mended,
That you have but slumbered here°
While these visions did appear.
And this weak and idle theme,
No more yielding but° a dream,   405
Gentles, do not reprehend.
If you pardon, we will mend.°
And, as I am an honest Puck,
If we have unearnèd luck
Now to scape the serpent's tongue,°   410
We will make amends ere long;
Else the Puck a liar call.
So, good night unto you all.
Give me your hands,° if we be friends,
And Robin shall restore amends.°   *[Exit.]* 415

393 *take his gait:* Go his way.   394 *several:* Separate.   402 *That...here:* I.e., that it is a "midsummer night's dream."   405 *No...but:* Yielding no more than.   407 *mend:* Improve.   410 *serpent's tongue:* I.e., hissing.   414 *Give...hands:* Applaud.   415 *restore amends:* Give satisfaction in return.

CONSIDERATIONS FOR CRITICAL THINKING AND WRITING

1. FIRST RESPONSE. Discuss the significance of the play's title. What expectations does it create for you?

2. Describe how the two settings, Athens and the nearby woods, reflect different social and physical environments as well as different types of behavior among the characters.

3. What is the symbolic function of the marriage of Theseus and Hippolyta? How is that function revealed in the scenes in which they appear?

4. Characterize the four young lovers. How individualized are their personalities? How does the extent of their characterizations suggest their function in the play?

5. What makes Bottom such a comic figure? How does his behavior shed light on the behavior of the other characters?

6. Consider how women — Hippolyta, Titania, Hermia, and Helena — are presented in the play. What characteristics do they have in common? How do they relate to the men in their lives?

7. Why does Puck describe "mortals" as "fools" (III.ii.115)? To what degree does this description fit the fairies as well?

8. How might Puck be regarded as the play's director as well as a central character?

9. How does the plot bring together the four groups of characters — Theseus and Hippolyta, the four lovers, the craftsmen, and the fairies — into a uni-

fied whole? Write a plot summary of the play that connects these four groups of characters. How does this summary resemble popular situation comedies that you've seen on television?

10. Choose a scene that you find particularly funny, and analyze how the humor is created. Describe how the scene contributes to the rest of the play.

11. What is the relationship between the play within the play, "Pyramus and Thisbe," and *A Midsummer Night's Dream*? How do the plot and theme of each serve as commentaries on each other?

12. Despite its comic scenes and happy ending, at various moments this play does raise the specter of potential tragedy. How seriously do you think we are meant to worry about the characters? What are your emotions about the young lovers as they struggle to sort things out in the woods? Discuss how this play might be transformed into a tragedy.

ESSAYS

KATIE ROIPHE (B. 1968)

As a relatively young essayist, Katie Roiphe has built a career around her response to the "ardent seventies feminism" of her mother's generation. (Her mother is Anne Roiphe, who has published seven books in twenty years on balancing being female and being a feminist.) As a recent Princeton graduate in 1993, Katie Roiphe published her first book, *The Morning After: Sex, Fear, and Feminism on Campus,* in which she questions "rape-crisis feminism." Roiphe's ideas have been the subject of much feminist debate ever since. (Essayist and critic Katha Pollitt later called her book "poorly argued and full of misrepresentations, slapdash research, and gossip," while political theorist Jean Bethke Elshtain called her "the voice of reason.") Her second book, *Last Night in Paradise: Sex and Morals at the Century's End* (1997), argues that safe sex messages say more about our moral health than our physical health. In "The Independent Woman (and Other Lies)," which appeared in *Esquire* in 1997, Roiphe questions another truism of seventies feminism, asking why a woman wouldn't want to find a man who will take care of her the way her father did.

The Independent Woman (and Other Lies)   1997

I was out to drinks with a man I'd recently met. "I'll take care of that," he said, sweeping up the check, and as he said it, I felt a warm glow of security, as if everything in my life was suddenly going to be taken care of. As the pink cosmopolitans glided smoothly across the bar, I thought for a moment of how nice it would be to live in an era when men *always* took care of the cosmopolitans. I pictured a lawyer with a creamy leather briefcase going off to work in the mornings and coming back home in the evenings to the townhouse he has

Katie Roiphe (1999), author of The Morning After: Sex, Fear, and Feminism on Campus, *a critique of modern feminism's focus on women's victimization.*

bought for me, where I have been ordering flowers, soaking in the bath, reading a nineteenth-century novel, and working idly on my next book. This fantasy of a Man in a Gray Flannel Suit° is one that independent, strong-minded women of the nineties are distinctly not supposed to have, but I find myself having it all the same. And many of the women I know are having it also.

Seen from the outside, my life is the model of modern female independence: I live alone, pay my own bills, and fix my stereo when it breaks down. But it sometimes seems like my independence is in part an elaborately constructed facade that hides a more traditional feminine desire to be protected and provided for. I admitted this once to my mother, an ardent seventies feminist, over Caesar salads at lunch, and she was shocked. I saw it on her face: *How could a daughter of mine say something like this?* I rushed to reassure her that I wouldn't dream of giving up my career, and it's true that I wouldn't. But when I think about marriage, somewhere deep in the irrational layers of my psyche, I still think of the man as the breadwinner. I feel as though I am working for "fulfillment," for "reward," for the richness of life promised by feminism, and that mundane things such as rent and mortgages and college tuitions are, ultimately, the man's responsibility — even though I know that they shouldn't be. "I just don't want to have to *think* about money," one of my most competent female friends said to me recently, and I knew exactly what she meant. Our liberated, postfeminist world seems to be filled with women who don't want to think about money and men who feel that they have to.

There are plenty of well-adjusted, independent women who never fantasize about the Man in the Gray Flannel Suit, but there are also a surprising number who do. Of course, there is a well-established tradition of women

The Man in the Gray Flannel Suit: A best-selling novel by Sloan Wilson published in 1955.

looking for men to provide for them that spans from Edith Wharton's *The House of Mirth* to Helen Gurley Brown's *Sex and the Single Girl* to Mona Simpson's *A Regular Guy*. You could almost say that this is the American dream for women: Find a man who can lift you out of your circumstances, whisk you away to Venice, and give you a new life.

In my mother's generation, a woman felt she had to marry a man with a successful career, whereas today she is supposed to focus on her own. Consider that in 1990, women received 42 percent of law degrees (up from 2.5 percent in 1960) and that as of 1992, women held 47 percent of lucrative jobs in the professions and management. And now that American women are more economically independent than ever before, now that we don't *need* to attach ourselves to successful men, many of us still seem to want to. I don't think, in the end, that this attraction is about bank accounts or trips to Paris or hundred-dollar haircuts; I think it's about the reassuring feeling of being protected and provided for, a feeling that mingles with love and attraction on the deepest level. It's strange to think of professional women in the nineties drinking café lattes and talking about men in the same way as characters in Jane Austen novels, appraising their prospects and fortunes, but many of us actually do.

A friend of mine, an editor at a women's magazine, said about a recent 5
breakup, "I just hated having to say, 'My boyfriend is a dog walker.' I hated the fact that he didn't have a real job." And then immediately afterward, she said, "I feel really awful admitting all of this." It was as if she had just told me something shameful, as if she had confessed to some terrible perversion. And I understand why she felt guilty. She was admitting to a sort of 1950s worldview that seemed as odd and unfashionable as walking down the street in a poodle skirt. But she is struggling with what defines masculinity and femininity in a supposedly equal society, with what draws us to men, what attracts us, what keeps us interested. She has no more reason to feel guilty than a man who says he likes tall blonds.

I've heard many women say that they wouldn't want to go out with a man who is much less successful than they are because "he would feel uncomfortable." But, of course, *he's* not the only one who would feel uncomfortable. What most of these women are really saying is that they themselves would feel uncomfortable. But why? Why can't the magazine editor be happy with the dog walker? Why does the woman at Salomon Brothers feel unhappy with the banker who isn't doing as well as she is? Part of it may have to do with the way we were raised. Even though I grew up in a liberal household in the seventies, I perceived early on that my father was the one who actually paid for things. As a little girl, I watched my father put his credit card down in restaurants and write checks and go to work every morning in a suit and tie, and it may be that this model of masculinity is still imprinted in my mind. It may be that there is a picture of our fathers that many of us carry like silver lockets around our necks: Why shouldn't we find a man who will take care of us the way our fathers did?

I've seen the various destructive ways in which this expectation can affect people's lives. Sam and Anna met at Brown. After they graduated, Anna went to Hollywood and started making nearly a million dollars a year in television production and Sam became an aspiring novelist who has never even filed a tax return. At first, the disparity in their styles of life manifested itself in trivial ways. "She would want to go to an expensive bistro," Sam, who is now twenty-seven, remembers, "and I would want to get a burrito for $4.25. We would go to the bistro and either she'd pay, which was bad, or I'd just eat salad and lots of bread, which was also bad." In college, they had been the kind of couple who stayed up until three in the morning talking about art and beauty and *The Brothers Karamazov,* but now they seemed to be spending a lot of time arguing about money and burritos. One night, when they went out with some of Anna's Hollywood friends, she slipped him eighty dollars under the table so that he could pretend to pay for dinner. Anna felt guilty. Sam was confused. He had grown up with a feminist mother who'd drummed the ideal of strong, independent women into his head, but now that he'd fallen in love with Anna, probably the strongest and most independent woman he'd ever met, she wanted him to pay for her dinner so badly she gave him money to do it. Anna, I should say, is not a particularly materialistic person; she is not someone who cares about Chanel suits and Prada bags. It's just that to her, money had become a luminous symbol of functionality and power.

The five-year relationship began to fall apart. Sam was not fulfilling the role of romantic lead in the script Anna had in her head. In a moment of desperation, Sam blurted out that he had made a lot of money on the stock market. He hadn't. Shortly afterward, they broke up. Anna started dating her boss, and she and Sam had agonizing long-distance phone calls about what had happened. "She kept telling me that she wanted me to be more of a man," Sam says. "She kept saying that she wanted to be taken care of." There was a certain irony to this situation, to this woman who was making almost a million dollars a year, sitting in her Santa Monica house, looking out at the ocean, saying that she just wanted a man who could take care of her.

There is also something appalling in this story, something cruel and hard and infinitely understandable. The strain of Anna's success and Sam's as of yet unrewarded talent was too much for the relationship. When Anna told Sam that she wanted him to be more masculine, part of what she was saying was that she wanted to feel more feminine. It's like the plight of the too-tall teenage girl who's anxiously scanning the dance floor for a fifteen-year-old boy who is taller than she is. A romantic might say, What about love? Love isn't supposed to be about dollars and cents and who puts their Visa card down at an expensive Beverly Hills restaurant. But this is a story about love in its more tarnished, worldly forms; it's about the balance of power, what men and women really want from one another, and the hidden mechanics of romance and attraction. In a way, what happened between my friends Sam and Anna is a parable of the times, of a generation of strong women who are looking for even stronger men.

I've said the same thing as Anna — "I need a man who can take care of me" — to more than one boyfriend, and I hear how it sounds. I recognize how shallow and unreasonable it seems. But I say it anyway. And, even worse, I actually feel it.

The mood passes. I realize that I can take care of myself. The relationship returns to normal, the boyfriend jokes that I should go to the bar at the Plaza to meet bankers, and we both laugh because we know that I don't really want to, but there is an undercurrent of resentment, eddies of tension, and disappointment that remain between us. This is a secret refrain that runs through conversations in bedrooms late at night, through phone wires, and in restaurants over drinks. One has to wonder why, at a moment in history when

10

women can so patently take care of themselves, do so many of us want so much to be taken care of?

The fantasy of a man who pays the bills, who works when you want to take time off to be with your kids or read *War and Peace,* who is in the end *responsible,* is one that many women have but fairly few admit to. It is one of those fantasies, like rape fantasies, that have been forbidden to us by our politics. But it's also deeply ingrained in our imaginations. All of girl culture tells us to find a man who will provide for us, a Prince Charming, a Mr. Rochester, a Mr. Darcy, and Rhett Butler.° These are the objects of our earliest romantic yearnings, the private desires of a whole country of little girls, the fairy tales that actually end up affecting our real lives. As the feminist film critic Molly Haskell says, "We never really escape the old-fashioned roles. They get inside our heads. Dependence has always been eroticized."

Many of the men I know seem understandably bewildered by the fact that women want to be independent only sometimes, only sort of, and only selectively. The same women who give eloquent speeches at dinner parties on the subject of "glass ceilings" still want men to pay for first dates, and this can be sort of perplexing for the men around them who are still trying to fit into the puzzle that the feminism of the seventies has created for them. For a long time, women have been saying that we don't want a double standard, but it sometimes seems that what many women want is simply a more subtle and refined version of a double standard: We want men to be the providers *and* to regard us as equals. This slightly unreasonable expectation is not exactly new. In 1963, a reporter asked Mary McCarthy° what women really wanted, and she answered, "They want everything. That's the trouble — they can't have everything. They can't possibly have all the prerogatives of being a woman and the privileges of being a man at the same time."

"We're spoiled," says Helen Gurley Brown, one of the world's foremost theorists on dating. "We just don't want to give up any of the good stuff." And she may have a point. In a world in which women compete with men, in which all of us are feeling the same drive to succeed, there is something reassuring about falling — if only for the length of a dinner — into traditional sex roles. You can just relax. You can take a rest from yourself. You can let the pressures and ambitions melt away and give in to the archaic fantasy: For just half an hour, you are just a pretty girl smiling at a man over a drink. I think that old-fashioned rituals, such as men paying for dates, endure precisely because of how much *has* actually changed; they cover up the fact that men and women *are* equal and that equality is not always, in all contexts and situations, comfortable or even desirable.

This may explain why I have been so ungratefully day-dreaming about the 15 Man in the Gray Flannel Suit thirty years after Betty Friedan published *The Feminine Mystique.* The truth is, the knowledge that I *can* take care of myself,

Mr. Rochester, a Mr. Darcy, and Rhett Butler: Respectively, the chief male characters in Charlotte Brontë's *Jane Eyre* (1847), Jane Austen's *Pride and Prejudice* (1813), and Margaret Mitchell's *Gone with the Wind* (1936).
Mary McCarthy (1912-1989): An American writer and intellectual, McCarthy published *The Group,* a novel about college women, in 1963, the same year that feminist Betty Friedan came out with *The Feminine Mystique.*

that I don't really need a man, is not without its own accompanying terrors. The idea that I could make myself into a sleek, self-sufficient androgyne is not all that appealing. Now that we have all of the rooms of our own that we need, we begin to look for that shared and crowded space. And it is this fear of independence, this fear of *not* needing a man, that explains the voices of more competent, accomplished corporate types than me saying to the men around them, "Provide for me, protect me." It may be one of the bad jokes that history occasionally plays on us: that the independence my mother's generation wanted so much for their daughters was something we could not entirely appreciate or want. It was like a birthday present from a distant relative — wrong size, wrong color, wrong style. And so women are left struggling with the desire to submit and not submit, to be dependent and independent, to take care of ourselves and be taken care of, and it's in the confusion of this struggle that most of us love and are loved.

For myself, I continue to go out with poets and novelists and writers, and with men who don't pay for dates or buy me dresses at Bergdorf's or go off to their offices in the morning, but the Man in the Gray Flannel Suit lives on in my imagination, perplexing, irrational, revealing of some dark and unsettling truth.

CONSIDERATIONS FOR CRITICAL THINKING AND WRITING

1. FIRST RESPONSE. If you are a female, do you share Roiphe's fantasy of being taken care of by a man? If you are a male, do you think many women share this fantasy? Why or why not? Explain why you are comfortable or uncomfortable with this fantasy.

2. To what extent do you think money is an issue in a romantic relationship? What do you think might be a possible solution to Anna's and Sam's problems (paragraphs 7–9)?

3. If being taken care of by a man is the secret wish of some contemporary women, what do you think is the equivalent secret wish for men?

4. Do you think Roiphe considers herself to be a feminist? Do you think she is a feminist? Why or why not?

5. This essay was originally published in *Esquire,* a men's magazine. Why do you think it was published there instead of, for example, in *Ms.?*

DEBORAH TANNEN (B. 1945)

Born in Brooklyn, New York, Deborah Tannen was educated at the State University of New York in Binghamton, Wayne State University, and the University of California at Berkeley, where she earned a Ph.D. in linguistics. A professor at Georgetown University, Tannen has written scholarly and popular articles and books on problems of communication among people of different genders, ethnicities, cultures, and classes. She is frequently interviewed in the media on these topics. Among her books that have enjoyed a wide readership are *You Just Don't Understand: Women and Men in Conversation* (1990), which includes the essay reprinted here; *Gender and Discourse* (1994), *Talking from 9 to 5* (1994); and *The Argument Culture: Moving from Debate to Dialogue* (1998).

Sex, Lies, and Conversation   *1990*

I was addressing a small gathering in a suburban Virginia living room — a women's group that had invited men to join them. Throughout the evening, one man had been particularly talkative, frequently offering ideas and anecdotes, while his wife sat silently beside him on the couch. Toward the end of the evening, I commented that women frequently complain that their husbands don't talk to them. This man quickly concurred. He gestured toward his wife and said, "She's the talker in our family." The room burst into laughter; the man looked puzzled and hurt. "It's true," he explained. "When I come home from work I have nothing to say. If she didn't keep the conversation going, we'd spend the whole evening in silence."

This episode crystallizes the irony that although American men tend to talk more than women in public situations, they often talk less at home. And this pattern is wreaking havoc with marriage.

The pattern was observed by political scientist Andrew Hacker in the late '70s. Sociologist Catherine Kohler Riessman reports in her new book *Divorce Talk* that most of the women she interviewed — but only a few of the men — gave lack of communication as the reason for their divorces. Given the current divorce rate of nearly 50 percent, that amounts to millions of cases in the United States every year — a virtual epidemic of failed conversation.

In my own research, complaints from women about their husbands most often focused not on tangible inequities such as having given up the chance for a career to accompany a husband to his, or doing far more than their share of daily life-support work like cleaning, cooking, social arrangements, and errands. Instead, they focused on communication: "He doesn't listen to me," "He doesn't talk to me." I found, as Hacker observed years before, that most wives want their husbands to be, first and foremost, conversational partners, but few husbands share this expectation of their wives.

In short, the image that best represents the current crisis is the stereotypical cartoon scene of a man sitting at the breakfast table with a newspaper held up in front of his face, while a woman glares at the back of it, wanting to talk.   5

Linguistic Battle of the Sexes

How can women and men have such different impressions of communication in marriage? Why the widespread imbalance in their interests and expectations?

In the April issue of *American Psychologist,* Stanford University's Eleanor Maccoby reports the results of her own and others' research showing that children's development is most influenced by the social structure of peer interactions. Boys and girls tend to play with children of their own gender, and their sex-separate groups have different organizational structures and interactive norms.

I believe these systematic differences in childhood socialization make talk between women and men like cross-cultural communication, heir to all the attraction and pitfalls of that enticing but difficult enterprise. My research on men's and women's conversations uncovered patterns similar to those described for children's groups.

914 | *Love and Its Complications*

For women, as for girls, intimacy is the fabric of relationships, and talk is the thread from which it is woven. Little girls create and maintain friendships by exchanging secrets; similarly, women regard conversation as the cornerstone of friendship. So a woman expects her husband to be a new and improved version of a best friend. What is important is not the individual subjects that are discussed but the sense of closeness, of a life shared, that emerges when people tell their thoughts, feelings, and impressions.

Bonds between boys can be as intense as girls', but they are based less on 10 talking, more on doing things together. Since they don't assume talk is the cement that binds a relationship, men don't know what kind of talk women want, and they don't miss it when it isn't there.

Boys' groups are larger, more inclusive, and more hierarchical, so boys must struggle to avoid the subordinate position in the group. This may play a role in women's complaints that men don't listen to them. Some men really don't like to listen, because being the listener makes them feel one-down, like a child listening to adults or an employee to a boss.

But often when women tell men, "You aren't listening," and the men protest, "I am," the men are right. The impression of not listening results from misalignments in the mechanics of conversation. The misalignment begins as soon as a man and a woman take physical positions. This became clear when I studied videotapes made by psychologist Bruce Dorval of children and adults talking to their same-sex best friends. I found that at every age, the girls and women faced each other directly, their eyes anchored on each other's faces. At every age, the boys and men sat at angles to each other and looked elsewhere in the room, periodically glancing at each other. They were obviously attuned to each other, often mirroring each other's movements. But the tendency of men to face away can give women the impression they aren't listening even when they are. A young woman in college was frustrated: Whenever she told her boyfriend she wanted to talk to him, he would lie down on the floor, close his eyes, and put his arm over his face. This signaled to her, "He's taking a nap." But he insisted he was listening extra hard. Normally, he looks around the room, so he is easily distracted. Lying down and covering his eyes helped him concentrate on what she was saying.

Analogous to the physical alignment that women and men take in conversation is their topical alignment. The girls in my study tended to talk at length about one topic, but the boys tended to jump from topic to topic. The second-grade girls exchanged stories about people they knew. The second-grade boys teased, told jokes, noticed things in the room, and talked about finding games to play. The sixth-grade girls talked about problems with a mutual friend. The sixth-grade boys talked about 55 different topics, none of which extended over more than a few turns.

Listening to Body Language

Switching topics is another habit that gives women the impression men aren't listening, especially if they switch to a topic about themselves. But the evidence of the 10th-grade boys in my study indicates otherwise. The 10th-grade boys sprawled across their chairs with bodies parallel and eyes straight ahead, rarely looking at each other. They looked as if they were riding in a car, staring out the windshield. But they were talking about their feelings. One boy was upset because a girl had told him he had a drinking problem, and the other was feeling alienated from all his friends.

Now, when a girl told a friend about a problem, the friend responded by asking probing questions and expressing agreement and understanding. But the boys dismissed each other's problems. Todd assured Richard that his drinking was "no big problem" because "sometimes you're funny when you're off your butt." And when Todd said he felt left out, Richard responded, "Why should you? You know more people than me." 15

Women perceive such responses as belittling and unsupportive. But the boys seemed satisfied with them. Whereas women reassure each other by implying, "You shouldn't feel bad because I've had similar experiences," men do so by implying, "You shouldn't feel bad because your problems aren't so bad."

There are even simpler reasons for women's impression that men don't listen. Linguist Lynette Hirschman found that women make more listener-noise, such as "mhm," "uhuh," and "yeah," to show "I'm with you." Men, she found, more often give silent attention. Women who expect a stream of listener-noise interpret silent attention as no attention at all.

Women's conversational habits are as frustrating to men as men's are to women. Men who expect silent attention interpret a stream of listener-noise as overreaction or impatience. Also, when women talk to each other in a close, comfortable setting, they often overlap, finish each other's sentences, and anticipate what the other is about to say. This practice, which I call "participatory listenership," is often perceived by men as interruption, intrusion, and lack of attention.

A parallel difference caused a man to complain about his wife, "She just wants to talk about her own point of view. If I show her another view, she gets mad at me." When most women talk to each other, they assume a conversationalist's job is to express agreement and support. But many men see their conversational duty as pointing out the other side of an argument. This is heard as disloyalty by women, and refusal to offer the requisite support. It is not that women don't want to see other points of view, but that they prefer them phrased as suggestions and inquiries rather than as direct challenges.

In his book *Fighting for Life,* Walter Ong points out that men use "agonistic" or warlike, oppositional formats to do almost anything; thus discussion becomes debate, and conversation a competitive sport. In contrast, women see conversation as a ritual means of establishing rapport. If Jane tells a problem and June says she has a similar one, they walk away feeling closer to each other. But this attempt at establishing rapport can backfire when used with men. Men take too literally women's ritual "troubles talk," just as women mistake men's ritual challenges for real attack. 20

The Sounds of Silence

These differences begin to clarify why women and men have such different expectations about communication in marriage. For women, talk creates intimacy. Marriage is an orgy of closeness: you can tell your feelings and thoughts, and still be loved. Their greatest fear is being pushed away. But men live in a hierarchical world, where talk maintains independence and status. They are on guard to protect themselves from being put down and pushed around.

This explains the paradox of the talkative man who said of his silent wife, "She's the talker." In the public setting of a guest lecture, he felt challenged to show his intelligence and display his understanding of the lecture. But at home, where he has nothing to prove and no one to defend against, he is free to remain silent. For his wife, being home means she is free from the worry that something she says might offend someone, or spark disagreement, or appear to be showing off; at home she is free to talk.

The communication problems that endanger marriage can't be fixed by mechanical engineering. They require a new conceptual framework about the role of talk in human relationships. Many of the psychological explanations that have become second nature may not be helpful, because they tend to blame either women (for not being assertive enough) or men (for not being in touch with their feelings). A sociolinguistic approach by which male-female conversation is seen as cross-cultural communication allows us to understand the problem and forge solutions without blaming either party.

Once the problem is understood, improvement comes naturally, as it did to the young woman and her boyfriend who seemed to go to sleep when she wanted to talk. Previously, she had accused him of not listening, and he had refused to change his behavior, since that would be admitting fault. But then she learned about and explained to him the differences in women's and men's habitual ways of aligning themselves in conversation. The next time she told him she wanted to talk, he began, as usual, by lying down and covering his eyes. When the familiar negative reaction bubbled up, she reassured herself that he really was listening. But then he sat up and looked at her. Thrilled, she asked why. He said, "You like me to look at you when we talk, so I'll try to do it." Once he saw their differences as cross-cultural rather than right and wrong, he independently altered his behavior.

Women who feel abandoned and deprived when their husbands won't lis- 25 ten to or report daily news may be happy to discover their husbands trying to adapt once they understand the place of small talk in women's relationships. But if their husbands don't adapt, the women may still be comforted that for men, this is not a failure of intimacy. Accepting the difference, the wives may look to their friends or family for that kind of talk. And husbands who can't provide it shouldn't feel their wives have made unreasonable demands. Some couples will still decide to divorce, but at least their decisions will be based on realistic expectations.

In these times of resurgent ethnic conflicts, the world desperately needs cross-cultural understanding. Like charity, successful cross-cultural communication should begin at home.

CONSIDERATIONS FOR CRITICAL THINKING AND WRITING

1. FIRST RESPONSE. Based on your own experience, do you agree that "American men tend to talk more than women in public situations [and] they often talk less at home"?

2. How does Tannen make clear that she is as sympathetic to men as she is to women in their struggles to communicate?

3. What does Tannen see as the essential differences between how men and women listen to each other?

4. Describe Tannen's purpose in writing this essay. How did you find it useful (or not) in understanding your own communications with the opposite sex?

5. How does the essay's style reveal that it was written more for a popular audience than a scholarly or academic one?

Personal Response

This casebook shows you how one student, Eric Hoffbauer, develops a formal essay responding to Katie Roiphe's essay "The Independent Woman (and Other Lies)" (p. 907). You may want to read Roiphe's essay, if you haven't yet done so. Eric was asked by his instructor to pay attention to how compelling he found Roiphe's essay and to try to identify specific points where he strongly agrees or disagrees with her argument. The instructor also asked the class to try to think about whether their own gender and political identities changed how they read Roiphe's essay—whether the effect of the writer depends on who the reader is.

A Sample First Response

After reading Roiphe's essay several times, Eric writes a first, informal response. His instructor asked him to write a brief response to the questions *"How did you respond to Roiphe's essay? Do you buy her argument? Why or why not?"* The class has been talking about "love in the new millennium" as they've worked through this chapter, and Eric also considers that larger theme in his first response. How would you answer those same questions?

> I've read Katie Roiphe's article a few times now, and I think she's done a good job of covering both sides of the argument. Maybe this means she is unsure about her stance on the topic of love in the '90s. She throws out a very strong opinion that women of her generation have an underlying and innate desire to be protected and taken care of. In the beginning of the essay she uses herself as an example of a woman tempted by the comfort and security of a man with financial means. In the end she sides with the independent woman. She shows herself to be ambivalent, or confused, and I think this weakens her objective in the essay.
>
> Another of the problems that I see in Roiphe's essay is that she bases much of her definition of protection, care, and

independence on money. It seemed that the emotions she was discussing were too intertwined with money. Maybe this just says
a lot about love these days, but I wonder if her definitions
apply for people outside of Roiphe's small cross-section of
American society. Her examples of women and couples are people
who are all from the same class, educational background, and
generation. I think her ideas of love and independence are
defined too much by money. I understand that the essay appeared
in a certain magazine, with a certain audience in mind, but
this doesn't excuse her generalizing in a way I think is wrong.

A Sample of Brainstorming

After his first response, Eric sits down to develop his ideas into a formal response paper. Before he starts to write, he gathers together notes on
the essay and reviews the information about reader-response strategies
(pp. 74–76) and the Reader-Response Questions in the Questions for Writing (p. 99). He then jots down his thoughts about what he wants to include
in his paper so that they'll be easier to organize later. In the course of
brainstorming, he realizes that he thinks that it *is* important that he's
responding from a male point of view—he also jots down the larger thematic issues that interest him (money, gender roles, class, his friends)
along with questions that he'd like to explore further.

Write a response essay from a male point of view.

The issue of equating security and protection with money
  It's a learned attitude.
  What underlies it?

Gender roles in American society
  Financial ability part of the definition
  What do men and women really want on a deeper level?

Class and generation as influences on the definition of love
  *Are these issues a reality for couples who aren't in the upper or upper-
  middle class?*
  Will they be an issue for me in 5 years or so?

My friends as example of another reality than Roiphe's

A Sample Student Response Paper

Eric starts his final draft of his reader-response paper with a personal
anecdote that raises — in a more coherent way — some of the questions that
Roiphe's essay raised for him, along with some analysis of his own answers

to these questions. He then moves to a brief summary of Roiphe's argument, along with personal commentary about some of her points. Note that he uses quotations from her essay to back his points. At the end of his essay, Eric moves to larger generalizations about contemporary culture and attitudes toward love, gender, and class. As you read Eric's essay, think about how successful his response is. Does he cover all ground equally well? Do his points move fluidly? Do you agree with what he says?

Eric Hoffbauer
Professor Jarvis
English 1102
April 20, 20--

Love Today:
What's Cash Got to Do with It?

I was out to dinner with a woman friend of mine
recently. When the check came, she offered to pay for
some of my meal (my credit card was at its limit) so I
begrudgingly accepted. Later that week, although she
insisted that I not worry about it, I felt driven to pay
her back and did. She accepted my money, and the cloud of
guilt that had been following me around for three days
was finally lifted. Why could I not accept her help without feeling guilty? What was inside me that compelled me
to always pull my own weight? I think that as some last
tenacious grasp at my masculinity I've always tried to
pay my way, even if my date offered to treat me. During
my upbringing in American society, the rules of gender
roles were imprinted, and the ideas of masculinity, independence, and money were linked. Equality between the
sexes is growing on a professional and financial level,
but traditional ideas of masculine and feminine financial
responsibilities and rights can impede if not ruin our
attempts at love.

According to Katie Roiphe, the nineties woman is in
somewhat of a quandary. In her article "The Independent
Woman (and Other Lies)," she explains that some of
today's successful and strong-minded women feel the
"more traditional feminine desire to be protected and
provided for" (para. 2). This may be the case, because
men these days feel similarly about their role. Even
today young men like myself still feel the urge and
pressure to become responsible financially for the well-

being of a family so much so that failure to achieve this
security results in feelings of guilt and threatens our
masculinity. Although it is impossible to know which gender started this backlash of traditional values, they
developed together under the misleading guidance of a
conservatively shifting American society. It is interesting to see that so much of Roiphe's definition of "being
protected and provided for, a feeling that mingles with
love and attraction on the deepest level" (4) is so tied
up in money. Many of Roiphe's examples of failed love
center around the woman's feeling that the man's
masculinity was in some way flawed. In each case, this
boils down to the man not making enough money.

   In the ancient history of sex roles, the man was
a provider and protector in a physical way; he shielded
his family from attackers and actual, physical danger.
As societies formed, the hunter-gatherer turned into
the wage laborer, yet for the most part the man has
remained the primary provider, only his physical actions
now manifest themselves in currency. In today's society
it is dangerously sexist to give the man the title of
protector. This role comes with a lot of historical baggage and shifts too much power to the man. It is disappointing and somewhat disturbing that after the struggles
the American woman has had to endure to get equal pay and
opportunity, she could still want a masculine provider.
This means the man would need to make more money than the
woman in any partnership, and we take two steps
backwards. Essentially Roiphe suggests that earning power
defines typical American gender roles. Where does this
leave the dog walker, the struggling talented writer, or
the jazz musician? I suppose if we bought into Roiphe's
ideas these men are considered emasculated failures,
which, perhaps, they are to some women. If tax brackets

determine love in our times, then I do not want any part
of love.

But perhaps the women about whom Roiphe writes, con-
flicted in their own views on independence and love, are
not to be taken as an honest representation of our society's relationship seekers. Although there are many women
who are in situations like those Roiphe describes, and
there are men who struggle with their roles, it is important to note that these people are from similar class and
educational backgrounds and are between 22 and 35. I know
plenty of people for whom love is not caught up in these
dilemmas of money and earning power. Take, for example,
my friend Pete, whose wedding I recently attended. Both
Pete and his new wife are working hard at their careers
but hardly earning what Roiphe's friends were earning.
On top of that his new wife has a 3-year-old boy from a
previous marriage, and they are expecting another child
in a few months. In this situation there cannot be only
one provider; both must work to make this marriage financially, and emotionally, successful. It will be a hard
road for them, but they are working together and sharing
the responsibility.

It is obvious that these people have a different
concept of and approach to love than did the characters
in Roiphe's essay. The most obvious difference is that
they are not upwardly mobile, young (white) urban professionals, as the people in Roiphe's essay seem to be. Is
it not possible, then, that Roiphe's dissatisfaction with
the "masculinity"--the earning power--of the men around her
is really a dissatisfaction with the way love plays out
in the upper class? The women, through their successes,
have a higher income bracket but not a lesser need for
love. It may be that these women, and the men they date,
are confusing financial stability with other, deeper,

Hoffbauer 4

more human needs. Women have the desire to feel safe and
secure, but so do men. If we can learn to separate these
nongendered needs from our ideas about money, masculinity, and femininity, perhaps then we won't think of the
women in Roiphe's essay as having retrograde, antifemi-
nist desires. They simply desire what every human
desires: security, protection, the freedom to pursue
one's dreams without financial constraint.

11

Life and Its Lessons

As we all know, life's lessons come in many forms and at unexpected moments. The stories, poems, plays, and essays included in this chapter all depict a lesson of sorts—even if what has been taught and what has been learned are not always clear (and they are not always the same thing). Ralph Ellison in "Battle Royal" and Andrew Hudgins in "Seventeen" both deal with a boy learning what it means to be grown up after a dramatic and violent encounter. Other selections—Arthur Miller's *Death of a Salesman,* for example—are less about an individual lesson being imparted than a family facing a less-than-kind world, and each member coming away changed by a set of circumstances. Essays by Gloria Naylor and by Gary Soto both recount the essayist's discovery of something about his or her self and identity, a discovery that changes the course of the writer's life. These are only a few of the connections that can be made between the selections in this chapter; as you read, you should think about who is learning what, how you could link each reading with another, and how you personally respond to the work in question. The lessons found in this literature will undoubtedly add to your own understanding that the lessons of life are complicated things—as well as an unending reservoir of material to write about.

FICTION

TONI CADE BAMBARA (1939–1995)

Raised in New York City's Harlem and Bedford-Stuyvesant communities, Toni Cade Bambara graduated from Queens College in 1959, studied in Florence and Paris, and earned her M.A. at City College of New York in

1964. She also studied dance, linguistics, and filmmaking and worked a variety of jobs in welfare, recreation, and community housing, in addition to teaching at various schools, including Rutgers University and Spelman College. She described her writing as "straight-up fiction . . . 'cause I value my family and friends, and mostly 'cause I lie a lot anyway." Her fiction has been collected in *Gorilla, My Love* (1972) and *The Sea Birds Are Still Alive* (1977), and in 1980 she published her first novel, *Salt Eaters,* followed by *If Blessing Comes* (1987). Her most recent books, *Deep Sightings and Rescue Missions* (1996) and *These Bones Are Not My Child* (1999), were published posthumously. A number of her screenplays have been produced, including *Epitaph for Willie* and *Tar Baby.* In the following story a serious lesson is prescribed with a healthy dose of humor.

The Lesson
1972

Back in the days when everyone was old and stupid or young and foolish and me and Sugar were the only ones just right, this lady moved on our block with nappy hair and proper speech and no makeup. And quite naturally we laughed at her, laughed the way we did at the junk man who went about his business like he was some big-time president and his sorry-ass horse his secretary. And we kinda hated her too, hated the way we did the winos who cluttered up our parks and pissed on our handball walls and stank up our hallways and stairs so you couldn't halfway play hide-and-seek without a goddamn gas mask. Miss Moore was her name. The only woman on the block with no first name. And she was black as hell, cept for her feet, which were fish-white and spooky. And she was always planning these boring-ass things for us to do, us being my cousin, mostly, who lived on the block cause we all moved North the same time and to the same apartment then spread out gradual to breathe. And our parents would yank our heads into some kinda shape and crisp up our clothes so we'd be presentable for travel with Miss Moore, who always looked like she was going to church, though she never did. Which is just one of the things the grownups talked about when they talked behind her back like a dog. But when she came calling with some sachet she'd sewed up or some gingerbread she'd made or some book, why then they'd all be too embarrassed to turn her down and we'd get handed over all spruced up. She'd been to college and said it was only right that she should take responsibility for the young ones' education, and she not even related by marriage or blood. So they'd go for it. Specially Aunt Gretchen. She was the main gofer in the family. You got some ole dumb shit foolishness you want somebody to go for, you send for Aunt Gretchen. She been screwed into the go-along for so long, it's a blood-deep natural thing with her. Which is how she got saddled with me and Sugar and Junior in the first place while our mothers were in a la-de-da apartment up the block having a good ole time.

So this one day Miss Moore rounds us all up at the mailbox and it's puredee hot and she's knockin herself out about arithmetic. And school suppose to let up in summer I heard, but she don't never let up. And the starch in my pinafore scratching the shit outta me and I'm really hating this nappy-head bitch and her goddamn college degree. I'd much rather go to the pool or to the show where it's cool. So me and Sugar leaning on the mailbox being surly, which is a Miss Moore word. And Flyboy checking out what everybody brought for lunch. And Fat Butt already wasting his peanut-butter-and-jelly sandwich like the pig he is. And Junebug punchin on Q.T.'s arm for potato chips. And Rosie Giraffe shifting from one hip to the other waiting for somebody to step on her foot or ask her if she from Georgia so she can kick ass, preferably Mercedes'. And Miss Moore asking us do we know what money is, like we a bunch of retards. I mean real money, she say, like it's only poker chips or monopoly papers we lay on the grocer. So right away I'm tired of this and say so. And would much rather snatch Sugar and go to the Sunset and terrorize the West Indian kids and take their hair ribbons and their money too. And Miss Moore files that remark away for next week's lesson on brotherhood, I can tell. And finally I say we oughta get to the subway cause it's cooler and besides we might meet some cute boys. Sugar done swiped her mama's lipstick, so we ready.

So we heading down the street and she's boring us silly about what things cost and what our parents make and how much goes for rent and how money ain't divided up right in this country. And then she gets to the part about we all poor and live in the slums, which I don't feature. And I'm ready to speak on that, but she steps out in the street and hails two cabs just like that. Then she hustles half the crew in with her and hands me a five-dollar bill and tells me to calculate 10 percent tip for the driver. And we're off. Me and Sugar and Junebug and Flyboy hangin out the window and hollering to everybody, putting lipstick on each other cause Flyboy a faggot anyway, and making farts with our sweaty armpits. But I'm mostly trying to figure how to spend this money. But they all fascinated with the meter ticking and Junebug starts laying bets as to how much it'll read when Flyboy can't hold his breath no more. Then Sugar lays bets as to how much it'll be when we get there. So I'm stuck. Don't nobody want to go for my plan, which is to jump out at the next light and run off to the first bar-b-que we can find. Then the driver tells us to get the hell out cause we there already. And the meter reads eighty-five cents. And I'm stalling to figure out the tip and Sugar say give him a dime. And I decide he don't need it bad as I do, so later for him. But then he tries to take off with Junebug foot still in the door so we talk about his mama something ferocious. Then we check out that we on Fifth Avenue and everybody dressed up in stockings. One lady in a fur coat, hot as it is. White folks crazy.

"This is the place," Miss Moore say, presenting it to us in the voice she uses at the museum. "Let's look in the windows before we go in."

"Can we steal?" Sugar asks very serious like she's getting the ground rules 5 squared away before she plays. "I beg your pardon," say Miss Moore, and we fall out. So she leads us around the windows of the toy store and me and Sugar screamin, "This is mine, that's mine, I gotta have that, that was made for me, I was born for that," till Big Butt drowns us out.

"Hey, I'm goin to buy that there."

"That there? You don't even know what it is, stupid."

"I do so," he say punchin on Rosie Giraffe. "It's a microscope."

"Whatcha gonna do with a microscope, fool?"

"Look at things." 10

"Like what, Ronald?" ask Miss Moore. And Big Butt ain't got the first notion. So here go Miss Moore gabbing about the thousands of bacteria in a drop of water and the somethinorother in a speck of blood and the million and one living things in the air around us is invisible to the naked eye. And what she say that for? Junebug go to town on that "naked" and we rolling. Then Miss Moore ask what it cost. So we all jam into the window smudgin it up and the price tag say $300. So then she ask how long'd take for Big Butt and Junebug to save up their allowances. "Too long," I say. "Yeh," adds Sugar, "outgrown it by that time." And Miss Moore say no, you never outgrow learning instruments. "Why, even medical students and interns and," blah, blah, blah. And we ready to choke Big Butt for bringing it up in the first damn place.

"This here costs four hundred eighty dollars," says Rosie Giraffe. So we pile up all over her to see what she pointin out. My eyes tell me it's a chunk of glass cracked with something heavy, and different-color inks dripped into the splits, then the whole thing put into a oven or something. But for $480 it don't make sense.

"That's a paperweight made of semi-precious stones fused together under tremendous pressure," she explains slowly, with her hands doing the mining and all the factory work.

"So what's a paperweight?" asks Rosie Giraffe.

"To weigh paper with, dumbbell," say Flyboy, the wise man from the East.   15

"Not exactly," say Miss Moore, which is what she say when you warm or way off too. "It's to weigh paper down so it won't scatter and make your desk untidy." So right away me and Sugar curtsy to each other and then to Mercedes who is more the tidy type.

"We don't keep paper on top of the desk in my class," say Junebug, figuring Miss Moore crazy or lyin one.

"At home, then," she say. "Don't you have a calendar and pencil case and a blotter and a letter-opener on your desk at home where you do your homework?" And she know damn well what our homes look like cause she nosys around in them every chance she gets.

"I don't even have a desk," say Junebug. "Do we?"

"No. And I don't get no homework neither," says Big Butt.   20

"And I don't even have a home," say Flyboy like he do at school to keep the white folks off his back and sorry for him. Send this poor kid to camp posters, is his specialty.

"I do," says Mercedes. "I have a box of stationery on my desk and a picture of my cat. My godmother bought the stationery and the desk. There's a big rose on each sheet and the envelopes smell like roses."

"Who wants to know about your smelly-ass stationery," say Rosie Giraffe fore I can get my two cents in.

"It's important to have a work area all your own so that . . ."

"Will you look at this sailboat, please," say Flyboy, cuttin her off and   25 pointin to the thing like it was his. So once again we tumble all over each other to gaze at this magnificent thing in the toy store which is just big enough to maybe sail two kittens across the pond if you strap them to the posts tight. We all start reciting the price tag like we in assembly. "Handcrafted sailboat of fiberglass at one thousand one hundred ninety-five dollars."

"Unbelievable," I hear myself say and am really stunned. I read it again for myself just in case the group recitation put me in a trance. Same thing. For some reason this pisses me off. We look at Miss Moore and she lookin at us, waiting for I dunno what.

"Who'd pay all that when you can buy a sailboat set for a quarter at Pop's, a tube of glue for a dime, and a ball of string for eight cents? It must have a motor and a whole lot else besides," I say. "My sailboat cost me about fifty cents."

"But will it take water?" say Mercedes with her smart ass.

"Took mine to Alley Pond Park once," say Flyboy. "String broke. Lost it. Pity."

"Sailed mine in Central Park and it keeled over and sank. Had to ask my 30 father for another dollar."

"And you got the strap," laugh Big Butt. "The jerk didn't even have a string on it. My old man wailed on his behind."

Little Q.T. was staring hard at the sailboat and you could see he wanted it bad. But he too little and somebody'd just take it from him. So what the hell. "This boat for kids, Miss Moore?"

"Parents silly to buy something like that just to get all broke up," say Rosie Giraffe.

"That much money it should last forever," I figure.

"My father'd buy it for me if I wanted it." 35

"Your father, my ass," say Rosie Giraffe getting a chance to finally push Mercedes.

"Must be rich people shop here," say Q.T.

"You are a very bright boy," say Flyboy. "What was your first clue?" And he rap him on the head with the back of his knuckles, since Q.T. the only one he could get away with. Though Q.T. liable to come up behind you years later and get his licks in when you half expect it.

"What I want to know is," I says to Miss Moore though I never talk to her, I wouldn't give the bitch that satisfaction, "is how much a real boat costs? I figure a thousand'd get you a yacht any day."

"Why don't you check that out," she says, "and report back to the group?" 40 Which really pains my ass. If you gonna mess up a perfectly good swim day least you could do is have some answers. "Let's go in," she say like she got something up her sleeve. Only she don't lead the way. So me and Sugar turn the corner to where the entrance is, but when we get there I kinda hang back. Not that I'm scared, what's there to be afraid of, just a toy store. But I feel funny, shame. But what I got to be shamed about? Got as much right to go in as anybody. But somehow I can't seem to get hold of the door, so I step away from Sugar to lead. But she hangs back too. And I look at her and she looks at me and this is ridiculous. I mean, damn, I have never ever been shy about doing nothing or going nowhere. But then Mercedes steps up and then Rosie Giraffe and Big Butt crowd in behind and shove, and next thing we all stuffed into the doorway with only Mercedes squeezing past us, smoothing out her jumper and walking right down the aisle. Then the rest of us tumble in like a glued-together jigsaw done all wrong. And people lookin at us. And it's like the time me and Sugar crashed into the Catholic church on a dare. But once we got in there and everything so hushed and holy and the candles and the bowin and the handkerchiefs on all the drooping heads, I just couldn't go through with the plan. Which was for me to run up to the altar and do a tap dance while Sugar played the nose flute and messed around in the holy water. And Sugar kept givin me the elbow. Then later teased me so bad I tied her up in the shower and turned it on and locked her in. And she'd be there till this day if

Aunt Gretchen hadn't finally figured I was lyin about the boarder takin a shower.

Same thing in the store. We all walkin on tiptoe and hardly touchin the games and puzzles and things. And I watched Miss Moore who is steady watchin us like she waitin for a sign. Like Mama Drewery watches the sky and sniffs the air and takes note of just how much slant is in the bird formation. Then me and Sugar bump smack into each other, so busy gazing at the toys, specially the sailboat. But we don't laugh and go into our fat-lady bump-stomach routine. We just stare at that price tag. Then Sugar run a finger over the whole boat. And I'm jealous and want to hit her. Maybe not her, but I sure want to punch somebody in the mouth.

"Watcha bring us here for, Miss Moore?"

"You sound angry, Sylvia. Are you mad about something?" Givin me one of them grins like she tellin a grown-up joke that never turns out to be funny. And she's lookin very closely at me like maybe she planning to do my portrait from memory. I'm mad, but I won't give her that satisfaction. So I slouch around the store bein very bored and say, "Let's go."

Me and Sugar at the back of the train watchin the tracks whizzin by large then small then getting gobbled up in the dark. I'm thinkin about this tricky toy I saw in the store. A clown that somersaults on a bar then does chin-ups just cause you yank lightly at his leg. Cost $35. I could see me askin my mother for a $35 birthday clown. "You wanna who that costs what?" she'd say, cocking her head to the side to get a better view of the hole in my head. Thirty-five dollars could buy new bunk beds for Junior and Gretchen's boy. Thirty-five dollars and the whole household could go visit Granddaddy Nelson in the country. Thirty-five dollars would pay for the rent and the piano bill too. Who are these people that spend that much for performing clowns and $1000 for toy sailboats? What kinda work they do and how they live and how come we ain't in on it? Where we are is who we are, Miss Moore always pointin out. But it don't necessarily have to be that way, she always adds then waits for somebody to say that poor people have to wake up and demand their share of the pie and don't none of us know what kind of pie she talking about in the first damn place. But she ain't so smart cause I still got her four dollars from the taxi and she sure ain't gettin it. Messin up my day with this shit. Sugar nudges me in my pocket and winks.

Miss Moore lines us up in front of the mailbox where we started from, 45 seem like years ago, and I got a headache for thinkin so hard. And we lean all over each other so we can hold up under the draggy-ass lecture she always finishes us off with at the end before we thank her for borin us to tears. But she just looks at us like she readin tea leaves. Finally she say, "Well, what did you think of F. A. O. Schwarz?"

Rosie Giraffe mumbles, "White folks crazy."

"I'd like to go there again when I get my birthday money," says Mercedes, and we shove her out the pack so she has to lean on the mailbox by herself.

"I'd like a shower. Tiring day," say Flyboy.

Then Sugar surprises me by sayin, "You know, Miss Moore, I don't think all of us here put together eat in a year what that sailboat costs." And Miss Moore lights up like somebody goosed her. "And?" she say, urging Sugar on. Only I'm standin on her foot so she don't continue.

"Imagine for a minute what kind of society it is in which some people can   50
spend on a toy what it would cost to feed a family of six or seven. What do you
think?"

"I think," say Sugar pushing me off her feet like she never done before,
cause I whip her ass in a minute, "that this is not much of a democracy if you
ask me. Equal chance to pursue happiness means an equal crack at the dough,
don't it?" Miss Moore is beside herself and I am disgusted with Sugar's treachery. So I stand on her foot one more time to see if she'll shove me. She shuts
up, and Miss Moore looks at me, sorrowfully I'm thinkin. And somethin weird
is goin on, I can feel it in my chest.

"Anybody else learn anything today?" lookin dead at me. I walk away and
Sugar has to run to catch up and don't even seem to notice when I shrug her
arm off my shoulder.

"Well, we got four dollars anyway," she says.

"Uh hunh."

"We could go to Hascombs and get half a chocolate layer and then go to   55
the Sunset and still have plenty money for potato chips and ice cream sodas."

"Un hunh."

"Race you to Hascombs," she say.

We start down the block and she gets ahead which is O.K. by me cause I'm
going to the West End and then over to the Drive to think this day through.
She can run if she want to and even run faster. But ain't nobody gonna beat
me at nuthin.

CONSIDERATIONS FOR CRITICAL THINKING AND WRITING

1. FIRST RESPONSE. How did you react to Bambara's serious social commentary in this story? Is it convincing? Preachy? Does it make you feel guilty?

2. What is the lesson Miss Moore tries to teach Sylvia? Is she successful?
   Invent an alternative title that captures for you the central meaning of the
   story.

3. What is the conflict in this story? Is there more than one? How are these
   conflicts resolved?

4. Write a paragraph characterizing Miss Moore's point of view about herself. Then write a descriptive paragraph of Miss Moore from Sylvia's point
   of view. Try to capture their voices in your descriptions.

5. The story begins with an adult narrator recalling her youth: "Back in the
   days when . . . ." Although that adult perspective is quickly replaced by the
   young girl's point of view, what do you think the adult narrator thinks of
   herself as a young girl?

6. Explain why the use of an editorial omniscient point of view in this story
   would be inappropriate.

7. How does Sylvia's use of language serve to characterize her?

8. How do you feel about Miss Moore at the end of the story compared with
   your feelings about her at the beginning? Why?

9. How do Sylvia and Sugar get along? What does this relationship reveal
   about Sylvia?

10. What do you think the last line of the story means? Does Sylvia think
    Sugar is smarter than she is because Sugar knew the answer to Miss

Moore's question and she didn't? Who else could the "nobody" in that line refer to besides Sugar?

11. CRITICAL STRATEGIES. Read the section on Marxist criticism (p. 68) in Chapter 3, "Applying a Critical Strategy," and consider how a Marxist critic might describe the theme of "The Lesson."

RALPH ELLISON (1914–1994)

Born in Oklahoma and educated at the Tuskegee Institute in Alabama, where he studied music, Ralph Ellison gained his reputation as a writer on the strength of his only published novel, *Invisible Man* (1952). He also published some scattered short stories and two collections of essays, *Shadow and Act* (1964) and *Going to the Territory* (1986). Although his writing was not extensive, it is important because Ellison wrote about race relations in the context of universal human concerns. *Invisible Man* is the story of a young black man who moves from the South to the North and discovers what it means to be black in America. "Battle Royal," published in 1947 as a short story, became the first chapter of *Invisible Man*. It concerns the beginning of the protagonist's long struggle for an adult identity in a world made corrupt by racial prejudice.

Battle Royal   1947

It goes a long way back, some twenty years. All my life I had been looking for something, and everywhere I turned someone tried to tell me what it was. I accepted their answers too, though they were often in contradiction and even self-contradictory. I was naive. I was looking for myself and asking everyone except myself questions which I, and only I, could answer. It took me a long time and much painful boomeranging of my expectations to achieve a realization everyone else appears to have been born with: That I am nobody but myself. But first I had to discover that I am an invisible man!

And yet I am no freak of nature, nor of history. I was in the cards, other things having been equal (or unequal) eighty-five years ago. I am not ashamed of my grandparents for having been slaves. I am only ashamed of myself for having at one time been ashamed. About eighty-five years ago they were told that they were free, united with others of our country in everything pertaining to the common good, and, in everything social, separate like the fingers of the hand. And they believed it. They exulted in it. They stayed in their place, worked hard, and brought up my father to do the same. But my grandfather is the one. He was an odd old guy, my grandfather, and I am told I take after him. It was he who caused the trouble. On his deathbed he called my father to him and said, "Son, after I'm gone I want you to keep up the good fight. I never told you, but our life is a war and I have been a traitor all my born days, a spy in the enemy's country ever since I gave up my gun back in the Reconstruction. Live with your head in the lion's mouth. I want you to overcome 'em with yeses, undermine 'em with grins, agree 'em to death and destruction, let 'em swoller you till they vomit or bust wide open." They thought the old man had gone out of his mind. He had been the meekest of men. The younger children were rushed from the room, the shades drawn and the flame of the lamp turned so low that it sputtered on the wick like the old man's breathing. "Learn it to the younguns," he whispered fiercely; then he died.

But my folks were more alarmed over his last words than over his dying. It was as though he had not died at all, his words caused so much anxiety. I was warned emphatically to forget what he had said and, indeed, this is the first time it has been mentioned outside the family circle. It had a tremendous effect upon me, however. I could never be sure of what he meant. Grandfather had been a quiet old man who never made any trouble, yet on his deathbed he had called himself a traitor and a spy, and he had spoken of his meekness as a dangerous activity. It became a constant puzzle which lay unanswered in the back of my mind. And whenever things went well for me I remembered my grandfather and felt guilty and uncomfortable. It was as though I was carrying out his advice in spite of myself. And to make it worse, everyone loved me for it. I was praised by the most lily-white men of the town. I was considered an example of desirable conduct—just as my grandfather had been. And what puzzled me was that the old man had defined it as *treachery*. When I was praised for my conduct I felt a guilt that in some way I was doing something that was really against the wishes of the white folks, that if they had understood they would have desired me to act just the opposite, that I should have been sulky and mean, and that that really would have been what they wanted, even though they were fooled and thought they wanted me to act as I did. It made me afraid that some day they would look upon me as a traitor and I would be lost. Still I was more afraid to act any other way because they didn't like that at all. The old man's words were like a curse. On my graduation day I delivered an oration in which I showed that humility was the secret, indeed, the very essence of progress. (Not that I believed this—how could I, remembering my grandfather?—I only believed that it worked.) It was a great success. Everyone praised me and I was invited to give the speech at a gathering of the town's leading white citizens. It was a triumph for our whole community.

It was in the main ballroom of the leading hotel. When I got there I discovered that it was on the occasion of a smoker, and I was told that since I was to be there anyway I might as well take part in the battle royal to be fought by some of my schoolmates as part of the entertainment. The battle royal came first.

All of the town's big shots were there in their tuxedoes, wolfing down the buffet foods, drinking beer and whiskey and smoking black cigars. It was a large room with a high ceiling. Chairs were arranged in neat rows around three sides of a portable boxing ring. The fourth side was clear, revealing a gleaming space of polished floor. I had some misgivings over the battle royal, by the way. Not from a distaste for fighting, but because I didn't care too much for the other fellows who were to take part. They were tough guys who seemed to have no grandfather's curse worrying their minds. No one could mistake their toughness. And besides, I suspected that fighting a battle royal might detract from the dignity of my speech. In those pre-invisible days I visualized myself as a potential Booker T. Washington. But the other fellows didn't care too much for me either, and there were nine of them. I felt superior to them in my way, and I didn't like the manner in which we were all crowded together into the servants' elevator. Nor did they like my being there. In fact, as the warmly lighted floors flashed past the elevator we had words over the fact that I, by taking part in the fight, had knocked one of their friends out of a night's work.

We were led out of the elevator through a rococo hall into an anteroom and told to get into our fighting togs. Each of us was issued a pair of boxing gloves and ushered out into the big mirrored hall, which we entered looking cautiously about us and whispering, lest we might accidentally be heard above the noise of the room. It was foggy with cigar smoke. And already the whiskey was taking effect. I was shocked to see some of the most important men of the town quite tipsy. They were all there—bankers, lawyers, judges, doctors, fire chiefs, teachers, merchants. Even one of the more fashionable pastors. Something we could not see was going on up front. A clarinet was vibrating sensuously and the men were standing up and moving eagerly forward. We were a small tight group, clustered together, our bare upper bodies touching and shining with anticipatory sweat; while up front the big shots were becoming increasingly excited over something we still could not see. Suddenly I heard the school superintendent, who had told me to come, yell, "Bring up the shines, gentlemen! Bring up the little shines!"

We were rushed up to the front of the ballroom, where it smelled even more strongly of tobacco and whiskey. Then we were pushed into place. I almost wet my pants. A sea of faces, some hostile, some amused, ringed around us, and in the center, facing us, stood a magnificent blonde—stark naked. There was dead silence. I felt a blast of cold air chill me. I tried to back away, but they were behind me and around me. Some of the boys stood with lowered heads, trembling. I felt a wave of irrational guilt and fear. My teeth chattered, my skin turned to goose flesh, my knees knocked. Yet I was strongly attracted and looked in spite of myself. Had the price of looking been blindness, I would have looked. The hair was yellow like that of a circus kewpie doll, the face heavily powdered and rouged, as though to form an abstract mask, the eyes hollow and smeared a cool blue, the color of a baboon's butt. I felt a desire to spit upon her as my eyes brushed slowly over her body. Her breasts were firm and round as the domes of East Indian temples, and I stood so close as to see the fine skin texture and beads of pearly perspiration glistening like dew around the pink and erected buds of her nipples. I wanted at one and the same time to run from the room, to sink through the floor, or go to her and cover her from my eyes and the eyes of the others with my body; to feel the soft thighs, to caress her and destroy her, to love her and murder her, to hide from her, and yet to stroke where below the small American flag tattooed upon her belly her thighs formed a capital V. I had a notion that of all in the room she saw only me with her impersonal eyes.

And then she began to dance, a slow sensuous movement; the smoke of a hundred cigars clinging to her like the thinnest of veils. She seemed like a fair bird-girl girdled in veils calling to me from the angry surface of some gray and threatening sea. I was transported. Then I became aware of the clarinet playing and the big shots yelling at us. Some threatened us if we looked and others if we did not. On my right I saw one boy faint. And now a man grabbed a silver pitcher from a table and stepped close as he dashed ice water upon him and stood him up and forced two of us to support him as his head hung and moans issued from his thick bluish lips. Another boy began to plead to go home. He was the largest of the group, wearing dark red fighting trunks much too small to conceal the erection which projected from him as though in answer to the insinuating low-registered moaning of the clarinet. He tried to hide himself with his boxing gloves.

And all the while the blonde continued dancing, smiling faintly at the big shots who watched her with fascination, and faintly smiling at our fear. I noticed a certain merchant who followed her hungrily, his lips loose and drooling. He was a large man who wore diamond studs in a shirtfront which swelled with the ample paunch underneath, and each time the blonde swayed her undulating hips he ran his hand through the thin hair of his bald head and, with his arms upheld, his posture clumsy like that of an intoxicated panda, wound his belly in a slow and obscene grind. This creature was completely hypnotized. The music had quickened. As the dancer flung herself about with a detached expression on her face, the men began reaching out to touch her. I could see their beefy fingers sink into the soft flesh. Some of the others tried to stop them as she began to move around the floor in graceful circles, as they gave chase, slipping and sliding over the polished floor. It was mad. Chairs went crashing, drinks were spilt, as they ran laughing and howling after her. They caught her just as she reached a door, raised her from the floor, and tossed her as college boys are tossed at a hazing, and above her red, fixed-smiling lips I saw the terror and disgust in her eyes, almost like my own terror and that which I saw in some of the other boys. As I watched, they tossed her twice and her soft breasts seemed to flatten against the air and her legs flung wildly as she spun. Some of the more sober ones helped her to escape. And I started off the floor, heading for the anteroom with the rest of the boys.

Some were still crying in hysteria. But as we tried to leave we were stopped 10 and ordered to get into the ring. There was nothing to do but what we were told. All ten of us climbed under the ropes and allowed ourselves to be blindfolded with broad bands of white cloth. One of the men seemed to feel a bit sympathetic and tried to cheer us up as we stood with our backs against the ropes. Some of us tried to grin. "See that boy over there?" one of the men said. "I want you to run across at the bell and give it to him right in the belly. If you don't get him, I'm going to get you. I don't like his looks." Each of us was told the same. The blindfolds were put on. Yet even then I had been going over my speech. In my mind each word was as bright as flame. I felt the cloth pressed into place, and frowned so that it would be loosened when I relaxed.

But now I felt a sudden fit of blind terror. I was unused to darkness. It was as though I had suddenly found myself in a dark room filled with poisonous cottonmouths. I could hear the bleary voices yelling insistently for the battle royal to begin.

"Get going in there!"

"Let me at that big nigger!"

I strained to pick up the school superintendent's voice, as though to squeeze some security out of that slightly more familiar sound.

"Let me at those black sonsabitches!" someone yelled. 15

"No, Jackson, no!" another voice yelled. "Here, somebody, help me hold Jack."

"I want to get at that ginger-colored nigger. Tear him limb from limb," the first voice yelled.

I stood against the ropes trembling. For in those days I was what they called ginger-colored, and he sounded as though he might crunch me between his teeth like a crisp ginger cookie.

Quite a struggle was going on. Chairs were being kicked about and I could hear voices grunting as with a terrific effort. I wanted to see, to see more desperately than ever before. But the blindfold was tight as a thick skin-puckering scab and when I raised my gloved hands to push the layers of white aside a voice yelled, "Oh, no you don't, black bastard! Leave that alone!"

"Ring the bell before Jackson kills him a coon!" someone boomed in the 20 sudden silence. And I heard the bell clang and the sound of the feet scuffling forward.

A glove smacked against my head. I pivoted, striking out stiffly as someone went past, and felt the jar ripple along the length of my arm to my shoulder. Then it seemed as though all nine of the boys had turned upon me at once. Blows pounded me from all sides while I struck out as best I could. So many blows landed upon me that I wondered if I were not the only blindfolded fighter in the ring, or if the man called Jackson hadn't succeeded in getting me after all.

Blindfolded, I could no longer control my motions. I had no dignity. I stumbled about like a baby or a drunken man. The smoke had become thicker and with each new blow it seemed to sear and further restrict my lungs. My saliva became like hot bitter glue. A glove connected with my head, filling my mouth with warm blood. It was everywhere. I could not tell if the moisture I felt upon my body was sweat or blood. A blow landed hard against the nape of my neck. I felt myself going over, my head hitting the floor. Streaks of blue light filled the black world behind the blindfold. I lay prone, pretending that I was knocked out, but felt myself seized by hands and yanked to my feet. "Get going, black boy! Mix it up!" My arms were like lead, my head smarting from blows. I managed to feel my way to the ropes and held on, trying to catch my breath. A glove landed in my mid-section and I went over again, feeling as though the smoke had become a knife jabbed into my guts. Pushed this way and that by the legs milling around me, I finally pulled erect and discovered that I could see the black, sweat-washed forms weaving in the smoky-blue atmosphere like drunken dancers weaving to the rapid drumlike thuds of blows.

Everyone fought hysterically. It was complete anarchy. Everybody fought everybody else. No group fought together for long. Two, three, four, fought one, then turned to fight each other, were themselves attacked. Blows landed below the belt and in the kidney, with the gloves open as well as closed, and with my eye partly opened now there was not so much terror. I moved carefully, avoiding blows, although not too many to attract attention, fighting from group to group. The boys groped about like blind, cautious crabs crouching to protect their mid-sections, their heads pulled in short against their shoulders, their arms stretched nervously before them, with their fists testing the smoke-filled air like the knobbed feelers of hypersensitive snails. In one corner I glimpsed a boy violently punching the air and heard him scream in pain as he smashed his hand against a ring post. For a second I saw him bent over holding his hand, then going down as a blow caught his unprotected head. I played one group against the other, slipping in and throwing a punch then stepping out of range while pushing the others into the melee to take the blows blindly aimed at me. The smoke was agonizing and there were no rounds, no bells at three minute intervals to relieve our exhaustion. The room spun round me, a swirl of lights, smoke, sweating bodies surrounded by tense white faces. I bled from both nose and mouth, the blood spattering upon my chest.

The men kept yelling, "Slug him, black boy! Knock his guts out!"

"Uppercut him! Kill him! Kill that big boy!" 25

Taking a fake fall, I saw a boy going down heavily beside me as though we were felled by a single blow, saw a sneaker-clad foot shoot into his groin as the two who had knocked him down stumbled upon him. I rolled out of range, feeling a twinge of nausea.

The harder we fought the more threatening the men became. And yet, I had begun to worry about my speech again. How would it go? Would they recognize my ability? What would they give me?

I was fighting automatically when suddenly I noticed that one after another of the boys was leaving the ring. I was surprised, filled with panic, as though I had been left alone with an unknown danger. Then I understood. The boys had arranged it among themselves. It was the custom for the two men left in the ring to slug it out for the winner's prize. I discovered this too late. When the bell sounded two men in tuxedoes leaped into the ring and removed the blindfold. I found myself facing Tatlock, the biggest of the gang. I felt sick at my stomach. Hardly had the bell stopped ringing in my ears than it clanged again and I saw him moving swiftly toward me. Thinking of nothing else to do I hit him smash on the nose. He kept coming, bringing the rank sharp violence of stale sweat. His face was a black blank of a face, only his eyes alive — with hate of me and aglow with a feverish terror from what had happened to us all. I became anxious. I wanted to deliver my speech and he came at me as though he meant to beat it out of me. I smashed him again and again, taking his blows as they came. Then on a sudden impulse I struck him lightly and as we clinched, I whispered, "Fake like I knocked you out, you can have the prize."

"I'll break your behind," he whispered hoarsely.

"For *them?*" 30

"For *me*, sonofabitch!"

They were yelling for us to break it up and Tatlock spun me half around with a blow, and as a joggled camera sweeps in a reeling scene, I saw the howling red faces crouching tense beneath the cloud of blue-gray smoke. For a moment the world wavered, unraveled, flowed, then my head cleared and Tatlock bounced before me. That fluttering shadow before my eyes was his jabbing left hand. Then falling forward, my head against his damp shoulder, I whispered,

"I'll make it five dollars more."

"Go to hell!"

But his muscles relaxed a trifle beneath my pressure and I breathed, 35 "Seven?"

"Give it to your ma," he said, ripping me beneath the heart.

And while I still held him I butted him and moved away. I felt myself bombarded with punches. I fought back with hopeless desperation. I wanted to deliver my speech more than anything else in the world, because I felt that only these men could judge truly my ability, and now this stupid clown was ruining my chances. I began fighting carefully now, moving in to punch him and out again with my greater speed. A lucky blow to his chin and I had him going too — until I heard a loud voice yell, "I got my money on the big boy."

Hearing this, I almost dropped my guard. I was confused: Should I try to win against the voice out there? Would not this go against my speech, and was not this a moment for humility, for nonresistance? A blow to my head as I danced about sent my right eye popping like a jack-in-the-box and settled my dilemma. The room went red as I fell. It was a dream fall, my body languid and fastidious as to where to land, until the floor became impatient and smashed up to meet me. A moment later I came to. An hypnotic voice said FIVE emphatically. And I lay there, hazily watching a dark red spot of my own blood shaping itself into a butterfly, glistening and soaking into the soiled gray world of the canvas.

When the voice drawled TEN I was lifted up and dragged to a chair. I sat dazed. My eye pained and swelled with each throb of my pounding heart and I wondered if now I would be allowed to speak. I was wringing wet, my mouth still bleeding. We were grouped along the wall now. The other boys ignored me as they congratulated Tatlock and speculated as to how much they would be paid. One boy whimpered over his smashed hand. Looking up front, I saw attendants in white jackets rolling the portable ring away and placing a small square rug in the vacant space surrounded by chairs. Perhaps, I thought, I will stand on the rug to deliver my speech.

Then the M.C. called to us, "Come on up here boys and get your money." 40 We ran forward to where the men laughed and talked in their chairs, waiting. Everyone seemed friendly now.

"There it is on the rug," the man said. I saw the rug covered with coins of all dimensions and a few crumpled bills. But what excited me, scattered here and there, were the gold pieces.

"Boys, it's all yours," the man said. "You get all you grab."

"That's right, Sambo," a blond man said, winking at me confidentially.

I trembled with excitement, forgetting my pain. I would get the gold and the bills, I thought. I would use both hands. I would throw my body against the boys nearest me to block them from the gold.

"Get down around the rug now," the man commanded, "and don't anyone 45 touch it until I give the signal."

"This ought to be good," I heard.

As told, we got around the square rug on our knees. Slowly the man raised his freckled hand as we followed it upward with our eyes.

I heard, "These niggers look like they're about to pray!"

Then, "Ready," the man said. "Go!"

I lunged for a yellow coin lying on the blue design of the carpet, touching 50 it and sending a surprised shriek to join those rising around me. I tried frantically to remove my hand but could not let go. A hot, violent force tore through my body, shaking me like a wet rat. The rug was electrified. The hair bristled up on my head as I shook myself free. My muscles jumped, my nerves jangled, writhed. But I saw that this was not stopping the other boys. Laughing in fear and embarrassment, some were holding back and scooping up the coins knocked off by the painful contortions of the others. The men roared above us as we struggled.

"Pick it up, goddamnit, pick it up!" someone called like a bass-voiced parrot. "Go on, get it!"

I crawled rapidly around the floor, picking up the coins, trying to avoid the coppers and to get greenbacks and the gold. Ignoring the shock by laughing, as I brushed the coins off quickly, I discovered that I could contain the electricity—a contradiction, but it works. Then the men began to push us onto the rug. Laughing embarrassedly, we struggled out of their hands and kept after the coins. We were all wet and slippery and hard to hold. Suddenly I saw a boy lifted into the air, glistening with sweat like a circus seal, and dropped, his wet back landing flush upon the charged rug, heard him yell and saw him literally dance upon his back, his elbows beating a frenzied tattoo upon the floor, his muscles twitching like the flesh of a horse stung by many flies. When he finally rolled off, his face was gray and no one stopped him when he ran from the floor amid booming laughter.

"Get the money," the M.C. called. "That's good hard American cash!"

And we snatched and grabbed, snatched and grabbed. I was careful not to come too close to the rug now, and when I felt the hot whiskey breath descend upon me like a cloud of foul air I reached out and grabbed the leg of a chair. It was occupied and I held on desperately.

"Leggo, nigger! Leggo!"   55

The huge face wavered down to mine as he tried to push me free. But my body was slippery and he was too drunk. It was Mr. Colcord, who owned a chain of movie houses and "entertainment palaces." Each time he grabbed me I slipped out of his hands. It became a real struggle. I feared the rug more than I did the drunk, so I held on, surprising myself for a moment by trying to topple *him* upon the rug. It was such an enormous idea that I found myself actually carrying it out. I tried not to be obvious, yet when I grabbed his leg, trying to tumble him out of the chair, he raised up roaring with laughter, and, looking at me with soberness dead in the eye, kicked me viciously in the chest. The chair leg flew out of my hand and I felt myself going and rolled. It was as though I had rolled through a bed of hot coals. It seemed a whole century would pass before I would roll free, a century in which I was seared through the deepest levels of my body to the fearful breath within me and the breath seared and heated to the point of explosion. It'll all be over in a flash, I thought as I rolled clear. It'll all be over in a flash.

But not yet, the men on the other side were waiting, red faces swollen as though from apoplexy as they bent forward in their chairs. Seeing their fingers coming toward me I rolled away as a fumbled football rolls off the receiver's fingertips, back into the coals. That time I luckily sent the rug sliding out of place and heard the coins ringing against the floor and the boys scuffling to pick them up and the M.C. calling, "All right, boys, that's all. Go get dressed and get your money."

I was limp as a dish rag. My back felt as though it had been beaten with wires.

When we had dressed the M.C. came in and gave us each five dollars, except Tatlock, who got ten for being last in the ring. Then he told us to leave. I was not to get a chance to deliver my speech, I thought. I was going out into the dim alley in despair when I was stopped and told to go back. I returned to the ballroom, where the men were pushing back their chairs and gathering in groups to talk.

The M.C. knocked on a table for quiet. "Gentlemen," he said, "we almost 60 forgot an important part of the program. A most serious part, gentlemen.

This boy was brought here to deliver a speech which he made at his graduation yesterday . . ."

"Bravo!"

"I'm told that he is the smartest boy we've got out there in Greenwood. I'm told that he knows more big words than a pocket-sized dictionary."

Much applause and laughter.

"So now, gentlemen, I want you to give him your attention."

There was still laughter as I faced them, my mouth dry, my eye throbbing. 65
I began slowly, but evidently my throat was tense, because they began shouting, "Louder! Louder!"

"We of the younger generation extol the wisdom of that great leader and educator," I shouted, "who first spoke these flaming words of wisdom: 'A ship lost at sea for many days suddenly sighted a friendly vessel. From the mast of the unfortunate vessel was seen a signal: "Water, water; we die of thirst!" The answer from the friendly vessel came back: "Cast down your bucket where you are." The captain of the distressed vessel, at last heeding the injunction, cast down his bucket, and it came up full of fresh sparkling water from the mouth of the Amazon River.' And like him I say, and in his words, 'To those of my race who depend upon bettering their condition in a foreign land, or who underestimate the importance of cultivating friendly relations with the Southern white man, who is his next-door neighbor, I would say: "Cast down your bucket where you are" — cast it down in making friends in every manly way of the people of all races by whom we are surrounded . . .'"

I spoke automatically and with such fervor that I did not realize that the men were still talking and laughing until my dry mouth, filling up with blood from the cut, almost strangled me. I coughed, wanting to stop and go to one of the tall brass, sand-filled spittoons to relieve myself, but a few of the men, especially the superintendent, were listening and I was afraid. So I gulped it down, blood, saliva, and all, and continued. (What powers of endurance I had during those days! What enthusiasm! What a belief in the rightness of things!) I spoke even louder in spite of the pain. But still they talked and still they laughed, as though deaf with cotton in dirty ears. So I spoke with greater emotional emphasis. I closed my ears and swallowed blood until I was nauseated. The speech seemed a hundred times as long as before, but I could not leave out a single word. All had to be said, each memorized nuance considered, rendered. Nor was that all. Whenever I uttered a word of three or more syllables a group of voices would yell for me to repeat it. I used the phrase "social responsibility" and they yelled:

"What's that word you say, boy?"

"Social responsibility," I said.

"What?" 70

"Social . . ."

"Louder."

". . . responsibility."

"More!"

"Respon —" 75

"Repeat!"

"— sibility."

The room filled with the uproar of laughter until, no doubt, distracted by having to gulp down my blood, I made a mistake and yelled a phrase I had often seen denounced in newspaper editorials, heard debated in private.

"Social . . ."

"What?" they yelled.   80

". . . equality—"

The laughter hung smokelike in the sudden stillness. I opened my eyes, puzzled. Sounds of displeasure filled the room. The M.C. rushed forward. They shouted hostile phrases at me. But I did not understand.

A small dry mustached man in the front row blared out, "Say that slowly, son!"

"What, sir?"

"What you just said!"   85

"Social responsibility, sir," I said.

"You weren't being smart, were you, boy?" he said, not unkindly.

"No, sir!"

"You sure that about 'equality' was a mistake?"

"Oh, yes, sir," I said. "I was swallowing blood."   90

"Well, you had better speak more slowly so we can understand. We mean to do right by you, but you've got to know your place at all times. All right, now, go on with your speech."

I was afraid. I wanted to leave but I wanted also to speak and I was afraid they'd snatch me down.

"Thank you, sir," I said, beginning where I had left off, and having them ignore me as before.

Yet when I finished there was a thunderous applause. I was surprised to see the superintendent come forth with a package wrapped in white tissue paper, and, gesturing for quiet, address the men.

"Gentlemen, you see that I did not overpraise this boy. He makes a good   95
speech and some day he'll lead his people in the proper paths. And I don't have to tell you that that is important in these days and times. This is a good, smart boy, and so to encourage him in the right direction, in the name of the Board of Education I wish to present him a prize in the form of this . . ."

He paused, removing the tissue paper and revealing a gleaming calfskin brief case.

". . . in the form of this first-class article from Shad Whitmore's shop."

"Boy," he said, addressing me, "take this prize and keep it well. Consider it a badge of office. Prize it. Keep developing as you are and some day it will be filled with important papers that will help shape the destiny of your people."

I was so moved that I could hardly express my thanks. A rope of bloody saliva forming a shape like an undiscovered continent drooled upon the leather and I wiped it quickly away. I felt an importance that I had never dreamed.

"Open it and see what's inside," I was told.   100

My fingers a-tremble, I complied, smelling the fresh leather and finding an official-looking document inside. It was a scholarship to the state college for Negroes. My eyes filled with tears and I ran awkwardly off the floor.

I was overjoyed; I did not even mind when I discovered that the gold pieces I had scrambled for were brass pocket tokens advertising a certain make of automobile.

When I reached home everyone was excited. Next day the neighbors came to congratulate me. I even felt safe from grandfather, whose deathbed curse usually spoiled my triumphs. I stood beneath his photograph with my brief case in hand and smiled triumphantly into his stolid black peasant's face. It was a face that fascinated me. The eyes seemed to follow everywhere I went.

That night I dreamed I was at a circus with him and that he refused to laugh at the clowns no matter what they did. Then later he told me to open my brief case and read what was inside and I did, finding an official envelope stamped with the state seal; and inside the envelope I found another and another, endlessly, and I thought I would fall of weariness. "Them's years," he said. "Now open that one." And I did and in it I found an engraved document containing a short message in letters of gold. "Read it," my grandfather said. "Out loud!"

"To Whom It May Concern," I intoned. "Keep This Nigger-Boy Running." 105
I awoke with the old man's laughter ringing in my ears.

(It was a dream I was to remember and dream again for many years after. But at that time I had no insight into its meaning. First I had to attend college.)

CONSIDERATIONS FOR CRITICAL THINKING AND WRITING

1. FIRST RESPONSE. Discuss how the protagonist's expectations are similar to what has come to be known as the American dream — the assumption that ambition, hard work, perseverance, intelligence, and virtue always lead to success. Do you believe in the American dream?

2. How does the first paragraph of the story sum up the conflict that the narrator confronts? In what sense is he "invisible"?

3. Why do his grandfather's last words cause so much anxiety in the family? What does his grandfather mean when he says, "I want you to overcome 'em with yeses, undermine 'em with grins, agree 'em to death"?

4. What is the symbolic significance of the naked blonde? What details reveal that she represents more than a sexual tease in the story?

5. How does the battle in the boxing ring and the scramble for money afterward suggest the kind of control whites have over blacks in the story?

6. Why is it significant that the town is named Greenwood and that the briefcase award comes from Shad Whitmore's shop? Can you find any other details that serve to reinforce the meaning of the story?

7. What is the narrator's perspective as an educated adult telling the story, in contrast to his assumptions and beliefs as a recent high-school graduate? How is this contrast especially evident in the speech before the "leading white citizens" of the town?

8. How can the dream at the end of the story be related to the major incidents that precede it?

9. Given the grandfather's advice, explain how "meekness" can be a "dangerous activity" and a weapon against oppression.

10. Imagine the story as told from a third-person point of view. How would this change the story? Do you think the story would be more or less effective told from a third-person point of view? Explain your answer.

11. CRITICAL STRATEGIES. Read the section on mythological criticism (pp. 72–74) in Chapter 3, "Applying a Critical Strategy," and discuss "Battle Royal" as an archetypal initiation story.

MARK HALLIDAY (B. 1949)

Born in Ann Arbor, Michigan, Mark Halliday earned a B.A. and an M.A. from Brown University and a Ph.D. from Brandeis University. A teacher at the University of Pennsylvania, his short stories and poems have appeared in a variety of periodicals, including *The Massachusetts Review, Michigan Quarterly Review, Chicago Review,* and *The New Republic.* His collection of poems, *Little Star,* was selected by the National Poetry Series for publication in 1987. He has also written a critical study on poet Wallace Stevens titled *Stevens and the Interpersonal* (1991).

Young Man on Sixth Avenue   *1995*

He was a young man in the big city. He was a young man in the biggest, the most overwhelming city—and he was not overwhelmed. For see, he strode across Fifth Avenue just before the light changed, and his head was up in the sharp New York wind and he was thriving upon the rock of Manhattan, in 1938. His legs were long and his legs were strong; there was no question about his legs; they were unmistakable in their length and strength; they were as bold and dependable as any American machine, moving him across Fifth just in time, his brown shoes attaining the sidewalk without any faltering, his gait unaware of the notion that legs might ever want to rest. Forty-ninth Street! He walked swiftly through the haste and blare, through the chilly exclamation points of taxis and trucks and people. He was a man! In America, '38, New York, two o'clock in the afternoon, sunlight chopping down between buildings, Forty-ninth Street. And his hair was so dark, almost black, and it had a natural wave in it recognized as a handsome feature by everyone, recognized universally, along with his dark blue eyes and strong jaw. Women saw him, they all had to see him, all the young women had to perceive him reaching the corner of Forty-ninth and Sixth, and they had to know he was a candidate. He knew they knew. He knew they knew he would *get* some of them, and he moved visibly tall with the tall potential of the not-finite twentieth-century getting that would be his inheritance; and young women who glanced at him on Sixth Avenue knew that he knew. They felt that they or their sisters would have to take him into account, and they touched their scarves a little nervously.

He was twenty-five years old, and this day in 1938 was the present. It was so obviously and totally the present, so unabashed and even garish with its presentness, beamingly right there right now like Rita Hayworth, all Sixth Avenue was in fact at two o'clock a thumping bright Rita Hayworth and the young man strode south irresistibly. If there was only one thing he knew, crossing Forty-eighth, it was that this day was the present, out of which uncounted glories could and must blossom—when?—in 1938, or in 1939, soon, or in the big brazen decade ahead, in 1940, soon; so he walked with fistfuls of futures that could happen in all his pockets.

And his wavy hair was so dark, almost black. And he knew the right restaurant for red roast beef, not too expensive. And in his head were some sharp ideas about Dreiser, and Thomas Wolfe, and John O'Hara.

On Forty-seventh between two buildings (buildings taller even than him) there was an unexpected zone of deep shade. He paused for half a second, and he shivered for some reason. Briskly then, briskly he moved ahead.

In the restaurant on Seventh Avenue he met his friend John for a witty late lunch. Everything was — the whole lunch was good. It was right. And what they said was both hilarious and notably well-informed. And then soon he was taking the stairs two at a time up to an office on Sixth for his interview. The powerful lady seemed to like his sincerity and the clarity of his eyes — a hard combination to beat! — and the even more powerful man in charge sized him up and saw the same things, and he got the job.

That job lasted three years, then came the War, then another job, then Judy, and the two kids, and a better job in Baltimore, and those years — those years. And those years. "Those years" — and the kids went to college with new typewriters. In the blue chair, with his work on his lapboard, after a pleasant dinner of macaroni and sausage and salad, he dozed off. Then he was sixty. Sixty? Then he rode back and forth on trains, Judy became ill, doctors offered opinions, comas were deceptive, Judy died. But the traffic on Coleytown Road next morning still moved casually too fast. And in a minute he was seventy-five and the phone rang with news that witty John of the great late lunches was dead. The house pulsed with silence.

Something undone? What? The thing that would have saved — what? Waking in the dark — maybe something unwritten, that would have made people say "*Yes* that's why you matter so much." Ideas about Wolfe. Dreiser. Or some lost point about John O'Hara.

Women see past him on the street in this pseudo-present and he feels they are so stupid and walks fierce for a minute but then his shoulders settle closer to his skeleton with the truth about these women: not especially stupid; only young. In this pseudo-present he blinks at a glimpse of that young man on Sixth Avenue, young man as if still out there in the exclamation of Sixth Avenue — that young man ready to stride across — but a taxi makes him step back to the curb, he'll have to wait a few more seconds, he can wait.

CONSIDERATIONS FOR CRITICAL THINKING AND WRITING

1. FIRST RESPONSE. Do you identify with the young man as he is described in the first paragraph? Is he appealing to you? Why or why not?

2. Why do you think this story opens in 1938? Why is the Manhattan setting important?

3. What is the conflict in the story?

4. Locate the climax in the story. Is there a resolution to the conflict? Explain.

5. How might paragraph 4 be described as an example of foreshadowing?

6. What does the plotting of this story suggest about the nature of the protagonist's life?

7. What do you think is the central point of this story?

8. CRITICAL STRATEGIES. Read the section on literary history criticism (pp. 67–68) in Chapter 3, "Applying a Critical Strategy." Based on that discussion, what do you think a literary historian might have to say about the relevance to the story of the American novelists Theodore Dreiser, Thomas

Wolfe, and John O'Hara mentioned in paragraphs 3 and 7? You may have to look up these writers in an encyclopedia or a dictionary of American literary biographies to answer this question.

HERMAN MELVILLE (1819–1891)

Hoping to improve his distressed financial situation, Herman Melville left New York and went to sea as a young common sailor. He returned to become an uncommon writer. His experiences at sea became the basis for his early novels: *Typee* (1846), *Omoo* (1847), *Mardi* (1849), *Redburn* (1849), and *White-Jacket* (1850). Ironically, with the publication of his masterpiece, *Moby-Dick* (1851), Melville lost the popular success he had enjoyed with his earlier books because his readers were not ready for its philosophical complexity. Although he wrote more, Melville's works were read less and slipped into obscurity. His final short novel, *Billy Budd,* was not published until the 1920s, when critics rediscovered him. In "Bartleby, the Scrivener," Melville presents a quiet clerk in a law office whose baffling "passive resistance" disrupts the life of his employer, a man who attempts to make sense of Bartleby's refusal to behave reasonably.

Bartleby, the Scrivener   *1853*
A Story of Wall Street

I am a rather elderly man. The nature of my avocations, for the last thirty years, has brought me into more than ordinary contact with what would seem an interesting and somewhat singular set of men, of whom, as yet, nothing, that I know of, has ever been written—I mean, the law-copyists, or scriveners. I have known very many of them, professionally and privately, and, if I pleased, could relate divers histories, at which good-natured gentlemen might smile, and sentimental souls might weep. But I waive the biographies of all other scriveners, for a few passages in the life of Bartleby, who was a scrivener, the strangest I ever saw, or heard of. While, of other law-copyists, I might write the complete life, of Bartleby nothing of that sort can be done. I believe that no materials exist, for a full and satisfactory biography of this man. It is an irreparable loss to literature. Bartleby was one of those beings of whom nothing is ascertainable, except from the original sources, and, in his case, those are very small. What my own astonished eyes saw of Bartleby, *that* is all I know of him, except, indeed, one vague report, which will appear in the sequel.

Ere introducing the scrivener, as he first appeared to me, it is fit I make some mention of myself, my *employés,* my business, my chambers, and general surroundings, because some such description is indispensable to an adequate understanding of the chief character about to be presented. Imprimis:° I am a

---

Imprimis: In the first place.

man who, from his youth upwards, has been filled with a profound conviction that the easiest way of life is the best. Hence, though I belong to a profession proverbially energetic and nervous, even to turbulence, at times, yet nothing of that sort have I ever suffered to invade my peace. I am one of those unambitious lawyers who never address a jury, or in any way draw down public applause; but, in the cool tranquillity of a snug retreat, do a snug business among rich men's bonds, and mortgages, and title-deeds. All who know me, consider me an eminently *safe* man. The late John Jacob Astor,° a personage little given to poetic enthusiasm, had no hesitation in pronouncing my first grand point to be prudence; my next, method. I do not speak it in vanity, but simply record the fact, that I was not unemployed in my profession by the late John Jacob Astor; a name which, I admit, I love to repeat; for it hath a rounded and orbicular sound to it, and rings like unto bullion. I will freely add, that I was not insensible to the late John Jacob Astor's good opinion.

Some time prior to the period at which this little history begins, my avocations had been largely increased. The good old office, now extinct in the State of New York, of a Master in Chancery, had been conferred upon me. It was not a very arduous office, but very pleasantly remunerative. I seldom lose my temper; much more seldom indulge in dangerous indignation at wrongs and outrages; but I must be permitted to be rash here and declare, that I consider the sudden and violent abrogation of the office of Master in Chancery, by the new Constitution, as a —— premature act; inasmuch as I had counted upon a life-lease of the profits, whereas I only received those of a few short years. But this is by the way.

My chambers were up stairs, at No. — Wall Street. At one end, they looked upon the white wall of the interior of a spacious skylight shaft, penetrating the building from top to bottom.

This view might have been considered rather tame than otherwise, deficient in what landscape painters call "life." But, if so, the view from the other end of my chambers offered, at least, a contrast, if nothing more. In that direction, my windows commanded an unobstructed view of a lofty brick wall, black by age and everlasting shade; which wall required no spyglass to bring out its lurking beauties, but, for the benefit of all near-sighted spectators, was pushed up to within ten feet of my window-panes. Owing to the great height of the surrounding buildings, and my chambers being on the second floor, the interval between this wall and mine not a little resembled a huge square cistern.

At the period just preceding the advent of Bartleby, I had two persons as copyists in my employment, and a promising lad as an office-boy. First, Turkey; second, Nippers; third, Ginger Nut. These may seem names, the like of which are not usually found in the Directory. In truth, they were nicknames, mutually conferred upon each other by my three clerks, and were deemed expressive of their respective persons or characters. Turkey was a short, pursy Englishman, of about my own age — that is, somewhere not far from sixty. In the morning, one might say, his face was of a fine florid hue, but after twelve o'clock, meridian — his dinner hour — it blazed like a grate full of Christmas coals; and continued blazing — but, as it were, with a gradual wane — till six o'clock, P.M., or thereabouts; after which, I saw no more of the proprietor of the face, which, gaining its meridian with the sun, seemed to set with it, to rise,

John Jacob Astor (1763-1848): An enormously wealthy American capitalist.

culminate, and decline the following day, with the like regularity and undiminished glory. There are many singular coincidences I have known in the course of my life, not the least among which was the fact, that, exactly when Turkey displayed his fullest beams from his red and radiant countenance, just then, too, at that critical moment, began the daily period when I considered his business capacities as seriously disturbed for the remainder of the twenty-four hours. Not that he was absolutely idle, or averse to business then; far from it. The difficulty was, he was apt to be altogether too energetic. There was a strange, inflamed, flurried, flighty recklessness of activity about him. He would be incautious in dipping his pen into his inkstand. All his blots upon my documents were dropped there after twelve o'clock, meridian. Indeed, not only would he be reckless, and sadly given to making blots in the afternoon, but, some days, he went further, and was rather noisy. At such times, too, his face flamed with augmented blazonry, as if cannel coal had been heaped on anthracite. He made an unpleasant racket with his chair; spilled his sand-box; in mending his pens, impatiently split them all to pieces, and threw them on the floor in a sudden passion; stood up, and leaned over his table, boxing his papers about in a most indecorous manner, very sad to behold in an elderly man like him. Nevertheless, as he was in many ways a most valuable person to me, and all the time before twelve o'clock, meridian, was the quickest, steadiest creature, too, accomplishing a great deal of work in a style not easily to be matched—for these reasons, I was willing to overlook his eccentricities, though, indeed, occasionally, I remonstrated with him. I did this very gently, however, because, though the civilest, nay, the blandest and most reverential of men in the morning, yet, in the afternoon, he was disposed, upon provocation, to be slightly rash with his tongue—in fact, insolent. Now, valuing his morning services as I did, and resolved not to lose them—yet, at the same time, made uncomfortable by his inflamed ways after twelve o'clock—and being a man of peace, unwilling by my admonitions to call forth unseemly retorts from him, I took upon me, one Saturday noon (he was always worse on Saturdays) to hint to him, very kindly, that, perhaps, now that he was growing old, it might be well to abridge his labors; in short, he need not come to my chambers after twelve o'clock, but, dinner over, had best go home to his lodgings, and rest himself till tea-time. But no; he insisted upon his afternoon devotions. His countenance became intolerably fervid, as he oratorically assured me—gesticulating with a long ruler at the other end of the room—that if his services in the morning were useful, how indispensable, then, in the afternoon?

"With submission, sir," said Turkey, on this occasion, "I consider myself your right-hand man. In the morning I but marshal and deploy my columns; but in the afternoon I put myself at their head, and gallantly charge the foe, thus"—and he made a violent thrust with the ruler.

"But the blots, Turkey," intimated I.

"True; but, with submission, sir, behold these hairs! I am getting old. Surely, sir, a blot or two of a warm afternoon is not to be severely urged against gray hairs. Old age—even if it blot the page—is honorable. With submission, sir, we *both* are getting old."

This appeal to my fellow-feeling was hardly to be resisted. At all events, I saw that go he would not. So, I made up my mind to let him stay, resolving, nevertheless, to see to it that, during the afternoon, he had to do with my less important papers.

Nippers, the second on my list, was a whiskered, sallow, and, upon the whole, rather piratical-looking young man, of about five-and-twenty. I always deemed him the victim of two evil powers—ambition and indigestion. The ambition was evinced by a certain impatience of the duties of a mere copyist, an unwarrantable usurpation of strictly professional affairs such as the original drawing up of legal documents. The indigestion seemed betokened in an occasional nervous testiness and grinning irritability, causing the teeth to audibly grind together over mistakes committed in copying; unnecessary maledictions, hissed, rather than spoken, in the heat of business; and especially by a continual discontent with the height of the table where he worked. Though of a very ingenious mechanical turn, Nippers could never get this table to suit him. He put chips under it, blocks of various sorts, bits of pasteboard, and at last went so far as to attempt an exquisite adjustment, by final pieces of folded blotting-paper. But no invention would answer. If, for the sake of easing his back, he brought the table-lid at a sharp angle well up towards his chin, and wrote there like a man using the steep roof of a Dutch house for his desk, then he declared that it stopped the circulation in his arms. If now he lowered the table to his waistbands, and stooped over it in writing, then there was a sore aching in his back. In short, the truth of the matter was, Nippers knew not what he wanted. Or, if he wanted anything, it was to be rid of a scrivener's table altogether. Among the manifestations of his diseased ambition was a fondness he had for receiving visits from certain ambiguous-looking fellows in seedy coats, whom he called his clients. Indeed, I was aware that not only was he, at times, considerable of a ward-politician, but he occasionally did a little business at the justices' courts, and was not unknown on the steps of the Tombs.° I have good reason to believe, however, that one individual who called upon him at my chambers, and who, with a grand air, he insisted was his client, was no other than a dun, and the alleged title-deed, a bill. But, with all his failings, and the annoyances he caused me, Nippers, like his compatriot Turkey, was a very useful man to me; wrote a neat, swift hand; and, when he chose, was not deficient in a gentlemanly sort of deportment. Added to this, he always dressed in a gentlemanly sort of way; and so, incidentally, reflected credit upon my chambers. Whereas, with respect to Turkey, I had much ado to keep him from being a reproach to me. His clothes were apt to look oily, a smell of eating-houses. He wore his pantaloons very loose and baggy in summer. His coats were execrable, his hat not to be handled. But while the hat was a thing of indifference to me, inasmuch as his natural civility and deference, as a dependent Englishman, always led him to doff it the moment he entered the room, yet his coat was another matter. Concerning his coats, I reasoned with him; but with no effect. The truth was, I suppose, that a man with so small an income could not afford to sport such a lustrous face and a lustrous coat at one and the same time. As Nippers once observed, Turkey's money went chiefly for red ink. One winter day, I presented Turkey with a highly respectable-looking coat of my own—a padded gray coat, of a most comfortable warmth, and which buttoned straight up from the knee to the neck. I thought Turkey would appreciate the favor, and abate his rashness and obstreperousness of afternoons. But no; I verily believe that buttoning himself up in so downy and blanket-like a coat had a pernicious effect upon him—upon the same principle that too much oats are bad for horses. In fact,

---

the Tombs: A jail in New York City.

precisely as a rash, restive horse is said to feel his oats, so Turkey felt his coat. It made him insolent. He was a man whom prosperity harmed.

Though, concerning the self-indulgent habits of Turkey, I had my own private surmises, yet, touching Nippers, I was well persuaded that, whatever might be his faults in other respects, he was, at least, a temperate young man. But indeed, nature herself seemed to have been his vintner, and, at his birth, charged him so thoroughly with an irritable, brandy-like disposition, that all subsequent potations were needless. When I consider how, amid the stillness of my chambers, Nippers would sometimes impatiently rise from his seat, and stooping over his table, spread his arms wide apart, seize the whole desk, and move it, and jerk it, with a grim, grinding motion on the floor, as if the table were a perverse voluntary agent, intent on thwarting and vexing him, I plainly perceive that, for Nippers, brandy-and-water were altogether superfluous.

It was fortunate for me that, owing to its peculiar cause — indigestion — the irritability and consequent nervousness of Nippers were mainly observable in the morning, while in the afternoon he was comparatively mild. So that, Turkey's paroxysms only coming on about twelve o'clock, I never had to do with their eccentricities at one time. Their fits relieved each other, like guards. When Nippers' was on, Turkey's was off; and *vice versa*. This was a good natural arrangement, under the circumstances.

Ginger Nut, the third on my list, was a lad, some twelve years old. His father was a carman, ambitious of seeing his son on the bench instead of a cart, before he died. So he sent him to my office, as student at law, errand-boy, cleaner, and sweeper, at the rate of one dollar a week. He had a little desk to himself, but he did not use it much. Upon inspection, the drawer exhibited a great array of the shells of various sorts of nuts. Indeed, to this quick-witted youth, the whole noble science of the law was contained in a nutshell. Not the least among the employments of Ginger Nut, as well as one which he discharged with the most alacrity, was his duty as cake and apple purveyor for Turkey and Nippers. Copying lawpapers being proverbially a dry, husky sort of business, my two scriveners were fain to moisten their mouths very often with Spitzenbergs, to be had at the numerous stalls nigh the Custom House and Post Office. Also, they sent Ginger Nut very frequently for that peculiar cake — small, flat, round, and very spicy — after which he had been named by them. Of a cold morning, when business was but dull, Turkey would gobble up scores of these cakes, as if they were mere wafers — indeed, they sell them at the rate of six or eight for a penny — the scrape of his pen blending with the crunching of the crisp particles in his mouth. Of all the fiery afternoon blunders and flurried rashness of Turkey, was his once moistening a ginger-cake between his lips, and clapping it on to a mortgage, for a seal. I came within an ace of dismissing him then. But he mollified me by making an oriental bow, and saying —

"With submission, sir, it was generous of me to find you in stationery on my own account."

Now my original business — that of a conveyancer and title hunter, and drawer-up of recondite documents of all sorts — was considerably increased by receiving the Master's office. There was now great work for scriveners. Not only must I push the clerks already with me, but I must have additional help.

In answer to my advertisement, a motionless young man one morning stood upon my office threshold, the door being open, for it was summer. I can see that figure now—pallidly neat, pitiably respectable, incurably forlorn! It was Bartleby.

After a few words touching his qualifications, I engaged him, glad to have among my corps of copyists a man of so singularly sedate an aspect, which I thought might operate beneficially upon the flighty temper of Turkey, and the fiery one of Nippers.

I should have stated before that ground-glass folding-doors divided my premises into two parts, one of which was occupied by my scriveners, the other by myself. According to my humor, I threw open these doors, or closed them. I resolved to assign Bartleby a corner by the folding-doors, but on my side of them, so as to have this quiet man within easy call, in case any trifling thing was to be done. I placed his desk close up to a small side-window in that part of the room, a window which originally had afforded a lateral view of certain grimy brickyards and bricks, but which, owing to subsequent erections, commanded at present no view at all, though it gave some light. Within three feet of the panes was a wall, and the light came down from far above, between two lofty buildings, as from a very small opening in a dome. Still further to a satisfactory arrangement, I procured a high green folding screen, which might entirely isolate Bartleby from my sight, though not remove him from my voice. And thus, in a manner, privacy and society were conjoined.

At first, Bartleby did an extraordinary quantity of writing. As if long famish- 20 ing for something to copy, he seemed to gorge himself on my documents. There was no pause for digestion. He ran a day and night line, copying by sunlight and by candle-light. I should have been quite delighted with his application, had he been cheerfully industrious. But he wrote on silently, palely, mechanically.

It is, of course, an indispensable part of a scrivener's business to verify the accuracy of his copy, word by word. Where there are two or more scriveners in an office, they assist each other in this examination, one reading from the copy, the other holding the original. It is a very dull, wearisome, and lethargic affair. I can readily imagine that, to some sanguine temperaments, it would be altogether intolerable. For example, I cannot credit that the mettlesome poet, Byron, would have contentedly sat down with Bartleby to examine a law document of, say five hundred pages, closely written in a crimpy hand.

Now and then, in the haste of business, it had been my habit to assist in comparing some brief document myself, calling Turkey or Nippers for this purpose. One object I had, in placing Bartleby so handy to me behind the screen, was, to avail myself of his services on such trivial occasions. It was on the third day, I think, of his being with me, and before any necessity had arisen for having his own writing examined, that, being much hurried to complete a small affair I had in hand, I abruptly called to Bartleby. In my haste and natural expectancy of instant compliance, I sat with my head bent over the original on my desk, and my right hand sideways, and somewhat nervously extended with the copy, so that, immediately upon emerging from his retreat, Bartleby might snatch it and proceed to business without the least delay.

In this very attitude did I sit when I called to him, rapidly stating what it was I wanted him to do—namely, to examine a small paper with me. Imagine my surprise, nay, my consternation, when, without moving from his privacy, Bartleby, in a singularly mild, firm voice, replied, "I would prefer not to."

I sat awhile in perfect silence, rallying my stunned faculties. Immediately it occurred to me that my ears had deceived me, or Bartleby had entirely misunderstood my meaning. I repeated my request in the clearest tone I could assume; but in quite as clear a one came the previous reply, "I would prefer not to."

"Prefer not to," echoed I, rising in high excitement, and crossing the room 25 with a stride. "What do you mean? Are you moonstruck? I want you to help me compare this sheet here — take it," and I thrust it towards him.

"I would prefer not to," said he.

I looked at him steadfastly. His face was leanly composed; his gray eye dimly calm. Not a wrinkle of agitation rippled him. Had there been the least uneasiness, anger, impatience, or impertinence in his manner; in other words, had there been anything ordinarily human about him, doubtless I should have violently dismissed him from the premises. But as it was, I should have as soon thought of turning my pale plaster-of-paris bust of Cicero out of doors. I stood gazing at him awhile, as he went on with his own writing, and then reseated myself at my desk. This is very strange, thought I. What had one best do? But my business hurried me. I concluded to forget the matter for the present, reserving it for my future leisure. So, calling Nippers from the other room, the paper was speedily examined.

A few days after this, Bartleby concluded four lengthy documents, being quadruplicates of a week's testimony taken before me in my High Court of Chancery. It became necessary to examine them. It was an important suit, and great accuracy was imperative. Having all things arranged, I called Turkey, Nippers, and Ginger Nut, from the next room, meaning to place the four copies in the hands of my four clerks, while I should read from the original. Accordingly, Turkey, Nippers, and Ginger Nut had taken their seats in a row, each with his document in his hand, when I called to Bartleby to join this interesting group.

"Bartleby! quick, I am waiting."

I heard a slow scrape of his chair legs on the uncarpeted floor, and soon he 30 appeared standing at the entrance of his hermitage.

"What is wanted?" said he, mildly.

"The copies, the copies," said I, hurriedly. "We are going to examine them. There" — and I held towards him the fourth quadruplicate.

"I would prefer not to," he said, and gently disappeared behind the screen.

For a few moments I was turned into a pillar of salt, standing at the head of my seated column of clerks. Recovering myself, I advanced towards the screen, and demanded the reason for such extraordinary conduct.

"*Why* do you refuse?" 35

"I would prefer not to."

With any other man I should have flown outright into a dreadful passion, scorned all further words, and thrust him ignominiously from my presence. But there was something about Bartleby that not only strangely disarmed me, but, in a wonderful manner, touched and disconcerted me. I began to reason with him.

"These are your own copies we are about to examine. It is labor saving to you, because one examination will answer for your four papers. It is common usage. Every copyist is bound to help examine his copy. Is it not so? Will you not speak? Answer!"

"I prefer not to," he replied in a flute-like tone. It seemed to me that, while I had been addressing him, he carefully revolved every statement that I made; fully comprehended the meaning; could not gainsay the irresistible conclusion; but, at the same time, some paramount consideration prevailed with him to reply as he did.

"You are decided, then, not to comply with my request—a request made 40 according to common usage and common sense?"

He briefly gave me to understand, that on that point my judgment was sound. Yes: his decision was irreversible.

It is not seldom the case that, when a man is browbeaten in some unprecedented and violently unreasonable way, he begins to stagger in his own plainest faith. He begins, as it were, vaguely to surmise that, wonderful as it may be, all the justice and all the reason is on the other side. Accordingly, if any disinterested persons are present, he turns to them for some reinforcement for his own faltering mind.

"Turkey," said I, "what do you think of this? Am I not right?"

"With submission, sir," said Turkey, in his blandest tone, "I think that you are."

"Nippers," said I, "what do *you* think of it?"   45

"I think I should kick him out of the office."

(The reader of nice perceptions will have perceived that, it being morning, Turkey's answer is couched in polite and tranquil terms, but Nippers replies in ill-tempered ones. Or, to repeat a previous sentence, Nippers' ugly mood was on duty, and Turkey's off.)

"Ginger Nut," said I, willing to enlist the smallest suffrage in my behalf, "what do *you* think of it?"

"I think, sir, he's a little *luny*," replied Ginger Nut, with a grin.

"You hear what they say," said I, turning towards the screen, "come forth 50 and do your duty."

But he vouchsafed no reply. I pondered a moment in sore perplexity. But once more business hurried me. I determined again to postpone the consideration of this dilemma to my future leisure. With a little trouble we made out to examine the papers without Bartleby, though at every page or two Turkey deferentially dropped his opinion, that this proceeding was quite out of the common; while Nippers, twitching in his chair with a dyspeptic nervousness, ground out, between his set teeth, occasional hissing maledictions against the stubborn oaf behind the screen. And for his (Nippers') part, this was the first and the last time he would do another man's business without pay.

Meanwhile Bartleby sat in his hermitage, oblivious to everything but his own peculiar business there.

Some days passed, the scrivener being employed upon another lengthy work. His late remarkable conduct led me to regard his ways narrowly. I observed that he never went to dinner; indeed, that he never went anywhere. As yet I had never, of my personal knowledge, known him to be outside of my office. He was a perpetual sentry in the corner. At about eleven o'clock though, in the morning, I noticed that Ginger Nut would advance toward the opening in Bartleby's screen, as if silently beckoned thither by a gesture invisible to me where I sat. The boy would then leave the office, jingling a few pence, and reappear with a handful of ginger-nuts, which he delivered in the hermitage, receiving two of the cakes for his trouble.

He lives, then, on ginger-nuts, thought I; never eats a dinner, properly speaking; he must be a vegetarian, then, but no; he never eats even vegetables, he eats nothing but ginger-nuts. My mind then ran on in reveries concerning the probable effects upon the human constitution of living entirely on ginger-nuts. Ginger-nuts are so called, because they contain ginger as one of their peculiar constituents, and the final flavoring one. Now, what was ginger? A hot, spicy thing. Was Bartleby hot and spicy? Not at all. Ginger, then, had no effect upon Bartleby. Probably he preferred it should have none.

Nothing so aggravates an earnest person as a passive resistance. If the individual so resisted be of a not inhumane temper, and the resisting one perfectly harmless in his passivity, then, in the better moods of the former, he will endeavor charitably to construe to his imagination what proves impossible to be solved by his judgment. Even so, for the most part, I regarded Bartleby and his ways. Poor fellow! thought I, he means no mischief; it is plain he intends no insolence; his aspect sufficiently evinces that his eccentricities are involuntary. He is useful to me. I can get along with him. If I turn him away, the chances are he will fall in with some less indulgent employer, and then he will be rudely treated, and perhaps driven forth miserably to starve. Yes. Here I can cheaply purchase a delicious self-approval. To befriend Bartleby; to humor him in his strange wilfulness, will cost me little or nothing, while I lay up in my soul what will eventually prove a sweet morsel for my conscience. But this mood was not invariable with me. The passiveness of Bartleby sometimes irritated me. I felt strangely goaded on to encounter him in new opposition—to elicit some angry spark from him answerable to my own. But, indeed, I might as well have essayed to strike fire with my knuckles against a bit of Windsor soap. But one afternoon the evil impulse in me mastered me, and the following little scene ensued:

"Bartleby," said I, "when those papers are all copied, I will compare them with you."

"I would prefer not to."

"How? Surely you do not mean to persist in that mulish vagary?"

No answer.

I threw open the folding-doors nearby, and turning upon Turkey and Nippers, exclaimed:

"Bartleby a second time says, he won't examine his papers. What do you think of it, Turkey?"

It was afternoon, be it remembered. Turkey sat glowing like a brass boiler; his bald head steaming; his hands reeling among his blotted papers.

"Think of it?" roared Turkey. "I think I'll just step behind his screen, and black his eyes for him!"

So saying, Turkey rose to his feet and threw his arms into a pugilistic position. He was hurrying away to make good his promise, when I detained him, alarmed at the effect of incautiously rousing Turkey's combativeness after dinner.

"Sit down, Turkey," said I, "and hear what Nippers has to say. What do you think of it, Nippers? Would I not be justified in immediately dismissing Bartleby?"

"Excuse me, that is for you to decide, sir. I think his conduct quite unusual, and, indeed, unjust, as regards Turkey and myself. But it may only be a passing whim."

"Ah," exclaimed I, "you have strangely changed your mind, then—you speak very gently of him now."

"All beer," cried Turkey; "gentleness is effects of beer—Nippers and I dined together to-day. You see how gentle *I* am, sir. Shall I go and black his eyes?"

"You refer to Bartleby, I suppose. No, not to-day, Turkey," I replied; "pray, put up your fists."

I closed the doors, and again advanced towards Bartleby. I felt additional 70 incentives tempting me to my fate. I burned to be rebelled against again. I remembered that Bartleby never left the office.

"Bartleby," said I, "Ginger Nut is away; just step around to the Post Office, won't you?" (it was but a three minutes' walk) "and see if there is anything for me."

"I would prefer not to."

"You *will* not?"

"I *prefer* not."

I staggered to my desk, and sat there in a deep study. My blind inveteracy 75 returned. Was there any other thing in which I could procure myself to be ignominiously repulsed by this lean, penniless wight?—my hired clerk? What added thing is there, perfectly reasonable, that he will be sure to refuse to do?

"Bartleby!"

No answer.

"Bartleby," in a louder tone.

No answer.

"Bartleby," I roared. 80

Like a very ghost, agreeably to the laws of magical invocation, at the third summons, he appeared at the entrance of his hermitage.

"Go to the next room, and tell Nippers to come to me."

"I prefer not to," he respectfully and slowly said, and mildly disappeared.

"Very good, Bartleby," said I, in a quiet sort of serenely-severe self-possessed tone, intimating the unalterable purpose of some terrible retribution very close at hand. At the moment I half intended something of the kind. But upon the whole, as it was drawing towards my dinner-hour, I thought it best to put on my hat and walk home for the day, suffering much from perplexity and distress of mind.

Shall I acknowledge it? The conclusion of this whole business was, that it 85 soon became a fixed fact of my chambers, that a pale young scrivener, by the name of Bartleby, had a desk there; that he copied for me at the usual rate of four cents a folio (one hundred words); but he was permanently exempt from examining the work done by him, that duty being transferred to Turkey and Nippers, out of compliment, doubtless, to their superior acuteness; moreover, said Bartleby was never, on any account, to be dispatched on the most trivial errand of any sort; and that even if entreated to take upon him such a matter, it was generally understood that he would "prefer not to"—in other words, that he would refuse point-blank.

As days passed on, I became considerably reconciled to Bartleby. His steadiness, his freedom from all dissipation, his incessant industry (except when he chose to throw himself into a standing revery behind his screen), his great stillness, his unalterableness of demeanor under all circumstances, made him a valuable acquisition. One prime thing was this—*he was always there*—first in the morning, continually through the day, and the last at night. I had a singular confidence in his honesty. I felt my most precious papers perfectly safe in his hands. Sometimes, to be sure, I could not, for the very soul of me, avoid falling into sudden spasmodic passions with him. For it was exceeding difficult to bear in mind all the time those strange peculiarities, privileges, and unheard-of exemptions, forming the tacit stipulations on Bartleby's part under which he remained in my office. Now and then, in the eagerness of dispatching pressing business, I would inadvertently summon Bartleby, in a short, rapid tone, to put his finger, say, on the incipient tie of a bit of red tape with which I was about compressing some papers. Of course, from behind the screen the usual answer, "I prefer not to," was sure to come; and then, how could a human creature, with the common infirmities of our nature, refrain from bitterly exclaiming upon such perverseness — such unreasonableness? However, every added repulse of this sort which I received only tended to lessen the probability of my repeating the inadvertence.

Here it must be said, that, according to the custom of most legal gentlemen occupying chambers in densely populated law buildings, there were several keys to my door. One was kept by a woman residing in the attic, which person weekly scrubbed and daily swept and dusted my apartments. Another was kept by Turkey for convenience sake. The third I sometimes carried in my own pocket. The fourth I knew not who had.

Now, one Sunday morning I happened to go to Trinity Church, to hear a celebrated preacher, and finding myself rather early on the ground I thought I would walk round to my chambers for a while. Luckily I had my key with me; but upon applying it to the lock, I found it resisted by something inserted from the inside. Quite surprised, I called out; when to my consternation a key was turned from within; and thrusting his lean visage at me, and holding the door ajar, the apparition of Bartleby appeared, in his shirt-sleeves, and otherwise in a strangely tattered *deshabille*, saying quietly that he was sorry, but he was deeply engaged just then, and — preferred not admitting me at present. In a brief word or two, he moreover added, that perhaps I had better walk round the block two or three times, and by that time he would probably have concluded his affairs.

Now, the utterly unsurmised appearance of Bartleby, tenanting my law-chambers of a Sunday morning, with his cadaverously gentlemanly *nonchalance*, yet withal firm and self-possessed, had such a strange effect upon me, that incontinently I slunk away from my own door, and did as desired. But not without sundry twinges of impotent rebellion against the mild effrontery of this unaccountable scrivener. Indeed, it was his wonderful mildness chiefly, which not only disarmed me, but unmanned me, as it were. For I consider that one, for the time, is sort of unmanned when he tranquilly permits his hired clerk to dictate to him, and order him away from his own premises. Furthermore, I was full of uneasiness as to what Bartleby could possibly be doing in my office in his shirt-sleeves, and in an otherwise dismantled condition of a Sunday morning. Was anything amiss going on? Nay, that was out of the question. It was not to be thought of for a moment that Bartleby was an immoral person. But what could he be doing there? — copying? Nay again, whatever might be his eccentricities, Bartleby was an eminently decorous person. He would be the last man to sit down to his desk in any state approaching to nudity. Besides, it was Sunday; and there was something about Bartleby that forbade the supposition that he would by any secular occupation violate the proprieties of the day.

Nevertheless, my mind was not pacified; and full of a restless curiosity, at 90 last I returned to the door. Without hindrance I inserted my key, opened it, and entered. Bartleby was not to be seen. I looked round anxiously, peeped behind his screen; but it was very plain that he was gone. Upon more closely examining the place, I surmised that for an indefinite period Bartleby must have ate, dressed, and slept in my office, and that too without plate, mirror, or bed. The cushioned seat of a rickety old sofa in one corner bore the faint impress of a lean, reclining form. Rolled away under his desk, I found a blanket; under the empty grate, a blacking box and brush; on a chair, a tin basin, with soap and a ragged towel; in a newspaper a few crumbs of ginger-nuts and a morsel of cheese. Yes, thought I, it is evident enough that Bartleby has been making his home here, keeping bachelor's hall all by himself. Immediately then the thought came sweeping across me, what miserable friendlessness and loneliness are here revealed! His poverty is great; but his solitude, how horrible! Think of it. Of a Sunday, Wall Street is deserted as Petra;° and every night of every day it is an emptiness. This building, too, which of week-days hums with industry and life, at nightfall echoes with sheer vacancy, and all through Sunday is forlorn. And here Bartleby makes his home; sole spectator of a solitude which he has seen all populous—a sort of innocent and transformed Marius brooding among the ruins of Carthage?°

For the first time in my life a feeling of overpowering stinging melancholy seized me. Before, I had never experienced aught but a not unpleasing sadness. The bond of a common humanity now drew me irresistibly to gloom. A fraternal melancholy! For both I and Bartleby were sons of Adam. I remembered the bright silks and sparkling faces I had seen that day, in gala trim, swan-like sailing down the Mississippi of Broadway; and I contrasted them with the pallid copyist, and thought to myself, Ah, happiness courts the light, so we deem the world is gay; but misery hides aloof, so we deem that misery there is none. These sad fancyings—chimeras, doubtless, of a sick and silly brain—led on to other and more special thoughts, concerning the eccentricities of Bartleby. Presentiments of strange discoveries hovered round me. The scrivener's pale form appeared to me laid out, among uncaring strangers, in its shivering winding-sheet.

Suddenly I was attracted by Bartleby's closed desk, the key in open sight left in the lock.

I mean no mischief, seek the gratification of no heartless curiosity, thought I; besides, the desk is mine, and its contents, too, so I will make bold to look within. Everything was methodically arranged, the papers smoothly placed. The pigeon-holes were deep, and removing the files of documents, I groped into their recesses. Presently I felt something there, and dragged it out. It was an old bandanna handkerchief, heavy and knotted. I opened it, and saw it was a saving's bank.

I now recalled all the quiet mysteries which I had noted in the man. I remembered that he never spoke but to answer; that, though at intervals he had considerable time to himself, yet I had never seen him reading—no, not even a newspaper; that for long periods he would stand looking out, at his pale window behind the screen, upon the dead brick wall; I was quite sure he never visited any refectory or eating-house; while his pale face clearly indicated that he never drank beer like Turkey; or tea and coffee even, like other men; that he

---

Petra: An ancient Arabian city whose ruins were discovered in 1812.
Marius . . . of Carthage: Gaius Marius (157–86 B.C.), an exiled Roman general, sought refuge in the African city-state of Carthage, which was destroyed by the Romans in the Third Punic War.

never went anywhere in particular that I could learn; never went out for a walk, unless, indeed, that was the case at present; that he had declined telling who he was, or whence he came, or whether he had any relatives in the world; that though so thin and pale, he never complained of ill-health. And more than all, I remembered a certain unconscious air of pallid — how shall I call it? — of pallid haughtiness, say, or rather an austere reserve about him, which had positively awed me into my tame compliance with his eccentricities, when I had feared to ask him to do the slightest incidental thing for me, even though I might know, from his long-continued motionlessness, that behind his screen he must be standing in one of those dead-wall reveries of his.

Revolving all these things, and coupling them with the recently discovered fact, that he made my office his constant abiding place and home, and not forgetful of his morbid moodiness; revolving all these things, a prudential feeling began to steal over me. My first emotions had been those of pure melancholy and sincerest pity; but just in proportion as the forlornness of Bartleby grew and grew to my imagination, did that same melancholy merge into fear, that pity into repulsion. So true it is, and so terrible, too, that up to a certain point the thought or sight of misery enlists our best affections; but, in certain special cases, beyond that point it does not. They err who would assert that invariably this is owing to the inherent selfishness of the human heart. It rather proceeds from a certain hopelessness of remedying excessive and organic ill. To a sensitive being, pity is not seldom pain. And when at last it is perceived that such pity cannot lead to effectual succor, common sense bids the soul be rid of it. What I saw that morning persuaded me that the scrivener was the victim of innate and incurable disorder. I might give alms to his body; but his body did not pain him; it was his soul that suffered, and his soul I could not reach.

I did not accomplish the purpose of going to Trinity Church that morning. Somehow, the things I had seen disqualified me for the time from churchgoing. I walked homeward, thinking what I would do with Bartleby. Finally, I resolved upon this — I would put certain calm questions to him the next morning, touching his history, etc., and if he declined to answer them openly and unreservedly (and I supposed he would prefer not), then to give him a twenty dollar bill over and above whatever I might owe him, and tell him his services were no longer required; but that if in any other way I could assist him, I would be happy to do so, especially if he desired to return to his native place, wherever that might be, I would willingly help to defray the expenses. Moreover, if, after reaching home, he found himself at any time in want of aid, a letter from him would be sure of a reply.

The next morning came.

"Bartleby," said I, gently calling to him behind his screen.

No reply.

"Bartleby," said I, in a still gentler tone, "come here; I am not going to ask you to do anything you would prefer not to do — I simply wish to speak to you."

Upon this he noiselessly slid into view.

"Will you tell me, Bartleby, where you were born?"

"I would prefer not to."

"Will you tell me *anything* about yourself?"

"I would prefer not to."

95

100

105

"But what reasonable objection can you have to speak to me? I feel friendly towards you."

He did not look at me while I spoke, but kept his glance fixed upon my bust of Cicero, which, as I then sat, was directly behind me, some six inches above my head.

"What is your answer, Bartleby?" said I, after waiting a considerable time for a reply, during which his countenance remained immovable, only there was the faintest conceivable tremor of the white attenuated mouth.

"At present I prefer to give no answer," he said, and retired into his hermitage.

It was rather weak in me I confess, but his manner, on this occasion, 110 nettled me. Not only did there seem to lurk in it a certain calm disdain, but his perverseness seemed ungrateful, considering the undeniable good usage and indulgence he had received from me.

Again I sat ruminating what I should do. Mortified as I was at his behavior, and resolved as I had been to dismiss him when I entered my office, nevertheless I strangely felt something superstitious knocking at my heart, and forbidding me to carry out my purpose, and denouncing me for a villain if I dared to breathe one bitter word against this forlornest of mankind. At last, familiarly drawing my chair behind his screen, I sat down and said: "Bartleby, never mind, then, about revealing your history; but let me entreat you, as a friend, to comply as far as may be with the usages of this office. Say now, you will help to examine papers tomorrow or next day: in short, say now, that in a day or two you will begin to be a little reasonable: — say so, Bartleby."

"At present I would prefer not to be a little reasonable," was his mildly cadaverous reply.

Just then the folding-doors opened, and Nippers approached. He seemed suffering from an unusually bad night's rest, induced by severer indigestion than common. He overheard those final words of Bartleby.

"*Prefer not,* eh?" gritted Nippers — "I'd *prefer* him, if I were you, sir," addressing me — "I'd *prefer* him; I'd give him preferences, the stubborn mule! What is it, sir, pray, that he *prefers* not to do now?"

Bartleby moved not a limb.   115

"Mr. Nippers," said I, "I'd prefer that you would withdraw for the present."

Somehow, of late, I had got into the way of involuntarily using this word "prefer" upon all sorts of not exactly suitable occasions. And I trembled to think that my contact with the scrivener had already and seriously affected me in a mental way. And what further and deeper aberration might it not yet produce? This apprehension had not been without efficacy in determining me to summary measures.

As Nippers, looking very sour and sulky, was departing, Turkey blandly and deferentially approached.

"With submission, sir," said he, "yesterday I was thinking about Bartleby here, and I think that if he would but prefer to take a quart of good ale every day, it would do much towards mending him, and enabling him to assist in examining his papers."

"So you have got the word, too," said I, slightly excited.   120

"With submission, what word, sir?" asked Turkey, respectfully crowding himself into the contracted space behind the screen, and by so doing, making me jostle the scrivener. "What word, sir?"

"I would prefer to be left alone here," said Bartleby, as if offended at being mobbed in his privacy.

"*That's* the word, Turkey," said I — "*that's* it."

"Oh, *prefer?* oh yes — queer word. I never use it myself. But, sir, as I was saying, if he would but prefer —"

"Turkey," interrupted I, "you will please withdraw."   125

"Oh certainly, sir, if you prefer that I should."

As he opened the folding-door to retire, Nippers at his desk caught a glimpse of me, and asked whether I would prefer to have a certain paper copied on blue paper or white. He did not in the least roguishly accent the word "prefer." It was plain that it involuntarily rolled from his tongue. I thought to myself, surely I must get rid of a demented man, who already has in some degree turned the tongues, if not the heads of myself and clerks. But I thought it prudent not to break the dismission at once.

The next day I noticed that Bartleby did nothing but stand at his window in his dead-wall revery. Upon asking him why he did not write, he said that he had decided upon doing no more writing.

"Why, how now? what next?" exclaimed I, "do no more writing?"

"No more."   130

"And what is the reason?"

"Do you not see the reason for yourself?" he indifferently replied.

I looked steadfastly at him, and perceived that his eyes looked dull and glazed. Instantly it occurred to me, that his unexampled diligence in copying by his dim window for the first few weeks of his stay with me might have temporarily impaired his vision.

I was touched. I said something in condolence with him. I hinted that of course he did wisely in abstaining from writing for a while; and urged him to embrace that opportunity of taking wholesome exercise in the open air. This, however, he did not do. A few days after this, my other clerks being absent, and being in a great hurry to dispatch certain letters by the mail, I thought that, having nothing else earthly to do, Bartleby would surely be less inflexible than usual, and carry these letters to the Post Office. But he blankly declined. So, much to my inconvenience, I went myself.

Still added days went by. Whether Bartleby's eyes improved or not, I could   135
not say. To all appearance, I thought they did. But when I asked him if they did, he vouchsafed no answer. At all events, he would do no copying. At last, in replying to my urgings, he informed me that he had permanently given up copying.

"What!" exclaimed I; "suppose your eyes should get entirely well — better than ever before — would you not copy then?"

"I have given up copying," he answered, and slid aside.

He remained as ever, a fixture in my chamber. Nay — if that were possible — he became still more of a fixture than before. What was to be done? He would do nothing in the office; why should he stay there? In plain fact, he had now become a millstone to me, not only useless as a necklace, but afflictive to bear. Yet I was sorry for him. I speak less than truth when I say that, on his own account, he occasioned me uneasiness. If he would but have named a single relative or friend, I would instantly have written, and urged their taking the poor fellow away to some convenient retreat. But he seemed alone, absolutely alone in the universe. A bit of wreck in the mid-Atlantic. At length, necessities connected with my business tyrannized over all other considerations. Decently as I could, I told Bartleby that in six days' time he must unconditionally leave the office. I warned him to take measures, in the interval, for procuring some other abode. I offered to assist him in this endeavor, if he himself would but take the first step towards a removal. "And when you finally quit me, Bartleby," added I, "I shall see that you go not away entirely unprovided. Six days from this hour, remember."

At the expiration of that period, I peeped behind the screen, and lo! Bartleby was there.

I buttoned up my coat, balanced myself; advanced slowly towards him, 140 touched his shoulder, and said, "The time has come; you must quit this place; I am sorry for you; here is money; but you must go."

"I would prefer not," he replied, with his back still towards me.

"You *must*."

He remained silent.

Now I had an unbounded confidence in this man's common honesty. He had frequently restored to me sixpences and shillings carelessly dropped upon the floor, for I am apt to be very reckless in such shirt-button affairs. The proceeding, then, which followed will not be deemed extraordinary.

"Bartleby," said I, "I owe you twelve dollars on account; here are thirty- 145 two, the odd twenty are yours — Will you take it?" and I handed the bills towards him.

But he made no motion.

"I will leave them here, then," putting them under a weight on the table. Then taking my hat and cane and going to the door, I tranquilly turned and added — "After you have removed your things from these offices, Bartleby, you will of course lock the door — since every one is now gone for the day but you — and if you please, slip your key underneath the mat, so that I may have it in the morning. I shall not see you again; so good-bye to you. If, hereafter, in your new place of abode, I can be of any service to you, do not fail to advise me by letter. Good-bye, Bartleby, and fare you well."

But he answered not a word; like the last column of some ruined temple, he remained standing mute and solitary in the middle of the otherwise deserted room.

As I walked home in a pensive mood, my vanity got the better of my pity. I could not but highly plume myself on my masterly management in getting rid of Bartleby. Masterly I call it, and such it must appear to any dispassionate thinker. The beauty of my procedure seemed to consist in its perfect quietness. There was no vulgar bullying, no bravado of any sort, no choleric hectoring, and striding to and fro across the apartment, jerking out vehement commands for Bartleby to bundle himself off with his beggarly traps. Nothing of the kind. Without loudly bidding Bartleby depart — as an inferior genius might have done — I *assumed* the ground that depart he must; and upon that assumption built all I had to say. The more I thought over my procedure, the more I was charmed with it. Nevertheless, next morning, upon awakening, I had my doubts — I had somehow slept off the fumes of vanity. One of the coolest and wisest hours a man has, is just after he awakes in the morning. My procedure seemed as sagacious as ever — but only in theory. How it would prove in practice — there was the rub. It was truly a beautiful thought to have assumed Bartleby's departure; but, after all, that assumption was simply my own, and none of Bartleby's. The great point was, not whether I had assumed that he would quit me, but whether he would prefer to do so. He was more a man of preferences than assumptions.

After breakfast, I walked down town, arguing the probabilities *pro* and *con*. One moment I thought it would prove a miserable failure, and Bartleby would be found all alive at my office as usual; the next moment it seemed certain that I should find his chair empty. And so I kept veering about. At the corner of Broadway and Canal Street, I saw quite an excited group of people standing in earnest conversation.

"I'll take odds he doesn't," said a voice as I passed.

"Doesn't go? — done!" said I, "put up your money."

I was instinctively putting my hand in my pocket to produce my own, when I remembered that this was an election day. The words I had overheard bore no reference to Bartleby, but to the success or non-success of some candidate for the mayoralty. In my intent frame of mind, I had, as it were, imagined that all Broadway shared in my excitement, and were debating the same question with me. I passed on, very thankful that the uproar of the street screened my momentary absent-mindedness.

As I had intended, I was earlier than usual at my office door. I stood listening for a moment. All was still. He must be gone. I tried the knob. The door was locked. Yes, my procedure had worked to a charm; he indeed must be vanished. Yet a certain melancholy mixed with this: I was almost sorry for my brilliant success. I was fumbling under the door mat for the key, which Bartleby was to have left there for me, when accidentally my knee knocked against a panel, producing a summoning sound, and in response a voice came to me from within — "Not yet; I am occupied."

It was Bartleby.

I was thunderstruck. For an instant I stood like the man who, pipe in mouth, was killed one cloudless afternoon long ago in Virginia, by summer lightning; at his own warm open window he was killed, and remained leaning out there upon the dreamy afternoon, till some one touched him, when he fell.

"Not gone!" I murmured at last. But again obeying that wondrous ascendancy which the inscrutable scrivener had over me, and from which ascendancy, for all my chafing, I could not completely escape, I slowly went down stairs and out into the street, and while walking round the block, considered what I should next do in this unheard-of perplexity. Turn the man out by an actual thrusting I could not; to drive him away by calling him hard names would not do; calling in the police was an unpleasant idea; and yet, permit him to enjoy his cadaverous triumph over me — this, too, I could not think of. What was to be done? or, if nothing could be done, was there anything further that I could *assume* in the matter? Yes, as before I had prospectively assumed that Bartleby would depart, so now I might retrospectively assume that departed he was. In the legitimate carrying out of this assumption, I might enter my office in a great hurry, and pretending not to see Bartleby at all, walk straight against him as if he were air. Such a proceeding would in a singular degree have the appearance of a home-thrust. It was hardly possible that Bartleby could withstand such an application of the doctrine of assumption. But upon second thoughts the success of the plan seemed rather dubious. I resolved to argue the matter over with him again.

"Bartleby," said I, entering the office, with a quietly severe expression, "I am seriously displeased. I am pained, Bartleby. I had thought better of you. I had imagined you of such a gentlemanly organization, that in any delicate dilemma a slight hint would suffice — in short, an assumption. But it appears I am deceived. Why," I added, unaffectedly starting, "you have not even touched that money yet," pointing to it, just where I had left it the evening previous.

He answered nothing.

"Will you, or will you not, quit me?" I now demanded in a sudden passion, advancing close to him.

"I would prefer *not* to quit you," he replied, gently emphasizing the *not*.

"What earthly right have you to stay here? Do you pay any rent? Do you pay my taxes? Or is this property yours?"

He answered nothing.

"Are you ready to go on and write now? Are your eyes recovered? Could you copy a small paper for me this morning? or help examine a few lines? or step round to the Post Office? In a word, will you do anything at all, to give a coloring to your refusal to depart the premises?"

He silently retired into his hermitage.

I was now in such a state of nervous resentment that I thought it but prudent to check myself at present from further demonstrations. Bartleby and I were alone. I remembered the tragedy of the unfortunate Adams and the still more unfortunate Colt° in the solitary office of the latter; and how poor Colt, being dreadfully incensed by Adams, and imprudently permitting himself to get wildly excited, was at unawares hurried into his fatal act — an act which certainly no man could possibly deplore more than the actor himself. Often it had occurred to me in my ponderings upon the subject that had that altercation taken place in the public street, or at a private residence, it would not have terminated as it did. It was the circumstance of being alone in a solitary office, up stairs, of a building entirely unhallowed by humanizing domestic associations — an uncarpeted office, doubtless, of a dusty, haggard sort of appearance — this it must have been, which greatly helped to enhance the irritable desperation of the hapless Colt.

But when this old Adam of resentment rose in me and tempted me concerning Bartleby, I grappled him and threw him. How? Why, simply by recalling the divine injunction: "A new commandment give I unto you, that ye love one another." Yes, this it was that saved me. Aside from higher considerations, charity often operates as a vastly wise and prudent principle — a great safeguard to its possessor. Men have committed murder for jealousy's sake, and anger's sake, and hatred's sake, and selfishness' sake, and spiritual pride's sake; but no man, that ever I heard of, ever committed a diabolical murder for sweet charity's sake. Mere self-interest, then, if no better motive can be enlisted, should, especially with high-tempered men, prompt all beings to charity and philanthropy. At any rate, upon the occasion in question, I strove to drown my exasperated feelings towards the scrivener by benevolently construing his conduct. Poor fellow, poor fellow! thought I, he don't mean anything; and besides, he has seen hard times, and ought to be indulged.

I endeavored, also, immediately to occupy myself, and at the same time to comfort my despondency. I tried to fancy, that in the course of the morning, at

Adams . . . Colt: Samuel Adams was killed by John C. Colt, brother of the gun maker, during a quarrel in 1842. After a sensational court case, Colt committed suicide just before he was to be hanged.

such time as might prove agreeable to him, Bartleby, of his own free accord, would emerge from his hermitage and take up some decided line of march in the direction of the door. But no. Half-past twelve o'clock came; Turkey began to glow in the face, overturn his inkstand, and become generally obstreperous; Nippers abated down into quietude and courtesy; Ginger Nut munched his noon apple; and Bartleby remained standing at his window in one of his profoundest dead-wall reveries. Will it be credited? Ought I to acknowledge it? That afternoon I left the office without saying one further word to him.

Some days now passed, during which, at leisure intervals I looked a little into "Edwards on the Will," and "Priestley on Necessity."° Under the circumstances, those books induced a salutary feeling. Gradually I slid into the persuasion that these troubles of mine, touching the scrivener, had been all predestined from eternity, and Bartleby was billeted upon me for some mysterious purpose of an all-wise Providence, which it was not for a mere mortal like me to fathom. Yes, Bartleby, stay there behind your screen, thought I; I shall persecute you no more; you are harmless and noiseless as any of these old chairs; in short, I never feel so private as when I know you are here. At last I see it, I feel it; I penetrate to the predestined purpose of my life. I am content. Others may have loftier parts to enact; but my mission in this world, Bartleby, is to furnish you with office-room for such period as you may see fit to remain.

I believe that this wise and blessed frame of mind would have continued 170 with me, had it not been for the unsolicited and uncharitable remarks obtruded upon me by my professional friends who visited the rooms. But thus it often is, that the constant friction of illiberal minds wears out at last the best resolves of the more generous. Though to be sure, when I reflected upon it, it was not strange that people entering my office should be struck by the peculiar aspect of the unaccountable Bartleby, and so be tempted to throw out some sinister observations concerning him. Sometimes an attorney, having business with me, and calling at my office, and finding no one but the scrivener there, would undertake to obtain some sort of precise information from him touching my whereabouts; but without heeding his idle talk, Bartleby would remain standing immovable in the middle of the room. So after contemplating him in that position for a time, the attorney would depart, no wiser than he came.

Also, when a reference was going on, and the room full of lawyers and witnesses, and business driving fast, some deeply-occupied legal gentleman present, seeing Bartleby wholly unemployed, would request him to run round to his (the legal gentleman's) office and fetch some papers for him. Thereupon, Bartleby would tranquilly decline, and yet remain idle as before. Then the lawyer would give a great stare, and turn to me. And what could I say? At last I was made aware that all through the circle of my professional acquaintance, a whisper of wonder was running round, having reference to the strange creature I kept at my office. This worried me very much. And as the idea came upon me of his possibly turning out a long-lived man, and keeping occupying my chambers, and denying my authority; and perplexing my visitors; and scandalizing my professional reputation; and casting a general gloom over the premises; keeping soul and body together to the last upon his savings (for

---

"*Edwards ... Necessity*": Jonathan Edwards, in *Freedom of the Will* (1754), and Joseph Priestley, in *Doctrine of Philosophical Necessity* (1777), both argued that human beings do not have free will.

doubtless he spent but half a dime a day), and in the end perhaps outlive me, and claim possession of my office by right of his perpetual occupancy: As all these dark anticipations crowded upon me more and more, and my friends continually intruded their relentless remarks upon the apparition in my room; a great change was wrought in me. I resolved to gather all my faculties together, and forever rid me of this intolerable incubus.

Ere revolving any complicated project, however, adapted to this end, I first simply suggested to Bartleby the propriety of his permanent departure. In a calm and serious tone, I commended the idea to his careful and mature consideration. But, having taken three days to meditate upon it, he apprised me, that his original determination remained the same; in short, that he still preferred to abide with me.

What shall I do? I now said to myself, buttoning up my coat to the last button. What shall I do? what ought I to do? what does conscience say I *should* do with this man, or, rather, ghost. Rid myself of him, I must; go, he shall. But how? You will not thrust him, the poor, pale, passive mortal — you will not thrust such a helpless creature out of your door? you will not dishonor yourself by such cruelty? No, I will not, I cannot do that. Rather would I let him live and die here, and then mason up his remains in the wall. What, then, will you do? For all your coaxing, he will not budge. Bribes he leaves under your own paperweight on your table; in short, it is quite plain that he prefers to cling to you.

Then something severe, something unusual must be done. What! surely you will not have him collared by a constable, and commit his innocent pallor to the common jail? And upon what ground could you procure such a thing to be done? — a vagrant, is he? What! he a vagrant, a wanderer, who refuses to budge? It is because he will *not* be a vagrant, then, that you seek to count him *as* a vagrant. That is too absurd. No visible means of support: there I have him. Wrong again: for indubitably he *does* support himself, and that is the only unanswerable proof that any man can show of his possessing the means so to do. No more, then. Since he will not quit me, I must quit him. I will change my offices; I will move elsewhere, and give him fair notice, that if I find him on my new premises I will then proceed against him as a common trespasser.

Acting accordingly, next day I thus addressed him: "I find these chambers [175] too far from the City Hall; the air is unwholesome. In a word, I propose to remove my offices next week, and shall no longer require your services. I tell you this now, in order that you may seek another place."

He made no reply, and nothing more was said.

On the appointed day I engaged carts and men, proceeded to my chambers, and having but little furniture, everything was removed in a few hours. Throughout, the scrivener remained standing behind the screen, which I directed to be removed the last thing. It was withdrawn; and, being folded up like a huge folio, left him the motionless occupant of a naked room. I stood in the entry watching him a moment, while something from within me upbraided me.

I re-entered, with my hand in my pocket — and — and my heart in my mouth.

"Good-bye, Bartleby; I am going — good-bye, and God some way bless you; and take that," slipping something in his hand. But it dropped upon the floor, and then — strange to say — I tore myself from him whom I had so longed to be rid of.

Established in my new quarters, for a day or two I kept the door locked, 180
and started at every footfall in the passages. When I returned to my rooms,
after any little absence, I would pause at the threshold for an instant, and
attentively listen, ere applying my key. But these fears were needless. Bartleby
never came nigh me.

I thought all was going well, when a perturbed-looking stranger visited
me, inquiring whether I was the person who had recently occupied rooms at
No. — Wall Street.

Full of forebodings, I replied that I was.

"Then, sir," said the stranger, who proved a lawyer, "you are responsible for
the man you left there. He refuses to do any copying; he refuses to do anything;
he says he prefers not to; and he refuses to quit the premises."

"I am very sorry, sir," said I, with assumed tranquillity, but an inward
tremor, "but, really, the man you allude to is nothing to me — he is no relation
or apprentice of mine, that you should hold me responsible for him."

"In mercy's name, who is he?" 185

"I certainly cannot inform you. I know nothing about him. Formerly I
employed him as a copyist; but he has done nothing for me now for some time
past."

"I shall settle him, then — good morning, sir."

Several days passed, and I heard nothing more; and, though I often felt a
charitable prompting to call at the place and see poor Bartleby, yet a certain
squeamishness, of I know not what, withheld me.

All is over with him, by this time, thought I, at last, when, through another
week, no further intelligence reached me. But, coming to my room the day
after, I found several persons waiting at my door in a high state of nervous
excitement.

"That's the man — here he comes," cried the foremost one, whom I recog- 190
nized as the lawyer who had previously called upon me alone.

"You must take him away, sir, at once," cried a portly person among them,
advancing upon me, and whom I knew to be the landlord of No. — Wall Street.
"These gentlemen, my tenants, cannot stand it any longer; Mr. B— ," pointing
to the lawyer, "has turned him out of his room, and he now persists in haunting the building generally, sitting upon the banisters of the stairs by day, and
sleeping in the entry by night. Everybody is concerned; clients are leaving the
offices; some fears are entertained of a mob; something you must do, and that
without delay."

Aghast at this torrent, I fell back before it, and would fain have locked
myself in my new quarters. In vain I persisted that Bartleby was nothing to
me — no more than to any one else. In vain — I was the last person known to
have anything to do with him, and they held me to the terrible account. Fearful, then, of being exposed in the papers (as one person present obscurely
threatened), I considered the matter, and, at length, said, that if the lawyer
would give me a confidential interview with the scrivener, in his (the lawyer's)
own room, I would, that afternoon, strive my best to rid them of the nuisance
they complained of.

Going up stairs to my old haunt, there was Bartleby silently sitting upon
the banister at the landing.

"What are you doing here, Bartleby?" said I.

"Sitting upon the banister," he mildly replied. 195

I motioned him into the lawyer's room, who then left us.

"Bartleby," said I, "are you aware that you are the cause of great tribulation to me, by persisting in occupying the entry after being dismissed from the office?"

No answer.

"Now one of two things must take place. Either you must do something, or something must be done to you. Now what sort of business would you like to engage in? Would you like to re-engage in copying for some one?"

"No; I would prefer not to make any change."   200

"Would you like a clerkship in a dry-goods store?"

"There is too much confinement about that. No, I would not like a clerkship; but I am not particular."

"Too much confinement," I cried, "why, you keep yourself confined all the time!"

"I would prefer not to take a clerkship," he rejoined, as if to settle that little item at once.

"How would a bar-tender's business suit you? There is no trying of the   205 eye-sight in that."

"I would not like it at all; though, as I said before, I am not particular."

His unwonted wordiness inspirited me. I returned to the charge.

"Well, then, would you like to travel through the country collecting bills for the merchants? That would improve your health."

"No, I would prefer to be doing something else."

"How, then, would going as a companion to Europe, to entertain some   210 young gentleman with your conversation — how would that suit you?"

"Not at all. It does not strike me that there is anything definite about that. I like to be stationary. But I am not particular."

"Stationary you shall be, then," I cried, now losing all patience, and, for the first time in all my exasperating connection with him, fairly flying into a passion. "If you do not go away from these premises before night, I shall feel bound — indeed, I *am* bound — to — to quit the premises myself!" I rather absurdly concluded, knowing not with what possible threat to try to frighten his immobility into compliance. Despairing of all further efforts, I was precipitately leaving him, when a final thought occurred to me — one which had not been wholly unindulged before.

"Bartleby," said I, in the kindest tone I could assume under such exciting circumstances, "will you go home with me now — not to my office, but my dwelling — and remain there till we can conclude upon some convenient arrangement for you at our leisure? Come, let us start now, right away."

"No: at present I would prefer not to make any change at all."

I answered nothing; but, effectually dodging every one by the sudden-   215 ness and rapidity of my flight, rushed from the building, ran up Wall Street towards Broadway, and, jumping into the first omnibus, was soon removed from pursuit. As soon as tranquillity returned, I distinctly perceived that I had now done all that I possibly could, both in respect to the demands of the landlord and his tenants, and with regard to my own desire and sense of duty, to benefit Bartleby, and shield him from rude persecution. I now strove to be entirely care-free and quiescent; and my conscience justified me in the attempt; though, indeed, it was not so successful as I could have wished. So fearful was I of being again hunted out by the incensed landlord and his exasperated tenants, that, surrendering my business to Nippers, for a few days, I drove about the upper part of the town and through the suburbs, in my rockaway; crossed over to Jersey City and Hoboken, and paid fugitive visits to Manhattanville and Astoria. In fact, I almost lived in my rockaway for the time.

When again I entered my office, lo, a note from the landlord lay upon the desk. I opened it with trembling hands. It informed me that the writer had sent to the police, and had Bartleby removed to the Tombs as a vagrant. Moreover, since I knew more about him than any one else, he wished me to appear at that place, and make a suitable statement of the facts. These tidings had a conflicting effect upon me. At first I was indignant; but, at last, almost approved. The landlord's energetic, summary disposition, had led him to adopt a procedure which I do not think I would have decided upon myself; and yet, as a last resort, under such peculiar circumstances, it seemed the only plan.

As I afterwards learned, the poor scrivener, when told that he must be conducted to the Tombs, offered not the slightest obstacle, but, in his pale, unmoving way, silently acquiesced.

Some of the compassionate and curious by-standers joined the party; and headed by one of the constables arm-in-arm with Bartleby, the silent procession filed its way through all the noise, and heat, and joy of the roaring thoroughfares at noon.

The same day I received the note, I went to the Tombs, or, to speak more properly, the Halls of Justice. Seeking the right officer, I stated the purpose of my call, and was informed that the individual I described was, indeed, within. I then assured the functionary that Bartleby was a perfectly honest man, and greatly to be compassionated, however unaccountably eccentric. I narrated all I knew, and closed by suggesting the idea of letting him remain in as indulgent confinement as possible, till something less harsh might be done — though, indeed, I hardly knew what. At all events, if nothing else could be decided upon, the almshouse must receive him. I then begged to have an interview.

Being under no disgraceful charge, and quite serene and harmless in all 220 his ways, they had permitted him freely to wander about the prison, and, especially, in the inclosed grass-platted yards thereof. And so I found him there, standing all alone in the quietest of the yards, his face towards a high wall, while all around, from the narrow slits of the jail windows, I thought I saw peering out upon him the eyes of murderers and thieves.

"Bartleby!"

"I know you," he said, without looking round — "and I want nothing to say to you."

"It was not I that brought you here, Bartleby," said I, keenly pained at his implied suspicion. "And to you, this should not be so vile a place. Nothing reproachful attaches to you by being here. And see, it is not so sad a place as one might think. Look, there is the sky, and here is the grass."

"I know where I am," he replied, but would say nothing more, and so I left him.

As I entered the corridor again, a broad meat-like man, in an apron, 225 accosted me, and, jerking his thumb over his shoulder, said — "Is that your friend?"

"Yes."

"Does he want to starve? If he does, let him live on the prison fare, that's all."

"Who are you?" asked I, not knowing what to make of such an unofficially speaking person in such a place.

"I am the grub-man. Such gentlemen as have friends here, hire me to provide them with something good to eat."

"Is this so?" said I, turning the turnkey. 230

He said it was.

"Well, then," said I, slipping some silver into the grub-man's hands (for so they called him), "I want you to give particular attention to my friend there; let him have the best dinner you can get. And you must be as polite to him as possible."

"Introduce me, will you?" said the grub-man, looking at me with an expression which seemed to say he was all impatience for an opportunity to give a specimen of his breeding.

Thinking it would prove of benefit to the scrivener, I acquiesced; and, asking the grub-man his name, went up with him to Bartleby.

"Bartleby, this is a friend; you will find him very useful to you." 235

"Your sarvant, sir, your sarvant," said the grub-man, making a low salutation behind his apron. "Hope you find it pleasant here, sir; nice grounds — cool apartments — hope you'll stay with us some time — try to make it agreeable. What will you have for dinner to-day?"

"I prefer not to dine to-day," said Bartleby, turning away. "It would disagree with me; I am unused to dinners." So saying, he slowly moved to the other side of the inclosure, and took up a position fronting the deadwall.

"How's this?" said the grub-man, addressing me with a stare of astonishment. "He's odd, ain't he?"

"I think he is a little deranged," said I, sadly.

"Deranged? deranged is it? Well, now, upon my word, I thought that 240
friend of yourn was a gentleman forger; they are always pale and genteel-like, them forgers. I can't help pity 'em — can't help it, sir. Did you know Monroe Edwards?" he added, touchingly, and paused. Then, laying his hand piteously on my shoulder, sighed, "he died of consumption at Sing-Sing. So you weren't acquainted with Monroe?"

"No, I was never socially acquainted with any forgers. But I cannot stop longer. Look to my friend yonder. You will not lose by it. I will see you again."

Some few days after this, I again obtained admission to the Tombs, and went through the corridors in quest of Bartleby; but without finding him.

"I saw him coming from his cell not long ago," said a turnkey, "may be he's gone to loiter in the yards."

So I went in that direction.

"Are you looking for the silent man?" said another turnkey, passing me. 245
"Yonder he lies — sleeping in the yard there. 'Tis not twenty minutes since I saw him lie down."

The yard was entirely quiet. It was not accessible to the common prisoners. The surrounding walls, of amazing thickness, kept off all sounds behind them. The Egyptian character of the masonry weighed upon me with its gloom. But a soft imprisoned turf grew under foot. The heart of the eternal pyramids, it seemed, wherein, by some strange magic, through the clefts, grass-seed, dropped by birds, had sprung.

Strangely huddled at the base of the wall, his knees drawn up, and lying on his side, his head touching the cold stones, I saw the wasted Bartleby. But nothing stirred. I paused; then went close up to him; stooped over, and saw that his dim eyes were open; otherwise he seemed profoundly sleeping. Something prompted me to touch him. I felt his hand, when a tingling shiver ran up my arm and down my spine to my feet.

The round face of the grub-man peered upon me now. "His dinner is ready. Won't he dine to-day, either? Or does he live without dining?"

"Lives without dining," said I, and closed the eyes.

"Eh! — He's asleep, ain't he?"   250

"With kings and counselors,"° murmured I.

There would seem little need for proceeding further in this history. Imagination will readily supply the meagre recital of poor Bartleby's interment. But, ere parting with the reader, let me say, that if this little narrative has sufficiently interested him, to awaken curiosity as to who Bartleby was, and what manner of life he led prior to the present narrator's making his acquaintance, I can only reply, that in such curiosity I fully share, but am wholly unable to gratify it. Yet here I hardly know whether I should divulge one little item of rumor, which came to my ear a few months after the scrivener's decease. Upon what basis it rested, I could never ascertain; and hence, how true it is I cannot now tell. But, inasmuch as this vague report has not been without a certain suggestive interest to me, however sad, it may prove the same with some others; and so I will briefly mention it. The report was this: that Bartleby had been a subordinate clerk in the Dead Letter Office at Washington, from which he had been suddenly removed by a change in the administration. When I think over this rumor, hardly can I express the emotions which seize me. Dead letters! does it not sound like dead men? Conceive a man by nature and misfortune prone to a pallid hopelessness, can any business seem more fitted to heighten it than that of continually handling these dead letters, and assorting them for the flames? For by the cart-load they are annually burned. Sometimes from out the folded paper the pale clerk takes a ring — the finger it was meant for, perhaps, moulders in the grave; a bank-note sent in swiftest charity — he whom it would relieve, nor eats nor hungers any more; pardon for those who died despairing; hope for those who died unhoping; good tidings for those who died stifled by unrelieved calamities. On errands of life, these letters speed to death.

Ah, Bartleby! Ah, humanity!

"With kings and counselors": From Job 3:13-14: "then had I been at rest, / With kings and counselors of the earth, / Which built desolate places for themselves."

CONSIDERATIONS FOR CRITICAL THINKING AND WRITING

1. FIRST RESPONSE. How does the lawyer's description of himself serve to characterize him? Why is it significant that he is a lawyer? Are his understandings and judgments about Bartleby and himself always sound?

2. Why do you think Turkey, Nippers, and Ginger Nut are introduced to the reader before Bartleby?

3. Describe Bartleby's physical characteristics. How is his physical description a foreshadowing of what happens to him?

4. How does Bartleby's "I would prefer not to" affect the routine of the lawyer and his employees?

5. What is the significance of the subtitle: "A Story of Wall Street"?

6. Who is the protagonist? Whose story is it?

7. Does the lawyer change during the story? Does Bartleby? Who is the antagonist?

8. What motivates Bartleby's behavior? Why do you think Melville withholds the information about the Dead Letter Office until the end of the story? Does this background adequately explain Bartleby?

9. Does Bartleby have any lasting impact on the lawyer?

10. Do you think Melville sympathizes more with Bartleby or with the lawyer?

11. Describe the lawyer's changing attitudes toward Bartleby.

12. Consider how this story could be regarded as a kind of protest with non-negotiable demands.

13. Discuss the story's humor and how it affects your response to Bartleby.

14. Trace your emotional reaction to Bartleby as he is revealed in the story.

15. CRITICAL STRATEGIES. Read the section on biographical criticism (pp. 62–64) in Chapter 3, "Applying a Critical Strategy," and use the library to learn about Melville's reputation as a writer at the time of his writing "Bartleby." How might this information produce a provocative biographical approach to the story?

JOYCE CAROL OATES (B. 1938)

Raised in upstate New York, Joyce Carol Oates earned degrees at Syracuse University and the University of Wisconsin. Both the range and volume of her writing are extensive. A writer of novels, plays, short stories, poetry, and literary criticism, she has published some eighty books. Oates has described the subject matter of her fiction as "real people in a real society," but her method of expression ranges from the realistic to the experimental. Her novels include *them* (1969), *Do with Me What You Will* (1973), *Childwold* (1976), *Bellefleur* (1980), *A Bloodsmoor Romance* (1982), *Marya: A Life* (1986), *You Must Remember This* (1987), and *Black Water* (1992). Among her collections of short stories are *Marriages and Infidelities* (1972); *Raven's Wing* (1986); *The Assignation* (1988); *Heat* (1991); *Haunted: Tales of the Grotesque* (1994); and *Will You Always Love Me? and Other Stories* (1996). In this story, Oates effectively creates a terrifying situation for her protagonist; she also invests the story with surprising compassion.

The Night Nurse   *1993*

Don't doubt there's a future. Rushing toward you.

It was flat pavement, a busy pedestrian mall between downtown streets where she was walking in the tattered sunshine of a moist April morning when without warning the sidewalk tilted to her left, and a sharp pain like a wasp's stinging attacked the calf of her left leg. Wide-eyed and astonished, too surprised at this time to be frightened, she did not scream. She was not the kind of person to scream, especially in a public place.

She fell heavily on her side. Her glasses went flying, her handsome leather handbag dropped from her fingers, the side of her face struck concrete. Her immediate thought was *I've been shot.* The pain was so sudden and so absolute.

Strangers hurried to help. They seemed, to the stricken woman, to be materializing out of the air, with remarkable swiftness and kindness. Afterward she would count herself lucky that she was a well-dressed, well-groomed Caucasian woman stricken in this particular pedestrian mall with its Bonwit's, its Waldenbooks, its gourmet food store and pricey boutiques, and not elsewhere on the fringes of downtown. She was lucky that her handbag wasn't taken from her in the confusion of her fall and that strangers perceived her as one of their kind and not someone diseased, homeless, threatening.

She would remember little of her collapse afterward except its suddenness. And the terrible helplessness of her body fallen to the pavement. An ambulance arrived, its deafening siren translating to her confused brain as a lurid neon-red color. White-clad youngish medics examined her, lifted her onto a stretcher. As in a dream she was being borne aloft. A crowd of curious, snatching eyes parted for her. Alive? Dead? Dying? No one, least of all the stricken woman, seemed to know. 5

And in the speeding ambulance delirious with pain and mounting terror, an incandescent bulb of pain in her left leg just below the knee but still she did not scream biting her lips to keep from screaming and thinking even at this time *I am behaving well, look how calm and civilized.* Then she was being carried into a room glaring with laser-lights, again the quick purposeful hands of strangers probed her, her blood pressure was taken and blood extracted from her limp arm and her voice faltered trying to explain to someone she could not see what had happened to her, the pain in her leg more terrible than any pain she'd known, and a tightness in her chest and shortness of breath but she did not break down sobbing nor did she ask *Am I dying? Will I die?* nor did she beg *Save me!* Her name was Grace Burkhardt and she was forty-four years old and she was a woman accustomed, as the chief administrator of a state arts council, to exercising authority but she seemed to remember none of these external facts as if they applied not to her but to another person and that person a stranger to her. She wanted to explain *I am in good health, I can't believe this has happened to me* as if to repudiate responsibility but she was fainting and could not speak. They would check her identification, they would contact her nearest-of-kin, they would rush her into surgery and all this would be done apart from her volition and so there was a perverse comfort in that — in knowing that, if she died, now, it would not be her fault.

Of course they saved her. Emergency surgery for a "massive" blood clot in her leg which, had it broken free and been carried to her heart, would have resulted in a pulmonary embolism. Grace Burkhardt, dead at the age of forty-four never regaining consciousness even to realize the future had been condensed into the present tense and all was over.

By degrees she woke moaning in the post-op room not knowing where she was but knowing that this was a place strange and frightening to her. And so cold! — she was shivering, her teeth chattering. She experienced a sensation of utter sick helplessness as if she were paralyzed. She could not recall the surgery, or having collapsed. She could not recall if she had been saved from death or was even now being prepared for death. Her vision was blurred as if she were underwater. A face floated near, a stranger's face that was at the same time familiar as a lost sister's.

Help me! she begged the face. *I'm so cold, I'm so frightened!*

The face was a woman's. The features were indistinct but the skin was 10 strangely flushed and shiny, like something not quite fully hatched. There was a smile, thin-lipped and tentative. No-color eyes. *Don't leave me, help! I'm so frightened!* Grace Burkhardt begged as like a large bubble playful and elusive the face rose, lifted lighter than air to disappear through the invisible ceiling.

Her nearest-of-kin was a married, older sister who drove forty miles from Rochester to be with her, staying through much of the day. As news of her "emergency surgery" spread among friends, acquaintances, colleagues at the arts council, there were telephone calls and the first of the floral deliveries. The public self, the self that was Grace Burkhardt, and not this woman in a hospital bed hooked to an IV gurney, her left leg raised and immobile swathed in bandages, struggled to emerge. You could not have guessed that Grace Burkhardt had survived a life-threatening collapse for, on the phone, she was wry, ironic, slightly embarrassed, determined to minimalize her condition. Her eyes were ringed with fatigue, her skin waxy-white, yet her voice maintained its usual timbre, or almost. Nothing meant more to her than to take back the control she'd lost back there in the pedestrian mall, to tell her story as if it were her own. For it was her own. *You wouldn't believe it! So suddenly. Yes, this morning. Yes, downtown. By ambulance. No, no warning. Yes, vascular surgery. A Dr. Rodman, do you know him? Yes, I'm lucky. I know. If it had to happen at all.*

Her sister finally took the telephone from her. She was protesting but too weak to prevail. Her head rang like the interior of a giant seashell. The pain in her leg was a balloon floating at a little distance from her — recognizable as her own, yet not *her. My name is Grace Burkhardt, my name is Grace Burkhardt* believing that this fact would save her. If anything would save her.

A powerful anti-coagulant drug was dripping into her veins to forestall more blood clots — that would save her.

The telephone messages. Daffodils, hyacinth, narcissus from the arts council staff, a potted pink azalea from a woman friend, another potted azalea so vividly crimson she could not look directly at it — these would save her. And the vascular surgeon who'd operated on her and saved her life, who came by the room to speak with her and with her sister. And her own doctor, an internist associated with the hospital who also dropped by on his rounds. And medical insurance forms, with which her sister helped her, and which, in a frail spidery hand, she signed. *You see? I'm fine, my mind hasn't been affected at all.*

And abruptly then, the day ended. This day that stretched dreamlike behind 15 Grace Burkhardt as if to the very horizon to a region she could not see, nor even recall. It was evening, and she was alone. A nurse came to examine her and to give her a barbiturate, a nurse's aide, a young cocoa-skinned woman, came to take away her bedpan discreetly covered with an aluminum lid, the light in her room was switched off. She called her sister's name not seeming to recall her sister's actual departure. Now alone, with no witness to admire her bravery, she tasted panic. Her left leg was swollen and stiff encased in bandages and elevated above the bed to reduce the condition the surgeon called "thrombophlebitis" which was the way, she understood, that death would enter her. The crepey-soft interior of her right elbow stung with a mysterious IV fluid dripping into a vein. Death would come as a lethal blood clot or death would come as a sudden massive hemorrhage that was the result of anti-coagulant medication. Though the stricken woman had not prayed in more than thirty years her parched lips moved silently *Help me through the night. Help me through the night.*

She felt a moment's rage at the injustice—that she, a good person, a woman known for her intelligence and her graciousness and her dependability in all things, a woman so widely liked, yes and respected, should be in this position, a life-threatening position. And trapped.

Help me through the night dear God, oh please!

As mercifully the contours of the room melted, the floor sank into darkness as into a pit, the powerful sleeping pill took her.

But then she woke, agitated and open-eyed as if she hadn't slept at all.

As if someone had called her name—"Grace Burkhardt."   20

There was a pinching sensation in her bladder, an urgent need to urinate. And such cold, why was the room so cold?—she woke shivering beneath a freezing sheet, a single-ply flannel blanket. The hospital by night was perceptibly cooler than by day. A ventilator rumbled, drafts of cold air passed over her. She'd been dreaming strangely and hadn't there been birds' wings flapping overhead stirring the air against her face . . .

"Grace Burkhardt."

The door had opened, now the door was closed. Someone had been in the room?—Grace tried to sit up, frightened, but was nearly immobilized. A sudden movement awakened pain, her heart's panicked throbbing that was pain, a sharp stinging in her right arm. Her eyes, mildly myopic, dulled with medication, moved blinking in the dark, this was an unfamiliar dark, she understood it was not her bedroom in her home nor any bedroom in her memory. The smell of disinfectant, the ventilator smell. The compression of space that was the size of a cell. She stared at the door a few yards away seeing a rim of light beneath it. For some moments she tried to remember where she was, and why such discomfort and pain, her leg elevated and held fast, her heartbeat so accelerated. As if pulling out of the dark a tangled dream of such complexity, the very effort was exhausting. She heard herself moan but the sound seemed to come from another part of the room. It was self-pity, it was terror and animal pain, it was not *her. I almost died, I'm in the hospital. I'm alone.* Struggling to sit up, to raise her head which swayed dangerously heavy on her shoulders, in a sudden mad terror of choking on her own tears and saliva and the mucus rapidly forming in her sinuses.

She fumbled to switch on her bedside light. Her sister had bought a traveler's digital clock in the gift shop downstairs—it was 2:55 A.M. She would never get through the night.

Yet she tried to calm herself. She was a patient in an excellent suburban 25 hospital, she could not possibly be in danger of dying. *Help me! Help me I'm alone* but she rang the bedside buzzer because she desperately needed a bedpan. The barbiturate had apparently knocked her out so completely, at 8:30 P.M., she hadn't wakened until the need to urinate was painful. And she needed an extra blanket. She rang the buzzer as she'd been instructed earlier to ring it and waited and there was no reply over the intercom so she rang it again and still there was no reply and so she counted twenty before ringing it again *Where are you? Isn't anyone there? Please help me* and this time a voice, a female voice, sounded over the intercom asking curtly what did she want and she explained her needs as clearly and politely as possible and the voice mumbled what sounded like *Yes ma'am* and was gone.

And now she waited. Waited and waited. It was three A.M., it was 3:10 A.M., it was 3:16 A.M. She could not get a comfortable position in the bed, her bladder so stricken, her leg at such an angle. Each second was agony. She tried to contract her lower body, her loins, as, as a small child, she'd tried to hold in the warm pee by pressing her thighs as tightly together as possible and not moving, hardly breathing. If she had an accident, urinating in the bed! — if that happened! All her life's history, all the striving of her very soul — to come to *that.* She felt a helpless child-anxiety she hadn't recalled for nearly forty years. The child-anxiety deep in the body of the adult. Remembering the agony of being trapped in some place (in the car, her father driving and unwilling to stop; in school assembly where she would have had to push her way out over the legs of her classmates enduring their jeering attention and the annoyance of her teacher) unable to get to a bathroom. The shame of it. The helplessness.

She rang the buzzer another, protracted time. Just as, thank God, the door was pushed open, and a nurse entered carrying a bedpan.

The night nurse, so short as to seem almost dwarfish. Hardly five feet tall. But round-bodied, with a moon face, peculiar flushed skin that was smooth and shiny as scar tissue; small close-set damp eyes; a thin pursed mouth. At a first glance the nurse might appear young but closer up she was obviously middle-aged, her eyes bracketed by fine white creases. "Here, lift up, like this, come *on* —" she issued instructions to the patient not so much coldly as mechanically, shoving the enamel bedpan beneath her buttocks, pulling down but not replacing the covers. Her manner was brisk and on the edge of impatience as if she and the patient had gone through this routine many times already and there was no need for coyness.

Grace's teeth were chattering with cold. She whispered, flinching under the nurse's unsmiling stare, "Thank you — very much." She could not help herself but began urinating immediately, as soon as the receptacle was in place, while the nurse was still in the room, though on her way out, turning away from Grace as if in disgust. No further words, no questioning of the patient if she needed anything else, no backwards glance. But Grace Burkhardt trapped in the bed was so grateful for this awkward receptacle, this adult-size potty, in which to empty her bursting bladder, she scarcely noticed the nurse's rudeness. If it was rudeness.

Her eyes smarted with the tears of gratitude and humility. Even the pain 30 in her leg seemed to subside. The panicky numbness in her brain. But how long she urinated, in a gush of scalding liquid, then a thinning stream, ceasing and beginning again, she did not know. Minutes? Actual minutes? Looking at the clock finally, when the last of the urine dripped from her, she saw it was 3:38 A.M.

Outside the room's single window it was night. Yet not true night for the room, being lighted now, was reflected in the glass; not as in a mirror but dimly, shapes without substance or color.

I could die here in this room. Others have died here.

She'd had a lover once who had been terrified of hospitals. An intelligent man, a reasonable man, yet, on the subject of hospitals, adamantly irrational. Hospitals are seething with germs, hospitals are where you die. Hospitals are where you have to entrust strangers with your life and you pay for the privilege.

A lover, and not a husband. So many years later, Grace could not clearly remember which of them had loved more deeply, which had been more hurt.

Now they lived a thousand miles apart, and kept in touch by telephone, a 35 few times a year. Thank God they no longer had any mutual friends who might tell him of her collapse, her emergency surgery. *Massive blood clot. Risk of embolism.* He knew her as a healthy, independent woman. Not the kind of woman you feel sorry for.

Now Grace was finished with the bedpan, and the sharp smell of urine pinched her nostrils, she waited for the night nurse, or an attendant, to come take it away. Surely they knew, at the nurses' station? — she hesitated to ring the buzzer again.

So she waited. It was 3:40 A.M., it was 3:50 A.M. Finally, shyly, she rang the buzzer. There was no reply over the intercom.

Maybe the night nurse was making rounds. Giving medication, checking patients. Maybe, routinely, she would be back in a few minutes. Maybe she would bring an extra blanket.

At four A.M. Grace rang the buzzer again. There was a sound of static or shrill voices, then silence. "Hello? Hello —" her voice was plaintive, faltering.

Could die here in this room. Others have died here. 40

The enamel bedpan was pressing into the soft flesh of her buttocks. The elevation of her leg, and its stiffness, made the pressure more intense.

And how cold the room was — freezing. A continual draft from the window and another, smelling of something dank, metallic, unclean, from the air vent overhead.

In desperation she wondered if she could remove the damned bedpan herself. But set it where? On the bedside table, only a few inches away? And what if she spilled it, as certainly she would? — it was impossible to lift herself and to remove the bedpan at the same time. And now her leg, the entire left side of her body, was throbbing with pain.

She rang the buzzer again, trying not to panic. Though the intercom was dead she begged for help — "Please, can you come? I need medication, I'm in pain. I need a blanket —"

If the night nurse withheld the painkiller from her, what would she do? 45

Don't be absurd. Why would a complete stranger want to hurt you resolved not to give in to panic though she was trapped in this cell of a room in this bed at the mercy of the nursing staff. Whom she knew it would be a mistake to antagonize, especially so early in her hospitalization — Dr. Rodman had told her she might have to be here a week or more, thrombophlebitis is a serious condition. And her sister, meaning well, had told her alarming tales of negligent and even hostile nurses and attendants at big-city hospitals as a way of assuring Grace that here, by contrast, in this suburban hospital, she would receive better treatment.

At night, the hospital seemed very different than it did by day. It was closed to visitors until 8:30 A.M. In a panicked fantasy, Grace imagined a fire, at once she could smell smoke, and she, here, trapped, crippled with pain, paralyzed. If she wrenched her leg free, would its wound be torn open? — would she begin to bleed? She shuddered, whimpering to herself. Trapped! Trapped on a bedpan! It was ludicrous, it was laughable! Her own urine sloshing beneath her, threatening to spill and soak the bed.

She thought she heard the door being opened, the doorknob turning — but no. If there were footsteps out in the corridor they were gone now.

Strange how the hospital was not much quieter at night. A different and more mysterious kind of sound prevailed — a ceaseless churning like a motor turning over, never quite starting; a deeper throbbing like a jazz downbeat, but arhythmic, irregular. Beyond the vibrating of the ventilator there were distant voices. Pleading, crying. *Help me. Help. Me. Help me.* The voices overlapped, drowning one another out.

When she stopped breathing to listen more closely, the voices faded.   50

Grace did not want to think whose voices these were.

It seemed to her that she could feel tiny blood clots forming in her afflicted leg, like rain at the point at which it turns to sleet. If a single one of these clots broke free into her bloodstream it would be carried to her heart, to her pulmonary artery, and kill her.

What it is, what finality — to fall to the ground, on dirty pavement, at the feet of strangers. Grace Burkhardt now knew.

She pressed the buzzer another time. The intercom remained dead.

"Help me! Where are you!"   55

She was agitated, on the brink of hysteria and yet, somehow, she was falling asleep. The room began to shift and lose its contours; the light rapidly fading as if sucked down a drain. The bedpan filled with cooling piss, *her* piss, began to melt, too, its hard enamel warmed by her body. She'd drawn the inadequate covers up to her chin and her eyes were starkly open waiting for the night nurse to return and suddenly she saw — was it possible? — the night nurse *was* back, had been back for some time, evidently? — standing motionless, watching her, just inside the door.

"Grace Burkhardt."

The nurse enunciated these syllables in a flat, nasal, ironic voice.

"Grace Burkhardt."

Grace whispered, frightened, "Yes? Do you know me?"   60

It was as if she'd never heard her own name before. Never heard its strangeness before.

The nurse's thin lips stretched in a smile. Her small close-set eyes shone with the opacity of glass marbles. "Do you know *me*, Grace Burkhardt?"

Grace stared. Quick as a thread pulled through the eye of a needle and out again she *knew* — knew the woman, or knew the girl the woman had been; but she remembered no name; and did not remember that face. She heard herself saying, quickly, "No. I've never been in this hospital before. I've never—" Her voice trailed off weakly.

There was an awkward pause. The nurse continued to stand motionless, arms folded tight across her breasts. Her peculiar shiny-smooth skin that looked like scar tissue, or like something incompletely hatched, was the color of spoiled cantaloupe. Her lips were bemused, childish in derision. "You wouldn't remember, Grace Burkhardt. No, not *you*."

The stricken woman lay trapped in bed. Her stiff throbbing leg, her arm 65 hooked to an IV apparatus. *She's mad, she's come to injure me* though smiling at the nurse, trying to smile. As if this was an ordinary exchange. Or might become so, if she smiled the right way, if she spoke the right words. "I—can't see very well. My glasses—my eyes— *Do* I know you?"

The nurse made a derisive laughing sound though her eyes showed no mirth. She jerked her chin at the bed—"You're finished there, eh? Grace Burkhardt? So you want *me* to take it away?"

Quickly, apologetically, Grace said, "If you would, please—"

"Registered nurses aren't required to touch bedpans."

"Then—an attendant? Could you call one?"

The nurse shook her head slowly. Bemused, disgusted. Still she stood 70 without moving, arms folded across her breasts. In that face, in those eyes, Grace saw—who? It had been years. Half her lifetime. *No! No I don't know you!* She whispered, pleading, "Please, I'm helpless. I need medication, I'm in pain. And this bedpan—"

"*You're* helpless. *You* need help. So what? 'Grace Burkhardt.'"

"Why do you keep saying my name? Do you know me?"

"Why don't you say *my* name? Don't you know *me*?"

Grace stared, and swallowed hard. *I am a good person, I am well-liked, respected.* Recalling how through the years of her career, in her several administrative positions at Wells College, and at the State University at Buffalo, and more recently on the New York State Council of the Arts, she'd been praised for her industry, her fair-mindedness, her diplomacy; her intelligence, her warmth, her inconspicuous competency. Hadn't she overheard, to her embarrassment, just the other day, two young women staff members at the arts council speaking of Grace Burkhardt warmly, comparing her favorably to her male predecessor. *I am an adult now, I am a professional woman, I am no one you know.* Grace heard herself saying in a voice of forced surprise, with a forced smile, "Harriet—? Is it—Zimmer?"

The nurse said curtly, "Zink. Harriet *Zink*." 75

"Of course. Harriet *Zink*."

Grace should have exclaimed what a coincidence, after so many years, twenty-five? twenty-six? so you became a nurse after all, you didn't give up, how wonderful, Harriet, I'm happy for you—remembering vaguely that Harriet Zink, one of her roommates for part of her freshman year at the State University at Albany had been enrolled in nursing school. But when she drew breath to speak a wave of nausea swept over her. She whispered, "—Please, I need help. My leg—the pain. And the bedpan—"

As if aroused by the word *pain*, the night nurse became more animated. She came closer to Grace, peering at her curiously, almost hungrily. Grace had not given Harriet Zink a thought, or hardly a thought, in twenty-six years, and now—what an irony! The mere face of Harriet Zink, with that childish moon face, now middle-aged—how repulsive! Grace recalled her ex-roommate's prominent front teeth, the peculiar blush of her skin, her unnerving manner that was both groveling and insolent—oh, unmistakable.

They'd lived on the fourth, top floor of Ailey Hall, one of the older residences south of campus near the university hospital. Entering freshman, class of 1967. They were of the same generation glancing at the other's third finger, left hand, to see if there was a wedding band. Neither wore one.

Harriet Zink was asking in a bright, mock-earnest voice, "How is Jilly Her- 80 man?" and Grace Burkhardt had to stop to think, "—Jilly Herman?" and Harriet Zink said impatiently, "Grace Burkhardt's roomie Jilly Herman — how is *she?*" Grace stared at her, perplexed. *I am dreaming this, am I dreaming this* trying not to show the fear she felt as Harriet Zink went on derisively, "The one with the cute blond curls, Jilly Herman," gesturing at her own steely-gray hair with exaggerated wriggly fingers, " — the one with the cute *ass.*"

Grace said, in a faltering voice, " — I haven't seen or heard from Jill Herman in twenty years." Though this was true it sounded weak, like a lie.

Harriet Zink said suspiciously, "You haven't? You expect me to believe that?" When Grace began to protest she cut her off with childish vehemence, "Oh no! I don't believe that! Gracie Burkhardt and Jilly Herman were *best friends.* I bet you still *are.*"

These words were mocking, singsong. Grace tried to maintain her smile which was strained and ghastly against her bared teeth. She explained that, after freshman year, she and Jill went their separate ways, speaking earnestly as if this exchange in the middle of the night in such circumstances was not at all extraordinary but normal, and no occasion for alarm. But Harriet Zink interrupted, "And what about Linda Mecky, and Sandy McGuire, and Dolly Slosson," spitting out these names Grace scarcely recalled, and had hardly given a thought to since graduation, " — Barbara West, Sue Ferguson — " the names of freshman girls who'd roomed on the fourth floor of the old sandstone residence hall in the fall of 1963.

There had been six rooms on the floor, all doubles except for the largest which was a triple to which Grace Burkhardt and Jill Herman and Harriet Zink were assigned. But Harriet Zink didn't arrive on campus until October, twelve days late; there'd been an "emergency crisis" in her family. (The residence advisor hinted that Harriet's mother had died, and there'd been other trouble besides. She warned the girls not to bring up the subject unless Harriet initiated it herself — which she was never to do.) By the time the mysterious Harriet Zink arrived at Ailey Hall, friendships and alliances had been formed among the fourth-floor girls in that quick, desperate way in which such relationships are formed in new, disorienting surroundings. There had not seemed space enough for another girl. There had not seemed any need for another girl. And there was the problem, too, of Harriet Zink.

I tried to be nice to you. I did what I could. How am I to blame. 85

Harriet Zink was demanding to know what of these other girls, and Grace Burkhardt was trying to explain she really knew nothing of them, she wasn't in contact with any of them, but Harriet Zink seemed not to believe her, and angry that she should be lying. Grace tried to explain that most of them had only been friends during freshman year and that had been a kind of accident, stuck away on the top floor of Ailey Hall so far from the center of campus life, she tried to evoke the shabby comedy of Ailey Hall with its falling plaster and its leaky windows and its cockroaches, but Harriet Zink kept interrupting, pursuing her own line of inquiry. "Do you remember what you did to me? You, and your friends?" Her face was heated and her small eyes brightly moist. There were half-moons of perspiration beneath the arms of her snug-fitting white nylon uniform and Grace remembered across the abyss of twenty-six years a snug-fitting clumsily homemade red plaid jumper of Harriet Zink's whose underarms were permanently stained. "Don't say you don't remember, Grace Burkhardt!"

Grace frowned, innocently perplexed. She was miserable in her bed, her leg pounding in pain, her head pounding, and, dear God, the sharp smell of urine penetrating the covers, had she spilled some of the urine into the bed, she bit her lip to keep from sobbing *I must not let her see I'm afraid of her, I must stay calm* shaking her head saying, "No, please, Harriet, I don't—" which brought the angry little woman closer to the bed, how like a dwarf she was, so short, and stouter now than she'd been at the age of eighteen, her face rounder, puffier, and that mouth made you think of a slug, always moving, working. Harriet Zink said in a tone of near-dignity, "I remember. I still dream about it sometimes."

Grace said softly, "Harriet, I'm sorry."

"Huh! How can you be sorry, if you don't remember?"

"Please, I'm in pain. If you could help me—"   90

"*I* was in pain. You didn't help *me*."

"—I need medication. Painkiller. Please. And this bedpan—please could you take it away—"

"I told you: registered nurses aren't required to take away bedpans. That's not our job."

You never took showers or baths. You wore your clothes until they were filthy. You smelled. You stank. You cried yourself to sleep every night. How am I to blame! Grace knew, yet didn't know: couldn't quite remember. It was so long ago, it was like a bad dream, not her own dream but another's. What exactly had happened between the time Harriet Zink, who like Grace Burkhardt was from a farming family in the central part of the state, and the weekend before Thanksgiving when she moved out of Ailey Hall, dropped out of nursing school. Disappeared. *I tried to be nice to you. I did what I could. How am I to blame!*

In a lowered, quavering voice Harriet Zink was saying, "You and Jill Her-   95
man, you wouldn't talk to me. I'd be there in the room and you'd send each other signals. Look right through me. Like I was dirt. If I came into the lounge you'd all stop talking and make like there was a bad smell. If I came into the cafeteria where you were all sitting you'd look away and freeze me out. You knew about my mother and how I cried at night and that was funny to you wasn't it. Everything about me was funny to you wasn't it. I was late starting classes and behind on all my work and you could see how scared I was, I couldn't sleep and I couldn't keep food down and all of you knew it, all twelve of you, but it was just a joke to you wasn't it—that I wanted to die."

Grace Burkhardt could not believe what she was hearing. She said, weakly, "Not me, Harriet. Not me. I tried—"

"Oh sure! You'd say to them sometimes, 'Let her alone.' Once in the downstairs lounge when they were laughing together you said to them, 'That's enough, it isn't funny, let her alone.' But you wouldn't say my name. You wouldn't ever say my name. It was like I was *it* to you. You wouldn't look at me even when we were alone together and if I talked to you, you'd just mumble something back and walk away. I could see in your face you felt sorry for me, sure, you pitied me like a leper, you thought you were so much better than me, you, 'Grace Burkhardt'! You tried to stop them from the worst of what they did but you didn't try hard *enough*."

"Harriet, I'm sorry. We were so young, then—so ignorant."

"You weren't ignorant. *You* were a scholarship student."

"We didn't mean to be cruel—"   100

"Yes you did! You meant to be cruel," Harriet Zink said, with angry satisfaction. "It made you happy, all of you, to be cruel."

"Harriet, no—"

Harriet Zink continued speaking in her low, accusing voice, her face now brightly flushed, recounting incidents Grace Burkhardt had long since forgotten, if indeed she'd ever known. She tried to remember how long pathetic Harriet Zink had actually roomed with her and Jill Herman before moving downstairs to a single room near the resident advisor's suite—that room kept in readiness for just such an emergency. *Yes, it's so. It made us happy. Our cruelty. Our loathing for the true freak among us.* After Harriet Zink dropped out of school, having failed more of her midterms, the girls of the fourth floor, including several nursing students to whom she'd been a particular embarrassment, had not missed her. Or, if they missed her, they did not dwell upon her absence. They did not consider its significance. It had nothing to do with them, did it?—*they* were normal, *they* were adjusting to college life. After Harriet Zink moved out of their room Grace and Jill cleaned it as they'd never cleaned it before, exhilarated, singing along with the Kingston Trio whose hit record Jill played repeatedly on her turntable, airing out the room, windows open to a bright dry autumn day, a breeze lifting papers on their desks. Gaily they vacuumed, they scrubbed. Their door was wide open to welcome their friends. *Sad to say, I'm on my way, won't be back for many a day* but their lifted voices, their shining eyes, were anything but sad. The third desk, in the corner, was bare. The third bed, beneath the tilt of the eave, was bare. Later, Grace would cover the bed with a beautiful afghan quilt knitted by her grandmother. The third desk was used by both girls. They were particularly grateful for the extra closet space.

Now Harriet Zink, middle-aged, squat body in her nurse's uniform solid as a little barrel, was leaning over Grace Burkhardt in her bed, saying, in disgust, "'Grace Burkhardt'—you were the evil one among them because you were the one who *knew*. I could see it in your face. And right now! You knew, but you wouldn't help me, you wouldn't be my friend."

Grace said stammering, "Harriet, I'm—I didn't—" her eyes brimming with   105 tears of shame, "—forgive me!" She was so frightened she'd leaned away from the angry woman and caused the IV needle to pop out of her vein.

There was a pause. Harriet Zink stared at Grace, leaning so close over her that Grace could see specks of hazel in the iris of her eyes; a glimmer of gold fillings in her mouth. Harriet was breathing harshly, like an overweight woman who has climbed a stairs too quickly. Yet her expression shifted suddenly, turned unexpectedly thoughtful. She said, with the air of one making a discovery, "Yes, I can forgive you, Grace Burkhardt. I'm a Christian woman. In my heart I'm empowered to forgive." She nodded gravely, as if, not knowing until this instant what she'd intended, what she would do, she was taking pleasure in it. "When I saw you here, Grace Burkhardt, and I thought, 'Am I strong enough to forgive that woman? Even with Jesus' help, am I strong enough?' I didn't know. But now I know. I *am* strong enough, I *can* forgive." She spoke with such sudden pride, it was as if sunshine flooded the room.

In this way, as a terrified Grace Burkhardt would not have anticipated, the siege ended.

For a long time after the night nurse left the room Grace lay unmoving too shocked to think even *How am I to blame! I tried, I did try* incredulous thinking *Evil—me? Of all people—me? The woman is a religious maniac.* She was too agitated to sleep yet somehow must have slept if only briefly and then waking opening her eyes wide and amazed that it was still night? still night? when in her dream she'd been staring into the sun as if in penance and her eyes were seared and aching.

She struggled to sit up. She could breathe better, sitting up. Her leg throbbed with pain, pain was like a wave that washed over her and through her leaving her exhausted but wakeful. The bedside lamp was still on. She'd thought the night nurse had turned it off. In the room's single window flat, ghostly reflections floated. She could not identify her own among them.

The night nurse, after her mad outburst, had treated Grace Burkhardt 110 kindly. Or, if not kindly, with a brisk businesslike efficiency. She'd replaced the needle in Grace's bruised right arm, and saw that the IV fluid was dripping into her vein. She called an aide, a young black girl, to bring an extra blanket and to carry away, at last, the bedpan. But, as she explained, she could not give Grace any of the painkiller Oxycodone prescribed for her by Dr. Rodman because the next dosage was scheduled for seven A.M. By that time the day staff would be on duty and another nurse would take care of her. Thank you, Grace murmured, thank you so much, Harriet, humbled and grateful as a chastened child but the night nurse merely shrugged as if embarrassed and then she was gone.

It was only 4:54 A.M. The extra blanket seemed not to make much difference — Grace was still shivering, the room was still very cold. There was a smell of something close, damp, unclean like mold. There was a faint smell of urine. *Help me, help* but Grace had already rung the buzzer and she understood that she'd already been helped and that there was no more help. She decided to sit up sleepless through the remainder of this terrible night though believing, with the resigned half-humor of the damned, that it would never end. Never would it be dawn and never the miraculous hour of seven A.M. and a respite from pain. Thinking, *I am not that strong. I am not evil, but I am not that strong. In her place, I could not forgive.* When she looked at the little digital clock her sister had brought her she saw it was 4:56 A.M.

CONSIDERATIONS FOR CRITICAL THINKING AND WRITING

1. FIRST RESPONSE. How is fear made central in the story? What purpose does it serve?

2. Discuss the effects of the setting. Pay particular attention to how the night is treated.

3. How is Grace characterized? Explain whether or not you find her sympathetic.

4. Choose a paragraph that you find especially descriptive and evocative. Explain how the paragraph achieves its effects.

5. What do you think is the major conflict in the story? To what extent is it resolved?

6. In what sense can Harriet be described as a lost sister to Grace (para. 8)?

7. Compare the physical descriptions of Grace and Harriet. How do they influence your response to the characters?

8. Locate what you take to be the scariest scene of the story and analyze how that scene achieves its emotional impact.

9. What do you think Grace and Harriet learn about themselves by the end of the story?

John Updike (1988), one of the most popular contemporary American novelists, during an interview at his publisher's office.

JOHN UPDIKE (B. 1932)

Born in Shillington, Pennsylvania, in 1932, John Updike graduated from Harvard University in 1954. He studied fine arts at Oxford University, and after returning from England in 1955, he worked on the staff of *The New Yorker* and began publishing his fiction. Since then Updike has published prodigiously, making his mark in fiction, poetry, and essay writing. Among his many awards are the National Book Award, the Pulitzer Prize, and the National Book Critics' Circle Award. His novels include *Rabbit, Run* (1960), *Rabbit Redux* (1971), *Rabbit Is Rich* (1981), and *Rabbit at Rest* (1990). His collections of stories include *Pigeon Feathers* (1962), *Museums and Women* (1972), and *Problems and Other Stories* (1981). His realistic stories brilliantly capture the small details of everyday life — and their significances.

A & P   *1961*

In walks these three girls in nothing but bathing suits. I'm in the third check-out slot, with my back to the door, so I don't see them until they're over by the bread. The one that caught my eye first was the one in the plaid green two-piece. She was a chunky kid, with a good tan and a sweet broad soft-looking can with those two crescents of white just under it, where the sun never seems to hit, at the top of the backs of her legs. I stood there with my hand on a box of HiHo crackers trying to remember if I rang it up or not. I ring it up again and the customer starts giving me hell. She's one of these cash-register-watchers, a witch about fifty with rouge on her cheekbones and no eyebrows, and I know it made her day to trip me up. She'd been watching cash registers for fifty years and probably never seen a mistake before.

By the time I got her feathers smoothed and her goodies into a bag — she gives me a little snort in passing, if she'd been born at the right time they would have burned her over in Salem — by the time I get her on her way the girls had circled around the bread and were coming back, without a pushcart, back my way along the counters, in the aisle between the checkouts and the Special bins. They didn't even have shoes on. There was this chunky one, with the two-piece — it was bright green and the seams on the bra were still sharp and her belly was still pretty pale so I guessed she just got it (the suit) — there was this one, with one of those chubby berry-faces, the lips all bunched together under her nose, this one, and a tall one, with black hair that hadn't quite frizzed right, and one of these sunburns right across under the eyes, and a chin that was too long — you know, the kind of girl other girls think is very "striking" and "attractive" but never quite makes it, as they very well know, which is why they like her so much — and then the third one, that wasn't quite so tall. She was the queen. She kind of led them, the other two peeking around and making their shoulders round. She didn't look around, not this queen, she just walked straight on slowly, on these long white prima-donna legs. She came down a little hard on her heels, as if she didn't walk in her bare feet that much, putting down her heels and then letting the weight move along to her toes as if she was testing the floor with every step, putting a little deliberate extra action into it. You never know for sure how girls' minds work (do you really think it's a mind in there or just a little buzz like a bee in a glass jar?) but you got the idea she had talked the other two into coming in here with her, and now she was showing them how to do it, walk slow and hold yourself straight.

She had on a kind of dirty-pink — beige maybe, I don't know — bathing suit with a little nubble all over it and, what got me, the straps were down. They were off her shoulders looped loose around the cool tops of her arms, and I guess as a result the suit had slipped a little on her, so all around the top of the cloth there was this shining rim. If it hadn't been there you wouldn't have known there could be anything whiter than those shoulders. With the straps pushed off, there was nothing between the top of the suit and the top of her head except just *her*, this clean bare plane of the top of her chest down from the shoulder bones like a dented sheet of metal tilted in the light. I mean, it was more than pretty.

She had sort of oaky hair that the sun and salt had bleached, done up in a bun that was unraveling, and a kind of prim face. Walking into the A & P with your straps down, I suppose it's the only kind of face you *can* have. She held her head so high her neck, coming up out of those white shoulders, looked kind of stretched, but I didn't mind. The longer her neck was, the more of her there was.

She must have felt in the corner of her eye me and over my shoulder Stokesie in the second slot watching, but she didn't tip. Not this queen. She kept her

5

eyes moving across the racks, and stopped, and turned so slow it made my stomach rub the inside of my apron, and buzzed to the other two, who kind of huddled against her for relief, and then they all three of them went up the cat-and-dog-food-breakfast-cereal-macaroni-rice-raisins-seasonings-spreads-spaghetti-soft-drinks-crackers-and-cookies aisle. From the third slot I look straight up this aisle to the meat counter, and I watched them all the way. The fat one with the tan sort of fumbled with the cookies, but on second thought she put the package back. The sheep pushing their carts down the aisle — the girls were walking against the usual traffic (not that we have one-way signs or anything) — were pretty hilarious. You could see them, when Queenie's white shoulders dawned on them, kind of jerk, or hop, or hiccup, but their eyes snapped back to their own baskets and on they pushed. I bet you could set off dynamite in an A & P and the people would by and large keep reaching and checking oatmeal off their lists and muttering "Let me see, there was a third thing, began with A, asparagus, no, ah, yes, applesauce!" or whatever it is they do mutter. But there was no doubt, this jiggled them. A few houseslaves in pin curlers even looked around after pushing their carts past to make sure what they had seen was correct.

You know, it's one thing to have a girl in a bathing suit down on the beach, where what with the glare nobody can look at each other much anyway, and another thing in the cool of the A & P, under the fluorescent lights, against all those stacked packages, with her feet paddling along naked over our checker-board green-and-cream rubber-tile floor.

"Oh Daddy," Stokesie said beside me. "I feel so faint."

"Darling," I said. "Hold me tight." Stokesie's married, with two babies chalked up on his fuselage already, but as far as I can tell that's the only difference. He's twenty-two, and I was nineteen this April.

"Is it done?" he asks, the responsible married man finding his voice. I forgot to say he thinks he's going to be manager some sunny day, maybe in 1990 when it's called the Great Alexandrov and Petrooshki Tea Company or something.

What he meant was, our town is five miles from a beach, with a big sum- 10
mer colony out on the Point, but we're right in the middle of town, and the women generally put on a shirt or shorts or something before they get out of the car into the street. And anyway these are usually women with six children and varicose veins mapping their legs and nobody, including them, could care less. As I say, we're right in the middle of town, and if you stand at our front doors you can see two banks and the Congregational church and the newspaper store and three real-estate offices and about twenty-seven old freeloaders tearing up Central Street because the sewer broke again. It's not as if we're on the Cape, we're north of Boston and there's people in this town haven't seen the ocean for twenty years.

The girls had reached the meat counter and were asking McMahon something. He pointed, they pointed, and they shuffled out of sight behind a pyramid of Diet Delight peaches. All that was left for us to see was old McMahon patting his mouth and looking after them sizing up their joints. Poor kids, I began to feel sorry for them, they couldn't help it.

Now here comes the sad part of the story, at least my family says it's sad, but I don't think it's so sad myself. The store's pretty empty, it being Thursday afternoon, so there was nothing much to do except lean on the register and wait for the girls to show up again. The whole store was like a pinball machine and I didn't know which tunnel they'd come out of. After a while they come around out of the far aisle, around the light bulbs, records at discount of the Caribbean Six or Tony Martin Sings or some such gunk you wonder they waste the wax on, sixpacks of candy bars, and plastic toys done up in cellophane that fall apart when a kid looks at them anyway. Around they come, Queenie still leading the way, and holding a little gray jar in her hands. Slots Three through Seven are unmanned and I could see her wondering between Stokes and me, but Stokesie with his usual luck draws an old party in baggy gray pants who stumbles up with four giant cans of pineapple juice (what do these bums *do* with all that pineapple juice? I've often asked myself). So the girls come to me. Queenie puts down the jar and I take it into my fingers icy cold. Kingfish Fancy Herring Snacks in Pure Sour Cream: 49¢. Now her hands are empty, not a ring or a bracelet, bare as God made them, and I wonder where the money's coming from. Still with that prim look she lifts a folded dollar bill out of the hollow at the center of her nubbled pink top. The jar went heavy in my hand. Really, I thought that was so cute.

Then everybody's luck begins to run out. Lengel comes in from haggling with a truck full of cabbages on the lot and is about to scuttle into that door marked MANAGER behind which he hides all day when the girls touch his eye. Lengel's pretty dreary, teaches Sunday school and the rest, but he doesn't miss that much. He comes over and says, "Girls, this isn't the beach."

Queenie blushes, though maybe it's just a brush of sunburn I was noticing for the first time, now that she was so close. "My mother asked me to pick up a jar of herring snacks." Her voice kind of startled me, the way voices do when you see the people first, coming out so flat and dumb yet kind of tony, too, the way it ticked over "pick up" and "snacks." All of a sudden I slid right down her voice into the living room. Her father and the other men were standing around in ice-cream coats and bow ties and the women were in sandals picking up herring snacks on toothpicks off a big glass plate and they were all holding drinks the color of water with olives and sprigs of mint in them. When my parents have somebody over they get lemonade and if it's a real racy affair Schlitz in tall glasses with "They'll Do It Every Time" cartoons stenciled on.

"That's all right," Lengel said. "But this isn't the beach." His repeating this 15 struck me as funny, as if it had just occurred to him, and he had been thinking all these years the A & P was a great big dune and he was the head lifeguard. He didn't like my smiling — as I say he doesn't miss much — but he concentrates on giving the girls that sad Sunday-school-superintendent stare.

Queenie's blush is no sunburn now, and the plump one in plaid, that I liked better from the back — a really sweet can — pipes up, "We weren't doing any shopping. We just came in for the one thing."

"That makes no difference," Lengel tells her, and I could see from the way his eyes went that he hadn't noticed she was wearing a two-piece before. "We want you decently dressed when you come in here."

"We *are* decent," Queenie says suddenly, her lower lip pushing, getting sore now that she remembers her place, a place from which the crowd that runs the A & P must look pretty crummy. Fancy Herring Snacks flashed in her very blue eyes.

"Girls, I don't want to argue with you. After this come in here with your shoulders covered. It's our policy." He turns his back. That's policy for you. Policy is what the kingpins want. What the others want is juvenile delinquency.

All this while, the customers had been showing up with their carts but, 20 you know, sheep, seeing a scene, they had all bunched up on Stokesie, who shook open a paper bag as gently as peeling a peach, not wanting to miss a word. I could feel in the silence everybody getting nervous, most of all Lengel, who asks me, "Sammy, have you rung up their purchase?"

I thought and said "No" but it wasn't about that I was thinking. I go through the punches, 4, 9, GROC. TOT — it's more complicated than you think, and after you do it often enough, it begins to make a little song, that you hear words to, in my case "Hello *(bing)* there, you *(gung)* hap-py *pee*-pul *(splat)!*" — the *splat* being the drawer flying out. I uncrease the bill, tenderly as you may imagine, it just having come from between the two smoothest scoops of vanilla I had ever known were there, and pass a half and a penny into her narrow pink palm, and nestle the herrings in a bag and twist its neck and hand it over, all the time thinking.

The girls, and who'd blame them, are in a hurry to get out, so I say "I quit" to Lengel quick enough for them to hear, hoping they'll stop and watch me, their unsuspected hero. They keep right on going, into the electric eye; the door flies open and they flicker across the lot to their car, Queenie and Plaid and Big Tall Goony-Goony (not that as raw material she was so bad), leaving me with Lengel and a kink in his eyebrow.

"Did you say something, Sammy?"

"I said I quit."

"I thought you did."   25

"You didn't have to embarrass them."

"It was they who were embarrassing us."

I started to say something that came out "Fiddle-de-doo." It's a saying of my grandmother's, and I know she would have been pleased.

"I don't think you know what you're saying," Lengel said.

"I know you don't," I said. "But I do." I pull the bow at the back of my 30 apron and start shrugging it off my shoulders. A couple customers that had been heading for my slot begin to knock against each other, like scared pigs in a chute.

Lengel sighs and begins to look very patient and old and gray. He's been a friend of my parents for years. "Sammy, you don't want to do this to your Mom and Dad," he tells me. It's true, I don't. But it seems to me that once you begin a gesture it's fatal not to go through with it. I fold the apron, "Sammy" stitched in red on the pocket, and put it on the counter, and drop the bow tie on top of it. The bow tie is theirs, if you've ever wondered. "You'll feel this for the rest of your life," Lengel says, and I know that's true, too, but remembering how he made the pretty girl blush makes me so scrunchy inside I punch the No Sale tab and the machine whirs "pee-pul" and the drawer splats out. One advantage to this scene taking place in summer, I can follow this up with a clean exit, there's no fumbling around getting your coat and galoshes, I just saunter into the electric eye in my white shirt that my mother ironed the night before, and the door heaves itself open, and outside the sunshine is skating around on the asphalt.

I look around for my girls, but they're gone, of course. There wasn't anybody but some young married screaming with her children about some candy they didn't get by the door of a powder-blue Falcon station wagon. Looking back in the big windows, over the bags of peat moss and aluminum lawn furniture stacked on the pavement, I could see Lengel in my place in the slot, checking the sheep through. His face was dark gray and his back stiff, as if he'd just had an injection of iron, and my stomach kind of fell as I felt how hard the world was going to be to me hereafter.

CONSIDERATIONS FOR CRITICAL THINKING AND WRITING

1. FIRST RESPONSE. Describe the setting. How accurate do you think Updike's treatment of the A & P is?

2. What kind of person is Sammy? How do his actions and speech constitute his own individual style?

3. Analyze the style of the first paragraph. How does it set the tone for the rest of the story?

4. What is the story's central conflict? Does it seem to be a serious or trivial conflict to you?

5. With what kind of values is Lengel associated? Do you feel any sympathy for him?

6. What do you think is Stoksie's function in the story?

7. Consider Sammy's treatment of the three girls. Do you think his account of them is sexist? Explain why or why not.

8. Locate the climax of the story. How does the climax affect your attitude toward Sammy?

9. How do you think the story would be different if it were told from another character's point of view instead of Sammy's?

10. Discuss the thematic significance of the story's final paragraph. Would you read the story differently if this last paragraph were eliminated?

POETRY

JULIA ALVAREZ (B. 1950)

Woman's Work   1996

Who says a woman's work isn't high art?
She'd challenge as she scrubbed the bathroom tiles.
Keep house as if the address were your heart.

We'd clean the whole upstairs before we'd start
downstairs. I'd sigh, hearing my friends outside.   5
Doing her woman's work was a hard art

to practice when the summer sun would bar
the floor I swept till she was satisfied.
She kept me prisoner in her housebound heart.

She'd shine the tines of forks, the wheels of carts,   10
cut lacy lattices for all her pies.
Her woman's work was nothing less than art.

And, I, her masterpiece since I was smart,
was primed, praised, polished, scolded and advised
to keep a house much better than my heart.   15

I did not want to be her counterpart!
I struck out . . . but became my mother's child:
a woman working at home on her art,
housekeeping paper as if it were her heart.

CONSIDERATIONS FOR CRITICAL THINKING AND WRITING

1. FIRST RESPONSE. Characterize the mother and daughter. How are they similar to one another?

2. How is the structure of this poem different from a conventional villanelle? How do these differences contribute to the speaker's description of "woman's work"?

3. How does the concluding quatrain make an important distinction between the mother and daughter while redefining "woman's work"?

WILLIAM BLAKE (1757–1827)

The Chimney Sweeper   *1789*

When my mother died I was very young,
And my father sold me while yet my tongue
Could scarcely cry "'weep! 'weep! 'weep! 'weep!"
So your chimneys I sweep, and in soot I sleep.

There's little Tom Dacre, who cried when his head,   5
That curled like a lamb's back, was shaved: so I said
"Hush, Tom! never mind it, for when your head's bare
You know that the soot cannot spoil your white hair."

And so he was quiet, and that very night,
As Tom was a-sleeping, he had such a sight!   10
That thousands of sweepers, Dick, Joe, Ned, and Jack,
Were all of them locked up in coffins of black.

And by came an Angel who had a bright key,
And he opened the coffins and set them all free;
Then down a green plain leaping, laughing, they run,   15
And wash in a river, and shine in the sun.

Then naked and white, all their bags left behind,
They rise upon clouds and sport in the wind;
And the Angel told Tom, if he'd be a good boy,
He'd have God for his father, and never want joy.   20

And so Tom awoke; and we rose in the dark,
And got with our bags and our brushes to work.
Though the morning was cold, Tom was happy and warm;
So if all do their duty they need not fear harm.

CONSIDERATIONS FOR CRITICAL THINKING AND WRITING

1. FIRST RESPONSE. Discuss the validity of this statement: "'The Chimney Sweeper' is a sentimental poem about a shameful eighteenth-century social problem; such a treatment of child abuse cannot be taken seriously."

2. Characterize the speaker in this poem, and describe his tone. Is his tone the same as the poet's? Consider especially lines 7, 8, and 24.

3. What is the symbolic value of the dream in lines 11 to 20?

4. Why is irony central to the meaning of this poem?

ANN CHOI (B. 1969)

The Shower   *1991*

In the sixth grade
your hands were not much smaller
than they are now,
the reach between your thumb
and last finger not quite   5
an octave. You did not complain
and learned to choose
your music carefully.

Sharing noodles after school
in your house full of trophies,   10
we spoke of things expiring
without our knowledge. How time
quickens and wraps around us,
makes us women in bright clothes
caught by the permanence of the ring   15
around your finger.

I am your friend, accustomed
to your diligence.
Soon you will marry and fill
a house with sounds of dishes   20
and of children whose weight
you will gain and lose,
whose small fingers will separate
to play staccato,
one brief note after another.   25

CONSIDERATIONS FOR CRITICAL THINKING AND WRITING

1. FIRST RESPONSE. How does the speaker characterize her friend? Which images seem especially revealing?

2. Discuss the sense of time as it moves through the poem.

3. Do you think this is a sad or a celebratory poem? Explain why.

JUDITH ORTIZ COFER (B. 1952)

Common Ground   *1987*

Blood tells the story of your life
in heartbeats as you live it;
bones speak in the language
of death, and flesh thins
with age when up   5
through your pores rises
the stuff of your origin.

        These days,
when I look in the mirror I see
my grandmother's stern lips   10
speaking in parentheses at the corners
of my mouth of pain and deprivation
I have never known. I recognize
my father's brows arching in disdain
over the objects of my vanity, my mother's   15
nervous hands smoothing lines
just appearing on my skin,
like arrows pointing downward
to our common ground.

CONSIDERATIONS FOR CRITICAL THINKING AND WRITING

1. FIRST RESPONSE. How do you interpret the title?
2. What is the relationship between the first and second stanzas?
3. What is the poem's tone? How do the diction and imagery create the tone?

JIM DANIELS (B. 1956)

Short-order Cook   *1985*

An average joe comes in
and orders thirty cheeseburgers and thirty fries.

I wait for him to pay before I start cooking.
He pays.
He ain't no average joe.   5

The grill is just big enough for ten rows of three.
I slap the burgers down
throw two buckets of fries in the deep frier
and they pop pop spit spit . . .
psss . . .   10
The counter girls laugh.

I concentrate.
It is the crucial point —
they are ready for the cheese:
my fingers shake as I tear off slices   15
toss them on the burgers/fries done/dump/
refill buckets/burgers ready/flip into buns/
beat that melting cheese/wrap burgers in plastic/
into paper bags/fries done/dump/fill thirty bags/
bring them to the counter/wipe sweat on sleeve   20
and smile at the counter girls.
I puff my chest out and bellow:
"Thirty cheeseburgers, thirty fries!"
They look at me funny.
I grab a handful of ice, toss it in my mouth   25
do a little dance and walk back to the grill.
Pressure, responsibility, success,
thirty cheeseburgers, thirty fries.

CONSIDERATIONS FOR CRITICAL THINKING AND WRITING

1. FIRST RESPONSE. What motivates this speaker?

2. What function do the three stanzas serve?

3. How do the varying line lengths contribute to the poem's meaning?

4. What is the effect of the slashes in lines 16–20?

5. What role do the counter girls play in the poem?

EMILY DICKINSON (1830–1886)

From all the Jails the Boys and Girls   *c. 1881*

From all the Jails the Boys and Girls
Ecstatically leap —
Beloved only Afternoon
That Prison doesn't keep

They storm the Earth and stun the Air,
A Mob of solid Bliss —
Alas — that Frowns should lie in wait
For such a Foe as this —

CONSIDERATIONS FOR CRITICAL THINKING AND WRITING

1. FIRST RESPONSE. What are the "Jails"? How are children characterized in this poem?

2. Comment on the effectiveness of the description in lines 5 and 6.

3. How might "Frowns" be read symbolically?

ROBERT FROST (1874–1963)

After Apple-Picking

1914

My long two-pointed ladder's sticking through a tree
Toward heaven still,
And there's a barrel that I didn't fill
Beside it, and there may be two or three
Apples I didn't pick upon some bough.   5
But I am done with apple-picking now.
Essence of winter sleep is on the night,
The scent of apples: I am drowsing off.
I cannot rub the strangeness from my sight
I got from looking through a pane of glass   10
I skimmed this morning from the drinking trough
And held against the world of hoary grass.
It melted, and I let it fall and break.
But I was well
Upon my way to sleep before it fell,   15
And I could tell
What form my dreaming was about to take.
Magnified apples appear and disappear,
Stem end and blossom end,
And every fleck of russet showing clear.   20
My instep arch not only keeps the ache,
It keeps the pressure of a ladder-round.
I feel the ladder sway as the boughs bend.
And I keep hearing from the cellar bin
The rumbling sound   25
Of load on load of apples coming in.
For I have had too much
Of apple-picking: I am overtired
Of the great harvest I myself desired.
There were ten thousand thousand fruit to touch,   30
Cherish in hand, lift down, and not let fall.
For all
That struck the earth,
No matter if not bruised or spiked with stubble,
Went surely to the cider-apple heap   35
As of no worth.
One can see what will trouble
This sleep of mine, whatever sleep it is.
Were he not gone,
The woodchuck could say whether it's like his   40
Long sleep, as I describe its coming on,
Or just some human sleep.

CONSIDERATIONS FOR CRITICAL THINKING AND WRITING

1. FIRST RESPONSE. How does this poem illustrate Frost's view that "Poetry provides the one permissible way of saying one thing and meaning another"? When do you first sense that the detailed description of apple picking is being used that way?

2. What comes after apple picking? What does the speaker worry about in the dream beginning in line 18?

3. Why do you suppose Frost uses apples rather than, say, pears or squash?

"Out, Out—"°   1916

The buzz-saw snarled and rattled in the yard
And made dust and dropped stove-length sticks of wood,
Sweet-scented stuff when the breeze drew across it.
And from there those that lifted eyes could count
Five mountain ranges one behind the other   5
Under the sunset far into Vermont.
And the saw snarled and rattled, snarled and rattled,
As it ran light, or had to bear a load.
And nothing happened: day was all but done.
Call it a day, I wish they might have said   10
To please the boy by giving him the half hour
That a boy counts so much when saved from work.
His sister stood beside them in her apron
To tell them "Supper." At the word, the saw,
As if to prove saws knew what supper meant,   15
Leaped out at the boy's hand, or seemed to leap—
He must have given the hand. However it was,
Neither refused the meeting. But the hand!
The boy's first outcry was a rueful laugh,
As he swung toward them holding up the hand   20
Half in appeal, but half as if to keep
The life from spilling. Then the boy saw all—
Since he was old enough to know, big boy
Doing a man's work, though a child at heart—
He saw all spoiled. "Don't let him cut my hand off—   25
The doctor, when he comes. Don't let him, sister!"
So. But the hand was gone already.
The doctor put him in the dark of ether.
He lay and puffed his lips out with his breath.
And then—the watcher at his pulse took fright.   30
No one believed. They listened at his heart.
Little—less—nothing!—and that ended it.
No more to build on there. And they, since they
Were not the one dead, turned to their affairs.

"*Out, Out*—": From Act V, Scene v, of Shakespeare's *Macbeth*.

CONSIDERATIONS FOR CRITICAL THINKING AND WRITING

1. FIRST RESPONSE. This narrative poem is about the accidental death of a boy. What is the purpose of the story? Some readers have argued that the final lines reveal the speaker's callousness and indifference. What do you think?

2. How does Frost's allusion to *Macbeth* contribute to the meaning of this poem? Does the speaker seem to agree with the view of life expressed in Macbeth's lines?

3. CRITICAL STRATEGIES. Read the section on Marxist criticism (p. 68) in Chapter 3, "Applying a Critical Strategy." How do you think a Marxist critic would interpret the family and events described in this poem?

NIKKI GIOVANNI (B. 1943)

Clouds   *1999*

```
I want to swim with hippos
      jump with salmon
         fly with geese
      land with robins
      walk with turtles                              5
   sleep with possum
   dress with penguins
   preen with peacocks
      fish with grizzlies
      hunt with lions                                10
forage with pigs for truffles
eat nuts with the squirrels
plant seeds with the wind
and ride on off with the clouds
         at the end                                  15
```

CONSIDERATIONS FOR CRITICAL THINKING AND WRITING

1. FIRST RESPONSE. How does the final line of this poem make all the difference in your understanding of it?

2. In what sense might this poem be a definition of heaven? What is your own definition?

MARILYN HACKER (B. 1942)

Groves of Academe   *1984*

The hour dragged on, and I was badly needing
coffee; that encouraged my perversity.
I asked the students of Poetry Writing,
"Tell me about the poetry you're reading."
There was some hair chewing and some nail biting.   5

Snowdrifts piled up around the university.
"I've really gotten into science fiction."
"I don't read much — it breaks my concentration.
I wouldn't want to influence my style."
"We taped some Sound Poems for the college station."   10
"When *I* give readings, should I work on diction?"
"Is it true that no really worthwhile
contemporary poets write in rhyme?"
"Do you think it would be a waste of time
to send my poems to *Vanity Fair*?   15
I mean — could they relate to my work there?"

CONSIDERATIONS FOR CRITICAL THINKING AND WRITING

1. FIRST RESPONSE. Characterize the speaker. How do the students compare?

2. What do the students' comments and questions in response to their teacher's request (line 4) reveal about themselves?

3. How does the speaker implicitly answer the question about poetic rhyme in lines 12 and 13?

MARK HALLIDAY (B. 1949)

Graded Paper   *1991*

On the whole this is quite successful work:
your main argument about the poet's ambivalence —
how he loves the very things he attacks —
is mostly persuasive and always engaging.
At the same time,   5
                    there are spots
where your thinking becomes, for me,
alarmingly opaque, and your syntax seems to jump
backwards through unnecessary hoops,
as on p. 2 where you speak of "precognitive awareness   10
not yet disestablished by the shell that encrusts
each thing that a person actually says"
or at the top of p. 5 where your discussion of
"subverbal undertow miming the subversion of self-belief
woven counter to desire's outreach"   15
leaves me groping for firmer footholds.
(I'd have said it differently,
or rather, said something else.)
And when you say that women "could not fulfill themselves" (p. 6)
"in that era" (only forty years ago, after all!)   20
are you so sure that the situation is so different today?
Also, how does Whitman bluff his way into
your penultimate paragraph? He is the *last* poet
I would have quoted in this context!

What plausible way of behaving   25
does the passage you quote represent? Don't you think
literature should ultimately reveal possibilities for *action*?

Please notice how I've repaired your use of semicolons.

And yet, despite what may seem my cranky response,
I do admire the freshness of   30
your thinking and your style; there is
a vitality here; your sentences thrust themselves forward
with a confidence as impressive as it is cheeky. . . .
You are not
         me, finally,   35
and though this is an awkward problem, involving
the inescapable fact that you are so young, so young
it is also a delightful provocation.

CONSIDERATIONS FOR CRITICAL THINKING AND WRITING

1. FIRST RESPONSE. What is the professor's biggest objection to the paper?
   What pleased him about it?
2. Discuss the speaker's voice and tone. Do you like or dislike the professor's
   comments? Explain why.
3. What do the comments reveal about the professor?

JUDY PAGE HEITZMAN (B. 1952)

The Schoolroom on the Second Floor of the Knitting Mill   *1991*

While most of us copied letters out of books,
Mrs. Lawrence carved and cleaned her nails.
Now the red and buff cardinals at my back-room window
make me miss her, her room, her hallway,
even the chimney outside   5
that broke up the sky.

In my memory it is afternoon.
Sun streams in through the door
next to the fire escape where we are lined up
getting our coats on to go out to the playground,   10
the tether ball, its towering height, the swings.
She tells me to make sure the line
does not move up over the threshold.
That would be dangerous.
So I stand guard at the door.   15
Somehow it happens
the way things seem to happen when we're not really looking,
or we are looking, just not the right way.
Kids crush up like cattle, pushing me over the line.

Judy is not a good leader is all Mrs. Lawrence says.   20
She says it quietly. Still, everybody hears.
Her arms hang down like sausages.
I hear her every time I fail.

CONSIDERATIONS FOR CRITICAL THINKING AND WRITING

1. FIRST RESPONSE. What do the images used to describe Mrs. Lawrence suggest about her personality and her teaching style?
2. Discuss the poem's tone. Why can't it be simply described as nostalgic?
3. Describe a teacher from your past who in your eyes was in some way similar to Mrs. Lawrence.

M. CARL HOLMAN (1919–1988)

Mr. Z   *1967*

Taught early that his mother's skin was the sign of error,
He dressed and spoke the perfect part of honor;
Won scholarships, attended the best schools,
Disclaimed kinship with jazz and spirituals;
Chose prudent, raceless views for each situation,   5
Or when he could not cleanly skirt dissension,
Faced up to the dilemma, firmly seized
Whatever ground was Anglo-Saxonized.

In diet, too, his practice was exemplary:
Of pork in its profane forms he was wary;   10
Expert in vintage wines, sauces and salads,
His palate shrank from cornbread, yams and collards.

He was as careful whom he chose to kiss:
His bride had somewhere lost her Jewishness,
But kept her blue eyes; an Episcopalian   15
Prelate proclaimed them matched chameleon.
Choosing the right addresses, here, abroad,
They shunned those places where they might be barred;
Even less anxious to be asked to dine
Where hosts catered to kosher accent or exotic skin.   20

And so he climbed, unclogged by ethnic weights,
An airborne plant, flourishing without roots.
Not one false note was struck — until he died:
His subtly grieving widow could have flayed
The obit writers, ringing crude changes on a clumsy phrase: 25
"One of the most distinguished members of his race."

CONSIDERATIONS FOR CRITICAL THINKING AND WRITING

1. FIRST RESPONSE. How does Mr. Z cope with being black in a white society? Do you empathize with him? Why or why not?
2. Discuss the irony of the final stanza and its relation to the poem's theme.

3. M. Carl Holman was a black poet. Would you read the poem any differently if the author had been white?

ANDREW HUDGINS (B. 1951)

Seventeen 1991

Ahead of me, the dog reared on its rope,
and swayed. The pickup took a hard left turn,
and the dog tipped off the side. He scrambled, fell,
and scraped along the hot asphalt
before he tumbled back into the air. 5
I pounded on my horn and yelled. The rope
snapped and the brown dog hurtled into the weeds.
I braked, still pounding on my horn. The truck
stopped too.

           We met halfway, and stared 10
down at the shivering dog, which flinched
and moaned and tried to flick its tail.
Most of one haunch was scraped away
and both hind legs were twisted. *You stupid shit!*
I said. He squinted at me. "Well now, bud— 15
you best watch what you say to me."
I'd never cussed a grown-up man before.
I nodded. I figured on a beating. He grinned.
"You so damn worried about that ole dog,
he's yours." He strolled back to his truck, 20
gunned it, and slewed off, spraying gravel.
The dog whined harshly.

           By the road,
gnats rose waist-high as I waded through
the dry weeds, looking for a rock. 25
I knelt down by the dog—tail flick—
and slammed the rock down twice. The first
blow did the job, but I had planned for two.
My hands swept up and down again. I grabbed
the hind legs, swung twice, and heaved the dog 30
into a clump of butterfly weed and vetch.
But then I didn't know that they had names,
those roadside weeds. His truck was a blue Ford,
the dog a beagle. I was seventeen.
The gnats rose, gathered to one loose cloud, 35
then scattered through coarse orange and purple weeds.

CONSIDERATIONS FOR CRITICAL THINKING AND WRITING

1. FIRST RESPONSE. Hudgins has described "Seventeen" as a "rite of passage." How does the title focus this idea?

2. What kind of language does Hudgins use to describe the injured dog (lines 1–14)? What is its effect?

3. Characterize the speaker and the driver of the pickup. What clues does the poem provide to the way each perceives the other?

4. Might killing the dog be understood as a symbolic action? Try to come up with more than one interpretation for the speaker's actions.

LANGSTON HUGHES (1902–1967)

Johannesburg Mines   *1925*

In the Johannesburg mines
There are 240,000
Native Africans working.
What kind of poem
Would you
Make out of that?
240,000 natives
Working in the
Johannesburg mines.

CONSIDERATIONS FOR CRITICAL THINKING AND WRITING

1. FIRST RESPONSE. What "kind of poem" does the speaker make out of the fact that 240,000 natives work in the mines of Johannesburg, South Africa? How do you respond to the speaker's direct address of you, the reader?

2. Describe the poem's tone.

3. What do you think is the poem's theme?

Theme for English B   *1949*

The instructor said,

> *Go home and write*
> *a page tonight.*
> *And let that page come out of you—*
> *Then, it will be true.*   5

I wonder if it's that simple?
I am twenty-two, colored, born in Winston-Salem.
I went to school there, then Durham, then here
to this college on the hill above Harlem.
I am the only colored student in my class.   10
The steps from the hill lead down into Harlem,
through a park, then I cross St. Nicholas,
Eighth Avenue, Seventh, and I come to the Y,
the Harlem Branch Y, where I take the elevator
up to my room, sit down, and write this page: 15

It's not easy to know what is true for you or me
at twenty-two, my age. But I guess I'm what
I feel and see and hear, Harlem, I hear you:

hear you, hear me — we two — you, me, talk on this page.
(I hear New York, too.) Me — who?   20
Well, I like to eat, sleep, drink, and be in love.
I like to work, read, learn, and understand life.
I like a pipe for a Christmas present,
or records — Bessie,° bop, or Bach.
I guess being colored doesn't make me *not* like   25
the same things other folks like who are other races.
So will my page be colored that I write?
Being me, it will not be white.
But it will be
a part of you, instructor.   30
You are white —
yet a part of me, as I am part of you.
That's American.
Sometimes perhaps you don't want to be a part of me.
Nor do I often want to be a part of you.   35
But we are, that's true!
As I learn from you,
I guess you learn from me —
although you're older — and white —
and somewhat more free.   40

This is my page for English B.

Bessie: Bessie Smith (1898–1937), a famous blues singer.

CONSIDERATIONS FOR CRITICAL THINKING AND WRITING

1. FIRST RESPONSE. Try to write "a page" in response to the instructor that, like the speaker's, captures who you are.

2. What complicates the writing assignment for the speaker? Does he fulfill the assignment? Explain why or why not.

3. What are the circumstances of the speaker's life? How does the speaker respond to the question "So will my page be colored that I write?" (line 27). Discuss the tone of lines 27–40.

4. Write a one-paragraph response to this poem as you think the speaker's instructor would in grading it.

MAXINE HONG KINGSTON (B. 1940)

Restaurant   *1981*

for Lilah Kan

The main cook lies sick on a banquette, and his assistant
has cut his thumb. So the quiche cook takes
their places at the eight-burner range, and you and I
get to roll out twenty-three rounds of pie
dough and break a hundred eggs, four at a crack,   5

and sift out shell with a China cap, pack
spinach in the steel sink, squish and squeeze
the water out, and grate a full moon of cheese.
Pam, the pastry chef, who is baking Choco-
late Globs (once called Mulattos) complains about the disco,   10
which Lewis, the salad man, turns up louder out of spite.
"Black so-called musician," "Broads. Whites."
The porters, who speak French, from the Ivory Coast,
sweep up droppings and wash the pans without soap.
We won't be out of here until three A.M. In this basement,   15
I lose my size. I am a bent-over
child, Gretel or Jill, and I can
lift a pot as big as a tub with both hands.
Using a pitchfork, you stoke the broccoli and bacon.
Then I find you in the freezer, taking   20
a nibble of a slab of chocolate as big as a table.
We put the quiches in the oven, then we are able
to stick our heads up out of the sidewalk into the night
and wonder at the clean diners behind glass in candlelight.

CONSIDERATIONS FOR CRITICAL THINKING AND WRITING

1. FIRST RESPONSE. How do the sounds of this poem contribute to the descriptions of what goes on in the restaurant kitchen? How do they contribute to the diners?

2. In what sense does the speaker "lose [her] size" in the kitchen? How would you describe her?

3. Examine the poem's rhymes. What effect do they have on your reading?

4. Describe the tone of the final line. How does it differ from the rest of the poem?

KATHARYN HOWD MACHAN (B. 1952)

Hazel Tells LaVerne   1976

last night
im cleanin out my
howard johnsons ladies room
when all of a sudden
up pops this frog   5
musta come from the sewer
swimmin aroun an tryin ta
climb up the sida the bowl
so i goes ta flushm down
but sohelpmegod he starts talkin   10
bout a golden ball
an how i can be a princess
me a princess
well my mouth drops

all the way to the floor   15
an he says
kiss me just kiss me
once on the nose
well i screams
ya little green pervert   20
an i hitsm with my mop
an has ta flush
the toilet down three times
me
a princess   25

CONSIDERATIONS FOR CRITICAL THINKING AND WRITING

1. FIRST RESPONSE. What do you imagine the situation and setting are for this poem? Do you like this revision of the fairy tale "The Frog Prince"?

2. What creates the poem's humor? How does Hazel's use of language reveal her personality? Is her treatment of the frog consistent with her character?

3. Although it has no punctuation, this poem is easy to follow. How does the arrangement of the lines organize Hazel's speech for clarity and emphasis?

4. What is the theme? Is it conveyed through denotative or connotative language?

5. Write what you think might be LaVerne's reply to Hazel. First, write La-Verne's response as a series of ordinary sentences, and then try editing and organizing them into poetic lines.

SAUNDRA SHARP

It's the Law: A Rap Poem   *1991*

You can learn about the state of the U.S.A.
By the laws we have on the books today.
The rules we break are the laws we make
The things that we fear, we legislate.

We got laws designed to keep folks in line   5
Laws for what happens when you lose your mind
Laws against stealing, laws against feeling,
The laws we have are a definite sign
That our vision of love is going blind.
(They probably got a law against this rhyme.)   10
Unh-hunh . . . . .

We got laws for cool cats & laws for dirty dogs
Laws about where you can park your hog
Laws against your mama and your papa, too
Even got a law to make the laws come true.   15

It's against the law to hurt an ol' lady,
It's against the law to steal a little baby,

The laws we make are what we do to each other
There is no law to make brother love brother
Hmmm   20

Now this respect thang is hard for some folks to do
They don't respect themselves
         so they can't respect you
This is the word we should get around —
These are the rules: we gonna run 'em on down.   25
Listen up!:

It ain't enough to be cute,
It ain't enough to be tough
You gotta walk tall
You gotta strut your stuff

You gotta learn to read, you gotta learn to write.   30
Get the tools you need to win this fight
Get your common sense down off the shelf
Start in the mirror . . . . Respect your Self!

When you respect yourself you keep your body clean
You walk tall, walk gentle, don't have to be mean   35
You keep your mind well fed, you keep a clear head
And you think 'bout who you let in your bed —
Unh-hunh . . . . . .

When you respect yourself you come to understand
That your body is a temple for a natural plan,   40
It's against that plan to use drugs or dope —
Use your heart and your mind when you need to cope . . .
It's the law!

We got laws that got started in '86
And laws made back when the Indians got kicked   45
If we want these laws to go out of favor
Then we've got to change our behavior

Change what!? you say, well let's take a look
How did the laws get on the books? Yeah.
I said it up front but let's get tougher   50
The laws we make are what we do to each other

If you never shoot at me then I don't need
A law to keep you from shooting at me, do you see?
There's a universal law that's tried and true
Says Don't do to me —   55
What you don't want done to you
Unh-hunh!
Don't do to me —
What you don't want done to you
It's the law!   60

CONSIDERATIONS FOR CRITICAL THINKING AND WRITING

1. FIRST RESPONSE. According to this rap poem, what do laws reveal "about the state of the U.S.A."?

2. How are the "laws" different from the "rules" prescribed in the middle stanzas of the poem?

3. What is the theme of this rap?

PATRICIA SMITH (B. 1955)

What It's Like to Be a Black Girl (For Those of You Who Aren't)   *1991*

First of all, it's being 9 years old and
feeling like you're not finished, like your
edges are wild, like there's something,
everything, wrong. it's dropping food coloring
in your eyes to make them blue and suffering   5
their burn in silence. it's popping a bleached
white mophead over the kinks of your hair and
primping in front of mirrors that deny your
reflection. it's finding a space between your
legs, a disturbance at your chest, and not knowing   10
what to do with the whistles. it's jumping
double dutch until your legs pop, it's sweat
and vaseline and bullets, it's growing tall and
wearing a lot of white, it's smelling blood in
your breakfast, it's learning to say fuck with   15
grace but learning to fuck without it, it's
flame and fists and life according to motown,
it's finally having a man reach out for you
then caving in
around his fingers.   20

CONSIDERATIONS FOR CRITICAL THINKING AND WRITING

1. FIRST RESPONSE. Describe the speaker's tone. How do you account for it?

2. How does the speaker characterize her life? What elements of it does she focus on?

3. Discuss the poem's final image. What sort of emotions does it evoke in you?

JEAN TOOMER (1894–1967)

Reapers   *1923*

Black reapers with the sound of steel on stones
Are sharpening scythes. I see them place the hones
In their hip-pockets as a thing that's done,

And start their silent swinging, one by one.
Black horses drive a mower through the weeds,
And there, a field rat, startled, squealing bleeds,
His belly close to ground. I see the blade,
Blood-stained, continue cutting weeds and shade.

CONSIDERATIONS FOR CRITICAL THINKING AND WRITING

1. FIRST RESPONSE. Is this poem primarily about harvesting or does it suggest something else? How do the sounds, particularly the rhyme, contribute to the meaning?

2. What is the poem's tone?

3. The reapers' work is described alliteratively as "silent swinging." How are the alliteration and assonance of lines 1–2 and 6 related to their meaning?

4. Why is Toomer's version of line 6 more effective than this one: "And there a startled, squealing field rat bleeds"?

DRAMA

JANE MARTIN

Jane Martin is a pseudonym. The author's identity is known only to a handful of administrators at the Actors Theatre of Louisville who handle permissions for productions and reprints of the play. *Rodeo* is one of eleven monologues in *Talking With.* . . . Martin has also published other plays including *Coup/Clucks* (1982), *What Mama Don't Know* (1988), and *Cementville* (1991).

Although only one character appears in *Rodeo*, the monologue is surprisingly moving as she describes what the rodeo once was, how it has changed, and what it means to her. At first glance the subject matter may not seem very promising for drama, but the character's energy, forthrightness, and colorful language transform seemingly trivial details into significant meanings.

Rodeo   *1981*

A young woman in her late twenties sits working on a piece of tack. Beside her is a Lone Star beer in the can. As the lights come up we hear the last verse of a Tanya Tucker song or some other female country-western vocalist. She is wearing old worn jeans and boots plus a long-sleeved workshirt with the sleeves rolled up. She works until the song is over and then speaks.

Big Eight: Shoot — Rodeo's just goin' to hell in a handbasket. Rodeo used to be somethin'. I loved it. I did. Once Daddy an' a bunch of 'em was foolin' around with some old bronc over to our place and this ol' red nose named

Cinch got bucked off and my Daddy hooted and said he had him a nine-year-old girl, namely me, wouldn't have no damn trouble cowboyin' that horse. Well, he put me on up there, stuck that ridin' rein in my hand, gimme a kiss, and said, "Now there's only one thing t' remember Honey Love, if ya fall off you jest don't come home." Well I stayed up. You gotta stay on a bronc eight seconds. Otherwise the ride don't count. So from that day on my daddy called me Big Eight. Heck! That's all the name I got anymore . . . Big Eight.

Used to be fer cowboys, the rodeo did. Do it in some open field, folks would pull their cars and pick-ups round it, sit on the hoods, some ranch hand'd bulldog him some rank steer and everybody'd wave their hats and call him by name. Ride us some buckin' stock, rope a few calves, git throwed off a bull, and then we'd jest git us to a bar and tell each other lies about how good we were.

Used to be a family thing. Wooly Billy Tilson and Tammy Lee had them five kids on the circuit. Three boys, two girls and Wooly and Tammy. Wasn't no two-beer rodeo in Oklahoma didn't have a Tilson entered. Used to call the oldest girl Tits. Tits Tilson. Never seen a girl that top-heavy could ride so well. Said she only fell off when the gravity got her. Cowboys used to say if she landed face down you could plant two young trees in the holes she'd leave. Ha! Tits Tilson.

Used to be people came to a rodeo had a horse of their own back home. Farm people, ranch people — lord, they *knew* what they were lookin' at. Knew a good ride from a bad ride, knew hard from easy. You broke some bones er spent the day eatin' dirt, at least ya got appreciated.

Now they bought the rodeo. Them. Coca-Cola, Pepsi Cola, Marlboro damn cigarettes. You know the ones I mean. Them. Hire some New York faggot t' sit on some ol' stuffed horse in front of a sagebrush photo n' smoke that junk. Hell, tobacco wasn't made to smoke, honey, it was made to chew. Lord wanted ya filled up with smoke he would've set ya on fire. Damn it gets me!

There's some guy in a banker's suit runs the rodeo now. Got him a pinky ring and a digital watch, honey. Told us we oughta have a watcha-macallit, choriographus or somethin', some ol' ballbuster used to be with the Ice damn Capades. Wants us to ride around dressed up like Mickey Mouse, Pluto, crap like that. Told me I had to haul my butt through the barrel race done up like Minnie damn Mouse in a tu-tu. Huh uh, honey! Them people is so screwed-up they probably eat what they run over in the road.

Listen, they got the clowns wearin' Astronaut suits! I ain't lyin'. You know what a rodeo clown does! You go down, fall off whatever — the clown runs in front of the bull so's ya don't git stomped. Pin-stripes, he got 'em in space suits tellin' jokes on a microphone. First horse see 'em, done up like the Star Wars went crazy. Best buckin' horse on the circuit, name of Piss 'N' Vinegar, took one look at them clowns, had him a heart attack and died. Cowboy was ridin' him got hisself squashed. Twelve hundred pounds of coronary arrest jes fell right through 'em. Blam! Vio con dios. Crowd thought that was funnier than the astronauts. I swear it won't be long before they're strappin' ice-skates on the ponies. Big crowds now. Ain't hardly no ranch people, no farm people, nobody I know. Buncha disco babies and dee-vorce lawyers—designer jeans and day-glo Stetsons. Hell, the whole bunch of 'em wears French perfume. Oh it smells like money now! Got it on the cable T and V—hey, you know what, when ya rodeo yer just bound to kick yerself up some dust—well now, seems like that fogs up the ol' TV camera, so they told us a while back that from now on we was gonna ride on some new stuff called Astro-dirt. Dust free. Artificial damn dirt, honey. Lord have mercy.

Banker Suit called me in the other day said "Lurlene . . ." "Hold it," I said, "Who's this Lurlene? Round here they call me Big Eight." "Well, Big Eight," he said, "My name's Wallace." "Well that's a real surprise t' me," I said, "Cause aroun' here everybody jes calls you Dumb-ass." My, he laughed real big, slapped his big ol' desk, an' then he said I wasn't suitable for the rodeo no more. Said they was lookin' fer another type, somethin' a little more in the showgirl line, like the Dallas Cowgirls maybe. Said the ridin' and ropin' wasn't the thing no more. Talked on about floats, costumes, dancin' choreog-aphy. If I was a man I woulda pissed on his shoe. Said he'd give me a lifetime pass though. Said I could come to his rodeo any time I wanted.

Rodeo used to be people ridin' horses for the pleasure of people who rode horses—made you feel good about what you could do. Rodeo wasn't worth no money to nobody. Money didn't have nothing to do with it! Used to be seven Tilsons riding in the rodeo. Wouldn't none of 'em dress up like Donald damn Duck so they quit. That there's the law of gravity!

There's a bunch of assholes in this country sneak around until they see ya havin' fun and then they buy the fun and start in sellin' it. See, they figure if ya love it, they can sell it. Well you look out, honey! They want to make them a dollar out of what you love. Dress *you* up like Minnie Mouse. Sell your rodeo. Turn *yer* pleasure into Ice damn Capades. You hear what I'm sayin'? You're jus' merchandise to them, sweetie. You're jus' merchandise to them.

Blackout.

CONSIDERATIONS FOR CRITICAL THINKING AND WRITING

1. FIRST RESPONSE. Big Eight is presented as an old-fashioned rodeo type. What associations or stereotypes do you have about such people? What assumptions do you make about them? How does the author use those expectations to heighten your understanding of Big Eight's character?

2. How has the rodeo changed from how it "used to be"? How do you account for those changes?

3. Comment on Big Eight's use of language. Why is it appropriate for her character?

4. How would you describe Big Eight's brand of humor? How does it affect your understanding of her?

5. How do your feelings about Big Eight develop during the course of the monologue?

6. What does the rodeo mean to Big Eight?

ARTHUR MILLER (B. 1915)

Arthur Miller was born in New York City to middle-class Jewish parents. His mother was a teacher and his father a clothing manufacturer. In 1938 he graduated from the University of Michigan, where he had begun writing plays. Six years later his first Broadway play, *The Man Who Had All the Luck,* closed after only a few performances, but *All My Sons* (1947) earned the admiration of both critics and audiences. This drama of family life launched his career, and his next play was even more successful. *Death of a Salesman* (1949) won a Pulitzer Prize and established his international reputation so that Miller, along with Tennessee Williams, became one of the most successful American playwrights of the 1940s and 1950s. During this period, his plays included an adaptation of Henrik Ibsen's *Enemy of the People* (1951), *The Crucible* (1953), and *A View from the Bridge* (1955). Among his later works are *The Misfits* (1961, a screenplay), *After the Fall* (1964), *Incident at Vichy* (1964), *The Price* (1968), *The Creation of the World and Other Business* (1972), *The Archbishop's Ceiling* (1976), *The American Clock* (1980), *Time Bends* (1987, essays), *The Ride down Mt. Morgan* (1991), and *Broken Glass* (1994).

In *Death of a Salesman* Miller's concerns and techniques are similar to those of social realism. His characters' dialogue sounds much like ordinary speech and deals with recognizable family problems ranging from feelings about one another to personal aspirations. Miller places his characters in a social context so that their behavior within the family suggests larger implications: The death of this salesman raises issues concerning the significance and value of the American dream of success.

Although such qualities resemble some of the techniques and concerns of realistic drama, Miller also uses other techniques to express Willy Loman's thoughts. In a sense, the play allows the audience to observe what goes on inside the protagonist's head. (At one point Miller was going to title the play *The Inside of His Head.*) When Willy thinks of the past, we see those events reenacted on stage in the midst of present events. This reenactment is achieved through the use of symbolic nonrealistic sets that appear or disappear as the stage lighting changes to reveal Willy's state of mind.

Death of a Salesman   1949

Certain private conversations in two acts and a requiem

CAST

Willy Loman	*Happy*
Linda	*Bernard*
Biff	*The Woman*

Charlie	*Stanley*
Uncle Ben	*Miss Forsythe*
Howard Wagner	*Letta*
Jenny	

SCENE: *The action takes place in Willy Loman's house and yard and in various places he visits in the New York and Boston of today.*

Throughout the play, in the stage directions, left and right mean stage left and stage right.

ACT I

A melody is heard, played upon a flute. It is small and fine, telling of grass and trees and the horizon. The curtain rises.

Before us is the Salesman's house. We are aware of towering, angular shapes behind it, surrounding it on all sides. Only the blue light of the sky falls upon the house and forestage; the surrounding area shows an angry glow of orange. As more light appears, we see a solid vault of apartment houses around the small, fragile-seeming home. An air of the dream clings to the place, a dream rising out of reality. The kitchen at center seems actual enough, for there is a kitchen table with three chairs, and a refrigerator. But no other fixtures are seen. At the back of the kitchen there is a draped entrance, which leads to the living-room. To the right of the kitchen, on a level raised two feet, is a bedroom furnished only with a brass bedstead and a straight chair. On a shelf over the bed a silver athletic trophy stands. A window opens onto the apartment house at the side.

Behind the kitchen, on a level raised six and a half feet, is the boys' bedroom, at present barely visible. Two beds are dimly seen, and at the back of the room a dormer window. (This bedroom is above the unseen living-room.) At the left a stairway curves up to it from the kitchen.

The entire setting is wholly or, in some places, partially transparent. The roof-line of the house is one-dimensional; under and over it we see the apartment buildings. Before the house lies an apron, curving beyond the forestage into the orchestra. This forward area serves as the back yard as well as the locale of all Willy's imaginings and of his city scenes. Whenever the action is in the present the actors observe the imaginary wall-lines, entering the house only through its door at the left. But in the scenes of the past these boundaries are broken, and characters enter or leave a room by stepping "through" a wall onto the forestage.

From the right, Willy Loman, the Salesman, enters, carrying two large sample cases. The flute plays on. He hears but is not aware of it. He is past sixty years of age, dressed quietly. Even as he crosses the stage to the doorway of the house, his exhaustion is apparent. He unlocks the door, comes into the kitchen, and thankfully lets his burden down, feeling the soreness of his palms. A word-sigh escapes his lips — it might be "Oh, boy, oh, boy." He closes the door, then carries his cases out into the living-room, through the draped kitchen doorway.

Linda, his wife, has stirred in her bed at the right. She gets out and puts on a robe, listening. Most often jovial, she has developed an iron repression of her exceptions to Willy's behavior — she more than loves him, she admires him, as though his mercurial nature, his temper, his massive dreams and little cruelties, served her only as sharp reminders of the turbulent longings within him, longings which she shares but lacks the temperament to utter and follow to their end.

Linda (*hearing Willy outside the bedroom, calls with some trepidation*): Willy!

Willy: It's all right. I came back.

Linda: Why? What happened? (*Slight pause.*) Did something happen, Willy?

Willy: No, nothing happened.

Linda: You didn't smash the car, did you?

Willy (*with casual irritation*): I said nothing happened. Didn't you hear me?

Linda: Don't you feel well?

Willy: I'm tired to the death. (*The flute has faded away. He sits on the bed beside her, a little numb.*) I couldn't make it. I just couldn't make it, Linda.

Linda (*very carefully, delicately*): Where were you all day? You look terrible.

Willy: I got as far as a little above Yonkers. I stopped for a cup of coffee. Maybe it was the coffee.

Linda: What?

Willy (*after a pause*): I suddenly couldn't drive any more. The car kept going off onto the shoulder, y'know?

Linda (*helpfully*): Oh. Maybe it was the steering again. I don't think Angelo knows the Studebaker.

Willy: No, it's me, it's me. Suddenly I realize I'm goin' sixty miles an hour and I don't remember the last five minutes. I'm—I can't seem to—keep my mind to it.

Linda: Maybe it's your glasses. You never went for your new glasses.

Willy: No, I see everything. I came back ten miles an hour. It took me nearly four hours from Yonkers.

Linda (*resigned*): Well, you'll just have to take a rest, Willy, you can't continue this way.

Willy: I just got back from Florida.

Linda: But you didn't rest your mind. Your mind is overactive, and the mind is what counts, dear.

Willy: I'll start out in the morning. Maybe I'll feel better in the morning. (*She is taking off his shoes.*) These goddam arch supports are killing me.

Linda: Take an aspirin. Should I get you an aspirin? It'll soothe you.

Willy (*with wonder*): I was driving along, you understand? And I was fine. I was even observing the scenery. You can imagine, me looking at scenery, on the road every week of my life. But it's so beautiful up there, Linda, the trees are so thick, and the sun is warm. I opened the windshield and just let the warm air bathe over me. And then all of a sudden I'm goin' off the road! I'm tellin' ya, I absolutely forgot I was driving. If I'd've gone the other way over the white line I might've killed somebody. So I went on again—and five minutes later I'm dreamin' again, and I nearly—(*He presses two fingers against his eyes.*) I have such thoughts, I have such strange thoughts.

Linda: Willy, dear. Talk to them again. There's no reason why you can't work in New York.

Willy: They don't need me in New York. I'm the New England man. I'm vital in New England.

Linda: But you're sixty years old. They can't expect you to keep traveling every week.

Willy: I'll have to send a wire to Portland. I'm supposed to see Brown and Morrison tomorrow morning at ten o'clock to show the line. Goddammit, I could sell them! *(He starts putting on his jacket.)*

Linda (taking the jacket from him): Why don't you go down to the place tomorrow and tell Howard you've simply got to work in New York? You're too accommodating, dear.

Willy: If old man Wagner was alive I'd a been in charge of New York now! That man was a prince, he was a masterful man. But that boy of his, that Howard, he don't appreciate. When I went north the first time, the Wagner Company didn't know where New England was!

Linda: Why don't you tell those things to Howard, dear?

Willy (encouraged): I will, I definitely will. Is there any cheese?

Linda: I'll make you a sandwich.

Willy: No, go to sleep. I'll take some milk. I'll be up right away. The boys in?

Linda: They're sleeping. Happy took Biff on a date tonight.

Willy (interested): That so?

Linda: It was so nice to see them shaving together, one behind the other, in the bathroom. And going out together. You notice? The whole house smells of shaving lotion.

Willy: Figure it out. Work a lifetime to pay off a house. You finally own it, and there's nobody to live in it.

Linda: Well, dear, life is a casting off. It's always that way.

Willy: No, no, some people — some people accomplish something. Did Biff say anything after I went this morning?

Linda: You shouldn't have criticized him, Willy, especially after he just got off the train. You mustn't lose your temper with him.

Willy: When the hell did I lose my temper? I simply asked him if he was making any money. Is that a criticism?

Linda: But, dear, how could he make any money?

Willy (worried and angered): There's such an undercurrent in him. He became a moody man. Did he apologize when I left this morning?

Linda: He was crestfallen, Willy. You know how he admires you. I think if he finds himself, then you'll both be happier and not fight any more.

Willy: How can he find himself on a farm? Is that a life? A farmhand? In the beginning, when he was young, I thought, well, a young man, it's good for him to tramp around, take a lot of different jobs. But it's more than ten years now and he has yet to make thirty-five dollars a week!

Linda: He's finding himself, Willy.

Willy: Not finding yourself at the age of thirty-four is a disgrace!

Linda: Shh!

Willy: The trouble is he's lazy, goddammit!

Linda: Willy, please!

Willy: Biff is a lazy bum!

Linda: They're sleeping. Get something to eat. Go on down.

Willy: Why did he come home? I would like to know what brought him home.

Linda: I don't know. I think he's still lost, Willy. I think he's very lost.

Willy: Biff Loman is lost. In the greatest country in the world a young man with such — personal attractiveness, gets lost. And such a hard worker. There's one thing about Biff — he's not lazy.

Linda: Never.

Willy (with pity and resolve): I'll see him in the morning; I'll have a nice talk with him. I'll get him a job selling. He could be big in no time. My God! Remember how they used to follow him around in high school? When he smiled at one of them their faces lit up. When he walked down the street . . . *(He loses himself in reminiscences.)*

Linda (trying to bring him out of it): Willy, dear, I got a new kind of American-type cheese today. It's whipped.

Willy: Why do you get American when I like Swiss?

Linda: I just thought you'd like a change —

Willy: I don't want a change! I want Swiss cheese. Why am I always being contradicted?

Linda (with a covering laugh): I thought it would be a surprise.

Willy: Why don't you open a window in here, for God's sake?

Linda (with infinite patience): They're all open, dear.

Willy: The way they boxed us in here. Bricks and windows, windows and bricks.

Linda: We should've bought the land next door.

Willy: The street is lined with cars. There's not a breath of fresh air in the neighborhood. The grass don't grow any more, you can't raise a carrot in the back yard. They should've had a law against apartment houses. Remember those two beautiful elm trees out there? When I and Biff hung the swing between them?

Linda: Yeah, like being a million miles from the city.

Willy: They should've arrested the builder for cutting those down. They massacred the neighborhood. *(Lost.)* More and more I think of those days, Linda. This time of year it was lilac and wisteria. And then the peonies would come out, and the daffodils. What fragrance in this room!

Linda: Well, after all, people had to move somewhere.

Willy: No, there's more people now.

Linda: I don't think there's more people. I think —

Willy: There's more people! That's what's ruining this country! Population is getting out of control. The competition is maddening! Smell the stink from that apartment house! And another one on the other side . . . How can they whip cheese?

On Willy's last line, Biff and Happy raise themselves up in their beds, listening.

Linda: Go down, try it. And be quiet.

Willy (turning to Linda, guiltily): You're not worried about me, are you, sweetheart?

Biff: What's the matter?

Happy: Listen!

Linda: You've got too much on the ball to worry about.

Willy: You're my foundation and my support, Linda.

Linda: Just try to relax, dear. You make mountains out of molehills.

Willy: I won't fight with him any more. If he wants to go back to Texas, let him go.

Linda: He'll find his way.

Willy: Sure. Certain men just don't get started till later in life. Like Thomas Edison, I think. Or B. F. Goodrich. One of them was deaf. *(He starts for the bedroom doorway.)* I'll put my money on Biff.

Linda: And Willy — if it's warm Sunday we'll drive in the country. And we'll open the windshield, and take lunch.

Willy: No, the windshields don't open on the new cars.

Linda: But you opened it today.

Willy: Me? I didn't. *(He stops.)* Now isn't that peculiar! Isn't that a remarkable —
   (He breaks off in amazement and fright as the flute is heard distantly.)

Linda: What, darling?

Willy: That is the most remarkable thing.

Linda: What, dear?

Willy: I was thinking of the Chevy. *(Slight pause.)* Nineteen twenty-eight . . .
   when I had that red Chevy — *(Breaks off.)* That funny? I coulda sworn I was
   driving that Chevy today.

Linda: Well, that's nothing. Something must've reminded you.

Willy: Remarkable. Ts. Remember those days? The way Biff used to simonize
   that car? The dealer refused to believe there was eighty thousand miles on
   it. *(He shakes his head.)* Heh! *(To Linda.)* Close your eyes, I'll be right up. *(He
   walks out of the bedroom.)*

Happy (to Biff): Jesus, maybe he smashed up the car again!

Linda (calling after Willy): Be careful on the stairs, dear! The cheese is on the
   middle shelf! *(She turns, goes over to the bed, takes his jacket, and goes out of the
   bedroom.)*

   *Light has risen on the boys' room. Unseen, Willy is heard talking to himself, "Eighty
   thousand miles," and a little laugh. Biff gets out of bed, comes downstage a bit, and
   stands attentively. Biff is two years older than his brother Happy, well built, but in
   these days bears a worn air and seems less self-assured. He has succeeded less, and
   his dreams are stronger and less acceptable than Happy's. Happy is tall, powerfully
   made. Sexuality is like a visible color on him, or a scent that many women have
   discovered. He, like his brother, is lost, but in a different way, for he has never
   allowed himself to turn his face toward defeat and is thus more confused and hard-
   skinned, although seemingly more content.*

Happy (getting out of bed): He's going to get his license taken away if he keeps
   that up. I'm getting nervous about him, y'know, Biff?

Biff: His eyes are going.

Happy: No, I've driven with him. He sees all right. He just doesn't keep his
   mind on it. I drove into the city with him last week. He stops at a green
   light and then it turns red and he goes. *(He laughs.)*

Biff: Maybe he's color-blind.

Happy: Pop? Why he's got the finest eye for color in the business. You know that.

Biff (sitting down on his bed): I'm going to sleep.

Happy: You're not still sour on Dad, are you, Biff?

Biff: He's all right, I guess.

Willy (underneath them, in the living-room): Yes, sir, eighty thousand miles —
   eighty-two thousand!

Biff: You smoking?

Happy (holding out a pack of cigarettes): Want one?

Biff (taking a cigarette): I can never sleep when I smell it.

Willy: What a simonizing job, heh!

Happy (with deep sentiment): Funny, Biff, y'know? Us sleeping in here again?
   The old beds. *(He pats his bed affectionately.)* All the talk that went across
   those two beds, huh? Our whole lives.

Biff: Yeah. Lotta dreams and plans.

Happy (with a deep and masculine laugh): About five hundred women would like to know what was said in this room.

They share a soft laugh.

Biff: Remember that big Betsy something — what the hell was her name — over on Bushwick Avenue?

Happy (combing his hair): With the collie dog!

Biff: That's the one. I got you in there, remember?

Happy: Yeah, that was my first time — I think. Boy, there was a pig! *(They laugh, almost crudely.)* You taught me everything I know about women. Don't forget that.

Biff: I bet you forgot how bashful you used to be. Especially with girls.

Happy: Oh, I still am, Biff.

Biff: Oh, go on.

Happy: I just control it, that's all. I think I got less bashful and you got more so. What happened, Biff? Where's the old humor, the old confidence? *(He shakes Biff's knee. Biff gets up and moves restlessly about the room.)* What's the matter?

Biff: Why does Dad mock me all the time?

Happy: He's not mocking you, he —

Biff: Everything I say there's a twist of mockery on his face. I can't get near him.

Happy: He just wants you to make good, that's all. I wanted to talk to you about Dad for a long time, Biff. Something's — happening to him. He — talks to himself.

Biff: I noticed that this morning. But he always mumbled.

Happy: But not so noticeable. It got so embarrassing I sent him to Florida. And you know something? Most of the time he's talking to you.

Biff: What's he say about me?

Happy: I can't make it out.

Biff: What's he say about me?

Happy: I think the fact that you're not settled, that you're still kind of up in the air . . .

Biff: There's one or two other things depressing him, Happy.

Happy: What do you mean?

Biff: Never mind. Just don't lay it all to me.

Happy: But I think if you just got started — I mean — is there any future for you out there?

Biff: I tell ya, Hap, I don't know what the future is. I don't know — what I'm supposed to want.

Happy: What do you mean?

Biff: Well, I spent six or seven years after high school trying to work myself up. Shipping clerk, salesman, business of one kind or another. And it's a measly manner of existence. To get on that subway on the hot mornings in summer. To devote your whole life to keeping stock, or making phone calls, or selling or buying. To suffer fifty weeks of the year for the sake of a two-week vacation, when all you really desire is to be outdoors, with your shirt off. And always to have to get ahead of the next fella. And still — that's how you build a future.

Happy: Well, you really enjoy it on a farm? Are you content out there?

Biff (with rising agitation): Hap, I've had twenty or thirty different kinds of jobs since I left home before the war, and it always turns out the same. I just realized it lately. In Nebraska when I herded cattle, and the Dakotas, and Arizona, and now in Texas. It's why I came home now, I guess, because I realized it. This farm I work on, it's spring there now, see? And they've got about fifteen new colts. There's nothing more inspiring or — beautiful than the sight of a mare and a new colt. And it's cool there now, see? Texas is cool now, and it's spring. And whenever spring comes to where I am, I suddenly get the feeling, my God, I'm not gettin' anywhere! What the hell am I doing, playing around with horses, twenty-eight dollars a week! I'm thirty-four years old, I oughta be makin' my future. That's when I come running home. And now, I get here, and I don't know what to do with myself. *(After a pause.)* I've always made a point of not wasting my life, and everytime I come back here I know that all I've done is to waste my life.

Happy: You're a poet, you know that, Biff? You're a — you're an idealist!

Biff: No, I'm mixed up very bad. Maybe I oughta get married. Maybe I oughta get stuck into something. Maybe that's my trouble. I'm like a boy. I'm not married. I'm not in business, I just — I'm like a boy. Are you content, Hap? You're a success, aren't you? Are you content?

Happy: Hell, no!

Biff: Why? You're making money, aren't you?

Happy (moving about with energy, expressiveness): All I can do now is wait for the merchandise manager to die. And suppose I get to be merchandise manager? He's a good friend of mine, and he just built a terrific estate on Long Island. And he lived there about two months and sold it, and now he's building another one. He can't enjoy it once it's finished. And I know that's just what I would do. I don't know what the hell I'm workin' for. Sometimes I sit in my apartment — all alone. And I think of the rent I'm paying. And it's crazy. But then, it's what I always wanted. My own apartment, a car, and plenty of women. And still, goddammit, I'm lonely.

Biff (with enthusiasm): Listen, why don't you come out West with me?

Happy: You and I, heh?

Biff: Sure, maybe we could buy a ranch. Raise cattle, use our muscles. Men built like we are should be working out in the open.

Happy (avidly): The Loman Brothers, heh?

Biff (with vast affection): Sure, we'd be known all over the counties!

Happy (enthralled): That's what I dream about, Biff. Sometimes I want to just rip my clothes off in the middle of the store and outbox that goddam merchandise manager. I mean I can outbox, outrun, and outlift anybody in that store, and I have to take orders from those common, petty sons-of-bitches till I can't stand it any more.

Biff: I'm tellin' you, kid, if you were with me I'd be happy out there.

Happy (enthused): See, Biff, everybody around me is so false that I'm constantly lowering my ideals . . .

Biff: Baby, together we'd stand up for one another, we'd have someone to trust.

Happy: If I were around you —

Biff: Hap, the trouble is we weren't brought up to grub for money. I don't know how to do it.

Happy: Neither can I!

Biff: Then let's go!

Happy: The only thing is — what can you make out there?

Biff: But look at your friend. Builds an estate and then hasn't the peace of mind to live in it.

Happy: Yeah, but when he walks into the store the waves part in front of him. That's fifty-two thousand dollars a year coming through the revolving door, and I got more in my pinky finger than he's got in his head.

Biff: Yeah, but you just said —

Happy: I gotta show some of those pompous, self-important executives over there that Hap Loman can make the grade. I want to walk into the store the way he walks in. Then I'll go with you, Biff. We'll be together yet, I swear. But take those two we had tonight. Now weren't they gorgeous creatures?

Biff: Yeah, yeah, most gorgeous I've had in years.

Happy: I get that any time I want, Biff. Whenever I feel disgusted. The trouble is, it gets like bowling or something. I just keep knockin' them over and it doesn't mean anything. You still run around a lot?

Biff: Naa. I'd like to find a girl — steady, somebody with substance.

Happy: That's what I long for.

Biff: Go on! You'd never come home.

Happy: I would! Somebody with character, with resistance! Like Mom, y'know? You're gonna call me a bastard when I tell you this. That girl Charlotte I was with tonight is engaged to be married in five weeks. *(He tries on his new hat.)*

Biff: No kiddin'!

Happy: Sure, the guy's in line for the vice-presidency of the store. I don't know what gets into me, maybe I just have an overdeveloped sense of competition or something, but I went and ruined her, and furthermore I can't get rid of her. And he's the third executive I've done that to. Isn't that a crummy characteristic? And to top it all, I go to their weddings! *(Indignantly, but laughing.)* Like I'm not supposed to take bribes. Manufacturers offer me a hundred-dollar bill now and then to throw an order their way. You know how honest I am, but it's like this girl, see. I hate myself for it. Because I don't want the girl, and, still, I take it and — I love it!

Biff: Let's go to sleep.

Happy: I guess we didn't settle anything, heh?

Biff: I just got one idea that I think I'm going to try.

Happy: What's that?

Biff: Remember Bill Oliver?

Happy: Sure, Oliver is very big now. You want to work for him again?

Biff: No, but when I quit he said something to me. He put his arm on my shoulder, and he said, "Biff, if you ever need anything, come to me."

Happy: I remember that. That sounds good.

Biff: I think I'll go to see him. If I could get ten thousand or even seven or eight thousand dollars I could buy a beautiful ranch.

Happy: I bet he'd back you. 'Cause he thought highly of you, Biff. I mean, they all do. You're well liked, Biff. That's why I say to come back here, and we both have the apartment. And I'm tellin' you, Biff, any babe you want . . .

Biff: No, with a ranch I could do the work I like and still be something. I just wonder though. I wonder if Oliver still thinks I stole that carton of basketballs.

Happy: Oh, he probably forgot that long ago. It's almost ten years. You're too sensitive. Anyway, he didn't really fire you.

Biff: Well, I think he was going to. I think that's why I quit. I was never sure whether he knew or not. I know he thought the world of me, though. I was the only one he'd let lock up the place.

Willy (below): You gonna wash the engine, Biff?

Happy: Shh!

Biff looks at Happy, who is gazing down, listening. Willy is mumbling in the parlor.

Happy: You hear that?

They listen. Willy laughs warmly.

Biff (growing angry): Doesn't he know Mom can hear that?

Willy: Don't get your sweater dirty, Biff!

A look of pain crosses Biff's face.

Happy: Isn't that terrible? Don't leave again, will you? You'll find a job here. You gotta stick around. I don't know what to do about him, it's getting embarrassing.

Willy: What a simonizing job!

Biff: Mom's hearing that!

Willy: No kiddin', Biff, you got a date? Wonderful!

Happy: Go on to sleep. But talk to him in the morning, will you?

Biff (reluctantly getting into bed): With her in the house. Brother!

Happy (getting into bed): I wish you'd have a good talk with him.

The light on their room begins to fade.

Biff (to himself in bed): That selfish, stupid . . .

Happy: Sh . . . Sleep, Biff.

Their light is out. Well before they have finished speaking, Willy's form is dimly seen below in the darkened kitchen. He opens the refrigerator, searches in there, and takes out a bottle of milk. The apartment houses are fading out, and the entire house and surroundings become covered with leaves. Music insinuates itself as the leaves appear.

Willy: Just wanna be careful with those girls, Biff, that's all. Don't make any promises. No promises of any kind. Because a girl, y'know, they always believe what you tell 'em, and you're very young, Biff, you're too young to be talking seriously to girls.

Light rises on the kitchen. Willy, talking, shuts the refrigerator door and comes downstage to the kitchen table. He pours milk into a glass. He is totally immersed in himself, smiling faintly.

Willy: Too young entirely, Biff. You want to watch your schooling first. Then when you're all set, there'll be plenty of girls for a boy like you. (*He smiles broadly at a kitchen chair.*) That so? The girls pay for you? (*He laughs.*) Boy, you must really be makin' a hit.

Willy is gradually addressing—physically—a point offstage, speaking through the wall of the kitchen, and his voice has been rising in volume to that of a normal conversation.

Willy: I been wondering why you polish the car so careful. Ha! Don't leave the hubcaps, boys. Get the chamois to the hubcaps. Happy, use newspaper on the windows, it's the easiest thing. Show him how to do it, Biff! You see, Happy? Pad it up, use it like a pad. That's it, that's it, good work. You're doin' all right, Hap. *(He pauses, then nods in approbation for a few seconds, then looks upward.)* Biff, first thing we gotta do when we get time is clip that big branch over the house. Afraid it's gonna fall in a storm and hit the roof. Tell you what. We get a rope and sling her around, and then we climb up there with a couple of saws and take her down. Soon as you finish the car, boys, I wanna see ya. I got a surprise for you, boys.

Biff (offstage): Whatta ya got, Dad?

Willy: No, you finish first. Never leave a job till you're finished — remember that. *(Looking toward the "big trees.")* Biff, up in Albany I saw a beautiful hammock. I think I'll buy it next trip, and we'll hang it right between those two elms. Wouldn't that be something? Just swingin' there under those branches. Boy, that would be . . .

Young Biff and Young Happy appear from the direction Willy was addressing. Happy carries rags and a pail of water. Biff, wearing a sweater with a block "S," carries a football.

Biff (pointing in the direction of the car offstage): How's that, Pop, professional?

Willy: Terrific. Terrific job, boys. Good work, Biff.

Happy: Where's the surprise, Pop?

Willy: In the back seat of the car.

Happy: Boy! *(He runs off.)*

Biff: What is it, Dad? Tell me, what'd you buy?

Willy (laughing, cuffs him): Never mind, something I want you to have.

Biff (turns and starts off): What is it, Hap?

Happy (offstage): It's a punching bag!

Biff: Oh, Pop!

Willy: It's got Gene Tunney's signature on it!

Happy runs onstage with a punching bag.

Biff: Gee, how'd you know we wanted a punching bag?

Willy: Well, it's the finest thing for the timing.

Happy (lies down on his back and pedals with his feet): I'm losing weight, you notice, Pop?

Willy (to Happy): Jumping rope is good too.

Biff: Did you see the new football I got?

Willy (examining the ball): Where'd you get a new ball?

Biff: The coach told me to practice my passing.

Willy: That so? And he gave you the ball, heh?

Biff: Well, I borrowed it from the locker room. *(He laughs confidentially.)*

Willy (laughing with him at the theft): I want you to return that.

Happy: I told you he wouldn't like it!

Biff (angrily): Well, I'm bringing it back!

Willy (stopping the incipient argument, to Happy): Sure, he's gotta practice with a regulation ball, doesn't he? *(To Biff.)* Coach'll probably congratulate you on your initiative!

Biff: Oh, he keeps congratulating my initiative all the time, Pop.

Willy: That's because he likes you. If somebody else took that ball there'd be an uproar. So what's the report, boys, what's the report?

Biff: Where'd you go this time, Dad? Gee we were lonesome for you.

Willy (pleased, puts an arm around each boy and they come down to the apron): Lonesome, heh?

Biff: Missed you every minute.

Willy: Don't say? Tell you a secret, boys. Don't breathe it to a soul. Someday I'll have my own business, and I'll never have to leave home any more.

Happy: Like Uncle Charley, heh?

Willy: Bigger than Uncle Charley! Because Charley is not—liked. He's liked, but he's not—well liked.

Biff: Where'd you go this time, Dad?

Willy: Well, I got on the road, and I went north to Providence. Met the Mayor.

Biff: The Mayor of Providence!

Willy: He was sitting in the hotel lobby.

Biff: What'd he say?

Willy: He said, "Morning!" And I said, "You got a fine city here, Mayor." And then he had coffee with me. And then I went to Waterbury. Waterbury is a fine city. Big clock city, the famous Waterbury clock. Sold a nice bill there. And then Boston—Boston is the cradle of the Revolution. A fine city. And a couple of other towns in Mass., and on to Portland and Bangor and straight home!

Biff: Gee, I'd love to go with you sometime, Dad.

Willy: Soon as summer comes.

Happy: Promise?

Willy: You and Hap and I, and I'll show you all the towns. America is full of beautiful towns and fine, upstanding people. And they know me, boys, they know me up and down New England. The finest people. And when I bring you fellas up, there'll be open sesame for all of us, 'cause one thing, boys: I have friends. I can park my car in any street in New England, and the cops protect it like their own. This summer, heh?

Biff and Happy (together): Yeah! You bet!

Willy: We'll take our bathing suits.

Happy: We'll carry your bags, Pop!

Willy: Oh, won't that be something! Me comin' into the Boston stores with you boys carryin' my bags. What a sensation!

Biff is prancing around, practicing passing the ball.

Willy: You nervous, Biff, about the game?

Biff: Not if you're gonna be there.

Willy: What do they say about you in school, now that they made you captain?

Happy: There's a crowd of girls behind him everytime the classes change.

Biff (taking Willy's hand): This Saturday, Pop, this Saturday—just for you, I'm going to break through for a touchdown.

Happy: You're supposed to pass.

Biff: I'm takin' one play for Pop. You watch me, Pop, and when I take off my helmet, that means I'm breakin' out. Then you watch me crash through that line!

Willy (kisses Biff): Oh, wait'll I tell this in Boston!

Bernard enters in knickers. He is younger than Biff, earnest and loyal, a worried boy.

Bernard: Biff, where are you? You're supposed to study with me today.

Willy: Hey, looka Bernard. What're you lookin' so anemic about, Bernard?

Bernard: He's gotta study, Uncle Willy. He's got Regents next week.

Happy (tauntingly, spinning Bernard around): Let's box, Bernard!

Bernard: Biff! *(He gets away from Happy.)* Listen, Biff, I heard Mr. Birnbaum say that if you don't start studyin' math, he's gonna flunk you, and you won't graduate. I heard him!

Willy: You better study with him, Biff. Go ahead now.

Bernard: I heard him!

Biff: Oh, Pop, you didn't see my sneakers! *(He holds up a foot for Willy to look at.)*

Willy: Hey, that's a beautiful job of printing!

Bernard (wiping his glasses): Just because he printed University of Virginia on his sneakers doesn't mean they've got to graduate him, Uncle Willy!

Willy (angrily): What're you talking about? With scholarships to three universities they're gonna flunk him?

Bernard: But I heard Mr. Birnbaum say—

Willy: Don't be a pest, Bernard! *(To his boys.)* What an anemic!

Bernard: Okay, I'm waiting for you in my house, Biff.

    Bernard goes off. The Lomans laugh.

Willy: Bernard is not well liked, is he?

Biff: He's liked, but he's not well liked.

Happy: That's right, Pop.

Willy: That's just what I mean. Bernard can get the best marks in school, y'understand, but when he gets out in the business world, y'understand, you are going to be five times ahead of him. That's why I thank Almighty God you're both built like Adonises.° Because the man who makes an appearance in the business world, the man who creates personal interest, is the man who gets ahead. Be liked and you will never want. You take me, for instance. I never have to wait in line to see a buyer. "Willy Loman is here!" That's all they have to know, and I go right through.

Biff: Did you knock them dead, Pop?

Willy: Knocked 'em cold in Providence, slaughtered 'em in Boston.

Happy (on his back, pedaling again): I'm losing weight, you notice, Pop?

    Linda enters, as of old, a ribbon in her hair, carrying a basket of washing.

Linda (with youthful energy): Hello, dear!

Willy: Sweetheart!

Linda: How'd the Chevy run?

Willy: Chevrolet, Linda, is the greatest car ever built. *(To the boys.)* Since when do you let your mother carry wash up the stairs?

Biff: Grab hold there, boy!

Happy: Where to, Mom?

Linda: Hang them up on the line. And you better go down to your friends, Biff. The cellar is full of boys. They don't know what to do with themselves.

Adonis: In Greek mythology a young man known for his good looks and favored by Aphrodite, goddess of love and beauty.

Biff: Ah, when Pop comes home they can wait!

Willy (laughs appreciatively): You better go down and tell them what to do, Biff.

Biff: I think I'll have them sweep out the furnace room.

Willy: Good work, Biff.

Biff (goes through wall-line of kitchen to doorway at back and calls down): Fellas! Everybody sweep out the furnace room! I'll be right down!

Voices: All right! Okay, Biff.

Biff: George and Sam and Frank, come out back! We're hangin' up the wash! Come on, Hap, on the double! *(He and Happy carry out the basket.)*

Linda: The way they obey him!

Willy: Well, that's training, the training. I'm tellin' you, I was sellin' thousands and thousands, but I had to come home.

Linda: Oh, the whole block'll be at that game. Did you sell anything?

Willy: I did five hundred gross in Providence and seven hundred gross in Boston.

Linda: No! Wait a minute, I've got a pencil. *(She pulls pencil and paper out of her apron pocket.)* That makes your commission . . . Two hundred — my God! Two hundred and twelve dollars!

Willy: Well, I didn't figure it yet, but . . .

Linda: How much did you do?

Willy: Well, I — I did — about a hundred and eighty gross in Providence. Well, no — it came to — roughly two hundred gross on the whole trip.

Linda (without hesitation): Two hundred gross. That's . . . *(She figures.)*

Willy: The trouble was that three of the stores were half closed for inventory in Boston. Otherwise I woulda broke records.

Linda: Well, it makes seventy dollars and some pennies. That's very good.

Willy: What do we owe?

Linda: Well, on the first there's sixteen dollars on the refrigerator —

Willy: Why sixteen?

Linda: Well, the fan belt broke, so it was a dollar eighty.

Willy: But it's brand new.

Linda: Well, the man said that's the way it is. Till they work themselves in, y'know.

> *They move through the wall-line into the kitchen.*

Willy: I hope we didn't get stuck on that machine.

Linda: They got the biggest ads of any of them!

Willy: I know, it's a fine machine. What else?

Linda: Well, there's nine-sixty for the washing machine. And for the vacuum cleaner there's three and a half due on the fifteenth. Then the roof, you got twenty-one dollars remaining.

Willy: It don't leak, does it?

Linda: No, they did a wonderful job. Then you owe Frank for the carburetor.

Willy: I'm not going to pay that man! That goddam Chevrolet, they ought to prohibit the manufacture of that car!

Linda: Well, you owe him three and a half. And odds and ends, comes to around a hundred and twenty dollars by the fifteenth.

Willy: A hundred and twenty dollars! My God, if business don't pick up I don't know what I'm gonna do!

Linda: Well, next week you'll do better.

Willy: Oh, I'll knock 'em dead next week. I'll go to Hartford. I'm very well liked in Hartford. You know, the trouble is, Linda, people don't seem to take to me.

They move onto the forestage.

Linda: Oh, don't be foolish.

Willy: I know it when I walk in. They seem to laugh at me.

Linda: Why? Why would they laugh at you? Don't talk that way, Willy.

Willy moves to the edge of the stage. Linda goes into the kitchen and starts to darn stockings.

Willy: I don't know the reason for it, but they just pass me by. I'm not noticed.

Linda: But you're doing wonderful, dear. You're making seventy to a hundred dollars a week.

Willy: But I gotta be at it ten, twelve hours a day. Other men — I don't know — they do it easier. I don't know why — I can't stop myself — I talk too much. A man oughta come in with a few words. One thing about Charley. He's a man of few words, and they respect him.

Linda: You don't talk too much, you're just lively.

Willy (smiling): Well, I figure, what the hell, life is short, a couple of jokes. *(To himself.)* I joke too much! *(The smile goes.)*

Linda: Why? You're —

Willy: I'm fat. I'm very — foolish to look at, Linda. I didn't tell you, but Christmas time I happened to be calling on F. H. Stewarts, and a salesman I know, as I was going in to see the buyer I heard him say something about — walrus. And I — I cracked him right across the face. I won't take that. I simply will not take that. But they do laugh at me. I know that.

Linda: Darling . . .

Willy: I gotta overcome it. I know I gotta overcome it. I'm not dressing to advantage, maybe.

Linda: Willy, darling, you're the handsomest man in the world —

Willy: Oh, no, Linda.

Linda: To me you are. *(Slight pause.)* The handsomest.

From the darkness is heard the laughter of a woman. Willy doesn't turn to it, but it continues through Linda's lines.

Linda: And the boys, Willy. Few men are idolized by their children the way you are.

Music is heard as behind a scrim, to the left of the house, The Woman, dimly seen, is dressing.

Willy (with great feeling): You're the best there is, Linda, you're a pal, you know that? On the road — on the road I want to grab you sometimes and just kiss the life outa you.

The laughter is loud now, and he moves into a brightening area at the left, where The Woman has come from behind the scrim and is standing, putting on her hat, looking into a "mirror" and laughing.

Willy: 'Cause I get so lonely — especially when business is bad and there's nobody to talk to. I get the feeling that I'll never sell anything again, that I won't make a living for you, or a business, a business for the boys. *(He talks through The Woman's subsiding laughter; The Woman primps at the "mirror.")* There's so much I want to make for —

The Woman: Me? You didn't make me, Willy. I picked you.

Willy (pleased): You picked me?

The Woman (who is quite proper-looking, Willy's age): I did. I've been sitting at that desk watching all the salesmen go by, day in, day out. But you've got such a sense of humor, and we do have such a good time together, don't we?

Willy: Sure, sure. *(He takes her in his arms.)* Why do you have to go now?

The Woman: It's two o'clock . . .

Willy: No, come on in! *(He pulls her.)*

The Woman: . . . my sisters'll be scandalized. When'll you be back?

Willy: Oh, two weeks about. Will you come up again?

The Woman: Sure thing. You do make me laugh. It's good for me. *(She squeezes his arm, kisses him.)* And I think you're a wonderful man.

Willy: You picked me, heh?

The Woman: Sure. Because you're so sweet. And such a kidder.

Willy: Well, I'll see you next time I'm in Boston.

The Woman: I'll put you right through to the buyers.

Willy (slapping her bottom): Right. Well, bottoms up!

The Woman (slaps him gently and laughs): You just kill me, Willy. *(He suddenly grabs her and kisses her roughly.)* You kill me. And thanks for the stockings. I love a lot of stockings. Well, good night.

Willy: Good night. And keep your pores open!

The Woman: Oh, Willy!

> *The Woman bursts out laughing, and Linda's laughter blends in. The Woman disappears into the dark. Now the area at the kitchen table brightens. Linda is sitting where she was at the kitchen table, but now is mending a pair of her silk stockings.*

Linda: You are, Willy. The handsomest man. You've got no reason to feel that—

Willy (coming out of The Woman's dimming area and going over to Linda): I'll make it all up to you, Linda, I'll—

Linda: There's nothing to make up, dear. You're doing fine, better than—

Willy (noticing her mending): What's that?

Linda: Just mending my stockings. They're so expensive—

Willy (angrily, taking them from her): I won't have you mending stockings in this house! Now throw them out!

> *Linda puts the stockings in her pocket.*

Bernard (entering on the run): Where is he? If he doesn't study!

Willy (moving to the forestage, with great agitation): You'll give him the answers!

Bernard: I do, but I can't on a Regents! That's a state exam! They're liable to arrest me!

Willy: Where is he? I'll whip him, I'll whip him!

Linda: And he'd better give back that football, Willy, it's not nice.

Willy: Biff! Where is he? Why is he taking everything?

Linda: He's too rough with the girls, Willy. All the mothers are afraid of him!

Willy: I'll whip him!

Bernard: He's driving the car without a license!

> *The Woman's laugh is heard.*

Willy: Shut up!

Linda: All the mothers—

Willy: Shut up!

Bernard (backing quietly away and out): Mr. Birnbaum says he's stuck up.

Willy: Get outa here!

Bernard: If he doesn't buckle down he'll flunk math! *(He goes off.)*

Linda: He's right, Willy, you've gotta —

Willy (exploding at her): There's nothing the matter with him! You want him to
  be a worm like Bernard? He's got spirit, personality . . .

> *As he speaks, Linda, almost in tears, exits into the living-room. Willy is alone in the
> kitchen, wilting and staring. The leaves are gone. It is night again, and the apart-
> ment houses look down from behind.*

Willy: Loaded with it. Loaded! What is he stealing? He's giving it back, isn't he?
  Why is he stealing? What did I tell him? I never in my life told him anything but decent things.

> *Happy in pajamas has come down the stairs; Willy suddenly becomes aware of
> Happy's presence.*

Happy: Let's go now, come on.

Willy (sitting down at the kitchen table): Huh! Why did she have to wax the floors
  herself? Everytime she waxes the floors she keels over. She knows that!

Happy: Shh! Take it easy. What brought you back tonight?

Willy: I got an awful scare. Nearly hit a kid in Yonkers. God! Why didn't I go to
  Alaska with my brother Ben that time! Ben! That man was a genius, that
  man was success incarnate! What a mistake! He begged me to go.

Happy: Well, there's no use in —

Willy: You guys! There was a man started with the clothes on his back and
  ended up with diamond mines!

Happy: Boy, someday I'd like to know how he did it.

Willy: What's the mystery? The man knew what he wanted and went out and
  got it! Walked into a jungle, and comes out, the age of twenty-one, and
  he's rich! The world is an oyster, but you don't crack it open on a mattress!

Happy: Pop, I told you I'm gonna retire you for life.

Willy: You'll retire me for life on seventy goddam dollars a week? And your
  women and your car and your apartment, and you'll retire me for life!
  Christ's sake, I couldn't get past Yonkers today! Where are you guys, where
  are you? The woods are burning! I can't drive a car!

> *Charley has appeared in the doorway. He is a large man, slow of speech, laconic,
> immovable. In all he says, despite what he says, there is pity, and, now, trepidation.
> He has a robe over pajamas, slippers on his feet. He enters the kitchen.*

Charley: Everything all right?

Happy: Yeah, Charley, everything's . . .

Willy: What's the matter?

Charley: I heard some noise. I thought something happened. Can't we do something about the walls? You sneeze in here, and in my house hats blow off.

Happy: Let's go to bed, Dad. Come on.

> *Charley signals to Happy to go.*

Willy: You go ahead, I'm not tired at the moment.

Happy (to Willy): Take it easy, huh? *(He exits.)*

Willy: What're you doin' up?

Charley (sitting down at the kitchen table opposite Willy): Couldn't sleep good. I had a heartburn.

Willy: Well, you don't know how to eat.

Charley: I eat with my mouth.

Willy: No, you're ignorant. You gotta know about vitamins and things like that.

Charley: Come on, let's shoot. Tire you out a little.

Willy (hesitantly): All right. You got cards?

Charley (taking a deck from his pocket): Yeah, I got them. Someplace. What is it with those vitamins?

Willy (dealing): They build up your bones. Chemistry.

Charley: Yeah, but there's no bones in a heartburn.

Willy: What are you talkin' about? Do you know the first thing about it?

Charley: Don't get insulted.

Willy: Don't talk about something you don't know anything about.

> *They are playing. Pause.*

Charley: What're you doin' home?

Willy: A little trouble with the car.

Charley: Oh. (*Pause.*) I'd like to take a trip to California.

Willy: Don't say.

Charley: You want a job?

Willy: I got a job, I told you that. (*After a slight pause.*) What the hell are you offering me a job for?

Charley: Don't get insulted.

Willy: Don't insult me.

Charley: I don't see no sense in it. You don't have to go on this way.

Willy: I got a good job. (*Slight pause.*) What do you keep comin' in here for?

Charley: You want me to go?

Willy (after a pause, withering): I can't understand it. He's going back to Texas again. What the hell is that?

Charley: Let him go.

Willy: I got nothin' to give him, Charley, I'm clean, I'm clean.

Charley: He won't starve. None a them starve. Forget about him.

Willy: Then what have I got to remember?

Charley: You take it too hard. To hell with it. When a deposit bottle is broken you don't get your nickel back.

Willy: That's easy enough for you to say.

Charley: That ain't easy for me to say.

Willy: Did you see the ceiling I put up in the living-room?

Charley: Yeah, that's a piece of work. To put up a ceiling is a mystery to me. How do you do it?

Willy: What's the difference?

Charley: Well, talk about it.

Willy: You gonna put up a ceiling?

Charley: How could I put up a ceiling?

Willy: Then what the hell are you bothering me for?

Charley: You're insulted again.

Willy: A man who can't handle tools is not a man. You're disgusting.

Charley: Don't call me disgusting, Willy.

Uncle Ben, carrying a valise and an umbrella, enters the forestage from around the right corner of the house. He is a stolid man, in his sixties, with a mustache and an authoritative air. He is utterly certain of his destiny, and there is an aura of far places about him. He enters exactly as Willy speaks.

Willy: I'm getting awfully tired, Ben.

Ben's music is heard. Ben looks around at everything.

Charley: Good, keep playing; you'll sleep better. Did you call me Ben?

Ben looks at his watch.

Willy: That's funny. For a second there you reminded me of my brother Ben.

Ben: I only have a few minutes. *(He strolls, inspecting the place. Willy and Charley continue playing.)*

Charley: You never heard from him again, heh? Since that time?

Willy: Didn't Linda tell you? Couple of weeks ago we got a letter from his wife in Africa. He died.

Charley: That so.

Ben (chuckling): So this is Brooklyn, eh?

Charley: Maybe you're in for some of his money.

Willy: Naa, he had seven sons. There's just one opportunity I had with that man . . .

Ben: I must make a train, William. There are several properties I'm looking at in Alaska.

Willy: Sure, sure! If I'd gone with him to Alaska that time, everything would've been totally different.

Charley: Go on, you'd froze to death up there.

Willy: What're you talking about?

Ben: Opportunity is tremendous in Alaska, William. Surprised you're not up there.

Willy: Sure, tremendous.

Charley: Heh?

Willy: There was the only man I ever met who knew the answers.

Charley: Who?

Ben: How are you all?

Willy (taking a pot, smiling): Fine, fine.

Charley: Pretty sharp tonight.

Ben: Is mother living with you?

Willy: No, she died a long time ago.

Charley: Who?

Ben: That's too bad. Fine specimen of a lady, Mother.

Willy (to Charley): Heh?

Ben: I'd hoped to see the old girl.

Charley: Who died?

Ben: Heard anything from Father, have you?

Willy (unnerved): What do you mean, who died?

Charley (taking a pot): What're you talkin' about?

Ben (looking at his watch): William, it's half-past eight!

Willy (as though to dispel his confusion he angrily stops Charley's hand): That's my build!

Charley: I put the ace —

Willy: If you don't know how to play the game I'm not gonna throw my money away on you!

Charley (rising): It was my ace, for God's sake!

Willy: I'm through, I'm through!

Ben: When did Mother die?

Willy: Long ago. Since the beginning you never knew how to play cards.

Charley (picks up the cards and goes to the door): All right! Next time I'll bring a deck with five aces.

Willy: I don't play that kind of game!

Charley (turning to him): You ought to be ashamed of yourself!

Willy: Yeah?

Charley: Yeah! *(He goes out.)*

Willy (slamming the door after him): Ignoramus!

Ben (as Willy comes toward him through the wall-line of the kitchen): So you're William.

Willy (shaking Ben's hand): Ben! I've been waiting for you so long! What's the answer? How did you do it?

Ben: Oh, there's a story in that.

Linda enters the forestage, as of old, carrying the wash basket.

Linda: Is this Ben?

Ben (gallantly): How do you do, my dear.

Linda: Where've you been all these years? Willy's always wondered why you—

Willy (pulling Ben away from her impatiently): Where is Dad? Didn't you follow him? How did you get started?

Ben: Well, I don't know how much you remember.

Willy: Well, I was just a baby, of course, only three or four years old—

Ben: Three years and eleven months.

Willy: What a memory, Ben!

Ben: I have many enterprises, William, and I have never kept books.

Willy: I remember I was sitting under the wagon in—was it Nebraska?

Ben: It was South Dakota, and I gave you a bunch of wild flowers.

Willy: I remember you walking away down some open road.

Ben (laughing): I was going to find Father in Alaska.

Willy: Where is he?

Ben: At that age I had a very faulty view of geography, William. I discovered after a few days that I was heading due south, so instead of Alaska, I ended up in Africa.

Linda: Africa!

Willy: The Gold Coast!

Ben: Principally diamond mines.

Linda: Diamond mines!

Ben: Yes, my dear. But I've only a few minutes—

Willy: No! Boys! Boys! *(Young Biff and Happy appear.)* Listen to this. This is your Uncle Ben, a great man! Tell my boys, Ben!

Ben: Why, boys, when I was seventeen I walked into the jungle, and when I was twenty-one I walked out. *(He laughs.)* And by God I was rich.

Willy (to the boys): You see what I been talking about? The greatest things can happen!

Ben (glancing at his watch): I have an appointment in Ketchikan Tuesday week.

Willy: No, Ben! Please tell about Dad. I want my boys to hear. I want them to know the kind of stock they spring from. All I remember is a man with a big beard, and I was in Mamma's lap, sitting around a fire, and some kind of high music.

Ben: His flute. He played the flute.

Willy: Sure, the flute, that's right!

New music is heard, a high, rollicking tune.

Ben: Father was a very great and a very wild-hearted man. We would start in Boston, and he'd toss the whole family into the wagon, and then he'd drive the team right across the country; through Ohio, and Indiana, Michigan, Illinois, and all the Western states. And we'd stop in the towns and sell the flutes that he'd made on the way. Great inventor, Father. With one gadget he made more in a week than a man like you could make in a lifetime.

Willy: That's just the way I'm bringing them up, Ben — rugged, well liked, all-around.

Ben: Yeah? *(To Biff.)* Hit that, boy — hard as you can. *(He pounds his stomach.)*

Biff: Oh, no, sir!

Ben (taking boxing stance): Come on, get to me. *(He laughs.)*

Willy: Go to it, Biff! Go ahead, show him!

Biff: Okay! *(He cocks his fists and starts in.)*

Linda (to Willy): Why must he fight, dear?

Ben (sparring with Biff): Good boy! Good boy!

Willy: How's that, Ben, heh?

Happy: Give him the left, Biff!

Linda: Why are you fighting?

Ben: Good boy! *(Suddenly comes in, trips Biff, and stands over him, the point of his umbrella poised over Biff's eye.)*

Linda: Look out, Biff!

Biff: Gee!

Ben (patting Biff's knee): Never fight fair with a stranger, boy. You'll never get out of the jungle that way. *(Taking Linda's hand and bowing):* It was an honor and a pleasure to meet you, Linda.

Linda (withdrawing her hand coldly, frightened): Have a nice — trip.

Ben (to Willy): And good luck with your — what do you do?

Willy: Selling.

Ben: Yes. Well . . . *(He raises his hand in farewell to all.)*

Willy: No, Ben, I don't want you to think . . . *(He takes Ben's arm to show him.)* It's Brooklyn, I know, but we hunt too.

Ben: Really, now.

Willy: Oh, sure, there's snakes and rabbits and — that's why I moved out here. Why, Biff can fell any one of these trees in no time! Boys! Go right over to where they're building the apartment house and get some sand. We're gonna rebuild the entire front stoop now! Watch this, Ben!

Biff: Yes, sir! On the double, Hap!

Happy (as he and Biff run off): I lost weight, Pop, you notice?

Charley enters in knickers, even before the boys are gone.

Charley: Listen, if they steal any more from that building the watchman'll put the cops on them!

Linda (to Willy): Don't let Biff . . .

> *Ben laughs lustily.*

Willy: You shoulda seen the lumber they brought home last week. At least a dozen six-by-tens worth all kinds a money.

Charley: Listen, if that watchman—

Willy: I gave them hell, understand. But I got a couple of fearless characters there.

Charley: Willy, the jails are full of fearless characters.

Ben (clapping Willy on the back, with a laugh at Charley): And the stock exchange, friend!

Willy (joining in Ben's laughter): Where are the rest of your pants?

Charley: My wife bought them.

Willy: Now all you need is a golf club and you can go upstairs and go to sleep. *(To Ben).* Great athlete! Between him and his son Bernard they can't hammer a nail!

Bernard (rushing in): The watchman's chasing Biff!

Willy (angrily): Shut up! He's not stealing anything!

Linda (alarmed, hurrying off left): Where is he? Biff, dear! *(She exits.)*

Willy (moving toward the left, away from Ben): There's nothing wrong. What's the matter with you?

Ben: Nervy boy. Good!

Willy (laughing): Oh, nerves of iron, that Biff!

Charley: Don't know what it is. My New England man comes back and he's bleedin', they murdered him up there.

Willy: It's contacts, Charley, I got important contacts!

Charley (sarcastically): Glad to hear it, Willy. Come in later, we'll shoot a little casino. I'll take some of your Portland money. *(He laughs at Willy and exits.)*

Willy (turning to Ben): Business is bad, it's murderous. But not for me, of course.

Ben: I'll stop by on my way back to Africa.

Willy (longingly): Can't you stay a few days? You're just what I need, Ben, because I—I have a fine position here, but I—well, Dad left when I was such a baby and I never had a chance to talk to him and I still feel—kind of temporary about myself.

Ben: I'll be late for my train.

> *They are at opposite ends of the stage.*

Willy: Ben, my boys—can't we talk? They'd go into the jaws of hell for me, see, but I—

Ben: William, you're being first-rate with your boys. Outstanding, manly chaps!

Willy (hanging on to his words): Oh, Ben, that's good to hear! Because sometimes I'm afraid that I'm not teaching them the right kind of—Ben, how should I teach them?

Ben (giving great weight to each word, and with a certain vicious audacity): William, when I walked into the jungle, I was seventeen. When I walked out I was twenty-one. And, by God, I was rich! *(He goes off into darkness around the right corner of the house.)*

Willy: . . . was rich! That's just the spirit I want to imbue them with! To walk into a jungle! I was right! I was right! I was right!

Ben is gone, but Willy is still speaking to him as Linda, in nightgown and robe, enters the kitchen, glances around for Willy, then goes to the door of the house, looks out, and sees him. Comes down to his left. He looks at her.

Linda: Willy, dear? Willy?

Willy: I was right!

Linda: Did you have some cheese? *(He can't answer.)* It's very late, darling. Come to bed, heh?

Willy (looking straight up): Gotta break your neck to see a star in this yard.

Linda: You coming in?

Willy: Whatever happened to that diamond watch fob? Remember? When Ben came from Africa that time? Didn't he give me a watch fob with a diamond in it?

Linda: You pawned it, dear. Twelve, thirteen years ago. For Biff's radio correspondence course.

Willy: Gee, that was a beautiful thing. I'll take a walk.

Linda: But you're in your slippers.

Willy (starting to go around the house at the left): I was right! I was! *(Half to Linda, as he goes, shaking his head.)* What a man! There was a man worth talking to. I was right!

Linda (calling after Willy): But in your slippers, Willy!

Willy is almost gone when Biff, in his pajamas, comes down the stairs and enters the kitchen.

Biff: What is he doing out there?

Linda: Sh!

Biff: God Almighty, Mom, how long has he been doing this?

Linda: Don't, he'll hear you.

Biff: What the hell is the matter with him?

Linda: It'll pass by morning.

Biff: Shouldn't we do anything?

Linda: Oh, my dear, you should do a lot of things, but there's nothing to do, so go to sleep.

Happy comes down the stairs and sits on the steps.

Happy: I never heard him so loud, Mom.

Linda: Well, come around more often; you'll hear him. *(She sits down at the table and mends the lining of Willy's jacket.)*

Biff: Why didn't you ever write me about this, Mom?

Linda: How would I write to you? For over three months you had no address.

Biff: I was on the move. But you know I thought of you all the time. You know that, don't you, pal?

Linda: I know, dear, I know. But he likes to have a letter. Just to know that there's still a possibility for better things.

Biff: He's not like this all the time, is he?

Linda: It's when you come home he's always the worst.

Biff: When I come home?

Linda: When you write you're coming, he's all smiles, and talks about the future, and—he's just wonderful. And then the closer you seem to come, the more shaky he gets, and then, by the time you get here, he's arguing, and he seems angry at you. I think it's just that maybe he can't bring himself to — to open up to you. Why are you so hateful to each other? Why is that?

Biff (evasively): I'm not hateful, Mom.

Linda: But you no sooner come in the door than you're fighting!

Biff: I don't know why. I mean to change. I'm tryin', Mom, you understand?

Linda: Are you home to stay now?

Biff: I don't know. I want to look around, see what's doin'.

Linda: Biff, you can't look around all your life, can you?

Biff: I just can't take hold, Mom. I can't take hold of some kind of a life.

Linda: Biff, a man is not a bird, to come and go with the springtime.

Biff: Your hair . . . (He touches her hair.) Your hair got so gray.

Linda: Oh, it's been gray since you were in high school. I just stopped dyeing it, that's all.

Biff: Dye it again, will ya? I don't want my pal looking old. (He smiles.)

Linda: You're such a boy! You think you can go away for a year and . . . You've got to get it into your head now that one day you'll knock on this door and there'll be strange people here —

Biff: What are you talking about? You're not even sixty, Mom.

Linda: But what about your father?

Biff (lamely): Well, I meant him too.

Happy: He admires Pop.

Linda: Biff, dear, if you don't have any feeling for him, then you can't have any feeling for me.

Biff: Sure I can, Mom.

Linda: No. You can't just come to see me, because I love him. (With a threat, but only a threat, of tears.) He's the dearest man in the world to me, and I won't have anyone making him feel unwanted and low and blue. You've got to make up your mind now, darling, there's no leeway any more. Either he's your father and you pay him that respect, or else you're not to come here. I know he's not easy to get along with — nobody knows that better than me — but . . .

Willy (from the left, with a laugh): Hey, hey, Biffo!

Biff (starting to go out after Willy): What the hell is the matter with him? (Happy stops him.)

Linda: Don't — don't go near him!

Biff: Stop making excuses for him! He always, always wiped the floor with you. Never had an ounce of respect for you.

Happy: He's always had respect for —

Biff: What the hell do you know about it?

Happy (surlily): Just don't call him crazy!

Biff: He's got no character — Charley wouldn't do this. Not in his own house — spewing out that vomit from his mind.

Happy: Charley never had to cope with what he's got to.

Biff: People are worse off than Willy Loman. Believe me, I've seen them!

Linda: Then make Charley your father, Biff. You can't do that, can you? I don't say he's a great man. Willy Loman never made a lot of money. His name was never in the paper. He's not the finest character that ever lived. But he's a human being, and a terrible thing is happening to him. So attention must be paid. He's not to be allowed to fall into his grave like an old dog. Attention, attention must be finally paid to such a person. You called him crazy —

Biff: I didn't mean —

Linda: No, a lot of people think he's lost his — balance. But you don't have to be very smart to know what his trouble is. The man is exhausted.

Happy: Sure!

Linda: A small man can be just as exhausted as a great man. He works for a company thirty-six years this March, opens up unheard-of territories to their trademark, and now in his old age they take his salary away.

Happy (indignantly): I didn't know that, Mom.

Linda: You never asked, my dear! Now that you get your spending money someplace else you don't trouble your mind with him.

Happy: But I gave you money last —

Linda: Christmas time, fifty dollars! To fix the hot water it cost ninety-seven fifty! For five weeks he's been on straight commission, like a beginner, an unknown!

Biff: Those ungrateful bastards!

Linda: Are they any worse than his sons? When he brought them business, when he was young, they were glad to see him. But now his old friends, the old buyers that loved him so and always found some order to hand him in a pinch — they're all dead, retired. He used to be able to make six, seven calls a day in Boston. Now he takes his valises out of the car and puts them back and takes them out again and he's exhausted. Instead of walking he talks now. He drives seven hundred miles, and when he gets there no one knows him any more, no one welcomes him. And what goes through a man's mind, driving seven hundred miles home without having earned a cent? Why shouldn't he talk to himself? Why? When he has to go to Charley and borrow fifty dollars a week and pretend to me that it's his pay? How long can that go on? How long? You see what I'm sitting here and waiting for? And you tell me he has no character? The man who never worked a day but for your benefit? When does he get the medal for that? Is this his reward — to turn around at the age of sixty-three and find his sons, who he loved better than his life, one a philandering bum —

Happy: Mom!

Linda: That's all you are, my baby! *(To Biff.)* And you! What happened to the love you had for him? You were such pals! How you used to talk to him on the phone every night! How lonely he was till he could come home to you!

Biff: All right, Mom. I'll live here in my room, and I'll get a job. I'll keep away from him, that's all.

Linda: No, Biff. You can't stay here and fight all the time.

Biff: He threw me out of this house, remember that.

Linda: Why did he do that? I never knew why.

Biff: Because I know he's a fake and he doesn't like anybody around who knows!

Linda: Why a fake? In what way? What do you mean?

Biff: Just don't lay it all at my feet. It's between me and him — that's all I have to say. I'll chip in from now on. He'll settle for half my pay check. He'll be all right. I'm going to bed. *(He starts for the stairs.)*

Linda: He won't be all right.

Biff (turning on the stairs, furiously): I hate this city and I'll stay here. Now what do you want?

Linda: He's dying, Biff.

Happy turns quickly to her, shocked.

Biff (after a pause): Why is he dying?
Linda: He's been trying to kill himself.
Biff (with great horror): How?
Linda: I live from day to day.
Biff: What're you talking about?
Linda: Remember I wrote you that he smashed up the car again? In February?
Biff: Well?
Linda: The insurance inspector came. He said that they have evidence. That all these accidents in the last year — weren't — weren't — accidents.
Happy: How can they tell that? That's a lie.
Linda: It seems there's a woman . . . *(She takes a breath as):*
    Biff (sharply but contained): What woman?
    Linda (simultaneously): . . . and this woman . . .
Linda: What?
Biff: Nothing. Go ahead.
Linda: What did you say?
Biff: Nothing. I just said what woman?
Happy: What about her?
Linda: Well, it seems she was walking down the road and saw his car. She says that he wasn't driving fast at all, and that he didn't skid. She says he came to that little bridge, and then deliberately smashed into the railing, and it was only the shallowness of the water that saved him.
Biff: Oh, no, he probably just fell asleep again.
Linda: I don't think he fell asleep.
Biff: Why not?
Linda: Last month . . . *(With great difficulty.)* Oh, boys, it's so hard to say a thing like this! He's just a big stupid man to you, but I tell you there's more good in him than in many other people. *(She chokes, wipes her eyes.)* I was looking for a fuse. The lights blew out, and I went down the cellar. And behind the fuse box — it happened to fall out — was a length of rubber pipe — just short.
Happy: No kidding?
Linda: There's a little attachment on the end of it. I knew right away. And sure enough, on the bottom of the water heater there's a new little nipple on the gas pipe.
Happy (angrily): That — jerk.
Biff: Did you have it taken off?
Linda: I'm — I'm ashamed to. How can I mention it to him? Every day I go down and take away that little rubber pipe. But, when he comes home, I put it back where it was. How can I insult him that way? I don't know what to do. I live from day to day, boys. I tell you, I know every thought in his mind. It sounds so old-fashioned and silly, but I tell you he put his whole life into you and you've turned your backs on him. *(She is bent over in chair, weeping, her face in her hands.)* Biff, I swear to God! Biff, his life is in your hands!
Happy (to Biff): How do you like that damned fool!
Biff (kissing her): All right, pal, all right. It's all settled now. I've been remiss. I know that, Mom. But now I'll stay, and I swear to you, I'll apply myself.

(Kneeling in front of her, in a fever of self-reproach.) It's just—you see, Mom, I don't fit in business. Not that I won't try. I'll try, and I'll make good.

Happy: Sure you will. The trouble with you in business was you never tried to please people.

Biff: I know, I—

Happy: Like when you worked for Harrison's. Bob Harrison said you were tops, and then you go and do some damn fool thing like whistling whole songs in the elevator like a comedian.

Biff (against Happy): So what? I like to whistle sometimes.

Happy: You don't raise a guy to a responsible job who whistles in the elevator!

Linda: Well, don't argue about it now.

Happy: Like when you'd go off and swim in the middle of the day instead of taking the line around.

Biff (his resentment rising): Well, don't you run off? You take off sometimes, don't you? On a nice summer day?

Happy: Yeah, but I cover myself!

Linda: Boys!

Happy: If I'm going to take a fade the boss can call any number where I'm supposed to be and they'll swear to him that I just left. I'll tell you something that I hate to say, Biff, but in the business world some of them think you're crazy.

Biff (angered): Screw the business world!

Happy: All right, screw it! Great, but cover yourself!

Linda: Hap, Hap!

Biff: I don't care what they think! They've laughed at Dad for years, and you know why? Because we don't belong in this nuthouse of a city! We should be mixing cement on some open plain, or—or carpenters. A carpenter is allowed to whistle!

Willy walks in from the entrance of the house, at left.

Willy: Even your grandfather was better than a carpenter. *(Pause. They watch him.)* You never grew up. Bernard does not whistle in the elevator, I assure you.

Biff (as though to laugh Willy out of it): Yeah, but you do, Pop.

Willy: I never in my life whistled in an elevator! And who in the business world thinks I'm crazy?

Biff: I didn't mean it like that, Pop. Now don't make a whole thing out of it, will ya?

Willy: Go back to the West! Be a carpenter, a cowboy, enjoy yourself!

Linda: Willy, he was just saying—

Willy: I heard what he said!

Happy (trying to quiet Willy): Hey, Pop, come on now . . .

Willy (continuing over Happy's line): They laugh at me, heh? Go to Filene's, go to the Hub, go to Slattery's, Boston. Call out the name Willy Loman and see what happens! Big shot!

Biff: All right, Pop.

Willy: Big!

Biff: All right!

Willy: Why do you always insult me?

Biff: I didn't say a word. *(To Linda.)* Did I say a word?

Linda: He didn't say anything, Willy.

Willy (going to the doorway of the living-room): All right, good night, good night.

Linda: Willy, dear, he just decided . . .

Willy (to Biff): If you get tired hanging around tomorrow, paint the ceiling I put up in the living-room.

Biff: I'm leaving early tomorrow.

Happy: He's going to see Bill Oliver, Pop.

Willy (interestedly): Oliver? For what?

Biff (with reserve, but trying, trying): He always said he'd stake me. I'd like to go into business, so maybe I can take him up on it.

Linda: Isn't that wonderful?

Willy: Don't interrupt. What's wonderful about it? There's fifty men in the City of New York who'd stake him. *(To Biff.)* Sporting goods?

Biff: I guess so. I know something about it and —

Willy: He knows something about it! You know sporting goods better than Spalding, for God's sake! How much is he giving you?

Biff: I don't know, I didn't even see him yet, but —

Willy: Then what're you talkin' about?

Biff (getting angry): Well, all I said was I'm gonna see him, that's all!

Willy (turning away): Ah, you're counting your chickens again.

Biff (starting left for the stairs): Oh, Jesus, I'm going to sleep!

Willy (calling after him): Don't curse in this house!

Biff (turning): Since when did you get so clean?

Happy (trying to stop them): Wait a . . .

Willy: Don't use that language to me! I won't have it!

Happy (grabbing Biff, shouts): Wait a minute! I got an idea. I got a feasible idea. Come here, Biff, let's talk this over now, let's talk some sense here. When I was down in Florida last time, I thought of a great idea to sell sporting goods. It just came back to me. You and I, Biff — we have a line, the Loman Line. We train a couple of weeks, and put on a couple of exhibitions, see?

Willy: That's an idea!

Happy: Wait! We form two basketball teams, see? Two water-polo teams. We play each other. It's a million dollars' worth of publicity. Two brothers, see? The Loman Brothers. Displays in the Royal Palms — all the hotels. And banners over the ring and the basketball court: "Loman Brothers." Baby, we could sell sporting goods!

Willy: That is a one-million-dollar idea!

Linda: Marvelous!

Biff: I'm in great shape as far as that's concerned.

Happy: And the beauty of it is, Biff, it wouldn't be like a business. We'd be out playin' ball again . . .

Biff (enthused): Yeah, that's . . .

Willy: Million-dollar . . .

Happy: And you wouldn't get fed up with it, Biff. It'd be the family again. There'd be the old honor, and comradeship, and if you wanted to go off for a swim or somethin' — well, you'd do it! Without some smart cooky gettin' up ahead of you!

Willy: Lick the world! You guys together could absolutely lick the civilized world.

Biff: I'll see Oliver tomorrow. Hap, if we could work that out . . .

Linda: Maybe things are beginning to —

Willy (wildly enthused, to Linda): Stop interrupting! *(To Biff.)* But don't wear sport jacket and slacks when you see Oliver.

Biff: No, I'll—

Willy: A business suit, and talk as little as possible, and don't crack any jokes.

Biff: He did like me. Always liked me.

Linda: He loved you!

Willy (to Linda): Will you stop! *(To Biff.)* Walk in very serious. You are not applying for a boy's job. Money is to pass. Be quiet, fine, and serious. Everybody likes a kidder, but nobody lends him money.

Happy: I'll try to get some myself, Biff. I'm sure I can.

Willy: I see great things for you kids, I think your troubles are over. But remember, start big and you'll end big. Ask for fifteen. How much you gonna ask for?

Biff: Gee, I don't know—

Willy: And don't say "Gee." "Gee" is a boy's word. A man walking in for fifteen thousand dollars does not say "Gee!"

Biff: Ten, I think, would be top though.

Willy: Don't be so modest. You always started too low. Walk in with a big laugh. Don't look worried. Start off with a couple of your good stories to lighten things up. It's not what you say, it's how you say it—because personality always wins the day.

Linda: Oliver always thought the highest of him—

Willy: Will you let me talk?

Biff: Don't yell at her, Pop, will ya?

Willy (angrily): I was talking, wasn't I?

Biff: I don't like you yelling at her all the time, and I'm tellin' you, that's all.

Willy: What're you, takin' over this house?

Linda: Willy—

Willy (turning on her): Don't take his side all the time, goddammit!

Biff (furiously): Stop yelling at her!

Willy (suddenly pulling on his cheek, beaten down, guilt ridden): Give my best to Bill Oliver—he may remember me. *(He exits through the living-room doorway.)*

Linda (her voice subdued): What'd you have to start that for? *(Biff turns away.)* You see how sweet he was as soon as you talked hopefully? *(She goes over to Biff.)* Come up and say good night to him. Don't let him go to bed that way.

Happy: Come on, Biff, let's buck him up.

Linda: Please, dear. Just say good night. It takes so little to make him happy. Come. *(She goes through the living-room doorway, calling upstairs from within the living-room.)* Your pajamas are hanging in the bathroom, Willy!

Happy (looking toward where Linda went out): What a woman! They broke the mold when they made her. You know that, Biff?

Biff: He's off salary. My God, working on commission!

Happy: Well, let's face it: he's no hot-shot selling man. Except that sometimes, you have to admit, he's a sweet personality.

Biff (deciding): Lend me ten bucks, will ya? I want to buy some new ties.

Happy: I'll take you to a place I know. Beautiful stuff. Wear one of my striped shirts tomorrow.

Biff: She got gray. Mom got awful old. Gee, I'm gonna go in to Oliver tomorrow and knock him for a—

Happy: Come on up. Tell that to Dad. Let's give him a whirl. Come on.

Biff (steamed up): You know, with ten thousand bucks, boy!

Happy (as they go into the living-room): That's the talk, Biff, that's the first time I've heard the old confidence out of you! *(From within the living-room, fading off.)* You're gonna live with me, kid, and any babe you want just say the word . . . *(The last lines are hardly heard. They are mounting the stairs to their parents' bedroom.)*

Linda (entering her bedroom and addressing Willy, who is in the bathroom. She is straightening the bed for him): Can you do anything about the shower? It drips.

Willy (from the bathroom): All of a sudden everything falls to pieces! Goddam plumbing, oughta be sued, those people. I hardly finished putting it in and the thing . . . *(His words rumble off.)*

Linda: I'm just wondering if Oliver will remember him. You think he might?

Willy (coming out of the bathroom in his pajamas): Remember him? What's the matter with you, you crazy? If he'd've stayed with Oliver he'd be on top by now! Wait'll Oliver gets a look at him. You don't know the average caliber any more. The average young man today — *(he is getting into bed)* — is got a caliber of zero. Greatest thing in the world for him was to bum around.

Biff and Happy enter the bedroom. Slight pause.

Willy (stops short, looking at Biff): Glad to hear it, boy.

Happy: He wanted to say good night to you, sport.

Willy (to Biff): Yeah. Knock him dead, boy. What'd you want to tell me?

Biff: Just take it easy, Pop. Good night. *(He turns to go.)*

Willy (unable to resist): And if anything falls off the desk while you're talking to him — like a package or something — don't you pick it up. They have office boys for that.

Linda: I'll make a big breakfast —

Willy: Will you let me finish? *(To Biff.)* Tell him you were in the business in the West. Not farm work.

Biff: All right, Dad.

Linda: I think everything —

Willy (going right through her speech): And don't undersell yourself. No less than fifteen thousand dollars.

Biff (unable to bear him): Okay. Good night, Mom. *(He starts moving.)*

Willy: Because you got a greatness in you, Biff, remember that. You got all kinds a greatness . . . *(He lies back, exhausted. Biff walks out.)*

Linda (calling after Biff): Sleep well, darling!

Happy: I'm gonna get married, Mom. I wanted to tell you.

Linda: Go to sleep, dear.

Happy (going): I just wanted to tell you.

Willy: Keep up the good work. *(Happy exits.)* God . . . remember that Ebbets Field game? The championship of the city?

Linda: Just rest. Should I sing to you?

Willy: Yeah. Sing to me. *(Linda hums a soft lullaby.)* When that team came out — he was the tallest, remember?

Linda: Oh, yes. And in gold.

Biff enters the darkened kitchen, takes a cigarette, and leaves the house. He comes downstage into a golden pool of light. He smokes, staring at the night.

Willy: Like a young god. Hercules — something like that. And the sun, the sun all around him. Remember how he waved to me? Right up from the field, with the representatives of three colleges standing by? And the buyers I brought, and the cheers when he came out — Loman, Loman, Loman! God Almighty, he'll be great yet. A star like that, magnificent, can never really fade away!

The light on Willy is fading. The gas heater begins to glow through the kitchen wall, near the stairs, a blue flame beneath red coils.

Linda (timidly): Willy dear, what has he got against you?
Willy: I'm so tired. Don't talk any more.

Biff slowly returns to the kitchen. He stops, stares toward the heater.

Linda: Will you ask Howard to let you work in New York?
Willy: First thing in the morning. Everything'll be all right.

Biff reaches behind the heater and draws out a length of rubber tubing. He is horrified and turns his head toward Willy's room, still dimly lit, from which the strains of Linda's desperate but monotonous humming rise.

Willy (staring through the window into the moonlight): Gee, look at the moon moving between the buildings!

Biff wraps the tubing around his hand and quickly goes up the stairs.

Curtain

ACT II

Music is heard, gay and bright. The curtain rises as the music fades away. Willy, in shirt sleeves, is sitting at the kitchen table, sipping coffee, his hat in his lap. Linda is filling his cup when she can.

Willy: Wonderful coffee. Meal in itself.
Linda: Can I make you some eggs?
Willy: No. Take a breath.
Linda: You look so rested, dear.
Willy: I slept like a dead one. First time in months. Imagine, sleeping till ten on a Tuesday morning. Boys left nice and early, heh?
Linda: They were out of here by eight o'clock.
Willy: Good work!
Linda: It was so thrilling to see them leaving together. I can't get over the shaving lotion in this house!
Willy (smiling): Mmm —
Linda: Biff was very changed this morning. His whole attitude seemed to be hopeful. He couldn't wait to get downtown to see Oliver.
Willy: He's heading for a change. There's no question, there simply are certain men that take longer to get — solidified. How did he dress?
Linda: His blue suit. He's so handsome in that suit. He could be a — anything in that suit!

Willy gets up from the table. Linda holds his jacket for him.

Willy: There's no question, no question at all. Gee, on the way home tonight I'd like to buy some seeds.

Linda (laughing): That'd be wonderful. But not enough sun gets back there. Nothing'll grow any more.

Willy: You wait, kid, before it's all over we're gonna get a little place out in the country, and I'll raise some vegetables, a couple of chickens . . .

Linda: You'll do it yet, dear.

Willy walks out of his jacket. Linda follows him.

Willy: And they'll get married, and come for a weekend. I'd build a little guest house. 'Cause I got so many fine tools, all I'd need would be a little lumber and some peace of mind.

Linda (joyfully): I sewed the lining . . .

Willy: I could build two guest houses, so they'd both come. Did he decide how much he's going to ask Oliver for?

Linda (getting him into the jacket): He didn't mention it, but I imagine ten or fifteen thousand. You going to talk to Howard today?

Willy: Yeah. I'll put it to him straight and simple. He'll just have to take me off the road.

Linda: And Willy, don't forget to ask for a little advance, because we've got the insurance premium. It's the grace period now.

Willy: That's a hundred . . . ?

Linda: A hundred and eight, sixty-eight. Because we're a little short again.

Willy: Why are we short?

Linda: Well, you had the motor job on the car . . .

Willy: That goddam Studebaker!

Linda: And you got one more payment on the refrigerator . . .

Willy: But it just broke again!

Linda: Well, it's old, dear.

Willy: I told you we should've bought a well-advertised machine. Charley bought a General Electric and it's twenty years old and it's still good, that son-of-a-bitch.

Linda: But, Willy—

Willy: Whoever heard of a Hastings refrigerator? Once in my life I would like to own something outright before it's broken! I'm always in a race with the junkyard! I just finished paying for the car and it's on its last legs. The refrigerator consumes belts like a goddam maniac. They time those things. They time them so when you finally paid for them, they're used up.

Linda (buttoning up his jacket as he unbuttons it): All told, about two hundred dollars would carry us, dear. But that includes the last payment on the mortgage. After this payment, Willy, the house belongs to us.

Willy: It's twenty-five years!

Linda: Biff was nine years old when we bought it.

Willy: Well, that's a great thing. To weather a twenty-five year mortgage is—

Linda: It's an accomplishment.

Willy: All the cement, the lumber, the reconstruction I put in this house! There ain't a crack to be found in it any more.

Linda: Well, it served its purpose.

Willy: What purpose? Some stranger'll come along, move in, and that's that. If only Biff would take this house, and raise a family . . . *(He starts to go.)* Good-by, I'm late.

Linda (suddenly remembering): Oh, I forgot! You're supposed to meet them for dinner.

Willy: Me?

Linda: At Frank's Chop House on Forty-eighth near Sixth Avenue.

Willy: Is that so! How about you?

Linda: No, just the three of you. They're gonna blow you to a big meal!

Willy: Don't say! Who thought of that?

Linda: Biff came to me this morning, Willy, and he said, "Tell Dad, we want to blow him to a big meal." Be there six o'clock. You and your two boys are going to have dinner.

Willy: Gee whiz! That's really somethin'. I'm gonna knock Howard for a loop, kid. I'll get an advance, and I'll come home with a New York job. Goddammit, now I'm gonna do it!

Linda: Oh, that's the spirit, Willy!

Willy: I will never get behind a wheel the rest of my life!

Linda: It's changing, Willy, I can feel it changing!

Willy: Beyond a question. G'by, I'm late. *(He starts to go again.)*

Linda (calling after him as she runs to the kitchen table for a handkerchief): You got your glasses?

Willy (feels for them, then comes back in): Yeah, yeah, got my glasses.

Linda (giving him the handkerchief): And a handkerchief.

Willy: Yeah, handkerchief.

Linda: And your saccharine?

Willy: Yeah, my saccharine.

Linda: Be careful on the subway stairs.

   She kisses him, and a silk stocking is seen hanging from her hand. Willy notices it.

Willy: Will you stop mending stockings? At least while I'm in the house. It gets me nervous. I can't tell you. Please.

   Linda hides the stocking in her hand as she follows Willy across the forestage in front of the house.

Linda: Remember, Frank's Chop House.

Willy (passing the apron): Maybe beets would grow out there.

Linda (laughing): But you tried so many times.

Willy: Yeah. Well, don't work hard today. *(He disappears around the right corner of the house.)*

Linda: Be careful!

   As Willy vanishes, Linda waves to him. Suddenly the phone rings. She runs across the stage and into the kitchen and lifts it.

Linda: Hello? Oh, Biff! I'm so glad you called, I just . . . Yes, sure, I just told him. Yes, he'll be there for dinner at six o'clock, I didn't forget. Listen, I was just dying to tell you. You know that little rubber pipe I told you about? That he connected to the gas heater? I finally decided to go down the cellar this morning and take it away and destroy it. But it's gone! Imagine? He took it away himself, it isn't there! *(She listens.)* When? Oh, then you took it. Oh — nothing, it's just that I'd hoped he'd taken it away himself. Oh,

I'm not worried, darling, because this morning he left in such high spirits, it was like the old days! I'm not afraid any more. Did Mr. Oliver see you? . . . Well, you wait there then. And make a nice impression on him, darling. Just don't perspire too much before you see him. And have a nice time with Dad. He may have big news too! . . . That's right, a New York job. And be sweet to him tonight, dear. Be loving to him. Because he's only a little boat looking for a harbor. *(She is trembling with sorrow and joy.)* Oh, that's wonderful, Biff, you'll save his life. Thanks, darling. Just put your arm around him when he comes into the restaurant. Give him a smile. That's the boy . . . Good-by, dear. . . . You got your comb? . . . That's fine. Good-by, Biff dear.

In the middle of her speech, Howard Wagner, thirty-six, wheels in a small type-writer table on which is a wire-recording machine and proceeds to plug it in. This is on the left forestage. Light slowly fades on Linda as it rises on Howard. Howard is intent on threading the machine and only glances over his shoulder as Willy appears.

Willy: Pst! Pst!

Howard: Hello, Willy, come in.

Willy: Like to have a little talk with you, Howard.

Howard: Sorry to keep you waiting. I'll be with you in a minute.

Willy: What's that, Howard?

Howard: Didn't you ever see one of these? Wire recorder.

Willy: Oh. Can we talk a minute?

Howard: Records things. Just got delivery yesterday. Been driving me crazy, the most terrific machine I ever saw in my life. I was up all night with it.

Willy: What do you do with it?

Howard: I bought it for dictation, but you can do anything with it. Listen to this. I had it home last night. Listen to what I picked up. The first one is my daughter. Get this. *(He flicks the switch and "Roll Out the Barrel" is heard being whistled.)* Listen to that kid whistle.

Willy: That is lifelike, isn't it?

Howard: Seven years old. Get that tone.

Willy: Ts, ts. Like to ask a little favor if you . . .

The whistling breaks off, and the voice of Howard's daughter is heard.

His Daughter: "Now you, Daddy."

Howard: She's crazy for me! *(Again the same song is whistled.)* That's me! Ha! *(He winks.)*

Willy: You're very good!

The whistling breaks off again. The machine runs silent for a moment.

Howard: Sh! Get this now, this is my son.

His Son: "The capital of Alabama is Montgomery; the capital of Arizona is Phoenix; the capital of Arkansas is Little Rock; the capital of California is Sacramento . . ." *(and on, and on).*

Howard (holding up five fingers): Five years old, Willy!

Willy: He'll make an announcer some day!

His Son (continuing): "The capital . . ."

Howard: Get that—alphabetical order! *(The machine breaks off suddenly.)* Wait a minute. The maid kicked the plug out.

Willy: It certainly is a —
Howard: Sh, for God's sake!
His Son: "It's nine o'clock, Bulova watch time. So I have to go to sleep."
Willy: That really is —
Howard: Wait a minute! The next is my wife.

    They wait.

Howard's Voice: "Go on, say something." *(Pause.)* "Well, you gonna talk?"
His Wife: "I can't think of anything."
Howard's Voice: "Well, talk — it's turning."
His Wife (shyly, beaten): "Hello." *(Silence.)* "Oh, Howard, I can't talk into this . . ."
Howard (snapping the machine off): That was my wife.
Willy: That is a wonderful machine. Can we —
Howard: I tell you, Willy, I'm gonna take my camera, and my bandsaw, and all
    my hobbies, and out they go. This is the most fascinating relaxation I ever
    found.
Willy: I think I'll get one myself.
Howard: Sure, they're only a hundred and a half. You can't do without it. Sup-
    posing you wanna hear Jack Benny, see? But you can't be at home at that
    hour. So you tell the maid to turn the radio on when Jack Benny comes on,
    and this automatically goes on with the radio . . .
Willy: And when you come home you . . .
Howard: You can come home twelve o'clock, one o'clock, any time you like,
    and you get yourself a Coke and sit yourself down, throw the switch, and
    there's Jack Benny's program in the middle of the night!
Willy: I'm definitely going to get one. Because lots of time I'm on the road, and
    I think to myself, what I must be missing on the radio!
Howard: Don't you have a radio in the car?
Willy: Well, yeah, but who ever thinks of turning it on?
Howard: Say, aren't you supposed to be in Boston?
Willy: That's what I want to talk to you about, Howard. You got a minute? *(He
    draws a chair in from the wing.)*
Howard: What happened? What're you doing here?
Willy: Well . . .
Howard: You didn't crack up again, did you?
Willy: Oh, no. No . . .
Howard: Geez, you had me worried there for a minute. What's the trouble?
Willy: Well, tell you the truth, Howard. I've come to the decision that I'd rather
    not travel any more.
Howard: Not travel! Well, what'll you do?
Willy: Remember, Christmas time, when you had the party here? You said
    you'd try to think of some spot for me here in town.
Howard: With us?
Willy: Well, sure.
Howard: Oh, yeah, yeah. I remember. Well, I couldn't think of anything for
    you, Willy.
Willy: I tell ya, Howard. The kids are all grown up, y'know. I don't need much
    any more. If I could take home — well, sixty-five dollars a week, I could
    swing it.
Howard: Yeah, but Willy, see I —

Willy: I tell ya why, Howard. Speaking frankly and between the two of us, y'know — I'm just a little tired.

Howard: Oh, I could understand that, Willy. But you're a road man, Willy, and we do a road business. We've only got a half-dozen salesmen on the floor here.

Willy: God knows, Howard, I never asked a favor of any man. But I was with the firm when your father used to carry you in here in his arms.

Howard: I know that, Willy, but —

Willy: Your father came to me the day you were born and asked me what I thought of the name of Howard, may he rest in peace.

Howard: I appreciate that, Willy, but there just is no spot here for you. If I had a spot I'd slam you right in, but I just don't have a single solitary spot.

He looks for his lighter. Willy has picked it up and gives it to him. Pause.

Willy (with increasing anger): Howard, all I need to set my table is fifty dollars a week.

Howard: But where am I going to put you, kid?

Willy: Look, it isn't a question of whether I can sell merchandise, is it?

Howard: No, but it's a business, kid, and everybody's gotta pull his own weight.

Willy (desperately): Just let me tell you a story, Howard —

Howard: 'Cause you gotta admit, business is business.

Willy (angrily): Business is definitely business, but just listen for a minute. You don't understand this. When I was a boy — eighteen, nineteen — I was already on the road. And there was a question in my mind as to whether selling had a future for me. Because in those days I had a yearning to go to Alaska. See, there were three gold strikes in one month in Alaska, and I felt like going out. Just for the ride, you might say.

Howard (barely interested): Don't say.

Willy: Oh, yeah, my father lived many years in Alaska. He was an adventurous man. We've got quite a little streak of self-reliance in our family. I thought I'd go out with my older brother and try to locate him, and maybe settle in the North with the old man. And I was almost decided to go, when I met a salesman in the Parker House. His name was Dave Singleman. And he was eighty-four years old, and he'd drummed merchandise in thirty-one states. And old Dave, he'd go up to his room, y'understand, put on his green velvet slippers — I'll never forget — and pick up his phone and call the buyers, and without ever leaving his room, at the age of eighty-four, he made his living. And when I saw that, I realized that selling was the greatest career a man could want. 'Cause what could be more satisfying than to be able to go, at the age of eighty-four, into twenty or thirty different cities, and pick up a phone, and be remembered and loved and helped by so many different people? Do you know? when he died — and by the way he died the death of a salesman, in his green velvet slippers in the smoker of the New York, New Haven, and Hartford, going into Boston — when he died, hundreds of salesmen and buyers were at his funeral. Things were sad on a lotta trains for months after that. (*He stands up. Howard has not looked at him.*) In those days there was personality in it, Howard. There was respect, and comradeship, and gratitude in it. Today, it's all cut and dried, and there's no chance for bringing friendship to bear — or personality. You see what I mean? They don't know me any more.

Howard (moving away, to the right): That's just the thing, Willy.

Willy: If I had forty dollars a week — that's all I'd need. Forty dollars, Howard.

Howard: Kid, I can't take blood from a stone, I —

Willy (desperation is on him now): Howard, the year Al Smith° was nominated, your father came to me and —

Howard (starting to go off): I've got to see some people, kid.

Willy (stopping him): I'm talking about your father! There were promises made across this desk! You mustn't tell me you've got people to see — I put thirty-four years into this firm, Howard, and now I can't pay my insurance! You can't eat the orange and throw the peel away — a man is not a piece of fruit! *(After a pause.)* Now pay attention. Your father — in 1928 I had a big year. I averaged a hundred and seventy dollars a week in commissions.

Howard (impatiently): Now, Willy, you never averaged —

Willy (banging his hand on the desk): I averaged a hundred and seventy dollars a week in the year of 1928! And your father came to me — or rather, I was in the office here — it was right over this desk — and he put his hand on my shoulder —

Howard (getting up): You'll have to excuse me, Willy, I gotta see some people. Pull yourself together. *(Going out.)* I'll be back in a little while.

On Howard's exit, the light on his chair grows very bright and strange.

Willy: Pull myself together! What the hell did I say to him? My God, I was yelling at him! How could I! *(Willy breaks off, staring at the light, which occupies the chair, animating it. He approaches this chair, standing across the desk from it.)* Frank, Frank, don't you remember what you told me that time? How you put your hand on my shoulder, and Frank . . . *(He leans on the desk and as he speaks the dead man's name he accidentally switches on the recorder, and instantly:)*

Howard's Son: ". . . of New York is Albany. The capital of Ohio is Cincinnati, the capital of Rhode Island is . . . " *(The recitation continues.)*

Willy (leaping away with fright, shouting): Ha! Howard! Howard! Howard!

Howard (rushing in): What happened?

Willy (pointing at the machine, which continues nasally, childishly, with the capital cities): Shut it off! Shut it off!

Howard (pulling the plug out): Look, Willy . . .

Willy (pressing his hands to his eyes): I gotta get myself some coffee. I'll get some coffee . . .

Willy starts to walk out. Howard stops him.

Howard (rolling up the cord): Willy, look . . .

Willy: I'll go to Boston.

Howard: Willy, you can't go to Boston for us.

Willy: Why can't I go?

Howard: I don't want you to represent us. I've been meaning to tell you for a long time now.

Willy: Howard, are you firing me?

Howard: I think you need a good long rest, Willy.

Willy: Howard —

Al Smith: Democratic candidate for president of the United States in 1928 who lost the election to Herbert Hoover.

Howard: And when you feel better, come back, and we'll see if we can work something out.

Willy: But I gotta earn money, Howard. I'm in no position to —

Howard: Where are your sons? Why don't your sons give you a hand?

Willy: They're working on a very big deal.

Howard: This is no time for false pride, Willy. You go to your sons and you tell them that you're tired. You've got two great boys, haven't you?

Willy: Oh, no question, no question, but in the meantime . . .

Howard: Then that's that, heh?

Willy: All right, I'll go to Boston tomorrow.

Howard: No, no.

Willy: I can't throw myself on my sons. I'm not a cripple!

Howard: Look, kid, I'm busy this morning.

Willy (grasping Howard's arm): Howard, you've got to let me go to Boston!

Howard (hard, keeping himself under control): I've got a line of people to see this morning. Sit down, take five minutes, and pull yourself together, and then go home, will ya? I need the office, Willy. *(He starts to go, turns, remembering the recorder, starts to push off the table holding the recorder.)* Oh, yeah. Whenever you can this week, stop by and drop off the samples. You'll feel better, Willy, and then come back and we'll talk. Pull yourself together, kid, there's people outside.

Howard exits, pushing the table off left. Willy stares into space, exhausted. Now the music is heard — Ben's music — first distantly, then closer, closer. As Willy speaks, Ben enters from the right. He carries valise and umbrella.

Willy: Oh, Ben, how did you do it? What is the answer? Did you wind up the Alaska deal already?

Ben: Doesn't take much time if you know what you're doing. Just a short business trip. Boarding ship in an hour. Wanted to say good-by.

Willy: Ben, I've got to talk to you.

Ben (glancing at his watch): Haven't the time, William.

Willy (crossing the apron to Ben): Ben, nothing's working out. I don't know what to do.

Ben: Now, look here, William. I've bought timberland in Alaska and I need a man to look after things for me.

Willy: God, timberland! Me and my boys in those grand outdoors!

Ben: You've a new continent at your doorstep, William. Get out of these cities, they're full of talk and time payments and courts of law. Screw on your fists and you can fight for a fortune up there.

Willy: Yes, yes! Linda, Linda!

Linda enters as of old, with the wash.

Linda: Oh, you're back?

Ben: I haven't much time.

Willy: No, wait! Linda, he's got a proposition for me in Alaska.

Linda: But you've got — *(To Ben.)* He's got a beautiful job here.

Willy: But in Alaska, kid, I could —

Linda: You're doing well enough, Willy!

Ben (to Linda): Enough for what, my dear?

Linda (frightened of Ben and angry at him): Don't say those things to him! Enough to be happy right here, right now. *(To Willy, while Ben laughs.)* Why must everybody conquer the world? You're well liked, and the boys love you, and someday— *(to Ben)*—why, old man Wagner told him just the other day that if he keeps it up he'll be a member of the firm, didn't he, Willy?

Willy: Sure, sure. I am building something with this firm, Ben, and if a man is building something he must be on the right track, mustn't he?

Ben: What are you building? Lay your hand on it. Where is it?

Willy (hesitantly): That's true, Linda, there's nothing.

Linda: Why? *(To Ben.)* There's a man eighty-four years old—

Willy: That's right, Ben, that's right. When I look at that man I say, what is there to worry about?

Ben: Bah!

Willy: It's true, Ben. All he has to do is go into any city, pick up the phone, and he's making his living and you know why?

Ben (picking up his valise): I've got to go.

Willy (holding Ben back): Look at this boy!

Biff, in his high school sweater, enters carrying suitcase. Happy carries Biff's shoulder guards, gold helmet, and football pants.

Willy: Without a penny to his name, three great universities are begging for him, and from there the sky's the limit, because it's not what you do, Ben. It's who you know and the smile on your face! It's contacts, Ben, contacts! The whole wealth of Alaska passes over the lunch table at the Commodore Hotel, and that's the wonder, the wonder of this country, that a man can end with diamonds here on the basis of being liked! *(He turns to Biff.)* And that's why when you get out on that field today it's important. Because thousands of people will be rooting for you and loving you. *(To Ben, who has again begun to leave.)* And Ben! when he walks into a business office his name will sound out like a bell and all the doors will open to him! I've seen it, Ben, I've seen it a thousand times! You can't feel it with your hand like timber, but it's there!

Ben: Good-by, William.

Willy: Ben, am I right? Don't you think I'm right? I value your advice.

Ben: There's a new continent at your doorstep, William. You could walk out rich. Rich! *(He is gone.)*

Willy: We'll do it here, Ben! You hear me? We're gonna do it here!

Young Bernard rushes in. The gay music of the Boys is heard.

Bernard: Oh, gee, I was afraid you left already!

Willy: Why? What time is it?

Bernard: It's half-past one!

Willy: Well, come on, everybody! Ebbets Field next stop! Where's the pennants? *(He rushes through the wall-line of the kitchen and out into the living-room.)*

Linda (to Biff): Did you pack fresh underwear?

Biff (who has been limbering up): I want to go!

Bernard: Biff, I'm carrying your helmet, ain't I?

Happy: I'm carrying the helmet.

Bernard: How am I going to get in the locker room?

Linda: Let him carry the shoulder guards. *(She puts her coat and hat on in the kitchen.)*

Bernard: Can I, Biff? 'Cause I told everybody I'm going to be in the locker room.

Happy: In Ebbets Field it's the clubhouse.

Bernard: I meant the clubhouse. Biff!

Happy: Biff!

Biff (grandly, after a slight pause): Let him carry the shoulder guards.

Happy (as he gives Bernard the shoulder guards): Stay close to us now.

> *Willy rushes in with the pennants.*

Willy (handing them out): Everybody wave when Biff comes out on the field. *(Happy and Bernard run off.)* You set now, boy?

> *The music has died away.*

Biff: Ready to go, Pop. Every muscle is ready.

Willy (at the edge of the apron): You realize what this means?

Biff: That's right, Pop.

Willy (feeling Biff's muscles): You're comin' home this afternoon captain of the All-Scholastic Championship Team of the City of New York.

Biff: I got it, Pop. And remember, pal, when I take off my helmet, that touch-down is for you.

Willy: Let's go! *(He is starting out, with his arm around Biff, when Charley enters, as of old, in knickers.)* I got no room for you, Charley.

Charley: Room? For what?

Willy: In the car.

Charley: You goin' for a ride? I wanted to shoot some casino.   •

Willy (furiously): Casino! *(Incredulously.)* Don't you realize what today is?

Linda: Oh, he knows, Willy. He's just kidding you.

Willy: That's nothing to kid about!

Charley: No, Linda, what's goin' on?

Linda: He's playing in Ebbets Field.

Charley: Baseball in this weather?

Willy: Don't talk to him. Come on, come on! *(He is pushing them out.)*

Charley: Wait a minute, didn't you hear the news?

Willy: What?

Charley: Don't you listen to the radio? Ebbets Field just blew up.

Willy: You go to hell! *(Charley laughs. Pushing them out.)* Come on, come on! We're late.

Charley (as they go): Knock a homer, Biff, knock a homer!

Willy (the last to leave, turning to Charley): I don't think that was funny, Charley. This is the greatest day of his life.

Charley: Willy, when are you going to grow up?

Willy: Yeah, heh? When this game is over, Charley, you'll be laughing out of the other side of your face. They'll be calling him another Red Grange. Twenty-five thousand a year.

Charley (kidding): Is that so?

Willy: Yeah, that's so.

Charley: Well, then, I'm sorry, Willy. But tell me something.

Willy: What?

Charley: Who is Red Grange?

Willy: Put up your hands. Goddam you, put up your hands!

Charley, chuckling, shakes his head and walks away, around the left corner of the stage. Willy follows him. The music rises to a mocking frenzy.

Willy: Who the hell do you think you are, better than everybody else? You don't know everything, you big, ignorant, stupid . . . Put up your hands!

Light rises, on the right side of the forestage, on a small table in the reception room of Charley's office. Traffic sounds are heard. Bernard, now mature, sits whistling to himself. A pair of tennis rackets and an overnight bag are on the floor beside him.

Willy (offstage): What are you walking away for? Don't walk away! If you're going to say something say it to my face! I know you laugh at me behind my back. You'll laugh out of the other side of your goddam face after this game. Touchdown! Touchdown! Eighty thousand people! Touchdown! Right between the goal posts.

Bernard is a quiet, earnest, but self-assured young man. Willy's voice is coming from right upstage now. Bernard lowers his feet off the table and listens. Jenny, his father's secretary, enters.

Jenny (distressed): Say, Bernard, will you go out in the hall?

Bernard: What is that noise? Who is it?

Jenny: Mr. Loman. He just got off the elevator.

Bernard (getting up): Who's he arguing with?

Jenny: Nobody. There's nobody with him. I can't deal with him any more, and your father gets all upset everytime he comes. I've got a lot of typing to do, and your father's waiting to sign it. Will you see him?

Willy (entering): Touchdown! Touch — *(He sees Jenny.)* Jenny, Jenny, good to see you. How're ya? Workin'? Or still honest?

Jenny: Fine. How've you been feeling?

Willy: Not much any more, Jenny. Ha, ha! *(He is surprised to see the rackets.)*

Bernard: Hello, Uncle Willy.

Willy (almost shocked): Bernard! Well, look who's here! *(He comes quickly, guiltily, to Bernard and warmly shakes his hand.)*

Bernard: How are you? Good to see you.

Willy: What are you doing here?

Bernard: Oh, just stopped by to see Pop. Get off my feet till my train leaves. I'm going to Washington in a few minutes.

Willy: Is he in?

Bernard: Yes, he's in his office with the accountant. Sit down.

Willy (sitting down): What're you going to do in Washington?

Bernard: Oh, just a case I've got there, Willy.

Willy: That so? *(Indicating the rackets.)* You going to play tennis there?

Bernard: I'm staying with a friend who's got a court.

Willy: Don't say. His own tennis court. Must be fine people, I bet.

Bernard: They are, very nice. Dad tells me Biff's in town.

Willy (with a big smile): Yeah, Biff's in. Working on a very big deal, Bernard.

Bernard: What's Biff doing?

Willy: Well, he's been doing very big things in the West. But he decided to establish himself here. Very big. We're having dinner. Did I hear your wife had a boy?

Bernard: That's right. Our second.

Willy: Two boys! What do you know!

Bernard: What kind of a deal has Biff got?

Willy: Well, Bill Oliver—very big sporting-goods man—he wants Biff very badly. Called him in from the West. Long distance, carte blanche, special deliveries. Your friends have their own private tennis court?

Bernard: You still with the old firm, Willy?

Willy (after a pause): I'm—I'm overjoyed to see how you made the grade, Bernard, overjoyed. It's an encouraging thing to see a young man really— really—Looks very good for Biff—very—*(He breaks off, then.)* Bernard— *(He is so full of emotion, he breaks off again.)*

Bernard: What is it, Willy?

Willy (small and alone): What—what's the secret?

Bernard: What secret?

Willy: How—how did you? Why didn't he ever catch on?

Bernard: I wouldn't know that, Willy.

Willy (confidentially, desperately): You were his friend, his boyhood friend. There's something I don't understand about it. His life ended after that Ebbets Field game. From the age of seventeen nothing good ever happened to him.

Bernard: He never trained himself for anything.

Willy: But he did, he did. After high school he took so many correspondence courses. Radio mechanics; television; God knows what, and never made the slightest mark.

Bernard (taking off his glasses): Willy, do you want to talk candidly?

Willy (rising, faces Bernard): I regard you as a very brilliant man, Bernard. I value your advice.

Bernard: Oh, the hell with the advice, Willy. I couldn't advise you. There's just one thing I've always wanted to ask you. When he was supposed to graduate, and the math teacher flunked him—

Willy: Oh, that son-of-a-bitch ruined his life.

Bernard: Yeah, but, Willy, all he had to do was go to summer school and make up that subject.

Willy: That's right, that's right.

Bernard: Did you tell him not to go to summer school?

Willy: Me? I begged him to go. I ordered him to go!

Bernard: Then why wouldn't he go?

Willy: Why? Why! Bernard, that question has been trailing me like a ghost for the last fifteen years. He flunked the subject, and laid down and died like a hammer hit him!

Bernard: Take it easy, kid.

Willy: Let me talk to you—I got nobody to talk to. Bernard, Bernard, was it my fault? Y'see? It keeps going around in my mind, maybe I did something to him. I got nothing to give him.

Bernard: Don't take it so hard.

Willy: Why did he lay down? What is the story there? You were his friend!

Bernard: Willy, I remember, it was June, and our grades came out. And he'd flunked math.

Willy: That son-of-a-bitch!

Bernard: No, it wasn't right then. Biff just got very angry, I remember, and he was ready to enroll in summer school.

Willy (surprised): He was?

Bernard: He wasn't beaten by it at all. But then, Willy, he disappeared from the block for almost a month. And I got the idea that he'd gone up to New England to see you. Did he have a talk with you then?

Willy stares in silence.

Bernard: Willy?

Willy (with a strong edge of resentment in his voice): Yeah, he came to Boston. What about it?

Bernard: Well, just that when he came back — I'll never forget this, it always mystifies me. Because I'd thought so well of Biff, even though he'd always taken advantage of me. I loved him, Willy, y'know? And he came back after that month and took his sneakers — remember those sneakers with "University of Virginia" printed on them? He was so proud of those, wore them every day. And he took them down in the cellar, and burned them up in the furnace. We had a fist fight. It lasted at least half an hour. Just the two of us, punching each other down the cellar, and crying right through it. I've often thought of how strange it was that I knew he'd given up his life. What happened in Boston, Willy?

Willy looks at him as at an intruder.

Bernard: I just bring it up because you asked me.

Willy (angrily): Nothing. What do you mean, "What happened?" What's that got to do with anything?

Bernard: Well, don't get sore.

Willy: What are you trying to do, blame it on me? If a boy lays down is that my fault?

Bernard: Now, Willy, don't get —

Willy: Well, don't — don't talk to me that way! What does that mean, "What happened?"

Charley enters. He is in his vest, and he carries a bottle of bourbon.

Charley: Hey, you're going to miss that train. (He waves the bottle.)

Bernard: Yeah, I'm going. (He takes the bottle.) Thanks, Pop. (He picks up his rackets and bag.) Good-by, Willy, and don't worry about it. You know. "If at first you don't succeed . . ."

Willy: Yes, I believe in that.

Bernard: But sometimes, Willy, it's better for a man just to walk away.

Willy: Walk away?

Bernard: That's right.

Willy: But if you can't walk away?

Bernard (after a slight pause): I guess that's when it's tough. (Extending his hand.) Good-by, Willy.

Willy (shaking Bernard's hand): Good-by, boy.

Charley (an arm on Bernard's shoulder): How do you like this kid? Gonna argue a case in front of the Supreme Court.

Bernard (protesting): Pop!

Willy (genuinely shocked, pained, and happy): No! The Supreme Court!

Bernard: I gotta run. 'By, Dad!

Charley: Knock 'em dead, Bernard!

> *Bernard goes off.*

Willy (as Charley takes out his wallet): The Supreme Court! And he didn't even mention it!

Charley (counting out money on the desk): He don't have to — he's gonna do it.

Willy: And you never told him what to do, did you? You never took any interest in him.

Charley: My salvation is that I never took any interest in any thing. There's some money — fifty dollars. I got an accountant inside.

Willy: Charley, look . . . *(With difficulty.)* I got my insurance to pay. If you can manage it — I need a hundred and ten dollars.

> *Charley doesn't reply for a moment; merely stops moving.*

Willy: I'd draw it from my bank but Linda would know, and I . . .

Charley: Sit down, Willy.

Willy (moving toward the chair): I'm keeping an account of everything, remember. I'll pay every penny back. *(He sits.)*

Charley: Now listen to me, Willy.

Willy: I want you to know I appreciate . . .

Charley (sitting down on the table): Willy, what're you doin'? What the hell is goin' on in your head?

Willy: Why? I'm simply . . .

Charley: I offered you a job. You can make fifty dollars a week. And I won't send you on the road.

Willy: I've got a job.

Charley: Without pay? What kind of a job is a job without pay? *(He rises.)* Now, look, kid, enough is enough. I'm no genius but I know when I'm being insulted.

Willy: Insulted!

Charley: Why don't you want to work for me?

Willy: What's the matter with you? I've got a job.

Charley: Then what're you walkin' in here every week for?

Willy (getting up): Well, if you don't want me to walk in here —

Charley: I am offering you a job.

Willy: I don't want your goddam job!

Charley: When the hell are you going to grow up?

Willy (furiously): You big ignoramus, if you say that to me again I'll rap you one! I don't care how big you are! *(He's ready to fight.)*

> *Pause.*

Charley (kindly, going to him): How much do you need, Willy?

Willy: Charley, I'm strapped. I'm strapped. I don't know what to do. I was just fired.

Charley: Howard fired you?

Willy: That snotnose. Imagine that? I named him. I named him Howard.

Charley: Willy, when're you gonna realize that them things don't mean anything? You named him Howard, but you can't sell that. The only thing you got in this world is what you can sell. And the funny thing is that you're a salesman, and you don't know that.

Willy: I've always tried to think otherwise, I guess. I always felt that if a man was impressive, and well liked, that nothing —

Charley: Why must everybody like you? Who liked J. P. Morgan? Was he impressive? In a Turkish bath he'd look like a butcher. But with his pockets on he was very well liked. Now listen, Willy, I know you don't like me, and nobody can say I'm in love with you, but I'll give you a job because — just for the hell of it, put it that way. Now what do you say?

Willy: I — I just can't work for you, Charley.

Charley: What're you, jealous of me?

Willy: I can't work for you, that's all, don't ask me why.

Charley (angered, takes out more bills): You been jealous of me all your life, you damned fool! Here, pay your insurance. *(He puts the money in Willy's hand.)*

Willy: I'm keeping strict accounts.

Charley: I've got some work to do. Take care of yourself. And pay your insurance.

Willy (moving to the right): Funny, y'know? After all the highways, and the trains, and the appointments, and the years, you end up worth more dead than alive.

Charley: Willy, nobody's worth nothin' dead. *(After a slight pause.)* Did you hear what I said?

Willy stands still, dreaming.

Charley: Willy!

Willy: Apologize to Bernard for me when you see him. I didn't mean to argue with him. He's a fine boy. They're all fine boys, and they'll end up big — all of them. Someday they'll all play tennis together. Wish me luck, Charley. He saw Bill Oliver today.

Charley: Good luck.

Willy (on the verge of tears): Charley, you're the only friend I got. Isn't that a remarkable thing? *(He goes out.)*

Charley: Jesus!

Charley stares after him a moment and follows. All light blacks out. Suddenly raucous music is heard, and a red glow rises behind the screen at right. Stanley, a young waiter, appears, carrying a table, followed by Happy, who is carrying two chairs.

Stanley (putting the table down): That's all right, Mr. Loman, I can handle it myself. *(He turns and takes the chairs from Happy and places them at the table.)*

Happy (glancing around): Oh, this is better.

Stanley: Sure, in the front there you're in the middle of all kinds a noise. Whenever you got a party, Mr. Loman, you just tell me and I'll put you back here. Y'know, there's a lotta people they don't like it private, because when they go out they like to see a lotta action around them because they're sick and tired to stay in the house by theirself. But I know you, you ain't from Hackensack. You know what I mean?

Happy (sitting down): So how's it coming, Stanley?

Stanley: Ah, it's a dog's life. I only wish during the war they'd a took me in the Army. I coulda been dead by now.

Happy: My brother's back, Stanley.

Stanley: Oh, he come back, heh? From the Far West.

Happy: Yeah, big cattle man, my brother, so treat him right. And my father's coming too.

Stanley: Oh, your father too!

Happy: You got a couple of nice lobsters?

Stanley: Hundred per cent, big.

Happy: I want them with the claws.

Stanley: Don't worry, I don't give you no mice. *(Happy laughs.)* How about some wine? It'll put a head on the meal.

Happy: No. You remember, Stanley, that recipe I brought you from overseas? With the champagne in it?

Stanley: Oh, yeah, sure. I still got it tacked up yet in the kitchen. But that'll have to cost a buck apiece anyways.

Happy: That's all right.

Stanley: What'd you, hit a number or somethin'?

Happy: No, it's a little celebration. My brother is — I think he pulled off a big deal today. I think we're going into business together.

Stanley: Great! That's the best for you. Because a family business, you know what I mean? — that's the best.

Happy: That's what I think.

Stanley: 'Cause what's the difference? Somebody steals? It's in the family. Know what I mean? *(Sotto voce.°)* Like this bartender here. The boss is goin' crazy what kinda leak he's got in the cash register. You put it in but it don't come out.

Happy (raising his head): Sh!

Stanley: What?

Happy: You notice I wasn't lookin' right or left, was I?

Stanley: No.

Happy: And my eyes are closed.

Stanley: So what's the — ?

Happy: Strudel's comin'.

Stanley (catching on, looks around): Ah, no, there's no —

> He breaks off as a furred, lavishly dressed girl enters and sits at the next table. Both follow her with their eyes.

Stanley: Geez, how'd ya know?

Happy: I got radar or something. *(Staring directly at her profile.)* Ooooooooo . . . Stanley.

Stanley: I think that's for you, Mr. Loman.

Happy: Look at that mouth. Oh, God. And the binoculars.

Stanley: Geez, you got a life, Mr. Loman.

Happy: Wait on her.

Stanley (going to the girl's table): Would you like a menu, ma'am?

Girl: I'm expecting someone, but I'd like a —

Happy: Why don't you bring her — excuse me, miss, do you mind? I sell champagne, and I'd like you to try my brand. Bring her a champagne, Stanley.

Girl: That's awfully nice of you.

Sotto voce: Softly, "under the breath" (Italian).

Happy: Don't mention it. It's all company money. *(He laughs.)*

Girl: That's a charming product to be selling, isn't it?

Happy: Oh, gets to be like everything else. Selling is selling, y'know.

Girl: I suppose.

Happy: You don't happen to sell, do you?

Girl: No, I don't sell.

Happy: Would you object to a compliment from a stranger? You ought to be on a magazine cover.

Girl (looking at him a little archly): I have been.

> *Stanley comes in with a glass of champagne.*

Happy: What'd I say before, Stanley? You see? She's a cover girl.

Stanley: Oh, I could see, I could see.

Happy (to the Girl): What magazine?

Girl: Oh, a lot of them. *(She takes the drink.)* Thank you.

Happy: You know what they say in France, don't you? "Champagne is the drink of the complexion" — Hya, Biff!

> *Biff has entered and sits with Happy.*

Biff: Hello, kid. Sorry I'm late.

Happy: I just got here. Uh, Miss — ?

Girl: Forsythe.

Happy: Miss Forsythe, this is my brother.

Biff: Is Dad here?

Happy: His name is Biff. You might've heard of him. Great football player.

Girl: Really? What team?

Happy: Are you familiar with football?

Girl: No, I'm afraid I'm not.

Happy: Biff is quarterback with the New York Giants.

Girl: Well, that is nice, isn't it? *(She drinks.)*

Happy: Good health.

Girl: I'm happy to meet you.

Happy: That's my name. Hap. It's really Harold, but at West Point they called me Happy.

Girl (now really impressed): Oh, I see. How do you do? *(She turns her profile.)*

Biff: Isn't Dad coming?

Happy: You want her?

Biff: Oh, I could never make that.

Happy: I remember the time that idea would never come into your head. Where's the old confidence, Biff?

Biff: I just saw Oliver —

Happy: Wait a minute. I've got to see that old confidence again. Do you want her? She's on call.

Biff: Oh, no. *(He turns to look at the Girl.)*

Happy: I'm telling you. Watch this. *(Turning to the Girl.)* Honey? *(She turns to him.)* Are you busy?

Girl: Well, I am . . . but I could make a phone call.

Happy: Do that, will you, honey? And see if you can get a friend. We'll be here for a while. Biff is one of the greatest football players in the country.

Girl (standing up): Well, I'm certainly happy to meet you.

Happy: Come back soon.

Girl: I'll try.

Happy: Don't try, honey, try hard.

The Girl exits. Stanley follows, shaking his head in bewildered admiration.

Happy: Isn't that a shame now? A beautiful girl like that? That's why I can't get married. There's not a good woman in a thousand. New York is loaded with them, kid!

Biff: Hap, look —

Happy: I told you she was on call!

Biff (strangely unnerved): Cut it out, will ya? I want to say something to you.

Happy: Did you see Oliver?

Biff: I saw him all right. Now look, I want to tell Dad a couple of things and I want you to help me.

Happy: What? Is he going to back you?

Biff: Are you crazy? You're out of your goddam head, you know that?

Happy: Why? What happened?

Biff (breathlessly): I did a terrible thing today, Hap. It's been the strangest day I ever went through. I'm all numb, I swear.

Happy: You mean he wouldn't see you?

Biff: Well, I waited six hours for him, see? All day. Kept sending my name in. Even tried to date his secretary so she'd get me to him, but no soap.

Happy: Because you're not showin' the old confidence, Biff. He remembered you, didn't he?

Biff (stopping Happy with a gesture): Finally, about five o'clock, he comes out. Didn't remember who I was or anything. I felt like such an idiot, Hap.

Happy: Did you tell him my Florida idea?

Biff: He walked away. I saw him for one minute. I got so mad I could've torn the walls down! How the hell did I ever get the idea I was a salesman there? I even believed myself that I'd been a salesman for him! And then he gave me one look and — I realized what a ridiculous lie my whole life has been! We've been talking in a dream for fifteen years. I was a shipping clerk.

Happy: What'd you do?

Biff (with great tension and wonder): Well, he left, see. And the secretary went out. I was all alone in the waiting-room. I don't know what came over me, Hap. The next thing I know I'm in his office — paneled walls, everything. I can't explain it. I — Hap, I took his fountain pen.

Happy: Geez, did he catch you?

Biff: I ran out. I ran down all eleven flights. I ran and ran and ran.

Happy: That was an awful dumb — what'd you do that for?

Biff (agonized): I don't know, I just — wanted to take something, I don't know. You gotta help me, Hap, I'm gonna tell Pop.

Happy: You crazy? What for?

Biff: Hap, he's got to understand that I'm not the man somebody lends that kind of money to. He thinks I've been spiting him all these years and it's eating him up.

Happy: That's just it. You tell him something nice.

Biff: I can't.

Happy: Say you got a lunch date with Oliver tomorrow.

Biff: So what do I do tomorrow?

Happy: You leave the house tomorrow and come back at night and say Oliver is thinking it over. And he thinks it over for a couple of weeks, and gradually it fades away and nobody's the worse.

Biff: But it'll go on forever!

Happy: Dad is never so happy as when he's looking forward to something!

Willy enters.

Happy: Hello, scout!

Willy: Gee, I haven't been here in years!

Stanley has followed Willy in and sets a chair for him. Stanley starts off but Happy stops him.

Happy: Stanley!

Stanley stands by, waiting for an order.

Biff (going to Willy with guilt, as to an invalid): Sit down, Pop. You want a drink?

Willy: Sure, I don't mind.

Biff: Let's get a load on.

Willy: You look worried.

Biff: N-no. *(To Stanley.)* Scotch all around. Make it doubles.

Stanley: Doubles, right. *(He goes.)*

Willy: You had a couple already, didn't you?

Biff: Just a couple, yeah.

Willy: Well, what happened, boy? *(Nodding affirmatively, with a smile.)* Everything go all right?

Biff (takes a breath, then reaches out and grasps Willy's hand): Pal . . . *(He is smiling bravely, and Willy is smiling too.)* I had an experience today.

Happy: Terrific, Pop.

Willy: That so? What happened?

Biff (high, slightly alcoholic, above the earth): I'm going to tell you everything from first to last. It's been a strange day. *(Silence. He looks around, composes himself as best he can, but his breath keeps breaking the rhythm of his voice.)* I had to wait quite a while for him, and—

Willy: Oliver.

Biff: Yeah, Oliver. All day, as a matter of cold fact. And a lot of—instances—facts, Pop, facts about my life came back to me. Who was it, Pop? Who ever said I was a salesman with Oliver?

Willy: Well, you were.

Biff: No, Dad, I was a shipping clerk.

Willy: But you were practically—

Biff (with determination): Dad, I don't know who said it first, but I was never a salesman for Bill Oliver.

Willy: What're you talking about?

Biff: Let's hold on to the facts tonight, Pop. We're not going to get anywhere bullin' around. I was a shipping clerk.

Willy (angrily): All right, now listen to me—

Biff: Why don't you let me finish?

Willy: I'm not interested in stories about the past or any crap of that kind because the woods are burning, boys, you understand? There's a big blaze going on all around. I was fired today.

Biff (shocked): How could you be?

Willy: I was fired, and I'm looking for a little good news to tell your mother, because the woman has waited and the woman has suffered. The gist of it is that I haven't got a story left in my head, Biff. So don't give me a lecture about facts and aspects. I am not interested. Now what've you got to say to me?

Stanley enters with three drinks. They wait until he leaves.

Willy: Did you see Oliver?

Biff: Jesus, Dad!

Willy: You mean you didn't go up there?

Happy: Sure he went up there.

Biff: I did. I — saw him. How could they fire you?

Willy (on the edge of his chair): What kind of a welcome did he give you?

Biff: He won't even let you work on commission?

Willy: I'm out! *(Driving.)* So tell me, he gave you a warm welcome?

Happy: Sure, Pop, sure!

Biff (driven): Well, it was kind of —

Willy: I was wondering if he'd remember you. *(To Happy.)* Imagine, man doesn't see him for ten, twelve years and gives him that kind of a welcome!

Happy: Damn right!

Biff (trying to return to the offensive): Pop, look —

Willy: You know why he remembered you, don't you? Because you impressed him in those days.

Biff: Let's talk quietly and get this down to the facts, huh?

Willy (as though Biff had been interrupting): Well, what happened? It's great news, Biff. Did he take you into his office or'd you talk in the waiting-room?

Biff: Well, he came in, see, and —

Willy (with a big smile): What'd he say? Betcha he threw his arm around you.

Biff: Well, he kinda —

Willy: He's a fine man. *(To Happy.)* Very hard man to see, y'know.

Happy (agreeing): Oh, I know.

Willy (to Biff): Is that where you had the drinks?

Biff: Yeah, he gave me a couple of — no, no!

Happy (cutting in): He told him my Florida idea.

Willy: Don't interrupt. *(To Biff.)* How'd he react to the Florida idea?

Biff: Dad, will you give me a minute to explain?

Willy: I've been waiting for you to explain since I sat down here! What happened? He took you into his office and what?

Biff: Well — I talked. And — and he listened, see.

Willy: Famous for the way he listens, y'know. What was his answer?

Biff: His answer was — *(He breaks off, suddenly angry.)* Dad, you're not letting me tell you what I want to tell you!

Willy (accusing, angered): You didn't see him, did you?

Biff: I did see him!

Willy: What'd you insult him or something? You insulted him, didn't you?

Biff: Listen, will you let me out of it, will you just let me out of it!

Happy: What the hell!

Willy: Tell me what happened!

Biff (to Happy): I can't talk to him!

A single trumpet note jars the ear. The light of green leaves stains the house, which holds the air of night and a dream. Young Bernard enters and knocks on the door of the house.

Young Bernard (frantically): Mrs. Loman, Mrs. Loman!

Happy: Tell him what happened!

Biff (to Happy): Shut up and leave me alone!

Willy: No, no! You had to go and flunk math!

Biff: What math? What're you talking about?

Young Bernard: Mrs. Loman, Mrs. Loman!

    Linda appears in the house, as of old.

Willy (wildly): Math, math, math!

Biff: Take it easy, Pop!

Young Bernard: Mrs. Loman!

Willy (furiously): If you hadn't flunked you'd've been set by now!

Biff: Now, look, I'm gonna tell you what happened, and you're going to listen to me.

Young Bernard: Mrs. Loman!

Biff: I waited six hours —

Happy: What the hell are you saying?

Biff: I kept sending in my name but he wouldn't see me. So finally he . . . *(He continues unheard as light fades low on the restaurant.)*

Young Bernard: Biff flunked math!

Linda: No!

Young Bernard: Birnbaum flunked him! They won't graduate him!

Linda: But they have to. He's gotta go to the university. Where is he? Biff! Biff!

Young Bernard: No, he left. He went to Grand Central.

Linda: Grand — You mean he went to Boston!

Young Bernard: Is Uncle Willy in Boston?

Linda: Oh, maybe Willy can talk to the teacher. Oh, the poor, poor boy!

    Light on house area snaps out.

Biff (at the table, now audible, holding up a gold fountain pen): . . . so I'm washed up with Oliver, you understand? Are you listening to me?

Willy (at a loss): Yeah, sure. If you hadn't flunked —

Biff: Flunked what? What're you talking about?

Willy: Don't blame everything on me! I didn't flunk math — you did! What pen?

Happy: That was awful dumb, Biff, a pen like that is worth —

Willy (seeing the pen for the first time): You took Oliver's pen?

Biff (weakening): Dad, I just explained it to you.

Willy: You stole Bill Oliver's fountain pen!

Biff: I didn't exactly steal it! That's just what I've been explaining to you!

Happy: He had it in his hand and just then Oliver walked in, so he got nervous and stuck it in his pocket!

Willy: My God, Biff!

Biff: I never intended to do it, Dad!

Operator's Voice: Standish Arms, good evening!

Willy (shouting): I'm not in my room!

Biff (frightened): Dad, what's the matter? *(He and Happy stand up.)*

Operator: Ringing Mr. Loman for you!

Willy: I'm not there, stop it!

Biff (horrified, gets down on one knee before Willy): Dad, I'll make good, I'll make good. *(Willy tries to get to his feet. Biff holds him down.)* Sit down now.

Willy: No, you're no good, you're no good for anything.

Biff: I am, Dad, I'll find something else, you understand? Now don't worry about anything. *(He holds up Willy's face.)* Talk to me, Dad.

Operator: Mr. Loman does not answer. Shall I page him?

Willy (attempting to stand, as though to rush and silence the Operator): No, no, no!

Happy: He'll strike something, Pop.

Willy: No, no . . .

Biff (desperately, standing over Willy): Pop, listen! Listen to me! I'm telling you something good. Oliver talked to his partner about the Florida idea. You listening? He—he talked to his partner, and he came to me . . . I'm going to be all right, you hear? Dad, listen to me, he said it was just a question of the amount!

Willy: Then you . . . got it?

Happy: He's gonna be terrific, Pop!

Willy (trying to stand): Then you got it, haven't you? You got it! You got it!

Biff (agonized, holds Willy down): No, no. Look, Pop. I'm supposed to have lunch with them tomorrow. I'm just telling you this so you'll know that I can still make an impression, Pop. And I'll make good somewhere, but I can't go tomorrow, see?

Willy: Why not? You simply—

Biff: But the pen, Pop!

Willy: You give it to him and tell him it was an oversight!

Happy: Sure, have lunch tomorrow!

Biff: I can't say that—

Willy: You were doing a crossword puzzle and accidentally used his pen!

Biff: Listen, kid, I took those balls years ago, now I walk in with his fountain pen? That clinches it, don't you see? I can't face him like that! I'll try elsewhere.

Page's Voice: Paging Mr. Loman!

Willy: Don't you want to be anything?

Biff: Pop, how can I go back?

Willy: You don't want to be anything, is that what's behind it?

Biff (now angry at Willy for not crediting his sympathy): Don't take it that way! You think it was easy walking into that office after what I'd done to him? A team of horses couldn't have dragged me back to Bill Oliver!

Willy: Then why'd you go?

Biff: Why did I go? Why did I go! Look at you! Look at what's become of you!

Off left, The Woman laughs.

Willy: Biff, you're going to lunch tomorrow, or—

Biff: I can't go. I've got no appointment!

Happy: Biff, for . . . !

Willy: Are you spiting me?

Biff: Don't take it that way! Goddammit!

Willy (strikes Biff and falters away from the table): You rotten little louse! Are you spiting me?

The Woman: Someone's at the door, Willy!

Biff: I'm no good, can't you see what I am?

Happy (separating them): Hey, you're in a restaurant! Now cut it out, both of you! *(The girls enter.)* Hello, girls, sit down.

> *The Woman laughs, off left.*

Miss Forsythe: I guess we might as well. This is Letta.

The Woman: Willy, are you going to wake up?

Biff (ignoring Willy): How're ya, miss, sit down. What do you drink?

Miss Forsythe: Letta might not be able to stay long.

Letta: I gotta get up very early tomorrow. I got jury duty. I'm so excited! Were you fellows ever on a jury?

Biff: No, but I been in front of them! *(The girls laugh.)* This is my father.

Letta: Isn't he cute? Sit down with us, Pop.

Happy: Sit him down, Biff!

Biff (going to him): Come on, slugger, drink us under the table. To hell with it! Come on, sit down, pal.

> *On Biff's last insistence, Willy is about to sit.*

The Woman (now urgently): Willy, are you going to answer the door!

> *The Woman's call pulls Willy back. He starts right, befuddled.*

Biff: Hey, where are you going?

Willy: Open the door.

Biff: The door?

Willy: The washroom . . . the door . . . where's the door?

Biff (leading Willy to the left): Just go straight down.

> *Willy moves left.*

The Woman: Willy, Willy, are you going to get up, get up, get up, get up?

> *Willy exits left.*

Letta: I think it's sweet you bring your daddy along.

Miss Forsythe: Oh, he isn't really your father!

Biff (at left, turning to her resentfully): Miss Forsythe, you've just seen a prince walk by. A fine, troubled prince. A hard-working, unappreciated prince. A pal, you understand? A good companion. Always for his boys.

Letta: That's so sweet.

Happy: Well, girls, what's the program? We're wasting time. Come on, Biff. Gather round. Where would you like to go?

Biff: Why don't you do something for him?

Happy: Me!

Biff: Don't you give a damn for him, Hap?

Happy: What're you talking about? I'm the one who —

Biff: I sense it, you don't give a good goddamn about him. *(He takes the rolled-up hose from his pocket and puts it on the table in front of Happy.)* Look what I found in the cellar, for Christ's sake. How can you bear to let it go on?

Happy: Me? Who goes away? Who runs off and —

Biff: Yeah, but he doesn't mean anything to you. You could help him — I can't! Don't you understand what I'm talking about? He's going to kill himself, don't you know that?

Happy: Don't I know it! Me!

Biff: Hap, help him! Jesus . . . help him . . . Help me, help me, I can't bear to look at his face! *(Ready to weep, he hurries out, up right.)*

Happy (starting after him): Where are you going?

Miss Forsythe: What's he so mad about?

Happy: Come on, girls, we'll catch up with him.

Miss Forsythe (as Happy pushes her out): Say, I don't like that temper of his!

Happy: He's just a little overstrung, he'll be all right!

Willy (off left, as The Woman laughs): Don't answer! Don't answer!

Letta: Don't you want to tell your father —

Happy: No, that's not my father. He's just a guy. Come on, we'll catch Biff, and, honey, we're going to paint this town! Stanley, where's the check! Hey, Stanley!

They exit. Stanley looks toward left.

Stanley (calling to Happy indignantly): Mr. Loman! Mr. Loman!

Stanley picks up a chair and follows them off. Knocking is heard off left. The Woman enters, laughing. Willy follows her. She is in a black slip; he is buttoning his shirt. Raw, sensuous music accompanies their speech.

Willy: Will you stop laughing? Will you stop?

The Woman: Aren't you going to answer the door? He'll wake the whole hotel.

Willy: I'm not expecting anybody.

The Woman: Whyn't you have another drink, honey, and stop being so damn self-centered?

Willy: I'm so lonely.

The Woman: You know you ruined me, Willy? From now on, whenever you come to the office, I'll see that you go right through to the buyers. No waiting at my desk any more, Willy. You ruined me.

Willy: That's nice of you to say that.

The Woman: Gee, you are self-centered! Why so sad? You are the saddest, self-centeredest soul I ever did see-saw. *(She laughs. He kisses her.)* Come on inside, drummer boy. It's silly to be dressing in the middle of the night. *(As knocking is heard.)* Aren't you going to answer the door?

Willy: They're knocking on the wrong door.

The Woman: But I felt the knocking. And he heard us talking in here. Maybe the hotel's on fire!

Willy (his terror rising): It's a mistake.

The Woman: Then tell him to go away!

Willy: There's nobody there.

The Woman: It's getting on my nerves, Willy. There's somebody standing out there and it's getting on my nerves!

Willy (pushing her away from him): All right, stay in the bathroom here, and don't come out. I think there's a law in Massachusetts about it, so don't come out. It may be that new room clerk. He looked very mean. So don't come out. It's a mistake, there's no fire.

The knocking is heard again. He takes a few steps away from her, and she vanishes into the wing. The light follows him, and now he is facing Young Biff, who carries a suitcase. Biff steps toward him. The music is gone.

Biff: Why didn't you answer?

Willy: Biff! What are you doing in Boston?

Biff: Why didn't you answer? I've been knocking for five minutes, I called you on the phone —

Willy: I just heard you. I was in the bathroom and had the door shut. Did anything happen home?

Biff: Dad — I let you down.

Willy: What do you mean?

Biff: Dad . . .

Willy: Biffo, what's this about? *(Putting his arm around Biff.)* Come on, let's go downstairs and get you a malted.

Biff: Dad, I flunked math.

Willy: Not for the term?

Biff: The term. I haven't got enough credits to graduate.

Willy: You mean to say Bernard wouldn't give you the answers?

Biff: He did, he tried, but I only got a sixty-one.

Willy: And they wouldn't give you four points?

Biff: Birnbaum refused absolutely. I begged him, Pop, but he won't give me those points. You gotta talk to him before they close the school. Because if he saw the kind of man you are, and you just talked to him in your way, I'm sure he'd come through for me. The class came right before practice, see, and I didn't go enough. Would you talk to him? He'd like you, Pop. You know the way you could talk.

Willy: You're on. We'll drive right back.

Biff: Oh, Dad, good work! I'm sure he'll change it for you!

Willy: Go downstairs and tell the clerk I'm checkin' out. Go right down.

Biff: Yes, sir! See, the reason he hates me, Pop — one day he was late for class so I got up at the blackboard and imitated him. I crossed my eyes and talked with a lithp.

Willy (laughing): You did? The kids like it?

Riff: They nearly died laughing!

Willy: Yeah? What'd you do?

Biff: The thquare root of thixthy twee is . . . *(Willy bursts out laughing; Biff joins him.)* And in the middle of it he walked in!

Willy laughs and The Woman joins in offstage.

Willy (without hesitation): Hurry downstairs and —

Biff: Somebody in there?

Willy: No, that was next door.

The Woman laughs offstage.

Biff: Somebody got in your bathroom!

Willy: No, it's the next room, there's a party —

The Woman (enters, laughing. She lisps this): Can I come in? There's something in the bathtub, Willy, and it's moving!

Willy looks at Biff, who is staring open-mouthed and horrified at The Woman.

Willy: Ah — you better go back to your room. They must be finished painting by now. They're painting her room so I let her take a shower here. Go back, go back . . . *(He pushes her.)*

The Woman (resisting): But I've got to get dressed, Willy, I can't —

Willy: Get out of here! Go back, go back . . . *(Suddenly striving for the ordinary.)* This is Miss Francis, Biff, she's a buyer. They're painting her room. Go back, Miss Francis, go back . . .

The Woman: But my clothes, I can't go out naked in the hall!

Willy (pushing her offstage): Get outa here! Go back, go back!

Biff slowly sits down on his suitcase as the argument continues offstage.

The Woman: Where's my stockings? You promised me stockings, Willy!

Willy: I have no stockings here!

The Woman: You had two boxes of size nine sheers for me, and I want them!

Willy: Here, for God's sake, will you get outa here!

The Woman (enters holding a box of stockings): I just hope there's nobody in the hall. That's all I hope. *(To Biff.)* Are you football or baseball?

Biff: Football.

The Woman (angry, humiliated): That's me too. G'night. *(She snatches her clothes from Willy, and walks out.)*

Willy (after a pause): Well, better get going. I want to get to the school first thing in the morning. Get my suits out of the closet. I'll get my valise. *(Biff doesn't move.)* What's the matter? *(Biff remains motionless, tears falling.)* She's a buyer. Buys for J. H. Simmons. She lives down the hall — they're painting. You don't imagine — *(He breaks off. After a pause.)* Now listen, pal, she's just a buyer. She sees merchandise in her room and they have to keep it looking just so . . . *(Pause. Assuming command.)* All right, get my suits. *(Biff doesn't move.)* Now stop crying and do as I say. I gave you an order. Biff, I gave you an order! Is that what you do when I give you an order? How dare you cry! *(Putting his arm around Biff.)* Now look, Biff, when you grow up you'll understand about these things. You mustn't — you mustn't overemphasize a thing like this. I'll see Birnbaum first thing in the morning.

Biff: Never mind.

Willy (getting down beside Biff): Never mind! He's going to give you those points. I'll see to it.

Biff: He wouldn't listen to you.

Willy: He certainly will listen to me. You need those points for the U. of Virginia.

Biff: I'm not going there.

Willy: Heh? If I can't get him to change that mark you'll make it up in summer school. You've got all summer to —

Biff (his weeping breaking from him): Dad . . .

Willy (infected by it): Oh, my boy . . .

Biff: Dad . . .

Willy: She's nothing to me, Biff. I was lonely, I was terribly lonely.

Biff: You — you gave her Mama's stockings! *(His tears break through and he rises to go.)*

Willy (grabbing for Biff): I gave you an order!

Biff: Don't touch me, you — liar!

Willy: Apologize for that!

Biff: You fake! You phony little fake! You fake! *(Overcome, he turns quickly and weeping fully goes out with his suitcase. Willy is left on the floor on his knees.)*

Willy: I gave you an order! Biff, come back here or I'll beat you! Come back here! I'll whip you!

> *Stanley comes quickly in from the right and stands in front of Willy.*

Willy (shouts at Stanley): I gave you an order . . .

Stanley: Hey, let's pick it up, pick it up, Mr. Loman. *(He helps Willy to his feet.)* Your boys left with the chippies. They said they'll see you home.

> *A second waiter watches some distance away.*

Willy: But we were supposed to have dinner together.

> *Music is heard, Willy's theme.*

Stanley: Can you make it?

Willy: I'll — sure, I can make it. *(Suddenly concerned about his clothes.)* Do I — I look all right?

Stanley: Sure, you look all right. *(He flicks a speck off Willy's lapel.)*

Willy: Here — here's a dollar.

Stanley: Oh, your son paid me. It's all right.

Willy (putting it in Stanley's hand): No, take it. You're a good boy.

Stanley: Oh, no, you don't have to . . .

Willy: Here — here's some more, I don't need it any more. *(After a slight pause.)* Tell me — is there a seed store in the neighborhood?

Stanley: Seeds? You mean like to plant?

> *As Willy turns, Stanley slips the money back into his jacket pocket.*

Willy: Yes. Carrots, peas . . .

Stanley: Well, there's hardware stores on Sixth Avenue, but it may be too late now.

Willy (anxiously): Oh, I'd better hurry. I've got to get some seeds. *(He starts off to the right.)* I've got to get some seeds, right away. Nothing's planted. I don't have a thing in the ground.

> *Willy hurries out as the light goes down. Stanley moves over to the right after him, watches him off. The other waiter has been staring at Willy.*

Stanley (to the waiter): Well, whatta you looking at?

> *The waiter picks up the chairs and moves off right. Stanley takes the table and follows him. The light fades on this area. There is a long pause, the sound of the flute coming over. The light gradually rises on the kitchen, which is empty. Happy appears at the door of the house, followed by Biff. Happy is carrying a large bunch of long-stemmed roses. He enters the kitchen, looks around for Linda. Not seeing her, he turns to Biff, who is just outside the house door, and makes a gesture with his hands, indicating "Not here, I guess." He looks into the living-room and freezes. Inside, Linda, unseen, is seated, Willy's coat on her lap. She rises ominously and quietly and moves toward Happy, who backs up into the kitchen, afraid.*

Happy: Hey, what're you doing up? *(Linda says nothing but moves toward him implacably.)* Where's Pop? *(He keeps backing to the right, and now Linda is in full view in the doorway to the living-room.)* Is he sleeping?

Linda: Where were you?

Happy (trying to laugh it off): We met two girls, Mom, very fine types. Here, we brought you some flowers. *(Offering them to her.)* Put them in your room, Ma.

She knocks them to the floor at Biff's feet. He has now come inside and closed the door behind him. She stares at Biff, silent.

Happy: Now what'd you do that for? Mom, I want you to have some flowers —

Linda (cutting Happy off, violently to Biff): Don't you care whether he lives or dies?

Happy (going to the stairs): Come upstairs, Biff.

Biff (with a flare of disgust, to Happy): Go away from me! *(To Linda.)* What do you mean, lives or dies? Nobody's dying around here, pal.

Linda: Get out of my sight! Get out of here!

Biff: I wanna see the boss.

Linda: You're not going near him!

Biff: Where is he? *(He moves into the living-room and Linda follows.)*

Linda (shouting after Biff): You invite him for dinner. He looks forward to it all day — *(Biff appears in his parents' bedroom, looks around, and exits.)* — and then you desert him there. There's no stranger you'd do that to!

Happy: Why? He had a swell time with us. Listen, when I — *(Linda comes back into the kitchen)* — desert him I hope I don't outlive the day!

Linda: Get out of here!

Happy: Now look, Mom . . .

Linda: Did you have to go to women tonight? You and your lousy rotten whores!

Biff re-enters the kitchen.

Happy: Mom, all we did was follow Biff around trying to cheer him up! *(To Biff.)* Boy, what a night you gave me!

Linda: Get out of here, both of you, and don't come back! I don't want you tormenting him any more. Go on now, get your things together! *(To Biff.)* You can sleep in his apartment. *(She starts to pick up the flowers and stops herself.)* Pick up this stuff, I'm not your maid any more. Pick it up, you bum, you!

Happy turns his back to her in refusal. Biff slowly moves over and gets down on his knees, picking up the flowers.

Linda: You're a pair of animals! Not one, not another living soul would have had the cruelty to walk out on that man in a restaurant!

Biff (not looking at her): Is that what he said?

Linda: He didn't have to say anything. He was so humiliated he nearly limped when he came in.

Happy: But, Mom, he had a great time with us —

Biff (cutting him off violently): Shut up!

Without another word, Happy goes upstairs.

Linda: You! You didn't even go in to see if he was all right!

Biff (still on the floor in front of Linda, the flowers in his hand; with self-loathing): No. Didn't. Didn't do a damned thing. How do you like that, heh? Left him babbling in a toilet.

Linda: You louse. You . . .

Biff: Now you hit it on the nose! *(He gets up, throws the flowers in the wastebasket.)* The scum of the earth, and you're looking at him!

Linda: Get out of here!

Biff: I gotta talk to the boss, Mom. Where is he?

Linda: You're not going near him. Get out of this house!

Biff (with absolute assurance, determination): No. We're gonna have an abrupt conversation, him and me.

Linda: You're not talking to him!

Hammering is heard from outside the house, off right. Biff turns toward the noise.

Linda (suddenly pleading): Will you please leave him alone?

Biff: What's he doing out there?

Linda: He's planting the garden!

Biff (quietly): Now? Oh, my God!

Biff moves outside, Linda following. The light dies down on them and comes up on the center of the apron as Willy walks into it. He is carrying a flashlight, a hoe, and handful of seed packets. He raps the top of the hoe sharply to fix it firmly, and then moves to the left, measuring off the distance with his foot. He holds the flashlight to look at the seed packets, reading off the instructions. He is in the blue of night.

Willy: Carrots . . . quarter-inch apart. Rows . . . one-foot rows. *(He measures it off.)* One foot. *(He puts down a package and measures off.)* Beets. *(He puts down another package and measures again.)* Lettuce. *(He reads the package, puts it down.)* One foot — *(He breaks off as Ben appears at the right and moves slowly down to him.)* What a proposition, ts, ts. Terrific, terrific. 'Cause she's suffered, Ben, the woman has suffered. You understand me? A man can't go out the way he came in, Ben, a man has got to add up to something. You can't, you can't — *(Ben moves toward him as though to interrupt.)* You gotta consider, now. Don't answer so quick. Remember, it's a guaranteed twenty-thousand-dollar proposition. Now look, Ben, I want you to go through the ins and outs of this thing with me. I've got nobody to talk to, Ben, and the woman has suffered, you hear me?

Ben (standing still, considering): What's the proposition?

Willy: It's twenty thousand dollars on the barrelhead. Guaranteed, gilt-edged, you understand?

Ben: You don't want to make a fool of yourself. They might not honor the policy.

Willy: How can they dare refuse? Didn't I work like a coolie to meet every premium on the nose? And now they don't pay off? Impossible!

Ben: It's called a cowardly thing, William.

Willy: Why? Does it take more guts to stand here the rest of my life ringing up a zero?

Ben (yielding): That's a point, William. *(He moves, thinking, turns.)* And twenty thousand — that *is* something one can feel with the hand, it is there.

Willy (now assured, with rising power): Oh, Ben, that's the whole beauty of it! I see it like a diamond, shining in the dark, hard and rough, that I can pick up and touch in my hand. Not like — like an appointment! This would not be another damned-fool appointment, Ben, and it changes all the aspects. Because he thinks I'm nothing, see, and so he spites me. But the funeral — *(Straightening up.)* Ben, that funeral will be massive! They'll come from Maine, Massachusetts, Vermont, New Hampshire! All the old-timers with the strange license plates — that boy will be thunder-struck, Ben, because he never realized — I am known! Rhode Island, New York, New Jersey — I am known, Ben, and he'll see it with his eyes once and for all. He'll see what I am, Ben! He's in for a shock, that boy!

Ben (coming to the edge of the garden): He'll call you a coward.

Willy (suddenly fearful): No, that would be terrible.

Ben: Yes. And a damned fool.

Willy: No, no, he mustn't, I won't have that! *(He is broken and desperate.)*

Ben: He'll hate you William.

The gay music of the Boys is heard.

Willy: Oh, Ben, how do we get back to all the great times? Used to be so full of light, and comradeship, the sleigh-riding in winter, and the ruddiness on his cheeks. And always some kind of good news coming up, always something nice coming up ahead. And never even let me carry the valises in the house, and simonizing, simonizing that little red car! Why, why can't I give him something and not have him hate me?

Ben: Let me think about it. *(He glances at his watch.)* I still have a little time. Remarkable proposition, but you've got to be sure you're not making a fool of yourself.

Ben drifts off upstage and goes out of sight. Biff comes down from the left.

Willy (suddenly conscious of Biff, turns and looks up at him, then begins picking up the packages of seeds in confusion): Where the hell is that seed? *(Indignantly.)* You can't see nothing out here! They boxed in the whole goddamn neighborhood!

Biff: There are people all around here. Don't you realize that?

Willy: I'm busy. Don't bother me.

Biff (taking the hoe from Willy): I'm saying good-by to you, Pop. *(Willy looks at him, silent, unable to move.)* I'm not coming back any more.

Willy: You're not going to see Oliver tomorrow?

Biff: I've got no appointment, Dad.

Willy: He put his arm around you, and you've got no appointment?

Biff: Pop, get this now, will you? Everytime I've left it's been a fight that sent me out of here. Today I realized something about myself and I tried to explain it to you and I—I think I'm just not smart enough to make any sense out of it for you. To hell with whose fault it is or anything like that. *(He takes Willy's arm.)* Let's just wrap it up, heh? Come on in, we'll tell Mom. *(He gently tries to pull Willy to left.)*

Willy (frozen, immobile, with guilt in his voice): No, I don't want to see her.

Biff: Come on! *(He pulls again, and Willy tries to pull away.)*

Willy (highly nervous): No, no, I don't want to see her.

Biff (tries to look into Willy's face, as if to find the answer there): Why don't you want to see her?

Willy (more harshly now): Don't bother me, will you?

Biff: What do you mean, you don't want to see her? You don't want them calling you yellow, do you? This isn't your fault; it's me, I'm a bum. Now come inside! *(Willy strains to get away.)* Did you hear what I said to you?

Willy pulls away and quickly goes by himself into the house. Biff follows.

Linda (to Willy): Did you plant, dear?

Biff (at the door, to Linda): All right, we had it out. I'm going and I'm not writing any more.

Linda (going to Willy in the kitchen): I think that's the best way, dear. 'Cause there's no use drawing it out, you'll just never get along.

Willy doesn't respond.

Biff: People ask where I am and what I'm doing, you don't know, and you don't care. That way it'll be off your mind and you can start brightening up again. All right? That clears it, doesn't it? *(Willy is silent, and Biff goes to him.)* You gonna wish me luck, scout? *(He extends his hand.)* What do you say?

Linda: Shake his hand, Willy.

Willy (turning to her, seething with hurt): There's no necessity to mention the pen at all, y'know.

Biff (gently): I've got no appointment, Dad.

Willy (erupting fiercely): He put his arm around . . . ?

Biff: Dad, you're never going to see what I am, so what's the use of arguing? If I strike oil I'll send you a check. Meantime forget I'm alive.

Willy (to Linda): Spite, see?

Biff: Shake hands, Dad.

Willy: Not my hand.

Biff: I was hoping not to go this way.

Willy: Well, this is the way you're going. Good-by.

Biff looks at him a moment, then turns sharply and goes to the stairs.

Willy (stops him with): May you rot in hell if you leave this house!

Biff (turning): Exactly what is it that you want from me?

Willy: I want you to know, on the train, in the mountains, in the valleys, wherever you go, that you cut down your life for spite!

Biff: No, no.

Willy: Spite, spite, is the word of your undoing! And when you're down and out, remember what did it. When you're rotting somewhere beside the railroad tracks, remember, and don't you dare blame it on me!

Biff: I'm not blaming it on you!

Willy: I won't take the rap for this, you hear?

Happy comes down the stairs and stands on the bottom step, watching.

Biff: That's just what I'm telling you!

Willy (sinking into a chair at the table, with full accusation): You're trying to put a knife in me — don't think I don't know what you're doing!

Biff: All right, phony! Then let's lay it on the line. *(He whips the rubber tube out of his pocket and puts it on the table.)*

Happy: You crazy —

Linda: Biff! *(She moves to grab the hose, but Biff holds it down with his hand.)*

Biff: Leave it there! Don't move it!

Willy (not looking at it): What is that?

Biff: You know goddam well what that is.

Willy (caged, wanting to escape): I never saw that.

Biff: You saw it. The mice didn't bring it into the cellar! What is this supposed to do, make a hero out of you? This supposed to make me sorry for you?

Willy: Never heard of it.

Biff: There'll be no pity for you, you hear it? No pity!

Willy (to Linda): You hear the spite!

Biff: No, you're going to hear the truth—what you are and what I am!

Linda: Stop it!

Willy: Spite!

Happy (coming down toward Biff): You cut it now!

Biff (to Happy): The man don't know who we are! The man is gonna know! *(To Willy.)* We never told the truth for ten minutes in this house!

Happy: We always told the truth!

Biff (turning on him): You big blow, are you the assistant buyer? You're one of the two assistants to the assistant, aren't you?

Happy: Well, I'm practically—

Biff: You're practically full of it! We all are! And I'm through with it. *(To Willy.)* Now hear this, Willy, this is me.

Willy: I know you!

Biff: You know why I had no address for three months? I stole a suit in Kansas City and I was in jail. *(To Linda, who is sobbing.)* Stop crying. I'm through with it.

Linda turns away from them, her hands covering her face.

Willy: I suppose that's my fault!

Biff: I stole myself out of every good job since high school!

Willy: And whose fault is that?

Biff: And I never got anywhere because you blew me so full of hot air I could never stand taking orders from anybody! That's whose fault it is!

Willy: I hear that!

Linda: Don't, Biff!

Biff: It's goddam time you heard that! I had to be boss big shot in two weeks, and I'm through with it!

Willy: Then hang yourself! For spite, hang yourself!

Biff: No! Nobody's hanging himself, Willy! I ran down eleven flights with a pen in my hand today. And suddenly I stopped, you hear me? And in the middle of that office building, do you hear this? I stopped in the middle of that building and I saw—the sky. I saw the things that I love in this world. The work and the food and time to sit and smoke. And I looked at the pen and said to myself, what the hell am I grabbing this for? Why am I trying to become what I don't want to be? What am I doing in an office, making a contemptuous, begging fool of myself, when all I want is out there, waiting for me the minute I say I know who I am! Why can't I say that, Willy? *(He tries to make Willy face him, but Willy pulls away and moves to the left.)*

Willy (with hatred, threateningly): The door of your life is wide open!

Biff: Pop! I'm a dime a dozen, and so are you!

Willy (turning on him now in an uncontrolled outburst): I am not a dime a dozen! I am Willy Loman, and you are Biff Loman!

Biff starts for Willy, but is blocked by Happy. In his fury, Biff seems on the verge of attacking his father.

Biff: I am not a leader of men, Willy, and neither are you. You were never anything but a hard-working drummer who landed in the ash can like all the rest of them! I'm one dollar an hour, Willy! I tried seven states and couldn't raise it. A buck an hour! Do you gather my meaning? I'm not bringing home any prizes any more, and you're going to stop waiting for me to bring them home!

Willy (directly to Biff): You vengeful, spiteful mutt!

> *Biff breaks from Happy. Willy, in fright, starts up the stairs. Biff grabs him.*

Biff (at the peak of his fury): Pop, I'm nothing! I'm nothing, Pop. Can't you understand that? There's no spite in it any more. I'm just what I am, that's all.

> *Biff's fury has spent itself, and he breaks down, sobbing, holding on to Willy, who dumbly fumbles for Biff's face.*

Willy (astonished): What're you doing? What're you doing? *(To Linda.)* Why is he crying?

Biff (crying, broken): Will you let me go, for Christ's sake? Will you take that phony dream and burn it before something happens? *(Struggling to contain himself, he pulls away and moves to the stairs.)* I'll go in the morning. Put him — put him to bed. *(Exhausted, Biff moves up the stairs to his room.)*

Willy (after a long pause, astonished, elevated): Isn't that — isn't that remarkable? Biff — he likes me!

Linda: He loves you, Willy!

Happy (deeply moved): Always did, Pop.

Willy: Oh, Biff! *(Staring wildly.)* He cried! Cried to me. *(He is choking with his love, and now cries out his promise.)* That boy — that boy is going to be magnificent!

> *Ben appears in the light just outside the kitchen.*

Ben: Yes, outstanding, with twenty thousand behind him.

Linda (sensing the racing of his mind, fearfully, carefully): Now come to bed, Willy. It's all settled now.

Willy (finding it difficult not to rush out of the house): Yes, we'll sleep. Come on. Go to sleep, Hap.

Ben: And it does take a great kind of a man to crack the jungle.

> *In accents of dread, Ben's idyllic music starts up.*

Happy (his arm around Linda): I'm getting married, Pop, don't forget it. I'm changing everything. I'm gonna run that department before the year is up. You'll see, Mom. *(He kisses her.)*

Ben: The jungle is dark but full of diamonds, Willy.

> *Willy turns, moves, listening to Ben.*

Linda: Be good. You're both good boys, just act that way, that's all.

Happy: 'Night, Pop. *(He goes upstairs.)*

Linda (to Willy): Come, dear.

Ben (with greater force): One must go in to fetch a diamond out.

Willy (to Linda, as he moves slowly along the edge of the kitchen, toward the door): I just want to get settled down, Linda. Let me sit alone for a little.

Linda (almost uttering her fear): I want you upstairs.

Willy (taking her in his arms): In a few minutes, Linda. I couldn't sleep right now. Go on, you look awful tired. *(He kisses her.)*

Ben: Not like an appointment at all. A diamond is rough and hard to the touch.

Willy: Go on now. I'll be right up.

Linda: I think this is the only way, Willy.

Willy: Sure, it's the best thing.

Ben: Best thing!

Willy: The only way. Everything is gonna be — go on, kid, get to bed. You look so tired.

Linda: Come right up.

Willy: Two minutes.

Linda goes into the living-room, then reappears in her bedroom. Willy moves just outside the kitchen door.

Willy: Loves me. *(Wonderingly.)* Always loved me. Isn't that a remarkable thing? Ben, he'll worship me for it!

Ben (with promise): It's dark there, but full of diamonds.

Willy: Can you imagine that magnificence with twenty thousand dollars in his pocket?

Linda (calling from her room): Willy! Come up!

Willy (calling into the kitchen): Yes! Yes. Coming! It's very smart, you realize that, don't you, sweetheart? Even Ben sees it. I gotta go, baby. 'By! 'By! *(Going over to Ben, almost dancing.)* Imagine? When the mail comes he'll be ahead of Bernard again!

Ben: A perfect proposition all around.

Willy: Did you see how he cried to me? Oh, if I could kiss him, Ben!

Ben: Time, William, time!

Willy: Oh, Ben, I always knew one way or another we were gonna make it, Biff and I!

Ben (looking at his watch): The boat. We'll be late. *(He moves slowly off into the darkness.)*

Willy (elegiacally, turning to the house): Now when you kick off, boy, I want a seventy-yard boot, and get right down the field under the ball, and when you hit, hit low and hit hard, because it's important, boy. *(He swings around and faces the audience.)* There's all kinds of important people in the stands, and the first thing you know . . . *(Suddenly realizing he is alone.)* Ben! Ben, where do I . . . ? *(He makes a sudden movement of search.)* Ben, how do I . . . ?

Linda (calling): Willy, you coming up?

Willy (uttering a gasp of fear, whirling about as if to quiet her): Sh! *(He turns around as if to find his way; sounds, faces, voices, seem to be swarming in upon him and he flicks at them, crying.)* Sh! Sh! *(Suddenly music, faint and high, stops him. It rises in intensity, almost to an unbearable scream. He goes up and down on his toes, and rushes off around the house.)* Shhh!

Linda: Willy?

There is no answer. Linda waits. Biff gets up off his bed. He is still in his clothes. Happy sits up. Biff stands listening.

Linda (with real fear): Willy, answer me! Willy!

There is the sound of a car starting and moving away at full speed.

Linda: No!

Biff (rushing down the stairs): Pop!

As the car speeds off, the music crashes down in a frenzy of sound, which becomes the soft pulsation of a single cello string. Biff slowly returns to his bedroom. He and Happy gravely don their jackets. Linda slowly walks out of her room. The music has developed into a dead march. The leaves of day are appearing over everything. Charley and Bernard, somberly dressed, appear and knock on the kitchen door. Biff and Happy slowly descend the stairs to the kitchen as Charley and Bernard enter. All stop a moment when Linda, in clothes of mourning, bearing a little bunch of roses, comes through the draped doorway into the kitchen. She goes to Charley and takes his arm. Now all move toward the audience, through the wall-line of the kitchen. At the limit of the apron, Linda lays down the flowers, kneels, and sits back on her heels. All stare down at the grave.

REQUIEM

Charley: It's getting dark, Linda.

Linda doesn't react. She stares at the grave.

Biff: How about it, Mom? Better get some rest, heh? They'll be closing the gate soon.

Linda makes no move. Pause.

Happy (deeply angered): He had no right to do that. There was no necessity for it. We would've helped him.

Charley (grunting): Hmmm.

Biff: Come along, Mom.

Linda: Why didn't anybody come?

Charley: It was a very nice funeral.

Linda: But where are all the people he knew? Maybe they blame him.

Charley: Naa. It's a rough world, Linda. They wouldn't blame him.

Linda: I can't understand it. At this time especially. First time in thirty-five years we were just about free and clear. He only needed a little salary. He was even finished with the dentist.

Charley: No man only needs a little salary.

Linda: I can't understand it.

Biff: There were a lot of nice days. When he'd come home from a trip; or on Sundays, making the stoop; finishing the cellar; putting on the new porch; when he built the extra bathroom; and put up the garage. You know something, Charley, there's more of him in that front stoop than in all the sales he ever made.

Charley: Yeah. He was a happy man with a batch of cement.

Linda: He was so wonderful with his hands.

Biff: He had the wrong dreams. All, all, wrong.

Happy (almost ready to fight Biff): Don't say that!

Biff: He never knew who he was.

Charley (stopping Happy's movement and reply. To Biff): Nobody dast blame this man. You don't understand: Willy was a salesman. And for a salesman, there is no rock bottom to the life. He don't put a bolt to a nut, he don't tell you the law or give you medicine. He's a man way out there in the blue, riding on a smile and a shoeshine. And when they start not smiling back — that's an earthquake. And then you get yourself a couple of spots on your hat, and you're finished. Nobody dast blame this man. A salesman is got to dream, boy. It comes with the territory.

Biff: Charley, the man didn't know who he was.

Happy (infuriated): Don't say that!

Biff: Why don't you come with me, Happy?

Happy: I'm not licked that easily. I'm staying right in this city, and I'm gonna beat this racket! *(He looks at Biff, his chin set.)* The Loman Brothers!

Biff: I know who I am, kid.

Happy: All right, boy. I'm gonna show you and everybody else that Willy Loman did not die in vain. He had a good dream. It's the only dream you can have — to come out number-one man. He fought it out here, and this is where I'm gonna win it for him.

Biff (with a hopeless glance at Happy, bends toward his mother): Let's go, Mom.

Linda: I'll be with you in a minute. Go on, Charley. *(He hesitates.)* I want to, just for a minute. I never had a chance to say good-by.

Charley moves away, followed by Happy. Biff remains a slight distance up and left of Linda. She sits there, summoning herself. The flute begins, not far away, playing behind her speech.

Linda: Forgive me, dear. I can't cry. I don't know what it is, but I can't cry. I don't understand it. Why did you ever do that? Help me, Willy, I can't cry. It seems to me that you're just on another trip. I keep expecting you. Willy, dear, I can't cry. Why did you do it? I search and search and I search, and I can't understand it, Willy. I made the last payment on the house today. Today, dear. And there'll be nobody home. *(A sob rises in her throat.)* We're free and clear. *(Sobbing more fully, released.)* We're free. *(Biff comes slowly toward her.)* We're free . . . We're free . . .

Biff lifts her to her feet and moves out up right with her in his arms. Linda sobs quietly. Bernard and Charley come together and follow them, followed by Happy. Only the music of the flute is left on the darkening stage as over the house the hard towers of the apartment buildings rise into sharp focus, and

The Curtain Falls

CONSIDERATIONS FOR CRITICAL THINKING AND WRITING

1. FIRST RESPONSE. How much do you think Willy Loman is to be blamed for his circumstances? Is he himself mostly at fault or is he a victim of some kind?

2. Discuss Willy's relationship with his sons. What kinds of conflicts does he have with them?

3. What distinguishes Biff and Happy from one another? To what extent do they serve as foils to one another?

4. Describe Linda's relationship with Willy. What sort of marriage do they have? Is she a static or a dynamic character?

5. What do the flashbacks reveal about Willy? Do you think they would enhance or detract from your enjoying a production of the play?

6. Why is being a salesman so important to Willy? What values does he associate with his work?

7. How does Willy define success for himself? Do the other characters share the same perspective?

8. Choose any two minor characters and analyze their function in the play.

9. How might the play be understood as an implicit commentary on the idea of the American Dream? Do you think the American Dream has changed very much since the play was first produced in 1949?

10. *Death of a Salesman* is now more than a half-century old and yet it is widely produced in contemporary playhouses throughout not only America but also many other parts of the world. What do you think it is about this play that keeps it alive?

ESSAYS

REGINA BARRECA (B. 1957)

Born in Brooklyn, New York, Regina Barreca was among the first women to attend Dartmouth College after it went coeducational in the 1970s. She went on to receive a degree from Cambridge University and a Ph.D. from the City University of New York. Her scholarly and popular work focuses primarily on the uses of humor in everyday life. Her books include *They Used to Call Me Snow White, But I Drifted* (1990), *Perfect Husbands (and Other Fairy Tales)* (1993), *Sweet Revenge* (1995), and *Too Much of a Good Thing Is Wonderful* (2000), a collection of her columns from the *Hartford Courant*, the *Orlando Sentinel*, and the *Chicago Tribune*, from which her essay "Envy" is reprinted. She is a professor of English at the University of Connecticut.

Envy   *1996*

"Envy," said a friend on a cold night over a glass of red wine, "is the one vice everybody has experienced. There are people who aren't gluttons, who aren't greedy, and even some who aren't particularly proud. But everybody," he said, leaning over the table and lowering his voice to emphasize the point, "everybody has been envious at some time in their life." I knew what he meant, given that the very day on which we were speaking was full of envy for me. Hell, I envied him as he spoke to me, what with his good job and happy family. Then I remembered that I also had a pretty good job and a pretty happy family. Why, when everything is going fairly well, do we still spend time envying others?

What do I envy? Like every woman over size 10, I envy women under size 10. Like every worker, I envy other people's bigger offices (complete with more windows with better views), better staff, preferred seating at restaurants over power lunches, and mythically proportioned expense accounts. I have foreign language envy: speaking only bad Sicilian and bad French-Canadian (and in these tongues knowing only how to say things you can't say in front of the kids), I routinely envy those fluent in German and Parisian French and Florentine Italian. I envy athletes who play graceful tennis, singers who effortlessly harmonize with Mary Chapin Carpenter, and dancers smooth enough to make George Steinbrenner look like Fred Astaire.

Penis envy I don't have, although I wouldn't mind some of the benefits awarded to those members: full access to the power structure, political influence, a decent credit line, and the ability to walk into a garage without the mechanic thinking, "Oh, good, now I can put that addition on my house," because I have a question about my transmission. (The best story I ever heard as an antidote to Freud concerns a little girl who, when seeing her naked infant brother for the first time, merely commented, "Isn't it a good thing, Mommy, that it isn't on his face?").

I content myself with envying those who are richer, cuter, taller, better, and nicer. I even envy those who are less envious, the ones who applaud the accomplishments of their rivals without a tightening of the fist of the heart. That generosity is characteristic of angels, and not even all of *them* can live up to it: As I remember, Milton's version of the story says that Lucifer took arms against God because of envy, declaring it "Better to reign in hell than serve in heaven."

My pal, I think, is right: Envy is pervasive. Envy is what makes you, when   5
an acquaintance is lustily telling you that she's dating a Greek god of a guy, ask, "Which one, Hades?" Envy makes you, when a co-worker brags about his son's success on the varsity team, say, "How nice. When I bought my new Cadillac last week, my car salesman's assistant had also been a football player." Envy keeps you from saying, "Good for you! You earned it!" even when someone has legitimately, honestly, and sweetly come by some success.

Envy feeds on itself and is a sort of greed with a vengeance. If Greed wants what's out there, Envy feels a sense of entitlement to what's inside. When Greed and Gluttony want something, they grab it and consume it; Pride says that if it can't have it, then it isn't worth wanting; Envy is destined to be perpetually in a state of longing, howling for what appears just out of reach like a shivering dog baying at the moon. Greed wants money, Pride wants fame, and Gluttony wants satisfaction, but Envy wants above all to breed more envy. Envy grows poor because others gain wealth; Envy grows sick because others are healthy; Envy grows gaunt watching others eat.

Snow White's stepmother felt envy after asking that magic mirror, "Who is the fairest of them all?" and hearing the wrong answer, and every kid whose parent says "no" declares himself a similar victim. "You don't want me to go out Saturday night only because you have to stay home," the teenager yells, and half a parent's heart might hear truth in that.

Iago in *Othello* was envious; maybe Hamlet was envious of the man who got to sleep with his mother; and certainly the Beach Boys envied the Beatles. The teacher who downgrades the smartass but nevertheless smart student might be driven by envy, and so might the boss who won't give her administrative assistant the raise she earned. "I got it the hard way," sniffs Envy, "Why should I make it easier for anybody else?"

Envy isn't Jealousy. In *Fatal Attraction*, for example, we meet the mistress who is jealous of the wife, and in *Disclosure* we meet the wife who's jealous of the mistress. These examples highlight the difference between jealousy and envy: the mistress and wife share exactly the same desire for precisely the same man. (These examples also highlight the fact that the Motion Picture Academy should create a category for the best actor in a But-Honey-She-Made-Me-Do-It role and that Michael Douglas should always get that award.) The women circling Douglas like two cheetahs around a kill on the Discovery Channel are jealous of one another and wish to replace one another. That's not the widely sweeping net of envy but the hook of jealousy.

The man who is envious of his neighbor's job, in contrast, probably does not want to steal that job away but instead wants to get a better one. He's envious of the ease with which he assumes his neighbor gets through the day; he doesn't covet his neighbor's wife, particularly, but he might covet his neighbor's 401K. If I envy a model's perfect thighs, I am all too well aware that on my body those thighs would look, to put it kindly, out of place. I don't want her thighs; I just wish mine were better.

The neighbor doesn't want the other guy's job, but he wants acknowledgement that he is equally accomplished. He wants to be number one, to be best, to be the winner. When only one can be declared a winner, that means that the rest of us are "also-rans," looking on from the sidelines, secretly hoping the leader will stumble and their fall will be our big break. It isn't pretty.

Envy is an especially embarrassing vice because it often seems petty. The big sins seem noble; envy creeps around coveting the nobility of a regal vice but never quite making it. When it's not wringing its hands, envy is busy pointing out the spot on the competition's tie. That the spots are there is undeniable, but the glee that envy takes in labeling them gives the game away.

Let's say my actress friend and I go to a movie. If all she can talk about is the awfulness of the heroine's accent, I have a fairly clear sense that envy is coloring her assessment. I can say in all honesty that I thought the performance good or bad, but she can't. Not if the actress is close to her "type." If I can't stand somebody's essay in a magazine, my husband might lightly point out that my distaste is surprising, given that the essayist's style is similar to mine.

Of course that's what's getting to me, and he knows it. Someone who loves you doesn't want you to feel envious because it makes everything else in your life seem unimportant. It seems to say, "If I only had her unfair advantages, then I'd be happy." Someone who loves you wants to hear, "I've got you, so how could I ever envy another person?" This is one reason envy is such a secret vice, and the fact of its secrecy is one of the reasons it is tricky to change.

But I owe a great deal to envy. The first piece I ever sent out for publication I wrote only because a girl I went to college with had two poems printed in a small literary journal that I happened to come across in a tiny bookstore on St. Mark's Place in Manhattan's East Village. There I was, flipping through these thin pages after cranking out another paper for graduate school and there was her name. It tripped some internal alarm signal, her name in print, and all my sirens were immediately set off. I had to do better. For God's sake, I had to do at least as well.

Buying the magazine, I took it home hidden under my jacket as if it were some controlled substance, and I smuggled it up to my typewriter where I read the guidelines for submission as though they were the answers to an exam. Which they were, in a way: my test was to be as good as this phantom rival.

To make a long story short, I got one poem published, one I wrote that night with my eyes more on her words than on my own. I'm sure she never read it; I no longer have any idea where she is or what she is doing, and I'm sure she never even gave me a quarter as much thought as I gave her. And I got only one poem published. I've never felt quite as if I've caught up. So I keep at it.

In a way, though, I am grateful for the spur of envy that night because it drove me on, took me down the dark road of my own ambition and gave me the necessary gall to toss a typed page on an editor's desk. If I hadn't been so envious, I might not have been able to face the blank page. I'm not convinced yet that envy doesn't have something to do with every word that's ever been written, and not only by me.

Perhaps fate has arranged for envy to have its best as well as worst uses, and, as is the case with most of fate's arrangements, we can benefit from those very things we are taught to condemn. Without envy we might escape the pain of comparison but forfeit the vital heat of competition; we might avoid some tingling sorrow but lose the pleasure of unforeseen accomplishment.

Maybe it's a good thing to think that the grass always looks greener on the 20 other side of the fence. Maybe without that belief, we would focus only on the fences, those walls boxing us in and trying to keep us in our place, built as high as they are wide and climbed only at great risk. It's scary to think about getting over them without a reason, and envy can provide a reason — perhaps not a good one, but nonetheless effective.

Envy refuses to allow us to be complacent inside the box of our own making, chides us to move up and out and away into new pastures, across fields of risk. Envy might entice us toward heartbreaking failure or dizzying success, but at least it moves us. That movement, that taking of risk, is what enables us to leave what is familiar and break new ground.

In having such power for good, envy itself is enviable.

CONSIDERATIONS FOR CRITICAL THINKING AND WRITING

1. FIRST RESPONSE. Does the author's confession that her envy of a college acquaintance drove her to send her writing out for publication lessen or strengthen the essay's arguments? Would you feel flattered or disturbed if you were that rival?

2. How do the various references to literature, film, and television enhance the essay's effectiveness?

3. The tone of the essay is a light and humorous one even though its subject is one of the seven deadly sins. Does the humor interfere with or underscore the seriousness of the issues raised?

4. Do you find the argument distinguishing envy from jealousy convincing? What other examples defining the differences between the two emotions can you imagine?

5. Do you agree with the author that it might be "a good thing to think that the grass always looks greener on the other side of the fence," or do you believe envy's negative effects outweigh its positive ones?

GLORIA NAYLOR (B. 1950)

Born in New York City to parents from the rural South, Gloria Naylor was educated at Brooklyn College and Yale University, where she earned a master's degree in Afro-American studies. An essayist and novelist, she has taught at George Washington University, the University of Pennsylvania,

New York University, and Princeton University. In addition to publishing widely in magazines and newspapers, she has written a number of books, including *The Women of Brewster County* (1982), *Linden Hills* (1985), *Mamma Day* (1988), and *Bailey's Cafe* (1992). This essay originally appeared in the *New York Times Magazine*. The title is supplied by the editor.

Taking Possession of a Word   *1986*

Language is the subject. It is the written form with which I've managed to keep the wolf away from the door and, in diaries, to keep my sanity. In spite of this, I consider the written word inferior to the spoken, and much of the frustration experienced by novelists is the awareness that whatever we manage to capture in even the most transcendent passages falls far short of the richness of life. Dialogue achieves its power in the dynamics of a fleeting moment of sight, sound, smell and touch.

I'm not going to enter the debate here about whether it is language that shapes reality or vice versa. That battle is doomed to be waged whenever we seek intermittent reprieve from the chicken and egg dispute. I will simply take the position that the spoken word, like the written word, amounts to a nonsensical arrangement of sounds or letters without a consensus that assigns "meaning." And building from the meanings of what we hear, we order reality. Words themselves are innocuous; it is the consensus that gives them true power.

I remember the first time I heard the word *nigger*. In my third-grade class, our math tests were being passed down the rows, and as I handed the papers to a little boy in back of me, I remarked that once again he had received a much lower mark than I did. He snatched his test from me and spit out that word. Had he called me a nymphomaniac or a necrophiliac, I couldn't have been more puzzled. I didn't know what a nigger was, but I knew that whatever it meant, it was something he shouldn't have called me. This was verified when I raised my hand, and in a loud voice repeated what he had said and watched the teacher scold him for using a "bad" word. I was later to go home and ask the inevitable questions that every black parent must face — "Mommy, what does 'nigger' mean?"

And what exactly did it mean? Thinking back, I realize that this could not have been the first time the word was used in my presence. I was part of a large extended family that had migrated from the rural South after World War II and formed a close-knit network that gravitated around my maternal grandparents. Their ground-floor apartment in one of the buildings they owned in Harlem was a weekend mecca for my immediate family, along with countless aunts, uncles and cousins who brought along assorted friends. It was a bustling and open house with assorted neighbors and tenants popping in and out to exchange bits of gossip, pick up an old quarrel or referee the ongoing checkers game in which my grandmother cheated shamelessly. They were all there to let down their hair and put up their feet after a week of labor in the factories, laundries and shipyards of New York.

Amid the clamor, which could reach deafening proportions — two or three   5
conversations going on simultaneously, punctuated by the sound of a baby's

crying somewhere in the back rooms or out on the street—there was still a rigid set of rules about what was said and how. Older children were sent out of the living room when it was time to get into the juicy details about "you-know-who" up on the third floor who had gone and gotten herself "p-r-e-g-n-a-n-t!" But my parents, knowing that I could spell well beyond my years, always demanded that I follow the others out to play. Beyond sexual misconduct and death, everything else was considered harmless for our young ears. And so among the anecdotes of the triumphs and disappointments in the various workings of their lives, the word nigger was used in my presence, but it was set within contexts and inflections that caused it to register in my mind as something else.

In the singular, the word was always applied to a man who had distinguished himself in some situation that brought their approval for his strength, intelligence or drive:

"Did Johnny *really* do that?"

"I'm telling you, that nigger pulled in $6,000 of overtime last year. Said he got enough for a down payment on a house."

When used with a possessive adjective by a woman—"my nigger"—it became a term of endearment for husband or boyfriend. But it could be more than just a term applied to a man. In their mouths it became the pure essence of manhood—a disembodied force that channeled their past history of struggle and present survival against the odds into a victorious statement of being: "Yeah, that old foreman found out quick enough—you don't mess with a nigger."

In the plural, it became a description of some group within the community that had overstepped the bounds of decency as my family defined it: Parents who neglected their children, a drunken couple who fought in public, people who simply refused to look for work, those with excessively dirty mouths or unkempt households were all "trifling niggers." This particular circle could forgive hard times, unemployment, the occasional bout of depression—they had gone through all of that themselves—but the unforgivable sin was a lack of self-respect.

A woman could never be a "nigger" in the singular, with its connotation of confirming worth. The noun "girl" was its closest equivalent in that sense, but only when used in direct address and regardless of the gender doing the addressing. "Girl" was a token of respect for a woman. The one-syllable word was drawn out to sound like three in recognition of the extra ounce of wit, nerve or daring that the woman had shown in the situation under discussion.

"G-i-r-l, stop. You mean you said that to his face?"

But if the word was used in a third-person reference or shortened so that it almost snapped out of the mouth, it always involved some element of communal disapproval. And age became an important factor in these exchanges. It was only between individuals of the same generation, or from an older person to a younger (but never the other way around), that "girl" would be considered a compliment.

I don't agree with the argument that use of the word *nigger* at this social stratum of the black community was an internalization of racism. The dynamics were the exact opposite: the people in my grandmother's living room took a word that whites used to signify worthlessness or degradation and rendered it impotent. Gathering there together, they transformed "nigger" to signify the varied and complex human beings they knew themselves to be. If the word was to disappear totally from the mouths of even the most liberal of white society, no one in that room was naïve enough to believe it would disappear from white minds. Meeting the word head-on, they proved it had absolutely nothing to do with the way they were determined to live their lives.

So there must have been dozens of times that the "nigger" was spoken in 15 front of me before I reached the third grade. But I didn't "hear" it until it was said by a small pair of lips that had already learned it could be a way to humiliate me. That was the word I went home and asked my mother about. And since she knew that I had to grow up in America, she took me in her lap and explained.

CONSIDERATIONS FOR CRITICAL THINKING AND WRITING

1. FIRST RESPONSE. What do you think is the purpose of Naylor's discussion of the word *nigger*? Why does she think it is important to address this offensive slang term?

2. What is the function of the essay's first two paragraphs? How are they different in tone from the rest of the essay?

3. What are the various contexts cited by Naylor that change the meaning of the term *nigger*?

4. What does Naylor mean when she writes that "the people in my grandmother's living room took a word that whites used to signify worthlessness or degradation and rendered it impotent" (para. 14)?

5. Discuss the significance and impact of the essay's final paragraph.

GARY SOTO (B. 1952)

Born in Fresno, California, Gary Soto earned a bachelor's degree from California State University at Fresno and an M.F.A. from the University of California at Irvine. A poet, essayist, and writer of children's books, Soto has published widely in magazines and literary journals. His poetry books include *Black Hair* (1985), *Home Course in Religion* (1991), and *Junior College* (1997). His children's titles include *Too Many Tamales* (1993), *Old Man and His Door* (1996), and *Big Bushy Mustache* (1998). The following essay originally appeared in the *Iowa Review*.

The Childhood Worries, or Why I Became a Writer 1995

As a boy growing up in Fresno I knew that disease lurked just beneath the skin, that it was possible to wake up in the morning unable to move your legs or arms or even your head, that stone on a pillow. Your eyeballs might still swim in their own liquids as they searched the ceiling, or beyond, toward heaven and whatever savage god did this to you. Frail and whimpering, you could lie in your rickety bed. You could hear the siren blast at the Sun-Maid Raisin plant, and answer that blast with your own chirp-like cry. But that was it for you, a boy now reduced to the dull activity of blinking. In the adjoining rooms, a chair scraped against the linoleum floor, the kitchen faucet ran over frozen chicken parts, the toilet flushed, the radio sputtered something in Spanish. But you were not involved. You lay useless in bed while your family prepared for the day.

Disease startled Uncle Johnnie first, a mole on his forearm having turned cancerous and bright as a red berry. He was living in Texas when he wrote my mother about his illness. We took him in in spring. He lived with us the last three months of his life, mostly lying ill on the couch, a space meant for my brother Rick and me. Before our uncle arrived, we jumped on that couch, me with a flea-like leap and my brother with the heavier bounce of a frog. Now he had the couch to himself, this uncle who was as tender as a pony.

I didn't have much memory to go on. At age six, I didn't lie in bed at night, arms folded behind my head, and savor the time when I was four and a half, a sprout of orneriness. I was too busy in my young body to consider my trail of footprints, all wiped out at the end of a day. But I recall Uncle Johnnie and the apple pie he bought me at Charlie's Market. My greed for sweetness grinned from my sticky mouth, and we devoured the pie as we strolled home, I walking backwards and looking at the market. Later I would return to that market and let my hands settle like small crabs on two candy bars. They opened and closed around them as I decided whether to take them, thus steal, thus let my mouth lather itself with the creamy taste of chocolate. Charlie was probably looking at me, wagging his large Armenian head at my stupidity. But that wasn't the point: I was deciding for myself whether I should sin and then worry about this sin, the wings of my bony shoulder blades less holy.

I recall also when our television was broken and my father pulled the tube out and took it to a repair shop. The TV was eyeless, just sprouts of wires and a smothering scent of dust. While Uncle Johnnie lay on the couch, I climbed into the back of the television set and pretended to be someone funny, one of the Three Stooges, and then someone scary, like Rodan° with his monstrous roar. My uncle watched me with a weary smile but no joy. I told him that I could be funny or scary, but in such a small space I couldn't play a horse or an Indian shot by the cavalry. He died that spring, all because of a cancerous mole, died after the tube was once again fitted into the television set. Then the couch returned to us.

For one summer disease scared me. My whiskery neighbor, whose name I   5
have forgotten, was a talker and addressed every growing plant, chicken, and dog in his dirt yard. When he got sick, his talk increased, as if he needed to get out all the words that he had intended to use in his old age. He had to use them then or never. One afternoon he came into our yard and showed me his fingernails, yellow and hard. He held them out quivering, as if he were going to do a hocus-pocus magic trick, and when he said it was cancer, I flinched. When I looked up into his face, pale as a fistful of straw, I saw that his eyes were large and bluish, his face already sinking in disease. I was eating grapes, feeding them into my mouth, and I didn't know what to do about his dying except to offer him some of my grapes. He laughed at this. He walked away, straight as any other man, and returned to his yard where he talked to himself and revved

---

Rodan: A gigantic bird in nuclear monster films.

up a boat engine clamped to a barrel. A scarf of smoke unfurled from the engine, and the blackish water boiled. He didn't seem to be getting anywhere.

That summer we did our rough living on the street, and our dogs did too. When my Uncle Junior's collie got hit by a car on Van Ness Avenue, I watched my uncle, a teenager with a flattop haircut, gather his dog into his arms. He was the bravest person I knew, for he hugged to his chest what he loved best. A few of the kids from Braly Street milled around; the barber came out of his shop, snapped his sheet as if in surrender, and stared at the commotion for a moment, his eyes the color of twilight itself.

Uncle Junior yelled at us to get away, but I shadowed him for a while, barefoot and pagan. He walked up the alley that ran along our dusty-white house. I didn't know then that he intended to wait out the last breaths and then bury his dog. I didn't know that months later at the end of this same alley we were walking down, a car would roll, its wheels in the air, the man inside dead and his hat as flat as cardboard. I would be excited. Like my uncle's collie, I panted, except from exhilaration, when the police asked if we knew the person. I pointed and said that he lived near the man with the motorboat engine and cancer.

This was the summer I began to worry about disease. My father was in road camp with my uncle Shorty. They'd gotten drunk and stolen a car, but I was behaving. I drank my milk, ate my Graham Crackers, and dutifully picked slivers from my palm, but despite my hygiene, I was involved in disease. One morning my brother woke with his throat pinched with a clot that made it difficult for him to swallow. He opened his mouth in the backyard light and, along with my mother, I looked in, worried that I would have to wallow in the same bedroom and, in time, the same disease. His mouth was like any other mouth, wet with a push of milky air. But our mother knew better: the tonsils would have to come out. Mine would have to come out, too, no matter how many times I swallowed, cried, and said, "See, Mom, I'm OK." She figured that if you do one son you might as well do two.

That night I stood by the window in our bedroom and ate M & M candies and wondered about Father and Uncle Shorty. They were in a sort of a prison camp, I knew. We had gone to see them, and father had shown me his hands, which were speckled white with paint. I rode on his knee, a camel ride of excitement because I was chewing gum and sunflower seeds at the same time. I asked him when he was coming home. Pretty soon, he answered. I didn't know that he and my uncle were painting rocks along the rural Kearny Boulevard and hoisting railroad ties that became bumpers in the gravel parking lots of Kearny Park.

I thought about them as I ate my M & Ms and touched my throat when I 10 swallowed the candy. Father wasn't there to help me. He was far away, it seemed, and I peered out the window toward the junkyard, with its silhouette of pipes, plumbing, and jagged sheet metal, the playground of my childhood. The summer wind picked up the metallic scent and whipped it about. When a sweep of headlights from the cars that turned from Van Ness onto Braly Street frisked the junkyard, the eyes of its German Shepherd watchdog glowed orange and stared at me. I ate my candy, one last taste of sweetness on the eve of blood and gagging.

When we arrived at the community hospital, I hugged my pajamas and coloring book. I glanced nervously down the corridor. I looked at the old people's yellow fingernails, clear signs of cancer, and I peeked in a lab where I knew that blood was drawn. My brother and I walked on each side of our mother. We were led to a room where there was another child sitting up in a crib-like bed, mute as a teddy bear. He spit red into a bowl, and I immediately knew this was a scary place.

After we settled into our room, I worried not about dying, but about the filthy act of baring my bottom to a bedpan. I was in a hospital gown, not my pajamas. I held out for hours, but when I couldn't stand it anymore, I told the nurse I had to use the bathroom. She wouldn't allow me to get up from bed. I started to cry, but she scolded me, and I knew better than to carry on because she had the instruments of pain. I told my brother not to laugh, but he was too scared to entertain the thought. I squatted on the bedpan and was letting my water flow when a blind, teenage girl walked past our open door, a ghost-like figure blowing down the corridor. A nurse was helping her along, step by hesitant step. I wanted to ask the nurse if she was blind forever, or would she one day peel off that bandage and smile at every bloodshot color in the precious world. I did my number and then looked over at the boy, now asleep and pale as an angel.

I don't recall my brother and me talking much at the hospital. I lay in bed, touching the plastic wrist band with my typed name. I closed my eyes. I tried to shut out the image of the "thing" they would take out of my throat, a kidney-bean sac no longer needed. I knew that my baby teeth would eventually loosen and come out, possibly when I was biting into a peach or an apple, but I was terrified that someone behind a white mask would probe my mouth.

A few hours later, my brother was wheeled away with tears brimming in his eyes. If my big brother had dime-sized tears in his eyes, than I, his little brother with just baby teeth, would have silver dollars rolling down my cheeks. I considered crying and sobbing as pitifully as I could manage, but who would listen? My mother was gone, a tiny egg of memory living inside my head. Now my brother was gone. I looked over to where the other boy was, but his parents had come and rescued him. I didn't have anything to do except thumb through my animal coloring book and imagine what crayons I would use on the deer, elephant, giraffe, and grinning hyena. This diversion helped. But then I was wheeled away.

This was the late '50s when almost every child's tonsils were routinely 15 clipped from his throat. I remember the room where a nurse in a mask lowered a disk-like mask onto my nose and mouth. She lowered it three times and each time said, "breathe in" as they basted my face with ether. I did what I was told until my consciousness receded like a wave, and I was in a room full of testing patterns, something like television when it was still too early for cartoons. They operated, and I bled into a bowl all night, it seemed, but happily drank 7-Up with no ice, a treat that didn't cost me anything except for hoarse speech for three days.

When Rick and I got home, we were pampered with ice cream and 7-Up, a lovely blast of carbonation which singed my nostrils. I believed that we might continue to live our remaining childhood that way with mounds of ice cream, 7-Up, and cooing words from our mother. But too soon that stopped, and we were back to the usual plates of *frijoles* and tortillas. At that time, while my father and uncle were in jail, my mother worked at Readi-Spud, peeling potatoes that scurried down troughs of icy water. She would give us over to Mrs.

Moreno, the mother of at least nine children and the jolliest woman in the western world. She laughed more than she spoke, and she spoke a lot. While in Mrs. Moreno's care, I became even more worried about disease because I knew roaches made a princely living in her cupboards.

Mrs. Moreno worked at a Chinese noodle factory and came to get Rick and me after work. One day, when we climbed into the back seat of her station wagon, her son Donald was standing in a cardboard tub of noodles. His feet pumped up and down and emitted a sucking sound with each marching step. When I asked Mrs. Moreno about dinner she was laughing because the baby on the front seat was crawling toward her breast. She giggled, "You like chow mein?" I slowly lowered my gaze to Donald's bare feet and felt sick.

They ate noodles right after we arrived, slurped them down so that the ends wiggled like worms into their suctioning mouths. My brother and I ate grapes and drank water. Later, all of us — eleven kids — played our version of "The Old Woman Who Lived in a Shoe." We climbed onto the roof and jumped off, a cargo of unkillable kids hitting the ground like sacks of flour. It may not have been that same evening, but I recall three babies at the end of a long, dirty hallway and some of the kids, the older ones, trying to knock them over with a real bowling ball. There was squealing and crying, but it was mostly laughter that cut through the cloistered air of a dank hallway, laughter coming even from Mrs. Moreno when one of the babies went down.

One untroubled afternoon Lloyd showed me a toy rifle, the kind that you had to crack in half to cock and which shot arrows tipped with red suction cups. He took one suction cup off, cocked the rifle, and shot the arrow into the flat spatula of his palm. "It doesn't hurt," he told me, and let me shoot the arrow repeatedly into my palm, the pressure of the arrow no more than a push. He recocked the rifle and fit the arrow into one of his nostrils. I automatically stepped back even though Lloyd was smiling. He was smiling just a moment before he pulled the trigger, before blood suddenly streamed from his nose and his eyes grew huge as two white moons and full of fright. He started crying and running around the house with the arrow in his nose, and I ran after him, almost crying. When his mother caught him by the arm, I raced out of the house, not wanting to get involved, and returned home, scared as I touched my own nose. I imagined the arrow in my own nose. I imagined blood spilling on the back porch. Later, just after I had finished dinner, I returned to Lloyd's house. He was at the table, with the threads of cotton balls hanging from his nostrils. The family was eating chow mein, piled like worms and wiggling down their throats.

The house was a poor, curled shoe, and it scared me because in its careless- 20 ness lurked disease and calamity. I recall standing at their stove and asking a teenage boy who had drifted inside the house, "What's that you're making?" I looked at a large, dented kettle containing a grayish soup which Arnold was stirring with a pencil. I peeked into the soup, sipped it with a large spoon, and saw small things wheeling in the water as he stirred them — a merry-go-round of meats, I thought. When he said, "pigeons," I looked closely and could see the plucked birds bob and rise, bob and rise, and with each rise I could see the slits of their closed eyes.

The Moreno place, however, was not nearly as scary as the hospital. There were no instruments of pain, unless you counted the hive of tapeworms that showed up later because I ate raw bacon, white strips we peeled like Band-Aids from the wrapper. The Morenos taught me this too; they said it was good, and I ate my share while sitting on the roof, the sunset a stain the color of bright, bright medicine. How I would need that sun! How I would need a cure for my worry, and a cure for my brother, who was sporting on the bottom of his foot a sliver the size of a chopstick.

At age six disease scared me, and so did Grandpa, who lived just down the alley from our house on Braly Street. When I went over to eat lunch—yet another pile of *frijoles* wrapped in a diaper-sized tortilla—he was at the kitchen table playing solitaire with a big chunk of his head missing. I backed out of the house, bristling with fear, because the only thing left was his face. He looked like the poker-face card in front of him: Jack of Bad Luck, or King of Almighty Mistakes? While I backed out of the screen door, Uncle Junior caught me from behind and nudged me into the kitchen. He told me that Grandpa was wearing a nylon stocking on his head, trying to grow his hair back. A stinky concoction of *yerba buena*° and earthly fuels smothered his crown and temples. I sat down and ate my beans while watching Grandpa eat from his plate. I asked him if his head would grow back; he was chewing a huge amount of food like a camel. I thought I would turn seven by the time he cleared his throat and heard his answer, which was, "Mi'jo,° you got beans on your shirt. Shaddup."

Two kittens died from distemper and then Pete, our canary, was devoured by mama cat. A stray dog showed up outside our yard with a piece of wood in its watery eye. I touched my own eye, pulling at a tiny string of sleep. Everything seemed ill and ominous. Even our house began to slip on its foundation, which excited me because the bathroom was now at a slant. The water in the tub slouched now that one side was higher. With a scoop of my hands, it was easy to force a tidal wave on the line of ants scurrying along the baseboard.

I looked around at family and friends who were hurt or dying, but I didn't know that a year later my father would die, his neck broken in an industrial accident. This would be in August, when we were settled in a new house the color of cement. He didn't live in that house more than a week, and then he was gone. The funeral didn't mean much to me. It was the scent of flowers and the wash of tears; it was a sympathetic squeeze of my shoulders and candies slipped into the pockets of my tweed coat, which was too small because it was borrowed. After his burial I recall eating donuts at my grandparents' house. When a doctor was called because Grandma was in hysterics, I didn't stop eating. I took what was rightly mine and devoured it in the dark, near the ugly claw-like crowns of a rose bush.

I didn't know what to think except that Father was out of prison and now ²⁵ in the earth forever. Because he wasn't returning, I began to play with his squeaky hand drill, boring into trees and fences. I liked the smell of the blond shavings and liked to think that maybe Father used the drill in prison. He mostly painted rocks, this much I was told, but I fantasized about how he might have used it in prison to get away. I saw him poking holes in a cement wall and then pushing over that wall to get Uncle Shorty in the adjacent cell. Uncle Johnnie was there, too, a ghost-like bundle of flesh on the cot. My father was going to save not only the both of them, but in the end himself as well.

Occasionally, we would visit my father's grave, where my mother cried and set flowers, half-shadowing the oval photo on his grave. What worried me was

---

yerba buena: A mint tea.   *Mi'jo:* My son (*mi hijo*).

not his death, but the gold-painted cannon on a hill that pointed at our Chevy when we drove through the cement gates. The cannon scared me because my vision of death was that when you died an angel would pick you up, place your head in the cannon, and give your neck a little twist. I was spooked by this cannon and wanted to ask my mother about it, but she was too busy in her sorrow for a straight answer. I kept quiet on the matter. I figured there was one cannon, like one God, and all graves rolled on a hill. In time, you were asked to put your head in a cannon and die as well.

I didn't realize that I was probably ill. Neither did I realize how I used my time when my mother would send me off to school. For weeks, I didn't go there. I stayed in an alley, kicking though the garbage and boredom, and returned home only after I assumed my classmates had finished with whatever the teacher had asked them to do. Sometimes I would take the drill and make holes, occasionally even in the lawn. But I had grown bored with this. I had discovered how I could make a huge noise. In the empty bedroom, the one my father and mother would have used, I spent hours with fistfuls of marbles. I bounced them off the baseboard, a ricochetting clatter that I imagined were soldiers getting their fill of death. The clatter of noise busied my mind with something like hate. If I had looked into a mirror, I would have seen this hate pleated on my forehead. If anyone, including my sister or brother, had smarted off to me, I had plans to get even. I would let them go to sleep and then blast them with marbles at close range as they inhaled a simple dream.

My mother was alone, and in her loneliness she often piled us into our Chevy and drove us over to my *nina's* house on the west side of Fresno, a place that was so scary that even the blacks were afraid. My *nina* — godmother — took in identical twin boys, same age as me but filthier. Their dirty hair was like the hair Woody Woodpecker wore. They were orphans. They were sadly nicknamed "Caca" and "Peepee," and for a while they made me feel good because I knew they were poorer than me. "Peepee, is your dad dead?" I would ask. "Caca, what grade are you in?" I would inquire. They shrugged their shoulders a lot and ran when they saw my *nina,* a woman you dared not play with. Every time we visited, I took a toy to show them — plastic plane, steel car, sock of marbles, and even my brother's glow-in-the-dark statue of Jesus. I wanted them to know that even though my father was dead, I still owned things. After a few visits I didn't have anything left to share, just a ten-foot link of rubber bands. This lack made me mad, and I began to pick on them, even beat them up, in a kind of Punch-and-Judy show in the dirt driveway. When we found out that the twins were scared of ghosts, my brother and Rachel, my *nina's* daughter, told them to sit and wait in the living room because their mother and father were going to pick them up. We gave them fistfuls of raisins. Rick and Rachel then ran outside, where they scraped a bamboo rake against the window. The twins looked at me, then the curtain that was dancing like ghosts from the blast of the window cooler. Their mouths stopped churning on those raisins and the gray light of the TV flashed briefly in their eyes. When I yelled, "*La llorona*° is outside," they jumped and ran from the house, poor, terrified "Caca" and "Peepee" living up to their names that early evening.

I often attended church, a place that was scarier than the hospital or the Moreno's house or grandfather's head. Mother said that Jesus had been a good

La llorona: The weeping woman; a ghost in a Mexican folk tale.

man, and he wanted peace and harmony in the hearts of all men. She said this while I looked at Jesus on his cross, poor Jesus who had nails and blood all over him. If they did that to someone who was so good I wondered what they might do to me. You see, I was turning out bad. I was so angry from having to worry all the time that I had become violent. Once I stuck a broken shaft of bottle in my brother's leg for going swimming without me. Blood ran down my knuckles, and I ran away amazed that it was so calming to hurt someone who was bigger. My mother beat me with a hanger for my violence and then made me eat dinner in the bathroom. I put my bowl first on the hamper, then moved it to my knees, because I wanted a better view of the faucet dripping water. In the bathroom, then, I began to worry about our wasting water. I counted the drips to a hundred. I swallowed and pictured in my mind a pagan baby sucking a rock for moisture. Later, after I was allowed out of the bathroom, I took a pair of pliers and tried to tighten the faucet. I managed only to scratch the chrome plating on the faucets, and I went to bed worrying that my mother would conclude that it was me. I closed my eyes and let the pagan baby swallow the rock.

I asked my mother if you ever had to stop worrying, or if you had to continue until you were old. I was already tired of having to learn about Jesus and the more important apostles. She answered yes and mumbled something about life not being easy. This was when I began to look at pictures in the medical dictionary: ringworms, rickets, TB, tongues with canker sores, and elephantiasis. With elephantiasis, the scariest disease, your legs swelled fat as water balloons and, I suspected, sloshed some evil liquids. I looked down at my own legs, those reeds of bone and marrow. They were skinny, but still I worried that my legs could swell and the rest of me, arms mainly, would stay thin, possibly from rickets which had made headway at school. I would be the second deformed kid on this street, the other being an older boy with one small arm that was shaped like a banana.

I knew the face of the boy in the iron lung. His hair was black and his eyes flat. He was motherless, for who could wrap a loving hug around a machine large as a barrel. I could hardly look at this boy. He might have shared my name, or my brother's name, or been related to the kid at school who had one leg shrunken from polio. I didn't like the idea of lying down for what might be forever. Still, I practiced what he lived by lying still on the couch until I fell asleep. When I woke I didn't know if I was at the new house or the old house, or if an angel had already picked me up and fit my head in the gold-painted cannon.

Then I worried about air and radiation and religious equations like the Trinity and, finally, the march of communists against our country. The hollowness in my face concerned my mother. She studied me when I did my homework at the kitchen table. She suspected that I might have ringworm because there were pale splotches on my face. It was only dirt, though, a film of dirt you could rub off with spit and a thumb.

My worry lessened when I began to understand that nothing could really hurt me. It was another summer and the beginning of the '60s. On our new street, which was green with lawns and squeaky with new trikes, I discovered my invincibility when I was running with new friends, barefoot, and with no shirt. I was particularly proud because I had hooked a screwdriver in a belt loop on my pants. I tripped and fell, and as I fell I worried for a moment, wondering if the screwdriver would drive its point into my belly. The fall was slow, like the build-up to my seven years, and the result would either be yes or no to my living.

The screwdriver kicked up sparks when it cut across the sidewalk. They were wonderful, these sparks that lasted no longer than a blink. Right then, with gravel pitted in my palm and my belly spanked by the fall, I rolled onto my back, cried, and knew that hurt and disease were way off, in another country, one that thanks to Jesus Almighty, I would never think to visit.

Considerations for Critical Thinking and Writing

1. FIRST RESPONSE. What do you think is the overall purpose of this essay? What do you think is Soto's central point in writing it?

2. In spite of all the disease, death, violence, chaos, filth, and anxiety that is described in this essay, why would it be inaccurate to describe the narrator as pessimistic?

3. Describe how the essay is organized. How does its structure contribute to its meaning?

4. Discuss the significance of the final two paragraphs. How would the tone and meaning of the essay shift if these two paragraphs were eliminated?

5. Comment on the essay's title. In what sense does the essay explain "Why I Became a Writer"?

Critical Analysis

This casebook shows how one student, Nancy Lager, drafts a formal analysis of the John Updike short story "A & P" (p. 981). You may want to read Updike's story if you haven't already. Nancy was told to think about what kind of lesson Sammy learns in the story, and how the formal elements of the story work to construct and reinforce the theme. As she read, she made notes in the margin about the different elements. Do you think one element—plot, character, setting, or something else—is ultimately more important to the story's effect? You may find it helpful, as Nancy did, to review the Questions for Writing about Fiction (p. 194) in Chapter 5.

A Sample First Response

After reading "A & P" twice, Nancy writes a first, informal response. Her instructor asked her to write a brief response to the questions *"What strikes you most in this story? What lesson do you think has been learned, and by whom?"* How would you answer those same questions?

The title for this story is strange. I didn't know what to make of it until my second reading (it's a grocery store!). Sammy's descriptions of the A & P seem accurate and they're pretty funny too. I liked the little details about the HiHo crackers, the rows of food, and the "rubber tile floor." Ugh! Sammy is like the guys I knew in high school who worked at McDonald's and Stop & Shop. They all made fun of those places. The customers and other employees got ragged too, so the story's setting seems very realistic to me.

I can also imagine everyone being upset and bothered by three girls coming into the store in their bathing suits.

Everywhere I go I see signs that say "NO SHIRT, NO SHOES, NO
SERVICE." Even in winter. But I think more is at stake in this
story than just service. Lengel is obviously the antagonist to
Sammy, and he is most directly connected to the policies associated with the store. In a sense, Lengel is the A & P because
he's the manager, so maybe the store can be seen as the antagonist too. That explains why Sammy quits--besides wanting to be
a hero, he quits the A & P policies. That way the emphasis on
the title makes sense.

A Sample of Brainstorming

Nancy had asked herself what the significance of Updike's title was
before reading the story; in the course of reading "A & P" and writing her
first response, she answered her question with the observation that the setting seemed particularly important to this narrative. This answer is only
the beginning of a tentative thesis, though, and she realized that she still
had to explain *how* the setting is important and *what exactly* in the text suggested its importance. Her brainstorming notes show her fleshing out her
support, with quotations from the story under headings that represent
what Nancy sees as three different aspects of the setting.

A & P

"usual traffic"

lights and tile

"electric eye"

shoppers like "sheep," "houseslaves," "pigs"

"Alexandrov and Petrooshki"—Russia

New England Town

typical: bank, church, etc.

traditional

conservative

proper

near Salem—witch trials

puritanical

intolerant

Lengel

"manager"

"doesn't miss that much" (like lady shopper)

Sunday school

"It's our policy"

spokesman for A & P values

A Sample Student Analysis

After her first response, Nancy is ready to turn her notes from reading and first response into a formal analysis. Notice how she opens with a thesis that clearly states what she wants to prove: that the setting of the story is "crucial" to our understanding of what happens. Notice also how she uses the quotations she'd found earlier to support her points. As you read her essay, think about what works and what doesn't in her analysis. Do you find her support persuasive? Could she have gone further with her observations?

Nancy Lager
Professor Taylor
English 102-12
April 1, 20--

                The A & P as a State of Mind

    The setting of John Updike's "A & P" is crucial to
our understanding of Sammy's decision to quit his job.
Although Sammy is the central character in the story and
we learn that he is a principled, good-natured nineteen-
year-old with a sense of humor, Updike seems to invest as
much effort in describing the setting as he does in
Sammy. The setting is the antagonist and plays a role
that is as important as Sammy's. The title, after all, is
not "Youthful Rebellion" or "Sammy Quits" but "A & P."
Even though Sammy knows that his quitting will make life
more difficult for him, he instinctively insists on
rejecting what the A & P comes to represent in the story.
When he rings up a "No Sale" and "saunter[s]" (985) out
of the store, he leaves behind not only a job but the
rigid state of mind associated with the A & P.

    Sammy's descriptions of the A & P present a setting
that is ugly, monotonous, and rigidly regulated. The fluorescent light is as blandly cool as the "checkerboard
green-and-cream rubber-tile floor" (983). We can see the
uniformity Sammy describes because we have all been in
chain stores. The "usual traffic" (983) moves in one
direction (except for the swimsuited girls, who move
against it), and everything is neatly ordered and categorized in tidy aisles. The dehumanizing routine of this
environment is suggested by Sammy's offhand references to
the typical shoppers as "sheep" (983), "houseslaves"
(983), and "pigs" (985). They seem to pace through the
store in a stupor; as Sammy tells us, not even dynamite
could move them.

Lager 2

The A & P is appropriately located "right in the middle" (983) of a proper, conservative, traditional New England town north of Boston. This location, coupled with the fact that the town is only five miles from Salem, the site of the famous seventeenth-century witch trials, suggests a narrow, intolerant social atmosphere in which there is no room for stepping beyond the boundaries of what is regarded as normal and proper. The importance of this setting can be appreciated even more if we imagine the action taking place in, say, a mellow suburb of southern California. In this prim New England setting, the girls in their bathing suits are bound to offend somebody's sense of propriety.

As soon as Lengel sees the girls, the inevitable conflict begins. He embodies the dull conformity represented by the A & P. As "manager," he is both the guardian and enforcer of "policy" (984). When he gives the girls "that sad Sunday-school-superintendent stare" (984), we know we are in the presence of the A & P version of a dreary bureaucrat who "doesn't miss that much" (984). He is as unsympathetic and unpleasant as the woman "with rouge on her cheeks and no eyebrows" who pounces on Sammy for ringing up her "HiHo crackers" (982) twice. Like the "electric eye" (985) in the doorway, her vigilant eyes allow nothing to escape their notice. For Sammy the logical extension of Lengel's "policy" is the half-serious notion that one day the A & P might be known as the "Great Alexandrov and Petrooshki Tea Company" (983). Sammy's connection between what he regards as mindless "policy" and Soviet oppression is obviously an exaggeration, but the reader is invited to entertain the similarities anyway.

The reason Sammy quits his job has less to do with defending the girls than with his own sense of what it

Lager 2

means to be a decent human being. His decision is not
an easy one. He doesn't want to make trouble or disap-
point his parents, and he knows his independence and
self-reliance (the other side of New England tradition)
will make life more complex for him. In spite of his own
hesitations, he finds himself blurting out "Fiddle-de-
doo" to Lengel's policies and in doing so knows that his
grandmother "would have been pleased" (985). Sammy's "No
Sale" rejects the crabbed perspective on life that Lengel
represents as manager of the A & P. This gesture is more
than just a negative, however, for as he punches in that
last entry on the cash register, "the machine whirs 'pee-
pul'" (985). His decision to quit his job at the A & P is
an expression of his refusal to regard policies as more
important than people.

12

The Natural and Unnatural

As we move into the twenty-first century, advancing technology and the increasing public exposure to "virtual" experiences and artifacts have thickened and complicated the distinction between the natural and the unnatural. The poems, stories, essays, and play in this chapter all touch on the difference between the world made by man and that constructed outside of human means. As you read the works in this chapter, you might want to consider what you know about the time and place from which a work has been produced—as well as what you know about the author. The works that focus on nature and were produced more than fifty years ago—by Emily Dickinson, Robert Frost, and Henry David Thoreau, for example—compare and contrast in interesting ways with those written more recently on the same theme—such as T. Coraghessan Boyle's "Carnal Knowledge" and Alden Nowlan's "The Bull Moose." Tim O'Brien's "How to Tell a True War Story" and Wilfred Owen's "Dulce et Decorum Est"—both on war, though two different ones with different horrors—speak directly to each other. You'll undoubtedly discover other connections as you read and bring your own knowledge of the natural and unnatural to bear on the literature.

FICTION

MARGARET ATWOOD (B. 1939)

Born in Ottawa, Ontario, Margaret Atwood was educated at the University of Toronto and Harvard University. She has been writing fiction and poetry since she was a child; along the way she has done odd jobs and been a screenwriter and a teacher. Among her collections of short stories are *Dancing Girls* (1977), *Bluebird's Egg* (1983), and *Wilderness Tips* (1991), from which "Death by Landscape" is taken. Her highly successful novels include *Surfacing* (1972), *The Handmaid's Tale* (1986), *Cat's Eye* (1989), *The Robber Bride* (1993), and *Alias Grace* (1995). She has also written more than a dozen books of poetry. Atwood has enhanced the appreciation of Canadian literature through her editing of *The New Oxford Book of Canadian Verse in English* (1982) and *The Oxford Book of Canadian Short Stories in English* (1986). Her own work closely examines the weight of the complex human relationships that complicate her characters' lives.

Death by Landscape 1991

Now that the boys are grown up and Rob is dead, Lois has moved to a condominium apartment in one of the newer waterfront developments. She is relieved not to have to worry about the lawn, or about the ivy pushing its muscular little suckers into the brickwork, or the squirrels gnawing their way into the attic and eating the insulation off the wiring, or about strange noises. This building has a security system, and the only plant life is in pots in the solarium.

Lois is glad she's been able to find an apartment big enough for her pictures. They are more crowded together than they were in the house, but this arrangement gives the walls a European look: blocks of pictures, above and beside one another, rather than one over the chesterfield, one over the fireplace, one in the front hall, in the old acceptable manner of sprinkling art around so it does not get too intrusive. This way has more of an impact. You know it's not supposed to be furniture.

None of the pictures is very large, which doesn't mean they aren't valuable. They are paintings, or sketches and drawings, by artists who were not nearly as well known when Lois began to buy them as they are now. Their work later turned up on stamps, or as silk-screen reproductions hung in the principals' offices of high schools, or as jigsaw puzzles, or on beautifully printed calendars sent out by corporations as Christmas gifts, to their less important clients. These artists painted mostly in the twenties and thirties and forties; they painted landscapes. Lois has two Tom Thomsons, three A. Y. Jacksons, a Lawren Harris. She has an Arthur Lismer, she has a J. E. H. MacDonald. She has a David Milne. They are pictures of convoluted tree trunks on an island of pink wave-smoothed stone, with more islands behind: of a lake with rough, bright, sparsely wooded cliffs; of a vivid river shore with a tangle of bush and two beached canoes, one red, one gray; of a yellow autumn woods with the ice-blue gleam of a pond half-seen through the interlaced branches.

It was Lois who'd chosen them. Rob had no interest in art, although he could see the necessity of having something on the walls. He left all the decorating decisions to her, while providing the money, of course. Because of this collection of hers, Lois's friends — especially the men — have given her the reputation of having a good nose for art investments.

But this is not why she bought the pictures, way back then. She bought them because she wanted them. She wanted something that was in them, 5 although she could not have said at the time what it was. It was not peace: she does not find them peaceful in the least. Looking at them fills her with a wordless unease. Despite the fact that there are no people in them or even animals, it's as if there is something, or someone, looking back out.

When she was thirteen, Lois went on a canoe trip. She'd only been on overnights before. This was to be a long one, into the trackless wilderness, as Cappie put it. It was Lois's first canoe trip, and her last.

Cappie was the head of the summer camp to which Lois had been sent ever since she was nine. Camp Manitou, it was called; it was one of the better ones, for girls, though not the best. Girls of her age whose parents could afford it were routinely packed off to such camps, which bore a generic resemblance to one another. They favored Indian names and had hearty, energetic leaders, who were called Cappie or Skip or Scottie. At these camps you learned to swim well and sail, and paddle a canoe, and perhaps ride a horse or play tennis. When you weren't doing these things you could do Arts and Crafts and turn out dingy, lumpish clay ashtrays for your mother — mothers smoked more, then — or bracelets made of colored braided string.

Cheerfulness was required at all times, even at breakfast. Loud shouting and the banging of spoons on the tables were allowed, and even encouraged, at ritual intervals. Chocolate bars were rationed, to control tooth decay and pimples. At night, after supper, in the dining hall or outside around a mosquito-infested campfire ring for special treats, there were singsongs. Lois can still remember all the words to "My Darling Clementine," and to "My Bonnie Lies over the Ocean," with acting-out gestures: a rippling of the hands for "the ocean," two hands together under the cheek for "lies." She will never be able to forget them, which is a sad thought.

Lois thinks she can recognize women who went to these camps, and were good at it. They have a hardness to their handshakes, even now; a way of standing, legs planted firmly and farther apart than usual; a way of sizing you up, to see if you'd be any good in a canoe — the front, not the back. They themselves would be in the back. They would call it the stern.

She knows that such camps still exist, although Camp Manitou does not. 10 They are one of the few things that haven't changed much. They now offer copper enameling, and functionless pieces of stained glass baked in electric ovens, though judging from the productions of her friends' grandchildren the artistic standards have not improved.

To Lois, encountering it in the first year after the war, Camp Manitou seemed ancient. Its log-sided buildings with the white cement in between the half-logs, its flagpole ringed with whitewashed stones, its weathered gray dock jutting out into Lake Prospect, with its woven rope bumpers and its rusty rings for tying up, its prim round flowerbed of petunias near the office door, must surely have been there always. In truth it dated only from the first decade of the century; it had been founded by Cappie's parents, who'd thought of camping as bracing to the character, like cold showers, and had been passed along to her as an inheritance, and an obligation.

Lois realized, later, that it must have been a struggle for Cappie to keep Camp Manitou going, during the Depression and then the war, when money did not flow freely. If it had been a camp for the very rich, instead of the merely well off, there would have been fewer problems. But there must have been enough Old Girls, ones with daughters, to keep the thing in operation, though not entirely shipshape: furniture was battered, painted trim was peeling, roofs leaked. There were dim photographs of these Old Girls dotted around the dining hall, wearing ample woolen bathing suits and showing their fat, dimpled legs, or standing, arms twined, in odd tennis outfits with baggy skirts.

In the dining hall, over the stone fireplace that was never used, there was a huge molting stuffed moose head, which looked somehow carnivorous. It was a sort of mascot; its name was Monty Manitou. The older campers spread the story that it was haunted, and came to life in the dark, when the feeble and undependable lights had been turned off or, due to yet another generator failure, had gone out. Lois was afraid of it at first, but not after she got used to it.

Cappie was the same: you had to get used to her. Possibly she was forty, or thirty-five, or fifty. She had fawn-colored hair that looked as if it was cut with a bowl. Her head jutted forward, jigging like a chicken's as she strode around the camp, clutching notebooks and checking things off in them. She was like their minister in church: both of them smiled a lot and were anxious because they wanted things to go well; they both had the same overwashed skins and stringy necks. But all this disappeared when Cappie was leading a singsong, or otherwise leading. Then she was happy, sure of herself, her plain face almost luminous. She wanted to cause joy. At these times she was loved, at others merely trusted.

There were many things Lois didn't like about Camp Manitou, at first. She 15 hated the noisy chaos and spoon-banging of the dining hall, the rowdy singsongs at which you were expected to yell in order to show that you were enjoying yourself. Hers was not a household that encouraged yelling. She hated the necessity of having to write dutiful letters to her parents claiming she was having fun. She could not complain, because camp cost so much money.

She didn't much like having to undress in a roomful of other girls, even in the dim light, although nobody paid any attention, or sleeping in a cabin with seven other girls, some of whom snored because they had adenoids or colds, some of whom had nightmares, or wet their beds and cried about it. Bottom bunks made her feel closed in, and she was afraid of falling out of top ones; she was afraid of heights. She got homesick, and suspected her parents of having a better time when she wasn't there than when she was, although her mother wrote to her every week saying how much they missed her. All this was when she was nine. By the time she was thirteen she liked it. She was an old hand by then.

Lucy was her best friend at camp. Lois had other friends in winter, when there was school and itchy woolen clothing and darkness in the afternoons, but Lucy was her summer friend.

She turned up the second year, when Lois was ten, and a Bluejay. (Chickadees, Bluejays, Ravens, and Kingfishers — these were the names Camp Manitou assigned to the different age groups, a sort of totemic clan system. In those days, thinks Lois, it was birds for girls, animals for boys: wolves, and so forth. Though some animals and birds were suitable and some were not. Never vultures, for instance; never skunks, or rats.)

Lois helped Lucy to unpack her tin trunk and place the folded clothes on the wooden shelves, and to make up her bed. She put her in the top bunk right above her, where she could keep an eye on her. Already she knew that Lucy was an exception, to a good many rules; already she felt proprietorial.

Lucy was from the United States, where the comic books came from, and the movies. She wasn't from New York or Hollywood or Buffalo, the only American cities Lois knew the names of, but from Chicago. Her house was on the lake shore and had gates to it, and grounds. They had a maid, all of the time. Lois's family only had a cleaning lady twice a week.

The only reason Lucy was being sent to this camp (she cast a look of minor scorn around the cabin, diminishing it and also offending Lois, while at the same time daunting her) was that her mother had been a camper here. Her mother had been a Canadian once, but had married her father, who had a patch over one eye, like a pirate. She showed Lois the picture of him in her wallet. He got the patch in the war. "Shrapnel," said Lucy. Lois, who was unsure about shrapnel, was so impressed she could only grunt. Her own two-eyed, unwounded father was tame by comparison.

"My father plays golf," she ventured at last.

"*Everyone* plays golf," said Lucy. "My *mother* plays golf."

Lois's mother did not. Lois took Lucy to see the outhouses and the swimming dock and the dining hall with Monty Manitou's baleful head, knowing in advance they would not measure up.

This was a bad beginning; but Lucy was good-natured, and accepted Camp Manitou with the same casual shrug with which she seemed to accept everything. She would make the best of it, without letting Lois forget that this was what she was doing.

However, there were things Lois knew that Lucy did not. Lucy scratched the tops off all her mosquito bites and had to be taken to the infirmary to be daubed with Ozonol. She took her T-shirt off while sailing, and although the counselor spotted her after a while and made her put it back on, she burnt spectacularly, bright red, with the X of her bathing-suit straps standing out in alarming white; she let Lois peel the sheets of whispery-thin burned skin off her shoulders. When they sang "Alouette" around the campfire, she did not know any of the French words. The difference was that Lucy did not care about the things she didn't know, whereas Lois did.

During the next winter, and subsequent winters, Lucy and Lois wrote to each other. They were both only children, at a time when this was thought to be a disadvantage, so in their letters they pretended to be sisters, or even twins. Lois had to strain a little over this, because Lucy was so blond, with translucent skin and large blue eyes like a doll's, and Lois was nothing out of the ordinary — just a tallish, thinnish, brownish person with freckles. They signed their letters LL, with the L's entwined together like the monograms on a towel. (Lois and Lucy, thinks Lois. How our names date us. Lois Lane, Superman's girlfriend, enterprising female reporter; "I Love Lucy." Now we are obsolete, and it's little Jennifers, little Emilys, little Alexandras, and Carolines and Tiffanys.)

They were more effusive in their letters than they ever were in person. They bordered their pages with X's and O's, but when they met again in the summers it was always a shock. They had changed so much, or Lucy had. It was like watching someone grow up in jolts. At first it would be hard to think up things to say.

But Lucy always had a surprise or two, something to show, some marvel to reveal. The first year she had a picture of herself in a tutu, her hair in a ballerina's knot on the top of her head; she pirouetted around the swimming dock, to show Lois how it was done, and almost fell off. The next year she had given that up and was taking horseback riding. (Camp Manitou did not have horses.) The next year her mother and father had been divorced, and she had a new stepfather, one with both eyes, and a new house, although the maid was the same. The next year, when they had graduated from Bluejays and entered Ravens, she got her period, right in the first week of camp. The two of them snitched some matches from their counselor, who smoked illegally, and made a small fire out behind the farthest outhouse, at dusk, using their flashlights. They could set all kinds of fires by now; they had learned how in Campcraft. On this fire they burned one of Lucy's used sanitary napkins. Lois is not sure why they did this, or whose idea it was. But she can remember the feeling of deep satisfaction it gave her as the white fluff singed and the blood sizzled, as if some wordless ritual had been fulfilled.

They did not get caught, but then they rarely got caught at any of their camp 30 transgressions. Lucy had such large eyes, and was such an accomplished liar.

This year Lucy is different again: slower, more languorous. She is no longer interested in sneaking around after dark, purloining cigarettes from the counselor, dealing in black-market candy bars. She is pensive, and hard to wake in the mornings. She doesn't like her stepfather, but she doesn't want to live with her real father either, who has a new wife. She thinks her mother may be having a love affair with a doctor; she doesn't know for sure, but she's seen them smooching in his car, out on the driveway, when her stepfather wasn't there. It serves him right. She hates her private school. She has a boyfriend, who is sixteen and works as a gardener's assistant. This is how she met him: in the garden. She describes to Lois what it is like when he kisses her — rubbery at first, but then your knees go limp. She has been forbidden to see him, and threatened with boarding school. She wants to run away from home.

Lois has little to offer in return. Her own life is placid and satisfactory, but there is nothing much that can be said about happiness. "You're so lucky," Lucy tells her, a little smugly. She might as well say *boring* because this is how it makes Lois feel.

Lucy is apathetic about the canoe trip, so Lois has to disguise her own excitement. The evening before they are to leave, she slouches into the campfire ring as if coerced, and sits down with a sigh of endurance, just as Lucy does.

Every canoe trip that went out of camp was given a special send-off by Cappie and the section leader and counselors, with the whole section in attendance. Cappie painted three streaks of red across each of her cheeks with a lipstick. They looked like three-fingered claw marks. She put a blue circle on her forehead with fountain-pen ink, and tied a twisted bandanna around her head and stuck a row of frazzle-ended feathers around it, and wrapped herself in a red-and-black Hudson's Bay blanket. The counselors, also in blankets but with only two streaks of red, beat on tom-toms made of round wooden cheese boxes with leather stretched over the top and nailed in place. Cappie was Chief Cappeosota. They all had to say "How!" when she walked into the circle and stood there with one hand raised.

Looking back on this, Lois finds it disquieting. She knows too much 35 about Indians: this is why. She knows, for instance, that they should not even be called Indians, and that they have enough worries without other people taking their names and dressing up as them. It has all been a form of stealing.

But she remembers, too, that she was once ignorant of this. Once she loved the campfire, the flickering of light on the ring of faces, the sound of the fake tom-toms, heavy and fast like a scared heartbeat; she loved Cappie in a red blanket and feathers, solemn, as a chief should be, raising her hand and saying, "Greetings, my Ravens." It was not funny, it was not making fun. She wanted to be an Indian. She wanted to be adventurous and pure, and aboriginal.

"You go on big water," says Cappie. This is her idea—all their ideas—of how Indians talk. "You go where no man has ever trod. You go many moons." This is not true. They are only going for a week, not many moons. The canoe route is clearly marked, they have gone over it on a map, and there are prepared campsites with names which are used year after year. But when Cappie says this—and despite the way Lucy rolls up her eyes—Lois can feel the water stretching out, with the shores twisting away on either side, immense and a little frightening.

"You bring back much wampum," says Cappie. "Do good in war, my braves, and capture many scalps." This is another of her pretenses: that they are boys, and bloodthirsty. But such a game cannot be played by substituting the word "squaw." It would not work at all.

Each of them has to stand up and step forward and have a red line drawn across her cheeks by Cappie. She tells them they must follow in the paths of their ancestors (who most certainly, thinks Lois, looking out the window of her apartment and remembering the family stash of daguerreotypes and sepia-colored portraits on her mother's dressing table, the stiff-shirted, black-coated, grim-faced men and the beflounced women with their severe hair and their corseted respectability, would never have considered heading off onto an open lake, in a canoe, just for fun).

At the end of the ceremony they all stood and held hands around the 40 circle, and sang taps. This did not sound very Indian, thinks Lois. It sounded like a bugle call at a military post, in a movie. But Cappie was never one to be much concerned with consistency, or with archeology.

After breakfast the next morning they set out from the main dock, in four canoes, three in each. The lipstick stripes have not come off completely, and still show faintly pink, like heating burns. They wear their white denim sailing hats, because of the sun, and thin-striped T-shirts, and pale baggy shorts with the cuffs rolled up. The middle one kneels, propping her rear end against the rolled sleeping bags. The counselors going with them are Pat and Kip. Kip is no-nonsense; Pat is easier to wheedle, or fool.

There are white puffy clouds and a small breeze. Glints come from the little waves. Lois is in the bow of Kip's canoe. She still can't do a J-stroke very well, and she will have to be in the bow or the middle for the whole trip. Lucy is behind her; her own J-stroke is even worse. She splashes Lois with her paddle, quite a big splash.

"I'll get you back," says Lois.

"There was a stable fly on your shoulder," Lucy says.

Lois turns to look at her, to see if she's grinning. They're in the habit of 45 splashing each other. Back there, the camp has vanished behind the first long point of rock and rough trees. Lois feels as if an invisible rope has broken. They're floating free, on their own, cut loose. Beneath the canoe the lake goes down, deeper and colder than it was a minute before.

"No horsing around in the canoe," says Kip. She's rolled her T-shirt sleeves up to the shoulder; her arms are brown and sinewy, her jaw determined, her stroke perfect. She looks as if she knows exactly what she is doing.

The four canoes keep close together. They sing, raucously and with defiance; they sing "The Quartermaster's Store," and "Clementine," and "Alouette." It is more like bellowing than singing.

After that the wind grows stronger, blowing slantwise against the bows, and they have to put all their energy into shoving themselves through the water.

Was there anything important, anything that would provide some sort of reason or clue to what happened next? Lois can remember everything, every detail; but it does her no good.

They stopped at noon for a swim and lunch, and went on in the afternoon. 50 At last they reached Little Birch, which was the first campsite for overnight. Lois and Lucy made the fire, while the others pitched the heavy canvas tents. The fireplace was already there, flat stones piled into a U. A burned tin can and a beer bottle had been left in it. Their fire went out, and they had to restart it. "Hustle your bustle," said Kip. "We're starving."

The sun went down, and in the pink sunset light they brushed their teeth and spat the toothpaste froth into the lake. Kip and Pat put all the food that wasn't in cans into a packsack and slung it into a tree, in case of bears.

Lois and Lucy weren't sleeping in a tent. They'd begged to be allowed to sleep out; that way they could talk without the others hearing. If it rained, they told Kip, they promised not to crawl dripping into the tent over everyone's legs: they would get under the canoes. So they were out on the point.

Lois tried to get comfortable inside her sleeping bag, which smelled of musty storage and of earlier campers, a stale salty sweetness. She curled herself up, with her sweater rolled up under her head for a pillow and her flashlight inside her sleeping bag so it wouldn't roll away. The muscles of her sore arms were making small pings, like rubber bands breaking.

Beside her Lucy was rustling around. Lois could see the glimmering oval of her white face.

"I've got a rock poking into my back," said Lucy.   55

"So do I," said Lois. "You want to go into the tent?" She herself didn't, but it was right to ask.

"No," said Lucy. She subsided into her sleeping bag. After a moment she said, "It would be nice not to go back."

"To camp?" said Lois.

"To Chicago," said Lucy. "I hate it there."

"What about your boyfriend?" said Lois. Lucy didn't answer. She was 60 either asleep or pretending to be.

There was a moon, and a movement of the trees. In the sky there were stars, layers of stars that went down and down. Kip said that when the stars were bright like that instead of hazy it meant bad weather later on. Out on the lake there were two loons, calling to each other in their insane, mournful voices. At the time it did not sound like grief. It was just background.

The lake in the morning was flat calm. They skimmed along over the glassy surface, leaving V-shaped trails behind them; it felt like flying. As the sun rose higher it got hot, almost too hot. There were stable flies in the canoes, landing on a bare arm or leg for a quick sting. Lois hoped for wind.

They stopped for lunch at the next of the named campsites, Lookout Point. It was called this because, although the site itself was down near the water on a flat shelf of rock, there was a sheer cliff nearby and a trail that led up to the top. The top was the lookout, although what you were supposed to see from there was not clear. Kip said it was just a view.

Lois and Lucy decided to make the climb anyway. They didn't want to hang around waiting for lunch. It wasn't their turn to cook, though they hadn't avoided much by not doing it, because cooking lunch was no big deal, it was just unwrapping the cheese and getting out the bread and peanut butter, but Pat and Kip always had to do their woodsy act and boil up a billy tin for their own tea.

They told Kip where they were going. You had to tell Kip where you were 65 going, even if it was only a little way into the woods to get dry twigs for kindling. You could never go anywhere without a buddy.

"Sure," said Kip, who was crouching over the fire, feeding driftwood into it. "Fifteen minutes to lunch."

"Where are they off to?" said Pat. She was bringing their billy tin of water from the lake.

"Lookout," said Kip.

"Be careful," said Pat. She said it as an afterthought, because it was what she always said.

"They're old hands," Kip said. 70

Lois looks at her watch: it's ten to twelve. She is the watch-minder; Lucy is careless of time. They walk up the path, which is dry earth and rocks, big rounded pinky-gray boulders or split-open ones with jagged edges. Spindly balsam and spruce trees grow to either side, the lake is blue fragments to the left. The sun is right overhead; there are no shadows anywhere. The heat comes up at them as well as down. The forest is dry and crackly.

It isn't far, but it's a steep climb and they're sweating when they reach the top. They wipe their faces with their bare arms, sit gingerly down on a scorching-hot rock, five feet from the edge but too close for Lois. It's a lookout all right, a sheer drop to the lake and a long view over the water, back the way they've come. It's amazing to Lois that they've traveled so far, over all that water, with nothing to propel them but their own arms. It makes her feel strong. There are all kinds of things she is capable of doing.

"It would be quite a dive off here," says Lucy.

"You'd have to be nuts," says Lois.

"Why?" says Lucy. "It's really deep. It goes straight down." She stands up 75 and takes a step nearer the edge. Lois gets a stab in her midriff, the kind she gets when a car goes too fast over a bump. "Don't," she says.

"Don't what?" says Lucy, glancing around at her mischievously. She knows how Lois feels about heights. But she turns back. "I really have to pee," she says.

"You have toilet paper?" says Lois, who is never without it. She digs in her shorts pocket.

"Thanks," says Lucy.

They are both adept at peeing in the woods: doing it fast so the mosquitoes don't get you, the underwear pulled up between the knees, the squat with the feet apart so you don't wet your legs, facing downhill. The exposed feeling of your bum, as if someone is looking at you from behind. The etiquette when you're with someone else is not to look. Lois stands up and starts to walk back down the path, to be out of sight.

"Wait for me?" says Lucy.   80

Lois climbed down, over and around the boulders, until she could not see Lucy; she waited. She could hear the voices of the others, talking and laughing, down near the shore. One voice was yelling, "Ants! Ants!" Someone must have sat on an ant hill. Off to the side, in the woods, a raven was croaking, a hoarse single note.

She looked at her watch: it was noon. This is when she heard the shout.

She has gone over and over it in her mind since, so many times that the first, real shout has been obliterated, like a footprint trampled by other footprints. But she is sure (she is almost positive, she is nearly certain) that it was not a shout of fear. Not a scream. More like a cry of surprise, cut off too soon. Short, like a dog's bark.

"Lucy?" Lois said. Then she called "Lucy!" By now she was clambering back up, over the stones of the path. Lucy was not up there. Or she was not in sight.

"Stop fooling around," Lois said. "It's lunchtime." But Lucy did not rise   85 from behind a rock or step out, smiling, from behind a tree. The sunlight was all around; the rocks looked white. "This isn't funny!" Lois said, and it wasn't, panic was rising in her, the panic of a small child who does not know where the bigger ones are hidden. She could hear her own heart. She looked quickly around; she lay down on the ground and looked over the edge of the cliff. It made her feel cold. There was nothing.

She went back down the path, stumbling; she was breathing too quickly; she was too frightened to cry. She felt terrible — guilty and dismayed, as if she had done something very bad, by mistake. Something that could never be repaired. "Lucy's gone," she told Kip.

Kip looked up from her fire, annoyed. The water in the billy can was boiling. "What do you mean, gone?" she said. "Where did she go?"

"I don't know," said Lois. "She's just gone."

No one had heard the shout, but then no one heard Lois calling, either. They had been talking among themselves, by the water.

Kip and Pat went up to the lookout and searched and called, and blew   90 their whistles. Nothing answered.

Then they came back down, and Lois had to tell exactly what had happened. The other girls all sat in a circle and listened to her. Nobody said anything. They all looked frightened, especially Pat and Kip. They were the leaders. You did not just lose a camper like this, for no reason at all.

"Why did you leave her alone?" said Kip.

"I was just down the path," said Lois. "I told you. She had to go to the bathroom." She did not say *pee* in front of people older than herself.

Kip looked disgusted.

"Maybe she just walked off into the woods and got turned around," said   95 one of the girls.

"Maybe she's doing it on purpose," said another.

Nobody believed either of these theories.

They took the canoes and searched around the base of the cliff, and peered down into the water. But there had been no sound of falling rock; there had been no splash. There was no clue, nothing at all. Lucy had simply vanished.

That was the end of the canoe trip. It took them the same two days to go back that it had taken coming in, even though they were short a paddler. They did not sing.

After that, the police went in a motorboat, with dogs; they were the Mounties and the dogs were German shepherds, trained to follow trails in the woods. But it had rained since, and they could find nothing. 100

Lois is sitting in Cappie's office. Her face is bloated with crying, she's seen that in the mirror. By now she feels numbed; she feels as if she has drowned. She can't stay here. It has been too much of a shock. Tomorrow her parents are coming to take her away. Several of the other girls who were on the canoe trip are also being collected. The others will have to stay, because their parents are in Europe, or cannot be reached.

Cappie is grim. They've tried to hush it up, but of course everyone in camp knows. Soon the papers will know too. You can't keep it quiet, but what can be said? What can be said that makes any sense? "Girl vanishes in broad daylight, without a trace." It can't be believed. Other things, worse things, will be suspected. Negligence, at the very least. But they have always taken such care. Bad luck will gather around Camp Manitou like a fog; parents will avoid it, in favor of other, luckier places. Lois can see Cappie thinking all this, even through her numbness. It's what anyone would think.

Lois sits on the hard wooden chair in Cappie's office, beside the old wooden desk, over which hangs the thumbtacked bulletin board of normal camp routine, and gazes at Cappie through her puffy eyelids. Cappie is now smiling what is supposed to be a reassuring smile. Her manner is too casual: she's after something. Lois has seen this look on Cappie's face when she's been sniffing out contraband chocolate bars, hunting down those rumored to have snuck out of their cabins at night.

"Tell me again," says Cappie, "from the beginning."

Lois has told her story so many times by now, to Pat and Kip, to Cappie, to the police, that she knows it word for word. She knows it, but she no longer believes it. It has become a story. "I told you," she said. "She wanted to go to the bathroom. I gave her my toilet paper. I went down the path, I waited for her. I heard this kind of shout . . ." 105

"Yes," says Cappie, smiling confidingly, "but before that. What did you say to one another?"

Lois thinks. Nobody has asked her this before. "She said you could dive off there. She said it went straight down."

"And what did you say?"

"I said you'd have to be nuts."

"Were you mad at Lucy?" says Cappie, in an encouraging voice. 110

"No," says Lois. "Why would I be mad at Lucy? I wasn't ever mad at Lucy." She feels like crying again. The times when she has in fact been mad at Lucy have been erased already. Lucy was always perfect.

"Sometimes we're angry when we don't know we're angry," says Cappie, as if to herself. "Sometimes we get really mad and we don't even know it. Sometimes we might do a thing without meaning to, or without knowing what will happen. We lose our tempers."

Lois is only thirteen, but it doesn't take her long to figure out that Cappie is not including herself in any of this. By *we* she means Lois. She is accusing Lois of pushing Lucy off the cliff. The unfairness of this hits her like a slap. "I didn't!" she says.

"Didn't what?" says Cappie softly. "Didn't what, Lois?"

Lois does the worst thing, she begins to cry. Cappie gives her a look like a 115 pounce. She's got what she wanted.

Later, when she was grown up, Lois was able to understand what this interview had been about. She could see Cappie's desperation, her need for a story, a real story with a reason in it; anything but the senseless vacancy Lucy had left for her to deal with. Cappie wanted Lois to supply the reason, to be the reason. It wasn't even for the newspapers or the parents, because she could never make such an accusation without proof. It was for herself: something to explain the loss of Camp Manitou and of all she had worked for, the years of entertaining spoiled children and buttering up parents and making a fool of herself with feathers stuck in her hair. Camp Manitou was in fact lost. It did not survive.

Lois worked all this out, twenty years later. But it was far too late. It was too late even ten minutes afterwards, when she'd left Cappie's office and was walking slowly back to her cabin to pack. Lucy's clothes were still there, folded on the shelves, as if waiting. She felt the other girls in the cabin watching her with speculation in their eyes. *Could she have done it? She must have done it.* For the rest of her life, she has caught people watching her in this way.

Maybe they weren't thinking this. Maybe they were merely sorry for her. But she felt she had been tried and sentenced, and this is what has stayed with her: the knowledge that she had been singled out, condemned for something that was not her fault.

Lois sits in the living room of her apartment, drinking a cup of tea. Through the knee-to-ceiling window she has a wide view of Lake Ontario, with its skin of wrinkled blue-gray light, and of the willows of Centre Island shaken by a wind, which is silent at this distance, and on this side of the glass. When there isn't too much pollution she can see the far shore, the foreign shore; though today it is obscured.

Possibly she could go out, go downstairs, do some shopping; there isn't 120 much in the refrigerator. The boys say she doesn't get out enough. But she isn't hungry, and moving, stirring from this space, is increasingly an effort.

She can hardly remember, now, having her two boys in the hospital, nursing them as babies; she can hardly remember getting married, or what Rob looked like. Even at the time she never felt she was paying full attention. She was tired a lot, as if she was living not one life but two: her own, and another, shadowy life that hovered around her and would not let itself be realized—the life of what would have happened if Lucy had not stepped sideways, and disappeared from time.

She would never go up north, to Rob's family cottage or to any place with wild lakes and wild trees and the calls of loons. She would never go anywhere near. Still, it was as if she was always listening for another voice, the voice of a person who should have been there but was not. An echo.

While Rob was alive, while the boys were growing up, she could pretend she didn't hear it, this empty space in sound. But now there is nothing much left to distract her.

She turns away from the window and looks at her pictures. There is the pinkish island, in the lake, with the intertwisted trees. It's the same landscape they paddled through, that distant summer. She's seen travelogues of this country, aerial photographs; it looks different from above, bigger, more hopeless: lake after lake, random blue puddles in dark green bush, the trees like bristles.

How could you ever find anything there, once it was lost? Maybe if they cut 125 it all down, drained it all away, they might find Lucy's bones, some time, wherever they are hidden. A few bones, some buttons, the buckle from her shorts.

But a dead person is a body; a body occupies space, it exists somewhere. You can see it; you put it in a box and bury it in the ground, and then it's in a box in the ground. But Lucy is not in a box, or in the ground. Because she is nowhere definite, she could be anywhere.

And these paintings are not landscape paintings. Because there aren't any landscapes up there, not in the old, tidy European sense, with a gentle hill, a curving river, a cottage, a mountain in the background, a golden evening sky. Instead there's a tangle, a receding maze, in which you can become lost almost as soon as you step off the path. There are no backgrounds in any of these paintings, no vistas; only a great deal of foreground that goes back and back, endlessly, involving you in its twists and turns of tree and branch and rock. No matter how far back in you go, there will be more. And the trees themselves are hardly trees; they are currents of energy, charged with violent color.

Who knows how many trees there were on the cliff just before Lucy disappeared? Who counted? Maybe there was one more, afterwards.

Lois sits in her chair and does not move. Her hand with the cup is raised halfway to her mouth. She hears something, almost hears it: a shout of recognition, or of joy.

She looks at the paintings, she looks into them. Every one of them is a pic- 130 ture of Lucy. You can't see her exactly, but she's there, in behind the pink stone island or the one behind that. In the picture of the cliff she is hidden by the clutch of fallen rocks towards the bottom, in the one of the river shore she is crouching beneath the overturned canoe. In the yellow autumn woods she's behind the tree that cannot be seen because of the other trees, over beside the blue silver of pond; but if you walked into the picture and found the tree, it would be the wrong one, because the right one would be further on.

Everyone has to be somewhere, and this is where Lucy is. She is in Lois's apartment, in the holes that open inwards on the wall, not like windows but like doors. She is here. She is entirely alive.

Considerations for Critical Thinking and Writing

1. FIRST RESPONSE. How might "Death by Landscape" be read as a ghost story?

2. How is Lois's condominium apartment contrasted with her previous home?

3. Why are the paintings in Lois's apartment important to her?

4. Describe Camp Manitou. What is the narrator's attitude toward it? How does Lois seem to feel about the camp as she recalls her experiences there?

5. What does Lucy's family background reveal about her? How are U.S. and Canadian cultures contrasted in the story?

6. Comment on Atwood's use of the present tense in paragraph 31. What effect is achieved here?

7. Compare the early descriptions of the weather and the lake at the start of the girls' canoe trip (beginning with paragraph 41) with the subsequent descriptions of the natural environment. How does your sense of the setting change?

8. Discuss the significance of the name "Lookout Point" (para. 63).

9. Why does Lois feel guilty after she discovers that Lucy is missing? How does Lucy's disappearance affect Lois's life?

10. In what sense is Lucy "entirely alive" (para. 131) in the paintings hanging in Lois's apartment?

11. Discuss the significance of the story's title. Choose an alternative title that sums up the story for you and explain why it does.

T. CORAGHESSAN BOYLE (B. 1948)

Born in Peekskill, New York, T. Coraghessan Boyle earned a doctorate at the University of Iowa and has taught at the University of Southern California. Among his literary awards is a National Endowment for the Arts Creative Writing Fellowship and the PEN/Faulkner Award for fiction. His fiction has appeared in a variety of periodicals including the *North American Review, The New Yorker, Harper's,* the *Atlantic Monthly,* and *Playboy.* His novels include *Water Music* (1981), *Budding Projects* (1984), *World's End* (1987), *East Is East* (1990), and *The Road to Wellville* (1993), recently made into a film. His short stories are collected in *Descent of Man* (1979), *Greasy Lake and Other Stories* (1985), *If the River Was Whiskey* (1989), and *Without a Hero and Other Stories* (1994), from which "Carnal Knowledge," a story characteristic of Boyle's ironic humor, is reprinted. His most recent collection is *T. C. Boyle Stories: The Collected Stories of T. Coraghessan Boyle* (1998).

Carnal Knowledge   1994

I'd never really thought much about meat. It was there in the supermarket in a plastic wrapper; it came between slices of bread with mayo and mustard and a dill pickle on the side; it sputtered and smoked on the grill till somebody flipped it over, and then it appeared on the plate, between the baked potato and the julienne carrots, neatly cross-hatched and floating in a puddle of red juice. Beef, mutton, pork, venison, dripping burgers, and greasy ribs — it was all the same to me, food, the body's fuel, something to savor a moment on the tongue before the digestive system went to work on it. Which is not to say I was totally unconscious of the deeper implications. Every once in a while I'd eat at home, a quartered chicken, a package of Shake 'n Bake, Stove Top stuffing, and frozen peas, and as I hacked away at the stippled yellow skin and pink flesh of the sanitized bird I'd wonder at the darkish bits of organ clinging to the ribs — what was that, liver? kidney? — but in the end it didn't make me any less fond of Kentucky Fried or Chicken McNuggets. I saw those ads in the magazines, too, the ones that showed the veal calves penned up in their own waste, their limbs atrophied and their veins so pumped full of antibiotics they couldn't control their bowels, but when I took a date to Anna Maria's, I could never resist the veal scallopini.

And then I met Alena Jorgensen.

It was a year ago, two weeks before Thanksgiving — I remember the date because it was my birthday, my thirtieth, and I'd called in sick and gone to the beach to warm my face, read a book, and feel a little sorry for myself. The Santa Anas were blowing and it was clear all the way to Catalina, but there was an edge to the air, a scent of winter hanging over Utah, and as far as I could see in either direction I had the beach pretty much to myself. I found a sheltered spot in a tumble of boulders, spread a blanket, and settled down to attack the pastrami on rye I'd brought along for nourishment. Then I turned to my book — a comfortingly apocalyptic tract about the demise of the planet — and let the sun warm me as I read about the denuding of the rain forest, the poisoning of the atmosphere, and the swift silent eradication of species. Gulls coasted by overhead. I saw the distant glint of jetliners.

I must have dozed, my head thrown back, the book spread open in my lap, because the next thing I remember, a strange dog was hovering over me and the sun had dipped behind the rocks. The dog was big, wild-haired, with one staring blue eye, and it just looked at me, ears slightly cocked, as if it expected a Milk-Bone or something. I was startled — not that I don't like dogs, but here was this woolly thing poking its snout in my face — and I guess that I must have made some sort of defensive gesture, because the dog staggered back a step and froze. Even in the confusion of the moment I could see that there was something wrong with this dog, an unsteadiness, a gimp, a wobble to its legs. I felt a mixture of pity and revulsion — had it been hit by a car, was that it? — when all at once I became aware of a wetness on the breast of my windbreaker, and an unmistakable odor rose to my nostrils: I'd been pissed on.

Pissed on. As I lay there unsuspecting, enjoying the sun, the beach, the solitude, this stupid beast had lifted its leg and used me as a pissoir — and now it was poised there on the edge of the blanket as if it expected a reward. A sudden rage seized me. I came up off the blanket with a curse, and it was only then that a dim apprehension seemed to seep into the dog's other eye, the brown one, and it lurched back and fell on its face, just out of reach. And then it lurched and fell again, bobbing and weaving across the sand like a seal out of water. I was on my feet now, murderous, glad to see that the thing was hobbled — it would simplify the task of running it down and beating it to death. 5

"Alf!" a voice called, and as the dog floundered in the sand, I turned and saw Alena Jorgensen poised on the boulder behind me. I don't want to make too much of the moment, don't want to mythologize it or clutter the scene with allusions to Aphrodite rising from the waves or accepting the golden apple from Paris, but she was a pretty impressive sight. Bare-legged, fluid, as tall and uncompromising as her Nordic ancestors, and dressed in a Gore-Tex bikini and hooded sweatshirt unzipped to the waist, she blew me away, in any event. Piss-spattered and stupified, I could only gape up at her.

"You bad boy," she said, scolding, "you get out of there." She glanced from the dog to me and back again. "Oh, you bad boy, what have you done?" she demanded, and I was ready to admit to anything, but it was the dog she was addressing, and the dog flopped over in the sand as if it had been shot. Alena skipped lightly down from the rock, and in the next moment, before I could protest, she was rubbing at the stain on my windbreaker with the wadded-up hem of her sweatshirt.

I tried to stop her — "It's all right," I said, "it's nothing," as if dogs routinely pissed on my wardrobe — but she wouldn't hear of it.

"No," she said, rubbing, her hair flying in my face, the naked skin of her thigh pressing unconsciously to my own, "no, this is terrible, I'm so embarrassed — Alf, you bad boy — I'll clean it for you, I will, it's the least — oh, look at that, it's stained right through to your T-shirt —"

I could smell her, the mousse she used in her hair, a lilac soap or perfume, 10 the salt-sweet odor of her sweat — she'd been jogging, that was it. I murmured something about taking it to the cleaner's myself.

She stopped rubbing and straightened up. She was my height, maybe even a fraction taller, and her eyes were ever so slightly mismatched, like the dog's: a deep earnest blue in the right iris, shading to sea-green and turquoise in the left. We were so close we might have been dancing. "Tell you what," she said, and her face lit with a smile, "since you're so nice about the whole thing, and most people wouldn't be, even if they knew what poor Alf has been through, why don't you let me wash it for you — and the T-shirt too?"

I was a little disconcerted at this point — I was the one who'd been pissed on, after all — but my anger was gone. I felt weightless, adrift, like a piece of fluff floating on the breeze. "Listen," I said, and for the moment I couldn't look her in the eye, "I don't want to put you to any trouble . . ."

"I'm ten minutes up the beach, and I've got a washer and dryer. Come on, it's no trouble at all. Or do you have plans? I mean, I could just pay for the cleaner's if you want . . ."

I was between relationships — the person I'd been seeing off and on for the past year wouldn't even return my calls — and my plans consisted of taking a solitary late-afternoon movie as a birthday treat, then heading over to my mother's for dinner and the cake with the candles. My Aunt Irene would be there, and so would my grandmother. They would exclaim over how big I was and how handsome and then they would begin to contrast my present self with my previous, more diminutive incarnations, and finally work themselves up to a spate of reminiscence that would continue unabated till my mother drove them home. And then, if I was lucky, I'd go out to a singles bar and make the acquaintance of a divorced computer programmer in her mid-thirties with three kids and bad breath.

I shrugged. "Plans? No, not really. I mean, nothing in particular." 15

Alena was housesitting a one-room bungalow that rose stumplike from the sand, no more than fifty feet from the tide line. There were trees in the yard behind it and the place was sandwiched between glass fortresses with crenellated decks, whipping flags, and great hulking concrete pylons. Sitting on the couch inside, you could feel the dull reverberation of each wave hitting the shore, a slow steady pulse that forever defined the place for me. Alena gave me a faded UC Davis sweatshirt that nearly fit, sprayed a stain remover on my T-shirt and windbreaker, and in a single fluid motion flipped down the lid of the washer and extracted two beers from the refrigerator beside it.

There was an awkward moment as she settled into the chair opposite me and we concentrated on our beers. I didn't know what to say. I was disoriented, giddy, still struggling to grasp what had happened. Fifteen minutes earlier I'd been dozing on the beach, alone on my birthday and feeling sorry for myself, and now I was ensconced in a cozy beach house, in the presence of Alena Jorgensen and her naked spill of leg, drinking a beer. "So what do you do?" she said, setting her beer down on the coffee table.

I was grateful for the question, too grateful maybe. I described to her at length how dull my job was, nearly ten years with the same agency, writing ad copy, my brain gone numb with disuse. I was somewhere in the middle of a blow-by-blow account of our current campaign for a Ghanian vodka distilled from calabash husks when she said, "I know what you mean," and told me she'd dropped out of veterinary school herself. "After I saw what they did to the animals. I mean, can you see neutering a dog just for our convenience, just because it's easier for us if they don't have a sex life?" Her voice grew hot. "It's the same old story, species fascism at its worst."

Alf was lying at my feet, grunting softly and looking up mournfully out of his staring blue eye, as blameless a creature as ever lived. I made a small noise of agreement and then focused on Alf. "And your dog," I said, "he's arthritic? Or is it hip dysplasia or what?" I was pleased with myself for the question — aside from "tapeworm," "hip dysplasia" was the only veterinary term I could dredge up from the memory bank, and I could see that Alf's problems ran deeper than worms.

Alena looked angry suddenly. "Don't I wish," she said. She paused to draw 20 a bitter breath. "There's nothing wrong with Alf that wasn't inflicted on him. They tortured him, maimed him, mutilated him."

"Tortured him?" I echoed, feeling the indignation rise in me — this beautiful girl, this innocent beast. "Who?"

Alena leaned forward and there was real hate in her eyes. She mentioned a prominent shoe company — spat out the name, actually. It was an ordinary name, a familiar one, and it hung in the air between us, suddenly sinister. Alf had been part of an experiment to market booties for dogs — suede, cordovan, patent leather, the works. The dogs were made to pace a treadmill in their booties, to assess wear; Alf was part of the control group.

"Control group?" I could feel the hackles rising on the back of my neck.

"They used eighty-grit sandpaper on the treads, to accelerate the process." Alena shot a glance out the window to where the surf pounded the shore; she bit her lip. "Alf was one of the dogs without booties."

I was stunned. I wanted to get up and comfort her, but I might as well have 25 been grafted to the chair. "I don't believe it," I said. "How could anybody —"

"Believe it," she said. She studied me a moment, then set down her beer and crossed the room to dig through a cardboard box in the corner. If I was moved by the emotion she'd called up, I was moved even more by the sight of her bending over the box in her Gore-Tex bikini; I clung to the edge of the chair as if it were a plunging roller coaster. A moment later she dropped a dozen file folders in my lap. The uppermost bore the name of the shoe company, and it was crammed with news clippings, several pages of a diary relating to plant operations and workers' shifts at the Grand Rapids facility, and a floor plan of the laboratories. The folders beneath it were inscribed with the names of cosmetics firms, biomedical research centers, furriers, tanners, meatpackers. Alena perched on the edge of the coffee table and watched as I shuffled through them.

"You know the Draize test?"

I gave her a blank look.

"They inject chemicals into rabbits' eyes to see how much it'll take before they go blind. The rabbits are in cages, thousands of them, and they take a needle and jab it into their eyes — and you know why, you know in the name of what great humanitarian cause this is going on, even as we speak?"

I didn't know. The surf pounded at my feet. I glanced at Alf and then back 30 into her angry eyes.

"Mascara, that's what. Mascara. They torture countless thousands of rabbits so women can look like sluts."

I thought the characterization a bit harsh, but when I studied her pale lashes and tight lipstickless mouth, I saw that she meant it. At any rate, the notion set her off, and she launched into a two-hour lecture, gesturing with her flawless hands, quoting figures, digging through her files for the odd photo of legless mice or morphine-addicted gerbils. She told me how she'd rescued Alf herself, raiding the laboratory with six other members of the Animal Liberation Front, the militant group in honor of which Alf had been named. At first, she'd been content to write letters and carry placards, but now, with the lives of so many animals at stake, she'd turned to more direct action: harassment, vandalism, sabotage. She described how she'd spiked trees with Earth-First!ers in Oregon, cut miles of barbed-wire fence on cattle ranches in Nevada, destroyed records in biomedical research labs up and down the coast and insinuated herself between the hunters and the bighorn sheep in the mountains of Arizona. I could only nod and exclaim, smile ruefully and whistle in a low "holy cow!" sort of way. Finally, she paused to level her unsettling eyes on me. "You know what Isaac Bashevis Singer said?"

We were on our third beer. The sun was gone. I didn't have a clue.

Alena leaned forward. " 'Every day is Auschwitz for the animals.' "

I looked down into the amber aperture of my beer bottle and nodded my 35 head sadly. The dryer had stopped an hour and a half ago. I wondered if she'd go out to dinner with me, and what she could eat if she did. "Uh, I was wondering," I said, "if . . . if you might want to go out for something to eat —"

Alf chose that moment to heave himself up from the floor and urinate on the wall behind me. My dinner proposal hung in the balance as Alena shot up off the edge of the table to scold him and then gently usher him out the door. "Poor Alf," she sighed, turning back to me with a shrug. "But listen, I'm sorry if I talked your head off — I didn't mean to, but it's rare to find somebody on your own wavelength."

She smiled. *On your own wavelength:* the words illuminated me, excited me, sent up a tremor I could feel all the way down in the deepest nodes of my reproductive tract. "So how about dinner?" I persisted. Restaurants were running through my head — would it have to be veggie? Could there be even a whiff of grilled flesh on the air? Curdled goat's milk and tabbouleh, tofu, lentil soup, sprouts: *Every day is Auschwitz for the animals.* "No place with meat, of course."

She just looked at me.

"I mean, I don't eat meat myself," I lied, "or actually, not anymore" — since the pastrami sandwich, that is — "but I don't really know any place that . . ." I trailed off lamely.

"I'm a Vegan," she said.   40

After two hours of blind bunnies, butchered calves and mutilated pups, I couldn't resist the joke. "I'm from Venus myself."

She laughed, but I could see she didn't find it all that funny. Vegans didn't eat meat or fish, she explained, or milk or cheese or eggs, and they didn't wear wool or leather — or fur, of course.

"Of course," I said. We were both standing there, hovering over the coffee table. I was beginning to feel a little foolish.

"Why don't we just eat here," she said.

The deep throb of the ocean seemed to settle in my bones as we lay there   45
in bed that night, Alena and I, and I learned all about the fluency of her limbs and the sweetness of her vegetable tongue. Alf sprawled on the floor beneath us, wheezing and groaning in his sleep, and I blessed him for his incontinence and his doggy stupidity. Something was happening to me — I could feel it in the way the boards shifted under me, feel it with each beat of the surf — and I was ready to go along with it. In the morning, I called in sick again.

Alena was watching me from bed as I dialed the office and described how the flu had migrated from my head to my gut and beyond, and there was a look in her eye that told me I would spend the rest of the day right there beside her, peeling grapes and dropping them one by one between her parted and expectant lips. I was wrong. Half an hour later, after a breakfast of brewer's yeast and what appeared to be some sort of bark marinated in yogurt, I found myself marching up and down the sidewalk in front of a fur emporium in Beverly Hills, waving a placard that read HOW DOES IT FEEL TO WEAR A CORPSE? in letters that dripped like blood.

It was a shock. I'd seen protest marches on TV, antiwar rallies and civil rights demonstrations and all that, but I'd never warmed my heels on the pavement or chanted slogans or felt the naked stick in my hand. There were maybe forty of us in all, mostly women, and we waved our placards at passing cars and blocked traffic on the sidewalk. One woman had smeared her face and hands with cold cream steeped in red dye, and Alena had found a ratty mink stole somewhere — the kind that features whole animals sewed together, snout to tail, their miniature limbs dangling — and she'd taken a can of crimson spray paint to their muzzles so that they looked freshly killed. She brandished this grisly banner on a stick high above her head, whooping like a savage and chanting, "Fur is death, fur is death," over and over again till it became a mantra for the crowd. The day was unseasonably warm, the Jaguars glinted in the sun and the palms nodded in the breeze, and no one, but for a single tight-lipped salesman glowering from behind the store's immaculate windows, paid the slightest bit of attention to us.

I marched out there on the street, feeling exposed and conspicuous, but marching nonetheless — for Alena's sake and for the sake of the foxes and martens and all the rest, and for my own sake too: with each step I took I could feel my consciousness expanding like a balloon, the breath of saintliness seeping steadily into me. Up to this point I'd worn suede and leather like anybody else, ankle boots and Air Jordans, a bombardier jacket I'd had since high school. If I'd drawn the line with fur, it was only because I'd never had any use for it. If I lived in the Yukon — and sometimes, drowsing through a meeting at work, I found myself fantasizing about it — I would have worn fur, no compunction, no second thoughts.

But not anymore. Now I was the protestor, a placard waver, now I was fighting for the right of every last weasel and lynx to grow old and die gracefully, now I was Alena Jorgensen's lover and a force to be reckoned with. Of course, my feet hurt and I was running sweat and praying that no one from work would drive by and see me there on the sidewalk with my crazy cohorts and denunciatory sign.

We marched for hours, back and forth, till I thought we'd wear a groove in 50 the pavement. We chanted and jeered and nobody so much as looked at us twice. We could have been Hare Krishnas, bums, antiabortionists, or lepers, what did it matter? To the rest of the world, to the uninitiated masses to whose sorry number I'd belonged just twenty-four hours earlier, we were invisible. I was hungry, tired, discouraged. Alena was ignoring me. Even the woman in red-face was slowing down, her chant a hoarse whisper that was sucked up and obliterated in the roar of traffic. And then, as the afternoon faded toward rush hour, a wizened silvery old woman who might have been an aging star or a star's mother or even the first dimly remembered wife of a studio exec got out of a long white car at the curb and strode fearlessly toward us. Despite the heat — it must have been eighty degrees at this point — she was wearing an ankle-length silver fox coat, a bristling shouldery wafting mass of peltry that must have decimated every burrow on the tundra. It was the moment we'd been waiting for.

A cry went up, shrill and ululating, and we converged on the lone old woman like a Cheyenne war party scouring the plains. The man beside me went down on all fours and howled like a dog. Alena slashed the air with her limp mink, and the blood sang in my ears. "Murderer!" I screamed, getting into it. "Torturer! Nazi!" The strings in my neck were tight. I didn't know what I was saying. The crowd gibbered. The placards danced. I was so close to the old woman I could smell her — her perfume, a whiff of mothballs from the coat — and it intoxicated me, maddened me, and I stepped in front of her to block her path with all the seething militant bulk of my one hundred eighty-five pounds of sinew and muscle.

I never saw the chauffeur. Alena told me afterward that he was a former kickboxing champion who'd been banned from the sport for excessive brutality. The first blow seemed to drop down from above, a shell lobbed from deep within enemy territory; the others came at me like a windmill churning in a storm. Someone screamed. I remember focusing on the flawless rigid pleats of the chauffeur's trousers, and then things got a bit hazy.

I woke to the dull thump of the surf slamming at the shore and the touch of Alena's lips on my own. I felt as if I'd been broken on the wheel, dismantled, and put back together again. "Lie still," she said, and her tongue moved against my swollen cheek. Stricken, I could only drag my head across the pillow and gaze into the depths of her parti-colored eyes. "You're one of us now," she whispered.

Next morning I didn't even bother to call in sick.

By the end of the week I'd recovered enough to crave meat, for which I felt 55
deeply ashamed, and to wear out a pair of vinyl huaraches on the picket line.
Together, and with various coalitions of antivivisectionists, militant Vegans,
and cat lovers, Alena and I tramped a hundred miles of sidewalk, spray-painted
inflammatory slogans across the windows of supermarkets and burger stands,
denounced tanners, furriers, poulterers, and sausage makers, and somehow
found time to break up a cockfight in Pacoima. It was exhilarating, heady, dangerous. If I'd been disconnected in the past, I was plugged in now. I felt righteous—for the first time in my life I had a cause—and I had Alena, Alena above
all. She fascinated me, fixated me, made me feel like a tomcat leaping in and
out of second-story windows, oblivious to the free-fall and the picket fence
below. There was her beauty, of course, a triumph of evolution and the happy
interchange of genes going all the way back to the cavemen, but it was more
than that—it was her commitment to animals, to the righting of wrongs, to
morality that made her irresistible. Was it love? The term is something I've
always had difficulty with, but I suppose it was. Sure it was. Love, pure and
simple. I had it, it had me.

"You know what?" Alena said one night as she stood over the miniature
stove, searing tofu in oil and garlic. We'd spent the afternoon demonstrating
out front of a tortilla factory that used rendered animal fat as a congealing
agent, after which we'd been chased three blocks by an overweight assistant
manager at Von's who objected to Alena's spray-painting MEAT IS DEATH over
the specials in the front window. I was giddy with the adolescent joy of it. I
sank into the couch with a beer and watched Alf limp across the floor to fling
himself down and lick at a suspicious spot on the floor. The surf boomed like
thunder.

"What?" I said.

"Thanksgiving's coming."

I let it ride a moment, wondering if I should invite Alena to my mother's
for the big basted bird stuffed with canned oysters and buttered bread crumbs,
and then realized it probably wouldn't be such a great idea. I said nothing.

She glanced over her shoulder. "The animals don't have a whole lot to be 60
thankful for, that's for sure. It's just an excuse for the meat industry to butcher
a couple million turkeys, is all it is." She paused; hot safflower oil popped in
the pan. "I think it's time for a little road trip," she said. "Can we take your
car?"

"Sure, but where are we going?"

She gave me her Gioconda smile. "To liberate some turkeys."

In the morning I called my boss to tell him I had pancreatic cancer and
wouldn't be in for a while, then we threw some things in the car, helped Alf
scrabble into the back seat, and headed up Route 5 for the San Joaquin Valley.
We drove for three hours through a fog so dense the windows might as well
have been packed with cotton. Alena was secretive, but I could see she was
excited. I knew only that we were on our way to rendezvous with a certain
"Rolfe," a longtime friend of hers and a big name in the world of ecotage and
animal rights, after which we would commit some desperate and illegal act, for
which the turkeys would be eternally grateful.

There was a truck stalled in front of the sign for our exit at Calpurnia
Springs, and I had to brake hard and jerk the wheel around twice to keep the

tires on the pavement. Alena came up out of her seat and Alf slammed into the armrest like a sack of meal, but we made it. A few minutes later we were gliding through the ghostly vacancy of the town itself, lights drifting past in a nimbus of fog, glowing pink, yellow, and white, and then there was only the blacktop road and the pale void that engulfed it. We'd gone ten miles or so when Alena instructed me to slow down and began to study the right-hand shoulder with a keen, unwavering eye.

The earth breathed in and out. I squinted hard into the soft drifting glow 65 of the headlights. "There, there!" she cried and I swung the wheel to the right, and suddenly we were lurching along a pitted dirt road that rose up from the blacktop like a goat path worn into the side of a mountain. Five minutes later Alf sat up in the back seat and began to whine, and then a crude unpainted shack began to detach itself from the vagueness around us.

Rolfe met us on the porch. He was tall and leathery, in his fifties, I guessed, with a shock of hair and rutted features that brought Samuel Beckett to mind. He was wearing gumboots and jeans and a faded lumberjack shirt that looked as if it had been washed a hundred times. Alf took a quick pee against the side of the house, then fumbled up the steps to roll over and fawn at his feet.

"Rolfe!" Alena called, and there was too much animation in her voice, too much familiarity, for my taste. She took the steps in a bound and threw herself in his arms. I watched them kiss, and it wasn't a fatherly-daughterly sort of kiss, not at all. It was a kiss with some meaning behind it, and I didn't like it. Rolfe, I thought: What kind of name is that?

"Rolfe," Alena gasped, still a little breathless from bouncing up the steps like a cheerleader, "I'd like you to meet Jim."

That was my signal. I ascended the porch steps and held out my hand. Rolfe gave me a look out of the hooded depths of his eyes and then took my hand in a hard calloused grip, the grip of the wood splitter, the fence mender, the liberator of hothouse turkeys and laboratory mice. "A pleasure," he said, and his voice rasped like sandpaper.

There was a fire going inside, and Alena and I sat before it and warmed our 70 hands while Alf whined and sniffed and Rolfe served Red Zinger tea in Japanese cups the size of thimbles. Alena hadn't stopped chattering since we stepped through the door, and Rolfe came right back at her in his woodsy rasp, the two of them exchanging names and news and gossip as if they were talking in code. I studied the reproductions of teal and widgeon that hung from the peeling walls, noted the case of Heinz vegetarian beans in the corner and the half-gallon of Jack Daniel's on the mantel. Finally, after the third cup of tea, Alena settled back in her chair—a huge old Salvation Army sort of thing with a soiled antimacassar—and said, "So what's the plan?"

Rolfe gave me another look, a quick predatory darting of the eyes, as if he weren't sure I could be trusted, and then turned back to Alena. "Hedda Gabler's Range-Fed Turkey Ranch," he said. "And no, I don't find the name cute, not at all." He looked at me now, a long steady assay. "They grind up the heads for cat food, and the neck, the organs, and the rest, that they wrap up in paper and stuff back in the body cavity like it was a war atrocity or something. Whatever did a turkey go and do to us to deserve a fate like that?"

The question was rhetorical, even if it seemed to have been aimed at me, and I made no response other than to compose my face in a look that wedded grief, outrage, and resolve. I was thinking of all the turkeys I'd sent to their doom, of the plucked wishbones, the pope's noses,° and the crisp browned skin I used to relish as a kid. It brought a lump to my throat, and something more: I realized I was hungry.

"Ben Franklin wanted to make them our national symbol," Alena chimed in, "did you know that? But the meat eaters won out."

"Fifty thousand birds," Rolfe said, glancing at Alena and bringing his incendiary gaze back to rest on me. "I have information they're going to start slaughtering them tomorrow, for the fresh-not-frozen market."

"Yuppie poultry," Alena's voice was drenched in disgust. 75

For a moment, no one spoke. I became aware of the crackling of the fire. The fog pressed at the windows. It was getting dark.

"You can see the place from the highway," Rolfe said finally, "but the only access is through Calpurnia Springs. It's about twenty miles—twenty-two point three, to be exact."

Alena's eyes were bright. She was gazing on Rolfe as if he'd just dropped down from heaven. I felt something heave in my stomach.

"We strike tonight."

Rolfe insisted that we take my car—"Everybody around here knows my 80 pickup, and I can't take any chances on a little operation like this"—but we did mask the plates, front and back, with an inch-thick smear of mud. We blackened our faces like commandos and collected our tools from the shed out back—tin snips, a crowbar, and two five-gallon cans of gasoline. "Gasoline?" I said, trying the heft of the can. Rolfe gave me a craggy look. "To create a diversion," he said. Alf, for obvious reasons, stayed behind in the shack.

If the fog had been thick in daylight, it was impenetrable now, the sky collapsed upon the earth. It took hold of the headlights and threw them back at me till my eyes began to water from the effort of keeping the car on the road. But for the ruts and bumps we might have been floating in space. Alena sat up front between Rolfe and me, curiously silent. Rolfe didn't have much to say either, save for the occasional grunted command: "Hang a right here"; "Hard left"; "Easy, easy." I thought about meat and jail and the heroic proportions to which I was about to swell in Alena's eyes and what I intended to do to her when we finally got to bed. It was 2:00 A.M. by the dashboard clock.

"Okay," Rolfe said, and his voice came at me so suddenly it startled me, "pull over here—and kill the lights."

We stepped out into the hush of night and eased the doors shut behind us. I couldn't see a thing, but I could hear the not-so-distant hiss of traffic on the highway, and another sound, too, muffled and indistinct, the gentle unconscious suspiration of thousands upon thousands of my fellow creatures. And I could smell them, a seething rancid odor of feces and feathers and naked scaly feet that crawled down my throat and burned my nostrils. "Whew," I said in a whisper, "I can smell them."

Rolfe and Alena were vague presences at my side. Rolfe flipped open the trunk and in the next moment I felt the heft of a crowbar and a pair of tin snips in my hand. "Listen, you, Jim," Rolfe whispered, taking me by the wrist in his iron grip and leading me half-a-dozen steps forward. "Feel this?"

I felt a grid of wire, which he promptly cut: *snip, snip, snip.* 85

---

pope's noses: Slang for the fleshy tail sections of turkeys and other poultry.

"This is their enclosure — they're out there in the day, scratching around in the dirt. You get lost, you follow this wire. Now, you're going to take a section out of this side, Alena's got the west side and I've got the south. Once that's done I signal with the flashlight and we bust open the doors to the turkey houses — they're these big low white buildings, you'll see them when you get close — and flush the birds out. Don't worry about me or Alena. Just worry about getting as many birds out as you can."

I was worried. Worried about everything, from some half-crazed farmer with a shotgun or AK-47 or whatever they carried these days, to losing Alena in the fog, to the turkeys themselves: How big were they? Were they violent? They had claws and beaks, didn't they? And how were they going to feel about me bursting into their bedroom in the middle of the night?

"And when the gas cans go up, you hightail it back to the car, got it?"

I could hear the turkeys tossing in their sleep. A truck shifted gears out on the highway. "I think so," I whispered.

"And one more thing — be sure to leave the keys in the ignition."   90

This gave me pause. "But—"

"The getaway." Alena was so close I could feel her breath on my ear. "I mean, we don't want to be fumbling around for the keys when all hell is breaking loose out there, do we?"

I eased open the door and reinserted the keys in the ignition, even though the automatic buzzer warned me against it. "Okay," I murmured, but they were already gone, soaked up in the shadows and the mist. At this point my heart was hammering so loudly I could barely hear the rustling of the turkeys — this is crazy, I told myself, it's hurtful and wrong, not to mention illegal. Spray-painting slogans was one thing, but this was something else altogether. I thought of the turkey farmer asleep in his bed, an entrepreneur working to make America strong, a man with a wife and kids and a mortgage . . . but then I thought of all those innocent turkeys consigned to death, and finally I thought of Alena, long-legged and loving, and the way she came to me out of the darkness of the bathroom and the boom of the surf. I took the tin snips to the wire.

I must have been at it half an hour, forty-five minutes, gradually working my way toward the big white sheds that had begun to emerge from the gloom up ahead, when I saw Rolfe's flashlight blinking off to my left. This was my signal to head to the nearest shed, snap off the padlock with my crowbar, fling open the doors, and herd a bunch of cranky suspicious gobblers out into the night. It was now or never. I looked twice round me and then broke for the near shed in an awkward crouching gait. The turkeys must have sensed that something was up — from behind the long white windowless wall there arose a watchful gabbling, a soughing of feathers that fanned up like a breeze in the treetops. *Hold on, you toms and hens,* I thought, *freedom is at hand.* A jerk of the wrist, and the padlock fell to the ground. Blood pounded in my ears, I took hold of the sliding door and jerked it open with a great dull booming reverberation — and suddenly, there they were, turkeys, thousands upon thousands of them, cloaked in white feathers under a string of dim yellow bulbs. The light glinted in their reptilian eyes. Somewhere a dog began to bark.

I steeled myself and sprang through the door with a shout, whirling the 95 crowbar over my head, "All right!" I boomed, and the echo gave it back to me a hundred times over, "this is it! Turkeys, on your feet!" Nothing. No response.

But for the whisper of rustling feathers and the alertly cocked heads, they might have been sculptures, throw pillows, they might as well have been dead and butchered and served up with yams and onions and all the trimmings. The barking of the dog went up a notch. I thought I heard voices.

The turkeys crouched on the concrete floor, wave upon wave of them, stupid and immovable; they perched in the rafters, on shelves and platforms, huddled in wooden stalls. Desperate, I rushed into the front rank of them, swinging my crowbar, stamping my feet, and howling like the wishbone plucker I once was. That did it. There was a shriek from the nearest bird and the others took it up till an unholy racket filled the place, and now they were moving, tumbling down from their perches, flapping their wings in a storm of dried excrement and pecked-over grain, pouring across the concrete floor till it vanished beneath them. Encouraged, I screamed again—"Yeeee-ha-ha-ha-ha!"—and beat at the aluminum walls with the crowbar as the turkeys shot through the doorway and out into the night.

It was then that the black mouth of the doorway erupted with light and the *ka-boom!* of the gas cans sent a tremor through the earth. *Run!* a voice screamed in my head, and the adrenaline kicked in and all of a sudden I was scrambling for the door in a hurricane of turkeys. They were everywhere, flapping their wings, gobbling and screeching, loosing their bowels in panic. Something hit the back of my legs and all at once I was down amongst them, on the floor, in the dirt and feathers and wet turkey shit. I was a roadbed, a turkey expressway. Their claws dug at my back, my shoulders, the crown of my head. Panicked now, choking on feathers and dust and worse, I fought to my feet as the big screeching birds launched themselves round me, and staggered out into the barnyard. "There! Who's that there?" a voice roared, and I was off and running.

What can I say? I vaulted turkeys, kicked them aside like so many footballs, slashed and tore at them as they sailed through the air. I ran till my lungs felt as if they were burning right through my chest, disoriented, bewildered, terrified of the shotgun blast I was sure would cut me down at any moment. Behind me the fire raged and lit the fog till it glowed blood-red and hellish. But where was the fence? And where the car?

I got control of my feet then and stood stock-still in a flurry of turkeys, squinting into the wall of fog. Was that it? Was that the car over there? At that moment I heard an engine start up somewhere behind me—a familiar engine with a familiar coughing gurgle in the throat of the carburetor—and then the lights blinked on briefly three hundred yards away. I heard the engine race and listened, helpless, as the car roared off in the opposite direction. I stood there a moment longer, forlorn and forsaken, and then I ran blindly off into the night, putting the fire and the shouts and the barking and the incessant mindless squawking of the turkeys as far behind me as I could.

When dawn finally broke, it was only just perceptibly, so thick was the fog. 100 I'd made my way to a blacktop road—which road and where it led I didn't know—and sat crouched and shivering in a clump of weed just off the shoulder. Alena wouldn't desert me, I was sure of that—she loved me, as I loved her; needed me, as I needed her—and I was sure she'd be cruising along the back roads looking for me. My pride was wounded, of course, and if I never laid eyes on Rolfe again I felt I wouldn't be missing much, but at least I hadn't been drilled full of shot, savaged by farm dogs, or pecked to death by irate turkeys. I was sore all over, my shin throbbed where I'd slammed into something substantial while vaulting through the night, there were feathers in my hair, and my face and arms were a mosaic of cuts and scratches and long trailing fissures of dirt. I'd been sitting there for what seemed like hours, cursing Rolfe, developing suspicions about Alena and unflattering theories about environmentalists in general, when finally I heard the familiar slurp and roar of my Chevy Citation cutting through the mist ahead of me.

Rolfe was driving, his face impassive. I flung myself into the road like a tattered beggar, waving my arms over my head and giving vent to my joy, and he very nearly ran me down. Alena was out of the car before it stopped, wrapping me up in her arms, and then she was bundling me into the rear seat with Alf and we were on our way back to the hideaway. "What happened?" she cried, as if she couldn't have guessed. "Where were you? We waited as long as we could."

I was feeling sulky, betrayed, feeling as if I was owed a whole lot more than a perfunctory hug and a string of insipid questions. Still, as I told my tale I began to warm to it—they'd got away in the car with the heater going, and I'd stayed behind to fight the turkeys, the farmers, and the elements, too, and if that wasn't heroic, I'd like to know what was. I looked into Alena's admiring eyes and pictured Rolfe's shack, a nip or two from the bottle of Jack Daniel's, maybe a peanut-butter-and-tofu sandwich, and then the bed, with Alena in it. Rolfe said nothing.

Back at Rolfe's, I took a shower and scrubbed the turkey droppings from my pores, then helped myself to the bourbon. It was ten in the morning and the house was dark—if the world had ever been without fog, there was no sign of it here. When Rolfe stepped out on the porch to fetch an armload of firewood, I pulled Alena down into my lap. "Hey," she murmured, "I thought you were an invalid."

She was wearing a pair of too-tight jeans and an oversize sweater with nothing underneath it. I slipped my hand inside the sweater and found something to hold on to. "Invalid?" I said, nuzzling at her sleeve. "Hell, I'm a turkey liberator, an ecoguerrilla, a friend of the animals and the environment, too."

She laughed, but she pushed herself up and crossed the room to stare out 105 the occluded window. "Listen, Jim," she said, "what we did last night was great, really great, but it's just the beginning." Alf looked up at her expectantly. I heard Rolfe fumbling around on the porch, the thump of wood on wood. She turned around to face me now. "What I mean is, Rolfe wants me to go up to Wyoming for a little bit, just outside of Yellowstone—"

Me? Rolfe wants me? There was no invitation in that, no plurality, no acknowledgment of all we'd done and meant to each other. "For what?" I said. "What do you mean?"

"There's this grizzly—a pair of them, actually—and they've been raiding places outside the park. One of them made off with the mayor's Doberman the other night and the people are up in arms. We—I mean Rolfe and me and some other people from the old Bolt Weevils in Minnesota?—we're going to go up there and make sure the Park Service—or the local yahoos—don't eliminate them. The bears, I mean."

My tone was corrosive. "You and Rolfe?"

"There's nothing between us, if that's what you're thinking. This has to do with animals, that's all."

"Like us?"

She shook her head slowly. "Not like us, no. We're the plague on this planet, don't you know that?"

Suddenly I was angry. Seething. Here I'd crouched in the bushes all night, covered in turkey crap, and now I was part of a plague. I was on my feet. "No, I don't know that."

She gave me a look that let me know it didn't matter, that she was already gone, that her agenda, at least for the moment, didn't include me and there was no use arguing about it. "Look," she said, her voice dropping as Rolfe slammed back through the door with a load of wood, "I'll see you in L.A. in a month or so, okay?" She gave me an apologetic smile. "Water the plants for me?"

An hour later I was on the road again. I'd helped Rolfe stack the wood beside the fireplace, allowed Alena to brush my lips with a good-bye kiss, and then stood there on the porch while Rolfe locked up, lifted Alf into the bed of his pickup, and rumbled down the rutted dirt road with Alena at his side. I watched till their brake lights dissolved in the drifting gray mist, then fired up the Citation and lurched down the road behind them. *A month or so:* I felt hollow inside. I pictured her with Rolfe, eating yogurt and wheat germ, stopping at motels, wrestling grizzlies, and spiking trees. The hollowness opened up, cored me out till I felt as if I'd been plucked and gutted and served up on a platter myself.

I found my way back through Calpurnia Springs without incident—there were no roadblocks, no flashing lights and grim-looking troopers searching trunks and back seats for a tallish thirty-year-old ecoterrorist with turkey tracks down his back—but after I turned onto the highway for Los Angeles, I had a shock. Ten miles up the road my nightmare materialized out of the gloom: red lights everywhere, signal flares and police cars lined up on the shoulder. I was on the very edge of panicking, a beat away from cutting across the median and giving them a run for it, when I saw the truck jackknifed up ahead. I slowed to forty, thirty, and then hit the brakes again. In a moment I was stalled in a line of cars and there was something all over the road, ghostly and white in the fog. At first I thought it must have been flung from the truck, rolls of toilet paper or crates of soap powder ruptured on the pavement. It was neither. As I inched closer, the tires creeping now, the pulse of the lights in my face, I saw that the road was coated in feathers, turkey feathers. A storm of them. A blizzard. And more: there was flesh there too, slick and greasy, a red pulp ground into the surface of the road, thrown up like slush from the tires of the car ahead of me, ground beneath the massive wheels of the truck. Turkeys. Turkeys everywhere.

The car crept forward. I flicked on the windshield wipers, hit the washer button, and for a moment a scrim of diluted blood obscured the windows and the hollowness opened up inside of me till I thought it would suck me inside out. Behind me, someone was leaning on his horn. A trooper loomed up out of the gloom, waving me on with the dead yellow eye of his flashlight. I thought of Alena and felt sick. All there was between us had come to this, expectations gone sour, a smear on the road. I wanted to get out and shoot myself, turn myself in, close my eyes, and wake up in jail, in a hair shirt, in a straitjacket, anything. It went on. Time passed. Nothing moved. And then, miraculously, a vision began to emerge from behind the smeared glass and the gray belly of the fog, lights glowing golden in the waste. I saw the sign, Gas / Food / Lodging, and my hand was on the blinker.

It took me a moment, picturing the place, the generic tile, the false cheer of the lights, the odor of charred flesh hanging heavy on the air, Big Mac, three-piece dark meat, carne asada, cheeseburger. The engine coughed. The lights glowed. I didn't think of Alena then, didn't think of Rolfe or grizzlies or the doomed bleating flocks and herds, or of the blind bunnies and cancerous mice — I thought only of the cavern opening inside me and how to fill it. "Meat," and I spoke the word aloud, talking to calm myself as if I'd awakened from a bad dream, "it's only meat."

CONSIDERATIONS FOR CRITICAL THINKING AND WRITING

1. FIRST RESPONSE. How do your own views of vegetarianism and animal rights' groups influence your response to this story?

2. Comment on how Boyle achieves humorous effects through his first-person narrator in the story's first paragraph.

3. How does Boyle's style reveal the narrator's character? Select several paragraphs to illustrate your points.

4. How does the narrator use irony? Select three instances of his use of irony, and discuss their effects and what they reveal about him.

5. How does Boyle create a genuinely comic character with Alf? What is the narrator's relationship with Alf?

6. Characterize Alena. Why is the narrator both attracted to her and puzzled by her?

7. How do you think the story would differ if it were told from Alena's point of view?

8. What is your response to Alena's descriptions of commercial experiments on animals? How does the narrator respond to them?

9. How does paragraph 93 explain the narrator's willingness to go along with the raid on the turkey farm?

10. Describe the narrator's response to Rolfe. How does Boyle make Rolfe into a comic figure?

11. What is the major conflict in the story? How is it resolved in the story's final paragraphs?

STEPHEN CRANE (1871–1900)

Born in Newark, New Jersey, Stephen Crane attended Lafayette College and Syracuse University and then worked as a free-lance journalist in New York City. He wrote newspaper pieces, short stories, poems, and novels for his entire, brief adult life. His first book, *Maggie: A Girl of the Streets* (1893), is a story about New York slum life and prostitution. His most famous novel, *The Red Badge of Courage* (1895), gives readers a vivid, convincing re-creation of Civil War battles, even though Crane had never been to war. However, Crane was personally familiar with the American West, where he traveled as a reporter. "The Bride Comes to Yellow Sky" includes some of the ingredients of a typical popular western — a confrontation between a marshal and a drunk who shoots up the town — but the story's theme is less predictable and more serious than the plot seems to suggest.

The Bride Comes to Yellow Sky   *1898*

I

The great Pullman was whirling onward with such dignity of motion that a glance from the window seemed simply to prove that the plains of Texas were pouring eastward. Vast flats of green grass, dull-hued spaces of mesquit and cactus, little groups of frame houses, woods of light and tender trees, all were sweeping into the east, sweeping over the horizon, a precipice.

A newly married pair had boarded this coach at San Antonio. The man's face was reddened from many days in the wind and sun, and a direct result of his new black clothes was that his brick-colored hands were constantly performing in a most conscious fashion. From time to time he looked down respectfully at his attire. He sat with a hand on each knee, like a man waiting in a barber's shop. The glances he devoted to other passengers were furtive and shy.

The bride was not pretty, nor was she very young. She wore a dress of blue cashmere, with small reservations of velvet here and there, and with steel buttons abounding. She continually twisted her head to regard her puff sleeves, very stiff, straight, and high. They embarrassed her. It was quite apparent that she had cooked, and that she expected to cook, dutifully. The blushes caused by the careless scrutiny of some passengers as she had entered the car were strange to see upon this plain, under-class countenance, which was drawn in placid, almost emotionless lines.

They were evidently very happy. "Ever been in a parlor-car before?" he asked, smiling with delight.

"No," she answered; "I never was. It's fine, ain't it?"   5

"Great! And then after a while we'll go forward to the diner, and get a big lay-out. Finest meal in the world. Charge a dollar."

"Oh, do they?" cried the bride. "Charge a dollar? Why, that's too much— for us—ain't it, Jack?"

"Not this trip, anyhow," he answered bravely. "We're going to go the whole thing."

Later he explained to her about the trains. "You see, it's a thousand miles from one end of Texas to the other; and this train runs right across it, and never stops but four times." He had the pride of an owner. He pointed out to her the dazzling fittings of the coach; and in truth her eyes opened wider as she contemplated the sea-green figured velvet, the shining brass, silver, and glass, the wood that gleamed as darkly brilliant as the surface of a pool of oil. At one end a bronze figure sturdily held a support for a separated chamber, and at convenient places on the ceiling were frescoes in olive and silver.

To the minds of the pair, their surroundings reflected the glory of their 10 marriage that morning in San Antonio; this was the environment of their new estate; and the man's face in particular beamed with an elation that made him appear ridiculous to the negro porter. This individual at times surveyed them from afar with an amused and superior grin. On other occasions he bullied them with skill in ways that did not make it exactly plain to them that they were being bullied. He subtly used all the manners of the most unconquerable kind of snobbery. He oppressed them; but of this oppression they had small knowledge, and they speedily forgot that infrequently a number of travelers covered them with stares of derisive enjoyment. Historically there was supposed to be something infinitely humorous in their situation.

"We are due in Yellow Sky at 3:42," he said, looking tenderly into her eyes.

"Oh, are we?" she said, as if she had not been aware of it. To evince surprise at her husband's statement was part of her wifely amiability. She took from a pocket a little silver watch; and as she held it before her, and stared at it with a frown of attention, the new husband's face shone.

"I bought it in San Anton' from a friend of mine," he told her gleefully.

"It's seventeen minutes past twelve," she said, looking up at him with a kind of shy and clumsy coquetry. A passenger, noting this play, grew excessively sardonic, and winked at himself in one of the numerous mirrors.

At last they went to the dining-car. Two rows of negro waiters, in glowing white suits, surveyed their entrance with the interest, and also the equanimity, of men who had been forewarned. The pair fell to the lot of a waiter who happened to feel pleasure in steering them through their meal. He viewed them with the manner of a fatherly pilot, his countenance radiant with benevolence. The patronage, entwined with the ordinary deference, was not plain to them. And yet, as they returned to their coach, they showed in their faces a sense of escape. 15

To the left, miles down a long purple slope, was a little ribbon of mist where moved the keening Rio Grande. The train was approaching it at an angle, and the apex was Yellow Sky. Presently it was apparent that, as the distance from Yellow Sky grew shorter, the husband became commensurately restless. His brick-red hands were more insistent in their prominence. Occasionally he was even rather absent-minded and far-away when the bride leaned forward and addressed him.

As a matter of truth, Jack Potter was beginning to find the shadow of a deed weigh upon him like a leaden slab. He, the town marshal of Yellow Sky, a man known, liked, and feared in his corner, a prominent person, had gone to San Antonio to meet a girl he believed he loved, and there, after the usual prayers, had actually induced her to marry him, without consulting Yellow Sky for any part of the transaction. He was now bringing his bride before an innocent and unsuspecting community.

Of course people in Yellow Sky married as it pleased them in accordance with a general custom; but such was Potter's thought of his duty to his friends, or of their idea of his duty, or of an unspoken form which does not control men in these matters, that he felt he was heinous. He had committed an extraordinary crime. Face to face with this girl in San Antonio, and spurred by his sharp impulse, he had gone headlong over all the social hedges. At San Antonio he was like a man hidden in the dark. A knife to sever any friendly duty, any form, was easy to his hand in that remote city. But the hour of Yellow Sky—the hour of daylight—was approaching.

He knew full well that his marriage was an important thing to his town. It could only be exceeded by the burning of the new hotel. His friends could not forgive him. Frequently he had reflected on the advisability of telling them by telegraph, but a new cowardice had been upon him. He feared to do it. And now the train was hurrying him toward a scene of amazement, glee, and reproach. He glanced out of the window at the line of haze swinging slowly in toward the train.

Yellow Sky had a kind of brass band, which played painfully, to the delight   20
of the populace. He laughed without heart as he thought of it. If the citizens
could dream of his prospective arrival with his bride, they would parade the
band at the station and escort them, amid cheers and laughing congratulations, to his adobe home.

He resolved that he would use all the devices of speed and plainscraft in
making the journey from the station to his house. Once within that safe
citadel, he could issue some sort of vocal bulletin, and then not go among the
citizens until they had time to wear off a little of their enthusiasm.

The bride looked anxiously at him. "What's worrying you, Jack?"

He laughed again. "I'm not worrying, girl; I'm only thinking of Yellow Sky."

She flushed in comprehension.

A sense of mutual guilt invaded their minds and developed a finer tender-   25
ness. They looked at each other with eyes softly aglow. But Potter often
laughed the same nervous laugh; the flush upon the bride's face seemed quite
permanent.

The traitor to the feelings of Yellow Sky narrowly watched the speeding
landscape. "We're nearly there," he said.

Presently the porter came and announced the proximity of Potter's home.
He held a brush in his hand, and, with all his airy superiority gone, he brushed
Potter's new clothes as the latter slowly turned this way and that way. Potter
fumbled out a coin and gave it to the porter, as he had seen others do. It was a
heavy and muscle-bound business, as that of a man shoeing his first horse.

The porter took their bag, and as the train began to slow they moved forward to the hooded platform of the car. Presently the two engines and their
long string of coaches rushed into the station of Yellow Sky.

"They have to take water here," said Potter, from a constricted throat and
in mournful cadence, as one announcing death. Before the train stopped his
eye had swept the length of the platform, and he was glad and astonished to
see there was none upon it but the station-agent, who, with a slightly hurried
and anxious air, was walking toward the water-tanks. When the train had
halted, the porter alighted first, and placed in position a little temporary step.

"Come on, girl," said Potter, hoarsely. As he helped her down they each   30
laughed on a false note. He took the bag from the negro, and bade his wife
cling to his arm. As they slunk rapidly away, his hang-dog glance perceived that
they were unloading the two trunks, and also that the station-agent, far ahead
near the baggage-car, had turned and was running toward him, making gestures. He laughed, and groaned as he laughed, when he noted the first effect of
his marital bliss upon Yellow Sky. He gripped his wife's arm firmly to his side,
and they fled. Behind them the porter stood, chuckling fatuously.

II

The California express on the Southern Railway was due at Yellow Sky in
twenty-one minutes. There were six men at the bar of the Weary Gentleman
saloon. One was a drummer° who talked a great deal and rapidly; three were
Texans who did not care to talk at that time; and two were Mexican sheep-
herders, who did not talk as a general practice in the Weary Gentleman saloon.
The barkeeper's dog lay on the board walk that crossed in front of the door.

drummer: Traveling salesman.

His head was on his paws, and he glanced drowsily here and there with the constant vigilance of a dog that is kicked on occasion. Across the sandy street were some vivid green grass-plots, so wonderful in appearance, amid the sands that burned near them in a blazing sun, that they caused a doubt in the mind. They exactly resembled the grass mats used to represent lawns on the stage. At the cooler end of the railway station, a man without a coat sat in a tilted chair and smoked his pipe. The fresh-cut bank of the Rio Grande circled near the town, and there could be seen beyond it a great plum-colored plain of mesquit.

Save for the busy drummer and his companions in the saloon, Yellow Sky was dozing. The new-comer leaned gracefully upon the bar, and recited many tales with the confidence of a bard who has come upon a new field.

"— and at the moment that the old man fell downstairs with the bureau in his arms, the old woman was coming up with two scuttles of coal, and of course —"

The drummer's tale was interrupted by a young man who suddenly appeared in the open door. He cried: "Scratchy Wilson's drunk, and has turned loose with both hands." The two Mexicans at once set down their glasses and faded out of the rear entrance of the saloon.

The drummer, innocent and jocular, answered: "All right, old man. S'pose 35 he has? Come in and have a drink, anyhow."

But the information had made such an obvious cleft in every skull in the room that the drummer was obliged to see its importance. All had become instantly solemn. "Say," said he, mystified, "what is this?" His three companions made the introductory gesture of eloquent speech; but the young man at the door forestalled them.

"It means, my friend," he answered, as he came into the saloon, "that for the next two hours this town won't be a health resort."

The barkeeper went to the door, and locked and barred it; reaching out of the window, he pulled in heavy wooden shutters, and barred them. Immediately a solemn, chapel-like gloom was upon the place. The drummer was looking from one to another.

"But, say," he cried, "what is this, anyhow? You don't mean there is going to be a gun-fight?"

"Don't know whether there'll be a fight or not," answered one man, 40 grimly; "but there'll be some shootin' — some good shootin'."

The young man who had warned them waved his hand. "Oh, there'll be a fight fast enough, if any one wants it. Anybody can get a fight out there in the street. There's a fight just waiting."

The drummer seemed to be swayed between the interest of a foreigner and a perception of personal danger.

"What did you say his name was?" he asked.

"Scratchy Wilson," they answered in chorus.

"And will he kill anybody? What are you going to do? Does this happen 45 often? Does he rampage around like this once a week or so? Can he break in that door?"

"No; he can't break down that door," replied the barkeeper. "He's tried it three times. But when he comes you'd better lay down on the floor, stranger. He's dead sure to shoot at it, and a bullet may come through."

Thereafter the drummer kept a strict eye upon the door. The time had not yet called for him to hug the floor, but, as a minor precaution, he sidled near the wall. "Will he kill anybody?" he said again.

The men laughed low and scornfully at the question.

"He's out to shoot, and he's out for trouble. Don't see any good in experimentin' with him."

"But what do you do in a case like this? What do you do?" 50

A man responded: "Why, he and Jack Potter—"

"But," in chorus the other men interrupted, "Jack Potter's in San Anton'."

"Well, who is he? What's he got to do with it?"

"Oh, he's the town marshal. He goes out and fights Scratchy when he gets on one of these tears."

"Wow!" said the drummer, mopping his brow. "Nice job he's got." 55

The voices had toned away to mere whisperings. The drummer wished to ask further questions, which were born of an increasing anxiety and bewilderment; but when he attempted them, the men merely looked at him in irritation and motioned him to remain silent. A tense waiting hush was upon them. In the deep shadows of the room their eyes shone as they listened for sounds from the street. One man made three gestures at the barkeeper; and the latter, moving like a ghost, handed him a glass and a bottle. The man poured a full glass of whisky, and set down the bottle noiselessly. He gulped the whisky in a swallow, and turned again toward the door in immovable silence. The drummer saw that the barkeeper, without a sound, had taken a Winchester from beneath the bar. Later he saw this individual beckoning to him, so he tiptoed across the room.

"You better come with me back of the bar."

"No thanks," said the drummer, perspiring; "I'd rather be where I can make a break for the back door."

Whereupon the man of bottles made a kindly but peremptory gesture. The drummer obeyed it, and, finding himself seated on a box with his head below the level of the bar, balm was laid upon his soul at sight of various zinc and copper fittings that bore a resemblance to armor-plate. The barkeeper took a seat comfortably upon an adjacent box.

"You see," he whispered, "this here Scratchy Wilson is a wonder with a 60 gun—a perfect wonder; and when he goes on the war-trail, we hunt our holes—naturally. He's about the last one of the old gang that used to hang out along the river here. He's a terror when he's drunk. When he's sober he's all right—kind of simple—wouldn't hurt a fly—nicest fellow in town. But when he's drunk—whoo!"

There were periods of stillness. "I wish Jack Potter was back from San Anton'," said the barkeeper. "He shot Wilson up once—in the leg—and he would sail in and pull out the kinks in this thing."

Presently they heard from a distance the sound of a shot, followed by three wild yowls. It instantly removed a bond from the men in the darkened saloon. There was a shuffling of feet. They looked at each other. "Here he comes," they said.

III

A man in a maroon-colored flannel shirt, which had been purchased for purposes of decoration, and made principally by some Jewish women on the East Side of New York, rounded a corner and walked into the middle of the main street of Yellow Sky. In either hand the man held a long, heavy, blue-black revolver. Often he yelled, and these cries rang through a semblance of a deserted village, shrilly flying over the roofs in a volume that seemed to have no relation to the ordinary vocal strength of a man. It was as if the surrounding stillness formed the arch of a tomb over him. These cries of ferocious challenge rang against walls of silence. And his boots had red tops with gilded imprints, of the kind beloved in winter by little sledding boys on the hillsides of New England.

The man's face flamed in a rage begot of whisky. His eyes, rolling, and yet keen for ambush, hunted the still doorways and windows. He walked with the creeping movement of the midnight cat. As it occurred to him, he roared menacing information. The long revolvers in his hands were as easy as straws; they were removed with an electric swiftness. The little fingers of each hand played sometimes in a musician's way. Plain from the low collar of the shirt, the cords of his neck straightened and sank, straightened and sank, as passion moved him. The only sounds were his terrible invitations. The calm adobes preserved their demeanor at the passing of this small thing in the middle of the street.

There was no offer of fight — no offer of fight. The man called to the sky. 65 There were no attractions. He bellowed and fumed and swayed his revolvers here and everywhere.

The dog of the barkeeper of the Weary Gentleman saloon had not appreciated the advance of events. He yet lay dozing in front of his master's door. At sight of the dog, the man paused and raised his revolver humorously. At sight of the man, the dog sprang up and walked diagonally away, with a sullen head, and growling. The man yelled, and the dog broke into a gallop. As it was about to enter the alley, there was a loud noise, a whistling, and something spat the ground directly before it. The dog screamed, and, wheeling in terror, galloped headlong in a new direction. Again there was a noise, a whistling, and sand was kicked viciously before it. Fear-stricken, the dog turned and flurried like an animal in a pen. The man stood laughing, his weapons at his hips.

Ultimately the man was attracted by the closed door of the Weary Gentleman saloon. He went to it and, hammering with a revolver, demanded drink.

The door remaining imperturbable, he picked a bit of paper from the walk, and nailed it to the framework with a knife. He then turned his back contemptuously upon this popular resort and, walking to the opposite side of the street and spinning there on his heel quickly and lithely, fired at the bit of paper. He missed it by a half inch. He swore at himself, and went away. Later he comfortably fusilladed the windows of his most intimate friend. The man was playing with this town; it was a toy for him.

But still there was no offer of fight. The name of Jack Potter, his ancient antagonist, entered his mind, and he concluded that it would be a glad thing if he should go to Potter's house, and by bombardment induce him to come out and fight. He moved in the direction of his desire, chanting Apache scalp-music.

When he arrived at it, Potter's house presented the same still front as had 70 the other adobes. Taking up a strategic position, the man howled a challenge. But this house regarded him as might a great stone god. It gave no sign. After a decent wait, the man howled further challenges, mingling with them wonderful epithets.

Presently there came the spectacle of a man churning himself into deepest rage over the immobility of a house. He fumed at it as the winter wind attacks a prairie cabin in the North. To the distance there should have gone the sound of a tumult like the fighting of two hundred Mexicans. As necessity bade him, he paused for breath or to reload his revolvers.

IV

Potter and his bride walked sheepishly and with speed. Sometimes they laughed together shamefacedly and low.

"Next corner, dear," he said finally.

They put forth the efforts of a pair walking bowed against a strong wind. Potter was about to raise a finger to point the first appearance of the new home when, as they circled the corner, they came face to face with a man in a maroon-colored shirt, who was feverishly pushing cartridges into a large revolver. Upon the instant the man dropped his revolver to the ground and, like lightning, whipped another from its holster. The second weapon was aimed at the bridegroom's chest.

There was a silence. Potter's mouth seemed to be merely a grave for his 75 tongue. He exhibited an instinct to at once loosen his arm from the woman's grip, and he dropped the bag to the sand. As for the bride, her face had gone as yellow as old cloth. She was a slave to hideous rites, gazing at the apparitional snake.

The two men faced each other at a distance of three paces. He of the revolver smiled with a new and quiet ferocity.

"Tried to sneak up on me," he said. "Tried to sneak up on me!" His eyes grew more baleful. As Potter made a slight movement, the man thrust his revolver venomously forward. "No, don't you do it, Jack Potter. Don't you move a finger toward a gun just yet. Don't you move an eyelash. The time has come for me to settle with you and I'm goin' to do it my own way, and loaf along with no interferin'. So if you don't want a gun bent on you, just mind what I tell you."

Potter looked at his enemy. "I ain't got a gun on me, Scratchy," he said. "Honest, I ain't." He was stiffening and steadying, but yet somewhere at the back of his mind a vision of the Pullman floated: the sea-green figured velvet, the shining brass, silver, and glass, the wood that gleamed as darkly brilliant as the surface of a pool of oil — all the glory of marriage, the environment of the new estate. "You know I fight when it comes to fighting, Scratchy Wilson; but I ain't got a gun on me. You'll have to do all the shootin' yourself."

His enemy's face went livid. He stepped forward, and lashed his weapon to and fro before Potter's chest. "Don't you tell me you ain't got no gun on you, you whelp. Don't tell me no lie like that. There ain't a man in Texas ever seen you without no gun. Don't take me for no kid." His eyes blazed with light, and his throat worked like a pump.

"I ain't takin' you for no kid," answered Potter. His heels had not moved 80 an inch backward. "I'm takin' you for a damn fool. I tell you I ain't got a gun, and I ain't. If you're goin' to shoot me up, you better begin now; you'll never get a chance like this again."

So much enforced reasoning had told on Wilson's rage; he was calmer. "If you ain't got a gun, why ain't you got a gun?" he sneered. "Been to Sunday-school?"

"I ain't got a gun because I've just come from San Anton' with my wife. I'm married," said Potter. "And if I'd thought there was going to be any galoots like you prowling around when I brought my wife home, I'd had a gun, and don't you forget it."

"Married!" said Scratchy, not at all comprehending.

"Yes, married. I'm married," said Potter, distinctly.

"Married?" said Scratchy. Seemingly for the first time, he saw the droop- 85 ing, drowning woman at the other man's side. "No!" he said. He was like a creature allowed a glimpse of another world. He moved a pace backward, and his arm, with the revolver, dropped to his side. "Is this the lady?" he asked.

"Yes; this is the lady," answered Potter.

There was another period of silence.

"Well," said Wilson at last, slowly, "I s'pose it's all off now."

"It's all off if you say so, Scratchy. You know I didn't make the trouble." Potter lifted his valise.

"Well, I 'low it's off, Jack," said Wilson. He was looking at the ground. 90 "Married!" He was not a student of chivalry; it was merely that in the presence of this foreign condition he was a simple child of the earlier plains. He picked up his starboard revolver, and, placing both weapons in their holsters, he went away. His feet made funnel-shaped tracks in the heavy sand.

CONSIDERATIONS FOR CRITICAL THINKING AND WRITING

1. FIRST RESPONSE. Think of a western you've read or seen: any of Larry McMurtry's books would work, such as *Lonesome Dove* or *Evening Star*. Compare and contrast the setting, characters, action, and theme in Crane's story with your western.

2. What is the nature of the conflict Marshal Potter feels on the train in Part I? Why does he feel that he committed a "crime" in bringing home a bride to Yellow Sky?

3. What is the function of the "drummer," the traveling salesman, in Part II?

4. How do Mrs. Potter and Scratchy Wilson serve as foils for each other? What does each represent in the story?

5. What is the significance of the setting?

6. How does Crane create suspense about what will happen when Marshal Potter meets Scratchy Wilson? Is suspense the major point of the story?

7. Is Scratchy Wilson too drunk, comical, and ineffective to be a sympathetic character? What is the meaning of his conceding that "I s'pose it's all off now" at the end of Part IV? Is he a dynamic or a static character?

8. What details seem to support the story's theme? Consider, for example, the descriptions of the bride's clothes and Scratchy Wilson's shirt and boots.

9. Explain why the heroes in western stories are rarely married and why Crane's use of marriage is central to his theme.

10. CRITICAL STRATEGIES. Read the section on gender strategies (pp. 70–71) in Chapter 3, "Applying a Critical Strategy." Explore the heterosexual and potentially homosexual issues that a gender critic might discover in the story.

NATHANIEL HAWTHORNE (1804–1864)

Born in Salem, Massachusetts, Nathaniel Hawthorne came from a family that traced its roots back to the Puritans. After graduating from Bowdoin College in 1825, he returned home to Salem, where for the next twelve years he read and taught himself how to write. He published his first collection of stories, *Twice-Told Tales*, in 1837, followed by a second edition in 1842, and *Mosses from an Old House* in 1846. In 1849 he lost his job at the Salem Custom House and focused on his writing. In addition to *The Scarlet Letter* (1850), he wrote *The House of Seven Gables* (1851); *The Blithedale Romance* (1852); *The Snow-Image, and Other Twice-Told Tales* (1852); a campaign biography of his Bowdoin classmate, *The Life of Franklin Pierce* (1852); and two collections of stories for children, *A Wonder Book* (1852) and *Tanglewood Tales* (1853).

The Birthmark   *1843*

In the latter part of the last century there lived a man of science, an eminent proficient in every branch of natural philosophy, who not long before our story opens had made experience of a spiritual affinity more attractive than any chemical one. He had left his laboratory to the care of an assistant, cleared his fine countenance from the furnace smoke, washed the stain of acids from his fingers, and persuaded a beautiful woman to become his wife. In those days when the comparatively recent discovery of electricity and other kindred mysteries of Nature seemed to open paths into the region of miracle, it was not unusual for the love of science to rival the love of woman in its depth and absorbing energy. The higher intellect, the imagination, the spirit, and even the heart might all find their congenial aliment in pursuits which, as some of their ardent votaries believed, would ascend from one step of powerful intelligence to another, until the philosopher should lay his hand on the secret of creative force and perhaps make new worlds for himself. We know not whether Aylmer possessed this degree of faith in man's ultimate control over Nature. He had devoted himself, however, too unreservedly to scientific studies ever to be weaned from them by any second passion. His love for his young wife might prove the stronger of the two; but it could only be by intertwining itself with his love of science, and uniting the strength of the latter to his own.

Such a union accordingly took place, and was attended with truly remarkable consequences and a deeply impressive moral. One day, very soon after their marriage, Aylmer sat gazing at his wife with a trouble in his countenance that grew stronger until he spoke.

"Georgiana," said he, "has it never occurred to you that the mark upon your cheek might be removed?"

"No, indeed," said she, smiling; but perceiving the seriousness of his manner, she blushed deeply. "To tell you the truth it has been so often called a charm that I was simple enough to imagine it might be so."

"Ah, upon another face perhaps it might," replied her husband; "but never   5 on yours. No, dearest Georgiana, you came so nearly perfect from the hand of

Nature that this slightest possible defect, which we hesitate whether to term a defect or a beauty, shocks me, as being the visible mark of earthly imperfection."

"Shocks you, my husband!" cried Georgiana, deeply hurt; at first reddening with momentary anger, but then bursting into tears. "Then why did you take me from my mother's side? You cannot love what shocks you!"

To explain this conversation it must be mentioned that in the center of Georgiana's left cheek there was a singular mark, deeply interwoven, as it were, with the texture and substance of her face. In the usual state of her complexion — a healthy though delicate bloom — the mark wore a tint of deeper crimson, which imperfectly defined its shape amid the surrounding rosiness. When she blushed it gradually became more indistinct, and finally vanished amid the triumphant rush of blood that bathed the whole cheek with its brilliant glow. But if any shifting motion caused her to turn pale, there was the mark again, a crimson stain upon the snow, in what Aylmer sometimes deemed an almost fearful distinctness. Its shape bore not a little similarity to the human hand, though of the smallest pygmy size. Georgiana's lovers were wont to say that some fairy at her birth hour had laid her tiny hand upon the infant's cheek, and left this impress there in token of the magic endowments that were to give her such sway over all hearts. Many a desperate swain would have risked life for the privilege of pressing his lips to the mysterious hand. It must not be concealed, however, that the impression wrought by this fairy sign manual varied exceedingly, according to the difference of temperament in the beholders. Some fastidious persons — but they were exclusively of her own sex — affirmed that the bloody hand, as they chose to call it, quite destroyed the effect of Georgiana's beauty, and rendered her countenance even hideous. But it would be as reasonable to say that one of those small blue stains which sometimes occur in the purest statuary marble would convert the Eve of Powers° to a monster. Masculine observers, if the birthmark did not heighten their admiration, contented themselves with wishing it away, that the world might possess one living specimen of ideal loveliness without the semblance of a flaw. After his marriage, — for he thought little or nothing of the matter before, — Aylmer discovered that this was the case with himself.

Had she been less beautiful, — if Envy's self could have found aught else to sneer at, — he might have felt his affection heightened by the prettiness of this mimic hand, now vaguely portrayed, now lost, now stealing forth again and glimmering to and fro with every pulse of emotion that throbbed within her heart; but seeing her otherwise so perfect, he found this one defect grow more and more intolerable with every moment of their united lives. It was the fatal flaw of humanity which Nature, in one shape or another, stamps ineffaceably on all her productions, either to imply that they are temporary and finite, or that their perfection must be wrought by toil and pain. The crimson hand expressed the ineludible gripe° in which mortality clutches the highest and purest of earthly mold, degrading them into kindred with the lowest, and even with the very brutes, like whom their visible frames return to dust. In this manner, selecting it as the symbol of his wife's liability to sin, sorrow, decay, and death, Aylmer's somber imagination was not long in rendering the birthmark a frightful object, causing him more trouble and horror than ever Georgiana's beauty, whether of soul or sense, had given him delight.

Eve of Powers: A statue by Hiram Powers (1805–1873), American sculptor.
gripe: Grip.

At all the seasons which should have been their happiest, he invariably and without intending it, nay, in spite of a purpose to the contrary, reverted to this one disastrous topic. Trifling as it at first appeared, it so connected itself with innumerable trains of thought and modes of feeling that it became the central point of all. With the morning twilight Aylmer opened his eyes upon his wife's face and recognized the symbol of imperfection; and when they sat together at the evening hearth his eyes wandered stealthily to her cheek, and beheld, flickering with the blaze of the wood fire, the spectral hand that wrote mortality where he would fain have worshiped. Georgiana soon learned to shudder at his gaze. It needed but a glance with the peculiar expression that his face often wore to change the roses of her cheek into a deathlike paleness, amid which the crimson hand was brought strongly out, like a bas-relief of ruby on the whitest marble.

Late one night when the lights were growing dim, so as hardly to betray   10
the stain on the poor wife's cheek, she herself, for the first time, voluntarily took up the subject.

"Do you remember, my dear Aylmer," said she, with a feeble attempt at a smile, "have you any recollection of a dream last night about this odious hand?"

"None! none whatever!" replied Aylmer, starting; but then he added, in a dry, cold tone, affected for the sake of concealing the real depth of his emotion, "I might well dream of it; for before I fell asleep it had taken a pretty firm hold of my fancy."

"And you did dream of it?" continued Georgiana hastily, for she dreaded lest a gush of tears should interrupt what she had to say. "A terrible dream! I wonder that you can forget it. Is it possible to forget this one expression? — 'It is in her heart now; we must have it out!' Reflect, my husband; for by all means I would have you recall that dream."

The mind is in a sad state when Sleep, the all-involving, cannot confine her specters within the dim region of her sway, but suffers them to break forth, affrighting this actual life with secrets that perchance belong to a deeper one. Aylmer now remembered his dream. He had fancied himself with his servant Aminadab, attempting an operation for the removal of the birthmark; but the deeper went the knife, the deeper sank the hand, until at length its tiny grasp appeared to have caught hold of Georgiana's heart; whence, however, her husband was inexorably resolved to cut or wrench it away.

When the dream had shaped itself perfectly in his memory, Aylmer sat in   15
his wife's presence with a guilty feeling. Truth often finds its way to the mind close muffled in robes of sleep, and then speaks with uncompromising directness of matters in regard to which we practice an unconscious self-deception during our waking moments. Until now he had not been aware of the tyrannizing influence acquired by one idea over his mind, and of the lengths which he might find in his heart to go for the sake of giving himself peace.

"Aylmer," resumed Georgiana solemnly, "I know not what may be the cost to both of us to rid me of this fatal birthmark. Perhaps its removal may cause cureless deformity; or it may be the stain goes as deep as life itself. Again: do we know that there is a possibility, on any terms, of unclasping the firm grip of this little hand which was laid upon me before I came into the world?"

"Dearest Georgiana, I have spent much thought upon the subject," hastily interrupted Aylmer. "I am convinced of the perfect practicability of its removal."

"If there be the remotest possibility of it," continued Georgiana, "let the attempt be made at whatever risk. Danger is nothing to me; for life, while this hateful mark makes me the object of your horror and disgust, — life is a burden which I would fling down with joy. Either remove this dreadful hand, or take my wretched life! You have deep science. All the world bears witness of it. You have achieved great wonders. Cannot you remove this little, little mark, which I cover with the tips of two small fingers? Is this beyond your power, for the sake of your own peace, and to save your poor wife from madness?"

"Noblest, dearest, tenderest wife," cried Aylmer rapturously, "doubt not my power. I have already given this matter the deepest thought — thought which might almost have enlightened me to create a being less perfect than yourself. Georgiana, you have led me deeper than ever into the heart of science. I feel myself fully competent to render this dear cheek as faultless as its fellow; and then, most beloved, what will be my triumph when I shall have corrected what Nature left imperfect in her fairest work! Even Pygmalion, when his sculptured woman assumed life, felt not greater ecstasy than mine will be."

"It is resolved, then," said Georgiana, faintly smiling. "And, Aylmer, spare 20 me not, though you should find the birthmark take refuge in my heart at last."

Her husband tenderly kissed her cheek — her right cheek — not that which bore the impress of the crimson hand.

The next day Aylmer apprised his wife of a plan that he had formed whereby he might have opportunity for the intense thought and constant watchfulness which the proposed operation would require; while Georgiana, likewise, would enjoy the perfect repose essential to its success. They were to seclude themselves in the extensive apartments occupied by Aylmer as a laboratory, and where, during his toilsome youth, he had made discoveries in the elemental powers of Nature that had roused the admiration of all the learned societies in Europe. Seated calmly in this laboratory, the pale philosopher had investigated the secrets of the highest cloud region and of the profoundest mines; he had satisfied himself of the causes that kindled and kept alive the fires of the volcano; and had explained the mystery of fountains, and how it is that they gush forth, some so bright and pure, and others with such rich medicinal virtues, from the dark bosom of the earth. Here, too, at an earlier period, he had studied the wonders of the human frame, and attempted to fathom the very process by which Nature assimilates all her precious influences from earth and air, and from the spiritual world, to create and foster man, her masterpiece. The latter pursuit, however, Aylmer had long laid aside in unwilling recognition of the truth — against which all seekers sooner or later stumble — that our great creative Mother, while she amuses us with apparently working in the broadest sunshine, is yet severely careful to keep her own secrets, and, in spite of her pretended openness, shows us nothing but results. She permits us, indeed, to mar, but seldom to mend, and, like a jealous patentee, on no account to make. Now, however, Aylmer resumed these half-forgotten investigations, — not, of course, with such hopes or wishes as first suggested them, but because they involved much physiological truth and lay in the path of his proposed scheme for the treatment of Georgiana.

As he led her over the threshold of the laboratory, Georgiana was cold and tremulous. Aylmer looked cheerfully into her face, with intent to reassure her, but was so startled with the intense glow of the birthmark upon the whiteness of her cheek that he could not restrain a strong convulsive shudder. His wife fainted.

"Aminadab! Aminadab!" shouted Aylmer, stamping violently on the floor.

Forthwith there issued from an inner apartment a man of low stature, but 25 bulky frame, with shaggy hair hanging about his visage, which was grimed with the vapors of the furnace. This personage had been Aylmer's under-worker during his whole scientific career, and was admirably fitted for that office by his great mechanical readiness, and the skill with which, while inca-pable of comprehending a single principle, he executed all the details of his master's experiments. With his vast strength, his shaggy hair, his smoky aspect, and the indescribable earthiness that encrusted him, he seemed to rep-resent man's physical nature; while Aylmer's slender figure, and pale, intellec-tual face, were no less apt a type of the spiritual element.

"Throw open the door of the boudoir, Aminadab," said Aylmer, "and burn a pastille."

"Yes, master," answered Aminadab, looking intently at the lifeless form of Georgiana; and then he muttered to himself, "If she were my wife, I'd never part with that birthmark."

When Georgiana recovered consciousness she found herself breathing an atmosphere of penetrating fragrance, the gentle potency of which had recalled her from her deathlike faintness. The scene around her looked like enchant-ment. Aylmer had converted those smoky, dingy, somber rooms, where he had spent his brightest years in recondite pursuits, into a series of beautiful apart-ments not unfit to be the secluded abode of a lovely woman. The walls were hung with gorgeous curtains, which imparted the combination of grandeur and grace that no other species of adornment can achieve; and as they fell from the ceiling to the floor, their rich and ponderous folds, concealing all angles and straight lines, appeared to shut in the scene from infinite space. For aught Georgiana knew, it might be a pavilion among the clouds. And Aylmer, excluding the sunshine, which would have interfered with his chemical processes, had supplied its place with perfumed lamps, emitting flames of var-ious hue, but all uniting in a soft, empurpled radiance. He now knelt by his wife's side, watching her earnestly, but without alarm; for he was confident in his science, and felt that he could draw a magic circle round her within which no evil might intrude.

"Where am I? Ah, I remember," said Georgiana faintly; and she placed her hand over her cheek to hide the terrible mark from her husband's eyes.

"Fear not, dearest!" exclaimed he. "Do not shrink from me! Believe me, 30 Georgiana, I even rejoice in this single imperfection, since it will be such a rap-ture to remove it."

"Oh, spare me!" sadly replied his wife. "Pray do not look at it again. I never can forget that convulsive shudder."

In order to soothe Georgiana, and, as it were, to release her mind from the burden of actual things, Aylmer now put in practice some of the light and playful secrets which science had taught him among its profounder lore. Airy figures, absolutely bodiless ideas, and forms of unsubstantial beauty came and danced before her, imprinting their momentary footsteps on beams of light. Though she had some indistinct idea of the method of these optical phenom-ena, still the illusion was almost perfect enough to warrant the belief that her husband possessed sway over the spiritual world. Then again, when she felt a wish to look forth from her seclusion, immediately, as if her thoughts were answered, the procession of external existence flitted across a screen. The scenery and the figures of actual life were perfectly represented, but with that bewitching, yet indescribable difference which always makes a picture, an image, or a shadow so much more attractive than the original. When wearied of this, Aylmer bade her cast her eyes upon a vessel containing a quantity of earth. She did so, with little interest at first; but was soon startled to perceive the germ of a plant shooting upward from the soil. Then came the slender stalk; the leaves gradually unfolded themselves; and amid them was a perfect and lovely flower.

"It is magical!" cried Georgiana. "I dare not touch it."

"Nay, pluck it," answered Aylmer: "pluck it, and inhale its brief perfume while you may. The flower will wither in a few moments and leave nothing save its brown seed vessels; but thence may be perpetuated a race as ephemeral as itself."

But Georgiana had no sooner touched the flower than the whole plant 35 suffered a blight, its leaves turning coal-black as if by the agency of fire.

"There was too powerful a stimulus," said Aylmer thoughtfully.

To make up for this abortive experiment, he proposed to take her portrait by a scientific process of his own invention. It was to be effected by rays of light striking upon a polished plate of metal. Georgiana assented; but, on looking at the result, was affrighted to find the features of the portrait blurred and indefinable; while the minute figure of a hand appeared where the cheek should have been. Aylmer snatched the metallic plate and threw it into a jar of corrosive acid.

Soon, however, he forgot these mortifying failures. In the intervals of study and chemical experiment he came to her flushed and exhausted, but seemed invigorated by her presence, and spoke in glowing language of the resources of his art. He gave a history of the long dynasty of the alchemists, who spent so many ages in quest of the universal solvent by which the golden principle might be elicited from all things vile and base. Aylmer appeared to believe that, by the plainest scientific logic, it was altogether within the limits of possibility to discover this long-sought medium; "but," he added, "a philosopher who should go deep enough to acquire the power would attain too lofty a wisdom to stoop to the exercise of it." Not less singular were his opinions in regard to the elixir vitae. He more than intimated that it was at his option to concoct a liquid that should prolong life for years, perhaps interminably; but that it would produce a discord in Nature which all the world, and chiefly the quaffer of the immortal nostrum, would find cause to curse.

"Aylmer, are you in earnest?" asked Georgiana, looking at him with amazement and fear. "It is terrible to possess such power, or even to dream of possessing it."

"Oh, do not tremble, my love," said her husband. "I would not wrong 40 either you or myself by working such inharmonious effects upon our lives; but I would have you consider how trifling, in comparison, is the skill requisite to remove this little hand."

At the mention of the birthmark, Georgiana, as usual, shrank as if a red-hot iron had touched her cheek.

Again Aylmer applied himself to his labors. She could hear his voice in the distant furnace-room giving directions to Aminadab, whose harsh, uncouth, misshapen tones were audible in response, more like the grunt or growl of a brute than human speech. After hours of absence, Aylmer reappeared and proposed that she should now examine his cabinet of chemical products and natural treasures of the earth. Among the former he showed her a small vial, in which, he remarked, was contained a gentle yet most powerful fragrance, capable of impregnating all the breezes that blow across a kingdom. They were of inestimable value, the contents of that little vial; and, as he said so, he threw some of the perfume into the air and filled the room with piercing and invigorating delight.

"And what is this?" asked Georgiana, pointing to a small crystal globe containing a gold-colored liquid. "It is so beautiful to the eye that I could imagine it the elixir of life."

"In one sense it is," replied Aylmer; "or rather, the elixir of immortality. It is the most precious poison that ever was concocted in this world. By its aid I could apportion the lifetime of any mortal at whom you might point your finger. The strength of the dose would determine whether he were to linger out years, or drop dead in the midst of a breath. No king on his guarded throne could keep his life if I, in my private station, should deem that the welfare of millions justified me in depriving him of it."

"Why do you keep such a terrific drug?" inquired Georgiana in horror.   45

"Do not mistrust me, dearest," said her husband, smiling; "its virtuous potency is yet greater than its harmful one. But see! here is a powerful cosmetic. With a few drops of this in a vase of water, freckles may be washed away as easily as the hands are cleansed. A stronger infusion would take the blood out of the cheek, and leave the rosiest beauty a pale ghost."

"Is it with this lotion that you intend to bathe my cheek?" asked Georgiana, anxiously.

"Oh, no," hastily replied her husband; "this is merely superficial. Your case demands a remedy that shall go deeper."

In his interviews with Georgiana, Aylmer generally made minute inquiries as to her sensations and whether the confinement of the rooms and the temperature of the atmosphere agreed with her. These questions had such a particular drift that Georgiana began to conjecture that she was already subjected to certain physical influences, either breathed in with the fragrant air or taken with her food. She fancied likewise, but it might be altogether fancy, that there was a stirring up of her system—a strange, indefinite sensation creeping through her veins, and tingling, half painfully, half pleasurably, at her heart. Still, whenever she dared to look into the mirror, there she beheld herself pale as a white rose and with the crimson birthmark stamped upon her cheek. Not even Aylmer now hated it so much as she.

To dispel the tedium of the hours which her husband found it necessary to   50 devote to the processes of combination and analysis, Georgiana turned over the volumes of his scientific library. In many dark old tomes she met with chapters full of romance and poetry. They were the works of the philosophers of the middle ages, such as Albertus Magnus, Cornelius Agrippa, Paracelsus, and the famous friar who created the prophetic Brazen Head. All these antique naturalists stood in advance of their centuries, yet were imbued with some of their credulity, and therefore were believed, and perhaps imagined themselves to have acquired from the investigation of Nature a power above Nature, and from physics a sway over the spiritual world. Hardly less curious and imaginative were the early volumes of the Transactions of the Royal Society, in which the members, knowing little of the limits of natural possibility, were continually recording wonders or proposing methods whereby wonders might be wrought.

But to Georgiana the most engrossing volume was a large folio from her husband's own hand, in which he had recorded every experiment of his scientific career, its original aim, the methods adopted for its development, and its final success or failure, with the circumstances to which either event was attributable. The book, in truth, was both the history and emblem of his ardent, ambitious, imaginative, yet practical and laborious life. He handled physical details as if there were nothing beyond them; yet spiritualized them all, and redeemed himself from materialism by his strong and eager aspiration towards the infinite. In his grasp the veriest clod of earth assumed a soul. Georgiana, as she read, reverenced Aylmer and loved him more profoundly than ever, but with a less entire dependence on his judgment than heretofore. Much as he had accomplished, she could not but observe that his most splendid successes were almost invariably failures, if compared with the ideal at which he aimed. His brightest diamonds were the merest pebbles, and felt to be so by himself, in comparison with the inestimable gems which lay hidden beyond his reach. The volume, rich with achievements that had won renown for its author, was yet as melancholy a record as ever mortal hand had penned. It was the sad confession and continual exemplification of the shortcomings of the composite man, the spirit burdened with clay and working in matter, and of the despair that assails the higher nature at finding itself so miserably thwarted by the earthly part. Perhaps every man of genius in whatever sphere might recognize the image of his own experience in Aylmer's journal.

So deeply did these reflections affect Georgiana that she laid her face upon the open volume and burst into tears. In this situation she was found by her husband.

"It is dangerous to read in a sorcerer's books," said he with a smile, though his countenance was uneasy and displeased. "Georgiana, there are pages in that volume which I can scarcely glance over and keep my senses. Take heed lest it prove as detrimental to you."

"It has made me worship you more than ever," said she.

"Ah, wait for this one success," rejoined he, "then worship me if you will. I 55 shall deem myself hardly unworthy of it. But come, I have sought you for the luxury of your voice. Sing to me, dearest."

So she poured out the liquid music of her voice to quench the thirst of his spirit. He then took his leave with a boyish exuberance of gaiety, assuring her that her seclusion would endure but a little longer, and that the result was already certain. Scarcely had he departed when Georgiana felt irresistibly impelled to follow him. She had forgotten to inform Aylmer of a symptom which for two or three hours past had begun to excite her attention. It was a sensation in the fatal birthmark, not painful, but which induced a restlessness throughout her system. Hastening after her husband, she intruded for the first time into the laboratory.

The first thing that struck her eye was the furnace, that hot and feverish worker, with the intense glow of its fire, which by the quantities of soot clustered above it seemed to have been burning for ages. There was a distilling apparatus in full operation. Around the room were retorts, tubes, cylinders, crucibles, and other apparatus of chemical research. An electrical machine stood ready for immediate use. The atmosphere felt oppressively close, and was tainted with gaseous odors which had been tormented forth by the processes of science. The severe and homely simplicity of the apartment, with its naked walls and brick pavement, looked strange, accustomed as Georgiana had become to the fantastic elegance of her boudoir. But what chiefly, indeed almost solely, drew her attention, was the aspect of Aylmer himself.

He was pale as death, anxious and absorbed, and hung over the furnace as if it depended upon his utmost watchfulness whether the liquid which it was distilling should be the draught of immortal happiness or misery. How different from the sanguine and joyous mien that he had assumed for Georgiana's encouragement!

"Carefully now, Aminadab; carefully, thou human machine; carefully, thou man of clay!" muttered Aylmer, more to himself than his assistant. "Now, if there be a thought too much or too little, it is all over."

"Ho! ho!" mumbled Aminadab. "Look, master! look!"   60

Aylmer raised his eyes hastily, and at first reddened, then grew paler than ever, on beholding Georgiana. He rushed towards her and seized her arm with a gripe that left the print of his fingers upon it.

"Why do you come hither? Have you no trust in your husband?" cried he impetuously. "Would you throw the blight of that fatal birthmark over my labors? It is not well done. Go, prying woman, go!"

"Nay, Aylmer," said Georgiana with the firmness of which she possessed no stinted endowment, "it is not you that have a right to complain. You mistrust your wife; you have concealed the anxiety with which you watch the development of this experiment. Think not so unworthily of me, my husband. Tell me all the risk we run, and fear not that I shall shrink; for my share in it is far less than your own."

"No, no, Georgiana!" said Aylmer impatiently; "it must not be."

"I submit," replied she calmly. "And, Aylmer, I shall quaff whatever   65 draught you bring me; but it will be on the same principle that would induce me to take a dose of poison if offered by your hand."

"My noble wife," said Aylmer, deeply moved, "I knew not the height and depth of your nature until now. Nothing shall be concealed. Know, then, that this crimson hand, superficial as it seems, has clutched its grasp into your being with a strength of which I had no previous conception. I have already administered agents powerful enough to do aught except to change your entire physical system. Only one thing remains to be tried. If that fails us we are ruined."

"Why did you hesitate to tell me this?" asked she.

"Because, Georgiana," said Aylmer in a low voice, "there is danger."

"Danger? There is but one danger—that this horrible stigma shall be left upon my cheek!" cried Georgiana. "Remove it, remove it, whatever be the cost, or we shall both go mad!"

"Heaven knows your words are too true," said Aylmer sadly. "And now,   70 dearest, return to your boudoir. In a little while all will be tested."

He conducted her back and took leave of her with a solemn tenderness which spoke far more than his words how much was now at stake. After his departure Georgiana became rapt in musings. She considered the character of Aylmer, and did it completer justice than at any previous moment. Her heart exulted, while it trembled, at his honorable love—so pure and lofty that it would accept nothing less than perfection nor miserably make itself contented with an earthlier nature than he had dreamed of. She felt how much more precious was such a sentiment than that meaner kind which would have borne with the imperfection for her sake, and have been guilty of treason to holy love by degrading its perfect idea to the level of the actual; and with her whole spirit she prayed that, for a single moment, she might satisfy his highest and deepest conception. Longer than one moment she well knew it could not be; for his spirit was ever on the march, ever ascending, and each instant required something that was beyond the scope of the instant before.

The sound of her husband's footsteps aroused her. He bore a crystal goblet containing a liquor colorless as water, but bright enough to be the draught of immortality. Aylmer was pale; but it seemed rather the consequence of a highly wrought state of mind and tension of spirit than of fear or doubt.

"The concoction of the draught has been perfect," said he, in answer to Georgiana's look. "Unless all my science have deceived me, it cannot fail."

"Save on your account, my dearest Aylmer," observed his wife, "I might wish to put off this birthmark of mortality by relinquishing mortality itself in preference to any other mode. Life is but a sad possession to those who have attained precisely the degree of moral advancement at which I stand. Were I weaker and blinder it might be happiness. Were I stronger, it might be endured hopefully. But, being what I find myself, methinks I am of all mortals the most fit to die."

"You are fit for heaven without tasting death!" replied her husband. "But 75 why do we speak of dying? The draught cannot fail. Behold its effect upon this plant."

On the window seat there stood a geranium diseased with yellow blotches, which had overspread all its leaves. Aylmer poured a small quantity of the liquid upon the soil in which it grew. In a little time, when the roots of the plant had taken up the moisture, the unsightly blotches began to be extinguished in a living verdure.

"There needed no proof," said Georgiana quietly. "Give me the goblet. I joyfully stake all upon your word."

"Drink, then, thou lofty creature!" exclaimed Aylmer, with fervid admiration. "There is no taint of imperfection on thy spirit. Thy sensible frame, too, shall soon be all perfect."

She quaffed the liquid and returned the goblet to his hand.

"It is grateful," said she, with a placid smile. "Methinks it is like water 80 from a heavenly fountain; for it contains I know not what of unobtrusive fragrance and deliciousness. It allays a feverish thirst that had parched me for many days. Now, dearest, let me sleep. My earthly senses are closing over my spirit like the leaves around the heart of a rose at sunset."

She spoke the last words with a gentle reluctance, as if it required almost more energy than she could command to pronounce the faint and lingering syllables. Scarcely had they loitered through her lips ere she was lost in slumber. Aylmer sat by her side, watching her aspect with the emotions proper to a man the whole value of whose existence was involved in the process now to be tested. Mingled with this mood, however, was the philosophic investigation characteristic of the man of science. Not the minutest symptom escaped him. A heightened flush of the cheek, a slight irregularity of breath, a quiver of the eyelid, a hardly perceptible tremor through the frame,—such were the details which, as the moments passed, he wrote down in his folio volume. Intense thought had set its stamp upon every previous page of that volume, but the thoughts of years were all concentrated upon the last.

While thus employed, he failed not to gaze often at the fatal hand, and not without a shudder. Yet once, by a strange and unaccountable impulse, he pressed it with his lips. His spirit recoiled, however, in the very act; and Georgiana, out of the midst of her deep sleep, moved uneasily and murmured as if in remonstrance. Again Aylmer resumed his watch. Nor was it without avail. The crimson hand, which at first had been strongly visible upon the marble paleness of Georgiana's cheek, now grew more faintly outlined. She remained not less pale than ever; but the birthmark, with every breath that came and went, lost somewhat of its former distinctness. Its presence had been awful; its departure was more awful still. Watch the stain of the rainbow fading out of the sky, and you will know how that mysterious symbol passed away.

"By Heaven! it is well-nigh gone!" said Aylmer to himself, in almost irrepressible ecstasy. "I can scarcely trace it now. Success! success! And now it is like the faintest rose color. The lightest flush of blood across her cheek would overcome it. But she is so pale!"

He drew aside the window curtain and suffered the light of natural day to fall into the room and rest upon her cheek. At the same time he heard a gross, hoarse chuckle, which he had long known as his servant Aminadab's expression of delight.

"Ah, clod! ah, earthly mass!" cried Aylmer, laughing in a sort of frenzy, "you have served me well! Matter and spirit — earth and heaven — have both done their part in this! Laugh, thing of the senses! You have earned the right to laugh." 85

These exclamations broke Georgiana's sleep. She slowly unclosed her eyes and gazed into the mirror which her husband had arranged for that purpose. A faint smile flitted over her lips when she recognized how barely perceptible was now that crimson hand which had once blazed forth with such disastrous brilliancy as to scare away all their happiness. But then her eyes sought Aylmer's face with a trouble and anxiety that he could by no means account for.

"My poor Aylmer!" murmured she.

"Poor? Nay, richest, happiest, most favored!" exclaimed he. "My peerless bride, it is successful! You are perfect!"

"My poor Aylmer," she repeated, with a more than human tenderness, "you have aimed loftily; you have done nobly. Do not repent that with so high and pure a feeling, you have rejected the best the earth could offer. Aylmer, dearest Aylmer, I am dying!"

Alas! it was too true! The fatal hand had grappled with the mystery of life, 90 and was the bond by which an angelic spirit kept itself in union with a mortal frame. As the last crimson tint of the birthmark — that sole token of human imperfection — faded from her cheek, the parting breath of the now perfect woman passed into the atmosphere, and her soul, lingering a moment near her husband, took its heavenward flight. Then a hoarse, chuckling laugh was heard again! Thus ever does the gross fatality of earth exult in its invariable triumph over the immortal essence which, in this dim sphere of half development, demands the completeness of a higher state. Yet, had Aylmer reached a profounder wisdom, he need not thus have flung away the happiness which would have woven his mortal life of the selfsame texture with the celestial. The momentary circumstance was too strong for him; he failed to look beyond the shadowy scope of time, and, living once for all in eternity, to find the perfect future in the present.

CONSIDERATIONS FOR CRITICAL THINKING AND WRITING

1. FIRST RESPONSE. Consider this story as an early version of our contemporary obsession with physical perfection. What significant similarities — and differences — do you find?

2. Is Aylmer evil? Is he simply a stock version of a mad scientist? In what sense might he be regarded as an idealist?

3. What does the birthmark symbolize? How does Aylmer's view of it differ from the other perspectives provided in the story? What is the significance of its handlike shape?

4. Does Aylmer love Georgiana? Why does she allow him to risk her life to remove the birthmark?

5. In what sense can Aylmer be characterized as guilty of the sin of pride?

6. How is Aminadab a foil for Aylmer?

7. What is the significance of the descriptions of Aylmer's laboratory?

8. What do Aylmer's other experiments reveal about the nature of his work? How do they constitute foreshadowings of what will happen to Georgiana?

9. What is the theme of the story? What point is made about what it means to be a human being?

10. Despite the risks to Georgiana, Aylmer conducts his experiments in the hope and expectation of achieving a higher good. He devotes his life to science, and yet he is an egotist. Explain.

11. Discuss the extent to which Georgiana is responsible for her own death.

SARAH ORNE JEWETT (1849–1909)

Born in South Berwick, Maine, Sarah Orne Jewett was educated at Miss Rayne's School and at Berwick Academy. She was steeped in the small-town rural life of northern New England and is famous for her local color treatments of the setting, character, dialect, and sensibilities of her region. By the time she was twenty-one years old, she was publishing in the *Atlantic Monthly*. In addition to a novel, *The Country Doctor* (1884), she published collections of short stories: *Deephaven* (1877), *A White Heron and Other Stories* (1886), and *The Country of the Pointed Firs* (1896). In recent years, Jewett's reputation has swelled as increasing numbers of readers have discovered the high quality of her fiction.

A White Heron   *1886*

I

The woods were already filled with shadows one June evening, just before eight o'clock, though a bright sunset still glimmered faintly among the trunks of the trees. A little girl was driving home her cow, a plodding, dilatory, provoking creature in her behavior, but a valued companion for all that. They were going away from the western light, and striking deep into the dark woods, but their feet were familiar with the path, and it was no matter whether their eyes could see it or not.

There was hardly a night the summer through when the old cow could be found waiting at the pasture bars; on the contrary, it was her greatest pleasure to hide herself away among the high huckleberry bushes, and though she wore a loud bell she had made the discovery that if one stood perfectly still it would not ring. So Sylvia had to hunt for her until she found her and call Co'! Co'! with never an answering Moo, until her childish patience was quite spent. If the creature had not given good milk and plenty of it, the case would have seemed very different to her owners. Besides, Sylvia had all the time there was, and very little use to make of it. Sometimes in pleasant weather it was a consolation to look upon the cow's pranks as an intelligent attempt to play hide and seek, and as the child had no playmates she lent herself to this amusement with a good deal of zest. Though this chase had been so long that the wary animal herself had given an unusual signal of her whereabouts, Sylvia had only laughed when she came upon Mistress Moolly at the swamp-side, and urged her affectionately homeward with a twig of birch leaves. The old cow was not inclined to wander farther, she even turned in the right direction for once as they left the pasture, and stepped along the road at a good pace. She was quite ready to be milked now, and seldom stopped to browse. Sylvia wondered what her grandmother would say because they were so late. It was a great while since she had left home at half past five o'clock, but everybody knew the difficulty of making this errand a short one. Mrs. Tilley had chased the horned torment too many summer evenings herself to blame any one else for lingering, and was only thankful as she waited that she had Sylvia, nowadays, to give such valuable assistance. The good woman suspected that Sylvia loitered occasionally on her own account; there never was such a child for straying about out-of-doors since the world was made! Everybody said that it was a good change for a little maid who had tried to grow for eight years in a crowded manufacturing town, but, as for Sylvia herself, it seemed as if she never had been alive at all before she came to live at the farm. She thought often with wistful compassion of a wretched dry geranium that belonged to a town neighbor.

"'Afraid of folks,'" old Mrs. Tilley said to herself, with a smile, after she had made the unlikely choice of Sylvia from her daughter's houseful of children, and was returning to the farm. "'Afraid of folks,' they said! I guess she won't be troubled no great with 'em up to the old place!" When they reached the door of the lonely house and stopped to unlock it, and the cat came to purr loudly, and rub against them, a deserted pussy, indeed, but fat with young robins, Sylvia whispered that this was a beautiful place to live in, and she never should wish to go home.

The companions followed the shady wood-road, the cow taking slow steps, and the child very fast ones. The cow stopped long at the brook to drink, as if the pasture were not half a swamp, and Sylvia stood still and waited, letting her bare feet cool themselves in the shoal water, while the great twilight moths struck softly against her. She waded on through the brook as the cow moved away, and listened to the thrushes with a heart that beat fast with pleasure. There was a stirring in the great boughs overhead. They were full of little birds and beasts that seemed to be wide-awake, and going about their world, or else saying good-night to each other in sleepy twitters. Sylvia herself felt sleepy as she walked along. However, it was not much farther to the house, and the air was soft and sweet. She was not often in the woods so late as this, and it made her feel as if she were a part of the gray shadows and the moving leaves. She was just thinking how long it seemed since she first came to the farm a year ago, and wondering if everything went on in the noisy town just the same as when she was there; the thought of the great red-faced boy who used to chase and frighten her made her hurry along the path to escape from the shadow of the trees.

Suddenly this little woods-girl is horror-stricken to hear a clear whistle not   5 very far away. Not a bird's whistle, which would have a sort of friendliness, but a boy's whistle, determined, and somewhat aggressive. Sylvia left the cow to whatever sad fate might await her, and stepped discreetly aside into the bushes, but she was just too late. The enemy had discovered her, and called out in a very cheerful and persuasive tone, "Halloa, little girl, how far is it to the road?" and trembling Sylvia answered almost inaudibly, "A good ways."

She did not dare to look boldly at the tall young man, who carried a gun over his shoulder, but she came out of her bush and again followed the cow, while he walked alongside.

"I have been hunting for some birds," the stranger said kindly, "and I have lost my way, and need a friend very much. Don't be afraid," he added gallantly. "Speak up and tell me what your name is, and whether you think I can spend the night at your house, and go out gunning early in the morning."

Sylvia was more alarmed than before. Would not her grandmother consider her much to blame? But who could have foreseen such an accident as this? It did not appear to be her fault, and she hung her head as if the stem of it were broken, but managed to answer, "Sylvy," with much effort when her companion again asked her name.

Mrs. Tilley was standing in the doorway when the trio came into view. The cow gave a loud moo by way of explanation.

"Yes, you'd better speak up for yourself, you old trial! Where'd she tucked 10 herself away this time, Sylvy?" Sylvia kept an awed silence; she knew by instinct that her grandmother did not comprehend the gravity of the situation. She must be mistaking the stranger for one of the farmer-lads of the region.

The young man stood his gun beside the door, and dropped a heavy gamebag beside it; then he bade Mrs. Tilley good-evening, and repeated his wayfarer's story, and asked if he could have a night's lodging.

"Put me anywhere you like," he said. "I must be off early in the morning, before day; but I am very hungry, indeed. You can give me some milk at any rate, that's plain."

"Dear sakes, yes," responded the hostess, whose long slumbering hospitality seemed to be easily awakened. "You might fare better if you went out on the main road a mile or so, but you're welcome to what we've got. I'll milk right off, and you make yourself at home. You can sleep on husks or feathers," she proffered graciously. "I raised them all myself. There's good pasturing for geese just below here towards the ma'sh. Now step round and set a plate for the gentleman, Sylvy!" And Sylvia promptly stepped. She was glad to have something to do, and she was hungry herself.

It was a surprise to find so clean and comfortable a little dwelling in this New England wilderness. The young man had known the horrors of its most primitive housekeeping, and the dreary squalor of that level of society which does not rebel at the companionship of hens. This was the best thrift of an old-fashioned farmstead, though on such a small scale that it seemed like a hermitage. He listened eagerly to the old woman's quaint talk, he watched Sylvia's pale face and shining gray eyes with ever growing enthusiasm, and insisted that this was the best supper he had eaten for a month; then, afterward, the new-made friends sat down in the doorway together while the moon came up.

Soon it would be berry-time, and Sylvia was a great help at picking. The cow was a good milker, though a plaguy thing to keep track of, the hostess gossiped frankly, adding presently that she had buried four children, so that Sylvia's mother, and a son (who might be dead) in California were all the children she had left. "Dan, my boy, was a great hand to go gunning," she explained sadly. "I never wanted for pa'tridges or gray squer'ls while he was to home. He's been a great wand'rer, I expect, and he's no hand to write letters. There, I don't blame him, I'd ha' seen the world myself if it had been so I could.

"Sylvia takes after him," the grandmother continued affectionately, after a minute's pause. "There ain't a foot o' ground she don't know her way over, and the wild creatur's counts her one o' themselves. Squer'ls she'll tame to come an' feed right out o' her hands, and all sorts o' birds. Last winter she got the jay-birds to bangeing here, and I believe she'd 'a' scanted herself of her own meals to have plenty to throw out amongst 'em, if I hadn't kep' watch. Anything but crows, I tell her, I'm willin' to help support, — though Dan he went an' tamed one o' them that did seem to have reason same as folks. It was round here a good spell after he went away. Dan an' his father they didn't hitch, — but he never held up his head ag'in after Dan had dared him an' gone off."

The guest did not notice this hint of family sorrows in his eager interest in something else.

"So Sylvy knows all about birds, does she?" he exclaimed, as he looked round at the little girl who sat, very demure but increasingly sleepy, in the moonlight. "I am making a collection of birds myself. I have been at it ever since I was a boy." (Mrs. Tilley smiled.) "There are two or three very rare ones I have been hunting for these five years. I mean to get them on my own ground if they can be found."

"Do you cage 'em up?" asked Mrs. Tilley doubtfully, in response to this enthusiastic announcement.

"Oh, no, they're stuffed and preserved, dozens and dozens of them," said the ornithologist, "and I have shot or snared every one myself. I caught a glimpse of a white heron three miles from here on Saturday, and I have followed it in this direction. They have never been found in this district at all. The little white heron, it is," and he turned again to look at Sylvia with the hope of discovering that the rare bird was one of her acquaintances.

But Sylvia was watching a hop-toad in the narrow footpath.

"You would know the heron if you saw it," the stranger continued eagerly. "A queer tall white bird with soft feathers and long thin legs. And it would have a nest perhaps in the top of a high tree, made of sticks, something like a hawk's nest."

Sylvia's heart gave a wild beat; she knew that strange white bird, and had once stolen softly near where it stood in some bright green swamp grass, away over at the other side of the woods. There was an open place where the sunshine always seemed strangely yellow and hot, where tall, nodding rushes grew, and her grandmother had warned her that she might sink in the soft black mud underneath and never be heard of more. Not far beyond were the salt marshes and beyond those was the sea, the sea which Sylvia wondered and dreamed about, but never had looked upon, though its great voice could often be heard above the noise of the woods on stormy nights.

"I can't think of anything I should like so much as to find that heron's nest," the handsome stranger was saying. "I would give ten dollars to anybody who could show it to me," he added desperately, "and I mean to spend my whole vacation hunting for it if need be. Perhaps it was only migrating, or had been chased out of its own region by some bird of prey."

Mrs. Tilley gave amazed attention to all this, but Sylvia still watched the 25 toad, not divining, as she might have done at some calmer time, that the creature wished to get to its hole under the doorstep, and was much hindered by the unusual spectators at that hour of the evening. No amount of thought, that night, could decide how many wished-for treasures the ten dollars, so lightly spoken of, would buy.

The next day the young sportsman hovered about the woods, and Sylvia kept him company, having lost her first fear of the friendly lad, who proved to be most kind and sympathetic. He told her many things about the birds and what they knew and where they lived and what they did with themselves. And he gave her a jack-knife, which she thought as great a treasure as if she were a desert-islander. All day long he did not once make her troubled or afraid except when he brought down some unsuspecting singing creature from its bough. Sylvia would have liked him vastly better without his gun; she could not understand why he killed the very birds he seemed to like so much. But as the day waned, Sylvia still watched the young man with loving admiration. She had never seen anybody so charming and delightful; the woman's heart, asleep in the child, was vaguely thrilled by a dream of love. Some premonition of that great power stirred and swayed these young foresters who traversed the solemn woodlands with soft-footed silent care. They stopped to listen to a bird's song; they pressed forward again eagerly, parting the branches—speaking to each other rarely and in whispers; the young man going first and Sylvia following, fascinated, a few steps behind, with her gray eyes dark with excitement.

She grieved because the longed-for white heron was elusive, but she did not lead the guest, she only followed, and there was no such thing as speaking first. The sound of her own unquestioned voice would have terrified her—it was hard enough to answer yes or no when there was need of that. At last evening began to fall, and they drove the cow home together, and Sylvia smiled with pleasure when they came to the place where she heard the whistle and was afraid only the night before.

II

Half a mile from home, at the farther edge of the woods, where the land was highest, a great pine-tree stood, the last of its generation. Whether it was left for a boundary mark, or for what reason, no one could say; the woodchoppers who had felled its mates were dead and gone long ago, and a whole forest of sturdy trees, pines and oaks and maples, had grown again. But the stately head of this old pine towered above them all and made a landmark for sea and shore miles and miles away. Sylvia knew it well. She had always believed that whoever climbed to the top of it could see the ocean; and the little girl had often laid her hand on the great rough trunk and looked up wistfully at those dark boughs that the wind always stirred, no matter how hot and still the air might be below. Now she thought of the tree with a new excitement, for why, if one climbed it at break of day, could not one see all the world, and easily discover whence the white heron flew, and mark the place, and find the hidden nest?

What a spirit of adventure, what wild ambition! What fancied triumph and delight and glory for the later morning when she could make known the secret! It was almost too real and too great for the childish heart to bear.

All night the door of the little house stood open, and the whippoorwills 30 came and sang upon the very step. The young sportsman and his old hostess were sound asleep, but Sylvia's great design kept her broad awake and watching. She forgot to think of sleep. The short summer night seemed as long as the winter darkness, and at last when the whippoorwills ceased, and she was afraid the morning would after all come too soon, she stole out of the house and followed the pasture path through the woods, hastening toward the open ground beyond, listening with a sense of comfort and companionship to the drowsy twitter of a half-awakened bird, whose perch she had jarred in passing. Alas, if the great wave of human interest which flooded for the first time this dull little life should sweep away the satisfactions of an existence heart to heart with nature and the dumb life of the forest!

There was the huge tree asleep yet in the paling moonlight, and small and hopeful Sylvia began with utmost bravery to mount to the top of it, with tingling, eager blood coursing the channels of her whole frame, with her bare feet and fingers, that pinched and held like bird's claws to the monstrous ladder reaching up, up, almost to the sky itself. First she must mount the white oak tree that grew alongside, where she was almost lost among the dark branches and the green leaves heavy and wet with dew; a bird fluttered off its nest, and a red squirrel ran to and fro and scolded pettishly at the harmless housebreaker. Sylvia felt her way easily. She had often climbed there, and knew that higher still one of the oak's upper branches chafed against the pine trunk, just where its lower boughs were set close together. There, when she made the dangerous pass from one tree to the other, the great enterprise would really begin.

She crept out along the swaying oak limb at last, and took the daring step across into the old pine-tree. The way was harder than she thought; she must reach far and hold fast, the sharp dry twigs caught and held her and scratched her like angry talons, the pitch made her thin little fingers clumsy and stiff as she went round and round the tree's great stem, higher and higher upward. The sparrows and robins in the woods below were beginning to wake and twitter to the dawn, yet it seemed much lighter there aloft in the pine-tree, and the child knew that she must hurry if her project were to be of any use.

The tree seemed to lengthen itself out as she went up, and to reach farther and farther upward. It was like a great main-mast to the voyaging earth; it must truly have been amazed that morning through all its ponderous frame as it felt this determined spark of human spirit creeping and climbing from higher branch to branch. Who knows how steadily the least twigs held themselves to advantage this light, weak creature on her way! The old pine must have loved his new dependent. More than all the hawks, and bats, and moths, and even the sweet-voiced thrushes, was the brave, beating heart of the solitary gray-eyed child. And the tree stood still and held away the winds that June morning while the dawn grew bright in the east.

Sylvia's face was like a pale star, if one had seen it from the ground, when the last thorny bough was past, and she stood trembling and tired but wholly triumphant, high in the tree-top. Yes, there was the sea with the dawning sun making a golden dazzle over it, and toward that glorious east flew two hawks with slow-moving pinions. How low they looked in the air from that height when before one had only seen them far up, and dark against the blue sky. Their gray feathers were as soft as moths; they seemed only a little way from the tree, and Sylvia felt as if she too could go flying away among the clouds. Westward, the woodlands and farms reached miles and miles into the distance; here and there were church steeples, and white villages; truly it was a vast and awesome world.

The birds sang louder and louder. At last the sun came up bewilderingly 35 bright. Sylvia could see the white sails of ships out at sea, and the clouds that were purple and rose-colored and yellow at first began to fade away. Where was the white heron's nest in the sea of green branches, and was this wonderful sight and pageant of the world the only reward for having climbed to such a giddy height? Now look down again, Sylvia, where the green marsh is set among the shining birches and dark hemlocks; there where you saw the white heron once you will see him again; look, look! a white spot of him like a single floating feather comes up from the dead hemlock and grows larger, and rises, and comes close at last, and goes by the landmark pine with steady sweep of wing and outstretched slender neck and crested head. And wait! wait! do not move a foot or a finger, little girl, do not send an arrow of light and consciousness from your two eager eyes, for the heron has perched on a pine bough not far beyond yours, and cries back to his mate on the nest, and plumes his feathers for the new day!

The child gives a long sigh a minute later when a company of shouting cat-birds comes also to the tree, and vexed by their fluttering and lawlessness the solemn heron goes away. She knows his secret now, the wild, light, slender bird that floats and wavers, and goes back like an arrow presently to his home in the green world beneath. Then Sylvia, well satisfied, makes her perilous way down again, not daring to look far below the branch she stands on, ready to cry sometimes because her fingers ache and her lamed feet slip. Wondering over and over again what the stranger would say to her, and what he would think when she told him how to find his way straight to the heron's nest.

"Sylvy, Sylvy!" called the busy old grandmother again and again, but nobody answered, and the small husk bed was empty, and Sylvia had disappeared.

The guest waked from a dream, and remembering his day's pleasure hurried to dress himself that it might sooner begin. He was sure from the way the shy little girl looked once or twice yesterday that she had at least seen the white heron, and now she must really be persuaded to tell. Here she comes now, paler than ever, and her worn old frock is torn and tattered, and smeared with pine pitch. The grandmother and the sportsman stand in the door together and question her, and the splendid moment had come to speak of the dead hemlock-tree by the green marsh.

But Sylvia does not speak after all, though the old grandmother fretfully rebukes her, and the young man's kind appealing eyes are looking straight in her own. He can make them rich with money; he has promised it, and they are poor now. He is so well worth making happy, and he waits to hear the story she can tell.

No, she must keep silence! What is it that suddenly forbids her and makes 40 her dumb? Has she been nine years growing, and now, when the great world for the first time puts out a hand to her, must she thrust it aside for a bird's sake? The murmur of the pine's green branches is in her ears, she remembers how the white heron came flying through the golden air and how they watched the sea and the morning together, and Sylvia cannot speak; she cannot tell the heron's secret and give its life away.

Dear loyalty, that suffered a sharp pang as the guest went away disappointed later in the day, that could have served and followed him and loved him as a dog loves! Many a night Sylvia heard the echo of his whistle haunting the pasture path as she came home with the loitering cow. She forgot even her sorrow at the sharp report of his gun and the piteous sight of thrushes and sparrows dropping silent to the ground, their songs hushed and their pretty feathers stained and wet with blood. Were the birds better friends than their hunter might have been,—who can tell? Whatever treasures were lost to her, woodlands and summer-time, remember! Bring your gifts and graces and tell your secrets to this lonely country child!

CONSIDERATIONS FOR CRITICAL THINKING AND WRITING

1. FIRST RESPONSE. What is the central conflict that Sylvia faces in the story? Did you anticipate her final decision? Why or why not?

2. What kind of mood is established in the first three paragraphs? How is country life presented?

3. What do you imagine life was like for Sylvia in the "noisy town" where she previously lived?

4. Why does Sylvia want to help the young hunter find the heron?

5. How does the hunter regard Sylvia and Mrs. Tilley? What sort of person is he?

6. How might the ornithologist and the white heron be read symbolically? What larger issues do they suggest?

7. Describe the use of point of view in the story. Why do you suppose Jewett handles the point of view as she does?

8. Read closely paragraphs 31–34. What significance do you find in Sylvia's climbing the tree to look for the heron?

9. Consult a dictionary to determine what the name "Sylvia" means. Why is it an especially appropriate name for her character?

10. What is your response to the story's final paragraph? Explain why you think the story would be more or less effective if the final paragraph were not there.

Tim O'Brien (b. 1946)

Born in Austin, Minnesota, Tim O'Brien was educated at Macalester College and Harvard University. He was drafted to serve in the Vietnam War and received a Purple Heart. His work is heavily influenced by his service in the war. His first book, *If I Die in a Combat Zone, Box Me up and Ship Me Home* (1973), is a blend of fiction and actual experiences during his tour of duty. *Going after Cacciato,* judged by many critics to be the best work of American fiction about the Vietnam War, won the National Book Award in 1978. He has also published four other novels, *Northern Lights* (1974), *The Nuclear Age* (1985), *In the Lake of the Woods* (1994), and *Tomcat in Love* (1998). "How to Tell a True War Story" is from a collection of interrelated stories titled *The Things They Carried* (1990). Originally published in *Esquire,* this story is at once grotesque and beautiful in its attempt to be true to experience.

How to Tell a True War Story   1987

This is true.

I had a buddy in Vietnam. His name was Bob Kiley, but everybody called him Rat.

A friend of his gets killed, so about a week later Rat sits down and writes a letter to the guy's sister. Rat tells her what a great brother she had, how strack° the guy was, a number one pal and comrade. A real soldier's soldier, Rat says. Then he tells a few stories to make the point, how her brother would always volunteer for stuff nobody else would volunteer for in a million years, dangerous stuff, like doing recon° or going out on these really badass night patrols. Stainless steel balls, Rat tells her. The guy was a little crazy, for sure, but crazy in a good way, a real daredevil, because he liked the challenge of it, he liked testing himself, just man against gook. A great, great guy, Rat says.

Anyway, it's a terrific letter, very personal and touching. Rat almost bawls writing it. He gets all teary telling about the good times they had together, how her brother made the war seem almost fun, always raising hell and lighting up villes° and bringing smoke to bear every which way. A great sense of humor, too. Like the time at this river when he went fishing with a whole damn crate of hand grenades. Probably the funniest thing in world history, Rat says, all that gore, about twenty zillion dead gook fish. Her brother, he had the right attitude. He knew how to have a good time. On Halloween, this real hot spooky night, the dude paints up his body all different colors and puts on this weird mask and goes out on ambush almost stark naked, just boots and balls and an M-16. A tremendous human being, Rat says. Pretty nutso sometimes, but you could trust him with your life.

---

strack: A strict military appearance.
doing recon: Reconnaissance, or exploratory survey of enemy territory.
villes: Villages.

And then the letter gets very sad and serious. Rat pours his heart out. He 5
says he loved the guy. He says the guy was his best friend in the world. They
were like soul mates, he says, like twins or something, they had a whole lot in
common. He tells the guy's sister he'll look her up when the war's over.

So what happens?

Rat mails the letter. He waits two months. The dumb cooze never writes
back.

A true war story is never moral. It does not instruct, nor encourage virtue,
nor suggest models of proper human behavior, nor restrain men from doing
the things they have always done. If a story seems moral, do not believe it. If at
the end of a war story you feel uplifted, or if you feel that some small bit of rectitude has been salvaged from the larger waste, then you have been made the
victim of a very old and terrible lie. There is no rectitude whatsover. There is no
virtue. As a first rule of thumb, therefore, you can tell a true war story by its
absolute and uncompromising allegiance to obscenity and evil. Listen to Rat
Kiley. *Cooze*, he says. He does not say *bitch*. He certainly does not say *woman*, or
girl. He says *cooze*. Then he spits and stares. He's nineteen years old — it's too
much for him — so he looks at you with those big gentle killer eyes and says
cooze, because his friend is dead, and because it's so incredibly sad and true:
she never wrote back.

You can tell a true war story if it embarrasses you. If you don't care for
obscenity, you don't care for the truth; if you don't care for the truth, watch
how you vote. Send guys to war, they come home talking dirty.

Listen to Rat: "Jesus Christ, man, I write this beautiful fucking letter, I 10
slave over it, and what happens? The dumb cooze never writes back."

The dead guy's name was Curt Lemon. What happened was, we crossed a
muddy river and marched west into the mountains, and on the third day we
took a break along a trail junction in deep jungle. Right away, Lemon and Rat
Kiley started goofing off. They didn't understand about the spookiness. They
were kids; they just didn't know. A nature hike, they thought, not even a war,
so they went off into the shade of some giant trees — quadruple canopy, no
sunlight at all — and they were giggling and calling each other motherfucker
and playing a silly game they'd invented. The game involved smoke grenades,
which were harmless unless you did stupid things, and what they did was pull
out the pin and stand a few feet apart and play catch under the shade of those
huge trees. Whoever chickened out was a motherfucker. And if nobody chickened out, the grenade would make a light popping sound and they'd be covered with smoke and they'd laugh and dance around and then do it again.

It's all exactly true.

It happened nearly twenty years ago, but I still remember that trail junction and the giant trees and a soft dripping sound somewhere beyond the
trees. I remember the smell of moss. Up in the canopy there were tiny white
blossoms, but no sunlight at all, and I remember the shadows spreading out
under the trees where Lemon and Rat Kiley were playing catch with smoke
grenades. Mitchell Sanders sat flipping his yo-yo. Norman Bowker and Kiowa
and Dave Jensen were dozing, or half-dozing, and all around us were those
ragged green mountains.

Except for the laughter things were quiet.

At one point, I remember, Mitchell Sanders turned and looked at me, not 15 quite nodding, then after a while he rolled up his yo-yo and moved away.

It's hard to tell what happened next.

They were just goofing. There was a noise, I suppose, which must've been the detonator, so I glanced behind me and watched Lemon step from the shade into bright sunlight. His face was suddenly brown and shining. A handsome kid, really. Sharp gray eyes, lean and narrow-waisted, and when he died it was almost beautiful, the way the sunlight came around him and lifted him up and sucked him high into a tree full of moss and vines and white blossoms.

In any war story, but especially a true one, it's difficult to separate what happened from what seemed to happen. What seems to happen becomes its own happening and has to be told that way. The angles of vision are skewed. When a booby trap explodes, you close your eyes and duck and float outside yourself. When a guy dies, like Lemon, you look away and then look back for a moment and then look away again. The pictures get jumbled; you tend to miss a lot. And then afterward, when you go to tell about it, there is always that surreal seemingness, which makes the story seem untrue, but which in fact represents the hard and exact truth as it seemed.

In many cases a true war story cannot be believed. If you believe it, be skeptical. It's a question of credibility. Often the crazy stuff is true and the normal stuff isn't because the normal stuff is necessary to make you believe the truly incredible craziness.

In other cases you can't even tell a true war story. Sometimes it's just 20 beyond telling.

I heard this one, for example, from Mitchell Sanders. It was near dusk and we were sitting at my foxhole along a wide, muddy river north of Quang Ngai. I remember how peaceful the twilight was. A deep pinkish red spilled out on the river, which moved without sound, and in the morning we would cross the river and march west into the mountains. The occasion was right for a good story.

"God's truth," Mitchell Sanders said. "A six-man patrol goes up into the mountains on a basic listening-post operation. The idea's to spend a week up there, just lie low and listen for enemy movement. They've got a radio along, so if they hear anything suspicious — anything — they're supposed to call in artillery or gunships, whatever it takes. Otherwise they keep strict field discipline. Absolute silence. They just listen."

He glanced at me to make sure I had the scenario. He was playing with his yo-yo, making it dance with short, tight little strokes of the wrist.

His face was blank in the dusk.

"We're talking hardass LP.° These six guys, they don't say boo for a solid 25 week. They don't got tongues. *All* ears."

"Right," I said.

"Understand me?"

"Invisible."

Sanders nodded.

"Affirm," he said. "Invisible. So what happens is, these guys get themselves 30 deep in the bush, all camouflaged up, and they lie down and wait and that's all

LP: Listening post.

they do, nothing else, they lie there for seven straight days and just listen. And man, I'll tell you—it's spooky. This is mountains. You don't *know* spooky till you been there. Jungle, sort of, except it's way up in the clouds and there's always this fog—like rain, except it's not raining—everything's all wet and swirly and tangled up and you can't see jack, you can't find your own pecker to piss with. Like you don't even have a body. Serious spooky. You just go with the vapors—the fog sort of takes you in. . . . And the sounds, man. The sounds carry forever. You hear shit nobody should *ever* hear."

Sanders was quiet for a second, just working the yo-yo, then he smiled at me. "So, after a couple days the guys start hearing this real soft, kind of wacked-out music. Weird echoes and stuff. Like a radio or something, but it's not a radio, it's this strange gook music that comes right out of the rocks. Faraway, sort of, but right up close, too. They try to ignore it. But it's a listening post, right? So they listen. And every night they keep hearing this crazyass gook concert. All kinds of chimes and xylophones. I mean, this is wilderness— no way, it can't be real—but there it *is,* like the mountains are tuned in to Radio Fucking Hanoi. Naturally they get nervous. One guy sticks Juicy Fruit in his ears. Another guy almost flips. Thing is, though, they can't report music. They can't get on the horn and call back to base and say, 'Hey, listen, we need some firepower, we got to blow away this weirdo gook rock band.' They can't do that. It wouldn't go down. So they lie there in the fog and keep their mouths shut. And what makes it extra bad, see, is the poor dudes can't horse around like normal. Can't joke it away. Can't even talk to each other except maybe in whispers, all hush-hush, and that just revs up the willies. All they do is listen."

Again there was some silence as Mitchell Sanders looked out on the river. The dark was coming on hard now, and off to the west I could see the mountains rising in silhouette, all the mysteries and unknowns.

"This next part," Sanders said quietly, "you won't believe."

"Probably not," I said.

"You won't. And you know why?"   35

"Why?"

He gave me a tired smile. "Because it happened. Because every word is absolutely dead-on true."

Sanders made a little sound in his throat, like a sigh, as if to say he didn't care if I believed it or not. But he did care. He wanted me to believe, I could tell. He seemed sad, in a way.

"These six guys, they're pretty fried out by now, and one night they start hearing voices. Like at a cocktail party. That's what it sounds like, this big swank gook cocktail party somewhere out there in the fog. Music and chitchat and stuff. It's crazy, I know, but they hear the champagne corks. They hear the actual martini glasses. Real hoity-toity, all very civilized, except this isn't civilization. This is Nam.

"Anyway, the guys try to be cool. They just lie there and groove, but after a 40 while they start hearing—you won't believe this—they hear chamber music. They hear violins and shit. They hear this terrific mama-san soprano. Then after a while they hear gook opera and a glee club and the Haiphong Boys Choir and a barbershop quartet and all kinds of weird chanting and Buddha-Buddha stuff. The whole time, in the background, there's still that cocktail party going on. All these different voices. Not human voices, though. Because it's the mountains. Follow me? The rock — it's *talking.* And the fog, too, and the grass and the goddamn mongooses. Everything talks. The trees talk politics, the monkeys talk religion. The whole country. Vietnam, the place talks.

"The guys can't cope. They lose it. They get on the radio and report enemy movement — a whole army, they say — and they order up the firepower. They get arty° and gunships. They call in air strikes. And I'll tell you, they fuckin' crash that cocktail party. All night long, they just smoke those mountains. They make jungle juice. They blow away trees and glee clubs and whatever else there is to blow away. Scorch time. They walk napalm up and down the ridges. They bring in the Cobras and F-4s, they use Willie Peter and HE° and incendiaries. It's all fire. They make those mountains burn.

"Around dawn things finally get quiet. Like you never even *heard* quiet before. One of those real thick, real misty days — just clouds and fog, they're off in this special zone — and the mountains are absolutely dead-flat silent. Like Brigadoon° — pure vapor, you know? Everything's all sucked up inside the fog. Not a single sound, except they still *hear* it.

"So they pack up and start humping. They head down the mountain, back to base camp, and when they get there they don't say diddly. They don't talk. Not a word, like they're deaf and dumb. Later on this fat bird colonel comes up and asks what the hell happened out there. What'd they hear? Why all the ordnance? The man's ragged out, he gets down tight on their case. I mean, they spent six trillion dollars on firepower, and this fatass colonel wants answers, he wants to know what the fuckin' story is.

"But the guys don't say zip. They just look at him for a while, sort of funny-like, sort of amazed, and the whole war is right there in that stare. It says everything you can't ever say. It says, man, you got *wax* in your ears. It says, poor bastard, you'll never know — wrong frequency — you don't *even* want to hear this. Then they salute the fucker and walk away, because certain stories you don't ever tell."

You can tell a true war story by the way it never seems to end. Not then, 45 not ever. Not when Mitchell Sanders stood up and moved off into the dark.

It all happened.

Even now I remember that yo-yo. In a way, I suppose, you had to be there, you had to hear it, but I could tell how desperately Sanders wanted me to believe him, his frustration at not quite getting the details right, not quite pinning down the final and definitive truth.

And I remember sitting at my foxhole that night, watching the shadows of Quang Ngai, thinking about the coming day and how we would cross the river and march west into the mountains, all the ways I might die, all the things I did not understand.

Late in the night Mitchell Sanders touched my shoulder.

"Just came to me," he whispered. "The moral, I mean. Nobody listens. 50 Nobody hears nothing. Like that fatass colonel. The politicians, all the civilian types, what they need is to go out on LP. The vapors, man. Trees and rocks — you got to *listen* to your enemy."

arty: Artillery.
Willie Peter and HE: White phosphorus, an incendiary substance, and high explosives.
Brigadoon: A fictional village in Scotland that only appears once every one hundred years; subject of a popular American musical (1947).

And then again, in the morning, Sanders came up to me. The platoon was preparing to move out, checking weapons, going through all the little rituals that preceded a day's march. Already the lead squad had crossed the river and was filing off toward the west.

"I got a confession to make," Sanders said. "Last night, man, I had to make up a few things."

"I know that."

"The glee club. There wasn't any glee club."

"Right."

"No opera." 55

"Forget it, I understand."

"Yeah, but listen, it's still true. Those six guys, they heard wicked sound out there. They heard sound you just plain won't believe."

Sanders pulled on his rucksack, closed his eyes for a moment, then almost smiled at me.

I knew what was coming but I beat him to it. 60

"All right," I said, "what's the moral?"

"Forget it."

"No, go ahead."

For a long while he was quiet, looking away, and the silence kept stretching out until it was almost embarrassing. Then he shrugged and gave me a stare that lasted all day.

"Hear that quiet, man?" he said. "There's your moral." 65

In a true war story, if there's a moral at all, it's like the thread that makes the cloth. You can't tease it out. You can't extract the meaning without unraveling the deeper meaning. And in the end, really, there's nothing much to say about a true war story, except maybe "Oh."

True war stories do not generalize. They do not indulge in abstraction or analysis.

For example: War is hell. As a moral declaration the old truism seems perfectly true, and yet because it abstracts, because it generalizes, I can't believe it with my stomach. Nothing turns inside.

It comes down to gut instinct. A true war story, if truly told, makes the stomach believe.

This one does it for me. I've told it before — many times, many versions — 70 but here's what actually happened.

We crossed the river and marched west into the mountains. On the third day, Curt Lemon stepped on a booby-trapped 105 round. He was playing catch with Rat Kiley, laughing, and then he was dead. The trees were thick; it took nearly an hour to cut an LZ for the dustoff.°

Later, higher in the mountains, we came across a baby VC° water buffalo. What it was doing there I don't know — no farms or paddies — but we chased it down and got a rope around it and led it along to a deserted village where we set for the night. After supper Rat Kiley went over and stroked its nose.

He opened up a can of C rations, pork and beans, but the baby buffalo wasn't interested.

LZ for the dustoff: Landing zone for a helicopter evacuation of a casualty.
VC: Vietcong (South Vietnamese communist guerrillas).

Rat shrugged.

He stepped back and shot it through the right front knee. The animal did 75
not make a sound. It went down hard, then got up again, and Rat took careful
aim and shot off an ear. He shot it in the hindquarters and in the little hump
at its back. He shot it twice in the flanks. It wasn't to kill; it was just to hurt. He
put the rifle muzzle up against the mouth and shot the mouth away. Nobody
said much. The whole platoon stood there watching, feeling all kinds of
things, but there wasn't a great deal of pity for the baby water buffalo. Lemon
was dead. Rat Kiley had lost his best friend in the world. Later in the week he
would write a long personal letter to the guy's sister, who would not write
back, but for now it was a question of pain. He shot off the tail. He shot away
chunks of meat below the ribs. All around us there was the smell of smoke and
filth, and deep greenery, and the evening was humid and very hot. Rat went to
automatic. He shot randomly, almost casually, quick little spurts in the belly
and butt. Then he reloaded, squatted down, and shot it in the left front knee.
Again the animal fell hard and tried to get up, but this time it couldn't quite
make it. It wobbled and went down sideways. Rat shot it in the nose. He bent
forward and whispered something, as if talking to a pet, then he shot it in the
throat. All the while the baby buffalo was silent, or almost silent, just a light
bubbling sound where the nose had been. It lay very still. Nothing moved
except the eyes, which were enormous, the pupils shiny black and dumb.

Rat Kiley was crying. He tried to say something, but then cradled his rifle
and went off by himself.

The rest of us stood in a ragged circle around the baby buffalo. For a time
no one spoke. We had witnessed something essential, something brand-new
and profound, a piece of the world so startling there was not yet a name for it.

Somebody kicked the baby buffalo.

It was still alive, though just barely, just in the eyes.

"Amazing," Dave Jensen said. "My whole life, I never seen anything like it." 80

"Never?"

"Not hardly. Not once."

Kiowa and Mitchell Sanders picked up the baby buffalo. They hauled it
across the open square, hoisted it up, and dumped it in the village well.

Afterward, we sat waiting for Rat to get himself together.

"Amazing," Dave Jensen kept saying. 85

"For sure."

"A new wrinkle. I never seen it before."

Mitchell Sanders took out his yo-yo.

"Well, that's Nam," he said. "Garden of Evil. Over here, man, every sin's
real fresh and original."

How do you generalize? 90

War is hell, but that's not the half of it, because war is also mystery and
terror and adventure and courage and discovery and holiness and pity and
despair and longing and love. War is nasty; war is fun. War is thrilling; war is
drudgery. War makes you a man; war makes you dead.

The truths are contradictory. It can be argued, for instance, that war is
grotesque. But in truth war is also beauty. For all its horror, you can't help but
gape at the awful majesty of combat. You stare out at tracer rounds unwind-
ing through the dark like brilliant red ribbons. You crouch in ambush as a
cool, impassive moon rises over the nighttime paddies. You admire the fluid

symmetries of troops on the move, the harmonies of sound and shape and proportion, the great sheets of metal-fire streaming down from a gunship, the illumination rounds, the white phosphorus, the purply black glow of napalm, the rocket's red glare. It's not pretty, exactly. It's astonishing. It fills the eye. It commands you. You hate it, yes, but your eyes do not. Like a killer forest fire, like cancer under a microscope, any battle or bombing raid or artillery barrage has the aesthetic purity of absolute moral indifference — a powerful, implacable beauty — and a true war story will tell the truth about this, though the truth is ugly.

To generalize about war is like generalizing about peace. Almost everything is true. Almost nothing is true. At its core, perhaps, war is just another name for death, and yet any soldier will tell you, if he tells the truth, that proximity to death brings with it a corresponding proximity to life. After a fire fight, there is always the immense pleasure of aliveness. The trees are alive. The grass, the soil — everything. All around you things are purely living, and you among them, and the aliveness makes you tremble. You feel an intense, out-of-the-skin awareness of your living self — your truest self, the human being you want to be and then become by the force of wanting it. In the midst of evil you want to be a good man. You want decency. You want justice and courtesy and human concord, things you never knew you wanted. There is a kind of largeness to it; a kind of godliness. Though it's odd, you're never more alive than when you're almost dead. You recognize what's valuable. Freshly, as if for the first time, you love what's best in yourself and in the world, all that might be lost. At the hour of dusk you sit at your foxhole and look out on a wide river turning pinkish red, and at the mountains beyond, and although in the morning you must cross the river and go into the mountains and do terrible things and maybe die, even so, you find yourself studying the fine colors on the river, you feel wonder and awe at the setting of the sun, and you are filled with a hard, aching love for how the world could be and always should be, but now is not.

Mitchell Sanders was right. For the common soldier, at least, war has the feel — the spiritual texture — of a great ghostly fog, thick and permanent. There is no clarity. Everything swirls. The old rules are no longer binding, the old truths no longer true. Right spills over into wrong. Order blends into chaos, love into hate, ugliness into beauty, law into anarchy, civility into savagery. The vapors suck you in. You can't tell where you are, or why you're there, and the only certainty is absolute ambiguity.

In war you lose your sense of the definite, hence your sense of truth itself, 95 and therefore it's safe to say that in a true war story nothing much is ever very true.

Often in a true war story there is not even a point, or else the point doesn't hit you until twenty years later, in your sleep, and you wake up and shake your wife and start telling the story to her, except when you get to the end you've forgotten the point again. And then for a long time you lie there watching the story happen in your head. You listen to your wife's breathing. The war's over. You close your eyes. You smile and think, Christ, what's the *point*?

This one wakes me up.

In the mountains that day, I watched Lemon turn sideways. He laughed and said something to Rat Kiley. Then he took a peculiar half step, moving from shade into bright sunlight, and the booby-trapped 105 round blew him into a tree. The parts were just hanging there, so Norman Bowker and I were ordered to shinny up and peel him off. I remember the white bone of an arm. I remember pieces of skin and something wet and yellow that must've been the intestines. The gore was horrible, and stays with me, but what wakes me up twenty years later is Norman Bowker singing "Lemon Tree" as we threw down the parts.

You can tell a true war story by the questions you ask. Somebody tells a story, let's say, and afterward you ask, "Is it true?" and if the answer matters, you've got your answer.

For example, we've all heard this one. Four guys go down a trail. A grenade sails out. One guy jumps on it and takes the blast and saves his three buddies.

Is it true?

The answer matters.

You'd feel cheated if it never happened. Without the grounding reality, it's just a trite bit of puffery, pure Hollywood, untrue in the way all such stories are untrue. Yet even if it did happen — and maybe it did, anything's possible — even then you know it can't be true, because a true war story does not depend upon that kind of truth. Happeningness is irrelevant. A thing may happen and be a total lie; another thing may not happen and be truer than the truth. For example: four guys go down a trail. A grenade sails out. One guy jumps on it and takes the blast, but it's a killer grenade and everybody dies anyway. Before they die, though, one of the dead guys says, "The fuck you do *that* for?" and the jumper says, "Story of my life, man," and the other guy starts to smile but he's dead.

That's a true story that never happened.

Twenty years later, I can still see the sunlight on Lemon's face. I can see him turning, looking back at Rat Kiley, then he laughed and took that curious half step from shade into sunlight, his face suddenly brown and shining, and when his foot touched down, in that instant, he must've thought it was the sunlight that was killing him. It was not the sunlight. It was a rigged 105 round. But if I could ever get the story right, how the sun seemed to gather around him and pick him up and lift him into a tree, if I could somehow recreate the fatal whiteness of that light, the quick glare, the obvious cause and effect, then you would believe the last thing Lemon believed, which for him must've been the final truth.

Now and then, when I tell this story, someone will come up to me afterward and say she liked it. It's always a woman. Usually it's an older woman of kindly temperament and humane politics. She'll explain that as a rule she hates war stories, she can't understand why people want to wallow in blood and gore. But this one she liked. Sometimes, even, there are little tears. What I should do, she'll say, is put it all behind me. Find new stories to tell.

I won't say it but I'll think it.

I'll picture Rat Kiley's face, his grief, and I'll think, *You dumb cooze.*

Because she wasn't listening.

It wasn't a war story. It was a love story. It was a ghost story.

But you can't say that. All you can do is tell it one more time, patiently, adding and subtracting, making up a few things to get at the real truth. No

Mitchell Sanders, you tell her. No Lemon, no Rat Kiley. And it didn't happen in the mountains, it happened in this little village on the Batangan Peninsula, and it was raining like crazy, and one night a guy named Stink Harris woke up screaming with a leech on his tongue. You can tell a true war story if you just keep on telling it.

In the end, of course, a true war story is never about war. It's about the special way that dawn spreads out on a river when you know you must cross the river and march into the mountains and do things you are afraid to do. It's about love and memory. It's about sorrow. It's about sisters who never write back and people who never listen.

CONSIDERATIONS FOR CRITICAL THINKING AND WRITING

1. FIRST RESPONSE. What implicit problem is created about the story by its first line, "This is true"? How is the notion of "truth" problematized throughout the story?

2. Why is Rat Kiley so upset over Curt Lemon's sister not writing back?

3. How are you affected by the descriptions of Curt Lemon being blown up in paragraphs 17, 98, and 105?

4. Analyze the story told about the six-man patrol in paragraphs 19–65. How is this story relevant to the rest of the plot?

5. What emotions did you feel as you read about the shooting of the water buffalo? How does paragraph 75 achieve these effects?

6. Explain what you think O'Brien means when he writes "After a fire fight, there is always the immense pleasure of aliveness" (para. 93).

7. Trace the narrator's comments about what constitutes a true war story. What do you think these competing and contradictory ideas finally add up to?

8. Characterize the narrator. Why must he repeatedly "keep on telling" his war story?

9. Consider O'Brien's use of profanity and violence in this story. Do you think they are essential or merely sensational?

10. CRITICAL STRATEGIES. Read the discussion concerning historical criticism (pp. 66–70) in Chapter 3, "Applying a Critical Strategy," and research American protests and reactions to the war in Vietnam. How are these responses relevant to O'Brien's story, particularly paragraphs 1–10 and 106–111?

POETRY

ELIZABETH BISHOP (1911–1979)

The Fish   *1946*

I caught a tremendous fish
and held him beside the boat
half out of water, with my hook
fast in a corner of his mouth.
He didn't fight.   5
He hadn't fought at all.

He hung a grunting weight,
battered and venerable
and homely. Here and there
his brown skin hung in strips   10
like ancient wall-paper,
and its pattern of darker brown
was like wall-paper:
shapes like full-blown roses
stained and lost through age.   15
He was speckled with barnacles,
fine rosettes of lime,
and infested
with tiny white sea-lice,
and underneath two or three   20
rags of green weed hung down.
While his gills were breathing in
the terrible oxygen
— the frightening gills,
fresh and crisp with blood,   25
that can cut so badly —
I thought of the coarse white flesh
packed in like feathers,
the big bones and the little bones,
the dramatic reds and blacks   30
of his shiny entrails,
and the pink swim-bladder
like a big peony.
I looked into his eyes
which were far larger than mine   35
but shallower, and yellowed,
the irises backed and packed
with tarnished tinfoil
seen through the lenses
of old scratched isinglass.   40
They shifted a little, but not
to return my stare.
— It was more like the tipping
of an object toward the light.
I admired his sullen face,   45
the mechanism of his jaw,
and then I saw
that from his lower lip
— if you could call it a lip —
grim, wet, and weapon-like,   50
hung five old pieces of fish-line,
or four and a wire leader
with the swivel still attached,
with all their five big hooks
grown firmly in his mouth.   55
A green line, frayed at the end
where he broke it, two heavier lines,

and a fine black thread
still crimped from the strain and snap
when it broke and he got away.   60
Like medals with their ribbons
frayed and wavering,
a five-haired beard of wisdom
trailing from his aching jaw.
I stared and stared   65
and victory filled up
the little rented boat,
from the pool of bilge
where oil had spread a rainbow
around the rusted engine   70
to the bailer rusted orange,
the sun-cracked thwarts,
the oarlocks on their strings,
the gunnels — until everything
was rainbow, rainbow, rainbow!   75
And I let the fish go.

CONSIDERATIONS FOR CRITICAL THINKING AND WRITING

1. FIRST RESPONSE. Which lines in this poem provide especially vivid details of the fish? What makes these descriptions effective?

2. How is the fish characterized? Is it simply a weak victim because it "didn't fight"?

3. Comment on lines 65–76. In what sense has "victory filled up" the boat, given that the speaker finally lets the fish go?

WILLIAM BLAKE (1757–1827)

The Lamb   1789

    Little Lamb, who made thee?
    Dost thou know who made thee?
Gave thee life, and bid thee feed
By the stream and o'er the mead;
Gave thee clothing of delight,   5
Softest clothing, wooly, bright;
Gave thee such a tender voice,
Making all the vales rejoice?
    Little Lamb, who made thee?
    Dost thou know who made thee?   10

    Little Lamb, I'll tell thee,
    Little Lamb, I'll tell thee:
He is callèd by thy name,
For he calls himself a Lamb.
He is meek, and he is mild;   15
He became a little child.

I a child, and thou a lamb,
We are callèd by his name.
  Little Lamb, God bless thee!
  Little Lamb, God bless thee!   20

CONSIDERATIONS FOR CRITICAL THINKING AND WRITING

1. FIRST RESPONSE. This poem is from Blake's *Songs of Innocence*. Describe its tone. How do the meter, rhyme, and repetition help to characterize the speaker's voice?

2. Why is it significant that the animal addressed by the speaker is a lamb? What symbolic value would be lost if the animal were, for example, a doe?

3. How does the second stanza answer the question raised in the first? What is the speaker's view of the creation?

The Tyger   *1794*

Tyger! Tyger! burning bright
In the forests of the night,
What immortal hand or eye
Could frame thy fearful symmetry?

In what distant deeps or skies   5
Burnt the fire of thine eyes?
On what wings dare he aspire?
What the hand dare seize the fire?

And what shoulder, and what art,
Could twist the sinews of thy heart?   10
And when thy heart began to beat,
What dread hand? and what dread feet?

What the hammer? what the chain?
In what furnace was thy brain?
What the anvil? what dread grasp   15
Dare its deadly terrors clasp?

When the stars threw down their spears,
And watered heaven with their tears,
Did he smile his work to see?
Did he who made the Lamb make thee?   20

Tyger! Tyger! burning bright
In the forests of the night,
What immortal hand or eye
Dare frame thy fearful symmetry?

CONSIDERATIONS FOR CRITICAL THINKING AND WRITING

1. FIRST RESPONSE. This poem from Blake's *Songs of Experience* is often paired with "The Lamb." Describe the poem's tone. Is the speaker's voice the same

here as in "The Lamb"? Which words are repeated, and how do they contribute to the tone?

2. What is revealed about the nature of the tiger by the words used to describe its creation? What do you think the tiger symbolizes?

3. Unlike in "The Lamb," more than one question is raised in "The Tyger." What are these questions? Are they answered?

4. Compare the rhythms in "The Lamb" and "The Tyger." Each basically uses a seven-syllable line, but the effects are very different. Why?

5. Using these two poems as the basis of your discussion, describe what distinguishes innocence from experience.

JAMES DICKEY (1923–1997)

Deer among Cattle

1981

Here and there in the searing beam
Of my hand going through the night meadow
They all are grazing

With pins of human light in their eyes.
A wild one also is eating   5
The human grass,

Slender, graceful, domesticated
By darkness, among the bred-
for-slaughter,

Having bounded their paralyzed fence   10
And inclined his branched forehead onto
Their green frosted table,

The only live thing in this flashlight
Who can leave whenever he wishes,
Turn grass into forest,   15

Foreclose inhuman brightness from his eyes
But stands here still, unperturbed,
In their wide-open country,

The sparks from my hand in his pupils
Unmatched anywhere among cattle,   20

Grazing with them the night of the hammer
As one of their own who shall rise.

CONSIDERATIONS FOR CRITICAL THINKING AND WRITING

1. FIRST RESPONSE. What images distinguish the deer from the cattle?

2. Do the words "domesticated" and "human" have positive or negative connotations in this poem? Explain your answer.

3. Discuss the possible implications of the last two lines. You may want to consider the speaker and his role in this tableau.

EMILY DICKINSON (1830–1886)

A Light exists in Spring

c. 1864

A Light exists in Spring
Not present on the Year
At any other period —
When March is scarcely here

A Color stands abroad   5
On Solitary Fields
That Science cannot overtake
But Human Nature feels.

It waits upon the Lawn,
It shows the furthest Tree   10
Upon the furthest Slope you know
It almost speaks to you.

Then as Horizons step
Or Noons report away
Without the Formula of sound   15
It passes and we stay —

A quality of loss
Affecting our Content
As Trade had suddenly encroached
Upon a Sacrament.   20

CONSIDERATIONS FOR CRITICAL THINKING AND WRITING

1. FIRST RESPONSE. Describe the poem's tone. Does it change from the beginning to the end?

2. What does the speaker associate with the spring light of March? Paraphrase each stanza. Which one reveals most clearly the nature of this light for you?

3. Discuss the meaning of the speaker's use of "Trade."

ROBERT FROST (1874–1963)

Design

1936

I found a dimpled spider, fat and white,
On a white heal-all,° holding up a moth
Like a white piece of rigid satin cloth —
Assorted characters of death and blight
Mixed ready to begin the morning right,   5
Like the ingredients of a witches' broth —
A snow-drop spider, a flower like a froth,
And dead wings carried like a paper kite.

2 *heal-all:* A common flower, usually blue, once used for medicinal purposes.

What had the flower to do with being white,
The wayside blue and innocent heal-all? 10
What brought the kindred spider to that height,
Then steered the white moth thither in the night?
What but design of darkness to appall? —
If design govern in a thing so small.

CONSIDERATIONS FOR CRITICAL THINKING AND WRITING

1. FIRST RESPONSE. What kinds of speculations are raised in the final two lines? Consider the meaning of the title. Is there more than one way to read it?

2. How does the division of the octave and sestet in this sonnet serve to organize the speaker's thoughts and feelings? What is the predominant rhyme? How does that rhyme relate to the poem's meaning?

3. CRITICAL STRATEGIES. Read the section on formalist criticism (pp. 60–62) in Chapter 3, "Applying a Critical Strategy." Which words seem especially rich in connotative meanings? Explain how they function in the sonnet.

THOMAS HARDY (1840–1928)

The Convergence of the Twain 1912

Lines on the Loss of the "Titanic"°

I

       In a solitude of the sea
       Deep from human vanity,
And the Pride of Life that planned her, stilly couches she.

II

       Steel chambers, late the pyres
       Of her salamandrine fires,° 5
Cold currents thrid,° and turn to rhythmic tidal lyres. *thread*

III

       Over the mirrors meant
       To glass the opulent
The sea-worm crawls — grotesque, slimed, dumb, indifferent.

IV

       Jewels in joy designed 10
       To ravish the sensuous mind
Lie lightless, all their sparkles bleared and black and blind.

V

       Dim moon-eyed fishes near
       Gaze at the gilded gear
And query: "What does this vaingloriousness down here?" 15

"*Titanic:*" A luxurious ocean liner, reputed to be unsinkable, which sank after hitting an iceberg on its maiden voyage in 1912. Only a third of the 2,200 passengers survived.
5 *salamandrine fires:* Salamanders were, according to legend, able to survive fire; hence, the ship's fires burned even though under water.

VI

      Well: while was fashioning
      This creature of cleaving wing,
The Immanent Will that stirs and urges everything

VII

      Prepared a sinister mate
      For her — so gaily great —   20
A Shape of Ice, for the time far and dissociate.

VIII

      And as the smart ship grew
      In stature, grace, and hue,
In shadowy silent distance grew the Iceberg too.

IX

      Alien they seemed to be: 25
      No mortal eye could see
The intimate welding of their later history,

X

      Or sign that they were bent
      By paths coincident
On being anon twin halves of one august event,   30

XI

      Till the Spinner of the Years
      Said "Now!" And each one hears,
And consummation comes, and jars two hemispheres.

Considerations for Critical Thinking and Writing

1. FIRST RESPONSE. Describe a contemporary disaster comparable to the *Titanic*. How was your response to it similar to or different from the speaker's response to the *Titanic*?

2. How do the words used to describe the ship in this poem reveal the speaker's attitude toward the *Titanic*?

3. The diction of the poem suggests that the *Titanic* and the iceberg participate in something like an arranged marriage. What specific words imply this?

4. Who or what causes the disaster? Does the speaker assign responsibility?

Margaret Holley (b. 1944)

Peepers   *1992*

One amber inch
of blinking berry-eyed
amphibian,

four fetal fingers
on each hand,   5
a honey and mud-brown

pulse of appetite
surprised into stillness,
folded in a momentary lump

of flying bat-fish   10
ready to jump
full-tilt into anything

— the whole strength
of its struggling length
you can hold in your hand.   15

Its poetry, a raucous
refrain of pleasure
in the April-warm pools

of rain, the insistent
chorus of whistles   20
jingles through night woods,

Females! It's time!
that confident come-on
to a whole wet population

of embraces, eggs, tadpoles   25
— all head and tail,
mind darting in every direction

until the articulating torso,
Ovidian bag of bones,
results in the "mature adult":   30

a rumpled face in the mirror
still sleeping through Basho's°
awakening plop,

re-enchanted daily
by the comforting slop   35
of burgeoning spring woods

and all this sexual chatter,
doing its best to make
the wet and silky season

last forever. Yet   40
as you lie dreaming mid-leap,
splayed in the sheets,

the future as a kind
but relentless scientist
feels around in your flesh   45

for the nerve of surprise;
he just loves
the look of wonder on your face,

---

32 *Basho:* Matsuo Bashō (1644–1694), a Japanese poet most famous for his haiku.

the world on your open lips
for the immensity　　　　　　　　　　　　　　　　　　　　50
that grips you,

Oh.

CONSIDERATIONS FOR CRITICAL THINKING AND WRITING

1. FIRST RESPONSE. What is the speaker's attitude toward what is described in this poem?

2. What is being described in lines 1–40? How does the subject shift in lines 40–52? What is the relationship between these two groups of lines?

3. The word "Peepers" only appears in the title, but are there images in the poem that connect to the title? What does the title mean?

4. What is the effect and significance of the final line?

GERARD MANLEY HOPKINS　(1844–1889)

Pied Beauty　　　　　　　　　　　　　　　　　　　　　　　1877

Glory be to God for dappled things —
　　For skies of couple-color as a brinded cow;
　　　　For rose-moles all in stipple upon trout that swim;
Fresh-firecoal chestnut-falls;° finches' wings;　　　　　　　*fallen chestnut*
　　Landscape plotted and pieced — fold, fallow, and plow;　　5
　　　　And all trades, their gear and tackle and trim.

All things counter, original, spare, strange;
　　Whatever is fickle, freckled (who knows how?)
　　　　With swift, slow; sweet, sour; adazzle, dim;
He fathers-forth whose beauty is past change:　　　　　　　10
　　　　　Praise him.

CONSIDERATIONS FOR CRITICAL THINKING AND WRITING

1. FIRST RESPONSE. Read the poem aloud. How do the sounds affect your understanding of it?

2. What does "pied" mean? How is this idea repeated throughout the poem?

3. Discuss the poem's images. What do they have in common?

4. Explain what you think is the poem's theme.

ALICE JONES　(B. 1949)

The Foot　　　　　　　　　　　　　　　　　　　　　　　1993

Our improbable support, erected
on the osseous architecture
of the calcaneus, talus, cuboid,

navicular, cuneiforms, metatarsals,
phalanges, a plethora of hinges,   5

all strung together by gliding
tendons, covered by the pearly
plantar fascia, then fat-padded
to form the sole, humble surface
of our contact with earth.   10

Here the body's broadest tendon
anchors the heel's fleshy base,
the finely wrinkled skin stretches
forward across the capillaried arch,
to the ball, a balance point.   15

A wide web of flexor tendons
and branched veins maps the dorsum,
fades into the stub-laden bone
splay, the stuffed sausage sacks
of toes, each with a tuft   20

of proximal hairs to introduce
the distal nail, whose useless
curve remembers an ancestor,
the vanished creature's wild
and necessary claw.   25

Considerations for Critical Thinking and Writing

1. FIRST RESPONSE. What is the effect of the diction? What sort of tone is
   established by the use of anatomical terms? How do the terms affect the
   rhythm?

2. Alice Jones has described the form of "The Foot" as "five stubby stanzas."
   Explain why the lines of this poem may or may not warrant this description
   of the stanzas.

3. CRITICAL STRATEGIES. Read the section on formalist criticism (pp. 60–62) in
   Chapter 3, "Applying a Critical Strategy." Describe the effect of the final
   stanza. How would your reading be affected if the poem ended after the
   comma in the middle of line 22?

John Keats (1795–1821)

To Autumn   *1819*

I
Season of mists and mellow fruitfulness,
    Close bosom-friend of the maturing sun;
Conspiring with him how to load and bless
    With fruit the vines that round the thatch-eves run;
To bend with apples the mossed cottage-trees,   5
    And fill all fruit with ripeness to the core;

To swell the gourd, and plump the hazel shells
 With a sweet kernel; to set budding more,
And still more, later flowers for the bees,
Until they think warm days will never cease,   10
 For summer has o'er-brimmed their clammy cells.

II
Who hath not seen thee oft amid thy store?
 Sometimes whoever seeks abroad may find
Thee sitting careless on a granary floor,
 Thy hair soft-lifted by the winnowing wind;   15
Or on a half-reaped furrow sound asleep,
 Drowsed with the fume of poppies, while thy hook°   *scythe*
 Spares the next swath and all its twinèd flowers:
And sometimes like a gleaner thou dost keep
 Steady thy laden head across a brook;   20
 Or by a cider-press, with patient look,
 Thou watchest the last oozings hours by hours.

III
Where are the songs of spring? Ay, where are they?
 Think not of them, thou hast thy music too, —
While barred clouds bloom the soft-dying day,   25
 And touch the stubble-plains with rosy hue;
Then in a wailful choir the small gnats mourn
 Among the river swallows,° borne aloft   *willows*
 Or sinking as the light wind lives or dies;
And full-grown lambs loud bleat from hilly bourn;°   *territory* 30
 Hedge-crickets sing; and now with treble soft
 The redbreast whistles from a garden-croft,
 And gathering swallows twitter in the skies.

Considerations for Critical Thinking and Writing

1. FIRST RESPONSE. How is autumn made to seem like a person in each stanza of this ode?

2. Which senses are most emphasized in each stanza?

3. How is the progression of time expressed in the ode?

4. How does the imagery convey tone? Which words have particularly strong connotative values?

5. What is the speaker's view of death?

Galway Kinnell (b. 1927)

Blackberry Eating   1980

I love to go out in late September
among the fat, overripe, icy, black blackberries
to eat blackberries for breakfast,

the stalks very prickly, a penalty
they earn for knowing the black art   5
of blackberry-making; and as I stand among them
lifting the stalks to my mouth, the ripest berries
fall almost unbidden to my tongue,
as words sometimes do, certain peculiar words
like *strengths* or *squinched*,   10
many-lettered, one-syllabled lumps,
which I squeeze, squinch open, and splurge well
in the silent, startled, icy, black language
of blackberry-eating in late September.

CONSIDERATIONS FOR CRITICAL THINKING AND WRITING

1. FIRST RESPONSE. What types of sounds does Kinnell use throughout this poem? What categories can you place them in? What is the effect of these sounds?

2. How do lines 4–6 fit into the poem? What does this prickly image add to the poem?

3. Explain what you think the poem's theme is.

4. Write an essay that considers the speaker's love of blackberry-eating along with the speaker's appetite for words. How are the two blended in the poem?

HERMAN MELVILLE (1819–1891)

The Maldive Shark   *1888*

About the Shark, phlegmatical one,
Pale sot of the Maldive sea,
The sleek little pilot-fish, azure and slim,
How alert in attendance be.
From his saw-pit of mouth, from his charnel of maw   5
They have nothing of harm to dread,
But liquidly glide on his ghastly flank
Or before his Gorgonian head;
Or lurk in the port of serrated teeth
In white triple tiers of glittering gates,   10
And there find a haven when peril's abroad,
An asylum in jaws of the Fates!

They are friends; and friendly they guide him to prey,
Yet never partake of the treat—
Eyes and brains to the dotard lethargic and dull,   15
Pale ravener of horrible meat.

CONSIDERATIONS FOR CRITICAL THINKING AND WRITING

1. FIRST RESPONSE. Describe the nature of the relationship between the shark and the pilot fish.

2. What is the effect of the use of personification in the poem?

3. Consider the poem's diction and how it serves to create a particular tone.

4. In a sentence try to articulate what you think is the theme of the poem.

N. Scott Momaday (b. 1934)

The Bear

1992

What ruse of vision,
escarping the wall of leaves,
    rending incision
into countless surfaces,

would cull and color   5
his somnolence, whose old age
    has outworn valor,
all but the fact of courage?

Seen, he does not come,
move, but seems forever there,   10
    dimensionless, dumb,
in the windless noon's hot glare.

More scarred than others
these years since the trap maimed him,
    pain slants his withers,   15
drawing up the crooked limb.

Then he is gone, whole,
without urgency, from sight,
    as buzzards control,
imperceptibly, their flight.   20

Considerations for Critical Thinking and Writing

1. First response. How is the bear depicted? In what sense do the images compete with one another?

2. What is the speaker's relationship to the bear? How does the speaker feel and think about it?

3. Discuss the tone of the image in lines 20–21. How does it make you feel about the bear?

4. Why is this poem more than a simple description of a bear? What thematic significance do you find in the poem?

Mary Oliver (b. 1935)

The Black Snake

When the black snake
flashed onto the morning road,
and the truck could not swerve —
death, that is how it happens.

Now he lies looped and useless   5
as an old bicycle tire.
I stop the car
and carry him into the bushes.

He is as cool and gleaming
as a braided whip, he is as beautiful and quiet   10
as a dead brother.
I leave him under the leaves

and drive on, thinking,
about *death:* its suddenness,
its terrible weight,   15
its certain coming. Yet under

reason burns a brighter fire, which the bones
have always preferred.
It is the story of endless good fortune.
It says to oblivion: not me!   20

It is the light at the center of every cell.
It is what sent the snake coiling and flowing forward
happily all spring through the green leaves before
he came to the road.

CONSIDERATIONS FOR CRITICAL THINKING AND WRITING

1. FIRST RESPONSE. What makes this such a vivid description of a snake? Discuss the poet's use of figurative language.
2. How is the snake used as a symbol of both death and life?
3. Explain whether or not you think this is an optimistic or pessimistic poem.

WILFRED OWEN (1893–1918)

Dulce et Decorum Est   *1920*

Bent double, like old beggars under sacks,
Knock-kneed, coughing like hags, we cursed through sludge,
Till on the haunting flares we turned our backs,
And towards our distant rest began to trudge.

Men marched asleep. Many had lost their boots,   5
But limped on, blood-shod. All went lame, all blind;
Drunk with fatigue; deaf even to the hoots
Of gas-shells dropping softly behind.

Gas! GAS! Quick, boys!—An ecstasy of fumbling,
Fitting the clumsy helmets just in time,   10
But someone still was yelling out and stumbling
And flound'ring like a man in fire or lime.—
Dim through the misty panes and thick green light,
As under a green sea, I saw him drowning.

In all my dreams before my helpless sight   15
He plunges at me, guttering, choking, drowning.

If in some smothering dreams, you too could pace
Behind the wagon that we flung him in,
And watch the white eyes writhing in his face,
His hanging face, like a devil's sick of sin,   20
If you could hear, at every jolt, the blood
Come gargling from the froth-corrupted lungs
Bitter as the cud
Obscene as cancer,
Of vile, incurable sores on innocent tongues, —   25
My friend, you would not tell with such high zest
To children ardent for some desperate glory,
The old lie: *Dulce et decorum est*
Pro patria mori.

CONSIDERATIONS FOR CRITICAL THINKING AND WRITING

1. FIRST RESPONSE. The Latin quotation in lines 28 and 29 is from Horace: "It is sweet and fitting to die for one's country." Owen served as a British soldier during World War I and was killed. Is this poem unpatriotic? What is its purpose?

2. Which images in the poem are most vivid? To which senses do they speak?

3. Describe the speaker's tone. What is his relationship to his audience?

4. How are the images of the soldiers in this poem different from the images that typically appear in recruiting posters?

5. CRITICAL STRATEGIES. Read the section on biographical criticism (pp. 62–64) in Chapter 3, "Applying a Critical Strategy," and use the library to learn about Owen's response to being a soldier during World War I. How might a biographical critic use this information to shed light on the poem?

ALDEN NOWLAN (1933–1983)

The Bull Moose   *1962*

Down from the purple mist of trees on the mountain,
lurching through forests of white spruce and cedar,
stumbling through tamarack swamps,
came the bull moose
to be stopped at last by a pole-fenced pasture.   5

Too tired to turn or, perhaps, aware
there was no place left to go, he stood with the cattle.
They, scenting the musk of death, seeing his great head
like the ritual mask of a blood god, moved to the other end
of the field, and waited.   10

The neighbors heard of it, and by afternoon
cars lined the road. The children teased him

with alder switches and he gazed at them
like an old, tolerant collie. The women asked
if he could have escaped from a Fair.   15

The oldest man in the parish remembered seeing
a gelded moose yoked with an ox for plowing.
The young men snickered and tried to pour beer
down his throat, while their girl friends took their pictures.

The bull moose let them stroke his tick-ravaged flanks,   20
let them pry open his jaws with bottles, let a giggling girl
plant a little purple cap
of thistles on his head.

When the wardens came, everyone agreed it was a shame
to shoot anything so shaggy and cuddlesome.   25
He looked like the kind of pet
women put to bed with their sons.

So they held their fire. But just as the sun dropped in the river
the bull moose gathered his strength
like a scaffolded king, straightened and lifted his horns   30
so that even the wardens backed away as they raised their rifles.
When he roared, people ran to their cars. All the young men
leaned on their automobile horns as he toppled.

CONSIDERATIONS FOR CRITICAL THINKING AND WRITING

1. FIRST RESPONSE. How does the speaker present the moose and the townspeople? How are the moose and townspeople contrasted? Discuss specific
   lines to support your response.

2. Explain how the symbols in this poem point to a conflict between humanity
   and nature. What do you think is the speaker's attitude toward this conflict?

3. CRITICAL STRATEGIES. Read the section on mythological criticism (pp. 72–74)
   in Chapter 3, "Applying a Critical Strategy," and write an essay on "The Bull
   Moose" that approaches the poem from a mythological perspective.

MARGE PIERCY (B. 1936)

A Work of Artifice   1973

The bonsai tree
in the attractive pot
could have grown eighty feet tall
on the side of a mountain
till split by lightning.   5
But a gardener
carefully pruned it.
It is nine inches high.
Every day as he
whittles back the branches   10

the gardener croons,
It is your nature
to be small and cozy,
domestic and weak;
how lucky, little tree,   15
to have a pot to grow in.
With living creatures
one must begin very early
to dwarf their growth:
the bound feet,   20
the crippled brain,
the hair in curlers,
the hands you
love to touch.

CONSIDERATIONS FOR CRITICAL THINKING AND WRITING

1. FIRST RESPONSE. What is a bonsai tree? How is it likened to a woman in this poem? At what point in the poem does the comparison become apparent?

2. What attitudes are revealed by the language of the gardener's song? Which words have especially strong connotative values?

3. The final two lines ("the hands you / love to touch") allude to a soap commercial. Explain the effect this allusion has on your understanding of the poem's theme.

WILLIAM STAFFORD (B. 1914)

Traveling through the Dark   *1962*

Traveling through the dark I found a deer
dead on the edge of the Wilson River road.
It is usually best to roll them into the canyon:
that road is narrow; to swerve might make more dead.

By glow of the tail-light I stumbled back of the car   5
and stood by the heap, a doe, a recent killing;
she had stiffened already, almost cold.
I dragged her off; she was large in the belly.

My fingers touching her side brought me the reason —
her side was warm; her fawn lay there waiting,   10
alive, still, never to be born.
Beside that mountain road I hesitated.

The car aimed ahead its lowered parking lights;
under the hood purred the steady engine.
I stood in the glare of the warm exhaust turning red;   15
around our group I could hear the wilderness listen.

I thought hard for us all — my only swerving —
then pushed her over the edge into the river.

CONSIDERATIONS FOR CRITICAL THINKING AND WRITING

1. FIRST RESPONSE. Notice the description of the car in this poem: the "glow of the tail-light," the "lowered parking lights," and how the engine "purred." How do these and other details suggest symbolic meanings for the car and the "recent killing"?

2. Discuss the speaker's tone. Does the speaker seem, for example, tough, callous, kind, sentimental, confused, or confident?

3. What is the effect of the last stanza's having only two lines rather than the established four lines of the previous stanzas?

4. Discuss the appropriateness of this poem's title. In what sense has the speaker "thought hard for us all"? What are those thoughts?

5. Is this a didactic poem?

WALT WHITMAN (1819–1892)

When I Heard the Learn'd Astronomer   *1865*

When I heard the learn'd astronomer,
When the proofs, the figures, were ranged in columns before me,
When I was shown the charts and diagrams, to add, divide, and measure
    them,
When I sitting heard the astronomer where he lectured with much applause
    in the lecture-room,
How soon unaccountable I became tired and sick,
Till rising and gliding out I wandered off by myself,
In the mystical moist night-air, and from time to time,
Looked up in perfect silence at the stars.

CONSIDERATIONS FOR CRITICAL THINKING AND WRITING

1. FIRST RESPONSE. Read the poem aloud. How do the last three lines sound compared to what precedes them? How does sound reinforce meaning in these lines?

2. How can the word "unaccountable" be read as a significant pun?

3. Compare the speaker's feelings in the second half of the poem with those of the first half. What has made the difference?

WILLIAM CARLOS WILLIAMS (1883–1963)

Spring and All   *1923*

By the road to the contagious hospital
under the surge of the blue
mottled clouds driven from the
northeast — a cold wind. Beyond, the
waste of broad, muddy fields   5
brown with dried weeds, standing and fallen

patches of standing water
and scattering of tall trees

All along the road the reddish
purplish, forked, upstanding, twiggy   10
stuff of bushes and small trees
with dead, brown leaves under them
leafless vines —

Lifeless in appearance, sluggish
dazed spring approaches —   15

They enter the new world naked,
cold, uncertain of all
save that they enter. All about them
the cold, familiar wind —

Now the grass, tomorrow   20
the stiff curl of wildcarrot leaf
One by one objects are defined —
It quickens: clarity, outline of leaf

But now the stark dignity of
entrance — Still, the profound change   25
has come upon them: rooted, the
grip down and begin to waken

Considerations for Critical Thinking and Writing

1. **First response.** Discuss how the imagery of this poem creates a powerful
   evocation of spring.
2. Why do you suppose the title of the poem isn't simply "Spring"?
3. Comment on Williams's use of punctuation throughout the poem. Why
   do you think there is not a final period?

DRAMA

William Seebring (b. 1956)

William Seebring grew up in an area of Ohio commonly referred to as
the Rustbelt and now widely regarded as the fast-food capital of the world.
After leaving a factory job where he assembled prototype emission control
systems for the automobile industry, Seebring drove a 1965 Pontiac Le-
Mans to Brooklyn, New York, where he took up structural drawing. Adopt-
ing the pseudonym Douglas Michael, Seebring published a series of
underground comic books titled *Tales from the Outerboroughs* as well as an
illustrated full-color travel guide to fictitious lands that was published by a
magazine catering to lonely hearts. After selling his Pontiac for a slightly

used Honda Accord, Seebring moved his family to upstate New York to raise chickens and adapt his comics into stage plays. Other plays include *Das Wolfkin,* a darkly comic fairy tale written in an invented language, and *The Geldings,* a Western spoof about cowboys without genitals. Under his assumed name, Seebring has dabbled in numerous pursuits, from literary agent to country and western songwriter.

The Original Last Wish Baby   *1995*

THE SETS

> *Aside from a podium, the action of the play is best staged with pools of lighting and minor propping.*

THE CAST

> *There are more than 40 characters, and almost all are speaking parts. However, the play can be performed with as few as four actors. A suggested breakdown of parts follows:*

Narrator

Actor #2: Executive, Specialist #1, Network Exec #1, Terry Collins, Customer #1, Glam Entertainment Marketeer, Newsboy, Phoney Last Wish Baby, Judge, Pundit #1, Surgeon #3, Right-to-Extended-Lifer #2, Congregant #2, Diner, Politician #1

Actor #3: Nurse, Mrs. Kornfeld, Product Demonstrator, Welda Mae Forms, Network Exec #3, Waitress, Glam Entertainment Exec, Pundit #3, Surgeon #2, Congregant #1, Corpse, Right-to-Extended-Lifer #1, Pollster

Actor #4: Doctor, Assistant, Man, Specialist #2, Network Exec #2, Customer #2, Glam Entertainment Pitchman, Guatemalan Cleaning Woman, Lawyer, Daryl Wayne Trebleau, Pundit #2, Surgeon #1, Maitre d', Preacher, Woman in Black, Politician #2

> *We hear "tha-dump, bump — tha-dump, bump." The steady, rhythmic beat of a human heart. A special light comes up on a podium and the Narrator at stage right. The Narrator opens a large storybook.*

Narrator: *The Original Last Wish Baby,* as researched, recorded, and revised by William Seebring. Cleveland, Ohio. Or, more specifically, the third-floor maternity room of the Holy Name Hospital on Cleveland's impoverished West Side where, at precisely seven-oh-one P.M. —

> *Turns page. We hear a baby crying.*

A baby was born. Not just any baby, but the infamous, original, Last Wish Baby. The baby born without a heart.

> *Lights up on a Doctor and Nurse. The Nurse is cradling a bundled infant.*

Doctor: What's this about a baby with no heart? Good heavens, that's impossible.
Nurse: Check for yourself, Doctor.
Doctor: Nothing, no pulse. Not a sound.

The bundled baby squirms in the Nurse's arms.

And yet, this baby clearly mimics life. A freak.
Nurse (softly): No. A miracle.
Doctor: What's that?
Nurse: A miracle . . . the baby is a miracle.
Doctor: A miracle? This is Cleveland. It'll be a miracle if the mother's insured.

Lights down on the maternity ward.

Narrator: Not only were the baby's parents uninsured, the identity of the
baby's father was unknown. However, the birth mother's name was given
as Welda Mae Forms, a thirty-one-year-old unemployed cosmetologist. At
the time, little else was known about Ms. Forms, but word of her remarkable progeny spread quickly from the maternity ward to the scrub rooms
to the hospital's administrative offices, where a larger picture began to
emerge.

Lights up on the hospital's administrative Executive and his Assistant.

Executive: A baby born without a heart? Sounds awful. Sounds *really* awful.
Assistant: Maybe not as bad as you think.
Executive: C'mon, Chet. How the hell do ya' window dress a missing heart?
God knows we've had our share of high-risk deliveries here at Holy
Name — little baby heads get smushed, tiny baby limbs get . . . it's messy,
terrible, makes me shudder. But delivering a baby and not the heart —
good God! *(Beat.)* What's our liability on something like that?
Assistant: Well, here's the thing, sir . . . the baby is alive.
Executive: Alive? Without a heart? But that's . . . that . . .
Assistant: Impossible? Yes. Nevertheless, it's —
Executive: What, some kind of weird, autoneuron tremors? Good God, is that
what passes for life these days?
Assistant: The baby is fully functioning, quite spirited, and has a healthy
appetite, I might add.
Executive: For how long? An hour, maybe two?
Assistant: Who can say? But even if the baby were to, God forbid. . . . Its short
life could, with the right spin, be played out as the most incredible P.R.
story of our time. What's more, the timing couldn't have been more . . .
fortuitous . . . sir.
Executive: What, the Sprach/Klockenheimer takeover?
Assistant: Precisely the kind of thing that could triple our name factor
overnight. A miracle . . . and it happened here, in *our* hospital, under the
care and guidance of *our* health care professionals. Think of it, sir. "Holy
Name, the get-well place where miracles happen."
Executive: "The get-well place where miracles happen.". . . Now there's a ball
with some bounce to it! Call Delores Childs at Channel Five. If we can
dazzle her, there's a good chance we could make the six o'clock news!
Assistant: She's on her way, sir.
Executive: Good boy. Oh, one other thing . . . the heart? Did anyone ever *find*
the heart?
Assistant: No. Actually, as far as we know, there never was a heart.

Lights down on the administrative offices.

Narrator: In point of fact, there was a heart. However, through one of those unfathomable anomalies which defy all logic yet govern most things, the heart was delivered separately by a surprised New Jersey woman on her way home from the store.

Lights up on a Man and Mrs. Kornfeld. Mrs. Kornfeld steps forward carrying a Nordstrom's bag and then stops to hail a taxi when something like a beefsteak tomato falls from her skirt. The man regards it.

Man: Yo, Miss . . . Lady! You dropped something.

Mrs. Kornfeld looks back.

Mrs. Kornfeld: Oh-my-god, what is it!

The thumping heart is heard. Lights fade on Mrs. Kornfeld as she bends to retrieve the heart.

Narrator: That something would soon be determined to be the baby's heart. However, at that particular moment, the New Jersey woman, later identified as Mrs. Sydney Kornfeld and soon to become known as "The Baby Heart Mom," was not yet aware of the miracle baby story unfolding in Cleveland.

Lights up on a Product Demonstrator with a Tupperware container, a beefsteak tomato, and a can of peaches.

As for Mrs. Kornfeld, she fortuitously retrieved the baby heart and returned immediately to her home in Paramus, where, as the demonstrator shall faithfully recreate, she placed the pulsating vital organ into a clear, air-tight, number-seven Tupperware container, which she then filled with a high-fructose, low-sodium, heavy syrup drained from a can of Libby's yellow-cling sliced peaches. After burping for a tight seal, Mrs. Kornfeld placed the container in the crisper drawer of her refrigerator where, according to product designers, the heart could have been stored indefinitely and would remain every bit as fresh and vigorous as the moment she delivered it.

Lights down on the Product Demonstrator.

Meanwhile, back in Cleveland, ever more adept medical specialists were brought in to examine the so-called miracle baby.

Lights up on the maternity ward as Two Medical Specialists look into a crib and we hear a giggling baby.

Specialist #1: Coo-chee-coo-chee-cooo.
Specialist #2: No pulse. No pressure. This baby doesn't have a heart.
Specialist #1: I'll be damned.
Specialist #2: And yet . . . this baby is alive.

The Hospital's Executive Assistant enters. He appears agitated.

Assistant: Doctors, please, the press conference. They're waiting.

Lights down on the maternity ward.

Lights up as the specialists and assistant take their places at a table facing the audience. The table skirt advertises the Holy Name Hospital and its new slogan. The Narrator assumes the role of reporter.

Questions for the doctors?

Narrator: Yes. A living baby without a heart? How is this possible?

Specialist #2: Technically, it's not.

Specialist #1: The baby should be dead.

Specialist #2: In fact, the baby could die any minute.

Assistant: It's a miracle is what it is! And it happened right here in our —

Narrator: What about the baby's mom?

Assistant: What about her?

Narrator: I'd like to hear her side of the story. I'd like to ask her a few questions.

Assistant (horrified): What, you mean *talk* with her?

Narrator: Why not?

Assistant: No reason, uh, well, actually — that's impossible. I'm sorry, we're just, she's just — she's in recovery right now.

Lights down on the press conference.

Narrator: In fact, Welda Mae Forms was not in recovery. The so-called Baby Mom was not only alert and well rested, she was, much to the dismay of hospital staffers, quite lucid and most outspoken.

Lights up on Welda Mae Forms, the Executive, and the Assistant. Welda paces like a trapped animal. The Executive and Assistant hover.

Welda Mae Forms: What the hell's going on here! And where's my damn kid! I come into this dump to pop off another slug, which is the last thing I need, and you-all got me strapped down so I can't even see Oprah — big as she is!

Executive: Ms. Forms, please, please calm down. There's something we have to tell you.

Welda Mae Forms: What, is my baby dead or deformed or some damn thing?

Assistant: Uh, well, Miss Forms, actually, it's *more* than that.

Welda Mae Forms: Huh? Was that a hard question, or are you really as stupid as you look? Listen-here, lapdog. Tell your fat-ass boss that as far as I'm concerned I could care less if the little maggot's dead or mutated — hell, I never wanted one tuh begin with. Tried to have it flushed out in one of them clinics, but them damn bible-thumpers chased me away —

Executive (aghast): You were going to . . . ! Cleveland's miracle baby . . . ?

Welda Mae Forms: So I figured I'd drown the slug in booze. Well, did it work or what?

Executive: Ms. Forms, you've got to understand. . . . You've made medical history here today.

Welda Mae Forms: Hee-doggie! Do tell, the little maggot's got three heads? Two weenies? Five titties? What?!

Assistant: This is insane. We can't put *that* before the public. She'll ruin everything!

Lights down on Welda Mae's hospital room.

Narrator: Meanwhile, at that very moment, the afternoon press conference was being fed via satellite to network studios in New York.

We hear the squelch of computer modems linking. Then lights up on a roomful of Network Execs.

Network Exec #1 (tears a fax from a machine): Can this be for real — a baby without a heart?!

Network Exec #2: The affiliate swears it's true.

Network Exec #3: Regardless, it's too late to break tonight.

Network Exec #1: Are you nuts! This stuff goes on immediately.

Network Exec #3: But, but we're airing a live feed from the White House!

Network Exec #2: Who cares? A baby without a heart! Now that's news!

Lights down on the Network Execs.

Narrator: And news it was. Within the hour, satellite-beaming reporters from around the world had descended on Cleveland like the plague, and every last one of them wanted one thing — a baby mom exclusive. Hospital officials acted with both haste and prudence.

Lights up on Welda Mae's hospital room. Welda is still under restraint.

Welda Mae Forms: Let me outta' here! You hear me? Let me out!

Terry Collins, a foppish man with a long scarf around his neck, enters and assesses Welda with dread.

Terry Collins (carefully): Hello, Ms. Forms.

Welda Mae Forms: Who are you? What do ya' want?

Terry Collins: My name is Terry Collins, and I've been hired to be your image consultant.

Welda Mae Forms: Oh yeah? Well, does that mean you can reach up there and change the channel on that pile a' crap TV? Because that's all I've been trying to get from the lazy turds in white that run around here all day. And do they listen? Hell no. Channel Five — wrestling. You get me Bone-Crusher on the tube and lay a six-pack of Huedey Gold 'side my pillow here and I'll be so happy I could pee green.

Terry Collins: Oh my, I see I have my work cut out for me.

Lights down on Welda's room.

Narrator: Terry Collins proved he was worth every penny of his hefty makeover fee. In short order, Ms. Welda Mae Forms was polished, enlightened, and coiffured. At long last, cameras were admitted into her room, and a nation known for its thirst of spectacle tuned in.

Lights up on Welda. She's no longer restrained, and her appearance has been transformed. Terry Collins stands in the shadows like a nervous stage mother.

Welda Mae Forms (her hands folded as if in prayer): With the Lord's help, my precious, precious baby will live. Of course, I can't begin to thank all you wonderful little people out there who have kept me and my baby in your thoughts and prayers. Bless you. Bless you all.

Lights down on Welda.

Narrator: With that one newsbit, the groundswell of public emotion became unquenchable. Overnight, Cleveland's miracle tot became America's most adored critical-list baby. There were news conferences every morning and afternoon, and updates on the baby's condition flashed every hour on the hour, but it wasn't enough. Americans not only wanted to know more: they wanted to know what more they could do. . . .

Lights up on a lunch counter somewhere deep in rural America.

Waitress: And they say that baby could die any moment.

Customer #1: Hate to see that baby die and me not knowing if they was *some-thing* I coulda' done.

Customer #2: By Gawd, I'd give my left nut for that sweet, little innocent lamb.

Waitress: Hell, Ross, baby don't need a go-nad. That baby needs a heart!

Customer #2: Can't give baby my heart. But I'd give that baby anything else. Anything a'tall.

Customer #1: You know, I hear baby likes to watch big-time wrestling! What say we call the hospital and see if we could buy that baby a brand-new color TV! Now wouldn't that make us all feel a sight better?

Lights down on the lunch counter.

Narrator: Calls from like-minded Americans jammed the hospital's switchboard. It was reported that in a single twenty-four-hour period more than twenty thousand color TVs were bought and delivered. Corporate America stood up and took note. Syndicate giant Glam Entertainment culled their best minds and put forward a most alluring concept.

Lights up on an executive board meeting. The Pitchman stands before an easel scrawled with dollar signs.

Glam Entertainment Pitchman: Every night we'll feature the baby's mom, what's her name —

Glam Entertainment Marketeer: Welda Mae Forms.

Glam Entertainment Exec: Welda Mae? Where do you gotta' go to get a name like that?

Glam Entertainment Marketeer: Welda, last stop before Zelda.

Glam Entertainment Pitchman: Whatever. We get her, and we call it "The Last Wish Baby Show." See, every night mom stands in front of the camera holding little baby no-heart in her arms like this, and she's pouting 'cause the docs are telling her how the baby's supposed to die any minute, but — and here's the kicker — before baby goes, baby's made this one last wish . . . get it? Baby's last wish — Last Wish Baby!

Eyes widen with delight. Lights down on the meeting.

Narrator: A deal was proffered and quickly struck with Ms. Forms and her people. That very night, "The Last Wish Baby Show" blew out the ratings board with a whopping seventy-five share. Even more notable, the show's seamless tie-in with corporate sponsors set an industry standard.

Lights up on Welda. She is clutching a cloth-wrapped bundle of baby in her arms.

Welda Mae Forms: Poor, poor baby. Baby doesn't have a heart. Doctors say baby might have to leave us all for heaven any minute now.

The baby cries.

What's that, Baby . . . ?

Welda leans in to the baby and then returns her gaze to the cameras.

Awww. Baby wishes some nice person out there would buy us a, uh . . . a Sony XRK-35 Digital Game System.

Narrator (as the studio announcer): That's right folks, the Sony game system could be Baby's Last Wish. Poor, poor baby. So open up that heart God so kindly gave you, and call the 1-800 number you see now on your screen.

Lights down on "The Last Wish Baby Show."

Lights up on Mrs. Kornfeld's kitchen as a Guatemalan Cleaning Woman removes a Tupperware container.

Meanwhile, in a certain kitchen in Paramus, New Jersey, a certain Guatemalan cleaning woman was wiping down a certain refrigerator when she made an unusual discovery.

Guatemalan Cleaning Woman: Eeeeee! Mios Dios! Eeeee!

Mrs. Kornfeld enters.

Mrs. Kornfeld: What? Que? Que esta? What the hell is it?

Guatemalan Cleaning Woman: Esta la corazón de la niño con *last wish!*

Mrs. Kornfeld: What? What are you talking about?

Guatemalan Cleaning Woman: Niño! Niño con last wish! Niño con last wish!

Mrs. Kornfeld: Baby? You mean *that* baby? That Last Wish Baby? The one on TV? Give me that! *(Studies the heart for a moment.)* Oh-my-God, it's alive! I have the baby heart! What should I do? What should I do?

Guatemalan Cleaning Woman: Llama de medico! Pronto! Pronto!

Mrs. Kornfeld: Call a doctor?! Are you crazy? This is big, really big! I'm calling Howard Stern!

Mrs. Kornfeld reaches for the phone. Lights down.

Narrator: Mrs. Kornfeld's call to the popular radio shock jock was quickly put through, and she not only revealed that she possessed what she believed was the Last Wish Baby's heart, but listeners also learned her cup size and that she enjoyed lesbian sex while a sophomore at Harley Dickerson University. Meanwhile, word of the whereabouts of the newly discovered baby heart spread fast and a race, of sorts, was on. EMS crews were the first on the scene, but no sooner had they readied the baby heart for shipment to Cleveland, when . . . the lawyers arrived.

Lights up on a Lawyer waving a writ.

Lawyer: Halt! Court order!

Lights down on the lawyer.

Narrator: Motions were made. Injunctions issued. Larger questions loomed. The battle for custody of the Last Wish Baby had begun.

We hear the thumping heart.

The hearing to determine the rightful custodial parents of the Last Wish Baby had barely opened when legal fees threatened to exceed even Ms. Welda Mae Forms's recently fatted purse strings. However, with the "Baby Show" still posting record ratings, Ms. Forms saw fit to make full use of her forum.

Lights up on Welda.

Welda Mae Forms (angelic): Poor, poor precious baby. Baby doesn't have a heart . . . know why? Hmmm? *(Bitter.)* 'Cause some East Coast floozy has got it and won't hand it over unless I give her half a' baby's royalties on the —

The baby cries. Welda looks at it.

Yeah, what do you want? *(A beat to compose herself.)* Awww, but of course, my sweet little precious baby.

Welda looks up and smiles for the camera.

Baby wishes there was some nice, pro-bono law firm out there who would take Baby's rightful mother's custody case and, when that was all settled and a certain individual from a certain so-called *Garden State* was financially ruined, that same nice law firm might just be retained to negotiate with those shysters at Glum Entertainment for a more favorable contract . . . idn't that what baby wants? Yes, baby's so sweet. I just hope and pray this won't be baby's last wish.

Lights down on Welda.

Narrator: But no sooner had Welda Mae and her people retained new legal counsel than a shocking courtroom revelation hit the newsstands.

Lights up on a Newsboy hawking his papers.

Newsboy: Read all about it! "Last Wish Baby Show" Hoax! Read all about it!

Lights down on the newsboy.

Narrator: Unsealed court documents alleged that "The Last Wish Baby Show" Baby was not the real Last Wish Baby, the baby born without a heart, but, rather, a sixteen-year-old unemployed actor with a glandular condition. Americans shuddered. Did this mean the Original Last Wish Baby was dead? Or, Heaven forbid, was there even an original Last Wish Baby in the first place? Congressional spouses convened a hearing and demanded answers.

Lights up on a hearing room. Welda Mae, the Hospital's Executive Assistant, and the Phoney Last Wish Baby are seated together under a glaring light. The Narrator serves as inquisitor.

Come forward. State your full name and occupation for the record, please.

Phoney Last Wish Baby: Look, pal, you can't nail this one on me! I'm not even equity! The only reason I signed on to this sham was 'cause the lady there got me tanked up, then threatened to put my nuts in the grinder if I didn't —

Welda Mae Forms: Shut your trap you little —

Phoney Last Wish Baby: Who are you calling little!? The only thing little around here is your heart! You wanna' know why her kid's got no heart? I'll tell ya' why —

Welda Mae Forms: How dare you! And you said you loved me!

Assistant: Stop it! Okay, look, it was all my fault. I agreed to pull the baby from the show, and I was the one who okayed it when the Forms woman wanted to hire the little guy. But I only went along with it 'cause the doctors insisted on keeping the baby in intensive care. That's the God's-honest truth. There really is a Last Wish Baby, there really is a baby without a heart! I can prove it! I swear to God, I can prove it!

Lights down on the hearing room.

Narrator: Needless to say, Americans were skeptical and demanded that proof. Thus, the following night, "The Last Wish Baby Show" aired live from the Holy Name Hospital's pediatric intensive care unit. Viewers held their breath as the Baby Mom ushered the cameras toward the swinging doors which led to Baby's chamber.

Lights up on a hospital corridor. Welda Mae and the Assistant are wearing scrubs. Welda Mae motions for the camera to follow her.

Welda Mae Forms: Shhh. Be quiet. This way, please.

Daryl Wayne Trebleau pushes his way toward Welda.

Assistant: Watch it, he's got a gun!

Blackout. Four shots are fired, and Welda screams. We then hear the high-pitched hum of the Emergency Broadcast System. Lights come up on the Narrator.

Narrator: Four shots, each one following its own fatal trajectory, were fired into the torso and cranial cavity of the woman most Americans knew only as the Last Wish Baby Mom.

Lights up on Daryl Wayne Trebleau as he faces forward and then turns for a profile.

The assailant was identified as Daryl Wayne Trebleau, a slope-shouldered itinerant floral designer from nearby Loraine, Ohio, and, purportedly, the man many believed to be the Last Wish Baby Dad.

Daryl steps forward as if on the witness stand.

Daryl Wayne Trebleau never uttered a single word in his own defense. Rather, he expressed himself through artfully designed floral arrangements.

Daryl holds up a floral bouquet.

Mr. Trebleau's "Not competent to stand trial bouquet" was a lovely and eloquent display of mums, gladioli, and forty-four magnum shell casings set in a handsome earthenware bowl. Meanwhile, in another court in another state, the judge in the custody hearing for the Last Wish Baby had reached a verdict.

Lights down on Daryl Wayne Trebleau. Lights up on a Judge.

Judge: As per the dictates of the honorable State of New Jersey, Court of Domestic Relations, I, Judge Maliss T. Ward Nunn, have found as follows: Said infant, herein-and-ever-after known as "The Original Last Wish Baby," shall be granted ward status of this court and thereby ordered to be joined immediately with heart. So be it, so help us God.

The Judge pounds his gavel. Lights down.

Narrator: With "The Last Wish Baby Show" having been abruptly pulled from the airwaves, no effort was made to appeal the Judge's decision. Thus, a medical team of the nation's leading cardiovascular surgeons were assembled to carry out the court's wishes and, with God's blessing, prolong the baby's life. Meanwhile, high-minded pontificators from the academic, medical, and legal communities pondered the implications of it all for the benefit of viewers at home.

Lights up on a television round-table show.

Pundit #1: The baby phenomenon speaks directly to who we are as a nation.

Pundit #2: And who we, as a nation, are not.

Pundit #3: Yes, who we are and who we are not.

Pundit #1: But *more* to who we are than who we are not.

Pundit #3: Then again, I think one could say this whole baby phenomenon says even more *still* to where we, as a nation, are going than where we, as a nation, have been.

Pundit #2: Or not been.

Pundit #1: Or not, not been.

Pundit #2: Or not been, not-been-not.

Pundit #3: Yes, not-been-not. But not, been-been, not-not, been-not-been.

Pundit #1: Been-not-been been-not. But not-been, been-not-been-been.

Pundit #2: Nor been.

Pundit #1: Nor been-been.

Narrator: We interrupt this program to bring you a special Last Wish Baby medical update. We take you now, *live,* directly to the Hoppenscotch Medical Center in Tarmac, New Jersey.

Lights down on the Pundits. Lights up on a team of Surgeons.

Surgeon #1: The operation to implant the baby heart into the Last Wish Baby was both a success and . . .

Surgeon #2: A failure.

Surgeon #1: The heart was successfully sutured and continues to pump vigorously. Unfortunately, the baby . . .

Surgeon #3: The baby, for reasons we do not fully understand, has ceased all other life-sustaining functions and appears to be in a rapid state of . . .

Surgeon #2: Decay.

Surgeon #1: Decay.

Surgeon #3: Decay.

Lights down on the Surgeons. We hear the thumping of the baby heart.

Narrator: There was no denying it. The Original Last Wish Baby, the baby born without a heart, was now and irretrievably a dead baby but — one with a very healthy heart. And that presented doctors and lawyers with an entirely new set of problems. For one, the baby could not be considered legally dead unless the heart were either stopped or removed. However, if the baby was not legally dead, then removing or stopping the heart would be, in a word, murder. Therefore, despite all appearances to the contrary, the Last Wish Baby was, in the eyes of the law, very much alive. Further, this being a democratic society, it did not take long for Americans to gaze upon their own dearly departed loved ones and find similar cause to stretch the definition of what constitutes life . . . and death.

The thumping fades. Lights up in a restaurant.

Maitre d': Chatterwok, party of four, your table is ready. Chatterwok, party of four —

A Diner wheels in a well-dressed Corpse on a two-wheeler. The Maitre d' is appalled.

Excusez-moi, monsieur! Excusez — Yo! What in God's name do you think you're doing?

Diner: Look here, buddy. . . . My wife may look a little ripe to you, but she's still getting mail, and *that,* in my opinion, qualifies her for your early bird special. Oh, and, uh, nonsmoking section, please.

Lights down on the restaurant.

Narrator: Suddenly, Americans became embroiled in an entirely new moral debate — when did life end? The question was not at all as simple as it sounded. After all, who in this country can say with any real certainty when life begins?

Lights up on a Preacher as he takes the pulpit with two swaying Congregants on either side.

Preacher: The Bible, my friends, is very specific with regard to one thing.
Congregant #1: Tell it now!
Preacher: No bones about it! It says so right here!
Congregant #2: Hallelujah!
Preacher: It says, "dust to dust"!
Congregant #1: Dust to dust!
Congregant #2: Hallelujah!
Preacher: Say it with me, everybody!
Preacher and Congregants: Dust to dust!

Lights down on the Preacher.

Narrator: With these words, the "Right to Extended Life" movement was born. Also known as "Antifuneralists," the movement cannily usurped the image of the Last Wish Baby and made it their own. Soon, that image was being bandied about as a symbol of protest in nearly every cemetery and crematorium in the country.

Lights up on a funeral as a Woman in Black stands over an open grave. The Narrator joins her and offers a shoulder in comfort.

Narrator: Bill was . . . he was a decent guy. A sensible guy. The kind of guy who let you know where he stood even when everything else around just got weirder and weirder —

Two Right to Extended Lifers enter and march around. They are wearing Last Wish Baby/Antifuneralist tee-shirts.

Right to Extended Lifer #1: Burial is murder! Burial is murder! Burial is murder!
Right to Extended Lifer #2: Save the undead! Save the undead! Save the undead!

The Woman in Black shrieks. Lights down on the funeral. The Woman and the Right to Extended Lifers exit. The Narrator remains downstage.

Narrator: Despite their innocent-looking symbol, the movement stressed confrontation. Funeral homes were fire-bombed. Morticians and embalmers were forced to conceal their identities. Even limo drivers were suspect. Many believed reason would prevail and took comfort in the fact that the movement failed to win mainstream support. However, the ranks of the Antifuneralists continued to swell as old members never died off and new recruits were always just a few shovelfuls away. Inevitably, highly paid political pollsters were the first to see the writing on the wall.

The Narrator backs off and returns to the podium. Lights up on a political party meeting of Politicians and their Pollster.

Politician #1: Speaking for my constituents, I say, cut the heart out of that damned baby and you kill the movement. It's that simple!

Pollster: You're dead wrong. Give them what they want. Embrace these people *now*, and they might remember you in the fall.

Politician #2: But that's insane. We'd be giving the right to vote to the dead!

Pollster: Dead, alive — c'mon, this is America — what's the difference?

Lights down on the political meeting.

Narrator: And so, in an historic Rose Garden ceremony, President Jesse "Mind, Body & Soul" Ventura signed the so-called Last Wish Baby Bill into law. The bill not only granted the living-impaired the right to vote but also guaranteed entitlements and protections historically denied to members of this community, a community long regarded by many narrow-minded Americans as sloven, listless, and, euphemistically speaking, somewhat aromatic. *(Beat.)*

As the years passed and the American political spectrum calcified, living-impaired voters inevitably sought a candidate from among their own ranks. Republican strategists boldly exhumed a former California vote-getter whose appeal cut across party lines and living tissue.

The cast steps forward and fervently wave small American flags.

During his first news conference as President, the newly reelected Ronald Reagan announced his plan to fund and build a massive protective shield, which he claimed would act as a deterrent to foreign aggression and help staunch the flow of illegal immigration.

They gradually lose their enthusiasm as we get some indication of a massive shield descending upon them. Lighting and/or perhaps a black scrim being lowered can achieve this effect.

When completed, the shield did more than defend American shores. It stood as a symbol to all that here was a nation entombed, whose people sought no light to guide them and silenced any sound which might stir them. *(Beat.)* Except one . . .

We hear the growing sound of the thump-thump-thumping of the baby heart.

The never-ceasing, ever-pumping, always-thumping heart of the Original Last Wish Baby.

The thumping continues as lights slowly fade to black.

End of Play.

CONSIDERATIONS FOR CRITICAL THINKING AND WRITING

1. FIRST RESPONSE. Though this play is certainly not realistic in style, how does it manage to capture certain contemporary American realities?

2. Why do you think Seebring includes "more than 40 characters" in his play?

3. Describe the function of the narrator. Why is his role essential?

4. What is the play's central conflict?

5. Choose a scene from the play and analyze what it contributes to the rest of the play and how it is related to it.

6. How did you respond to the play's humor?

7. What aspects of American life does Seebring satirize in the play? What serious issues are included that make this satire a play concerned with social commentary a swell as humor?

8. Discuss the meaning of the play's title. Can you think of appropriate alternative titles?

9. William Seebring wrote his own biographical headnote (p. 1177) for this textbook. Read it again. How does his description of himself anticipate and parallel the tone of *The Original Last Wish Baby*?

ESSAYS

HENRY DAVID THOREAU (1817–1862)

Born in Concord, Massachusetts, Henry David Thoreau graduated from Harvard University in 1837 and briefly worked a series of jobs, including teaching and helping out at his father's backyard pencil factory. Eventually, he settled into working about fifty days a year as a land surveyor so that he could devote himself to reading and writing. He published two books during his life, *A Week on the Concord and Merrimac Rivers* (1849) and *Walden* (1854). A number of collections of his essays were also published posthumously. His close observations of and meditations on nature, initially recorded in his voluminous journals, have made him one of the most popular nineteenth-century American authors. "Life without Principle" stands as a kind of summary statement about Thoreau's insistence upon the necessity for living a life in tune with nature rather than an unnatural life driven by societal expectations. Though most of the writing for "Life without Principle" was completed in 1854, the essay was not published in the *Atlantic Monthly* until 1863.

Life without Principle   *1863*

At a lyceum, not long since, I felt that the lecturer had chosen a theme too foreign to himself, and so failed to interest me as much as he might have done. He described things not in or near to his heart, but toward his extremities and superficies. There was, in this sense, no truly central or centralizing thought in the lecture. I would have had him deal with his privatest experience, as the poet does. The greatest compliment that was ever paid me was when one asked me what I *thought*, and attended to my answer. I am surprised, as well as delighted, when this happens, it is such a rare use he would make of me, as if he were acquainted with the tool. Commonly, if men want anything of me, it is only to know how many acres I make of their land, — since I am a surveyor, — or, at most, what trivial news I have burdened myself with. They never will go to law for my meat; they prefer the shell. A man once came a considerable distance to ask me to lecture on Slavery; but on conversing with him, I found that he and his clique expected seven eighths of the lecture to be theirs, and only one eighth mine; so I declined. I take it for granted, when I am invited to lecture anywhere, — for I have had a little experience in that business, — that there is a desire to hear what *I think* on some subject, though I may be the greatest fool in the country, — and not that I should say pleasant things merely, or such as the audience will assent to; and I resolve, accordingly, that I will give them a strong dose of myself. They have sent for me, and engaged to pay for me, and I am determined that they shall have me, though I bore them beyond all precedent.

So now I would say something similar to you, my readers. Since *you* are my readers, and I have not been much of a traveler, I will not talk about people a thousand miles off, but come as near home as I can. As the time is short, I will leave out all the flattery, and retain all the criticism.

Let us consider the way in which we spend our lives.

This world is a place of business. What an infinite bustle! I am awaked almost every night by the panting of the locomotive. It interrupts my dreams. There is no sabbath. It would be glorious to see mankind at leisure for once. It is nothing but work, work, work. I cannot easily buy a blank-book to write thoughts in; they are commonly ruled for dollars and cents. An Irishman, seeing me making a minute° in the fields, took it for granted that I was calculating my wages. If a man was tossed out of a window when an infant, and so made a cripple for life, or scared out of his wits by the Indians, it is regretted chiefly because he was thus incapacitated for — business! I think that there is nothing, not even crime, more opposed to poetry, to philosophy, ay, to life itself, than this incessant business.

There is a coarse and boisterous money-making fellow in the outskirts of   5 our town, who is going to build a bank-wall under the hill along the edge of his meadow. The powers have put this into his head to keep him out of mischief, and he wishes me to spend three weeks digging there with him. The result will be that he will perhaps get some more money to hoard, and leave for his heirs to spend foolishly. If I do this, most will commend me as an industrious and hard-working man; but if I choose to devote myself to certain labors which yield more real profit, though but little money, they may be inclined to look on me as an idler. Nevertheless, as I do not need the police of meaningless labor to regulate me, and do not see anything absolutely praiseworthy in this fellow's undertaking any more than in many an enterprise of our own or foreign governments, however amusing it may be to him or them, I prefer to finish my education at a different school.

If a man walk in the woods for love of them half of each day, he is in danger of being regarded as a loafer; but if he spends his whole day as a speculator, shearing off those woods and making earth bald before her time, he is esteemed an industrious and enterprising citizen. As if a town had no interest in its forests but to cut them down!

Most men would feel insulted if it were proposed to employ them in throwing stones over a wall, and then in throwing them back, merely that they might earn their wages. But many are no more worthily employed now. For instance: just after sunrise, one summer morning, I noticed one of my neighbors walking

---

minute: A note.

beside his team, which was slowly drawing a heavy hewn stone swung under the axle, surrounded by an atmosphere of industry, — his day's work begun, — his brow commenced to sweat, — a reproach to all sluggards and idlers, — pausing abreast the shoulders of his oxen, and half turning round with a flourish of his merciful whip, while they gained their length on him. And I thought, Such is the labor which the American Congress exists to protect, — honest, manly toil, — honest as the day is long, — that makes his bread taste sweet, and keeps society sweet, — which all men respect and have consecrated; one of the sacred band, doing the needful but irksome drudgery. Indeed, I felt a slight reproach, because I observed this from a window, and was not abroad and stirring about a similar business. The day went by, and at evening I passed the yard of another neighbor, who keeps many servants, and spends much money foolishly, while he adds nothing to the common stock, and there I saw the stone of the morning lying beside a whimsical structure intended to adorn this Lord Timothy Dexter's° premises, and the dignity forthwith departed from the teamster's labor, in my eyes. In my opinion, the sun was made to light worthier toil than this. I may add that his employer has since run off, in debt to a good part of the town, and, after passing through Chancery,° has settled somewhere else, there to become once more a patron of the arts.

The ways by which you may get money almost without exception lead downward. To have done anything by which you earned money *merely* is to have been truly idle or worse. If the laborer gets no more than the wages which his employer pays him, he is cheated, he cheats himself. If you would get money as a writer or lecturer, you must be popular, which is to go down perpendicularly. Those services which the community will most readily pay for, it is most disagreeable to render. You are paid for being something less than a man. The State does not commonly reward a genius any more wisely. Even the poet-laureate would rather not have to celebrate the accidents of royalty. He must be bribed with a pipe° of wine; and perhaps another poet is called away from his muse to gauge that very pipe. As for my own business, even that kind of surveying which I could do with most satisfaction my employers do not want. They would prefer that I should do my work coarsely and not too well, ay, not well enough. When I observe that there are different ways of surveying, my employer commonly asks which will give him the most land, not which is most correct. I once invented a rule for measuring cord-wood, and tried to introduce it in Boston; but the measurer there told me that the sellers did not wish to have their wood measured correctly, — that he was already too accurate for them, and therefore they commonly got their wood measured in Charlestown before crossing the bridge.

The aim of the laborer should be, not to get his living, to get "a good job," but to perform well a certain work; and, even in a pecuniary sense, it would be economy for a town to pay its laborers so well that they would not feel that they were working for low ends, as for a livelihood merely, but for scientific, or even moral ends. Do not hire a man who does your work for money, but him who does it for love of it.

It is remarkable that there are few men so well employed, so much to their 10 minds, but that a little money or fame would commonly buy them off from

---

Dexter's: A rich merchant from Massachusetts who had elaborately decorated gardens.
Chancery: Bankruptcy court.
pipe: A cask.

their present pursuit. I see advertisements for *active* young men, as if activity were the whole of a young man's capital. Yet I have been surprised when one has with confidence proposed to me, a grown man, to embark in some enterprise of his, as if I had absolutely nothing to do, my life having been a complete failure hitherto. What a doubtful compliment this to pay me! As if he had met me halfway across the ocean beating up against the wind, but bound nowhere, and proposed to me to go along with him! If I did, what do you think the underwriters would say? No, no! I am not without employment at this stage of the voyage. To tell the truth, I saw an advertisement for able-bodied seamen, when I was a boy, sauntering in my native port, and as soon as I came of age I embarked.

The community has no bribe that will tempt a wise man. You may raise money enough to tunnel a mountain, but you cannot raise money enough to hire a man who is minding *his own* business. An efficient and valuable man does what he can, whether the community pay him for it or not. The inefficient offer their inefficiency to the highest bidder, and are forever expecting to be put into office. One would suppose that they were rarely disappointed.

Perhaps I am more than usually jealous with respect to my freedom. I feel that my connection with and obligation to society are still very slight and transient. Those slight labors which afford me a livelihood, and by which it is allowed that I am to some extent serviceable to my contemporaries, are as yet commonly a pleasure to me, and I am not often reminded that they are a necessity. So far I am successful. But I foresee that if my wants should be much increased, the labor required to supply them would become a drudgery. If I should sell both my forenoons and afternoons to society, as most appear to do, I am sure that for me there would be nothing left worth living for. I trust that I shall never thus sell my birthright for a mess of pottage. I wish to suggest that a man may be very industrious, and yet not spend his time well. There is no more fatal blunderer than he who consumes the greater part of his life getting his living. All great enterprises are self-supporting. The poet, for instance, must sustain his body by his poetry, as a steam planing-mill feeds its boilers with the shavings it makes. You must get your living by loving. But as it is said of the merchants that ninety-seven in a hundred fail, so the life of men generally, tried by this standard, is a failure, and bankruptcy may be surely prophesied.

Merely to come into the world the heir of a fortune is not to be born, but to be still-born, rather. To be supported by the charity of friends, or a government-pension,— provided you continue to breathe,— by whatever fine synonyms you describe these relations, is to go into the almshouse. On Sundays the poor debtor goes to church to take an account of stock, and finds, of course, that his outgoes have been greater than his income. In the Catholic Church, especially, they go into Chancery, make a clean confession, give up all, and think to start again. Thus men will lie on their backs, talking about the fall of man, and never make an effort to get up.

As for the comparative demand which men make on life, it is an important difference between two, that the one is satisfied with a level success, that his marks can all be hit by pointblank shots, but the other, however low and unsuccessful his life may be, constantly elevates his aim, though at a very slight angle to the horizon. I should much rather be the last man,— though, as the Orientals say, "Greatness doth not approach him who is forever looking down; and all those who are looking high are growing poor."

It is remarkable that there is little or nothing to be remembered written   15
on the subject of getting a living; how to make getting a living not merely honest and honorable, but altogether inviting and glorious; for if *getting* a living is
not so, then living is not. One would think, from looking at literature, that
this question had never disturbed a solitary individual's musings. Is it that
men are too much disgusted with their experience to speak of it? The lesson of
value which money teaches, which the Author of the Universe has taken so
much pains to teach us, we are inclined to skip altogether. As for the means of
living, it is wonderful how indifferent men of all classes are about it, even
reformers, so called, — whether they inherit, or earn, or steal it. I think that
Society has done nothing for us in this respect, or at least has undone what she
has done. Cold and hunger seem more friendly to my nature than those methods which men have adopted and advise to ward them off.

The title *wise* is, for the most part, falsely applied. How can one be a wise
man, if he does not know any better how to live than other men? — if he is only
more cunning and intellectually subtle? Does Wisdom work in a treadmill? or
does she teach how to succeed *by her example*? Is there any such thing as wisdom not applied to life? Is she merely the miller who grinds the finest logic? It
is pertinent to ask if Plato got his *living* in a better way or more successfully
than his contemporaries, — or did he succumb to the difficulties of life like
other men? Did he seem to prevail over some of them merely by indifference,
or by assuming grand airs? or find it easier to live, because his aunt remembered him in her will? The ways in which most men get their living, that is, live,
are mere make-shifts, and a shirking of the real business of life, — chiefly
because they do not know, but partly because they do not mean, any better.

The rush to California,° for instance, and the attitude, not merely of merchants, but of philosophers and prophets, so called, in relation to it, reflect the
greatest disgrace on mankind. That so many are ready to live by luck, and so
get the means of commanding the labor of others less lucky, without contributing any value to society! And that is called enterprise! I know of no more
startling development of the immortality of trade, and all the common modes
of getting a living. The philosophy and poetry and religion of such a mankind
are not worth the dust of a puff-ball. The hog that gets his living by rooting,
stirring up the soil so, would be ashamed of such company. If I could command the wealth of all the worlds by lifting my finger, I would not pay *such* a
price for it. Even Mahomet knew that God did not make this world in jest. It
makes God to be a moneyed gentleman who scatters a handful of pennies in
order to see mankind scramble for them. The world's raffle! A subsistence in
the domains of Nature a thing to be raffled for! What a comment, what a
satire, on our institutions! The conclusion will be, that mankind will hang
itself upon a tree. And have all the precepts in all the Bibles taught men only
this? and is the last and most admirable invention of the human race only an
improved muck-rake? Is this the ground on which Orientals and Occidentals
meet? Did God direct us so to get our living, digging where we never planted, —
and He would, perchance, reward us with lumps of gold?

God gave the righteous man a certificate entitling him to food and raiment, but the unrighteous man found a facsimile of the same in God's coffers,
and appropriated it, and obtained food and raiment like the former. It is one

California: The California gold rush of 1849.

of the most extensive systems of counterfeiting that the world has seen. I did not know that mankind were suffering for want of gold. I have seen a little of it. I know that it is very malleable, but not so malleable as wit. A grain of gold will gild a great surface, but not so much as a grain of wisdom.

The gold-digger in the ravines of the mountains is as much a gambler as his fellow in the saloons of San Francisco. What difference does it make whether you shake dirt or shake dice? If you win, society is the loser. The gold-digger is the enemy of the honest laborer, whatever checks and compensations there may be. It is not enough to tell me that you worked hard to get your gold. So does the Devil work hard. The way of transgressors may be hard in many respects. The humblest observer who goes to the mines sees and says that gold-digging is of the character of a lottery; the gold thus obtained is not the same thing with the wages of honest toil. But, practically, he forgets what he has seen, for he has seen only the fact, not the principle, and goes into trade there, that is, buys a ticket in what commonly proves another lottery, where the fact is not so obvious.

After reading Howitt's account° of the Australian gold-diggings one 20 evening, I had in my mind's eye, all night, the numerous valleys, with their streams, all cut up with foul pits, from ten to one hundred feet deep, and half a dozen feet across, as close as they can be dug, and partly filled with water, — the locality to which men furiously rush to probe for their fortunes, — uncertain where they shall break ground, — not knowing but the gold is under their camp itself, — sometimes digging one hundred and sixty feet before they strike the vein, or then missing it by a foot, — turned into demons, and regardless of each others' rights, in their thirst for riches, — whole valleys, for thirty miles, suddenly honeycombed by the pits of the miners, so that even hundreds are drowned in them, — standing in water, and covered with mud and clay, they work night and day, dying of exposure and disease. Having read this, and partly forgotten it, I was thinking, accidentally, of my own unsatisfactory life, doing as others do; and with that vision of the diggings still before me, I asked myself why *I* might not be washing some gold daily, though it were only the finest particles, — why *I* might not sink a shaft down to the gold within me, and work that mine. *There* is a Ballarat, a Bendigo for you, — what though it were a sulky-gully?° At any rate, I might pursue some path, however solitary and narrow and crooked, in which I could walk with love and reverence. Wherever a man separates from the multitude, and goes his own way in this mood, there indeed is a fork in the road, though ordinary travelers may see only a gap in the paling. His solitary path across-lots will turn out the *higher way* of the two.

Men rush to California and Australia as if the true gold were to be found in that direction; but that is to go to the very opposite extreme to where it lies. They go prospecting farther and farther away from the true lead, and are most unfortunate when they think themselves most successful. Is not our *native* soil auriferous?° Does not a stream from the golden mountains flow through our native valley? and has not this for more than geologic ages been bringing down the shining particles and forming the nuggets for us? Yet, strange to tell, if a digger steal away, prospecting for this true gold, into the unexplored solitudes

---

Howitt's account: William Howitt's *Land, Labor, and Gold* (1855).
Ballarat, a Bendigo . . . a sulky-gully: Ballarat and Bendigo were two gold-digging sites in Australia; a sulky-gully was an unproductive site.
auriferous: Producing gold.

around us, there is no danger that any will dog his steps, and endeavor to supplant him. He may claim and undermine the whole valley even, both the cultivated and the uncultivated portions, his whole life long in peace, for no one will ever dispute his claim. They will not mind his cradles or his toms. He is not confined to a claim twelve feet square, as at Ballarat, but may mine anywhere, and wash the whole wide world in his tom.

Howitt says of the man who found the great nugget which weighed twenty-eight pounds, at the Bendigo diggings in Australia: "He soon began to drink; got a horse, and rode all about, generally at full gallop, and, when he met people, called out to inquire if they knew who he was, and then kindly informed them that he was 'the bloody wretch that had found the nugget.' At last he rode full speed against a tree, and nearly knocked his brains out." I think, however, there was no danger of that, for he had already knocked his brains out against the nugget. Howitt adds, "He is a hopelessly ruined man." But he is a type of the class. They are all fast men. Hear some of the names of the places where they dig: "Jackass Flat," — "Sheep's-Head Gully," — "Murderer's Bar," etc. Is there no satire in these names? Let them carry their ill-gotten wealth where they will, I am thinking it will still be "Jackass Flat," if not "Murderer's Bar," where they live.

The last resource of our energy has been the robbing of graveyards on the Isthmus of Darien,° an enterprise which appears to be but in its infancy; for, according to late accounts, an act has passed its second reading in the legislature of New Granada,° regulating this kind of mining; and a correspondent of the *Tribune* writes: "In the dry season, when the weather will permit of the country being properly prospected, no doubt other rich *guacas* [that is, graveyards] will be found." To emigrants he says: "Do not come before December; take the Isthmus route in preference to the Boca del Toro one; bring no useless baggage, and do not cumber yourself with a tent; but a good pair of blankets will be necessary; a pick, shovel, and axe of good material will be almost all that is required:" advice which might have been taken from the "Burker's Guide."° And he concludes with this line in Italics and small capitals: "*If you are doing well at home,* STAY THERE," which may fairly be interpreted to mean, "If you are getting a good living by robbing graveyards at home, stay there."

But why go to California for a text? She is the child of New England, bred at her own school and church.

It is remarkable that among all the preachers there are so few moral teachers. The prophets are employed in excusing the ways of men. Most reverend seniors, the *illuminati* of the age, tell me, with a gracious, reminiscent smile, betwixt an aspiration and a shudder, not to be too tender about these things, — to lump all that, that is, make a lump of gold of it. The highest advice I have heard on these subjects was groveling. The burden of it was, — It is not worth your while to undertake to reform the world in this particular. Do not ask how your bread is buttered; it will make you sick, if you do, — and the like. A man had better starve at once than lose his innocence in the process of getting his bread. If within the sophisticated man there is not an unsophisticated one, then he is but one of the Devil's angels. As we grow old, we live more coarsely, we relax a little in our disciplines, and, to some extent, cease to obey our finest

Isthmus of Darien: Panama.
New Granada: Columbia.
"Burker's Guide": A figurative guide to stealing bodies from cemeteries for dissection.

instincts. But we should be fastidious to the extreme of sanity, disregarding the gibes of those who are more unfortunate than ourselves.

In our science and philosophy, even, there is commonly no true and absolute account of things. The spirit of sect and bigotry has planted its hoof amid the stars. You have only to discuss the problem, whether the stars are inhabited or not, in order to discover it. Why must we daub the heavens as well as the earth? It was an unfortunate discovery that Dr. Kane was a Mason, and that Sir John Franklin was another.° But it was a more cruel suggestion that possibly that was the reason why the former went in search of the latter. There is not a popular magazine in this country that would dare to print a child's thought on important subjects without comment. It must be submitted to the D. D.'s.° I would it were the chicka-dee-dees.

You come from attending the funeral of mankind to attend to a natural phenomenon. A little thought is sexton to all the world.

I hardly know an *intellectual* man, even, who is so broad and truly liberal that you can think aloud in his society. Most with whom you endeavor to talk soon come to a stand against some institution in which they appear to hold stock, — that is, some particular, not universal, way of viewing things. They will continually thrust their own low roof, with its narrow skylight, between you and the sky, when it is the unobstructed heavens you would view. Get out of the way with your cobwebs, wash your windows, I say! In some lyceums they tell me that they have voted to exclude the subject of religion. But how do I know what their religion is, and when I am near to or far from it? I have walked into such an arena and done my best to make a clean breast of what religion I have experienced, and the audience never suspected what I was about. The lecture was as harmless as moonshine to them. Whereas, if I had read to them the biography of the greatest scamps in history, they might have thought that I had written the lives of the deacons of their church. Ordinarily, the inquiry is, Where did you come from? or, Where are you going? That was a more pertinent question which I overheard one of my auditors put to another once, — "What does he lecture for?" It made me quake in my shoes.

To speak impartially, the best men that I know are not serene, a world in themselves. For the most part, they dwell in forms, and flatter and study effect only more finely than the rest. We select granite for the underpinning of our houses and barns; we build fences of stone; but we do not ourselves rest on an underpinning of granitic truth, the lowest primitive rock. Our sills are rotten. What stuff is the man made of who is not coexistent in our thought with the purest and subtilest truth? I often accuse my finest acquaintances of an immense frivolity; for, while there are manners and compliments we do not meet, we do not teach one another the lessons of honesty and sincerity that the brutes do, or of steadiness and solidity that the rocks do. The fault is commonly mutual, however; for we do not habitually demand any more of each other.

That excitement about Kossuth,° consider how characteristic, but superfi- 30 cial it was! — only another kind of politics or dancing. Men were making speeches to him all over the country, but each expressed only the thought, or the want of thought, of the multitude. No man stood on truth. They were

---

It . . . another: Kane died trying to save Franklin in the Arctic not realizing that Franklin was already dead before he set out on his rescue mission.
D. D.'s: Doctors of Divinity.
Kossuth: Lajos Kossuth (1802–1894) was a Hungarian revolutionary hero celebrated in the American newspapers in 1851.

merely banded together, as usual one leaning on another, and all together on nothing; as the Hindoos made the world rest on an elephant, the elephant on a tortoise, and the tortoise on a serpent, and had nothing to put under the serpent. For all fruit of that stir we have the Kossuth hat.

Just so hollow and ineffectual, for the most part, is our ordinary conversation. Surface meets surface. When our life ceases to be inward and private, conversation degenerates into mere gossip. We rarely meet a man who can tell us any news which he has not read in a newspaper, or been told by his neighbor; and, for the most part, the only difference between us and our fellow is that he has seen the newspaper, or been out to tea, and we have not. In proportion as our inward life fails, we go more constantly and desperately to the post-office. You may depend on it, that the poor fellow who walks away with the greatest number of letters proud of his extensive correspondence has not heard from himself this long while.

I do not know but it is too much to read one newspaper a week. I have tried it recently, and for so long it seems to me that I have not dwelt in my native region. The sun, the clouds, the snow, the trees say not so much to me. You cannot serve two masters. It requires more than a day's devotion to know and to possess the wealth of a day.

We may well be ashamed to tell what things we have read or heard in our day. I do not know why my news should be so trivial, — considering what one's dreams and expectations are, why developments should be so paltry. The news we hear, for the most part, is not news to our genius. It is the stalest repetition. You are often tempted to ask why such stress is laid on a particular experience which you have had, — that, after twenty-five years, you should meet Hobbins, Registrar of Deeds, again on the sidewalk. Have you not budged an inch, then? Such is the daily news. Its facts appear to float in the atmosphere, insignificant as the sporules of fungi, and impinge on some neglected *thallus,* or surface of our minds, which affords a basis for them, and hence a parasitic growth. We should wash ourselves clean of such news. Of what consequence, though our planet explode, if there is no character involved in the explosion? In health we have not the least curiosity about such events. We do not live for idle amusement. I would not run round a corner to see the world blow up.

All summer, and far into the autumn, perchance, you unconsciously went by the newspapers and the news, and now you find it was because the morning and the evening were full of news to you. Your walks were full of incidents. You attended, not to the affairs of Europe, but to your own affairs in Massachusetts fields. If you chance to live and move and have your being in that thin stratum in which the events that make the news transpire, — thinner than the paper on which it is printed, — then these things will fill the world for you; but if you soar about or dive below that plane, you cannot remember nor be reminded of them. Really to see the sun rise or go down every day, so to relate ourselves to a universal fact, would preserve us sane forever. Nations! What are nations? Tartars, and Huns, and Chinamen! Like insects, they swarm. The historian strives in vain to make them memorable. It is for want of a man that there are so many men. It is individuals that populate the world. Any man thinking may say with the Spirit of Lodin,° —

Lodin: Thoreau meant to write Loda, a character from James Macpherson's poems of Ossian; the verse is a version of Loda's speech in one of the poems.

"I look down from my height on nations,
   And they become ashes before me; —
   Calm is my dwelling in the clouds;
   Pleasant are the great fields of my rest."

Pray, let us live without being drawn by dogs, Esquimaux-fashion, tearing 35
over hill and dale, and biting each other's ears.

Not without a slight shudder at the danger, I often perceive how near I
had come to admitting into my mind the details of some trivial affair, — the
news of the street; and I am astonished to observe how willing men are to lumber their minds with such rubbish, — to permit idle rumors and incidents of
the most insignificant kind to intrude on ground which should be sacred to
thought. Shall the mind be a public arena, where the affairs of the street and
the gossip of the tea-table chiefly are discussed? Or shall it be a quarter of
heaven itself, — an hypæthral° temple, consecrated to the service of the gods? I
find it so difficult to dispose of the few facts which to me are significant, that I
hesitate to burden my attention with those which are insignificant, which only
a divine mind could illustrate. Such is, for the most part, the news in newspapers and conversation. It is important to preserve the mind's chastity in this
respect. Think of admitting the details of a single case of the criminal court
into our thoughts, to stalk profanely through their very *sanctum sanctorum*° for
an hour, ay, for many hours! to make a very bar-room of the mind's inmost
apartment, as if for so long the dust of the street had occupied us, — the very
street itself, with all its travel, its bustle, and filth, had passed through our
thoughts' shrine! Would it not be an intellectual and moral suicide? When I
have been compelled to sit spectator and auditor in a court room for some
hours, and have seen my neighbors, who were not compelled, stealing in from
time to time, and tiptoeing about with washed hands and faces, it has
appeared to my mind's eye, that, when they took off their hats, their ears suddenly expanded into vast hoppers for sound, between which even their narrow
heads were crowded. Like the vanes of windmills, they caught the broad but
shallow stream of sound, which, after a few titillating gyrations in their coggy
brains, passed out the other side. I wondered if, when they got home, they were
as careful to wash their ears as before their hands and faces. It has seemed to
me, at such a time, that the auditors and the witnesses, the jury and the counsel, the judge and the criminal at the bar, — if I may presume him guilty before
he is convicted, — were all equally criminal, and a thunderbolt might be expected to descend and consume them all together.

By all kinds of traps and signboards, threatening the extreme penalty of
the divine law, exclude such trespassers from the only ground which can be
sacred to you. It is so hard to forget what it is worse than useless to remember!
If I am to be a thoroughfare, I prefer that it be of the mountain-brooks, the
Parnassian streams,° and not the town-sewers. There is inspiration, that gossip
which comes to the ear of the attentive mind from the courts of heaven. There
is the profane and stale revelation of the bar-room and the police court. The
same ear is fitted to receive both communications. Only the character of the
hearer determines to which it shall be open, and to which closed. I believe that

---

hypæthral: Outdoors.
sanctum sanctorum: Holy of holies.
Parnassian streams: Springs of inspiration.

the mind can be permanently profaned by the habit of attending to trivial things, so that all our thoughts shall be tinged with triviality. Our very intellect shall be macadamized,° as it were, — its foundation broken into fragments for the wheels of travel to roll over; and if you would know what will make the most durable pavement, surpassing rolled stones, spruce blocks, and asphaltum, you have only to look into some of our minds which have been subjected to this treatment so long.

If we have thus desecrated ourselves, — as who has not? — the remedy will be wariness and devotion to reconsecrate ourselves, and make once more a fane of the mind. We should treat our minds, that is, ourselves, as innocent and ingenuous children, whose guardians we are, and be careful what objects and what subjects we thrust on their attention. Read not the Times. Read the Eternities. Conventionalities are at length as bad as impurities. Even the facts of science may dust the mind by their dryness, unless they are in a sense effaced each morning, or rather rendered fertile by the dews of fresh and living truth. Knowledge does not come to us by details, but in flashes of light from heaven. Yes, every thought that passes through the mind helps to wear and tear it, and to deepen the ruts, which, as in the streets of Pompeii, evince how much it has been used. How many things there are concerning which we might well deliberate whether we had better know them, — had better let their peddling-carts be driven, even at the slowest trot or walk, over that bridge of glorious span by which we trust to pass at last from the farthest brink of time to the nearest shore of eternity! Have we no culture, no refinement, — but skill only to live coarsely and serve the Devil? — to acquire a little worldly wealth, or fame, or liberty, and make a false show with it, as if we were all husk and shell, with no tender and living kernel to us? Shall our institutions be like those chestnut-burs which contain abortive nuts, perfect only to prick the fingers?

America is said to be the arena on which the battle of freedom is to be fought; but surely it cannot be freedom in a merely political sense that is meant. Even if we grant that the American has freed himself from a political tyrant, he is still the slave of an economical and moral tyrant. Now that the republic — the *res-publica* — has been settled, it is time to look after *res-privata*, — the private state, — to see, as the Roman senate charged its consuls, "*ne quid res-*PRIVATA *detrimenti caperet*," that the *private* state receive no detriment.

Do we call this the land of the free? What is it to be free from King George 40 and continue the slaves of King Prejudice? What is it to be born free and not to live free? What is the value of any political freedom, but as a means to moral freedom? Is it a freedom to be slaves, or a freedom to be free, of which we boast? We are a nation of politicians, concerned about the outmost defenses only of freedom. It is our children's children who may perchance be really free. We tax ourselves unjustly. There is a part of us which is not represented. It is taxation without representation. We quarter troops, we quarter fools and cattle of all sorts upon ourselves. We quarter our gross bodies on our poor souls, till the former eat up all the latter's substance.

With respect to a true culture and manhood, we are essentially provincial still, not metropolitan, — mere Jonathans.° We are provincial, because we do not find at home our standards; because we do not worship truth, but the

---

macadamized: John McAdam (1756–1836) invented a process for paving roads.
Jonathans: A term for Americans.

reflection of truth; because we are warped and narrowed by an exclusive devotion to trade and commerce and manufactures and agriculture and the like, which are but means, and not the end.

So is the English Parliament provincial. Mere country-bumpkins, they betray themselves, when any more important question arises for them to settle, the Irish question, for instance, — the English question why did I not say? Their natures are subdued to what they work in. Their "good breeding" respects only secondary objects. The finest manners in the world are awkwardness and fatuity when contrasted with a finer intelligence. They appear but as the fashions of past days, — mere courtliness, knee-buckles and small-clothes, out of date. It is the vice, but not the excellence of manners, that they are continually being deserted by the character; they are cast-off clothes or shells, claiming the respect which belonged to the living creature. You are presented with the shells instead of the meat, and it is no excuse generally, that, in the case of some fishes, the shells are of more worth than the meat. The man who thrusts his manners upon me does as if he were to insist on introducing me to his cabinet of curiosities, when I wished to see himself. It was not in this sense that the poet Decker called Christ "the first true gentleman that ever breathed." I repeat that in this sense the most splendid court in Christendom is provincial, having authority to consult about Transalpine interests only, and not the affairs of Rome. A prætor or proconsul would suffice to settle the questions which absorb the attention of the English Parliament and the American Congress.

Government and legislation: these I thought were respectable professions. We have heard of heaven-born Numas, Lycurguses, and Solons,° in the history of the world, whose *names* at least may stand for ideal legislators; but think of legislating to *regulate* the breeding of slaves, or the exportation of tobacco! What have divine legislators to do with the exportation or the importation of tobacco? what humane ones with the breeding of slaves? Suppose you were to submit the question to any son of God, — and has He no children in the nineteenth century? is it a family which is extinct? — in what condition would you get it again? What shall a State like Virginia say for itself at the last day, in which these have been the principal, the staple productions? What ground is there for patriotism in such a State? I derive my facts from statistical tables which the States themselves have published.

A commerce that whitens° every sea in quest of nuts and raisins, and makes slaves of its sailors for this purpose! I saw, the other day, a vessel which had been wrecked, and many lives lost, and her cargo of rags, juniper-berries, and bitter almonds were strewn along the shore. It seemed hardly worth the while to tempt the dangers of the sea between Leghorn and New York for the sake of a cargo of juniper-berries and bitter almonds. America sending to the Old World for her bitters! Is not the sea-brine, is not shipwreck, bitter enough to make the cup of life go down here? Yet such, to a great extent, is our boasted commerce; and there are those who style themselves statesmen and philosophers who are so blind as to think that progress and civilization depend on precisely this kind of interchange and activity, — the activity of flies about a molasses-hogshead. Very well, observes one, if men were oysters. And very well, answer I, if men were mosquitoes.

Numas . . . Solons: Legislators of Rome, Sparta, and Athens, respectively.
whitens: Fills with sails.

Lieutenant Herndon, whom our Government sent to explore the Amazon,   45
and, it is said, to extend the area of slavery, observed that there was wanting
there "an industrious and active population, who know what the comforts of
life are, and who have artificial wants to draw out the great resources of the
country." But what are the "artificial wants" to be encouraged? Not the love of
luxuries, like the tobacco and slaves of, I believe, his native Virginia, nor the ice
and granite and other material wealth of our native New England; nor are "the
great resources of a country" that fertility or barrenness of soil which produces
these. The chief want, in every State that I have been into, was a high and
earnest purpose in its inhabitants. This alone draws out "the great resources" of
Nature, and at last taxes her beyond her resources; for man naturally dies out of
her. When we want culture more than potatoes, and illumination more than
sugar-plums, then the great resources of a world are taxed and drawn out, and
the result, or staple production, is, not slaves, nor operatives,° but men, — those
rare fruits called heroes, saints, poets, philosophers, and redeemers.

In short, as a snow-drift is formed where there is a lull in the wind, so, one
would say, where there is a lull of truth, an institution springs up. But the
truth blows right on over it, nevertheless, and at length blows it down.

What is called politics is comparatively something so superficial and inhuman, that practically I have never fairly recognized that it concerns me at all.
The newspapers, I perceive, devote some of their columns specially to politics
or government without charge; and this, one would say, is all that saves it; but
as I love literature and to some extent the truth also, I never read those
columns at any rate. I do not wish to blunt my sense of right so much. I have
not got to answer for having read a single President's Message. A strange age of
the world this, when empires, kingdoms, and republics come a-begging to a
private man's door, and utter their complaints at his elbow! I cannot take up a
newspaper but I find that some wretched government or other, hard pushed,
and on its last legs, is interceding with me, the reader, to vote for it, — more
importunate than an Italian beggar; and if I have a mind to look at its certificate, made, perchance, by some benevolent merchant's clerk, or the skipper
that brought it over, for it cannot speak a word of English itself, I shall probably read of the eruption of some Vesuvius, or the overflowing of some Po, true
or forged, which brought it into this condition. I do not hesitate, in such a
case, to suggest work, or the almshouse; or why not keep its castle in silence, as
I do commonly? The poor President, what with preserving his popularity and
doing his duty, is completely bewildered. The newspapers are the ruling power.
Any other government is reduced to a few marines at Fort Independence.° If a
man neglects to read the Daily Times, government will go down on its knees to
him, for this is the only treason in these days.

Those things which now most engage the attention of men, as politics
and the daily routine, are, it is true, vital functions of human society, but
should be unconsciously performed, like the corresponding functions of the
physical body. They are *infra*-human, a kind of vegetation. I sometimes awake
to a half-consciousness of them going on about me, as a man may become
conscious of some of the processes of digestion in a morbid state, and so have
the dyspepsia, as it is called. It is as if a thinker submitted himself to be rasped
by the great gizzard of creation. Politics is, as it were, the gizzard of society, full

operatives: Factory workers.
Fort Independence: In Boston's harbor.

of grit and gravel, and the two political parties are its two opposite halves, — sometimes split into quarters, it may be, which grind on each other. Not only individuals, but states, have thus a confirmed dyspepsia, which expresses itself, you can imagine by what sort of eloquence. Thus our life is not altogether a forgetting, but also, alas! to a great extent, a remembering, of that which we should never have been conscious of, certainly not in our waking hours. Why should we not meet, not always as dyspeptics, to tell our bad dreams, but sometimes as *eu*peptics,° to congratulate each other on the ever-glorious morning? I do not make an exorbitant demand, surely.

eupeptics: Healthy people.

CONSIDERATIONS FOR CRITICAL THINKING AND WRITING

1. FIRST RESPONSE. This essay was originally delivered as a lecture. How does Thoreau's style sometimes indicate this essay's origins?

2. In what sense does Thoreau keep to his promise to "leave out all the flattery, and retain all the criticism" (para. 2) in his essay?

3. Describe Thoreau's attitudes toward work and money. Do you share his values? Why or why not?

4. What do you think of Thoreau's assertion that "I believe that the mind can be permanently profaned by the habit of attending to trivial things, so that all our thoughts shall be tinged with triviality" (para. 37)?

5. Try imitating Thoreau's pithy style (e.g., "where there is a lull of truth, an institution springs up") by writing something striking about an aspect of contemporary American life.

EDWARD HOAGLAND (B. 1932)

Born in New York City and raised in Connecticut, Edward Hoagland graduated from Harvard University in 1955 and wrote three novels in the early stages of his career. Later, however, he concentrated on writing essays about nature (including human nature) and taught at Brown, Columbia, and Rutgers Universities as well as Sarah Lawrence College and the University of Iowa. Among his many collections of essays are *The Courage of Turtles* (1970), the source of the essay reprinted here; *Walking the Dead Diamond River* (1973); *Red Wolves and Black Bears* (1976); *The Edward Hoagland Reader;* and *Tigers & Ice* (1999).

The Courage of Turtles   *1970*

Turtles are a kind of bird with the governor turned low. With the same attitude of removal, they cock a glance at what is going on, as if they need only to fly away. Until recently they were also a case of virtue rewarded, at least in the town where I grew up, because, being humble creatures, there were plenty of them. Even when we still had a few bobcats in the woods the local snapping turtles, growing up to forty pounds, were the largest carnivores. You would see them through the amber water, as big as greeny wash basins at the bottom of the pond, until they faded into the inscrutable mud as if they hadn't existed at all.

When I was ten I went to Dr. Green's Pond, a two-acre pond across the road. When I was twelve I walked a mile or so to Taggart's Pond, which was lusher, had big water snakes and a waterfall; and shortly after that I was bicycling way up to the adventuresome vastness of Mud Pond, a lake-sized body of water in the reservoir system of a Connecticut city, possessed of cat-backed little islands and empty shacks and a forest of pines and hardwoods along the shore. Otters, foxes and mink left their prints on the bank; there were pike and perch. As I got older, the estates and forgotten back lots in town were parceled out and sold for nice prices, yet, though the woods had shrunk, it seemed that fewer people walked in the woods. The new residents didn't know how to find them. Eventually, exploring, they did find them, and it required some ingenuity and doubling around on my part to go for eight miles without meeting someone. I was grown by now, I lived in New York, and that's what I wanted on the occasional weekends when I came out.

Since Mud Pond contained drinking water I had felt confident nothing untoward would happen there. For a long while the developers stayed away, until the drought of the mid-1960s. This event, squeezing the edges in, convinced the local water company that the pond really wasn't a necessity as a catch basin, however; so they bulldozed a hole in the earthen dam, bulldozed the banks to fill in the bottom, and landscaped the flow of water that remained to wind like an English brook and provide a domestic view for the houses which were planned. Most of the painted turtles of Mud Pond, who had been inaccessible as they sunned on their rocks wound up in boxes in boy's closets within a matter of days. Their footsteps in the dry leaves gave them away as they wandered forlornly. The snappers and the little musk turtles, neither of whom leave the water except once a year to lay their eggs, dug into the drying mud for another siege of hot weather, which they were accustomed to doing whenever the pond got low. But this time it was low for good; the mud baked over them and slowly entombed them. As for the ducks, I couldn't stroll in the woods and not feel guilty, because they were crouched beside every stagnant pothole, or were slinking between the bushes with their heads tucked into their shoulders so that I wouldn't see them. If they decided I had, they beat their way through the screen of trees, striking their wings dangerously, and wheeled about with that headlong, magnificent velocity to locate another poor puddle.

I used to catch possums and black snakes as well as turtles, and I kept dogs and goats. Some summers I worked in a menagerie with the big personalities of the animal kingdom, like elephants and rhinoceroses. I was twenty before these enthusiasms began to wane, and it was then that I picked turtles as the particular animal I wanted to keep in touch with. I was allergic to fur, for one thing, and turtles need minimal care and not much in the way of quarters. They're personable beasts. They see the same colors we do and they seem to see just as well, as one discovers in trying to sneak up on them. In the laboratory they unravel the twists of a maze with the hot-blooded rapidity of a mammal. Though they can't run as fast as a rat, they improve on their errors just as quickly, pausing at each crossroads to look left and right. And they rock rhythmically in place, as we often do, although they are hatched from eggs, not the womb. (A common explanation psychologists give for our pleasure in rocking quietly is that it recapitulates our mother's heartbeat *in utero*.)

Snakes, by contrast, are dryly silent and priapic. They are smooth movers, 5 legalistic, unblinking, and they afford the humor which the humorless do. But they make challenging captives; sometimes they don't eat for months on a point of order — if the light isn't right, for instance. Alligators are sticklers too. They're like war-horses, or German shepherds, and with their bar-shaped, vertical pupils adding emphasis, they have the *idée fixe* of eating, eating even when they choose to refuse all food and stubbornly die. They delight in tossing a salamander up towards the sky and grabbing him in their long mouths as he comes down. They're so eager that they get the jitters, and they're too much of a proposition for a casual aquarium like mine. Frogs are depressingly defenseless: that moist, extensive back, with the bones almost sticking through. Hold a frog and you're holding its skeleton. Frogs' tasty legs are the staff of life to many animals — herons, raccoons, ribbon snakes — though they themselves are hard to feed. It's not an enviable role to be the staff of life, and after frogs you descend down the evolutionary ladder a big step to fish.

Turtles cough, burp, whistle, grunt and hiss, and produce social judgments. They put their heads together amicably enough, but then one drives the other back with the suddenness of two dogs who have been conversing in tones too low for an onlooker to hear. They pee in fear when they're first caught, but exercise both pluck and optimism in trying to escape, walking for hundreds of yards within the confines of their pen, carrying the weight of that cumbersome box on legs which are cruelly positioned for walking. They don't feel that the contest is unfair; they keep plugging, rolling like sailorly souls — a bobbing, infirm gait, a brave, sea-legged momentum — stopping occasionally to study the lay of the land. For me, anyway, they manage to contain the rest of the animal world. They can stretch out their necks like a giraffe, or loom underwater like an apocryphal hippo. They browse on lettuce thrown on the water like a cow moose which is partly submerged. They have a penguin's alertness, combined with a build like a Brontosaurus when they rise up on tiptoe. Then they hunch and ponderously lunge like a grizzly going forward.

Baby turtles in a turtle bowl are a puzzle in geometrics. They're as decorative as pansy petals, but they are also self-directed building blocks, propping themselves on one another in different arrangements, before upending the tower. The timid individuals turn fearless, or vice versa. If one gets a bit arrogant he will push the others off the rock and afterwards climb down into the water and cling to the back of one of those he has bullied, tickling him with his hind feet until he bucks like a bronco. On the other hand, when this same milder-mannered fellow isn't exerting himself, he will stare right into the face of the sun for hours. What could be more lionlike? And he's at home in or out of the water and does lots of metaphysical tilting. He sinks and rises, with an infinity of levels to choose from; or, elongating himself, he climbs out on the land again to perambulate, sits boxed in his box, and finally slides back in the water, submerging into dreams.

I have five of these babies in a kidney-shaped bowl. The hatchling, who is a painted turtle, is not as large as the top joint of my thumb. He eats chicken gladly. Other foods he will attempt to eat but not with sufficient perseverance to succeed because he's so little. The yellow-bellied terrapin is probably a yearling,

and he eats salad voraciously, but not meat, fish, or fowl. The Cumberland terrapin won't touch salad or chicken but eats fish and all of the meats except
bacon. The little snapper, with a black crenelated shell, feasts on any kind of
meat, but rejects greens and fish. The fifth of the turtles is African. I acquired
him only recently and don't know him well. A mottled brown, he unnerves the
green turtles, dragging their food off to his lairs. He doesn't seem to want to be
green — he bites the algae off his shell, hanging meanwhile at daring, steep, head-
first angles.

The snapper was a Ferdinand until I provided him with deeper water. Now
he snaps at my pencil with his downturned and fearsome mouth, his swollen
face like a napalm victim's. The Cumberland has an elliptical red mark on the
side of his green-and-yellow head. He is benign by nature and ought to be as
elegant as his scientific name (*Pseudemys scripta elegans*), except he has contracted a disease of the air bladder which has permanently inflated it; he floats
high in the water at an undignified slant and can't go under. There may have
been internal bleeding, too, because his carapace is stained along its ridge.
Unfortunately, like flowers, baby turtles often die. Their mouths fill up with a
white fungus and their lungs with pneumonia. Their organs clog up from the
rust in the water, or diet troubles, and, like a dying man's, their eyes and heads
become too prominent. Toward the end, the edge of the shell becomes flabby
as felt and folds around them like a shroud.

While they live they're like puppies. Although they're vivacious, they 10
would be a bore to be with all the time, so I also have an adult wood turtle
about six inches long. Her shell is the equal of any seashell for sculpturing,
even a Cellini shell; it's like an old, dusty, richly engraved medallion dug out of
a hillside. Her legs are salmon-orange bordered with black and protected by
canted, heroic scales. Her plastron — the bottom shell — is splotched like a mar-
gay cat's coat, with black ocelli on a yellow background. It is convex to make
room for the female organs inside, whereas a male's would be concave to help
him fit tightly on top of her. Altogether, she exhibits every camouflage color
on her limbs and shells. She has a turtleneck, a tail like an elephant's, wise old
pachydermous hind legs and the face of a turkey — except that when I carry her
she gazes at the passing ground with a hawk's eyes and mouth. Her feet fit to
the fingers of my hand, one to each one, and she rides looking down. She can
walk on the floor in perfect silence, but usually she lets her shell knock porten-
tously, like a footstep, so that she resembles some grand, concise, slow-moving
id. But if an earthworm is presented, she jerks swiftly ahead, poises above it
and strikes like a mongoose, consuming it with wild vigor. Yet she will climb
on my lap to eat bread or boiled eggs.

If put into a creek, she swims like a cutter, nosing forward to intercept a
strange turtle and smell him. She drifts with the current to go downstream,
maneuvering behind a rock when she wants to take stock, or sinking to the
nether levels, while bubbles float up. Getting out, choosing her path, she will
proceed a distance and dig into a pile of humus, thrusting herself to the
coolest layer at the bottom. The hole closes over her until it's as small as a
mouse's hole. She's not as aquatic as a musk turtle, not quite as terrestrial as
the box turtles in the same woods, but because of her versatility she's marvelous, she's everywhere. And though she breathes the way we breathe, with
scarcely perceptible movements of her chest, sometimes instead she pumps her
throat ruminatively, like a pipe smoker sucking and puffing. She waits and

blinks, pumping her throat, turning her head, then sets off like a loping tiger in slow motion, hurdling the jungly lumber, the pea vine and twigs. She estimates angles so well that when she rides over the rocks, sliding down a drop-off with her rugged front legs extended, she has the grace of a rodeo mare.

But she's well off to be with me rather than at Mud Pond. The other turtles have fled—those that aren't baked into the bottom. Creeping up the brooks to sad, constricted marshes, burdened as they are with that box on their backs, they're walking into a setup where all their enemies move thirty times faster than they. It's like the nightmare most of us have whimpered through, where we are weighted down disastrously while trying to flee; fleeing our home ground, we try to run.

I've seen turtles in still worse straits. On Broadway, in New York, there is a penny arcade which used to sell baby terrapins that were scrawled with bon mots in enamel paint, such as KISS ME BABY. The manager turned out to be a wholesaler as well, and once I asked him whether he had any larger turtles to sell. He took me upstairs to a loft room devoted to the turtle business. There were desks for the paper work and a series of racks that held shallow tin bins atop one another, each with several hundred babies crawling around in it. He was a smudgy-complexioned, serious fellow and he did have a few adult terrapins, but I was going to school and wasn't planning to buy; I'd only wanted to see them. They were aquatic turtles, but here they went without water, presumably for weeks, lurching about in those dry bins like handicapped citizens, living on gumption. An easel where the artist worked stood in the middle of the floor. She had a palette and a clip attachment for fastening the babies in place. She wore a smock and a beret, and was homely, short and eccentric-looking, with funny black hair, like some of the ladies who show their paintings in Washington Square in May. She had a cold, she was smoking, and her hand wasn't very steady, although she worked quickly enough. The smile that she produced for me would have looked giddy if she had been happier, or drunk. Of course the turtles' doom was sealed when she painted them, because their bodies inside would continue to grow but their shells would not. Gradually, invisibly, they would be crushed. Around us their bellies—two thousand belly shells—rubbed on the bins with a mournful, momentous hiss.

Somehow there were so many of them I didn't rescue one. Years later, however, I was walking on First Avenue when I noticed a basket of living turtles in front of a fish store. They were as dry as a heap of old bones in the sun; nevertheless, they were creeping over one another gimpily, doing their best to escape. I looked and was touched to discover that they appeared to be wood turtles, my favorites, so I bought one. In my apartment I looked closer and realized that in fact this was a diamond-back terrapin, which was bad news. Diamondbacks are tidewater turtles from brackish estuaries, and I had no sea water to keep him in. He spent his days thumping interminably against the baseboards, pushing for an opening through the wall. He drank thirstily but would not eat and had none of the hearty, accepting qualities of wood turtles. He was morose, paler in color, sleeker and more Oriental in the carved ridges and rings that formed his shell. Though I felt sorry for him, finally I found his unrelenting presence exasperating. I carried him, struggling in a paper bag, across town to the Morton Street Pier on the Hudson. It was August but gray and windy. He was very surprised when I tossed him in; for the first time in our association, I think, he was afraid. He looked afraid as he bobbed about on top of the water, looking up at me from ten feet below. Though we were both accustomed to his resistance and rigidity, seeing him still pitiful, I recognized that I must have done the wrong thing. At least the river was salty, but it was also bottomless; the waves were too rough for him, and the tide was coming in, bumping him against the pilings underneath the pier. Too late, I realized that he wouldn't be able to swim to a peaceful inlet in New Jersey, even if he could figure out which way to swim. But since, short of diving in after him, there was nothing I could do, I walked away.

CONSIDERATIONS FOR CRITICAL THINKING AND WRITING

1. FIRST RESPONSE. How do you explain the title? In what sense are turtles courageous?

2. Why does the real estate development of Mud Pond make the narrator feel "guilty"? How is guilt also a factor (for the reader) as a result of the narrator's description of the painted turtles in paragraph 13?

3. Why does the narrator prefer turtles to other animals? How do you feel about turtles after reading the essay?

4. Choose an animal that is not described in the essay and try describing it in an interesting manner as the narrator does, for example, in paragraph 6.

5. How do you think the final paragraph is related to the rest of the essay? What do you take to be the predominant tone and theme of the essay?

An Author in Depth

This casebook shows you how one student, Michael Weitz, moves through the stages of writing about an author in depth—in his case, Emily Dickinson. His instructor had asked him to write an analysis (about 750 words) on any topic that could be traced in three or four poems by Emily Dickinson. As you read multiple works by the same author, you'll begin to recognize situations, events, characters, issues, perspectives, styles, and strategies—even recurring words or phrases—that provide a kind of signature, making the poem in some way identifiable with that particular writer. Previous knowledge of a writer's work and background information about an author and her historical and cultural moment can set up useful expectations in a reader. Michael read the following introduction to Emily Dickinson and a number of her poems in order to find a thematic grouping that he wanted to analyze. After reading the introduction, he had a good sense of the general issues that Dickinson deals with in her work. As you read about Dickinson, think about what you would want to explore further.

EMILY DICKINSON (1830–1886)

Emily Dickinson grew up in a prominent and prosperous household in Amherst, Massachusetts. Along with her younger sister Lavinia and older brother Austin, she experienced a quiet and reserved family life headed by her father, Edward Dickinson. In a letter to Austin at law school, she once described the atmosphere in her father's house as "pretty much all sobriety." Her mother, Emily Norcross Dickinson, was not as powerful a presence in her life; she seems not to have been

Daguerreotype of Emily Dickinson at seventeen, the only authenticated likeness of the poet. Reprinted by permission of the Amherst College Library.

as emotionally accessible as Dickinson would have liked. Her daughter is said to have characterized her as not the sort of mother "to whom you hurry when you are troubled." Both parents raised Dickinson to be a cultured Christian woman who would one day be responsible for a family of her own. Her father attempted to protect her from reading books that might "joggle" her mind, particularly her religious faith, but Dickinson's individualistic instincts and irreverent sensibilities created conflicts that did not allow her to fall into step with the conventional piety, domesticity, and social duty prescribed by her father and the orthodox Congregationalism of Amherst.

The Dickinsons were well known in Massachusetts. Her father was a lawyer and served as the treasurer of Amherst College (a position Austin eventually took up as well), and her grandfather was one of the college's founders. Although nineteenth-century politics, economics, and social issues do not appear in the foreground of her poetry, Dickinson lived in a family environment that was steeped in them: Her father was an active town official and served in the General Court of Massachusetts, the state senate, and the U. S. House of Representatives.

Dickinson, however, withdrew not only from her father's public world but also from almost all social life in Amherst. She refused to see most people, and aside from a single year at South Hadley Female Seminary (now Mount Holyoke College), one excursion to Philadelphia and Washington, and several brief trips to Boston to see a doctor about eye problems, she lived all her life in her father's house. She dressed only in white and developed a reputation as a reclusive eccentric. Dickinson selected her own society carefully and frugally. Like her poetry, her relationship to the world was intensely reticent. Indeed, during the last twenty years of her life she rarely left the house.

Though Dickinson never married, she had significant relationships with several men who were friends, confidantes, and mentors. She also enjoyed an intimate relationship with her friend Susan Huntington Gilbert, who became her sister-in-law by marrying Austin. Susan and her husband lived next door and were extremely close with Dickinson. Biographers have attempted to find in a number of her relationships the source for the passion of some of her love poems and letters. Several possibilities have been put forward as the person she addressed in three letters as "Dear Master": Benjamin Newton, a clerk in her father's office who talked about books with her; Samuel Bowles, editor of the *Springfield Republican* and friend of the family; the Reverend Charles Wadsworth, a Presbyterian preacher with a reputation for powerful sermons; and an old friend and widower, Judge Otis P. Lord. Despite these speculations, no biographer has been able to identify definitively the object of Dickinson's love. What matters, of course, is not with whom she was in love — if, in fact, there was any single person — but that she wrote about such passions so intensely and convincingly in her poetry.

Choosing to live life internally within the confines of her home, Dickinson brought her life into sharp focus. For she also chose to live within the limitless expanses of her imagination, a choice she was keenly aware of and which she described in one of her poems this way: "I dwell in Possibility — ." Her small circle of domestic life did not impinge on her creative sen-

Manuscript page for "What Soft—Cherubic Creatures—," taken from one of Dickinson's forty fascicles—small booklets hand-sewn with white string that contained her poetry as well as other miscellaneous writings. These fascicles are important for Dickinson scholars, as this manuscript page makes clear: Her style to some extent resists translation into the conventions of print. Courtesy of the Amherst College Library.

sibilities. Like Henry David Thoreau, she simplified her life so that doing without was a means of being within. In a sense she redefined the meaning of deprivation because being denied something—whether it was faith, love, literary recognition, or some other desire—provided a sharper, more intense understanding than she would have experienced had she achieved what she wanted: "'Heaven,'" she wrote, "is what I cannot reach!" This poem, along with many others, such as "Water, is taught by thirst" and "Success is counted sweetest / By those who ne'er succeed," suggests just how persistently she saw deprivation as a way of sensitizing herself to the value of what she was missing. For Dickinson hopeful expectation was always more satisfying than achieving a golden moment. Perhaps that's one reason she was so attracted to John Keats's poetry.

Today, Dickinson is regarded as one of America's greatest poets, but when she died at the age of fifty-six after devoting most of her life to writing poetry, her nearly two thousand poems — only a dozen of which were published, anonymously, during her lifetime — were unknown except to a small number of friends and relatives. Dickinson was not recognized as a major poet until the twentieth century, when modern readers ranked her as a major new voice whose literary innovations were unmatched by any other nineteenth-century poet in the United States.

Dickinson neither completed many poems nor prepared them for publication. She wrote her drafts on scraps of paper, grocery lists, and the backs of recipes and used envelopes. Early editors of her poems took the liberty of making them more accessible to nineteenth-century readers when several volumes of selected poems were published in the 1890s. The poems were made to appear like traditional nineteenth-century verse by assigning them titles, rearranging their syntax, normalizing their grammar, and regularizing their capitalizations. Instead of dashes editors used standard punctuation; instead of the highly elliptical telegraphic lines so characteristic of her poems editors added articles, conjunctions, and prepositions to make them more readable and in line with conventional expectations. In addition, the poems were made more predictable by organizing them into categories such as friendship, nature, love, and death. Not until 1955, when Thomas Johnson published Dickinson's complete works in a form that attempted to be true to her manuscript versions, did readers have the opportunity to see the full range of her style and themes.

Like that of Robert Frost, Dickinson's popular reputation has sometimes relegated her to the role of a New England regionalist who writes quaint uplifting verses that touch the heart. In 1971 that image was mailed first class all over the country by the U. S. Postal Service. In addition to issuing a commemorative stamp featuring a portrait of Dickinson, the Postal Service affixed the stamp to a first-day-of-issue envelope that included an engraved rose and one of her poems. Here's the poem chosen from among the nearly two thousand she wrote:

If I can stop one Heart from breaking   *c. 1864*

If I can stop one Heart from breaking
I shall not live in vain
If I can ease one Life the Aching
or cool one Pain

Or help one fainting Robin
Unto his Nest again
I shall not live in Vain.

   This is typical not only of many nineteenth-century popular poems but of the kind of verse that can be found in contemporary greeting cards. The speaker tells us what we imagine we should think about and makes the point simply with a sentimental image of a "fainting Robin." To point out that robins don't faint or that altruism isn't necessarily the only rule of conduct by which one should live one's life is to make trouble for this poem. Moreover, its use of language is unexceptional; the metaphors used, like that robin, are a bit weary. If this poem were characteristic of Dickinson's poetry, the U.S. Postal Service probably would not have been urged to issue a stamp in her honor, nor would you be reading her poems in this anthology or many others. Here's a poem by Dickinson that is more typical of her writing:

If I shouldn't be alive　　　　　　　　　　　　　　　　*c. 1860*

If I shouldn't be alive
When the Robins come,
Give the one in Red Cravat,
A Memorial crumb.

If I couldn't thank you,
Being fast asleep,
You will know I'm trying
With my Granite lip!

   This poem is more representative of Dickinson's sensibilities and techniques. Although the first stanza sets up a rather mild concern that the speaker might not survive the winter (a not uncommon fear for those who fell prey to pneumonia, for example, during Dickinson's time), the concern can't be taken too seriously — a gentle humor lightens the poem when we realize that all robins have red cravats and are therefore the speaker's favorite. Furthermore, the euphemism that describes the speaker "Being fast asleep" in line 6 makes death seem not so threatening after all. But the sentimental expectations of the first six lines — lines that could have been written by any number of popular nineteenth-century writers — are dashed by the penultimate word of the last line. "Granite" is the perfect word here because it forces us to reread the poem and to recognize that it's not about feeding robins or offering a cosmetic treatment of death; rather, it's a bone-chilling description of a corpse's lip that evokes the cold, hard texture and grayish color of tombstones. These lips will never say "thank you" or anything else.

   Instead of the predictable rhymes and sentiments of "If I can stop one Heart from breaking," this poem is unnervingly precise in its use of language and tidily points out how much emphasis Dickinson places on an individual word. Her use of near rhyme with "asleep" and "lip" brilliantly mocks a euphemistic approach to death by its jarring dissonance. This is a better poem, not because it's grim or about death, but because it demonstrates Dickinson's skillful use of language to produce a shocking irony.

Dickinson found irony, ambiguity, and paradox lurking in the simplest and commonest experiences. The materials and subject matter of her poetry are quite conventional. Her poems are filled with robins, bees, winter light, household items, and domestic duties. These materials represent the range of what she experienced in and around her father's house. She used them because they constituted so much of her life and, more important, because she found meanings latent in them. Though her world was simple, it was also complex in its beauties and its terrors. Her lyric poems capture impressions of particular moments, scenes, or moods, and she characteristically focuses on topics such as nature, love, immortality, death, faith, doubt, pain, and the self.

Though her materials were conventional, her treatment of them was innovative because she was willing to break whatever poetic conventions stood in the way of the intensity of her thought and images. Her conciseness, brevity, and wit are tightly packed. Typically she offers her observations via one or two images that reveal her thought in a powerful manner. She once characterized her literary art by writing "My business is circumference." Her method is to reveal the inadequacy of declarative statements by evoking qualifications and questions with images that complicate firm assertions and affirmations. In one of her poems she describes her strategies this way: "Tell all the Truth but tell it slant —/ Success in Circuit lies." This might well stand as a working definition of Dickinson's aesthetics and is embodied in the following poem:

The Thought beneath so slight a film —   c. 1860

The Thought beneath so slight a film —
Is more distinctly seen —
As laces just reveal the surge —
Or Mists — the Apennine°   *Italian mountain range*

Paradoxically, "Thought" is more clearly understood precisely because a slight "film" — in this case language — covers it. Language, like lace, enhances what it covers and reveals it all the more — just as a mountain range is more engaging to the imagination if it is covered in mists rather than starkly presenting itself. Poetry for Dickinson intensifies, clarifies, and organizes experience.

Dickinson's poetry is challenging because it is radical and original in its rejection of most traditional nineteenth-century themes and techniques. Her poems require active engagement from the reader because she seems to leave out so much with her elliptical style and remarkable contracting metaphors. But these apparent gaps are filled with meaning if we are sensitive to her use of devices such as personification, allusion, symbolism, and startling syntax and grammar. Since her use of dashes is sometimes puzzling, it helps to read her poems aloud to hear how carefully the words are arranged. What might initially seem intimidating on a silent page can surprise the reader with meaning when heard. It's also worth keeping in mind that Dickinson was not always consistent in her views and that they can change from poem to poem, depending on how she felt at a given moment. For example, her definition of religious belief in "'Faith' is a fine invention" (p. 1217) reflects an ironically detached wariness in contrast to the faith embraced in "I never saw a Moor—" (p. 1218). Dickinson was less interested in absolute answers to questions than she was in examining and exploring their "circumference."

Because Dickinson's poems are all relatively brief (none is longer than fifty lines), they invite browsing and sampling, but perhaps a useful way into their highly metaphoric and witty world is this "how to" poem that reads almost like a recipe:

To make a prairie it takes a clover and one bee   *date unknown*

To make a prairie it takes a clover and one bee,
One clover, and a bee,
And revery.
The revery alone will do,
If bees are few.

This quiet but infinite claim for a writer's imagination brings together the range of ingredients in Dickinson's world of domestic and ordinary natural details. Not surprisingly, she deletes rather than adds to the recipe, because the one essential ingredient is the writer's creative imagination. *Bon appétit.*

CHRONOLOGY

1830	Born December 10 in Amherst, Massachusetts.
1840	Starts her first year at Amherst Academy.
1847–48	Graduates from Amherst Academy and enters South Hadley Female Seminary (now Mount Holyoke College).
1855	Visits Philadelphia and Washington, D.C.
1857	Emerson lectures in Amherst.
1862	Starts corresponding with Thomas Wentworth Higginson, asking for advice about her poems.

1864	Visits Boston for eye treatments.
1870	Higginson visits her in Amherst.
1873	Higginson visits her for a second and final time.
1874	Her father dies in Boston.
1875	Her mother suffers from paralysis.
1882	Her mother dies.
1886	Dies on May 15 in Amherst, Massachusetts.
1890	First edition of her poetry, edited by Mabel Loomis Todd and Thomas Wentworth Higginson, is published.
1955	Thomas H. Johnson publishes *The Poems of Emily Dickinson* in three volumes, thereby making available her poetry known to that date.

After reading the background information on Dickinson, Michael used the following Questions for Writing about an Author in Depth to identify the theme he wanted to focus on when looking for a group of poems to write about. He knew the answers to the first and second questions from his background reading and was particularly interested in Dickinson's interest in religious faith. He picked this topic out of interest, but he could as easily have looked for poems that focus on love, nature, domestic life, or writing as well as other topics. What especially intrigued him was some of the information he read about Dickinson, her sternly religious father, and the orthodox nature of the religious values of her hometown of Amherst, Massachusetts. Since this paper was not a research paper, he did not pursue these issues beyond the level of the general remarks provided in an introduction to her poetry (though he might have). He did, however, use this biographical and historical information as a means of framing his search for poems that were related to one another. In doing so he discovered consistent concerns along with contradictory themes that became the basis of his paper. The following questions can help you listen to how *any* writer's works can speak to each other and to you. What topic would you want to focus on in an in-depth paper on Emily Dickinson?

QUESTIONS FOR WRITING
ABOUT AN AUTHOR IN DEPTH

1. What topics reappear in the writer's work? What seem to be the major concerns of the author?

2. Does the author have a definable world view that can be discerned from work to work? Is, for example, the writer liberal, conservative, apolitical, or religious?

3. What social values come through in the author's work? Does he or she seem to identify with a particular group or social class?

4. Is there a consistent voice or point of view from work to work? Is it a persona or the author's actual self?

5. How much of the author's own life experiences and historical moment make their way into the works?

6. Does the author experiment with style from work to work, or are the works mostly consistent with one another?

7. Can the author's work be identified with a literary tradition, such as *carpe diem* poetry, that aligns his or her work with that of other writers?

8. What is distinctive about the author's writing? Is the language innovative? Are the themes challenging? Are the voices conventional? Is the tone characteristic?

9. Could you identify another work by the same author without a name being attached to it? What are the distinctive features that allow you to do so?

10. Do any of the writer's works seem *not* to be by that writer? Why?

11. What other writers are most like this author in style and content? Why?

12. Has the writer's work evolved over time? Are there significant changes or developments? Are there new ideas and styles, or do the works remain largely the same?

13. How would you characterize the writing habits of the writer? Is it possible to anticipate what goes on in different works, or are you surprised by their content or style?

14. Can difficult or ambiguous passages in a work be resolved by referring to a similar passage in another work?

15. What does the writer say about his or her own work? Do you trust the teller or the tale? Which do you think is more reliable?

Religious Faith in Four Poems by Emily Dickinson

After identifying religion as his topic, Michael begins to read poems by Dickinson. He chooses the following four—"'Faith' is a fine invention," "I know that He exists," "I never saw a Moor—," and "Apparently with no surprise." In all four of these poems, religion emerges as a central topic linked to a number of issues including faith, immortality, skepticism, and the nature of God. Michael takes careful notes on these poems using the Questions for Writing about an Author in Depth as well as the Questions for Writing about Poetry (p. 274).

"Faith" is a fine invention   *c. 1860*

"Faith" is a fine invention
When Gentlemen can *see*—
But *Microscopes* are prudent
In an Emergency.

I know that He exists

I know that He exists.
Somewhere — in Silence —
He has hid his rare life
From our gross eyes.

'Tis an instant's play.   5
'Tis a fond Ambush —
Just to make Bliss
Earn her own surprise!

But — should the play
Prove piercing earnest —   10
Should the glee-glaze —
In Death's — stiff — stare —

Would not the fun
Look too expensive!
Would not the jest —   15
Have crawled too far!

I never saw a Moor —

I never saw a Moor —
I never saw the Sea —
Yet know I how the Heather looks
And what a Billow be.

I never spoke with God
Nor visited in Heaven —
Yet certain am I of the spot
As if the Checks were given —

Apparently with no surprise

Apparently with no surprise
To any happy Flower
The Frost beheads it at its play —
In accidental power —
The blond Assassin passes on —
The Sun proceeds unmoved
To measure off another Day
For an Approving God.

A Sample First Response

After reading the poems carefully, Michael writes a first, informal response. His instructor didn't assign a topic but told the class to try to make some connections between the poems they had chosen as a way toward thinking about their thesis. By the end of his first response, Michael has decided to write about Dickinson's conflicting attitudes toward religion.

These four poems all have to do with God and religious
faith. The introduction said that this was an important issue
for Dickinson, and these poems get at that. Though I know the
poems' dates are only approximate, I thought that I might see a
chronological development from doubt to faith. "'Faith' is a
fine invention" (1860) and "I know that He exists" (1862) are
filled with skepticism and a kind of ironic treatment of faith.
So when I read "I never saw a Moor—" (1865), I figured that
Dickinson later turned to a more religious view of life. But
then "Apparently with no surprise" (1884) killed that idea
because the "Approving God" there seems brutal and indifferent
to life. I can't go with a chronological change, so I'll emphasize that Dickinson had conflicting attitudes toward religion--
both positive and negative. The negatives in these poems
certainly seem stronger than the positives. Dickinson sounds
almost angry that faith isn't enough to believe in God. She
cared about religion, but it was not enough for her.

A Sample of Brainstorming

Once Michael has a topic, he is ready to try to organize what he wants to say about each of the poems and how they read against each other. He uses brainstorming to jot down some notes about each poem—basically, what happens—along with notes about the poetic elements, such as word choice, that seem particularly important. By the end of his brainstorming he's come up with a strategy for his paper—to set up "I never saw a Moor—" as a traditional poem against which to read the other three poems he has chosen.

"Faith is a fine invention"

—*only an invention*

—*what's proper*

—*not realistic when it really matters in an emergency*

— negative definition

"I know that He exists"

— God can't be seen

— a kind of game of hide and seek

— surprise!

— but what if death is final

— bad joke, a jest

— "crawled"—a low down joke?

"I never saw a Moor —"

— hasn't seen a moor or ocean, but speaker can imagine or see them

— logic: like the moor and ocean we have not seen, we still believe they're there

— certainty of faith

"Apparently with no surprise"

— frost kills

— God approves—"accidental power"

— deadly routine

— another bad surprise

STRATEGY

— set up "Moor" as traditional faith poem

— use other 3 poems to show her doubts are dominant

Sample Student In-Depth Analysis

After his first response and brainstorming, Michael is ready to write his formal analysis. As you read his essay, notice how he moves from an overarching thesis statement that considers Dickinson's take on religious faith throughout her work into an examination of each poem's variations on the theme. Also pay attention to the careful way in which he uses textual evidence to support his points. What do you think of Michael's final paper? What makes it persuasive — or fail to be persuasive?

Michael Weitz

Professor Pearl

English 270

May 5, 20--

Religious Faith in Four Poems by Emily Dickinson

Throughout much of her poetry, Emily Dickinson wres-
tles with complex notions of God, faith, and religious
devotion. She adheres to no consistent view of religion:
Rather, her poetry reveals a vision of God and faith that
is constantly evolving. Dickinson's gods range from the
strict and powerful Old Testament father to a loving
spiritual guide to an irrational and ridiculous imaginary
figure. Through these varying images of God, Dickinson
portrays contrasting images of the meaning and validity
of religious faith. Her work reveals competing attitudes
toward religious devotion as conventional religious piety
struggles with a more cynical perception of God and religious worship.

Dickinson's "I never saw a Moor--" reveals a vision
of traditional religious sensibilities. Although the
speaker readily admits that "I never spoke with God / Nor
visited in Heaven" (lines 5, 6), her devout faith in a
supreme being does not waver. The poem appears to be a
straightforward profession of true faith stemming from
the argument that the proof of God's existence is the
universe's existence. Dickinson's imagery therefore
evolves from the natural to the supernatural, first
establishing her convictions that moors and seas exist,
in spite of her lack of personal contact with either.
This leads to the foundation of her religious faith,
again based not on physical experience but on intellectual convictions. The speaker professes that she believes
in the existence of Heaven even without conclusive evidence: "Yet certain am I of the spot / As if the Checks

were given--" (7, 8). But the appearance of such idealistic views of God and faith in "I never saw a Moor--" are
transformed in Dickinson's other poems into a much more
skeptical vision of the validity of religious piety.

While faith is portrayed as an authentic and deeply
important quality in "I never saw a Moor--," Dickinson's
"'Faith' is a fine invention" portrays faith as much less
essential. Faith is defined in the poem as "a fine invention" (1) suggesting that it is created by man for man
and therefore is not a crucial aspect of the natural universe. Thus the strong idealistic faith of "I never saw a
Moor--" becomes discredited in the face of scientific
rationalism. The speaker compares religious faith with
actual microscopes, both of which are meant to enhance
one's vision in some way. But "Faith" is useful only
"When Gentlemen can see--" (2) already; "In an Emergency"
(4), when one ostensibly cannot see, "Microscopes are
prudent" (3). Dickinson pits religion against science,
suggesting that science, with its tangible evidence and
rational attitude, is a more reliable lens through which
to view the world. Faith is irreverently reduced to a
mere invention and one that is ultimately less useful
than microscopes or other scientific instruments.

Rational, scientific observations are not the only
contributing factor to the portrayal of religious skepticism in Dickinson's poems; nature itself is seen to be
incompatible in some ways with conventional religious
ideology. In "Apparently with no surprise," the speaker
recognizes the inexorable cycle of natural life and death
as a morning frost kills a flower. But the tension in
this poem stems not from the "happy Flower" (2) struck
down by the frost's "accidental power" (4) but from the
apparent indifference of the "Approving God" (8) who con-
dones this seemingly cruel and unnecessary death. God is

seen as remote and uncompromising, and it is this perceived distance between the speaker and God that reveals
the increasing absurdity of traditional religious faith.
The speaker understands that praying to God or believing
in religion cannot change the course of nature, and as a
result feels so helplessly distanced from God that religious faith becomes virtually meaningless.

Dickinson's religious skepticism becomes even more
explicit in "I know that He exists," in which the speaker
attempts to understand the connection between seeing God
and facing death. In this poem Dickinson characterizes
God as a remote and mysterious figure; the speaker mockingly asserts, "I know that He exists" (1), even though
"He has hid his rare life / From our gross eyes" (3, 4).
The skepticism toward religious faith revealed in this
poem stems from the speaker's recognition of the paradoxical quest that people undertake to know and to see God.
A successful attempt to see God, to win the game of hide-
and-seek that He apparently is orchestrating, results
inevitably in death. With this recognition the speaker
comes to view religion as an absurd and reckless game in
which the prize may be "Bliss" (7) but more likely is
"Death's--stiff--stare--" (12). For to see God and to
meet one's death as a result certainly suggests that the
game of trying to see God (the so-called "fun" [13]) is
much "too expensive" (14) and that religion itself is a
"jest" (15) that, like the serpent in Genesis, has
"crawled too far" (16).

Ultimately, the vision of religious faith that Dickinson describes in her poems is one of suspicion and cyn-
icism. She cannot reconcile the physical world to the
spiritual existence that Christian doctrine teaches, and
as a result the traditional perception of God becomes
ludicrous. "I never saw a Moor--" does attempt to sustain

a conventional vision of religious devotion, but Dickinson's poems overall are far more likely to suggest that
God is elusive, indifferent, and often cruel, thus under-
mining the traditional vision of God as a loving father
worthy of devout worship. Thus, not only religious faith
but also those who are religiously faithful become tar-
gets for Dickinson's irreverent criticism of conventional
belief.

13

Culture and Identity

It is a safe, if sweeping, generalization to say that every piece of literature has something to say about the theme of culture and identity. The cultural identity of a writer always — consciously or not — permeates the writing he or she produces. The stories, poems, plays, and essays in this chapter, however, deal *explicitly* with the twin, often inextricable themes of culture and identity — and many, though by no means all, are autobiographical in nature. As you read, try to identify what each writer has to say about the role culture plays in shaping identity, and think about what you yourself bring to the mix as a reader.

FICTION

ISABEL ALLENDE (B. 1942)

Isabel Allende was born in Peru to an intensely political family. Her father, a Chilean diplomat, suddenly and mysteriously disappeared when she was very young. After high school she worked as a secretary in the Department of Information of the United Nations Food and Agriculture organization in Chile. She subsequently developed a weekly television program and wrote for magazines. In 1973 her father's first cousin Salvadore Allende, the president of Chile, was assassinated. To escape the repressive political climate, she moved to Venezuela in 1975, where she worked as a journalist, taught school, and began writing her first novel based on her exile. An English translation of *House of Spirits* appeared in 1985 and made her one of the most internationally popular women writers from Latin America. Her other translated novels include *Of Love and Shadows*

(1987), *Eva Luna* (1989), *The Infinite Plan* (1993), *Aphrodite: A Memoir of the Senses* (1998), and *Daughter of Fortune* (1999). Though her characters are often faced with terrible choices generated by repressive social conditions, Allende creates strong characters — particularly women — who take courageous risks.

The Judge's Wife   1989

TRANSLATED BY NICK CAISTOR

Nicolas Vidal always knew he would lose his head over a woman. So it was foretold on the day of his birth, and later confirmed by the Turkish woman in the corner shop the one time he allowed her to read his fortune in the coffee grounds. Little did he imagine though that it would be on account of Casilda, Judge Hidalgo's wife. It was on her wedding day that he first glimpsed her. He was not impressed, preferring his women dark-haired and brazen. This ethereal slip of a girl in her wedding gown, eyes filled with wonder, and fingers obviously unskilled in the art of rousing a man to pleasure, seemed to him almost ugly. Mindful of his destiny, he had always been wary of any emotional contact with women, hardening his heart and restricting himself to the briefest of encounters whenever the demands of manhood needed satisfying. Casilda, however, appeared so insubstantial, so distant, that he cast aside all precaution and, when the fateful moment arrived, forgot the prediction that usually weighed in all his decisions. From the roof of the bank, where he was crouching with two of his men, Nicolas Vidal peered down at this young lady from the capital. She had a dozen equally pale and dainty relatives with her, who spent the whole of the ceremony fanning themselves with an air of utter bewilderment, then departed straight away, never to return. Along with everyone else in the town, Vidal was convinced the young bride would not withstand the climate, and that within a few months the old women would be dressing her up again, this time for her funeral. Even if she did survive the heat and the dust that filtered in through every pore to lodge itself in the soul, she would be bound to succumb to the fussy habits of her confirmed bachelor of a husband. Judge Hidalgo was twice her age, and had slept alone for so many years he didn't have the slightest notion of how to go about pleasing a woman. The severity and stubbornness with which he executed the law even at the expense of justice had made him feared throughout the province. He refused to apply any common sense in the exercise of his profession, and was equally harsh in his condemnation of the theft of a chicken as of a premeditated murder. He dressed formally in black, and, despite the all-pervading dust in this godforsaken town, his boots always shone with beeswax. A man such as he was never meant to be a husband, and yet not only did the gloomy wedding-day prophecies remain unfulfilled, but Casilda emerged happy and smiling from three pregnancies in rapid succession. Every Sunday at noon she would go to mass with her husband, cool and collected beneath her Spanish mantilla, seemingly untouched by our pitiless summer, as wan and frail-looking as on the day of her arrival: a perfect example of delicacy and refinement. Her loudest words were a soft-spoken greeting; her most expressive gesture was a graceful nod of the head. She was such an airy, diaphanous creature that a moment's carelessness might mean she disappeared altogether. So slight an impression did she make that the changes noticeable in the Judge were all the more remarkable. Though outwardly he remained the same — he still dressed as black as a crow and was as stiff-necked and brusque as ever — his judgments in court altered dramatically. To general amazement, he found the youngster who robbed the Turkish shopkeeper innocent, on the grounds that she had been selling him short for years, and the money he had taken could therefore be seen as compensation. He also refused to punish an adulterous wife, arguing that since her husband himself kept a mistress he did not have the moral authority to demand fidelity. Word in the town had it that the Judge was transformed the minute he crossed the threshold at home: that he flung off his gloomy apparel, rollicked with his children, chuckled as he sat Casilda on his lap. Though no one ever succeeded in confirming these rumors, his wife got the credit for his newfound kindness, and her reputation grew accordingly. None of this was of the slightest interest to Nicolas Vidal, who as a wanted man was sure there would be no mercy shown him the day he was brought in chains before the Judge. He paid no heed to the talk about Doña Casilda, and the rare occasions he glimpsed her from afar only confirmed his first impression of her as a lifeless ghost.

Born thirty years earlier in a windowless room in the town's only brothel, Vidal was the son of Juana the Forlorn and an unknown father. The world had no place for him. His mother knew it, and so tried to wrench him from her womb with sprigs of parsley, candle butts, douches of ashes, and other violent purgatives, but the child clung to life. Once, years later, Juana was looking at her mysterious son and realized that, while all her infallible methods of aborting might have failed to dislodge him, they had none the less tempered his soul to the hardness of iron. As soon as he came into the world, he was lifted in the air by the midwife who examined him by the light of an oil lamp. She saw he had four nipples.

"Poor creature: he'll lose his head over a woman," she predicted, drawing on her wealth of experience.

Her words rested on the boy like a deformity. Perhaps a woman's love would have made his existence less wretched. To atone for all her attempts to kill him before birth, his mother chose him a beautiful first name, and an imposing family name picked at random. But the lofty name of Nicolas Vidal was no protection against the fateful cast of his destiny. His face was scarred from knife fights before he reached his teens, so it came as no surprise to decent folk that he ended up a bandit. By the age of twenty, he had become the leader of a band of desperadoes. The habit of violence toughened his sinews. The solitude he was condemned to for fear of falling prey to a woman lent his face a doleful expression. As soon as they saw him, everyone in the town knew from his eyes, clouded by tears he would never allow to fall, that he was the son of Juana the Forlorn. Whenever there was an outcry after a crime had been committed in the region, the police set out with dogs to track him down, but after scouring the hills invariably returned empty-handed. In all honesty they preferred it that way, because they could never have fought him. His gang gained such a fearsome reputation that the surrounding villages and estates paid to keep them away. This money would have been plenty for his men, but Nicolas Vidal kept them constantly on horseback in a whirlwind of death and destruction so they would not lose their taste for battle. Nobody dared take them on. More than once, Judge Hidalgo had asked the government to send troops to reinforce the police, but after several useless forays the soldiers returned to their barracks and Nicolas Vidal's gang to their exploits. On one occasion only did Vidal come close to falling into the hands of justice, and then he was saved by his hardened heart.

Weary of seeing the laws flouted, Judge Hidalgo resolved to forget his 5 scruples and set a trap for the outlaw. He realized that to defend justice he was committing an injustice, but chose the lesser of two evils. The only bait he could find was Juana the Forlorn, as she was Vidal's sole known relative. He had her dragged from the brothel where by now, since no clients were willing to pay for her exhausted charms, she scrubbed floors and cleaned out the lavatories. He put her in a specially made cage which was set up in the middle of the Plaza de Armas, with only a jug of water to meet her needs.

"As soon as the water's finished, she'll start to squawk. Then her son will come running, and I'll be waiting for him with the soldiers," Judge Hidalgo said.

News of this torture, unheard of since the days of slavery, reached Nicolas Vidal's ears shortly before his mother drank the last of the water. His men watched as he received the report in silence, without so much as a flicker of emotion on his blank lone wolf's face, or a pause in the sharpening of his dagger blade on a leather strap. Though for many years he had had no contact with Juana, and retained few happy childhood memories, this was a question of honor. No man can accept such an insult, his gang reasoned as they got guns and horses ready to rush into the ambush and, if need be, lay down their lives. Their chief showed no sign of being in a hurry. As the hours went by tension mounted in the camp. The perspiring, impatient men stared at each other, not daring to speak. Fretful, they caressed the butts of their revolvers and their horses' manes, or busied themselves coiling their lassos. Night fell. Nicolas Vidal was the only one in the camp who slept. At dawn, opinions were divided. Some of the men reckoned he was even more heartless than they had ever imagined, while others maintained their leader was planning a spectacular ruse to free his mother. The one thing that never crossed any of their minds was that his courage might have failed him, for he had always proved he had more than enough to spare. By noon, they could bear the suspense no longer, and went to ask him what he planned to do.

"I'm not going to fall into his trap like an idiot," he said.

"What about your mother?"

"We'll see who's got more balls, the Judge or me," Nicolas Vidal coolly 10 replied.

By the third day, Juana the Forlorn's cries for water had ceased. She lay curled on the cage floor, with wildly staring eyes and swollen lips, moaning softly whenever she regained consciousness, and the rest of the time dreaming she was in hell. Four armed guards stood watch to make sure nobody brought her water. Her groans penetrated the entire town, filtering through closed shutters or being carried by the wind through the cracks in doors. They got stuck in corners, where dogs worried at them, and passed them on in their howls to the newly born, so that whoever heard them was driven to distraction. The Judge couldn't prevent a steady stream of people filing through the square to show their sympathy for the old woman, and was powerless to stop the prostitutes going on a sympathy strike just as the miners' fortnight holiday was beginning. That Saturday, the streets were thronged with lusty workmen desperate to unload their savings, who now found nothing in town apart from the spectacle of the cage and this universal wailing carried mouth to mouth down from the river to the coast road. The priest headed a group of Catholic ladies to plead with Judge Hidalgo for Christian mercy and to beg him to spare the poor old innocent woman such a frightful death, but the man of the law bolted his door and refused to listen to them. It was then they decided to turn to Doña Casilda.

The Judge's wife received them in her shady living room. She listened to their pleas looking, as always, bashfully down at the floor. Her husband had not been home for three days, having locked himself in his office to wait for Nicolas Vidal to fall into his trap. Without so much as glancing out of the window, she was aware of what was going on, for Juana's long-drawn-out agony had forced its way even into the vast rooms of her residence. Doña Casilda waited until her visitors had left, dressed her children in their Sunday best, tied a black ribbon round their arms as a token of mourning, then strode out with them in the direction of the square. She carried a food hamper and a bottle of fresh water for Juana the Forlorn. When the guards spotted her turning the corner, they realized what she was up to, but they had strict orders, and barred her way with their rifles. When, watched now by a small crowd, she persisted, they grabbed her by the arms. Her children began to cry.

Judge Hidalgo sat in his office overlooking the square. He was the only person in the town who had not stuffed wax in his ears, because his mind was intent on the ambush and he was straining to catch the sound of horses' hoofs, the signal for action. For three long days and nights he put up with Juana's groans and the insults of the townspeople gathered outside the courtroom, but when he heard his own children start to wail he knew he had reached the bounds of his endurance. Vanquished, he walked out of the office with his three days' beard, his eyes bloodshot from keeping watch, and the weight of a thousand years on his back. He crossed the street, turned into the square and came face to face with his wife. They gazed at each other sadly. In seven years, this was the first time she had gone against him, and she had chosen to do so in front of the whole town. Easing the hamper and the bottle from Casilda's grasp, Judge Hidalgo himself opened the cage to release the prisoner.

"Didn't I tell you he wouldn't have the balls?" laughed Nicolas Vidal when the news reached him.

His laughter turned sour the next day, when he heard that Juana the Forlorn had hanged herself from the chandelier in the brothel where she had spent her life, overwhelmed by the shame of her only son leaving her to fester in a cage in the middle of the Plaza de Armas. 15

"That Judge's hour has come," said Vidal.

He planned to take the Judge by surprise, put him to a horrible death, then dump him in the accursed cage for all to see. The Turkish shopkeeper sent him word that the Hidalgo family had left that same night for a seaside resort to rid themselves of the bitter taste of defeat.

The Judge learned he was being pursued when he stopped to rest at a wayside inn. There was little protection for him there until an army patrol could arrive, but he had a few hours' start, and his motor car could outrun the gang's horses. He calculated he could make it to the next town and summon help there. He ordered his wife and children into the car, put his foot down on the accelerator, and sped off along the road. He ought to have arrived with time to spare, but it had been ordained that Nicolas Vidal was that day to meet the woman who would lead him to his doom.

Overburdened by the sleepless nights, the townspeople's hostility, the blow to his pride, and the stress of this race to save his family, Judge Hidalgo's heart gave a massive jolt, then split like a pomegranate. The car ran out of control, turned several somersaults and finally came to a halt in the ditch. It took Doña Casilda some minutes to work out what had happened. Her husband's advancing years had often led her to think what it would be like to be left a widow, yet she had never imagined he would leave her at the mercy of his enemies. She wasted little time dwelling on her situation, knowing she must act at once to get her children to safety. When she gazed around her, she almost burst into tears. There was no sign of life in the vast plain baked by a scorching sun, only barren cliffs beneath an unbounded sky bleached colorless by the fierce light. A second look revealed the dark shadow of a passage or cave on a distant slope, so she ran towards it with two children in her arms and the third clutching her skirts.

One by one she carried her children up the cliff. The cave was a natural   20
one, typical of many in the region. She peered inside to be certain it wasn't the den of some wild animal, sat her children against its back wall, then, dry-eyed, kissed them good-bye.

"The troops will come to find you a few hours from now. Until then, don't for any reason whatsoever come out of here, even if you hear me screaming — do you understand?"

Their mother gave one final glance at the terrified children clinging to each other, then clambered back down to the road. She reached the car, closed her husband's eyes, smoothed back her hair and settled down to wait. She had no idea how many men were in Nicolas Vidal's gang, but prayed there were a lot of them so it would take them all the more time to have their way with her. She gathered strength pondering on how long it would take her to die if she determined to do it as slowly as possible. She willed herself to be desirable, luscious, to create more work for them and thus gain time for her children.

Casilda did not have long to wait. She soon saw a cloud of dust on the horizon and heard the gallop of horses' hoofs. She clenched her teeth. Then, to her astonishment, she saw there was only one rider, who stopped a few yards from her, gun at the ready. By the scar on his face she recognized Nicolas Vidal, who had set out all alone in pursuit of Judge Hidalgo, as this was a private matter between the two men. The Judge's wife understood she was going to have to endure something far worse than a lingering death.

A quick glance at her husband was enough to convince Vidal that the Judge was safely out of his reach in the peaceful sleep of death. But there was his wife, a shimmering presence in the plain's glare. He leapt from his horse and strode over to her. She did not flinch or lower her gaze, and to his amazement he realized that for the first time in his life another person was facing him without fear. For several seconds that stretched to eternity, they sized each other up, trying to gauge the other's strength, and their own powers of resistance. It gradually dawned on both of them that they were up against a formidable opponent. He lowered his gun. She smiled.

Casilda won each moment of the ensuing hours. To all the wiles of seduc- 25 tion known since the beginning of time she added new ones born of necessity to bring this man to the heights of rapture. Not only did she work on his body like an artist, stimulating his every fiber to pleasure, but she brought all the delicacy of her spirit into play on her side. Both knew their lives were at stake, and this added a new and terrifying dimension to their meeting. Nicolas Vidal had fled from love since birth, and knew nothing of intimacy, tenderness, secret laughter, the riot of the senses, the joy of shared passion. Each minute brought the detachment of troops and the noose that much nearer, but he gladly accepted this in return for her prodigious gifts. Casilda was a passive, demure, timid woman who had been married to an austere old man in front of whom she had never even dared appear naked. Not once during that unforgettable afternoon did she forget that her aim was to win time for her children, and yet at some point, marveling at her own possibilities, she gave herself completely, and felt something akin to gratitude towards him. That was why, when she heard the soldiers in the distance, she begged him to flee to the hills. Instead, Nicolas Vidal chose to fold her in a last embrace, thus fulfilling the prophecy that had sealed his fate from the start.

Considerations for Critical Thinking and Writing

1. FIRST RESPONSE. Do you think it is fate that drives this plot or something else? How do you account for Nicolas Vidal's behavior?

2. How is Judge Hidalgo affected by his marriage to Casilda? What kind of judge is he?

3. Discuss how issues of justice are important to this story.

4. Characterize Vidal. How has his relationship with his mother influenced his life?

5. Why do you think Casilda "gave herself completely [to Vidal], and felt something akin to gratitude towards him" (para. 25)?

6. To what extent is this story about each character's ability to be courageous?

7. Describe the story's central conflict. Is there a resolution?

8. Explain what you think is the story's theme.

9. How is the cultural context of the story an important element for understanding and appreciating it?

Alison Baker (B. 1953)

Born in Pennsylvania, Alison Baker was raised in Indiana and has subsequently lived in Chicago, Maine, and Utah. After graduating from Reed College, she worked in a hospital as a library assistant and earned a master's degree in library science. She now lives and writes in Oregon. Her stories are collected in *How I Came West and Why I Stayed* (1993) and in *Loving*

Wanda Beaver: Novella and Stories (1995). "Better Be Ready 'Bout Half Past Eight" originally appeared in the *Atlantic Monthly* and was awarded first prize in the 1994 competition for the O. Henry Awards. Baker describes her fiction writing as "a comforting way of revising both my own past and the apparent present, as well as foretelling the unlikeliest of much-to-be-desired futures."

Better Be Ready 'Bout Half Past Eight   *1993*

"I'm changing sex," Zach said.

Byron looked up from his lab notebook. "For the better, I hope."

"This is something I've never discussed with you," Zach said, stepping back and leaning against the office door. "I need to. Do you want to get a beer or something?"

"I have to transcribe this data," Byron said. "What do you need to discuss?"

"My sexuality," Zach said. "The way I feel trapped in the wrong body."   5

"Well, I suppose you were right," Byron said.

"Right?" Zach said.

"Not to discuss it with me," Byron said. "It's none of my business, is it?"

"We've been friends a long time," Zach said.

"Have you always felt this way?" Byron said.   10

Zach nodded. "I didn't know it was this I was feeling," he said. "But I've been in therapy for over a year now, and I'm sure."

"You've been seeing Terry about *this*?"

Byron had given Zach the name of Terry Wu, whom he himself had once consulted professionally.

Zach nodded again.

"He's terrific. He knew the first time he met me what I was."   15

"What were you?" Byron said.

"A woman," Zach said.

Had he missed any signs? Byron sat frowning at the computer screen. Then he stood, shoved his hands into his pockets, and stared out the window. He could see the sky and the top of the snow-covered hills. On this floor all the windows started at chin level, so you couldn't see the parking lot or the ground outside; you could see only distances, clouds, and sections of sunrise.

He walked up and down the hall for a while. The surrounding labs buzzed with action, students leaning intently over whirring equipment, technicians laughing over coffee. Secretaries clopped through the hall and said, "Hi, Dr. Glass," when they passed him. He could ignore them, because he had a reputation for being absentminded; he was absorbed in his research, or perhaps in a new poem. He was well known, particularly in scientific circles, for his poetry. He edited the poetry column of a major scientific research journal. He judged many poetry-writing competitions, and he had edited anthologies.

What had he missed?   20

Worrying about it was useless. Zach's sexuality wasn't his concern. "Just as long as it doesn't interfere with work," he would say. "I can't have people's personal lives taking over the lab."

But in fact he didn't believe in the separation of work and home. "If your love life's screwed up, you're probably going to screw up the science," he'd said more than once when he sent a sobbing technician home, or gave a distraught graduate student the name of a counselor. As a result, his workers did sacrifice, to some extent, their personal lives; they came in on weekends or at night to see to an experiment. The dictum, even if artificial, seemed to work.

"Go on home," he imagined himself saying to Zach, patting him on the shoulder. "Come back when it's all over."

But that wouldn't work. For one thing, the fretting wouldn't end. For another thing, Zach wouldn't be Zach when he came back. He would be a woman Byron had never met.

"He's putting you on," Emily said. She was sitting at the table, ostensibly 25 editing a paper on the synthesis of mRNA at the transcriptional level in the Drosophila Per protein, but whenever the spoon Byron held approached Toby's mouth, her own mouth opened in anticipation.

"Nope," Byron said, spooning more applesauce from the jar. "He wanted to tell me before he started wearing makeup."

"If Zach thinks that's the definition of women, he's headed for trouble," Emily said. "I suppose he's shaving his legs and getting silicone implants too."

"Not to mention waxing his bikini line," Byron said.

"Oh, God," Emily said, laughing. "I don't want to hear any more." She handed Byron a washcloth, and Byron carefully wiped applesauce off Toby's chin. "How would you know you were the wrong sex?"

"Women's intuition?" Byron said.   30

"Very attractive," he said the next morning, when Zach walked into the lab wearing eye shadow.

"Don't make fun of me, okay?" Zach said.

Byron felt embarrassed. "I didn't mean anything," he said. "I mean, it's subtle and everything."

Zach looked pleased. "I've been practicing," he said. "You know what? My younger brother wears more makeup than I do. Is this a crazy world or what?"

"Yeah," Byron said. He'd met Zach's brother, whose makeup was usually 35 black. "Are you doing this gradually? Or are you sort of going cold turkey? I mean, will you come in in nylons and spike heels some morning?"

"Babe," Zach said, "I've been getting hormones for six months. Don't you notice anything different?"

He put his hands on his hips and turned slowly around, and Byron saw discernible breasts pushing up the cloth of Zach's rugby shirt. Byron felt a little faint, but he managed to say, "You're wearing a bra."

Zach went over to look in the mirror behind the door. He stood on tiptoe, staring intently at his breasts for a moment, and then, as he took his lab coat off the hook, he said, "God, I'm starting to feel good."

"You are?" was all Byron could manage. He was wondering how to say, without hurting Zach's new feelings, Don't call me babe.

All day he tried not to look at Zach's breasts, but there they were, right in 40 front of him, as Zach bent over the bench, or peered into the microscope, or leaned back with his hands behind his neck, staring at the ceiling, thinking.

"I'm heading out," Byron said to Sarah in midafternoon.

"Are you okay?" she said, looking up from the bench. "You look a little peaked."

"I'm fine," Byron said. "I'll be back in the morning."

But once out in the parking lot, sitting in his car, he could think of no place he wanted to go. He hung on to the steering wheel and stared at the Mercedes in front of him, which had a Utah license plate that read IMAQT. A woman, of course.

Well, it's not *my* life, he thought. Nothing has changed for me.   45

"I haven't had this much trouble with breasts since I was sixteen," he said to Emily as they sat at the kitchen table watching the sunset.

"How big are they?" Emily said.

"Jesus, I don't know," Byron said.

"Bigger than mine?" she said.

Byron looked at Emily's breasts, which were bigger since she'd had Toby.   50
"No," he said. "But I think they've just started."

"You mean he'll keep taking hormones till they're the size he wants?" Emily said. "I should do that."

"You know," Byron said, "what I don't understand is why it bothers me so much. You'd think he's doing it to spite me."

"Going to meetings will be more expensive," she said.

"What do you mean?" Byron said.

"Honey," Emily said, "if Zach's a woman, you won't be sharing a room.   55
Will you?"

"Oh," Byron said. "Do you think it will make that much difference?"

"You're already obsessed with his breasts," Emily said. "Wait till he's fully equipped."

Byron leaned his head on his hand. He hadn't even *thought* about the surgical procedure.

"I think you're letting this come between us," Zach said the next day.

"What?" Byron said.   60

"We've been friends a long time. I don't want to lose that."

"Zach," Byron said, "I don't see how things can stay the same."

"But I'm still the same person," Zach said.

Byron was not at all sure of that. "Well, how's it going?" he finally said.

Zach seemed pleased to be asked. He sat down on the desk and folded his   65
arms. "Really well," he said. "The surgeon says the physiological changes are right on schedule. I'm scheduled for surgery starting next month."

"Starting?" Byron said.

"I'm going to have a series of operations," Zach said. "Over several months. Cosmetic surgery for the most part."

"Zach," Byron said, "maybe it's none of my business, but don't you feel—" He cast about for the right way to say it. "Won't the operations make you feel, uh, mutilated?"

Zach shook his head. "That's what it's all about," he said. "They won't. To tell you the truth, in the past year or two I've come to feel as if my penis is an alien growth on my body. It's my *enemy*, Byron. This surgery's going to liberate me."

Byron crossed his legs. "I don't think I can relate to that," he said.   70

"I know," Zach said. "My support group says nobody really understands."

"Your support group?" Byron said.

"Women who've had the operation," Zach said, "or are in the process. We meet every week."

"How many are there?"

"More than you'd think," Zach said.   75

"So," Byron said. "Are you — I mean, should I call you 'she' now?"

Zach grinned. "I've been calling myself 'she' for a while. But so far nobody outside my group has."

"Well," Byron said. He tried to look at Zach and smile, but he couldn't do both at once. He smiled first, and then looked. "I'll work on it," he said. "But it's not exactly easy for me either, you know."

"I know," Zach said. "I really appreciate your trying to understand." He stood up. "Back to work," he said. "Oh." He turned around with his hand on the doorknob. "I'm changing my name, too. As of next month I'll be Zoe."

"Zoe," Byron said.   80

"It means 'life,'" Zach said. "Mine is finally beginning."

"It means 'life,'" Byron said mincingly to Toby as he pulled the soggy diaper out from under him. "'Life,' for Christ's sake."

Toby smiled.

"What's he been for thirty-eight years — dead?" Byron said. He dried Toby and sprinkled him with powder, smoothing it into the soft creases. As he lifted Toby's feet to slide a clean diaper underneath him, a stream of pee arced gracefully into the air and hit Byron in the chest, leaving a trail of droplets across Toby's powdered thighs.

"Oh, geez," Byron said. "Couldn't you wait ten seconds?" He reached for   85
the washcloth and wiped the baby off. Then he wiggled the little penis between his thumb and forefinger. "You know what you are, don't you?" he said, leaning over and peering into Toby's face. "A little man. No question about that."

Toby laughed.

After he'd put Toby into the crib, Byron went into the bathroom, pulling his T-shirt off. He caught sight of himself in the mirror and stood still. With the neckband of the shirt stuck on his head, framing his face, the shirt hung from his head like a wig of green hair.

He took his glasses off to blur the details and moved close to the mirror, looking at the line of his jaw. Was his jaw strong? Some women who had what were called "strong features" were quite attractive. Byron's mother used to say that Emily was built like a football player, but Byron had always thought she was sexy.

He put his glasses on and stepped back, bending his knees so that only his shoulders showed in the glass. With long hair around his face, and a few hormones to change his shape a little, he'd make a terrific woman.

He opened the medicine cabinet and took out one of Emily's lipsticks. He   90
leaned forward and spread it on his mouth, and as he pressed his lips together, a woman's face materialized in the mirror. Byron's heart came to a standstill.

It was his mother.

"It was the weirdest thing," he said. "I never looked like her before. Never."

"You never cross-dressed before," Zach said, continuing to stare at the computer screen. "What's going on with this data?"

"Of course I never cross-dressed," Byron said. "I still don't cross-dress. I just happened to look in the mirror when my shirt was on my head."

Zach looked up at him and grinned. "And there she was," he said. "You would be amazed what we find out about ourselves when we come to terms with our sexuality." 95

"Oh, for God's sake," Byron said. "I was taking my shirt off. I wasn't coming to terms with anything."

"That's fairly obvious," Zach said, tapping at the keyboard.

"Jesus!" Byron said. "Do those hormones come complete with bitchiness? Or is your period starting?"

Zach stared at him. "I can't believe you said that," he said.

Byron couldn't believe he'd said it either, but he went on. "Everything's 100 sexuality with you these days," he said crossly. "I'm trying to tell you about my mother and you tell me it's my goddamn sexuality."

Zach stood up and stepped away from the desk. "Look," he said, folding his arms, "it's called the Tiresias° syndrome. You're jealous because I understand both sexes. By cross-dressing — whether you go around in Emily's underwear or just pretend you've got a wig on — you're trying to identify with me."

For a long moment Byron was unable to move. "What?" he finally said.

"You can't handle talking about the things that really matter, can you?" Zach said. "As soon as we get close to personal feelings, you back off."

"Feelings," Byron said.

"You're a typical man when it comes to emotions," Zach said. 105

"And you're a typical woman," Byron said.

Zach shook his head. "You are in trouble, boy."

"*I'm* in trouble?" Byron said. "Looks to me like you're the one with the problem."

"That's the difference between us," Zach said. "I'm taking steps to correct my problem. You won't even admit yours."

"My problem is you," Byron said. "You are a fucking prick." 110

"Not for long," Zach said.

"Once a prick, always a prick," Byron shouted.

After Zach walked out the door, Byron sat down at his desk and stared at the data Zach had pulled up on the screen, but its sense eluded him. Finally he spun his chair around and put his feet up on the bookcase behind him, and reached for a legal pad.

He always wrote his poetry on long yellow legal pads. He had once tried to jot down some poetic thoughts on the computer, but they had slipped out of his poem and insinuated themselves into a new idea for a research project, which in fact developed into a grant proposal that was later funded. The experience had scared him.

He stared up at the slice of sky that was visible from where he sat, and held 115 the legal pad on his lap for more than an hour, during which time he wrote down thirteen words. When Sarah stuck her head into the office and said, "See you tomorrow," he put the pad down and left work for the day.

Driving home, he thought about his dead mother, Melba Glass. She had never liked Emily, but once Byron was married, his mother stopped saying

---

Tiresias: A blind prophet from Greek legend.

snide things about her. She asked them instead. "Honey," she'd say, "isn't Emily a little *strident*?"

"What do you mean, 'strident'?" Byron would snarl, and she would say she'd meant nothing at all, really, young women were just *different* these days. Byron would narrow his eyes at her, but later, when he'd driven his mother to the train station and waved her off, the idea would come back to him. Emily *was* vociferous in her opinions. And not particularly tolerant of her mother-in-law's old-fashioned tendencies.

"Why doesn't your mother *drive*?" she'd say.

"Why should she?" he'd say. "She never needed to."

"She needs to now, doesn't she?" Emily would say.   120

"Why should she?" Byron would repeat, and for a couple of days he would react to everything Emily said as if she were being highly unreasonable, and *strident*.

What would Emily say if he told her that his dead mother had appeared to him? Worse, that he had appeared to himself as his dead mother?

Emily would lean over Toby's crib in the dark. "I'll be Don Ameche in a taxi, honey," she'd sing. "Better be ready 'bout half past eight."

"How are you? Three of you now. Ha!" Terry Wu said.

"Three of me?" Byron said.   125

"You have a little baby?" Terry said.

"Oh! Toby! Terrific! And Emily. I see. Sure, we're fine. Really. Everything's terrific."

A concerned look seized Terry Wu's face. "Do you protest too much?" he said, and he leaned forward, pressing his fingertips together.

"Protest?" Byron said. "That's not why I'm here."

"Maybe no, maybe yes," Terry said, but he leaned back again.   130

"No, it's my, uh, colleague. You know, Zach."

"Ah," Terry said.

"I seem obsessed," Byron said weakly.

"You are obsessed with your colleague?"

"With his sex," Byron said.   135

"*His* sex?" Terry said.

Byron felt himself blushing. "I can't get used to the idea that he's a woman."

Terry nodded again. "Each one is a mystery."

"No, it's just—why didn't I know?"

"Did you know your wife was pregnant when she conceived?"   140

"What does that have to do with it?" Byron said.

"Well," Terry said, "you were there when it happened, in fact you did the deed, and yet you didn't know about it."

"Terry, I think that's something else."

Terry shrugged. "Are you in love with your colleague?"

"Of course not." He was becoming angry. "What are you getting at?"   145

"I am trying to elicit a coherent statement from you," Terry said. "So far all you have managed to tell me is that you are obsessed with your colleague and are not in love with her. I am having trouble following your flight of ideas."

"Look." Byron stared down at his feet. "Someone whom I have known for more than twenty years has overnight turned into a woman. It's shaken my understanding of reality. I can no longer trust what I see before my eyes."

"Yet you call yourself a scientist," Terry said thoughtfully. "It is simply a matter of surgery and hormonal therapy, isn't it? Changing one form into another by a well-documented protocol?"

Byron stared at him. "That's not what I mean," he said.

Terry clasped his hands together happily. "Yet a magical process is in- 150 volved as well! An invisible and powerful force! Something that is beyond our understanding! But" — he put his hands on his desk and stared into Byron's eyes — "even your poetic license will not allow you to accept it?"

"My poetic license?" Byron said.

"Are man and woman so different, so unrelated, that no transformation is possible? It's this Western culture," Terry said in disgust. "In my country, people exchange sexes every day."

Byron wondered if he had understood Terry correctly.

"Suppose your little baby comes to you in twenty years and says, 'Daddy, I am now Chinese.' Will you disown the child, after twenty years of paternity? No! He will still be the son you love."

"Chinese?" Byron said. 155

"I fear our time is up," Terry said. He stood up and held his hand out. Byron stood too, and shook it. "Good to see you again. Would you like to resume these discussions on a regular basis? I can see you at this time every week."

"I don't think so," Byron said. "I just wanted this one consultation."

"Glad to be of service," Terry said. "No charge, no charge. Professional courtesy. Someday I may need an experiment!" He chuckled. "Or a poem."

"A shower?" Byron said.

"Isn't it a kick?" Emily said. "Gifts like garter belts and strawberry douches." 160

"That's sick," he said.

"Oh, come on, honey. His men friends are invited too." She put down the screwdriver she'd been using to put together Toby's Baby Bouncer and leaned over to kiss Byron's knee. "It'll be fun."

"Why don't we just play red rover?" Byron said. "All the girls can stand on one side and yell, 'Let Zach come on over.'"

"You act as if you've lost your best friend," Emily said.

"I *am* losing him. I've known him for twenty years and suddenly I find out 165 he's the opposite of what I thought he was."

"Ah," Emily said, and she sat back against the sofa. "Here we go. Men and women are the exact opposite."

"Don't you start," he said. "I don't need an attack on the home front."

"I'm supposed to comfort you, I suppose," Emily said. "Sympathize with you because your good buddy's going over to the enemy."

"Well?" Byron said. "Aren't you secretly glad? Having a celebration? Let- ting him in on all your girlish secrets?"

Emily shook her head. "We're talking about a human being who has suf- 170 fered for forty years, and you're jealous because we're giving him some lacy underpants? You're welcome to some of mine, if that's what you want." She smiled at him.

"Suffered?" Byron said. "The dire fate of living in a male body? A fate worse than death, clearly."

"Why are you attacking *me*?" Emily said.

"I'm not attacking you," he said. "I'm just upset." He scooted closer to her and put his arms around her, laying his head against her breasts. "What if I lost you, too?"

"Sweetheart," Emily said, "you're stuck with me for the duration."

"I hope so," Byron said. He turned his head and pressed his face against 175 her. "I certainly hope so." His voice, caught in her cleavage, sounded very far away.

"Nearly twenty years ago," Byron said softly, holding Toby in his arms as he rocked in the dark, "when Daddy and Uncle Zach were very young —"

Toby, who was gazing at his eyes as he spoke, flung out a fist.

"He was still Uncle Zach at the time," Byron said. He tucked the fist into his armpit. "Anyway, we used to ride out to the quarries outside Bloomington to go swimming. You've never been swimming, but it's a lot like bobbing around in Mummy's uterus."

Toby's eyes closed.

"We used to ride our bikes out there after we'd finished our lab work," 180 Byron said. "Riding a bike in the summertime in southern Indiana is a lot like swimming too. The air is so full of humidity you can hardly push the sweat out your pores.

"So we would ride out there in the late afternoon, and hide our bikes in the trees, and go out to our favorite jumping-off place," Byron said. "And Daddy and Uncle Zach would take off all their clothes, and get a running start, and jump right off the edge of the cliff into space!"

Toby made a sound.

"Yes, the final frontier," Byron said. "And we would hit the water at the same instant, and sink nearly to the bottom of the bottomless pit, and bob up without any breath. It was so cold."

He frowned. What kind of story was this to tell his son? Toby was asleep now, but in a few years he'd complain. He'd want plot, and character development.

"That was poetry, son," Byron whispered. He stood up and laid the sleep- 185 ing baby on his stomach in the crib. Tomorrow morning Emily would put Toby in his new Baby Bouncer, and Toby Glass would begin to move through the world on his own.

"What are you giving her?" Sarah said.

"Who?" Byron said, looking up from his calculations.

"Zoe," Sarah said. "We're giving her silk underwear from Frederick's of Hollywood. Do you know her bra size?"

"Sarah," Byron said, pushing his chair back and crossing his arms, "why on earth would I know Zach's bra size?"

"Oooh," Sarah said. "Touchy, aren't we? You *are* friends." She stood there 190 watching him as if, Byron thought, she was daring him to deny it.

"There are some things you just don't discuss in the locker room," he said.

"Oh," Sarah said. "Well, what are you getting her?"

"I haven't thought about it," Byron said.

"Don't you think you *ought* to think about it?"

It was his mother's voice, and for a moment Byron thought his mother 195 had spoken, there in his office. It was just what she would have said. She would look at him over her glasses, a long, questioning look. "Why not something personal? Intimate? You two have known each other a long time."

"Mom, you don't get something intimate for another guy," he would say.

"Oh, Byron, Byron. You should be more flexible, dear. You sound like your father." Every time she had said it she meant it as a reproach, but Byron was always rather pleased.

He wished sadly that he *could* talk to his mother. She never even knew that he had a son of his own. He looked at the picture of Toby on the desk and thought, she would be disappointed to see how much he looks like Emily's father.

He pictured her sitting in the chair beside his desk, her legs crossed. She had had very nice legs. She always insisted on buying expensive stockings at Dellekamps'. "When I worked at Du Pont," she told him more than once, holding out her foot and gazing at her delicately pointed toes, "they gave us all the stockings we wanted, but they were nylon."

"Mom," Byron said aloud, "I don't want to give him anything."   200

And as if he had disappointed her again, he saw her sadly pick up her purse from the floor and stand up.

"Just let me tell you this, Byron," she said. "If you don't support Zoe at this time in her life, you'll regret it forever."

She stepped toward him, shaking her finger at him.

"Forever, Byron."

He sighed, and looked at the legal pad lying in wait on the desk. His   205
mother had once told him she used to write poetry, but he had never read any of it.

"I wonder what happened to all my mother's poems," Byron said.

Emily looked up from the paper she was reading and stared at him thoughtfully, chewing on the end of her red pencil. "It wasn't very *good* poetry," she said.

"How do you know?" he said.

She frowned. "Byron, sometimes I think you live in a cocoon."

"You read it?" Byron said in amazement.   210

"Sure," she said. "You know, little poems about love, flowers, the moon." She shook her head, looking at the paper in her lap. "This guy should try poetry," she said.

"Why didn't she let me read it?" Byron said. He glanced at the television screen, where a woman was talking about teenage reproductive strategies in abusive households. "Em. What happened to it?"

"She threw it away," Emily said. "She thought it was too embarrassing to keep."

"Why did she talk to *you* about it?" Byron said.

"We had to talk about something," Emily said.   215

"Maybe your mother is right," Byron said. "Maybe I have no idea what's going on in the world." He peered into the rearview mirror at Toby, who was snoring softly in his car seat and paying no attention.

Byron had thought in the beginning that being a scientist would increase his understanding of the world, and the world's understanding of itself. But instead, as his work grew more specialized over the years and his exper-

tise became narrower, his brain seemed to be purging its data banks of extraneous information and shutting down, one after another, his receptors for external stimuli. He had been so caught up in chronicling the minuscule changes
taking place in the gels and tubes of his laboratory that the universe had
changed its very nature without his even noticing. The world had a new
arrangement that everyone else seemed to understand very well; even his poetry
had simply served to keep him self-absorbed, oblivious of what must be reality.

Actually, he rather liked the idea of living in a cocoon while the world
became a wilder and more exotic place. Sirens wailed, cars throbbing with bass
notes roared past him with mere children at the wheel, dead women appeared
in mirrors, and men changed into women; but Byron and Toby Glass putted
across town safe and snug inside a cocoon.

"What do *I* know?" Byron thought. "What *do* I know?"

"Can I help you?" said a heavily scented woman with beige hair. Her lips 220
were a carnivorous shade of red, and her eyelids were a remarkable magenta.

"I'm looking for a gift," Byron said.

"For Baby's mother?" the woman said.

"Who?" Byron said.

"Baby's mother," she said, and with a long scarlet fingernail she poked at
the Snugli where Toby Glass was sleeping peacefully against Byron's stomach.

"Oh," Byron said. "No. This is for a shower." 225

"Oh, I love showers!" the woman said. "What kind?"

"Sort of a coming-out shower."

"We don't see many of those," she said. She turned to survey her wares.
"Are you close to the young lady?"

"I used to be," Byron said. "But she's changed."

"*Plus ça change,*" the woman said. "Something to remember you by. Some- 230
thing in leather?"

"Well, I don't know," Byron said, nervously stroking the warm curve of
Toby's back. "I thought maybe stockings?"

The woman frowned. "You mean like pantyhose?"

"I guess not," he said.

"I know." The woman tapped Byron's lower lip with the red fingernail.
"Follow me." She led him to the back of the store and leaned down to pull
open a drawer. "For our discerning customers. A Merry Widow." She held up a
lacy black item covered with ribbons and zippers.

"Wow," Byron said. "I didn't know they still made those." 235

"They are *hot,*" the saleswoman said. She held it up against her body.
"Imagine your friend in this!"

"I can't," Byron said.

"Do you know her bra size?" the woman asked.

"I'm not sure it's final yet," Byron said.

"Oh," the woman said. "Well. Maybe some perfume." Byron followed her 240
back to the front of the store, where she waved her hand grandly at a locked
glass cabinet. "These are very fine perfumes, from the perfume capitals of the
world. Paris, Hong Kong, Aspen. This one is very popular—La Différence."

"That's good," Byron said. "I'll take some of that."

"Oh, excellent choice!" The woman patted his cheek before she reached
into her cleavage and drew out a golden key to unlock the perfume cabinet.

"While Ginny rings that up, would you like to try on some of our makeup?" said another salesperson.

"No, thanks," Byron said.

The woman pouted at him. "You *should*," she said. "Lots of men wear it. 245 Girls go crazy for it." She patted a stool in front of the counter. "Sit down."

Byron sat, and she removed his glasses. "You'll look *terrific*," she said. She leaned toward him, her lips parted, and gently massaged his eyelid with a colorful finger. " 'Scuse me while I kiss the sky," she sang softly, stroking the other one. Then she drew on his eyelid with a long black instrument. "This is Creem-So-Soft," she told him. "It is *so* easy to put on." She drew it across the other eyelid, and finally she brushed his eyelashes with a little brush and stood back. "There," she said. "You are a *killer*."

Toby began to gasp into Byron's shirt. The makeup woman swooped down. "Oooh," she said. "Little booper's making hungry noises." She lifted her eyes to Byron. "Bet I can stall him."

"You can?" Byron said.

"Babies *love* this," she said. She maneuvered Toby out of the Snugli and sat him down facing her on Byron's lap. She began to sketch on his face with the Creem-So-Soft while Toby stared silently at her nose. "There!" She picked Toby up and held him for Byron to examine.

Toby beamed and waved his limbs. He was adorned with a black mous- 250 tache and a pointy black goatee.

"Oh, how darling," Ginny said, coming back from the cash register. "Will this be cash or charge?"

Byron looked at the bill she handed him. "Charge," he said. "I thought this store went out of business a long time ago."

"Lots of people say that," Ginny said.

"What have you done to the baby?" Emily said when Byron walked in the door.

"Babies like this," Byron said. "It's a preview of what he'll look like in 255 twenty years."

"He's going to be a beatnik?" Emily said. She took Toby from Byron's arms. "Don't you think you're rushing things a little?"

Byron sighed. "They grow up so fast," he said. He kissed the top of Toby's head, and then kissed Emily. "How do you like the new me?"

Emily looked at him. "Did you get your hair cut?" she said.

"Em, I'm wearing makeup," Byron said.

"Oh," she said. "So you are." She held Toby up and sniffed at his bottom. 260 "Daddy didn't change your dipes," she said, and she carried him off to his room.

Byron went into the bathroom to look at himself. His eyelids were a very bright purple. He picked up Emily's Barn Red lipstick and carefully covered his lips with it. Then he took off his glasses.

"You know who you look like?" Emily said, appearing beside him in the mirror. "Your mother. Honest to God. If you had one of those curly little perms, you could pass for your own mother." She peered into the mirror, stretching her upper lip with her forefinger. "Do you think I should shave my moustache?"

"No," Byron said. "It's sexy." He slid his hands under her arms and over her breasts. "Let's go to bed."

"No, thanks," Emily said. She picked up her Creem-So-Soft and started to outline her eyes. "I have no desire to sleep with your mother."

"You never did like my mother," Byron said.   265

"Not a lot," Emily said.

"I think I'll go over to the lab," Byron said. He kissed her cheek, leaving a large red lip print.

"Hold still," Emily said. She wet a washcloth, and as she scrubbed his lips he had a sudden vision of his mother scrubbing at grape juice the same way thirty-five years ago. "There. Now you look like my husband again."

He looked in the mirror. His stinging lips were still pinker than normal. "Is wearing makeup always so painful?"

"Always," she said. "We do it for love."   270

Byron liked weekends at the lab. He liked weekdays, too, when students and technicians wandered in and out of one another's labs borrowing chemicals, and all the world seemed engaged in analyzing the structures and chemical interactions of various tissues. But weekends, when the offices were empty and the halls were quiet, and only the odd student padded back and forth from the bathroom, had a cozy, private feeling. Byron could think better in the silence, and he felt close to other scientists, who had given up time in the outside world to bend lovingly over their benches and peer into microscopes, hoping to add to the world's slim store of truth. Both the lab work he did and the poetry he wrote on weekends seemed to spring from a deeper level: a place of intuition and hope that was inaccessible when he was distracted by bustle. On weekends he caught glimpses of the world he hoped to find, where poetry and science were one, and could explain the meaning of life.

"The meaning of life," he said aloud, and wrote it down on his legal pad. Then he turned and typed it on the keyboard, and it appeared in amber letters on the screen in front of him. He smiled and pushed back in his chair, and put his feet on the desk. Poem or experiment? Either one!

He felt that he was on the threshold of an important discovery.

"Why are you doing this?"

Byron opened his eyes. It was Zoe, leaning against the doorjamb. It was   275 definitely and absolutely Zoe; she could no longer be mistaken for a man. He stared at her; what *was* it? The hair, the clothes, the jaw, the way the arms were folded: all were utterly familiar. What had happened?

"The makeup," Zoe said. She shook her head. "You're trying to be something you're not."

He had forgotten about the purple eye shadow and the mascara, but he said, "How do you know what I'm not?"

"It's just that you're so conservative," Zoe said.

"No," he said. "I'm really quite wild. I'm just handicapped by my many fears."

"You?" Zoe said.   280

He nodded. "But you're wild through and through."

Zoe shook her head. "I'm conservative at the core. That's always been my major problem." She gazed out the window at the white hills. "You know the only thing I regret? I'll never have any children now."

"You could adopt."

She shook her head. "They won't have my genes."

"You never really know your children anyway," Byron said.   285

Zoe sighed. "Tell me honestly. Did Emily teach you how to put that eyeliner on?"

Byron smiled. "No," he said. "In fact she learned from me."

Zoe narrowed her eyes and stared at him for a moment, and then sat down on a stool. "I'm thinking of going to law school."

"Are you serious?" he said. "You'd leave the lab?"

"Sure. Patents is the way to go."   290

"You'd leave me?"

Zoe reached over and seized the tablet. "Poetry, poetry, poetry," she said. "Always with you it's the poetry. Anyone would think you're too distracted to work."

"You think any of this is easy?" Byron said.

"None of it," she said, and they sat together for a while without talking. "Are you coming to my shower?"

"Aren't showers supposed to be a surprise?" Byron said.   295

Zoe shrugged. "I hate surprises. I told Sarah she could give me a shower only if she invited men, too."

"I got you a gift." Byron was surprised to feel suddenly shy. "But is there anything you'd really like?"

"Will you come see me in the hospital?"

Byron nodded.

Zoe smiled. "Actually, you look good in makeup," she said. "It redefines   300
your features. You look stronger."

"It's the same old me, though," Byron said. "I'm not any stronger than before."

"I really am thinking of law school," Zoe said. "I need to change my life."

"Changing your sex isn't enough?"

"No. That's who I've been all along."

"Oh," Byron said, and all at once he felt very sad, and exhausted. He put   305
his feet up on the desk, and they sat there in silence, gazing at the part of the world they could see through the window.

After a while he told Zoe about Toby's trip to Dellekamps'. "And then," he said, "I'm sitting on a bench in the mall giving him his bottle, and I look up and these two old ladies are staring at him. 'That is dis*gust*ing,' one of them says. And then the other one gasps and grabs her arm and points at me. And they both back away looking horrified."

Zoe began to laugh.

"And then a man and a little girl walk by, and the little girl says, 'Daddy, is that a homeless person?' And the father says, 'No, dear, that's a man with problems.'"

"Oh," Zoe gasped, holding her ribs.

Byron wiped the tears from his own cheeks, and when he looked at his   310
hand, he saw that it was smeared with mascara. "I had no idea," he said, "no idea why these people were saying these things. I'd forgotten about my makeup. And Toby just looked normal to me."

"Stop," Zoe said, bending over and clutching her stomach.

"And finally a man comes up to me with his hands on his hips and says, 'You ought to be ashamed.'"

"I'm dying," Zoe croaked. "I can't breathe. Oh." She jumped from the stool and ran through the door. "I have to pee."

"You," Byron called after her, "should be ashamed." He listened to the squeegeeing of her sneakers as she ran down the empty hall, and to the familiar creak of the hinges as she pushed open the door to the men's room.

"Glad you could make it, glad you could make it," Terry Wu said, shaking Byron's hand vigorously.

"Did you doubt that I would?" Byron said.

"You're a busy man," Terry said. "So often the cells can't wait." He leaned forward and whispered, "I am giving her a vibrator." Aloud, he said, "The muscles of the calves ache when one first wears high heels."

"That is so true," Emily said. She smiled at Terry Wu and pulled Byron away. "That guy gives me the creeps," she said.

"Honey, you're being xenophobic," Byron said. "Things are different in his country."

They pushed their way through the crowd, Byron cupping one hand protectively around Toby's head to keep him from being squashed in his Snugli.

"There you are!" Sarah appeared in front of them. "Isn't the turnout great?" She waved her arm at the crowd.

Emily hugged her. "Did you get it?" she said.

Sarah nodded. "I never spent that much on a bra in my life."

"How did you know what size to get?" Byron asked.

"I asked her," Sarah said. She led them over to where Zoe stood beside a gift-covered table. "Here are the Glasses!"

"I'm so glad you could come," Zoe said. She kissed Emily on the cheek and prodded Toby's bottom with a glistening red-tipped forefinger. "How's my little beatnik godbaby?"

"Zoe, you look gorgeous," Emily said. "Really. You look so — you."

"Next I'm going to have electrolysis on my facial hair," Zoe said.

"You look pretty good as you are," Byron said. He wondered when the time would come that Zoe would kiss *his* cheek. "I bought you some perfume, but I ended up giving it to Emily."

"Thank goodness," Zoe said. "I'm allergic to everything but La Différence, anyway."

"One of these days," Byron said, "I'll write you a poem."

"He's never done that for me." Emily waved her hand at the table in front of them. "Look at all this loot."

They stared at the pile of presents. "I can't wait to open them," Zoe said. "I've always wanted a shower."

"Isn't it wonderful to get what you always wanted?" Byron put his arm through hers and squeezed it, and he could feel her breast against his triceps as she squeezed back, her muscles hardening briefly against his own.

He felt a rush of pleasure. On his left Emily reached for a bacon-wrapped chicken liver; on his right his oldest friend in the world gently disengaged her arm from his to touch the hands of the dozens of people who had come to wish her well; and from his shoulders, like a newly discovered organ of delight, hung the little bag full of Toby Glass.

Toby Glass, who could grow up to be anything!

The musicians in the string quartet hired for the occasion began to tune their instruments, leaning toward each other, listening, nodding gravely. The cellist moved her stool a little closer to the violinist; the violinist held her instrument away from her neck as she shook back her long red hair, and then replaced it firmly under her chin. Suddenly, as if spontaneously, each player lifted her bow and held it poised in the air for a long moment, until at some prearranged and invisible signal they plunged their bows toward the strings of their various instruments and began to play.

CONSIDERATIONS FOR CRITICAL THINKING AND WRITING

1. FIRST RESPONSE. "You would be amazed what we find out about ourselves when we come to terms with our sexuality" (para. 95). Reflect on this observation made by Zach/Zoe and respond to it.

2. Describe Byron's assumptions about what constitutes femininity and masculinity.

3. How does Byron react to Zach's announcement about his sex change operation?

4. Trace Byron's gradual shift in attitude toward Zach/Zoe.

5. How does Baker challenge readers' assumptions about gender roles?

6. Byron struggles with his interests in science and poetry. How is this related to the story's central conflict?

7. What do you think is Emily's function in the story?

8. Analyze the significance of the final paragraph. Given that most of the story consists of dialogue, why do you suppose there is none in this paragraph?

9. Compare the opening line of this story with several others in this anthology, and discuss how their respective writers attempt to engage their readers' interest.

NATHANIEL HAWTHORNE (1804–1864)

A biographical note on Nathaniel Hawthorne appears on page 1122.

Young Goodman Brown   1835

Young Goodman Brown came forth at sunset into the street at Salem village; but put his head back, after crossing the threshold, to exchange a parting kiss with his young wife. And Faith, as the wife was aptly named, thrust her own pretty head into the street, letting the wind play with the pink ribbons of her cap while she called to Goodman Brown.

"Dearest heart," whispered she, softly and rather sadly, when her lips were close to his ear, "prithee put off your journey until sunrise and sleep in your own bed tonight. A lone woman is troubled with such dreams and such thoughts that she's afeared of herself sometimes. Pray tarry with me this night, dear husband, of all nights in the year."

"My love and my Faith," replied young Goodman Brown, "of all nights in the year, this one night must I tarry away from thee. My journey, as thou callest it, forth and back again, must needs be done 'twixt now and sunrise. What, my sweet, pretty wife, dost thou doubt me already, and we but three months married?"

"Then God bless you!" said Faith, with the pink ribbons; "and may you find all well when you come back."

"Amen!" cried Goodman Brown. "Say thy prayers, dear Faith, and go to bed at dusk, and no harm will come to thee." 5

So they parted; and the young man pursued his way until, being about to turn the corner by the meeting-house, he looked back and saw the head of Faith still peeping after him with a melancholy air, in spite of her pink ribbons.

"Poor little Faith!" thought he, for his heart smote him. "What a wretch am I to leave her on such an errand! She talks of dreams, too. Methought as she spoke there was trouble in her face, as if a dream had warned her what work is to be done tonight. But no, no; 't would kill her to think it. Well, she's a blessed angel on earth; and after this one night I'll cling to her skirts and follow her to heaven."

With this excellent resolve for the future, Goodman Brown felt himself justified in making more haste on his present evil purpose. He had taken a dreary road, darkened by all the gloomiest trees of the forest, which barely stood aside to let the narrow path creep through, and closed immediately behind. It was all as lonely as could be; and there is this peculiarity in such a solitude, that the traveler knows not who may be concealed by the innumerable trunks and the thick boughs overhead; so that with lonely footsteps he may yet be passing through an unseen multitude.

"There may be a devilish Indian behind every tree," said Goodman Brown to himself; and he glanced fearfully behind him as he added, "What if the devil himself should be at my very elbow!"

His head being turned back, he passed a crook of the road, and, looking forward again, beheld the figure of a man, in grave and decent attire, seated at the foot of an old tree. He arose at Goodman Brown's approach and walked onward side by side with him. 10

"You are late, Goodman Brown," said he. "The clock of the Old South was striking as I came through Boston, and that is full fifteen minutes agone."

"Faith kept me back a while," replied the young man, with a tremor in his voice, caused by the sudden appearance of his companion, though not wholly unexpected.

It was now deep dusk in the forest, and deepest in that part of it where these two were journeying. As nearly as could be discerned, the second traveler was about fifty years old, apparently in the same rank of life as Goodman Brown, and bearing a considerable resemblance to him, though perhaps more in expression than features. Still they might have been taken for father and son. And yet, though the elder person was as simply clad as the younger, and as simple in manner too, he had an indescribable air of one who knew the world, and who would not have felt abashed at the governor's dinner table or in King William's court, were it possible that his affairs should call him thither. But the only thing about him that could be fixed upon as remarkable was his staff, which bore the likeness of a great black snake, so curiously wrought that it might almost be seen to twist and wriggle itself like a living serpent. This, of course, must have been an ocular deception, assisted by the uncertain light.

"Come, Goodman Brown," cried his fellow-traveler, "this is a dull pace for the beginning of a journey. Take my staff, if you are so soon weary."

"Friend," said the other, exchanging his slow pace for a full stop, "having 15 kept covenant by meeting thee here, it is my purpose now to return whence I came. I have scruples touching the matter thou wot'st° of."

"Sayest thou so?" replied he of the serpent, smiling apart. "Let us walk on, nevertheless, reasoning as we go; and if I convince thee not thou shalt turn back. We are but a little way in the forest yet."

"Too far! too far!" exclaimed the goodman, unconsciously resuming his walk. "My father never went into the woods on such an errand, nor his father before him. We have been a race of honest men and good Christians since the days of the martyrs; and shall I be the first of the name of Brown that ever took this path and kept—"

"Such company, thou wouldst say," observed the elder person, interpreting his pause. "Well said, Goodman Brown! I have been as well acquainted with your family as with ever a one among the Puritans; and that's no trifle to say. I helped your grandfather, the constable, when he lashed the Quaker woman so smartly through the streets of Salem; and it was I that brought your father a pitch-pine knot, kindled at my own hearth, to set fire to an Indian village, in King Philip's war.° They were my good friends, both; and many a pleasant walk have we had along this path, and returned merrily after midnight. I would fain be friends with you for their sake."

"If it be as thou sayest," replied Goodman Brown, "I marvel they never spoke of these matters; or, verily, I marvel not, seeing that the least rumor of the sort would have driven them from New England. We are a people of prayer, and good works to boot, and abide no such wickedness."

"Wickedness or not," said the traveler with the twisted staff, "I have a very 20 general acquaintance here in New England. The deacons of many a church have drunk the communion wine with me; the selectmen of divers towns make me their chairman; and a majority of the Great and General Court are firm supporters of my interest. The governor and I, too—But these are state secrets."

"Can this be so?" cried Goodman Brown, with a stare of amazement at his undisturbed companion. "Howbeit, I have nothing to do with the governor and council; they have their own ways, and are no rule for a simple husbandman like me. But, were I to go on with thee, how should I meet the eye of that good old man, our minister, at Salem village? Oh, his voice would make me tremble both Sabbath day and lecture day."

Thus far the elder traveler had listened with due gravity; but now burst into a fit of irrepressible mirth, shaking himself so violently that his snakelike staff actually seemed to wriggle in sympathy.

"Ha! ha! ha!" shouted he again and again; then composing himself, "Well, go on, Goodman Brown, go on; but, prithee, don't kill me with laughing."

"Well, then, to end the matter at once," said Goodman Brown, considerably nettled, "there is my wife, Faith. It would break her dear little heart; and I'd rather break my own."

---

wot'st: Know
King Philip's war (1675–1676): War between the colonists and an alliance of Indian tribes led by Metacan (also known as Metacomet), leader of the Wampanoags, who was called King Philip by the colonists.

"Nay, if that be the case," answered the other, "e'en go thy ways, Goodman 25 Brown. I would not for twenty old women like the one hobbling before us that Faith should come to any harm."

As he spoke he pointed his staff at a female figure on the path, in whom Goodman Brown recognized a very pious and exemplary dame, who had taught him his catechism in youth, and was still his moral and spiritual adviser, jointly with the minister and Deacon Gookin.

"A marvel, truly that Goody Cloyse should be so far in the wilderness at nightfall," said he. "But with your leave, friend, I shall take a cut through the woods until we have left this Christian woman behind. Being a stranger to you, she might ask whom I was consorting with and whither I was going."

"Be it so," said his fellow-traveler. "Betake you to the woods, and let me keep the path."

Accordingly the young man turned aside, but took care to watch his companion, who advanced softly along the road until he had come within a staff's length of the old dame. She, meanwhile, was making the best of her way, with singular speed for so aged a woman, and mumbling some indistinct words—a prayer, doubtless—as she went. The traveler put forth his staff and touched her withered neck with what seemed the serpent's tail.

"The devil!" screamed the pious old lady. 30

"Then Goody Cloyse knows her old friend?" observed the traveler, confronting her and leaning on his writhing stick.

"Ah, forsooth, and is it your worship indeed?" cried the good dame. "Yea, truly is it, and in the very image of my old gossip, Goodman Brown, the grandfather of the silly fellow that now is. But—would your worship believe it?—my broomstick hath strangely disappeared, stolen, as I suspect, by that unhanged witch, Goody Cory, and that, too, when I was all anointed with the juice of smallage, and cinquefoil, and wolfsbane—"

"Mingled with fine wheat and the fat of a newborn babe," said the shape of old Goodman Brown.

"Ah, your worship knows the recipe," cried the old lady, cackling aloud. "So, as I was saying, being all ready for the meeting, and no horse to ride on, I made up my mind to foot it; for they tell me there is a nice young man to be taken into communion tonight. But now your good worship will lend me your arm, and we shall be there in a twinkling."

"That can hardly be," answered her friend. "I may not spare you my arm, 35 Goody Cloyse; but here is my staff, if you will."

So saying, he threw it down at her feet, where, perhaps, it assumed life, being one of the rods which its owner had formerly lent to the Egyptian magi. Of this fact, however, Goodman Brown could not take cognizance. He had cast up his eyes in astonishment, and, looking down again, beheld neither Goody Cloyse nor the serpentine staff, but his fellow-traveler alone, who waited for him as calmly as if nothing had happened.

"That old woman taught me my catechism," said the young man; and there was a world of meaning in this simple comment.

They continued to walk onward, while the elder traveler exhorted his companion to make good speed and persevere in the path, discoursing so aptly that his arguments seemed rather to spring up in the bosom of his auditor than to be suggested by himself. As they went, he plucked a branch of maple to serve for a walking stick, and began to strip it of the twigs and little boughs, which were wet with evening dew. The moment his fingers touched them they became strangely withered and dried up as with a week's sunshine. Thus the pair proceeded, at a good free pace, until suddenly, in a gloomy hollow of the road, Goodman Brown sat himself down on the stump of a tree and refused to go any farther.

"Friend," he said, stubbornly, "my mind is made up. Not another step will I budge on this errand. What if a wretched old woman do choose to go to the devil when I thought she was going to heaven: is that any reason why I should quit my dear Faith and go after her?"

"You will think better of this by and by," said his acquaintance, compos- 40 edly. "Sit here and rest yourself a while; and when you feel like moving again, there is my staff to help you along."

Without more words, he threw his companion the maple stick, and was as speedily out of sight as if he had vanished into the deepening gloom. The young man sat a few moments by the roadside, applauding himself greatly, and thinking with how clear a conscience he should meet the minister in his morning walk, nor shrink from the eye of good old Deacon Gookin. And what calm sleep would be his that very night, which was to have been spent so wickedly, but so purely and sweetly now, in the arms of Faith! Amidst these pleasant and praiseworthy meditations, Goodman Brown heard the tramp of horses along the road, and deemed it advisable to conceal himself within the verge of the forest, conscious of the guilty purpose that had brought him thither, though now so happily turned from it.

On came the hoof tramps and the voices of the riders, two grave old voices, conversing soberly as they drew near. These mingled sounds appeared to pass along the road, within a few yards of the young man's hiding-place; but, owing doubtless to the depth of the gloom at that particular spot, neither the travelers nor their steeds were visible. Though their figures brushed the small boughs by the wayside, it could not be seen that they intercepted, even for a moment, the faint gleam from the strip of bright sky athwart which they must have passed. Goodman Brown alternately crouched and stood on tiptoe, pulling aside the branches and thrusting forth his head as far as he durst without discerning so much as a shadow. It vexed him the more, because he could have sworn, were such a thing possible, that he recognized the voices of the minister and Deacon Gookin, jogging along quietly, as they were wont to do, when bound to some ordination or ecclesiastical council. While yet within hearing, one of the riders stopped to pluck a switch.

"Of the two, reverend sir," said the voice like the deacon's, "I had rather miss an ordination dinner than tonight's meeting. They tell me that some of our community are to be here from Falmouth and beyond, and others from Connecticut and Rhode Island, besides several of the Indian powwows, who, after their fashion, know almost as much deviltry as the best of us. Moreover, there is a goodly young woman to be taken into communion."

"Mighty well, Deacon Gookin!" replied the solemn old tones of the minister. "Spur up, or we shall be late. Nothing can be done, you know, until I get on the ground."

The hoofs clattered again; and the voices, talking so strangely in the empty 45 air, passed on through the forest, where no church had ever been gathered or solitary Christian prayed. Whither, then, could these holy men be journeying so deep into the heathen wilderness? Young Goodman Brown caught hold of a tree for support, being ready to sink down on the ground, faint and overburdened with the heavy sickness of his heart. He looked up to the sky, doubting whether there really was a heaven above him. Yet there was the blue arch, and the stars brightening in it.

"With heaven above and Faith below, I will yet stand firm against the devil!" cried Goodman Brown.

While he still gazed upward into the deep arch of the firmament and had lifted his hands to pray, a cloud, though no wind was stirring, hurried across the zenith and hid the brightening stars. The blue sky was still visible, except directly overhead, where this black mass of cloud was sweeping swiftly northward. Aloft in the air, as if from the depths of the cloud, came a confused and doubtful sound of voices. Once the listener fancied that he could distinguish the accents of townspeople of his own, men and women, both pious and ungodly, many of whom he had met at the communion table, and had seen others rioting at the tavern. The next moment, so indistinct were the sounds, he doubted whether he had heard aught but the murmur of the old forest, whispering without a wind. Then came a stronger swell of those familiar tones, heard daily in the sunshine at Salem village, but never until now from a cloud of night. There was one voice, of a young woman, uttering lamentations, yet with an uncertain sorrow, and entreating for some favor, which, perhaps, it would grieve her to obtain; and all the unseen multitude, both saints and sinners, seemed to encourage her onward.

"Faith!" shouted Goodman Brown, in a voice of agony and desperation; and the echoes of the forest mocked him, crying, "Faith! Faith!" as if bewildered wretches were seeking her all through the wilderness.

The cry of grief, rage, and terror was yet piercing the night, when the unhappy husband held his breath for a response. There was a scream, drowned immediately in a louder murmur of voices, fading into far-off laughter, as the dark cloud swept away, leaving the clear and silent sky above Goodman Brown. But something fluttered lightly down through the air and caught on the branch of a tree. The young man seized it, and beheld a pink ribbon.

"My Faith is gone!" cried he after one stupefied moment. "There is no good 50 on earth; and sin is but a name. Come, devil; for to thee is this world given."

And, maddened with despair, so that he laughed loud and long, did Goodman Brown grasp his staff and set forth again, at such a rate that he seemed to fly along the forest path rather than to walk or run. The road grew wilder and drearier and more faintly traced, and vanished at length, leaving him in the heart of the dark wilderness, still rushing onward with the instinct that guides mortal man to evil. The whole forest was peopled with frightful sounds — the creaking of the trees, the howling of wild beasts, and the yell of Indians; while sometimes the wind tolled like a distant church bell, and sometimes gave a broad roar around the traveler, as if all Nature were laughing him to scorn. But he was himself the chief horror of the scene, and shrank not from its other horrors.

"Ha! ha! ha!" roared Goodman Brown when the wind laughed at him. "Let us hear which will laugh loudest. Think not to frighten me with your deviltry. Come witch, come wizard, come Indian powwow, come devil himself, and here comes Goodman Brown. You may as well fear him as he fear you."

In truth, all through the haunted forest there could be nothing more frightful than the figure of Goodman Brown. On he flew among the black pines, brandishing his staff with frenzied gestures, now giving vent to an inspiration of horrid blasphemy, and now shouting forth such laughter as set all the echoes of the forest laughing like demons around him. The fiend in his own shape is less hideous than when he rages in the breast of man. Thus sped the demoniac on his course, until, quivering among the trees, he saw a red light before him, as when the felled trunks and branches of a clearing have been set on fire, and throw up their lurid blaze against the sky, at the hour of midnight. He paused, in a lull of the tempest that had driven him onward, and heard the swell of what seemed a hymn, rolling solemnly from a distance with the weight of many voices. He knew the tune; it was a familiar one in the choir of the village meeting-house. The verse died heavily away, and was lengthened by a chorus, not of human voices, but of all the sounds of the benighted wilderness pealing in awful harmony together. Goodman Brown cried out, and his cry was lost to his own ear by its unison with the cry of the desert.

In the interval of silence he stole forward until the light glared full upon his eyes. At one extremity of an open space, hemmed in by the dark wall of the forest, arose a rock, bearing some rude, natural resemblance either to an altar or a pulpit, and surrounded by four blazing pines, their tops aflame, their stems untouched, like candles at an evening meeting. The mass of foliage that had overgrown the summit of the rock was all on fire, blazing high into the night and fitfully illuminating the whole field. Each pendent twig and leafy festoon was in a blaze. As the red light arose and fell, a numerous congregation alternately shone forth, then disappeared in shadow, and again grew, as it were, out of the darkness, peopling the heart of the solitary woods at once.

"A grave and dark-clad company," quoth Goodman Brown.   55

In truth they were such. Among them, quivering to and fro between gloom and splendor, appeared faces that would be seen next day at the council board of the province, and others which, Sabbath after Sabbath, looked devoutly heavenward, and benignantly over the crowded pews, from the holiest pulpits in the land. Some affirm that the lady of the governor was there. At least there were high dames well known to her, and wives of honored husbands, and widows, a great multitude, and ancient maidens, all of excellent repute, and fair young girls, who trembled lest their mothers should espy them. Either the sudden gleams of light flashing over the obscure field bedazzled Goodman Brown, or he recognized a score of the church members of Salem village famous for their especial sanctity. Good old Deacon Gookin had arrived, and waited at the skirts of that venerable saint, his revered pastor. But, irreverently consorting with these grave, reputable, and pious people, these elders of the church, these chaste dames and dewy virgins, there were men of dissolute lives and women of spotted fame, wretches given over to all mean and filthy vice, and suspected even of horrid crimes. It was strange to see that the good shrank not from the wicked, nor were the sinners abashed by the saints. Scattered also among their pale-faced enemies were the Indian priests, or powwows, who had often scared their native forest with more hideous incantations than any known to English witchcraft.

"But where is Faith?" thought Goodman Brown; and, as hope came into his heart, he trembled.

Another verse of the hymn arose, a slow and mournful strain, such as the pious love, but joined to words which expressed all that our nature can conceive of sin, and darkly hinted at far more. Unfathomable to mere mortals is the lore of fiends. Verse after verse was sung; and still the chorus of the desert swelled between like the deepest tone of a mighty organ; and with the final peal of that dreadful anthem there came a sound, as if the roaring wind, the rushing streams, the howling beasts, and every other voice of the unconcerted wilderness were mingling and according with the voice of guilty man in homage to the prince of all. The four blazing pines threw up a loftier flame, and obscurely discovered shapes and visages of horror on the smoke wreaths above the impious assembly. At the same moment the fire on the rock shot redly forth and formed a glowing arch above its base, where now appeared a figure. With reverence be it spoken, the figure bore no slight similitude, both in garb and manner, to some grave divine of the New England churches.

"Bring forth the converts!" cried a voice that echoed through the field and rolled into the forest.

At the word, Goodman Brown stepped forth from the shadow of the trees 60 and approached the congregation, with whom he felt a loathful brotherhood by the sympathy of all that was wicked in his heart. He could have well-nigh sworn that the shape of his own dead father beckoned him to advance, looking downward from a smoke wreath, while a woman, with dim features of despair, threw out her hand to warn him back. Was it his mother? But he had no power to retreat one step, nor to resist, even in thought, when the minister and good old Deacon Gookin seized his arms and led him to the blazing rock. Thither came also the slender form of a veiled female, led between Goody Cloyse, that pious teacher of the catechism, and Martha Carrier, who had received the devil's promise to be queen of hell. A rampant hag was she. And there stood the proselytes beneath the canopy of fire.

"Welcome, my children," said the dark figure, "to the communion of your race. Ye have found thus young your nature and your destiny. My children, look behind you!"

They turned; and flashing forth, as it were, in a sheet of flame, the fiend worshipers were seen; the smile of welcome gleamed darkly on every visage.

"There," resumed the sable form, "are all whom ye have reverenced from youth. Ye deemed them holier than yourselves and shrank from your own sin, contrasting it with their lives of righteousness and prayerful aspirations heavenward. Yet here are they all in my worshiping assembly. This night it shall be granted you to know their secret deeds: how hoary-bearded elders of the church have whispered wanton words to the young maids of their households; how many a woman, eager for widows' weeds, has given her husband a drink at bedtime and let him sleep his last sleep in her bosom; how beardless youths have made haste to inherit their fathers' wealth; and how fair damsels—blush not, sweet ones—have dug little graves in the garden, and bidden me, the sole guest, to an infant's funeral. By the sympathy of your human hearts for sin ye shall scent out all the places—whether in church, bedchamber, street, field, or forest—where crime has been committed, and shall exult to behold the whole earth one stain of guilt, one mighty blood spot. Far more than this. It shall be yours to penetrate, in every bosom, the deep mystery of sin, the fountain of all wicked arts, and which inexhaustibly supplies more evil impulses than human power—than my power at its utmost—can make manifest in deeds. And now, my children, look upon each other."

They did so; and, by the blaze of the hell-kindled torches, the wretched man beheld his Faith, and the wife her husband, trembling before that unhallowed altar.

"Lo, there ye stand, my children," said the figure, in a deep and solemn 65
tone, almost sad with its despairing awfulness, as if his once angelic nature
could yet mourn for our miserable race. "Depending upon one another's
hearts, ye had still hoped that virtue were not all a dream. Now are ye unde-
ceived. Evil is the nature of mankind. Evil must be your only happiness. Welcome again, my children, to the communion of your race."

"Welcome," repeated the fiend worshipers, in one cry of despair and
triumph.

And there they stood, the only pair, as it seemed, who were yet hesitating
on the verge of wickedness in this dark world. A basin was hollowed, naturally,
in the rock. Did it contain water, reddened by the lurid light? or was it blood?
or, perchance, a liquid flame? Herein did the shape of evil dip his hand and
prepare to lay the mark of baptism upon their foreheads, that they might be
partakers of the mystery of sin, more conscious of the secret guilt of others,
both in deed and thought, than they could now be of their own. The husband
cast one look at his pale wife, and Faith at him. What polluted wretches would
the next glance show them to each other, shuddering alike at what they disclosed and what they saw!

"Faith! Faith!" cried the husband, "look up to heaven, and resist the
wicked one."

Whether Faith obeyed he knew not. Hardly had he spoken when he found
himself amid calm night and solitude, listening to a roar of the wind which
died heavily away through the forest. He staggered against the rock, and felt it
chill and damp; while a hanging twig, that had been all on fire, besprinkled his
cheek with the coldest dew.

The next morning young Goodman Brown came slowly into the street of 70
Salem village, staring around him like a bewildered man. The good old minister was taking a walk along the graveyard to get an appetite for breakfast
and meditate his sermon, and bestowed a blessing, as he passed, on Goodman Brown. He shrank from the venerable saint as if to avoid an anathema.
Old Deacon Gookin was at domestic worship, and the holy words of his prayer
were heard through the open window. "What God doth the wizard pray to?"
quoth Goodman Brown. Goody Cloyse, that excellent old Christian, stood
in the early sunshine at her own lattice, catechizing a little girl who had
brought her a pint of morning's milk. Goodman Brown snatched away the
child as from the grasp of the fiend himself. Turning the corner by the
meeting-house, he spied the head of Faith, with the pink ribbons, gazing anxiously forth, and bursting into such joy at sight of him that she skipped along
the street and almost kissed her husband before the whole village. But Goodman Brown looked sternly and sadly into her face, and passed on without a
greeting.

Had Goodman Brown fallen asleep in the forest and only dreamed a wild
dream of a witch-meeting?

Be it so if you will; but, alas! it was a dream of evil omen for young Goodman Brown. A stern, a sad, a darkly meditative, a distrustful, if not a desperate
man did he become from the night of that fearful dream. On the Sabbath day,
when the congregation were singing a holy psalm, he could not listen because
an anthem of sin rushed loudly upon his ear and drowned all the blessed
strain. When the minister spoke from the pulpit with power and fervid elo-

quence, and, with his hand on the open Bible, of the sacred truths of our religion, and of saintlike lives and triumphant deaths, and of future bliss or misery unutterable, then did Goodman Brown turn pale, dreading lest the roof should thunder down upon the gray blasphemer and his hearers. Often, awaking suddenly at midnight, he shrank from the bosom of Faith; and at morning or eventide, when the family knelt down at prayer, he scowled and muttered to himself, and gazed sternly at his wife, and turned away. And when he had lived long, and was borne to his grave a hoary corpse, followed by Faith, an aged woman, and children and grandchildren, a goodly procession, besides neighbors not a few, they carved no hopeful verse upon his tombstone, for his dying hour was gloom.

CONSIDERATIONS FOR CRITICAL THINKING AND WRITING

1. FIRST RESPONSE. Try to summarize "Young Goodman Brown" with a tidy moral. Is it possible? What makes this story complex?

2. What is the significance of Young Goodman Brown's name?

3. What is the symbolic value of the forest in this story? How are the descriptions of the forest contrasted with those of Salem village?

4. Characterize Young Goodman Brown at the beginning of the story. Why does he go into the forest? What does he mean when he says "Faith kept me back a while" (para. 12)?

5. What function do Faith's ribbons have in the story?

6. What foreshadows Young Goodman Brown's meeting with his "fellow-traveler" (para. 14)? Who is he? How do we know that Brown is keeping an appointment with a supernatural being?

7. The narrator describes the fellow-traveler's staff wriggling like a snake but then says, "This, of course, must have been an ocular deception, assisted by the uncertain light" (para. 13). What is the effect of this and other instances of ambiguity in the story?

8. What does Young Goodman Brown discover in the forest? What does he come to think of his ancestors, the church and state, Goody Cloyse, and even his wife?

9. Is Salem populated by hypocrites who cover hideous crimes with a veneer of piety and respectability? Do Faith and the other characters Brown sees when he returns from the forest appear corrupt to you?

10. Near the end of the story the narrator asks, "Had Goodman Brown fallen asleep in the forest and only dreamed a wild dream of a witch-meeting?" (para. 71). Was it a dream, or did the meeting actually happen? How does the answer to this question affect your reading of the story? Write an essay giving an answer to the narrator's question.

11. How is Young Goodman Brown changed by his experience in the forest? Does the narrator endorse Brown's unwillingness to trust anyone?

12. Consider the story as a criticism of the village's hypocrisy.

13. CRITICAL STRATEGIES. Read the section on psychological criticism (pp. 64–66) in Chapter 3, "Applying a Critical Strategy," and discuss this story as an inward, psychological journey in which Young Goodman Brown discovers the power of blackness in himself but refuses to acknowledge that dimension of his personality.

RUTH PRAWER JHABVALA (B. 1927)

Born in Cologne, Germany, Ruth Prawer Jhabvala fled with her family in 1939 to England and became a British citizen in 1948. In 1951 she completed a master's degree at London University and married an architect from India, where the couple subsequently lived for nearly a quarter of a century. Currently, she lives in New York and continues to visit her husband's native land. Jhabvala's writings include many novels, such as *Amrita* (1956), *The Householder* (1960), *Three Continents* (1988), and *Shards of Memory* (1995). Among her volumes of collected stories is *Out of India: Selected Stories* (1986), and *East into Upper East: Plain Tales from New York and New Delhi* (1998). She has also written many popular screenplays including *A Passage to India*, *A Room with a View*, *Howards End*, and *Remains of the Day*. "The Englishwoman" reflects a topic frequently found in her writings: a person living in an adopted culture.

The Englishwoman   1972

The Englishwoman — her name is Sadie — was fifty-two years old when she decided to leave India. She could hardly believe it. She felt young and free. At fifty-two! Her bag is packed and she is running away. She is eloping, leaving everything behind her — husband, children, grandchildren, thirty years of married life. Her heart is light and so is her luggage. It is surprising how few things she has to take with her. Most of her clothes are not worth taking. These last years she has been mostly wearing dowdy cotton frocks sewn by a little turbaned tailor. She still has a few saris, but she is not taking them with her. She doesn't ever intend to wear those again.

The person who is crying the most at her impending departure is Annapurna, her husband's mistress. Annapurna has a very emotional nature. She looks into the packed bag; like Sadie, she is surprised by its meager contents. "Is that all you are taking with you?" she asks. Sadie answers, "It's all I've got." Annapurna breaks into a new storm of tears.

"But that's good," Sadie urges. "Not to accumulate things, to travel light, what could be better?"

"Oh, you're so spiritual," Annapurna tells her, wiping her eyes on the other's sleeve. "Really, you are far more Indian than I am."

"Nonsense," Sadie says, and she means it. What nonsense.   5

But it is true that if Indian means "spiritual" — as so many people like to believe — then Annapurna is an exception. She is a very, very physical sort of person. She is stout, with a tight glowing skin, and shining eyes and teeth, and hair glossy with black dye. She loves clothes and jewelry and rich food. Although she is about the same age as the Englishwoman, she is far more vigorous, and when she moves, her sari rustles and her bracelets jingle.

"But are you really going?"

Annapurna keeps asking this question. And Sadie keeps asking it of herself too. But they ask it in two very different ways. Annapurna is shocked and grieved (yes, grieved — she loves the Englishwoman). But Sadie is incredulous with happiness. Can it really be true? she keeps asking herself: I'm going? I'm leaving India? Her heart skips with joy and she has difficulty in repressing her smiles. She doesn't want anyone to suspect her feelings. She is ashamed of her own callousness — and yet she goes on smiling, more and more, and happiness wells up in her like a spring.

Last week she went to say good-bye to the children. They are both settled in Bombay now with their families. Dev, her son, has been married for two years and has a baby girl; Monica, the daughter, has three boys. Dev has a fine job with an advertising company; and Monica is working too, for she has too much drive to be content with just staying at home. She calls herself a go-go girl and that is what she is, charging around town interviewing people for the articles she writes for a women's magazine, talking in the latest slang current in Bombay, throwing parties of which she herself is the life and soul. Monica looks quite Indian — her eyes are black, her skin glows; she is really more like Annapurna than like the Englishwoman, who is gaunt and pale.

Although so gay, Monica also likes to have serious discussions. She 10 attempted to have such a discussion with her mother. She said, "But, Mummy, *why* are you going?" and she looked at her with the special serious face she has for serious moments.

Sadie didn't know what to answer. What could she say? But she had to say something, or Monica would be hurt. So she too became solemn, and she explained to her daughter that when people get older they begin to get very homesick for the place in which they were born and grew up and that this home-sickness becomes worse and worse till in the end life becomes almost unbearable. Monica understood what she said and sympathized with it. She made plans how they would all come and visit her in England. She promised that when the boys became bigger, she would send them to her for long holidays. She was now in full agreement with her mother's departure, so Sadie was glad she told her what she did. She was prepared to tell Dev the same thing if he asked her, but he didn't ask. He and his wife were rather worried in those days because there was an out-break of chicken pox in their apartment building and they were afraid Baby might catch it. But they too promised frequent visits to her in England.

Only Annapurna is still crying. She looks at Sadie's little suitcase and cries, and then she looks at Sadie and cries. She keeps asking, "But why, *why?*" Sadie tries to tell her what she told Monica, but Annapurna waves her aside; for her it is not a good enough reason, and she is right. Sadie herself knows it isn't. She asks wouldn't Sadie miss all of them and their love for her, and wouldn't she miss the life she has lived and the place in which she has lived it, her whole past, everything she has been and done for thirty years? Thirty years! she cries, again and again, appalled — and Sadie too is appalled, it is such a long time. Annapurna says that an Indian wife also yearns for her father's house, and at the beginning of her marriage she is always waiting to go off there to visit; but as the years progress and she becomes deeper and deeper embedded in her husband's home, these early memories fade till they are noth-ing more but a sweet sensation enshrined in the heart. Sadie knows that what Annapurna is saying is true, but also that it does not in the least apply in her own case, because her feelings are not ones of gentle nostalgia.

The Englishwoman doesn't like to remember the early years when she first came to live here. It is as if she wished to disown her happiness then. How she loved everything! She never gave a backward glance to home or England. Her husband's family enjoyed and abetted her attempts to become Indian. A whole lot of them — mother-in-law, sisters-in-law, aunts, cousins, and friends — would cram into the family car (with blue silk curtains discreetly drawn to shield them from view) and drive to the bazaar to buy saris for Sadie. She was never much consulted about their choice, and when they got home, she was tugged this way and that while they argued with each other about the best way to drape it round her. When they had finished, they stood back to admire, only instead of admiring they often could not help smiling at her appearance. She didn't care. Yes, she knew she was too tall for the sari, and too thin, and too English, but she loved wearing it and to feel herself Indian. She also made attempts to learn Hindi, and this too amused everyone, and they never tired of making her repeat certain words and going into peals of laughter at her pronunciation. Everyone, all the ladies of the household, had a lot of fun. They were healthy, rich, and gay. They were by no means a tradition-bound family, and although their life in the house did have something of the enclosed, languorous quality of purdah living, the minds flowering within it were full of energy and curiosity. The mother-in-law herself, at that time well over sixty, spent a lot of her time reading vernacular novels, and she also attempted to write some biographical sketches of her own, describing life in a high-caste household of the 1880s. She took to smoking cigarettes quite late in life and liked them so much that she ended up as a chain-smoker. When Sadie thinks of her, it is as if she can still see her reclining on an embroidered mat spread on the floor, one elbow supported on a bolster, some cushions at her back, reading a brown tattered little volume through her glasses and enveloping herself in clouds of scented cigarette smoke.

Annapurna often speaks about those days. Annapurna was a relative, some sort of cousin. She had run away from her husband (who drank and, it was whispered, went in for unnatural practices) and had come to live with them in the house. When Annapurna speaks about those distant times, she does so as if everyone were still alive and all of them as young and gay as they were then. Often she says, "If only Srilata" — or Radhika — or Raksha — or Chandralekha — "were here now, how she would laugh!" But Srilata died of typhoid twenty years ago; Raksha married a Nepalese general and has gone to live in Katmandu; Chandralekha poisoned herself over an unhappy love affair. To Annapurna, however, it is as if everyone is still there, and she recalls and brings to life every detail of a distant event so that to Sadie too it begins to appear that she can hear the voices of those days. Till Annapurna returns to the present and — with an outstretched hand, her plump palm turned up to heaven — she acknowledges that they are all gone and many of them are dead; and she turns and looks at the Englishwoman and says, "And now you are going too," and her eyes are full of reproach.

It may seem strange that the mistress should reproach the wife, but Annapurna is within her rights to do so. For so many years now it is she who has taken over from the Englishwoman all the duties of a wife. There has never been any bitterness or jealousy between them. On the contrary, Sadie has always been grateful to her. She knows that before her husband became intimate with Annapurna, he used to go to other women. He *had* to go, he was such a healthy man and needed women as strong and healthy as he was; these were often young prostitutes. But for a long time now he has been content with Annapurna. He has put on an enormous amount of weight in these last years. It is Annapurna's fault, she feeds him too well and panders to his passion for good food. His meals are frequent and so heavy that, in between them, he is not capable of moving. He lies on a couch arranged for him on a veranda and breathes heavily. Sometimes he puffs at a hookah which stands within easy reach. He lies there for hours while Annapurna sits on the other end of the couch and entertains him with lively gossip. He enjoys that, but doesn't mind at all if she has no time for him. When he feels like talking, he summons one of the servants to come and squat on the carpet near his couch.

When Sadie first knew him, as a student at Oxford, he was a slim boy with burning eyes and a lock of hair on his forehead. He was always smiling and always on the go. He loved being a student, and though he never managed to graduate, got a lot out of it. He gave breakfast parties and had his own wine merchant and a red car in which he drove up to London several times a week; he was always discovering new pleasures, like hampers from Fortnum and Mason's and champagne parties on the river. Sadie had grown up in rather an austere atmosphere. Her family were comfortably off but had high principles of self-restraint and preferred lofty thought to lavish living. Sadie herself — a serious girl, a spare, stringent, high-bred English beauty — thought she had the same principles, but the young Indian made her see another side to her nature. When he went back to India, it was impossible to stay behind. She followed him, married him, and loved him even more than she had done in England. He belonged here so completely. Sometimes Sadie didn't see him for days on end — when he went on shooting parties and other expeditions with his friends — but she didn't mind. She stayed at home with the other women and enjoyed life as much as he did. There were summer nights when they all sat out in the garden by the fountain, and Chandralekha, who had a very sweet voice, sang sad songs from the hills while Radhika accompanied her on a lutelike instrument; and the moon shone, and Annapurna cut up mangoes for all of them, and the smell of these mangoes mingled with that exuding from the flowering bushes in a mixture so pungent, so heady that when the Englishwoman recalls those nights now, it is always by their scent that they become physical and present to her.

Annapurna and Sadie's husband play cards every evening. They play for money and Annapurna usually loses and then she gets cross; she always refuses to pay up, and the next evening they conveniently forget her debt and start again from scratch. But if he loses, then she insists on immediate payment: she laughs in triumph and, holding out her hand, opens and shuts it greedily and shouts, "Come on, pay up!" She also calls to Sadie and the servants to witness his discomfiture: those evenings are always merry. But sooner or later, and often in the middle of a game, she falls asleep. Once Annapurna is asleep, everything is very quiet. The servants turn off the lights and go to their quarters; the husband sits on his couch and looks out into the garden and takes a few puffs at his hookah; Sadie is upstairs in her bedroom. Nothing stirs, there isn't a sound, until the husband gives a loud sigh as he heaves himself up. He wakes Annapurna and they support each other up the stairs to their bedroom, where they sink onto their large soft bed and are asleep immediately and totally until it is morning. It is a long time before Sadie can get to sleep. She walks up and down the room. She argues with herself to and fro, and her mind heaves in turmoil like a sea in storm. The fact that everything else is calm and sleeping exacerbates her restlessness. She longs for some response, for something or someone other than herself to be affected by what is going on within her. But there is only silence and sleep. She steps out of her room and onto the veranda. The garden is in imperfect darkness, dimly and fitfully lit by the moon. Occasionally — very, very occasionally — a bird wakes up and rustles in a tree.

It was during these hours of solitude that she came to her decision to leave. To others — and, at the actual moment of making it, even to herself — it seemed like a sudden decision, but in fact, looking back, she realizes that she has been preparing for it for twenty years. She can even mark the exact day, twenty years ago, when first she knew that she did not want to go on living here. It was when her son was sick with one of those sudden mysterious illnesses that so often attack children in India. He lay burning in the middle of a great bed, with his eyes full of fever; he was very quiet except for an occasional groan. All the women in the house had gathered round his bedside and all were giving advice and different remedies. Some sat on chairs, some on the floor; the mother-in-law squatted cross-legged on the end of his bed, her spectacles on her nose, smoking cigarettes and turning the pages of a novel; from time to time she made soothing noises at Dev and squeezed his ankles. Annapurna sat by his side and rubbed ice on his head. Every time Dev groaned they all said, "Oh, poor Baba, poor Baba." The servants moved in and out; they too said, "Oh, poor Baba" and looked at him pityingly. The Englishwoman remembered the sickbeds of her own childhood, how she lay for hours comfortable and bored with nothing to do except watch the tree outside the window and the fat wet raindrops squashing against and sliding down the windowpane. The only person who ever came in was her mother when it was time for her medicine. But Dev wouldn't have liked that. He wanted everyone with him, and if one of the aunts was out of the room for too long a time, he would ask for her in a weak voice and someone would have to go and fetch her.

Sadie went out onto the veranda. But it was no better there. The day was one of those murky yellow ones when the sun is stifled in vapors of dust. She felt full of fears, for Dev and for herself, as if they were both being sucked down by — what was it? The heat? The loving women inside? The air, thick as a swamp in which fevers breed? She longed to be alone with her sick child in some cool place. But she knew this was not possible and that they belonged here in this house crammed full with relatives and choking under a yellow sky. She could never forget the despair of that moment, though in the succeeding years there were many like it. But that was the first.

As she stood there on the veranda, she saw her husband arrive home. He 20 was a very bright spot in that murky day. He was dressed in a starched white kurta with little jewels for buttons, and his face was raised towards her as she stood up on the veranda and he was smiling. He was no longer the slim boy she had first known but neither was he as fat as he is today: no, he was in the prime of life then, and what a prime! He came bounding up the outside staircase towards her and said, "How is he?"

"How can he be," she answered, "with all of them in there."

Surprised at her tone, he stopped smiling and looked at her anxiously. Her anger mounted, and there were other things mixed in with it now: not only the heat and the overcrowded room but also that he was so sleek and smiling and young while she — oh, she felt worn-out, wrung-out, and knew she looked it.

She thought of the prostitutes he went to. It seemed to her that she could see and smell their plump, brown, wriggling young bodies, greasy with scented oil.

In a shaking voice she said, "They're stifling that poor boy—they won't let him breathe. No one seems to have the least idea of hygiene."

He knew it was more than she was saying and continued to look at her anxiously. "Are you ill?" he asked, and put out his hand to feel her forehead. When she drew back, he asked, "What is it?" full of sympathy.

They had been speaking in low voices, but all the same, from inside the 25 crowded room, Annapurna had sensed that something was wrong. She left the bedside and came out to join them. She looked inquiringly at Sadie's husband. They were not yet lovers at that time, but there was that instinctive understanding between them that there was between all the members of that household.

"She is not well," he said.

"I *am* well! I'm perfectly well!" Sadie burst into tears. She had no control over this. Furiously she wiped the foolish tears from her cheeks.

Both of them melted with tenderness. Annapurna folded her in an embrace; the husband stroked her back. When she struggled to get free, they thought it was a new outbreak of anguish and redoubled their attentions. At last she cried, "It's so *hot!*" and indeed she could hardly breathe, and perspiration ran down her in runnels from being squashed against fat Annapurna. Then Annapurna let her go. They both stood and looked at her full of anxiety for her; and these two round, healthy, shining faces looking at her with love, *pitying* her, were so unbearable to her that, to prevent herself from bursting into the tears that she despised but that they, she knew, not only awaited but even expected, she turned, and, hurrying along the veranda that ran like a gallery all round the house, she hid herself in her bedroom and locked the door. They followed and knocked urgently and begged to be allowed to enter. She refused to open. She could hear them discussing her outside the door: they were full of understanding, they realized that people did get upset like this and that then it was the duty of others to soothe and help them.

She was always being soothed and helped. She is still being soothed and helped. Annapurna has taken everything out of her suitcase and is repacking it in what she considers is a better way. She has had special shoe bags sewn. As a matter of fact, she would like to have a completely new outfit of clothes made for her. She says how will it look if Sadie arrives with nothing better than those few shabby rags in that little suitcase. Sadie thinks to herself, look to whom? She knows almost no one there: a few distant relatives, one old school friend; she hasn't been there for thirty years, she has no contacts, no correspondence— and yet she is going home! Home! And again happiness rushes over her in waves, and she takes a deep breath to be able to bear it.

"And not a single piece of jewelry," Annapurna grumbles.   30

Sadie laughs. She has given it all away long ago to Monica and to Dev's wife, and very glad she was to get rid of all those heavy costly gold ornaments. They were her share of the family jewels, but she never knew what to do with them. Certainly she couldn't wear them—she was always too thin and pale to be able to carry off these pieces fit for a barbarian queen; so she had left them lying around for years in a cupboard till Annapurna had taken them away from her to lock up in a safe.

"At least *one* piece you could have let me keep for you," Annapurna now says. "Then you would have had something to show them. What will they think of us?"

"What will *who* think?" Sadie asks, and the idea of the distant relatives and her poor school friend (Clare, still unmarried and still teaching) having any thoughts on the subject of what properties she has brought back with her from India makes her laugh again. And there is a lightheartedness in her laughter that hasn't been there for a long time, and Annapurna hears it and is hurt by it.

They are both hurt by her attitude. It has been years since Sadie saw her husband so upset; but then it has been years since anything really upset him. He has led a very calm life lately. Not that his life was not always calm and comfortable, but there were times in his younger days when he, like everyone else in the house, had his outbursts. She particularly remembers one he had with his sister Chandralekha. Actually, at that time, the whole house was in upheaval. Chandralekha had formed an unfortunate attachment to a man nobody approved of. They were not a rigid family that way — there had been several love matches — but it seemed Chandralekha's choice was entirely unsuitable. Sadie had met the man, who struck her as intelligent and of a strong character. In fact, she thought Chandralekha had shown excellent taste. But when she told her husband so, he waved her aside and said she didn't understand. And it was true, she didn't, everything that went on in the house during those days was a mystery to her. Oh, she understood vaguely what it was all about — the man was of *low birth,* and all his virtues of character and self-made position could not wipe that stain away — but the passions that were aroused, the issues that were thought to be at stake, were beyond her comprehension. Yet she could see that all of them were suffering deeply, and Chandralekha was in a torment of inner conflict (indeed, she later committed suicide).

One day Chandralekha came in carrying a dish of sweet rice which she had made herself. She said, "Just wait till you taste this," and she lovingly ladled a spoonful onto her brother's plate. He began to eat with relish, but quite suddenly he pushed the plate away and began to cry out loud. Everyone at once knew why, of course. The only person who was surprised was Sadie — both at the suddenness of the outburst and at the lengths to which he went. He banged his head against the wall, flung himself on the ground at Chandralekha's feet, and at one point he snatched up a knife and held it at his own throat and had to have it wrested away from him by all the women there surrounding him. "The children, the children!" he kept crying, and at first Sadie thought he meant their own children, Monica and Dev, and she couldn't understand what was threatening them; but everyone else knew he meant Chandralekha's children who were yet unborn but who would be born, and, if she married this man, born with polluted blood. Sadie didn't know how that scene ended; she went away and locked herself up in her bedroom. She covered her ears with her hands to shut out the noise and cries that echoed through the house.

When he learned of her decision to leave, Sadie's husband begged and pleaded with her in the same way he had done with Chandralekha all those years ago. The Englishwoman felt embarrassed and ashamed for him. He looked so ridiculous, being so heavy and fat, with his great bulk heaving and emitting cries like those of an hysterical woman. No one else found him ridiculous — on the contrary, the servants and Annapurna were deeply affected by his strong emotions and tried to comfort him. But he wouldn't be comforted till in the end his passion spent itself. Then he became resigned and even quite practical and sent for his lawyer to make a settlement. He was very generous toward his wife, and indeed keeps pressing her to accept more and is distressed because she doesn't need it. So now she feels ashamed not of him but of herself and her own lack of feeling.

It is her last night in India. As usual, her husband and Annapurna are playing cards together. When she joins them, they look at her affectionately and treat her like a guest. Annapurna offers tea, sherbet, limewater, and is distressed when she declines all these suggestions. She is always distressed by the fact that Sadie needs less food than she does. She says, "How can you live like that?" After a moment's thought, she adds, "How will you live *there*? Who will look after you and see that you don't starve yourself to death?" When Sadie looks at her, it is as she feared: tears are again flowing down Annapurna's cheeks. A sob also breaks from out of her bosom. It is echoed by another sob: Sadie looks up and sees that tears are also trickling down her husband's face. Neither of them speaks, and in fact they go on playing cards. The Englishwoman lowers her eyes away from them; she sits there, silent, prim, showing no emotion. She hopes they think she *has* no emotion; she does her best to hide it — the happiness that will not be suppressed, even at the sight of their tears.

Annapurna has had enough of playing. She flings down the cards (she has been losing). She wipes her tears away with her forearm, like a child, yawns, sighs, says, "Well, time to go to bed" in resignation. He says, "Yes, it's time," with the same sigh and the same resignation. They have accepted the Englishwoman's departure; it grieves them, but they submit to it, as human beings have to submit to everything, such as old age and disease and loss of every kind. They walk upstairs slowly, leaning on each other.

When Sadie goes up to her own room, she is almost running in her excitement. She looks in the mirror and is surprised at the drained face that looks back at her. She doesn't feel like that at all — no, she feels the way she used to, so that now she expects her bright eyes back again and her pink cheeks. She turns away from the mirror, laughing at her own foolishness; and she can hear her own laughter and it is just the way it used to be. She knows she won't sleep tonight. She doesn't want to sleep. She loves this feeling of excitement and youth and pacing the room with her heart beating and wild thoughts storming in her head. The servants have turned out the lights downstairs and gone to bed. The lights are out in her husband's and Annapurna's room too; they must be fast asleep side by side on their bed.

The Englishwoman can't see the moon, but the garden is lit up by some 40 sort of faint silver light. She can make out the fountain with the stone statue, and the lime trees, and the great flowering bush of queen of the night; there is the bench where they used to sit in the evenings when Chandralekha sang in her sweet voice. But as she goes on looking, the moonlit scene brightens until it is no longer that silver garden but English downs spreading as far as the eye can see, yellow on one side, green on another. The green side is being rained upon by mild soft rain coming down like a curtain, and the yellow side is being shone upon by a sun as mild and soft as that rain. On a raised knoll in the foreground there is an oak tree with leaves and acorns, and she is standing by this tree; and as she stands there, on that eminence overlooking the downs, strong winds blow right through her. They are as cold and fresh as the waters of a mountain torrent. They threaten to sweep her off her feet so that she has to plant herself down very firmly and put out her hand to support herself against the trunk of the tree (she can feel the rough texture of its bark). She raises her face, and her hair — not *her* hair but the shining hair of her youth — flies wild and free in that strong wind.

Considerations for Critical Thinking and Writing

1. First Response. Why do you think Sadie feels elated about leaving India? Is it the country, her family, or something else she wants to leave behind?

2. What qualities do you associate with Indian culture? The narrator suggests that many people think "Indian means 'spiritual'" (para. 6). Explain why you agree or disagree with this popular assumption. How do your ideas about India affect your reading of the story?

3. How does Annapurna serve as a foil to Sadie?

4. How does Sadie explain her reasons for leaving India to her daughter? Why isn't Sadie's explanation adequate for Annapurna?

5. Describe Sadie's early years in India. Why doesn't she like to recall those years?

6. Characterize Sadie's husband. What attracted her to him? How does she feel about him now?

7. Why does Sadie feel uncomfortable in her husband's household? What causes her to change her attitude toward her husband and Indian culture? Where is this turning point for Sadie in the story?

8. What does Chandralekha's story reveal about life in India? How does her story affect Sadie?

9. What is the effect of the narrator's referring to Sadie as "the English-woman"? Discuss the significance of the title.

10. How does Sadie think life in England will contrast with her life in India? Do you think her expectations about England are realistic? Explain your response.

11. Given the sense of England provided by Sadie, how do you think Annapurna would experience life there?

Charles Johnson (b. 1948)

Born in Evanston, Illinois, Charles Johnson was educated at Southern Illinois University and the State University of New York at Stony Brook. He has worked as a cartoonist and a journalist, and now teaches creative writing at the University of Washington. His writings often reflect a deep commitment to African American experience. His novels include *Faith and the Good Thing* (1974), *Oxherding Tale* (1982), *Middle Passage* (1990), and *Dreamer: A Novel* (1999), which won the National Book Award. He has also published *Being and Race: Black Writing Since 1970* (1988), a collection of essays, and *The Sorcerer's Apprentice* (1986), a collection of short stories.

Exchange Value   1982

Me and my brother, Loftis, came in by the old lady's window. There was some kinda boobytrap — boxes of broken glass — that shoulda warned us Miss Bailey wasn't the easy mark we made her to be. She been living alone for twenty years in 4-B down the hall from Loftis and me, long before our folks died — a hincty, halfbald West Indian woman with a craglike face, who kept her door barricaded, shutters closed, and wore the same sorry-looking outfit — black wingtip shoes, cropfingered gloves in winter, and a man's floppy hat — like maybe she dressed half-asleep or in a dark attic. Loftis, he figured Miss Bailey had some grandtheft dough stashed inside, jim, or leastways a shoebox full of money, 'cause she never spent a nickel on herself, not even for food, and only left her place at night.

Anyway, we figured Miss Bailey was gone. Her mailbox be full, and Pookie White, who run the Thirty-ninth Street Creole restaurant, he say she ain't dropped by in days to collect the handouts he give her so she can get by. So here's me and Loftis, tipping around Miss Bailey's blackdark kitchen. The floor be littered with fruitrinds, roaches, old food furred with blue mold. Her dirty dishes be stacked in a sink feathered with cracks, and it looks like the old lady been living, lately, on Ritz crackers and Department of Agriculture (Welfare Office) peanut butter. Her toilet be stopped up, too, and, on the bathroom floor, there's five Maxwell House coffee cans full of shit. Me, I was closing her bathroom door when I whiffed this evil smell so bad, so thick, I could hardly breathe, and what air I breathed was stifling, like solid fluid in my throatpipes, like broth or soup. "Cooter," Loftis whisper, low, across the room, "you smell that?" He went right on sniffing it, like people do for some reason when something be smelling stanky, then took out his headrag and held it over his mouth. "Smells like something crawled up in here and died!" Then, head low, he slipped his long self into the living room. Me, I stayed by the window, gulping for air, and do you know why?

You oughta know, up front, that I ain't too good at this gangster stuff, and I had a real bad feeling about Miss Bailey from the get-go. Mama used to say it was Loftis, not me, who'd go places — I see her standing at the sideboard by the sink now, big as a Frigidaire, white flour to her elbows, a washtowel over her shoulder, while we ate a breakfast of cornbread and syrup. Loftis, he graduated fifth at DuSable High School, had two gigs and, like Papa, he be always wanting the things white people had out in Hyde Park, where Mama did daywork sometimes. Loftis, he be the kind of brother who buys *Esquire*, sews Hart, Schaffner & Marx labels in Robert Hall suits, talks properlike, packs his hair with Murray's; and he took classes in politics and stuff at the Black People's Topographical Library in the late 1960s. At thirty, he make his bed military-style, reads *Black Scholar* on the bus he takes to the plant, and, come hell or high water, plans to make a Big Score. Loftis, he say I'm 'bout as useful on a hustle — or when it comes to getting ahead — as a headcold, and he says he has to count my legs sometimes to make sure I ain't a mule, seeing how, for all my eighteen years, I can't keep no job and sorta stay close to home, watching TV, or reading *World's Finest* comic books, or maybe just laying dead, listening to music, imagining I see faces or foreign places in water stains on the wallpaper, 'cause some days, when I remember Papa, then Mama, killing theyselves for chump change — a pitiful li'l bowl of porridge — I get to thinking that even if I ain't had all I wanted, maybe I've had, you know, all I'm ever gonna get.

"Cooter," Loftis say from the living room. "You best get in here quick."

Loftis, he'd switched on Miss Bailey's bright, overhead living room lights, 5 so for a second I couldn't see and started coughing — the smell be so powerful it hit my nostrils like coke — and when my eyes cleared, shapes come forward in the light, and I thought for an instant like I'd slipped in space. I seen why Loftis called me, and went back two steps. See, 4-B's so small if you ring Miss Bailey's doorbell, the toilet'd flush. But her living room, webbed in dust, be filled to the max with dollars of all denominations, stacks of stock in General Motors, Gulf Oil, and 3M Company in old White Owl cigar boxes, battered purses, or bound in pink rubber bands. It be like the kind of cubbyhole kids play in, but filled with . . . *things:* everything, like a world inside the world, you take it from me, so like picturebook scenes of plentifulness you could seal yourself off in here and settle forever. Loftis and me both drew breath suddenly. There be unopened cases of Jack Daniel's, three safes cemented to the floor, hundreds of matchbooks, unworn clothes, a fuel-burning stove, dozens of wedding rings, rubbish, World War II magazines, a carton of a hundred canned sardines, mink stoles, old rags, a birdcage, a bucket of silver dollars, thousands of books, paintings, quarters in tobacco cans, two pianos, glass jars of pennies, a set of bagpipes, an almost complete Model A Ford dappled with rust, and, I swear, three sections of a dead tree.

"Damn!" My head be light; I sat on an upended peach crate and picked up a bottle of Jack Daniel's.

"Don't you touch *anything!*" Loftis, he panting a little; he slap both hands on a table. "No until we inventory this stuff."

"Inventory? Aw, Lord, Loftis," I say, "something ain't *right* about this stash. There could be a curse on it. . . ."

"Boy, sometime you act weak-minded."

"For real, Loftis, I got a feeling. . . ." 10

Loftis, he shucked off his shoes, and sat down heavily on the lumpy arm of a stuffed chair. "Don't say *anything.*" He chewed his knuckles, and for the first time Loftis looked like he didn't know his next move. "Let me think, okay?" He squeezed his nose in a way he has when thinking hard, sighed, then stood up and say, "There's something you better see in that bedroom yonder. Cover up your mouth."

"Loftis, I ain't going in there."

He look at me right funny then. "She's a miser, that's all. She saves things."

"But a tree?" I say. "Loftis, a *tree* ain't normal!"

"Cooter, I ain't gonna tell you twice." 15

Like always, I followed Loftis, who swung his flashlight from the plant — he a night watchman — into Miss Bailey's bedroom, but me, I'm thinking how trippy this thing is getting, remembering how, last year, when I had a paper route, the old lady, with her queer, crablike walk, pulled my coat for some change in the hallway, and when I give her a handful of dimes, she say, like one of them spooks on old-time radio, "Thank you, Co-o-oter," then gulped the coins down like aspirin, no lie, and scurried off like a hunchback. Me, I wanted no parts of this squirrely old broad, but Loftis, he holding my wrist now, beaming his light onto a low bed. The room had a funny, museumlike smell.

Real sour. It was full of dirty laundry. And I be sure the old lady's stuff had a terrible string attached when Loftis, looking away, lifted her bedsheets and a knot of black flies rose. I stepped back and held my breath. Miss Bailey be in her long-sleeved flannel nightgown, bloated, like she'd been blown up by a bicycle pump, her old face caved in with rot, flyblown, her fingers big and colored like spoiled bananas. Her wristwatch be ticking softly beside a half-eaten hamburger. Above the bed, her wall had roaches squashed in little swirls of bloodstain. Maggots clustered in her eyes, her ears, and one fist-sized rat hissed inside her flesh. My eyes snapped shut. My knees failed; then I did a Hollywood faint. When I surfaced, Loftis, he be sitting beside me in the living room, where he'd drug me, reading a wrinkled, yellow article from the *Chicago Daily Defender.*

"Listen to this," Loftis say. "'Elnora Bailey, forty-five, a Negro housemaid in the Highland Park home of Henry Conners, is the beneficiary of her employer's will. An old American family, the Conners arrived in this country on the *Providence* shortly after the voyage of the *Mayflower.* The family flourished in the early days of the 1900s.' . . ." He went on, getting breath: "'A distinguished and wealthy industrialist, without heirs or a wife, Conners willed his entire estate to Miss Bailey of 3347 North Clark Street for her twenty years of service to his family.' . . ." Loftis, he give that Geoffrey Holder laugh of his, low and deep; then it eased up his throat until it hit a high note and tipped his head back onto his shoulders. "Cooter, that was before we was born! Miss Bailey kept this in the Bible next to her bed."

Standing, I braced myself with one hand against the wall. "She didn't earn it?"

"Naw." Loftis, he folded the paper—"Not one penny"—and stuffed it in his shirt pocket. His jaw looked tight as a horseshoe. "Way *I* see it," he say, "this was her one shot in a lifetime to be rich, but being country, she had backward ways and blew it." Rubbing his hands, he stood up to survey the living room. "Somebody's gonna find Miss Bailey soon, but if we stay on the case—Cooter, don't square up on me now—we can tote everything to our place before daybreak. Best we start with the big stuff."

"But why didn't she *use* it, huh? Tell me that?"   20

Loftis, he don't pay me no mind. When he gets an idea in his head, you can't dig it out with a chisel. How long it took me and Loftis to inventory, then haul Miss Bailey's queer old stuff to our crib, I can't say, but that cranky old ninnyhammer's hoard come to $879,543 in cash money, thirty-two bank books (some deposits be only $5), and me, I wasn't sure I was dreaming or what, but I suddenly flashed on this feeling, once we left her flat, that all the fears Loftis and me had about the future be gone, 'cause Miss Bailey's property was the past—the power of that fellah Henry Conners trapped like a bottle spirit—which we could live off, so it was the future, too, pure potential: can *do.* Loftis got to talking on about how that piano we pushed home be equal to a thousand bills, jim, which equals, say, a bad TEAC A-3340 tape deck, or a down payment on a deuce-and-a-quarter. Its value be (Loftis say) that of a universal standard of measure, relational, unreal as number, so that tape deck could turn, magically, into two gold lamé suits, a trip to Tijuana, or twenty-five blow jobs from a ho—we had $879,543 worth of wishes, if you can deal with that. Be like Miss Bailey's stuff is raw energy, and Loftis and me, like wizards, could transform her stuff into anything else at will. All we had to do, it seemed to me, was decide exactly what to exchange it for.

While Loftis studied this over (he looked funny, like a potato trying to say something, after the inventory, and sat, real quiet, in the kitchen), I filled my pockets with fifties, grabbed me a cab downtown to grease, yum, at one of them high-hat restaurants in the Loop. . . . But then I thought better of it, you know, like I'd be out of place — just another jig putting on airs — and scarfed instead at a ribjoint till both my eyes bubbled. This fat lady making fish-burgers in the back favored an old hardleg baby-sitter I once had, a Mrs. Paine who made me eat ocher, and I wanted so bad to say, "Loftis and me Got Ovuh," but I couldn't put that in the wind, could I, so I hatted up. Then I copped a boss silk necktie, cashmere socks, and a whistle-slick maxi leather jacket on State Street, took cabs *every*where, but when I got home that evening, a funny, Pandora-like feeling hit me. I took off the jacket, boxed it — it looked trifling in the hallway's weak light — and, tired, turned my key in the door. I couldn't get in. Loftis, he'd changed the lock and, when he finally let me in, looking vaguer, crabby, like something out of the Book of Revelations, I seen this elaborate, booby-trapped tunnel of cardboard and razor blades behind him, with a two-foot space just big enough for him or me to crawl through. That wasn't all. Two bags of trash from the furnace room downstairs be sitting inside the door. Loftis, he give my leather jacket this evil look, hauled me inside, and hit me upside my head.

"How much this thing set us back?"

"Two fifty." My jaws got tight; I toss him my receipt. "You want me to take it back? Maybe I can get something else. . . ."

Loftis, he say, not to me, but to the receipt, "Remember the time Mama 25 give me that ring we had in the family for fifty years? And I took it to Merchandise Mart and sold it for a few pieces of candy?" He hitched his chair forward and sat with his elbows on his knees. "That's what you did, Cooter. You crawled into a Clark bar." He commence to rip up my receipt, then picked up his flashlight and keys. "As soon as you buy something you *lose* the power to buy something." He button up his coat with holes in the elbows, showing his blue shirt, then turned 'round at the tunnel to say, "Don't touch Miss Bailey's money, or drink her splo, or do *any*thing until I get back."

"Where you going?"

"To work. It's Wednesday, ain't it?"

"You going to work?"

"Yeah."

"You got to go *really*? Loftis," I say, "what you brang them bags of trash in 30 here for?"

"It ain't trash!" He cut his eyes at me. "There's good clothes in there. Mr. Peterson tossed them out, he don't care, but I saw some use in them, that's all."

"Loftis . . ."

"Yeah?"

"What we gonna do with all this money?"

Loftis pressed his fingers to his eyelids, and for a second he looked caged, 35 or like somebody'd kicked him in his stomach. Then he cut me some slack: "Let me think on it tonight — it don't pay to rush — then we can TCB, okay?"

Five hours after Loftis leave for work, that old blister Mr. Peterson, our landlord, he come collecting rent, find Mrs. Bailey's body in apartment 4-B, and phoned the fire department. Me, I be folding my new jacket in tissue paper to keep it fresh, adding the box to Miss Bailey's unsunned treasures when two paramedics squeezed her on a long stretcher through a crowd in the hallway. See, I had to pin her from the stairhead, looking down one last time at this dizzy old lady, and I seen something in her face, like maybe she'd been poor as Job's turkey for thirty years, suffering that special Negro fear of using up what little we get in this life—Loftis, he call that entropy—believing in her belly, and for all her faith, jim, that there just ain't no more coming tomorrow from grace, or the Lord, or from her own labor, like she can't kill nothing, and won't nothing die . . . so when Conners will her his wealth, it put her through changes, she be spellbound, possessed by the promise of life, panicky about depletion, and locked now in the past 'cause *every* purchase, you know, has to be a poor buy: a loss of life. Me, I wasn't worried none. Loftis, he got a brain trained by years of talking trash with people in Frog Hudson's barbershop on Thirty-fifth Street. By morning, I knew, he'd have some kinda wheeze worked out.

But Loftis, he don't come home. Me, I got kinda worried. I listen to the hi-fi all day Thursday, only pawing outside to peep down the stairs, like that'd make Loftis come sooner. So Thursday go by; and come Friday the head's out of kilter—first there's an ogrelike belch from the toilet bowl, then water bursts from the bathroom into the kitchen—and me, I can't call the super (How do I explain the tunnel?), so I gave up and quit bailing. But on Saturday, I could smell greens cooking next door. Twice I almost opened Miss Bailey's sardines, even though starving be less an evil than eating up our stash, but I waited till it was dark and, with my stomach talking to me, stepped outside to Pookie White's, lay a hard-luck story on him, and Pookie, he give me some jambalaya and gumbo. Back home in the living room, finger-feeding myself, barricaded in by all that hope-made material, the Kid felt like a king in his counting room, and I copped some Zs in an armchair till I heard the door move on its hinges, then bumping in the tunnel, and a heavy-footed walk thumped into the bedroom.

"Loftis!" I rubbed my eyes. "You back?" It be Sunday morning. Six-thirty sharp. Darkness dissolved slowly into the strangeness of twilight, with the rays of sunlight surging at exactly the same angle they fall each evening, as if the hour be an island, a moment outside time. Me, I'm afraid Loftis gonna fuss 'bout my not straightening up, letting things go. I went into the bathroom, poured water in the one-spigot washstand—brown rust come bursting out in flakes—and rinsed my face. "Loftis, you supposed to be home four days ago. Hey," I say, toweling my face, "you okay?" How come he don't answer me? Wiping my hands on the seat of my trousers, I tipped into Loftis's room. He sleeping with his mouth open. His legs be drawn up, both fists clenched between his knees. He'd kicked his blanket on the floor. In his sleep, Loftis laughed, or moaned, it be hard to tell. His eyelids, not quite shut, show slits of white. I decided to wait till Loftis wake up for his decision, but turning, I seen his watch, keys, and what looked in the first stain of sunlight to be a carefully wrapped piece of newspaper on his nightstand. The sunlight swelled to a bright shimmer, focusing the bedroom slowly like solution do a photographic image in the developer. And then something so freakish went down I ain't sure it took place. Fumble-fingered, I unfolded the paper, and inside be a blemished penny. It be like suddenly somebody slapped my head from behind. Taped on the penny be a slip of paper, and on the paper be the note "Found while walking down Devon Avenue." I hear Loftis mumble like he trapped in a nightmare. "Hold tight," I whisper. "It's all right." Me, I wanted to tell Loftis how Miss Bailey looked four days ago, that maybe it didn't have to be like that for us — did it? — because we could change. Couldn't we? Me, I pull his packed sheets over him, wrap up the penny, and, when I locate Miss Bailey's glass jar in the living room, put it away carefully, for now, with the rest of our things.

CONSIDERATIONS FOR CRITICAL THINKING AND WRITING

1. FIRST RESPONSE. Comment on Cooter's concern early on that "something ain't right about this stash. There could be a curse on it" (para. 8).

2. How is Miss Bailey incidentally characterized throughout the story? Why does she hoard everything?

3. Compare Loftis's and Cooter's characters prior to their finding Miss Bailey's cache.

4. How do Loftis and Cooter react differently to their new-found wealth?

5. What does Loftis mean when he tells Cooter, "As soon as you buy something you *lose* the power to buy something" (25)?

6. How does Cooter explain Miss Bailey's hoarding in paragraph 36?

7. Explain how race is connected to the central conflict in the story.

8. Discuss the significance of the title. How do you read its meaning in relation to the plot and theme of the story?

9. Analyze the final paragraph. What do you think the future holds for Loftis and Cooter?

KATHERINE MANSFIELD (1888–1923)

Born in New Zealand, Katherine Mansfield moved to London when she was a young woman and began writing short stories. Her first collection, *In a German Pension,* appeared in 1911. Subsequent publications, which include *Bliss and Other Stories* (1920) and *The Garden Party* (1922), secured her reputation as an important writer. The full range of her short stories is available in *The Collected Short Stories of Katherine Mansfield* (1945). Mansfield tends to focus her stories on intelligent, sensitive protagonists who undergo subtle but important changes in their lives. In "Miss Brill," an aging Englishwoman spends the afternoon in a park located in an unnamed French vacation town watching the activities of the people around her. Through those observations, Mansfield characterizes Miss Brill and permits us to see her experience a moment that changes her view of the world as well as of herself.

Miss Brill   1922

Although it was so brilliantly fine — the blue sky powdered with gold and great spots of light like white wine splashed over the Jardins Publiques — Miss Brill was glad that she had decided on her fur. The air was motionless, but when you opened your mouth there was just a faint chill, like a chill from a glass of iced water before you sip, and now and again a leaf came drifting—from nowhere, from the sky. Miss Brill put up her hand and touched her fur. Dear little thing! It was nice to feel it again. She had taken it out of its box that afternoon, shaken out the moth-powder, given it a good brush, and rubbed the life back into the dim little eyes. "What has been happening to me?" said the sad little eyes. Oh, how sweet it was to see them snap at her again from the red eiderdown! . . . But the nose, which was of some black composition, wasn't at all firm. It must have had a knock, somehow. Never mind—a little dab of black sealing-wax when the time came—when it was absolutely necessary. . . . Little rogue! Yes, she really felt like that about it. Little rogue biting its tail just by her left ear. She could have taken it off and laid it on her lap and stroked it. She felt a tingling in her hands and arms, but that came from walking, she supposed. And when she breathed, something light and sad—no, not sad, exactly—something gentle seemed to move in her bosom.

There were a number of people out this afternoon, far more than last Sunday. And the band sounded louder and gayer. That was because the Season had begun. For although the band played all the year round on Sundays, out of season it was never the same. It was like some one playing with only the family to listen; it didn't care how it played if there weren't any strangers present. Wasn't the conductor wearing a new coat, too? She was sure it was new. He scraped with his foot and flapped his arms like a rooster about to crow, and the bandsmen sitting in the green rotunda blew out their cheeks and glared at the music. Now there came a little "flutey" bit—very pretty!—a little chain of bright drops. She was sure it would be repeated. It was; she lifted her head and smiled.

Only two people shared her "special" seat: a fine old man in a velvet coat, his hands clasped over a huge carved walking-stick, and a big old woman, sitting upright, with a roll of knitting on her embroidered apron. They did not speak. This was disappointing, for Miss Brill always looked forward to the conversation. She had become really quite expert, she thought, at listening as though she didn't listen, at sitting in other people's lives just for a minute while they talked around her.

She glanced, sideways, at the old couple. Perhaps they would go soon. Last Sunday, too, hadn't been as interesting as usual. An Englishman and his wife, he wearing a dreadful Panama hat and she button boots. And she'd gone on the whole time about how she ought to wear spectacles; she knew she needed them; but that it was no good getting any; they'd be sure to break and they'd never keep on. And he'd been so patient. He'd suggested everything—gold rims, the kind that curved round your ears, little pads inside the bridge. No, nothing would please her. "They'll always be sliding down my nose!" Miss Brill had wanted to shake her.

The old people sat on the bench, still as statues. Never mind, there was always the crowd to watch. To and fro, in front of the flower-beds and the band rotunda, the couples and groups paraded, stopped to talk, to greet, to buy a handful of flowers from the old beggar who had his tray fixed to the railings. Little children ran among them, swooping and laughing; little boys with big white silk bows under their chins, little girls, little French dolls, dressed up in velvet and lace. And sometimes a tiny staggerer came suddenly rocking into the open from under the trees, stopped, stared, as suddenly sat down "flop," until its small high-stepping mother, like a young hen, rushed scolding to its rescue. 5

Other people sat on the benches and green chairs, but they were nearly always the same, Sunday after Sunday, and—Miss Brill had often noticed—there was something funny about nearly all of them. They were odd, silent, nearly all old, and from the way they stared they looked as though they'd just come from dark little rooms or even—even cupboards!

Behind the rotunda the slender trees with yellow leaves down drooping, and through them just a line of sea, and beyond the blue sky with gold-veined clouds.

Tum-tum-tum tiddle-um! tiddle-um! tum tiddley-um tum ta! blew the band.

Two young girls in red came by and two young soldiers in blue met them, and they laughed and paired and went off arm-in-arm. Two peasant women with funny straw hats passed, gravely, leading beautiful smoke-colored donkeys. A cold, pale nun hurried by. A beautiful woman came along and dropped her bunch of violets, and a little boy ran after to hand them to her, and she took them and threw them away as if they'd been poisoned. Dear me! Miss Brill didn't know whether to admire that or not! And now an ermine toque and a gentleman in grey met just in front of her. He was tall, stiff, dignified, and she was wearing the ermine toque she'd bought when her hair was yellow. Now everything, her hair, her face, even her eyes, was the same color as the shabby ermine, and her hand, in its cleaned glove, lifted to dab her lips, was a tiny yellowish paw. Oh, she was so pleased to see him—delighted! She rather thought they were going to meet that afternoon. She described where she'd been—everywhere, here, there, along by the sea. The day was so charming—didn't he agree? And wouldn't he, perhaps? . . . But he shook his head, lighted a cigarette, slowly breathed a great deep puff into her face, and, even while she was still talking and laughing, flicked the match away and walked on. The ermine toque was alone; she smiled more brightly than ever. But even the band seemed to know what she was feeling and played more softly, played tenderly, and the drum beat, "The Brute! The Brute!" over and over. What would she do? What was going to happen now? But as Miss Brill wondered, the ermine toque turned, raised her hand as though she'd seen some one else, much nicer, just over there, and pattered away. And the band changed again and played more quickly, more gaily than ever, and the old couple on Miss Brill's seat got up and marched away, and such a funny old man with long whiskers hobbled along in time to the music and was nearly knocked over by four girls walking abreast.

Oh, how fascinating it was! How she enjoyed it! How she loved sitting here, watching it all! It was like a play. It was exactly like a play. Who could believe the sky at the back wasn't painted? But it wasn't till a little brown dog trotted on solemn and then slowly trotted off, like a little "theatre" dog, a little dog that had been drugged, that Miss Brill discovered what it was that made it so exciting. They were all on the stage. They weren't only the audience, not only looking on; they were acting. Even she had a part and came every Sunday. No doubt somebody would have noticed if she hadn't been there; she was part of the performance after all. How strange she'd never thought of it like that before! And yet it explained why she made such a point of starting from home at just the same time each week—so as not to be late for the performance— and it also explained why she had quite a queer, shy feeling at telling her English pupils how she spent her Sunday afternoons. No wonder! Miss Brill nearly laughed out loud. She was on the stage. She thought of the old invalid gentleman to whom she read the newspaper four afternoons a week while he slept in the garden. She had got quite used to the frail head on the cotton pillow, the hollowed eyes, the open mouth, and the high pinched nose. If he'd been dead she mightn't have noticed for weeks; she wouldn't have minded. But suddenly he knew he was having the paper read to him by an actress! "An actress!" The old head lifted; two points of light quivered in the old eyes. "An actress—are ye?" And Miss Brill smoothed the newspaper as though it were the manuscript of her part and said gently: "Yes, I have been an actress for a long time."

The band had been having a rest. Now they started again. And what they 10 played was warm, sunny, yet there was just a faint chill—a something, what was it?—not sadness—no, not sadness—a something that made you want to sing. The tune lifted, lifted, the light shone; and it seemed to Miss Brill that in another moment all of them, all the whole company, would begin singing. The young ones, the laughing ones who were moving together, they would begin, and the men's voices, very resolute and brave, would join them. And then she too, she too, and the others on the benches—they would come in with a kind of accompaniment—something low, that scarcely rose or fell, something so beautiful—moving. . . . And Miss Brill's eyes filled with tears and she looked smiling at all the other members of the company. Yes, we understand, we understand, she thought—though what they understood she didn't know.

Just at that moment a boy and a girl came and sat down where the old couple had been. They were beautifully dressed; they were in love. The hero and heroine, of course, just arrived from his father's yacht. And still soundlessly singing, still with that trembling smile, Miss Brill prepared to listen.

"No, not now," said the girl. "Not here, I can't."

"But why? Because of that stupid old thing at the end there?" asked the boy. "Why does she come here at all—who wants her? Why doesn't she keep her silly old mug at home?"

"It's her fu-fur which is so funny," giggled the girl. "It's exactly like a fried whiting."

"Ah, be off with you!" said the boy in an angry whisper. Then: "Tell me, ma 15 petite chère——"

"No, not here," said the girl. "Not *yet*."

On her way home she usually bought a slice of honey-cake at the baker's. It was her Sunday treat. Sometimes there was an almond in her slice, some-times not. It made a great difference. If there was an almond it was like carry-ing home a tiny present—a surprise—something that might very well not have been there. She hurried on the almond Sundays and struck the match for the kettle in quite a dashing way.

But today she passed the baker's by, climbed the stairs, went into the little dark room—her room like a cupboard—and sat down on the red eiderdown. She sat there for a long time. The box that the fur came out of was on the bed. She unclasped the necklet quickly; quickly, without looking, laid it inside. But when she put the lid on she thought she heard something crying.

CONSIDERATIONS FOR CRITICAL THINKING AND WRITING

1. FIRST RESPONSE. There is almost no physical description of Miss Brill in the story. What do you think she looks like? Develop a detailed description that would be consistent with her behavior.

2. How does the calculated omission of Miss Brill's first name contribute to her characterization?

3. What details make Miss Brill more than a stock characterization of a frail old lady?

4. What do Miss Brill's observations about the people she encounters reveal about her?

5. What is the conflict in the story? Who or what is the antagonist?

6. Locate the climax of the story. How is it resolved?

7. What is the purpose of the fur piece? What is the source of the crying in the final sentence of the story?

8. Is Miss Brill a static or a dynamic character?

9. Describe Miss Brill's sense of herself at the end of the story.

10. Discuss the function of the minor characters mentioned in the story. Analyze how Katherine Mansfield used them to reveal Miss Brill's character.

POETRY

Jimmy Santiago Baca (b. 1952)

Green Chile   *1989*

I prefer red chile over my eggs
and potatoes for breakfast.
Red chile *ristras*° decorate my door,   a braided string of peppers
dry on my roof, and hang from eaves.
They lend open-air vegetable stands   5
historical grandeur, and gently swing
with an air of festive welcome.
I can hear them talking in the wind,
haggard, yellowing, crisp, rasping
tongues of old men, licking the breeze.   10

     But grandmother loves green chile.
When I visit her,
she holds the green chile pepper
in her wrinkled hands.
Ah, voluptuous, masculine,   15
an air of authority and youth simmers
from its swan-neck stem, tapering to a flowery
collar, fermenting resinous spice.
A well-dressed gentleman at the door
my grandmother takes sensuously in her hand,   20
rubbing its firm glossed sides,
caressing the oily rubbery serpent,
with mouth-watering fulfillment,
fondling its curves with gentle fingers.

Its bearing magnificent and taut   25
as flanks of a tiger in mid-leap,
she thrusts her blade into
and cuts it open, with lust
on her hot mouth, sweating over the stove,
bandanna round her forehead,   30
mysterious passion on her face
and she serves me green chile con carne
between soft warm leaves of corn tortillas,
with beans and rice — her sacrifice
to her little prince.   35
I slurp from my plate
with last bit of tortilla, my mouth burns
and I hiss and drink a tall glass of cold water.

All over New Mexico, sunburned men and women
drive rickety trucks stuffed with gunny-sacks   40
of green chile, from Belen, Veguita, Willard, Estancia,
San Antonio y Socorro, from fields
to roadside stands, you see them roasting green chile
in screen-sided homemade barrels, and for a dollar a bag,
we relive this old, beautiful ritual again and again.   45

CONSIDERATIONS FOR CRITICAL THINKING AND WRITING

1. FIRST RESPONSE. What's the difference between red and green chiles in this
   poem? Find the different images the speaker uses to draw a distinction
   between the two.

2. What kinds of images are used to describe the grandmother's preparation
   of green chile? What is the effect of those images?

3. Try writing a description — in poetry or prose — that uses vivid images to
   evoke a powerful response (either positive or negative) to a particular food.

DIANE BURNS (B. 1957)

Sure You Can Ask Me a Personal Question   *1981*

How do you do?
   No, I am not Chinese.
No, not Spanish.
   No, I am American Indi — uh, Native American.
No, not from India.   5
   No, not Apache.
No, not Navajo.
   No, not Sioux.
No, we are not extinct.
   Yes, Indin.   10
Oh?

So that's where you got those high cheekbones.
Your great grandmother, huh?
   An Indian Princess, huh?
Hair down to there?   15
   Let me guess. Cherokee?
Oh, so you've had an Indian friend?
   That close?
Oh, so you've had an Indian lover?
   That tight?   20
Oh, so you've had an Indian servant?
   That much?
Yeah, it was awful what you guys did to us.
   It's real decent of you to apologize.
No, I don't know where you can get peyote.   25
   No, I don't know where you can get Navajo rugs real cheap.
No, I didn't make this. I bought it at Bloomingdales.
   Thank you. I like your hair too.
I don't know if anyone knows whether or not Cher is really Indian.
   No, I didn't make it rain tonight.   30
Yeah. Uh-huh. Spirituality.
   Uh-huh. Yeah. Spirituality. Uh-huh. Mother
Earth. Yeah. Uh-huh. Uh-huh. Spirituality.
   No, I didn't major in archery.
Yeah, a lot of us drink too much.   35
   Some of us can't drink enough.
This ain't no stoic look.
   This is my face.

CONSIDERATIONS FOR CRITICAL THINKING AND WRITING

1. FIRST RESPONSE. What sort of person do you imagine the speaker is addressing?

2. Discuss the poem's humor. Does it also have a serious theme? Explain.

3. What is the effect of the repeated phrases throughout the poem?

EMILY DICKINSON (1830–1886)

Much Madness is divinest Sense —   *c. 1862*

Much Madness is divinest Sense —
To a discerning Eye —
Much Sense — the starkest Madness —
'Tis the Majority
In this, as All, prevail —
Assent — and you are sane —
Demur — you're straightway dangerous —
And handled with a Chain —

CONSIDERATIONS FOR CRITICAL THINKING AND WRITING

1. FIRST RESPONSE. Thomas Wentworth Higginson's wife once referred to Dickinson as the "partially cracked poetess of Amherst." Assuming that Dickinson had some idea of how she was regarded by the "Majority," how might this poem be seen as an insight into her life?

2. Discuss the conflict between the individual and society in this poem. Which images are used to describe each? How do these images affect your attitudes about them?

3. Comment on the effectiveness of the poem's final line.

CHITRA BANERJEE DIVAKARUNI (B. 1956)

Indian Movie, New Jersey   1990

Not like the white filmstars, all rib
and gaunt cheekbone, the Indian sex-goddess
smiles plumply from behind a flowery
branch. Below her brief red skirt, her thighs
are satisfying-solid, redeeming   5
as tree trunks. She swings her hips
and the men-viewers whistle. The lover-hero
dances in to a song, his lip-sync
a little off, but no matter, we
know the words already and sing along.   10
It is safe here, the day
golden and cool so no one sweats,
roses on every bush and the Dal Lake
clean again.
              The sex-goddess switches   15
to thickened English to emphasize
a joke. We laugh and clap. Here
we need not be embarrassed by words
dropping like lead pellets into foreign ears.
The flickering movie-light   20
wipes from our faces years of America, sons
who want mohawks and refuse to run
the family store, daughters who date
on the sly.
              When at the end the hero   25
dies for his friend who also
loves the sex-goddess and now can marry her,
we weep, understanding. Even the men
clear their throats to say, "What *qurbani!*°   *sacrifice*
What *dosti!*"° After, we mill around   *friendship* 30
unwilling to leave, exchange greetings
and good news: a new gold chain, a trip
to India. We do not speak

of motel raids, canceled permits, stones
thrown through glass windows, daughters and sons   35
raped by Dotbusters.°
              In this dim foyer
we can pull around us the faint, comforting smell
of incense and *pakoras,*° can arrange   *fried appetizers*
our children's marriages with hometown boys and girls,   40
open a franchise, win a million
in the mail. We can retire
in India, a yellow two-storied house
with wrought-iron gates, our own
Ambassador car. Or at least   45
move to a rich white suburb, Summerfield
or Fort Lee, with neighbors that will
talk to us. Here while the film-songs still echo
in the corridors and restrooms, we can trust
in movie truths: sacrifice, success, love and luck,   50
the America that was supposed to be.

36 *Dotbusters:* New Jersey gangs that attack Indians.

CONSIDERATIONS FOR CRITICAL THINKING AND WRITING

1. FIRST RESPONSE. Why does the speaker feel comfortable at the movies? How
   is the world inside the theater different from life outside in New Jersey?
2. Explain the differences portrayed by the speaker between life in India and
   life in New Jersey. What connotative values are associated with each location in the poem?
3. Discuss the irony in the final two lines.

GREGORY DJANIKIAN (B. 1949)

When I First Saw Snow   *1989*

Tarrytown, N.Y.

Bing Crosby was singing "White Christmas"
        on the radio, we were staying at my aunt's house
        waiting for papers, my father was looking for a job.
We had trimmed the tree the night before,
        sap had run on my fingers and for the first time   5
        I was smelling pine wherever I went.
Anais, my cousin, was upstairs in her room
        listening to Danny and the Juniors.
Haigo was playing Monopoly with Lucy, his sister,
        Buzzy, the boy next door, had eyes for her   10
        and there was a rattle of dice, a shuffling
        of Boardwalk, Park Place, Marvin Gardens.
There were red bows on the Christmas tree.

It had snowed all night.
My boot buckles were clinking like small bells   15
    as I thumped to the door and out
    onto the gray planks of the porch dusted with snow.
The world was immaculate, new,
    even the trees had changed color,
    and when I touched the snow on the railing   20
    I didn't know what I had touched, ice or fire.
I heard, "I'm dreaming . . ."
I heard, "At the hop, hop, hop . . . oh, baby."
I heard "B & O" and the train in my imagination
    was whistling through the great plains.   25
And I was stepping off,
I was falling deeply into America.

CONSIDERATIONS FOR CRITICAL THINKING AND WRITING

1. FIRST RESPONSE. Which images do you find especially vivid for establishing the poem's tone?

2. What is the speaker's attitude toward America? How do you interpret the final line: "I was falling deeply into America"?

3. Discuss what you think is the poem's theme.

PAUL LAURENCE DUNBAR (1872–1906)

We Wear the Mask   *1896*

We wear the mask that grins and lies,
It hides our cheeks and shades our eyes, —
This debt we pay to human guile;
With torn and bleeding hearts we smile,
And mouth with myriad subtleties.   5

Why should the world be overwise,
In counting all our tears and sighs?
Nay, let them only see us, while
    We wear the mask.

We smile, but, O great Christ, our cries   10
To thee from tortured souls arise.
We sing, but oh the clay is vile
Beneath our feet, and long the mile;
But let the world dream otherwise,
    We wear the mask!   15

CONSIDERATIONS FOR CRITICAL THINKING AND WRITING

1. FIRST RESPONSE. What does the mask symbolize? What kind of behavior does it represent?

2. Dunbar was a black man. Does awareness of that fact affect your reading of the poem? Explain why or why not.

GEORGE ELIOT (MARY ANN EVANS / 1819–1880)

In a London Drawingroom   1865

The sky is cloudy, yellowed by the smoke.
For view there are the houses opposite,
Cutting the sky with one long line of wall
Like solid fog: far as the eye can stretch
Monotony of surface and of form   5
Without a break to hang a guess upon.
No bird can make a shadow as it flies,
For all its shadow, as in ways o'erhung
By thickest canvas, where the golden rays
Are clothed in hemp. No figure lingering   10
Pauses to feed the hunger of the eye
Or rest a little on the lap of life.
All hurry on and look upon the ground
Or glance unmarking at the passersby.
The wheels are hurrying, too, cabs, carriages   15
All closed, in multiplied identity.
The world seems one huge prison-house and court
Where men are punished at the slightest cost,
With lowest rate of color, warmth, and joy.

CONSIDERATIONS FOR CRITICAL THINKING AND WRITING

1. FIRST RESPONSE. How does this poem make you feel about life in London?
2. Though this poem focuses on a London street scene, what does it reveal about the speaker?
3. Why do you suppose the title is "In a London Drawingroom" rather than, say, "A London Street"?

T. S. ELIOT (1888–1965)

The Love Song of J. Alfred Prufrock   1917

S'io credesse che mia risposta fosse
A persona che mai tornasse al mondo,
Questa fiamma staria senza più scosse.
Ma perciocchè giammai di questo fondo
Non tornò vivo alcun, s'i'odo il vero,
Senza tema d'infamia ti rispondo. °

Epigraph: *S'io credesse . . . rispondo:* Dante's *Inferno,* XXVII, 58–63. In the Eighth Chasm of the Inferno, Dante and Virgil meet Guido da Montefeltro, one of the False Counselors, who is punished by being enveloped in an eternal flame. When Dante asks Guido to tell his life story, the spirit replies: "If I thought that my answer were to one who might ever return to the world, this flame would shake no more; but since from this depth none ever returned alive, if what I hear is true, I answer you without fear of infamy."

Let us go then, you and I,
When the evening is spread out against the sky
Like a patient etherized upon a table;
Let us go, through certain half-deserted streets,
The muttering retreats   5
Of restless nights in one-night cheap hotels
And sawdust restaurants with oyster-shells:
Streets that follow like a tedious argument
Of insidious intent
To lead you to an overwhelming question . . .   10

Oh, do not ask, "What is it?"
Let us go and make our visit.

In the room the women come and go
Talking of Michelangelo.

The yellow fog that rubs its back upon the window panes,   15
The yellow smoke that rubs its muzzle on the window panes
Licked its tongue into the corners of the evening,
Lingered upon the pools that stand in drains,
Let fall upon its back the soot that falls from chimneys,
Slipped by the terrace, made a sudden leap,   20
And seeing that it was a soft October night,
Curled once about the house, and fell asleep.

And indeed there will be time°
For the yellow smoke that slides along the street,
Rubbing its back upon the window panes;   25
There will be time, there will be time
To prepare a face to meet the faces that you meet;
There will be time to murder and create,
And time for all the works and days° of hands
That lift and drop a question on your plate: 30
Time for you and time for me,
And time yet for a hundred indecisions,
And for a hundred visions and revisions,
Before the taking of a toast and tea.

In the room the women come and go   35
Talking of Michelangelo.

And indeed there will be time
To wonder, "Do I dare?" and, "Do I dare?" —
Time to turn back and descend the stair,
With a bald spot in the middle of my hair —   40
(They will say: "How his hair is growing thin!")
My morning coat, my collar mounting firmly to the chin,
My necktie rich and modest, but asserted by a simple pin —
(They will say: "But how his arms and legs are thin!")

23 *there will be time:* An allusion to Ecclesiastes 3:1–8: "To everything there is a season, and a time to every purpose under heaven…." 29 *works and days:* Hesiod's eighth-century B.C. poem *Works and Days* gave practical advice on how to conduct one's life in accordance with the seasons.

Do I dare   45
Disturb the universe?
In a minute there is time
For decisions and revisions which a minute will reverse.

    For I have known them all already, known them all:
Have known the evenings, mornings, afternoons,   50
I have measured out my life with coffee spoons;
I know the voices dying with a dying fall
Beneath the music from a farther room.
    So how should I presume?

    And I have known the eyes already, known them all —   55
The eyes that fix you in a formulated phrase.
And when I am formulated, sprawling on a pin,
When I am pinned and wriggling on the wall,
Then how should I begin
To spit out all the butt-ends of my days and ways?   60
    And how should I presume?

    And I have known the arms already, known them all —
Arms that are braceleted and white and bare
(But in the lamplight, downed with light brown hair!)
    Is it perfume from a dress   65
    That makes me so digress?
Arms that lie along a table, or wrap about a shawl.
    And should I then presume?
    And how should I begin?

    Shall I say, I have gone at dusk through narrow streets,   70
And watched the smoke that rises from the pipes
Of lonely men in shirtsleeves, leaning out of windows? . . .

I should have been a pair of ragged claws
Scuttling across the floors of silent seas.

    And the afternoon, the evening, sleeps so peacefully!   75
Smoothed by long fingers,
Asleep . . . tired . . . or it malingers,
Stretched on the floor, here beside you and me.
Should I, after tea and cakes and ices,
Have the strength to force the moment to its crisis?   80
But though I have wept and fasted, wept and prayed,
Though I have seen my head (grown slightly bald) brought in upon a platter,°
I am no prophet — and here's no great matter;
I have seen the moment of my greatness flicker,
And I have seen the eternal Footman hold my coat, and snicker,   85
    And in short, I was afraid.

    And would it have been worth it, after all,
After the cups, the marmalade, the tea,
Among the porcelain, among some talk of you and me,

---

82 *head . . . upon a platter:* At Salome's request, Herod had John the Baptist decapitated and
had the severed head delivered to her on a platter (see Matt. 14:1–12 and Mark 6:17–29).

Would it have been worth while   90
To have bitten off the matter with a smile,
To have squeezed the universe into a ball°
To roll it toward some overwhelming question,
To say: "I am Lazarus,° come from the dead,
Come back to tell you all, I shall tell you all" —   95
If one, settling a pillow by her head,
    Should say: "That is not what I meant at all;
      That is not it, at all."

    And would it have been worth it, after all,
Would it have been worth while,   100
After the sunsets and the dooryards and the sprinkled streets,
After the novels, after the teacups, after the skirts that trail along the floor —
And this, and so much more? —
It is impossible to say just what I mean!
But as if a magic lantern threw the nerves in patterns on a screen: 105
Would it have been worth while
If one, settling a pillow or throwing off a shawl,
And turning toward the window, should say:
    "That is not it at all,
      That is not what I meant, at all."   110

No! I am not Prince Hamlet, nor was meant to be;
Am an attendant lord,° one that will do
To swell a progress,° start a scene or two   *state procession*
Advise the prince: withal, an easy tool,
Deferential, glad to be of use,   115
Politic, cautious, and meticulous;
Full of high sentence, but a bit obtuse;
At times, indeed, almost ridiculous —
Almost, at times, the Fool.

I grow old . . . I grow old . . .   120
I shall wear the bottoms of my trowsers rolled.

    Shall I part my hair behind? Do I dare to eat a peach?
I shall wear white flannel trowsers, and walk upon the beach.
I have heard the mermaids singing, each to each.

I do not think that they will sing to me.   125

I have seen them riding seaward on the waves,
Combing the white hair of the waves blown back
When the wind blows the water white and black.

We have lingered in the chambers of the sea
By seagirls wreathed with seaweed red and brown,   130
Till human voices wake us, and we drown.

---

92 *squeezed the universe into a ball:* See Marvell's "To His Coy Mistress" (p. 230), lines 41–42: "Let us roll all our strength and all / Our sweetness up into one ball." 94 *Lazarus:* The brother of Mary and Martha who was raised from the dead by Jesus (John 11:1–44). In Luke 16:19–31, a rich man asks that another Lazarus return from the dead to warn the living about their treatment of the poor. 112 *attendant lord:* Like Polonius in Shakespeare's *Hamlet*.

CONSIDERATIONS FOR CRITICAL THINKING AND WRITING

1. What does J. Alfred Prufrock's name connote? How would you characterize him?

2. What do you think is the purpose of the epigraph from Dante's *Inferno*?

3. What is it that Prufrock wants to do? How does he behave? What does he think of himself? Which parts of the poem answer these questions?

4. Who is the "you" of line 1 and the "we" in the final lines?

5. Discuss the imagery in the poem. How does the imagery reveal Prufrock's character? Which images seem especially striking to you?

MARTÍN ESPADA (B. 1957)

Coca-Cola and Coco Frío   1993

On his first visit to Puerto Rico,
island of family folklore,
the fat boy wandered
from table to table
with his mouth open.   5
At every table, some great-aunt
would steer him with cool spotted hands
to a glass of Coca-Cola.
One even sang to him, in all the English
she could remember, a Coca-Cola jingle   10
from the forties. He drank obediently, though
he was bored with this potion, familiar
from soda fountains in Brooklyn.

Then, at a roadside stand off the beach, the fat boy
opened his mouth to coco frío, a coconut   15
chilled, then scalped by a machete
so that a straw could inhale the clear milk.
The boy tilted the green shell overhead
and drooled coconut milk down his chin;
suddenly, Puerto Rico was not Coca-Cola   20
or Brooklyn, and neither was he.

For years afterward, the boy marveled at an island
where the people drank Coca-Cola
and sang jingles from World War II
in a language they did not speak,   25
while so many coconuts in the trees
sagged heavy with milk, swollen
and unsuckled.

CONSIDERATIONS FOR CRITICAL THINKING AND WRITING

1. FIRST RESPONSE. What has drinking coco frío taught this boy about Puerto Rico?

2. How does the poem's title set up the central conflict in the poem?

3. Discuss the meaning of lines 26–28. How are they related to the poem's theme?

RUTH FAINLIGHT (B. 1931)

Flower Feet   1989

(SILK SHOES IN THE WHITWORTH ART GALLERY,
MANCHESTER, ENGLAND)

Real women's feet wore these objects
that look like toys or spectacle cases stitched
from bands of coral, jade, and apricot silk
embroidered with twined sprays of flowers.
Those hearts, tongues, crescents, and disks, leather   5
shapes an inch across, are the soles of shoes
no wider or longer than the span of my ankle.

If the feet had been cut off and the raw stumps
thrust inside the openings, surely
it could not hurt more than broken toes, twisted   10
back and bandaged tight. An old woman,
leaning on a cane outside her door
in a Chinese village, smiled to tell how
she fought and cried, how when she stood on points
of pain that gnawed like fire, nurse and mother   15
praised her tottering walk on flower feet.
Her friends nodded, glad the times had changed.
Otherwise, they would have crippled their daughters.

CONSIDERATIONS FOR CRITICAL THINKING AND WRITING

1. FIRST RESPONSE. Why did the Chinese bind girls' and women's feet? Are
   there any contemporary equivalents in other cultures?

2. How is the speaker's description of the process of binding feet in lines 8 to
   16 different from the description of the shoes in lines 1 to 7?

3. Describe the poem's tone. Does it remain the same throughout the poem
   or does it change? Explain your response.

CAROLYN FORCHÉ (B. 1950)

The Colonel   May 1978

What you have heard is true. I was in his house. His wife carried a
tray of coffee and sugar. His daughter filed her nails, his son
went out for the night. There were daily papers, pet dogs, a pistol
on the cushion beside him. The moon swung bare on its black
cord over the house. On the television was a cop show. It was in   5
English. Broken bottles were embedded in the walls around the
house to scoop the kneecaps from a man's legs or cut his hands
to lace. On the windows there were gratings like those in liquor
stores. We had dinner, rack of lamb, good wine, a gold bell was
on the table for calling the maid. The maid brought green man-   10
goes, salt, a type of bread. I was asked how I enjoyed the country.

There was a brief commercial in Spanish. His wife took everything away. There was some talk then of how difficult it had
become to govern. The parrot said hello on the terrace. The
colonel told it to shut up, and pushed himself from the table.   15
My friend said to me with his eyes: say nothing. The colonel
returned with a sack used to bring groceries home. He spilled
many human ears on the table. They were like dried peach halves.
There is no other way to say this. He took one of them in his
hands, shook it in our faces, dropped it into a water glass. It   20
came alive there. I am tired of fooling around he said. As for the
rights of anyone, tell your people they can go fuck themselves.
He swept the ears to the floor with his arm and held the last of
his wine in the air. Something for your poetry, no? he said. Some
of the ears on the floor caught this scrap of his voice. Some of   25
the ears on the floor were pressed to the ground.

CONSIDERATIONS FOR CRITICAL THINKING AND WRITING

1. FIRST RESPONSE. How does this poem make you feel? Is it consistent
   throughout? How do the images contribute to its effects?

2. What kind of horror is described here? Characterize the colonel.

3. What makes this prose poem not a typical prose passage? How is it organized differently?

4. What poetic elements can you find in it?

5. What is the tone of the final two sentences?

LANGSTON HUGHES (1902–1967)

Dinner Guest: Me   *1965*

I know I am
The Negro Problem
Being wined and dined,
Answering the usual questions
That come to white mind   5
Which seeks demurely
To probe in polite way
The why and wherewithal
Of darkness U.S.A. —
Wondering how things got this way   10
In current democratic night,
Murmuring gently
Over *fraises du bois,*
"I'm so ashamed of being white."

The lobster is delicious,   15
The wine divine,
And center of attention
At the damask table, mine.

To be a Problem on
Park Avenue at eight   20
Is not so bad.
Solutions to the Problem,
Of course, wait.

CONSIDERATIONS FOR CRITICAL THINKING AND WRITING

1. FIRST RESPONSE. What does the speaker satirize in this description of a dinner party? Do you think this "Problem" exists today?

2. Why is line 9, "Of darkness U.S.A. —," especially resonant?

3. What effects are created by the speaker's diction?

4. Discuss the effects of the rhymes in lines 15–23.

JULIO MARZÁN (B. 1946)
Ethnic Poetry   *1994*

The ethnic poet said: "The earth is maybe
a huge maraca / and the sun a trombone /
and life / is to move your ass / to slow beats."
The ethnic audience roasted a suckling pig.

The ethnic poet said: "Oh thank Goddy, Goddy /   5
I be me, my toenails curled downward /
deep, deep, deep into Mama earth."
The ethnic audience shook strands of sea shells.

The ethnic poet said: "The sun was created black /
so we should imagine light / and also dream /   10
a walrus emerging from the broken ice."
The ethnic audience beat on sealskin drums.

The ethnic poet said: "Reproductive organs /
Eagles nesting California redwoods /
Shut up and listen to my ancestors."   15
The ethnic audience ate fried bread and honey.

The ethnic poet said: "Something there is that
doesn't love a wall / That sends
the frozen-ground-swell under it."
The ethnic audience deeply understood humanity.   20

CONSIDERATIONS FOR CRITICAL THINKING AND WRITING

1. FIRST RESPONSE. What is the implicit definition of ethnic poetry in this poem?

2. The final stanza quotes lines from Robert Frost's "Mending Wall" (p. 121). Read the entire poem. Why do you think Marzán chooses these lines and this particular poem as one kind of ethnic poetry?

3. What is the poem's central irony? Pay particular attention to the final line. What is being satirized here?

4. CRITICAL STRATEGIES. Read the section on the literary canon (pp. 58-60) in Chapter 3, "Applying a Critical Strategy," and consider how the formation of the literary canon is related to the theme of "Ethnic Poetry."

JANICE MIRIKITANI (B. 1942)

Recipe   *1987*

Round Eyes

Ingredients: scissors, Scotch magic transparent tape,
                eyeliner — water based, black.
                Optional: false eyelashes.

Cleanse face thoroughly.   5

For best results, powder entire face, including eyelids.
    (lighter shades suited to total effect desired)

With scissors, cut magic tape $\frac{1}{16}$" wide, $\frac{3}{4}$"–$\frac{1}{2}$" long —
depending on length of eyelid.

Stick firmly onto mid-upper eyelid area   10
    (looking down into handmirror facilitates finding
    adequate surface)

If using false eyelashes, affix first on lid, folding any
excess lid over the base of eyelash with glue.

Paint black eyeliner on tape and entire lid.   15

Do not cry.

CONSIDERATIONS FOR CRITICAL THINKING AND WRITING

1. FIRST RESPONSE. Discuss your response to the poem's final line.

2. What is the effect of the very specific details of this recipe?

3. Why is "false eyelashes" a particularly resonant phrase in the context of this poem?

4. Try writing your own "recipe" in poetic lines — one that makes a commentary concerning a social issue that you feel strongly about.

PABLO NERUDA (1904–1973)

Sweetness, Always   *1958*

TRANSLATED BY ALASTAIR REID

Why such harsh machinery?
Why, to write down the stuff
and people of every day,

must poems be dressed up in gold,
in old and fearful stone? 5
I want verses of felt or feather
which scarcely weigh, mild verses
with the intimacy of beds
where people have loved and dreamed.
I want poems stained 10
by hands and everydayness.

Verses of pastry which melt
into milk and sugar in the mouth,
air and water to drink,
the bites and kisses of love. 15
I long for eatable sonnets,
poems of honey and flour.

Vanity keeps prodding us
to lift ourselves skyward
or to make deep and useless 20
tunnels underground.
So we forget the joyous
love-needs of our bodies.
We forget about pastries.
We are not feeding the world. 25

In Madras a long time since,
I saw a sugary pyramid,
a tower of confectionery —
one level after another,
and in the construction, rubies, 30
and other blushing delights,
medieval and yellow.

Someone dirtied his hands
to cook up so much sweetness.

Brother poets from here 35
and there, from earth and sky,
from Medellín, from Veracruz,
Abyssinia, Antofagasta,
do you know the recipe for honeycombs?

Let's forget all about that stone. 40

Let your poetry fill up
the equinoctial pastry shop
our mouths long to devour —
all the children's mouths
and the poor adults' also. 45
Don't go on without seeing,
relishing, understanding
all these hearts of sugar.

Don't be afraid of sweetness.

With us or without us,   50
sweetness will go on living
and is infinitely alive,
forever being revived,
for it's in a man's mouth,
whether he's eating or singing,   55
that sweetness has its place.

CONSIDERATIONS FOR CRITICAL THINKING AND WRITING

1. FIRST RESPONSE. What kinds of poems does the speaker call for and prefer?
2. What do you think the speaker means in line 49: "Don't be afraid of
   sweetness"?
3. Why do you think Neruda makes the central metaphor of the poem food?

OCTAVIO PAZ (1914–1998)

The Street   *1963*

A long silent street.
I walk in blackness and I stumble and fall
and rise, and I walk blind, my feet
stepping on silent stones and dry leaves.
Someone behind me also stepping on stones, leaves: 5
if I slow down, he slows;
if I run, he runs. I turn: nobody.
Everything dark and doorless.
Turning and turning among these corners
which lead forever to the street   10
where nobody waits for, nobody follows me,
where I pursue a man who stumbles
and rises and says when he sees me: nobody.

CONSIDERATIONS FOR CRITICAL THINKING AND WRITING

1. FIRST RESPONSE. How might this poem be considered as a dream?
2. If you were to change all the verbs in the poem to the past tense, how would
   the poem's tone be changed?
3. How would the poem's effect be altered if it ended with line 11?

WYATT PRUNTY (B. 1947)

Elderly Lady Crossing on Green   *1993*

And give her no scouts doing their one good deed
Or sentimental cards to wish her well
During Christmas time or gallstone time —
Because there was a time, she'd like to tell,

She drove a loaded V8 powerglide   5
And would have run you flat as paint
To make the light before it turned on her,
Make it as she watched you faint

When looking up you saw her bearing down
Eyes locking you between the wheel and dash,   10
And you either scrambled back where you belonged
Or jaywalked to eternity, blown out like trash

Behind the grease spot where she braked on you. . . .
Never widow, wife, mother, or a bride,
And nothing up ahead she's looking for   15
But asphalt, the dotted line, the other side,

The way she's done a million times before,
With nothing in her brief to tell you more
Than she's a small tug on the tidal swell
Of her own sustaining notion that she's doing well.   20

CONSIDERATIONS FOR CRITICAL THINKING AND WRITING

1. FIRST RESPONSE. Does the description of the elderly lady in the poem
   undercut your expectations about her created by the title? Is this poem sentimental, ironic, or something else?

2. In what ways is this elderly woman "doing well" (line 20)? Does the poem
   suggest any ways in which she's not?

3. Describe the effect produced by the first line's beginning with "And . . . ."
   Why is this a fitting introduction to this elderly lady?

MARY JO SALTER (B. 1954)

Welcome to Hiroshima   *1985*

is what you first see, stepping off the train:
a billboard brought to you in living English
by Toshiba Electric. While a channel
silent in the TV of the brain

projects those flickering re-runs of a cloud   5
that brims its risen columnful like beer
and, spilling over, hangs its foamy head,
you feel a thirst for history: what year

it started to be safe to breathe the air,
and when to drink the blood and scum afloat   10
on the Ohta River. But no, the water's clear,
they pour it for your morning cup of tea

in one of the countless sunny coffee shops
whose plastic dioramas advertise
mutations of cuisine behind the glass: 15
a pancake sandwich; a pizza someone tops

with a maraschino cherry. Passing by
the Peace Park's floral hypocenter (where
how bravely, or with what mistaken cheer,
humanity erased its own erasure),   20

you enter the memorial museum
and through more glass are served, as on a dish
of blistered grass, three mannequins. Like gloves
a mother clips to coatsleeves, strings of flesh

hang from their fingertips; or as if tied   25
to recall a duty for us, *Reverence*
the dead whose mourners too shall soon be dead,
but all commemoration's swallowed up

in questions of bad taste, how re-created
horror mocks the grim original,   30
and thinking at last *They should have left it all*
you stop. This is the wristwatch of a child.

Jammed on the moment's impact, resolute
to communicate some message, although mute,
it gestures with its hands at eight-fifteen   35
and eight-fifteen and eight-fifteen again

while tables of statistics on the wall
update the news by calling on a roll
of tape, death gummed on death, and in the case
adjacent, an exhibit under glass   40

is glass itself: a shard the bomb slammed in
a woman's arm at eight-fifteen, but some
three decades on — as if to make it plain
hope's only as renewable as pain,

and as if all the unsung   45
debasements of the past may one day come
rising to the surface once again —
worked its filthy way out like a tongue.

Considerations for Critical Thinking and Writing

1. FIRST RESPONSE. Describe the tone of the poem's final line. How does it make you feel?

2. Describe the scene set by the first five stanzas. Is the speaker in "Welcome to Hiroshima" feeling welcome? Welcoming the reader?

3. How is the commemoration of the atomic bombing of Hiroshima "swallowed up in questions of bad taste" (lines 28–29) in this poem? Pick out specific images, and describe your reaction to them.

4. Do the speaker's emotions change through the course of the poem? Explain whether or not you think this is a hopeful or pessimistic poem.

GARY SOTO (B. 1952)

Mexicans Begin Jogging   *1995*

At the factory I worked
In the fleck of rubber, under the press
Of an oven yellow with flame,
Until the border patrol opened
Their vans and my boss waved for us to run.   5
"Over the fence, Soto," he shouted,
And I shouted that I was American.
"No time for lies," he said, and pressed
A dollar in my palm, hurrying me
Through the back door.   10

Since I was on his time, I ran
And became the wag to a short tail of Mexicans —
Ran past the amazed crowds that lined
The street and blurred like photographs, in rain.
I ran from that industrial road to the soft   15
Houses where people paled at the turn of an autumn sky.
What could I do but yell *vivas*
To baseball, milkshakes, and those sociologists
Who would clock me
As I jog into the next century   20
On the power of a great, silly grin.

CONSIDERATIONS FOR CRITICAL THINKING AND WRITING

1. FIRST RESPONSE. What ironies are present in this poem?
2. Soto was born and raised in Fresno, California. How does this fact affect your reading of the first stanza?
3. In what different ways does the speaker become "the wag" (line 12) in this poem? (You may want to look up the word to consider all possible meanings.)
4. Explain lines 17–21. What serious point is being made in these humorous lines?

WILLIAM BUTLER YEATS (1865–1939)

The Lake Isle of Innisfree   *1890*

I will arise and go now, and go to Innisfree,
And a small cabin build there, of clay and wattles° made;
Nine bean rows will I have there, a hive for the honey bee,
        And live alone in the bee-loud glade.

And I shall have some peace there, for peace comes dropping slow,   5
Dropping from the veils of the morning to where the cricket sings;

wattles: sticks and branches used to support roofs and walls.

There midnight's all a glimmer, and noon a purple glow,
    And evening full of the linnet's° wings.   *songbird*

I will arise and go now, for always night and day
I hear lake water lapping with low sounds by the shore;   10
While I stand on the roadway, or on the pavements gray,
    I hear it in the deep heart's core.

Considerations for Critical Thinking and Writing

1. FIRST RESPONSE. Why does the speaker want to get away from where he is now and move to Innisfree?

2. How does the speaker use imagery to make Innisfree an attractive alternative to his current life?

DRAMA

David Henry Hwang (b. 1957)

Born in Los Angeles, David Henry Hwang is the son of immigrant Chinese American parents; his father worked as a banker, and his mother was a professor of piano. Educated at Stanford University, from which he earned his B.A. in English in 1979, he became interested in theater after attending plays at the American Conservatory in San Francisco. His marginal interest in a law career quickly gave way to his involvement in the engaging world of live theater. By his senior year, he had written and produced his first play, *FOB* (an acronym for "fresh off the boat"), which marked the beginning of a meteoric rise as a playwright. After a brief stint as a writing teacher at a Menlo Park high school, Hwang attended the Yale University School of Drama from 1980 to 1981. Although he didn't stay to complete a degree, he studied theater history before leaving for New York City, where he thought the professional theater would provide a richer education than the student workshops at Yale.

In New York Hwang's work received a warm reception. In 1980 an off-Broadway production of *FOB* won an Obie Award for the best new play of the season. The play incorporates many of Hwang's characteristic concerns as a playwright. Growing up in California as a Chinese Ameri-

PHOTO: *Reprinted by permission of Michal Daniel.*

can made him politically conscious during his college years in the late 1970s; this interest in his Chinese roots is evident in the central conflicts of *FOB*, which focuses on a Chinese immigrant's relationship with two Chinese American students he meets in Los Angeles. The immigrant quickly learns that he is expected to abandon much of his Chinese identity if he is to fit into mainstream American culture. The issues that arise between East and West are played out with comic effect in a Western theater but enriched and complicated by Hwang's innovative use of a Chinese theatrical tradition that portrays major characters as figures from Chinese mythology.

Chinese American life is also the focus of *The Dance and the Railroad* and *Family Devotions,* both produced off-Broadway in 1981. *The Dance and the Railroad,* set in the nineteenth century, focuses on two immigrant Chinese men working on the transcontinental railroad and attempting to sort out their pasts while confronting new identities and uncertain futures in America. Hwang mirrors the characters' conflicts in the play's form by creating a mixture of Eastern and Western theater and incorporating the nonrealistic modes of Chinese opera. *Family Devotions* examines an established affluent Chinese American family in the twentieth century through the lens of a television sitcom. The problems faced by immigrants living hyphenated lives are comically played out through the interaction of a visiting Communist uncle from China and his great-nephew, who struggles to find an authentic identity amid his family's materialism and Christianity. Hwang's early plays are populated with Chinese Americans attempting to find the center of their own lives as they seesaw between the conventions, traditions, and values of East and West.

Hwang's next two dramas, produced in 1983, consist of two one-act plays set in Japan. Together they are titled *Sound and Beauty,* but each has its own title — *The House of Sleeping Beauties* and *The Sound of a Voice.* In these plays Hwang moves away from tales of Chinese American immigrants and themes of race and assimilation to stories about tragic love based on Japanese materials. Although Hwang was successful in having additional plays produced in the mid-1980s and won prestigious fellowships from the Guggenheim Foundation and the National Endowment for the Arts, it was not until 1988, when *M. Butterfly* was produced on Broadway, that he achieved astonishing commercial success as well as widespread acclaim. His awards for this play include the Outer Critics' Circle Award for best Broadway play, the Drama Desk Award for best new play, the John Gassner Award for best American play, and the Tony Award for best play of the year. By the end of 1988, Hwang was regarded by many critics as the most talented young playwright in the United States, and since then *M. Butterfly* has been staged in theaters around the world.

According to Hwang, *M. Butterfly* was inspired by newspaper accounts of an espionage trial. In his "Playwright's Notes" he cites an excerpt from the *New York Times* for May 11, 1986. Hwang takes this fascinating true story of espionage and astonishing sexual misidentification and transforms it into a complex treatment of social, political, racial, cultural, and sexual issues that has dazzled both audiences and readers with its remarkable eroticism, insights, and beauty.

M. Butterfly   *1988*

THE CHARACTERS

Rene Gallimard
Song Liling
Marc/Man No. 2/Consul Sharpless
Renee/Woman at Party/Pinup Girl
Comrade Chin/Suzuki/Shu-Fang
Helga
Toulon/Man No. 1/Judge
Dancers

TIME AND PLACE

> *The action of the play takes place in a Paris prison in the present, and, in recall, during the decade 1960–1970 in Beijing, and from 1966 to the present in Paris.*

PLAYWRIGHT'S NOTES

> *A former French diplomat and a Chinese opera singer have been sentenced to six years in jail for spying for China after a two-day trial that traced a story of clandestine love and mistaken sexual identity. . . .*
> *Mr. Boursicot was accused of passing information to China after he fell in love with Mr. Shi, whom he believed for twenty years to be a woman.*
> — The New York Times, *May 11, 1986*

> *This play was suggested by international newspaper accounts of a recent espionage trial. For purposes of dramatization, names have been changed, characters created, and incidents devised or altered, and this play does not purport to be a factual record of real events or real people.*

> *I could escape this feeling*
> *With my China girl . . .*
> *— David Bowie & Iggy Pop*

ACT I

Scene I

M. Gallimard's prison cell. Paris. 1988.

Lights fade up to reveal Rene Gallimard, sixty-five, in a prison cell. He wears a comfortable bathrobe and looks old and tired. The sparsely furnished cell contains a wooden crate, upon which sits a hot plate with a kettle and a portable tape recorder. Gallimard sits on the crate staring at the recorder, a sad smile on his face.

Upstage Song, who appears as a beautiful woman in traditional Chinese garb, dances a traditional piece from the Peking Opera, surrounded by the percussive clatter of Chinese music.

Then, slowly, lights and sound cross-fade; the Chinese opera music dissolves into a Western opera, the "Love Duet" from Puccini's Madame Butterfly. *Song continues dancing, now to the Western accompaniment. Though her movements are the same, the difference in music now gives them a balletic quality.*

Gallimard rises, and turns upstage towards the figure of Song, who dances without acknowledging him.

Gallimard: Butterfly, Butterfly . . .

He forces himself to turn away, as the image of Song fades out, and talks to us.

Gallimard: The limits of my cell are as such: four-and-a-half meters by five. There's one window against the far wall; a door, very strong, to protect me from autograph hounds. I'm responsible for the tape recorder, the hot plate, and this charming coffee table.

When I want to eat, I'm marched off to the dining room — hot, steaming slop appears on my plate. When I want to sleep, the light bulb turns itself off — the work of fairies. It's an enchanted space I occupy. The French — we know how to run a prison.

But, to be honest, I'm not treated like an ordinary prisoner. Why? Because I'm a celebrity. You see, I make people laugh.

I never dreamed this day would arrive. I've never been considered witty or clever. In fact, as a young boy, in an informal poll among my grammar school classmates, I was voted "least likely to be invited to a party." It's a title I managed to hold on to for many years. Despite some stiff competition.

But now, how the tables turn! Look at me: the life of every social function in Paris. Paris? Why be modest: My fame has spread to Amsterdam, London, New York. Listen to them! In the world's smartest parlors. I'm the one who lifts their spirits!

With a flourish, Gallimard directs our attention to another part of the stage.

Scene II

A party. 1988.

Lights go up on a chic-looking parlor, where a well-dressed trio, two men and one woman, make conversation. Gallimard also remains lit; he observes them from his cell.

Woman: And what of Gallimard?

Man 1: Gallimard?

Man 2: Gallimard!

Gallimard (to us): You see? They're all determined to say my name, as if it were some new dance.

Woman: He still claims not to believe the truth.

Man 1: What? Still? Even since the trial?

Woman: Yes. Isn't it mad?

Man 2 (laughing): He says . . . it was dark . . . and she was very modest!

> *The trio break into laughter.*

Man 1: So—what? He never touched her with his hands?

Man 2: Perhaps he did, and simply misidentified the equipment. A compelling case for sex education in the schools.

Woman: To protect the National Security—the Church can't argue with that.

Man 1: That's impossible! How could he not know?

Man 2: Simple ignorance.

Man 1: For twenty years?

Man 2: Time flies when you're being stupid.

Woman: Well, I thought the French were ladies' men.

Man 2: It seems Monsieur Gallimard was overly anxious to live up to his national reputation.

Woman: Well, he's not very good-looking.

Man 1: No, he's not.

Man 2: Certainly not.

Woman: Actually, I feel sorry for him.

Man 2: A toast! To Monsieur Gallimard!

Woman: Yes! To Gallimard!

Man 1: To Gallimard!

Man 2: Vive la différence!

> *They toast, laughing. Lights down on them.*

SCENE III

> *M. Gallimard's cell.*

Gallimard (smiling): You see? They toast me. I've become a patron saint of the socially inept. Can they really be so foolish? Men like that—they should be scratching at my door, begging to learn my secrets! For I, Rene Gallimard, you see, I have known, and been loved by . . . the Perfect Woman.

> Alone in this cell, I sit night after night, watching our story play through my head, always searching for a new ending, one which redeems my honor, where she returns at last to my arms. And I imagine you—my ideal audience—who come to understand and even, perhaps just a little, to envy me.

> *He turns on his tape recorder. Over the house speakers, we hear the opening phrases of* Madame Butterfly.

Gallimard: In order for you to understand what I did and why, I must introduce you to my favorite opera: *Madame Butterfly*. By Giacomo Puccini. First produced at La Scala, Milan, in 1904, it is now beloved throughout the Western world.

As Gallimard describes the opera, the tape segues in and out to sections he may be describing.

Gallimard: And why not? Its heroine, Cio-Cio-San, also known as Butterfly, is a feminine ideal, beautiful and brave. And its hero, the man for whom she gives up everything, is — *(He pulls out a naval officer's cap from under his crate, pops it on his head, and struts about.)* — not very good-looking, not too bright, and pretty much a wimp: Benjamin Franklin Pinkerton of the U.S. Navy. As the curtain rises, he's just closed on two great bargains: one on a house, the other on a woman — call it a package deal.

Pinkerton purchased the rights to Butterfly for one hundred yen — in modern currency, equivalent to about . . . sixty-six cents. So, he's feeling pretty pleased with himself as Sharpless, the American consul, arrives to witness the marriage.

Marc, wearing an official cap to designate Sharpless, enters and plays the character.

Sharpless/Marc: Pinkerton!

Pinkerton/Gallimard: Sharpless! How's it hangin'? It's a great day, just great. Between my house, my wife, and the rickshaw ride in from town, I've saved nineteen cents just this morning.

Sharpless: Wonderful. I can see the inscription on your tombstone already: "I saved a dollar, here I lie." *(He looks around.)* Nice house.

Pinkerton: It's artistic. Artistic, don't you think? Like the way the shoji screens slide open to reveal the wet bar and disco mirror ball? Classy, huh? Great for impressing the chicks.

Sharpless: "Chicks"? Pinkerton, you're going to be a married man!

Pinkerton: Well, sort of.

Sharpless: What do you mean?

Pinkerton: This country — Sharpless, it is okay. You got all these geisha girls running around —

Sharpless: I know! I live here!

Pinkerton: Then, you know the marriage laws, right? I split for one month, it's annulled!

Sharpless: Leave it to you to read the fine print. Who's the lucky girl?

Pinkerton: Cio-Cio-San. Her friends call her Butterfly. Sharpless, she eats out of my hand!

Sharpless: She's probably very hungry.

Pinkerton: Not like American girls. It's true what they say about Oriental girls. They want to be treated bad!

Sharpless: Oh, please!

Pinkerton: It's true!

Sharpless: Are you serious about this girl?

Pinkerton: I'm marrying her, aren't I?

Sharpless: Yes — with generous trade-in terms.

Pinkerton: When I leave, she'll know what it's like to have loved a real man. And I'll even buy her a few nylons.

Sharpless: You aren't planning to take her with you?

Pinkerton: Huh? Where?

Sharpless: Home!

Pinkerton: You mean, America? Are you crazy? Can you see her trying to buy rice in St. Louis?

Sharpless: So, you're not serious.

Pause.

Pinkerton/Gallimard (as Pinkerton): Consul, I am a sailor in port. *(As Gallimard.)* They then proceed to sing the famous duet, "The Whole World Over."

The duet plays on the speakers. Gallimard, as Pinkerton, lip-syncs his lines from the opera.

Gallimard: To give a rough translation: "The whole world over, the Yankee travels, casting his anchor wherever he wants. Life's not worth living unless he can win the hearts of the fairest maidens, then hotfoot it off the premises ASAP." *(He turns towards Marc.)* In the preceding scene, I played Pinkerton, the womanizing cad, and my friend Marc from school . . . *(Marc bows grandly for our benefit.)* played Sharpless, the sensitive soul of reason. In life, however, our positions were usually—no, always—reversed.

SCENE IV

École Nationale.° Aix-en-Provence. 1947.

Gallimard: No, Marc, I think I'd rather stay home.

Marc: Are you crazy?! We are going to Dad's condo in Marseilles! You know what happened last time?

Gallimard: Of course I do.

Marc: Of course you don't! You never know. . . . They stripped, Rene!

Gallimard: Who stripped?

Marc: The girls!

Gallimard: Girls? Who said anything about girls?

Marc: Rene, we're a buncha university guys goin' up to the woods. What are we gonna do—talk philosophy?

Gallimard: What girls? Where do you get them?

Marc: Who cares? The point is, they come. On trucks. Packed in like sardines. The back flips open, babes hop out, we're ready to roll.

Gallimard: You mean, they just—?

Marc: Before you know it, every last one of them—they're stripped and splashing around my pool. There's no moon out, they can't see what's going on, their boobs are flapping, right? You close your eyes, reach out—it's grab bag, get it? Doesn't matter whose ass is between whose legs, whose teeth are sinking into who. You're just in there, going at it, eyes closed, on and on for as long as you can stand. *(Pause.)* Some fun, huh?

Gallimard: What happens in the morning?

Marc: In the morning, you're ready to talk some philosophy. *(Beat.)* So how 'bout it?

Gallimard: Marc, I can't . . . I'm afraid they'll say no—the girls. So I never ask.

Marc: You don't have to ask! That's the beauty—don't you see? They don't have to say yes. It's perfect for a guy like you, really.

Gallimard: You go ahead . . . I may come later.

Marc: Hey, Rene—it doesn't matter that you're clumsy and got zits—they're not looking!

Gallimard: Thank you very much.

École Nationale: National School.

Marc: Wimp.

> *Marc walks over to the other side of the stage, and starts waving and smiling at women in the audience.*

Gallimard (to us): We now return to my version of *Madame Butterfly* and the events leading to my recent conviction for treason.

> *Gallimard notices Marc making lewd gestures.*

Gallimard: Marc, what are you doing?

Marc: Huh? *(Sotto voce.)* Rene, there're a lotta great babes out there. They're probably lookin' at me and thinking, "What a dangerous guy."

Gallimard: Yes — how could they help but be impressed by your cool sophistication?

> *Gallimard pops the Sharpless cap on Marc's head, and points him offstage. Marc exits, leering.*

Scene V

> *M. Gallimard's cell.*

Gallimard: Next, Butterfly makes her entrance. We learn her age — fifteen . . . but very mature for her years.

> *Lights come up on the area where we saw Song dancing at the top of the play. She appears there again, now dressed as Madame Butterfly, moving to the "Love Duet." Gallimard turns upstage slightly to watch, transfixed.*

Gallimard: But as she glides past him, beautiful, laughing softly behind her fan, don't we who are men sigh with hope? We, who are not handsome, nor brave, nor powerful, yet somehow believe, like Pinkerton, that we deserve a Butterfly. She arrives with all her possessions in the folds of her sleeves, lays them all out, for her man to do with as he pleases. Even her life itself — she bows her head as she whispers that she's not even worth the hundred yen he paid for her. He's already given too much, when we know he's really had to give nothing at all.

> *Music and lights on Song out. Gallimard sits at his crate.*

Gallimard: In real life, women who put their total worth at less than sixty-six cents are quite hard to find. The closest we come is in the pages of these magazines. *(He reaches into his crate, pulls out a stack of girlie magazines, and begins flipping through them.)* Quite a necessity in prison. For three or four dollars, you get seven or eight women.

I first discovered these magazines at my uncle's house. One day, as a boy of twelve. The first time I saw them in his closet . . . all lined up — my body shook. Not with lust — no, with power. Here were women — a shelf-ful — who would do exactly as I wanted.

> *The "Love Duet" creeps in over the speakers. Special comes up, revealing, not Song this time, but a pinup girl in a sexy negligee, her back to us. Gallimard turns upstage and looks at her.*

Girl: I know you're watching me.

Gallimard: My throat . . . it's dry.

Girl: I leave my blinds open every night before I go to bed.

Gallimard: I can't move.

Girl: I leave my blinds open and the lights on.

Gallimard: I'm shaking. My skin is hot, but my penis is soft. Why?

Girl: I stand in front of the window.

Gallimard: What is she going to do?

Girl: I toss my hair, and I let my lips part . . . barely.

Gallimard: I shouldn't be seeing this. It's so dirty. I'm so bad.

Girl: Then, slowly, I lift off my nightdress.

Gallimard: Oh, god. I can't believe it. I can't —

Girl: I toss it to the ground.

Gallimard: Now, she's going to walk away. She's going to —

Girl: I stand there, in the light, displaying myself.

Gallimard: No. She's — why is she naked?

Girl: To you.

Gallimard: In front of a window? This is wrong. No —

Girl: Without shame.

Gallimard: No, she must . . . like it.

Girl: I like it.

Gallimard: She . . . she wants me to see.

Girl: I want you to see.

Gallimard: I can't believe it! She's getting excited!

Girl: I can't see you. You can do whatever you want.

Gallimard: I can't do a thing. Why?

Girl: What would you like me to do . . . next?

> *Lights go down on her. Music off. Silence, as Gallimard puts away his magazines. Then he resumes talking to us.*

Gallimard: Act Two begins with Butterfly staring at the ocean. Pinkerton's been called back to the U.S., and he's given his wife a detailed schedule of his plans. In the column marked "return date," he's written "when the robins nest." This failed to ignite her suspicions. Now, three years have passed without a peep from him. Which brings a response from her faithful servant, Suzuki.

> *Comrade Chin enters, playing Suzuki.*

Suzuki: Girl, he's a loser. What'd he ever give you? Nineteen cents and those ugly Day-Glo stockings? Look, it's finished! Kaput! Done! And you should be glad! I mean, the guy was a woofer! He tried before, you know — before he met you, he went down to geisha central and plunked down his spare change in front of the usual candidates — everyone else gagged! These are hungry prostitutes, and they were not interested, get the picture? Now, stop slathering when an American ship sails in, and let's make some bucks — I mean, yen! We are broke!

Now, what about Yamadori? Hey, hey — don't look away — the man is a prince — figuratively, and, what's even better, literally. He's rich, he's handsome, he says he'll die if you don't marry him — and he's even willing to overlook the little fact that you've been deflowered all over the place by a foreign devil. What do you mean, "But he's Japanese"? What do you think you are? You think you've been touched by the whitey god? He was a sailor with dirty hands!

Suzuki stalks offstage.

Gallimard: She's also visited by Consul Sharpless, sent by Pinkerton on a minor errand.

Marc enters, as Sharpless.

Sharpless: I hate this job.

Gallimard: This Pinkerton—he doesn't show up personally to tell his wife he's abandoning her. No, he sends a government diplomat . . . at taxpayers' expense.

Sharpless: Butterfly? Butterfly? I have some bad—I'm going to be ill. Butterfly, I came to tell you—

Gallimard: Butterfly says she knows he'll return and if he doesn't she'll kill herself rather than go back to her own people. *(Beat.)* This causes a lull in the conversation.

Sharpless: Let's put it this way . . .

Gallimard: Butterfly runs into the next room, and returns holding—

Sound cue: a baby crying. Sharpless, "seeing" this, backs away.

Sharpless: Well, good. Happy to see things going so well. I suppose I'll be going now. Ta ta. Ciao. *(He turns away. Sound cue out.)* I hate this job. *(He exits.)*

Gallimard: At that moment, Butterfly spots in the harbor an American ship—the *Abramo Lincoln!*

Music cue: "The Flower Duet." Song, still dressed as Butterfly, changes into a wedding kimono, moving to the music.

Gallimard: This is the moment that redeems her years of waiting. With Suzuki's help, they cover the room with flowers—

Chin, as Suzuki, trudges onstage and drops a lone flower without much enthusiasm.

Gallimard: —and she changes into her wedding dress to prepare for Pinkerton's arrival.

Suzuki helps Butterfly change. Helga enters, and helps Gallimard change into a tuxedo.

Gallimard: I married a woman older than myself—Helga.

Helga: My father was ambassador to Australia. I grew up among criminals and kangaroos.

Gallimard: Hearing that brought me to the altar—

Helga exits.

Gallimard: —where I took a vow renouncing love. No fantasy woman would ever want me, so, yes, I would settle for a quick leap up the career ladder. Passion, I banish, and in its place—practicality!

But my vows had long since lost their charm by the time we arrived in China. The sad truth is that all men want a beautiful woman, and the uglier the man, the greater the want.

Suzuki makes final adjustments of Butterfly's costume, as does Gallimard of his tuxedo.

Gallimard: I married late, at age thirty-one. I was faithful to my marriage for eight years. Until the day when, as a junior-level diplomat in puritanical

Peking, in a parlor at the German ambassador's house, during the "Reign of a Hundred Flowers,"° I first saw her . . . singing the death scene from *Madame Butterfly*.

Suzuki runs offstage.

Scene VI

German ambassador's house. Beijing. 1960.
   The upstage special area now becomes a stage. Several chairs face upstage, representing seating for some twenty guests in the parlor. A few "diplomats"—Renee, Marc, Toulon—in formal dress enter and take seats.
   Gallimard also sits down, but turns towards us and continues to talk. Orchestral accompaniment on the tape is now replaced by a simple piano. Song picks up the death scene from the point where Butterfly uncovers the hara-kiri knife.

Gallimard: The ending is pitiful. Pinkerton, in an act of great courage, stays home and sends his American wife to pick up Butterfly's child. The truth, long deferred, has come up to her door.

Song, playing Butterfly, sings the lines from the opera in her own voice—which, though not classical, should be decent.

Song: "Con onor muore / chi non puo serbar / vita con onore."
Gallimard (*simultaneously*): "Death with honor / Is better than life / Life with dishonor."

The stage is illuminated; we are now completely within an elegant diplomat's residence. Song proceeds to play out an abbreviated death scene. Everyone in the room applauds. Song, shyly, takes her bows. Others in the room rush to congratulate her. Gallimard remains with us.

Gallimard: They say in opera the voice is everything. That's probably why I'd never before enjoyed opera. Here . . . here was a Butterfly with little or no voice—but she had the grace, the delicacy . . . I believed this girl. I believed her suffering. I wanted to take her in my arms—so delicate, even I could protect her, take her home, pamper her until she smiled.

Over the course of the preceding speech, Song has broken from the upstage crowd and moved directly upstage of Gallimard.

Song: Excuse me. Monsieur . . . ?

Gallimard turns upstage, shocked.

Gallimard: Oh! Gallimard. Mademoiselle . . . ? A beautiful . . .
Song: Song Liling.
Gallimard: A beautiful performance.
Song: Oh, please.
Gallimard: I usually—
Song: You make me blush. I'm no opera singer at all.
Gallimard: I usually don't like *Butterfly*.
Song: I can't blame you in the least.
Gallimard: I mean, the story—

Reign of a Hundred Flowers: A brief period in 1957 when freedom of expression was allowed in China.

Song: Ridiculous.

Gallimard: I like the story, but . . . what?

Song: Oh, you like it?

Gallimard: I . . . what I mean is, I've always seen it played by huge women in so much bad makeup.

Song: Bad makeup is not unique to the West.

Gallimard: But, who can believe them?

Song: And you believe me?

Gallimard: Absolutely. You were utterly convincing. It's the first time —

Song: Convincing? As a Japanese woman? The Japanese used hundreds of our people for medical experiments during the war, you know. But I gather such an irony is lost on you.

Gallimard: No! I was about to say, it's the first time I've seen the beauty of the story.

Song: Really?

Gallimard: Of her death. It's a . . . a pure sacrifice. He's unworthy, but what can she do? She loves him . . . so much. It's a very beautiful story.

Song: Well, yes, to a Westerner.

Gallimard: Excuse me?

Song: It's one of your favorite fantasies, isn't it? The submissive Oriental woman and the cruel white man.

Gallimard: Well, I didn't quite mean . . .

Song: Consider it this way: what would you say if a blonde homecoming queen fell in love with a short Japanese businessman? He treats her cruelly, then goes home for three years, during which time she prays to his picture and turns down marriage from a young Kennedy. Then, when she learns he has remarried, she kills herself. Now, I believe you would consider this girl to be a deranged idiot, correct? But because it's an Oriental who kills herself for a Westerner — ah! — you find it beautiful.

Silence.

Gallimard: Yes . . . well . . . I see your point . . .

Song: I will never do Butterfly again, Monsieur Gallimard. If you wish to see some real theater, come to the Peking Opera sometime. Expand your mind.

Song walks offstage. Other guests exit with her.

Gallimard (to us): So much for protecting her in my big Western arms.

Scene VII

M. Gallimard's apartment. Beijing. 1960.
Gallimard changes from his tux into a casual suit. Helga enters.

Gallimard: The Chinese are an incredibly arrogant people.

Helga: They warned us about that in Paris, remember?

Gallimard: Even Parisians consider them arrogant. That's a switch.

Helga: What is it that Madame Su says? "We are a very old civilization." I never know if she's talking about her country or herself.

Gallimard: I walk around here, all I hear every day, everywhere is how *old* this culture is. The fact that "old" may be synonymous with "senile" doesn't occur to them.

Helga: You're not going to change them. "East is east, west is west, and . . ." whatever that guy said.

Gallimard: It's just that—silly. I met . . . at Ambassador Koening's tonight—you should've been there.

Helga: Koening? Oh god, no. Did he enchant you all again with the history of Bavaria?

Gallimard: No. I met, I suppose, the Chinese equivalent of a diva. She's a singer in the Chinese opera.

Helga: They have an opera, too? Do they sing in Chinese? Or maybe—in Italian?

Gallimard: Tonight, she did sing in Italian.

Helga: How'd she manage that?

Gallimard: She must've been educated in the West before the Revolution. Her French is very good also. Anyway, she sang the death scene from *Madame Butterfly*.

Helga: Madame Butterfly! Then I should have come. *(She begins humming, floating around the room as if dragging long kimono sleeves.)* Did she have a nice costume? I think it's a classic piece of music.

Gallimard: That's what *I* thought, too. Don't let her hear you say that.

Helga: What's wrong?

Gallimard: Evidently the Chinese hate it.

Helga: She hated it, but she performed it anyway? Is she perverse?

Gallimard: They hate it because the white man gets the girl. Sour grapes if you ask me.

Helga: Politics again? Why can't they just hear it as a piece of beautiful music? So, what's in their opera?

Gallimard: I don't know. But, whatever it is, I'm sure it must be *old*.

Helga exits.

Scene VIII

Chinese opera house and the streets of Beijing. 1960.
The sound of gongs clanging fills the stage.

Gallimard: My wife's innocent question kept ringing in my ears. I asked around, but no one knew anything about the Chinese opera. It took four weeks, but my curiosity overcame my cowardice. This Chinese diva—this unwilling Butterfly—what did she do to make her so proud?

The room was hot, and full of smoke. Wrinkled faces, old women, teeth missing—a man with a growth on his neck, like a human toad. All smiling, pipes falling from their mouths, cracking nuts between their teeth, a live chicken pecking at my foot—all looking, screaming, gawking . . . at her.

The upstage area is suddenly hit with a harsh white light. It has become the stage for the Chinese opera performance. Two dancers enter, along with Song. Gallimard stands apart, watching. Song glides gracefully amidst the two dancers. Drums suddenly slam to a halt. Song strikes a pose, looking straight at Gallimard. Dancers exit. Light change. Pause, then Song walks right off the stage and straight up to Gallimard.

Song: Yes. You. White man. I'm looking straight at you.

Gallimard: Me?

Song: You see any other white men? It was too easy to spot you. How often does a man in my audience come in a tie?

Song starts to remove her costume. Underneath, she wears simple baggy clothes. They are now backstage. The show is over.

Song: So, you are an adventurous imperialist?

Gallimard: I . . . thought it would further my education.

Song: It took you four weeks. Why?

Gallimard: I've been busy.

Song: Well, education has always been undervalued in the West, hasn't it?

Gallimard (laughing): I don't think that's true.

Song: No, you wouldn't. You're a Westerner. How can you objectively judge your own values?

Gallimard: I think it's possible to achieve some distance.

Song: Do you? *(Pause.)* It stinks in here. Let's go.

Gallimard: These are the smells of your loyal fans.

Song: I love them for being my fans, I hate the smell they leave behind. I too can distance myself from my people. *(She looks around, then whispers in his ear.)* "Art for the masses" is a shitty excuse to keep artists poor. *(She pops a cigarette in her mouth.)* Be a gentleman, will you? And light my cigarette.

Gallimard fumbles for a match.

Gallimard: I don't . . . smoke.

Song (lighting her own): Your loss. Had you lit my cigarette, I might have blown a puff of smoke right between your eyes. Come.

They start to walk about the stage. It is a summer night on the Beijing streets. Sounds of the city play on the house speakers.

Song: How I wish there were even a tiny café to sit in. With cappuccinos, and men in tuxedos and bad expatriate jazz.

Gallimard: If my history serves me correctly, you weren't even allowed into the clubs in Shanghai before the Revolution.

Song: Your history serves you poorly, Monsieur Gallimard. True, there were signs reading "No dogs and Chinamen." But a woman, especially a delicate Oriental woman — we always go where we please. Could you imagine it otherwise? Clubs in China filled with pasty, big-thighed white women, while thousands of slender lotus blossoms wait just outside the door? Never. The clubs would be empty. *(Beat.)* We have always held a certain fascination for you Caucasian men, have we not?

Gallimard: But . . . that fascination is imperialist, or so you tell me.

Song: Do you believe everything I tell you? Yes. It is always imperialist. But sometimes . . . sometimes, it is also mutual. Oh — this is my flat.

Gallimard: I didn't even —

Song: Thank you. Come another time and we will further expand your mind.

Song exits. Gallimard continues roaming the streets as he speaks to us.

Gallimard: What was that? What did she mean, "Sometimes . . . it is mutual"? Women do not flirt with me. And I normally can't talk to them. But tonight, I held up my end of the conversation.

SCENE IX

> *Gallimard's bedroom. Beijing. 1960.*
> *Helga enters.*

Helga: You didn't tell me you'd be home late.

Gallimard: I didn't intend to. Something came up.

Helga: Oh? Like what?

Gallimard: I went to the . . . to the Dutch ambassador's home.

Helga: Again?

Gallimard: There was a reception for a visiting scholar. He's writing a six-volume treatise on the Chinese revolution. We all gathered that meant he'd have to live here long enough to actually write six volumes, and we all expressed our deepest sympathies.

Helga: Well, I had a good night too. I went with the ladies to a martial arts demonstration. Some of those men — when they break those thick boards — (*she mimes fanning herself*) whoo-whoo!

> *Helga exits. Lights dim.*

Gallimard: I lied to my wife. Why? I've never had any reason to lie before. But what reason did I have tonight? I didn't do anything wrong. That night, I had a dream. Other people, I've been told, have dreams when angels appear. Or dragons, or Sophia Loren in a towel. In my dream, Marc from school appeared.

> *Marc enters, in a nightshirt and cap.*

Marc: Rene! You met a girl!

> *Gallimard and Marc stumble down the Beijing streets. Night sounds over the speakers.*

Gallimard: It's not that amazing, thank you.

Marc: No! It's so monumental, I heard about it halfway around the world in my sleep!

Gallimard: I've met girls before, you know.

Marc: Name one. I've come across time and space to congratulate you. (*He hands Gallimard a bottle of wine.*)

Gallimard: Marc, this is expensive.

Marc: On those rare occasions when you become a formless spirit, why not steal the best?

> *Marc pops open the bottle, begins to share it with Gallimard.*

Gallimard: You embarrass me. She . . . there's no reason to think she likes me.

Marc: "Sometimes, it is mutual"?

Gallimard: Oh.

Marc: "Mutual"? "Mutual"? What does that mean?

Gallimard: You heard?

Marc: It means the money is in the bank, you only have to write the check!

Gallimard: I am a married man!

Marc: And an excellent one too. I cheated after . . . six months. Then again and again, until now — three hundred girls in twelve years.

Gallimard: I don't think we should hold that up as a model.

Marc: Of course not! My life — it is disgusting! Phooey! Phooey! But, you — you are the model husband.

Gallimard: Anyway, it's impossible. I'm a foreigner.

Marc: Ah, yes. She cannot love you, it is taboo, but something deep inside her heart . . . she cannot help herself . . . she must surrender to you. It is her destiny.

Gallimard: How do you imagine all this?

Marc: The same way you do. It's an old story. It's in our blood. They fear us, Rene. Their women fear us. And their men — their men hate us. And, you know something? They are all correct.

> *They spot a light in a window.*

Marc: There! There, Rene!

Gallimard: It's her window.

Marc: Late at night — it burns. The light — it burns for you.

Gallimard: I won't look. It's not respectful.

Marc: We don't have to be respectful. We're foreign devils.

> *Enter Song, in a sheer robe, her face completely swathed in black cloth. The "One Fine Day" aria creeps in over the speakers. With her back to us, Song mimes attending to her toilette. Her robe comes loose, revealing her white shoulders.*

Marc: All your life you've waited for a beautiful girl who would lay down for you. All your life you've smiled like a saint when it's happened to every other man you know. And you see them in magazines and you see them in movies. And you wonder, what's wrong with me? Will anyone beautiful ever want me? As the years pass, your hair thins and you struggle to hold on to even your hopes. Stop struggling, Rene. The wait is over. *(He exits.)*

Gallimard: Marc? Marc?

> *At that moment, Song, her back still towards us, drops her robe. A second of her naked back, then a sound cue: a phone ringing, very loud. Blackout, followed in the next beat by a special up on the bedroom area, where a phone now sits. Gallimard stumbles across the stage and picks up the phone. Sound cue out. Over the course of his conversation, area lights fill in the vicinity of his bed. It is the following morning.*

Gallimard: Yes? Hello?

Song (offstage): Is it very early?

Gallimard: Why, yes.

Song (offstage): How early?

Gallimard: It's . . . it's 5:30. Why are you — ?

Song (offstage): But it's light outside. Already.

Gallimard: It is. The sun must be in confusion today.

> *Over the course of Song's next speech, her upstage special comes up again. She sits in a chair, legs crossed, in a robe, telephone to her ear.*

Song: I waited until I saw the sun. That was as much discipline as I could manage for one night. Do you forgive me?

Gallimard: Of course . . . for what?

Song: Then I'll ask you quickly. Are you really interested in the opera?

Gallimard: Why, yes. Yes I am.

Song: Then come again next Thursday. I am playing *The Drunken Beauty.* May I count on you?

Gallimard: Yes. You may.

Song: Perfect. Well, I must be getting to bed. I'm exhausted. It's been a very long night for me.

Song hangs up; special on her goes off. Gallimard begins to dress for work.

SCENE X

Song Liling's apartment. Beijing. 1960.

Gallimard: I returned to the opera that next week, and the week after that . . . she keeps our meetings so short — perhaps fifteen, twenty minutes at most. So I am left each week with a thirst which is intensified. In this way, fifteen weeks have gone by. I am starting to doubt the words of my friend Marc. But no, not really. In my heart, I know she has . . . an interest in me. I suspect this is her way. She is outwardly bold and outspoken, yet her heart is shy and afraid. It is the Oriental in her at war with her Western education.

Song (offstage): I will be out in an instant. Ask the servant for anything you want.

Gallimard: Tonight, I have finally been invited to enter her apartment. Though the idea is almost beyond belief, I believe she is afraid of me.

Gallimard looks around the room. He picks up a picture in a frame, studies it. Without his noticing, Song enters, dressed elegantly in a black gown from the twenties. She stands in the doorway looking like Anna May Wong.°

Song: That is my father.

Gallimard (surprised): Mademoiselle Song . . .

She glides up to him, snatches away the picture.

Song: It is very good that he did not live to see the Revolution. They would, no doubt, have made him kneel on broken glass. Not that he didn't deserve such a punishment. But he is my father. I would've hated to see it happen.

Gallimard: I'm very honored that you've allowed me to visit your home.

Song curtseys.

Song: Thank you. Oh! Haven't you been poured any tea?

Gallimard: I'm really not —

Song (to her offstage servant): Shu-Fang! Cha! Kwai-lah! *(To Gallimard.)* I'm sorry. You want everything to be perfect —

Gallimard: Please.

Song: — and before the evening even begins —

Gallimard: I'm really not thirsty.

Song: — it's ruined.

Gallimard (sharply): Mademoiselle Song!

Song sits down.

Song: I'm sorry.

Anna May Wong (1905–1961): Chinese American actor known for her exotic beauty and most often cast as a villain.

Gallimard: What are you apologizing for now?

   Pause; Song starts to giggle.

Song: I don't know!

   Gallimard laughs.

Gallimard: Exactly my point.

Song: Oh, I am silly. Light-headed. I promise not to apologize for anything else
   tonight, do you hear me?

Gallimard: That's a good girl.

   Shu-Fang, a servant girl, comes out with a tea tray and starts to pour.

Song (to Shu-Fang): No! I'll pour myself for the gentleman!

   Shu-Fang, staring at Gallimard, exits.

Gallimard: You have a beautiful home.

Song: No, I . . . I don't even know why I invited you up.

Gallimard: Well, I'm glad you did.

   Song looks around the room.

Song: There is an element of danger to your presence.

Gallimard: Oh?

Song: You must know.

Gallimard: It doesn't concern me. We both know why I'm here.

Song: It doesn't concern me either. No . . . well perhaps . . .

Gallimard: What?

Song: Perhaps I am slightly afraid of scandal.

Gallimard: What are we doing?

Song: I'm entertaining you. In my parlor.

Gallimard: In France, that would hardly—

Song: France. France is a country living in the modern era. Perhaps even ahead
   of it. China is a nation whose soul is firmly rooted two thousand years in
   the past. What I do, even pouring the tea for you now . . . it has . . . implications. The walls and windows say so. Even my own heart, strapped inside
   this Western dress . . . even it says things—things I don't care to hear.

   *Song hands Gallimard a cup of tea. Gallimard puts his hand over both the teacup
   and Song's hand.*

Gallimard: This is a beautiful dress.

Song: Don't.

Gallimard: What?

Song: I don't even know if it looks right on me.

Gallimard: Believe me—

Song: You are from France. You see so many beautiful women.

Gallimard: France? Since when are the European women—?

Song: Oh! What am I trying to do, anyway?!

   Song runs to the door, composes herself, then turns towards Gallimard.

Song: Monsieur Gallimard, perhaps you should go.

Gallimard: But . . . why?

Song: There's something wrong about this.

Gallimard: I don't see what.

Song: I feel . . . I am not myself.

Gallimard: No. You're nervous.

Song: Please. Hard as I try to be modern, to speak like a man, to hold a Western woman's strong face up to my own . . . in the end, I fail. A small, frightened heart beats too quickly and gives me away. Monsieur Gallimard, I'm a Chinese girl. I've never . . . never invited a man up to my flat before. The forwardness of my actions makes my skin burn.

Gallimard: What are you afraid of? Certainly not me, I hope.

Song: I'm a modest girl.

Gallimard: I know. And very beautiful. *(He touches her hair.)*

Song: Please — go now. The next time you see me, I shall again be myself.

Gallimard: I like you the way you are right now.

Song: You are a cad.

Gallimard: What do you expect? I'm a foreign devil.

> *Gallimard walks downstage. Song exits.*

Gallimard (to us): Did you hear the way she talked about Western women? Much differently than the first night. She does — she feels inferior to them — and to me.

SCENE XI

> *The French embassy. Beijing. 1960.*
>   *Gallimard moves towards a desk.*

Gallimard: I determined to try an experiment. In *Madame Butterfly*, Cio-Cio-San fears that the Western man who catches a butterfly will pierce its heart with a needle, then leave it to perish. I began to wonder: Had I, too, caught a butterfly who would writhe on a needle?

> *Marc enters, dressed as a bureaucrat, holding a stack of papers. As Gallimard speaks, Marc hands papers to him. He peruses, then signs, stamps, or rejects them.*

Gallimard: Over the next five weeks, I worked like a dynamo. I stopped going to the opera, I didn't phone or write her. I knew this little flower was waiting for me to call, and, as I wickedly refused to do so, I felt for the first time that rush of power — the absolute power of a man.

> *Marc continues acting as the bureaucrat, but he now speaks as himself.*

Marc: Rene! It's me.

Gallimard: Marc — I hear your voice everywhere now. Even in the midst of work.

Marc: That's because I'm watching you — all the time.

Gallimard: You were always the most popular guy in school.

Marc: Well, there's no guarantee of failure in life like happiness in high school. Somehow I knew I'd end up in the suburbs working for Renault and you'd be in the Orient picking exotic women off the trees. And they say there's no justice.

Gallimard: That's why you were my friend?

Marc: I gave you a little of my life, so that now you can give me some of yours. *(Pause.)* Remember Isabelle?

Gallimard: Of course I remember! She was my first experience.

Marc: We all wanted to ball her. But she only wanted me.

Gallimard: I had her.

Marc: Right. You balled her.

Gallimard: You were the only one who ever believed me.

Marc: Well, there's a good reason for that. *(Beat.)* C'mon. You must've guessed.

Gallimard: You told me to wait in the bushes by the cafeteria that night. The next thing I knew, she was on me. Dress up in the air.

Marc: She never wore underwear.

Gallimard: My arms were pinned to the dirt.

Marc: She loved the superior position. A girl ahead of her time.

Gallimard: I looked up, and there was this woman . . . bouncing up and down on my loins.

Marc: Screaming, right?

Gallimard: Screaming, and breaking off the branches all around me, and pounding my butt up and down into the dirt.

Marc: Huffing and puffing like a locomotive.

Gallimard: And in the middle of all this, the leaves were getting into my mouth, my legs were losing circulation, I thought, "God. So this is *it?*"

Marc: You thought that?

Gallimard: Well, I was worried about my legs falling off.

Marc: You didn't have a good time?

Gallimard: No, that's not what I — I had a great time!

Marc: You're sure?

Gallimard: Yeah. Really.

Marc: 'Cuz I wanted you to have a good time.

Gallimard: I did.

> *Pause.*

Marc: Shit. *(Pause.)* When all is said and done, she was kind of a lousy lay, wasn't she? I mean, there was a lot of energy there, but you never knew what she was doing with it. Like when she yelled "I'm coming!" — hell, it was so loud, you wanted to go, "Look, it's not that big a deal."

Gallimard: I got scared. I thought she meant someone was actually coming. *(Pause.)* But, Marc?

Marc: What?

Gallimard: Thanks.

Marc: Oh, don't mention it.

Gallimard: It was my first experience.

Marc: Yeah. You got her.

Gallimard: I got her.

Marc: Wait! Look at that letter again!

> *Gallimard picks up one of the papers he's been stamping, and rereads it.*

Gallimard (to us): After six weeks, they began to arrive. The letters.

> *Upstage special on Song, as Madame Butterfly. The scene is underscored by the "Love Duet."*

Song: Did we fight? I do not know. Is the opera no longer of interest to you? Please come — my audiences miss the white devil in their midst.

> *Gallimard looks up from the letter, towards us.*

Gallimard (to us): A concession, but much too dignified. *(Beat; he discards the letter.)* I skipped the opera again that week to complete a position paper on trade.

The bureaucrat hands him another letter.

Song: Six weeks have passed since last we met. Is this your practice — to leave friends in the lurch? Sometimes I hate you, sometimes I hate myself, but always I miss you.

Gallimard (to us): Better, but I don't like the way she calls me "friend." When a woman calls a man her "friend," she's calling him a eunuch or a homosexual. *(Beat; he discards the letter.)* I was absent from the opera for the seventh week, feeling a sudden urge to clean out my files.

Bureaucrat hands him another letter.

Song: Your rudeness is beyond belief. I don't deserve this cruelty. Don't bother to call. I'll have you turned away at the door.

Gallimard (to us): I didn't. *(He discards the letter; bureaucrat hands him another.)* And then finally, the letter that concluded my experiment.

Song: I am out of words. I can hide behind dignity no longer. What do you want? I have already given you my shame.

Gallimard gives the letter back to Marc, slowly. Special on Song fades out.

Gallimard (to us): Reading it, I became suddenly ashamed. Yes, my experiment had been a success. She was turning on my needle. But the victory seemed hollow.

Marc: Hollow?! Are you crazy?

Gallimard: Nothing, Marc. Please go away.

Marc (exiting, with papers): Haven't I taught you anything?

Gallimard: "I have already given you my shame." I had to attend a reception that evening. On the way, I felt sick. If there is a God, surely he would punish me now. I had finally gained power over a beautiful woman, only to abuse it cruelly. There must be justice in the world. I had the strange feeling that the ax would fall this very evening.

Scene XII

Ambassador Toulon's residence. Beijing. 1960.
   Sound cue: party noises. Light change. We are now in a spacious residence.
Toulon, the French ambassador, enters and taps Gallimard on the shoulder.

Toulon: Gallimard? Can I have a word? Over here.

Gallimard (to us): Manuel Toulon. French ambassador to China. He likes to think of us all as his children. Rather like God.

Toulon: Look, Gallimard, there's not much to say. I've liked you. From the day you walked in. You were no leader, but you were tidy and efficient.

Gallimard: Thank you, sir.

Toulon: Don't jump the gun. Okay, our needs in China are changing. It's embarrassing that we lost Indochina. Someone just wasn't on the ball there. I don't mean you personally, of course.

Gallimard: Thank you, sir.

Toulon: We're going to be doing a lot more information-gathering in the future. The nature of our work here is changing. Some people are just going to have to go. It's nothing personal.

Gallimard: Oh.

Toulon: Want to know a secret? Vice-Consul LeBon is being transferred.

Gallimard (to us): My immediate superior!

Toulon: And most of his department.

Gallimard (to us): Just as I feared! God has seen my evil heart —

Toulon: But not you.

Gallimard (to us): — and he's taking her away just as . . . *(To Toulon.)* Excuse me, sir?

Toulon: Scare you? I think I did. Cheer up, Gallimard. I want you to replace LeBon as vice-consul.

Gallimard: You — ? Yes, well, thank you, sir.

Toulon: Anytime.

Gallimard: I . . . accept with great humility.

Toulon: Humility won't be part of the job. You're going to coordinate the revamped intelligence division. Want to know a secret? A year ago, you would've been out. But the past few months, I don't know how it happened, you've become this new aggressive confident . . . thing. And they also tell me you get along with the Chinese. So I think you're a lucky man, Gallimard. Congratulations.

They shake hands. Toulon exits. Party noises out. Gallimard stumbles across a darkened stage.

Gallimard: Vice-consul? Impossible! As I stumbled out of the party, I saw it written across the sky: There is no God. Or, no — say that there is a God. But that God . . . understands. Of course! God who creates Eve to serve Adam, who blesses Solomon with his harem but ties Jezebel to a burning bed° — that God is a man. And he understands! At age thirty-nine, I was suddenly initiated into the way of the world.

SCENE XIII

Song Liling's apartment. Beijing. 1960.
Song enters, in a sheer dressing gown.

Song: Are you crazy?

Gallimard: Mademoiselle Song —

Song: To come here — at this hour? After . . . after eight weeks?

Gallimard: It's the most amazing —

Song: You bang on my door? Scare my servants, scandalize the neighbors?

Gallimard: I've been promoted. To vice-consul.

Pause.

Song: And what is that supposed to mean to me?

Gallimard: Are you my Butterfly?

God who creates Eve . . . burning bed: Eve, Adam, Solomon, and Jezebel are biblical characters. See Gen. 2:18–25; I Kings 11:1–8; and II Kings 9:11–37.

Song: What are you saying?
Gallimard: I've come tonight for an answer: are you my Butterfly?
Song: Don't you know already?
Gallimard: I want you to say it.
Song: I don't want to say it.
Gallimard: So, that is your answer?
Song: You know how I feel about—
Gallimard: I do remember one thing.
Song: What?
Gallimard: In the letter I received today.
Song: Don't.
Gallimard: "I have already given you my shame."
Song: It's enough that I even wrote it.
Gallimard: Well, then—
Song: I shouldn't have it splashed across my face.
Gallimard: —if that's all true—
Song: Stop!
Gallimard: Then what is one more short answer?
Song: I don't want to!
Gallimard: Are you my Butterfly? *(Silence; he crosses the room and begins to touch her hair.)* I want from you honesty. There should be nothing false between us. No false pride.

> *Pause.*

Song: Yes, I am. I am your Butterfly.
Gallimard: Then let me be honest with you. It is because of you that I was promoted tonight. You have changed my life forever. My little Butterfly, there should be no more secrets: I love you.

> *He starts to kiss her roughly. She resists slightly.*

Song: No . . . no . . . gently . . . please, I've never . . .
Gallimard: No?
Song: I've tried to appear experienced, but . . . the truth is . . . no.
Gallimard: Are you cold?
Song: Yes. Cold.
Gallimard: Then we will go very, very slowly.

> *He starts to caress her; her gown begins to open.*

Song: No . . . let me . . . keep my clothes . . .
Gallimard: But . . .
Song: Please . . . it all frightens me. I'm a modest Chinese girl.
Gallimard: My poor little treasure.
Song: I am your treasure. Though inexperienced, I am not . . . ignorant. They teach us things, our mothers, about pleasing a man.
Gallimard: Yes?
Song: I'll do my best to make you happy. Turn off the lights.

> *Gallimard gets up and heads for a lamp. Song, propped up on one elbow, tosses her hair back and smiles.*

Song: Monsieur Gallimard?
Gallimard: Yes, Butterfly?

Song: "Vieni, vieni!"
Gallimard: "Come, darling."
Song: "Ah! Dolce notte!"
Gallimard: "Beautiful night."
Song: "Tutto estatico d'amor ride il ciel!"
Gallimard: "All ecstatic with love, the heavens are filled with laughter."

> *He turns off the lamp. Blackout.*

ACT II

SCENE I

> *M. Gallimard's cell. Paris. 1988.*
>   *Lights up on Gallimard. He sits in his cell, reading from a leaflet.*

Gallimard: This, from a contemporary critic's commentary on *Madame Butter-fly:* "Pinkerton suffers from . . . being an obnoxious bounder whom every man in the audience itches to kick." Bully for us men in the audience! Then, in the same note: "Butterfly is the most irresistibly appealing of Puccini's 'Little Women.' Watching the succession of her humiliations is like watching a child under torture." *(He tosses the pamphlet over his shoulder.)* I suggest that, while we men may all want to kick Pinkerton, very few of us would pass up the opportunity to *be* Pinkerton.

> *Gallimard moves out of his cell.*

SCENE II

> *Gallimard and Butterfly's flat. Beijing. 1960.*
>   *We are in a simple but well-decorated parlor. Gallimard moves to sit on a sofa, while Song, dressed in a cheongsam,° enters and curls up at his feet.*

Gallimard (to us): We secured a flat on the outskirts of Peking. Butterfly, as I was calling her now, decorated our "home" with Western furniture and Chinese antiques. And there, on a few stolen afternoons or evenings each week, Butterfly commenced her education.
Song: The Chinese men — they keep us down.
Gallimard: Even in the "New Society"?
Song: In the "New Society," we are all kept ignorant equally. That's one of the exciting things about loving a Western man. I know you are not threatened by a woman's education.
Gallimard: I'm no saint, Butterfly.
Song: But you come from a progressive society.
Gallimard: We're not always reminding each other how "old" we are, if that's what you mean.
Song: Exactly. We Chinese — once, I suppose, it is true, we ruled the world. But so what? How much more exciting to be part of the society ruling the world today. Tell me — what's happening in Vietnam?

---

cheongsam: A fitted dress with side slits in the skirt.

Gallimard: Oh, Butterfly — you want me to bring my work home?

Song: I want to know what you know. To be impressed by my man. It's not the particulars so much as the fact that you're making decisions which change the shape of the world.

Gallimard: Not the world. At best, a small corner.

Toulon enters, and sits at a desk upstage.

Scene III

> *French embassy. Beijing. 1961.*
> *Gallimard moves downstage, to Toulon's desk. Song remains upstage, watching.*

Toulon: And a more troublesome corner is hard to imagine.

Gallimard: So, the Americans plan to begin bombing?

Toulon: This is very secret, Gallimard: yes. The Americans don't have an embassy here. They're asking us to be their eyes and ears. Say Jack Kennedy signed an order to bomb North Vietnam, Laos. How would the Chinese react?

Gallimard: I think the Chinese will squawk —

Toulon: Uh-huh.

Gallimard: — but, in their hearts, they don't even like Ho Chi Minh.°

> *Pause.*

Toulon: What a bunch of jerks. Vietnam was *our* colony. Not only didn't the Americans help us fight to keep them, but now, seven years later, they've come back to grab the territory for themselves. It's very irritating.

Gallimard: With all due respect, sir, why should the Americans have won our war for us back in fifty-four if we didn't have the will to win it ourselves?

Toulon: You're kidding, aren't you?

> *Pause.*

Gallimard: The Orientals simply want to be associated with whoever shows the most strength and power. You live with the Chinese, sir. Do you think they like Communism?

Toulon: I live in China. Not with the Chinese.

Gallimard: Well, I —

Toulon: *You* live with the Chinese.

Gallimard: Excuse me?

Toulon: I can't keep a secret.

Gallimard: What are you saying?

Toulon: Only that I'm not immune to gossip. So, you're keeping a native mistress? Don't answer. It's none of my business. *(Pause.)* I'm sure she must be gorgeous.

Gallimard: Well . . .

Toulon: I'm impressed. You had the stamina to go out into the streets and hunt one down. Some of us have to be content with the wives of the expatriate community.

Gallimard: I do feel . . . fortunate.

Ho Chi Minh (1890–1969): First president of North Vietnam (1945–1969).

Toulon: So, Gallimard, you've got the inside knowledge — what *do* the Chinese think?

Gallimard: Deep down, they miss the old days. You know, cappuccinos, men in tuxedos —

Toulon: So what do we tell the Americans about Vietnam?

Gallimard: Tell them there's a natural affinity between the West and the Orient.

Toulon: And that you speak from experience?

Gallimard: The Orientals are people too. They want the good things we can give them. If the Americans demonstrate the will to win, the Vietnamese will welcome them into a mutually beneficial union.

Toulon: I don't see how the Vietnamese can stand up to American firepower.

Gallimard: Orientals will always submit to a greater force.

Toulon: I'll note your opinions in my report. The Americans always love to hear how "welcome" they'll be. *(He starts to exit.)*

Gallimard: Sir?

Toulon: Mmmm?

Gallimard: This . . . rumor you've heard.

Toulon: Uh-huh?

Gallimard: How . . . widespread do you think it is?

Toulon: It's only widespread within this embassy. Where nobody talks because everybody is guilty. We were worried about you, Gallimard. We thought you were the only one here without a secret. Now you go and find a lotus blossom . . . and top us all. *(He exits.)*

Gallimard (to us): Toulon knows! And he approves! I was learning the benefits of being a man. We form our own clubs, sit behind thick doors, smoke — and celebrate the fact that we're still boys. *(He starts to move downstage, towards Song.)* So, over the —

Suddenly Comrade Chin enters. Gallimard backs away.

Gallimard (to Song): No! Why does she have to come in?

Song: Rene, be sensible. How can they understand the story without her? Now, don't embarrass yourself.

Gallimard moves down center.

Gallimard (to us): Now, you will see why my story is so amusing to so many people. Why they snicker at parties in disbelief. Please — try to understand it from my point of view. We are all prisoners of our time and place. *(He exits.)*

Scene IV

Gallimard and Butterfly's flat. Beijing. 1961.

Song (to us): 1961. The flat Monsieur Gallimard rented for us. An evening after he has gone.

Chin: Okay, see if you can find out when the Americans plan to start bombing Vietnam. If you can find out what cities, even better.

Song: I'll do my best, but I don't want to arouse his suspicions.

Chin: Yeah, sure, of course. So, what else?

Song: The Americans will increase troops in Vietnam to 170,000 soldiers with 120,000 militia and 11,000 American advisors.

Chin *(writing):* Wait, wait, 120,000 militia and —
Song: —11,000 American —
Chin: —American advisors. *(Beat.)* How do you remember so much?
Song: I'm an actor.
Chin: Yeah. *(Beat.)* Is that how come you dress like that?
Song: Like what, Miss Chin?
Chin: Like that dress! You're wearing a dress. And every time I come here, you're wearing a dress. Is that because you're an actor? Or what?
Song: It's a . . . disguise, Miss Chin.
Chin: Actors, I think they're all weirdos. My mother tells me actors are like gamblers or prostitutes or —
Song: It helps me in my assignment.

> *Pause.*

Chin: You're not gathering information in any way that violates Communist Party principles, are you?
Song: Why would I do that?
Chin: Just checking. Remember: when working for the Great Proletarian State, you represent our Chairman Mao in every position you take.
Song: I'll try to imagine the Chairman taking my positions.
Chin: We all think of him this way. Good-bye, comrade. *(She starts to exit.)* Comrade?
Song: Yes?
Chin: Don't forget: there is no homosexuality in China!
Song: Yes, I've heard.
Chin: Just checking. *(She exits.)*
Song *(to us):* What passes for a woman in modern China.

> *Gallimard sticks his head out from the wings.*

Gallimard: Is she gone?
Song: Yes, Rene. Please continue in your own fashion.

Scene V

> *Beijing. 1961–1963.*
> *Gallimard moves to the couch where Song still sits. He lies down in her lap, and she strokes his forehead.*

Gallimard *(to us):* And so, over the years 1961, '62, '63, we settled into our routine, Butterfly and I. She would always have prepared a light snack and then, ever so delicately, and only if I agreed, she would start to pleasure me. With her hands, her mouth . . . too many ways to explain, and too sad, given my present situation. But mostly we would talk. About my life. Perhaps there is nothing more rare than to find a woman who passionately listens.

> *Song remains upstage, listening, as Helga enters and plays a scene downstage with Gallimard.*

Helga: Rene, I visited Dr. Bolleart this morning.
Gallimard: Why? Are you ill?

Helga: No, no. You see, I wanted to ask him . . . that question we've been discussing.

Gallimard: And I told you, it's only a matter of time. Why did you bring a doctor into this? We just have to keep trying — like a crapshoot, actually.

Helga: I went, I'm sorry. But listen: he says there's nothing wrong with me.

Gallimard: You see? Now, will you stop — ?

Helga: Rene, he says he'd like you to go in and take some tests.

Gallimard: Why? So he can find there's nothing wrong with both of us?

Helga: Rene, I don't ask for much. One trip! One visit! And then, whatever you want to do about it — you decide.

Gallimard: You're assuming he'll find something defective!

Helga: No! Of course not! Whatever he finds — if he finds nothing, we decide what to do about nothing! But go!

Gallimard: If he finds nothing, we keep trying. Just like we do now.

Helga: But at least we'll know! *(Pause.)* I'm sorry. *(She starts to exit.)*

Gallimard: Do you really want me to see Dr. Bolleart?

Helga: Only if you want a child, Rene. We have to face the fact that time is running out. Only if you want a child. *(She exits.)*

Gallimard (to Song): I'm a modern man, Butterfly. And yet, I don't want to go. It's the same old voodoo. I feel like God himself is laughing at me if I can't produce a child.

Song: You men of the West — you're obsessed by your odd desire for equality. Your wife can't give you a child, and *you're* going to the doctor?

Gallimard: Well, you see, she's already gone.

Song: And because this incompetent can't find the defect, you now have to subject yourself to him? It's unnatural.

Gallimard: Well, what is the "natural" solution?

Song: In Imperial China, when a man found that one wife was inadequate, he turned to another — to give him his son.

Gallimard: What do you — ? I can't . . . marry you, yet.

Song: Please. I'm not asking you to be my husband. But I am already your wife.

Gallimard: Do you want to . . . have my child?

Song: I thought you'd never ask.

Gallimard: But, your career . . . your —

Song: Phooey on my career! That's your Western mind, twisting itself into strange shapes again. Of course I love my career. But what would I love most of all? To feel something inside me — day and night — something I know is yours. *(Pause.)* Promise me . . . you won't go to this doctor. Who is this Western quack to set himself as judge over the man I love? I know who is a man, and who is not. *(She exits.)*

Gallimard (to us): Dr. Bolleart? Of course I didn't go. What man would?

SCENE VI

Beijing. 1963.
    Party noises over the house speakers. Renee enters, wearing a revealing gown.

Gallimard: 1963. A party at the Austrian embassy. None of us could remember the Austrian ambassador's name, which seemed somehow appropriate.

(To Renee.) So, I tell the Americans, Diem° must go. The U.S. wants to be respected by the Vietnamese, and yet they're propping up this nobody seminarian as her president. A man whose claim to fame is his sister-in-law imposing fanatic "moral order" campaigns? Oriental women — when they're good, they're very good, but when they're bad, they're Christians.

Renee: Yeah.

Gallimard: And what do you do?

Renee: I'm a student. My father exports a lot of useless stuff to the Third World.

Gallimard: How useless?

Renee: You know. Squirt guns, confectioner's sugar, Hula Hoops . . .

Gallimard: I'm sure they appreciate the sugar.

Renee: I'm here for two years to study Chinese.

Gallimard: Two years!

Renee: That's what everybody says.

Gallimard: When did you arrive?

Renee: Three weeks ago.

Gallimard: And?

Renee: I like it. It's primitive, but . . . well, this is the place to learn Chinese, so here I am.

Gallimard: Why Chinese?

Renee: I think it'll be important someday.

Gallimard: You do?

Renee: Don't ask me when, but . . . that's what I think.

Gallimard: Well, I agree with you. One hundred percent. That's very farsighted.

Renee: Yeah. Well of course, my father thinks I'm a complete weirdo.

Gallimard: He'll thank you someday.

Renee: Like when the Chinese start buying Hula Hoops?

Gallimard: There're a billion bellies out there.

Renee: And if they end up taking over the world — well, then I'll be lucky to know Chinese too, right?

    Pause.

Gallimard: At this point, I don't see how the Chinese can possibly take —

Renee: You know what I *don't* like about China?

Gallimard: Excuse me? No — what?

Renee: Nothing to do at night.

Gallimard: You come to parties at embassies like everyone else.

Renee: Yeah, but they get out at ten. And then what?

Gallimard: I'm afraid the Chinese idea of a dance hall is a dirt floor and a man with a flute.

Renee: Are you married?

Gallimard: Yes. Why?

Renee: You wanna . . . fool around?

    Pause.

Gallimard: Sure.

Renee: I'll wait for you outside. What's your name?

Diem: Ngo Dinh Diem (1901–1963), president of South Vietnam (1955–1963), assassinated in a coup d'état supported by the United States.

Gallimard: Gallimard. Rene.

Renee: Weird. I'm Renee too. *(She exits.)*

Gallimard (to us): And so, I embarked on my first extra-extramarital affair. Renee was picture perfect. With a body like those girls in the magazines. If I put a tissue paper over my eyes, I wouldn't have been able to tell the difference. And it was exciting to be with someone who wasn't afraid to be seen completely naked. But is it possible for a woman to be *too* uninhibited, *too* willing, so as to seem almost too . . . masculine?

Chuck Berry° blares from the house speakers, then comes down in volume as Renee enters, toweling her hair.

Renee: You have a nice weenie.

Gallimard: What?

Renee: Penis. You have a nice penis.

Gallimard: Oh. Well, thank you. That's very . . .

Renee: What—can't take a compliment?

Gallimard: No, it's very . . . reassuring.

Renee: But most girls don't come out and say it, huh?

Gallimard: And also . . . what did you call it?

Renee: Oh. Most girls don't call it a "weenie," huh?

Gallimard: It sounds very—

Renee: Small, I know.

Gallimard: I was going to say, "young."

Renee: Yeah. Young, small, same thing. Most guys are pretty, uh, sensitive about that. Like, you know, I had a boyfriend back home in Denmark. I got mad at him once and called him a little weeniehead. He got so mad! He said at least I should call him a great big weeniehead.

Gallimard: I suppose I just say "penis."

Renee: Yeah. That's pretty clinical. There's "cock," but that sounds like a chicken. And "prick" is painful, and "dick" is like you're talking about someone who's not in the room.

Gallimard: Yes. It's a . . . bigger problem than I imagined.

Renee: I—I think maybe it's because I really don't know what to do with them—that's why I call them "weenies."

Gallimard: Well, you did quite well with . . . mine.

Renee: Thanks, but I mean, really *do* with them. Like, okay, have you ever looked at one? I mean, really?

Gallimard: No, I suppose when it's part of you, you sort of take it for granted.

Renee: I guess. But, like, it just hangs there. This little . . . flap of flesh. And there's so much fuss that we make about it. Like, I think the reason we fight wars is because we wear clothes. Because no one knows—between the men, I mean—who has the biggest . . . weenie. So, if I'm a guy with a small one, I'm going to build a really big building or take over a really big piece of land or write a really long book so the other men don't know, right? But, see, it never really works, that's the problem. I mean, you conquer the country, or whatever, but you're still wearing clothes, so there's no way to prove absolutely whose is bigger or smaller. And that's what we call a civilized

Chuck Berry: Influential American rock 'n' roll musician whose first recording came out in 1955.

society. The whole world run by a bunch of men with pricks the size of pins. *(She exits.)*

Gallimard (to us): This was simply not acceptable.

A high-pitched chime rings through the air. Song, dressed as Butterfly, appears in the upstage special. She is obviously distressed. Her body swoons as she attempts to clip the stems of flowers she's arranging in a vase.

Gallimard: But I kept up our affair, wildly, for several months. Why? I believe because of Butterfly. She knew the secret I was trying to hide. But, unlike a Western woman, she didn't confront me, threaten, even pout. I remembered the words of Puccini's *Butterfly:*

Song: "Noi siamo gente avvezza / alle piccole cose / umili e silenziose."

Gallimard: "I come from a people / Who are accustomed to little / Humble and silent." I saw Pinkerton and Butterfly, and what she would say if he were unfaithful . . . nothing. She would cry, alone, into those wildly soft sleeves, once full of possessions, now empty to collect her tears. It was her tears and her silence that excited me, every time I visited Renee.

Toulon (offstage): Gallimard!

Toulon enters. Gallimard turns towards him. During the next section, Song, up center, begins to dance with the flowers. It is a drunken, reckless dance, where she breaks small pieces off the stems.

Toulon: They're killing him.

Gallimard: Who? I'm sorry? What?

Toulon: Bother you to come over at this late hour?

Gallimard: No . . . of course not.

Toulon: Not after you hear my secret. Champagne?

Gallimard: Um . . . thank you.

Toulon: You're surprised. There's something that you've wanted, Gallimard. No, not a promotion. Next time. Something in the world. You're not aware of this, but there's an informal gossip circle among intelligence agents. And some of ours heard from some of the Americans —

Gallimard: Yes?

Toulon: That the U.S. will allow the Vietnamese generals to stage a coup . . . and assassinate President Diem.

The chime rings again. Toulon freezes. Gallimard turns upstage and looks at Butterfly, who slowly and deliberately clips a flower off its stem. Gallimard turns back towards Toulon.

Gallimard: I think . . . that's a very wise move!

Toulon unfreezes.

Toulon: It's what you've been advocating. A toast?

Gallimard: Sure. I consider this a vindication.

Toulon: Not exactly. "To the test. Let's hope you pass."

They drink. The chime rings again. Toulon freezes. Gallimard turns upstage, and Song clips another flower.

Gallimard (to Toulon): The test?

Toulon (unfreezing): It's a test of everything you've been saying. I personally think the generals probably will stop the Communists. And you'll be a hero. But if anything goes wrong, then your opinions won't be worth a pig's ear. I'm sure that won't happen. But sometimes it's easier when they don't listen to you.

Gallimard: They're your opinions too, aren't they?

Toulon: Personally, yes.

Gallimard: So we agree.

Toulon: But my opinions aren't on that report. Yours are. Cheers.

Toulon turns away from Gallimard and raises his glass. At that instant Song picks up the vase and hurls it to the ground. It shatters. Song sinks down amidst the shards of the vase, in a calm, childlike trance. She sings softly, as if reciting a child's nursery rhyme.

Song (repeat as necessary): "The whole world over, the white man travels, setting anchor, wherever he likes. Life's not worth living, unless he finds, the finest maidens, of every land . . . "

Gallimard turns downstage towards us. Song continues singing.

Gallimard: I shook as I left his house. That coward! That worm! To put the burden for his decisions on my shoulders!

I started for Renee's. But no, that was all I needed. A schoolgirl who would question the role of the penis in modern society. What I wanted was revenge. A vessel to contain my humiliation. Though I hadn't seen her in several weeks, I headed for Butterfly's.

Gallimard enters Song's apartment.

Song: Oh! Rene . . . I was dreaming!

Gallimard: You've been drinking?

Song: If I can't sleep, then yes, I drink. But then, it gives me these dreams which — Rene, it's been almost three weeks since you visited me last.

Gallimard: I know. There's been a lot going on in the world.

Song: Fortunately I am drunk. So I can speak freely. It's not the world, it's you and me. And an old problem. Even the softest skin becomes like leather to a man who's touched it too often. I confess I don't know how to stop it. I don't know how to become another woman.

Gallimard: I have a request.

Song: Is this a solution? Or are you ready to give up the flat?

Gallimard: It may be a solution. But I'm sure you won't like it.

Song: Oh well, that's very important. "Like it?" Do you think I "like" lying here alone, waiting, always waiting for your return? Please — don't worry about what I may not "like."

Gallimard: I want to see you . . . naked.

Silence.

Song: I thought you understood my modesty. So you want me to — what — strip? Like a big cowboy girl? Shiny pasties on my breasts? Shall I fling my kimono over my head and yell "ya-hoo" in the process? I thought you respected my shame!

Gallimard: I believe you gave me your shame many years ago.

Song: Yes — and it is just like a white devil to use it against me. I can't believe it. I thought myself so repulsed by the passive Oriental and the cruel white man. Now I see — we are always most revolted by the things hidden within us.

Gallimard: I just mean—
Song: Yes?
Gallimard: —that it will remove the only barrier left between us.
Song: No, Rene. Don't couch your request in sweet words. Be yourself—a cad—
and know that my love is enough, that I submit—submit to the worst you
can give me. *(Pause.)* Well, come. Strip me. Whatever happens, know that
you have willed it. Our love, in your hands. I'm helpless before my man.

Gallimard starts to cross the room.

Gallimard: Did I not undress her because I knew, somewhere deep down, what
I would find? Perhaps. Happiness is so rare that our mind can turn somersaults to protect it.
    At the time, I only knew that I was seeing Pinkerton stalking towards
his Butterfly, ready to reward her love with his lecherous hands. The image
sickened me, pulled me to my knees, so I was crawling towards her like a
worm. By the time I reached her, Pinkerton . . . had vanished from my
heart. To be replaced by something new, something unnatural, that flew in
the face of all I'd learned in the world—something very close to love.

He grabs her around the waist; she strokes his hair.

Gallimard: Butterfly, forgive me.
Song: Rene . . .
Gallimard: For everything. From the start.
Song: I'm . . .
Gallimard: I want to—
Song: I'm pregnant. *(Beat.)* I'm pregnant. *(Beat.)* I'm pregnant.

    Beat.

Gallimard: I want to marry you!

SCENE VII

Gallimard and Butterfly's flat. Beijing. 1963.
    Downstage, Song paces as Comrade Chin reads from her notepad. Upstage,
Gallimard is still kneeling. He remains on his knees throughout the scene, watching it.

Song: I need a baby.
Chin (from pad): He's been spotted going to a dorm.
Song: I need a baby.
Chin: At the Foreign Language Institute.
Song: I need a baby.
Chin: The room of a Danish girl. . . . What do you mean, you need a baby?!
Song: Tell Comrade Kang—last night, the entire mission, it could've ended.
Chin: What do you mean?
Song: Tell Kang—he told me to strip.
Chin: Strip?!
Song: Write!
Chin: I tell you, I don't understand nothing about this case anymore. Nothing.
Song: He told me to strip, and I took a chance. Oh, we Chinese, we know how
    to gamble.
Chin (writing): " . . . told him to strip."

Song: My palms were wet, I had to make a split-second decision.
Chin: Hey! Can you slow down?!

   Pause.

Song: You write faster, I'm the artist here. Suddenly, it hit me — "All he wants is for her to submit. Once a woman submits, a man is always ready to become 'generous.'"
Chin: You're just gonna end up with rough notes.
Song: And it worked! He gave in! Now, if I can just present him with a baby. A Chinese baby with blond hair — he'll be mine for life!
Chin: Kang will never agree! The trading of babies has to be a counterrevolutionary act!
Song: Sometimes, a counterrevolutionary act is necessary to counter a counterrevolutionary act.

   Pause.

Chin: Wait.
Song: I need one . . . in seven months. Make sure it's a boy.
Chin: This doesn't sound like something the Chairman would do. Maybe you'd better talk to Comrade Kang yourself.
Song: Good. I will.

   Chin gets up to leave.

Song: Miss Chin? Why, in the Peking Opera, are women's roles played by men?
Chin: I don't know. Maybe, a reactionary remnant of male —
Song: No. *(Beat.)* Because only a man knows how a woman is supposed to act.

   Chin exits. Song turns upstage, towards Gallimard.

Gallimard (calling after Chin): Good riddance! *(To Song.)* I could forget all that betrayal in an instant, you know. If you'd just come back and become Butterfly again.
Song: Fat chance. You're here in prison, rotting in a cell. And I'm on a plane, winging my way back to China. Your President pardoned me of our treason, you know.
Gallimard: Yes, I read about that.
Song: Must make you feel . . . lower than shit.
Gallimard: But don't you, even a little bit, wish you were here with me?
Song: I'm an artist, Rene. You were my greatest . . . acting challenge. *(She laughs.)* It doesn't matter how rotten I answer, does it? You still adore me. That's why I love you, Rene. *(She points to us.)* So — you were telling your audience about the night I announced I was pregnant.

   Gallimard puts his arms around Song's waist. He and Song are in the positions they were in at the end of Scene VI.

Scene VIII

   Same.

Gallimard: I'll divorce my wife. We'll live together here, and then later in France.

Song: I feel so . . . ashamed.

Gallimard: Why?

Song: I had begun to lose faith. And now, you shame me with your generosity.

Gallimard: Generosity? No, I'm proposing for very selfish reasons.

Song: Your apologies only make me feel more ashamed. My outburst a moment ago!

Gallimard: Your outburst? What about my request?!

Song: You've been very patient dealing with my . . . eccentricities. A Western man, used to women freer with their bodies —

Gallimard: It was sick! Don't make excuses for me.

Song: I have to. You don't seem willing to make them for yourself.

> *Pause.*

Gallimard: You're crazy.

Song: I'm happy. Which often looks like crazy.

Gallimard: Then make me crazy. Marry me.

> *Pause.*

Song: No.

Gallimard: What?

Song: Do I sound silly, a slave, if I say I'm not worthy?

Gallimard: Yes. In fact you do. No one has loved me like you.

Song: Thank you. And no one ever will. I'll see to that.

Gallimard: So what is the problem?

Song: Rene, we Chinese are realists. We understand rice, gold, and guns. You are a diplomat. Your career is skyrocketing. Now, what would happen if you divorced your wife to marry a Communist Chinese actress?

Gallimard: That's not being realistic. That's defeating yourself before you begin.

Song: We conserve our strength for the battles we can win.

Gallimard: That sounds like a fortune cookie!

Song: Where do you think fortune cookies come from!

Gallimard: I don't care.

Song: You do. So do I. And we should. That is why I say I'm not worthy. I'm worthy to love and even to be loved by you. But I am not worthy to end the career of one of the West's most promising diplomats.

Gallimard: It's not that great a career! I made it sound like more than it is!

Song: Modesty will get you nowhere. Flatter yourself, and you flatter me. I'm flattered to decline your offer. *(She exits.)*

Gallimard (to us): Butterfly and I argued all night. And, in the end, I left, knowing I would never be her husband. She went away for several months — to the countryside, like a small animal. Until the night I received her call.

> *A baby's cry from offstage. Song enters, carrying a child.*

Song: He looks like you.

Gallimard: Oh! *(Beat; he approaches the baby.)* Well, babies are never very attractive at birth.

Song: Stop!

Gallimard: I'm sure he'll grow more beautiful with age. More like his mother.

Song: "Chi vide mai / a bimbo del Giappon . . ."

Gallimard: "What baby, I wonder, was ever born in Japan" — or China, for that matter —

Song: "*. . . occhi azzurrini?*"
Gallimard: "With azure eyes" — they're actually sort of brown, wouldn't you say?
Song: "*E il labbro.*"
Gallimard: "And such lips!" *(He kisses Song.)* And such lips.
Song: "*E i ricciolini d'oro schietto?*"
Gallimard: "And such a head of golden" — if slightly patchy — "curls?"
Song: I'm going to call him "Peepee."
Gallimard: Darling, could you repeat that because I'm sure a rickshaw just flew
   by overhead.
Song: You heard me.
Gallimard: "Song Peepee"? May I suggest Michael, or Stephan, or Adolph?
Song: You may, but I won't listen.
Gallimard: You can't be serious. Can you imagine the time this child will have
   in school?
Song: In the West, yes.
Gallimard: It's worse than naming him Ping Pong or Long Dong or —
Song: But he's never going to live in the West, is he?

   Pause.

Gallimard: That wasn't my choice.
Song: It is mine. And this is my promise to you: I will raise him, he will be our
   child, but he will never burden you outside of China.
Gallimard: Why do you make these promises? I want to be burdened! I want a
   scandal to cover the papers!
Song (to us): Prophetic.
Gallimard: I'm serious.
Song: So am I. His name is as I registered it. And he will never live in the West.

   Song exits with the child.

Gallimard (to us): Is it possible that her stubbornness only made me want her
   more? That drawing back at the moment of my capitulation was the most
   brilliant strategy she could have chosen? It is possible. But it is also possible that by this point she could have said, could have done . . . anything,
   and I would have adored her still.

Scene IX

   Beijing. 1966.
   A driving rhythm of Chinese percussion fills the stage.

Gallimard: And then, China began to change. Mao became very old, and his
   cult became very strong. And, like many old men, he entered his second
   childhood. So he handed over the reins of state to those with minds like
   his own. And children ruled the Middle Kingdom° with complete caprice.
   The doctrine of the Cultural Revolution° implied continuous anarchy.
   Contact between Chinese and foreigners became impossible. Our flat was
   confiscated. Her fame and my money now counted against us.

Middle Kingdom: The royal domain of China during its feudal period.   *Cultural Revolution:*
The reform campaign of 1965-1967 to purge counterrevolutionary thought in China that
challenged Mao Zedong.

Two dancers in Mao suits and red-starred caps enter, and begin crudely mimicking revolutionary violence, in an agitprop fashion.

Gallimard: And somehow the American war went wrong too. Four hundred thousand dollars were being spent for every Viet Cong° killed; so General Westmoreland's° remark that the Oriental does not value life the way Americans do was oddly accurate. Why weren't the Vietnamese people giving in? Why were they content instead to die and die and die again?

Toulon enters. Percussion and dancers continue upstage.

Toulon: Congratulations, Gallimard.
Gallimard: Excuse me, sir?
Toulon: Not a promotion. That was last time. You're going home.
Gallimard: What?
Toulon: Don't say I didn't warn you.
Gallimard: I'm being transferred . . . because I was wrong about the American war?
Toulon: Of course not. We don't care about the Americans. We care about your mind. The quality of your analysis. In general, everything you've predicted here in the Orient . . . just hasn't happened.
Gallimard: I think that's premature.
Toulon: Don't force me to be blunt. Okay, you said China was ready to open to Western trade. The only thing they're trading out there are Western heads. And, yes, you said the Americans would succeed in Indochina. You were kidding, right?
Gallimard: I think the end is in sight.
Toulon: Don't be pathetic. And don't take this personally. You were wrong. It's not your fault.
Gallimard: But I'm going home.
Toulon: Right. Could I have the number of your mistress? *(Beat.)* Joke! Joke! Eat a croissant for me.

Toulon exits. Song, wearing a Mao suit, is dragged in from the wings as part of the upstage dance. They "beat" her, then lampoon the acrobatics of the Chinese opera, as she is made to kneel onstage.

Gallimard (simultaneously): I don't care to recall how Butterfly and I said our hurried farewell. Perhaps it was better to end our affair before it killed her.

Gallimard exits. Percussion rises in volume. The lampooning becomes faster, more frenetic. At its height, Comrade Chin walks across the stage with a banner reading: "The Actor Renounces His Decadent Profession!" She reaches the kneeling Song. At the moment Chin touches Song's chin, percussion stops with a thud. Dancers strike poses.

Chin: Actor-oppressor, for years you have lived above the common people and looked down on their labor. While the farmer ate millet—
Song: I ate pastries from France and sweetmeats from silver trays.
Chin: And how did you come to live in such an exalted position?
Song: I was a plaything for the imperialists!

Viet Cong: Member of the National Liberation Front of South Vietnam, against which U.S. forces were fighting.   *General Westmoreland:* William Westmoreland (b. 1914), commander of American troops in Vietnam from 1964 to 1968.

Chin: What did you do?

Song: I shamed China by allowing myself to be corrupted by a foreigner . . .

Chin: What does this mean? The People demand a full confession!

Song: I engaged in the lowest perversions with China's enemies!

Chin: What perversions? Be more clear!

Song: I let him put it up my ass!

    Dancers look over, disgusted.

Chin: Aaaa-ya! How can you use such sickening language?!

Song: My language . . . is only as foul as the crimes I committed . . .

Chin: Yeah. That's better. So — what do you want to do . . . now?

Song: I want to serve the people!

    Percussion starts up, with Chinese strings.

Chin: What?

Song: I want to serve the people!

    Dancers regain their revolutionary smiles, and begin a dance of victory.

Chin: What?!

Song: I want to serve the people!!

    Dancers unveil a banner: "The Actor Is Re-Habilitated!" Song remains kneeling before Chin, as the dancers bounce around them, then exit. Music out.

SCENE X

    A commune. Hunan Province. 1970.

Chin: How you planning to do that?

Song: I've already worked four years in the fields of Hunan, Comrade Chin.

Chin: So? Farmers work all their lives. Let me see your hands.

    Song holds them out for her inspection.

Chin: Goddamn! Still so smooth! How long does it take to turn you actors into good anythings? Hunh. You've just spent too many years in luxury to be any good to the Revolution.

Song: I served the Revolution.

Chin: Serve the Revolution? Bullshit! You wore dresses! Don't tell me — I was there. I saw you! You and your white vice-consul! Stuck up there in your flat, living off the People's Treasury! Yeah, I knew what was going on! You two . . . homos! Homos! Homos! *(Pause; she composes herself.)* Ah! Well . . . you will serve the people, all right. But not with the Revolution's money. This time, you use your own money.

Song: I have no money.

Chin: Shut up! And you won't stink up China anymore with your pervert stuff. You'll pollute the place where pollution begins — the West.

Song: What do you mean?

Chin: Shut up! You're going to France. Without a cent in your pocket. You find your consul's house, you make him pay your expenses —

Song: No.

Chin: And you give us weekly reports! Useful information!

Song: That's crazy. It's been four years.

Chin: Either that, or back to rehabilitation center!

Song: Comrade Chin, he's not going to support me! Not in France! He's a white man! I was just his plaything—

Chin: Oh yuck! Again with the sickening language? Where's my stick?

Song: You don't understand the mind of a man.

> *Pause.*

Chin: Oh no? No I don't? Then how come I'm married, huh? How come I got a man? Five, six years ago, you always tell me those kind of things, I felt very bad. But not now! Because what does the Chairman say? He tells us *I'm* now the smart one, you're now the nincompoop! *You're* the blockhead, the harebrain, the nitwit! You think you're so smart? You understand "The Mind of a Man"? Good! Then *you* go to France and be a pervert for Chairman Mao!

> *Chin and Song exit in opposite directions.*

Scene XI

> *Paris. 1968–1970.*
> *Gallimard enters.*

Gallimard: And what was waiting for me back in Paris? Well, better Chinese food than I'd eaten in China. Friends and relatives. A little accounting, regular schedule, keeping track of traffic violations in the suburbs. . . . And the indignity of students shouting the slogans of Chairman Mao at me—in French.

Helga: Rene? Rene? *(She enters, soaking wet.)* I've had a . . . problem.

> *(She sneezes.)*

Gallimard: You're wet.

Helga: Yes, I . . . coming back from the grocer's. A group of students, waving red flags, they—

> *Gallimard fetches a towel.*

Helga: —they ran by, I was caught up along with them. Before I knew what was happening—

> *Gallimard gives her the towel.*

Helga: Thank you. The police started firing water cannons at us. I tried to shout, to tell them I was the wife of a diplomat, but—you know how it is . . . *(Pause.)* Needless to say, I lost the groceries. Rene, what's happening to France?

Gallimard: What's—? Well, nothing, really.

Helga: Nothing?! The storefronts are in flames, there's glass in the streets, buildings are toppling—and I'm wet!

Gallimard: Nothing! . . . that I care to think about.

Helga: And is that why you stay in this room?

Gallimard: Yes, in fact.

Helga: With the incense burning? You know something? I hate incense. It smells so sickly sweet.

Gallimard: Well, I hate the French. Who just smell—period!

Helga: And the Chinese were better?

Gallimard: Please — don't start.

Helga: When we left, this exact same thing, the riots —

Gallimard: No, no . . .

Helga: Students screaming slogans, smashing down doors —

Gallimard: Helga —

Helga: It was all going on in China, too. Don't you remember?!

Gallimard: Helga! Please! *(Pause.)* You have never understood China, have you? You walk in here with these ridiculous ideas, that the West is falling apart, that China was spitting in our faces. You come in, dripping of the streets, and you leave water all over my floor. *(He grabs Helga's towel, begins mopping up the floor.)*

Helga: But it's the truth!

Gallimard: Helga, I want a divorce.

    Pause; Gallimard continues mopping the floor.

Helga: I take it back. China is . . . beautiful. Incense, I like incense.

Gallimard: I've had a mistress.

Helga: So?

Gallimard: For eight years.

Helga: I knew you would. I knew you would the day I married you. And now what? You want to marry her?

Gallimard: I can't. She's in China.

Helga: I see. You know that no one else is ever going to marry me, right?

Gallimard: I'm sorry.

Helga: And you want to leave. For someone who's not here, is that right?

Gallimard: That's right.

Helga: You can't live with her, but still you don't want to live with me.

Gallimard: That's right.

    Pause.

Helga: Shit. How terrible that I can figure that out. *(Pause.)* I never thought I'd say it. But, in China, I was happy. I knew, in my own way, I knew that you were not everything you pretended to be. But the pretense — going on your arm to the embassy ball, visiting your office and the guards saying, "Good morning, good morning, Madame Gallimard" — the pretense . . . was very good indeed. *(Pause.)* I hope everyone is mean to you for the rest of your life. *(She exits.)*

Gallimard (to us): Prophetic.

    Marc enters with two drinks.

Gallimard (to Marc): In China, I was different from all other men.

Marc: Sure. You were white. Here's your drink.

Gallimard: I felt . . . touched.

Marc: In the head? Rene, I don't want to hear about the Oriental love goddess. Okay? One night — can we just drink and throw up without a lot of conversation?

Gallimard: You still don't believe me, do you?

Marc: Sure I do. She was the most beautiful, et cetera, et cetera, blasé, blasé.

    Pause.

Gallimard: My life in the West has been such a disappointment.

Marc: Life in the West is like that. You'll get used to it. Look, you're driving me away. I'm leaving. Happy, now? *(He exits, then returns.)* Look, I have a date tomorrow night. You wanna come? I can fix you up with —

Gallimard: Of course. I would love to come.

Pause.

Marc: Uh — on second thought, no. You'd better get ahold of yourself first.

He exits; Gallimard nurses his drink.

Gallimard (to us): This is the ultimate cruelty, isn't it? That I can talk and talk and to anyone listening, it's only air — too rich a diet to be swallowed by a mundane world. Why can't anyone understand? That in China, I once loved, and was loved by, very simply, the Perfect Woman.

Song enters, dressed as Butterfly in wedding dress.

Gallimard (to Song): Not again. My imagination is hell. Am I asleep this time? Or did I drink too much?

Song: Rene!

Gallimard: God, it's too painful! That you speak?

Song: What are you talking about? Rene — touch me.

Gallimard: Why?

Song: I'm real. Take my hand.

Gallimard: Why? So you can disappear again and leave me clutching at the air? For the entertainment of my neighbors who — ?

Song touches Gallimard.

Song: Rene?

Gallimard takes Song's hand. Silence.

Gallimard: Butterfly? I never doubted you'd return.

Song: You hadn't . . . forgotten — ?

Gallimard: Yes, actually, I've forgotten everything. My mind, you see — there wasn't enough room in this hard head — not for the world *and* for you. No, there was only room for one. *(Beat.)* Come, look. See? Your bed has been waiting, with the Klimt° poster you like, and — see? The *xiang lu*° you gave me?

Song: I . . . I don't know what to say.

Gallimard: There's nothing to say. Not at the end of a long trip. Can I make you some tea?

Song: But where's your wife?

Gallimard: She's by my side. She's by my side at last.

Gallimard reaches to embrace Song. Song sidesteps, dodging him.

Gallimard: Why?!

Song (to us): So I did return to Rene in Paris. Where I found —

Gallimard: Why do you run away? Can't we show them how we embraced that evening?

Song: Please. I'm talking.

Gallimard: You have to do what I say! I'm conjuring you up in *my* mind!

Klimt: Gustav Klimt (1863–1918), Austrian painter in the art nouveau style, whose most famous painting is *The Kiss; xiang lu:* Incense burner.

Song: Rene, I've never done what you've said. Why should it be any different in your mind? Now split — the story moves on, and I must change.

Gallimard: I welcomed you into my home! I didn't have to, you know! I could've left you penniless on the streets of Paris! But I took you in!

Song: Thank you.

Gallimard: So . . . please . . . don't change.

Song: You know I have to. You know I will. And anyway, what difference does it make? No matter what your eyes tell you, you can't ignore the truth. You already know too much.

Gallimard exits. Song turns to us.

Song: The change I'm going to make requires about five minutes. So I thought you might want to take this opportunity to stretch your legs, enjoy a drink, or listen to the musicians. I'll be here, when you return, right where you left me.

Song goes to a mirror in front of which is a wash basin of water. She starts to remove her makeup as stagelights go to half and houselights come up.

ACT III

Scene I

A courthouse in Paris. 1986.

    As he promised, Song has completed the bulk of his transformation onstage by the time the houselights go down and the stagelights come up full. As he speaks to us, he removes his wig and kimono, leaving them on the floor. Underneath, he wears a well-cut suit.

Song: So I'd done my job better than I had a right to expect. Well, give him some credit, too. He's right — I was in a fix when I arrived in Paris. I walked from the airport into town, then I located, by blind groping, the China-town district. Let me make one thing clear: whatever else may be said about the Chinese, they are stingy! I slept in doorways three days until I could find a tailor who would make me this kimono on credit. As it turns out, maybe I didn't even need it. Maybe he would've been happy to see me in a simple shift and mascara. But . . . better safe than sorry.

    That was 1970, when I arrived in Paris. For the next fifteen years, yes, I lived a very comfy life. Some relief, believe me, after four years on a fucking commune in Nowheresville, China. Rene supported the boy and me, and I did some demonstrations around the country as part of my "cultural exchange" cover. And then there was the spying.

Song moves upstage, to a chair. Toulon enters as a judge, wearing the appropriate wig and robes. He sits near Song. It's 1986, and Song is testifying in a courtroom.

Song: Not much at first. Rene had lost all his high-level contacts. Comrade Chin wasn't very interested in parking-ticket statistics. But finally, at my urging, Rene got a job as a courier, handling sensitive documents. He'd photograph them for me, and I'd pass them on to the Chinese embassy.

Judge: Did he understand the extent of his activity?

Song: He didn't ask. He knew that I needed those documents, and that was enough.

Judge: But he must've known he was passing classified information.

Song: I can't say.

Judge: He never asked what you were going to do with them?

Song: Nope.

    Pause.

Judge: There is one thing that the court—indeed, that all of France—would like to know.

Song: Fire away.

Judge: Did Monsieur Gallimard know you were a man?

Song: Well, he never saw me completely naked. Ever.

Judge: But surely, he must've . . . how can I put this?

Song: Put it however you like. I'm not shy. He must've felt around?

Judge: Mmmmm.

Song: Not really. I did all the work. He just laid back. Of course we did enjoy more . . . complete union, and I suppose he *might* have wondered why I was always on my stomach, but. . . . But what you're thinking is, "Of course a wrist must've brushed . . . a hand hit . . . over twenty years!" Yeah. Well, Your Honor, it was my job to make him think I was a woman. And chew on this: it wasn't all that hard. See, my mother was a prostitute along the Bundt before the Revolution. And, uh, I think it's fair to say she learned a few things about Western men. So I borrowed her knowledge. In service to my country.

Judge: Would you care to enlighten the court with this secret knowledge? I'm sure we're all very curious.

Song: I'm sure you are. *(Pause.)* Okay, Rule One is: Men always believe what they want to hear. So a girl can tell the most obnoxious lies and the guys will believe them every time—"This is my first time"—"That's the biggest I've ever seen"—or *both,* which, if you really think about it, is not possible in a single lifetime. You've maybe heard those phrases a few times in your own life, yes, Your Honor?

Judge: It's not my life, Monsieur Song, which is on trial today.

Song: Okay, okay, just trying to lighten up the proceedings. Tough room.

Judge: Go on.

Song: Rule Two: As soon as a Western man comes into contact with the East— he's already confused. The West has sort of an international rape mentality towards the East. Do you know rape mentality?

Judge: Give us your definition, please.

Song: Basically, "Her mouth says no, but her eyes say yes."

    The West thinks of itself as masculine—big guns, big industry, big money—so the East is feminine—weak, delicate, poor . . . but good at art, and full of inscrutable wisdom—the feminine mystique.

    Her mouth says no, but her eyes say yes. The West believes the East, deep down, *wants* to be dominated—because a woman can't think for herself.

Judge: What does this have to do with my question?

Song: You expect Oriental countries to submit to your guns, and you expect Oriental women to be submissive to your men. That's why you say they make the best wives.

Judge: But why would that make it possible for you to fool Monsieur Gallimard? Please — get to the point.

Song: One, because when he finally met his fantasy woman, he wanted more
than anything to believe that she was, in fact, a woman. And second, I am
an Oriental. And being an Oriental, I could never be completely a man.

Pause.

Judge: Your armchair political theory is tenuous, Monsieur Song.

Song: You think so? That's why you'll lose in all your dealings with the East.

Judge: Just answer my question: did he know you were a man?

Pause.

Song: You know, Your Honor, I never asked.

SCENE II

Same.

Music from the "Death Scene" from Butterfly *blares over the house speakers.
It is the loudest thing we've heard in this play.*

Gallimard enters, crawling towards Song's wig and kimono.

Gallimard: Butterfly? Butterfly?

Song remains a man, in the witness box, delivering a testimony we do not hear.

Gallimard (to us): In my moment of greatest shame, here, in this courtroom —
with that . . . person up there, telling the world. . . . What strikes me especially is how shallow he is, how glib and obsequious . . . completely . . .
without substance! The type that prowls around discos with a gold
medallion stinking of garlic. So little like my Butterfly.

   Yet even in this moment my mind remains agile, flip-flopping like a
man on a trampoline. Even now, my picture dissolves, and I see that . . .
witness . . . talking to me.

Song suddenly stands straight up in his witness box, and looks at Gallimard.

Song: Yes. You. White man.

*Song steps out of the witness box, and moves downstage towards Gallimard. Light
change.*

Gallimard (to Song): Who? Me?

Song: Do you see any other white men?

Gallimard: Yes. There're white men all around. This is a French courtroom.

Song: So you are an adventurous imperialist. Tell me, why did it take you so
long? To come back to this place?

Gallimard: What place?

Song: This theater in China. Where we met many years ago.

Gallimard (to us): And once again, against my will, I am transported.

*Chinese opera music comes up on the speakers. Song begins to do opera moves, as
he did the night they met.*

Song: Do you remember? The night you gave your heart?

Gallimard: It was a long time ago.

Song: Not long enough. A night that turned your world upside down.

Gallimard: Perhaps.

Song: Oh, be honest with me. What's another bit of flattery when you've already given me twenty years' worth? It's a wonder my head hasn't swollen to the size of China.

Gallimard: Who's to say it hasn't?

Song: Who's to say? And what's the shame? In pride? You think I could've pulled this off if I wasn't already full of pride when we met? No, not just pride. Arrogance. It takes arrogance, really — to believe you can will, with your eyes and your lips, the destiny of another. *(He dances.)* C'mon. Admit it. You still want me. Even in slacks and a button-down collar.

Gallimard: I don't see what the point of —

Song: You don't? Well maybe, Rene, just maybe — I want you.

Gallimard: You do?

Song: Then again, maybe I'm just playing with you. How can you tell? *(Reprising his feminine character, he sidles up to Gallimard.)* "How I wish there were even a small café to sit in. With men in tuxedos, and cappuccinos, and bad expatriate jazz." Now you want to kiss me, don't you?

Gallimard (pulling away): What makes you — ?

Song: — so sure? See? I take the words from your mouth. Then I wait for you to come and retrieve them. *(He reclines on the floor.)*

Gallimard: Why?! Why do you treat me so cruelly?

Song: Perhaps I *was* treating you cruelly. But now — I'm being nice. Come here, my little one.

Gallimard: I'm not your little one!

Song: My mistake. It's I who am *your* little one, right?

Gallimard: Yes, I —

Song: So come get your little one. If you like, I may even let you strip me.

Gallimard: I mean, you were! Before . . . but not like this!

Song: I was? Then perhaps I still am. If you look hard enough. *(He starts to remove his clothes.)*

Gallimard: What — what are you doing?

Song: Helping you to see through my act.

Gallimard: Stop that! I don't want to! I don't —

Song: Oh, but you asked me to strip, remember?

Gallimard: What? That was years ago! And I took it back!

Song: No. You postponed it. Postponed the inevitable. Today, the inevitable has come calling.

> *From the speakers, cacophony: Butterfly mixed in with Chinese gongs.*

Gallimard: No! Stop! I don't want to see!

Song: Then look away.

Gallimard: You're only in my mind! All this is in my mind! I order you! To stop!

Song: To what? To strip? That's just what I'm —

Gallimard: No! Stop! I want you — !

Song: You want me?

Gallimard: To stop!

Song: You know something, Rene? Your mouth says no, but your eyes say yes. Turn them away. I dare you.

Gallimard: I don't have to! Every night, you say you're going to strip, but then I beg you and you stop!

Song: I guess tonight is different.

Gallimard: Why? Why should that be?

Song: Maybe I've become frustrated. Maybe I'm saying "Look at me, you fool!" Or maybe I'm just feeling . . . sexy. *(He is down to his briefs.)*

Gallimard: Please. This is unnecessary. I know what you are.

Song: You do? What am I?

Gallimard: A—a man.

Song: You don't really believe that.

Gallimard: Yes I do! I knew all the time somewhere that my happiness was temporary, my love a deception. But my mind kept the knowledge at bay. To make the wait bearable.

Song: Monsieur Gallimard—the wait is over.

> *Song drops his briefs. He is naked. Sound cue out. Slowly, we and Song come to the realization that what we had thought to be Gallimard's sobbing is actually his laughter.*

Gallimard: Oh god! What an idiot! Of course!

Song: Rene—what?

Gallimard: Look at you! You're a man! *(He bursts into laughter again.)*

Song: I fail to see what's so funny!

Gallimard: "You fail to see—!" I mean, you never did have much of a sense of humor, did you? I just think it's ridiculously funny that I've wasted so much time on just a man!

Song: Wait. I'm not "just a man."

Gallimard: No? Isn't that what you've been trying to convince me of?

Song: Yes, but what I mean—

Gallimard: And now, I finally believe you, and you tell me it's not true? I think you must have some kind of identity problem.

Song: Will you listen to me?

Gallimard: Why?! I've been listening to you for twenty years. Don't I deserve a vacation?

Song: I'm not just any man!

Gallimard: Then, what exactly are you?

Song: Rene, how can you ask—? Okay, what about this?

> *He picks up Butterfly's robes, starts to dance around. No music.*

Gallimard: Yes, that's very nice. I have to admit.

> *Song holds out his arm to Gallimard.*

Song: It's the same skin you've worshipped for years. Touch it.

Gallimard: Yes, it does feel the same.

Song: Now—close your eyes.

> *Song covers Gallimard's eyes with one hand. With the other, Song draws Gallimard's hand up to his face. Gallimard, like a blind man, lets his hands run over Song's face.*

Gallimard: This skin, I remember. The curve of her face, the softness of her cheek, her hair against the back of my hand . . .

Song: I'm your Butterfly. Under the robes, beneath everything, it was always me. Now, open your eyes and admit it—you adore me. *(He removes his hand from Gallimard's eyes.)*

Gallimard: You, who knew every inch of my desires — how could you, of all people, have made such a mistake?

Song: What?

Gallimard: You showed me your true self. When all I loved was the lie. A perfect lie, which you let fall to the ground — and now, it's old and soiled.

Song: So — you never really loved me? Only when I was playing a part?

Gallimard: I'm a man who loved a woman created by a man. Everything else — simply falls short.

Pause.

Song: What am I supposed to do now?

Gallimard: You were a fine spy, Monsieur Song, with an even finer accomplice. But now I believe you should go. Get out of my life!

Song: Go where? Rene, you can't live without me. Not after twenty years.

Gallimard: I certainly can't live with you — not after twenty years of betrayal.

Song: Don't be stubborn! Where will you go?

Gallimard: I have a date . . . with my Butterfly.

Song: So, throw away your pride. And come . . .

Gallimard: Get away from me! Tonight, I've finally learned to tell fantasy from reality. And, knowing the difference, I choose fantasy.

Song: I'm your fantasy!

Gallimard: You? You're as real as hamburger. Now get out! I have a date with my Butterfly and I don't want your body polluting the room! *(He tosses Song's suit at him.)* Look at these — you dress like a pimp.

Song: Hey! These are Armani slacks and — ! *(He puts on his briefs and slacks.)* Let's just say . . . I'm disappointed in you, Rene. In the crush of your adoration, I thought you'd become something more. More like . . . a woman.

But no. Men. You're like the rest of them. It's all in the way we dress, and make up our faces, and bat our eyelashes. You really have so little imagination!

Gallimard: You, Monsieur Song? Accuse me of too little imagination? You, if anyone, should know — I am pure imagination. And in imagination I will remain. Now get out!

Gallimard bodily removes Song from the stage, taking his kimono.

Song: Rene! I'll never put on those robes again! You'll be sorry!

Gallimard (to Song): I'm already sorry! *(Looking at the kimono in his hands.)* Exactly as sorry . . . as a Butterfly.

Scene III

M. Gallimard's prison cell. Paris. 1988.

Gallimard: I've played out the events of my life night after night, always searching for a new ending to my story, one where I leave this cell and return forever to my Butterfly's arms.

Tonight I realize my search is over. That I've looked all along in the wrong place. And now, to you, I will prove that my love was not in vain — by returning to the world of fantasy where I first met her.

He picks up the kimono; dancers enter.

Gallimard: There is a vision of the Orient that I have. Of slender women in cheongsams and kimonos who die for the love of unworthy foreign devils. Who are born and raised to be the perfect women. Who take whatever punishment we give them, and bounce back, strengthened by love, unconditionally. It is a vision that has become my life.

Dancers bring the washbasin to him and help him make up his face.

Gallimard: In public, I have continued to deny that Song Liling is a man. This brings me headlines, and is a source of great embarrassment to my French colleagues, who can now be sent into a coughing fit by the mere mention of Chinese food. But alone, in my cell, I have long since faced the truth.

And the truth demands a sacrifice. For mistakes made over the course of a lifetime. My mistakes were simple and absolute — the man I loved was a cad, a bounder. He deserved nothing but a kick in the behind, and instead I gave him . . . all my love.

Yes — love. Why not admit it all? That was my undoing, wasn't it? Love warped my judgment, blinded my eyes, rearranged the very lines on my face . . . until I could look in the mirror and see nothing but . . . a woman.

Dancers help him put on the Butterfly wig.

Gallimard: I have a vision. Of the Orient. That, deep within its almond eyes, there are still women. Women willing to sacrifice themselves for the love of a man. Even a man whose love is completely without worth.

Dancers assist Gallimard in donning the kimono. They hand him a knife.

Gallimard: Death with honor is better than life . . . life with dishonor. *(He sets himself center stage, in a seppuku position.)* The love of a Butterfly can withstand many things — unfaithfulness, loss, even abandonment. But how can it face the one sin that implies all others? The devastating knowledge that, underneath it all, the object of her love was nothing more, nothing less than . . . a man. *(He sets the tip of the knife against his body.)* It is 1988. And I have found her at last. In a prison on the outskirts of Paris. My name is Rene Gallimard — also known as Madame Butterfly.

Gallimard turns upstage and plunges the knife into his body, as music from the "Love Duet" blares over the speakers. He collapses into the arms of the dancers, who lay him reverently on the floor. The image holds for several beats. Then a tight special up on Song, who stands as a man, staring at the dead Gallimard. He smokes a cigarette; the smoke filters up through the lights. Two words leave his lips.

Song: Butterfly? Butterfly?

Smoke rises as lights fade slowly to black.

CONSIDERATIONS FOR CRITICAL THINKING AND WRITING

1. FIRST RESPONSE. Do you think Gallimard is a sympathetic or despicable character? Does he have any redeeming qualities? Explain why or why not.

2. In addition to Gallimard, which other characters in the play reveal prejudices of one kind or another? What is the nature of these prejudices?

3. How does Gallimard's response to Song's letters reveal his attitudes toward her?

4. What purpose do Marc and Helga serve in the play?

5. What are some of the explanations for Gallimard's belief that Song is a woman? Which is the most plausible?

6. Why does Gallimard link magazine centerfold models with Asian women?

7. How does the structure of the play help to reinforce its themes?

8. Discuss the role reversal that takes place in the final scene.

9. Is *M. Butterfly* a comedy or a tragedy or something else?

10. Some critics have faulted *M. Butterfly* for the heavy-handed way in which Hwang links Western sexism to the events in Vietnam rather than letting the audience draw its own conclusions. Do you think the play is too polemical? Does the story carry its themes effectively from your point of view?

11. CRITICAL STRATEGIES. Read the section on gender criticism (pp. 70–72) in Chapter 3, "Applying a Critical Strategy," and discuss how the characters' ideas about gender — and, in particular, their ideas about what constitutes masculine and feminine behavior — are created by cultural institutions and conditioning.

ESSAYS

HELEN BAROLINI (B. 1925)

Born and raised in Syracuse, New York, Helen Barolini has written extensively about the lives of Italian American women in the United States. Among her books are *Umbertina* (1979), *The Dream Book: An Anthology of Writings by Italian American Women* (1985), *Love in the Middle Ages* (1986), and *Chiaroscuro: Essays of Identity*, from which "How I Learned Italian" is reprinted.

How I Learned to Speak Italian   1997

He was a patient man. His sloping shoulders curved with a bearing that spoke more of resistance and steadfastness than of resignation; his ruffled hair was graying, his eyes were mild and gray behind the glasses that were the badge of his work — he set type and proofread for *La Gazzetta*. It was because of his job at that weekly Italian-language newspaper in Syracuse that I met Mr. de Mascoli. In my last year at the university I found it wasn't Spanish that interested me, after all, but Italian. However, at that point I couldn't switch my language requirement; I would have to keep Spanish and do Italian on my own. I went to the *Gazzetta* to put in a want ad for a tutor. Instead I found Mr. de Mascoli willing to teach me.

And why Italian? Because during that last year before graduation I had met an Italian student who had come over on a Fulbright grant to study at Syracuse University. Knowing him awakened in me unsuspected longings for that Mediterranean world of his which I suddenly, belatedly, realized could also be mine. I became conscious of an Italian background that had been left deliberately vague and in abeyance by my parents who, though children of Italian immigrants, had so homogenized into standard American that their only trace of identity was an Italian surname, often misspelled and always mispronounced.

I knew nothing of Italian. It was not a popular subject at home. We had just come out of World War II in which Italy had been our enemy, and my father was at once scornful and touchy about Italy's role in that conflict. And even before that we had never been part of the Italian community of the North Side, my parents having selected their first, then second, homes on James Street, a thoroughfare of great mansions receding eastward into large, comfortable homes, then more modest two-families until, finally, it became the commercial area of Eastwood. I did not learn until recently that I had grown up on the street named for Henry James's° grandfather, an early developer of the barren tracts from which Syracuse grew and from which Henry enjoyed his income.

My parents' aspirations were away from the old Italian neighborhoods and into something better. My father made a significant leap into the American mainstream when he became a member of both the Rotary Club and the Syracuse Yacht and Country Club where he and my mother golfed and I spent aimless summers.

It never occurred to my father to speak his own father's language to my two brothers or to me, and so we grew up never conversing with our only two living grandparents, my father's father and my mother's mother, and so never knowing them. My grandfather came to call each Christmas, my father's birthday; he sat uneasily in the sunroom with his overcoat on, took the shot of scotch he was offered, and addressed the same phrase to me each year: "Youa gooda gehl?" Then he'd hand me a nickel. There was a feeling of strain in the performance. My father was a man of substance, his was not.

With my grandmother there was a brief ritual phrase in her dialect mouthed by us children when we went to the old Queen Anne–style house in Utica where my mother and all her brothers and sisters grew up. My grandmother was always in the kitchen, dressed in black, standing at a large black coal range stirring soup or something. My brothers and I, awkward in the presence of her foreignness, would be pushed in her direction by our mother during those holiday visits and told, "Go say hello to Gramma."

We'd go to the strange old woman who didn't look like any of the grandmothers of our friends or like any of those on the covers of the *Saturday Evening Post* around Thanksgiving time. Gramma didn't stuff a turkey or make candied sweet potatoes and pumpkin pies. She made chicken soup filled with tiny pale meatballs and a bitter green she grew in her backyard along with broad beans and basil, things that were definitely un-American in those days. Her smell was like that of the cedar closet in our attic. She spoke strange words with a raspy sound.

Henry James (1843–1916): American novelist and critic.

When we stepped into her kitchen to greet her she smiled broadly and tweaked our cheeks. We said in a rush the phrase our mother taught us. We didn't know what it meant. I think we never asked. And if we had known it meant "how are you?" what difference would it have made? What further knowledge would we have had of the old woman in the shapeless black garment, with her wisps of gray hair falling out of the thick knob crammed with large old-fashioned tortoiseshell hairpins? None. We were strangers. Yet she is part of my most fundamental sense of who I am.

When on a visit upstate recently I had occasion to drive through Cazenovia, a village on the shores of Lake Cazenovia, it appeared to me as if in a dream. I saw again the lakeshore meadow that has always remained indelibly imprinted on my mind from childhood, but which I had thought must have vanished from the real world. That meadow, now called Gypsy Bay Park, was the site of family picnics to which we and Aunt Mary's family proceeded from Syracuse, while the other contingent (which was by far the greater number, my mother's three brothers, two other sisters and all their families, plus our grandmother) came from Utica. Cazenovia was the approximate halfway point, and there in the meadow on the lake the cars would all pull up and baskets of food would be unloaded for the great summer reunion.

My father drove a car that had a front fold-up seat which I was allowed to 10 stand at and hold onto while looking straight out the window at the roadway, pretending that I was the driver guiding us all to the lake. I always made it, and the weather was always fine.

And so we met in a landscape which, today, I would never have expected to glimpse again in its original state. Whenever, over the years, I would think back to the picnics in Cazenovia, I would imagine the locale filled with new housing developments or fast food chains on the lakeshore. But no, the meadow was still green with grass, still fringed with trees bending toward the water, still free of picnic tables, barbecue grills on metal stands, and overflowing trash cans. It was the same as when I was five years old and the gathering took on the mythic quality that it still retains for me.

It was Gramma who had decreed this annual outing. When two of her daughters married and moved from Utica, she had made known her wish: that the family should meet each summer when travel was easier and eat together *al fresco*. It was her pleasure to have all her children, and their children, convene in the meadow, and spend the day eating, singing, playing cards, gossiping, throwing ball, making jokes and toasts. It was a celebration of her progeny of which she, long widowed, was the visible head, the venerable ancestor, the symbol of the strong-willed adventurer who had come from the Old World to make a new life and to prosper.

She was monumental. I can see her still, an imposing figure, still dressed in black although it was summer, seated on a folding camp chair (just for her) under the shade of a large, leafy elm tree. She sat there as silently as a Sioux chief and was served food, given babies to kiss, and paid homage to all day. The others spread around her, sitting on blankets on the grass, or on the running boards of their Oldsmobiles and Buicks. What made my grandmother so intriguing was the mystery of her. For, despite its gaiety, the family picnic was also a time of puzzlement for me. Who was this stranger in black with whom I could not speak? What was her story? What did she know?

What I knew of my grandmother I heard from my mother: she believed in good food on the table and good linens on the bed. Everything else was fripperies, and she had the greatest scorn for those who dieted or got their nourishment through pills and potions. She knew you are what you eat and she loved America for the great range of foods that it provided to people like her, used to so little, used to making do. She could not tolerate stinginess; she lived with her eldest son and his family of eleven and did all the gardening and cooking, providing a generous table.

She founded the family well-being on food. She had gotten up early, baked 15 bread, or used the dough for a crusty white pizza sprinkled with oil, oregano, and red pepper or with onions and potatoes, olives and anchovies—but never with tomato sauce for that disguised the taste of good bread dough and made it soggy and soft. She provided these pizzas, or *panini,* to the mill workers whose wives were too lazy or too improvident to do it themselves. She kept the men's orders all in her mind; she had great powers of concentration and her memory took the place of jotted-down notes. She never got an order wrong. From workers' lunches, she expanded into a small grocery store. Soon she was importing foodstuffs from Italy. Eventually, what she turned over to her sons was one of the largest wholesale food companies in central New York.

At those picnics my cousins were older than I, mostly young people in their teens and twenties. The boys wore knickerbockers and played banjos or ukeleles and the girls wore white stockings and sleeveless frocks. My uncles played cards and joked among themselves; the women arranged and served endless platters of food. Somebody was always taking snapshots, and I have many of them in a large album that has survived a dozen moves.

My grandmother stayed regally under her tree like a tribal queen, and mounds of food were placed around her like offerings. Her daughters and daughters-in-law kept up a steady parade of passing the foods they had been preparing all week: fried chicken, salames, prosciutto, roasted sweet peppers, fresh tomatoes sliced with mozzarella and basil, eggplant fritters, zucchini *imbottiti,* platters of corn, huge tubs of fresh salad greens, caciotto cheese, rounds of fresh, crusty bread, every kind of fruit, and biscotti galore. It was as if my grandmother's Thanksgiving took place not in bleak November, but on a summer day when there would be sun on her shoulders, flowers blooming and cool breezes off the lake, blue skies above, and the produce of her backyard garden abundantly present. She lived with the memory of the picnic through the long upstate winter, and by the time spring had come she would go out to plant the salad greens and put in the stakes for the broad beans and tomatoes, planting and planning for the coming picnic.

We were about fifty kin gathered in that meadow, living proof of the family progress. Gramma's sons and daughters vied to offer her their services, goods, and offspring—all that food, those cars, the well-dressed young men who would go to college. And Butch, an older cousin, would take me by the hand to the water's edge and I'd be allowed to wade in Cazenovia's waters which were always tingling cold and made me squeal with delicious shock.

And yet with all that, for all the good times and good food and the happy chattering people who fussed over me and my brothers, I still felt a sense of strangeness, a sense of my parents' tolerating with an edge of disdain this Old

World *festa* only for the sake of the old lady. When I asked my mother why Gramma looked so strange and never spoke to us, I was told, she came from the Old Country . . . she doesn't speak our language. She might as well have been from Mars.

I never remember hearing our own mother speak to her mother, although she must have, however briefly. I only recall my astonishment at Mother's grief when Gramma died and we went to Utica for the funeral. How could mother really feel so bad about someone she had never really talked to? Was it just because she was expected to cry? Or was she crying for the silence that had lain like a chasm between them? 20

Mother was a smartly dressed, very American lady, who played golf and bridge and went to dances. She seemed to us to have nothing to do with the old woman in a kitchen where, at one time, a dozen and more people had sat around the long, oilcloth-covered table. Nor did my father, with his downtown meetings and busy manner, seem to have any connection with his own father, who was called the Old Man and wore baggy pants and shuffled like a movie comedian.

There was no reason for me or my brothers to think, as we were growing up, that we were missing anything by not speaking Italian. We knew that our father spoke it, because at Christmas when the Old Man came to call, we'd overhear long streams of it and laugh at the queerness of it in our home. My mother, no, could never have been said to speak or know Italian, only some dialect phrases. But in my father reposed the tongue of his fathers; and it hadn't been important to him (or to us) that we have it.

What had I to do with any of those funny types I'd see on the North Side the few times I accompanied my mother there for shopping? We didn't speak or eat Italian at home with the exception of the loaf of Italian bread my father brought home every day from the Columbus Bakery. Occasionally my mother would prepare an Italian dinner for her mostly Irish friends, and then she'd have to go to the North Side where the Italians lived and had their own pungent grocery stores to find the pasta or the imported cheese and oil she needed. I hated to accompany her; the smell from barrels of dried and salted baccalà or of ripe provolone hanging by cords from the ceiling was as great an affront to my nose as the sound of the raspy Italian dialect spoken in the store was to my ears. That it all seemed crude and degrading was something I had absorbed from my parents in their zeal to advance themselves. It was the rather touching snobbery of second-generation Italian Americans toward those who were, in their view, "just off the boat."

But it was on the North Side that the *Gazzetta* offices were located, so I had to go there. And there I met Mr. de Mascoli. I could have grown up in Syracuse and lived there all my life without ever knowing that the *Gazzetta* existed. It took the Italian student to make me aware of the Italian paper, the beauty of Italian, and a lot of other things, too.

My father, as a Rotary project, had invited the Italian student (and a Colombian and a Venezuelan, also) home for Thanksgiving dinner to give them a taste of real America. What happened during that curious cultural exchange was not so much a forging of ties with America for the Italian and the South Americans, as an awareness in myself of my own Latin bloodline and a longing to see from where and what I originated. At Thanksgiving dinner it wasn't Pilgrims and Plymouth I thought of but Catullus. The Latin poets I read in my college courses connected me to the Italian student who was 25 already a *dottore*° from an Italian university and was saying things in a sharply funny, ironic way—a way no American spoke. It was strange that my awakening came at an all-American celebration through the medium of a tall, lean-faced student of forestry who was relating to my father in good English his experience during the war as an interpreter for the British troops pushing up through the Gothic Line to Florence.

Florence! I had never given thought to that fabled place, but in that instant I longed to see it. In my immediate conversion, I who knew nothing of Italy or Italians, not even how to pronounce Marconi's° first name, became aligned forever with the Italianness that had lain unplumbed and inert in me. My die was cast, over the native American bird, Yankee creamed onions, and Hubbard squash, across parents who would have been horrified to know it.

I was attracted to the Italian student, and he to me. When we started seeing each other, he was critical of my not knowing his language. "I know French and Spanish," I said. He was not impressed.

"Your language should have been Italian," he said sternly.

"I've had Latin, so it shouldn't be so hard to learn," I replied.

"Try this." He handed me his copy of the *Gazzetta*. It was the first time I 30 had seen the paper, seen Italian. I couldn't make any sense of the unfamiliar formations like *gli* and *sgombero*, the double *z*'s and the verb endings. I was filled with dismay, but I decided to learn and I thought it could be done easily, right at home. After all, my father knew Italian.

"No use in learning a language like that," my father said dismissively when I approached him. "Spanish is more useful. Even Portuguese will get you further than Italian."

Further where? Toward the foreign service in Brazil? But that was not my direction.

Learning Italian became something stronger than just pleasing the Italian student. I began to recall things like my mother saying that just before her death Gramma had called for a sip of the mountain spring water near her Calabrian village. That was her last wish, her last memory; she had left Calabria at the age of seventeen with a husband of almost forty and had never gone back. But sixty years later as she lay dying in Utica it was only the water of her native hills that she wanted and called for.

I wanted to go see where she came from. I wanted to be able to talk to the Old Man who still came each Christmas, and to tell him who I really was besides a gooda gehl and to find out who he was.

I went deliberately to the *Gazzetta* on the North Side to find an Italian 35 teacher rather than to the university's Italian department because, when I called the department, I was answered by a professor who said, giving his name twice, "Pay-chay or Pace speaking." As if one could choose between the Italian name and the anglicized version. For me, even then, there was only one way he could have said his name and if he didn't understand that he was not the teacher I wanted. Mr. de Mascoli was.

He was like Pinocchio's stepfather, a gentle Geppetto. And he was genuinely pleased that I should want to learn Italian. He would give me lessons in his home each evening after supper, he said. He wanted no payment. He had come from the hard, mountainous, central part of Italy called the Abruzzo. He

---

dottore: Holder of a doctoral degree.
Marconi: Guglielmo Marconi (1874–1937), Italian engineer and inventor of wireless telegraphy.

arrived in America in the late 1920s, not as an illiterate laborer, but as an ideal-ist, a political emigré out of sympathy with the fascist regime. And he had been educated. He had a profound love for his homeland, and it was love which made him want to give me its language.

I accepted his offer. And I thought of all the fine things I would send him in return when I got to Italy—the finest olive oil and parmesan cheese for his wife; the nougat candy called *torrone* for his children; and for him an elegantly bound volume of Dante. I would send him copies of Italian newspapers and magazines because he had told me confidentially that, yes, *La Gazzetta* was really the *porcheria*° everyone said it was. But bad as it was, it kept the language alive among the people on the North Side. When it was gone, what would they have?

I went to Mr. de Mascoli's home each night in the faded old Chevy my father passed on to me for getting to the university. The first night I arrived for my lessons I wore a full-skirted, almost ankle-length black watch tartan skirt my father had brought me from a trip to Chicago. It was topped by a wasp-waisted buttoned to the neck lime-green jacket. It was the New Look that Dior had just introduced to signal the end of wartime restrictions on fabric and style, and I felt very elegant, then too elegant as Mr. de Mascoli led me down a hall to his kitchen. We sat at the table in the clean white kitchen which showed no sign of the meal he and his wife and children had just eaten. Mrs. de Mascoli, a short, pudgy, youngish woman, made a brief appearance and greeted me cordially. I could hear she was American, but she had neither the education nor the ascetic and dedicated air of her husband. She spoke the kind of rough-hewn English one heard on the North Side. In her simple, friendly way she, too, was pleased that I was coming for Italian lessons.

In their clean white kitchen I spent a whole winter conjugating verbs, learning the impure *s* and the polite form of address. I began to speak Mr. de Mascoli's native language. I learned with a startled discomfit that my surname had a meaning and could be declined. *Mollica* was not only a family name but a noun of the feminine gender meaning crumb, or the soft inner part of the loaf as distinct from the good, hard outer crust. The name had always been a bane to me since teachers, salesgirls, or camp counselors were never able to say it. I would always have to repeat it and spell it as they stuttered and stumbled, mangling and mouthing it in ludicrous ways. It was my cross, and then I learned it meant crumb.

I began to fantasize: what if, like the draft that changed Alice's size, I ₄₀ could find a DRINK ME! that would switch me from a hard-to-pronounce crumb to something fine like Miller? Daisy Miller, Maud Miller. Even Henry. I'd be a different person immediately. In fact, for the first time I'd be a person in my own right, not just a target for discriminatory labels and jokes.

From years of Latin I could see how my name was related to all those words meaning "soft": mollify, mollescent (the down side of tumescent), mol-lusk. (A moll, as in Moll Flanders,° was something else!)

The Italian minces no meanings: *mollare*, the verb, means to slacken; from that, the adjective *molle* means not only soft or limber, but flabby, pliant, even wanton. From *molle* comes *mollica*, and then, *mollizia*, that intriguing word meaning effeminacy and suggesting its counterpart, *malizia*, which signifies cunning malice. But I was marked from the start by softness not cunning.

---

porcheria: A botched mess.
Moll Flanders: Main character in *The Fortunes and Misfortunes of Moll Flanders* (1721) by Daniel Defoe. She is a harlot, thief, and convict before she reforms and lives an honest life.

And what must have been the lewd cracks my father was prey to with a name from which so many allusions to soft and limp could be made?

A molleton, or *molletone* in Italian, is literally a swanskin, or a soft skin. Is this, I asked myself, why I was so hypersensitive, and thin-skinned? Because I came from a genetic line that was so incongruously delicate among the smoldering emotions of south Italy that they became identified forever after by a surname that told all? Were my forebears a soft touch, too soft for their own good in a place where basic fiber and guts would have been more pressingly urgent than skin like a swan?

What if I had been not Miss Softbread but, say, Sally Smith of the hard edge, a name evoking the manly English smith at his forge with all the honorable tradition and advantage *that* entailed? How my life might have advanced! I wondered about translating my name to Krumm; being female had an advantage—I could marry a right-sounding name. But then I'd have to abandon my Italian lessons and the plan to go to Italy and the Italian student.

I continued my lessons. At home I practiced singing in Italian with my opera records as I followed words in the libretti. In the high-flown phrases of operatic lingo I began to form myself a language as remote as could be from the grandmother's dialect or the North Side, but, I thought with satisfaction, very grand and eloquent.

"Ardo per voi, forestier innamorato," I sang in the sunroom along with Ezio Pinza. *"Ma perchè così straziarmi,"* I said to Mr. de Mascoli one night, right out of Rossini's *Mosè,* when he plied me with verbs. Or, rhetorically, *"O! Qual portento è questo?"* I expressed no everyday thought but something compounded of extreme yearning, sacrifice, tribulation, or joy. In the speech of grand opera everything becomes grander, and I felt so, too, as I sang all the roles. It was as if I were learning Elizabethan or Chaucerian English to visit contemporary London as I memorized my lines preparatory to leaving for Italy. I had worked and saved for a year to get there.

When I went to say goodbye to Mr. de Mascoli, he seemed sad and stooped. We had often spoken of the harshness many Italians had suffered in their own land and how they had had to emigrate, leaving with nothing, not even a proper language to bolster them. I told him I would write to him in Italian and send him news of his country. He said, "My country is a poor and beautiful place. I do not hate her."

"And I never will!" I answered.

I went to Italy thinking to rejoin the Italian student, who had already returned to his country, but that is another story: he turned out to have always been married. It wasn't the end of the world for me. I was in Italy and everything else was just beginning.

I studied in Perugia, I wrote articles for the Syracuse *Herald-Journal,* I saw Italy. I surpassed my initial Italian lessons and acquired a Veneto accent when I met and married Italian poet and journalist Antonio Barolini. He had courted me reading from a book of his poetry that included an ode to Catullus with the lovely lines (to be put on my gravestone):

ora la fanciulla è sogno,
sogno il poeta e l'amore . . .

(now the girl is a dream,
a dream the poet and love . . .)

Thus I acquired another Italian surname. Like the wine? some people inquire at introductions. Yes, I say even though they're confusing me with Bardolino. But having been born bread, I like that union with wine.

We lived some years in Italy before Antonio was sent to New York as the U.S. correspondent for *La Stampa*. We found a house outside the city, and it was there, finally, that I thought again of Mr. de Mascoli. The unlikely link to the printer was a May Day pageant given at my children's country day school. As the children frolicked on the lush green lawn, they sang a medley of spring songs, ending with an English May Day carol whose refrain was:

> For the Lord knows when we shall meet again
> To be Maying another year.

It struck me with great sadness. I thought of the Italian student, of my grandmother and the mountain spring she had never returned to, of Mr. de Mascoli and his gentle patience, of all the lost opportunities and combinations of all our lives.

I had never written to Mr. de Mascoli from Italy or sent him the fine gifts I had promised. That night I made a package of the Italian papers and magazines we had at home along with some of my husband's books and sent them to the printer in Syracuse with a letter expressing my regret for the delay and an explanation of what had happened in my life since I had last seen him more than ten years before.

The answer came from his wife. On a floral thank-you note (which I still 55 have) with the printed line, *It was so thoughtful of you,* she had written: "It is almost three years that I lost my husband and a son a year later which I think I will never get over it. I miss them very much . . . it was our wish to go back to Italy for a trip but all in vain. The books you sent will be read by my sister-in-law who reads very good Italian, not like me, I'm trying hard to read but don't understand it as well as her, but she explains to me. Like my husband to you . . ."

I thought of time that passed and the actions that remained forever stopped, undone. The May Day carol kept coming back to me:

> For the Lord knows when we shall meet again
> To be Maying another year.

And if not Maying, all the other things we'd planned to do for ourselves, for others. And then the others are no longer here. A few years after that May Day, Antonio died suddenly in Rome. He is buried far away in his Vicenza birthplace while I continue to live outside of New York, alone now, since our daughters are married and gone. Life does not permit unrelenting sadness. May goes but comes back each year. And though some shadow of regret remains for all the words left unsaid and acts left undone, there will be other words, other acts . . .

I often think of how my life, my husband's, and the lives of our three daughters were so entwined with the language that Mr. de Mascoli set out to give me so long ago. Despite his efforts and my opera records, I am still the child of my mother tongue. I still speak Italian with an upstate tonality; my daughters do much better. Though Italian couldn't root perfectly in me, it did in them: the eldest is chair of the Italian department at an Ivy League university; the middle one lives and teaches in Italy, a perfect *signora*; and the youngest has classes in Italian for the children of her town.

Occasionally I visit Susanna in Italy, but it's long between trips and each visit is short. The country has changed: Mr. de Mascoli's Italy is no longer a poor country of peasants pushed into war and ruinous defeat by a dictator, but a prosperous industrial nation. Susi married an Italian artist from Urbino and they have two sons, Beniamino and Anselmo, with whom I speak Italian for they speak no English.

Now I am called *Nonna*. I never knew the word with which to address my own grandmother when I was a child standing mute and embarrassed in front of her. Now, if it weren't too late, I would call her *Nonna*, too. We could speak to each other and I'd hear of the spring in Calabria.

How unexpected it all turned out . . . how long a progress as the seed of a long-ago infatuation found its right ground and produced its bloom. None of it did I foresee when I sat in his tidied white kitchen and learned with Mr. de Mascoli how to speak Italian.

CONSIDERATIONS FOR CRITICAL THINKING AND WRITING

1. FIRST RESPONSE. How do the narrator's parents react to their Italian parents? How do you respond to your own ethnic origins?
2. The grandmother, we're told, "founded the family well-being on food" (para. 15). How is food used in the essay to characterize her?
3. What sort of relationship does the narrator have with her parents? How are they different from her grandparents?
4. What prompts the narrator to explore her "Italianness"? What role does Mr. de Mascoli play in her life? How is he used to structure the essay?
5. How do the final six paragraphs concerning the biographical details of the narrator's adult life affect your understanding of the essay and your emotional response to it?

JUDITH ORTIZ COFER (B. 1952)

Born in Hormigueros, Puerto Rico, Judith Ortiz Cofer grew up in New Jersey and was educated at Augusta College and Florida Atlantic University. She is currently an English professor at the University of Georgia. Her books include poetry, *Terms of Survival* (1987) and *Reaching for the Mainland* (1987); a novel, *The Line of the Sun* (1989); and essays, *Silent Dancing* (1990) and *The Latin Deli: Prose and Poetry* (1993), from which "Advanced Biology" is reprinted. Her latest book is *The Year of Our Revolution: New and Selected Stories and Poems* (1998).

Advanced Biology   *1993*

As I lay out clothes for the trip to Miami to do a reading from my recently published novel, then on to Puerto Rico to see my mother, I take a close look at my travel wardrobe — the tailored skirts in basic colors easily coordinated with my silk blouses — I have to smile to myself remembering what my mother had said about my conservative outfits when I visited her the last time — that I looked like the Jehovah's Witnesses who went from door to door in her pueblo trying to sell tickets to heaven to the die-hard Catholics. I would scare people she said. They would bolt their doors if they saw me approaching with my brief-case. As for her, she dresses in tropical colors – a red skirt and parakeet-yellow blouse look good on her tan skin, and she still has a good enough figure that she can wear a tight, black cocktail dress to go dancing at her favorite club, *El Palacio,* on Saturday nights. And, she emphasizes, still make it to the 10 o'clock mass on Sunday. Catholics can have fun and still be saved, she has often pointed out to me, but only if you pay your respects to God and all His Court with the necessary rituals. She has never accepted my gradual slipping out of the faith in which I was so strictly brought up.

As I pack my clothes into the suitcase, I recall our early days in Paterson, New Jersey, where we lived for most of my adolescence while my father was alive and stationed in Brooklyn Yard in New York. At that time, my mother's views on everything from clothing to (the forbidden subject) sex were ruled by the religious fervor that she had developed as a shield against the cold foreign city. These days we have traded places in a couple of areas since she has "gone home" after my father's death, and "gone native." I chose to attend college in the United States and make a living as an English teacher and, lately, on the lecture circuit as a novelist and poet. But, though our lives are on the surface radically different, my mother and I have affected each other reciprocally over the past twenty years; she has managed to liberate herself from the rituals, mores, and traditions that "cramp" her style, while retaining her femininity and "Puertoricanness," while I struggle daily to consolidate my opposing cul-tural identities. In my adolescence, divided into my New Jersey years and my Georgia years, I received an education in the art of cultural compromise.

In Paterson in the 1960s I attended a public school in our neighborhood. Still predominantly white and Jewish, it was rated very well academically in a city where the educational system was in chaos, deteriorating rapidly as the best teachers moved on to suburban schools following the black and Puerto Rican migration into, and the white exodus from, the city proper.

The Jewish community had too much at stake to make a fast retreat; many of the small businesses and apartment buildings in the city's core were owned by Jewish families of the World War II generation. They had seen worse things happen than the influx of black and brown people that was scaring away the Italians and the Irish. But they too would gradually move their families out of the best apartments in their buildings and into houses in East Paterson, Fair-lawn, and other places with *lawns.* It was how I saw the world then; either you lived without your square of grass or you bought a house to go with it. But for most of my adolescence, I lived among the Jewish people of Paterson. We rented an apartment owned by the Milsteins, proprietors also of the deli on the bottom floor. I went to school with their children. My father took his busi-ness to the Jewish establishments, perhaps because these men symbolized "dignified survival" to him. He was obsessed with privacy, and could not stand the personal turns conversations almost always took when two or more Puerto Ricans met casually over a store counter. The Jewish men talked too, but they concentrated on externals. They asked my father about his job, politics, his opinion on Vietnam, Lyndon Johnson. And my father, in his quiet voice, answered their questions knowledgeably. Sometimes before we entered a store, the cleaners, or a shoe-repair shop, he would tell me to look for the blue-inked numbers on the owner's left forearm. I would stare at these numbers, now usually faded enough to look like veins in the wrong place. I would try to make them out. They were a telegram from the past, I later decided, informing the future of the deaths of millions. My father discussed the Holocaust with me in the same hushed tones my mother used to talk about God's Mysterious Ways. I could not reconcile both in my mind. This conflict eventually led to my first serious clash with my mother over irreconcilable differences between the "real world" and religious doctrine.

It had to do with the Virgin Birth.   5

And it had to do with my best friend and study partner, Ira Nathan, the acknowledged scientific genius at school. In junior high school it was almost a requirement to be "in love" with an older boy. I was an eighth grader and Ira was in the ninth grade that year and preparing to be sent away to some prep school in New England. I chose him as my boyfriend (in the eyes of my classmates, if a girl spent time with a boy that meant they were "going together") because I needed tutoring in biology — one of his best subjects. I ended up having a crush on him after our first Saturday morning meeting at the library. Ira was my first exposure to the wonders of an analytical mind.

The problem was the subject. Biology is a dangerous topic for young teenagers who are themselves walking laboratories, experimenting with interesting combinations of chemicals every time they make a choice. In my basic biology class, we were looking at single-cell organisms under the microscope, and watching them reproduce in slow-motion films in a darkened classroom. Though the process was as unexciting as watching a little kid blow bubbles, we were aroused by the concept itself. Ira's advanced class was dissecting fetal pigs. He brought me a photograph of his project, inner organs labeled neatly on the paper the picture had been glued to. My eyes refused to budge from the line drawn from "genitals" to a part of the pig it pertained to. I felt a wave of heat rising from my chest to my scalp. Ira must have seen my discomfort, though I tried to keep my face behind the black curtain of my hair, but as the boy-scientist, he was relentless. He actually traced the line from label to pig with his pencil.

"All mammals reproduce sexually," he said in a teacherly monotone.

The librarian, far off on the other side of the room, looked up at us and frowned. Logically, it was not possible that she could have heard Ira's pronouncement, but I was convinced that the mention of sex enhanced the hearing capabilities of parents, teachers and librarians by one hundred percent. I blushed more intensely, and peeked through my hair at Ira.

He was holding the eraser of his pencil on the pig's blurry sexual parts 10 and smiling at me. His features were distinctly Eastern European. I had recently seen the young singer Barbra Streisand on the Red Skelton show and had been amazed at how much similarity there was in their appearances. She could have been his sister. I was particularly attracted to the wide mouth and strong nose. No one that I knew in school thought that Ira was attractive, but his brains had long ago overshadowed his looks as his most impressive attribute. Like Ira, I was also a straight A student and also considered odd because I was one of the few Puerto Ricans on the honor roll. So it didn't surprise anyone that Ira and I had drifted toward each other. Though I could not have articulated it then, Ira was seducing me with his No. 2 pencil and the laboratory photograph of his fetal pig. The following Saturday, Ira brought in his advanced biology book and showed me the transparencies of the human anatomy in full color that I was not meant to see for a couple more years. I was shocked. The cosmic jump between paramecium and the human body was almost too much for me to take in. These were the first grown people I had ever seen naked and they revealed too much.

"Human sexual reproduction can only take place when the male's sperm is introduced into the female womb and fertilization of the egg takes place," Ira stated flatly.

The book was open to the page labeled "The Human Reproductive System." Feeling that my maturity was being tested, as well as my intelligence, I found my voice long enough to contradict Ira.

"There has been one exception to this, Ira." I was feeling a little smug about knowing something that Ira obviously did not.

"Judith, there are no exceptions in biology, only mutations, and adaptations through evolution." He was smiling in a superior way.

"The Virgin Mary had a baby without . . ." I couldn't say *having sex* in the same breath as the name of the Mother of God. I was totally unprepared for the explosion of laughter that followed my timid statement. Ira had crumped in his chair and was laughing so hard that his thin shoulders shook. I could hear the librarian approaching. Feeling humiliated, I started to put my books together. Ira grabbed my arm.

"Wait, don't go," he was still giggling uncontrollably, "I'm sorry. Let's talk a little more. Wait, give me a chance to explain."

Reluctantly, I sat down again mainly because the librarian was already at our table, hands on hips, whispering angrily: "If you *children* cannot behave in this *study area*, I will have to ask you to leave." Ira and I both apologized, though she gave him a nasty look because his mouth was still stretched from ear to ear in a hysterical grin.

"Listen, listen. I'm sorry that I laughed like that. I know you're Catholic and you believe in the Virgin Birth (he bit his lower lip trying to regain his composure), but it's just not biologically possible to have a baby without . . . (he struggled for control) . . . losing your virginity."

I sank down on my hard chair. "Virginity." He had said another of the forbidden words. I glanced back at the librarian who was keeping her eye on us. I was both offended and excited by Ira's blasphemy. How could he deny a doctrine that people had believed in for 2,000 years? It was part of my prayers every night. My mother talked about *La Virgen* as if she were our most important relative.

Recovering from his fit of laughter, Ira kept his hand discreetly on my elbow as he explained in the seductive language of the scientific laboratory how babies were made, and how it was impossible to violate certain natural laws.

"Unless God wills it," I argued feebly.

"There is no God," said Ira, and the last shred of my innocence fell away as I listened to his arguments backed up by irrefutable scientific evidence.

Our meetings continued all that year, becoming more exciting with every chapter in his biology book. My grades improved dramatically since one-celled organisms were no mystery to a student of advanced biology. Ira's warm, moist hand often brushed against mine under the table at the library, and walking home one bitter cold day, he asked me if I would wear his Beta club pin. I nodded and when we stepped inside the hallway of my building where he removed his thick mittens which his mother had knitted, he pinned the blue enamel B to my collar. And to the hissing of the steam heaters, I received a serious kiss from Ira. We separated abruptly when we heard Mrs. Milstein's door open.

"Hello, Ira."

"Hello, Mrs. Milstein."

"And how is your mother? I haven't seen Fritzie all week. She's not sick, is she?"

"She's had a mild cold, Mrs. Milstein. But she is steadily improving." Ira's diction became extremely precise and formal when he was in the presence of adults. As an only child and a prodigy, he had to live up to very high standards.

"I'll call her today," Mrs. Milstein said, finally looking over at me. Her eyes fixed on the collar of my blouse which was, I later saw in our hall mirror, sticking straight up with Ira's pin attached crookedly to the edge.

"Good-bye, Mrs. Milstein."

"Nice to see you, Ira."

Ira waved awkwardly to me as he left. Mrs. Milstein stood in the humid hallway of her building watching me run up the stairs.

Our "romance" lasted only a week; long enough for Mrs. Milstein to call Ira's mother, and for Mrs. Nathan to call my mother. I was subjected to a lecture on moral behavior by my mother, who, carried away by her anger and embarrassed that I had been seen kissing a boy (understood: a boy who was not even Catholic), had begun a chain of metaphors for the loss of virtue that was on the verge of the tragi/comical:

"A *perdida*, a cheap item," she said trembling before me as I sat on the edge of my bed, facing her accusations, "a girl begins to look like one when she allows herself to be *handled* by men."

"Mother . . ." I wanted her to lower her voice so that my father, sitting at the kitchen table reading, would not hear. I had already promised her that I would confess my sin that Saturday and take communion with a sparkling clean soul. I had not been successful at keeping the sarcasm out of my voice. Her fury was fueled by her own bitter litany.

"A dirty joke, a burden to her family . . ." She was rolling with her Spanish now; soon the Holy Mother would enter into the picture for good measure. "It's not as if I had not taught you better. Don't you know that those people do not have the example of the Holy Virgin Mary and her Son to follow and that is why they do things for the wrong reasons. Mrs. Nathan said she did not want her son messing around with you — not because of the wrongness of it — but because it would interfere with his studies!" She was yelling now. "She's afraid that he will (she crossed herself at the horror of the thought) make you pregnant! "

"We could say an angel came down and put a baby in my stomach, Mother." She had succeeded in dragging me into her field of hysteria. She grabbed my arm and pulled me to my feet.

"I do not want you associating any more than necessary with people who do not have God, do you hear me?"

"They have a god!" I was screaming now too, trying to get away from her suffocating grasp: "They have an intelligent god who doesn't ask you to believe that a woman can get pregnant without having sex!" That's when she slapped me. She looked horrified at what she had instinctively done.

"Nazi," I hissed, out of control by then too, "I bet you'd like to send Ira and his family to a concentration camp!" At that time I thought that was the harshest thing I could have said to anyone. I was certain that I had sentenced my soul to eternal damnation the minute the words came out of my mouth; but my cheek was burning from the slap and I wanted to hurt her. Father walked into my room at that moment looking shocked at the sight of the two of us entangled in mortal combat.

"Please, please," his voice sounded agonized. I ran to him and he held me 40 in his arms while I cried my heart out on his starched white shirt. My mother, also weeping quietly, tried to walk past us, but he pulled her into the circle. After a few moments, she put her trembling hand on my head.

"We are a family," my father said, "there is only the three of us against the world. Please, please . . ." But he did not follow the "please" with any suggestions as to what we could do to make things right in a world that was as confusing to my mother as it was to me.

I finished the eighth grade in Paterson, but Ira and I never got together to study again. I sent his Beta club pin back to him via a mutual friend. Once in a while I saw him in the hall or the playground. But he seemed to be in the clouds, where he belonged. In the fall, I was enrolled at St. Joseph's Catholic High School where everyone believed in the Virgin Birth, and I never had to take a test on the human reproductive system. It was a chapter that was not emphasized.

In 1968, the year Paterson, like many U.S. cities, exploded in racial violence, my father moved us to Augusta, Georgia, where two of his brothers had retired from the army at Fort Gordon. They had convinced him that it was a healthier place to rear teenagers. For me it was a shock to the senses, like moving from one planet to another: where Paterson had concrete to walk on and gray skies, bitter winters, and a smorgasbord of an ethnic population, Georgia was red like Mars, and Augusta was green — exploding in colors in more gardens of azaleas and dogwood and magnolia trees — more vegetation than I imagined was possible anywhere not tropical like Puerto Rico. People seemed to come in two basic colors: black and blond. And I could barely understand my teachers when they talked in a slowed-down version of English like one of those old 78-speed recordings played at 33. But I was placed in all advanced classes and one of them was biology. This is where I got to see my first real fetal pig which my assigned lab partner had chosen. She picked it up gingerly by the ends of the plastic bag in which it was stored: "Ain't he cute?" she asked. I nodded, nearly fainting from the overwhelming combination of the smell of formaldehyde and my sudden flashback to my brief but intense romance with Ira Nathan.

"What you want to call him?" My partner unwrapped our specimen on the table, and I surprised myself by my instant recall of Ira's chart. I knew all the parts. In my mind's eye I saw the pencil lines, the labeled photograph. I had had an excellent teacher.

"Let's call him Ira." 45

"That's a funny name, but OK." My lab partner, a smart girl destined to become my mentor in things Southern, then gave me a conspiratorial wink and pulled out a little perfume atomizer from her purse.

She sprayed Ira from snout to tail with it. I noticed this operation was taking place at other tables too. The teacher had conveniently left the room a few minutes before. I was once again stunned—almost literally knocked out by a fist of smell: "What is it?"

"*Intimate,*" my advanced biology partner replied smiling.

And by the time our instructor came back to the room, we were ready to delve into this mystery of muscle and bone; eager to discover the secrets that lie just beyond fear a little past loathing; of acknowledging the corruptibility of the flesh, and our own fascination with the subject.

As I finish packing, the telephone rings and it's my mother. She is reminding me to be ready to visit relatives, to go to a dance with her, and, of course, to attend a couple of the services at the church. It is the feast of the Black Virgin, revered patron saint of our home town in Puerto Rico. I agree to everything, and find myself anticipating the eclectic itinerary. Why not allow Evolution and Eve, Biology and the Virgin Birth? Why not take a vacation from logic? I will not be away for too long, I will not let myself be tempted to remain in the sealed garden of blind faith; I'll stay just long enough to rest myself from the exhausting enterprise of leading the examined life.

CONSIDERATIONS FOR CRITICAL THINKING AND WRITING

1. FIRST RESPONSE. How does Cofer receive "an education in the art of cultural compromise"? Have you ever had a similar experience?

2. What do you think is the connection between Cofer's description of her mother's style of dress, as well as her account of the Jewish neighbors, and her primary story about her relationship with Ira?

3. What is Cofer's attitude toward religion? Is she closer to Ira's or her mother's view of religion? Why?

4. Do you agree with Cofer that religion and "the examined life" are mostly incompatible?

5. What do you think is the purpose of Cofer's essay? How is the structure of her essay held together by its theme?

GEORGE ORWELL (1903–1950)

George Orwell was the pen name of Eric Arthur Blair, born in Bengal, India, and the son of an English civil servant. After attending Eton in England, he became an officer with the Indian Imperial Police in Burma from 1922 to 1927. Orwell was deeply suspicious of the methods and values of the colonial system and returned to England and Europe in the late twenties to pursue a writing career. Much of his work is strongly autobiographical. *Down and Out in Paris and London* (1933) describes his marginal existence trying to make a living, while *Homage to Catalonia* (1938) concerns his involvement in the Spanish Civil War. Among his most highly regarded novels are *Animal Farm* (1945) and *1984* (1949), which explore and satirize the nature of totalitarian threats to humanity. One of five collections of essays, *Shooting an Elephant* (1950) includes the piece reprinted here, though it was first published in 1936.

Shooting an Elephant   1936

In Moulmein, in Lower Burma, I was hated by large numbers of people—the only time in my life that I have been important enough for this to happen to me. I was subdivisional police officer of the town, and in an aimless, petty kind of way anti-European feeling was very bitter. No one had the guts to raise a riot, but if a European woman went through the bazaars alone somebody would probably spit betel juice over her dress. As a police officer I was an obvious target and was baited whenever it seemed safe to do so. When a nimble Burman tripped me up on the football field and the referee (another Burman) looked the other way, the crowd yelled with hideous laughter. This happened more than once. In the end the sneering yellow faces of young men that met me everywhere, the insults hooted after me when I was at a safe distance, got badly on my nerves. The young Buddhist priests were the worst of all. There were several thousands of them in the town and none of them seemed to have anything to do except stand on street corners and jeer at Europeans.

All this was perplexing and upsetting. For at that time I had already made up my mind that imperialism was an evil thing and the sooner I chucked up my job and got out of it the better. Theoretically—and secretly, of course—I was all for the Burmese and all against the oppressors, the British. As for the job I was doing, I hated it more bitterly than I can perhaps make clear. In a job like that you see the dirty work of Empire at close quarters. The wretched prisoners huddling in the stinking cages of the lockups, the grey, cowed faces of the long-term convicts, the scarred buttocks of the men who had been flogged with bamboos—all these oppressed me with an intolerable sense of guilt. But I could get nothing into perspective. I was young and ill-educated and I had had to think out my problems in the utter silence that is imposed on every Englishman in the East. I did not even know that the British Empire is dying, still less did I know that it is a great deal better than the younger empires that are going to supplant it. All I knew was that I was stuck between my hatred of the empire I served and my rage against the evil-spirited little beasts who tried to make my job impossible. With one part of my mind I thought of the British Raj° as an unbreakable tyranny, as something clamped down, in *saecula saeculorum,*° upon the will of prostrate peoples; with another part I thought that the greatest joy in the world would be to drive a bayonet into a Buddhist priest's guts. Feelings like these are the normal by-products of imperialism; ask any Anglo-Indian official, if you can catch him off duty.

One day something happened which in a roundabout way was enlightening. It was a tiny incident in itself, but it gave me a better glimpse than I had had before of the real nature of imperialism—the real motives for which despotic governments act. Early one morning the subinspector at a police station the other end of town rang me up on the phone and said that an elephant was ravaging the bazaar. Would I please come and do something about it? I did not know what I could do, but I wanted to see what was happening and I got on to a pony and started out. I took my rifle, an old .44 Winchester and much too small to kill an elephant, but I thought the noise might be useful *in terrorem.*° Various Burmans stopped me on the way and told me about the ele-

Raj: The British government in India.
saecula saeculorum: Forever and ever (Latin).
in terrorem: As a warning (Latin).

phant's doings. It was not, of course, a wild elephant, but a tame one which had gone "must."° It had been chained up, as tame elephants always are when their attack of "must" is due, but on the previous night it had broken its chain and escaped. Its mahout, the only person who could manage it when it was in that state, had set out in pursuit, but had taken the wrong direction and was now twelve hours' journey away, and in the morning the elephant had suddenly reappeared in the town. The Burmese population had no weapons and were quite helpless against it. It had already destroyed somebody's bamboo hut, killed a cow, and raided some fruit stalls and devoured the stock; also it had met the municipal rubbish van and, when the driver jumped out and took to his heels, had turned the van over and inflicted violences upon it.

The Burmese subinspector and some Indian constables were waiting for me in the quarter where the elephant had been seen. It was a very poor quarter, a labyrinth of squalid bamboo huts, thatched with palm-leaf, winding all over a steep hillside. I remember that it was a cloudy, stuffy morning at the beginning of the rains. We began questioning the people as to where the elephant had gone and, as usual, failed to get any definite information. That is invariably the case in the East; a story always sounds clear enough at a distance, but the nearer you get to the scene of events the vaguer it becomes. Some of the people said that the elephant had gone in one direction, some said that he had gone in another, some professed not even to have heard of any elephant. I had almost made up my mind that the whole story was a pack of lies, when we heard yells a little distance away. There was a loud, scandalized cry of "Go away, child! Go away this instant!" and an old woman with a switch in her hand came round the corner of a hut, violently shooing away a crowd of naked children. Some more women followed, clicking their tongues and exclaiming; evidently there was something that the children ought not to have seen. I rounded the hut and saw a man's dead body sprawling in the mud. He was an Indian, a black Dravidian° coolie, almost naked, and he could not have been dead many minutes. The people said that the elephant had come suddenly upon him round the corner of the hut, caught him with its trunk, put its foot on his back, and ground him into the earth. This was the rainy season and the ground was soft, and his face had scored a trench a foot deep and a couple of yards long. He was lying on his belly with arms crucified and head sharply twisted to one side. His face was coated with mud, the eyes wide open, the teeth bared and grinning with an expression of unendurable agony. (Never tell me, by the way, that the dead look peaceful. Most of the corpses I have seen looked devilish.) The friction of the great beast's foot had stripped the skin from his back as neatly as one skins a rabbit. As soon as I saw the dead man I sent an orderly to a friend's house nearby to borrow an elephant rifle. I had already sent back the pony, not wanting it to go mad with fright and throw me if it smelled the elephant.

The orderly came back in a few minutes with a rifle and five cartridges, and   5 meanwhile some Burmans had arrived and told us that the elephant was in the paddy fields below, only a few hundred yards away. As I started forward practically the whole population of the quarter flocked out of the houses and followed me. They had seen the rifle and were all shouting excitedly that I was

"must": Sexual heat.
Dravidian: A southern Indian.

going to shoot the elephant. They had not shown much interest in the elephant when he was merely ravaging their homes, but it was different now that he was going to be shot. It was a bit of fun to them, as it would be to an English crowd; besides they wanted the meat. It made me vaguely uneasy. I had no intention of shooting the elephant—I had merely sent for the rifle to defend myself if necessary—and it is always unnerving to have a crowd following you. I marched down the hill, looking and feeling a fool, with the rifle over my shoulder and an ever-growing army of people jostling at my heels. At the bottom, when you got away from the huts, there was a metalled road and beyond that a miry waste of paddy fields a thousand yards across, not yet ploughed but soggy from the first rains and dotted with coarse grass. The elephant was standing eight yards from the road, his left side towards us. He took not the slightest notice of the crowd's approach. He was tearing up bunches of grass, beating them against his knees to clean them and stuffing them into his mouth.

I had halted on the road. As soon as I saw the elephant I knew with perfect certainty that I ought not to shoot him. It is a serious matter to shoot a working elephant—it is comparable to destroying a huge and costly piece of machinery—and obviously one ought not to do it if it can possibly be avoided. And at that distance, peacefully eating, the elephant looked no more dangerous than a cow. I thought then and I think now that his attack of "must" was already passing off; in which case he would merely wander harmlessly about until the mahout came back and caught him. Moreover, I did not in the least want to shoot him. I decided that I would watch him for a little while to make sure that he did not turn savage again, and then go home.

But at that moment, I glanced round at the crowd that had followed me. It was an immense crowd, two thousand at the least and growing every minute. It blocked the road for a long distance on either side. I looked at the sea of yellow faces above the garish clothes—faces all happy and excited over this bit of fun, all certain that the elephant was going to be shot. They were watching me as they would watch a conjuror about to perform a trick. They did not like me, but with the magical rifle in my hands I was momentarily worth watching. And suddenly I realized that I should have to shoot the elephant after all. The people expected it of me and I had got to do it; I could feel their two thousand wills pressing me forward, irresistibly. And it was at this moment, as I stood there with the rifle in my hands, that I first grasped the hollowness, the futility of the white man's dominion in the East. Here was I, the white man with his gun, standing in front of the unarmed native crowd—seemingly the leading actor of the piece; but in reality I was only an absurd puppet pushed to and fro by the will of those yellow faces behind. I perceived in this moment that when the white man turns tyrant it is his own freedom that he destroys. He becomes a sort of hollow, posing dummy, the conventionalized figure of a sahib. For it is the condition of his rule that he shall spend his life in trying to impress the "natives," and so in every crisis he has got to do what the "natives" expect of him. He wears a mask, and his face grows to fit it. I had got to shoot the elephant. I had committed myself to doing it when I sent for the rifle. A sahib has got to act like a sahib; he has got to appear resolute, to know his own mind and do definite things. To come all that way, rifle in hand, with two thousand people marching at my heels, and then to trail feebly away, having done nothing—no, that was impossible. The crowd would laugh at me. And my whole life, every white man's life in the East, was one long struggle not to be laughed at.

But I did not want to shoot the elephant. I watched him beating his bunch of grass against his knees, with that preoccupied grandmotherly air that elephants have. It seemed to me that it would be murder to shoot him. At that age I was not squeamish about killing animals, but I had never shot an elephant and never wanted to. (Somehow it always seems worse to kill a *large* animal.) Besides, there was the beast's owner to be considered. Alive, the elephant was worth at least a hundred pounds; dead, he would only be worth the value of his tusks, five pounds, possibly. But I had got to act quickly. I turned to some experienced-looking Burmans who had been there when we arrived, and asked them how the elephant had been behaving. They all said the same thing: He took no notice of you if you left him alone, but he might charge if you went too close to him.

It was perfectly clear to me what I ought to do. I ought to walk up to within, say, twenty-five yards of the elephant and test his behavior. If he charged, I could shoot; if he took no notice of me, it would be safe to leave him until the mahout came back. But also I knew that I was going to do no such thing. I was a poor shot with a rifle and the ground was soft mud into which one would sink at every step. If the elephant charged and I missed him, I should have about as much chance as a toad under a steamroller. But even then I was not thinking particularly of my own skin, only of the watchful yellow faces behind. For at that moment, with the crowd watching me, I was not afraid in the ordinary sense, as I would have been if I had been alone. A white man mustn't be frightened in front of "natives"; and so, in general, he isn't frightened. The sole thought in my mind was that if anything went wrong those two thousand Burmans would see me pursued, caught, trampled on, and reduced to a grinning corpse like that Indian up the hill. And if that happened it was quite probable that some of them would laugh. That would never do. There was only one alternative. I shoved the cartridges into the magazine and lay down on the road to get a better aim.

The crowd grew very still, and a deep, low, happy sigh, as of people who see 10 the theatre curtain go up at last, breathed from innumerable throats. They were going to have their bit of fun after all. The rifle was a beautiful German thing with cross-hair sights. I did not then know that in shooting an elephant one would shoot to cut an imaginary bar running from ear-hole to ear-hole. I ought, therefore, as the elephant was sideways on, to have aimed straight at his ear-hole; actually I aimed several inches in front of this, thinking the brain would be further forward.

When I pulled the trigger I did not hear the bang or feel the kick—one never does when a shot goes home—but I heard the devilish roar of glee that went up from the crowd. In that instant, in too short a time, one would have thought, even for the bullet to get there, a mysterious, terrible change had come over the elephant. He neither stirred nor fell, but every line of his body had altered. He looked suddenly stricken, shrunken, immensely old, as though the frightful impact of the bullet had paralyzed him without knocking him down. At last, after what seemed a long time—it might have been five seconds, I dare say—he sagged flabbily to his knees. His mouth slobbered. An enormous senility seemed to have settled upon him. One could have imagined him thousands of years old. I fired again into the same spot. At the second shot he did not collapse but climbed with desperate slowness to his feet and stood weakly upright, with legs sagging and head drooping. I fired a third time. That was the shot that did for him. You could see the agony of it jolt his whole body and knock the last remnant of strength from his legs. But in falling he seemed for a moment to rise, for as his hind legs collapsed beneath him he seemed to tower upward like a huge rock toppling, his trunk reaching skywards like a tree. He trumpeted, for the first and only time. And then down he came, his belly towards me, with a crash that seemed to shake the ground even where I lay.

I got up. The Burmans were already racing past me across the mud. It was obvious that the elephant would never rise again, but he was not dead. He was breathing very rhythmically with long rattling gasps, his great mound of a side painfully rising and falling. His mouth was wide open. I could see far down into caverns of pale pink throat. I waited a long time for him to die, but his breathing did not weaken. Finally, I fired my two remaining shots into the spot where I thought his heart must be. The thick blood welled out of him like red velvet, but still he did not die. His body did not even jerk when the shots hit him, the tortured breathing continued without a pause. He was dying, very slowly and in great agony, but in some world remote from me where not even a bullet could damage him further. I felt I had got to put an end to that dreadful noise. It seemed dreadful to see the great beast lying there, powerless to move and yet powerless to die, and not even to be able to finish him. I sent back for my small rifle and poured shot after shot into his heart, and down his throat. They seemed to make no impression. The tortured gasps continued as steadily as the ticking of a clock.

In the end I could not stand it any longer and went away. I heard later that it took him half an hour to die. Burmans were bringing dahs° and baskets even before I left, and I was told they had stripped his body almost to the bones by the afternoon.

Afterwards, of course, there were endless discussions about the shooting of the elephant. The owner was furious, but he was only an Indian and could do nothing. Besides, legally I had done the right thing, for a mad elephant has to be killed, like a mad dog, if its owner fails to control it. Among the Europeans opinion was divided. The older men said I was right, the younger men said it was a damn shame to shoot an elephant for killing a coolie, because the elephant was worth more than any damn Coringhee coolie. And afterwards I was very glad that the coolie had been killed; it put me legally in the right and it gave me sufficient pretext for shooting the elephant. I often wondered whether any of the others grasped that I had done it solely to avoid looking a fool.

dahs: Knives.

CONSIDERATIONS FOR CRITICAL THINKING AND WRITING

1. FIRST RESPONSE. How did the narrator feel about the Burmese people when he was a policeman? How has his perspective changed as he recounts his story of shooting an elephant?

2. How do the Burmese regard the English? What do you think is the source of tension between the English and the Burmese?

3. Why does the narrator shoot the elephant? Are his reasons primarily personal or political?

4. Comment on Orwell's observations that "A white man mustn't be frightened in front of 'natives'; and so, in general, he isn't frightened" (para. 9).

5. What do you think is the theme of this essay?

Cultural Analysis

This casebook shows you how one student, Holly Furdyna, uses a number of cultural documents to contextualize a poem by Julia Alvarez, "Queens, 1963." Her instructor has asked the class to practice cultural criticism; you may want to review, as she did, the discussion of cultural criticism in Chapter 3 (pp. 69–70). Cultural criticism does not replace the need for close reading—close readings allow us to appreciate and understand the literary art of a text, how the formal elements work together. Holly's instructor asked her class to start with formal analysis before moving on to larger cultural issues; they read the following background on Julia Alvarez and "Queens, 1963" before they moved to the cultural documents that come later in this casebook. As you read the poem and the information on Alvarez, pay attention to the moments in the text that raise questions about its historical and cultural context—questions you well may not have answers for.

JULIA ALVAREZ (B. 1950)

Although Julia Alvarez was born in New York City, she lived in the Dominican Republic until she was ten years old. She returned to New York after her father, a physician, was connected to a plot to overthrow the dictatorship of Rafael Trujillo, and the family had to flee. Growing up in Queens was radically different from the Latino Caribbean world she experienced during her early childhood. A new culture and new language sensitized Alvarez to her surroundings and her use of language so that emigration from the Dominican Republic to Queens was

Photo: Reprinted by permission of Daniel Cima.

the beginning of her movement toward becoming a writer. Alvarez quotes the Polish poet Czeslow Milosz's assertion that "Language is the only homeland" to explain her own sense that what she really settled into was not so much the United States as the English language.

Her fascination with English continued into high school and took shape in college as she became a serious writer—first at Connecticut College from 1967 to 1969 and then at Middlebury College, where she earned her B.A. in 1971. At Syracuse University she was awarded the American Academy of Poetry Prize and, in 1975, earned an M.A. in creative writing. Since then she has worked as a writer-in-residence for the Kentucky Arts Commission, the Delaware Arts Council, and the Arts Council of Fayetteville, North Carolina, working in schools and community organizations. She has taught at California State College, College of Sequoias, Phillips Andover Academy, the University of Vermont, George Washington University, the University of Illinois, and, since 1988, at Middlebury College where she is a professor of literature and creative writing.

Alvarez's poetry has been widely published in journals and magazines ranging from *The New Yorker* to *Mirabella* to *The Kenyon Review*. Her book of poems, *Homecoming* (1984; second edition, 1986), uses simple—yet incisive—language to explore issues related to love, domestic life, and work. Her second book of poetry, *The Other Side/El Otro Lado* (1995), is a bilingual collection of meditations on her childhood memories of immigrant life that served to shape her adult identity and sensibilities.

In addition to her two volumes of poetry, Alvarez has also published three novels. The first, *How the García Girls Lost Their Accents* (1991), is a collection of fifteen separate but interrelated stories that cover thirty years of the lives of the García sisters from the late 1950s to the late 1980s. Drawing upon her own experiences, Alvarez describes the sisters fleeing the Dominican Republic and growing up as Latinas in the United States as well as their relationship to the country they left behind. Alvarez's second novel, *In the Time of the Butterflies* (1994), is a fictional account of a true story concerning four sisters who opposed Trujillo's dictatorship. Three of the sisters were murdered in 1960 by the government, and the fourth surviving sister recounts the events of their personal and political lives that led up to her sisters' deaths. Shaped by the history of Dominican freedom and tyranny, the novel also explores the sisters' relationships to each other and their country.

In *¡Yo!* (1997), her third novel, Alvarez focuses on Yolanda, one of the García sisters from her first novel, who is now a writer. Written in the different voices of Yo's friends and family members, this fractured narrative constructs a complete picture of a woman who uses her relationships as fodder for fiction; a woman who is selfish, aggravating, and finally lovable—and who is deeply embedded in American culture while remaining aware of her Dominican roots. Alvarez's most recent book, *Something to Declare* (1998), is a collection of essays that describes her abiding concerns about how to respond to competing cultures.

In "Queens, 1963" Alvarez remembers the neighborhood she lived in
when she was thirteen years old and how "Everyone seemed more American / than we, newly arrived." The tensions that arose when new immigrants and ethnic groups moved onto the block were mirrored in many
American neighborhoods in 1963. Indeed, the entire nation was made
keenly aware of such issues as antisegregation when demonstrations were
organized across the South and a massive march on Washington in support of civil rights for African Americans drew hundreds of thousands of
demonstrators who listened to Martin Luther King Jr. deliver his electrify-
ing "I have a dream" speech. But the issues were hardly resolved, as evidenced by 1963's two best-selling books: *Happiness Is a Warm Puppy* and
Security Is a Thumb and a Blanket, by Charles M. Schulz of "Peanuts" cartoon
fame. The popularity of these books is, perhaps, understandable given the
tensions that moved across the country and which seemed to culminate on
November 22, 1963, when President Kennedy was assassinated in Dallas,
Texas. These events are not mentioned in "Queens, 1963," but they are certainly part of the context that helps us to understand Alvarez's particular
neighborhood.

Queens, 1963   *1995*

Everyone seemed more American
than we, newly arrived,
foreign dirt still on our soles.
By year's end, a sprinkler waving
like a flag on our mowed lawn,   5
we were melted into the block,
owned our own mock Tudor house.
Then the house across the street
sold to a black family.
Cop cars patrolled our block   10
from the Castellucci's at one end
to the Balakian's on the other.
We heard rumors of bomb threats,
a burning cross on their lawn.
(It turned out to be a sprinkler.)   15
Still the neighborhood buzzed.
The barber's family, Haralambides,
our left side neighbors, didn't want trouble.
They'd come a long way to be free!
Mr. Scott, the retired plumber,   20
and his plump midwestern wife,
considered moving back home
where white and black got along
by staying where they belonged.
They had cultivated our street   25

like the garden she'd given up
on account of her ailing back,
bad knees, poor eyes, arthritic hands.
She went through her litany daily.
Politely, my mother listened —   30
¡Ay, Mrs. Scott, qué pena!°
— her Dominican good manners
still running on automatic.
The Jewish counselor next door,
had a practice in her house;   35
clients hurried up her walk
ashamed to be seen needing.
(I watched from my upstairs window,
gloomy with adolescence,
and guessed how they too must have   40
hypocritical old world parents.)
Mrs. Bernstein said it was time
the neighborhood opened up.
As the first Jew on the block,
she remembered the snubbing she got   45
a few years back from Mrs. Scott.
But real estate worried her,
our houses' plummeting value.
She shook her head as she might
at a client's grim disclosures.   50
Too bad the world works this way.
The German girl playing the piano
down the street abruptly stopped
in the middle of a note.
I completed the tune in my head   55
as I watched *their* front door open.
A dark man in a suit
with a girl about my age
walked quickly into a car.
My hand lifted but fell   60
before I made a welcoming gesture.
On her face I had seen a look
from the days before we had melted
into the United States of America.
It was hardness mixed with hurt.   65
It was knowing she never could be
the right kind of American.
A police car followed their car.
Down the street, curtains fell back.
Mrs. Scott swept her walk   70
as if it had just been dirtied.
Then the German piano commenced
downward scales as if tracking
the plummeting real estate.

31 *qué pena!*: What a shame!

One by one I imagined the houses   75
sinking into their lawns,
the grass grown wild and tall
in the past tense of this continent
before the first foreigners owned
any of this free country.   80

CONSIDERATIONS FOR CRITICAL THINKING AND WRITING

1. FIRST RESPONSE. What nationalities live in this neighborhood in the New York City borough of Queens? Are they neighborly to each other?

2. In line 3, why do you suppose Alvarez writes "foreign dirt still on our soles" rather than "foreign soil still on our shoes"? What does Alvarez's particular word choice suggest about her feelings for her native country?

3. Characterize the speaker. How old is she? How does she feel about having come from the Dominican Republic? About living in the United States?

4. Do you think this poem is optimistic or pessimistic about racial relations in the United States? Explain your answer by referring to specific details in the poem.

CULTURAL AND HISTORICAL DOCUMENTS

After reading the biographical information about Alvarez and making sure that she understands how the poetic elements work together in "Queens, 1963," Holly is ready to do outside reading in order to fill in the cultural context for the text. Her instructor asked the class to read the following documents: an excerpt from an interview with Alvarez on growing up as an immigrant in New York City, an advertisement showing typical row houses, a newspaper article that summarizes the Chamber of Commerce's perspective of Queens in 1963, an excerpt from a television script for *All in the Family* (set in Queens), and a photograph of a civil rights demonstration at a Queens construction site. These documents offer some possible approaches to understanding the culture contemporary to "Queens, 1963." As you read each document, use the questions that follow to think about what each brings to your understanding of the poem.

MARNY REQUA (B. 1971)

From an Interview with Julia Alvarez   1997

M.R. What was it like when you came to the United States?

J.A. When we got to Queens, it was really a shock to go from a totally Latino, *familia* Caribbean world into this very cold and kind of forbidding one in which we didn't speak the language. I didn't grow up with a tradition of writing or reading books at all. People were always telling stories but it wasn't a tradition of literary . . . reading a book or doing something solitary like that. Coming to this country I discovered books, I discovered that it was a way to enter into a portable homeland that you could carry around in your head. You didn't have to suffer what was going on around you. I found in books a place to go. I became interested in language because I was learning a language intentionally at the age of ten. I was wondering, "Why is it that word and not another?" which any writer has to do with their language. I always say I came to English late but to the profession early. By high school I was pretty set: that's what I want to do, be a writer.

M.R. Did you have culture shock returning to the Dominican Republic as you were growing up?

J.A. The culture here had an effect on me — at the time this country was coming undone with protests and flower children and drugs. Here I was back in the Dominican Republic and I wouldn't keep my mouth shut. I had my own ideas and I had my own politics, and it, I just didn't gel anymore with the family. I didn't quite feel I ever belonged in this North American culture and I always had this nostalgia that when I went back I'd belong, and then I found out I didn't belong there either.

M.R. Was it a source of inspiration to have a foot in both cultures?

J.A. I only came to that later. [Then], it was a burden because I felt torn. I wanted to be part of one culture and then part of the other. It was a time when the model for the immigrant was that you came and you became an American and you cut off your ties and that was that. My parents had that frame of mind, because they were so afraid, and they were "Learn your English" and "Become one of them," and that left out so much. Now I see the richness. Part of what I want to do with my work is that complexity, that richness. I don't want it to be simplistic and either/or.

From "The Politics of Fiction," Frontera magazine 5 (1997)

CONSIDERATIONS FOR CRITICAL THINKING AND WRITING

1. What do you think Alvarez means when she describes books as "a portable homeland that you could carry around in your head"?

2. Why is it difficult for Alvarez to feel that she belongs in either the Dominican or the North American culture?

3. Alvarez says that in the 1960s "the model for the immigrant was that you came and you became an American and you cut off your ties and that was that." Do you think this model has changed in the 1990s in the United States? Explain your response.

4. How might this interview alter your understanding of "Queens, 1963"? What light is shed, for example, on the speaker's feeling that her family "melted into the block" in line 6?

An Advertisement for Tudor Row Houses   *1920*

GIBSON'S
MODEL STUCCO HOME DEVELOPMENT
AT ELMHURST MANOR
WITH AUTO DRIVEWAYS

The Perfect Low Priced American Home
Designed and constructed for the Homeseeker
who desires the best at the least cost

The Ideal Home Place for the Children
Well Drained, Sewered, Convenient to Schools
Churches, Stores and Amusements

W. R. GIBSON
BUILDER AND DEVELOPER
OFFICE AND BUILDINGS
Burnside Avenue and Thirty-Seventh Street
Elmhurst Manor, L. I.
PHONE NEWTOWN 2073

From *Queen's Burough New York City, 1910–1920*

CONSIDERATIONS FOR CRITICAL THINKING AND WRITING

1. This advertisement from a publication of the Queens Chamber of Commerce shows row houses as the "Ideal Home Place." Write a paragraph
   describing how the details in the photograph make you feel about living
   there.

2. Compare the neighborhood in this picture with the neighborhood Alvarez describes in "Queens, 1963." How might the physical characteristics of such a neighborhood have changed between 1920 and 1963? What factors might have influenced such a change?

3. How does this advertisement shed light on "Queens, 1963"?

Queens: "The 'Fair' Borough"   1963

This newspaper account anticipates the opening of the 1964 World's Fair in Queens.

Cariello Glorifies Queens as Example of Gracious Living

The borough of Queens "truly represents the full flowering of advanced urban living," Borough President Mario J. Cariello says.

His encomium is in a brightly colored eight-page brochure entitled "The 'Fair' Borough." Mr. Cariello's foreword says the brochure was prepared "to reacquaint our residents" with the borough's history and present stature when they play host to "millions of visitors to the World's Fair."

Twenty-five thousand copies have been printed by photo-offset at a competitive bid cost of $1,600. The money came from the Borough President's special expense fund for proclamations, certificates and the like, a spokesman said yesterday.

A section on current "Data about Queens," compiled by the Queens Chamber of Commerce, says the borough has "such beautiful rural home communities as Forest Hills, Jamaica Estates, Kew Gardens, Jackson Heights, Flushing and Douglaston."

The booklet includes a map of 44 communities, a list of bus routes, a description of the Borough President's functions, the text of the 1657 Flushing Remonstrance as "the first declaration of religious freedom by a group of free citizens in America," a picture of the borough flag, and a brief history.

From the *New York Times,* July 18, 1963

CONSIDERATIONS FOR CRITICAL THINKING AND WRITING

1. Based on the newspaper article, how would you describe the probable tone of the eight-page brochure about Queens?

2. After reading Alvarez's poem about Queens, do you see any irony in the title of the brochure, "The 'Fair' Borough"? Explain why or why not.

3. What is left out of Borough President Cariello's account of Queens? Why do you suppose its focus is very different from that of "Queens, 1963"?

4. Try writing a dialogue between the Borough president and Alvarez on the subject of Queens as a representation of "the full flowering of advanced urban living." If you prefer, write an essay on this topic instead.

"Talkin' about Prejudice" in Queens

All in the Family, created by Norman Lear, was produced for nine seasons from 1971 to 1979, and at the height of its popularity, an estimated one-third of all Americans regularly viewed the program. Although this famous series has ceased production, reruns have preserved its popularity. The show's main character, Archie Bunker — a resident of a row house in a working-class Queens neighborhood — is so well known that his name has been used to describe anyone who is loud, stubborn, and blindly preju-diced. The basic conflict of the series centers on the verbal skirmishes that occur when Archie's middle-aged, working-class biases are challenged by his son-in-law Mike's liberal views. One reason for the show's popularity during its original run was that it mirrored so many issues of its time, such as racism, sexism, politics, religion, and alternative life-styles. The follow-ing excerpt is from the first episode of *All in the Family.*

NORMAN LEAR (B. 1922)

Meet the Bunkers 1971

CHARACTERS

Archie Bunker
Edith Bunker, Archie's wife
Michael Stivic, the Bunkers' son-in-law
Gloria Stivic, the Bunkers' daughter
Lionel, a neighbor

In this scene, Lionel, a black neighbor of the Bunkers, appears at the door on the heels of a dinner conversation in which Archie has fervently denied but amply demonstrated his prejudices. Earlier we learn from Lionel that Archie likes to ask him what he wants to study when he goes to college so that Lionel will say, "Ahm gwana be a 'lectical ingineer." Lionel obliges Archie because he believes that by giving "people what they want," he indeed can become an electrical engineer. He also enjoys watching Archie fall for his put-ons.

Mike: Hey, Lionel. How you doin'? Come on in. You know, in a way we were just talking about you.
Gloria: Michael!
Archie: Talkin' about prejudice, I'm glad you're here Lionel. *(Gets up and goes to living room.)*
Lionel: Yes, sir. Mr. Bunker, sir. *(Hands flowers to Edith.)* These are for you, Mrs. Bunker. A present from an admirer.
Edith (overwhelmed): For me? Oh my goodness, I ain't had a present for ten years.
Gloria: I wonder who it's from.
Archie (coming back to table): There's something I want to ask you, Lionel.
Gloria: Wait a minute, Daddy. Let her open her gift first.

Archie: She waited ten years; another minute ain't gonna kill her! *(Puts gift on table, takes Lionel to living room.)* Come here, Lionel. Let me ask your opinion of somethin' there, Lionel. When you started doin' odd jobs in the neighborhood, wasn't I one of the first guys to throw a little work your way — by the way, didya fix the TV up in the bedroom?

Lionel: Sure did, Mr. Bunker. *(Lionel nods. Archie slips him some change.)*

Archie: Swell. Good boy . . . Here, put this in your pocket.

Edith: Cheaper than a repairman, believe me.

Archie: Is anybody talkin' to you . . . Now, Lionel you could say by throwin' you these little jobs, in a way I was helpin' you get some money so you can get through college so's you can become . . .

Lionel: A 'lectical ingineer.

Archie (loves it): Yeah. Ya hear that?

Mike (impatient): Archie, ask your question already!

Archie: Will you keep your drawers on? Hey, by the way, that's a pretty nice looking suit you got on there. I mean it's classy, it's quiet. Where'd you get it?

Lionel: Up in Harlem.

Archie (looks): Nah.

Lionel: Now I got two more, but one's in yellow with stripes, the other one's in purple with checks. You know, for when I'm with *my* people.

Archie: Well, anyway Lionel, I'd say you know me pretty good, wouldn't you?

Lionel: Oh, yes, sir. I got a bead on you, all right. I know you real good.

Archie: Good, good.

Mike (crossing to living room): Alright, alright, let's get to the point. Lionel, what he wants to know, is if you think he's prejudiced.

Lionel (feigning innocence): Prejudiced?

Archie: Yeah.

Lionel: Prejudiced against who?

Mike: Against Black People.

Lionel: Against Black People! Mr. Bunker! That's the most ridiculous thing I ever heard!

> *Archie turns proudly to the others.*

Archie: There, you see that, wise guy. *(Turns to Mike.)* You thought you knew him. You thought you knew me. Oh these liberals — they're supposed to be so sensitive, ya know. I'll tell you where this guy's sensitive, Lionel — right in his tochas. *(Archie goes to dining room table.)*

Lionel (surprise): Where?

Mike: It's a Yiddish word. It means — *(points to buttocks).*

Lionel: Oh, I know where it's at. I was just wonderin', Mr. Bunker — what's with the Jewish word?

Archie: I hear them. We got a couple of Hebes working down the building.

Lionel: Does he use words like that very often?

Mike: Now and then.

Archie: I told ya, I work with a couple of Jews.

Lionel: Beggin' your pardon, Mr. Bunker, but you wouldn't happen to be one of them, would you?

Archie (no humor about this): What??

Lionel: I mean people don't use Jewish words just like that, do they, Mike?

Mike (crossing to table, sits): No, not in my experience.

Archie: Maybe people don't but *I* do! And I ain't no Yid!

Mike: Come to think of it . . . when your father was visiting last year . . . wasn't his name Davie, or somethin'?

Archie: David, my father's name is David.

Mike: Yeah, David. And your mother's name . . . uh . . . Sarah, wasn't it?

Archie (to Lionel): Sarah, my mother's name is Sarah — So what?

Lionel: David and Sarah, two Jewish names.

Archie: David and Sarah. Two names right out of the Bible — which is got nothin' to do with the Jews.

Lionel: You don't wanna get up tight about it, Mr. Bunker. There's nothing to be ashamed of being Jewish.

Archie: But I ain't Jewish!

Mike: Look at that — see the way he uses his hands when he argues. A very Semitic gesture.

Archie: What do you know about it, you dumb Polack.

Mike: All right, I'm a Polack.

Archie: You sure are! You're a Polack Joke!

Mike: Okay, I don't mind, so I'm Polish. I don't mind. I'm proud of it!

Lionel: There you are, Mr. Bunker. Now you oughta be proud that you're Jewish.

Archie (whining): But I ain't Jewish.

Edith: I didn't know you was Jewish.

Archie: What the hell are you talking about? You, of all people, should *know* that I ain't Jewish.

Edith: You *are* talking with your hands.

Lionel: See, the Jews tend to be emotional.

Archie (blowing): Now listen to me, Lionel. I'm going to give it to you just once more and that's all. I am not Jewish.

Lionel: Yes, Sir, Mr. Bunker. But even if you are, it doesn't change things between you and me. I mean I'm not gonna throw away nine years of friendship over a little thing like that. So long, everybody. *(He exits.)*

All: Bye, Lionel!

Archie watches him go and turns to others. They resume eating quickly.

Archie: Well, I hate a smart aleck kid, and I don't care what color he is!

Applause. Fade to black.

CONSIDERATIONS FOR CRITICAL THINKING AND WRITING

1. What kinds of assumptions does Archie make about Lionel because he is black? How does Lionel use Archie's prejudices to satirize him?

2. Some critics have insisted that *All in the Family* negatively affected society because the series presents a bigot who is likable, thereby characterizing his racial prejudices as funny and acceptable rather than harmful and repugnant. Do you think Archie is a dangerous character because his prejudices are presented humorously? Explain why or why not.

3. Compare and contrast how racial prejudice is treated in this script and in "Queens, 1963." Which treatment do you find more effective? Explain why.

4. How do the script and the poem suggest what it was like to be Jewish in Queens in the 1960s? Write an essay that explores how each work treats Jewishness. Consider whether these treatments are simplistic and reductive or complex and subtle.

A Civil Rights Demonstration 1963

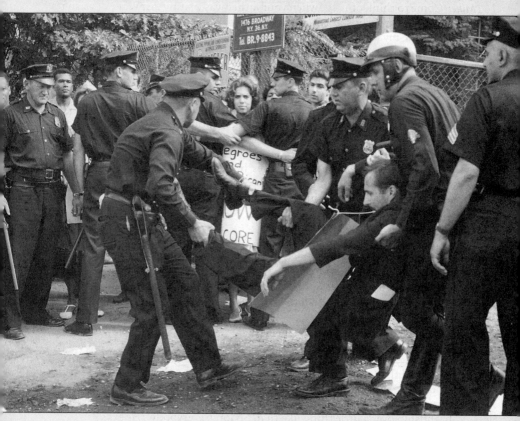

In this photograph police remove a Congress of Racial Equality (CORE) demonstrator from a Queens construction site. Demonstrators blocked the delivery entrance to the site because they wanted more African Americans and Puerto Ricans hired in the building-trade industry. Reprinted by permission of AP/Wide World Photos.

CONSIDERATIONS FOR CRITICAL THINKING AND WRITING

1. Discuss the role played by the police in this photograph and in "Queens, 1963." What attitudes toward the police do the photograph and the poem display?

2. How do you think the Scotts and Mrs. Bernstein would have responded to this photograph in 1963?

3. Compare the tensions in "Queens, 1963" to those depicted in this picture. How do the speaker's private reflections relate to this public protest?

A Sample First Response

After Holly has read the poem and has a sense of its context, she is ready to think about identifying a topic for her paper. She uses informal writing to begin to sift through the issues raised by the material she has read so far and the moments in the poem that struck her most. Notice that her focus is on the poem; even when you're practicing a cultural analysis of a literary text, the literature should always remain central. By the end of her first response, she has realized that she wants her paper to focus on the tension between assimilation and individuality, both in the small world described in Alvarez's poem and in the larger, historical America of 1963.

The poem shows the power of conformity in 1960s America (as advertised in the real estate poster from the 1920s) as superficial and insincere by using the symbols that represent America or conformity. I think her use of the sprinkler image waving like a flag, and then being mistaken for a burning cross, makes a particularly powerful statement both about people's desire for conformity and about their intolerance. The newspaper article about Queens adds to the ironies Alvarez highlights in her poem by describing Queens as a historical bastion of freedom and good values.

Alvarez portrays the complex interactions between people of different ethnicities and religions, using brief quotations to point to their intolerance for difference. An example of this is Mrs. Bernstein's implied statement, "Too bad the world works this way," which seems to reveal both a wish for more acceptance and a resigned or complacent feeling about race relations. Alvarez's word-choice is at times very evocative of the mixed feelings around racial and immigration issues; the word melt, which describes assimilation into American culture, is portrayed as desirable but is also ominous. If something melts, it loses its integrity, its self.

A Sample of Brainstorming

Once Holly has identified a topic, she is ready to collect different ideas and to organize them into a rough order in preparation for writing her paper. She uses brainstorming to think through a more developed thesis, along with rough notes about the moments in the text that she wants to use as evidence for her observations. Notice that the lines between text and context become blurry in a cultural analysis; she can use the documents and the poem equally well as evidence, as both are in some way products of the same historical moment.

Thesis?   *"Queens, 1963" reveals the ironies of the American ideal of conformity by showing that ideal interacting with a neighborhood made up of families from different ethnic or religious backgrounds. Poem implies dangers of this ideal in context of racial tensions in country at that time, and ends on a note of ambiguity between optimism about racial relations lending "complexity and richness" to society as well as to individuals, and pessimism about racial relations.*

Show how ideal is represented: poster, sprinklers image, homes all the same.

But ideal is undermined by real intolerance, symbolized by sprinkler/burning cross, ambiguous or intolerant statements of neighbors.

2 issues: people's intolerance and denial of it (e.g., Archie Bunker and Mrs. Bernstein); and the desire of immigrants to assimilate and cut off their ties, to forget the culture they came from, to "melt" into the USA. (discuss ambiguities of word "melt" and include Alvarez's statement about not belonging in either culture.

Conclusion: discuss whether poem is pessimistic or optimistic about race relations. Last image of wilderness before humanity is ambiguous. Could be complexity and diversity of wilderness as a metaphor for social diversity and richness. But also implies wish for humanity to disappear b/c they're hopelessly unable to get along.

A Sample Student Cultural Analysis

After her first response and brainstorming, Holly is ready to write her cultural analysis. As you read her essay, notice how she starts with the ad for row houses — it summarizes for her the fantasy of conformity that she sees Alvarez writing against in "Queens, 1963." Notice also how she pays attention throughout her paper to the formal elements of the poem and to the language and imagery that the poet uses. By the end of her argument, Holly has come to the conclusion that it isn't clear which side of the issue the poem comes down on. What do you think of Holly's argument? Would you have argued a different point, or come to a different conclusion, using the materials in this casebook?

Holly Furdyna

Literature 213

Professor Miller

December 2, 20--

                    Beneath the Surface of Conformity:
                      Julia Alvarez's "Queens, 1963"

A real estate agency's advertisement from the 1920s features a drawing of a street in Queens on which every
house is identical. The ad describes the homes as "ideal"
and "the perfect low priced American home." The poster
could be seen as an advertisement not just for homes but
for conformity--for the ideal of a neighborhood in which
all the houses are the same and, implicitly, so are the
families who live in them. But Alvarez's poem reveals the
ironies and dangers of this ideal by confronting it in
the context of the racial prejudices of Queens in 1963.

     The poem begins with the family's first impression
upon immigrating to the United States and moving into
Queens: "Everyone seemed more American / than we, newly
arrived, / foreign dirt still on our soles." The impression seems to contain an implicit wish already: to be
more American, like the others. Alvarez speaks elsewhere
of this wish to assimilate common to immigrants of her
parents' generation. In an interview for Frontera magazine she says, "The model for the immigrant was that you
came and you cut off your ties and that was that." Her
poem implies the urgency behind this wish by its quick
cut from "foreign dirt still on our soles" (which is an
evocative pun) to the next lines: "By year's end, a
sprinkler waving / like a flag on our mowed lawn, /
we were melted into the block, / owned our own mock
Tudor house" (4-7). The sprinkler, in this neighborhood,
has assumed the status of a symbol of patriotism and
Americanism, just as the mowed lawn and the mock, or

copied, houses have come to signify certain American
values.

But when a black family moves in across the street,
someone sees the sprinkler as a burning cross. The
implicit coupling of the flag--one analogy for the sprin-
kler--with a burning cross is one of Alvarez's strategies
for revealing the dark underside of American values. She
implies that this neighborhood saw no discrepancy between
its patriotism, values of conformity and manicured lawns,
and its racial prejudices. Alvarez even indicates that
people somewhat denied their own prejudices or accepted
them without a thought that they might be morally wrong;
these attitudes are exemplified by the character of
Archie Bunker in the sit-com All in the Family, who
reveals his racial prejudices by trying to deny them.
Similarly, in "Queens, 1963," Mrs. Bernstein, a Jewish
woman in the neighborhood, remembers "the snubbing she
got" (45) when she arrived but admits to being worried
about the state of the neighborhood now that that black
family has moved in. She says, "Too bad the world works
this way" (51), which implies a resigned or complacent
acceptance of the intolerance that is the status quo.

The simultaneous denial and perpetuation of racial
prejudice seems to have been a widespread phenomenon
at that time (and perhaps still is). In a newspaper
article from 1963 titled "The 'Fair' Borough," Queens
was described as a historical bastion of freedom and
American values. The description, read in the context of
the poem, only increases the power of the ironies Alvarez
highlights. We see in the poem strong negative reactions
to the arrival of a black family in the neighborhood that
the Smiths, perhaps the most blatantly prejudiced neighbors, "cultivated" like a garden. This description of the
street leads us to see, as Mrs. Smith implicitly saw, the

Furdyna 3

"respectable" (white, or near-white) families as the
healthy desired plants, and the new black family as an
invasive weed. This image recalls the image in the third
line, of "foreign dirt still on our soles." Together,
these images create the sense of the foreign land--home-
land really--as a place from which the immigrants have
been uprooted, but which was perhaps the only environment
in which they can truly grow and flower.

But in addition to the idea of the uprootedness of
immigrant families, Alvarez portrays the desire of immigrants to shake the foreign soil off of their soles, to
"melt" into American culture. Although this "melting" was
desirable to immigrant families, the verb itself, melt,
conveys an ominous impression of assimilation. When something melts, it loses its integrity and individuality,
blending into its environment. Alvarez says in the interview for Frontera that after moving from the Dominican
Republic and assimilating, somewhat, into American culture she felt torn, or spread thin, between cultures, as
if she didn't belong in either.

Throughout, the poem creates a sense of indecision
and ambiguity of feelings about living between cultures
and about which behaviors and attitudes to adopt. When
Alvarez, as a child, sees the "dark man in a suit /
with a girl about [her] age" (57-58) come out of the
house across the street, her first impulse is to wave,
but before she waves something tells her not to, some
unspoken rule of this new prejudiced culture: "My hand
lifted but fell / before I made a welcoming gesture"
(60-61). I think the speaker of the poem remains in
this "in-between" state of ambiguous feeling in which
she accepts her parents' desire to assimilate while
maintaining an awareness that something is not right
about it.

The poem ends on an image that crystallizes this
indecision:

> One by one I imagined the houses
> sinking into their lawns,
> the grass grown wild and tall
> in the past tense of this continent
> before the first foreigners owned
> any of this free country. (75-80)

Alvarez's ambiguous "I imagined" can be understood as a
wish or as something like a fear. The image of the houses
sinking into their lawns may convey a sense of ruin,
implying that the attempt to mingle cultures and conform
to one is doomed. Or it may convey a sense of fertility,
a return to the soil of <u>this</u> continent, out of which a
new "multi-culture" may be cultivated. Alvarez emphasizes
in these lines the fact that every American was at one
time a "foreigner," including the first "Native Americans" who probably trekked across the Bering Strait from
northeastern Asia. Her ambiguity of feeling is maintained
by her pointing to this fact and describing the land of
America's past as "wild" and "free," which it is not any
longer, as the whole poem has been illustrating. It is
unclear whether, in the end, Alvarez means to express
optimism or pessimism about race relations in the United
States. The wild freedom of "the past tense of this continent" may be seen, optimistically, as a kind of "ecologi-
cally" interdependent human society. But this image
evokes also the sense of hopelessness and inevitable
ruin. It may even be read as a wish for a place devoid of
human life, where irrational politics and prejudices have
no power and do not even exist. In these last lines
Alvarez reveals not the ironies of conformity, as the
sprinkler image showed, but the dangers.

Glossary of Literary Terms

Accent The emphasis, or STRESS, given a syllable in pronunciation. We say "*syl*-lable" not "syl*la*ble," "*em*phasis" not "em*pha*sis." Accents can also be used to emphasize a particular word in a sentence: Is she con*tent* with the *con*tents of the *yel*low *pack*age? See also METER.

Act A major division in the action of a play. The ends of acts are typically indicated by lowering the curtain or turning up the houselights. Playwrights frequently employ acts to accommodate changes in time, setting, characters onstage, or mood. In many full-length plays, acts are further divided into scenes, which often mark a point in the action when the location changes or when a new character enters. See also SCENE.

Allegory A narration or description usually restricted to a single meaning because its events, actions, characters, settings, and objects represent specific abstractions or ideas. Although the elements in an allegory may be interesting in themselves, the emphasis tends to be on what they ultimately mean. Characters may be given names such as Hope, Pride, Youth, and Charity; they have few if any personal qualities beyond their abstract meanings. These personifications are not symbols because, for instance, the meaning of a character named Charity is precisely that virtue. See also SYMBOL.

Alliteration The repetition of the same consonant sounds in a sequence of words, usually at the beginning of a word or stressed syllable: "*desc*ending *dew* *d*rops"; "*l*uscious *l*emons." Alliteration is based on the sounds of letters, rather than the spelling of words; for example, "*k*een" and "*c*ar" alliterate, but "*c*ar" and "*c*ite" do not. Used sparingly, alliteration can intensify ideas by emphasizing key words, but when used too self-consciously, it can be distracting, even ridiculous, rather than effective. See also ASSONANCE, CONSONANCE.

Allusion A brief reference to a person, place, thing, event, or idea in history or literature. Allusions conjure up biblical authority, scenes from Shakespeare's plays, historic figures, wars, great love stories, and anything else that might enrich an author's work. Allusions imply reading and cultural experiences shared by the writer and reader, functioning as a kind of shorthand whereby the recalling of something outside the work supplies an emotional or intellectual context, such as a poem about current racial struggles calling up the memory of Abraham Lincoln.

Ambiguity Allows for two or more simultaneous interpretations of a word, phrase, action, or situation, all of which can be supported by the context of a work. Deliberate ambiguity can contribute to the effectiveness and richness of a work, for example, in the open-ended conclusion to Hawthorne's "Young Goodman Brown." However, unintentional ambiguity obscures meaning and can confuse readers.

Anagram A word or phrase made from the letters of another word or phrase, as "heart" is an anagram of "earth." Anagrams have often been considered merely an exercise of one's ingenuity, but sometimes writers use anagrams to conceal proper names or veiled messages, or to suggest important connections between words, as in "hated" and "death."

Anapestic meter See FOOT.

Antagonist The character, force, or collection of forces in fiction or drama that opposes the PROTAGONIST and gives rise to the conflict of the story; an opponent of the protagonist, such as Claudius in Shakespeare's play *Hamlet*. See also CHARACTER, CONFLICT.

Antihero A protagonist who has the opposite of most of the traditional attributes of a hero. He or she may be bewildered, ineffectual, deluded, or merely pathetic. Often what antiheroes learn, if they learn anything at all, is that the world isolates them in an existence devoid of God and absolute values. Yossarian from Joseph Heller's *Catch-22* is an example of an antihero. See also CHARACTER.

Apostrophe An address, either to someone who is absent and therefore cannot hear the speaker or to something nonhuman that cannot comprehend. Apostrophe often provides a speaker the opportunity to think aloud.

Approximate rhyme See RHYME.

Archetype A term used to describe universal symbols that evoke deep and sometimes unconscious responses in a reader. In literature, characters, images, and themes that symbolically embody universal meanings and basic human experiences, regardless of when or where they live, are considered archetypes. Common literary archetypes include stories of quests, initiations, scapegoats, descents to the underworld, and ascents to heaven. See also MYTHOLOGICAL CRITICISM.

Aside In drama, a speech directed to the audience that supposedly is not audible to the other characters onstage at the time. When Hamlet first appears onstage, for example, his aside "A little more than kin, and less than kind!" gives the audience a strong sense of his alienation from King Claudius. See also SOLILOQUY.

Assonance The repetition of internal vowel sounds in nearby words that do not end the same, for example, "asleep under a tree," or "each evening." Similar endings result in rhyme, as in "asleep in the deep." Assonance is a strong means of emphasizing important words in a line. See also ALLITERATION, CONSONANCE.

Ballad Traditionally, a ballad is a song, transmitted orally from generation to generation, that tells a story and that eventually is written down. As such, ballads usually cannot be traced to a particular author or group of authors. Typically, ballads are dramatic, condensed, and impersonal narratives, such as "Bonny Barbara Allan." A **literary ballad** is a narrative poem that is written in deliberate imitation of the language, form, and spirit of the traditional ballad, such as Keats's "La Belle Dame sans Merci." See also BALLAD STANZA, QUATRAIN.

Ballad stanza A four-line stanza, known as a QUATRAIN, consisting of alternating eight- and six-syllable lines. Usually only the second and fourth lines rhyme (an *abcb* pattern). Coleridge adopted the ballad stanza in "The Rime of the Ancient Mariner."

All in a hot and copper sky
The bloody Sun, at noon,
Right up above the mast did stand,
No bigger than the Moon.

See also BALLAD, QUATRAIN.

Biographical criticism An approach to literature which suggests that knowledge of the author's life experiences can aid in the understanding of his or her work. While biographical information can sometimes complicate one's interpretation of a work, and some formalist critics (such as the New Critics) disparage the use of the author's biography as a tool for textual interpretation, learning about the life of the author can often enrich a reader's appreciation for that author's work. See also CULTURAL CRITICISM, FORMALIST CRITICISM, NEW CRITICISM.

Blank verse Unrhymed iambic pentameter. Blank verse is the English verse form closest to the natural rhythms of English speech and therefore is the most common pattern found in traditional English narrative and dramatic poetry from Shakespeare to the early twentieth century. Shakespeare's plays use blank verse extensively. See also IAMBIC PENTAMETER.

Cacophony Language that is discordant and difficult to pronounce, such as this line from John Updike's "Player Piano": "never my numb plunker fumbles." Cacophony ("bad sound") may be unintentional in the writer's sense of music, or it may be used consciously for deliberate dramatic effect. See also EUPHONY.

Caesura A pause within a line of poetry that contributes to the rhythm of the line. A caesura can occur anywhere within a line and need not be indicated by punctuation. In scanning a line, caesuras are indicated by a double vertical line (‖). See also METER, RHYTHM, SCANSION.

Canon Those works generally considered by scholars, critics, and teachers to be the most important to read and study, which collectively constitute the "masterpieces" of literature. Since the 1960s, the traditional English and American literary canon, consisting mostly of works by white male writers, has been rapidly expanding to include many female writers and writers of varying ethnic backgrounds.

Carpe diem The Latin phrase meaning "seize the day." This is a very common literary theme, especially in lyric poetry, which emphasizes that life is short, time is fleeting, and that one should make the most of present pleasures. Robert Herrick's poem "To the Virgins, to Make Much of Time" employs the *carpe diem* theme.

Catharsis Meaning "purgation," *catharsis* describes the release of the emotions of pity and fear by the audience at the end of a tragedy. In his *Poetics*,

Aristotle discusses the importance of catharsis. The audience faces the misfortunes of the protagonist, which elicit pity and compassion. Simultaneously, the audience also confronts the failure of the protagonist, thus receiving a frightening reminder of human limitations and frailties. Ultimately, however, both these negative emotions are purged, because the tragic protagonist's suffering is an affirmation of human values rather than a despairing denial of them. See also TRAGEDY.

Character, characterization A character is a person presented in a dramatic or narrative work, and characterization is the process by which a writer makes that character seem real to the reader. A **hero** or **heroine,** often called the PROTAGONIST, is the central character who engages the reader's interest and empathy. The ANTAGONIST is the character, force, or collection of forces that stands directly opposed to the protagonist and gives rise to the conflict of the story. A **static character** does not change throughout the work, and the reader's knowledge of that character does not grow, whereas a **dynamic character** undergoes some kind of change because of the action in the plot. A **flat character** embodies one or two qualities, ideas, or traits that can be readily described in a brief summary. They are not psychologically complex characters and therefore are readily accessible to readers. Some flat characters are recognized as **stock characters;** they embody stereotypes such as the "dumb blonde" or the "mean stepfather." They become types rather than individuals. **Round characters** are more complex than flat or stock characters, and often display the inconsistencies and internal conflicts found in most real people. They are more fully developed, and therefore are harder to summarize. Authors have two major methods of presenting characters: **showing** and **telling. Showing** allows the author to present a character talking and acting, and lets the reader infer what kind of person the character is. In **telling,** the author intervenes to describe and sometimes evaluate the character for the reader. Characters can be convincing whether they are presented by showing or by telling, as long as their actions are motivated. **Motivated action** by the characters occurs when the reader or audience is offered reasons for how the characters behave, what they say, and the decisions they make. **Plausible action** is action by a character in a story that seems reasonable, given the motivations presented. See also PLOT.

Chorus In Greek tragedies (especially those of Aeschylus and Sophocles), a group of people who serve mainly as commentators on the characters and events. They add to the audience's understanding of the play by expressing traditional moral, religious, and social attitudes. The role of the chorus in dramatic works evolved through the sixteenth century, and the chorus occasionally is still used by modern playwrights such as T. S. Eliot in *Murder in the Cathedral.* See also DRAMA.

Cliché An idea or expression that has become tired and trite from overuse, its freshness and clarity having worn off. Clichés often anesthetize readers, and are usually a sign of weak writing. See also SENTIMENTALITY, STOCK RESPONSES.

Climax See PLOT.

Closet drama A play that is written to be read rather than performed onstage. In this kind of drama, literary art outweighs all other considerations. See also DRAMA.

Colloquial Refers to a type of informal diction that reflects casual, conversational language and often includes slang expressions. See also DICTION.

Comedy A work intended to interest, involve, and amuse the reader or audience, in which no terrible disaster occurs and that ends happily for the main characters. **High comedy** refers to verbal wit, such as puns, whereas **low comedy** is generally associated with physical action and is less intellectual. **Romantic comedy** involves a love affair that meets with various obstacles (like disapproving parents, mistaken identities, deceptions, or other sorts of misunderstandings) but overcomes them to end in a blissful union. Shakespeare's comedies, such as *A Midsummer Night's Dream,* are considered romantic comedies.

Comic relief A humorous scene or incident that alleviates tension in an otherwise serious work. In many instances these moments enhance the thematic significance of the story in addition to providing laughter. When Hamlet jokes with the gravediggers we laugh, but something hauntingly serious about the humor also intensifies our more serious emotions.

Conflict The struggle within the plot between opposing forces. The PROTAGONIST engages in the conflict with the ANTAGONIST, which may take the form of a character, society, nature, or an aspect of the protagonist's personality. See also CHARACTER, PLOT.

Connotation Associations and implications that go beyond the literal meaning of a word, which derive from how the word has been commonly used and the associations people make with it. For example, the word *eagle* connotes ideas of liberty and freedom that have little to do with the word's literal meaning. See also DENOTATION.

Consonance A common type of near rhyme that consists of identical consonant sounds preceded by different vowel sounds: *home, same; worth, breath.* See also RHYME.

Contextual symbol See SYMBOL.

Controlling metaphor See METAPHOR.

Convention A characteristic of a literary genre (often unrealistic) that is understood and accepted by audiences because it has come, through usage and time, to be recognized as a familiar technique. For example, the division of a play into acts and scenes is a dramatic convention, as are soliloquies and asides. FLASHBACKS and FORESHADOWING are examples of literary conventions.

Conventional symbol See SYMBOL.

Cosmic irony See IRONY.

Couplet Two consecutive lines of poetry that usually rhyme and have the same meter. A **heroic couplet** is a couplet written in rhymed iambic pentameter.

Crisis A turning point in the action of a story that has a powerful effect on the protagonist. Opposing forces come together decisively to lead to the climax of the plot. See also PLOT.

Cultural criticism An approach to literature that focuses on the historical as well as social, political, and economic contexts of a work. Popular culture—mass produced and consumed cultural artifacts ranging from advertising to popular fiction to television to rock music—is given equal emphasis as "high culture." Cultural critics use widely eclectic strategies such as new historicism, psychology, gender studies, and deconstructionism to analyze not only literary texts but everything from radio talk shows, comic strips, calendar art, commercials, to travel guides and baseball cards. See also HISTORICAL CRITICISM, MARXIST CRITICISM, POSTCOLONIAL CRITICISM.

Dactylic meter See FOOT.

Deconstructionism An approach to literature which suggests that literary works do not yield fixed, single meanings, because language can never say exactly what we intend it to mean. Deconstructionism seeks to destabilize meaning by examining the gaps and ambiguities of the language of a text. Deconstructionists pay close attention to language in order to discover and describe how a variety of possible readings are generated by the elements of a text. See also NEW CRITICISM.

Denotation The dictionary meaning of a word. See also CONNOTATION.

Dénouement A French term meaning "unraveling" or "unknotting," used to describe the resolution of the plot following the climax. See also PLOT, RESOLUTION.

Dialect A type of informational diction. Dialects are spoken by definable groups of people from a particular geographic region, economic group, or social class. Writers use dialect to contrast and express differences in educational, class, social, and regional backgrounds of their characters. See also DICTION.

Dialogue The verbal exchanges between characters. Dialogue makes the characters seem real to the reader or audience by revealing firsthand their thoughts, responses, and emotional states. See also DICTION.

Diction A writer's choice of words, phrases, sentence structures, and figurative language, which combine to help create meaning. **Formal diction** consists of a dignified, impersonal, and elevated use of language; it follows the rules of syntax exactly and is often characterized by complex words and lofty tone. **Middle diction** maintains correct language usage, but is less elevated than formal diction; it reflects the way most educated people speak. **Informal diction** represents the plain language of everyday use, and often includes idiomatic expressions, slang, contractions, and many simple, common words. **Poetic diction** refers to the way poets sometimes employ an elevated diction that deviates significantly from the common speech and writing of their time, choosing words for their supposedly inherent poetic qualities. Since the eighteenth century, however, poets have been incorporating all kinds of diction in their work and so there is no longer an automatic distinction between the language of a poet and the language of everyday speech. See also DIALECT.

Didactic poetry Poetry designed to teach an ethical, moral, or religious lesson. Michael Wigglesworth's Puritan poem *Day of Doom* is an example of didactic poetry.

Doggerel A derogatory term used to describe poetry whose subject is trite and whose rhythm and sounds are monotonously heavy-handed.

Drama Derived from the Greek word *dram,* meaning "to do" or "to perform," the term *drama* may refer to a single play, a group of plays ("Jacobean drama"), or to all plays ("world drama"). Drama is designed for performance in a theater; actors take on the roles of characters, perform indicated actions, and speak the dialogue written in the script. **Play** is a general term for a work of dramatic literature, and a **playwright** is a writer who makes plays.

Dramatic irony See IRONY.

Dramatic monologue A type of lyric poem in which a character (the speaker) addresses a distinct but silent audience imagined to be present in the poem in such a way as to reveal a dramatic situation and, often unintentionally, some aspect of his or her temperament or personality. See also LYRIC.

Dynamic character See CHARACTER.

Editorial omniscience See NARRATOR.

Electra complex The female version of the Oedipus complex. *Electra complex* is a term used to describe the psychological conflict of a daughter's unconscious rivalry with her mother for her father's attention. The name comes from the Greek legend of Electra, who avenged the death of her father, Agamemnon, by plotting the death of her mother. See also OEDIPUS COMPLEX, PSYCHOLOGICAL CRITICISM.

Elegy A mournful, contemplative lyric poem written to commemorate someone who is dead, often ending in a consolation. Tennyson's *In Memoriam,* written on the death of Arthur Hallam, is an elegy. *Elegy* may also refer to a serious meditative poem produced to express the speaker's melancholy thoughts. See also LYRIC.

End rhyme See RHYME.

End-stopped line A poetic line that has a pause at the end. End-stopped lines reflect normal speech patterns and are often marked by punctuation. The first line of Keats's "Endymion" is an example of an end-stopped line; the natural pause coincides with the end of the line, and is marked by a period:

A thing of beauty is a joy forever.

English sonnet See SONNET.

Enjambment In poetry, when one line ends without a pause and continues into the next line for its meaning. This is also called a **run-on line.** The transition between the first two lines of Wordsworth's poem "My Heart Leaps Up" demonstrates enjambment:

My heart leaps up when I behold
  A rainbow in the sky:

Envoy See SESTINA.

Epic A long narrative poem, told in a formal, elevated style, that focuses on a serious subject and chronicles heroic deeds and events important to a culture or nation. Milton's *Paradise Lost,* which attempts to "justify the ways of God to man," is an epic. See also NARRATIVE POEM.

Epigram A brief, pointed, and witty poem that usually makes a satiric or humorous point. Epigrams are most often written in couplets, but take no prescribed form.

Epiphany In fiction, when a character suddenly experiences a deep realization about himself or herself; a truth which is grasped in an ordinary rather than a melodramatic moment.

Escape literature See FORMULA LITERATURE.

Euphony *Euphony* ("good sound") refers to language that is smooth and musically pleasant to the ear. See also CACOPHONY.

Exact rhyme See RHYME.

Exposition A narrative device, often used at the beginning of a work, that provides necessary background information about the characters and their circumstances. Exposition explains what has gone on before, the relationships between characters, the development of a theme, and the introduction of a conflict. See also FLASHBACK.

Extended metaphor See METAPHOR.

Eye rhyme See RHYME.

Falling action See PLOT.

Falling meter See METER.

Farce A form of humor based on exaggerated, improbable incongruities. Farce involves rapid shifts in action and emotion, as well as slapstick comedy and extravagant dialogue. Malvolio, in Shakespeare's *Twelfth Night*, is a farcical character.

Feminine rhyme See RHYME.

Feminist criticism An approach to literature that seeks to correct or supplement what may be regarded as a predominantly male-dominated critical perspective with a feminist consciousness. Feminist criticism places literature in a social context and uses a broad range of disciplines, including history, sociology, psychology, and linguistics, to provide a perspective sensitive to feminist issues. Feminist theories also attempt to understand representation from a woman's point of view and to explain women's writing strategies as specific to their social conditions. See also GAY AND LESBIAN CRITICISM, GENDER CRITICISM, SOCIOLOGICAL CRITICISM.

Figures of speech Ways of using language that deviate from the literal, denotative meanings of words in order to suggest additional meanings or effects. Figures of speech say one thing in terms of something else, such as when an eager funeral director is described as a vulture. See also METAPHOR, SIMILE.

First-person narrator See NARRATOR.

Fixed form A poem that may be categorized by the pattern of its lines, meter, rhythm, or stanzas. A sonnet is a fixed form of poetry because by definition it must have fourteen lines. Other fixed forms include LIMERICK, SESTINA, and VILLANELLE. However, poems written in a fixed form may not always fit into categories precisely, because writers sometimes vary traditional forms to create innovative effects. See also OPEN FORM.

Flashback A narrated scene that marks a break in the narrative in order to inform the reader or audience member about events that took place before the opening scene of a work. See also EXPOSITION.

Flat character See CHARACTER.

Foil A character in a work whose behavior and values contrast with those of another character in order to highlight the distinctive temperament of that character (usually the protagonist). In Shakespeare's *Hamlet,* Laertes acts as a foil to Hamlet, because his willingness to act underscores Hamlet's inability to do so.

Foot The metrical unit by which a line of poetry is measured. A foot usually consists of one stressed and one or two unstressed syllables. An *iambic foot,* which consists of one unstressed syllable followed by one stressed syllable ("away"), is the most common metrical foot in English poetry. A *trochaic foot* consists of one stressed syllable followed by an unstressed syllable ("lovely"). An *anapestic foot* is two unstressed syllables followed by one stressed one ("understand"). A *dactylic foot* is one stressed syllable followed by two unstressed ones ("desperate"). A *spondee* is a foot consisting of two stressed syllables ("dead set"), but is not a sustained metrical foot and is used mainly for variety or emphasis. See also IAMBIC PENTAMETER, LINE, METER.

Foreshadowing The introduction early in a story of verbal and dramatic hints that suggest what is to come later.

Form The overall structure or shape of a work, which frequently follows an established design. Forms may refer to a literary type (narrative form, short story form) or to patterns of meter, lines, and rhymes (stanza form, verse form). See also FIXED FORM, OPEN FORM.

Formal diction See DICTION.

Formalist criticism An approach to literature that focuses on the formal elements of a work, such as its language, structure, and tone. Formalist critics offer intense examinations of the relationship between form and meaning in a work, emphasizing the subtle complexity in how a work is arranged. Formalists pay special attention to diction, irony, paradox, metaphor, and symbol, as well as larger elements such as plot, characterization, and narrative technique. Formalist critics read literature as an independent work of art rather than as a reflection of the author's state of mind or as a representation of a moment in history. Therefore, anything outside of the work, including historical influences and authorial intent, is generally not examined by formalist critics. See also NEW CRITICISM.

Formula literature Often characterized as "escape literature," formula literature follows a pattern of conventional reader expectations. Romance novels, westerns, science fiction, and detective stories are all examples of formula literature; while the details of individual stories vary, the basic ingredients of each kind of story are the same. Formula literature offers happy endings (the hero "gets the girl," the detective cracks the case), entertains wide audiences, and sells tremendously well.

Found poem An unintentional poem discovered in a nonpoetic context, such as a conversation, news story, or advertisement. Found poems serve as reminders that everyday language often contains what can be considered poetry, or that poetry is definable as any text read as a poem.

Free verse Also called *open form poetry,* free verse refers to poems characterized by their nonconformity to established patterns of meter, rhyme, and stanza. Free verse uses elements such as speech patterns, grammar, emphasis, and breath pauses to decide line breaks, and usually does not rhyme. See OPEN FORM.

Gay and lesbian criticism An approach to literature that focuses on how homosexuals are represented in literature, how they read literature, and whether sexuality, as well as gender, is culturally constructed or innate. See also FEMINIST CRITICISM, GENDER CRITICISM.

Gender criticism An approach to literature that explores how ideas about men and women—what is masculine and feminine—can be regarded as socially constructed by particular cultures. Gender criticism expands categories and definitions of what is masculine or feminine and tends to regard sexuality as more complex than merely masculine or feminine, heterosexual or homosexual. See also FEMINIST CRITICISM, GAY AND LESBIAN CRITICISM.

Genre A French word meaning kind or type. The major genres in literature are poetry, fiction, drama, and essays. Genre can also refer to more specific types of literature such as comedy, tragedy, epic poetry, or science fiction.

Haiku A style of lyric poetry borrowed from the Japanese that typically presents an intense emotion or vivid image of nature, which, traditionally, is designed to lead to a spiritual insight. Haiku is a fixed poetic form, consisting of seventeen syllables organized into three unrhymed lines of five, seven, and five syllables. Today, however, many poets vary the syllabic count in their haiku. See also FIXED FORM.

Hamartia A term coined by Aristotle to describe "some error or frailty" that brings about misfortune for a tragic hero. The concept of hamartia is closely related to that of the tragic flaw: both lead to the downfall of the protagonist in a tragedy. Hamartia may be interpreted as an internal weakness in a character (like greed or passion or HUBRIS); however, it may also refer to a mistake that a character makes that is based not on a personal failure, but on circumstances outside the protagonist's personality and control. See also TRAGEDY.

Hero, heroine See CHARACTER.

Heroic couplet See COUPLET.

High comedy See COMEDY.

Historical criticism An approach to literature that uses history as a means of understanding a literary work more clearly. Such criticism moves beyond both the facts of an author's personal life and the text itself in order to examine the social and intellectual currents in which the author composed the work. See also CULTURAL CRITICISM, MARXIST CRITICISM, NEW HISTORICISM, POSTCOLONIAL CRITICISM.

Hubris or Hybris Excessive pride or self-confidence that leads a protagonist to disregard a divine warning or to violate an important moral law. In tragedies, hubris is a very common form of hamartia. See also HAMARTIA, TRAGEDY.

Hyperbole A boldly exaggerated statement that adds emphasis without intending to be literally true, as in the statement "He ate everything in the house." Hyperbole (also called **overstatement**) may be used for serious, comic, or ironic effect. See also FIGURES OF SPEECH.

Iambic meter See FOOT.

Iambic pentameter A metrical pattern in poetry which consists of five iambic feet per line. (An iamb, or iambic foot, consists of one unstressed syllable followed by a stressed syllable.) See also FOOT, METER.

Image A word, phrase, or figure of speech (especially a SIMILE or a METAPHOR) that addresses the senses, suggesting mental pictures of sights, sounds, smells, tastes, feelings, or actions. Images offer sensory impressions to the reader and also convey emotions and moods through their verbal pictures. See also FIGURES OF SPEECH.

Implied metaphor See METAPHOR.

In medias res See PLOT.

Informal diction See DICTION.

Internal rhyme See RHYME.

Irony A literary device that uses contradictory statements or situations to reveal a reality different from what appears to be true. It is ironic for a firehouse to burn down, or for a police station to be burglarized. **Verbal irony** is a figure of speech that occurs when a person says one thing but means the opposite. **Sarcasm** is a strong form of verbal irony that is calculated to hurt someone through, for example, false praise. **Dramatic irony** creates a discrepancy between what a character believes or says and what the reader or audience member knows to be true. **Tragic irony** is a form of dramatic irony found in tragedies such as *Oedipus the King*, in which Oedipus searches for the person responsible for the plague that ravishes his city and ironically ends up hunting himself. **Situational irony** exists when there is an incongruity between what is expected to happen and what actually happens due to forces beyond human comprehension or control. The suicide of the seemingly successful main character in Edwin Arlington Robinson's poem "Richard Cory" is an example of situational irony. **Cosmic irony** occurs when a writer uses God, destiny, or fate to dash the hopes and expectations of a character or of humankind in general. In cosmic irony, a discrepancy exists between what a character aspires to and what universal forces provide. Stephen Crane's poem "A Man Said to the Universe" is a good example of cosmic irony, because the universe acknowledges no obligation to the man's assertion of his own existence.

Italian sonnet See SONNET.

Limerick A light, humorous style of fixed form poetry. Its usual form consists of five lines with the rhyme scheme *aabba*; lines 1, 2, and 5 contain three feet, while lines 3 and 4 usually contain two feet. Limericks range in subject matter from the silly to the obscene, and since Edward Lear popularized them in the nineteenth century, children and adults have enjoyed these comic poems. See also FIXED FORM.

Limited omniscience See POINT OF VIEW.

Line A sequence of words printed as a separate entity on the page. In poetry, lines are usually measured by the number of feet they contain. The names for various line lengths are as follows:

monometer: one foot	pentameter: five feet
dimeter: two feet	hexameter: six feet
trimeter: three feet	heptameter: seven feet
tetrameter: four feet	octameter: eight feet

The number of feet in a line, coupled with the name of the foot, describes the metrical qualities of that line. See also END-STOPPED LINE, ENJAMBMENT, FOOT, METER.

Literary ballad See BALLAD.

Literary symbol See SYMBOL.

Low comedy See COMEDY.

Lyric A type of brief poem that expresses the personal emotions and thoughts of a single speaker. It is important to realize, however, that although the lyric is uttered in the first person, the speaker is not necessarily the poet. There are many varieties of lyric poetry, including the DRAMATIC MONOLOGUE, ELEGY, HAIKU, ODE, and SONNET forms.

Marxist criticism An approach to literature that focuses on the ideological content of a work — its explicit and implicit assumptions and values about matters such as culture, race, class, and power. Marxist criticism, based largely on the writings of Karl Marx, typically aims at not only revealing and clarifying ideological issues but also correcting social injustices. Some Marxist critics use literature to describe the competing socioeconomic interests that too often advance capitalist interests such as money and power rather than socialist interests such as morality and justice. They argue that literature and literary criticism are essentially political because they either challenge or support economic oppression. Because of this strong emphasis on the political aspects of texts, Marxist criticism focuses more on the content and themes of literature than on its form. See also CULTURAL CRITICISM, HISTORICAL CRITICISM, SOCIOLOGICAL CRITICISM.

Masculine rhyme See RHYME.

Melodrama A term applied to any literary work that relies on implausible events and sensational action for its effect. The conflicts in melodramas typically arise out of plot rather than characterization; often a virtuous individual must somehow confront and overcome a wicked oppressor. Usually, a melodramatic story ends happily, with the protagonist defeating the antagonist at the last possible moment. Thus, melodramas entertain the reader or audience with exciting action while still conforming to a traditional sense of justice. See SENTIMENTALITY.

Metaphor A metaphor is a figure of speech that makes a comparison between two unlike things, without using the word *like* or *as*. Metaphors assert the identity of dissimilar things, as when Macbeth asserts that life *is* a "brief candle." Metaphors can be subtle and powerful, and can transform people, places, objects, and ideas into whatever the writer imagines them to be. An **implied metaphor** is a more subtle comparison; the terms being compared are not so specifically explained. For example, to describe a stubborn man unwilling to leave, one could say that he was "a mule standing his ground." This is a fairly explicit metaphor; the man is being compared to a mule. But to say that the man "brayed his refusal to leave" is to create an implied metaphor, because the subject (the man) is never overtly identified as a mule. Braying is associated with the mule, a notoriously stubborn creature, and so the comparison between the stubborn man and the mule is sustained. Implied metaphors can slip by inattentive readers who are not sensitive to such carefully chosen, highly concentrated language. An **extended metaphor** is a sustained comparison in which part or all of a poem consists of a series of related metaphors. Robert Francis's poem "Catch" relies on an extended metaphor that compares poetry to playing catch. A **controlling metaphor** runs through an entire work and determines the form or nature of that work. The controlling metaphor in Anne Bradstreet's poem "The Author to Her Book" likens her book to a child. **Synecdoche** is a kind of metaphor in which a part of something is used to signify the whole, as when a gossip is called a "wagging tongue," or when ten ships are called "ten sails." Sometimes, synecdoche refers to the whole being used to signify the part, as in the phrase "Boston won the baseball game." Clearly, the entire city of Boston did not participate in the game; the whole of Boston is being used to signify the individuals who played and won the game. **Metonymy** is a type of metaphor in which something closely associated with a subject is substituted for it. In this way, we speak of the "silver screen" to mean motion pictures, "the crown" to stand for the king, "the White House" to stand for the activities of the president. See also FIGURES OF SPEECH, PERSONIFICATION, SIMILE.

Meter When a rhythmic pattern of stresses recurs in a poem, it is called *meter.* Metrical patterns are determined by the type and number of feet in a line of verse; combining the name of a line length with the name of a foot concisely describes the meter of the line. **Rising meter** refers to metrical feet which move from unstressed to stressed sounds, such as the iambic foot and the anapestic foot. **Falling meter** refers to metrical feet which move from stressed to unstressed sounds, such as the trochaic foot and the dactylic foot. See also ACCENT, FOOT, IAMBIC PENTAMETER, LINE.

Metonymy See METAPHOR.

Middle diction See DICTION.

Motivated action See CHARACTER.

Mythological criticism An approach to literature that seeks to identify what in a work creates deep universal responses in readers, by paying close attention to the hopes, fears, and expectations of entire cultures. Mythological critics (sometimes called *archetypal critics*) look for underlying, recurrent patterns in literature that reveal universal meanings and basic human experiences for readers regardless of when and where they live. These critics attempt to explain how archetypes (the characters, images, and themes that symbolically embody universal meanings and experiences) are embodied in literary works in order to make larger connections that explain a particular work's lasting appeal. Mythological critics may specialize in areas such as classical literature, philology, anthropology, psychology, and cultural history, but they all emphasize the assumptions and values of various cultures. See also ARCHETYPE.

Naive narrator See NARRATOR.

Narrative poem A poem that tells a story. A narrative poem may be short or long, and the story it relates may be simple or complex. See also BALLAD, EPIC.

Narrator The voice of the person telling the story, not to be confused with the author's voice. With a **first-person narrator,** the *I* in the story presents the point of view of only one character. The reader is restricted to the perceptions, thoughts, and feelings of that single character. For example, in Melville's "Bartleby, the Scrivener," the lawyer is the first-person narrator of the story. First-person narrators can play either a major or a minor role in the story they are telling. An **unreliable narrator** reveals an interpretation of events that is somehow different from the author's own interpretation of those events. Often, the unreliable narrator's perception of plot, characters, and setting becomes the actual subject of the story, as in Melville's "Bartleby, the Scrivener." Narrators can be unreliable for a number of reasons: they might lack self-knowledge (like Melville's lawyer), they might be inexperienced, they might even be insane. **Naive narrators** are usually characterized by youthful innocence, such as Mark Twain's Huck Finn or J. D. Salinger's Holden Caulfield. An **omniscient narrator** is an all-knowing narrator who is not a character in the story and who can move from place to place and pass back and forth through time, slipping into and out of characters as no human being possibly could in real life. Omniscient narrators can report the thoughts and feelings of the characters, as well as their words and actions. The narrator of *The Scarlet Letter* is an omniscient narrator. **Editorial omniscience** refers to an intrusion by the narrator in order to evaluate a character for a reader, as when the narrator of *The Scarlet Letter* describes Hester's relationship to the Puritan community. Narration that allows the characters' actions and thoughts to speak for themselves is called **neutral omniscience.** Most modern writers use neutral omniscience so that readers can reach their own conclusions. **Limited omniscience** occurs when an author restricts a narrator to the single perspective of either a major or minor character. The way people, places, and events appear to that character is the way they appear to the reader. Sometimes a limited omniscient narrator can see into more than one character, particularly in a work that focuses on two characters alternately from one chapter to the next. Short stories, however, are frequently limited to a single character's point of view. See also PERSONA, POINT OF VIEW, STREAM-OF-CONSCIOUSNESS TECHNIQUE.

Near rhyme See RHYME.

Neutral omniscience See NARRATOR.

New Criticism An approach to literature made popular between the 1940s and the 1960s that evolved out of formalist criticism. New Critics suggest that detailed analysis of the language of a literary text can uncover important layers of meaning in that work. New Criticism consciously downplays the historical influences, authorial intentions, and social contexts that surround texts in order to focus on explication — extremely close textual analysis. Critics such as John Crowe Ransom, I. A. Richards, and Robert Penn Warren are commonly associated with New Criticism. See also FORMALIST CRITICISM.

New historicism An approach to literature that emphasizes the interaction between the historic context of the work and a modern reader's understanding and interpretation of the work. New historicists attempt to describe the culture of a period by reading many different kinds of texts and paying close attention to many different dimensions of a culture, including political, economic, social, and aesthetic concerns. They regard texts not simply as a reflection of the culture that produced them but also as productive of that culture playing an active role in the social and political conflicts of an age. New historicism acknowledges and then explores various versions of "history," sensitizing us to the fact that the history on which we choose to focus is colored by being reconstructed from our present circumstances. See also HISTORICAL CRITICISM.

Objective point of view See POINT OF VIEW.

Octave A poetic stanza of eight lines, usually forming one part of a sonnet. See also SONNET, STANZA.

Ode A relatively lengthy lyric poem that often expresses lofty emotions in a dignified style. Odes are characterized by a serious topic, such as truth, art, freedom, justice, or the meaning of life; their tone tends to be formal. There is no prescribed pattern that defines an ode; some odes repeat the same pattern in each stanza, while others introduce a new pattern in each stanza. See also LYRIC.

Oedipus complex A Freudian term derived from Sophocles' tragedy *Oedipus the King*. It describes a psychological complex that is predicated on a boy's unconscious rivalry with his father for his mother's love and his desire to eliminate his father in order to take his father's place with his mother. The female equivalent of this complex is called the **Electra complex.** See also ELECTRA COMPLEX, PSYCHOLOGICAL CRITICISM.

Off rhyme See RHYME.

Omniscient narrator See NARRATOR.

One-act play A play that takes place in a single location and unfolds as one continuous action. The characters in a one-act play are presented economically and the action is sharply focused. See also DRAMA.

Onomatopoeia A term referring to the use of a word that resembles the sound it denotes. *Buzz, rattle, bang,* and *sizzle* all reflect onomatopoeia. Onomatopoeia can also consist of more than one word; writers sometimes create lines or whole passages in which the sound of the words helps to convey their meanings.

Open form Sometimes called "free verse," open form poetry does not conform to established patterns of METER, RHYME, and STANZA. Such poetry derives its rhythmic qualities from the repetition of words, phrases, or grammatical structures, the arrangement of words on the printed page, or by some other means. The poet E. E. Cummings wrote open form poetry;

his poems do not have measurable meters, but they do have rhythm. See also FIXED FORM.

Organic form Refers to works whose formal characteristics are not rigidly predetermined but follow the movement of thought or emotion being expressed. Such works are said to grow like living organisms, following their own individual patterns rather than external fixed rules that govern, for example, the form of a SONNET.

Overstatement See HYPERBOLE.

Oxymoron A condensed form of paradox in which two contradictory words are used together, as in "sweet sorrow" or "original copy." See also PARADOX.

Paradox A statement that initially appears to be contradictory but then, on closer inspection, turns out to make sense. For example, John Donne ends his sonnet "Death, Be Not Proud" with the paradoxical statement "Death, thou shalt die." To solve the paradox, it is necessary to discover the sense that underlies the statement. Paradox is useful in poetry because it arrests a reader's attention by its seemingly stubborn refusal to make sense.

Paraphrase A prose restatement of the central ideas of a poem, in your own language.

Parody A humorous imitation of another, usually serious, work. It can take any fixed or open form, because parodists imitate the tone, language, and shape of the original in order to deflate the subject matter, making the original work seem absurd. Anthony Hecht's poem "Dover Bitch" is a famous parody of Matthew Arnold's well-known "Dover Beach." Parody may also be used as a form of literary criticism to expose the defects in a work. But sometimes parody becomes an affectionate acknowledgment that a well-known work has become both institutionalized in our culture and fair game for some fun. For example, Peter De Vries's "To His Importunate Mistress" gently mocks Andrew Marvell's "To His Coy Mistress."

Persona Literally, a *persona* is a mask. In literature, a *persona* is a speaker created by a writer to tell a story or to speak in a poem. A persona is not a character in a story or narrative, nor does a persona necessarily directly reflect the author's personal voice. A persona is a separate self, created by and distinct from the author, through which he or she speaks. See also NARRATOR.

Personification A form of metaphor in which human characteristics are attributed to nonhuman things. Personification offers the writer a way to give the world life and motion by assigning familiar human behaviors and emotions to animals, inanimate objects, and abstract ideas. For example, in Keats's "Ode on a Grecian Urn," the speaker refers to the urn as an "unravished bride of quietness." See also METAPHOR.

Petrarchan sonnet See also SONNET.

Picture poem A type of open form poetry in which the poet arranges the lines of the poem so as to create a particular shape on the page. The shape of the poem embodies its subject; the poem becomes a picture of what the poem is describing. Michael McFee's "In Medias Res" is an example of a picture poem. See also OPEN FORM.

Plausible action See CHARACTER.

Play See DRAMA.

Playwright See DRAMA.

Plot An author's selection and arrangement of incidents in a story to shape the action and give the story a particular focus. Discussions of plot include not just what happens, but also how and why things happen the way they do. Stories that are written in a **pyramidal pattern** divide the plot into three essential parts. The first part is the **rising action,** in which complication creates some sort of conflict for the protagonist. The second part is the **climax,** the moment of greatest emotional tension in a narrative, usually marking a turning point in the plot at which the rising action reverses to become the falling action. The third part, the **falling action** (or RESOLUTION) is characterized by diminishing tensions and the resolution of the plot's conflicts and complications. *In medias res* is a term used to describe the common strategy of beginning a story in the middle of the action. In this type of plot, we enter the story on the verge of some important moment. See also CHARACTER, CRISIS, RESOLUTION, SUBPLOT.

Poetic diction See DICTION.

Point of view Refers to who tells us a story and how it is told. What we know and how we feel about the events in a work are shaped by the author's choice of point of view. The teller of the story, the narrator, inevitably affects our understanding of the characters' actions by filtering what is told through his or her own perspective. The various points of view that writers draw upon can be grouped into two broad categories: (1) the third-person narrator uses *he, she,* or *they* to tell the story and does not participate in the action; and (2) the first-person narrator uses *I* and is a major or minor participant in the action. In addition, a second-person narrator, *you,* is also possible, but is rarely used because of the awkwardness of thrusting the reader into the story, as in "You are minding your own business on a park bench when a drunk steps out and demands your lunch bag." An **objective point of view** employs a third-person narrator who does not see into the mind of any character. From this detached and impersonal perspective, the narrator reports action and dialogue without telling us directly what the characters think and feel. Since no analysis or interpretation is provided by the narrator, this point of view places a premium on dialogue, actions, and details to reveal character to the reader. See also NARRATOR, STREAM-OF-CONSCIOUSNESS TECHNIQUE.

Postcolonial criticism An approach to literature that focuses on the study of cultural behavior and expression in relationship to the colonized world. Postcolonial criticism refers to the analysis of literary works written by writers from countries and cultures that at one time have been controlled by colonizing powers — such as Indian writers during or after British colonial rule. Postcolonial criticism also refers to the analysis of literary works written about colonial cultures by writers from the colonizing country. Many of these kinds of analyses point out how writers from colonial powers sometimes misrepresent colonized cultures by reflecting more their own values. See also CULTURAL CRITICISM, HISTORICAL CRITICISM, MARXIST CRITICISM.

Problem play Popularized by Henrik Ibsen, a problem play is a type of drama that presents a social issue in order to awaken the audience to it. These plays usually reject romantic plots in favor of holding up a mirror that reflects not simply what the audience wants to see but what the playwright sees in them. Often, a problem play will propose a solution to the problem that does not coincide with prevailing opinion. The term is also used to refer to certain Shakespeare plays that do not fit the categories of tragedy, comedy, or romance. See also DRAMA.

Prologue The opening speech or dialogue of a play, especially a classic Greek play, that usually gives the exposition necessary to follow the subsequent action. Today the term also refers to the introduction to any literary work. See also DRAMA, EXPOSITION.

Prose poem A kind of open form poetry that is printed as prose and represents the most clear opposite of fixed form poetry. Prose poems are densely compact and often make use of striking imagery and figures of speech. See also FIXED FORM, OPEN FORM.

Prosody The overall metrical structure of a poem. See also METER.

Protagonist The main character of a narrative; its central character who engages the reader's interest and empathy. See also CHARACTER.

Psychological criticism An approach to literature that draws upon psycho-analytic theories, especially those of Sigmund Freud or Jacques Lacan to understand more fully the text, the writer, and the reader. The basis of this approach is the idea of the existence of a human unconscious—those impulses, desires, and feelings about which a person is unaware but which influence emotions and behavior. Critics use psychological approaches to explore the motivations of characters and the symbolic meanings of events, while biographers speculate about a writer's own motivations—conscious or unconscious—in a literary work. Psychological approaches are also used to describe and analyze the reader's personal responses to a text.

Pun A play on words that relies on a word's having more than one meaning or sounding like another word. Shakespeare and other writers use puns extensively, for serious and comic purposes; in *Romeo and Juliet* (III.i.101), the dying Mercutio puns, "Ask for me tomorrow and you shall find me a grave man." Puns have serious literary uses, but since the eighteenth century, puns have been used almost purely for humorous effect. See also COMEDY.

Pyramidal pattern See PLOT.

Quatrain A four-line stanza. Quatrains are the most common stanzaic form in the English language; they can have various meters and rhyme schemes. See also METER, RHYME, STANZA.

Reader-response criticism An approach to literature that focuses on the reader rather than the work itself, by attempting to describe what goes on in the reader's mind during the reading of a text. Hence, the consciousness of the reader—produced by reading the work—is the actual subject of reader-response criticism. These critics are not after a "correct" reading of the text or what the author presumably intended; instead, they are interested in the reader's individual experience with the text. Thus, there is no single definitive reading of a work, because readers create rather than discover absolute meanings in texts. However, this approach is not a rationale for mistaken or bizarre readings, but an exploration of the possibilities for a plurality of readings. This kind of strategy calls attention to how we read and what influences our readings, and what that reveals about ourselves.

Recognition The moment in a story when previously unknown or withheld information is revealed to the protagonist, resulting in the discovery of the truth of his or her situation and, usually, a decisive change in course for that character. In *Oedipus the King*, the moment of recognition comes when Oedipus finally realizes that he has killed his father and married his mother.

Resolution The conclusion of a plot's conflicts and complications. The resolution, also known as the **falling action**, follows the climax in the plot. See also DÉNOUEMENT, PLOT.

Revenge tragedy See TRAGEDY.

Reversal The point in a story when the protagonist's fortunes turn in an unexpected direction. See also PLOT.

Rhyme The repetition of identical or similar concluding syllables in different words, most often at the ends of lines. Rhyme is predominantly a function of sound rather than spelling; thus, words that end with the same vowel sounds rhyme, for instance, *day, prey, bouquet, weigh,* and words with the same consonant ending rhyme, for instance *vain, feign, rein, lane*. Words do not have to be spelled the same way or look alike to rhyme. In fact, words may look alike but not rhyme at all. This is called **eye rhyme**, as with *bough* and *cough*, or *brow* and *blow*. **End rhyme** is the most common form of rhyme in poetry; the rhyme comes at the end of the lines.

> It runs through the reeds
>   And away it proceeds,
> Through meadow and glade,
>   In sun and in shade.

The **rhyme scheme** of a poem describes the pattern of end rhymes. Rhyme schemes are mapped out by noting patterns of rhyme with small letters: the first rhyme sound is designated *a*, the second becomes *b*, the third *c*, and so on. Thus, the rhyme scheme of the stanza above is *aabb*. **Internal rhyme** places at least one of the rhymed words within the line, as in "Dividing and gliding and sliding" or "In mist or cloud, on mast or shroud." **Masculine rhyme** describes the rhyming of single-syllable words, such as *grade* or *shade*. Masculine rhyme also occurs where rhyming words of more than one syllable, when the same sound occurs in a final stressed syllable, as in *defend* and *contend, betray* and *away*. **Feminine rhyme** consists of a rhymed stressed syllable followed by one or more identical unstressed syllables, as in *butter, clutter; gratitude, attitude; quivering, shivering*. All the examples so far have illustrated **exact rhymes**, because they share the same stressed vowel sounds as well as sharing sounds that follow the vowel. In **near rhyme** (also called **off rhyme, slant rhyme,** and **approximate rhyme**), the sounds are almost but not exactly alike. A common form of near rhyme is CONSONANCE, which consists of identical consonant sounds preceded by different vowel sounds: *home, same; worth, breath*.

Rhyme scheme See RHYME.

Rhythm A term used to refer to the recurrence of stressed and unstressed sounds in poetry. Depending on how sounds are arranged, the rhythm of a poem may be fast or slow, choppy or smooth. Poets use rhythm to create pleasurable sound patterns and to reinforce meanings. Rhythm in prose arises from pattern repetitions of sounds and pauses that create looser rhythmic effects. See also METER.

Rising action See PLOT.

Rising meter See METER.

Romantic comedy See COMEDY.

Round character See CHARACTER.

Run-on line See ENJAMBMENT.

Sarcasm See IRONY.

Satire The literary art of ridiculing a folly or vice in order to expose or correct it. The object of satire is usually some human frailty; people, institutions, ideas, and things are all fair game for satirists. Satire evokes attitudes of amusement, contempt, scorn, or indignation toward its faulty subject in the hope of somehow improving it. See also IRONY, PARODY.

Scansion The process of measuring the stresses in a line of verse in order to determine the metrical pattern of the line. See also LINE, METER.

Scene In drama, a scene is a subdivision of an ACT. In modern plays, scenes usually consist of units of action in which there are no changes in the setting or breaks in the continuity of time. According to traditional conventions, a scene changes when the location of the action shifts or when a new character enters. See also ACT, CONVENTION, DRAMA.

Script The written text of a play, which includes the dialogue between characters, stage directions, and often other expository information. See also DRAMA, EXPOSITION, PROLOGUE, STAGE DIRECTIONS.

Sentimentality A pejorative term used to describe the effort by an author to induce emotional responses in the reader that exceed what the situation warrants. Sentimentality especially pertains to such emotions as pathos and sympathy; it cons readers into falling for the mass murderer who is devoted to stray cats, and it requires that readers do not examine such illogical responses. Clichés and stock responses are the key ingredients of sentimentality in literature. See also CLICHÉ, STOCK RESPONSES.

Sestet A stanza consisting of exactly six lines. See also STANZA.

Sestina A type of fixed form poetry consisting of thirty-six lines of any length divided into six sestets and a three-line concluding stanza called an ENVOY. The six words at the end of the first sestet's lines must also appear at the ends of the other five sestets, in varying order. These six words must also appear in the envoy, where they often resonate important themes. An example of this highly demanding form of poetry is Elizabeth Bishop's "Sestina." See also SESTET.

Setting The physical and social context in which the action of a story occurs. The major elements of setting are the time, the place, and the social environment that frames the characters. Setting can be used to evoke a mood or atmosphere that will prepare the reader for what is to come, as in Nathaniel Hawthorne's short story "Young Goodman Brown." Sometimes, writers choose a particular setting because of traditional associations with that setting that are closely related to the action of a story. For example, stories filled with adventure or romance often take place in exotic locales.

Shakespearean sonnet See SONNET.

Showing See CHARACTER.

Simile A common figure of speech that makes an explicit comparison between two things by using words such as *like, as, than, appears,* and *seems:* "A sip of Mrs. Cook's coffee is like a punch in the stomach." The effectiveness of this simile is created by the differences between the two things compared. There would be no simile if the comparison were stated this way: "Mrs. Cook's coffee is as strong as the cafeteria's coffee." This is a literal translation because Mrs. Cook's coffee is compared with something like it — another kind of coffee. See also FIGURES OF SPEECH, METAPHOR.

Situational irony See IRONY.

Slant rhyme See RHYME.

Sociological criticism An approach to literature that examines social groups, relationships, and values as they are manifested in literature. Sociological approaches emphasize the nature and effect of the social forces that shape power relationships between groups or classes of people. Such readings treat literature as either a document reflecting social conditions or a product of those conditions. The former view brings into focus the social milieu; the latter emphasizes the work. Two important forms of sociological criticism are Marxist and feminist approaches. See also FEMINIST CRITICISM, MARXIST CRITICISM.

Soliloquy A dramatic convention by means of which a character, alone onstage, utters his or her thoughts aloud. Playwrights use soliloquies as a convenient way to inform the audience about a character's motivations and state of mind. Shakespeare's Hamlet delivers perhaps the best known of all soliloquies, which begins: "To be or not to be." See also ASIDE, CONVENTION.

Sonnet A fixed form of lyric poetry that consists of fourteen lines, usually written in iambic pentameter. There are two basic types of sonnets, the Italian and the English. The **Italian sonnet,** also known as the **Petrarchan sonnet,** is divided into an octave, which typically rhymes *abbaabba,* and a sestet, which may have varying rhyme schemes. Common rhyme patterns in the sestet are *cdecde, cdcdcd,* and *cdccdc.* Very often the octave presents a situation, attitude, or problem that the sestet comments upon or resolves, as in John Keats's "On First Looking into Chapman's Homer." The **English sonnet,** also known as the **Shakespearean sonnet,** is organized into three quatrains and a couplet, which typically rhyme *abab cdcd efef gg.* This rhyme scheme is more suited to English poetry because English has fewer rhyming words than Italian. English sonnets, because of their four-part organization, also have more flexibility with respect to where thematic breaks can occur. Frequently, however, the most pronounced break or turn comes with the concluding couplet, as in Shakespeare's "Shall I compare thee to a

summer's day?" See also COUPLET, IAMBIC PENTAMETER, LINE, OCTAVE, QUA-
TRAIN, SESTET.

Speaker The voice used by an author to tell a story or speak a poem. The
speaker is often a created identity, and should not automatically be equated
with the author's self. See also NARRATOR, PERSONA, POINT OF VIEW.

Spondee See FOOT.

Stage directions A playwright's written instructions about how the actors
are to move and behave in a play. They explain in which direction characters
should move, what facial expressions they should assume, and so on. See
also DRAMA, SCRIPT.

Stanza In poetry, *stanza* refers to a grouping of lines, set off by a space, that
usually has a set pattern of meter and rhyme. See also LINE, METER, RHYME.

Static character See CHARACTER.

Stock character See CHARACTER.

Stock responses Predictable, conventional reactions to language, characters,
symbols, or situations. The flag, motherhood, puppies, God, and peace are
common objects used to elicit stock responses from unsophisticated audiences. See also CLICHÉ, SENTIMENTALITY.

Stream-of-consciousness technique The most intense use of a central consciousness in narration. The stream-of-consciousness technique takes a
reader inside a character's mind to reveal perceptions, thoughts, and feelings on a conscious or unconscious level. This technique suggests the flow
of thought as well as its content; hence, complete sentences may give way to
fragments as the character's mind makes rapid associations free of conventional logic or transitions. James Joyce's novel *Ulysses* makes extensive use of
this narrative technique. See also NARRATOR, POINT OF VIEW.

Stress The emphasis, or accent, given a syllable in pronunciation. See also
ACCENT.

Style The distinctive and unique manner in which a writer arranges words to
achieve particular effects. Style essentially combines the idea to be expressed with the individuality of the author. These arrangements include
individual word choices as well as matters such as the length of sentences,
their structure, tone, and use of irony. See also DICTION, IRONY, TONE.

Subplot The secondary action of a story, complete and interesting in its own
right, that reinforces or contrasts with the main plot. There may be more
than one subplot, and sometimes as many as three, four, or even more, running through a piece of fiction. Subplots are generally either analogous to
the main plot, thereby enhancing our understanding of it, or extraneous to
the main plot, to provide relief from it. See also PLOT.

Suspense The anxious anticipation of a reader or an audience as to the outcome of a story, especially concerning the character or characters with
whom sympathetic attachments are formed. Suspense helps to secure and
sustain the interest of the reader or audience throughout a work.

Symbol A person, object, image, word, or event that evokes a range of additional meaning beyond and usually more abstract than its literal signifi-

cance. Symbols are educational devices for evoking complex ideas without having to resort to painstaking explanations that would make a story more like an essay than an experience. **Conventional symbols** have meanings that are widely recognized by a society or culture. Some conventional symbols are the Christian cross, the Star of David, a swastika, or a nation's flag. Writers use conventional symbols to reinforce meanings. Kate Chopin, for example, emphasizes the spring setting in "The Story of an Hour" as a way of suggesting the renewed sense of life that Mrs. Mallard feels when she thinks herself free from her husband. A **literary** or **contextual symbol** can be a setting, character, action, object, name, or anything else in a work that maintains its literal significance while suggesting other meanings. Such symbols go beyond conventional symbols; they gain their symbolic meaning within the context of a specific story. For example, the white whale in Melville's *Moby-Dick* takes on multiple symbolic meanings in the work, but these meanings do not automatically carry over into other stories about whales. The meanings suggested by Melville's whale are specific to that text; therefore, it becomes a contextual symbol. See also ALLEGORY.

Synecdoche See METAPHOR.

Syntax The ordering of words into meaningful verbal patterns such as phrases, clauses, and sentences. Poets often manipulate syntax, changing conventional word order, to place certain emphasis on particular words. Emily Dickinson, for instance, writes about being surprised by a snake in her poem "A narrow Fellow in the Grass," and includes this line: "His notice sudden is." In addition to the alliterative hissing *s*-sounds here, Dickinson also effectively manipulates the line's syntax so that the verb *is* appears unexpectedly at the end, making the snake's hissing presence all the more "sudden."

Telling See CHARACTER.

Tercet A three-line stanza. See also STANZA, TRIPLET.

Terza rima An interlocking three-line rhyme scheme: *aba, bcb, cdc, ded,* and so on. Dante's *The Divine Comedy* and Frost's "Acquainted with the Night" are written in terza rima. See also RHYME, TERCET.

Theme The central meaning or dominant idea in a literary work. A theme provides a unifying point around which the plot, characters, setting, point of view, symbols, and other elements of a work are organized. It is important not to mistake the theme for the actual subject of the work; the theme refers to the abstract concept that is made concrete through the images, characterization, and action of the text. In nonfiction, however, the theme generally refers to the main topic of the discourse.

Thesis The central idea of an essay. The thesis is a complete sentence (although sometimes it may require more than one sentence) that establishes the topic of the essay in clear, unambiguous language.

Tone The author's implicit attitude toward the reader or the people, places, and events in a work as revealed by the elements of the author's style. Tone may be characterized as serious or ironic, sad or happy, private or public, angry or affectionate, bitter or nostalgic, or any other attitudes and feelings that human beings experience. See also STYLE.

Tragedy A story that presents courageous individuals who confront powerful forces within or outside themselves with a dignity that reveals the breadth and depth of the human spirit in the face of failure, defeat, and even death. Tragedies recount an individual's downfall; they usually begin high and end low. Shakespeare is known for his tragedies, including *Macbeth, King Lear, Othello,* and *Hamlet.* The **revenge tragedy** is a well-established type of drama that can be traced back to Greek and Roman plays, particularly through the Roman playwright Seneca (c. 3 B.C.–A.D. 63). Revenge tragedies basically consist of a murder that has to be avenged by a relative of the victim. Typically, the victim's ghost appears to demand revenge, and invariably madness of some sort is worked into subsequent events, which ultimately end in the deaths of the murderer, the avenger, and a number of other characters. Shakespeare's *Hamlet* subscribes to the basic ingredients of revenge tragedy, but it also transcends these conventions because Hamlet contemplates not merely revenge but suicide and the meaning of life itself. A **tragic flaw** is an error or defect in the tragic hero that leads to his downfall, such as greed, pride, or ambition. This flaw may be a result of bad character, bad judgment, an inherited weakness, or any other defect of character. **Tragic irony** is a form of dramatic irony found in tragedies such as *Oedipus the King,* in which Oedipus ironically ends up hunting himself. See also COMEDY, DRAMA.

Tragic flaw See TRAGEDY.

Tragic irony See IRONY, TRAGEDY.

Tragicomedy A type of drama that combines certain elements of both tragedy and comedy. The play's plot tends to be serious, leading to a terrible catastrophe, until an unexpected turn in events leads to a reversal of circumstance, and the story ends happily. Tragicomedy often employs a romantic, fast-moving plot dealing with love, jealousy, disguises, treachery, intrigue, and surprises, all moving toward a melodramatic resolution. Shakespeare's *Merchant of Venice* is a tragicomedy. See also COMEDY, DRAMA, MELODRAMA, TRAGEDY.

Triplet A tercet in which all three lines rhyme. See also TERCET.

Trochaic meter See FOOT.

Understatement The opposite of hyperbole, *understatement* (or litotes) refers to a figure of speech that says less than is intended. Understatement usually has an ironic effect, and sometimes may be used for comic purposes, as in Mark Twain's statement, "The reports of my death are greatly exaggerated." See also HYPERBOLE, IRONY.

Unreliable narrator See NARRATOR.

Verbal irony See IRONY.

Verse A generic term used to describe poetic lines composed in a measured rhythmical pattern, that are often, but not necessarily, rhymed. See also LINE, METER, RHYME, RHYTHM.

Villanelle A type of fixed form poetry consisting of nineteen lines of any length divided into six stanzas: five tercets and a concluding quatrain. The first and third lines of the initial tercet rhyme; these rhymes are repeated in each subsequent tercet (*aba*) and in the final two lines of the quatrain (*abaa*). Line 1 appears in its entirety as lines 6, 12, and 18, while line 3 reappears as lines 9, 15, and 19. Dylan Thomas's "Do not go gentle into that good night" is a villanelle. See also FIXED FORM, QUATRAIN, RHYME, TERCET.

Well-made play A realistic style of play that employs conventions including plenty of suspense created by meticulous plotting. Well-made plays are tightly and logically constructed, and lead to a logical resolution that is favorable to the protagonist. This dramatic structure was popularized in France by Eugène Scribe (1791–1861) and Victorien Sardou (1831–1908) and was adopted by Henrik Ibsen. See also CHARACTER, PLOT.

Acknowledgments (continued from p. iv)

Anonymous. "A Nineteenth-Century Husband's Letter to His Wife," translated by Hans Panofsky. Original German text in the Archive of the Leo Baeck Institute, New York. Reprinted by permission of the Leo Baeck Institute and Margaret A. Panofsky.

Margaret Atwood. "Bored" from *Morning in the Burned House* by Margaret Atwood. Copyright © 1995 by Margaret Atwood. Used by permission of Houghton Mifflin Company and by written permission of McClelland & Stewart, Inc., *The Canadian Publishers*. All rights reserved. "Death by Landscape" from *Wilderness Tips* by Margaret Atwood. Copyright © 1991 by O.W. Toad Limited. Used by permission of Doubleday, a Division of Random House, Inc., and by written permission of McClelland & Stewart, Inc., *The Canadian Publishers*.

Jimmy Santiago Baca. "Green Chile" from *Black Mesa Poems*. Copyright © 1989 by Jimmy Santiago Baca. Reprinted by permission of New Directions Publishing Corp.

Alison Baker. "Better Be Ready 'Bout Half Past Eight" from *How I Came West and Why I Stayed* by Alison Baker. Copyright © 1993 by Allison Baker. Reprinted by permission of Brandt & Brandt Literary Agents, Inc.

Toni Cade Bambara. "The Lesson" from *Gorilla, My Love* by Toni Cade Bambara. Copyright © 1972 by Toni Cade Bambara. Reprinted by permission of Random House, Inc.

Helen Barolini. "How I Learned to Speak Italian" from *Chiaroscuro: Essays of Identity* by Helen Barolini (Madison: University of Wisconsin Press, 1999), pp. 25-37. Originally published in *Southwest Review* (Winter 1997). Reprinted by permission of *Southwest Review*.

Regina Barreca. "Envy" from *Too Much of a Good Thing Is Wonderful* by Regina Barreca. Copyright © 2000 by Regina Barreca. "Nighttime Fires" from *The Minnesota Review* (Fall, 1986). Both poems reprinted by permission of the author.

Elizabeth Bishop. "The Fish" from *The Complete Poems 1927–1979* by Elizabeth Bishop. Copyright © 1979, 1983 by Alice Helen Methfessel. Reprinted by permission of Farrar, Straus and Giroux, LLC.

Robert Bly. "The Man Who Didn't Know What Was His" from *Morning Poems* by Robert Bly (New York: HarperCollins, 1997). Copyright © 1997 by Robert Bly. Reprinted by permission of George Borchardt, Inc., for the author.

T. Coraghessan Boyle. "Carnal Knowledge" from *Without a Hero* by T. Coraghessan Boyle. Copyright © 1994 by T. Coraghessan Boyle. Used by permission of Viking Penguin, a Division of Penguin Putnam Inc.

Gwendolyn Brooks. "The Mother" from *Blacks*. Copyright © 1991 by Gwendolyn Brooks Blakely. Reprinted by permission of the author.

Diane Burns. "Sure You Can Ask Me a Personal Question" from *Riding the One-Eyed Ford* by Diane Burns. Reprinted in Lawana Trout, ed., *Native American Literature* (NTC/Contemporary Publishing Group, 1999). Used with permission of NTC/Contemporary Publishing Group Inc.

Edgar Rice Burroughs. Excerpt from *Tarzan of the Apes* by Edgar Rice Burroughs. Copyright ©1912 by Frank A. Munsey Company, used by permission of Edgar Rice Burroughs, Inc.

Raymond Carver. "Popular Mechanics" from *What We Talk about When We Talk about Love* by Raymond Carver. Copyright © 1981 by Raymond Carver. Reprinted by permission of Alfred A. Knopf, a Division of Random House, Inc.

Linda Chavez. "Demystifying Multiculturalism" from *National Review,* February 21, 1994. Copyright © 1994 by National Review, Inc., 215 Lexington Avenue, New York, NY 10016. Reprinted by permission.

John Cheever. "Reunion" from *The Stories of John Cheever* by John Cheever. Copyright © 1962 by John Cheever. Reprinted by permission of Alfred A. Knopf, a Division of Random House, Inc.

Anton Chekhov. "The Lady with the Pet Dog" from *The Portable Chekhov* by Anton Chekhov, edited by Avrahm Yarmolinsky. Copyright © 1947, © 1968 by Viking Penguin, Inc. Renewed © 1975 by Avrahm Yarmolinsky. Used by permission of Viking Penguin, a Division of Penguin Putnam Inc.

Ann Choi. "The Shower" from *The Asian American Literary Reader* 4 (1991) by permission of the poet.

Judith Ortiz Cofer. "Advanced Biology" from *The Latin Deli: Prose and Poetry* by Judith Ortiz Cofer. Copyright © 1993 by Judith Ortiz Cofer. Reprinted by permission of The University of Georgia Press. "Common Ground" by Judith Ortiz Cofer is reprinted with permission from the publisher of *Silent Dancing: A Partial Remembrance of a Puerto Rican Childhood* (Houston: Arte Público Press–University of Houston, 1990).

K. C. Cole. "Calculated Risks" from *The Universe and the Teacup: The Mathematics of Truth and Beauty* by K. C. Cole. Copyright © 1998 by K. C. Cole. Reprinted by permission of Harcourt, Inc.

Colette. "The Hand" from *The Collected Stories of Colette,* edited by Robert Phelps, and translated by Matthew Ward. Translation copyright © 1983 by Farrar, Straus and Giroux, Inc. Reprinted by permission of Farrar, Straus and Giroux, LLC.

Bernard Cooper, "A Clack of Tiny Sparks: Remembrances of a Gay Boyhood." Copyright © 1990 by *Harper's Magazine*. All rights reserved. Reproduced from the January 1991 issue by special permission.

Sally Croft. "Home-Baked Bread" from *Light Year '86*. Reprinted by permission of the author.

E. E. Cummings. "in Just-," Copyright © 1923, 1951, © 1991 by the Trustees for the E. E. Cummings Trust. Copyright © 1976 by George James Firmage. "l(a," Copyright © 1958, 1986, 1991 by the Trustees for the E. E. Cummings Trust. "since feeling is first," Copyright © 1926, 1954, © 1991 by the Trustees for the E. E. Cummings Trust, Copyright © 1985 by George James Firmage. From *Complete Poems: 1904–1962* by E. E. Cummings, edited by George J. Firmage. Used by permission of Liveright Publishing Corporation.

Jim Daniels. "Short-Order Cook" from *Places/Everyone*. Winner of the 1985 Brittingham Prize in Poetry. Copyright © 1985. Reprinted by permission of The University of Wisconsin Press.

James Dickey. "Deer Among Cattle" from *Poems, 1957–1967,* Copyright © 1978 by James Dickey, Wesleyan University Press. Reprinted by permission of University Press of New England.

Emily Dickinson. "A Bird came down the Walk—," "A Light exists in Spring," "A narrow Fellow in the Grass," "From all the Jails the Boys and Girls," "I never saw a Moor—," "If I shouldn't be alive," and "Much Madness is divinest Sense—," from *The Poems of Emily Dickinson,* Ralph W. Franklin, ed., Cambridge, Mass.: The Belknap Press of Harvard University Press, Copyright © 1951, 1955, 1979 by the President and Fellows of Harvard College. Reprinted by permission of the publishers and the Trustees of Amherst College.

Chitra Banerjee Divakaruni. "Indian Movie, New Jersey" from the *Indiana Review,* 1990. Copyright © by Chitra Banerjee Divakaruni. Reprinted by permission of the author.

Gregory Djanikian. "When I First Saw Snow." Reprinted from Gregory Djanikian: *Falling Deeply into America* by permission of Carnegie Mellon University Press. Copyright © 1989 by Gregory Djanikian.

Andre Dubus. "Killings" from *Finding a Girl in America* by Andre Dubus. Copyright © 1980 by Andre Dubus. Reprinted by permission of David R. Godine, Publisher, Inc.

George Eliot, "In a London Drawingroom" from the George Eliot and George Henry Lewes Collection, Beinecke Rare Book and Manuscript Library, Yale University. Reprinted in *George Eliot, Collected Poems,* ed. Lucien Jenkins. Skoob Books LTD, London, 1989. Reprinted by permission.

Ralph Ellison. "Battle Royal" from *Invisible Man* by Ralph Ellison. Copyright © 1948 by Ralph Ellison. Reprinted by permission of Random House, Inc.

Louise Erdrich. "I'm a Mad Dog Biting Myself for Sympathy." Copyright © 1990 by Louise Erdrich. Reprinted with permission of the Wylie Agency, Inc. No changes shall be made to the text of this work without the express written consent of the Wylie Agency, Inc. No further use of this material shall be made without the express written consent of the Wylie Agency, Inc.

Martín Espada. "Coca-Cola and Coco Frío" from *City of Coughing and Dead Radiators* by Martín Espada. Copyright © 1993 by Martín Espada. Used by permission of W. W. Norton & Company, Inc. "Latin Night at the Pawnshop" from *Rebellion Is the Circle of a Lover's Hands* by Martín Espada. Curbstone Press, 1990. Reprinted by permission of Curbstone Press. Distributed by Consortium.

Ruth Fainlight. "Flower Feet" from *Selected Poems* by Ruth Fainlight. Copyright © 1989 by Ruth Fainlight. Originally appeared in *The New Yorker.* Reprinted by permission of the author.

William Faulkner, "A Rose for Emily" from *Collected Stories of William Faulkner* by William Faulkner. Copyright © 1930 and renewed 1958 by William Faulkner. "Barn Burning" from *Collected Stories of William Faulkner* by William Faulkner. Copyright © 1950 by Random House, Inc., and renewed 1977 by Jill Faulkner Summers. Reprinted by permission of Random House, Inc.

Kenneth Fearing. "AD" from *Kenneth Fearing Complete Poems,* ed. by Robert Ryely (Orono, ME: National Poetry Foundation, 1997). Reprinted by permission of the National Poetry Foundation.

Carolyn Forché. "The Colonel" from *The Country Between Us* by Carolyn Forché. Copyright © 1981 by Carolyn Forché. Originally appeared in *Women's International Resource Exchange.* Reprinted by permission of HarperCollins Publishers, Inc.

Robert Francis. "Catch" from *The Orb Weaver.* Copyright © 1960 by Robert Francis, Wesleyan University Press. Reprinted by permission of University Press of New England.

Robert Frost. "Acquainted with the Night" and "Design" from *The Poetry of Robert Frost,* edited by Edward Connery Lathem. Copyright © 1928, 1969 by Henry Holt and Co., Copyright © 1936, 1956 by Robert Frost, Copyright © 1964, 1970 by Lesley Frost Ballantine. Reprinted by permission of Henry Holt & Company, LLC.

Dagoberto Gilb. "Love in L.A." from *The Magic of Blood* by Dagoberto Gilb. Copyright © 1993 by the University of New Mexico Press. Story originally published in *Buffalo.* Reprinted by permission of the University of New Mexico Press.

Nikki Giovanni. "Clouds" from *Blues: For All the Changes* by Nikki Giovanni. Copyright © 1999 by Nikki Giovanni. Reprinted by permission of HarperCollins Publishers, Inc. William Morrow.

Gail Godwin. "A Sorrowful Woman," published in 1971 by *Esquire* Magazine. Copyright © 1971 by Gail Godwin. Reprinted by permission of John Hawkins & Associates, Inc.

Marilyn Hacker. "Groves of Academe" from *Winter Numbers* by Marilyn Hacker. Copyright © 1994 by Marilyn Hacker. Used by permission of the author and W. W. Norton & Company, Inc.

Rachel Hadas. "The Red Hat" from *Halfway Down the Hall,* Copyright © 1998 by Rachel Hadas, Wesleyan University Press. Reprinted by permission of University Press of New England.

Donald Hall. "Letter with No Address" from *Without* by Donald Hall. Copyright © 1998 by Donald Hall. Reprinted by permission of Houghton Mifflin Company. All rights reserved.

Mark Halliday. "Graded Paper" from *The Michigan Quarterly Review.* "Young Man on Sixth Avenue" from *The Pushcart Prize XXI: 1997 Best of the Small Presses* (Pushcart Press, 1996), pp. 358–60. Originally appeared in *Chicago Review* 1995. Copyright © 1995 by Mark Halliday. Reprinted by permission of the author.

Lorraine Hansberry. *A Raisin in the Sun.* Copyright © 1959 by Robert Nemiroff, as an unpublished work. Copyright © 1959, 1966, 1984 by Robert Nemiroff. Reprinted by permission of Random House, Inc.

Robert Hass. "A Story About the Body" from *Human Wishes* by Robert Hass. Copyright © 1989 by Robert Hass. Reprinted by permission of HarperCollins Publishers, Inc.

William Hathaway. "Oh, Oh" from *Light Year '86.* This poem was originally published in *The Cincinnati Poetry Review.* Reprinted by permission of the author.

Robert Hayden. "Those Winter Sundays," Copyright © 1966, by Robert Hayden, from *Angle of Ascent: New and Selected Poems* by Robert Hayden. Used by permission of Liveright Publishing Corporation.

Judy Page Heitzman, "The Schoolroom on the Second Floor of the Knitting Mill." Copyright © 1991 by Judy Page Heitzman. Originally appeared in *The New Yorker,* December 2, 1992. Reprinted by permission of the author.

Robert Morgan. "Mountain Graveyard" from *Sigodlin*, Copyright © 1990 by Robert Morgan, Wesleyan University Press. Reprinted by permission of University Press of New England.

Bharati Mukherjee. "A Father" from *Darkness* by Bharati Mukherjee. Copyright © 1985 by Bharati Mukherjee. Reprinted by permission of the author.

Alice Munro. "An Ounce of Cure" originally published in *Dance of the Happy Shades* by Alice Munro; originally published by McGraw-Hill Ryerson Limited, Copyright © 1968. Reprinted by permission of The Writers Shop and McGraw-Hill Ryerson. All rights reserved.

Joan Murray. "Play-By-Play." Reprinted by permission from *The Hudson Review*, Vol. XLIX, No. 4 (Winter 1997). Copyright © 1997 by Joan Murray.

Gloria Naylor. "Taking Possession of a Word." Copyright © 1986 by Gloria Naylor. Reprinted by permission of Sterling Lord Literistic, Inc.

Pablo Neruda. "Juventud" from *Neruda & Vallejo: Selected Poems*. Ed. Robert Bly. Beacon Press, 1993. Reprinted by permission of Carmen Balcells Literary Agency, Barcelona, Spain, on behalf of the Pablo Neruda Foundation of Chile. "Youth", trans. Robert Bly, from *Neruda & Vallejo: Selected Poems*. Ed. Robert Bly. Beacon Press, 1993. Reprinted by permission of Robert Bly. "Youth" from *Canto General, Fiftieth Anniversary Edition* by Pablo Neruda, translated/edited by Jack Schmitt. Copyright © 1991 Fundacion Pablo Neruda. Reprinted by permission of the publisher, the University of California Press. "Sweetness, Always" from *Extravagaria* by Pablo Neruda, translated by Alastair Reid. Translation Copyright © 1974 by Alastair Reid. Reprinted by permission of Farrar, Straus and Giroux, LLC.

Fae Myenne Ng. "A Red Sweater." Originally appeared in *The American Voice*, 1987. Reprinted by permission of Donadio & Olson, Inc. Copyright © 1987 by Fae Myenne Ng.

Alden Nowlan. "The Bull Moose" from *An Exchange of Gifts* by Alden Nowlan. Copyright © 1985 by Alden Nowlan. Reprinted by permission of Stoddart Publishing Co. Limited.

Joyce Carol Oates. "The Night Nurse," published in *Ploughshares* Vol. 19, #4 (Winter 1993–94). Copyright © 1994 by The Ontario Review, Inc. Reprinted by permission of John Hawkins & Associates, Inc.

Tim O'Brien. "How to Tell a True War Story." Copyright © 1987 by Tim O'Brien. Originally published in *Esquire* Magazine. Reprinted by permission of the author.

Flannery O'Connor. "Good Country People" from *A Good Man Is Hard to Find and Other Stories*. Copyright © 1955 by Flannery O'Connor and renewed 1983 by Regina O'Connor. Reprinted by permission of Harcourt, Inc.

Sharon Olds. "Rite of Passage" and "Sex without Love" from *The Dead and the Living* by Sharon Olds. Copyright © 1983 by Sharon Olds. Reprinted by permission of Alfred A. Knopf, a Division of Random House, Inc.

Mary Oliver. "The Black Snake" from *Twelve Moons* by Mary Oliver. Copyright © 1972, 1973, 1974, 1976, 1977, 1978, 1979 by Mary Oliver. Reprinted by permission of Little, Brown and Company (Inc).

George Orwell. "Shooting an Elephant" from *Shooting an Elephant and Other Essays* by George Orwell, Copyright © 1950 by Sonia Brownell Orwell and renewed 1978 by Sonia Pitt-Rivers, reprinted by permission of Harcourt, Inc., and by permission of Bill Hamilton as the Literary Executor of the Estate of the late Sonia Brownell Orwell, Martin Secker & Warburg Ltd.

Wilfred Owen. "Dulce et Decorum Est" from *The Collected Poems of Wilfred Owen*. Copyright © 1963 by Chatto & Windus, Ltd. Reprinted by permission of New Directions Publishing Corp.

Octavio Paz. "The Street" from *Early Poems 1935–1955*. Reprinted by permission of Indiana University Press.

Marge Piercy. "A Work of Artifice" and "The Secretary Chant" from *Circles on the Water* by Marge Piercy. Copyright © 1982 by Marge Piercy. Reprinted by permission of Alfred A. Knopf, a Division of Random House, Inc.

Sylvia Plath. "Daddy" from *The Collected Poems of Sylvia Plath*, ed. Ted Hughes. Copyright © 1960, 1965, 1971, 1981 by the Estate of Sylvia Plath. Editorial material Copyright © 1981 by Ted Hughes. Also from *Ariel* by Sylvia Plath, Copyright © 1963 by Ted Hughes. Reprinted by permission of Faber & Faber, Ltd. and HarperCollins Publishers, Inc.

Wyatt Prunty. "Elderly Lady Crossing on Green" from *The Run of the House*, page 18. Copyright © 1989. The Johns Hopkins University Press.

Marny Requa. From an Interview with Julia Alvarez, from "The Politics of Fiction," *Frontera* 5 (1997): n. pdg. Online. Internet. 29 Jan. 1997. Reprinted with the permission of the author.

Alberto Ríos. "Seniors" from *Five Indiscretions*. Copyright © 1985 by Alberto Ríos. Reprinted by permission of the author.

Theodore Roethke. "My Papa's Waltz," Copyright © 1942 by Hearst Magazines, Inc. From *The Collected Poems of Theodore Roethke* by Theodore Roethke, published by Doubleday & Company, Inc. Copyright © 1966 by Beatrice Roethke. Used by permission of Doubleday, a division of Random House, Inc.

Katie Roiphe. "The Independent Woman (and Other Lies)," *Esquire*, February 1997. Copyright © 1997 by Katie Roiphe. Reprinted by permission of International Creative Management, Inc.

Mary Jo Salter. "Welcome to Hiroshima" from *Henry Purcell in Japan* by Mary Jo Salter. Copyright © 1984 by Mary Jo Salter. Reprinted by permission of Alfred A. Knopf, a Division of Random House, Inc.

Indira Sant. "Household Fires" from *Sixteen Modern Indian Poems*, ed. A.K. Ramanujan and Vinay Dharwadker, Copyright © 1989. Reprinted by permission of *Daedalus*, Journal of the American Academy of Arts and Sciences, from the issue entitled "Another India," Fall 1989, Vol. 118, No. 4.

William Seebring. *The Original Last Wish Baby*. Copyright © 1995 by Douglas Michael. Reprinted by permission. CAUTION: Professionals and amateurs are hereby warned that *The Original Last Wish Baby* is subject to a royalty. The play is fully protected under the copyright laws of the United States of America, the British Empire, including Canada, and all other countries covered by the International Copyright Union and the Universal Copyright Convention. All rights, including professional, amateur, motion picture, radio and/or television broadcast, and any other form of electronic transmission are strictly reserved by the author. No portion of the play may be published, reprinted in any publication, or copied for any reason without the permission of the author, c/o the author's agent. No performances, professional, stock or amateur, of this play may be given without the written permission of the author. All inquiries should be addressed to Frieda Fishbein Associates, P.O. Box 723, Bedford, NY 10506; (914) 234-7232.

William Shakespeare. Introduction and Footnotes to accompany *Hamlet, Prince of Denmark* and *An Introduction to Shakespeare* edited by Hardin Craig and David Bevington. Copyright © 1973, 1975 by Scott, Foresman and Company. *A Midsummer Night's Dream* from *The Complete Works of Shakespeare*, 4th ed. by David Bevington. Copyright © 1992 by HarperCollins Publishers, Inc. Reprinted by permission of Addison-Wesley Educational Publishers, Inc.

Saundra Sharp. "It's the Law: A Rap Poem" from *Typing in the Dark* by Saundra Sharp. Copyright © 1991 by Saundra Sharp. Published by Harlem River Press, an imprint of Writers and Readers Publishing, Inc. Reprinted by permission.

Patricia Smith. "What It's Like to Be a Black Girl (For Those of You Who Aren't)" from *Life According to Motown* by Patricia Smith. Copyright © 1991 by Patricia Smith. Reprinted by permission of the author.

Cathy Song. "The White Porch" and "The Youngest Daughter" from *Picture Bride*. Copyright © 1983 by Yale University Press. Reprinted by permission of Yale University Press.

Sophocles, "Oedipus the King" from *Three Theban Plays* by Sophocles, translated by Robert Fagles. Translation Copyright © 1982 by Robert Fagles. Used by permission of Viking Penguin, a Division of Penguin Putnam Inc.

Gary Soto. "Behind Grandma's House" and "Mexicans Begin Jogging" from *New and Selected Poems* by Gary Soto Copyright © 1995, published by Chronicle Books, San Francisco. Used with permission of Chronicle Books. "The Childhood Worries, or Why I Became a Writer." Text Copyright © 1995 by Gary Soto. Used with permission of the Author and BookStop Literary Agency. All rights reserved.

Wole Soyinka. "Telephone Conversation" from *Ibadan* 10, (November 1960), p. 34. Reprinted by permission of the author.

William Stafford. "Traveling through the Dark," Copyright © 1962, 1998 by the Estate of William Stafford. Reprinted from *The Way It Is: New and Selected Poems* with the permission of Graywolf Press, Saint Paul, Minnesota.

Timothy Steele. "Waiting for the Storm" from *Sapphics and Uncertainties: Poems, 1970–1986* by Timothy Steele. University of Arkansas Press, 1995. Reprinted by permission of the University of Arkansas Press.

Deborah Tannen. "Sex, Lies, and Conversation" from *You Just Don't Understand* by Deborah Tannen. Copyright © 1990 by Deborah Tannen. Reprinted by permission of HarperCollins Publishers, Inc. William Morrow.

Joan Templeton. "Is *A Doll House* a Feminist Text?" excerpted from "The *Doll House* Backlash: Criticism, Feminism, and Ibsen." Reprinted by permission of the Modern Language Association of America from *PMLA* 104. Copyright © 1989 by the Modern Language Association of America.

Dylan Thomas. "Do not go gentle into that good night" and "The Hand That Signed the Paper" from *The Poems of Dylan Thomas*. Copyright © 1939 by New Directions Publishing Corporation. Reprinted by permission of New Directions Publishing Corp.

Jean Toomer. "Reapers" from *Cane* by Jean Toomer. Copyright © 1923 by Boni & Liveright, renewed 1951 by Jean Toomer. Used by permission of Liveright Publishing Corporation.

Carol Strongin Tufts. "A Psychoanalytic Reading of Nora," excerpted from "Recasting *A Doll House*: Narcissism as Character Motivation in Ibsen's Play." Originally published in *Comparative Drama* (Summer 1986). Reprinted by permission of the editors of *Comparative Drama*.

David Updike. "Summer" from *Out on the Marsh* by David Updike. Copyright © 1988 by David Updike. Reprinted by permission of David R. Godine, Publisher, Inc.

John Updike. "A & P" from *Pigeon Feathers and Other Stories* by John Updike. Copyright © 1962 by John Updike. Originally appeared in *The New Yorker*. "Dog's Death" from *Midpoint and Other Poems* by John Updike. Copyright © 1969 by John Updike. "Player Piano" from *Collected Poems 1953–1993* by John Updike. Copyright © 1993 by John Updike. All works reprinted by permission of Alfred A. Knopf, a Division of Random House, Inc.

Karen Van Der Zee. Chapters 11 and 12 of *A Secret Sorrow*. Copyright © 1981 by Karen Van Der Zee. All rights reserved. Reproduction with the permission of the publisher, Harlequin Books S.A.

Fay Weldon. "IND AFF, or Out of Love in Sarajevo." Copyright © 1988 by Fay Weldon. First published in *The Observer* magazine (7 August 1988). Reprinted by permission of the author.

E. B. White. "Once More to the Lake" from *One Man's Meat* by E. B. White, text Copyright © 1941 by E. B. White. Reprinted by permission of Tilbury House, Publishers, Gardiner, Maine.

Richard Wilbur. "A Late Aubade" from *Walking to Sleep: New Poems and Translations*. Copyright © 1968 and renewed by Richard Wilbur, reprinted by permission of Harcourt, Inc. First appeared in *The New Yorker*.

Tennessee Williams. *The Glass Menagerie*. Copyright © 1945 by Tennessee Williams and Edwina D. Williams. Copyright renewed 1973 by Tennessee Williams. Reprinted by permission of Random House, Inc.

William Carlos Williams. "Poem" and "Spring and All" from *Collected Poems 1909–1939, Volume I.* Copyright © 1938 by New Directions Publishing Corp. Reprinted by permission of New Directions Publishing Corp.

Barry Witham and John Lutterbie. "A Marxist Approach to *A Doll House*." Reprinted by permission of the Modern Language Association of America from *Approaches to Teaching Ibsen's* A Doll House, edited by Yvonne Shafer. Copyright © 1985 by the Modern Language Association of America.

Tobias Wolff, "Powder" from *The Night in Question* by Tobias Wolff. Copyright © 1996 by Tobias Wolff. Reprinted by permission of Alfred A. Knopf, a Division of Random House, Inc.

Mitsuye Yamada. "A Bedtime Story" from *Camp Notes and Other Writings* by Mitsuye Yamada. Copyright © 1992 by Mitsuye Yamada. Reprinted by permission of Rutgers University Press.

Index of First Lines

Index of Authors and Titles